Abnormal Child and Adolescent Psychology

Abnormal Child and Adolescent Psychology is a comprehensive introduction to the field. It covers theoretical and methodological foundations and examines the characteristics, epidemiology, etiology, developmental course, assessment, and treatment of disorders of childhood and adolescence. At the heart of the text is the partnership of the developmental psychopathology perspective, which analyzes problems of youth within a developmental context, and a traditional clinical/disorder approach, which underscores the symptoms, causes, and treatments of disorders. Woven throughout the text is the view that behavior stems from the continuous interaction of multiple influences, that the problems of the young are intricately tied to their social and cultural contexts, and that empirical approaches and the scientific method provide the best avenue for understanding the complexity of human behavior.

This edition explores the latest areas of research and tackles important contemporary topics, including:

- how to best classify and diagnose problems
- the Research Domain Criteria (RDoC) framework
- the roles of genetics and early brain development and their interaction with the environment
- the complex roles of family and peers; sex/gender; and culture, ethnicity, and race in psychopathology
- progress in early intervention and prevention
- improvements in accessibility and dissemination of evidence-based treatments
- social issues such as poverty, child maltreatment, substance use, bullying/victimization, and terrorism and war

This edition also features a new full-color design and over 200 color figures, tables, and photos. The text is written in a clear and engaging style and is approachable for students with varying academic backgrounds and experiences. It is rich in case descriptions that allow students to examine problems through the lens of youth and their families. The "Accent" boxes foster discussion of current interest topics such as infant mental health, scientific evidence regarding vaccines and autism, suicidality in sexual minority youth, and the impact of stigmatization. The "Looking Forward" sections focus students' attention on the central concepts to be addressed, while the "Looking Back" sections provide students with a synopsis of the chapter for further study and reflection. **The text is also supplemented with online resources for students and instructors.**

Allen C. Israel, Professor Emeritus, University at Albany, State University of New York, USA.

Jennifer Weil Malatras, Clinical Assistant Professor, University at Albany, State University of New York, USA.

Rita Wicks-Nelson, Professor Emeritus, West Virginia University Institute of Technology, USA.

Abnormal Child and Adolescent Psychology

International Student Edition

Ninth Edition

Allen C. Israel, Jennifer Weil Malatras,
and Rita Wicks-Nelson

Routledge
Taylor & Francis Group

NEW YORK AND LONDON

Ninth edition published 2022
by Routledge
605 Third Avenue, New York, NY 10158

and by Routledge
4 Park Square, Milton Park, Abingdon, Oxon OX14 4RN

Routledge is an imprint of the Taylor & Francis Group, an informa business

© 2022 Taylor & Francis

Eighth edition published by Pearson 2015

ISBN: 978-1-032-15720-7 (ISE pb)

Typeset in ITC Officina Sans
by Newgen Publishing UK

Not for distribution in North America

Brief Contents

Contents

Contents

Contents

Contents

Contents

Contents

Contents

About the Authors

Allen C. Israel served as professor of psychology at the University at Albany, State University of New York and held the roles of director of clinical training and director of graduate studies. He has authored numerous scholarly articles in refereed journals and chapters in edited books. He serves on government boards concerned with services for children, adults, and families with mental health, developmental, and substance use challenges.

Jennifer Weil Malatras is a clinical assistant professor of psychology at the University at Albany, State University of New York and associate director for child services at the University's Psychological Services Center. She has authored articles in peer-reviewed journals and has contributed to multiple resources on child psychology and parenting. She has served on statewide workgroups aimed at enhancing outcomes and models of care for children and families.

Rita Wicks-Nelson earned a PhD in psychology at the State University of New York at Stony Brook. She has taught at Stony Brook, the State University of New York College at Old Westbury, and West Virginia Institute of Technology. She conducted research on children's development and worked as a clinical psychologist with youth and adults.

Preface

An historical perspective allows us to see that we have considerably increased our knowledge about human development in general and disordered behavior more specifically. During the last few decades, in particular, we have made considerable progress in understanding the problems of children and adolescents and how they and their families might be assisted. Of course, there is much yet to be learned and the needs of youth are considerable, so the study of young people is an especially worthwhile enterprise. We hope that this text makes clear the challenge and excitement of the endeavor.

Now in its updated ninth edition, *Abnormal Child and Adolescent Psychology* has enjoyed enormous success. It has been gratifying for us to know that it continues to make a substantial contribution to the field. At the inception of this text (initially entitled "Behavior Disorders of Children"), relatively few comprehensive books were available in the field. Just as important was the need for a text that emphasized certain themes that we considered critical to the study of problems of youth. These themes have stood the test of time, have evolved, and have become more widely and subtly recognized as essential. Indeed, their early incorporation into the text undoubtedly accounts in part for its ongoing success.

Theme 1: Developmental Psychopathology

At the heart of the text is the partnership of the developmental psychopathology perspective and the more traditional (usual) clinical/disorder approach. The latter underscores description of the symptoms, causes, and treatments of disorders of young people. The developmental psychopathology perspective assumes that problems of youth must be viewed within a developmental context. The developmental psychopathology perspective is articulated in early chapters of the book and guides discussion of specific disorders in subsequent chapters.

A primary assumption of developmental psychopathology is the belief that normal and disturbed behavior are related and are best viewed as occurring along a dynamic pathway of growth and experience, with connections to the past and to the future. This proposition is reflected in the text in several ways. Consideration is given to the timing and processes of normal development and how these may go awry in psychopathology. We also take seriously the assumption that behavioral development cannot be readily parsed by age, and thus we employ a broad time frame for discussing psychological problems in childhood and adolescence. Understanding these problems is enhanced by anchoring them in the early years of life and linking them to outcomes in adulthood.

Theme 2: Multiple Transactional Influences

A second theme woven throughout the text is the view that behavioral problems result from transactions among variables. With few—if any—exceptions, behavior stems from multiple influences and their continuous interactions. Biological structure and function, genetic transmission, cognition, emotion, social interaction, and numerous aspects of the immediate and broader environment play complex roles in generating and maintaining psychological and behavioral functioning. Those who study developmental psychopathology are committed to the difficult task of understanding and integrating these multiple influences—efforts that are addressed throughout the text.

Theme 3: The Individual in Context

Following from this, a third theme emphasizes that the problems of the young are intricately tied to the social and cultural contexts in which they experience life. Children and adolescents are embedded in a circle of social and environmental influences involving family, peer, school, neighborhood, societal, and cultural circumstances. At any one time, youth bring their personal attributes to these circumstances, are affected by them, and in turn, influence other people and situations. Meaningful analysis of psychological problems thus requires that the individual be considered in context. Such aspects as family interactions, friendships, gender, educational opportunity, poverty, ethnicity, race, and cultural values all come into play.

Theme 4: The Empirical Approach

A fourth major theme is a bias toward the empirical approach. Prudent and insightful thinking is required in both figuring out the puzzles of behavioral problems and applying acquired knowledge. We believe that empirical approaches and the theoretical frameworks that rely on scientific method provide the best avenue for understanding the complexity of human behavior. Research findings thus are a central component of the book and inform our understanding of the problems experienced by youth and how the lives of young people might be improved.

Theme 5: The Person at the Center

Concern for the optimal development of the child or adolescent is given important emphasis throughout this text. While there is no doubt that empirical studies further our understanding of development, it is helpful to examine problems from a more personal viewpoint. Thus, by also viewing problems through the lens of the experience of troubled youth and their families, students better come to understand how psychopathology is manifested, what needs a youth may have, how intervention can help a child, and a plethora of other factors. The many case descriptions in the text are vital in bringing forth the personal. So also are the several other individual accounts, quotations, and photographs. Real life is singularly captured by the hyperactive child who realizes that he is considered a "bad boy," the sister who believes she has become a better person through caring for her intellectually challenged brother, and the parents who report being "jolted" by a TV description of a youth whose problems were similar to those of their undiagnosed child.

Organization of the Text

As a relatively comprehensive introduction to the field, *Abnormal Child and Adolescent Psychology* includes theoretical and methodological foundations of the field and devotes most discussion to specific problems of youth—that is, to the characteristics, epidemiology, developmental course, etiology, assessment, treatment, and prevention of psychopathology.

Although we have not formally divided the chapters into broader sections, they are conceptualized as three units.

The first unit, consisting of Chapters 1 through 5, presents the foundation for subsequent discussion. A broad overview of the field is presented, including basic concepts, historical context, developmental influences, theoretical perspectives, research methodology, classification and diagnosis, assessment, prevention, and treatment approaches. These chapters draw heavily on the psychological literature and also recognize the multidisciplinary nature of the study and treatment of youth. We assume that readers have some background in psychology, but we have made an effort to serve those with relatively limited background or experience.

The second unit, consisting of Chapters 6 through 15, addresses major disorders. There is considerable organizational consistency across these chapters. For most disorders, classification, clinical description, epidemiology, developmental course, etiology, assessment, and prevention/treatment are discussed in that order. At the same time, flexible organization is a guiding principle so that the complexity inherent in specific chapter topics is not sacrificed.

- Chapter 6 (anxiety and obsessive-compulsive disorders), Chapter 7 (trauma- and stressor-related disorders), and Chapter 8 (mood disorders) focus on internalizing disorders.
- Chapter 9 (conduct problems) and Chapter 10 (attention-deficit/hyperactivity disorder) discuss disorders frequently described as externalizing disorders.
- Specific and pervasive developmental problems are presented in Chapter 11 (communication and learning disorders), Chapter 12 (intellectual disability), and Chapter 13 (autism spectrum disorder and schizophrenia).
- Chapter 14 (basic physical functions) and Chapter 15 (medical conditions) focus on health- and medical-related problems.

The third unit consists of an Epilogue, which rounds out and extends what has gone before. The Epilogue highlights some current and evolving concerns for children and adolescents. It is intended as a starting point for further thought and interest.

Content: Highlights and Updates

It almost goes without saying that the study of the psychopathology of youth must include judicious consideration of recent and emerging research and issues. Such consideration is reflected by the provision of new information throughout the text. The updated content not only points to new findings and issues but, importantly, it also confirms or extends previous findings in various ways. Moreover, in reviewing new information we have been especially sensitive to topics that are currently of high interest and concern. The following are notable instances of highlighted and updated topics.

- This edition of the text captures the heightened interest in how best to classify and diagnose psychological problems. It includes diagnostic criteria and information from the most recent version of the DSM (DSM-5) and gives appreciable attention to how the dimensional approach has informed and is likely to continue to inform developments in the classification of psychopathology of youth. Also, the current edition includes discussion of the Research Domain Criteria (RDoC) being developed through the National Institute of Mental Health.
- The substantial progress in understanding the causes of psychopathology is exemplified across chapters. Special attention is given to the complex interplay of multiple influences on child and adolescent adjustment.
- Similarly, continued and updated consideration is given to neurobiological findings, particularly as advances in technology have allowed greater understanding of the roles of genetics and early brain development in the etiology of various disorders.
- Consonant with advances in the field, genetic processes and new findings that implicate gene effects and their interaction with the environment receive greater attention.
- Receiving particular attention are the complex roles of the family and peers within the transaction of multiple influences on the development of problems in children and adolescents.
- The developmental course and outcome of major disorders continues to have high priority.
- Attention is given to the role of sex/gender in psychopathology—both to differences in prevalence, symptoms, and outcome as well as to factors that may underlie them.
- Continued and increased attention is given to the various roles of culture, ethnicity, and race in psychopathology. An example is how cultural considerations may influence assessment and treatment.
- Continued progress being made in the prevention of disorder is reflected in new findings and extended discussion. Early intervention efforts—such as for specific learning disorders and autism spectrum disorder—can be viewed as merging prevention and treatment.
- Examples of specific individual and family treatments are generously interwoven throughout the chapters, with an emphasis on evidence-based intervention.
- Increased attention is also given to efforts to improve accessibility of evidence-based treatments, to how such treatments can be disseminated from research to "real-world"

settings, and to the role that technology may play in these efforts.
- Consideration is given to specific problems that remain of high societal interest—such as poverty, child maltreatment, substance use, bullying/victimization, and terrorism and war.
- Also updated and/or expanded is discussion of issues that have been or still are particularly controversial. These include, for example, debates over inappropriate or excessive use of medication in children, discredited claims of a link between vaccines and autism spectrum disorder, and more generally the attention given to evolving approaches to classification and diagnosis.

Features: Some Old, Some New

Based on developments in the literature, we have created two separate chapters (Anxiety and Obsessive-Compulsive Disorders and Trauma- and Stressor-Related Disorders). As will be obvious to users of the previous edition, we have, however, retained the basic organization of the chapters, which appears to work well. Similarly, specific features of the book continue to emphasize for students a person-oriented, applied perspective. The text is rich in case descriptions and in accounts of assessment and treatment. An additional feature, the Accents, allows for detailed discussion of particular topics of interest, for example, infant mental health, scientific evidence regarding vaccines and autism, suicidality in sexual minority youth, and the impact of stigmatization. Further, the text continues to be rich in illustrations including figures, tables, photos, and drawings.

Other features of the text are especially aimed at facilitating student learning. Continued in this edition is Looking Forward, which focuses students' attention at the beginning of each chapter on the central issues to be addressed. Looking Forward roughly follows the organization of the chapter and sets the stage for the overview at the chapter's end, referred to as Looking Back. In addition, important or new terms in each chapter appear in bold in the text and also are listed as Key Terms at the conclusion of the chapter. Finally, several supplementary teaching and learning materials (see below) add to the value of *Abnormal Child and Adolescent Psychology* for both students and instructors.

Supplementary Teaching and Learning Materials

Please visit the online resources at www.routledge.com/ 9780367252632

Acknowledgments

The reviewers of the eighth edition of the book were indispensable for the many comments and suggestions for improvement they provided. We would like to thank: Michael Gascoigne, Shelly Haslam, Grant King, and Sandi Tait-McCutcheon.

Thanks to the Routledge/Taylor & Francis team: Georgette Enriquez, Charlotte Mapp, Abigail Stanley, Kelly Winter, Rachel Carter, Geraldine Lyons, and Penelope Kent.

In addition, we want to express our sincere appreciation to our families, friends, and colleagues who have provided support, advice, and input throughout the process of the current and previous editions of this book. In particular, we would like to thank Kevin Haworth for his contributions to the current edition. We are also each especially grateful for our parents and the support and encouragement they provided over the years.

Finally, our collaboration on this book and as colleagues has been one of appreciation, equality, and friendship and for that we are grateful.

Allen C. Israel
Jennifer Weil Malatras
Rita Wicks-Nelson

CHAPTER 1
Introduction

Looking Forward

After reading this chapter, you should be able to discuss:

- How psychological disorders are defined and identified
- Prevalence of psychological disorders
- The relationship between developmental level and psychological disorders

- The relationship between gender and psychological disorders
- Historical influences on understanding psychological disorders
- Current study and practice of abnormal child and adolescent psychology

To be young is to bounce balls as high as the heavens, gobble up fairytales, walk tightropes without falling, love friends with glee, and peer at the wondrous future.

To be young is to feel ignorant and useless, to be alone and unlovable, to ride the waves of ups and downs and unending insecurities.

The early years of life have long been described in extremes of emotions, behaviors, and encounters. In fact, most individuals who look back on their own youth not only admit to some of the extremes—but also to a sizable portion of more moderate experiences. And they frequently view their youth as a special time of growth and opportunity. It is against this backdrop that we embark on the study of the psychological problems of childhood and adolescence.

This book is written for those who ask questions about and have concerns regarding less-than-optimal development of youth. It addresses definitions, characteristics, origins, development, diagnosis, prevention, and amelioration of maladaptive functioning. We anticipate, and hope, that you will find this field of study as satisfying as we do. It is an area of study that encompasses both humanitarian concerns for young people and scientific intrigue.

Recent decades have been a particularly promising time to study behavioral and psychological disturbance. The current need for increased understanding, prevention, and treatment is substantial, and is recognized in many parts of the world. At the same time, research into the development of youth continues to grow by leaps and bounds, with contributions from many disciplines. As is usually true in science, increased knowledge and improved methods have led to new questions and paradoxes. This combination of new understandings, new questions, and new avenues of inquiry gives both promise and enthusiasm to the study of the problems of young people.

Defining and Identifying Abnormality

Behavioral repertoires come in endless varieties, and many kinds of disorders are discussed in this text (see Accent: "Some Faces of Problem Behavior"). Various labels have been applied to such problems: abnormal behavior, behavioral disturbance, emotional disorder, psychological deficit, mental illness, psychopathology, maladaptive behavior, developmental disorder, and so forth. Moreover, systems have been constructed to categorize problems and to offer guidelines to professionals for identifying abnormality. Underlying this effort are complex issues in defining and distinguishing psychopathology.

ACCENT Some Faces of Problem Behavior

Four-year-old **Joey** had been kicked out of preschool, where he had sat on the floor and stared, refused to talk, and hit any child who touched him. If the teacher insisted that he participate in activities, he screamed, cried, and banged his arms and legs on the floor. Similar behaviors occurred at home. Joey rarely talked or showed emotion, and he slept fitfully, banged his head against the wall, and rocked back and forth (adapted from Morgan, 1999, pp. 3–4).

Lakeshia had always been considered a slow learner but these difficulties had sometimes been beneath the "radar screen" of her teachers, perhaps in part because she was quiet and well-behaved. She repeated second grade and had a tutor, but by the time she was in fifth grade, Lakeshia was failing all her subjects. An evaluation indicated low-average to borderline overall intelligence and ratings of attention and learning problems in the clinically borderline range (adapted from Hathaway, Dooling-Litfin, & Edwards, 2006, pp. 402–405).

Nine-year-old **Mateo**'s mother described him as a bright and active child who would "lose his head if it weren't attached to his body." In school, he was easily distracted, fidgety,

and had to be redirected frequently by his teacher. Although he had average academic skills, he had difficulty following instructions, would often fail to finish work, was easily bored, and often seemed to guess rather than take the time to think about his answers. While he enjoyed spending time with other children, he seemed socially immature and had trouble making friends. His classmates were often frustrated with him for interrupting or intruding on their games.

Anne had begun to worship Satan and noted that praying to Satan brought her relief from distress. Anne had dyed her hair black, dusted her face with white powder, and looked like a character in a vampire story rather than a 14-year-old. Anne reported that she had difficulty falling asleep because she worried about her grades and her parents' divorce, for which she believed she was partly responsible. She found it hard to concentrate in school, was irritable, and had lost weight. She had no energy, no longer enjoyed activities with friends, and spent most of her time in her room. Anne denied any intent or plan for suicide, involvement with cults, or drug use (adapted from Morgan, 1999, pp. 35–37).

The criteria for abnormality are primarily based on how a person is acting or what a person is saying and only rarely include a specific known marker for disorder. Of course, most of us would agree that problems are evident when individuals do not acquire speech, are unable to feed themselves, or see and hear things that others do not. But less dramatic instances are harder to judge and a fine line can exist between what is considered disordered and what is normal. Young people of specific ages display behaviors that may or may not be considered signs of disturbance, such as noncompliance with parental rules, social withdrawal, high activity level, fearfulness, sadness, and delayed reading skills. Thus, we must ask, "When do we consider behaviors abnormal?" and "How can we distinguish everyday problems from more serious indications of psychopathology?" There are no simple answers to these questions, but it is informative to consider several factors that enter into judgments about psychological or behavioral disturbances.

Atypical and Harmful Behavior

Psychological problems frequently are viewed as atypical, odd, or abnormal—all of which imply that they deviate from the average. Indeed, "ab" means "away" or "from," whereas "normal" refers to the average or standard. However, being atypical, in itself, hardly defines psychopathology. People who display exceptionally

high intelligence and social competence are generally considered fortunate, and their "oddness" is looked upon with favor. The deviations we are considering are assumed to be harmful in some way to the individual. The American Psychiatric Association (2013), for example, defines disorder as a syndrome of clinically significant behavioral, cognitive, or emotional disturbances that reflect dysfunction in underlying mental processes, and that is associated with distress or disability in important areas of functioning.

Abnormality or psychopathology is viewed as interfering with adaptation, that is, with individuals fitting the circumstances of their lives. Psychopathology hinders or prevents the young person from negotiating developmental tasks, whether acquiring language skills, emotional control, or satisfactory social relationships. Disorder may be viewed as residing *within* the individual. Alternatively, it can be regarded as the individual's reactions to circumstances—with the interface of the person with other people or environmental conditions. The latter, more appropriate, perspective emphasizes that behavior is inextricably linked with the larger world in which it is embedded.

Developmental Standards

Developmental level is always important in judging behavior, but it is especially important for children and adolescents

The behavior that is expected of or considered appropriate for a child varies across cultures. (ESB Professional/Shutterstock (left) and robertharding/Alamy Stock Photo (right).)

because they change so rapidly. Judgments about behavior rely on **developmental norms**, which describe the typical rates of growth, sequences of growth, and forms of physical skills, language, cognition, emotion, and social behavior. These serve as developmental standards from which to evaluate the possibility that "something is wrong."

Behavior can be judged as anomalous relative to these norms in a number of ways, as indicated in Table 1.1. Delayed development, or failure to keep up with typical developmental change, indicates that something is awry. Children sometimes may achieve developmental norms and then regress, or return, to behavior typically seen in younger individuals.

Several other signs are noteworthy. These include atypical frequency, intensity, or duration of behavior, as well as the display of behavior in inappropriate situations. It is not unusual for a child to display fear, for example, but fearfulness may be a problem if it occurs excessively, is extremely intense, does not weaken over time, or is shown in harmless situations. Concern might also be expressed for the youth whose behavior abruptly changes, as when an outgoing adolescent turns solitary, or when a child displays several questionable behaviors. All of these

Table 1.1 Behavioral Indicators of Disorder

Developmental delay
Developmental regression or deterioration
Extremely high or low frequency of behavior
Extremely high or low intensity of behavior
Behavioral difficulty persisting over time
Behavior inappropriate to the situation
Abrupt changes in behavior
Several problem behaviors
Behavior qualitatively different from normal

indications of disturbance are quantitative differences from developmental norms.

Yet another manifestation that may signal the need for help is behavior that appears qualitatively different from the norm. That is, the behavior—or the sequence in which it develops—is not seen in normal growth. For instance, most children are socially responsive to their caretakers soon after birth, but children diagnosed as autistic display atypical unresponsive behaviors, such as lack of normal eye contact. Qualitatively different behaviors frequently indicate a pervasive problem in development.

Culture and Race/Ethnicity

The term **culture** encompasses the idea that groups of people are organized in specific ways, live in specific environmental niches, and share specific attitudes, beliefs, values, practices, and behavioral standards. Culture is a way of life that is transmitted from generation to generation. It is unsurprising, then, that although many disorders are found across cultures—that is, they are universal—there are some cross-cultural differences. Rates of disorders have been found to vary and disorders may be expressed in subtly different ways (Canino & Alegría, 2008; Rutter, 2011). An example of the latter is anxiety disorder; it appears to be universal but may be expressed more through bodily symptoms in Asian and Latino groups than in European Americans (Serafica & Vargas, 2006).

Cultural analyses describe the many ways in which cultures shape normal and abnormal development and also conceptualize, explain, and treat psychopathology (Chen & Liu, 2016). **Cultural norms** have broad influence on expectations, judgments, and beliefs about the behavior of youth. Children in the United States, for example, are expected to show less self-control and less deference to adults than children in some other parts of the world (Weisz et al., 1995). Weisz and his colleagues found that teachers in Thailand reported more conduct problems among their students than teachers in the United States, but trained observers reported just the opposite for the two student groups. The researchers suggested that Thai teachers may hold students to a more demanding behavioral standard—and thus see more problems and more readily label them.

The influence of culture can be seen not only in terms of expectations, but also in terms of parental attitudes and behaviors. For example, Majdandžić and colleagues (2018) compared levels of challenging parenting behaviors in Dutch and Australian parents of preschoolers. Challenging parenting behavior (CPB) refers to parenting practices that encourage children to push their limits by taking reasonable risks, being appropriately assertive, and by confidently exploring unfamiliar situations. Higher levels of CPB have been found to be associated with decreased risk for childhood anxiety problems. The results of the investigation illustrated cultural differences, but also alert us to the likely complexity of influences (see Table 1.2). Australian mothers appear to express lower levels of CPB than Australian fathers and Dutch fathers and mothers. Consistent with previous research, higher levels of CPB were associated with fewer anxiety symptoms and anxiety disorders for all groups.

Discussions of cultural issues regarding abnormality are often framed in terms of ethnicity and race. **Ethnicity** denotes common customs, values, language, or traits that are associated with national origin or geographic area. **Race**, a distinction based on physical characteristics, can also be associated with shared customs, values, and the like. Ethnic or racial groups embedded within a heterogeneous society may show different rates of psychopathology, express psychopathology somewhat differently, and hold beliefs and standards different from those of the dominant cultural group (Anderson & Mayes, 2010). Even when parenting behaviors are similar in dominant and ethnic groups, the effects on offspring may be dissimilar due to the different values held by these groups (Eichelsheim et al., 2010).

An example of ethnic difference in the United States is provided by comparisons between European American and Asian American parents concerning the achievement behavior of their children (Ly, 2008). In general, compared to European American parents, Asian American parents assign greater importance to the child's effort—for example, in academic success—than to

Table 1.2 Mean Challenging Parenting Behavior*

Parent	Culture	
	Australian	Dutch
Mother	3.11	3.28
Father	3.20	3.47

Note: * As measured by the Challenging Parenting Behavior Questionnaire (CPBQ4-6).

Source: Adapted from Majdandžić et al., 2018.

the child's ability. However, there are relatively few cultural comparisons of families with children with disability. As part of one such study, parents were asked to rate the success of their intellectually disabled children's performance on a task and also rate the degree to which performance was due to ability and effort. The Asian American parents viewed their children as less successful (real differences did not exist), held lower expectations for future success, and attributed performance to lower ability and lower effort. They also reported different emotional reactions to their children's performance. Although this study had limitations (e.g., families were volunteers), it demonstrates the need for sensitivity to possible ethnic/racial differences in the study of psychopathology of young people.

Other Standards: Gender and Situations

Expectations based on gender also contribute to defining problem behavior. **Gender norms** significantly influence development; they affect emotions, behaviors, opportunities, and choices. In most societies, males are expected to be relatively more aggressive, dominant, active, and adventurous, while females are expected to be more passive, dependent, quiet, sensitive, and emotional. These gender stereotypes play a role in judgments about normality. We would probably be less inclined to worry about the hypersensitive, shy girl and the excessively dominant boy than about their opposite-sex counterparts.

Judgments of deviance or normality of behavior also take into account **situational norms**—what is expected in specific settings or social situations. Energetic running may be quite acceptable on a playground but not allowed in a library. Norms for social interaction can be quite subtle; for example, how a statement is voiced can either compliment or insult another person. Individuals in all cultures are expected to learn what is acceptable and to act in certain ways in certain situations, given their age and gender. When they do not, their competence or societal adjustment may be questioned.

The Role of Others

Youth, especially young children, hardly ever refer themselves for clinical evaluation, thereby declaring a problem. The identification and labeling of a problem is more likely to occur when others become concerned—for example, when parents worry about their child's social isolation or when a teacher is troubled about a child's inability to learn.

Referral of youth to mental health professionals thus may have as much or more to do with the characteristics of parents, teachers, or family physicians as with the young people themselves (Briggs-Gowan et al., 2000; Verhulst & van der Ende, 1997). Indeed, disagreement often exists among adults as to whether a child or adolescent "has a problem." This may in part be due to different adults being exposed to different child behaviors but adult attitudes, sensitivity, tolerance, and ability to cope all play a role in identifying disorders.

Changing Views of Abnormality

Finally, judgments about abnormality are not set in stone. Examples abound. In the 1800s, masturbation was considered a sign of disturbance or a behavior that could cause insanity (Rie, 1971). Nail biting was once seen as a sign of degeneration (Anthony, 1970). Excessive intellectual activity in young women was believed by some to lead to mental problems (Silk et al., 2000). Today these views are not given credence.

Many factors undoubtedly contribute to change in judgments about abnormality (see Figure 1.1). Enhanced knowledge and theoretical modifications have played a role. So has transition in cultural beliefs and values. For example, eating disorders, once found almost exclusively in Western societies, have increased worldwide in the past decades, perhaps due, in part, to wider adoption of the modern Western preference for slender body size (Pike & Dunne, 2015).

In summary, psychopathology cannot simply be defined as an entity carried around within a person. It is most appropriately viewed as a judgment that a person's behavior, emotion, or thinking are atypical, dysfunctional, and harmful in some way—a judgment involving knowledge about development, cultural and ethnic influences, social norms, and the people making the judgment.

How Common Are Psychological Problems?

The prevalence of behavioral or psychological disorder suggests the extent to which prevention, treatment, and research are needed. However, frequency depends on several factors, most importantly how a disorder is defined and the criteria set for identification. Rates of disorder can vary with the measures used and whether parents, teachers, or youth themselves are the source of information. Characteristics of the population examined— regarding, for example, age, gender, and clinic versus community populations—can make a difference in prevalence (Merikangas & Hommer, 2019).

Given such complexity, considerable disparity is found in rates of problems. A systematic review of studies published from 1985 to 2012, which included several countries, indicated that the prevalence of any mental disorder in youth was estimated at 13.4% (Polanczyk et al., 2015). National surveys in the United States, of serious emotional disorders in children and adolescents indicate rates of between about 4.8% to 8.9% (Merikangas & Hommer, 2019). The American Psychological Association (2007) cited 10% of youth as having a serious mental health problem and another 10% as having mild to moderate problems. Many of the youth reported as having a problem are identified as displaying symptoms of more than one disorder. In addition, there is evidence that by young adulthood, most individuals have experienced some type of mental problem at some time (Copeland et al., 2011).

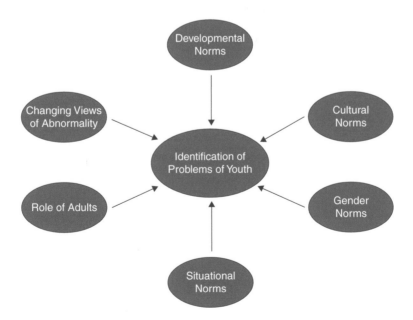

Figure 1.1 Several factors enter into judgments about normality and abnormality.

ACCENT Infant Mental Health

Despite long interest in very early-occurring problems, the idea that infants could have mental health problems had been puzzling to and even resisted by some individuals. Perhaps the notion of innocent infancy seemed mismatched to maladjustment, stigma, and mental illness. Or perhaps infant mental health problems were thought impossible as long as infants were viewed as having limited emotional and cognitive capacity (Tronick & Beeghly, 2011).

Increased understanding of the very early years of life has notably contributed to interest in and acceptance of the idea of infant mental health. The age range considered by those studying infant mental health has expanded in recent years (Egger & Emde, 2011; Zeanah & Zeanah, 2019). In pediatrics—the medical specialty focusing on children—"infant" typically refers to the first year of life. In the mental health field, birth to 3 years was initially taken as the span of interest; this age range has been extended to age 5 or so. In many respects, we can expect continuities between the mental health of very young and older children, but some aspects of infant mental health, if not unique, are sufficiently different to merit special comment. Here, we note four of these.

First, concern for infants historically has emphasized the importance of early interpersonal relationships and how the development of very young children strongly depends on the caregiving context (Rosenblum, Dayton, & Muzik, 2019; Zeanah & Zeanah, 2019). Early descriptions of infant mental health appeared in case reports of infant symptoms originating from emotional deprivation in orphanages, disturbances in attachment relationships, and rearing by parents with

psychological disorder (Egger & Emde, 2011; Humphreys, King, & Gotlib, 2019). The child's relationship with caregivers remains important in the field.

Second, of particular concern is the need for reliable and valid criteria for identifying and categorizing mental health problems for very young children (Egger & Emde, 2011). Methods and systems used with older children are largely viewed as insufficiently sensitive to developmental differences, and those currently used for infants as requiring improvement.

Third, the role of primary health care practitioners is noteworthy. Most all infants/toddlers are seen by general physicians, pediatricians, or various other health care providers as part of "well-child" visits (Gleason, 2019). These practitioners frequently are the first professionals to hear about feeding and sleep problems, delayed motor or language milestones, and behavioral difficulties. It is thus imperative that they have general knowledge of infant mental health principles and practices, including screenings for symptoms, and a good working relationship with families and mental health professionals.

Fourth, prevention of disorder is inherent in infant mental health. The relief of symptoms is critical, of course, but because infants change so rapidly high priority must be given to their future development. In addition, research shows that early prevention is especially effective. Thus, treatment goes hand in hand with prevention of future difficulties, and there is a call for efforts to support policies and programs that promote the well-being of infants and very young children (Nagle, 2019; Nelson & Mann, 2010).

Although research of prevalence has highlighted the age range from childhood through adolescence, problems in preschoolers often received less attention. During the last few decades, the field of infant mental health has emerged as a multidimensional effort to better understand and enhance the development of very young children (Zeanah & Zeanah, 2019). (See Accent: "Infant Mental Health.")

Concern has been expressed that societal change during the last several decades has resulted in an increased risk of disorders for the young. Some change and its cause are obvious; for example, medical advances have increased the survival of infants born prematurely or with physical problems, and these infants have relatively high rates of behavioral and learning

difficulties. However, due to limited research, variations across studies, and methodological issues, it has been difficult to draw overall conclusions about such historical or so-called **secular trends**.

The work of Sawyer and colleagues (2018) is an example of research on secular trends. These investigators used data collected in national surveys in Australia in 1998 and 2013–2014 to examine trends in the prevalence of major depressive disorder, attention-deficit/hyperactivity disorder and conduct disorder. In both surveys, the participants were randomly selected from all 6- to 17-year-olds in Australia, and disorders were assessed using a well-established structured diagnostic interview completed by parents. There was little change in the overall prevalence

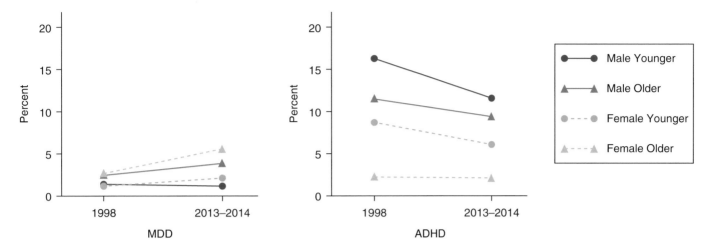

Figure 1.2 Change in prevalence as function of type of disorder, sex, and age. MDD = Major Depressive Disorder. ADHD = Attention-deficit/hyperactivity disorder. (Adapted from Sawyer et al., 2018)

of mental disorders between 1998 (12.5%) and 2013 to 2014 (11.1%). There were some changes in prevalence for some disorders. Most of these changes were small in magnitude. Changes in prevalence also differed depending on sex, age, and sociodemographic factors. Figure 1.2 illustrates examples of difference in changes in prevalence as a function of type of disorder, sex, and age. The authors report a persisting pattern of higher prevalence among children living in single-parent and low-income households.

Overall, research findings are mixed regarding secular trends in young people, with some studies but not all showing increases and some indicating decreases (Collishaw et al., 2004; Polanczyk et al., 2015; Sawyer et al., 2018; Tick, van der Ende, & Verhulst, 2008; Twenge et al., 2010). Moreover, research methodologies differ and results often are complex with regard to types of problems, gender, social class, family, and the like (Merikangas, 2018; Sellers et al., 2019). Continued concern is certainly appropriate, as understanding trends in frequency of problems and what might contribute to change can be valuable in prevention and intervention.

Whether or not problems are increasing, there is little doubt that young people have substantial needs. Yet their mental health problems too often go unrecognized in schools, primary health facilities, and other settings (Hoagwood, 2005). In addition, many youth with diagnosable disorders do not receive adequate treatment (Federal Interagency Forum on Child and Family Statistics, 2011; Ghandour et al., 2019). As we will see, appreciable progress has been made in the development of effective interventions, however challenges remain in implementing and providing access to these interventions. Efforts continue to improve dissemination of effective treatments to underserved communities, to reach youth and families who may

be reluctant to engage in the therapeutic process, to integrate interventions into the health care delivery system, and in various ways to improve systems of service delivery (Chorpita, Becker, & Higa-McMillan, 2019; Cuijpers et al., 2017; Hoagwood et al., 2017).

There are several reasons for concern about this situation. Surely, no one wants to see young people suffer the pain or lowered quality of life associated with psychopathology. Moreover, early disturbances can interfere with subsequent developmental processes, leading to an accumulation of problems. Half of all adults with mental illness reported having symptoms by age 14, so that the study of psychopathology of youth has implications across the lifespan (From Discovery to Cure, 2010). Furthermore, mental health problems in young people adversely influence families and the broader society, as reflected in health care expenditures and other economic and social costs (Lynch & Dickerson, 2019). Indeed, according to the World Health Organization, many of the disorders that carry the heaviest burden of adult death and disability in the developed areas of the world are related to mental health and are often first observed in youth (Merikangas, Nakamura, & Kessler, 2009).

How Are Developmental Level and Disorder Related?

Of concern to professionals and parents alike is whether and how psychological difficulties are related to developmental level. Some relationship does exist between specific problems and the age at which they usually first appear or are

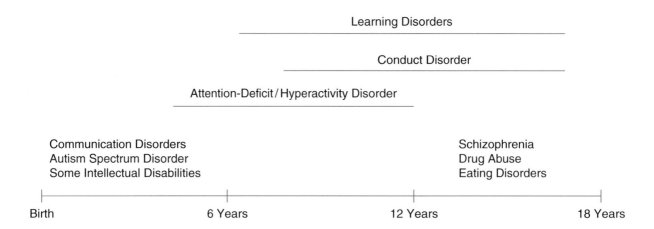

Figure 1.3 The age ranges during which some specific disorders typically first occur, are identified, or are most likely to be observed.

identified. Figure 1.3 depicts the age association for several disturbances. The reason for the link is sometimes obvious. Chronological age is correlated with developmental level, which, in turn, makes some disorders more likely than others. For instance, developmental speech problems appear when children are first acquiring language skills. But other aspects of onset may be less obvious. Actual onset can occur gradually, with symptoms and social impairment escalating over time. For some disorders, time of onset varies according to gender. Moreover, the time at which a disorder is said to occur may depend on extraneous circumstances. For example, although more severe cases of intellectual disability are identified early in life, most are recognized during the school years when classroom demands call attention to children's abilities to learn.

Taking these distinctions into account, information about developmental level and disorder is helpful in several ways. Knowing the usual age of onset can point to etiology. Very early occurrence suggests genetic and/or prenatal etiology, whereas later onset directs attention to additional developmental influences. Knowing the typical age of onset also serves as a guide to judging the severity or outcome of a disorder: cases that occur especially early are likely to be more severe. For example, the onset of drug use is common in adolescence; if it occurs earlier, it is especially associated with substance use disorders and other social and mental problems later in life (SAMHSA, 2013; Wills & Dishion, 2004). In addition, parents, teachers, and other adults who are aware of the usual timing of disorder may be more sensitive to the signs of specific problems in youth. In turn, this can lead to preventing the disorder or facilitating early treatment, an outcome thought to aid in reducing the severity or the persistence of disorder and the secondary problems that often are associated with psychological problems (McGorry et al., 2010).

Table 1.3 Gender Prevalence for Some Disorders of Youth

HIGHER FOR MALES		
Autism spectrum disorder	Attention-deficit hyperactivity disorder	
Oppositional disorder	Conduct disorder	
Drug abuse	Language disorder	
Intellectual disability	Reading disability	
HIGHER FOR FEMALES		
Anxieties and fears	Depression	Eating disorder

How Are Gender and Disorder Related?

For decades, the role of gender in psychopathology in the young was neglected (Crick & Zahn-Waxler, 2003). Several fascinating findings have now emerged. Consistent over the years is the finding of gender differences in the overall rates of many disturbances, with males being more frequently affected than females (Rutter & Sroufe, 2000). Gender differences have been found across time and in many different countries (Merikangas & Hommer, 2019; Seedat et al., 2009). Table 1.3 shows the findings for several specific disorders. But the picture actually is much more complex.

Some gender differences are related to age. For example, males are particularly vulnerable to neurodevelopmental disorders that occur early in life, whereas females are more vulnerable to emotional problems and eating disorders that more commonly are seen at adolescence (Rutter, Caspi, & Moffitt, 2003). As shown in Figure 1.4, gender differences may exist not only in the rates of disorder but also in developmental change for externalizing problems (e.g., aggression, delinquency) and internalizing problems (e.g., anxiety, depression). In addition, problems may be

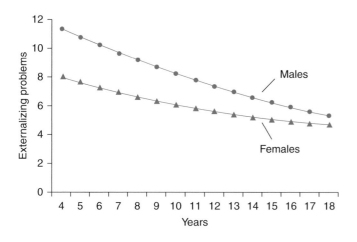
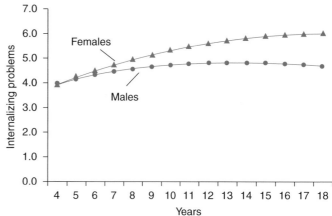

Figure 1.4 The presence and developmental change for externalizing and internalizing problems in youth age 4 to 18 years. Externalizing problems drop with age for both genders, while internalizing problems rise for females. (From Bongers, Koot, vander Ende, & Verhulst, 2003)

expressed differently according to gender. For example, males tend to display overt physical aggression while females may be more likely to exhibit indirect or relational aggression by harmful gossip or rumor spreading (Björkqvist, 2018; Zalecki & Hinshaw, 2004). The severity, causes, and consequences of some disorders may also vary with gender. There is still much to learn about gender differences and methodological issues must be considered.

Methodological Issues, True Differences

To some extent, reported gender differences may result from methodological practices. In the past, a bias existed for studying males, and an emphasis on one gender over the other can result in mistaken inferences about gender differences. Misleading reports of gender differences also can result from females or males being more willing to report certain problems, for example, girls being more willing to speak of emotional difficulties.

Gender-specific prevalence of disorders also can be an artifact of referral bias when clinical samples are studied. Clinical samples are biased toward boys, partly because help is sought for disruptive behavior and this behavior is more often exhibited by boys than girls. Thus, boys with reading problems may be referred over girls with reading problems due to boys' higher rates of disruptive behaviors (Shaywitz, Fletcher, & Shaywitz, 1996). Although boys probably do have more reading problems, referral bias can give misleadingly high rates of disorder.

The bias in clinic samples may affect gender rates in another, more indirect, way (Hartung & Widiger, 1998). When more boys are seen in mental health facilities, they become the subject of more research. In turn, the disorders are described in the way boys express the symptoms, which may not be identical to the symptom picture in girls. When these descriptions (criteria) are used for identifying the disorder, fewer girls will fit the symptom picture and be identified. For example, this possibility is thought to be

relevant to attention-deficit hyperactivity disorder in girls (Greven et al., 2018; Waschbusch & King, 2006).

Although methodological issues caution us to examine research carefully, the weight of the evidence does point to some real gender differences. To what might they be attributed? Both biological and psychosocial influences, observed prenatally onward, might reasonably underlie gender-specific psychopathology (Rutter et al., 2003; Zahn-Waxler et al., 2006). Differential biological vulnerabilities and strengths may exist. Biological differences between the sexes—in sex chromosomes, sex hormones, and brain structure and function—play a fundamental role in gender development and differences. Biological maturity occurs later in boys, and the X and Y chromosomes are likely related to specific disorders in complicated ways. In addition, biological sex differences may exist in response to stress and in emotion, which we would expect to be relevant to psychological disturbances.

At the same time, boys and girls are differentially exposed to risk and to protective experiences associated with psychopathology. Consider the following examples. From infancy onward, boys suffer a higher rate of traumatic brain injury, which increases their risk of intellectual impairments (Anderson et al., 2001). Boys are more often physically victimized by peers, an event that is related to a variety of behavioral and emotional problems (Hanish & Guerra, 2002). Girls are more likely to have inappropriate sexual encounters. More generally, there are gender differences in sociability, friendships, and interaction with parents and teachers (Auyeung et al., 2009; Rutter et al., 2003). Boys and girls also experience different sex-role expectations for how they should express emotion, control behavior, and the like. It is also worth noting that gender may affect psychological responses to circumstances, for example, to chaotic environments and family problems (Cicchetti & Sroufe, 2000; Leinonen, Solantaus, & Punamäki, 2003). We might expect that these gender-differentiated experiences would result in gender differences in psychopathology.

Investigation of gender effects has the potential to inform us about the causes, prevention, and treatment of abnormal behavior. More generally, we have seen that what may appear to be simple issues regarding the psychopathology of children and adolescents often is multifaceted. Despite the complexities, progress is being made in understanding the needs of the young. This relatively recent circumstance is illuminated in the next section.

Historical Influences

Humans have long speculated on behavioral dysfunction, but early interest focused primarily on adulthood. Some analyses suggest that this was partly because children were not considered very different from adults and because they had high death rates that hindered parental attachment and interest (Ariès, 1962). However, at least by the seventeenth century, children were viewed as having physical, psychological, and educational needs that required nourishment, nurturance, and instruction (Pollock, 2001). By the early eighteenth century, they were variously seen as either stained with original sin, as innately innocent and needy of protection, or as blank slates upon which experience would write. By the end of the nineteenth century, adolescence was conceived as a distinct period of transition between childhood and adulthood that entailed specific change, challenge, and opportunity (Demos & Demos, 1972). Differing and often conflicting views of childhood and adolescence continue to this day, undoubtedly influencing perspectives on problem behaviors and how abnormality should be treated.

Progress in the Nineteenth Century

The nineteenth century brought efforts to record the growth and abilities of the young, as well as progress in understanding disturbed development and behavior. By this time, two explanations of adult mental illness had long been recognized: demonology and somatogenesis. **Demonology** is the belief that behavior results from a person's being possessed or otherwise influenced by evil spirits or demons. Both adults and youth acting in unusual, bizarre, or problematic ways were often thought to be possessed by evil spirits. Closely associated with religion, demonology tended to cast suffering individuals as wicked or evil in themselves. Although demonology is still espoused in some cultures, it is largely rejected in scientifically advanced societies.

Somatogenesis is the belief that mental disorder can be attributed to bodily malfunction or imbalance. This perspective was advocated by Hippocrates, considered the father of medicine, when little was known about the workings of the human body.

Although the influence of somatogenesis has waxed and waned, it has remained a hardy hypothesis. By the late nineteenth century, a dominant assumption regarding psychopathology was that inheritance, and degeneration that began in childhood, led to irreversible disease, which could be transmitted to the next generation (Costello & Angold, 2001). Today, due to advances in the biological sciences, somatogenesis is a dominant view that garners much enthusiasm.

Efforts to identify and classify mental illness progressed by the late nineteenth century. Emil Kraepelin, in 1883, published a classification system in which he tried to establish a biological basis for mental disorder. Kraepelin recognized that particular symptoms tended to group together—to occur in **syndromes**—and therefore he thought they might have a common physical cause. He viewed each disorder as distinct from others in origin, symptoms, course, and outcome (Widiger & Clark, 2000). Eventually his work would be the basis of modern classification systems for mental disorders.

Although the study of youth generally lagged behind the study of adults, the first records of childhood disorders appeared early in the nineteenth century (Rie, 1971). By the end of the century, a few efforts had been made to classify children's disturbances, and causes had been proposed. Aggression, psychoses, hyperactivity, and "masturbatory insanity" in youth were all noted, with mental retardation receiving by far the most attention (Bernstein, 1996). An optimistic remedial approach to mental retardation began in Europe and spread to the United States—only to give way later to custodial institutionalization that would not be rectified for many decades.

Meanwhile, around the beginning of the twentieth century, several developments began to fundamentally alter how children and adolescents were viewed, ideas about how their development might go awry, and how they might be treated (Table 1.4). Professional and scientific activities were interwoven with progressive efforts regarding young people, females, and weak and ill members of society (Silk et al., 2000).

Sigmund Freud and Psychoanalytic Theory

One of these developments was the rise of **psychoanalytic theory** and its associated treatment, psychoanalysis. Sigmund Freud's theory was the first modern systematic attempt to understand mental disorders in psychological terms. The term **psychogenesis** refers to the belief that mental problems are caused by psychological variables. As a young neurologist, Freud became convinced, based on his study of adults, that unconscious childhood conflicts and crises were the keys to understanding behavior.

Freud proposed three structures of the mind whose goals and tasks made conflict inevitable: the id, ego, and superego. Thus, anxiety could be generated as a danger signal to the ego—the

Table 1.4 Some Early Historical Landmarks

1896	The first child clinic in the United States was established at the University of Pennsylvania by Lightner Witmer.
1905	Alfred Binet and Theophil Simon developed the first intelligence tests to identify children who could benefit from special educational efforts.
1905	Sigmund Freud's *Three Essays on the Theory of Sexuality* described a startlingly different view of childhood development.
1908	In *A Mind That Found Itself*, Clifford Beers recounted his mental breakdown and advocated an enlightened view of mental disorders, initiating the mental hygiene and child guidance movements.
1909	G. Stanley Hall invited Sigmund Freud to lecture on psychoanalysis at Clark University in Worcester, Massachusetts.
1909	William Healy and Grace Fernald established the Juvenile Psychopathic Institute in Chicago, which would become the model for the child guidance clinics.
1911	The Yale Clinic of Child Development was established for child development research under the guidance of Arnold Gesell.
1913	John B. Watson introduced behaviorism in his essay "Psychology as a Behaviorist Views It."
1917	William Healy and Augusta Bronner established the Judge Baker Guidance Center in Boston.
1922	The National Committee on Mental Hygiene and the Commonwealth Fund initiated a demonstration program of child guidance clinics.
1924	The American Orthopsychiatric Association was established.
1928–1929	Longitudinal studies of child development began at Berkeley and Fels Research Institute.
1935	Leo Kanner authored *Child Psychiatry*, the first child psychiatry text published in the United States.

problem-solving part of the mind—that id impulses unacceptable to the superego were seeking to gain consciousness. Freud proposed that to protect itself from awareness of unacceptable impulses, the ego creates defense mechanisms that distort or deny the impulses. Although defense mechanisms can be adaptive, they may also generate psychological symptoms.

The psychoanalytic perspective rests on a psychosexual stage theory of development. As the child develops, the focus of psychological energy passes from one bodily zone to the next, leading the child through five fixed stages—oral, anal, phallic, latency, and genital. The first three stages involve particular crises that are crucial for later development. During the oral stage, the child must be weaned; during the anal stage, the child must be toilet trained; during the phallic stage, the child must resolve the crisis brought on by the desire to possess the opposite-sex parent (the Oedipal conflict for the boy, the Electra conflict for the girl). For Freud, the basic personality was laid down during these first three stages—by age 6 or 7—and healthy development was hindered by failure to resolve the crisis during each stage. (See Accent: "Little Hans: A Classic Psychoanalytic Case.")

In *Three Essays on the Theory of Sexuality*, published in 1905, and in his 1909 lectures at Clark University in Worcester, Massachusetts, Freud introduced his radical ideas about the importance of childhood to adult development (Evans & Koelsch, 1985; Rie, 1971). His views were controversial from the start and are criticized on several grounds. For example, they rested primarily on impressions from case studies, involved large

Both Sigmund Freud and his daughter, Anna Freud, were influential in the development of the psychodynamic conceptualizations of childhood disorders. (Chronicle/Alamy Stock Photo)

inferences from what he observed to what he interpreted as existing, and were difficult to test. Freud's ideas nevertheless had enormous influence (Eisenberg, 2001).

Classical psychoanalytic theory has been modified by a number of workers. Some minimized sexual forces and emphasized social influences, among them Erik Erikson who proposed an influential theory of psychosocial development. Freud's daughter, Anna, elaborated his ideas and applied them to children (Fonagy & Target, 2003). By the 1930s, Freud's ideas provided a framework

ACCENT Little Hans: A Classic Psychoanalytic Case

Freud's well-known case of "Little Hans" illustrates both the concept of symptoms arising from defense mechanisms and the phallic stage of development. Although the analysis is widely rejected today, the case served as a model for the psychoanalytic interpretation of childhood phobias (Freud, 1953/1909).

Hans was very affectionate toward his mother and enjoyed "cuddling" with her. When Hans was almost 5, he returned from a daily walk with his nursemaid frightened, crying, and wanting to cuddle with his mother. The next day, when the mother herself took him for a walk, Hans expressed a fear of being bitten by a horse, and that evening he insisted on cuddling with his mother. He cried about having to go out the next day and expressed considerable fear concerning horses.

These worsening symptoms were interpreted by Freud as reflecting the child's conflict over the sexual impulses he had toward his mother and fear of castration by his father.

Hans's ego employed three defense mechanisms to keep the unacceptable impulses unconscious or distorted. First, Hans's wish to attack his father, the rival for his mother's affection, was *repressed* in memory. The next step was *projection* of the unacceptable impulses onto the father: Hans believed that his father wished to attack him, rather than the other way around. The final step was *displacement*, wherein the perceived dangerousness of the father was displaced onto a horse. According to Freud, the choice of the horse as a symbol of the father was due to numerous associations of horses with Hans's father. For example, the black muzzles and blinders of horses were viewed as symbolic of the father's mustache and eyeglasses. The fear Hans displaced onto horses permitted the child's ambivalent feelings toward his father to be resolved. He could now love his father. In addition, perceiving horses as the source of anxiety allowed Hans to avoid anxiety by simply avoiding horses (Kessler, 1988).

for conceptualizing child, adolescent, and adult behavior. They helped to establish psychiatry as a major discipline in the study and treatment of childhood disorders. In 1935, Leo Kanner authored the first child psychiatry text published in the United States.

Modification of traditional psychoanalysis has occurred over the decades (Fonagy & Target, 2003; Gabbard, 2000). Some basic concepts have been altered, newer forms of therapy have evolved, and research on infant and child development has been considered. Current psychoanalytic psychotherapy emphasizes affect, interpersonal relations, past experiences, and recurring themes in the client's functioning, with the goal of fostering psychological capacities and resources (Shedler, 2010). Although the overall influence of psychoanalytic theory has waned, among its many contributions are an emphasis on psychological causation, mental processes, unconscious motivation, anxiety and other emotions, infant and childhood experiences, and the child–parent relationship.

Behaviorism and Social Learning Theory

In 1913, John B. Watson's essay "Psychology as a Behaviorist Views It" introduced **behaviorism** in the United States. Unlike Freud, Watson placed little value on describing developmental stages and on early psychological conflicts. Instead, he drew on theories of learning to emphasize that most behavior, adaptive or maladaptive, could be explained by learning experiences. Widely quoted is the following statement, which reflected his belief in the power of experience to shape children's development:

John B. Watson was a highly influential figure in the application of the behavioral perspective. (Photo by George Rinhart/Corbis via Getty Images)

Give me a dozen healthy infants, well-formed, and my own specified world to bring them up in and I'll guarantee to take any one at random and train him to become any type of specialist I might select—doctor, lawyer, merchant, chief and yes, even beggar-man and thief, regardless of his talents, penchants, tendencies, abilities, vocations, and race of his ancestors.

Watson, 1930, p. 104

Among the models that Watson drew on was classical conditioning, described earlier by Pavlov, whose animal studies demonstrated learning that occurred through the pairing of new with old stimuli. In addition to placing a strong emphasis on learning and environment, Watson was committed to testing ideas by experimental methods, as were other behaviorists (Horowitz, 1992).

E. L. Thorndike (1905) made an early contribution to behaviorism by formulating the Law of Effect. Simply put, this law states that behavior is shaped by its consequences. If the consequence is satisfying, the behavior will be strengthened in the future; if the consequence is unpleasant, the behavior will be weakened. Thorndike considered the Law of Effect a fundamental principle of learning and teaching; later researchers substantiated his idea. Of special note is B. F. Skinner, who is widely known for his work on operant learning—that is, for investigating and writing on the application of behavioral consequences to the shaping of behavior (Skinner, 1948, 1953, 1968). Skinner can be viewed as Watson's descendant in his emphasis on learning, the environment, and experimental methods (Horowitz, 1992).

Behaviorism, like psychoanalytic theory, thrived in the United States during the first half of the twentieth century. Its impact on behavioral disorders came gradually as learning principles were applied to behavior. Albert Bandura (1977) expanded the learning approach through his study of how humans learn from others. His work on observational learning, which highlighted the social context and cognition, became a major influence (Grusec, 1992).

Learning is, of course, fundamental to human functioning, and its application to many facets of problem behavior is widespread (Jacob & Pelham, 2000). Learning approaches can improve the lives of young people experiencing emotional, cognitive, and social disorders. The explicit application of learning principles to the assessment and treatment of behavioral problems is referred to as behavior modification or behavior therapy. Approaches that emphasize the combination of learning principles and the social context and/or cognition are referred to as **social learning** or **cognitive–behavioral perspectives**.

Mental Hygiene and Child Guidance Movements

The twentieth century saw another important thread being woven in different settings. Despite early interest in adult psychopathology, much remained to be done, and treatment often consisted of custodial care. The **mental hygiene movement** aimed to increase understanding, improve treatment, and prevent disorder from occurring at all.

In 1908, Clifford Beers wrote an account, *A Mind That Found Itself*, of the insensitive and ineffective treatment he had received as a mental patient. Beers proposed reform, and he obtained support from renowned professionals, including Adolf Meyer. Offering a "commonsense" approach to studying the patient's environment and to counseling, Meyer viewed the individual as integrated across thought, emotion, and biological functioning (Cicchetti, 2006). He also advocated a new professional role—the psychiatric social worker (Achenbach, 1982). Beers's efforts led to the establishment of the National Committee for Mental Hygiene to study mental dysfunction, support treatment, and encourage prevention. In part because childhood experiences were viewed as influencing adult mental health, children became the focus of attention in the **child guidance movement** (Rie, 1971).

In 1896, at the University of Pennsylvania, Lightner Witmer had set up the first child psychology clinic in the United States (McReynolds, 1987; Ross, 1972). This clinic primarily assessed and treated children who had learning difficulties. Witmer also founded the journal *Psychological Clinic* and began a hospital school for long-term observation of children. He related psychology to education, sociology, and other disciplines.

An interdisciplinary approach was taken by psychiatrist William Healy and psychologist Grace Fernald in Chicago in 1909, when they founded the Juvenile Psychopathic Institute. The approach of this institution, which focused on delinquent children, became the model for child guidance (Santostefano, 1978). Freudian theory was integrated with educational, medical, and religious approaches in child guidance clinics (Costello & Angold, 2001). Healy and his wife, psychologist Augusta Bronner, opened the Judge Baker Guidance Center in Boston in 1917, and several other child clinics subsequently followed. The clinics began to treat cases of personality and emotional problems, and flourished in the 1920s and 1930s. Some of these clinics are still providing services to youth. In 1924, the child guidance movement became formally represented in the newly formed American Orthopsychiatric Association, which today includes a variety of professionals concerned about children and adolescents.

Scientific Study of Youth

It was also during the early twentieth century that systematic study of youth became widespread. In 1918, barely a handful of psychologists and psychiatrists were full-time scholars of childhood; by 1930 more than 600 such professionals could be counted (Smuts, 2006). Perhaps the most influential figure in this endeavor was G. Stanley Hall (Cravens, 1992). Among other things, he collected data on the problems of youth in order to understand mental disorder, crime, social disorder, and the like

G. Stanley Hall contributed to the early scientific study of youth and served as the first president of the American Psychological Association. (Corbis/Bettmann)

(White, 1992). Hall wrote extensively on youth, trained students who later became leaders in the field, and as president of Clark University invited Freud to lecture in 1909. He also helped establish the American Psychological Association, of which he was the first president.

At about the same time, an important event occurred in Europe: Alfred Binet and Theophil Simon were asked to design a test to identify children who were in need of special education (Siegler, 1992). Their 1905 Binet–Simon test became the basis for the development of intelligence tests, and it encouraged efforts to measure other psychological attributes.

Another outstanding figure was Arnold Gesell, who meticulously recorded the physical, motor, and social behavior of young children in his laboratory at Yale University (Thelen & Adolph, 1992). He charted developmental norms, created an extensive film archive of child behavior, and was a strong advocate for optimal rearing conditions for youth.

Around 1920, child study began to benefit from several longitudinal research projects that evaluated youth as they developed over many years. Research centers existed at the universities of California, Colorado, Michigan, Minnesota, Ohio, and Washington; other research centers were at Fels Research Institute, Columbia Teachers College, Johns Hopkins University, and the Iowa Child Welfare Station. Knowledge about normal development began to accumulate that eventually was applied to the study of child and adolescent disorders. (See Accent: "Mrs. Hillis: Improving Corn, Hogs, and Children in Iowa.") Some of these institutes still operate, albeit in different forms, while others closed their doors after several decades; all had tremendous influence on scientific study of the young (Smuts, 2006).

ACCENT Mrs. Hillis: Improving Corn, Hogs, and Children in Iowa

The establishment of the Iowa Child Welfare Research Station was sparked by Mrs. Cora Bussey Hillis, who demonstrated how advocacy for children can go hand in hand with advocacy for science (Cravens, 1993; Sears, 1975). Mrs. Hillis, a clubwoman married to an attorney, had considerable social and political influence. Life's tragedies, particularly the loss of three of her five children, directed and reinforced her passionate interest in child welfare.

Mrs. Hillis was aware of the respected agricultural station of the college in Ames, Iowa. In her mind's eye, she saw a comparable child welfare station that would be devoted to research, teaching, and dissemination of knowledge. The center would focus on problems in children's development and health. Researchers and professionals would be trained to work directly with children and parents. A body of knowledge would be constructed and disseminated to the public as rapidly as possible. Mrs. Hillis had faith that if research could "improve corn and hogs it could also improve children" (Sears, 1975, p. 17).

Working closely with Mrs. Hillis on the project was Carl Emil Seashore, a psychologist and admirer of G. Stanley Hall, who was dean of the graduate school at the State University of Iowa, in Iowa City. These two dominant, stubborn individuals did not always agree on the goals for the Station, and they faced many obstacles, including difficulty in obtaining Iowa legislative support (Cravens, 1993). In 1917—after years of advocacy with women's clubs, education groups, and politicians—Mrs. Hillis achieved her dream when the Station opened at the Iowa City campus. It was a site of prolific and leading research on children's physical, mental, and social development for almost 60 years.

Current Study and Practice

Today, the study and practice of abnormal child and adolescent psychology reflect the diverse historical theories, movements, and events that were set into motion in the early decades of the twentieth century. Some of the early approaches and occurrences are presently more significant than others and many new influences have come into play. Thus, both older and more recent assumptions, concepts, and knowledge give shape to a dynamic and multidisciplinary field.

The primary goals of the field are to identify, describe, and classify psychological disorder; to reveal the causes of disturbance; and to treat and prevent disorder. Highly valuable in meeting these aims is the developmental psychopathology perspective, which is discussed in Chapter 2 of this text. Here, we briefly note some premises that we view as central to the field, as well as issues relevant to working with young people and their families.

- With few, if any, exceptions, psychological problems stem from multiple causes that must be reckoned with if we are truly to understand, prevent, and ameliorate such problems.
- Normal and abnormal behavior go hand in hand, and we must study one in order to understand the other.
- The complexity of human behavior calls for systematic conceptualization, observation, data collection, and hypothesis testing.
- Continued efforts are needed to develop, verify, and disseminate treatment and prevention programs.
- Whether they are in treatment, prevention, or research settings, young people have a right to high-quality care that is sensitive to their developmental level, family role, and societal status.
- Advocacy for the well-being of youth is appropriate, particularly because of their relative lack of maturity and social influence.

Working with Youth and Their Families

Professionals interact with children, adolescents, and their families in many settings—research-based, medical, educational, and legal, to name a few. The focus of the present discussion is the clinical setting.

Interdisciplinary Efforts
More than one professional is often involved in clinical activities with a young person. Among these are psychologists, psychiatrists, social workers, and special education teachers.

The majority of psychologists working with child and adolescent problems have specialized in clinical psychology; others may have specialized in school, developmental, or educational psychology. They usually hold a doctoral degree (Ph.D. or Psy.D.). Psychology has sturdy roots in the laboratory and an interest in both normal and abnormal behavior. Psychologists thus receive training in research, and have direct contact in assessing and treating individuals. Psychiatrists, on the other hand, hold a doctorate in medicine (M.D.); they are physicians who have specialized in the treatment of mental disturbance. Although psychiatrists function in ways similar to those of psychologists, they are more likely to view psychopathology as a medical dysfunction and to employ medical treatments, especially pharmacological treatments.

Social workers generally hold a master's degree (M.A.) in social work. Like psychologists and psychiatrists, they may counsel and conduct therapy, but their special focus is more broadly working with the family and other social systems in which young people are enmeshed.

Special education teachers, who usually have obtained a master's degree, emphasize the importance of providing optimal educational experiences. They are able to plan and implement individualized educational programs, thus contributing to interventions for many disorders.

Young people with problems also come to the attention of nurses, physicians, teachers in regular classrooms, and workers in the legal system. Indeed, these professionals may be the first to hear about a problem. Substantial coordination among professionals and agencies is thus often necessary and valuable.

The Role of Parents and Families
Professional contact with youth typically involves some, often crucial, communication with families, usually with one or more parents. Families differ in their needs, including needs for support, basic education about psychopathology, and information about the availability of services. Depending on the presenting problem, the young person's developmental level, and various aspects of the clinical situation, parents and families may play various roles in actual intervention (Forgatch & Gewirtz, 2017; Kendall et al., 2017; Shirk, Stiles, & Leonard, 2018). As consultants, they have unique information about their child and can offer a valuable perspective of the situation. They may serve as collaborators with mental health professionals in carrying out treatment for their offspring—in effect, serving as cotherapists. When they are more directly involved in the difficulties, parents may participate as coclients with their child or adolescent.

Unsurprisingly, parents vary in the knowledge they have about mental health and in their motivation and ability to participate. They may seek consultation for many reasons: concern for their sons and daughters, the relief of their own worries, or fulfillment of school or court referrals. Some may have inappropriate goals or believe that the outcome of treatment depends only on the mental health worker. Despite these and other issues, however, many parents form a cooperative and constructive alliance with the mental health worker. Such differences likely affect the outcome of interventions (Hughes et al., 2018; Weisz & Kazdin, 2017).

Whatever the situation and setting, parental involvement is usually recommended, although the type of services to families depends on whether needs are best met by education, support, skills training, psychotherapy, and the like (Hoagwood, 2005). The optimal degree of parental involvement in child-centered therapy also must be evaluated. For example, parents who are themselves anxious may require additional coaching or other interventions so as to promote the child's coping and not inadvertently maintain their child's anxieties (Kendall et al., 2017).

Working with Young Clients

The relative immaturity, inexperience, and vulnerability of children and adolescents require special considerations. Knowledge about and attitudes toward mental health may be quite variable among children. Gender differences also may exist. In a Scottish adolescent sample, Williams and Pow (2007) found negative attitudes were more common in boys, who reported less knowledge of, and less desire for, information about mental health.

Young children may lack the ability to identify problems, and they most frequently enter treatment at the suggestion or coercion of adults. Adolescents often have more input into the decision to seek clinical services, but many are sensitive about autonomy, and this issue requires special attention (Cicchetti & Rogosch, 2002). Efforts by the mental health worker to create a **therapeutic alliance** with the client—that is, to forge a trusting personal bond and collaboration on treatment—may increase the chance of a successful outcome (Green, 2006; Weisz & Kazdin, 2017).

In working with youth, knowledge and mindfulness of normal development and developmental issues are essential for evaluating problems and planning intervention (Cicchetti & Toth, 2017; De Los Reyes, Augenstein, & Lipton, 2019; Shirk et al., 2018). We have seen that developmental norms serve as a guide to judging whether behaviors should be of concern. Moreover, optimal growth requires that young people master developmental tasks (e.g., school achievement, forming friendships), progress that often is hindered by psychological disturbance. For example, an anxious child with good cognitive skills can develop academic deficits stemming from fears of and withdrawal from classroom activities. Treatment planning may thus need to address not only the anxiety but also the academic problems. In addition, choice of treatment techniques must be developmentally sensitive. For young children, play or modeling techniques may be more appropriate than methods that rely on verbal interactions and more advanced cognitive skills. On the other hand, the development of more complex thinking during adolescence makes the success of cognitive approaches more likely.

Finally, youth have basic rights that must be recognized and protected. This is often a complex and challenging task (Belitz, 2018; Fried & Fisher, 2019). Ethical standards set by the American Psychological Association (2017) address issues regarding both clinical and research activities. The guidelines concerning intervention include the rights to informed consent to treatment, to participate in deciding the goals of treatment, and to receive confidential care. With young clients, developmental level enters into determining the exact ways in which these considerations play out. For example, the principle of **informed consent** requires that the client consent to participate with full understanding of the rationale for treatment, how treatment will proceed, and the potential benefits and risks. In addition to developmental considerations, there are legal issues regarding consent. Children cannot legally give consent and parental or guardian consent is required. This requirement can sometimes be waived, for instance, to allow a minor living apart from parents to consent to receive treatment.

When they treat young people, mental health workers often face a unique mix of ethical and legal issues. Consider the following situation of providing treatment for Aaron.

AARON Clinical, Legal, and Ethical Considerations

Mrs. Schulz, recently divorced, is seeking therapy for her 6-year-old son, Aaron. The father has shared custody and is responsible for treatment costs. He insists that Aaron is fine and does not need therapy. Mr. Schulz suggests that the problem lies with his ex-wife. The therapist, believing that Aaron requires treatment, is in a bind. Apart from legal issues of consent needed to see a child, she recognizes that proceeding without the father's consent might well lead to his undermining treatment. She must decide what is in the best interests of the child in the long run. She wishes that she had involved the father from the beginning.

Adapted from Schetky, 2000, p. 2944

The right to confidentiality also can present challenges for mental health workers. For example, the possibility that the client may harm others or him- or herself can demand a break in confidentiality or additional action. Confidentiality is also an issue when child abuse is suspected. Mental health professionals must report this circumstance, whether or not it threatens the therapeutic relationship. In such instances, professionals must understand and meet legal requirements and must inform families of the kinds of things that must be reported. Ethical and legal dilemmas regarding psychological disorders are not uncommon in working with clients, but they are of special concern when they involve young people who are limited in speaking for themselves.

Looking Back

Defining and Identifying Abnormality

- Behaviors are judged as abnormal on the basis of their being atypical, harmful, and inappropriate. Standards for behavior depend on developmental, cultural, gender, and situational norms.
- Adult attitudes, sensitivities, and tolerance play a role in identifying disturbances in young people, and what is considered as abnormal may change over time.

How Common Are Psychological Problems?

- The estimated prevalence of psychopathology can vary depending on several factors. Estimates are generally around 20% for U.S. children and adolescents. There has been recent increased attention to the prevalence of problems in infants and preschoolers.
- There is some suggestion that rates of disorders among youth are increasing, however findings are mixed.
- Providing high-quality services to all youth and families who are in need remains an ongoing challenge and effort.

How Are Developmental Level and Disorder Related?

- Some association exists between the onset or identification of specific disorders and age/developmental level, due in part to the timing of the child's emerging abilities and environmental demands placed on the child. Onset may occur gradually, however.

How Are Gender and Disorder Related?

- Gender differences occur in the rates of disorder, with boys exhibiting higher rates for many disorders. Other important gender differences exist, for example, in the timing, developmental change, and expression of problems.
- Although methodological factors, including bias inherent in clinical samples, probably account in part for reported gender differences, numerous biological and psychosocial factors underlie true gender differences.

Historical Influences

- Early interest in psychopathology focused on adults, with problems attributed to demonology or somatogenesis.
- The nineteenth century saw progress in identifying and classifying mental illness. Several childhood disorders were identified, and biological causation held sway.
- The early decades of the twentieth century brought new knowledge and understanding through psychoanalytic theory, behaviorism and social learning theory, the mental hygiene and child guidance movements, and increased scientific study of youth.

Current Study and Practice

- The current study and practice of the psychopathology of youth is shaped both by past and more recent efforts. Emphasis is given to multiple causation, the relation between normal and abnormal behavior, scientific approaches, effective treatment and prevention, and advocacy.
- Working with youth often involves multidisciplinary approaches. Parents, who may play various roles in intervention, are important to its success. Regarding young clients, consideration must be given to attitudes, developmental abilities and needs, and ethical and legal requirements.

Key Terms

developmental norms *3*

culture, cultural norms *3*

ethnicity *4*

race *4*

gender norms *4*

situational norms *4*

secular trends *6*

demonology *10*

somatogenesis *10*

syndromes *10*

psychoanalytic theory *10*

psychogenesis *10*

behaviorism *12*

social learning perspective *13*

cognitive–behavioral perspective *13*

mental hygiene and child guidance movements *13*

therapeutic alliance *16*

informed consent *16*

CHAPTER 2
The Developmental Psychopathology Perspective

Looking Forward

After reading this chapter, you should be able to discuss:

- Paradigms, theories, and models in the study of psychopathology
- The developmental psychopathology perspective
- The concept of development

- How causation is variously conceptualized
- Pathways of development
- Aspects of risk, vulnerability, and resilience
- Continuity and change in psychological disorders
- Examples of how normal and abnormal development go hand in hand

Hardly a day passes without each of us wondering about many aspects of development and behavior. We want to know how our father manages to be consistently helpful, why our friends' personalities differ so much, what led a classmate to suddenly drop out of school, and whether a talented actor will be able to stop abusing drugs. Generally, the more usual the behavior or situation, the fewer questions we have, and the more easily answered they seem. It is the unexpected that is more likely to confound us—especially when a behavior appears to be problematic or harmful in some way.

The ability to explain abnormality is of critical interest to those who investigate psychopathology and those who treat it. Although it is possible to treat and prevent disturbances without fully understanding them, increased knowledge significantly aids these efforts. Behavioral scientists also are committed to more generally exploring an array of fundamental questions about human functioning. In this chapter, we present a framework for conceptualizing aspects of psychological disturbances of young people.

ELIZABETH No Obvious Explanation

Elizabeth Fellows was referred to a therapist by her physician, who outlined concerns about a possible eating disorder. Elizabeth's mother, who had taken her to the physician, was worried. Not only had she heard Elizabeth vomiting in the bathroom on three occasions, but Elizabeth also had dropped all of her friends and stayed home in her bedroom. Mrs. Fellows reported that until approximately six months ago, Elizabeth had seemed fairly normal to her. Since then, Elizabeth had spent more and more time by herself, dropping even Katie,

with whom she had been friends since kindergarten. Elizabeth had been a straight A student; now she was earning Bs and Cs. Mrs. Fellows acknowledged that 10th grade had been a difficult one, but she felt that Elizabeth's personality was changing. Mrs. Fellows was unable to remember any single event that had occurred in the past six months that might explain her daughter's behavior.

Adapted from Morgan, 1999, p. 46

Perspectives, Theories, Models

Much of today's understanding of both normal and abnormal behavior comes from applying the assumptions and methods of science. The writings of Thomas Kuhn (1962) and others have made us aware that science is not a completely objective endeavor. Like all of us, scientists must think about and deal with a complex world. To study and understand phenomena, scientists adopt a perspective—a view, an approach, or cognitive set. When investigators share a perspective, it may be termed a **paradigm**. Paradigms typically include assumptions and concepts, as well as ways to evaluate these.

There are several benefits to adopting a particular view. A perspective helps make sense of the puzzling and complex universe. It guides the kinds of questions we ask, what we select for investigation, what we decide to observe and how we observe it, and how we interpret and make sense of the information we collect. A perspective influences how a problem is approached, investigated, and interpreted.

There are also disadvantages in taking a perspective—mostly related to the fact that acting on a certain view sets some limitations. When we ask certain questions, we may preclude others. When we observe some things, we do not examine others. When we choose particular methods and instruments to detect certain phenomena, we undoubtedly miss other phenomena. We limit the ways in which we might interpret and think about new information. Taking a perspective is a trade-off—albeit one that, on balance, is more beneficial than detrimental.

Theories

Closely related to the process of taking a perspective—and sharing its benefits and limitations—is the process of theory construction. Simply put, a **theory** is a formal, integrated set of principles or propositions that explains phenomena. Although the term "theories" may be used casually to mean a hunch or educated guess, scientific theories are supported by accepted evidence that often has accumulated gradually. Moreover, theories provide formal propositions that can be tested, thereby advancing knowledge. Because they provide concepts and formal propositions that can be tested, theories are highly valued by researchers and clinicians.

As we saw in Chapter 1, biological, psychoanalytic, and behavior/social learning explanations of psychopathology were rooted in concepts developed in the early twentieth century. Currently, numerous theories that vary in scope offer explanations of child and adolescent problems. They focus on emotion, self-regulation, brain functioning, higher-level cognition, family interaction, and many other facets of functioning.

Models

In addition to having a theory to guide the study of psychopathology, it is often helpful to employ a model—a representation or description—of the phenomenon of study. Of particular current interest are models that encourage us to simultaneously consider the numerous factors that influence the development of psychopathology.

At the heart of **interactional models** is the assumption that these influences are not likely to act independently, but rather to interrelate to produce an outcome. One such approach, the **vulnerability-stress model**, conceptualizes the multiple causes of psychopathology as the working together of a vulnerability factor(s) and a stress factor(s). In this model, both vulnerability (also referred to as diathesis) and stress are necessary. They may be biological, psychological, or social factors—although vulnerability often has been considered as biological and stress as environmental. For example, a child's presumed biological susceptibility for anxiety may interact with the stress of parental divorce, resulting in child problems. Interactional models have contributed much to our understanding of psychopathology. It is recognized that the relationships among influences is often not unidirectional.

Transactional models describe this reciprocal relationship between influences. For example, a highly stressed mother harshly tells her young son that he cannot have cookies from the supermarket shelf; the defiant young son screams and has a tantrum; the mother becomes angry and frustrated and threatens the child with physical punishment. Transactional models are widely employed in the study of both normal and abnormal development. The basic assumption is that development is the result of ongoing, reciprocal transactions between the individual and the environmental context. The individual is viewed as an active agent who brings a history of past experience that has shaped her or his current functioning.

Transactional models fall into the domain of **systems models** in that they incorporate several levels, or systems, of functioning in which development is viewed as occurring over time as the systems interact or enter into ongoing transactions with each other. For example, a biopsychosocial model may integrate brain and genetic functioning, behavior, and several aspects of the social environment. In such a model, change at one level/system of functioning is assumed to influence other levels/systems. Another example of a systems model is the ecological model, which places the individual within a network of environmental influences and assumes transactions between the person and these influences, as well as among the several levels of the environment. Throughout this text, we have opportunity to see how various models facilitate the study of problem behavior.

The Developmental Psychopathology Perspective: An Overview

Since the 1970s, the **developmental psychopathology perspective** that we call upon in this text has rapidly become influential in the study of psychological disorders of youth. This perspective integrates the understanding and study of normal developmental processes with those of child and adolescent psychopathology (Hayden & Durbin, 2019; Hinshaw, 2017). It is interested in the origins and developmental course of disordered behavior, as well as individual adaptation and competence. Central to the approach was the coming together of developmental psychology and clinical child/adolescent psychology and psychiatry (Cicchetti, 1984, 1989). Developmental psychology has traditionally taken normal development as its subject matter; it is especially focused on understanding universal principles of how people grow and change during their lifetime. The primary interest of clinical psychology and psychiatry is in identifying the symptoms of psychological disorders, understanding the causes of disorders, and alleviating the difficulties. In addition to these disciplines, contributions to developmental psychopathology come from a variety of other areas, including the biological sciences, sociology, and philosophy (Hinshaw, 2017).

Developmental psychopathology is a systems framework for understanding disordered behavior in relation to normal development. Rather than imposing specific theoretical explanations, it is a way of combining various theories or approaches around a core of developmental knowledge, issues, and questions (Achenbach, 1990). Individuals working within a developmental psychopathology framework may be informed by cognitive, behavioral, psychodynamic, family, genetic, or other theories. In any case, however, several assumptions are central to the developmental psychopathology perspective. We turn to these after first examining the concept of development.

Concept of Development

The concept of **development** can seem deceptively simple. Most people would probably offer growth as a synonym, with growth meaning not only bigger but also better. And many would recognize that development requires time. However, any definition that stops here would fall far short of a full description of development.

Although many different depictions and explanations have been proposed, there is some consensus among theorists on the essence of development (e.g., Cicchetti & Toth, 2009; Cummings, Davies, & Campbell, 2000; Sroufe, 2009).

- Development refers to change over the lifespan that results from ongoing transactions of an individual with biological, psychological, and sociocultural variables, which themselves are changing.
- Although quantitative change in development is noteworthy—for example, an increase in the number of a child's social interactions—qualitative change is more salient—for example, a change in the features or qualities of social interactions.
- Early development of the biological, motor, physical, cognitive, emotional, and social systems follows a general course. Within each system, structures and functions become more finely differentiated and also integrated. Integration occurs across systems as well, enhancing organization and complexity.
- Development proceeds in a coherent pattern, so that for each person, current functioning is connected both to past and future functioning. Development thus can be thought of as proceeding along pathways or trajectories of more or less complexity. In youth, developmental pathways are relatively open and flexible, but there is some narrowing of possibilities over time.
- Over the lifespan, developmental change may produce higher modes of functioning and the attainment of goals, but change is not inevitably positive. Physical aging in adulthood brings decrements in functioning, and maladaptive behavior can develop at any time during the lifespan.

With the concept of development serving as a backdrop, we now turn to four overlapping issues that are central to the developmental psychopathology approach: the search for causal factors and processes; pathways of development; risk and resilience; and continuity of problems over time.

Searching for Causal Factors and Processes

There is a long history of trying to explain the causes, or etiology, of abnormal development in relatively simple ways. An example is the basic **medical model**. This model considers disorders to be discrete entities—things, if you will—that result from specific and limited biological causes within the individual and tend to ignore context. This explanatory approach was reinforced in the early 1900s by the realization that the microorganism that caused syphilis sometimes affected the brain, thereby causing mental disturbance. Now we realize that a single cause seldom, if ever, accounts for most psychological or behavioral outcomes. (In fact, this is also true for many physical illnesses; for example, biological, psychological, and social factors appear to contribute to cardiac disease.) Thus, as is commonly acknowledged, the understanding of outcome rests on identifying multiple variables concerning both the developing person and contextual factors.

A full account of causation requires, however, more than identification of contributory factors. Developmental psychopathologists seek to understand how causal factors work together and what the underlying processes or mechanisms might be.

In conceptualizing causation, it is useful to distinguish between direct and indirect causes. When a **direct effect** operates, variable X leads straight to the outcome. An **indirect effect** is operating when variable X influences one or more other variables that, in turn, lead to the outcome. Establishing indirect effects is usually more difficult as the path of influences may be complex. Consider, for example, the reported association between parental alcohol use and children's adjustment problems. Might one or more variables underlie this link? Keller, Cummings, and Davies (2005) were interested in the possible role of marital conflict and ineffective parenting. The results of their study suggested that problem drinking led to marital conflict that, through parenting difficulties, led to child problems. The findings supported the hypothesis that, given parental alcohol problems, marital conflict and ineffective parenting are mediators of child difficulties. The term **mediator** refers to a factor or variable that explains or brings about an outcome, more specifically, by indirect means. The identification of mediators is crucial to understanding causal processes.

So also is the identification of moderators. A **moderator** is a variable that influences the direction or the strength of the relationship between an independent (or predictor) variable and a dependent (or criterion) variable. For example, suppose that boys and girls are exposed to the same treatment but that the outcome is more positive for boys than for girls. Here, it appears that gender moderates the relationship between treatment and outcome. Or to take another example, if cultural context moderates the influence of an experience, outcome may differ in some way for children of different cultural backgrounds. (See Accent: "A Possible Moderating Influence of Culture.")

In examining causation, it is also useful to make a distinction among necessary, sufficient, and contributing causes. A **necessary cause** must be present in order for the disorder to occur. A **sufficient cause** can, in and of itself, be responsible for the disorder. In Down syndrome, which is characterized by intellectual disability, known genetic anomalies are both necessary (they must be present) and sufficient (other factors are not required). By contrast, in the debilitating disorder of schizophrenia, brain dysfunction is thought to be necessary but perhaps not sufficient. Brain abnormality is implicated in schizophrenia, but other factors must be present in order for the condition to arise. It is also important to recognize that **contributing causes** can be operating; these are not necessary or sufficient. In some disorders, several factors may contribute by adding or multiplying their effects to reach a threshold to produce the problem.

ACCENT A Possible Moderating Influence of Culture

Parents in many countries report or endorse the use of mild physical discipline—such as spanking, slapping, grabbing, or restraining—in certain situations, although differences exist in the degree to which they use or accept such practices (Deater-Deckard, Dodge, & Sorbring, 2005; Lansford et al., 2004, 2005). In general, such punishment is correlated with aggression or acting out in childhood and adolescence. Evidence exists, however, that the link between physical punishment and acting out may be moderated by the cultural context.

Lansford and her colleagues (2005) hypothesized that acting-out behavior would be reduced in cultures in which physical discipline was viewed as more normative. They assessed cultural normativeness by parent and child perceptions of physical discipline. Their hypothesis was supported in the study of six different countries (Thailand, China, Philippines, India, Kenya, and Italy). Consonant with this finding, some research in the United States indicates that physical punishment is more normative in

African American than European American families, and also that the link between physical discipline and child aggression/acting out may be weaker in African American families.

These moderating effects can be variously interpreted. For example, if parental behavior is viewed as normative, the punished child may be less likely to feel rejected, an outcome generally related to child adjustment. Or the child may be more likely to perceive physical punishment as a reflection of parental concern for their offspring. Indeed, there is evidence that firm parenting is seen as less intrusive in African American families (Anderson & Mayes, 2010). Whatever underlies the moderating effect, Lansford and colleagues warn that their findings should not be taken as encouraging physical punishment, which was generally associated with child aggression and also with other maladjustment. The results do suggest, however, the value of examining the possible moderating role of cultural context.

The search for causation, as we will see in Chapter 4, may employ various research strategies and designs. No matter what the approach, a strength of the developmental psychopathology perspective is its focus on understanding the mix of causal processes. We now further examine concepts and assumptions that contribute to this quest.

Pathways of Development

The developmental psychopathology perspective assumes that abnormal behavior does not appear out of the blue. Rather, it emerges gradually as the child and environmental influences transact (Cummings, Davies, & Campbell, 2000; Hayden & Durbin, 2019). Development is characterized as involving progressive adaptations or maladaptations to changing circumstances. It can be viewed

as a pathway over time that is forged by cascades of changing circumstances and reactions. Thus, development is not cast in stone; rather, it is open or probabilistic. New situations, or new reactions to ongoing circumstances, can bring about redirection.

One way to better understand psychopathology is to describe and understand pathways of adaptation and maladaptation. For example, we can examine research efforts that focused on general developmental trajectories across the adolescent years (Compas, Hinden, & Gerhardt, 1995). Figure 2.1 presents the five trajectories and briefly describes each one. Path 1 is characterized by stable good adaptation. This pathway is associated with relatively low exposure to negative circumstances, and the adolescents show positive self-worth and few problems. Path 2 indicates stable maladaptation, whereby youth who already are having problems experience adversities and inadequate resources to relieve them. The remaining paths involve significant change

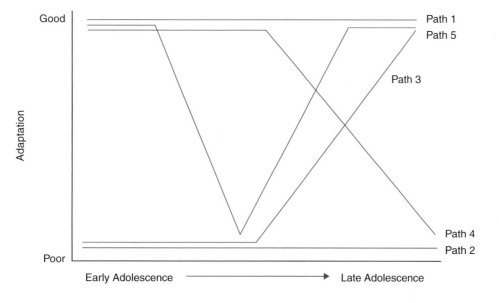

Path 1 Stable Adaptation	Few environmental adversities; few behavior problems; good self-worth.
Path 2 Stable Maladaptation	Chronic environmental adversities. Example: aggressive, antisocial behavior maintained.
Path 3 Reversal of Maladaptation	Important life change creates new opportunity. Example: military career affords opportunity.
Path 4 Decline of Adaptation	Environmental or biological shifts bring adversity. Example: family divorce contributes to maladaptation.
Path 5 Temporal Maladaptation	Can reflect transient experimental risk taking. Example: use of illegal drugs.

Figure 2.1 Five developmental pathways during adolescence. (Adapted from Compas, Hinden, & Gerhardt, 1995. Copyright 1995 by *Annual Reviews*; reprinted with permission)

Mick Stevens/Cartoon Collections

in developmental direction during adolescence. Path 3 shows maladaptation that turns into positive outcome, due at least in some cases to environmental opportunity. Path 4 indicates an initial adaptation that, due to adversities, ends with decline. Path 5 depicts a temporary decline and a bouncing back to adaptive behavior, as might occur, for example, in experimental short-term drug use. An obvious aspect of these trajectories is that adaptation level at any given time does not necessarily predict later functioning.

Substantial progress is being made in mapping developmental trajectories with regard to specific problems or disorders, as we will see in later chapters. Both stable and changing pathways are commonly observed, even for a single problem. For example, childhood aggression appears stable into adulthood for some individuals but ceases with the transition into adolescence for others (Hinshaw, 2017).

Equifinality and Multifinality

The transactional and probabilistic nature of development is recognized in the principles of equifinality and multifinality. A simplified illustration of these concepts is provided in Figure 2.2. **Equifinality** refers to the fact that diverse factors can be associated with the same outcome. For example, some children may inherit a trait that puts them at risk, others may be exposed to harsh and ineffective discipline, while others may affiliate with a deviant peer group. Each of these influences sets them on a pathway to the development of antisocial behavior. In other words, children can have different experiences, or follow different pathways, and yet develop the same problems.

The second principle, **multifinality**, refers to the fact that an experience may function differently depending on a host of other influences that may lead to different outcomes. For example, children may grow up in a home with a depressed parent. Some of these children will themselves later meet the criteria for a diagnosis of depression, others may develop anxiety disorders, and others may exhibit aggressive and antisocial behaviors. Simply put, children can have similar experiences and yet end up with different problems or no difficulties at all.

This illustration in Figure 2.2 is simplified in that the depiction of equifinality presents the influences as singular and separate, whereas a more accurate depiction is one of different combinations of multiple influences, interacting with each other in a variety of ways, yielding different development pathways to a similar outcome. Similarly, with regard to multifinality, rather than having a single problem, young people who experience a particular adverse influence are likely to display differing combinations of problems from different domains or meet the diagnostic criteria for a variety of disorders.

The principles of equifinality and multifinality are a reflection of a common theme in the development of behavior: enormous

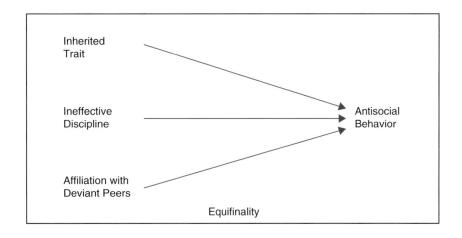

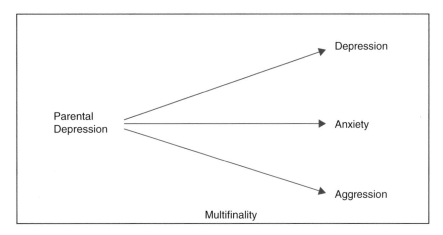

Figure 2.2 Examples of how both equifinality and multifinality operate in development.

complexity usually must be addressed in terms of what is likely to happen along life's pathways. In this regard, the concepts of risk and resilience contribute further to understanding the development of psychological problems.

Risk, Vulnerability, and Resilience

Risk and Vulnerability

Risks are variables that precede and increase the chance of psychological impairments. Substantial investigation points to several important aspects of risk (Compas, Gruhn, & Bettis, 2017; Liaw & Brooks-Gunn, 1994; Pungello et al., 2010; Shanahan et al., 2008).

- Although a single risk certainly can have an impact, multiple risks are particularly harmful.

- Risks tend to cluster; for instance, children at risk due to low parental education are more likely to reside in disadvantaged communities.
- The effects of many risk factors appear nonspecific, a finding reflected in the principle of multifinality. This is not always the case, however, and further research is needed.
- Risk factors may be different for the onset of a disorder than for the persistence of the disorder.
- A risk may increase the likelihood of future risks by increasing the child's susceptibility for problems or adversely affecting the environmental context.
- The intensity, duration, and timing of a risk can make a difference.

A central aim of risk research is to understand how risk is translated into psychopathology (Price & Zwolinski, 2010; Schroeder, Slopen, & Mittal, 2020). Initially, it is necessary to identify risk factors, and numerous risks have been recognized

ACCENT The Timing of Risky Experiences

An important theoretical and practical concern in developmental psychopathology is to better understand when and how experiences have different effects depending on the age or developmental level of the individual.

The timing of an event can make a difference for several reasons (Rutter, 1989, 2006). Among these, the effects of experience on the nervous system may be different depending on the developmental level of the nervous and other biological systems. Similarly, the effect of experience can vary with age-related psychological functioning, for example, the child's ability to think adaptively about an adverse event. Whether an experience is normative or nonnormative may also matter. Normative events happen to most people at more or less predictable time (e.g., puberty between ages 11 and 14) whereas nonnormative events occur only to certain persons at atypical times (e.g., very early or late onset of puberty). Nonnormative events may be problematic because they put the individual "out of sync" with, for example, social expectations and supports.

Historically, there has been a strong interest in the proposition that early influences may be especially powerful.

O'Connor and Parfitt (2009) describe three developmental models that illustrate how early adverse experience has been conceptualized. The *sensitive period* model predicts that exposure to risk during a specific window of time may have permanent effects, whereas the same exposure at a different time has little or no influence. Research has shown that sensitive periods operate in normal development in animals. However, the applicability of this model, particularly the notion of permanent effects, to human development may be limited. The *developmental programming* model proposes that some features of the individual can be set, or programmed, by early environmental occurrences, and that these features persist into the future. For example, early trauma may program a child's biological reactivity to stressful events, which is preserved over time. The *life-course model* proposes that early experience can have long-term consequences but only when the experience is maintained, reinforced, or accentuated in some way. A major idea here is that early risk can lead to poor adaptation, which increases the probability of subsequent maladaptation.

as operating across cultures. They are associated with biological, cognitive, psychosocial, and other domains (Table 2.1). Some of these factors appear to reside in the youth's tendency to respond maladaptively to life circumstances, and the term **vulnerability** often is applied to this subset of risk factors. Vulnerability may be inborn (e.g., genetic conditions) or acquired (e.g., learned ways of thinking), and although somewhat enduring can be modified.

Given the complexities of development, it is appropriate to view risk within a transactional model that includes both environmental circumstances and the individual. An example of this approach is shown in Figure 2.3. This conceptual model relates risky life experiences (stressors) to psychopathology (Grant et al., 2003). The risky experiences are major or minor events that can be acute, occurring suddenly and perhaps disastrously (e.g., a damaging accident), or they can be chronic, persisting over time (e.g., poverty). The model proposes that these experiences produce a variety of processes in the individual—biological, psychological, and social—that mediate, or lead to, psychopathology. In addition, the relationship between stressors and child mediators can be moderated by attributes of the child or the environment. For example, the child's age, gender, or sensitivity to the environment can influence the strength of this relationship. Finally, this model recognizes two-way influences

between the components, thereby reflecting the dynamic processes of development.

Resilience

The topic of resilience has been a central component of a developmental psychopathology perspective from the outset of this approach. Over time, the study of resilience has changed and definitions have become more multilevel and dynamic (Masten & Cicchetti, 2016). In a broad sense, **resilience** is defined by relatively positive outcome in the face of significantly adverse or traumatic experiences. Resilience speaks to differences in response to risk, in the ability to resist or overcome life's adversities (Masten & Cicchetti, 2016; Werner, 1995).

Resilience can be manifested as the absence of psychopathology, a low level of symptoms, or in terms of competence regarding meeting common developmental tasks or cultural age-expectations despite unfavorable life circumstances. Table 2.2 provides examples of these common developmental tasks.

As with research on risk, investigation of resilience has evolved over time (Masten & Cicchetti, 2016). The initial interest in resilience led to descriptions of why some individuals succumb to adversities while others rise above threat. As research

Table 2.1 Examples of Developmental Risk Factors

Hereditary influence; gene abnormalities
Prenatal or birth complications
Below average intelligence or learning difficulty
Psychological/social: difficult temperament, poor regulation of emotion and behavior, social incompetence, peer rejection
Poor parenting and family abuse, neglect, disorganization, conflict, psychopathology, stress
Poverty
Disorganized neighborhood
Racial, ethnic, or gender injustice
Nonnormative stressful events such as early death of a parent, natural catastrophes, armed conflict, or war

Source: Based in part on Coie et al., 1993.

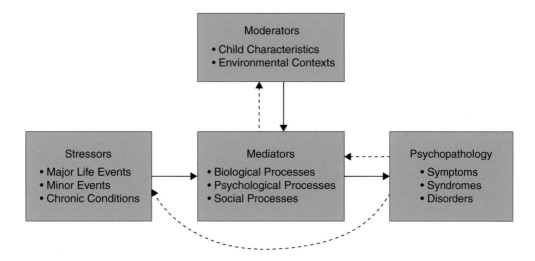

Figure 2.3 A model of the relation between adversities (stressors) and psychopathology. (Adapted from Grant et al., 2003)

Table 2.2 Examples of Developmental Tasks

Developmental Period	Task
Infancy	Forming attachment to caregivers
	Learning to communicate by gesture
	and language
Toddler/Preschool	Learning family's language
	Self-control and compliance
	Playing with other children
Early school years	Adjusting to school
	Learning to read and write
	Getting along with peers
Adolescence	Adjusting to physical maturation
	Forming cohesive sense of self
	Forming close friendships/relationships
	Following rules and laws

Source: Adapted from Table 1.1 in Masten, 2015.

ANN AND AMY The "Ordinary Magic" of Resilience

Ann and Amy were from different family circumstances, and at 6 years of age their functioning was dissimilar. Ann was from an affluent family background, with parents who had an intact marriage and optimally managed both child-rearing and emotional relations with Ann. Amy, on the other hand, was from more difficult circumstances, with a single-parent father who had experienced an acrimonious divorce. During assessment at age 6, Ann was well-adjusted, whereas Amy evidenced problems in the clinical range. However, over the next several years, Amy was able to take advantage of her social and athletic skills to develop good social relations with classmates, and her parents (ex-spouses) learned ways to interact much more amicably as they faced custody-related decisions and problems. For example, Amy's noncustodial mother gradually came to contribute faithfully to child support, even though she had remarried and had another child. An assessment conducted when both Ann and Amy were 10 years of age indicated that Ann, whose family circumstances had continued to be stable, supportive, and positive, still scored as well-adjusted, but Amy now also scored as well-adjusted and above average in social competence.

Adapted from Cummings et al., 2000, p. 40

evolved, conceptualizations shifted from viewing resilience as a fixed trait of the individual to viewing resilience as a multifaceted developmental process. An early groundbreaking study was conducted with children born in 1955 on the Hawaiian island of Kauai (Werner & Smith, 1982, 2001). A high-risk group was identified on the basis of early exposure to at least four risk factors. In late adolescence, most of the high-risk children had developed behavioral and/or learning problems, but one-third of the youth were successfully negotiating life. The resilience of these youth originated from three broad categories: personal attributes, family characteristics, and support from outside the family. This trio of categories has been found in many investigations, and can be thought of as sources of protective factors—that is, factors that counter risk factors operating in the situation. The sources of resilience are well-recognized factors that are beneficial to most children, a finding that Masten (2015) has referred to as the "ordinary magic" of resilience.

Resilience has implicated a wide range of influences that contribute to variations in outcomes among children exposed to adversities. These are referred to as **promotive** or **protective factors**. Table 2.3 provides examples of the influences that contribute to the development of resilience. Some of these are attributes of the individual—for example, skills in problem solving and self-regulation. Such attributes focus on resilience viewed as residing within the individual; however, other influences can derive from the family, community, or larger societal factors.

Resilience can be regarded as the opposite of vulnerability (Ingram & Price, 2010). Figure 2.4 depicts resilience and vulnerability at opposite ends of a vulnerability continuum that interacts with varying levels of (environmental) stress. At the resilience end of the continuum, more stress is required for disorder to occur. With vulnerability, even low stress can result in mild disorder, and severity of disorder increases as stress level rises.

Research on resilience has gone beyond identifying correlates or protective factors to searching for underlying processes. Much attention is currently being given to biological processes. Central to this work is the study of coping with stress (Feder, Nestler, & Charney, 2009; Perry, 2017). Individual genetic composition plays a role in a person's response to stress, and the complex interplay of genes and exposure to stress helps shape biological processes and brain development thought to be relevant to resilience (Elbau, Cruceanu, & Binder, 2019).

Resilience is an ongoing, complex process (Masten & Cicchetti, 2016). Whether any particular variable protects an at-risk child may depend on the situation. Or resilience may occur in some

Table 2.3 Example of Influences Contributing to Resilience in Young People

Problem-solving skills
Skills in self-regulation
Positive views of self
Achievement motivation
Perceived self-efficacy and control
Active coping strategies
Close, caring family relationships
Supportive relationships with adults in the community
Friends or romantic partners
Spirituality, finding meaning in life

Sources: Adapted from Cicchetti, 2010b; and Sapienza & Masten, 2011.

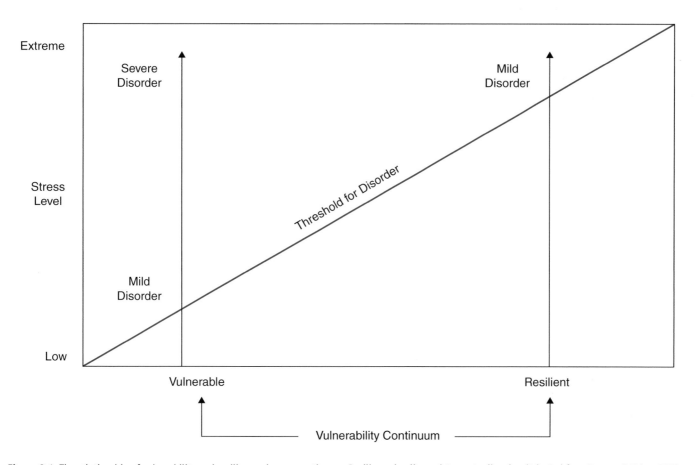

Figure 2.4 The relationship of vulnerability and resilience along a continuum. Resilience implies resistance to disorder. (Adapted from Ingram & Price, 2010. Copyright 2010 by Guilford Press; reprinted with permission)

risk situations (e.g., family conflict) and not others (e.g., peer pressure). Further, an at-risk youth may show positive outcome in some domains of functioning (e.g., emotional) and not others (e.g., academic achievement). In addition, for any individual, resilience may be modified over time with changing circumstances that alter strengths and vulnerabilities. Indeed, increased interest exists in how positive functioning is maintained over time, cascades from one functional domain to another (e.g., from early academic competence to later social competence), or spreads from one level to another (e.g., from the biological to psychosocial or vice versa). Advances in the understanding of resilience are immensely important to the prevention of psychopathology and to optimizing the development of youth.

Continuity of Disorder

Inherent in the developmental psychopathology perspective is an interest in understanding continuity and change over time.

Development is defined in terms of change, and humans certainly are malleable. But there are limits to malleability and we can expect to see both change and continuity in an individual. When a young handsome man reaches old age, he may still be attractive compared to his peers, but his face will be both different from and similar to its earlier appearance. We can generally expect the same for psychological functioning.

When the issue of continuity or change is applied to the study of psychological disorders, a basic question is, "Does a difficulty at an earlier time in life carry over to later life?" This question is important for understanding the development of problems, and it has implications for treatment and prevention. Treatment is desirable for any disturbance that causes discomfort and maladaptation, but problems that persist warrant increased concern. Moreover, knowing that early problems predict later disturbance puts high priority on efforts to intervene early in the process.

What is known about the continuity of problems or disorders? Given the transactional quality of development, it is unsurprising that the answer is not simple and is still being investigated. Considering the wide array of problems, both continuity and discontinuity have been observed and we cannot assume that the young merely grow out of psychopathology. Some disorders, such as the sleep and eating problems of very young children, are likely to cease. Among those that tend to persist are intellectual deficiencies related to genetic abnormalities, autism, and schizophrenia. The picture is especially complex for still other problems. Antisocial behavior often carries over; for example, children who rank high in aggression compared to their peers maintain this high ranking in adolescence (Hinshaw, 2017). But this does not hold for all individuals, and some may no longer display aggression.

The concepts of heterotypic and homotypic continuity are a central part of conceptualizing the issue of continuity over time. Investigators have recognized that the expression of a problem may change in form with development; that is, **heterotypic continuity** may occur. Hyperactivity in an 8-year-old that is manifest by restless, fidgety movement may present itself by inability to relax during the teen years and adulthood. As well, we would expect that depression in early childhood would be expressed somewhat differently from depression in adolescence or adulthood. **Homotypic continuity** also may be observed, however; that is, how a problem is expressed may be relatively stable over time.

In general, continuity of problems can be anticipated to vary with the length of time being examined, the kinds of psychopathology or symptoms, and other variables. A host of questions can be asked about which variables predict continuity of problems. Do symptoms that are severe rather than mild forecast continuity? Is continuity more likely when a child simultaneously displays more than one disorder? Is gender related to continuity and, if so, with regard to all or only some disorders? Many of these questions are being addressed by researchers, which will be discussed later in this text.

Also under investigation are the processes responsible for carrying psychopathology forward in time. Several such processes that have been demonstrated or proposed are briefly described below. It is important, however, to remember that individual processes do not operate in isolation, but likely interrelate in a complex manner that evolves over the course of development (Hinshaw, 2017; Rutter, 2006; Sroufe, Coffino, & Carlson, 2010). Continuity may be sustained by environmental constancy—as when poor parental care or poor schooling persists and continues to negatively affect development. Genetic predisposition may be involved, and early problems or experiences can affect the development of the brain and other biological systems in ways that make continuity likely. Another process concerns the construction of mental representations or views of the social environment. Based on their experiences, people set up expectations and the

like and tend to act in accordance with such representations, thus bringing continuity to their behavior. In addition, continuity can result from a chain of negative circumstances or interactional behavior patterns. For example, continuity may stem from children's being channeled into environments that perpetuate a maladaptive style—as when an ill-tempered boy limits opportunity by dropping out of school, thereby creating frustrating situations, to which he responds with more irritability, lack of control, and the like (Caspi, Elder, & Bem, 1987).

We should note that our present discussion of continuity and change focuses on whether a disorder, or symptoms of a disorder, in youth is observed at a later time in the person's life. A related question is whether early disorder predicts other kinds of problems later in life (Copeland et al., 2009). This important issue is addressed in subsequent chapters that examine specific disorders.

Normal Development, Problematic Outcomes

So far in this chapter, we have discussed core aspects of the developmental psychopathology perspective. We now briefly examine select areas of development in order to illustrate how normal developmental processes and less-than-optimal outcomes go hand in hand. These areas are attachment, temperament, emotion, and social cognitive processing. These examples also describe development as involving the overlap and interdependence of the biological, social, emotional, and cognitive domains of functioning.

Attachment

From infancy onward, virtually all children and their caregivers seem biologically prepared to interact in ways that foster their relationship. Most parents are remarkably sensitive in understanding and responding to their babies' signals and needs. Infants, in turn, are sensitive to parental emotional–social signals. Such synchronous interactions are the basis for the special social–emotional bond called early **attachment**, which develops gradually and becomes evident when the child is 7 to 9 months of age.

Recognizing that Freudian theory gave importance to the mother–child relationship, Bowlby (1969) emphasized that behaviors that facilitate attachment—smiling, crying, eye contact, proximity to caretakers, and the like—were biologically "wired" into the human species to ensure that infants would be nurtured and protected by caregivers. These behaviors are regarded as a component of an attachment system, which protects

Infants and their caregivers are predisposed to interact in ways that foster attachment. (wavebreakmedia/Shutterstock)

against high levels of threat or fear in stressful situations and also enhances the infant's exploration of novel and challenging situations (Fearon et al., 2016).

Bowlby viewed attachment as part of the ongoing transactions between a child and major caregivers, which help shape developmental pathways to adaptive or less adaptive outcomes. He and subsequent workers proposed that the child's attachment experiences result in internal representations, or expectations, about the caregiver's availability and responsiveness. Expectations regarding the trustworthiness of caregivers affect the child's ability to regulate emotion and cope with stress and are tied to the acquisition of confidence and self-worth—all of which are carried into future relationships and behavior.

Attachment has been examined across the lifespan but especially in early development. In infancy, attachment is frequently studied with Ainsworth's procedure, the Strange Situation. Here, a caregiver (usually the mother), the infant, and a stranger interact in a comfortable room. The caregiver leaves and returns several times, while the child's behavior is observed in this potentially threatening situation. Initial research indicated that many infants could be categorized as displaying **secure attachment** or one of two types of **insecure attachment** (Fearon et al., 2016). Securely attached infants, when distressed by caregiver separation, seek contact with her upon her return,

react positively, and use the caregiver as a secure base from which they venture forth to explore the environment. Insecurely attached infants fail to use the caregiver as a resource to cope with stress. They tend either to give fewer signals of distress and ignore the caregiver (the avoidant type) or display distress and make ineffective attempts to seek contact with the caregiver (the resistant type). The development of one pattern of attachment over another depends on child characteristics, caregiver sensitivity to the infant's needs, and the broader social context (Meins et al., 2001).

Later research suggested a pattern of **disorganized attachment** (Fearon et al., 2016; Green & Goldwyn, 2002). This pattern reflects the lack of a consistent strategy to organize behavior under stressful situations. Infants seem apprehensive and they display contradictory behaviors that may be misdirected and atypical (Table 2.4). The pattern is associated with child maltreatment and poor parenting (Shumaker, Deutsch, & Brenninkmeyer, 2009), and found at much greater frequency in high-risk than low-risk families (Juffer, Bakermans-Kranenburg, & van IJzendoorn, 2005). It is hypothesized that the child may experience the parent as frightening, unavailable, or threatening—and the child's behavior may become disorganized in the face of this circumstance.

Some research suggests an alternative to thinking about attachment in terms of categories. Instead, individual differences in attachment might be conceptualized as existing along two dimensions—attachment-related avoidance and attachment-related resistance (a combination of resistance and disorganization indicators). Thus, a child's attachment could be described by positions on two dimensions—high (or low) on both attachment dimensions or high on one dimension and low on the other (Fearon et al., 2016; Fraley & Spieker, 2003).

In later childhood and adolescence, the attachment system includes peer and romantic relationships, and measurement shifts to procedures that include self-reports and interviews about the child–parent relationship. Early attachment experiences are thought to carry over to later relationship, and parents still play a critical role. The concepts of secure and insecure attachment are still relevant and research continues to investigate issues of change in attachment over time (Fearon et al., 2016).

Table 2.4 Some Indications of Disorganized/Disoriented Attachment

Infant displays contradictory behaviors, such as seeking contact with the caregiver and also avoiding the caregiver.
Movements and expressions are undirected, misdirected, incomplete, or interrupted.
Movements and expressions are frozen or appear as in "slow motion."
Infant appears apprehensive regarding the caregiver.
Disorganization or disorientation is obvious in disoriented wandering, confused or dazed expression, or multiple rapid changes of affect.

Source: Adapted from Lyons-Ruth, Zeanah, & Benoit, 2003. (Copyright 2003 by Guilford Press; reprinted with permission)

The relationship of attachment patterns to other behaviors has been extensively investigated. Secure attachment has been associated with adaptive behavior in childhood and adolescence, such as competence and positive peer interactions (Groh et al., 2014). In contrast, insecure attachment and especially disorganized attachment are linked to several maladaptive behaviors—aggression, anxiety, substance use, delinquency, academic deficits, low self-esteem, poor peer interaction, unusual or bizarre classroom behavior, and dissociative behaviors (Brumariu & Kerns, 2010; Fearon et al., 2010; Groh et al., 2012; Madigan et al., 2013).

The association of early attachment status and later behavior is modest in strength and is not always found. However, attachment theory is a dominant approach to understanding the influence of early close relationships on current or later psychological functioning. In this regard, attachment can serve as a risk or protective factor and as a part of a broader developmental model of psychopathology (Fearon et al., 2016; Rutter, Kreppner, & Sonuga-Barke, 2009; Sroufe et al., 2010).

Temperament

The word "**temperament**" generally refers to early-emerging basic dispositions that are the product of complex interactions between biological and environmental factors over time. The concept of temperament is an old one, going back to the classical Greek era. Current interest can be traced to Chess and Thomas's study of New York City children (1972, 1977). These investigators recognized environmental influences on the development of behavior, but they were struck by individual differences in how infants behaved from the first days of life. On the basis of parental interviews and actual observations, Chess and Thomas were able to demonstrate that young babies had distinct individual differences in temperament that were somewhat stable over time.

Chess and Thomas defined temperament in terms of nine dimensions of behavioral style that included reactivity to stimuli, regulation of bodily function, mood, and adaptability to change. They also identified three basic temperamental categories or styles: easy, slow-to-warm, and difficult. The last temperament—characterized in part by intense reactivity and negative mood—has especially been associated with social and psychological disturbance (Nigg, 2006; Stifter & Dollar, 2016).

Chess and Thomas avoided simplistic notions about temperament and development. They suggested that early biologically-based temperamental differences occur in the presence of parents who themselves differ in how they react to and manage their children. Parental responding, in turn, influences child reactions, which affects parental reactions, and so on—all of which occurs within the broader context of a changing environment. The investigators proposed that temperament is malleable and that final outcome depends on **goodness-of-fit**, that is, how the child's behavioral tendencies fit with parental characteristics and other environmental circumstances. Their case description of Carl demonstrates that a good match can facilitate adaptation.

Chess and Thomas's basic insight into temperament has stood the test of time. Temperament continues to be conceptualized and investigated from both dimensional and categorical approaches. Also, temperament is viewed as individual differences in behavioral style that are thought to develop into later psychological outcomes through biological and environmental interaction. Early temperament is moderately stable over time and can predict later temperament and later psychological outcomes. The role of biology in temperamental difference is examined through research employing measures such as cardiac functioning, neural activity, and brain structure and function (Hardee et al., 2013; Stifter & Dollar, 2016). Parenting practices and parental affect and stress have been associated with changes in

CARL A Case of Goodness-of-Fit

[Early] in life Carl had been one of our most extreme "difficult child" temperamental types, with intense, negative reactions to new situations and slow adaptability only after many exposures. This was true whether it was the first bath or first solid foods in infancy, the beginning of nursery school and elementary school, first birthday parties, or the first shopping trip. Each experience evoked stormy responses, with loud crying and struggling to get away. However, his parents learned to anticipate Carl's reactions, knew that if they were patient, presented only one or a few new situations at a time, and gave Carl the opportunity for repeated exposure to the new, he would finally adapt positively. ... His parents recognized that the difficulties in raising Carl were due to his temperament and not to their being "bad parents." The father even looked on his son's shrieking and turmoil as a sign of "lustiness." As a result of this positive parent–child interaction Carl never became a behavior problem even though the "difficult" child as a group is significantly at higher risk for disturbed development.

Chess & Thomas, 1977, pp. 220–221

Table 2.5 Three General Dimensions of Temperament

Emotionality	Refers to aspects of emotion such as the quality of mood (positive/negative or anger, fear, sadness), intensity of emotion, and temporal variations in expression of emotion.
Activity level	Reflects an individual's level and intensity of motor activity.
Attention/Regulatory Behaviors	Regulation describes the process that increases, decreases or maintains emotional and behavioral reactivity and attention is viewed as essential to the development of this ability. Attention includes aspects such as attention span and attention focusing.

Source: Adapted from Stifter & Dollar, 2016.

temperament, demonstrating the role of environmental processes (Aktar et al., 2018; Planalp & Goldsmith, 2020; van den Akker et al., 2010).

As research on temperament has proceeded, different dimensions or categories of temperament have been presented. Much of contemporary research has viewed the structure of temperament as dimensional. Stifter and Dollar (2016), in reviewing different models of temperament, suggest that these approaches coalesce around three general dimensions: emotionality, activity level, and attention/regulatory behaviors (Table 2.5). Research has supported associations between temperament and the development of psychopathology and our discussion of specific disorders in later chapters will touch on these findings.

Nigg (2006) suggested two perspectives of temperament and psychopathology. One considers problem behavior as an extreme of normal temperament. For example, attention-deficit/hyperactivity disorder (ADHD) may reflect the extreme of temperamental tendencies for impulsivity and inattention. The second perspective views temperament as a risk or protective factor, depending on the specific temperamental tendency and circumstance.

It is noteworthy that temperament has been included in a broader consideration of children's susceptibility and malleability to environmental circumstances. Specifically, it has been proposed that difficult temperament is associated with an increased sensitivity to the environment regardless of the quality of the environment. (See Accent: "Sensitivity to Context: For Better or Worse.")

ACCENT Sensitivity to Context: For Better or Worse

As already noted, children with difficult temperament have been reported as having especially negative outcomes to environmental adversities. These youth are considered to be highly reactive and are regarded as a high-risk group. However, some investigators have argued for a more nuanced perspective. They propose that reactivity is linked to a more general sensitivity to environmental context, for better or worse. In other words, highly reactive youth are more malleable to a variety of experiences (Belsky, Bakermans-Kranenburg, & Van IJzendoorn, 2007; Ehrlich, Miller, & Chen, 2016; Ellis et al., 2011). An obvious implication of this proposal— sometimes referred to as the **differential susceptibility hypothesis**—is that certain children with particular characteristics (genetic predisposition, temperament) should not only be more reactive than other youth to adversities but *also* to advantageous environments.

In a test of the hypothesis, Bradley and Corwyn (2008) looked at the interaction of child temperament and measures of parenting as related to externalizing problems in young children. Based on infant assessment, the children were categorized as exhibiting easy, average, or difficult temperament. Parenting behavior was measured by observation of the mother interacting with the child on several occasions. Assessment of problem behavior was based on teacher ratings of the children when they were in first grade. Overall, the hypothesis was supported. Figure 2.5 indicates the findings with regard to three child temperaments and mother's sensitivity. The children with difficult temperament had the highest problem scores with low-sensitivity mothers (poor parenting) but the lowest problem scores with high-sensitivity mothers (good parenting). The same pattern occurred with two other measures of parenting. Thus, children with difficult temperament appeared more susceptible than other youth to the kind of parenting they received, for better or worse.

(continued)

(continued)

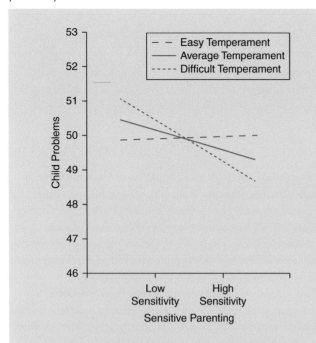

Figure 2.5 The interaction of child temperament and parenting. The findings suggest that children with difficult temperament were more affected by both low-sensitivity and high-sensitivity parenting. (Adapted from Bradley & Corwyn, 2008. Copyright 2008 by John Wiley & Sons; reprinted with permission)

Several additional investigations, using various measures, provide support for the hypothesis of differential susceptibility to the environment (Bakermans-Kranenburg & van IJzendoorn, 2015; Boyce, 2016; Ellis et al., 2011; Essex et al., 2011; Obradović et al., 2010). Genetic studies are quite striking: individuals possessing the gene of interest are more negatively affected by adversity and more positively affected by a supportive situation than other persons. The genetic findings suggest that differential susceptibility has a biological basis, but findings also suggest the gene × environment interactions (van IJzendoorn & Bakermans-Kranenburg, 2015).

Further testing of the differential susceptibility hypothesis has implications for child development (Belsky & Pluess, 2009). For example, if children with difficult temperament are more susceptible not only to low-quality parenting/child care but also to high-quality parenting/child care, supportive environments may be especially beneficial for them (Belsky & van IJzendoorn, 2017).

Emotion and Its Regulation

Emotionality is an element of temperament, but emotion is not identical to temperament and is deserving of further discussion. Human emotion is evident early in life and is rapidly entwined with social development. Early on, infants express basic emotions such as joy, sadness, disgust, and fear; in the second year of life, more complex emotions become obvious, such as shame and guilt (Rosenblum, Dayton, & Muzik, 2019). Appropriate emotional responses to others also appear early; for example, the social smile is evident by 2 months. By 12–18 months, infants display social referencing by using the expressions of others to guide their own responses; for instance, in approaching or avoiding an object. Two- and 3-year-olds are able to name and talk about basic emotions and exert some control over emotional expression. Ages 2 to 5 appear to be an important period in the development of connections between emotion and cognition (Izard et al., 2002). Further progress in emotional development continues during the periods of middle childhood and adolescence, increasingly interfacing with rapidly developing cognitive abilities and the widening of the young person's social world (Dollar & Calkins, 2019).

Complex biological processes are an important basis for the development of emotion. But childhood emotional development is also rooted in the interaction of biological influences and a social context (Cole, 2016; Dollar & Calkins, 2019; Noroña et al., 2018). The caregiving context plays a primary role during the first years of life. Infants' emotions communicate their needs to their caregivers and infants' social smiles and cooing promote social engagement from adults. Over the course of development, the social context comes to include other family and social influences as well as the broader cultural context.

There are a number of ways in which the concept of **emotion** is understood. Emotion is often described through three measurement systems: (1) self-report—private "feelings" of sadness, joy, anger, disgust, and the like; (2) physiological—autonomic nervous system arousal and bodily reactions such as rapid heartbeat; and (3) behavioral—overt behavioral expressions such as smiles, scowls, and drooping shoulders. Emotions may be viewed as relatively brief or as more general mood states that vary in intensity and that are experienced as positive or negative.

The concept of emotion can also be framed in terms of the development of emotional competence. The complex construct of emotional competence is often divided into three domains: emotion expressiveness, emotion understanding, and emotion regulation (Cole, 2016).

From their facial expressions, it appears that very young children experience basic emotions such as happiness and unhappiness. The regulation of emotion is acquired gradually, and for some children much more easily than for others. (Left image: Courtesy of Jennifer Weil Malatras; right image: Shutterstock)

Emotion Expressiveness

Emotion expressiveness is typically defined as the ability to respond to circumstances with a full range of emotions that communicate effectively (achieve goals), flexibly (appropriate to situation), and appropriately (social norms). To evidence emotional competence requires the ability to modulate the expression of emotion. The capacity to express emotion begins early. During the first year of life, infants express emotions through nonverbal means (e.g., facial expressions and movements of their whole body) and later through beginning to use gestures. Beginning in the second year of life, children begin to employ simple use of words to express their emotions and this verbal mode of communication continues to evolve over the course of typical development (Cole, 2016). Effective emotion expressiveness is important for the development of other domains of emotional competence.

Emotion Understanding

The construct of **emotion understanding** addresses a number of skills that involve the knowledge of one's own and other's emotions (Cole, 2016). These include awareness (clear recognition of one's own emotions), emotion perception (accurate decoding of facial and vocal aspects of emotions expressed by others), knowledge of rules (awareness of cultural rules of how emotion is, or is not, expressed), understanding that another person may have a different emotional reaction than one's own, and empathy (understanding other's emotions and responding on their behalf).

The understanding of emotion is important to child competence and adjustment (Cole, 2016; Eisenberg, Spinard, & Eggum, 2010a). In one study, for example, emotion knowledge

and social problems in 5- to 7-year-olds were examined (Schultz et al., 2001). Emotion knowledge was defined in terms of the children's ability to identify (1) emotional expressions on other's faces and (2) the emotion that would be experienced by a person in particular circumstances. As predicted, children who showed low levels of emotion knowledge tended to have social problems and withdrawal two years later. Other research demonstrates a link between difficulty in understanding emotion and later academic or psychological problems (Fine et al., 2003; Trentacosta & Fine, 2010). It is important to remember that the impact of emotion understanding does not occur in isolation, but likely interacts with other aspects of emotional competence such as emotion regulation (Di Maggio, Zappulla, & Pace, 2016).

Emotion Regulation

A large body of research has developed regarding the relationship of emotion regulation to various aspects of adjustment (Cole, 2016). Numerous definitions of the construct of emotion regulation have been offered within both the theoretical and empirical literatures. A general sense of emotion regulation that emerges from these efforts might define **emotion regulation** as behaviors, skills, or strategies that modulate, inhibit, or enhance emotional experiences and expressions (Cole, Hall, & Hajal, 2017; Dollar & Calkins, 2019). Very young children can learn to respond to distress by engaging in self-soothing (e.g., sucking on their hands) or averting their gaze from the source of distress and to elicit caregiver support and assistance. As children's cognitive and social abilities increase, they are better able to initiate and sustain self-distraction. Children develop a greater repertoire of emotion-regulation strategies

JARED Extreme Emotion Dysregulation

Eight-year-old Jared was referred for inpatient treatment following repeated meltdowns. These extreme outbursts would occur when he was given classwork he didn't like. Jared would physically attack teachers, throw objects, and would refuse any attempts at comforting or distraction. With hospitalization there was an initial "honeymoon" period. However, Jared soon became increasingly aggressive because he did not want to participate in the evening activity. Part of his behavioral treatment plan called for the use of a time-out procedure, but Jared refused the usual procedure. Time out was implemented in a special "quiet room" where Jared screamed and cursed for almost an hour. Another shorter outburst occurred a few days later under similar circumstances. The third time, Jared was able to manage his irritability and emotional distress with a 10-minute time out. Following discharge Jared was placed in a self-contained class in his home school district and the parent training that was begun while he was in the inpatient unit was continued in the community.

Adapted from Carlson, 2020, p. 16

(e.g., shift attention, create images or recall memories, reappraise a situation, take action) and show greater autonomy in their execution of emotion regulatory strategies.

Emotion Dysregulation

When emotion regulation is considered in the context of psychopathology, the focus often shifts to a consideration of emotion dysregulation. **Emotion dysregulation** refers to dysfunctional patterns of emotional regulation (Cole et al., 2017). Emotion dysregulation is not the absence of emotion regulation. Rather, the emotion-regulation strategies that a person employs may aid in achieving an immediate goal or sense of well-being, but may impede longer-term functioning and goals. For example, a young person may regulate their emotions when confronting a novel or challenging social situation and avoid or escape from the situation. As a result, they may feel an immediate reduction in anxiety and a sense of relief. However, long-term social functioning and the development of positive coping strategies may be compromised. Cole and colleagues (2017) also suggest that emotion dysregulation can be distinguished from competent patterns of regulation in the following ways:

- Emotions endure and regulation is ineffective
- Emotions interfere with appropriate behavior
- Emotions are inappropriate to the context
- Emotions change too abruptly or slowly

Emotion dysregulation is a central aspect of the conceptualization of many disorders, part of the description of several disorders in the dominant diagnostic system, and a prominent feature of newly developing approaches to classifying and studying psychopathology (see Chapter 5). We will see throughout our discussion in later chapters that research has identified relationships between emotion-regulation difficulties and multiple forms of adjustment difficulties (Beauchaine & Cicchetti, 2019) including anxiety disorders, mood disorders, conduct disorder, ADHD, eating disorders, and posttraumatic stress disorder. The case of Jared provides one such clinical example.

Social Cognitive Processing

In contrast to feeling states that motivate and guide behavior, the cognitive domain of functioning has to do with knowing or understanding through higher-order thinking processes. Multiple aspects of cognition include attention, memory, explanatory style, interpretation bias, and cognitive flexibility. Here, we only consider one aspect of cognition: **social cognitive processing**.

Social cognitive processing has to do with thinking about the social world. It focuses on how individuals take in, understand, and interpret social situations—and how behavior is then affected (Lemerise & Arsenio, 2000). Of immediate concern to our discussion is the role that interpretation of the social situation can play in maladaptive behavior. To take an example, numerous studies indicate that children and adolescents who display more than average aggression or who have been rejected by their peers tend to interpret the behaviors of others as hostile (Dodge et al., 2015b; Martinelli et al., 2018). That is, they appear to have a bias to attribute hostility to others, especially when provoked.

It is noteworthy that although social information processing emphasizes cognition, emotion is viewed as playing an integral role (Arsenio & Lemerise, 2004; Dodge & Rabiner, 2004). Cognition and emotion may interact in various and increasingly complex ways over the course of development (Cole, 2016; Lemerise & Arsenio, 2000). For example, poor understanding of emotion likely plays a role in a child's misperceptions of social cues (Denham et al., 2002). Also, a youth who is already emotionally aroused may be highly prone to misperceptions. The finding that arousal of negative emotions in highly aggressive boys can increase their attribution of hostile intent to others is one such example (de Castro et al., 2003). Alternatively, the perception of hostility in others can arouse feelings of negative emotions. As these examples demonstrate, research on social cognitive processing contributes to our understanding of how thinking and emotions are united in the interchange between individuals and their environments (Cole, 2016; Rutter & Sroufe, 2000).

Cognitive processing of the social context influences much human functioning. For an everyday example, consider that children's perception of their parents' interaction with them or with each other is related to parental influence on the children

and youth's adjustment (Berzenski & Yates, 2013; Fosco & Grych, 2007; Gomez et al., 2001). Regarding psychological problems, specific beliefs and attributions about the world and the self appear to operate in depression, anxiety, and negative peer relationships, among other difficulties.

Inherent in the topics we have just examined—attachment, temperament, emotion, and social cognition processing—is the assumption that development is rooted in both biological and experiential factors and their transactions with the child or adolescent. Influences on the development of psychopathology are further explored in Chapter 3.

Looking Back

Perspectives, Theories, Models

- Perspectives (paradigms), theories, and models are critical to the scientific study of human development.
- Theories, which consist of formal propositions to explain phenomena, are highly valued because they permit the testing of hypotheses.
- Interactional and transactional models presume that several factors, working together, underlie psychopathology.

Developmental Psychopathology Perspective: An Overview

- The developmental psychopathology perspective explores psychological disturbances with respect to several core developmental issues. A systems framework for organizing other perspectives or theories of psychopathology, it integrates normal and maladaptive development.

Concept of Development

- Development refers to change over time resulting from transactions of an individual with biological, psychological, and sociocultural factors. Development follows a general course and proceeds in a coherent pattern.

Searching for Causal Factors and Processes

- A major goal of developmental psychopathology is to uncover the multiple causes of psychological disorders and underlying processes.
- It is helpful to differentiate direct and indirect influences; mediating and moderating influences; and necessary, sufficient, and contributing causes.

Pathways of Development

- Development proceeds along complex probabilistic pathways, as reflected in the principles of equifinality and multifinality.

Risk, Vulnerability, and Resilience

- Risk factors increase the chance of psychopathology; many kinds have been identified.
- Among important aspects of risk are the number; general or specific effects; and intensity, duration, and timing of risks. Early risk may be particularly influential.
- Vulnerability refers to individual attributes that may act as risk factors.
- Risk is best conceptualized within a transactional model.
- Resilience refers to relatively positive outcome in the face of adversity or risk. Protective or promotive factors that confer resilience include individual, family, and extrafamilial variables.
- When viewed as attributes of the individual, resilience can be considered as the opposite of vulnerability.

Continuity of Disorder

- Continuity of disorder over time varies, but it cannot be assumed that most children outgrow psychopathology. Both homotypic and heterotypic continuity are observed. Among the processes that underlie continuity are environmental stability, biological mechanisms, and psychological functioning.

Normal Development, Problematic Outcomes

- Patterns of early socioemotional attachment between children and their caregivers have been described. Secure attachment is associated with later positive outcome; insecure and disorganized/disoriented patterns are associated with unfavorable outcome.
- Temperament generally refers to early-emerging basic dispositions that are the product of interactions between biological and environmental factors. Temperament can be viewed as a risk or protective factor.

- Emotion is evident early in infancy and develops rapidly in childhood. Emotion expression, understanding, and regulation are central in adaptive and maladaptive development.
- Various aspects of cognition are central to typical and atypical development. Cognitive processing of the social world is implicated in several forms of psychological problems. For example, highly aggressive children may have a cognitive bias to view the world as hostile.

Key Terms

paradigm *20*
theory *20*
interactional models *20*
vulnerability-stress model *20*
transactional models *20*
systems models *20*
developmental psychopathology perspective *21*
development *21*
medical model *21*
direct effect, indirect effect *22*
mediator *22*
moderator *22*
necessary, sufficient, contributing causes *22*
equifinality *24*
multifinality *24*
risk *25*

vulnerability *26*
resilience *26*
promotive/protective factors *28*
heterotypic continuity, homotypic continuity *30*
attachment *30*
secure, insecure, disorganized attachment *31*
temperament *32*
goodness-of-fit *32*
differential susceptibility hypothesis *33*
emotion *34*
emotion expressiveness *35*
emotion understanding *35*
emotion regulation *35*
emotion dysregulation *36*
social cognitive processing *36*

CHAPTER 3

Biological and Environmental Contexts of Psychopathology

Looking Forward

After reading this chapter, you should be able to discuss:

- Brain and nervous system development, structure, and function
- Pre-, peri-, and postnatal risks to the nervous system
- The genetic context of development, including genetic research

- Basic learning/cognitive processes and their role in development
- An ecological model of sociocultural influences on development
- The family context of development
- Influences of peers on development
- Community and societal contexts of development

The aim of this chapter is to consider the major biological and environmental contexts of the development of psychological problems. We discuss the nervous system and brain, genetics, learning and cognition, and the social/cultural contexts of development. Basic information is provided and emphasis is placed on influences on behavioral and psychological disorders.

Brain and Nervous System

Brain Development: Biology and Experience

The development of the brain and nervous system is, arguably, among the most fascinating of all developmental processes. Much early growth is biologically guided but the influence of experience is critical.

The nervous system begins to develop shortly after conception when a group of cells called the neural plate thickens, folds inward, and forms the neural tube. The rapidly developing cells migrate to fixed locations. The brain contains millions of multifunctioning cells, the glial cells, and **neurons** that are specialized to chemically transmit impulses within the nervous system and to and from other body parts. These cells continue to become more interconnected and functional, and nerve fibers become sheathed in **myelin**, a white substance that increases

the efficiency of communication in the brain. Both before and after birth, an excess of neurons and connections are produced, apparently setting the brain up to ensure flexibility (Rapoport & Gogtay, 2008). Different brain areas develop more rapidly than others. For example, the enormous growth of connections among neurons that are related to vision and hearing peaks a few months after birth, but occurs much more slowly in the frontal part of the brain involved in complex, flexible thinking (Thompson-Schill, Ramscar, & Chrysikou, 2009).

Adolescence is a time of notable brain maturation (Luciana, 2013; Powers & Casey, 2015). Change occurs in brain chemistry; connections between brain regions proliferate; the amount of gray matter (cell bodies) decreases in the front part of the brain whereas white matter increases, reflecting continuing myelination. As with earlier brain development, these changes have implications for psychological and behavioral functioning.

The development of the brain results from both intrinsic biological programming and experience, that is, activity-dependent processes. Both before and after birth the shaping of the brain involves the mechanism of **pruning**, whereby unneeded cells and connections are eliminated. For example, brain regions important in the visual system of animals rely in part on pruning, a process that requires experience with patterned visual input (Grossman et al., 2003). In humans, pruning is thought to underlie the decrease in gray matter that occurs in adolescence. Enormous

"Young man, go to your room and stay there until your cerebral cortex matures."

Barbara Smaller/The New Yorker Collection/Cartoon Bank/

progress has been made in understanding developmental change in the structures and functioning of the human brain, including both biological and environmental influences (Beauchaine, Zisner, & Hayden, 2019).

Structure

The brain and spinal cord together form the **central nervous system**. The nerves outside the central nervous system that transmit messages to and from it compose the **peripheral nervous system**, which has two subsystems. One of these, the somatic system, involves the sensory organs and muscles and is engaged in sensing and voluntary movement. The other, the autonomic system, helps involuntary regulation of arousal and the emotions. The branches of the autonomic system either increase arousal (sympathetic system) or work to slow arousal and maintain bodily functioning (parasympathetic system). The entire nervous system communicates within itself, and is in close communication with the **endocrine system**, a collection of glands intricately involved in bodily functions through the release of hormones.

The brain—a wrinkled mass atop the spinal cord—has three major interconnected divisions. The **hindbrain** includes the pons, medulla, and cerebellum. Among other functions, the pons relays information and the medulla helps regulate heart function and breathing. The cerebellum is involved in movement and cognitive processing. A small area called the **midbrain** contains fibers that connect the hindbrain and upper brain regions. It also shares with the hindbrain netlike connections, the reticular activating system, which influences arousal states such as waking and sleeping. Sometimes the midbrain and hindbrain are called the brain stem (Figure 3.1).

The third major division, the **forebrain**, consists chiefly of two cerebral hemispheres, the outer surface of which is referred to as the cortex. The hemispheres are connected to each other by the corpus callosum, and each hemisphere has four lobes. The cerebral hemispheres are involved in a wide range of activities, such as sensory processing, motor control, and higher mental functioning that includes information processing, learning, and memory.

Situated below the cerebral hemispheres and deep in the brain are several subcortical structures. The thalamus is involved in processing and relaying information between the cerebral hemispheres and other parts of the central nervous system. The hypothalamus regulates basic urges such as hunger, thirst, and sexual activity. The multistructured limbic system, which includes the hippocampus and amygdala, plays a central role in memory and emotion.

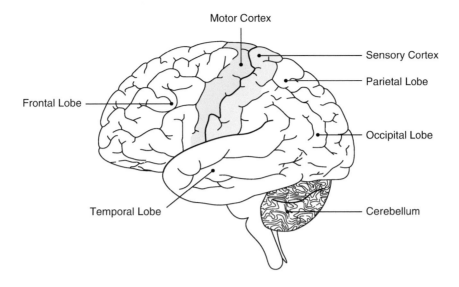

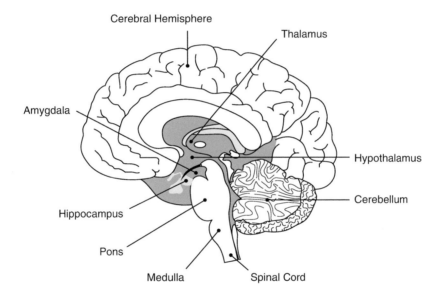

Figure 3.1 The outer view (top) and cross-sectional view (bottom) of the human brain.

Neurotransmission

Although neurons vary in size, shape, and chemistry, they all have three major parts: a multifunctional **cell body**, **dendrites**, and an **axon**. Communication between neurons occurs across a **synapse**, the small gap between the cells (the synaptic gap, or cleft). The dendrites of a neuron receive chemical messages from other neurons that result in an electric impulse being sent down the axon. When the impulse reaches the end of the axon, packets of chemicals—the **neurotransmitters**—are released. They cross the synaptic gap and are taken up by the receptor sites on the dendrites of the receiving neuron. The receiving neuron, in turn, generates new electrical impulses (Figure 3.2). Among the major neurotransmitters are dopamine, serotonin, norepinephrine, glutamate, and GABA, whose role in brain functioning is being intensely investigated.

The complexity of communication is hard even to imagine. Neurons may make thousands of connections to other neurons, and neurotransmitters may travel multiple pathways to receptor sites. Neurotransmitters can act to excite or inhibit neurons, that is, make them more or less likely to fire an impulse. Communication is far from helter-skelter, however. Brain regions work together, forming pathways, or circuits, that are associated with different neurotransmitters and functions.

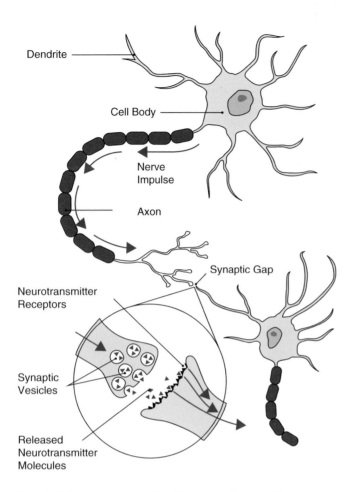

Dendrite

Cell Body

Nerve
Impulse

Axon

Synaptic Gap

Neurotransmitter
Receptors

Synaptic
Vesicles

Released
Neurotransmitter
Molecules

Figure 3.2 Messages are transmitted in a neuron from dendrites, to the cell body, to the axon, and then, through the release of neurotransmitters, across the synaptic gap to other neurons.

Nervous System and Risk for Disordered Functioning

The nervous system is a major aspect of the constitutional factors that influence psychological functioning and behavior. Impaired functioning can result from inheritance or from early-occurring abnormalities of the genetic processes that guide nervous system development. Thus, dysfunction can be "wired in" from the beginning. However, harm can also be attributed to events that occur during pregnancy (prenatal), at about the time of birth (perinatal), or during later development (postnatal).

Prenatal Influences

Numerous prenatal influences can put the developing child at risk. Among these are poor maternal diet and health. Research also shows that maternal stress can alter the fetal biological system, including the brain, in ways that can affect susceptibility to later psychological problems (Doyle et al., 2017; O'Conner, Monk, & Fitelson, 2014; Slade & Sadler, 2019).

At one time, it was believed that the fetus was protected from most harmful substances, or **teratogens**, that might enter the mother's bloodstream. We now know that a variety of agents can be detrimental. Potentially harmful drugs include alcohol, cocaine, and opiates. Radiation, environmental contaminants—such as lead, mercury, and polychlorinated biphenyls (PCBs)—and many maternal diseases—such as rubella, syphilis, gonorrhea, and AIDS—also can be harmful. Teratogens are associated with malformation, low birthweight, fetal death, and functional and behavioral impairment (Boris et al., 2019; Doyle & Mattson, 2019; Perera et al., 2011).

Teratogens are thought to interfere with brain cell formation and migration, as well as other developmental processes (Doyle et al., 2017; Lebel, Roussotte, & Sowell, 2011). Perhaps unsurprisingly, the amount of exposure to a teratogen makes a difference in outcome. So does the timing of exposure during gestation. In general, specific structures and systems are most sensitive to harm when they are rapidly developing (Talge, Neal, & Glover, 2007). It is thought that the genetic endowment of the developing organism can act as a risk or protective factor regarding the effects of teratogens or maternal stress.

The adverse consequence of prenatal exposure is exemplified by **Fetal Alcohol Syndrome (FAS)**, which lies at the most severe end of a spectrum of defects associated with maternal alcohol consumption. Suspected for many years before it was documented, FAS is characterized by abnormal brain development, neurological signs such as impaired motor skills and unusual gait, retarded growth, and birth defects (American Academy of Pediatrics, 2000; Doyle et al., 2017). Specific facial abnormalities also are observed. These include small eyes, a thin upper lip, and a smooth philtrum (flattening or absence of the usual indentation under the nose) (Astley et al., 2009). MRI imaging has revealed effects on multiple regions of the brain, with the most common findings being reduced brain volume and malformations of the corpus callosum (Lebel et al., 2011). A variety of psychological difficulties including lower intelligence, specific cognitive impairments, learning disabilities, stereotypic behavior, sleep problems, hyperactivity, disruptive behavior disorders, and depression also often accompany FAS. The effects of maternal alcohol use vary with several factors, including the amount of alcohol exposure, timing of exposure, mother's age and health, and fetal susceptibility. Environmental risk factors such as socioeconomic status, family placement, and parental psychopathology impact outcomes. FAS symptoms can be pervasive and persistent, and many children without the full-blown syndrome are impaired with lesser alcohol-related symptoms (Chasnoff et al., 2010; Doyle et al., 2017).

While recognizing the adverse effects of prenatal alcohol and other teratogens, we must regard research results cautiously. It is, of course, unacceptable to conduct controlled experiments in which pregnant women are exposed to harmful agents, and the feasible research strategies make it challenging to establish causality. Because teratogens tend to cluster, it is difficult to distinguish the impact of one teratogen from another. For

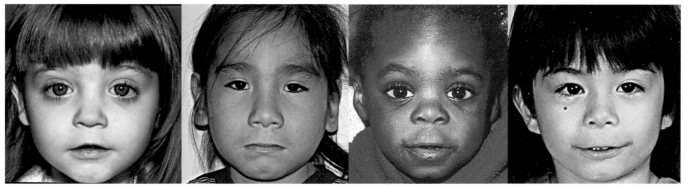

Examples of the FAS facial phenotype (small eyes, smooth philtrum, and thin upper lip) across four races: (A) Caucasian, (B) Native American, (C) African American, (D) Asian American. (Copyright 2020 Susan (Astley) Hemingway, Ph.D., University of Washington)

example, prenatal use of illicit substances is often associated with alcohol and cigarette use. Further, prenatal substance abuse is associated with poverty, which can influence children's development both prenatally *and* during the child's subsequent development, making it difficult to establish the timing of influence (Brown et al., 2004).

These difficulties require carefully designed research. Lavigne and colleagues (2010), for example, studied the effects of maternal tobacco smoking, which has been shown to carry risk. Knowing that women who smoke are different from nonsmokers in several ways, including in parenting behaviors and psychopathology, the researchers controlled for possible effects of several variables. Smoking was then no longer associated with child behavior problems. In addition to carefully designed human studies, research on prenatal influences has benefitted from work with animals, which allows intentional exposure to teratogens and the testing of causal hypotheses.

Perinatal and Postnatal Influences

Developmental risks are associated with birth. Excessive medication given to the mother, unusual delivery, and anoxia (lack of oxygen) can result in neurological problems in the newborn.

Preterm delivery (birth less than 37 weeks into gestation) and low birthweight (less than 2,500 grams or approximately 5.5 pounds) are associated with death and a variety of developmental problems, including behavioral and cognitive/academic difficulties (Johnson et al., 2011; Shah, Browne, & Poehlmann-Tynan, 2019). In the United States, the overall rate of prematurity is about 10%, with considerable variation across race/ethnic groups (Martin et al., 2018). Comparable rates are reported worldwide, with particularly high rates in developing countries (Shah et al., 2019). The earlier an infant is born and the lower the birthweight, the greater the risk. A relationship between low birthweight and structural brain abnormalities has been shown from infancy through adolescence with some risks persisting into adulthood (Nagy, Lagercrantz, & Hutton, 2011; Shah et al., 2019).

Developmental outcome depends on the interplay of biological and psychosocial factors.

Postnatal effects on the nervous system can result from malnutrition, injury, illness, or exposure to chemicals. For example, air pollution may affect neuropsychological development (Suades-Gonzalez et al., 2015), and exposure of children to lead, even at low levels, appears to have a negative impact on brain processes involved in attention, cognition, and behavior (Doyle et al., 2017; Marcus, Fulton, & Clarke, 2010; Winter & Sampson, 2017).

When brain damage occurs in youth, a major concern is the degree to which the resulting problems can be remediated. At issue is the **plasticity**, or flexibility, of the brain to recover. There is evidence that the young, immature nervous system is relatively adept at restoring itself or at transferring functions to undamaged brain areas. Plasticity has been shown especially in vision, audition, motor, and language functioning (Rapoport & Gogtay, 2008). For example, brain damage to the language areas of the brain results in less impairment in childhood than in adulthood. On the other hand, damage to the immature brain may set up a cascade of negative effects on future brain development, and deficits may become apparent over time (P. Arnett et al., 2017). The timing, extent, severity, and region of damage, as well as the kind and amount of environmental support and therapy provided, are among the factors that influence recuperation.

Genetic Context

The study of genetic influences seeks to establish the extent of genetic influence on attributes, discover the genes involved, understand how the genes operate, and reveal the paths from genes to characteristics (Plomin & Davis, 2009). Evidence for genetic influence has been established for many attributes and psychological disorders, and progress is being made in the discovery of the underlying genetic processes. As we shall see in our discussion of various disorders, it is particularly important to be aware that multiple genes, and their interplay

43

with environmental influences, are implicated in the expression of complex human characteristics (e.g., intelligence) and psychological disorders. Here we provide a somewhat brief overview of these complex processes.

The basic genetic material is contained in all body cells. It consists of **chromosomes** containing **DNA** (deoxyribonucleic acid), functional segments of which are called **genes**. At conception, billions of chromosome combinations are possible for any one individual, and other genetic mechanisms result in even greater variability. Chromosomes may exchange genes, break and reattach to each other, and change by mutation, which is spontaneous alteration of the DNA molecule.

In some cases, early genetic processes result in structural defects in the chromosomes or a lack or excess of the 23 pairs of chromosomes found in most human cells. These "errors" may be inherited but many are new occurrences. In either case, the consequence can be dire, and can result in the death of the early-developing organism. Less severe outcomes include a variety of medical syndromes involving physical, intellectual, and psychological abnormalities. These instances are certainly of interest to mental health workers, although most individual differences relevant to psychopathology involve more subtle genetic processes, many of which implicate inheritance.

Genes act indirectly and in complex ways to guide the biochemistry of cells (Beauchaine, Gatzke-Kopp, & Gizer, 2017). Any single gene may affect many bodily processes and, as well, interact with other genes and environmental factors. As applied to an individual, the term *genetic code* refers to the order in which four nucleotides (adenine, thymine, guanine, and cytosine) appear in particular regions of a gene. This sequence is the basis for the **transcription**, or synthesis, of messenger RNA, a molecule that carries the information to other parts of the cell, where it plays a role in the **translation** of the code into the manufacture of proteins (Figure 3.3).

The genetic code is critical in determining protein manufacture, and so are processes that regulate coding (Plomin & Davis, 2009). Regulation is a complex process. Indeed, only a part of each gene (the exon) codes for proteins, and a larger part is engaged in regulatory mechanisms. Moreover, about half of the RNA that is transcribed is not messenger RNA but is instead involved in the activation or suppression of the protein-coding DNA. There is increasing evidence for the influence of both the internal and external environments on the processes of transcription, translation, and gene expression. As even this brief description makes clear, the path from individual genetic endowment—the **genotype**—to the observable characteristics of the person—the **phenotype**—is indirect and incredibly intricate. In the following discussion, we introduce some of the major concepts, strategies, and findings of genetics research with a focus on psychopathology.

Epigenetics and Gene Expression

A further indication of the complexity of genetic influence is provided by an examination of epigenetics. The term **epigenetics** refers to changes in gene expression that are environmentally mediated (i.e. regulated, activated, silenced, etc.) (Beauchaine et al., 2017a). These changes in gene expression occur through reversible modifications of the genome that help regulate gene function without changing the actual genetic code. Several epigenetic processes are being investigated. Widely studied are specific chemical changes in the DNA molecule (methylation) and in the histone proteins that are wrapped with DNA in the cell nucleus. Such DNA changes make it more or less likely that a gene will be expressed or suppressed. These modifications can be passed on during usual cell duplication (mitosis) and also during the formation of the ova and sperm (meiosis), which means they can be inherited (Hill & Roth, 2016).

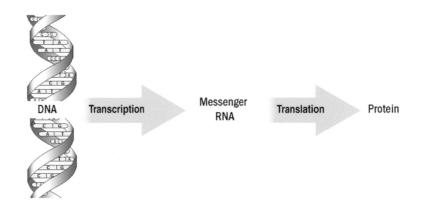

Figure 3.3 The sequence of nucleotides (T, A, C, G) in DNA in the cell nucleus is transcribed to messenger RNA and then the information is translated for the production of proteins.

In recent years, it has become increasingly recognized that epigenetic change can occur in response to the environment. Correlational research with humans and controlled studies with animals indicate that diet/nutrition, exposure to environmental toxins, in utero stress, exposure to adverse child rearing, and other experiences can result in epigenetic change (Beauchaine et al., 2017a; Roth & Sweatt, 2011; Scorza et al., 2019).

Epigenetic processes hold enormous promise of helping to elucidate gene–environment interaction, developmental phenomena, and mental disorder. Prenatal and early postnatal life appear to be periods of particular vulnerability to epigenetic effects (Roth, 2013). For example, it has been demonstrated in animal studies that the quality of early maternal care can induce methylation of DNA. The contribution of epigenetic mechanisms to a wide range of disorders is being explored, including FAS, autism, depression, aggression and conduct problems, and attention-deficit/hyperactivity disorder (ADHD) (Barker, Walton, & Cecil, 2018; Hill & Roth, 2016; Ramsey, 2010; Shulha et al., 2012).

Single-Gene Inheritance

Gregor Mendel, a monk who experimented with plants in a monastery garden in Moravia in the mid-nineteenth century, is credited with discoveries crucial to modern genetics. Among Mendel's contributions are descriptions of the inheritance of certain characteristics that are influenced by a single gene. He correctly hypothesized that each parent carries two hereditary factors (later called genes), but passes on only one to the offspring. A gene can be **dominant**—its transmission by either parent leads to the display of traits associated with it—or **recessive**—only its transmission by both parents results in associated traits. Dominant and recessive patterns of inheritance, as well as the sex-linked pattern, described later in this text, are involved in the inheritance of many human attributes and disorders.

In general, the effects of single genes are quite predictable, and often result in individuals either having or not having the relevant phenotype. One way to establish single-gene influence on a specific disorder is to identify a person with the disorder—the **index case** or the **proband**—and determine whether a known pattern of single-gene inheritance runs in the family.

Quantitative Methods—Behavioral Genetics

As important as single-gene effects are, multiple genes are more often implicated in complex human characteristics, such as intelligence, and in psychological disorders. Each of these multiple genes are inherited in the usual patterns, but each has relatively small influence—which combines to create a larger effect (Plomin, 2005; Plomin & Crabbe, 2000). The genes may vary in the size of their influence, interact with each other, and be interchangeable in some instances. Any one gene thus may not be sufficient or necessary for a disorder, and indeed may be carried by a person without the disorder. Multiple genes working together result in a range of phenotypes, varying from lesser to greater display of the characteristic. Multigenic influence is less predictable, or more probabilistic, than single-gene inheritance.

Research into multiple-gene influence relies on a combination of evidence from a variety of **quantitative genetic methods**. This research approach is also often referred to as **behavioral genetics**. Family, twin, and adoption studies are important in establishing genetic influence on an attribute (Table 3.1). Quantitative genetic methods allow the assessment of **heritability**, the degree to which genetic influence accounts for variance in behavior among individuals in the population studied. Overall results suggest that heritability for psychological disorders or dimensions rarely exceeds 50% (Plomin & Davis, 2009). This means that substantial variation in attributes has a basis in other biological factors, the environment, or some interplay of genes with these other influences.

Table 3.1 Behavioral Genetic Methods: Family, Twin, and Adoption Studies

Family studies These evaluate the likelihood of family members displaying the same or similar attributes as the index case. If genetic influence is operating, family members who are genetically closer to the index case should be more likely than those less close to display the attribute. However, this pattern is also consistent with family psychosocial influence.

Twin studies Comparison is made between monozygotic twins, who share 100% of their genes, and dizygotic twins, who share on average 50% of their genes. Genetic influence is suggested when monozygotic twins are more concordant (similar to each other) than dizygotic twins.

Adoption studies Adopted and nonadopted individuals and their families are compared in various ways. For adopted children with a disorder, the rate of a disorder can be examined in their biological families and adoptive families. Higher rate in the former indicates genetic influence.

Another strategy starts with biological parents with a disorder and examines the rate of the disorder in their offspring who were adopted by nonrelated families. This rate can be compared to the rate in the biological children of the adoptive parents. A higher rate in the adopted children indicates genetic effects.

Quantitative genetic research also provides information on the contribution of environmental influences and how genes work together. Both shared and nonshared environmental influences are recognized. **Shared environmental influences** refer to influences that contribute to family members developing in similar ways. Examples might be exposure to intellectual stimulation, environmental toxins, or divorce, which similarly affect siblings. **Nonshared environmental influences** refer to influences that are different for children growing up in the same family and result in siblings being different from each other. Examples might be the effects of differential treatment of siblings by the parents or of siblings having different friends or teachers.

Although quantitative research methods can examine a single attribute, multivariate designs focus on two or more attributes. These designs make it possible to estimate the degree to which genetic and environmental factors that influence one attribute also influence another. For example, depression and antisocial symptoms have been found to share some common genetic liability (Caspi et al., 2014; Plomin, Kovacs, & Haworth, 2007). In these instances, the disorders share so-called "generalist" genes or a higher-order psychopathology factor conferring a more general vulnerability. However, nonshared genes and/or environmental influences make the disorders different from each other (Lahey et al., 2011). Overall, multivariate studies and other sophisticated quantitative analyses permit the evaluation of models of genetic transmission and of the interaction of genetic and environmental influences (Beauchaine et al., 2017a).

Molecular Genetic Methods

Molecular genetics is a rapidly expanding field that seeks to discover the specific genes and DNA sequence differences on those genes associated with a disorder, the biochemicals coded by the genes, and how these biochemicals are involved in behavior. In research with humans, the methods of linkage analysis and association analysis are central (Beauchaine et al., 2017a; Kornilov & Grigorenko, 2016).

The aim of **linkage analysis** is to reveal the location of a problematic gene, that is, the specific chromosome and the place on the chromosome. This strategy takes advantage of the fact that genes on the same chromosome, especially when located close to each other, are generally transmitted together to the offspring. The strategy also takes advantage of genetic markers—segments of DNA with a known chromosome location. Genetic data are collected from families and searches are made for genetic markers with a known chromosome location. Linkage analysis determines whether a specific disorder appears among family members in the same pattern as the genetic marker. If it does, it can be presumed that a gene that influences the disorder is located on

the same chromosome as the marker and is close to the marker. Thus, the approximate genetic address for the disorder is revealed. Vulnerability for most disorders involves multiple genes and, thus, multiple chromosomal loci are likely involved (Beauchaine et al., 2017a).

Association analysis searches for genes in a different way. This method tests whether a particular form of a gene is associated with a trait or disorder in the population. A comparison is made between the genetic material of persons with a specific disorder and that from a matched control group. The focus may be a particular gene—called a candidate gene—that is suspect, based on theory or past research. As an example, the candidate genes DRD4 and the DAT1 have been found to be associated with impulsivity and ADHD (Neuhaus & Beauchaine, 2017). Association analysis is more suitable than linkage analysis to identify multiple genes that have relatively small influence on a disorder or trait (Beauchaine et al., 2017a; Plomin & Davis, 2009). For some disturbances, a very large number of genes appear to be involved, indicating a sizable task for genetic investigators.

Advanced genetic technology has improved the search for genes. **Genome-wide linkage** and **genome-wide association analyses** enable researchers to scan across the genomes of individuals or large portions of the genome. These analyses, which require large samples, are able to examine millions of DNA sequences. Of critical interest are small variations in the nucleotides of the DNA molecule. In addition, these methods can examine variations in the number of duplications and deletions of segments of DNA (copy number variations). Variations in nucleotides or in copy number that appear more often in individuals with a disorder suggest a possible causal role.

Gene–Environment Interplay

Although we have already noted that genetic and environmental influences work together, it is important to examine this interplay in greater detail. Of substantial importance are gene–environment interactions and gene–environment correlations. These occurrences have been increasingly recognized in developmental processes.

Gene–environment interaction (G × E) refers to the interdependence of genetic and environmental factors with regard to impact on the expression of a trait. G × E is posited when the effect of the environment depends on the genome and, vice versa, the effect of the genome depends on the environment. Thus from the genetic perspective, G × E refers to differential sensitivity to experience due to differences in genotype.

A renowned example is the interaction of variations in the 5-HTTLPR gene and reactions to stressful life events. Caspi and colleagues (2003) found that individuals carrying a particular form of the gene, but not another form, are more likely to react to adverse life events so that they suffer symptoms of depression in later life. Many subsequent studies have found the same impact of the relationship between this variant of the 5-HTTLPR gene and adverse life events on depression (e.g., Starr et al., 2014). Another example of G × E is provided by research on the interaction of the DRD4 gene and parenting. Children with a particular variant of this gene who experienced insensitive parenting assessed at 10 months of age displayed greater externalizing behavior (e.g., non-compliance, aggression) two years later than children who did not have this variant of the DRD4 gene. Moreover, although children with this variant displayed the most externalizing behavior if they experienced insensitive parenting, they also exhibited the least externalizing behavior if they experienced highly sensitive parenting (Bakermans-Kranenburg & van IJzendoorn, 2006, 2011). Such compelling instances call attention to the influence of gene–environment interaction, and there is much current interest in this process (Beauchaine et al., 2017a; Belsky & Pluess, 2016; Golds, deKruiff, & MacBeth, 2020).

Gene–environment correlation (GE) refers to situations in which genetic differences affect exposure to environments. Three kinds of GE correlations have been described: passive, reactive, and active (Table 3.2). *Passive* GE correlations stem from parents transmitting both their genes and gene-related rearing environments to their offspring. *Reactive* GE correlations reflect both the child's genetic endowment and reactions from others to the child's gene-related characteristics. *Active* GE correlations are based on both the child's genetic endowment and the child's active selection of gene-related experiences. The importance of GE correlations is that they inform us that a person's experiences are not independent of genetic influences. In fact, there is considerable evidence that genetic influences play a role in determining the experiences a person will have—and thus the

risks and protections that will be encountered (Beauchaine et al., 2017a; Jaffee, 2016).

Learning and Cognition

Learning and cognition are inextricably intertwined with development. The abilities to learn and think not only become more advanced over time, but also facilitate other kinds of development as the child transacts with the environment. Our present discussion of this topic is introductory, and the vital role that learning and cognition play in psychopathology is woven throughout the text.

Classical Conditioning

Pavlov focused attention on the process of **classical conditioning** by demonstrations that hungry dogs, which normally salivate when food is present, could learn to salivate to neutral stimuli presented just prior to the presentation of food. In classical conditioning, the individual learns to respond to a stimulus that previously did not elicit the response. Many aspects of this kind of learning have been described. For example, once a new response (the conditioned response) is acquired, it can generalize to similar situations and can have far-reaching effects on emotion and behavior.

Historically, two early studies based on classical conditioning had a notable impact on the application of learning to problem behavior. (See Accent: "Albert and Peter: Two Historic Cases.") The now-famous case of little Albert was an early illustration of the conditioning of fear, whereas the case of Peter demonstrated that fearful responses could be eliminated by the application of classical conditioning principles.

Table 3.2 Types of Gene–Environment Correlations Demonstrating How Genetic Predisposition and Aspects of the Environment Are Linked

PASSIVE	A family's environment is influenced by the genetic predisposition of the parents. The child experiences this environment and *also* shares the genetic predisposition of the parents. This mechanism occurs at birth and is "passive" in the sense that the child has relatively little active input.
Example:	*The child who has a genetic propensity for a high activity level also experiences a high-activity family environment.*
REACTIVE	A child evokes reactions from other people on the basis of her or his genetic predisposition, so that the child's genetic propensities are linked to environmental experiences.
Example:	*Others react to the child's gene-based high activity level.*
ACTIVE	A child, particularly as he or she grows older, selects or creates environments on the basis of his or her genetic predisposition.
Example:	*The child with a genetic propensity for high activity level engages in activities requiring high activity rather than restrained, quiet activities such as reading.*

Source: Adapted from Plomin, 1994. Copyright 1994 by Sage; reprinted with permission.

ACCENT Albert and Peter: Two Historic Cases

As reported by Watson and Rayner (1920), Albert, an 11-month-old child, initially showed no fear reactions to a variety of objects, including a white rat. He did, however, exhibit fear when a loud sound was produced by the striking of a steel bar. Watson and Rayner attempted to condition fear of the white rat by producing the loud clanging sound each time Albert reached for the animal. After several of these pairings, Albert reacted with crying and avoidance when the rat was presented without the noise. It was later shown that the infant's fear generalized to other furry objects. Thus, it appeared that fear could be learned through classical conditioning. Interestingly, upon the completion of the study, Albert's whereabouts became a mystery until Beck, Levinson, and Irons (2009), after a lengthy effort, presented evidence to show that Albert probably lived for a short period of time on the grounds of Johns Hopkins University, the site of the study and where his mother was employed. He lived only to age 6, however; his life was cut short by illness, probably meningitis. Albert's legacy is the role he played in a demonstration that helped shape the early development of the discipline of psychology, including raising ethical questions about conditioning fear in children.

The landmark study by Mary Cover Jones (1924) described the treatment of Peter, a boy nearing 3 years of age, who exhibited fear of furry objects. Jones first attempted to treat Peter by placing him in the presence of a rabbit, along with children who liked the rabbit and petted it. The treatment appeared to be working but was interrupted when Peter became ill for nearly two months. Just prior to his return to treatment, he was also frightened by a large dog. With Peter's fear back at its original level, Jones decided to treat Peter with a counterconditioning procedure, which involved allowing Peter to eat some of his favorite foods while the animal was moved progressively closer. In this way, the feared stimulus was associated with pleasantness. The procedure was apparently successful in reducing the boy's fears, and he was ultimately able to hold the animal by himself. Although this study has methodological weaknesses, it stimulated the development of treatments for psychological disturbance based on the principles of classical conditioning.

Operant Learning

A second basic type of learning is **operant learning**, which was set forth in Thorndike's Law of Effect recognizing that a positive consequence of a behavior will strengthen the behavior while a negative consequence will weaken it. The work of B. F. Skinner was especially influential. Operant, or instrumental, conditioning emphasizes the consequences of behavior. Behavior is acquired, strengthened, weakened, maintained, eliminated, or emitted in some circumstances but not in others through reinforcement, punishment, and other learning processes (Table 3.3). Operant learning is ubiquitous; through it, knowledge is acquired and adaptive and maladaptive behaviors are shaped.

Table 3.3 Some Fundamental Operant Conditioning Processes

Term	Definition	Example
Positive reinforcement	A stimulus is presented following a response (contingent upon the response), increasing the frequency of that response.	Praise following good behavior increases the likelihood of good behavior.
Negative reinforcement	A stimulus is withdrawn contingent on a response, increasing the frequency of that response.	Removal of a mother's demands following a child's tantrum increases the likelihood of tantrums.
Extinction	A weakening of a learned response is produced when the reinforcement that followed it no longer occurs.	Parents ignore bad behavior, and it decreases.
Punishment	A response is followed by either an unpleasant stimulus or the removal of a pleasant stimulus, thereby decreasing the frequency of the response.	A parent scolds a child for hitting, and the child stops hitting; food is removed from the table after a child spits, and the spitting stops.
Generalization	A response is made to a new stimulus that is different from, but similar to, the stimulus present during learning.	A child has a stern uncle with a mustache and develops fear of all men with mustaches.
Discrimination	A stimulus comes to signal that a certain response is likely to be followed by a particular consequence.	An adult's smile indicates that a child's request is likely to be granted.
Shaping	A desired behavior that is not in the child's repertoire is taught by rewarding responses that are increasingly similar to (successive approximations of) the desired response.	A mute child is taught to talk by initially reinforcing any sound, then a sound somewhat like a word, and so on.

The principles of operant conditioning have been applied to a broad range of behavioral problems with regard to their etiology, maintenance, and especially treatment. The specific applications of these procedures, discussed in succeeding chapters of this book, all share the assumption that problem behavior can be changed through a learning process and with a particular focus on the consequences of behavior (De Meyer et al., 2019).

Observational Learning

Observational learning is another fundamental way through which individuals change due to experience. A wide range of behaviors can be acquired by observing others perform them—from jumping rope, to cooperation or aggression, to social skills. As with other forms of learning, observational learning can lead to both the acquisition and the removal of problem behaviors. Early work by Bandura (1997) and his colleagues, as well as subsequent research, demonstrated how problem behaviors may be acquired through the observation of a model.

Although observational learning may seem simple, it is actually quite complex. Children can learn new responses by watching a model. However, they are more likely to display the responses if they observe the model being reinforced for the behavior and are less likely to display them if they observe the model being punished. As with other kinds of basic learning processes, observational learning can generalize. A child who observes another child being scolded for shouting may become quiet in other ways (inhibition). The observation of shooting and fighting on television may lead a child to exhibit other forms of aggression, such as verbal abuse and physical roughness (disinhibition). In neither case is the exact behavior of the model imitated; rather, a class of behaviors becomes either less likely or more likely to occur because of observation of the model.

Whether imitation is specific or generalized, complex cognitive processes are required for observational learning to occur (Bandura, 1977). The child must attend to salient features of the model's behavior, organize and encode this information, and store the information in memory. The child's imitation of the model in the near or far future depends on several factors, including recall of the information and expectation that the behavior will garner desired consequences. Observational learning is central in the social learning perspective, which recognizes that what children observe influences their understanding of the world and their behavior.

Cognitive Processes

Various approaches to cognition focus on how individuals mentally process information and think about the world. Briefly put, individuals perceive their experiences, construct concepts or schemas that represent experience, store information in memory, and employ their understanding to think about and act in the world. Among the many higher-order mental operations involved are perception, attention, memory, and mental manipulation of information. Different facets of cognition are implicated in many different kinds of problems—intellectual disabilities, specific learning disabilities, aggression, anxiety, and attention deficits, to name a few. The present discussion examines one cognitive viewpoint, the cognitive-behavioral perspective, which has contributed substantially to both understanding and treating problems of youth.

Cognitive-Behavioral Perspective
The **cognitive-behavioral perspective** incorporates cognition, emotion, behavior, and social factors. It is assumed that behaviors are learned and maintained by the interaction of internal cognitions and emotions with external environmental events. Cognitive factors influence whether the individual pays attention to environmental events, how the person perceives events, and whether these events affect future behavior. A basic hypothesis is that maladaptive cognitions are related to maladaptive behavior. As an example of support for this assumption, maladaptive thoughts and beliefs have been found among phobic and anxious children. For instance, in test situations, children with test anxiety frequently report more off-task thoughts, more negative self-evaluations, and fewer positive self-evaluations (Ollendick & King, 1998).

Kendall and colleagues suggest one way to distinguish the complex cognitive functions that contribute to the development, maintenance, and treatment of psychopathology (Kendall, 2006; Kendall et al., 1997b). *Cognitive structures* are schema for representing information stored in memory. Constructed over time from experience, they screen new experiences and can trigger other cognitive operations. *Cognitive content* refers to the actual content of the cognitive structures stored in memory. *Cognitive processes* refer to how people perceive and interpret experience. The combination of cognitive structures, content, and processes—interacting with actual events—results in *cognitive products*. (See Accent: "Thinking About Missteps.")

Kendall (2006) also recognizes the important difference between cognitive deficiencies and cognitive distortions. *Cognitive deficiencies* refer to an absence of thinking. The lack of forethought and planning exhibited by an impulsive child is an example of cognitive deficiency. *Cognitive distortions* are inaccurate thought processes that are dysfunctional. Depressed children viewing themselves as less capable than their peers even though others do not hold this view is an example of cognitive distortion.

Cognitive-behavioral therapy aims, through behavior-based procedures and structured sessions, to modify maladaptive

ACCENT Thinking About Missteps

Kendall (2006) offers an interesting—albeit less than pleasant—example of the workings of cognition. Consider, he suggests, the experience of what you would say to yourself if you stepped on something a dog had deposited on a lawn. For many people, a cognitive *structure* representing this event might automatically trigger a self-statement of dismay: "Oh sh--!" This statement reflects *cognitive content*. Individuals who respond thusly might then proceed to cognitively *process* the event in quite different ways, which is significant to the outcome. Some might think about social embarrassment (Did anyone see me?); others might have self-denigrating thoughts (I can't even walk!); still others might give little

attention to the experience and nonchalantly walk on. Subsequent to processing the event, individuals would draw conclusions about the event; for example, they might make causal attributions. These are cognitive *products*. Some individuals might attribute the problem to themselves (I can't do anything right!); others might blame whoever allowed the dog access to the lawn (I bet the guy knew someone would step in it!). As noted by Kendall, all of these processes are involved in a person making sense of experience. It is not so much an event itself but cognitions surrounding the event that influence the emotional and behavioral consequences for the person.

cognitive structures, deficiencies, and distortions. The particular ways in which the approach both conceptualizes and treats specific disorders of youth are presented throughout this text.

Sociocultural Context: An Overview

Development, whether adaptive or maladaptive, occurs within and is influenced by an elaborate sociocultural context (Kearney & Haskins, 2020). Although there are various ways to conceptualize this context, ecological models have grown in importance. (Ecology refers to the interrelationship of organisms and their environments.)

Figure 3.4 presents one way in which young people are perceived to be embedded within, and interacting with, numerous domains of overlapping, transactional environmental influences or systems. The youth is surrounded by three contexts—family, community, and society/culture—each of which consists of structures, institutions, values, rules, relationships, and other aspects that influence development. The arrows in the figure emphasize the potential interactions among the systems. For example, a child both is influenced by and influences peers, who may influence and be influenced by the child's parents and the school. In general, we would expect proximal contexts—the inner circles—to have relatively more direct impact on the child than more distal contexts. It would also be anticipated that the nature and importance of any one domain would vary with the developmental level of the individual, an obvious example being an increase in peer influence from infancy into adolescence. This model serves as a backdrop for further discussion of select aspects of sociocultural influences on development.

The Family Context

For many reasons, the family has been considered a critical force in development of the young. Family relationships and experiences are dominant from the first days of life and endure in some way over the lifespan of most individuals. The family plays a major role in socializing the child to behave in culturally acceptable ways and in transmitting cultural values and traditions. Families are also the conduit of food, shelter, neighborhood residence, education, and other opportunities to experience the world. The family may function as a mediator or moderator in development, and provide either risk or protection.

Although many kinds of family relationships are considered influential, including sibling and grandparent interactions, the parent–child relationship is considered dominant for most youth. It is worth noting that the family is most appropriately viewed as a complex, interacting system. Not only do parents affect children and each other, but children also influence parents in subtle and not-so-subtle ways.

Parenting

Various adults can fill the parental role (e.g., mothers, fathers, grandparents, alone or in combination). Historically, the influence of mothers has received much more attention than the influence of fathers (Cassano et al., 2006; Fabiano & Caserta, 2018). Mothers have been considered primary in day-to-day care, nurturance, management, and other aspects of child development—and have been more implicated in, and sometimes blamed for, the disturbances of their offspring. Nevertheless, recent decades have witnessed increased attention to fathers; including the roles fathers play in the development of psychopathology (Brouillard

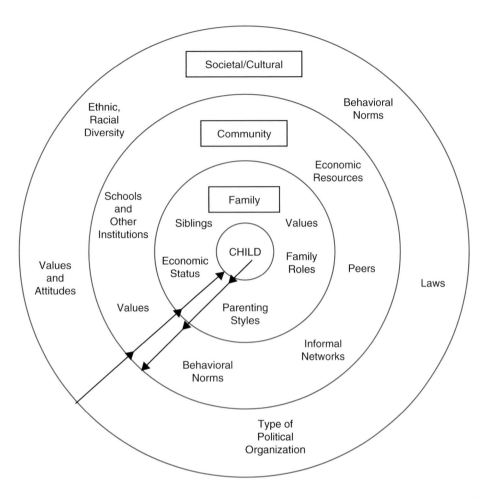

Figure 3.4 Youth are embedded in, and interact with, a number of contexts that are influenced by each other. (Based in part on Belsky, 1980; Bronfenbrenner, 1977; and Lynch & Cicchetti, 1998)

et al., 2018; E. K. Hughes et al., 2018; Tichovolsky et al., 2018). In the United States, the view of fathers as breadwinners harks back to the industrial revolution (Lamb, 2010). Around the time of the Great Depression (1930), emphasis was given to the father as a model of masculinity important to sex-role development of their sons. By the 1970s, greater emphasis was given to fathers as providers of custodial care and emotional involvement. It is recognized today that fathers assume several roles—breadwinners, role models, companions, protectors, teachers, and the like—although the importance of these roles may vary across fathers and social/cultural groups (Waller, 2010). It appears, however, that fathers' emotional involvement and guidance are highly valued today.

Due perhaps in part to their different roles, fathers and mothers may interact somewhat differently with their children, but sensitive fathering predicts positive child development just as sensitive mothering does. Paternal influence on the child may be direct or may operate indirectly, for instance, through interaction of the father with the mother. As one indication of recent greater involvement of fathers in the parenting role, the percentage of fathers who are stay-at-home dads was 7% in 2016 (up from 4% in 1989) and 17% of 2016 stay-at-home parents were fathers (up from 10% in 1989). In addition, 57% of fathers (comparable to 58% of mothers) said that "parenting is extremely important to their identity" (Livingston & Parker, 2019).

In any event, current understanding of parental roles and influences must consider that although today's fathers appear more involved with their children than in past times, it is also the case that many live apart from their children. A substantial number of children live apart from a parent (particularly a father) due to family divorce/relationship dissolution, incarceration, and other circumstances (Azar, Goslin, & Patallo, 2019; Humphreys, 2019; Poehlmann-Tynan et al., 2019). The percentage of children, under 18 years old, living with two parents, mother-only, father-only, or with other relatives (primarily grandparents) in 2019 and 1970 is illustrated in Figure 3.5. As can be seen in the figure, there has been an appreciable decrease in the number of children living in two-parent homes. (There was a steady decrease through

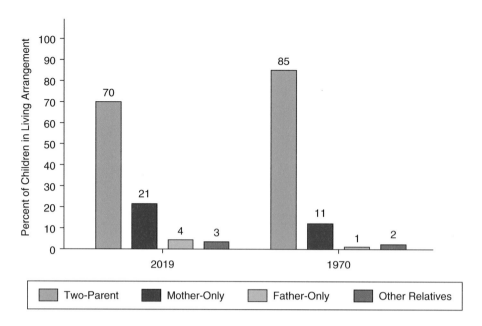

Figure 3.5 Living arrangements of children under 18 years old. (U.S. Census Bureau, 2019a)

the mid-1990s and a leveling off between then and 2019.) There were race/ethnicity differences in the percentage of children living in two-parent homes. In 2019, 75% of white children, 42% of black children, and 68% of Hispanic children were living in two-parent homes (U.S. Census Bureau, 2019).

Parenting Behaviors and Styles

The study of parenting is a multifaceted and complex undertaking (Bornstein, 2016; Lee, 2018). There are multiple ways in which one can approach the topic of parenting. Many of the efforts we will encounter during our explanation of various disorders address parenting behaviors. **Parenting behaviors** are particular actions employed by parents that can facilitate or hinder adaptive development. Positive examples of these behaviors include modeling appropriate behavior, giving clear directions or instructions, providing appropriate consequences for a child's actions, monitoring a child's behavior, and avoiding coercive interactions.

The quality of the relationship between parents and their offspring, beginning with early attachment, is believed to be crucial to development and adjustment. Examining the relatively characteristic ways in which parents deal with and manage their offspring is another way of studying parenting (Maccoby, 1992; Wood et al., 2003). Such **parenting styles** can be viewed as sets of attitudes, goals, and patterns of parenting practices that affect outcomes for children and adolescents (Pinquart, 2017a, 2017b).

Two major dimensions historically have been central in parent–child relationships. One dimension is degree of control, or discipline, and the other is degree of warmth, or acceptance.

Figure 3.6 presents the four parenting styles according to these dimensions. Authoritative parenting generally is associated with the most favorable child attributes. Authoritative parents assume control; set rules and expect their children to abide by the rules; follow through with consequences; and are simultaneously warm, accepting, and considerate of the needs of their offspring. Their children, in turn, tend to be independent, socially responsible, prosocial, and self-confident. In contrast, children of authoritarian, indulgent/permissive, and neglectful parents are thought to be at greater risk for less-than-optimal behaviors, including aggression, withdrawal, dependence, low self-esteem, irresponsibility, antisocial behaviors, anxiety, and school problems (e.g., Steinberg et al., 1994; Wood et al., 2003).

The dimensions of control and warmth continue to be important in the study of parenting practices, and much has also been learned about the effects of parent sensitivity, parent harshness, and parent monitoring (Warren et al., 2010). In considering parental practices, it is worthwhile to bear in mind the following issues (Eisenberg et al., 2010b; Eiser et al., 2005; O'Connor et al., 2006). *First*, effective parenting involves consideration of each youth's needs, as well as developmental level. Appropriate control for a 7-year-old child would not be expected to apply to a 15-year-old. *Second*, parenting practices may in part be a response to the child's characteristics as well as other relationships and circumstances in the family. *Third*, the extent to which the analysis of parenting practices holds across cultures and situations is noteworthy. For example, authoritative parenting may be less appropriate when local cultural values differ from those of mainstream culture in the United States. And in the

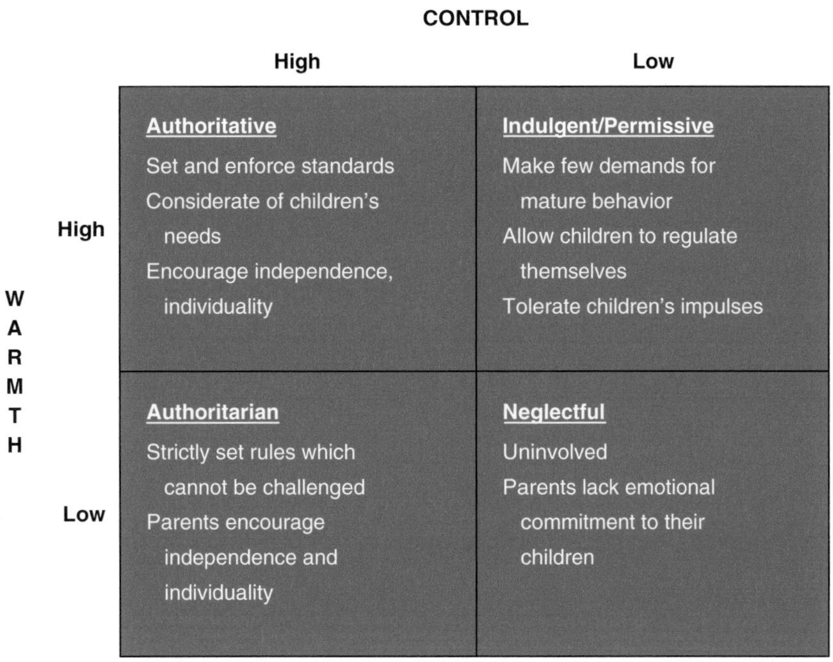

CONTROL

		High	Low
W A R M T H	**High**	**Authoritative** Set and enforce standards Considerate of children's needs Encourage independence, individuality	**Indulgent/Permissive** Make few demands for mature behavior Allow children to regulate themselves Tolerate children's impulses
	Low	**Authoritarian** Strictly set rules which cannot be challenged Parents encourage independence and individuality	**Neglectful** Uninvolved Parents lack emotional commitment to their children

Figure 3.6 Patterns of parental behavior. (Based in part on Maccoby & Martin, 1983. Copyright 1993 by John Wiley & Sons; reprinted with permission)

United States authoritarian parenting may protect children who are reared in disadvantaged environments.

Parent Psychopathology

The relationship between parent psychopathology and child adjustment has received considerable attention. Perhaps unsurprising, parent disturbance is a risk factor. Maternal depression, anxiety, and substance abuse are among several disorders linked to problems in offspring (Boris et al., 2019; Lawrence, Murayama, & Creswell, 2019; Murray, Halligan, & Cooper, 2019; Weissman et al., 2016). Although research on the association of father and child psychopathology lagged until more recently, it is clear that paternal problems also carry risk for children and adolescents (Brouillard et al., 2018; Flouri, 2010; Tichovolsky et al., 2018). Paternal antisocial behavior, substance abuse, ADHD, and depression are among the disorders implicated in child adjustment.

In general, both genetic transmission and environmental factors underlie the association of parent and offspring psychopathology. Children may inherit a genetic predisposition that increases risk and/or be affected by a risky family environment. As we have seen in our previous discussion of gene–environment correlation, genetic influence transmitted from parent to child may go hand in hand with the kind of family environment set up by the parent. But even when the child does not inherit vulnerability genes, parent psychopathology may negatively influence parenting, cause family stress, and otherwise create a less-than-optimal rearing environment.

Changes in Family Structure

In research about the family, it has often been assumed that families consist of parents and children together in the home. In fact, families have always been more varied. Even so, by most standards, dramatic changes have occurred in family structure during the last few decades in the United States and similar countries. Children are living in a variety of family types including two married parents, two cohabiting non-married parents, two same-sex parents, single parent, and adoptive, blended, extended families (Azar et al., 2019).

Divorce and Relationship Dissolution

That many marriages end in divorce is well documented. The divorce rate in the United States increased dramatically in the 1960s and 1970s, reaching a peak about 1980. This trend has leveled off and perhaps declined in recent years. Yet, it has been estimated that more than eight million children in the United States live with a divorced parent (U.S. Census Bureau, 2018a). However compelling, this statistic does not fully capture the problem. Many children experience considerable stress prior to the divorce. Some go through periodic separation and discord in families in which divorce petitions are filed and withdrawn. Others experience more than one divorce or the comings and goings of nonmarried partners. Moreover, divorce and subsequent reconstitution of the family are not static events, but rather are a series of family transitions that modify the lives of children (Amato, 2010; Azar et al., 2019; Hetherington & Stanley-Hagan, 1999).

Children and adolescents from divorced and remarried families are at increased risk for developing adjustment problems (Amato, 2010; Hetherington & Kelly, 2002; Schroeder & Smith-Boydston, 2017). There is, nonetheless, considerable variability in outcome. Indeed, the vast majority of children from divorced or remarried families function in the normal range, and some youth experience positive outcomes. Through divorce, some move out of highly conflicted and violent situations, may move into less stressful and more supportive circumstances, and may actually experience opportunities for the development of exceptional competencies (Amato & Keith, 1991; Hetherington & Kelly, 2002; Hetherington & Stanley-Hagan, 1999). However, these findings should not lead us to ignore the clinical significance of the adjustment problems experienced by some young people. An important question, worthy of continuing investigation, is what accounts for increased risk for youth who develop adjustment difficulties and for the resilience of those who do not (Azar et al., 2019).

The effects of family composition/parent absence are not simple and are likely modified by factors such as parent adjustment, quality of family relationships, the child's age and gender, and the availability of both parents to the child (Braver, Ellman, & Fabricius, 2003; Jaffee et al., 2003; Schroeder & Smith-Boydston, 2017). Furthermore, there are cultural and ethnic differences in how family is defined. The presence of extended family in the household, for example, is more likely among African American families than among European American families, as is an informal network of kin and friends available to function in parental roles (Emery & Kitzmann, 1995).

Hetherington and her colleagues (Hetherington, Bridges, & Insabella, 1998) suggest a model, based on a set of interrelated risks, to explain the links between divorce/remarriage and a child's adjustment. As Figure 3.7 shows, adjustment to marital transitions encompasses complex interactions among a large number of influences. To add to the complexity, while the process of family transitions is occurring, children and the developmental tasks they face are also changing (O'Connor, 2003). In addition, ethnic and cultural influences are salient in this process. With such complexities in mind, we turn to an examination of some of the influences likely to affect the adjustment of children and adolescents to marital transitions.

A central aspect of the divorce process is the interaction among family members, particularly the ongoing relationship between the two parents. Indeed, the degree of family conflict is considered to be a primary influence on the adjustment of children (Cummings & Davies, 2010; Kelly, 2000; Schroeder & Smith-Boydston, 2017; Xerxa et al., 2020). Also, following divorce, the ongoing relationship between the parents, stepparents, or significant others and between each parent or stepparent and the child contributes to complicated family transitions that affect the child (Hakvoort et al., 2011; Hetherington et al., 1998; O'Hara et al., 2019; van der Wal, Finkenauer, & Visser, 2019).

Preexisting individual characteristics also contribute to a child's adjustment. Individual attributes of adults (e.g., antisocial behavior, depression) place some parents at risk for marital discord and multiple marital transitions, and also impact the adult's ability to parent effectively. Individual characteristics of the youth may

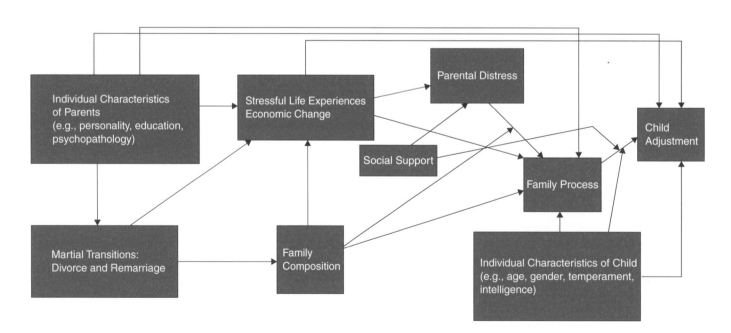

Figure 3.7 A transactional model of the predictors of children's adjustment following divorce and remarriage. (From Hetherington, Bridges, & Insabella, 1998)

also contribute to adjustment. For example, children with an easy temperament may be better able to cope with the disruptions. Those with a difficult temperament may be more likely to elicit negative responses from their stressed parents and to have greater difficulty adapting to parental negativity and marital transitions. They may be less capable of eliciting the support of other people around them (Hetherington et al., 1998).

The relationship between parental characteristics, child characteristics, and the ongoing divorce process is complex. For example, the child's prior level of adjustment may have resulted in part from the marital friction that contributed to the divorce. In turn, the challenges of parenting a difficult child may have contributed to the marital difficulty and divorce. Furthermore, the parental characteristics that played a role in the divorce, as well as child behavior problems, may be influenced by common genetic contributions (Amato, 2010; Musci et al., 2016; Salvatore et al., 2017). Shared genes may contribute, for example, to the likelihood of parent antisocial behavior (a risk for divorce) and acting-out problems in children and adolescents.

A variety of other factors such as the child's gender, custody arrangements, post-divorce parental contact, timing/developmental stage, and economic consequences of divorce likely affect this complex process. Furthermore, divorce may result in a number of stressful family life changes, such as more frequent moves and changes in schools. Much of the impact of these divorce-related circumstances on child functioning may be mediated by their effect on family processes in general and on the stability of the family environment in particular (Sun & Li, 2011; Them, Israel, Ivanova, & Chalmers, 2003). (See Accent: "Family Stability.") Such stress and other changes can contribute to dysfunctional family relations (e.g., conflict) and interfere with effective parenting (Beck et al., 2010; Hetherington et al., 1998). Within this context, however, it is important to remember that positive experiences such as a stable family environment, good parent–child communication, and supportive relationships with another adult may serve as protective factors for young people experiencing divorce-related events (Doyle et al., 2003; King, 2009; Velez et al., 2011).

ACCENT Family Stability

Family stability is an aspect of the family environment that often emerges in the discussion of children's development and adjustment, with higher levels of stability associated with better outcomes. What is meant by "family stability"? Often, it is conceptualized in terms of the stability of family structure—for example, maintaining a household with a nuclear family structure as compared to separation or divorce. While this view is reasonable, it is also possible to consider a broader notion of family stability.

In an attempt to offer a broader conceptualization, Israel and colleagues (Israel, Roderick, & Ivanova, 2002; Ivanova & Israel, 2006; Sheppard, Malatras, & Israel, 2010) have suggested a model of family stability that encompasses two components. The first component, *global family stability*, addresses changes in family structure, such as those that may be associated with divorce, as well as family life changes described as accompanying events such as divorce or parental death (Hetherington & Stanley-Hagan, 1999; Tremblay & Israel, 1998). Family life changes may include, for example, changes in residence, schools, and household composition (who lives in the child's home). The term *global* is used to describe these structural and family life changes as they are deemed more distal from the youth's daily experiences and are less easily controlled by the child or parent.

The second component, *molecular family stability*, refers to the predictability and consistency of family activities and routines. These may include daily routines such as those that occur at bed or mealtimes; activities that children engage in with the family on a regular basis, such as weekend activities or religious observances; or activities that do not involve family members but are arranged and supported by the family, such as extracurricular activities or time with friends. It is expected that differences exist in how families achieve stability—one family may have regular mealtime routines while another regularly participates in joint outings and activities—and also that families may create stability in different ways over time, perhaps adjusting to the developmental level of the child. Moreover, molecular family stability is conceptualized as a parenting skill and as a component of stability that is more proximal to the youth's daily experiences and more accessible to intervention. Thus, professionals may be able to work with families to develop predictable and regular family activities and routines that may help create a sense of stability within the context of a family environment that may be otherwise disrupted. Molecular family stability has, indeed, been demonstrated to be associated with adjustment (Israel et al., 2002; Ivanova & Israel, 2006; Sokolowski & Israel, 2008).

(continued)

(continued)

The creation of a stable family environment is likely to be important to all children and families and may be particularly so for those undergoing multiple transitions. Such transitions occur frequently for families experiencing separation, divorce, and remarriage, for example. Other life circumstances also may present challenges. One example suggested by recent circumstances is the transitions and challenges faced by U.S. military families experiencing deployment of a parent. The model of family stability offered by Israel and colleagues may be one way of helping to understand the potential impact of military deployment on families and children (Sheppard et al., 2010). Military deployment may, for example, be associated with the family life changes that are part of the concept of global family stability (e.g., changes of residence or household residents). On the other hand, aspects of military life for some families may protect against such instability (e.g., military housing on a base with other military families).

The military deployment process can be viewed as having several transitions for families—preparing for deployment, deployment, sustaining the family while the parent is away, preparation for redeployment home, and the period following the return home. These transitions may be repeated if the service member has multiple deployments away from home. The multiple phases of the deployment cycle may present challenges with regard to maintaining typical family activities and routines (molecular family stability). This may be the case during actual deployment and also with regard to the challenges that the service member/parent and family may face after the service member returns home. The ability of the parents to create stability in the family environment may be one factor influencing the adjustment of children in families facing the challenges associated with military deployment.

Parental Incarceration

Unfortunately, for an appreciable number of children, disruptions in family structure, family activities, and parenting occur as a result of a parent being incarcerated (Poehlmann-Tynan et al., 2019). During 2017–2018, an estimated 7.4% of children in the United States had a parent or guardian who served time in jail (National Survey of Children's Health, 2019).

The changes experienced are often part of a sequence of arrest, jailing, sentencing to incarceration to a jail or prison and, perhaps, release back into the community. Again, it is not best to think in terms of a discrete legal event, but to consider parental incarceration as a process from potential pre-arrest stress on the family, through arrest, through potential repeated separations from and re-entries into the home.

Children with incarcerated parents, on average, are more likely to experience multiple risk factors and stress exposures including poverty, parental unemployment, neighborhood violence, homelessness, domestic violence, and parental psychopathology. Some of these risks may occur prior to incarceration. Given the association of these multiple risk factors with parental incarceration the relationship between incarceration and child outcomes is likely to be a complex one. However, research suggests that children with an incarcerated parent have been found to experience multiple adverse outcomes. Parental incarceration has been found to be associated with a variety of psychological problems and, in particular, problems such as aggression, oppositional/defiant behavior, and antisocial behavior in children. In addition, negative effects on children's cognitive and academic functioning has been noted (Poehlmann-Tynan et al., 2019; Turney, 2017).

Foster Care

In an attempt to maintain an adaptive parenting and family environment, it is sometimes necessary to remove children from their homes and place them in **foster care** settings. Children may be placed in a variety of foster care settings including nonrelative and relative foster family homes, group homes, emergency shelters, residential facilities, and pre-adoptive homes (Child Welfare Information Gateway, 2019a). The percentage of placements in various foster care settings in 2017 is illustrated in Figure 3.8.

Although it is ordinarily preferable for children and adolescents to remain with their birth families, substitute care is not always avoidable. Substitute placement occurs involuntarily or voluntarily when families are unable to care for their offspring. In earlier times in the United States and other countries, these youth were placed in institutions and had few connections to their families. Concerns about harmful effects of institutionalization led to family foster care (Fisher et al., 2016). Although the goal often was to return children to their biological families, many youth remained in foster care for long periods of time, some until they reached the legal age to be independent. Further, although foster care placements certainly can have positive influences, they also can be inadequate and the rate of disruption is high, with children being moved from placement to placement. In an effort to improve this situation, the federal government enacted the Adoption and Safe Families Act (ASFA) in 1997. ASFA brought substantial change in foster care. Here, we discuss two aspects of efforts to improve the foster care system.

First, because youth in foster care are at risk for psychological problems, **treatment foster care** programs have been created

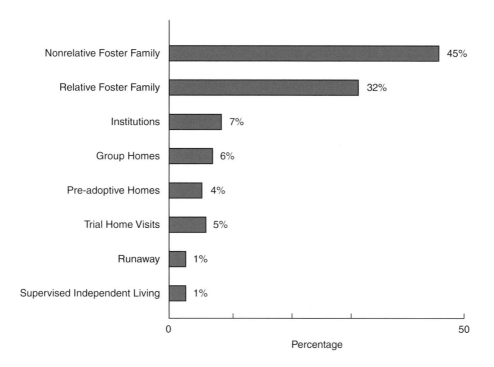

Figure 3.8 Percentage of children in various foster care placements, 2017. (Adapted from Child Welfare Information Gateway, 2019a)

(Buchanan, Chamberlain, & Smith, 2017; Dore & Mullin, 2006; Fisher et al., 2016). Prior to the child's being placed in their care, foster parents understand that the child requires mental health services and that they will serve as agents of change. An example of treatment foster care is described in Chapter 9 (p. 223), in which multidimensional treatment foster care was designed specifically for delinquent youth (Buchanan et al., 2017). In such programs, special training and help are given to foster parents; links may be forged with community mental health services; and foster parents may work with the child's family to facilitate reunion with the child.

The work of Linares and colleagues (2006) also illustrates the potential benefits of providing specific training to parents of high-risk children in foster care. Parent training intervention was provided to biological and foster parent *pairs* of maltreated (primarily neglected) 3- to 10-year-olds who had been placed in foster care. It was reasoned that training in pairs would facilitate cooperation and communication between families and avoid fragmented services. The Incredible Years (IY) parent training program (pp. 220–221) was employed, based on evidence of its effectiveness in teaching parenting skills and in reducing child problems. A separate co-parenting component addressed communication, conflict resolution, and cooperative parenting of the child. There were significant differences between intervention families and control families at the end of treatment and at a three-month follow-up. Both sets of intervention families exhibited significant gains and at the follow-up reported a trend for fewer child problems.

A second challenge for the foster care system is the exiting of foster care. Among other priorities of the ASFA is the provision of a permanent home for every youth in foster care. Within a specified time, each child must either be returned to the biological family, or be adopted, or be permanently placed with a foster family, which can include relatives or legal guardians. The ASFA provides the states with a financial incentive for permanency planning/adoption of children in temporary foster care. In some circumstances, it may be difficult to attain this goal. Administrative entities, including child welfare agencies, attorneys, and the courts, can be overloaded, yet face the challenge of providing, in a timely manner, safe and stable permanent families for children (Child Welfare Information Gateway, 2019b). And the task is substantial; for example, in 2017, there were about 443,000 children in foster care (Child Welfare Information Gateway, 2019a). Many of these youth have experienced chaotic or traumatized lives and require special behavioral, educational, or medical care (Fisher et al., 2016).

Nevertheless, the goal of finding a permanent family for youth in foster care has met with some success. Of those exiting foster care in 2017, 49% were reunited with parents or primary caretakers, 24% were adopted, 7% went to live with other relatives, 10% went to live with a guardian, and 8% were emancipated (Child Welfare Information Gateway, 2019a).

It is noteworthy, however, that finding families for older children may be particularly difficult. The median age of exiting foster care was 7.8 years of age in 2017 and from 2007 to 2017 there was a decrease in the median age of exiting foster care (Child Welfare Information Gateway, 2019a). Moreover, those who leave foster care because they reach the age of emancipation are too often left without sufficient social, educational, and financial support (Child Welfare Information Gateway, 2019b; Howard & Berzin, 2011).

Peer Influences

From infancy onward, individuals relate socially to each other and peer relations are likely to grow in influence. The peer group provides a unique developmental context that influences immediate and long-term social and cognitive growth (Bukowski, Laurson, & Rubin, 2018; Schroeder & Smith-Boydston, 2017). Areas in which peer interactions may play a unique and/or essential role include the development of sociability, empathy, cooperation, and morality; negotiation of conflict and competition; control of aggression; and socialization of sexuality and gender roles. Peer relations may ensure the development of social competence in the face of adversity, thereby preventing or reducing the likelihood of disorder (Arbel, Perrone, & Margolin, 2018; Chen & Liu, 2016; Masten & Cicchetti, 2016). They may also be associated with the presence of disorder.

Individual child characteristics—emotional, cognitive, and social—enter into the development of peer relationships (Hay, Payne, & Chadwick, 2004). So also do other social relationships. Early attachment experiences in the family are thought to be related to peer relationships and social competence (Booth-LaForce & Groh, 2018). Parental hostility, coercion, lack of involvement, and authoritarian/restrictive styles are associated

Peer interactions provide a unique and essential opportunity to develop certain skills. (Monkey Business Images/Shutterstock)

with child aggression and peer rejection (Dekovic & Janssens, 1992; Dishion & Patterson, 2016). Teachers also can play a role in shaping peers' attitudes toward one another (Ryan & Shin, 2018; Vollet, Kindermann, &Skinner, 2017), and neighborhood characteristics can influence the nature of peer relations (Brody et al., 2001; Deutsch et al., 2012; Smith, Faulk, & Sizer, 2016).

The multifaceted nature of peer relationships is appreciated (Bukowski & Adams, 2005). Early research primarily focused on overall peer status, that is, on whether the peer group accepted, rejected, or neglected the target child. Additional interest has been directed at particular relationships, such as that between bullies and their victims (Espelage & Hong, 2019). The nature and role of friendship also has received attention (Bukowski, Laursen, & Hoza, 2010; Markovic & Bowker, 2017; Prinstein & Giletta, 2016). A close friendship is viewed as a mutual relationship that, among other positive aspects, can serve as protection against risk factors, including the risk of being excluded, rejected, or neglected by classmates. Unsurprisingly, children tend to select friends who have similar interests or are similarly adjusted. Whereas this can strengthen positive attitudes and behaviors, it also can magnify and encourage psychological difficulties and deviant behavior.

An extreme instance of such negative outcome was described in the analyses of the relationship of two students who engaged in a murderous rampage at Columbine High School (Cullen, 2009; Larkin, 2007). Although complex circumstances undoubtedly led to the event, it was suggested that the adolescent boys desperately needed each other, reinforced each other, and could not have carried out the attack alone.

One of the most commonly cited reasons for interest in peer relationships is their association with later adjustment. Children who experience peer rejection, who are withdrawn and socially isolated, or who associate with deviant peers are at risk for later difficulties (Prinstein & Giletta, 2016; van Lier & Koot, 2010). Indeed, difficult peer relationships often underlie children's referrals to mental health centers and are reported among children with a variety of disorders. There is a bidirectional association of peer difficulties with adjustment problems. Not only do peer difficulties contribute to the development of behavioral disorders, but the presence of disorder may also adversely affect peer relationships (Achenbach & Rescorla, 2001).

How is the association of early peer problems with later psychological disturbances to be understood? It is possible that, in some instances, the relationship is not causal, that some unidentified general tendency independently causes both peer and other difficulties. When a causal link is suspected, one hypothesis is that a child's initial tendencies and social experiences enter into a negative transaction with peers that leads the child to behave in ways that perpetuate peer rejection and other difficulties.

Community and Societal Contexts

School Influences

The school is one of the most central contexts in children's lives. Although a primary function of the school is to teach intellectual skills and knowledge, mental health services are often provided in schools, and schools are expected to guide additional aspects of development (Holt, Green, & Guzman, 2019; Pianta, 2016). Schools help socialize youth to societal norms and values, shape motivation to achieve, and contribute to socioemotional growth and mental health. School influences operate through distal factors such as district resources and educational policy and proximal influences such as classroom climate, instruction, and social relationships.

The structure and organization of schools can be more or less conducive to healthy development. Consider, for example, that today's educational system often requires children to move into middle schools in early adolescence. Thus, at a time of notable biological and other social change, children must also adapt to new school demands. These frequently include more unsupervised time, less parent–teacher communication, and exposure to a wider assortment of peers (Stormshak et al., 2011). The transition to middle school can be a risky time.

Social relationships are a crucial component of school life. Schools are the locale for important peer interactions—for supportive friendships, rejection and bullying, and social cliques. Among the many factors that might affect these interactions is variations in school settings (Pianta, 2016). For example, school size, division of students into educational tracts, and opportunity for informal social contact all might have influence.

Student–teacher relationships are often critical to young people, many of whom remember in adulthood their most favored or "hated" teachers. Such relationships may play a role in positive normative development, operate as a risk factor, or serve as protection against risk (O'Connor, Dearing, & Collins, 2011; Pianta, 2016; Sointu et al., 2017). Perhaps unsurprising, high-quality relationships are associated with positive child outcomes, whereas conflicted relationships are linked with unfavorable behavioral and academic outcomes (Archambault, Vanderbossche-Makombo, & Fraser, 2017; Crosnoe et al., 2010).

Successful completion of school is widely viewed as contributing to positive development, but success is not realized by many youth. Low socioeconomic status, academic failure, behavioral problems, and lack of family support are among the factors associated with dropping out of school or repeating a grade level (Mattison, 2000). Unfortunately, large inequities often exist between schools attended by students from upper class backgrounds and schools attended by children of lower social class and minority backgrounds. In contrast, concerns have emerged regarding excessive pressure on students to excel. These generally occur in affluent contexts. Such pressure is among the top four high-risk factors for adolescents' adjustment, along with exposure to poverty, trauma, and discrimination (Luthar, Kumar, & Zillmer, 2020).

Of course, schools do not have control over all the determinants of student success, but there is consensus that schools have some responsibility to both children's cognitive development and their social and emotional growth. Some schools have incorporated social and emotional learning programs aimed at preventing problems such as academic failure and substance abuse, enhancing social competence, and providing students the opportunity to contribute to their social environments (Durlak et al., 2011; Holt et al., 2019).

Socioeconomic Status and Poverty

Socioeconomic status (SES), or social class, is indexed by factors such as income, educational achievement, and occupational level, which correlate with one another. Virtually all societies are stratified according to social class, and social class is marked by differences in many facets of life—environmental conditions, social interactions, values, attitudes, expectations, and opportunities.

Although good adjustment and psychological problems occur in all social classes, the relatively higher risk associated with lower social class has led to an emphasis on the effects of poverty. Young people who live in families of low SES experience increased risk for negative outcomes such as developmental delay, learning disabilities, school failure, and behavioral and psychological problems (van Oort et al., 2011; Piccolo & Noble, 2019; Wadsworth et al., 2016). Unfortunately, poverty rates in the United States are higher in young people than in other age groups. In 2018, 18% of youth under age 18 lived in families below the poverty line (U.S. Census Bureau, 2018b). Rates varied considerably by race and Hispanic origin. The percentage of families living in poverty in 2018 by race/ethnicity is presented in Table 3.4.

In discussing the impact of family income on children's achievements and verbal ability, Duncan and Brooks-Gunn (2000) pointed to the probable importance of poverty's *persistence*, *depth*, and *timing*. Poverty that persists over time, is severe, and occurs early in the child's life has the most negative effects.

Table 3.4 Percentage of Families Living in Poverty, 2018

All families	7.3
White, non-Hispanic alone	5.9
Asian alone	7.5
Hispanic or Latino alone	16.5
Black or African American alone	18.5
American Indian and Alaskan Native alone	19.6
Two or more races	12.5

Source: U.S. Census Bureau, 2018c.

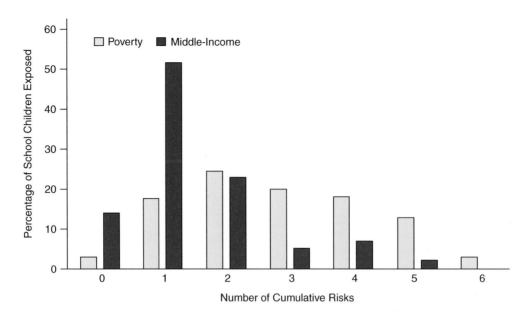

Figure 3.9 Percentage of poor and nonpoor school children exposed to cumulative physical and psychosocial environmental risks. (From Evans, 2004)

In addition, exposure to multiple risks that accumulate over time is related to developmental outcome (Evans, 2004). Figure 3.9 shows a striking difference in the number of cumulative risks experienced by poor and middle-class children in the third to fifth grades. Poor children are more likely to have exposure to unsafe levels of lead, pesticides, and air pollution; inadequate water supplies; and poor sanitation. They are more likely to live in crowded homes with structural defects, rodent infestation, and other safety hazards.

Family processes undoubtedly play a crucial role in mediating the influence of poverty. Although family genetics may be implicated, additional influences are involved (Evans, 2004; Pungello et al., 2010; Wadsworth et al., 2016). Children growing up in poor homes often lack learning resources such as books, appropriate toys, and computers. Parenting in low SES homes tends to be harsher and less sensitive and responsive compared with that in middle-class (less stressed) homes, where parents give relatively more time, effort, and verbal attention to their young children. In addition, the stress of being poor may increase the likelihood of parent–child conflict, and it is likely that family separation and lower marital quality are also linked to poverty.

The many-faceted effects of poverty influence development through varied pathways (A. B. Miller et al., 2018; Wadsworth et al., 2016). The impact of poverty on brain development is one such pathway (Piccolo & Noble, 2019). For example, Hair and colleagues (2015) reasoned that living in poverty often involves heightened stress and reduced environmental stimulation—both of which have been shown to affect neural functioning. Drawing on a database of youth 4 to 18 years of age, the investigators showed an association between poverty and the volume of gray matter of the frontal lobe, temporal lobe, and hippocampus, even when controlling for other factors such as parental health and education. Although the study does not definitely establish a causal pathway, it suggests one mechanism through which the environment may put poor youth at risk for numerous negative outcomes.

Neighborhood

There has been appreciable interest on the impact of community influences on child and adolescent development (Jennings & Perez, 2017; Leventhal & Brooks-Gunn, 2000; Warner & Settersten, 2017). Interest in community influences is not entirely distinct from considerations of the impact of poverty on development. Most investigations of the impact of neighborhood have focused on low-income neighborhoods. Such neighborhoods also face multiple other challenges including inadequate housing, crowding, and high levels of violence and crime. Although it would be a mistake to assume that such neighborhoods are identical, all too often they provide a developmental context that is far from optimal.

Various community-influenced outcomes have received attention including distress, anxiety, and depression, health-risk behaviors, and sexual-risk behaviors (Barker et al., 2019; Cambron et al., 2018; James et al., 2018; Snedker & Herting, 2016). However, the greatest attention has been to the impact of community influences on antisocial and delinquent behaviors (Criss et al., 2017; Jennings & Perez, 2017; Li et al., 2017).

Leventhal and Brooks-Gunn discussed a conceptualization of the mechanisms or pathways of community influences (Figure 3.10).

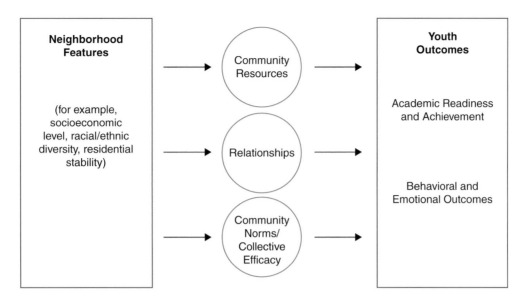

Figure 3.10 Three proposed mechanisms or pathways linking community characteristics to outcomes for youth. (Based on Leventhal & Brooks-Gunn, 2000)

- One pathway is *community resources*, which includes opportunities for learning offered in schools, libraries, and museums; quality day care; medical services; and employment.
- The second pathway focuses on *relationships*, especially within the family. It includes parents' personal characteristics; parenting styles and supervision; support networks for parents; and physical and organizational features of the home such as cleanliness, safety, and regular schedules and routines.
- The third pathway, *community norms/collective efficacy*, refers to the extent to which communities are organized to maintain behavioral norms and order. To varying degrees formal institutions or informal networks monitor or supervise the behavior of individuals and watch for physical risks that might exist. The neighborhood scrutinizes child and adolescent behavior, the availability of illegal substances, and violence, crime, and similar activities.

As suggested by the Leventhal and Brooks-Gunn conceptualization, youth outcomes are not the product of a single influence. Research indicates that the interplay of various aspects of community, family factors, peer influences, and individual variables contribute to adjustment. For example, Jennings and colleagues (2011) analyzed data collected from sixth through eighth grade for over 5,000 youths. Measure of neighborhood problems (including drug and alcohol availability and use, poor supervision, and inadequate police presence), individual variables (e.g., alcohol use, peer alcohol use, depression), and demographics (e.g., age, sex, race, household composition) all were related to youth physical aggression. However, neighborhood problems significantly predicted physical aggression over time, even after

controlling for individual and demographic influences. Similarly, Criss and colleagues (2017) studied a sample of 206 adolescents from predominantly low-income families. Their findings indicated that high levels of neighborhood violence and danger were related to high levels of youth antisocial behavior. Interestingly, and indicative of the interplay between influences, positive, warm, and supportive parent–adolescent relationship quality and higher levels of peer prosocial behavior reduced the negative impact of neighborhood problems on adolescent antisocial behavior. Aspects of community can also serve as protective influences. Donnelly and colleagues (2016) analyzed data from over 2,000 youth to examine the influence of neighborhood collective efficacy (social cohesion and shared expectations for social control) on adolescent adjustment. Youth who grew up in neighborhoods with high collective efficacy experienced fewer symptoms of anxiety and depression during adolescence than youth from neighborhoods with low collective efficacy. Thus, aspects of neighborhoods can present risk or facilitate positive development. (See Accent: "Changing Neighborhoods.")

Culture, Race/Ethnicity, and Immigrant Status

All of the contexts we have already discussed operate within a still larger cultural context consisting of a society's beliefs and values, social structures, social roles and norms, and ways of "doing business."

Influences stemming from cultural factors may have broad positive or negative effects. For example, certain practices in the United States may inadvertently foster conduct problems in youth. A case in point concerns the exposure of youth to high levels of aggressive and violent content in media. Decades of research

Very poor neighborhoods often provide a context that is less than optimal for the development of youth. (Andrew Burton/Getty Images)

indicate that observing such television, film, video games, and the internet can contribute to increased risk for aggressive behavior and decreased prosocial behavior in children (Anderson et al., 2017; Bushman & Anderson, 2015; Krahé, 2012).

Risk stemming from the cultural context may be particularly high for individuals whose ethnic/racial background is other than mainstream. Indigenous groups deal with unique historical issues and matters of **acculturation**, that is, modifications in culture resulting from cultures coming into contact with each other. In many countries, Indigenous groups have higher rates of poverty, psychopathology, health problems, educational disadvantages, and the like (Juster et al., 2016). In the United States, the poverty rate for Native Americans is high (U.S. Census Bureau, 2018a), and youth in these communities experience numerous risk factors and have high rates of problems such as symptoms of depression and PTSD, suicide attempts, substance abuse, disruptive behavior, and juvenile delinquency (Brockie et al., 2015; Hawkins, Cummins, & Marlatt, 2004; Hautala & Sittner, 2019; Stiffman et al., 2007; Storck et al., 2009).

In the United States, ethnic/racial diversity has grown enormously in the last few decades, and Hispanic children made up approximately 25% of the child population in 2018 (Federal Interagency Forum on Child and Family Statistics, 2019). Children of immigrants—whether foreign or U.S. born—require special

consideration. It is estimated that in 2019 in the United States about 26% of youth age 18 and under lived with an immigrant parent (U.S. Census Bureau, 2019a). Immigrant parents may lack proficiency in the English language and be economically limited. Moreover, they may be undocumented, a situation that threatens cultural integration and opportunity. Although the national background of these families varies greatly, immigrant children generally are at risk for poverty, low educational attainment, and adjustment problems.

Children of immigrants may experience a variety of stressors including poor English language skills and struggles with acculturation. Minority and immigrant groups also commonly face prejudice and discrimination, and devaluation by others may be perceived relatively early in life. Prejudice and discrimination not only reduce opportunity but also have other influences. For example, negative prejudgment and stereotyping of African American and Latino students may adversely affect their academic performance (Brown & Chu, 2012; Cohen et al., 2009; English, Lambert, & Ialongo, 2016). Discrimination and perceived racism have been associated with aggression, antisocial acts, anxiety, and depression in African American and other minority children and adolescents (Huatala & Sitner, 2019; Nyborg & Curry, 2003; Priest et al., 2013). Among the variables that may protect these youth from some negative outcomes are racial identity—the

ACCENT Changing Neighborhoods

There has been a variety of evidence suggesting risk associated with living in areas characterized by poverty, crime, and violence. There may be multiple reasons why families living in high-risk neighborhoods do not move to safer and more affluent neighborhoods. Families may prefer their current neighborhoods for reasons such as family and friends, cultural factors, and proximity to work. However, there also may be economic and other barriers that influence the decision whether or not to move.

Research conducted as part of the Moving to Opportunity project (Bergman et al., 2019; Chetty, Hendren, & Katz, 2016) offered randomly selected families living in high-poverty housing assistance in relocating to lower-poverty neighborhoods. The assistance consisted of financial assistance in the form of housing vouchers and other services such as customized search assistance and landlord engagement to help reduce barriers to moving.

Among the families offered this assistance 54% moved to lower-poverty and higher-opportunity neighborhoods as compared to 14% of the control group. Families who moved expressed high levels of neighborhood satisfaction and indicated that their move was facilitated by provision of concrete services and emotional support that was individualized and specific to each family.

Of particular interest were findings regarding the long-term impact of moving to higher-opportunity areas on the children in these families. Moving to a lower-poverty neighborhood before the age of 13 resulted in higher rates of college attendance, higher earnings, and reduced rates of single parenthood. There was a slightly negative impact on young people who moved during adolescence. This may be due to disruptions in important aspects of the adolescents' lives or may suggest that the duration of exposure to different neighborhood environments is an important determinant of long-term outcomes.

degree to which they identify with their ethnic/racial group—and racial socialization—being reared to be aware of the meaning of being a member of one's racial/ethnic group and being proud of one's heritage (Anderson & Mayes, 2010; Jones & Neblett, 2017; Rucker, Neblett, & Anyiwo, 2014; Yasui et al., 2015; Wang & Huguley, 2012).

Multiple investigators emphasize the need to consider the effects of the unique experiences of youth of minority ethnic and racial background on development (Anderson & Mayes, 2010; Hope, Hoggard, & Thomas, 2015; Masten & Cicchetti, 2016; Wadsworth et al., 2016). It is suggested that developmental models for nonmainstream youth include the possible influences of prejudice, discrimination, acculturation, racial socialization and identity, and cultural values. (We would add to this the need for

similar consideration of other youth who, due to handicapping conditions or sexual orientation, experience more than a usual share of devaluation and prejudice.)

Finally, we should note the disadvantages often experienced by minority groups in seeking and receiving mental and other health services (Cummings et al., 2017; Pina, Polo, & Huey, 2019). In addition to inaccessible or inadequate services in needy communities, professionals in multicultural settings may lack the awareness of cultural differences and the skills and openness to others required for productive work. To facilitate cultural competence, the American Psychological Association (Clauss-Ehlers et al., 2019) has published guidelines for training, practice, and other aspects of serving multicultural communities. There is little doubt that the need is substantial.

Looking Back

Brain and Nervous System

- Early brain development depends on the interaction of biological programming and experience.
- The various parts of the nervous system and brain function as a whole, with specific areas playing primary roles in specific functions. Communication occurs through complex neurotransmission among neurons.

Nervous System and Risk for Disordered Functioning

- Damage to the brain can result from genetic, prenatal, perinatal, and postnatal events. Numerous prenatal risks have been identified, and their effects depend on several variables.
- The capacity of young people to recover from brain damage is not easy to predict.

Genetic Context

- The basic genetic material consists of chromosomal DNA residing in all body cells. Transcription and translation of the genetic code are affected by the internal and external environment.
- Epigenetic modifications of DNA play a role in gene expression.
- Genetic influences on development occur through single-gene and multiple-gene processes. Such influences are studied through a variety of quantitative (family, twin, and adoption studies) and molecular (linkage and association) analyses.
- Hereditary influences, as well as shared and nonshared environmental effects, have been demonstrated for many disorders.
- The interplay of genetic and environmental influences is shown in gene–environment interactions and gene–environment correlations.

Learning and Cognition

- Learning and cognition are critical to development. Classical conditioning, operant learning, observational learning, and higher-order cognitive processes play major roles in the development and treatment of psychological disorders.

Sociocultural Context: An Overview

- The sociocultural context of development consists of overlapping transactional domains of influences that include family, peers, community, societal, and cultural influences.

The Family Context

- Family interaction is complex, with fathers and mothers and other adults performing overlapping but not identical roles.
- Parenting is a multifaceted and complex process. Parenting behaviors such as modeling, monitoring a child's behavior, and providing instruction, directions, and consequences for a child's actions facilitate or hinder adaptive development. Studies of parenting styles suggest that an authoritative, warm style generally fosters favorable development. Parent psychopathology is a developmental risk factor.
- Divorce is best conceptualized as a complex process of family transition that heightens developmental risk. Its effects depend on multiple variables. Similar considerations apply to parental incarceration, and foster care.

Peer Influences

- Peers influence each other in many, perhaps unique, ways through friendship and other relationships. Poor peer relationships in childhood are associated with problematic behavior in childhood and later life.

Community and Societal Contexts

- School resources, culture, and relationships are a central context for the development of youth. Schools teach intellectual skills and knowledge as well as many aspects of social development.
- Low socioeconomic status and the poverty associated with it disadvantage children in many areas of development. Poor children are exposed to multiple physical and psychosocial risks. The effects of poverty are mediated in part by family factors.
- Young people are influenced by the neighborhoods in which they reside. Neighborhood influences operate through community resources, family relationships, and community norms/efficacy.
- The broad cultural context influences development through family and community variables. Indigenous, minority, and immigrant groups often experience the risks of poverty, prejudice, and discrimination, as well as lesser availability of adequate mental health care.

Key Terms

neurons *39*

myelin *39*

pruning *39*

central nervous system *40*

peripheral nervous system *40*

endocrine system *40*

hindbrain, midbrain, forebrain *40*

cell body, dendrites, axons *41*

synapse *41*

neurotransmitters *41*

teratogens *42*

Fetal Alcohol Syndrome (FAS) *42*

brain plasticity *43*

chromosomes *44*

DNA *44*

genes *44*

transcription *44*

translation *44*

genotype, phenotype *44*

epigenetics *44*

dominant genes, recessive genes *45*

index case, proband *45*

quantitative genetic methods, behavioral genetics *45*

heritability *45*

shared and nonshared environmental influences *46*

linkage analysis *46*

association analysis *46*

genome-wide linkage and association analyses *46*

gene–environment interaction *46*

gene–environment correlation *47*

classical conditioning *47*

operant learning *48*

observational learning *49*

cognitive-behavioral perspective *49*

parenting behaviors *52*

parenting styles *52*

foster care *56*

treatment foster care *56*

acculturation *62*

CHAPTER 4
Research: Its Role and Methods

Looking Forward

After reading this chapter, you should be able to discuss:

- The aim of science and the roles of observation and measurement
- Reliability and validity of research results

- The case study, correlational methods, the experiment, and single-subject designs
- Cross-sectional, longitudinal, and accelerated longitudinal designs
- Qualitative research
- Ethical issues in research

As a discipline, psychology is committed to the view that science can provide the most complete and valid information about human functioning, behavior, and development. Although common sense tells us much about behavior, science aims to go beyond common sense to develop systematic, reliable, and accurate knowledge. The general purpose of science is to describe and explain phenomena.

The word *science* comes from the Latin word for "knowledge," or "to know," but specifically refers to knowledge gained by particular methods of inquiry. We might know the world from reading literature or listening to music, but we would not consider knowledge gained in this way to be scientific knowledge. Scientific understanding derives from systematic formulation of a problem, observation and collection of data, and interpretation of findings by what is considered acceptable procedures. Despite some misgivings—and even warnings of danger—about the scientific study of humans, we have come to value what science can tell us about ourselves.

Fundamentals of Research

The numerous major questions relevant to developmental psychopathology are progressively being addressed by scientific investigations (Figure 4.1). Of course, these general questions are transformed into countless more specific queries. To answer them, it is sometimes necessary only to describe phenomena, that is, count the number of cases of particular disorders and describe the symptoms of disorders. At other times, it is necessary to determine the conditions under which a phenomenon occurs and to discover its relationship to other variables. Frequently, the quest is to determine cause-and-effect relationships.

We previously have noted that researchers rarely, if ever, simply pose questions and then try to answer them in an intellectual vacuum. They are guided by already established information, concepts, perspectives, or theories, and by their own inclinations. Theoretical concepts and assumptions guide research goals, choice of variables, procedures, analyses, and conclusions. But there is always at least a touch of subjectivity and creativity in the posing of research questions and in deciding how best to seek answers.

It is common to try to test specific hypotheses derived from theoretical notions. **Hypothesis testing** is valuable because it tends to build knowledge systematically rather than haphazardly. Any one investigation rarely proves that a hypothesis is either correct or incorrect; instead, it provides evidence for or against the hypothesis. In turn, a hypothesis that is supported serves as evidence for the accuracy and explanatory power of the underlying theory. An unsupported hypothesis, in contrast, serves to disprove, limit, or redirect the theory. Together, observations and theory advance scientific understanding.

Just as researchers ask a variety of questions and pose hypotheses, they work in a variety of settings, ranging from the natural environments of the home or community to controlled

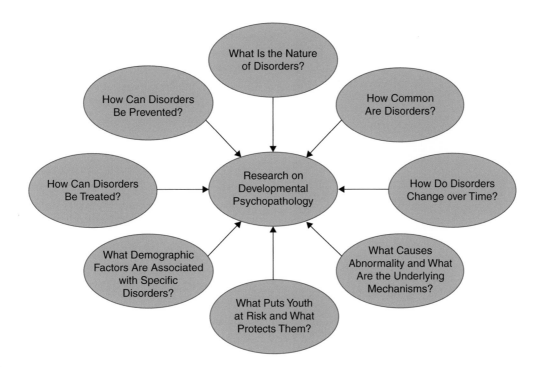

Figure 4.1 Some of the major questions for research on developmental psychopathology.

laboratory settings. Different strategies and designs are used, depending on the purposes of the research—and on ethics and practicality, too. In all cases, however, careful consideration must be given to selection of participants, observation and measurement, reliability, and validity.

Selection of Participants

For good reason, research reports require the description of the participants and the way they were selected. This information is important in judging the adequacy of investigations and interpretations of the findings.

Investigations of development and abnormal psychology are typically interested in drawing general conclusions about a population of interest. Because it is rarely possible to study an entire population, the next best choice is to examine a representative sample. Representativeness is best achieved by **random selection** of participants from the population, that is, by choosing each participant by chance. Even this goal may not be feasible; for example, it is impossible to randomly select a sample from *all* preschoolers or *all* children with intellectual disability. However, efforts can be made to approximate representativeness, and the extent to which it is achieved affects the interpretation of the research findings.

In the study of psychological disorders, research participants are often drawn from clinics, hospitals, and other facilities serving youth with problems. Such clinic populations are unlikely to represent the entire population of young people with disorders. They may exclude children whose families cannot afford treatment or for whom help was not sought due to denial, shame, fear, or high levels of adult tolerance. Clinic populations can also *over*represent youth who experience more serious symptoms or who act out or otherwise concern people. Such **selection bias** has important implications. For instance, working with clinic populations rather than general populations, or boys rather than girls, might affect how disorders are defined. The characteristics of research participants and the way that participants are chosen are critical in planning and drawing conclusions from research investigations.

Observation and Measurement

At the heart of scientific endeavors are observation and measurement, both of which can be challenging to behavioral scientists. Whereas it is relatively simple to observe and measure overt action, thought and emotion are more elusive. In any case, the scientist must provide an **operational definition** of the behavior or concept being studied. That is, some observable and measurable operation must be selected to define the behavior or concept. Aggression might be operationalized as the frequency with which children actually shove or threaten their playmates; depression might be operationalized by a score on a scale that measures adolescent reports of feelings of sadness and hopelessness.

Direct observation allows the researcher to systematically measure behavior as it is occurring. (Courtesy of Jennifer Weil Malatras)

In the attempt to tap all sources of information, behavioral scientists make many kinds of observations and measurements. They directly observe overt behavior in naturalistic or laboratory settings; employ standardized tests; record physiological functioning of the brain, sensory organs, or heart; ask people to report or rate their own behavior, feelings, and thoughts; and collect the reports of others about the subject of investigation. Increasingly, highly technical genetic methods to study chromosomes and neuroscience procedures to image the brain have become additional sources of information.

Whatever the measure, it should be valid, that is, be an accurate indicator of the attribute of interest. There are several kinds of **validity** (Table 4.1). For instance, construct validity exists if a questionnaire about anxiety gets at what is accepted as the underlying concept or meaning of anxiety. The observations also must be **reliable**, that is, the data would be similar, or consistent, if measurements were taken again under similar circumstances. Numerous considerations and practices are required to ensure objective, accurate, and dependable observation and measurement.

Consider, for example, a study that used naturalistic observation to investigate childhood depression (Dadds et al., 1992). **Naturalistic observation** consists of directly observing individuals in their "real world," at times simply to describe naturally occurring behavior and at other times to answer specific questions or to test hypotheses. In this study, a comparison was made of parent–child interaction in families that had a child who was referred to a clinic for either depression, conduct disorder, or depression/conduct disorder. The families, and a group of nonclinic families, were videotaped during a typical evening meal. The videotaped behavior was then independently coded by observers who were trained to use a carefully constructed observation system, the Family Observation Schedule. This instrument provided 20 categories for parent and child behaviors—among them smiling, frowning, praising, and complaining. The reliability of measurement was then examined to determine whether the taped behaviors were coded in a consistent way by the independent coders. Such **interobserver reliability** is known to be generally higher when the observation schedule is optimally specific and clear. In this study, interobserver reliability was checked by an additional observer, who coded one-third of the tapes. The investigation also benefitted from the observers' having no knowledge of each family's clinical status, that is, the problems displayed by the children. Nor did the observers know the hypotheses being tested. Such **observer "blindness"** decreased the chance that the observers would be biased by such information. All of these features—a well-constructed observational measure, observer training, a check on the reliability of the coding, and blind observation—addressed important standards for measurement in research.

Reliability of Research Results

The concepts of reliability and validity apply to the results of research as well. The findings of a research study are assumed to

Table 4.1 Some Types of Validity Pertaining to Measurement

Content Validity	Refers to whether the content of a measure corresponds to the content of the attribute of interest
Construct Validity	Refers to whether a measure corresponds to the construct (concept) underlying the attribute of interest
Face Validity	Refers to whether a measure, on its surface, seems appropriate to the attribute of interest
Concurrent Validity	Refers to whether the scores on a measure correlate with scores on another acceptable measure of the attribute of interest
Predictive Validity	Refers to whether the scores on a measure predict later scores on another acceptable measure of the attribute of interest or other outcomes of interest

"Miss Rogers, Sally Green. Is it true my son's research project is
'the effect of too much television on a typical ten-year-old?'"

David Sipress/The New Yorker Collection/Cartoon Bank

report a "truth" about the world. The scientific method assumes that truth repeats itself, given identical or similar conditions; consequently, it can be observed again by others. Replication of findings is thus an important component of scientific work. If the same truth is not reported under similar conditions, the original finding is considered unreliable or inconsistent, and it remains questionable. The need for reliability, or repeatability, of results places a burden on researchers to be clear and concise as they conceptualize and conduct their study, and to communicate their findings so that others may replicate and judge their work.

Validity of Research Results

Whereas reliability refers to the consistency or repeatability of results, validity refers to the correctness, soundness, or appropriateness of scientific findings. The validity of research findings is a complex matter; in general, validity must be judged in terms of the purpose of the research and the way the results are used. Of major concern are internal and external validity.

The purpose of much research is to offer an explanation for phenomena. **Internal validity** refers to the extent to which the explanation is judged to be correct or sound. Many factors pose a threat to internal validity, depending on the methods and research designs employed (Shadish, Cook, & Campbell, 2002). Given the purpose of the research, as well as practical and ethical considerations, investigators do well to select methods and conduct research so as to maximize internal validity. In general,

the extent to which alternative explanations can be ruled out determines the certainty that the offered explanation is valid.

External validity addresses generalizability, the extent to which the results of an investigation apply to other populations and situations. Although researchers are virtually always interested in generalizability, it cannot be assumed. Findings based on European American children in the United States may or may not hold for children of Mexican American ancestry; findings from research with animals may or may not apply to humans; findings from highly controlled studies conducted in controlled settings may or may not hold in real-world settings. The question of generalizability is rarely, if ever, completely answered but evidence for external validity increases as various populations, settings, and methods are used.

Basic Methods of Research

There are many ways to approach and conduct research. Investigations may focus on a single person or on one or more groups of individuals. Researchers may exert comparatively more or less control over the procedures and settings. The time frame of the study may be relatively brief, or it may last several years. Nevertheless, all research methods have strengths and weaknesses, and the choice of one over another reasonably depends on the purpose and other aspects of the investigation. Moreover, conclusions are impressive when they are based on a convergence of findings from investigations that employ different methods.

There is no single way to conceptualize or categorize research methods. One useful distinction is between **descriptive** (or **nonexperimental)**, and **experimental methods**. The general purpose of descriptive methods is to portray a phenomenon of interest. Observations are made and analyzed in a variety of ways. The attributes and life of a single child may be described; the behaviors of groups of adolescents who vary in some way may be compared. Frequently the relationship of two or more variables of interest is described. Nonexperimental methods are widely employed, and they may involve sophisticated correlational and multivariate statistical analysis to study complex relationships.

Experimental studies can be viewed as randomized or quasi-experimental (Shadish et al., 2002). **Randomized experiments** are highly esteemed because they come closest to establishing cause-and-effect relationships. They require that a manipulation (A) be made, followed by an examination of the effects (B). A causal relationship exists when variation in A is related to variation in B and alternative explanations of this relationship are unlikely. Crucial to ruling out alternative explanations are random assignment of participants to the manipulation, as well as experimenter control of the procedures and extraneous factors.

Quasi-experimental studies are similar to randomized experiments in that they include a manipulation and various controls. However, participants are not randomly assigned to the manipulation. This difference reduces the confidence with which causal explanations can be made. Take, for example, a hypothetical study in which families of diagnosed children volunteer for parent training and subsequently are compared to similar families who do not receive the treatment. If the training group performed better, can it be concluded that the training is effective? Perhaps the volunteer parents had better skills to begin with or were more motivated than the no-treatment parents to perform well. In fact, we cannot rule out the possibility that something besides treatment caused the effect. There are ways, however, to strengthen the argument for causation. Had each group been measured before and then after the manipulation, and had the training group made greater pre-post gains than the no-treatment group, we would have evidence for the effectiveness of the training.

With the distinctions in mind between descriptive and experimental methods, we next examine four basic research methods common in the study of developmental psychopathology.

CURTIS Oppositional Defiant Disorder: A Case for Behavioral Parent Training

Curtis was an 8-year-old Caucasian male referred to the clinic by his previous therapist because of continued defiance at home and at school despite therapy. Curtis was 140 lb., and his body mass index placed him in the "overweight" range. Both parents reported that Curtis would "get upset" (e.g., yell, refuse to listen, or argue) two to three times a day and that he would remain defiant and noncompliant "for hours following a tantrum." Curtis's parents also reported that he had problems following directions, he talked back to his parents, and he intimidated his two sisters (3 and 9 years old) by acting as if he would hurt them.

Curtis had no close friends at school, and had recently received poor grades, although historically his teachers had not had concerns about his academic achievement. Medical and developmental history was unremarkable, and the family denied a history of trauma. Curtis was not prescribed any medications. There was an immediate family history of depression and anxiety. Curtis's parents were separated at the time of the intake, although behavioral problems predated their separation. Curtis underwent a psychological assessment that included a clinical interview with Curtis and his parents, parent- and teacher-report questionnaires, objective psychological testing, a structured interview for anxiety, and classroom observations.

Psychological testing did not provide evidence of underlying attention deficits or impulsivity. Curtis had some symptoms of separation anxiety, specifically in separating from his mother; however, he did not meet criteria for separation anxiety disorder. Curtis had average intelligence with high average verbal intelligence and oral language abilities at the 99th percentile. Further, academic problems were a function of noncompliance with schoolwork rather than underlying learning difficulties. In summary, results of the assessment indicated diagnoses of oppositional defiant disorder (moderate) and anxiety disorder (unspecified).

Based on the results of the psychological assessment, the evaluator recommended that Curtis and his parents participate in behavioral parent training to help his parents effectively reduce his oppositional and defiant behavior.

Adapted from Stokes et al., 2017

Case Studies

The **case study** is a descriptive, nonexperimental method commonly used in investigations of psychological disorders. It focuses on an individual—describing the background, present and past life circumstances, functioning, and characteristics of the person. Case studies can tell us something about the nature, course, correlates, outcomes, and possible etiology of psychological problems. In addition, they can bridge the gap that all too often exists between clinical practice and research endeavors (Kazdin, 2011).

The case of Curtis is an abridged version of a case study of a boy referred for treatment to address oppositional and defiant behavior. Curtis and his parents participated in treatment employing parent training in behavior management and rewards for appropriate behavior. At the end of treatment, Curtis's behavior improved. His parents reported he rarely displayed defiant behavior at home or at school, his compliance had improved, and his anxiety had diminished. Curtis no longer met criteria for a diagnosis of Oppositional Defiant Disorder.

The primary goal of this case report was to illustrate an approach to treating children with considerable problems and to emphasize that treatment must be tailored to each child's needs (Stokes et al., 2017). Case studies can meet such a goal, for one of their strengths is the power to illustrate (Kazdin, 2016). They can richly describe phenomena, even phenomena so rare that they would be difficult to study in other ways. They can provide hypotheses to be tested by other methods as well as demonstrations that run counter to acceptable ideas. The weaknesses of the case study concern reliability and validity. The descriptions of life events often go back in time, raising questions about their reliability and accuracy. When case studies go beyond description to interpretations, there are few guidelines to judge the validity of the interpretations. Moreover, since only one person is examined, the findings cannot be generalized confidently to others. Despite weaknesses, however, the descriptive case study has a long history in the study of psychopathology and continues to make contributions.

Correlational Studies

Correlational studies are nonexperimental investigations that describe the relations between two or more factors without exposing the participants to a manipulation. They may be conducted in the natural environment or in the laboratory in a variety of ways, and can involve many variables in complex research designs. Statistical procedures are employed to determine the strength and nature of the relationship.

Here we only examine the basic aspects of the method. In its simplest form, the question asked is, "Are factors X and Y related, and, if so, in what direction are they related, and how strongly?" After the researchers select an appropriate sample, they obtain a measure of variable X and of variable Y from each participant. Statistical analysis of these two sets of scores is then performed. In this case, the Pearson product–moment coefficient, r, could be computed.

The value of Pearson r, which always ranges between +1.00 and −1.00, indicates the direction and the strength of the relationship.[1] Direction is indicated by the sign of the coefficient. A positive sign (+) means that high scores on the X variable tend to be associated with high scores on the Y variable, and that low scores on X tend to be related to low scores on Y. This relationship is referred to as a **positive correlation** (or direct correlation). A negative sign (-) indicates that high scores on X tend to be related to low scores on Y, and that low scores on X tend to be related to high scores on Y. This is a **negative correlation** (also called an indirect, or inverse, correlation).

The strength or magnitude of a correlation is reflected in the absolute value of the coefficient. The strongest relationship is expressed by an r of +1.00 or −1.00. As the absolute value of the coefficient value decreases, the relationship becomes weaker. A coefficient of .00 indicates no relationship at all and the scores on one variable tell us nothing about the scores on the other variable.

Suppose that an investigator explored the association of secure attachment in infancy with childhood adjustment. For each participant, the researcher obtained a measure of secure attachment in infancy and a measure of adjustment in childhood. The hypothetical data appear in Table 4.2. Pearson r for the data

Table 4.2 Data from a Hypothetical Study of Infant Secure Attachment and Childhood Adjustment. The Pearson r Value is +0.82, which Indicates a Strong Positive Relationship between the Variables

Child	Variable X attachment score	Variable Y childhood adjustment score
Daniel	2	5
Nicky	3	4
Sara	4	12
Beth	7	16
Jessica	9	10
Alia	11	22
Brent	13	18

was calculated, and its value is +0.82. How would this finding be interpreted? The positive sign indicates that children who scored higher on secure attachment tended to score higher on later adjustment. The magnitude of the coefficient indicates that the relationship is strong (since 1.00 is a perfect positive relationship).

When a correlation exists, knowing a person's score on one variable allows us to predict the person's performance on the other variable. It does not, however, permit us automatically to draw a cause-and-effect conclusion. One problem is that of directionality. If a positive correlation were found between parenting behaviors and child adjustment, it is possible that parenting caused child maladjustment or, alternatively, that child maladjustment caused parents to behave in a certain way. The direction of causation is unclear. The problem can sometimes be solved by examining the nature of the variables. For example, if a correlation between insecure early attachment and later childhood problems exists, it is impossible for later adjustment to cause early insecure attachment.

However, even when directionality is not a problem, a correlation may be caused by one or more unknown variables. Perhaps children's social competence is responsible for both the quality of their early attachment and their later social adjustment. To evaluate this possibility, social competence could be measured and a statistical technique could be applied to partial out, or hold constant, its effects. To the extent that the correlation remains, it is not explained by social competence. As helpful as partialing techniques are in ruling out the effects of other possible causal factors, an investigator can never be sure that all possible causative variables have been evaluated.

Despite the aforementioned weaknesses, research designs that employ correlational analysis are of considerable value in abnormal psychology. They are useful when an investigator wants to determine whether any relationships exist among variables before advancing specific hypotheses. They can be invaluable when the variable of interest cannot be manipulated—due to ethical or other considerations—such as maltreatment, social class, drug use, or genetic differences.

In addition, techniques such as structural modeling, too complicated to discuss here, permit researchers to explore complex relationships and to have more confidence in their hypotheses about cause and effect. The researcher hypothesizes specific patterns of relationships among the variables being studied. Statistical techniques are then employed to determine how well the collected data fit the model that the researcher specified. Examples of the use of this and other methods based on correlations to address questions about psychological disturbance appear throughout this text. (See Accent: "Experiments of Nature.")

Randomized Experiments

The randomized experiment is sometimes referred to as the "true" experiment in that it is the strongest method for inferring causal links between variables. A controlled manipulation (the **independent variable**) is presented to participants who are randomly assigned to different conditions. The outcome of the manipulation is measured (the **dependent variable**), and

ACCENT Experiments of Nature

Despite their name, **experiments of nature** are not experiments in the usual sense of this word and do not involve a manipulation. The condition of interest may not even be manipulable by researchers. These studies examine naturally occurring events and contrast a condition of interest with a condition in a comparison group (Kim & Steiner, 2016). Correlational and other statistical analyses may be used to evaluate the relationships of interest.

A noteworthy example is the investigation of the effects of institutionalization on children's development. There is a lengthy history of comparing children who reside in orphanages with children who had been adopted from orphanages or had never been institutionalized. These studies indicate an adverse effect of institutionalization on intellectual development, academic achievement, physical health, and social-emotional functioning (Merz et al., 2016; Woodhouse, Miah, & Rutter, 2018). Lengthy institutionalization and poor quality of orphanages are associated with worse outcomes (McCall & Groark, 2015).

Like all research methods, experiments of nature have weaknesses and strengths (Thapar & Rutter, 2019). Regarding the effects of institutionalization, a major weakness is the potential selection bias inherent in the groups. For example, children who are adopted from orphanages may have had fewer difficulties even prior to leaving than children who remained behind. Such a selection bias complicates the interpretation of the findings. Despite weaknesses, however, natural experiments have enriched our understanding of life circumstances that cannot readily be manipulated by researchers.

differences among the conditions are then evaluated. With the exception of the independent variable, the groups are treated as similarly as possible so that group differences can be attributed to the independent variable. In addition, random assignment of participants to groups makes it likely that any differences are not caused by initial group disparity but by the manipulation itself.

To illustrate the experiment, we draw on an early report of the Abecedarian Project, a research project of historic interest because it was among the first efforts to ask whether at-risk children could benefit from a child-centered, intellectually stimulating environment provided as part of a day care service (Campbell et al., 2001; Ramey & Campbell, 1984). Potential participants were identified through prenatal clinics and the local social service department. Families were identified as at-risk on the basis of a survey, and selected before or soon after the birth of the participant child. The investigators then paired the families according to similarity on the High Risk Index, and the children from each pair were randomly assigned to one of two conditions, either the treatment or the control group (Ramey & Campbell, 1984).

The independent variable was the provision of the educational program. Children in the treatment group began day care by 3 months of age, and their development was tracked until they reached 54 months. The educational program included language, motor, social, and cognitive components, varying somewhat with the child's age. Control-group children did not attend the day care center and were not exposed to the educational program. Efforts were made to otherwise equate their experiences with those of the treatment group: they were given similar nutritional supplements, pediatric care, and supportive social services. The dependent variable was standardized developmental or intelligence tests administered to all the children twice annually.

The test results revealed that beginning at 18 months, children in the treatment group scored higher than children in the control group, and this difference was **statistically significant**.[2] Figure 4.2 shows one way of examining the findings. It indicates that at 24, 36, and 48 months, the educationally treated children were much less likely to obtain intelligence scores at or below 85 than were the control children. The researchers concluded that the educational program resulted in intellectual benefits for the treated at-risk youth.

Is this conclusion justified; that is, does the study have internal validity? The method by which the subjects were selected and assigned makes it unlikely that the results simply reflect group differences that existed prior to the study. Moreover, efforts were made to treat the experimental and control groups similarly except for the independent variable. To the degree that this was accomplished, it can be argued that the study is internally valid and that the results are due to the treatment. With regard to this issue, caution is appropriate, however. When research is

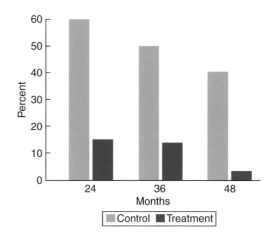

Figure 4.2 Percentage of Stanford–Binet IQ scores at or below 85 at three ages for treatment and control subjects. (From Ramey & Campbell, 1984)

conducted in the laboratory, it is relatively easy to control the experiences of the groups. In an experiment such as Ramey and Campbell's, the degree of control and thus internal validity are less clear.

An additional issue concerns the actual collection of data. It appears that those who gave the standardized tests might have known the group to which each child had been assigned, raising the question of bias in data collection. At the same time, the individual testers had been randomly assigned to testing sessions, a procedure that could offset possible bias.

What about external validity, or generalizability, of the findings? External validity is enhanced by the intervention actually being conducted in a day care center, the setting in which the program likely would be used. However, the positive effects of treatments may not accrue when they are employed in circumstances other than those in which they were initially demonstrated. (See Accent: "Translational Research: From Lab to Real-World Settings.")

The purpose of our discussion of the Abecedarian Project is to illustrate the randomized experiment, but it is noteworthy that the project is a landmark investigation of early educational intervention (Pungello et al., 2010). The participants in the study were followed into young adulthood, and long-terms benefits were demonstrated (Campbell & Ramey, 1994; Campbell et al., 2001, 2014). The project also was depicted in the television documentary *My Brilliant Brain* (The Carolina Abecedarian Project-FPG Child Development, 2008).

Single-Case Experimental Designs

Single-case experimental designs involve a manipulation with a single (or a few) participant(s). They are sometimes referred to as time-series designs because measures of the dependent variable

ACCENT Translational Research: From Lab to Real-World Settings

The issue of generalizability of treatment is part of a more general concern about the gap between research and the application of knowledge (Palinkas, 2018). This concern has been addressed by various professional and government groups. The National Institutes of Health (NIH) has been especially influential in guiding efforts to link basic research to applications in the real world, with the goal of improving human health (Guerra, Graham, & Tolan, 2011). The NIH call for **translational research** has been conceptualized as a two-step model or as two types of research.

As applied to mental health, Type 1 research—often referred to as "bench to bedside"—focuses on basic research to identify problems, etiology, and the design and testing of interventions to improve well-being. Much progress has been made in recent years in such efforts. This includes research demonstrations of beneficial effects on youth of a range of interventions and preventions (Prinstein et al., 2019). However, numerous investigations show that these benefits may not accrue in clinical practice. Perhaps real-world clinical cases may be more complex, or the application of empirically tested interventions may differ substantially, for example, by being less organized or structured. To remedy the situation, it is suggested that researchers build the characteristics of real-world settings into the designs and evaluations of interventions and implement empirically based interventions with appropriate flexibility (Kendall & Frank, 2018).

In addition, given the prevalence of disorder in youth and the lack of access to care, there is much need to successfully move evidence-based mental health care to a broader scale, that is, from "bedside to community." Type 2 translational research focuses on the broad scale adoption, implementation, and sustainability of evidence-based interventions by community systems that deliver care (Guerra et al., 2011). Researchers have begun to develop a science of implementation. Although still in relatively early stages, crucial components of implementation are being studied and advanced (Hoagwood et al., 2017). These components include the decision by a service agency to adopt an evidence-based program; the training and evaluation of practitioners; the organizational change usually required, such as commitment to the program and "unfreezing" of current practices; and the evaluation and maintenance of the new program in the community. Substantial government and private resources, as well as professional efforts, are being invested in system-level implementation.

are repeated across time periods. The designs are frequently used to evaluate the effects of clinical interventions (Nestor & Schutt, 2019). External validity is not strong, because generalization from a single participant cannot be confidently made. It can be enhanced, however, by repeating the study with different subjects or in different settings. The issue of internal validity can be approached with the use of specific design features that control for the possibility of alternative explanations (Gast, Blair, & Ledford, 2018).

Reversal Designs

In the ABA reversal design, a problem behavior is carefully defined and measured across time periods, during which the subject is exposed to different conditions. During the first period (A), measures are taken of the behavior prior to intervention. This baseline measure serves as a standard against which change can be evaluated. In the next period (B), the intervention is carried out while the behavior is measured in the identical way. The intervention is then removed; that is, there is a return to the same condition as during baseline (A).

Figure 4.3 gives a hypothetical example of the ABA design. Appropriate play behavior occurs at low frequency during the baseline, increases during the treatment phase B, and decreases when the intervention is removed in the second A phase. In studies in which behavior improves during intervention, particularly if clinical treatment is the aim, a fourth period, during which the successful intervention is reintroduced, must be added. Typically, the relevant behaviors show improvement again.

The ABA design is limited in that the intervention may make reversal of the targeted behavior unlikely. For example, when treatment results in increased academic skill, a child may not display decreases in the skill when intervention is removed. From a treatment standpoint, this is a positive outcome; from a research standpoint, there is no way to demonstrate that the intervention caused the positive behavior. In other instances, the researcher may hesitate to remove a manipulation once it is associated with positive change, so that a definite demonstration of its effects is lacking.

Multiple Baseline Designs

When reversal designs are inappropriate, multiple baseline designs may be suitable. Multiple baselines are recorded, which may represent different behaviors of a participant, the same behavior of a participant in different settings, the same behavior of a few different participants, and so on. Intervention is then presented

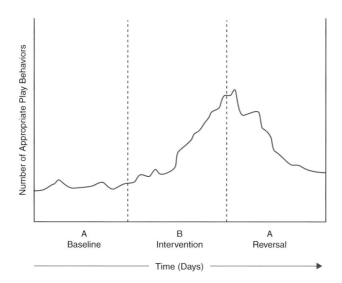

Figure 4.3 Hypothetical example of the ABA design.

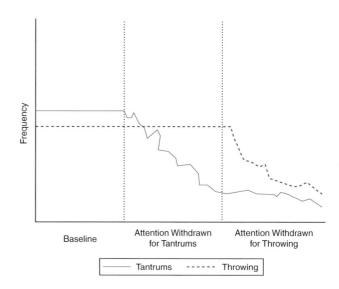

Figure 4.4 Frequency of tantrums and throwing across the phases of a hypothetical multiple baseline, single-subject experiment.

to observe the effects on one of the baselines but not the others. If effects are found, they likely are due to intervention rather than extraneous factors. In this way, multiple baseline designs provide some basis for internal validity (Gast et al., 2018).

Consider, for example, the multiple baseline design in which two behaviors by a single child are recorded across time. After baselines are established for both behaviors, the intervention is made for only one behavior. During the next phase, the intervention is applied to the other behavior as well. A clinician may hypothesize, say, that a child's temper tantrums and throwing of objects are maintained by adult attention to these behaviors. Withdrawal of attention would thus be expected to reduce the behaviors. Support for the hypothesis can be seen in Figure 4.4, a hypothetical graph of the frequency of both behaviors across time periods. Because behavior change follows the pattern of the treatment procedure, it is likely that withdrawal of attention and not some other variable caused the change.

In another commonly used multiple baseline design, baselines are recorded for multiple participants, and intervention follows different timelines (Tate & Perdices, 2019). Figure 4.5 demonstrates a hypothetical study in which intervention is provided to increase the verbalization of nonverbal developmentally delayed children. Here, baselines are recorded for two children and Child 1 is then provided the treatment, successively followed by treatment for Child 2. Similar patterns of change for both children upon introduction of the intervention increases confidence that the treatment actually caused improvement.

There are numerous other single-case experimental designs (Kazdin, 2016). They all permit the researcher-clinician to test hypotheses while working with a single or a few participants and,

in the case of treatment, to focus on the youth of immediate concern. Moreover, although control of extraneous factors is more easily affected in the laboratory, single-case research is relatively easy to conduct in natural environments (Morgan & Morgan, 2001). The method thus has the potential to capture actual clinic practice.

To summarize, the research methods we have discussed in this section vary in several ways, and each has weaknesses and strengths. Nonexperimental methods are appropriate for describing phenomena and are especially useful when a manipulation is not feasible. Experimental methods best meet the standards of internal validity and best permit causal inferences to be drawn. The choice of research method depends on the purpose of the investigation, as well as practical and ethical considerations. Scientific endeavors are enriched by the availability of various methods, which are employed in numerous approaches to understanding psychopathology. (See Accent: "Epidemiological Research: More than Counting Noses.")

Time Frames in Research

In addition to the distinctions among research methods described above, investigations differ with regard to time.

Cross-Sectional Research

In this approach, participants are observed at one point in time, as if a snapshot were being taken. Group comparisons are frequently made between groups that differ in age or

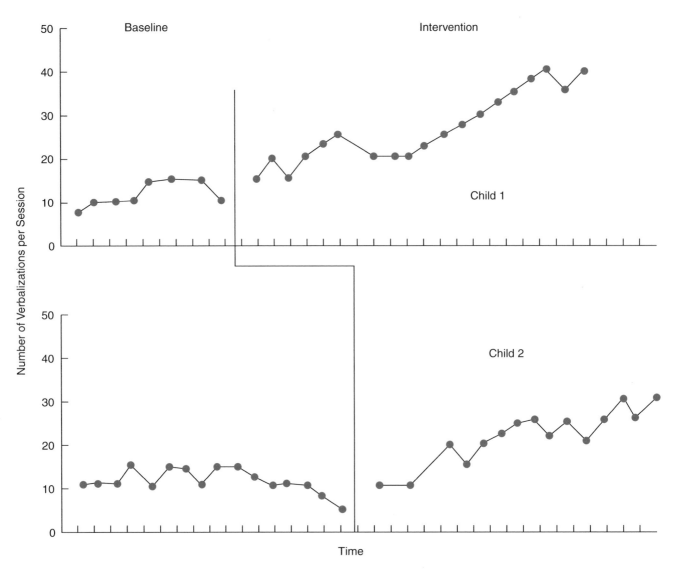

Figure 4.5 Number of verbalizations of two children across the phases of a hypothetical multiple baseline experiment.

developmental status. For instance, aggression displayed by 6-, 10-, and 14-year-olds might be compared. **Cross-sectional research** is relatively inexpensive and efficient, and has contributed significantly to understanding development and psychological problems.

Nevertheless, tracing developmental change with cross-sectional research is problematic and can be misleading. If older youth display more aggression, it might be concluded that aggression "naturally" increases with development. But this conclusion may not be warranted. What we are seeing is an *age difference*, which is not necessarily *developmental change*. Perhaps specific experiences of the age groups are responsible for the findings. The 14-year-olds might have received

more reinforcement for displaying aggression during a time period characterized by greater exposure to violence and aggression.

Retrospective Longitudinal Research

Consistent with the meaning of the word *retrospective*, **retrospective longitudinal research** goes back in time. Youth may be identified on some variable of interest—such as a specific disorder—and information about their earlier characteristics and life experiences is then collected. One type of study that is frequently retrospective is the **case-control study**, in which a group that has been diagnosed with a disorder is compared with

ACCENT Epidemiological Research: More than Counting Noses

Epidemiology can be defined as the quantitative study of the distribution and causes of disorder in human populations (Scott et al., 2018). The approach has a basis in medicine and public health, and initially focused on investigating infectious diseases. Cases of disorder are identified in large populations, or representative samples of the populations, and several kinds of data about the disorders may be collected and analyzed.

One goal of epidemiology is to monitor the frequency of disorders in populations, including how frequency may change over time. Frequency may be measured in several ways. Incidence refers to the number of new cases that appear in a particular time period, often in one year. Prevalence refers to the presence of a disorder in a population at a particular time; for example, the number of cases or proportion of the population can be determined. Lifetime prevalence refers to the number or proportion of people in a population who have had the disorder at any time during their life. The focus on general populations rather than on clinical samples is especially valuable in that it reduces the likelihood of selection bias inherent in clinical samples. "Counting noses" is valuable in that it informs us about the need for treatment, whether a disorder is increasing or decreasing, and the like. But epidemiology does more than simply count noses (Costello, Egger, & Angold, 2005a).

By associating the frequency of disorder with specific characteristics of populations—that is, determining how cases of disorder are distributed in a population—epidemiology provides information pertinent to risk and causation. For example, the revelation that prevalence of eating disorder in populations increases at adolescence, especially in females, puts emphasis on causal questions regarding timing and gender. That is, what is there about adolescence and about being female that puts individuals at risk?

Epidemiology seeks to understand what groups of people are at high risk for a disorder, what factors or other dysfunctions are correlated with the disorder, what the causes and modes of transmission are, and how the disorder can be prevented or reduced. Epidemiologists interested in young people are applying the developmental perspective, for example, by studying disorders longitudinally from the time of risk to onset of disorder to outcome (Costello & Angold, 2016). The epidemiological approach is important in furthering the understanding of genetic effects and gene–environment causation, an area of research requiring large to very large representative samples (Lahey, D'Onofrio, & Waldman, 2009). The approach thus broadly contributes to understanding, preventing, and treating psychological problems of youth.

---

a group without the disorder. The purpose of this follow-back method is to seek hypotheses about the predictors or causes of the observed disturbance. In retrospective studies, caution is warranted by possible unreliability of the data because old records and memories of the past may be sketchy, biased, or mistaken. Nevertheless, the discovery of a relationship of earlier-occurring variables with the disorder can suggest risk or causal factors.

Prospective Longitudinal Research

In **prospective longitudinal research**, individuals are observed and then evaluated with repeated observations as time passes. In "seeing" development as it occurs, the method can uniquely answer questions about the nature and course of development. For instance, children with language disabilities can be tested at specific time intervals to discern how the deficits change as the children develop. Comparison with a group showing no language problems would be valuable. Prospective longitudinal research can be informative with regard to numerous questions. Youth

who experience birth complications, an early traumatic event, or risks associated with poverty can be assessed over periods of time to determine factors related to their development. Girls and boys diagnosed with ADHD can be followed into adulthood to ascertain possible gender difference in outcome and the variables implicated.

This method is highly valued, but there are several drawbacks. The studies are expensive and require investigators to commit to a project for many years. Retaining participants over long periods of time may be difficult, and the loss of participants can bias the sample when dropouts are more transient, less psychologically oriented, or less healthy than those who continue. Another problem is that repeated testing of participants may make them test-wise, but attempting to control for this by changing test instruments makes it difficult to compare earlier and later findings. In addition, in planning long-term studies, researchers must take educated guesses about which variables to observe along the way, and they may miss relevant factors. For example, in discussing their 30-year longitudinal project, Sroufe and colleagues (2005) noted that in hindsight they would have included measures of neurophysiological functioning that might have provided valuable information.

Finally, in interpreting longitudinal results, it is important to consider possible societal changes. If individuals were followed from birth in 2000 through 2020, their development might be different, due to historical factors, from that of persons followed from birth in 2020 through 2040. The groups would likely have different experiences, for example, in the social environment or educational opportunity. These possible generational, or cohort, effects must be considered in interpreting longitudinal studies.

Accelerated Longitudinal Research

To overcome some of the weaknesses of the cross-sectional and prospective longitudinal methods, researchers interested in developmental change can conduct **accelerated longitudinal research**, which combines the two approaches in a variety of designs. Take, for example, a hypothetical study in which groups of children of different ages are studied over a relatively short time span. At Time I, children ages 3, 6, and 9 years are examined in a cross-sectional study. Similar examination of the same children occurs again three years later at Time II, and again another three years later at Time III. Figure 4.6 depicts the study. From reading down the columns of the figure, cross-sectional comparisons can be made at three different times. In addition, as is apparent by reading from left to right across the figure, the children (A, B, and C) are studied longitudinally over a six-year period (2014–2020). The age range in the investigation is thus 12 years (from 3 to 15 years), although the study is completed in six years.

Various comparisons can provide a wealth of information from such a design. To consider a possibility, if anxiety were found to

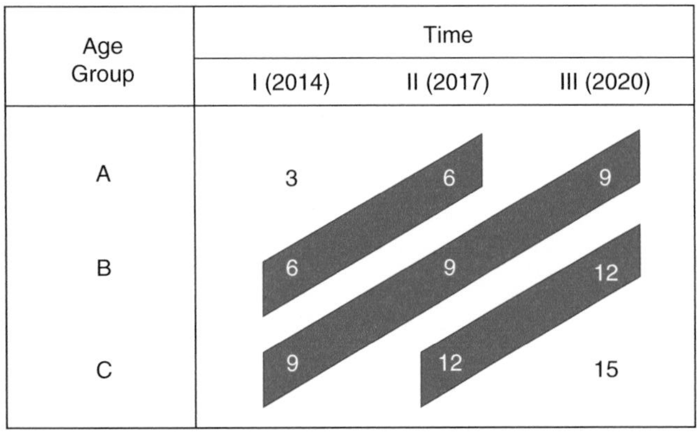

increase with age at Times I, II, and III (cross-sectional analyses) and also across time for each group of children (the longitudinal analyses), evidence would be strong for developmental change over the entire age range. Moreover, by comparing anxiety at age 6, or 9, or 12 (as shaded in the figure), the impact of societal conditions could also be evaluated. It might be found, for example, that anxiety at age 9 increased from the year 2014 to 2017 to 2020. Since only one age is involved, this increase is not developmental and likely indicates a change in societal conditions during the years under investigation. Thus, accelerated longitudinal designs can be a powerful way to separate age differences and developmental changes, while taking generational effects into consideration.

Qualitative Research

Most of the research on psychopathology of youth is quantitative. That is, the various methods collect and analyze numerical data that represent the world in some way (Yoshikawa et al., 2013). Quantitative research is essential to the empirical or positivistic paradigm that underlies much of the scientific progress made in modern times (Eisner, 2003). This perspective favors theory-guided objective measurement done by objective investigators in controlled situations.

In contrast, **qualitative research** collects and analyzes non-numerical information and favors methods such as in-depth interviews, intensive case studies, and life histories rather than controlled laboratory and experimental manipulations (Flick, 2018). Naturalistic observation is also important, with observations often recorded in narrative forms rather than with a restrictive coding of categories. Participant observation, in which the observer engages in and becomes part of the setting, is valued as a way to collect credible data and to optimize understanding. All these methods are consistent with the assumptions and values of qualitative research, which emphasize real-world contexts and the belief that human behavior and development can best be understood from a personal frame of reference when individuals have the opportunity to speak about their beliefs, attitudes, and experience (Levitt et al., 2018).

It is not unusual to collect large amounts of written data in qualitative research. Once collected, the narrative data are conceptualized, analyzed, and interpreted. This process may entail coding or categorizing statements or written observations. The categories are often viewed as arising naturally from the data rather than being based on predetermined expectations or constructed coding systems. What gets coded, how the coding is accomplished, and how data are interpreted vary with the approach and aims of the study. Quantification of data is minimal and statistical analysis may have little, if any, role.

Age Group	Time		
	I (2014)	II (2017)	III (2020)
A	3	6	9
B	6	9	12
C	9	12	15

Figure 4.6 Schema of an accelerated longitudinal research design in which children of different ages are examined cross-sectionally and longitudinally.

Like other strategies, qualitative methods have weaknesses and strengths. Sample size is often small, huge amounts of data can be difficult and costly to analyze, and questions are raised about reliability, validity, and generalizability. At the same time, with its focus on the individual in context, qualitative research can increase basic knowledge, suggest hypotheses for further testing, and illustrate and enrich quantitative findings.

Examples of Qualitative Studies

Some of the topics that have been examined with qualitative methods are life experiences of individuals diagnosed in childhood as having a learning disability, parents' and siblings' adjustment to having a family member with a disability, parents' experiences regarding their child's life-threatening illness, disadvantaged parents' attitudes about family ties, and adolescent attitudes toward their society (Fiese & Bickman, 1998; Flaton, 2006; Krahn, Hohn, & Kime, 1995; McNulty, 2003; Torney-Purta, 2009; Waller, 2010).

As an example of the strategy, consider a study of parents' experiences as participants in a support program called Parent to Parent (Ainbinder et al., 1998). The specific purpose of the program was to provide support for parents who had a child with disabilities, such as intellectual disability or chronic illness. Each parent was matched with a trained supporting parent who had a child with a similar disability and who provided information and emotional support, usually by telephone. One of the ways in which the program was evaluated was through a qualitative, semi-structured interview with participating parents, which explored the impact and meaning of being matched with a supportive parent. The transcribed telephone interviews were coded and categorized according to themes that emerged from the telephone conversations. Among the themes were the way the program was helpful, reasons for program failure, skills and information learned by the parents, and personal growth of the parents. The following from the parent interviews exemplifies learning by the parent:

> I wanted some reassurance that [our daughter] is likely to have most of the same things everybody else has, as far as you know, going to school and having friends, going out and doing things. And [our supporting Parent's] daughter's involved in a lot of things. She's got a good life. And that gave me a great deal of hope about the future of our daughter, that she can have a good life, too.
>
> p. 104

Overall, the data indicated that talking, sharing, comparing, and learning with others who are perceived as similar can enhance coping and adaptability. The qualitative analysis of Parent to Parent provided understanding of the strengths and weaknesses of the program in a way that other data, collected from quantitative surveys, had not provided.

Combining Qualitative and Quantitative Methods

Qualitative and quantitative strategies have often been viewed as adversarial (Schiff, 2019), and yet they are not necessarily at odds with each other and are often employed together. The combination of the approaches can be valuable in addressing many questions and issues (Yoshikawa et al., 2013). For example, research on culture and child rearing requires observation of behaviors and activities relevant to child rearing, as well as understanding the goals and beliefs underlying these activities. Quantitative methods can be suitable to determine the prevalence of certain child-rearing practices, and qualitative methods may be particularly fitting to reveal the goals of child rearing held by the culture. To take another example, a study of friendship drew on quantitative data to show that in late adolescence girls and boys reported equal support from friends; however, qualitative findings indicated that the meaning and function of friend support was different for girls and boys. In general, quantitative procedures provide more traditional data collection and hypothesis testing whereas qualitative procedures provide flexible, broad-scope investigation.

Ethical Issues

Scientific research is enormously beneficial, but it brings concerns about the welfare and rights of participants. Underlying such concerns is sensitivity to individual rights—both ethical and legal—and to past documented abuse of research participants. One well-known instance in which the problem of abuse was raised involved research into the natural course of hepatitis. From the 1950s to the 1970s, children with intellectual disability who resided in the Willowbrook school in the state of New York were deliberately infected with hepatitis in order to study the disease (Glantz, 1996). Although specific instances like this of past abuse in biomedical research appear especially egregious, ethical issues in all areas require continuous attention.

For many years, government agencies and professional organizations have published ethical guidelines for research. Philosophical underpinnings were presented in the *Belmont Report: Ethical Principles and Guidelines for the Protection of Human Subjects of Research*, which led to the Code of Federal Regulations pertaining to human research participants (National Commission, 1979). The American Psychological Association's *Ethical Principles of Psychologists and Code of Conduct* addresses the multiple professional roles of psychologists, including that of the researcher (American Psychological Association, 2010, 2016). The guidelines of the Society for Research in Child Development specifically address research with youth. Table 4.3 shows an abridged version of these standards (two additional Principles concern scientific and personal misconduct of the researcher). There is considerable overlap in the guidelines adopted by different agencies and disciplines.

Depending on funding and the setting, research proposals may be reviewed by federally mandated **Institutional Review Boards (IRBs)**, or by local review boards. IRBs consider such issues as the scientific soundness of the proposed research, voluntary consent of the participants, and potential harm and benefits to the participants (U.S. Department of Health and Human Services, 2018). Particular consideration is given to vulnerable persons, including youth, individuals with intellectual disability, and the economically disadvantaged. Whether or not an official review is required, adhering to ethical standards is a mandate for all researchers. Although doing as mandated may seem quite simple, ethical concerns are often complex. The following discussion covers a few major issues.

Voluntary Informed Consent

Fundamental to most ethical guidelines is the voluntary consent of individuals to participate, given that they understand the investigation. The requirement of voluntary **informed consent**, which is viewed as a component of respect due all participants,

Table 4.3 Ethical Standards for Research with Children

Principle 1	**Nonharmful Procedures.** No research operation that may physically or psychologically harm the child should be used. The least stressful operation should be used. Doubts about harmfulness should be discussed with consultants.
Principle 2	**Informed Consent.** The child's consent or assent should be obtained. The child should be informed of features of the research that may affect his or her willingness to participate. When research participants are infants, their parents should be informed. If consent would make the research impossible, it may be ethically conducted under certain circumstances; judgments should be made with Institutional Review Boards.
Principle 3	**Parental Consent.** Informed consent of parents, guardians, and those acting *in loco parentis* (e.g., school superintendents) similarly should be obtained, preferably in writing.
Principle 4	**Additional Consent.** Informed consent should be obtained of persons, such as teachers, whose interaction with the child is the subject of the research.
Principle 5	**Incentives.** Incentives to participate in the research must be fair and not unduly exceed incentives the child normally experiences.
Principle 6	**Deception.** If deception or withholding information is considered essential, colleagues must agree with this judgment. Participants should be told later of the reason for the deception. Efforts should be made to employ deception methods that have no known negative effects.
Principle 7	**Anonymity.** Permission should be gained for access to institutional records, and anonymity of information should be preserved.
Principle 8	**Mutual Responsibilities.** There should be clear agreement as to the responsibilities of all parties in the research. The investigator must honor all promises and commitments.
Principle 9	**Jeopardy.** When, in the research, information comes to the investigator's attention about circumstances that may jeopardize the child's welfare, the information must be discussed with parents or guardians and experts who can arrange for assistance to the child.
Principle 10	**Unforeseen Consequences.** When research procedures result in unforeseen, undesirable consequences for the participant, the consequences should be corrected and the procedures redesigned.
Principle 11	**Confidentiality.** The identity of participants and information about them should be kept confidential. When confidentiality might be threatened, this possibility and methods to prevent it should be explained as part of the procedures of obtaining informed consent.
Principle 12	**Informing Participants.** Immediately after data collection, any misconceptions that might have arisen should be clarified. General findings should be given to the participants, appropriate to their understanding. When scientific or humane reasons justify withholding information, efforts should be made to ensure that withholding has no damaging consequences.
Principle 13	**Reporting Results.** Investigators' words may carry unintended weight; thus, caution should be used in reporting results, giving advice, and making evaluative statements.
Principle 14	**Implications of Findings.** Investigators should be mindful of the social, political, and human implications of the research, and especially careful in the presentations of findings.

Source: Summarized from the Society for Research in Child Development, 2007; www.srcd.org/ethicalstandards.html

often calls for written consent. Among other things, participants should know the purpose of the research, procedures, risks and benefits, and their option to refuse participation or to withdraw at any time (Hoagwood & Cavaleri, 2010). They should have the competence to understand the information and to judge risk and benefits. It is presumed that immaturity hinders children's ability to fully understand these issues and make informed decisions. Thus, until children have reached the legal age of consent, usually age 18, consent on their behalf is required from their parents or guardians (Fried & Fisher, 2017).

Like some other standards, the American Psychological Association's standard allows some exceptions to this guideline, such as for research on educational curricula that would likely create no stress or harm. In addition, it recommends that persons not of legal age should nevertheless be asked to assent, or agree, to participate. For adolescents, consent generally involves assent from the youth and consent from the parent. Descriptions of the research need to be tailored to the developmental level of the person. For example, Miller (1998) suggests that the following information might appropriately be conveyed to the young child: a general idea of what will happen ("play a game"), where it will occur ("in Mr. Smith's office"), how many people will be involved ("just you and me"), how long it will take ("about 20 minutes"), whether others will do the same thing ("lots of kids from the class will be doing this"), whether a reward will be offered ("get a little prize at the end"), and the opportunity to assent ("Would you like to come?"). Obviously, with infants and toddlers, informed consent is an unreasonable expectation, and parental or guardian consent is usually sufficient.

Confidentiality

Research involves the participants giving personal information of some sort, whether they complete surveys or tests, describe their feelings, or allow others to observe their behavior. The principle of **confidentiality** assumes that participants have the right to control the degree to which personal information can be disclosed to others. It is often necessary for the researcher to know the identity of the participants who provide specific information. However, information can be kept confidential by numbering or otherwise coding individual reports, securing storage of data, and limiting access to data (Hoagwood & Cavaleri, 2010).

Several issues arise when the participants are children or adolescents (Fried & Fisher, 2017). Parents, schools, and other agencies involved may be interested in the course and outcome of the research. The researcher can limit the information given to parents, as in cases in which disclosure can put the child at risk. On the other hand, in some instances, the sharing of information might potentially benefit the young person, for example, in research on adolescent use of illicit drugs. Investigators may reveal information when participants appear in danger of harming themselves or others. Participating youth, parents, and relevant

agencies should understand the limits of confidentiality prior to the investigation.

Balancing It All: Harm and Good

A critical ethical principle is that no serious harm—physical, psychological, legal, or economic—should be done to participants. Research that, for instance, engages children in aggressive acts or exposes them to aggressive models raises questions of possible harm. Children also participate in research on the effects of medications, which can entail complex ethical dilemmas. Clearly, it is necessary to guard against the potential for harm, a principle that is referred to as **nonmaleficence**.

Moreover, the ethical principle of **beneficence**, based on respect for each individual, requires that benefits be maximized. It is not always possible for individuals to benefit personally from the research that they participate in, but a risk–benefit ratio should be considered (Hoagwood & Cavaleri, 2010). In general, when greater benefit to the participant is likely, greater risk of

When a youth participates in research, informed consent by a parent or guardian, and possibly by the youth, should usually be obtained. What constitutes informed consent by a child is a complex issue. (Courtesy of Jennifer Weil Malatras)

harm is more acceptable. Obviously, this guideline has limits in that risk of serious harm is virtually never acceptable.

In the final analysis, judgments about what is ethical often involve balancing several factors. Indeed, IRBs were instituted to aid in finding a balance between society's need for knowledge and participants' need for protection in research (Hayes, 2003). The individual's competence to understand and voluntarily consent, the risk of harm, and the possibility of benefit all play a crucial role in guiding ethical standards. Like other ethical concerns, the ethics of research can never be a completely settled matter, and ongoing discussion and tension are appropriate. Reasonable balance must be maintained, however, if beneficial research is to go forward.

Notes

1   Pearson r is one of several correlation coefficients that could be calculated, depending on the nature and complexity of the study. The general procedures and interpretations described here apply to other correlation coefficients.
2   Statistical significance concerns the probability that a finding is not due to mere chance. A common convention is that a statistically significant finding would occur by chance only five or fewer times were the study repeated 100 times. Statistical significance tests can be applied to many kinds of research methods.

Looking Back

Fundamentals of Research

- The aim of science is to describe phenomena and offer explanations for them.
- Scientific knowledge is based on systematic formulation, observation, and interpretation of findings. Hypothesis testing builds knowledge systematically and is tied to the advancement of theory.
- The selection of research participants is critical. Random selection best ensures that a sample represents the population from which it is drawn.
- Observation and measurement are accomplished in various ways in various settings. The behavior or concept being studied must be operationalized. Efforts should be made to achieve reliable and valid measurements.
- Reliability (consistency) of research results is important, as is validity (correctness) of findings. Internal validity is the degree to which alternative explanations for results can be confidently ruled out. External validity refers to generalizability of findings to other populations and settings.

Basic Methods of Research

- Numerous research methods are employed, each suited to particular purposes and each having weaknesses and strengths. Research methods can be categorized as descriptive (nonexperimental) or experimental, the latter of which can be viewed as randomized or quasi-experimental.
- Case studies can provide compelling descriptions; correlational methods provide information about the relationships among variables.
- Randomized experiments and single-subject experiments best meet the standards for establishing causality.

Time Frames in Research

- The cross-sectional strategy examines groups of people at a particular point in time; it is not a strong tool for evaluating developmental change.
- Retrospective longitudinal research goes back in time; it can generate hypotheses. The prospective longitudinal strategy, which makes repeated observations forward over time, is valued for tracing development.
- Accelerated longitudinal designs combine the cross-sectional and prospective longitudinal approaches to permit examination of developmental change, age differences, and the influence of generational effects.

Qualitative Research

- Qualitative research places high value on individuals' perception of their experiences in their natural environments. Data are collected through in-depth interviews, life histories, and the like. This strategy and the quantitative strategy—which values control, manipulation, and quantitative measures—are often seen as adversarial but can be complementary.

Ethical Issues

- Ethical issues in the conduct of research are addressed by several government agencies and professional organizations. Youth and those with mental disabilities require special protection.
- Central to ethical guidelines are voluntary informed consent, confidentiality, and assessment of risks and benefits to the participant.

Key Terms

hypothesis testing *66*

random selection *67*

selection bias *67*

operational definition *67*

validity *68*

reliability 68

naturalistic observation *68*

interobserver reliability *68*

observer blindness *68*

internal validity *69*

external validity *69*

descriptive (nonexperimental) methods *70*

experimental methods *70*

randomized experiments *70*

quasi-experimental studies *70*

case study *71*

correlational studies *71*

positive correlation *71*

negative correlation *71*

experiments of nature *72*

independent variable *72*

dependent variable *72*

statistical significance *73*

single-case experimental designs *73*

translational research *74*

cross-sectional research *76*

retrospective longitudinal research *76*

case-control study *76*

epidemiology *77*

prospective longitudinal research *77*

accelerated longitudinal research *78*

qualitative research *78*

Institutional Review Boards (IRBs) *80*

informed consent *80*

confidentiality *81*

nonmaleficence *81*

beneficence *81*

CHAPTER 5
Classification, Assessment, and Intervention

Looking Forward

After reading this chapter, you should be able to discuss:

- Processes of classification and diagnosis
- DSM, empirical, and Research Domain approaches to classifying psychological problems

- How assessment is conducted and various approaches to assessment
- Various approaches to prevention
- Various modes and strategies of treatment

Before beginning our discussion of specific disorders, it is important to consider how disorders of childhood and adolescence are defined, grouped, evaluated, and treated. In this chapter we will introduce the processes of classification, assessment, and intervention.

The terms *classification*, *taxonomy*, and *diagnosis* refer to the process of description and grouping. **Classification** and **taxonomy** are terms that refer to the delineation of major categories or dimensions of disorders. **Diagnosis** usually refers to assigning a category of a classification system to an individual. **Assessment** refers to evaluating youth, in part to assist the processes of classification and diagnosis and in part to direct intervention. All of these entwined processes are intricately related to the clinical and scientific aspects of child and adolescent disorders.

Classification and Diagnosis

Classification systems are employed to systematically describe a phenomenon. Biologists have classification systems for living organisms, and physicians classify physical dysfunction. Similarly, systems exist to classify psychological dysfunction. These systems describe categories or dimensions. A **category** is a discrete grouping, for example, anxiety disorder, into which an individual's symptoms are judged to fit or not fit. In contrast, the term **dimension** implies that an attribute is continuous and can occur to various degrees. Thus, for example, a child may exhibit high, moderate, or low levels of anxiety.

Any classification system must have clearly defined categories or dimensions. In other words, the criteria for defining a category or dimension must be explicitly stated. Clear and explicit definitions allow for good communication among professionals. Also, one must be able to clearly discriminate diagnostic groupings from one another. It must be demonstrated, too, that a category or dimension actually exists. That is, the features used to describe a category or dimension must occur together regularly, in one or more situations or as measured by one or more methods.

Classification systems must be reliable and valid. These terms were applied to research methods in Chapter 4. When applied to classification or diagnosis, the terms retain the general meanings of consistency and correctness but are used in somewhat different ways.

Interrater reliability refers to whether different diagnosticians use the same category to describe a person's behavior. For example, it addresses the question, "Is Maria's behavior called separation anxiety by two or more professionals who observe it?" **Test–retest reliability** asks whether the use of a category is stable over some reasonable period of time. For example, is Sean's difficulty, originally diagnosed as Oppositional Defiant Disorder, diagnosed as the same disorder when he returns for a second evaluation? These definitions of reliability also can be applied to dimensional approaches. Is the child's position on a dimension relatively the same as judged by two professionals or over time?

The **validity** of diagnostic systems is also a central concern. To be valid, a diagnosis should provide us with more information than we had when we originally defined the category or dimension. Thus, diagnoses should give us information about the etiology of a disorder, the course of development that the disorder is expected to take, response to treatment, or some additional clinical features of the problem. Does the diagnosis of Conduct Disorder, for example, tell us something about this disorder that is different from other disorders? Does the diagnosis tell us something about what causes this problem? Does it tell us what is likely to happen to youth who have this disorder and what treatments are likely to help? Does it tell us additional things about these young people or their backgrounds? The question of validity is thus largely one of whether we know anything we did not already know when we defined the category or dimension. Another important aspect of validity is whether our description of a disorder is accurate. Is the way we have described and classified this disorder the way it actually exists? Answering this question is often not an easy matter.

Finally, the **clinical utility** of a classification system is judged by how complete and useful it is. A diagnostic system that describes all the concerns that come to the attention of clinicians in a manner that is useful to them is more likely to be employed.

The DSM Approach

The most widely used classification system in the United States is the American Psychiatric Association's *Diagnostic and Statistical Manual of Mental Disorders* (DSM). The *International Classification of Diseases* (ICD) developed by the World Health Organization is an alternative system that is widely employed. An 11th edition is expected to be available soon (World Health Organization, 2019). There has been some concern that the DSM coverage of disorders has not given sufficient attention to younger children (Bufford et al., 2016). The **Diagnostic Classification of Mental Health and Developmental Disorders of Infancy and Early Childhood, Revised (DC: 0–5)**, one response to this concern, is a system developed to classify mental disorders of very young children (Zero to Three, 2016). We will focus our discussion on the DSM because it is the dominant system in the United States.

The DSM is often referred to as a **clinically derived classification** system. Clinically derived classification systems are based on the consensus of clinicians that certain characteristics occur together. These have been described as "top down" approaches (Achenbach, 2000). Committees of experts propose concepts of disorders and then choose diagnostic criteria for defining disorders. It is from these criteria that the development of assessments and evaluations proceed.

The DSM is also a **categorical approach** to classification; a person either does or does not meet the criteria for a diagnosis. In a categorical approach the difference between normal and abnormal is one of *kind* rather than one of *degree*. This approach also suggests that distinctions can be made between *qualitatively* different types of disorders.

The DSM is an outgrowth of the original psychiatric taxonomy developed by Kraepelin in 1883. There have been a number of revisions of the DSM system. The most recent revision is the DSM-5. The DSM-5 provides information regarding a large number of disorders. These disorders are organized into groups of related disorders. Disorders within a grouping (chapter) or, indeed, disorders in adjacent chapters are thought to be similar with regard to symptoms or with regard to factors such as genetic, neural, or environmental risks; cognitive or emotional processes; or response to treatment.

A description and diagnostic criteria are provided for each disorder. In addition, there is accompanying text material that provides information about features that may be associated with a disorder (e.g., low self-esteem) and information regarding cultural, age, and gender features; probable course of the disorder; prevalence; familial patterns; and so on (American Psychiatric Association, 2013).

Historically, the classification of abnormal behavior focused primarily on adult disorders and there was no extensive classification scheme for child and adolescent disorders (Silk et al., 2000). By the 1960s, it had become obvious that a more extensive system was needed. In response, the DSM-II, III, III-R, and IV expanded appreciably the number of categories specific to children and adolescents and a section of disorders "usually first diagnosed in infancy, childhood, or adolescence" was introduced. In addition, some "adult" diagnoses (e.g., anxiety disorders, mood disorders, schizophrenia, sleep disorders) could be used for children and adolescents. The DSM-5 no longer has a separate grouping of "disorders usually first diagnosed in infancy, childhood, or adolescence." Attention is still given to disorders experienced by children and adolescents; however, the disorders previously included in this section, like all other disorders, are placed within chapters of related disorders. For example, separation anxiety disorder is described in the chapter on anxiety disorders and attention-deficit/hyperactivity disorder (ADHD) is described in the chapter on neurodevelopmental disorders.

Thus, the DSM approach provides criteria for the diagnosis of and information related to specific disorders. From this a clinician working with a particular youth could derive a diagnosis thought to capture the youth's problems (e.g., conduct disorder, separation anxiety disorder). In addition to providing a diagnosis, it is suggested that the clinician may wish to indicate other information that may be relevant in working with this youth. This can include other difficulties that may be the focus of clinical attention (e.g., academic problems) or any current medical condition (e.g., arthritis or diabetes) that may be relevant to understanding or treating the youth. In addition, psychosocial or

KEVIN Seeking a Diagnosis

Kevin is a 9-year-old third-grader. He was brought to the clinic after his teacher repeatedly called home about his worsening behavior in school. The teacher described Kevin as likeable and friendly, but also said that, among other things, he repeatedly disrupted the class with his antics, hummed and made noises, blurted out answers, and had to be constantly reminded to stay in his seat. He was full of energy on the playground, but seemed to have few playmates and was often last to be chosen for teams. When playing games such as softball, he might be in the outfield concentrating on things in the sky or interesting pebbles on the ground. Although he seemed very bright, Kevin seldom completed his assignments in class. Despite his mother's report of considerable time and effort being spent on getting Kevin to concentrate on and complete his homework, papers sent home were seldom returned and homework was forgotten or left crumpled in his book bag.

At home Kevin is always on the go, his play is noisy and he leaves a trail of toys in his wake. Chores are left uncompleted or not done at all. Kevin's mother describes him as "the sweetest boy imaginable," but also as a "real handful."

A physical examination indicates that Kevin is healthy, well nourished, and in good physical condition except for several scrapes, bruises, and healed lacerations. The only significant medical history is a broken wrist at age 3 that resulted from a fall from a high wall that Kevin had managed to climb. Kevin's birth and early development were normal, and he reached developmental milestones at a normal or early time.

To illustrate how one might make a DSM diagnosis and provide other information, here is a diagnosis and some additional information relevant to Kevin's case that might be provided by his clinician.

Diagnosis: Attention-Deficit/Hyperactivity Disorder, Combined Presentation
Other Difficulties: Academic Problem
Related Medical Conditions: None
Psychosocial or Environmental Problems: Impending school expulsion
Overall Adjustment: Serious impairment in schoolwork, moderate impairment in social relationships
Adapted from Frances & Ross, 2001, pp. 8–11

environmental problems that might affect diagnosis, treatment, or prognosis (e.g., death of a family member or housing problems) might be noted. In certain circumstances the clinician might also be called upon to provide a judgment of the young person's overall level of functioning or disability. Including such information can help provide a fuller view of the problems of a particular young person. This is illustrated by the application of such an approach to a young boy, Kevin.

Considering the DSM Approach
The development of the DSM approach to classification has been an ongoing process (American Psychiatric Association, 2013; Regier et al., 2009). Over time, efforts have been made to improve the DSM system (Widiger et al., 1991). However, clinical, scientific, conceptual, and political issues have and continue to be raised (Angold & Costello, 2009; Beauchaine & Klein, 2017; Bufford et al., 2016; Egger & Emde, 2011; Follette & Houts, 1996; Jensen & Mrazek, 2006; Lilienfeld & Treadway, 2016; Rutter, 2011; Silverman & Mayes, 2018; Sonuga-Barke, 2020). Because the DSM is currently the dominant approach, it is important to consider some of the concerns regarding this system of classification.

For example, greater attention to the disorders of children and adolescents can be seen as a positive development. However,

there is, at the same time, concern about the proliferation of categories and the very comprehensiveness of the DSM system (Houts, 2002; Rutter, 2011). Furthermore, there is a concern with setting too liberal a cutoff between "disorder" and "normal"—the problem of false positives—classifying children within the normal range of development as having a disorder (Wakefield, 2016). This raises the fundamental question (Follette & Houts, 1996; Silk et al., 2000) that perhaps we have over-defined pathological behavior—in other words, too broadly defined children's behavior as deviant (cf. Richters & Cicchetti, 1993).

The issue of reliability has been another concern. Reliability has been a major consideration that has guided the development of the DSM. In earlier versions, disagreements between diagnosticians resulted from inadequate criteria for making a diagnosis. Thus, efforts were made starting with the DSM-III to improve interrater reliability by replacing general descriptions of disorders with clearer and more delineated diagnostic criteria based on a listing of symptoms. This approach, of more structured diagnostic rules, has improved communication among clinicians and researchers and has increased inter-clinician agreement in diagnosis. As would be expected, however, reliability still varies and may depend on the specific disorder and the nature and source of information (Leyfer & Brown, 2011). Reliability may also be affected by characteristics of the youth such as gender or ethnicity, or characteristics of the clinician. Furthermore, evidence of higher levels of reliability has typically been obtained under research conditions in which diagnosticians are given special training and employ procedures different from those likely to be used in typical clinical practice (APA Working Group on Psychoactive Medications for Children and Adolescents, 2006; Nathan & Langenbucher, 1999; Pottick et al., 2007; Valo & Tannock, 2010).

It has been argued that diagnostic research has focused too heavily on issues of reliability and clarity of communication. Although these issues are clearly important, it is also crucial for the DSM to provide an accurate representation of the nature of disorders. Whether a system is useful or helpful for clinicians, a question of utility, is different from whether it is a good description of the true nature of clinically significant differences in psychological functioning—a question of validity (Beauchaine & Klein, 2017; Knapp & Jensen, 2006).

Indeed, many of the questions raised to guide the future development of classification are questions of the validity of the current system. For example, validity would be indicated if research discovered treatments or etiologies that were *specific to particular disorders*. However, many treatments have been reported as being effective in treating several DSM disorders (Brown, 2017; Marchette & Weisz, 2017). Similarly, research studies have challenged the assumption that different disorders have entirely distinct environmental or genetic/neurobiological basis factors (Beauchaine, Gatzke-Kopp, & Gizer, 2017; Franić et al., 2010; Hoppen & Chalder, 2018; Lilienfeld & Treadway, 2016; Mikami, Miller, & Lerner, 2019). For example, adversity, maltreatment, and impairment of social functioning have been demonstrated to be contributing factors to a variety of disorders. Similarly, it has been found that disorders such as anxiety and depression, and depression and conduct problems, may share genetic and neurobiological influences. The term **"transdiagnostic"** has been employed to describe treatments that have been shown to be effective for two or more disorders or etiological influences that impact multiple disorders.

A frequently expressed concern regarding the validity of the current DSM is a basic concern with its categorical approach. Is this categorical (yes or no) approach accurate or might a dimensional (more continuous) view of disorder better reflect the true nature of clinical phenomena? The term **"dimension"** refers to a quantitative rather than qualitative approach to thinking about disorders. For example, research has supported the validity of three presentations (previously referred to as subtypes) of ADHD. However, Hudziak and his colleagues (1998) conducted structured diagnostic assessments in a large community sample of adolescent female twins. Their findings again supported the existence of the presentations but suggested that the presentations were best conceptualized as three dimensions (continuously distributed

between clinical and nonclinical levels) rather than three distinct categories. This and other research (Craske, 2012; Shaw et al., 2011) suggest the importance of considering a dimensional conceptualization of disorders.

In addition, researchers point out that the practice of dichotomizing continuous symptoms to form two categories— disorder and non-disorder—results in reduced statistical power and may lead to misleading research outcomes. An illustration of this is provided by an example of the use of diagnosis in treatment research. Individuals with eating disorders were randomly assigned to either a treatment or self-help control condition. The presence or absence of a diagnosis of Bulimia Nervosa at the end of treatment was used as the outcome measure. The researchers did not find significant outcome differences between the two treatment groups using this categorical approach to assess outcome. However, when a dimensional approach—the frequency of binges and purges—was used to determine outcome, a significant group difference did emerge (American Psychiatric Association, 2011).

An important aspect of challenges regarding the validity of the DSM approach involves the concept of **comorbidity**. The term comorbidity is used to describe the situation in which individuals meet the criteria for more than one disorder. The use of the term is controversial and some prefer the term **co-occurrence** (Lilienfeld, Waldman, & Israel, 1994; Widiger & Clark, 2000). Comorbidity typically implies the simultaneous existence of two or more distinct disorders in the same individual. Such co-occurrence is frequently reported (see Accent: "Co-occurrence: A Common Circumstance") and has led some to question the DSM approach to classification. Do these youth have multiple distinct disorders, or are there other ways of understanding the many difficulties that they are experiencing?

There are multiple ways to interpret a situation in which a child or an adolescent meets the diagnostic criteria for more than one disorder (Angold, Costello, & Erkanli, 1999; Beauchaine & Cicchetti, 2016; Carson & Rutter, 1991). It may be that many disorders have mixed patterns of symptoms. For example, a mixture of depression and anxiety may characterize mood disorders. Another alternative is that there are **transdiagnostic** processes that impact dysfunction across diagnostic categories. That is, some of the same risk factors lead to the development of multiple disorders (e.g., difficulties in emotion regulation contribute to both anxiety and conduct problems). Or perhaps the presence of one disorder creates an increased risk for developing the other disorder. A related idea is that the second problem is a later stage in a developmental progression in which earlier problems may or may not be retained, even as additional difficulties develop. For example, for some children and adolescents, a diagnosis of Oppositional Defiant Disorder is followed by a diagnosis of Conduct Disorder. It has been suggested, by some, that for these young people the diagnoses may represent a developmental pattern of a single common condition.

ACCENT Co-occurrence: A Common Circumstance

Children and adolescents who are evaluated by professionals in clinic or school settings often present with several different problems. These problems frequently fit the criteria for a number of different disorders, and thus clinicians often give these children or adolescents more than one diagnosis. How best to conceptualize these instances of co-occurrence or comorbidity is an ongoing concern. The description of Samuel that follows illustrates this common circumstance.

SAMUEL

A Case of Co-occurring Disorders

Samuel, an 11-year-old child, was referred to a clinic for attempted suicide after he had consumed a mixture of medicines, prescribed to his mother, in an attempt to kill himself. Samuel had slept for almost two days, when he was finally awakened by his mother and brought to the hospital.

Samuel lived in an inner-city neighborhood and since second grade had been in repeated trouble for stealing and breaking into empty homes. He had academic difficulties, was assigned to a special reading class, and was truant from school on a number of occasions. His mother may have experienced several major depressive episodes, sometimes drank heavily, and may have relied on prostitution for income. Samuel's father had not been in contact with the mother since Samuel was born.

At his interview, Samuel appeared sad and cried at one point. He reported having severe "blue periods," the most recent of which had been continuous for the past month. During these periods he thought that he might be better off dead. Samuel also reported that he had recently started to wake up in the middle of the night and had been avoiding his usual neighborhood "gang."

Samuel was given a diagnosis of Major Depressive Disorder, and a diagnosis of Persistent Depressive Disorder/Dysthymia (a chronic form of depression) was also considered. In addition he received a diagnosis of Conduct Disorder, Childhood Onset Type, and a diagnosis of Specific Learning Disorder with impairment in reading.

Adapted from Rapoport & Ismond, 1996

These are only some of the possible ways to explain "comorbidity." The issues involved in understanding co-occurrence of disorders are complex, and at present the solution to this issue remains unclear. However, the frequency of co-occurrence and the conceptual issues it raises are at the heart of how best to conceptualize child and adolescent psychopathology and discussions of the current DSM approach (Beauchaine & Cicchetti, 2016; Lilienfeld & Treadway, 2016; Rutter, 2011).

Finally, as mentioned earlier, there have been a number of other concerns expressed regarding the DSM approach to classification. One such concern is that the DSM promotes a disease/medical model that overly emphasizes biological etiology and treatment, and that conceptualizes disorder as being within the child rather than resulting from multiple causes and from the interaction of the child and the environment (Carrey & Ungar, 2007; Cicchetti, 2010a; Silk et al., 2000; Sroufe, 1997).

Concern has also been expressed regarding the limited degree of attention to issues of developmental level, cultural context, and gender in the DSM (Achenbach, 2000; Beauchaine & Klein, 2017; Hudziak et al., 2007; Silk et al., 2000). In DSM-5, differences in age-, gender-, and culture-related expressions of symptoms have been added for some diagnoses. The DSM-5 also does include, in the text that accompanies each set of diagnostic criteria and elsewhere, sections that address developmental, cultural, and gender-related features. This textual material may alert clinicians to variations associated with developmental level, culture, and gender. Nevertheless, diagnostic criteria are largely the same for both sexes and for all ages and cultures.

This approach may have important consequences. For example, it has been pointed out that if one applies a set of fixed cutpoints (number of symptoms needed for diagnosis) to diagnostic criteria, disorders may appear to have prevalence rates that vary with age and gender (Achenbach, 2000; Hudziak et al., 2007). The same applies to cultural differences. We could ask, however, whether these are real differences in rates of disorders. For example, the DSM indicates that ADHD occurs more frequently in males. This sex difference in diagnosis led the literature on ADHD to be based largely on males. However, even non-deviant boys exhibit higher rates of behaviors characteristic of ADHD than do girls. Thus, the sex difference in ADHD might be an artifact of higher base rates of these behaviors in boys. If these sex differences in base rates in the population were considered in setting diagnostic cutpoints (e.g., slightly decreasing the number of required criteria for girls), would gender differences in prevalence of ADHD still emerge? Hudziak and colleagues (2005) employed a measure that contained

DSM ADHD items (the Conners' Rating Scales—CRS) but also provided sex norms. These researchers used the CRS to measure ADHD and used the sex-specific norms to determine which children were statistically deviant on ADHD scales. This approach resulted in as many girls as boys meeting the criteria for ADHD—nearly equal prevalence for boys and girls. By contrast, if DSM criteria (where diagnostic thresholds do not differ by sex) were used, many girls who were impaired failed to meet diagnostic criteria. In a similar way, reported declines in the rates of ADHD diagnoses with age may also be an artifact of the age-related decline in base rates of ADHD behaviors.

In addition to affecting estimates of prevalence, the issue of whether to have fixed or variable cutoffs or criteria based on sex, age-related, or cultural considerations has implications for who will be identified as needing services. In some cases "fixed" cutoffs may, as illustrated above, result in failing to identify individuals who may benefit from services. Under other circumstances individuals whose behavior may not be deviant might be designated as having a disorder.

Throughout our exploration of the development of psychopathology, we will see that research suggests that the potentially complex interactions of culture, context, and behavior deserve attention and that diagnostic and classification systems will need to pay increasing attention to issues of cultural and developmental context (Achenbach, 2017; Beauchaine & Klein, 2017; Lewis-Fernández et al., 2010; Rescorla et al., 2007, 2011).

As we have mentioned, one of the major concerns with the DSM classification is its categorical approach. Approaches to classification that consider problems of children and adolescents dimensionally do exist. We turn now to an examination of empirically based approaches to classification.

Empirical Approaches to Classification

The **empirical approach to classification** is an alternative to the clinical approach to taxonomy. It is based on the use of statistical techniques to identify patterns of behavior that are interrelated. The general procedure is for a parent or some other respondent to indicate the presence or absence of specific behaviors by the youth. The information from these responses is quantified in some way. For example, the respondent marks a "0" if the youth does not exhibit a certain characteristic, a "1" if the youth displays a moderate degree of the characteristic, and a "2" if the characteristic is clearly present. Such information is obtained for a large number of young people. Statistical techniques such as factor analysis are then employed, and groups of items that tend to occur together are identified. These groups are referred to as factors or clusters. The term **syndrome** is also often employed to describe behaviors that tend to occur together,

whether they are identified by empirical or clinical judgment procedures. Thus, rather than relying on clinicians' views about which behaviors tend to occur together, researchers can employ empirical and statistical procedures as the basis for developing a classification scheme.

Substantial evidence exists for two **broadband syndromes**, or general clusters of behaviors or characteristics (Achenbach et al., 2016). One of these clusters is commonly given the label **internalizing**. Descriptions such as anxious, shy, withdrawn, and depressed are some of the characteristics associated with this grouping. The second grouping is commonly labeled **externalizing**. Fighting, temper tantrums, disobedience, and destructiveness are frequently associated with this pattern. The Achenbach System of Empirically Based Assessment (ASEBA) is among the measures used to derive these two broadband clusters (Achenbach & Rescorla, 2001).

In addition to the two broadband *Internalizing* and *Externalizing syndromes*, research with these instruments has identified empirically defined, less general, or **narrowband syndromes**. These eight syndromes for school-age youth are described in Table 5.1. There is strong research support for these eight syndromes across diverse societies (Ivanova et al., 2019). Every child who is evaluated receives a score on each of the syndromes, resulting in a profile of syndrome scores for a particular child (see Figure 5.1). This approach to classification evaluates each young person on several dimensions.

Thus, this approach to classification differs from the clinical approach of the DSM in several ways. One important difference between the two approaches is how groupings are defined and formed (empirically versus clinical consensus). A second important difference is that the empirical approach to classification views problems as dimensional rather than categorical. It suggests that differences between individuals are quantitative rather than qualitative and that the difference between normal and pathological is one of degree rather than one of kind (Achenbach, 2000). Also, since every child obtains scores on every dimension/syndrome, many patterns of co-occurring problems are possible and expected. This approach to conceptualizing a youth's problems differs from the comorbidity perspective described in the DSM approach.

Empirically based classifications also employ data from **normative samples** as a frame of reference for judging the problems of an individual youth. For example, using the ASEBA measures, a youth's scores can be compared with norms for non-referred youth or with norms for other young people referred for mental health services. In addition, the youth is evaluated as compared to norms for youth of the same age and gender. Norms are also available for reports by different types of informants (youth, parent, teacher) and for multiple cultures (Achenbach, 2017; Achenbach & Rescorla, 2001).

Table 5.1 Eight Narrowband Syndromes Common to the ASEBA School-Age Measures—With Sample Items

INTERNALIZING SYNDROMES		
Anxious/Depressed	**Withdrawn/Depressed**	**Somatic Complaints**
Cries a lot	Rather be alone	Overtired
Fearful, anxious	Shy, timid	Aches, pains
Feels worthless	Withdrawn	Stomachaches
MIXED SYNDROMES		
Social Problems	**Thought Problems**	**Attention Problems**
Lonely	Hears things	Can't concentrate
Gets teased	Sees things	Can't sit still
Not liked	Strange ideas	Impulsive
EXTERNALIZING SYNDROMES		
Rule-Breaking Behavior	**Aggressive Behavior**	
Lacks guilt	Mean to others	
Bad friends	Destroys others' things	
Steals at home	Gets in fights	

Source: Adapted from Achenbach & Rescorla, 2001. Copyright 2001 by University of Vermont, Research Center for Children, Youth & Families; reprinted with permission.

It is worth noting that, in addition to the dimensions/syndromes described above and outlined in Table 5.1, the Achenbach instruments can be scored to yield scales that correspond to some DSM categories (Achenbach, Dumenci, & Rescorla, 2003; Achenbach & Rescorla, 2007). These DSM-oriented scales are one way that the two approaches might be compared.

The Research Domain Criteria

The National Institute of Mental Health (NIMH) more recently launched another alternative to the DSM approach to classification. This initiative is known as the **Research Domain Criteria (RDoC)**. The goal of this initiative is "to understand the nature of mental health and illness in terms of varying degrees of dysfunctions in general psychological/biological systems" (NIMH, 2019). While not stated as an immediate goal, the RDoC initiative is viewed by proponents as an ongoing effort to develop a research-based system that would eventually replace the current DSM/ICD classification systems and serve as a framework for clinical assessment and the development of more precise and effective treatments (Cuthbert, 2014; Insel et al., 2010; Sanislow et al., 2010).

In addition to its strong emphasis on research, the RDoC conceptualization differs from current classification systems in two major ways. First, the RDoC defines disorder in terms of underlying *systems* rather than by lists of observable *symptoms*. The RDoC is formulated as a matrix. One dimension of that matrix describes domains of functioning/underlying systems. These domains describe neurobiological and psychological systems underlying typical and atypical development—normal to abnormal outcomes. The RDoC matrix contains six such domains of functioning and, within each, several constructs that comprise the different aspects of each domain. The six domains of functioning and examples of the related constructs are described in Table 5.2.

The second dimension of the matrix includes descriptions of how the systems, described in the domains and constructs, may be studied. The RDoC suggests that systems be measured across multiple levels of analysis, ranging from genes, molecules, cells, circuits, physiology, and behavior, to self-reports. The RDoC formulation also includes useful paradigms or tasks for examining the research questions (for further information see www.nimh.nih.gov/research-priorities/rdoc/units/index.shtml).

Thus, an important distinction between the RDoC and DSM approaches to classification is that the RDoC focuses on measures of underlying systems rather than on lists of observable symptoms (the DSM approach). A second, major way in which the RDoC approach differs from traditional diagnostic approaches such as the DSM is that the RDoC conceptualization is dimensional rather than categorical. As indicated above, the RDoC explores basic dimensions of functioning that span the full range of human behavior. Thus, normal to abnormal is viewed as a matter of degree. In addition, the RDoC approach views constructs as dimensions that cut across traditional diagnostic boundaries. For example, it might be expected that a specific construct within the negative

Table 5.2 The RDoC Domains of Function with Examples of Related Constructs

Negative valence systems (e.g., potential threat/anxiety, loss)
Positive valence systems (e.g., responsiveness to reward, reward learning)
Cognitive systems (e.g., attention, working memory)
Social processes (e.g., affiliation and attachment, social communication)
Arousal/regulatory systems (e.g., arousal, sleep-wakefulness)
Sensorimotor systems (e.g., motor actions, habits-sensorimotor)

Source: Adapted from NIMH, 2019.

valence systems (e.g., potential threat) would be relevant to understanding both anxiety and conduct problems as well as other disorders. Thus, the focus of the RDoC approach is on dimensions of underlying systems rather than on distinct categories/disorders.

The RDoC approach addresses some of the concerns with the current dominant diagnostic approaches. However, it has been noted that the RDoC initiative may be relatively insensitive to context—the role of the social/environmental context in which the various domains unfold and to developmental context or how the various domains develop over time (De Los Reyes et al., 2020; Hayden & Durbin, 2019; Lilienfeld & Treadway, 2016). The challenges of applying the RDoC approach to the problems of youth, in particular, will need to be part of ongoing efforts (Beauchaine & Hinshaw, 2020; Garber & Bradshaw, 2020).

Stigmatization and the Impact of Labels

As we have already noted, classification and diagnosis are intended to facilitate understanding and treatment of psychological problems. Although classification is intended as a scientific and clinical enterprise, it can be seen as a social process. The **diagnostic label** places the youth in a subgroup of individuals and this has implications for how the young person may be viewed and treated by others. If this impact is negative, this may be due, in part, to the stigma associated with mental illness. **Stigmatization** refers to stereotyping, prejudice, discrimination, and self-degradation that may be associated with membership in a socially devalued group. (See Accent: "The Impact of Stigmatization.")

Any negative impact of a diagnostic label may actually detract from the original purpose of categorizing—that of helping young people (Hinshaw, 2005). When attempting to define a mental disorder (American Psychiatric Association, 2013) it is important to remember that formal classification is intended to categorize disorders, not people (Cantwell, 1980). Thus, it is correct, for example, to say, "Billy Greene has autism." However, it is incorrect to say "Billy Greene, the autistic child."

It is important to be aware of the potential negative effects of the labeling process. Labels can contribute to a variety of unintended consequences. Overgeneralization is one concern. It may incorrectly be assumed that all young people labeled with ADHD, for example, are more alike than they actually are. Such an assumption readily leads to neglect of the individual child or adolescent. Labels also may produce negative perceptions of young people. For example, Walker and colleagues (2008) presented vignettes of a child labeled as having ADHD, depression, or asthma to a large sample of young people ages 8–18. Other than the disorder designation, the description of the child was the same. Children with ADHD or depression were viewed as more likely to engage in antisocial behavior and violence than the children described as having asthma.

Also, expectations regarding a youth may be biased by the presence of a label. Others may act in a manner that is guided by such expectations, influencing the youth to behave in a manner consistent with those expectations. The negative expectation that may be transmitted by labels is suggested by the findings of a study by Briggs and colleagues (1994). Adults read vignettes of a 6-year-old child engaged in aggressive behavior on a school playground. The stories varied regarding the family history of the child (normal, mother dying of cancer, sexually abused). After reading the vignette, the adults completed a questionnaire about their expectations regarding the behavior of the child. Results indicated that the adults had different expectations regarding the sexually abused child; for example, they believed that the sexually abused child would have more behavior problems and lesser achievement than either of the other two children.

Labels may not always produce negative expectations, however. Some suggest that labels provide an "explanation" for the child's problematic behavior. When an adult understands why the child is behaving in this manner, the adult may be less likely to have negative reactions and may have more appropriate expectations for the child. A study by Wood and Valdez-Menchaca (1996) illustrates that labels do not always lead to negative expectations. Adults interacted with four children, one of whom had previously been diagnosed with a language disorder (LD). The adults were randomly assigned to one of two conditions: The first was a non-label condition in which the child with LD was not identified, and the second was a label condition in which the child with LD was identified. Adults in the non-label group ranked the child with LD as significantly less likeable, less productive, and less academically competent than the other children. Adults in the label group did not. They had observed the same inappropriate behaviors as the adults in the non-label group but they appeared to be more accepting of such behavior.

ACCENT The Impact of Stigmatization

The stigma associated with mental illness is increasingly realized to be a central issue by those concerned for the well-being of children, adolescents, and their families (Corrigan & Nieweglowski, 2019; Martinez & Hinshaw, 2016; Mukolo, Heflinger, & Wallston, 2010). Stigmatization may affect youth in multiple ways. It may affect both youth with a disorder and youth whose parents have a mental disorder.

Stigmatization is often thought of as involving three dimensions: negative stereotypes, devaluation, and discrimination. Stereotyping means that a young person with a disorder may be viewed in terms of negative traits or attributes such as being dangerous or incompetent. Devaluing may lead to separation from others and loss of status. Discrimination refers to actions that limit the young person's rights and power. In addition, the youth may internalize negative evaluations and develop a negative view of his or her abilities and even him- or herself. Research suggests a number of other ways that stigmatization affects youth. For example, a young person with a disorder may experience a variety of negative social experiences, be denigrated, and be rejected by peers. The young person may also experience a similar impact of stigmatization in interactions with adults and even professionals. Also, the youth's parents may be blamed for their child's difficulties. This, along with the stigma associated with the young person's disorder, may reduce the likelihood that the family will seek help (Pescosolido et al., 2008).

We also know that parental psychopathology is a risk factor for future child psychopathology. The stigma associated with mental disorders may prevent parents with a disorder from seeking help and thereby increase their children's risk. Also, the stigma associated with the parent's disorder may inhibit open family discussion and thereby further increase risk, limiting support for the children and perhaps leading them to blame themselves for their parents' or family's difficulties. There also may be increased risk if the parent and family feel the need to conceal the parent's difficulties, thereby reducing access to social support.

Understanding stigmatization and its impact is clearly a complex and difficult issue. Education regarding child psychopathology and the issue of stigmatization is clearly part of the solution. However, a broader effort is needed to overcome stigmatization (Martinez & Hinshaw, 2016). As Hinshaw (2005) has stated,

> For children and adolescents, stigma processes occur in families, schools, and communities; the notion of "fit" between child and setting is crucial for the diagnosis of the child as mentally disturbed. Hence, community tolerance and acceptance of developmental disorders—and community facilitation of accommodation for youth with special educational needs—are essential components of fostering academic, social, and life competence. (p. 726)

Finally, concern has been voiced that diagnostic labeling minimizes attention to the interpersonal and social context in which the child's behavior exists (Silk et al., 2000; Sroufe, 1997). Traditional diagnostic categories ignore the fact that a young person's problems "belong" to at least one other person—the one who is identifying or reporting the problems (Algozzine, 1977; Lilly, 1979). As we shall see throughout this book, there is much evidence that the way a youth is described and viewed may reflect as much on the individual doing the describing as it does on the behavior of the child or adolescent.

Many experts involved in the study and treatment of young people are concerned about potential negative consequences of diagnostic labels, and these experts advocate for various ways to reduce the possible harmful effects. Categorization, however, is embedded in our thinking and contributes to the advancement of our knowledge. Completely discarding categorization is neither desirable nor possible. Thus, it is important to improve

classification systems and, at the same time, to be sensitive to social factors inherent in the use of categories, the social status imparted by a label, and the impact of labels on the young person and the family (Adelman, 1996; Hinshaw, 2010).

Assessment

Evaluating child and adolescent problems is a complex process. By the time a young person comes to the attention of a clinician, the presenting problem is usually, if not always, multifaceted. But because assessment is the first part of any contact, the professional's knowledge of the problem is limited. Both of these factors, as well as common sense and caution, argue that the best interests of the young person are most likely served by a comprehensive assessment of multiple facets of the young person and his or her environment.

ALICIA An Initial Assessment

The parents of 6-year-old Alicia were seeking assistance in understanding her problems and ways to help their daughter improve her adjustment at home and school and with her peers. The parents described Alicia as impulsive, moody, and having difficulty in school. The initial information provided by the parents indicated that several male relatives on the mother's side of the family were diagnosed with intellectual disabilities and that one of these relatives had been diagnosed with a fragile X chromosomal disorder. The clinician hypothesized that Alicia might be a fragile X carrier because females are carriers for the defective gene associated with the syndrome. Based on initial information, the clinician also hypothesized that Alicia might have ADHD and/or a learning disability.

Information was gathered from several sources: the parents (interview, rating scales, daily behavioral logs, observation of parent–child interactions), the teacher (rating scales, academic performance and test scores), and Alicia herself (interview, direct observation, psychoeducational testing). Information obtained during the assessment revealed that Alicia had many characteristics of females who carry the fragile X chromosome. This was discussed with the parents and referral for a genetic evaluation revealed that this was

indeed the case. The assessment also indicated that Alicia met the diagnostic criteria for ADHD and that she had a specific learning disorder.

In addition, evaluation revealed that Alicia's parents provided a structured yet stimulating environment for her. Alicia had friends, successfully engaged in age-appropriate activities, and felt loved by her parents. She also realized that her impulsive behavior created problems for herself and her family. Positive aspects of the case were Alicia's desire to please and her good social skills, warm and loving parents, and supportive home and school environments.

The assessment led to intervention strategies that included a change in Alicia's class placement and resource support, support for the family, referral to a support group for parents of children with fragile X syndrome, behavior management techniques for the parents, and brief individual work with Alicia to help her recognize her strengths and cope with her difficulties. The clinician indicated that Alicia would likely adapt and continue to develop successfully, but further assessment and intervention might be needed as new challenges were encountered.

Adapted from Schroeder & Smith-Boydston, 2017, pp. 55–56

Conducting a Comprehensive Assessment

As we shall see throughout our discussion, behavioral disorders in youth are complex, often encompassing a variety of components rather than a single problem behavior. Furthermore, these problems typically arise from, and are maintained by, multiple influences. Such influences include biological factors; aspects of the young person's behavioral, cognitive, and social functioning; and influences of the family and other social systems such as peers and school. Thus, an assessment must be comprehensive in evaluating a variety of potential presenting problems, measuring a variety of aspects of youth themselves, and assessing multiple contexts and other individuals.

Information must be obtained from a number of sources (e.g., the youth, parents, teachers) to assess problems that may vary by context or that may be displayed differently in the presence of different individuals (De Los Reyes et al., 2015). A child may behave differently at home, in school, and in playing with his or her peers. Also, observers may view the same or similar behaviors differently. A mother who is depressed and experiencing life stresses may be less able to tolerate minor deviations from expected behavior. Such differences in perception may be important both in understanding the presenting problems and

in planning interventions. Assessment thus requires the use of multiple and varied methods as well as familiarity with assessment instruments for individuals of many different ages. The process requires considerable skill and sensitivity.

Assessment may be best accomplished by a team of clinicians carefully trained in the administration and interpretation of specific procedures and instruments. It is desirable for clinicians to employ **evidence-based assessment**—procedures that rely on empirical evidence and theory to guide their selection and support their validity (Achenbach, 2017; De Los Reyes & Langer, 2018; McLeod et al., 2019; Youngstrom et al., 2017). As we will see later in this chapter when we discuss empirically supported treatments, such evidence-based practice is an ongoing goal for researchers and clinicians.

Because assessment is usually conducted immediately on contact with the young person or family, it demands special sensitivity to anxiety, shyness, manipulation, and the like as well as to family and cultural values. If treatment ensues, assessment should be a continuous process, so that new information can be gleaned and the ongoing effects of treatment can be ascertained. In this way, the clinician remains open to nuances and can avoid rigid judgments about a multifaceted and complex phenomenon.

The Interview

The General Clinical Interview

The **general clinical interview** is clearly the most common method of assessment. Information on all areas of functioning is obtained by interviewing the child or adolescent and various other people in the social environment (Sattler & Garro, 2014b; Watkins et al., 1995).

Whether the young person will be interviewed alone will probably vary with age. An older child or adolescent generally is more capable and is more likely to provide valuable information. Nevertheless, clinicians often elect to interview even a very young child in order to obtain their own impressions. Preschool and grade school children can provide valuable information if appropriate developmental considerations are used to tailor the interview to the individual child (Bierman & Schwartz, 1986; Kamphaus & Frick, 1996; Sattler & Garro, 2014b). For example, an adult-like face-to-face interview may be intimidating for a young child, so a more successful technique may be to model the interview after a familiar play or school task.

Most clinicians seek information concerning the nature of the problem, past and recent history, present conditions, feelings and perceptions, attempts to solve the problem, and expectations concerning treatment. The general clinical interview is used not only to determine the nature of the presenting problem and perhaps to help formulate a diagnosis but also to gather information that allows the clinician to conceptualize the case and to plan an appropriate therapeutic intervention.

The general clinical interview is usually described as open-ended or unstructured. Because such interviews are most often conducted in the context of a therapeutic interaction and are employed along with a variety of other assessment instruments, it has been difficult to evaluate reliability and validity.

Structured and Semi-Structured Diagnostic Interviews

Structured and semi-structured diagnostic interviews have arisen in part to create interviews that are likely to be more reliable. They also have been developed for the more limited purpose of deriving a diagnosis based on a particular classification scheme, such as the DSM; for use in research; or in order to screen large populations for the prevalence of disorders. These interviews can be conducted with the youth and/or parent(s). Improving such interviews remains an ongoing goal and reliability varies for different disorders and depending on the source (parent or youth) of the information (Duncan et al., 2019).

In the unstructured general clinical interview, there are no particular questions that the clinician must ask, no designated format, and no stipulated method to record information. That is not to say that there are no guidelines or agreed-on procedures for conducting an effective interview. Indeed, there is an extensive literature on effective interviewing (McConaughy, 2005; Sattler

& Garro, 2014a, 2014b). However, unstructured interviews are intended to give the clinician great latitude. In contrast, structured diagnostic interviews consist of a set of questions that the interviewer asks the young person. There are rules for how the interview is to be conducted, and explicit guidelines for recording and scoring the responses (McClellan & Werry, 2000; Schroeder & Smith-Boydston, 2017). The Anxiety Disorders Interview for Children Schedule (ADIS C/P; Albano & Silverman, 2017), the Diagnostic Interview for Children and Adolescents (DICA; Reich, 2000), and the Schedule for Affective Disorders and Schizophrenia for School-Age Children (K-SADS; Ambrosini, 2000) are examples of these diagnostic interviews.

Problem Checklists and Self-Report Instruments

Problem checklists and rating scales were described in our discussion of classification (p. 89). There are a wide variety of such instruments. Some are for general use—such as the Child Behavior Checklist (Achenbach & Rescorla, 2001) and the Behavior Assessment System for Children (Reynolds & Kamphaus, 2015). Others are used with particular populations. The Conners Rating Scales (Conners, 2008), for instance, can be particularly useful when ADHD needs to be assessed.

A considerable empirical literature suggests that these instruments may be valuable tools for clinicians and researchers (Achenbach, 2017; Schroeder & Smith-Boydston, 2107). The ASEBA family of instruments mentioned earlier (pp. 89–90) is an example of problem checklists (Achenbach & Rescorla, 2001). These instruments are widely employed in research and clinical settings. The Child Behavior Checklist (CBCL) is completed by the parents of youth 6 to 18 years of age. The Teacher Report Form (TRF) is a parallel instrument completed by teachers of youth 6 to 18 years old, and the Youth Self-Report (YSR) is completed by youth who are 11 to 18 years of age. Parallel measures for younger children, the CBCL for Ages 1.5 to 5 and the C-TRF (Caregiver–Teacher Report Form) are also available (Achenbach & Rescorla, 2000). In addition, the functioning of the parent(s) can be assessed through Adult Self-Report (ASR) to describe oneself and the Adult Behavior Checklist (ABCL) to describe one's partner (Achenbach & Rescorla, 2015).

Rating scales completed by different informants may help the clinician gain a fuller appreciation of the clinical picture and of potential situational aspects of the child's problem (Achenbach, 2017). For example, Figure 5.1 illustrates the differences in responses of a young girl's mother and father. Differing perceptions of two informants may provide important information to a clinician. For example, the CBCL, TRF, and YSR make it possible to compare multiple informants' reports about the child with respect to a common set of problem items and dimensions. When two or more respondents use these instruments to describe a child or adolescent, a statistic can be computed indicating the degree of agreement. This degree of agreement for a particular youth can then be compared with the degree of agreement between comparable informants for a large representative sample. Thus, it is possible to know whether the degree of agreement between Tommy's mother and his teacher is less than, similar to, or greater than the average mother–teacher agreement about boys in Tommy's age range. This information is likely to be valuable to the clinician in conceptualizing the presenting problems. Information from reports by different informants also may be helpful to the therapeutic process. For example, parents can learn about differences in how their child is perceived.

As indicated earlier in our discussion of empirical approaches to classification (pp. 89–90), problem checklists such as the ASEBA instruments allow comparison to **normative samples** as a frame of reference for judging the problems of an individual youth. For the CBCL, TRF, and YSR, for example, there are two sets of norms against which to compare an individual child's or adolescent's scores. A youth's scores can be compared with norms for non-referred youth or with norms for other young people referred for mental health services. There are separate norms for each sex in

particular age ranges, as rated by each type of informant. Thus, there are separate parent informant CBCL norms for boys 6 to 11, boys 12 to 18, girls 6 to 11, and girls 12 to 18, and separate similar norms for teacher and for youth informants (Achenbach & Rescorla, 2001). A youth's scores can also be evaluated with respect to norms from multiple cultures (Achenbach, 2017).

To evaluate the behavior problems of an 11-year-old boy named Jason, for example, one could compare Jason's scores on the empirically based syndromes derived from his parents' reports with two sets of norms: norms of parent reports for non-referred 11-year-old boys and norms of parent reports for clinic-referred 11-year-old boys. Scores based on Jason's teacher's TRF could be compared with two similar sets of norms of teachers' reports for 11-year-old boys. And scores based on Jason's own YSR could be compared with norms of responses of non-referred and clinic-referred boys of his age.

A general rating scale may thus help a clinician judge the child's adjustment relative to appropriate norms. This procedure can help to evaluate the appropriateness of the referral. Once a particular presenting problem is identified, the clinician might

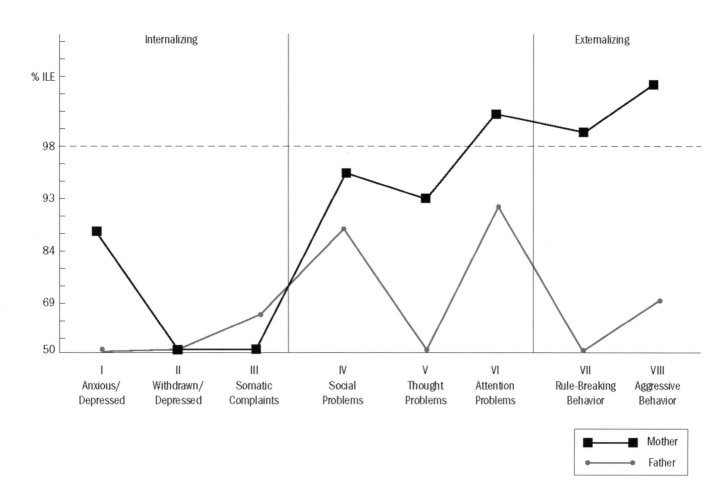

Figure 5.1 Profiles of an 11-year-old girl based on Child Behavior Checklists completed by her mother and father.

also use a rating scale designed for a more specific problem (e.g., ADHD, anxiety, or depression).

In addition, the clinician or researcher may also draw on an array of **self-report measures**. Here, too, there are general measures and there are measures to assess specific problems such as anxiety and depression (Kovacs, 2011; March, 2013). Instruments also are available to assess constructs related to adjustment such as self-control and self-concept (Connell, 1985; Harter, 1985). Many of these measures will be described in later chapters that focus on particular child and adolescent problems.

Parents and other adults may also be asked to complete self-report instruments about themselves. These instruments, such as the ASR, evaluate a wide array of aspects of adult functioning. Alternatively, they may assess specific problems, for example, a parent's own anxiety or depression. Other measures may assess one or more of a wide array of aspects of adult functioning. For instance, the feelings, attitudes, and beliefs of adults, particularly with respect to the child or adolescent, may be assessed (e.g., the Stability of Activities in the Family Environment—Israel, Roderick, & Ivanova, 2002; the Parenting Stress Index—Abidin, 2012), or aspects of the family environment may be measured (e.g., the Family Environment Scale—Moos & Moos, 1994; and the Parent–Adolescent Relationship Questionnaire—Robin, Koepke, & Moye, 1990). Such assessment can provide important information about the social environment and factors that may influence problem behavior. The use of such measures acknowledges that the presenting problem is complex and exists in a social context.

Observational Assessment

Early attempts to observe children's behavior used diaries or continuous observations and narrations that were deliberately nonselective (Wright, 1960). From this tradition evolved observations of a more focused, pinpointed set of behaviors that could be reliably coded by observers (Bijou et al., 1969). Such structured observations continue to be a potentially important aspect of the assessment process (Pelsch et al., 2017; Sattler & Pillai Riddell, 2014a). They involve watching and systematically observing the behavior of a youth or parent, or some other aspect of the young person's environment as it occurs.

Behavioral observations are frequently made in the child's natural environment, although situations are sometimes created in clinic or laboratory settings to approximate naturally occurring interactions. Observations can include reports of single, relatively simple, and discrete behaviors of the child; interactions of the child and peers; and complex systems of interactions among family members (Achenbach, 2013; Eyberg et al., 2013; Israel, Pravder, & Knights, 1980; Kaugars et al., 2011; Reid, 1978; Reynolds & Kamphaus, 2015). Clearly, ongoing interactions are more difficult to observe and code than are the behaviors of a single individual; however, they are likely to be theoretically and clinically relevant.

The first step in any behavioral observation system involves explicitly pinpointing and defining behaviors. Observers are trained to use the system and note whether a particular behavior or sequence of behaviors occurs. Research indicates that a number of factors affect reliability as well as validity and clinical utility of observational systems (Sattler & Pillai Riddell, 2014b). For example, the complexity of the observational system and changes over time in the observers' use of the system (observer drift) are two such factors. Reactivity (a change in an individual's behavior when the individual knows that he or she is being observed) is often cited as the greatest impediment to the utility of direct observation. Careful training, periodic monitoring of observers' use of the system, and use of observers already in the situation (e.g., teachers) are some recommended ways to reduce distortions in the information obtained from direct observation.

Behavioral observations are the most direct method of assessment and require the least inference. The difficulty and expense involved in training and maintaining reliable observers is probably the primary obstacle to their common use in non-research contexts. Since direct observation has long been considered the hallmark of assessment from a behavioral perspective, attempts have been made to create systems that are more amenable to widespread use (Sargent et al., 2020). Direct observation is, however, just one aspect of a multimethod approach to behavioral assessment that can include self-monitoring of behavior, interviews, ratings and checklists, and self-report instruments.

Projective Tests

At one time the most common form of psychological test employed to assess children was the projective test. These tests are less commonly used today, in large part because of debates regarding lack of empirical norms, reliability, and validity (Anastasi & Urbina, 1997; Erickson, Lilienfeld, & Vitacco, 2007; Kleiger, 2001; Lilienfeld, Wood, & Garb, 2000; Sattler, 2014).

Projective tests were derived from the psychoanalytic notion of projection as a defense mechanism: one way the ego deals with unacceptable impulses is to project them onto some external object. It is assumed that the impulses cannot be expressed directly. Therefore, many projective tests present an ambiguous stimulus, allowing the individual to project "unacceptable" thoughts and impulses, as well as other defense mechanisms onto the stimulus. Some clinicians employ projective tests in a manner that involves less psychodynamic inference (Chandler, 2003; McGrath & Carroll, 2012). For example, the young person may see an ambiguous stimulus in terms of past

Figure 5.2 Drawings similar to those employed in the CAT.

experiences and present desires and thus be prompted to report these. Analyses that examine formal aspects of a test response—for example, the distance between human figures that the child draws—may also be used. Interpretations are then made on the basis of this response style rather than on the content of the response.

Projective tests may ask a child to interpret an image or to create his or her own picture. Examples of projective tests include the Rorschach test, in which the youth is asked what he or she sees in each of ten inkblots. The most commonly used methods for scoring and interpretation are based on characteristics of the response, such as the portion of the blot responded to (location), factors such as color and shading (determinants), and the nature of what is seen in the blot (content) (Exner & Weiner, 1995). The Draw-a-Person test (Koppitz, 1984) asks the child to draw a picture of a person and then a second person of the opposite sex. Then, the child is asked to tell a story about the person drawn. The Children's Apperception Test (CAT) (Bellak & Bellak, 1982; Bellak & Abrams, 1997), and the Roberts Apperception Test for Children (Roberts, 2005) provide the young person with pictures for which he or she is asked to make up a story. Figure 5.2 presents pictures similar to those used in the CAT.

Intellectual–Educational Assessment

The evaluation of intellectual and academic functioning is an important part of almost all clinical assessments. Intellectual functioning is a central defining feature for disorders such as intellectual disability and specific learning disorders, but it may also contribute to and be affected by a wide array of behavioral problems. Compared with most other assessment instruments, tests of intellectual functioning tend to have better normative data, reliability, and validity. Although our present discussion of these instruments is brief, we will consider additional information in later chapters.

Intelligence Tests

By far the most commonly employed assessment devices for evaluating intellectual functioning are tests of general intelligence. The Stanford–Binet (Roid & Barram, 2004); the Wechsler tests—the Wechsler Preschool and Primary Scale of Intelligence (Wechsler, 2012) and the Wechsler Intelligence Scale for Children (Wechsler, 2014a); and the Kaufman Assessment Battery for Children (Kaufman & Kaufman, 2004) are some of the intelligence tests widely used in clinical settings. All are individually administered and yield an **intelligence (IQ) score.** The average score is 100, and an individual score reflects how far above or below the average person of his or her age an individual has scored.

Intelligence tests have long been the subject of controversy. Questions have arisen regarding the nature of intelligence and the tests developed to assess intelligence. As a result, how intelligence is conceptualized and how it is measured continue to evolve (Flanagan & McDonough, 2018; Wasserman, 2018). There are also concerns that intelligence tests may be culturally biased and have the potential to contribute to educational and social injustices. Although intelligence tests are popular and useful in predicting a variety of outcomes, continued concern with legal, ethical, and practical issues demand that they be used cautiously and that efforts be made to insure that intellectual assessments are conducted in a way that is sensitive to cultural and language issues (Ortiz et al., 2018; Sattler, Dumont, & Coalson, 2016; Wasserman, 2018).

Developmental Scales

Assessment of intellectual functioning in very young children, and particularly in infants, requires a special kind of assessment instrument. A popular measure is the Bayley Scales of Infant and Toddler Development (Bayley, 2005). The Bayley can be used to assess children from 1 to 42 months of age and includes scales that assess multiple aspects of development. Performance on developmental tests yields a **developmental index** rather than an intelligence score. Unlike intelligence tests, which place considerable emphasis on language and abstract reasoning abilities, developmental scales place considerable emphasis on sensorimotor skills and simple social skills. For example, the Bayley examines the ability to sit, walk, place objects, attend to visual and auditory stimuli, smile, and imitate adults. Perhaps because they tap somewhat different abilities, there is only a low correlation between developmental scales, particularly when they are administered early, and measures of intellectual functioning later in childhood. Early developmental test scores may, however, be better predictors of later intellectual functioning for children with serious developmental disabilities (Hodapp & Dykens, 2019).

Ability and Achievement Tests

In addition to assessing a youth's general intellectual functioning, it is often necessary or helpful to assess a child or adolescent's functioning in a particular area. **Ability and achievement tests** have been developed for this purpose (Katz & Brown, 2019). The Wide Range Achievement Test (Wilkinson & Robertson, 2017), the Woodcock-Johnson Tests of Achievement (Shrank, Mather, & McGraw, 2014), and the Wechsler Individual Achievement Test (Wechsler, 2009) are examples of measures of academic achievement. Assessment of specific abilities and achievement levels may be particularly important to professionals working with children who have learning and school-related problems (Sattler et al., 2014).

Assessment of Physical Functioning

General Physical Assessment

Assessment of physical functioning can provide several kinds of information valuable to understanding disordered behavior. Family and child histories and physical examinations may reveal genetic problems that are treatable by environmental manipulation. For example, phenylketonuria (PKU) is a recessive gene condition that is affected by dietary treatment. Avoidance of phenylalanine in the child's diet prevents most of the cognitive problems usually associated with the condition. In addition, diseases and defects may be diagnosed that affect important areas of functioning either directly (e.g., a urinary tract infection causing problems in toilet training) or indirectly (e.g., a sickly child being overprotected by parents). Also, signs of atypical or lagging physical development may be an early indication of developmental disorders that eventually influence many aspects of behavior.

Psychophysiological Assessment

Changes in physiological systems are associated with a wide range of problems (Aldao & De Los Reyes, 2015). Thus, **psychophysiological assessments** are often conducted in circumstances where a child or adolescent's arousal level is of concern. Because of the equipment that is necessary, such assessments are more common in research settings than in general clinical practice. Evaluation of heart rate, muscle tension, and respiration rate are examples of these assessments. Measures of electrical activity in the autonomic nervous system, such as skin conductance, or in the central nervous system, such as the electroencephalogram (EEG), are also often aspects of psychophysiological assessments.

Assessment of Nervous System Functioning

The assessment of the nervous system is particularly important to understanding a wide array of disorders (Ernst et al., 2015; Goldstein & Reynolds, 2011; Uddin & Karlsgodt, 2018). These assessment techniques potentially provide information regarding the etiology of disorder and also benefit treatment research by providing information regarding the mechanisms through which treatments, particularly medications, have their effects (Fleck et al., 2010; Pliszka, 2011). Assessment of the nervous system is also an important aspect of evaluating outcomes for young people who experience brain injury (Sattler & Mrazik, 2014). The assessment of nervous system–behavior relationships requires the coordinated efforts of neurologists, psychologists, and other professional workers.

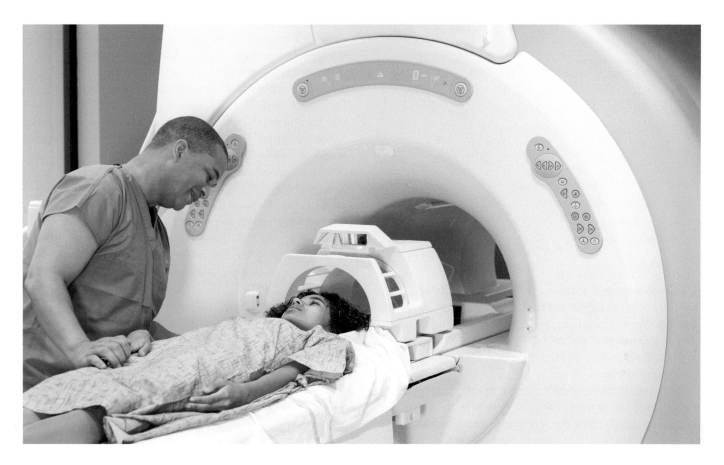

The use of brain imaging technologies has improved our ability to assess brain structure and function. (DigitalVision/Getty Images)

Neurological Assessment A number of procedures that directly assess the integrity of the nervous system fall into the category of **neurological assessment**. To record an electroencephalograph (EEG) or an event-related potential (ERP), electrodes are placed on the young person's scalp. Activity of the brain cortex in general or during a time when the youth is engaged in information-processing tasks is recorded. EEG/ERP activation patterns have contributed to the understanding of brain functioning in a number of populations, including young people at risk for anxiety and mood disorders and youth with learning and language disorders, ADHD, and autism (Bress, Meyer, & Hajcak, 2015; Faja & Dawson, 2017; Moser et al., 2015; Rothenberger, 2009).

Technologies such as **brain imaging** techniques have vastly improved our ability to assess brain structure and function. For example, **magnetic resonance imaging (MRI)** methods are noninvasive procedures that produce images of brain structure. A set of methods often referred to as structural or volumetric MRI makes use of magnet and radiowaves to create a 3D computer image of brain regions. Evolving MRI technology continues to improve our ability to assess brain structure and function (Batalle, Edmunds, & O'Muircheartaigh, 2018).

Functional magnetic resonance imaging (fMRI) uses the same technology as structural MRI and produces images by tracking subtle changes in oxygen in different parts of the brain. When particular parts of the brain are called on to perform some task, these regions receive increased blood flow and thus increased oxygen. The MRI scanner detects these changes and produces pictures of the brain that indicate areas of activity.

Other techniques help reveal brain activity. **Positron emission tomography (PET) scans**, for example, determine the rate of activity of different parts of the brain by assessing the use of oxygen and glucose, which fuel brain activity. The more active a particular part of the brain is, the more oxygen and glucose it uses. After a small amount of radioactive substance has been injected into the bloodstream, amounts of radiation appearing in different areas of the brain are measured while the person engages in a particular task. Many images are taken of the brain, to create a color-coded picture that indicates different levels of activity in different parts of the brain.

Table 5.3 Some Domains Evaluated in Neuropsychological Assessment

Attention
Memory
New learning
Language comprehension and expression
Executive functions (e.g., planning, inhibition, abstract reasoning)
Visual–spatial function
Motor and visual–motor function
General intelligence
Academic achievement

Neuropsychological Evaluations Tests that assess attributes such as general intellectual abilities, attention, memory, language functions, learning, and sensorimotor skills contribute the process of **neuropsychological evaluation**. Inferences are made about brain functioning on the basis of the individual's performance on these assessment tasks.

Neuropsychological evaluations have a number of uses. For example, they may be used to describe changes in psychological functioning that may arise out of alterations in the central nervous system or other disorders or conditions. They also may be used to assess changes over time and to develop a prognosis; for example, evaluating recovery from head injury. Neuropsychological evaluations also may provide guidelines for treatment planning (Flanagan & McDonough, 2018; McCaffrey, Lynch, & Westervelt, 2011).

The current interest in neuropsychological evaluation is attributable, at least in part, to increased sensitivity to the needs and legal requirements of providing services to children with special needs—some of whom exhibit problems presumed to have a neurological etiology. Also, due to advances in medicine, increasing numbers of children survive known or suspected neurological trauma. The increase in survival rates of infants born prematurely is one example. Children with cancer who receive treatment that includes the injection of substances into the spinal column and radiation to the head are another example.

Neuropsychological evaluation appreciates the need for broadly based assessment. Examples of multidimensional collections of neuropsychological instruments are the Halstead–Reitan Neuropsychological Test Battery for Children (Reitan & Wolfson, 1993), the Nebraska Neuropsychological Children's Battery (Golden, 1997), and the NEPSY-II (Korkman, Kirk, & Kemp, 2007). As the term *battery* implies, these instruments consist of several subtests or scales, each intended to assess one or more

abilities. The use of a broad spectrum of tests is the usual strategy employed in neuropsychological approaches to assessment. The spectrum may be fixed batteries like the examples just mentioned, or flexible batteries based on combinations of existing tests (Reynolds & Mayfield, 2011). Table 5.3 lists some of the domains that are assessed by these various tests. The importance of these various domains of functioning will become apparent as we discuss specific disorders.

Neuropsychological evaluation of children (pediatric neuropsychology) is still a relatively young field. Part of this ongoing effort is the development of instruments that derive from evolving research on cognitive development, neurological development, and brain–behavior relationships and that include reference to normative child development data (Miller & Maricle, 2018; Pavuluri & Sweeney, 2008; Reynolds & Mayfield, 2011; Yeates et al., 2007).

Intervention: Prevention and Treatment

Intervention is an umbrella term applied to both systematic prevention and treatment of psychological difficulty. **Prevention** refers to interventions targeting individuals who are not yet experiencing a clinical disorder, that is, those in the general population or those at risk for disorder. For example, an eating disorder prevention program may be offered to all middle school students or only to some students at particular risk based on early signs of unusual eating habits or weight concerns. On the other hand, **treatment** traditionally describes interventions for individuals already experiencing clinical levels of some problem (or symptoms that approach diagnostic levels). For example, young people who are diagnosed with Obsessive-Compulsive Disorder may receive a combination of medication and behavioral strategies to treat their problems.

Figure 5.3 illustrates one way of conceptualizing the variety of intervention strategies employed to assist youth and their families. In this model, formulated by Weisz, Sandler, Durlak, and Anton (2005), the upper semicircle contains various intervention strategies. The interventions are arrayed from the most universally applicable at the left to the most narrowly focused at the right and with prevention strategies to the left and treatment strategies to the right. The lower semicircle presents a sample of the range of potential settings in which interventions may be offered. The intervention settings are arrayed from the least restrictive on the left to the most restrictive on the right.

The concentric circles in the middle of the figure are meant to indicate that an individual youth's strengths are supported by family and community connections influenced by cultural and ethnic differences. The various intervention strategies shown

INTERVENTIONS

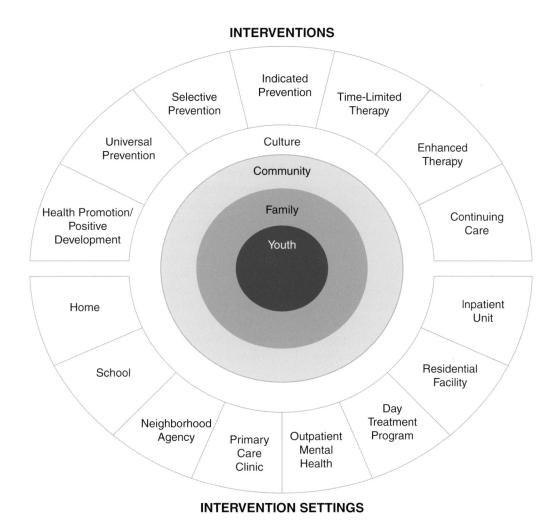

INTERVENTION SETTINGS

Figure 5.3 A model of interventions and intervention settings. (Adapted from Weisz et al., 2005)

Note: Primary strengths reside in youth, families, communities, and cultures (center), supported and protected by effective interventions (examples in upper semicircle), delivered within an array of life settings (examples in lower semicircle).

in the figure are viewed as complementary to one another and in combination may be used to assist a particular youth or population at different points in time. Multiple interventions may be delivered in the same setting, or interventions may be delivered in multiple settings.

Both prevention and treatment programs may be delivered in the home, the school, or a neighborhood agency. Treatment also may be delivered in specialized settings such as an outpatient mental health clinic. It is sometimes necessary to remove youth from their family home and provide treatment in residential settings (e.g., group homes, therapeutic camping programs, facilities that are part of the juvenile justice system) or inpatient hospital units. These settings are usually considered only for severe problems. The problems may be so difficult to treat that if the youth continue to reside at home, there is not enough contact

or control for a successful outcome. Concern may also exist that youth may harm themselves or others and, therefore, that closer supervision is necessary. Children or adolescents may also be removed from the home because circumstances there are highly problematic, suggesting that successful interventions could not be achieved at home. Unfortunately, the lack of availability of alternative placements or appropriate funding can result in young people being placed in institutional settings when interventions in the home, with additional support provided to the family, or in less restrictive environments, such as foster homes, might be successful. Typically, professionals strive to use interventions that allow youth to remain at home and that permit families to stay intact. On the other hand, treatment in residential settings is often undertaken when other modes of intervention have not proven successful.

As discussed in Chapter 1, the beginning of the twentieth century brought notable progress to the United States regarding the mental and social problems of young people. Currently, there is enthusiasm and commitment to promoting the prevention and treatment of psychological dysfunction in children and adolescents. Also, there is increased awareness of the need for increased attention to cultural issues and the needs of ethnic minority youth (Chu & Leino, 2017; Huey & Polo, 2017; Pina, Polo, & Huey, 2019). In this discussion we provide a general sense of what may be involved in the intervention process. In the chapters that follow, we examine various multi-component interventions for specific disorders.

Prevention

In the United States, interest in prevention can be traced to the early twentieth-century writings of Clifford Beers, the mental hygiene movement, and the creation of the child guidance clinics (Coie, Miller-Johnson, & Bagwell, 2000; Heller, 1996). However, progress did not come easily. Mental health professionals were trained for treatment, not prevention, and high priority was given to funding the care of individuals already experiencing mental health problems rather than to preventing future problems. Some professionals expressed doubts about the basis for prevention, since the etiology of psychological disorders is often multifactorial and difficult to establish. Moreover, the general public sometimes resisted specific prevention efforts— such as sex education and drug programs—because they were thought to intrude on parental prerogatives or values (Enzer & Heard, 2000).

Several arguments may be made for increasing prevention efforts. From a humanitarian viewpoint, prevention is clearly desirable because it averts discomfort and suffering. Practical considerations also argue for prevention. There are likely not enough (and may never be enough) professionals to treat mental disorders, intervention is less likely to be available to certain groups of people, and treatment is quite costly. In addition, increased understanding of risk and protective factors in psychopathology provides a firmer basis for prevention efforts. Importantly, evidence suggesting possible beneficial effects of prevention programs has been accumulating (Costello, 2016; Dodge, 2020; Sandler et al., 2014; Wakschlag et al., 2019; Weisz et al., 2005).

Conceptualizing Prevention

Caplan is usually credited with being a catalyst for the preventive approach in mental health (Lorian, 2000). Based on the public health assumption that major diseases have been controlled only by preventive efforts, Caplan's (1964) three-prong model has served as a general framework for thinking about prevention.

In this model, prevention is viewed as primary, secondary, or tertiary. *Primary prevention*, which attempts to stave off disorders in the first place, involves both general health enhancement and prevention of specific dysfunction. *Secondary prevention* is usually defined as the effort to shorten the duration of existing cases through early referral, diagnosis, and treatment. It is a "nipping in the bud" strategy. *Tertiary prevention* is an after-the-fact strategy that aims to reduce problems that are residual to disorders. It might seek to minimize the negative impact of labeling a child as learning disabled, to rehabilitate an adolescent who has suffered a severe mental disorder, or to ward off relapse after treatment.

Caplan's model and the terms he used are still employed. However, somewhat different approaches also have been put forth. Many conceptualizations tend to emphasize preventive efforts occurring prior to the full onset of disorders or problems (rather than tertiary programs). The Institute of Medicine, a part of the National Academy of Sciences, proposed three components (Munoz, Mrazek, & Haggerty, 1996), which are evident in Figure 5.3.

1. **Universal prevention strategies** are targeted to entire populations for which greater than average risk has not been identified in individuals. Hypothetical examples are encouraging parents to read to their children to avoid learning problems, and promoting exercise and proper diet to avoid obesity.
2. **Selective prevention strategies** (also called **high-risk prevention strategies**) are targeted to individuals who are at higher than average risk for disorder. Intervention might be directed toward individuals or subgroups with biological risks, high stress, family dysfunction, or poverty.
3. **Indicated prevention strategies** are targeted to high-risk individuals who show minimal symptoms or signs forecasting a disorder, or who have biological markers for a disorder but do not meet the criteria for the disorder.

It is noteworthy that the Institute of Medicine's influential model did not include efforts designed to foster wellness—health promotion and positive development (Munoz et al., 1996). As exemplified in Figure 5.3, other workers include the promotion of mental health and well-being in prevention. They recommend promoting characteristics such as individual competencies, self-esteem, social connections to others, security, optimism, and persistence so as to prevent the development of disorder (Albee, 1996; Costello, 2016; Cowen, 1994; Tolan, 2014). In this regard, it has been noted that many mental disorders are linked to poverty, sexism, and racism and that such social ills must be confronted. The American Psychological Association's Task Force on Prevention: Promoting Strength, Resilience, and Health in

Young People endorsed the broader wellness approach (Weissberg et al., 2003).

Diversity of Prevention Programs

Given the several components of prevention, it is unsurprising that interventions vary tremendously in aims, focus, and setting. Programs to enhance positive development require input from fields such as human development, mental health, community planning, social policy, and the like. A developmental psychopathology approach is valuable in pointing to the interplay of multiple factors that facilitate optimal growth and resilience (Hinshaw, 2017). Prevention programs for children have involved various intervention agents such as mental health professionals, teachers, parents, and college students (Durlak & Wells, 1997). While universal prevention programs do exist, many prevention interventions target at-risk populations, for example, families experiencing divorce and youth exposed to poverty-related stress (Sandler et al., 2020; Wadsworth et al., 2018).

A distinction can be made between programs that focus on preventing a potential array of negative outcomes and programs that focus on specific symptoms of disorders. The former include, for example, interventions with economically disadvantaged children to prevent the varied cognitive, social, and emotional adversities associated with poverty (Wadsworth et al., 2018). Programs focusing more on specific psychopathology include, for example, interventions for deterring the development of depression or conduct-disordered behaviors (Forgatch & Gewirtz, 2017; Rohde, 2017; Webster-Stratton & Reid, 2017).

Treatment

Clinicians are likely to be called on to treat children and adolescents whose problems are multifaceted. For example, a youth may simultaneously have problems involving anxiety and depression, social problems with peers, and academic difficulties. Indeed, it is likely that a young person will have multiple presenting problems. Furthermore, presenting problems may vary with situation and may be more broadly defined to include other individuals. Thus, clinical attention often will be directed not only to the child or adolescent but also to family members and perhaps school personnel and peers. Treatment is therefore likely to contain multiple elements that address different aspects of the clinical problem.

There are a number of ways to conceptualize treatment approaches. For example, a clinician's theoretical conceptualization of the presenting problem and of the process by which change occurs will influence how treatment is provided. Thus, a psychologist whose conceptualization of the disorder emphasizes environmental influences and contingencies is likely to consider treatments that include both the youth and significant others and that focus on modifying environmental stimuli and the consequences of behavior. Meanwhile, a psychologist whose conceptualization emphasizes cognitive processes is likely to consider interventions aimed at modifying particular cognitions, and a psychologist whose conceptualization emphasizes interpersonal processes or family dynamics is likely to consider treatments that focus on these aspects of a problem. Nevertheless, many professionals realize that psychological problems are subject to multiple influences and that treatment may involve multiple components.

As seen in Figure 5.3, treatment can also be conceptualized in terms of the length of treatment required and the number of strategies employed. Treatment may involve a limited number of sessions (e.g., 20) and a standard treatment protocol, it may be enhanced by booster sessions and supplemental strategies, or it may require a variety of strategies used in an ongoing way over an extended period.

Psychological Treatment Modes

The mode in which treatment is delivered is another aspect of treatment efforts. Treatment may be delivered in a variety of modes (e.g., individual therapy, family therapy). Indeed, one or more modes of treatment can be employed to assist a particular child or adolescent.

Individual and Group Psychotherapy Therapists may see the young client in individual one-to-one sessions. A therapist working with a child or adolescent with an anxiety disorder may, for example, help the young person to understand the problem and teach the youth active ways of confronting and coping with the anxiety. These sessions may resemble the verbal interchanges and activities of adult sessions or, particularly with young children, may employ play as the primary mode of interaction between the therapist and the child. Alternatively, various forms of individually focused treatment may be delivered in a group rather than in an individual format. The same assumptions and methods that guide individual therapies may be used. The group format may be selected in order to serve larger numbers of children and adolescents. Another advantage of this choice is that groups offer the opportunity for socialization experiences not present in the individual mode. Group treatment also may be more appealing to young people because it is less threatening; demonstrates that peers, too, have difficulties; and often includes opportunities for activities not likely to occur in a one-to-one relationship with an adult therapist.

Play Therapy The need to alter treatment procedures to fit the young child's level of cognitive and emotional development is

The use of play as a mode of therapy is common with younger children. Play allows for the establishment of rapport, but it also provides a means of communication more age-appropriate than verbal forms of therapy. (Phanie/Alamy Stock Photo)

one factor that has produced nonverbal modes of working with children. The use of play as a therapeutic vehicle is a common mode of treatment with young children. This is consistent with the importance of play in their development (Schaefer & Drewes, 2011). Rather than relying exclusively on abstract verbal interactions, the therapist uses play to facilitate communication. Play may also be a more familiar way for the child to interact with an adult and may help make the child feel at ease. A therapist may use puppets and dolls, have the child draw or paint, employ specially created board games, or use children's books that tell the story of children with similar difficulties. In this manner, most practitioners use play as a part of therapy. Another option is to use play itself as a therapeutic vehicle and **play therapy** as a more structured and distinct approach to treatment. Two well-known perspectives on play therapy are derived from the psychodynamic and the client-centered perspectives (Nash & Schaefer, 2011).

Early psychoanalytic therapists agreed that child patients required a different mode of treatment than the highly verbal, free association mode used in adult psychoanalysis. Melanie Klein (1932) gave the child's play a prominent role in the therapeutic process and used it as the basis for psychoanalytic interpretation. In contrast, Anna Freud viewed play as only one potential mode of expression and placed less emphasis on symbolic interpretation of play. For example, she disagreed with Klein that a child opening a woman's handbag was symbolically expressing curiosity regarding the contents of the mother's womb. She suggested that, rather, the child might be responding to a previous experience in which someone brought a gift in a similar receptacle (Freud, 1946). Anna Freud's position on play, which included interpretation, but also focused on external realities, tended to become the dominant view (Levy, 2011).

Another major influence on the evolution of play therapy was the work of Virginia Axline, who developed her approach from the client-centered perspective associated with Carl Rogers. The basic principles outlined by Axline (1947) remain the guidelines for contemporary client-centered play therapy (Sweeney & Landreth, 2011). The therapist adjusts his or her communication style to create the appropriate accepting, permissive, and nondirective therapeutic environment. The use of play with young children helps to create such an environment.

Family Therapy and Parent Training Clinicians may also work with the young person's parents or family. We will see that working with the family can take many forms. Here we highlight a few examples.

Including members of the family as part of the therapeutic process is consistent with the understanding that a clinical problem exists in a social context and that the family is a very important part of that context. Clinicians who treat adolescents with eating disorders, for example, frequently work with the entire family to change maladaptive family interaction patterns that may contribute to the maintenance of eating disorders (Le Grange & Eisler, 2017; Le Grange & Robin, 2017). Similarly, clinicians working with youth who have significant conduct problems, such as juvenile offending and substance abuse, may seek to develop critical competencies and establish adaptive relationships by involving the family as well as other social systems in the treatment process (Henggeler & Schaeffer, 2017; Waldron, Brody, & Hops, 2017).

Another common therapeutic tool is **parent training**. Many professionals have taken the position that producing changes in the way that the parents manage the young person is central to change in the child or adolescent's behavior. This viewpoint is consistent with the observation that the parent's perception, as well as the child's actual behavior, results in the child being referred for treatment. Siblings of the referred youth may have similar problems; this is another reason that it may be helpful to

Treatment may involve the youth, parent(s), and other family members. (Photographee.eu/Shutterstock)

work with the entire family or provide parents with a general set of parenting skills.

Parent training procedures have been applied to a wide array of child and adolescent problems. A number of approaches have emerged, and popular books presenting these approaches appear on the shelves of bookstores everywhere. However, in terms of systematic applications and research, much of the work has come from the social learning/behavioral approach.

Behavioral parent training has received a great deal of clinical and research attention. Efforts have focused on teaching parents to identify and monitor behaviors and to manage the consequences, or contingencies, that they apply to their children's behavior. Parent training approaches also include skills such as verbal communication and expression of emotion. In addition, parent training programs attempt to consider the impact of stressors such as socioeconomic disadvantage, single-parent status, social isolation, and parental depression on the effectiveness of treatment. Parent training is frequently employed as part of a multifaceted approach to treatment, and specific cultural adaptations may be implemented (Huey & Polo, 2017; Martinez & Eddy, 2005; Sanders & Turner, 2017). Other components may include additional therapeutic work with the parent, direct work with the child, or work with the teacher and the school (Kazdin, 2017; Webster-Stratton & Reid, 2017).

Treatment Strategies

A therapist employing one of the modes of treatment described above also is likely to make use of a number of treatment strategies as a way of delivering that mode of treatment to the young person and her or his family. The most commonly used strategy to deliver services probably remains the tradition of regular office visits with a therapist. However, as illustrated in Table 5.4, a variety of strategies have begun to be developed to provide treatment content to youth and their families. The array of available treatment strategies is likely to continue to evolve as professionals consider effective use of technology in their efforts to assist youth and their families (Comer et al., 2017; Cuijpers et al., 2017).

Pharmacological Treatment

Pharmacological treatments (medications) are another mode of intervention that is employed for a variety of childhood and

Table 5.4 Examples of Alternative Strategies for Providing Treatment Content to Youth and Families

Embedding illustrations of core principles and skills in video vignettes for parents
Embedding concepts and lessons in stories or videos for youth
Therapists as coaches for parents as they interact with their children in real time
Building intervention into summer camp programs
Employing traveling therapists who function in the youth's environment
Teaching skills to foster care providers
Teaching skills to parents through easily readable books with accompanying electronic media
Delivering training and intervention through the internet and related technologies

Source: Adapted, in part, from Weisz & Kazdin, 2017.

adolescent disorders. Medications that affect mood, thought processes, or overt behavior are known as **psychotropic** or **psychoactive**, and treatment that uses medication is called **psychopharmacological treatment**.

The decision whether to use psychopharmacological treatment is, in part, determined by the nature of the presenting problem. However, other considerations such as possible side effects and a family's comfort with using medication need to be considered and discussed. Racial/ethnic and income differences contribute to the rates of psychotropic medication use in young people. For example, Leslie and colleagues (2003) reported that among a large sample of families receiving publicly funded services, caregivers of African American and Latino children were less likely to report use of such medication than caregivers of white children. Higher income and private insurance also were associated with a greater likelihood of psychotropic medication use.

Children and adolescents have been increasingly treated with psychotropic medications and, while the use of psychotropic medications can be a helpful component of treatment, concern is frequently expressed regarding this trend. In particular, there often are concerns and special considerations expressed regarding the treatment of preschool-age children with psychotropic medications (Gleason & Humphreys, 2018; Luby & Whalen, 2019; Zito et al., 2000). Research regarding the efficacy and safety of many of these medications for children and adolescents often lags behind their use. Controversy exists regarding so-called "off-label" use of medications with children and adolescents. The term **"off-label"** refers to the use of a medication for a problem, age group, or dosage for which official approval has not been granted (Geller, 2019; Sharma et al., 2016). Thus, ethical and practical concerns remain as research continues to address issues of safety and effectiveness (Garcia, Logan, & Gonzalez-Heydrich, 2012; Ray et al., 2019; Scahill & Rojas, 2019). Such research is needed to guide the appropriate use of psychotropic medications as part of intervention plans, particularly for young people with serious difficulties.

Evidence-Based Assessment/Intervention

In subsequent chapters in this text, as part of our discussion of various disorders of youth, we examine assessments and interventions for specific disorders. Interventions and assessments for which there is empirical support are emphasized—that is, assessments, prevention programs, and treatments that have been deemed worthy through scientific evaluation. The terms **evidence-based assessment** and **evidence-based interventions** are used to describe practices for which such evidence exists. The development of evidence-based practice is an evolving effort (Hunsley & Mash, 2018; Roberts et al., 2017; Southam-Gerow & Prinstein, 2014). This approach follows from one of the themes of this text, an orientation toward empirical approaches and the methods of science.

This same emphasis, along with an increasing demand that professionals be held accountable for the effectiveness of the services they offer, was among the considerations that led professional organizations to identify such practices. Also, as part of this evolving effort, criteria have been proposed to designate practices as evidence-based. For example, Kazdin and Weisz's (2017) description exemplifies the criteria for evidence-based interventions.

- The population studied is carefully specified
- Participants are randomly assigned to conditions
- Treatment manuals that document intervention procedures are employed
- Multiple outcome measures are employed including measurement of the problems targeted in treatment. If raters are employed they are naive as to conditions.
- There are statistically significant post-treatment differences between the treatment and comparison group
- Outcome effects are replicated (ideally by a second/independent research team)

A growing number of evidence-based interventions and assessments have been identified and throughout the remaining chapters our discussion is sensitive to the need for assessments and interventions for which empirical evidence is strongest. As noted in Chapter 4, a continuing concern, however, revolves around the question of the applicability and transportability of practices from the research setting to implementation in typical community service settings. The task of disseminating evidence-based practices that were developed in research settings to

settings where children and families receive services is clearly an important focus of evolving efforts to help children and adolescents (Atkins et al., 2016; Jensen-Doss, Walsh, & Ringle, 2018; Weisz & Kazdin, 2017; Williams & Beidas, 2019). This effort is part of a larger concern with how best to think about and provide assistance to all children and families in need of mental health services (Chorpita, 2019; Kazdin, 2019).

Looking Back

- Classification, assessment, and intervention are interrelated processes and are intricately related to the clinical and scientific aspects of child and adolescent disorders.

Classification and Diagnosis

- Classification systems must have clearly defined categories or dimensions that can be discriminated from each other. Classification systems must be reliable and valid. Diagnostic systems are also judged by their clinical utility.
- The DSM, the system most commonly employed in the United States, is a clinically derived system and a categorical approach to classification. Clinically derived classification relies on consensus among clinicians regarding disorders and their definition.
- The current version of the DSM organizes disorders into groups (chapters) of related disorders. The disorders within a group are thought to be similar with respect to considerations such as risk factors, cognitive and emotional processes, or response to treatment.
- Over time, efforts have been made to improve the DSM system. These efforts included greater coverage of child and adolescent disorders, more highly structured rules for diagnosis, and attempts to draw on research in a more consistent fashion.
- Although reliability of the DSM has been improved by more structured diagnostic rules, there is still variation across categories, and reliability may be affected by the conditions under which information is obtained and diagnoses are made. The question of validity has received considerable attention, and the validity of various aspects of the DSM system is an ongoing concern.
- The problem of comorbidity— children or adolescents meeting the criteria for more than one disorder—presents particular challenges.

- The development of the DSM approach continues to face criticisms regarding issues of age/developmental level, gender, and cultural context as well as concerns based on other clinical and scientific grounds.
- Empirical approaches to classification rely on behavior checklists and statistical analyses, and are associated with dimensional rather than categorical approaches to classification.
- The Achenbach instruments, including the Child Behavior Checklist, Teacher Report Form, and Youth Self-Report, are examples of checklists employed in the empirical approach. There is good support for the existence of two broad syndromes—externalizing and internalizing—and support for narrower syndromes within each general syndrome.
- The Research Domain Criteria (RDoC) is an ongoing initiative that differs from the DSM/ICD approach by focusing on underlying systems rather than on observable symptoms and on dimensions of underlying systems rather than on categories/disorders.
- Critics of diagnostic systems remind us of the possible dangers of labeling children and adolescents and of the potential impact of stigmatization.

Assessment

- Conducting a comprehensive assessment is necessary, not only for classification and diagnosis but also for planning and executing appropriate interventions. The complex process of assessment requires a multifaceted approach.
- Information from multiple informants can reveal the possible influence of situational differences on behavior and differences due to the respondent's perspective.
- The general clinical interview is the most common form of assessment. Structured interviews are often organized to provide information for a DSM diagnosis.
- Problem checklists can sample a wide range of behavior problems or focus on those problems particular to a specific

disorder. These checklists may enable the clinician to compare a young person's behavior with appropriate norms and to examine issues such as situational aspects of a youth's behavior and the perceptions of various informants.

- Self-report measures are available for both the young person and the relevant adults in the child's or adolescent's life. These instruments can be used to assess constructs directly related to the presenting problem (e.g., anxiety, depression) or related constructs of potential interest (e.g., self-concept, self-control, parenting stress, family environment).

- Observation of behavior is central to a behavioral/cognitive-behavioral approach and is a direct method of assessment. The challenge of implementing observation systems in general clinical practice is an obstacle to their widespread use.

- Projective tests are probably less commonly used than they once were, as a result of questions concerning their reliability and validity.

- Intellectual–educational assessments are conducted for a wide range of presenting problems. These assessments evaluate general intelligence and developmental levels, as well as specific abilities and achievement. Although intelligence tests are popular, they are in many ways controversial and they should be used and interpreted with caution.

- Assessment of physical functioning, especially of the nervous system, is important for understanding a wide array of problems. Methods include case histories, medical examinations, the EEG, and several brain imaging techniques, such as the MRI, fMRI, and PET scan. Much attention has also been given to neuropsychological testing as a means of indirectly assessing known or suspected problems in central nervous system functioning.

Intervention: Prevention and Treatment

- Intervention strategies can range from the most universally applicable to the most narrowly focused. Interventions may be implemented in a range of settings.

- The Institute of Medicine model of prevention describes three types of prevention strategies: universal, selective/high-risk, and indicated strategies. Other models not only include those strategies, but also add broad health promotion and wellness approaches.

- Treatment of children and adolescents usually includes several elements, because young people are likely to have multiple problems. Treatments are likely to include family members and may need to incorporate school personnel and peers as well.

- Various modes and settings for treatment of young people and their families are available. Psychotherapy may be conducted with a single child or adolescent or in groups. Play can be an important aspect of therapy, especially with younger clients. Treatments often include family members, focus on the family as a unit, or incorporate parent training in child management skills. Psychotropic medications have increasingly been employed in the treatment of child and adolescent disorders. Treatment may take place in a variety of settings including the clinician's office, schools, and various residential facilities.

- Demand for professionals to be accountable for the effectiveness of their services along with an increasing emphasis on empiricism has led professional organizations to develop evidence-based assessments and interventions.

Key Terms

classification *84*

taxonomy *84*

diagnosis *84*

assessment *84*

category *84*

dimension *84, 87*

interrater reliability *84*

test–retest reliability *84*

validity *84*

clinical utility *85*

Diagnostic and Statistical Manual of Mental Disorders (DSM) *85*

International Classification of Diseases (ICD) *85*

Diagnostic Classification: 0–5 *85*

clinically derived classification *85*

categorical approach *85*

transdiagnostic *87*

comorbidity *87*

co-occurrence *87*

empirical approach to classification *89*

syndrome *89*

broadband syndrome *89*

internalizing syndrome/behaviors *89*

externalizing syndrome/behaviors *89*

narrowband syndrome *89*

normative sample *89, 95*

Research Domain Criteria (RDoC) *90*

diagnostic label *91*

stigmatization *91, 92*

evidence-based assessment *93*

general clinical interview *94*

structured/semi-structured diagnostic interview *94*

problem checklist *94*

self-report measure *96*

behavioral observation *96*

intelligence (IQ) score *97*

developmental index *98*

ability/achievement test *98*

psychophysiological assessment *98*

neurological assessment *99*

brain imaging *99*

magnetic resonance imaging (MRI) *99*

functional magnetic resonance imaging (fMRI) *99*

positron emission tomography (PET) scan *99*

neuropsychological evaluation *100*

intervention *100*

prevention *100*

treatment *100*

universal prevention strategies *102*

selective/high-risk prevention strategies *102*

indicated prevention strategies *102*

play therapy *104*

parent training *104*

psychotropic/psychoactive *106*

psychopharmacological treatment *106*

off-label *106*

evidence-based assessment/intervention *106*

CHAPTER 6

Anxiety and Obsessive-Compulsive Disorders

Looking Forward

After reading this chapter, you should be able to discuss:

- Internalizing disorders
- How anxiety, fears, and worries are defined and experienced and how anxiety disorders are classified
- Features of each of the different disorders
- The epidemiology and developmental course of the different disorders

- Biological and psychosocial influences related to the development of anxiety and obsessive-compulsive disorders
- Assessment strategies for a youth presenting with anxiety and obsessive-compulsive difficulties
- Psychological and pharmacological treatments and prevention of anxiety and obsessive-compulsive disorders

This chapter begins our examination of specific problems and disorders. The children and adolescents discussed in this and the next two chapters are variously described as anxious, fearful, withdrawn, timid, depressed, and the like. They seem to be very unhappy and to lack self-confidence. These young people are often said to have emotional difficulties that they take out on themselves; thus, their problems are often termed **internalizing disorders**.

An Introduction to Internalizing Disorders

Empirical efforts to classify child and adolescent behavior disorders have clearly found support for a broad syndrome composed of internalizing problems (see Chapter 5). Some suggest that this general grouping of emotional/internalizing disorders best describes the clinical picture (Watson, O'Hara, & Stuart, 2008). Alternatively, the focus might be on multiple specific disorders. Thus, terms such as phobias, obsessions and compulsions, anxiety disorders, depression, and mood disorders are the focus within clinical classification systems such as the DSM.

However, the relationship among, or the ability to distinguish between, the more specific clinical diagnostic categories is often

discussed. Thus, for example, there is the question of whether, in children and adolescents, the various anxiety diagnoses described in the DSM represent clearly distinct disorders. Why is this the case? While this is a complex issue, there are a number of key related concerns. For example, risk factors have been found to contribute to a variety of disorders. That is, a particular risk factor may not be associated with one particular disorder, but may contribute to the development of several different disorders (Beauchaine, Gatzke-Kopp, & Gizer, 2017; Weems & Silverman, 2017).

Another, related, concern is the high rate of co-occurrence of internalizing disorders. Considerable evidence indicates that a given child or adolescent often meets the criteria for more than one of the different disorders (Angold, Costello, & Erkanli, 1999; Kessler et al., 2009; Klein, Goldstein, & Finsaas, 2017; Ricketts, Bose, & Piacentini, 2017; Weems & Silverman, 2017). The phenomenon of an individual's meeting the criteria for more than one disorder, which is often termed comorbidity, was discussed in Chapter 5. The dilemma is an appreciable one.

It has also been suggested that instead of thinking in terms of separate disorders, it might be helpful to think of one or more general dispositions toward the development of internalizing difficulties (Vaidyanathan, Patrick, & Cuthbert, 2009). Particular environments or experiences shape this general disposition into a particular pattern of symptoms, or disorder (Williamson et al., 2005). Cultural differences may be one influence that operates in this manner. For example, it is not clear that there are differences among cultural groups in the overall prevalence of anxiety disorders. However, cultural differences in the prevalence of specific anxiety disorders and types of symptoms are reported (Anderson & Mayes, 2010; Austin & Chorpita, 2004; Pina & Silverman, 2004; Trosper et al., 2012). For example, higher rates of separation anxiety disorder and of somatic/physiological symptoms in Hispanic than in European American children have been cited (Ginsburg & Silverman, 1996; Varela et al., 2004). The strong value that Hispanic cultures place on familial interdependence (collectivism) and on empathizing with others and remaining agreeable (simpatia) may contribute to shaping a general anxious disposition to this particular expression of anxiety.

Defining and Classifying Anxiety Disorders

What do we mean when we say that someone is anxious? Barlow (2002) suggests that

> **anxiety** *seems best characterized as a future-oriented emotion, characterized by perceptions of uncontrollability and unpredictability over potentially aversive events and a rapid shift in attention to the focus of potentially dangerous events or one's own affective response to these events. (p. 104)*

Fear and anxiety have much in common, and the terms are at times used interchangeably. However, a distinction is often made between **fear** as a reaction to an immediate/present threat characterized by an alarm reaction, and anxiety as a future-oriented emotion characterized by an elevated level of apprehension and lack of control. In general, anxiety and fear are viewed as a complex pattern of three types of reactions to a perceived threat (Barrios & O'Dell, 1998; Lang, 1984). This tripartite model describes overt behavioral responses (e.g., running away, trembling voice, eyes closing), cognitive responses (e.g., thoughts of being scared, self-deprecatory thoughts, images of bodily harm), and physiological responses (e.g., changes in heart rate and respiration, muscle tension, stomach upset).

In contrast to the complex combination of three components that define fear and anxiety, **worry**—thoughts about possible negative outcomes that are intrusive and difficult to control—is viewed as a cognitive component of anxiety (Barlow, 2002; Vasey & Daleiden, 1994).

One of the challenges facing clinicians is to decide whether the anxiety exhibited by a child or adolescent is normal and

perhaps transitory, or atypical and persistent (Albano, Chorpita, & Barlow, 2003; Bosquet & Egeland, 2006). Anxiety is a basic human emotion. It can serve an adaptive function by alerting the young person to novel or threatening situations. Anxiety is thus part of normal developmental processes by which the young person learns, for example, to identify and cope with arousal, develop competencies, and become more autonomous. Thus, young children learn to cope with the dark and separation, while adolescents deal with the anxieties of beginning high school and dating. What then do we know about typical fear, worry, and anxiety?

Fears and anxieties are quite common in children. It is only when these are persistent, are intense, interfere with functioning, or are developmentally inappropriate that they may require clinical attention.

Normal Fears, Worries, and Anxieties

General Prevalence
Several classic studies of general populations indicate that children exhibit a surprisingly large number of fears, worries, and anxieties (Jersild & Holmes, 1935; Lapouse & Monk, 1959; MacFarlane, Allen, & Honzik, 1954). Parents may underestimate the prevalence of fears in their children, particularly older children who are increasingly

Fears and anxieties are quite common in children. It is only when these are persistent, are intense, interfere with functioning, or are developmentally inappropriate, they may require clinical attention. (Megapress/Alamy Stock Photo)

able to mask their emotions (Gullone, 2000). It is important to understand the frequency and intensity of childhood anxiety behaviors so as to better assess, diagnose, and treat anxiety that may impair development (Bufferd, Dougherty, & Olino, 2019).

Gender, Age, and Cultural Differences
Most research suggests that girls exhibit a greater number of fears than boys. This difference is clearer in older children and less clear in preschool and elementary school children. Studies generally suggest greater fear intensity in girls as well (Gullone, 2000). Findings of sex differences probably should be interpreted with caution because gender-role expectations may, in part, be responsible for differences between boys and girls in displaying and admitting to fears (Ginsburg & Silverman, 2000).

It is commonly reported that both the number and the intensity of fears experienced by children decline with age (Gullone, 2000). Worry becomes prominent in children at about 7 years of age and becomes more complex and varied as children develop.

Certain fears appear to be more common at particular ages: for example, fear of strangers at 6 to 9 months, fear of imaginary creatures during the second year, fear of the dark among

4-year-olds, and social fears and fear of failure in older children and adolescents (Gullone, 2000; Miller, Barrett, & Hampe, 1974). Similarly, preschoolers may worry about imaginary threats, young children about their physical safety, and older children and adolescents about social situations and their competence. Thus, threats to young people's well-being are a prominent worry across age (Silverman, La Greca, & Wasserstein, 1995). Changes in the content of fears and worries likely reflect ongoing cognitive, social, and emotional development.

Cross-cultural examinations of common fears suggest similarities across cultures. The Fear Survey Schedule for Children (FSSC-R; Ollendick, 1983) is an inventory of fear stimuli and situations. The FSSC-R has been translated into a number of different languages. The most common fears were similar across different countries and cultures and girls were found to score higher than boys (Fonseca, Yule, & Erol, 1994).

Classification of Anxiety Disorders

Most authorities would not usually view age-appropriate anxieties as requiring clinical attention unless they were quite intense or continued longer than expected. However, if the fear or anxiety,

ACCENT Culture, Ethnicity, and Disorder

Culture and ethnicity affect child and adolescent psychopathology in many ways. For example, certain disorders (e.g., social anxiety) may be more prevalent in certain cultures or ethnic groups. What, then, do prevalence findings tell us about the development of anxiety disorders?

Whether or not there are differences in prevalence, there may be cultural/ethnic differences in anxiety presentation. For example, certain symptoms (e.g., somatic symptoms) may be more common in certain cultures or ethnic groups. Also, the way in which symptoms are expressed should be considered. For example, the content of anxious cognitions may vary.

How does consideration of culture and ethnicity help us understand the development of anxiety disorders? Are certain risk factors, for example, more prevalent in certain groups or in the communities in which they reside? Are there cultural differences in parenting that increase the risk for, or serve as, protective factors against the development of these disorders? Also, discrimination and/or the process of acculturation may be stresses that can contribute to anxiety or challenge developing coping skills.

Appreciation of the necessity for culturally sensitive assessment has increased. Instruments that were developed

in one cultural context may not accurately assess anxiety in a different cultural context or ethnic group. Also, symptoms may not group into different factors in the same way for all cultural or ethnic groups. This may be due in part, as suggested above, to the differences in the ways in which anxiety presents. But this may also be due to differences in how anxiety is thought about and understood by members of different cultural groups. Language may also be an important consideration in conducting an assessment. Differences may emerge in assessment findings depending on the language employed in interviews or assessment instruments.

There has also been an increasing sensitivity to treatment issues. Adapting effective treatment programs to better fit particular cultures suggests that such adaptations may increase the effectiveness of these treatments and make them more acceptable to members of different cultural groups. It is also important to appreciate that there may be important ethnic/cultural differences in the likelihood of young people and their families seeking treatment. Increasing the use of and access to effective interventions serves the larger goal of helping children, adolescents, and their families. Clearly, these considerations apply not only to anxiety disorders, but also to many, if not all, of the disorders considered in future chapters.

even though short-lived, creates sufficient discomfort or interferes with functioning, intervention may be justified. Furthermore, anxiety disorders, if left untreated, may follow a chronic course and be associated with additional difficulties for at least some children (Kendall et al., 2018; Kertz et al., 2019; Pliszka, 2011). How, then, do we define and classify disorders of childhood and adolescence in which anxiety is an important feature?

The DSM Approach

The DSM describes a number of anxiety and related disorders. The DSM anxiety disorders chapter includes Separation Anxiety Disorder, Specific Phobia, Social Anxiety Disorder (Social Phobia), Selective Mutism, Panic Disorder, Agoraphobia, and Generalized Anxiety Disorder. A child or adolescent can be diagnosed with one or more of the anxiety disorders included in the DSM. We will define and discuss each of these disorders in our examination of specific disorders. The definitions of most of these anxiety disorders involve similar processes such as apprehension of objects or situations, and avoidant/anxiety-reducing behaviors.

The Empirical Approach

Empirical systems that are based on statistical procedures have yielded subcategories of internalizing disorders that include anxiety-related problems. Within the broad category of internalizing disorders, for example, Achenbach (Achenbach & Rescorla, 2001) describes an anxious/depressed syndrome (see Table 6.1). There is not, however, a separate anxiety syndrome or other narrower syndromes that correspond to the specific anxiety disorders of the DSM. This suggests that in youth, various anxiety and depression symptoms tend to occur together. Other internalizing syndromes, such as "somatic complaints" (e.g., feeling dizzy, having stomachaches) and "withdrawn/depressed" (e.g., refusing to talk, feeling withdrawn), also contain symptoms that are likely to be part of anxiety and related difficulties.

Epidemiology of Anxiety Disorders

Anxiety disorders are among the most common disorders experienced by children and adolescents. Estimates of prevalence may vary considerably. Prevalence rates of 2.5 to 12% or even higher are often cited (Kessler et al., 2009; Merikangas & Hommer, 2019; Polanczyk et al., 2015; Rapee, Schniering, & Hudson, 2009). Young people are likely to meet the criteria for more than one anxiety disorder. Also, evidence suggests that an appreciable

Table 6.1 Behavior Problems Included in the Anxious/Depressed Syndrome

Cries a lot	Fearful, anxious
Fears	Feels too guilty
Fears school	Self-conscious
Fears doing bad	Feels hurt when criticized
Must be perfect	Talks or thinks of suicide
Feels unloved	Anxious to please
Feels worthless	Fears mistakes
Nervous, tense	Worries

Source: From Achenbach & Rescorla, 2001. Copyright 2001 by University of Vermont, Research Center for Children, Youth & Families; reprinted with permission.

portion of anxious youth is likely to continue to meet the criteria for one or more anxiety disorders from childhood to adolescence, and through young adulthood. These youth are also likely to develop other problems (Kendall et al., 2010; Rapee, Schniering, & Hudson, 2009).

Research suggests that girls are slightly more likely than boys to have an anxiety disorder (Collishaw et al., 2010; Costello, Egger, & Angold, 2005b). It is unclear as to whether there are overall differences in the prevalence of anxiety disorders in different ethnic groups. Literature, however, suggests cultural and ethnic differences in how anxiety is expressed. Thus, there may be differences with regard to the prevalence of specific disorders (e.g., separation anxiety, social anxiety) across ethnic groups (Anderson & Mayes, 2010; Austin & Chorpita, 2004; Roberts, Ramsay Roberts, & Xing, 2006; Weems & Silverman, 2017).

Specific Phobias

Phobias, as contrasted with developmentally appropriate fears, are of concern because they are excessive, cannot be reasoned away, are beyond voluntary control, lead to avoidance, and interfere with functioning (Miller et al., 1974).

Diagnostic Criteria

The essential feature of the diagnosis of **Specific Phobia** is a marked fear of, or anxiety regarding, a specific object or situation (e.g., animals, heights). In addition, the diagnosis requires the following:

- An immediate anxiety response occurs almost every time the person is exposed to the phobic stimulus.
- The person must either avoid the anxiety situation(s) or endure any exposure with anxiety or distress.
- The fear or anxiety is out of proportion to the actual risk.
- The fear or anxiety is persistent (six or more months).

In addition to these main features, the fear must produce considerable distress or must interfere significantly with the young person's normal routine, academic functioning, or social relationships. The DSM acknowledges developmental differences by noting that in children anxiety may be expressed by crying, tantrums, freezing, or clinging.

Description

Behaviorally, youth with specific phobias try to avoid the situation or object that they fear. For example, children who have an extreme fear of dogs may refuse to go outside. When confronted with a large dog, they may "freeze" or run to their parents for protection. In addition, young people may describe feelings of tension, panic, or disgust regarding the phobic object. Often young persons' reactions include thoughts of catastrophic events that may occur upon exposure to the phobic situation. Physical reactions such as nausea, rapid heart rate, and difficulty in breathing may also occur. Any or all of these reactions may occur even when contact with the feared situation is merely anticipated. Thus, young persons' phobias not only restrict their own activities, but also are likely to change the lifestyle and activities of the family as a whole.

Epidemiology

Specific phobias are among the most commonly diagnosed anxiety disorders in children and adolescents. Although estimates vary somewhat, prevalence rates of up to 10% have been reported. Specific phobias are often more prevalent in girls than in boys, but such gender differences may be more prominent for some types of phobias (e.g., animal phobias) than others. Information regarding ethnic, age, and socioeconomic differences is limited (Costello, Egger, & Angold, 2005a; Kim et al., 2010; Silverman & Moreno, 2005).

Youth with specific phobias usually have more than one phobia and are likely to meet the criteria for other disorders. Additional diagnoses include other anxiety disorders, depression and mood disorders, and externalizing disorders such as oppositional defiant disorder. In a community sample of adolescents, Essau and colleagues (2000) report that nearly half of the young people with a specific phobia met the criteria for another anxiety disorder, and depressive and somatoform disorders (physical symptoms in the absence of a known physical pathology) were also common. In addition, Verduin and Kendall (2003) report that nearly half of a clinical sample of youth whose primary diagnosis was another anxiety disorder also met the criteria for a specific phobia.

Developmental Course

A large proportion of specific phobias are thought to begin in early to middle childhood. These phobias are commonly believed to be relatively benign, and improvement is expected over time with or without treatment. However, there is reason to question this perception and to think in terms of continuity over time (Silverman & Moreno, 2005; Sterba, Prinstein, & Cox, 2007). Findings from Essau and colleagues' (2000) sample of German adolescents, for example, suggest that, for some young people, phobic symptoms persist over time and are associated with impaired functioning. This finding is consistent with reports of phobic adults that suggest that specific phobias are likely to begin in childhood and may, for some individuals, persist into adulthood (Kendler et al., 1992b;

CARLOS A Specific Phobia

Carlos, a 9-year-old Hispanic American boy, presented at a child anxiety clinic with an avoidance of buttons. The problem began in kindergarten when Carlos was 5 years old. Carlos was working on an art project that involved buttons and ran out of buttons. He described being asked to come to the front of the classroom to get additional buttons from a large bowl on the teacher's desk. In reaching for the buttons, his hand slipped and all the buttons in the bowl fell on him. Carlos reported being distressed at that moment and both he and his mother report an increasing avoidance of buttons since that time. As time progressed it became more difficult for Carlos to handle buttons. Carlos also reported that he viewed buttons contacting his body as disgusting (e.g., "buttons are gross"). This led to interference in several aspects of Carlos's and his family's life such as not being able to dress himself and difficulty concentrating in school as a result of preoccupation with not touching his school uniform buttons or anything touched by his buttoned shirt.

Adapted from Silverman & Moreno, 2005, pp. 834–835

Öst, 1987). A reasonable suggestion, therefore, is that specific phobias are likely to begin during childhood and, for at least some individuals, they may persist over time.

Social Anxiety Disorder (Social Phobia)

Diagnostic Criteria

The criteria for diagnosing a social anxiety disorder (social phobia) are parallel to those employed in diagnosing a specific phobia. However, here the concern is with anxiety related to social or evaluative situations rather than with a specific object or nonsocial situation. Thus, the essential feature of **social anxiety disorder** (**social phobia**) is a marked or persistent fear of acting in an embarrassing or humiliating way in social or performance situations.

As was the case with specific phobias, the criteria acknowledge developmental differences by noting that children may express anxiety differently than adults. Furthermore, to distinguish social anxiety disorder from other aspects of social development, children receiving the diagnosis would experience social anxiety with peers and not just with adults.

In addition to these main features, the social anxiety must interfere significantly with the young person's normal routine, academic functioning, or social relationships, or must produce marked distress. Also, the anxiety/phobia must have duration of at least six months.

Description

Youth with social anxiety fear social activities and situations such as speaking, reading, writing or performing in public, initiating or maintaining conversations, speaking to authority figures, and interacting in informal social situations (Beidel, Turner, & Morris, 1999).

The behavioral component of this social anxiety is most frequently manifested by the avoidance of situations that involve social interactions or evaluation. Young people may avoid even everyday and seemingly mundane activities, such as eating in public. Albano, Chorpita, and Barlow (2003) describe a teenage girl who spent every lunch period in a bathroom stall in order to avoid the school cafeteria. In the cognitive realm, concerns about being embarrassed or negatively evaluated are common for these young people. They are likely to focus their thoughts on negative attributes that they perceive in themselves, to negatively evaluate their performance, and to interpret others responses as critical or disapproving even when this is not the case. Somatic symptoms such as restlessness, blushing, and sweating and complaints of illness and stomachaches are common physiological symptoms reported in youth with social anxiety disorder (Ginsburg, Riddle, & Davies, 2006).

Because these young people try to avoid social situations, they may miss school and may be unlikely to participate in recreational activities. For example, younger children may not attend birthday parties or participate in Scout meetings, whereas adolescents are unlikely to attend school events, such as club meetings or dances, or to date. At least some of these young people may therefore feel lonely and have few, or low-quality, friendships (Parker et al., 2006).

Youth with social anxiety disorder often report feelings of lesser self-worth, as well as of sadness and loneliness. Over time they may also experience lesser educational achievement (Ginsburg, LaGreca, & Silverman, 1998; Velting & Albano, 2001). The potential consequences for a young person are thus quite broad.

LOUIS Social Anxiety Disorder and Its Consequences

Louis, a 12-year-old white male, was referred by his school counselor because of periodic episodes of school refusal, social withdrawal, and excessive need for reassurance. On an almost daily basis Louis would claim he could not remain in the classroom. He would generally be sent to the nurse or counselor's office until his mother came and took him home early. Louis had few friends and rarely participated in social activities that involved other children. Louis found parties, eating in public, and using public restrooms particularly difficult. Spanish class was also particularly difficult because of regular assignments to read aloud or to carry on conversations with classmates. Louis's mother described him as always having been excessively fearful, timid, scared of everything, and needing constant reassurance. The mother herself had a history of anxiety problems, was fearful of meeting new people, and had little social contact, saying "it's basically just Louis and me." Louis received the diagnoses of Social Anxiety Disorder and Generalized Anxiety Disorder.

Adapted from Silverman & Ginsburg, 1998, pp. 260–261

BRUCE Selective Mutism

Bruce, an 8-year-old boy from a two-parent household with several siblings, was referred for treatment. His mother reported that he spoke only to his immediate family members and not to extended family, teachers, or peers. Bruce had been prescribed Prozac by his psychiatrist and was stabilized on the medication for three months. It is particularly challenging to conduct an assessment and get the child to serve as the primary informant in cases such as Bruce's. By gathering information from multiple informants, observations, and getting Bruce to participate nonverbally in some assessment tasks, an assessment was completed and Bruce met criteria for selective mutism and social anxiety disorder. Bruce's mother reported that he had spoken in school on only one occasion—shortly after he began taking Prozac he said one short phrase

in class when he was frustrated. She also reported that he was not teased by peers, but reported instead that classmates spoke for him if they noticed he needed something. In other settings his immediate family spoke for him, and Bruce would not speak, even to his immediate family, in public places. At the clinic, during the assessment, he spoke with his family, but only behind closed doors and without the therapist present.

A 21-session cognitive-behavioral treatment program was provided for Bruce and family members. By the end of treatment Bruce's symptoms were greatly improved and he no longer met the criteria for selective mutism. Treatment gains were maintained at a six-month follow-up.

Adapted from Reuther et al., 2011

Selective Mutism and Social Anxiety

A young kindergarten girl, Amy, does not speak in school or with her peers. She has been this way since beginning preschool. Amy and others like her (see Bruce: Selective Mutism) might be given a diagnosis of Selective Mutism (SM).

Young people with **Selective Mutism** do not talk in specific social situations. These situations, such as the classroom or play activities, are ones in which their peers typically do talk or in which talking is important to development. Mutism occurs despite the fact that the youth speak in other situations. For example, they may speak easily with family members if no one else is present. The reported average age of onset is between about 2.5 and 4 years of age, but may go unrecognized until the child enters school at about age 5 (Viana, Beidel, & Rabian, 2009). These youth are typically described as shy, withdrawn, fearful, and clingy (American Psychiatric Association, 2013). Some also display language problems and stubborn, disobedient, and oppositional behavior (Cohan et al., 2008; Ford et al., 1998).

SM is thought to develop as a function of a complex interplay of environmental and genetic influences (Viana et al., 2009). Some evidence suggests that SM might be conceptualized as an extreme form of social anxiety (Chavira et al., 2007; Standart & Le Couteur, 2003). For example, a majority, and perhaps as many as 90 to 100%, of children with SM also meet diagnostic criteria for social anxiety disorder (Black & Uhde, 1995; Manassis et al., 2003). There is also some support for the idea that children with SM are more socially anxious than children with social anxiety disorder who are not selectively mute. The relationship between

SM and social anxiety disorder remains unclear (Viana et al., 2009; Yeganeh et al., 2003). However, clinicians who work with young people with SM may need to consider their clients' potentially severe levels of social anxiety and possible oppositional behavior and language problems in planning treatments.

Epidemiology

Social anxiety disorder is estimated to be present in approximately 1 to 2% of children, and about 3 to 4% of adolescents, with estimates of about 9% lifetime prevalence for adolescents (Costello et al., 2005a; Hirshfeld-Becker, 2010; Kessler et al., 2009). It is also a common diagnosis in clinic populations. Last and colleagues (1992) report that 14.9% of youth, assessed at an anxiety disorders clinic, were given a primary diagnosis of Social Anxiety Disorder, and 32.4% had a lifetime history of the disorder. On the basis of reports of young people seen in clinics and retrospective reports, middle to late adolescence is the typical age of onset (Chavira & Stein, 2005; Strauss & Last, 1993). This finding is consistent with the developmental considerations discussed below. Although social anxiety disorder is most frequently diagnosed in adolescents, it can occur earlier (Bernstein et al., 2008; Costello et al., 2005b). Prevalence probably increases with age, and the disorder may be under-recognized, particularly in adolescents (Chavira & Stein, 2005). One reason that the problem may be under-recognized is that young people with social anxiety disorder may minimize their problems in order to present themselves in a desirable way (DiBartolo et al., 1998). This tendency would be consistent

Table 6.2 Comorbid Diagnoses of Children with Social Anxiety Disorder

Comorbid Diagnosis	Percentage
Generalized anxiety disorder	73
Separation anxiety disorder	51
Specific phobia	36
Attention-deficit/hyperactivity disorder	9
Conduct disorder	4
Dysthymia	4
Major depressive disorder	2
Obsessive-compulsive disorder	2
Oppositional defiant disorder	2
Posttraumatic stress disorder	2

Source: Adapted from Bernstein et al., 2008.

with a concern about negative evaluation. Slightly higher rates are reported for girls, but it is not clear whether there are sex differences in the prevalence of social anxiety disorder (Chavira & Stein, 2005; Ford et al., 2003).

Most young people with social anxiety disorder also meet the criteria for one or more other disorders (Bernstein et al., 2008; Chavira & Stein, 2005). As with Louis, another anxiety disorder is the most common additional diagnosis. For example, in a sample of children, 7–10 years of age, diagnosed with social anxiety disorders, 84% met criteria for at least one other anxiety disorder. On average, children met the criteria for about two co-occurring disorders (Bernstein et al., 2008). Table 6.2 illustrates the percentages of the various co-occurring disorders in this sample. Adolescents, in particular, may meet the criteria for a major depressive disorder.

Developmental Course

Social anxiety disorder can be viewed within the context of developmental factors (Hayward et al., 2008; Velting & Albano, 2001). In young children between the ages of 6 months and 3 years, stranger anxiety and separation anxiety are common. The self-consciousness that is an essential part of what we mean by social anxiety disorder, however, does not develop until later. The abilities to see oneself as a social object and to feel embarrassment may emerge at about 4 or 5 years of age. Envisioning the perspective of other people and then experiencing concern over their possible negative evaluation probably do not emerge until about 8 years of age. By late childhood or early adolescence, these cognitive developmental prerequisites, and the awareness that one's appearance and behavior can be the basis for others' evaluations, are in place. So, for example, Westenberg and

colleagues (2004) assessed fears among a sample of children and adolescents (8 to 18 years of age) from the Netherlands. Fears of social and achievement evaluation increased with age, and these age-related changes in fears were associated with level of social-cognitive maturity.

By late childhood or early adolescence, youth are regularly required to perform tasks that have a social-evaluative component. They are, for example, expected to speak in class, engage in group activities, and perform in athletic or musical events. Responsibility for initiating and arranging social activities is also shifting. Parents are no longer likely to be highly involved in arranging social interactions. Young adolescents also may be expected to engage in different social activities such as attending school dances and dating. The combination of these social demands and the development of self-awareness can set the stage for the emergence of social anxiety. Social anxiety disorder may be thought to evolve from anxiety that is typical in this developmental period but that is magnified for some young people by individual differences and social demands (Gazelle, 2010; Neal & Edelmann, 2003; Parker et al., 2006).

Because adolescence is a period during which social anxieties are quite common, it may be particularly difficult to distinguish between normal and abnormal social anxiety. Interpretation of severity, defined in the DSM diagnostic criteria by phrases such as "almost invariably," "marked distress," "intense anxiety," and "interferes significantly," becomes particularly important in this age group (Clark et al., 1994). The view that some level of social anxiety is common during adolescence is supported by research data (Velting & Albano, 2001). For example, Essau, Conradt, and Peterman (1999) found that approximately 51% of a community sample of youth between the ages of 12 and 17 reported at least one specific social

Adolescence is a period during which involvement in a variety of social activities is expected. Some young people find these social demands particularly difficult. (Stephen Oliver/Alamy Stock Photo)

"Mommy and Daddy still love you, but we're going to try living thirteen inches apart for a while."

CartoonCollections.com

Paul Karasik/Cartoon Collections

fear. However, only some smaller proportion of youth develops more general and clinical level problems (Chavira & Stein, 2005).

Separation Anxiety

We have chosen to describe separation anxiety followed by a discussion of school refusal because much of what has been written about the problem of school refusal and its etiology has derived from a separation anxiety perspective. In addition, given that compulsory education laws require all children to attend school, it seems likely that many children with separation anxiety would also have problems with school attendance.

Diagnosis and Classification

The DSM category of **Separation Anxiety Disorder** (SAD) is intended to describe anxiety regarding separation from a major attachment figure and/or home. The anxiety experienced by the young person exceeds what might be expected given their developmental level. Diagnostic criteria include eight symptoms describing various concerns about separation from, being alone without, or worry of harm befalling, major attachment figures. One of the eight symptoms specifically addresses reluctance or refusal to go to school. These separation concerns are accompanied by persistent and excessive worry or distress and related sleep and physical problems (e.g., headaches, abdominal complaints, nausea, vomiting).

For a child to receive the diagnosis of SAD, the DSM requires the presence of three or more symptoms for at least four weeks and the problems must cause significant distress or impairment in social, school, or other areas of functioning.

Description

Young children experiencing separation anxiety may be clingy and follow their parents around. They may express general fear or apprehension, experience nightmares, or complain of somatic symptoms (e.g., headaches, stomachaches, nausea, palpitations). Older children may complain about not feeling well, think about illness or tragedy that might befall them or their caregivers, become apathetic and depressed, and be reluctant to leave home or to participate in activities with their peers. Some young people may threaten to harm themselves. This threat is usually viewed as a means of escaping or avoiding separation, and serious suicidal behavior is rare.

Epidemiology

Estimates of the prevalence of SAD in community samples typically range from about 3 to 12% of young people. SAD is one of the most common anxiety disorders in children younger than 12. Prevalence is higher in children than in adolescents and the disorder is uncommon in older adolescents (American Psychiatric Association, 2013). Children and adolescents with SAD often also meet diagnostic criteria for other disorders. Generalized Anxiety Disorder seems to be the most common other diagnosis received (Last, Strauss, & Francis, 1987; Verduin & Kendall, 2003). The status of sex and of ethnic differences in prevalence remains unclear (Ford et al., 2003; Suveg et al., 2005). Some studies report a greater prevalence of SAD among girls than among boys, but others report no sex differences. Clinical samples suggest no ethnic differences in rates, but there is some suggestion of greater rates in community samples of African American youth.

Developmental Course

Anxiety concerning separation from a primary caregiver is part of the normal developmental process in infants. From the first year of life through the preschool years, children typically exhibit periodic distress and worry when they are separated from their parents or other individuals to whom they have an attachment. Indeed, the absence of any separation distress may indicate an insecure attachment. Even in older children, it is not uncommon for expectations, beliefs, and prior separation experiences to lead to feelings of homesickness when the children are separated from their parents. Such distress is viewed as problematic only when distress about separation persists beyond the expected age or is excessive.

KENNY Separation Anxiety

Kenny, a 10-year-old boy, lived with his parents and his two half-siblings from his mother's previous marriage. His parents brought him to an anxiety disorders clinic because he was extremely fearful and had refused to go to school during the past several months. Kenny was also unable to be in other situations in which he was separated from his parents—such as when playing in the backyard, at Little League practice, and staying with a sitter. When separated from his parents, Kenny cried, had tantrums, or threatened to hurt himself (e.g., jump from the school window). Kenny also exhibited high levels of anxiety, a number of specific fears, significant depressive symptomatology (e.g., sad mood, guilt about his problems, occasional wishes to be dead, and periodic early awakening). Kenny's separation problems appeared to have begun about a year earlier when his father was having drinking problems and was away from home for prolonged periods of time. Kenny's separation problems gradually worsened over the year.

Adapted from Last, 1988, pp. 12–13

For children with separation anxiety, symptoms often progress from milder to more severe. For example, a child's complaints of nightmares may lead to the parents allowing the child to sleep in their bed on an intermittent basis. This often rapidly progresses to the child sleeping with one or both parents on a regular basis (Albano et al., 2003). Most children appear to recover from SAD (Kearney et al., 2003); however, in some, the symptoms may persist and they may develop a later disorder, with depression being particularly common (Last et al., 1996). In adolescents, separation anxiety, if present, may be the precursor of more serious problems (Blagg & Yule, 1994; Tonge, 1994).

School Refusal

Definition

Some children and adolescents exhibit excessive anxiety regarding school attendance. When these young people do not attend school, their condition is typically termed **school refusal**. School refusal is not a DSM diagnosis; however, reluctance or refusal to go to school is one of the eight symptoms listed for the DSM diagnosis of SAD, and some youth who exhibit school refusal do receive this diagnosis. However, since a young person need present with only three of the eight listed symptoms to receive the diagnosis of SAD, not all young people with SAD exhibit school refusal. In addition, not all school refusers show separation anxiety (Kearney, Eisen, & Silverman, 1995; Last & Strauss, 1990). Although the most common conceptualization of school refusal attributes the problem to separation anxiety, some young people may fear a particular aspect of the school experience, in which case they might be diagnosed under the specific phobia or social anxiety disorder categories. For example, a youth may fear going to school because of anxiety regarding academic performance, evaluation, speaking in public, conflict with peers, or meeting new people.

Thus, it is best not to view all cases of school refusal as being similar or as having a single cause. Indeed, school refusal should probably be considered heterogeneous and multicausal (Suveg et al., 2005). One suggestion is that it might be more useful to classify school refusal by the function that the behavior serves—by a **functional analysis**—rather than by symptoms (Kearney, 2018). Some youth may refuse to go to or stay in school due to avoidance of school-related distress (e.g., riding the school bus) that provoke negative affect, such as anxiety and depression. Also, occasions that require social interactions and activities that involve evaluation are likely to occur during the school day. Another function of school refusal might be to escape from these situations. Alternatively, children and adolescents who refuse to attend school may receive attention from others. For these young people school refusal behaviors (e.g., complaints of illness) may elicit attention from parents. Finally, youth who refuse to go to school may receive positive reinforcement for such behavior in the form of tangible reinforcers such as being able to watch television or play video games, or they may be served special treats. Using a functional analysis approach, treatment programs can be designed that address one or more functions that school refusal behavior serves for a particular young person.

Description

A certain degree of anxiety and fear about school is common for children and adolescents, but some exhibit excessive anxiety regarding school attendance. The behaviors, thoughts, and somatic complaints characteristic of separation anxiety are often part of the picture of school refusal. Young people, particularly adolescents, may also show signs of depression. They are often absent from school on a regular basis, may fall behind in their

Refusing to go to school and/or to be separated from parents is a common reason for referral for psychological services. (Sean Locke Photography/Shutterstock)

academic work, and sometimes have to repeat a grade. In addition, because they miss opportunities for social experiences, they are likely to experience difficulties with their peers as well. School refusal can be a serious problem that causes considerable distress for both the youth and his or her caregivers and that may also interfere with the young person's development. Clinical reports suggest that onset of these problems often follows some life stress, such as a death, an illness, a change of school, or a move to a new neighborhood.

Refusing to go to school and/or to be separated from parents is a common reason for referral for psychological services.

School refusal is often differentiated from **truancy**. Truants are usually described as unlikely to be excessively anxious or fearful about attending school. They typically are absent on an intermittent basis, often without parental knowledge. The school refuser, in contrast, is usually absent for continuous extended periods, during which time the parents are aware that the youth is at home. Truants are often described as poor students who exhibit other conduct problems, such as stealing and lying. There is considerable disagreement as to whether truancy or school attendance problems associated with conduct problems and antisocial behaviors should be included in the concept of school refusal (King & Bernstein, 2001).

Epidemiology and Developmental Course

School refusal is usually estimated to occur in 1 to 2% of the general population and in about 5% of all clinic-referred cases; it is equally common in boys and girls (Suveg et al., 2005). School refusal can be found in youth of all ages. Like SAD, however, it seems more likely to occur at major transition points. There is the suggestion that, in younger children, the problem is likely to be related to separation anxiety, but children in middle-age groups or early adolescence are likely to have complex and mixed presentations of anxiety and depressive disorders. Prognosis seems best for children under the age of 10 years, and treatment seems to be particularly difficult for older youth and those who are also depressed (Bernstein et al., 2001; Blagg & Yule, 1994). If problems are left untreated, serious long-term consequences may result (Suveg et al., 2005).

In working with school refusers, the majority of clinicians of all orientations stress the importance of getting the young person back to school (Blagg & Yule, 1994; King, Ollendick, & Gullone, 1990). Successful strategies take an active approach to the problem, finding a way of getting the young person back to school even if this is difficult or requires the threat of legal intervention. Applying cognitive-behavioral interventions that include exposure to fearful situations, teaching the youth coping skills, and incorporating training and advice for parents and teachers have shown promise in achieving both regular school attendance and overall improvement in functioning (Elliott & Place, 2019; Suveg et al., 2005).

Generalized Anxiety Disorder

Phobias, social anxiety, separation anxiety, and school refusal represent relatively focused anxiety difficulties. However, anxiety is sometimes experienced in a less focused manner.

Diagnostic Criteria

Generalized Anxiety Disorder (GAD) is characterized by excessive anxiety and worry about a number of events or activities. The child or adolescent finds these anxieties or worries difficult to control. Thus, a youth with generalized anxiety will experience excessive anxiety and worry that is not confined to a specific type of situation. Unlike the youth with social anxiety, where the focus may be on social and performance situations, or the youth with separation anxiety, where the focus may be on separation from home or familiar people, the distress the youth with generalized anxiety feels is not limited to a specific type of situation.

The DSM diagnostic criteria require that this generalized anxiety and worry are associated with one or more of six symptoms:

1. restlessness, feeling keyed up or on edge
2. being easily fatigued
3. difficulty concentrating
4. irritability
5. muscle tension
6. disturbed sleep.

Some of these symptoms must be present most days for the past six months, and the symptoms must cause significant distress or impairment in important areas of the young person's functioning. The DSM acknowledges some developmental difference in that a child need only display one or more (contrasted with three for adults) of the six symptoms listed above. Although GAD is the way that generalized anxiety is defined by the DSM, various questions remain about how to understand and define generalized anxiety in children and adolescents (Ellis & Hudson, 2010), and how similar these symptoms are to those used to diagnose depression (Costello et al., 2005b; Kendall, Hedtke, & Aschenbrand, 2006).

Description

Clinicians frequently describe children and adolescents who worry excessively and exhibit extensive fearful behavior. They are often described as "little worriers." These intense worries are not due to some specific recent stress and are not focused on any particular object or situation, but rather occur in regard to a number of general life circumstances and are not due to a specific recent stress. These youth also seem excessively concerned with their competence and performance in a number of areas (e.g., academics, peer relations, sports) to the point of being perfectionistic and setting unreasonably high standards for themselves. They may also worry about things like family finances and natural disasters. They repeatedly seek approval and reassurance, and exhibit nervous habits (e.g., nail biting) and sleep disturbances. Physical complaints such as headaches and stomachaches are common (Albano et al., 2003; American Psychiatric Association, 2013). The description of John captures the clinical picture of GAD.

Epidemiology

Epidemiological studies of nonclinic samples suggest that GAD is a relatively common problem. Estimates, among youth of all ages, vary from about 2 to 14% and the disorder is common among youth seen in clinic settings (Benjamin et al., 2011; Canino et al., 2004; Cohen et al., 1993b; Lavigne et al., 2009).

The disorder is sometimes reported to be more common in girls, but there are also reports of no sex differences in prevalence. The median age of onset is estimated to be about 10 years of age. The number and intensity of symptoms seem to increase with age (Ford et al., 2003; Keller et al., 1992; Kendall et al., 2006).

Children and adolescents who meet the diagnostic criteria for GAD are likely to meet the diagnostic criteria for additional disorders (Masi et al., 2004), and rates of such co-occurrence seem higher for youth with GAD than for those with other diagnoses (Silverman & Ginsburg, 1998). Depression, separation anxiety, and phobias are common co-occurring disorders (Masi et al., 2004; Verduin & Kendall, 2003).

GAD may be over-diagnosed in children (American Psychiatric Association, 2013), and some have questioned whether it is a distinct disorder. What is now considered the separate disorder of GAD might instead be an indication of a dimension of general constitutional vulnerability toward anxiety or emotional reactivity (Flannery-Schroeder, 2004). It may be that professional help is sought when youth with high levels of this dimension of general vulnerability exhibit other anxiety or internalizing disorders (Beidel, Silverman, & Hammond-Laurence, 1996).

JOHN Generalized Anxiety Disorder

Like his mother, John had a very low opinion of himself and his abilities ... and found it difficult to cope with the "scary things" inside himself. His main problem had to do with the numerous fears that he had and the panic attacks that overtook him from time to time. He was afraid of the dark, of ghosts, of monsters, of being abandoned, of being alone, of strangers, of war, of guns, of knives, of loud noises, and of snakes. ... Like his mother again, he had many psychosomatic complaints involving his bladder, his bowels, his kidneys, his intestines, and his blood. ... He also suffered from insomnia and would not or could not go to sleep until his mother did. ... He was also afraid to sleep alone or to sleep without a light, and regularly wet and soiled himself. He was often afraid but could not say why and was also fearful of contact with others.

Anthony, 1981, pp. 163–164

Developmental Course

GAD does not seem transitory (Keller et al., 1992). Symptoms may persist for several years (Cohen, Cohen, & Brook, 1993a). Persistence may be particularly likely for those with more severe symptoms. A greater number of severe overanxious symptoms, increased impairment, and an increased risk of alcohol use have been reported among adolescents with this disorder (Clark et al., 1994; Kendall et al., 2006; Strauss, 1994).

An examination of developmental differences in co-occurring disorders provides some interesting information (Masi et al., 2004; Strauss et al., 1988). For example, although rates of co-occurrence are high for youth of all ages, young children seem more likely to receive a concurrent diagnosis of separation anxiety disorder, and adolescents a concurrent diagnosis of depression or social anxiety disorder. These findings may suggest a developmental difference in how generalized anxiety is experienced. Alternatively, since separation anxiety is generally more common in young children and depression and social anxiety are more common in adolescents, these findings may also be viewed as consistent with questions, raised above, about whether GAD is a distinct disorder or an indication of a dimension of heightened general vulnerability.

Panic Attacks and Panic Disorder

Intense, discrete experiences of extreme anxiety that seem to arise quickly and often, are known as panic attacks, and are another way that adolescents and children experience anxiety.

Diagnostic Criteria

A distinction is made between panic attacks and panic disorder.

Panic Attacks

A **panic attack** is a discrete period of intense fear or terror that has a sudden onset and reaches a peak quickly—within a few minutes. The DSM describes the 13 physical and cognitive

symptoms listed below. Four or more of these symptoms must be present during an episode:

1. cardiac reactions (e.g., rapid heart rate)
2. sweating
3. shaking or trembling
4. feeling short of breath or smothering
5. feeling as if choking
6. feeling chest discomfort or pain
7. feelings of abdominal distress or nausea
8. feeling faint or lightheaded
9. feeling chill or flushed
10. feeling numbness or tingling (parathesias)
11. feelings of unreality (derealization) or of being detached from oneself (depersonalization)
12. fear of "going crazy" or of losing control
13. fear of dying.

Panic attacks are typically differentiated by the presence or absence of triggers. Unexpected (uncued) panic attacks occur spontaneously or "out of the blue" with no apparent situational trigger. In contrast, expected (cued) panic attacks have an obvious trigger or cue. Expected panic attacks may occur, for example, when the person is exposed to or anticipates a feared object or situation (e.g., a dog) or when the person encounters situations in which panic attacks previously occurred. Panic attacks are not themselves a disorder within the DSM system, but they may occur in the context of a variety of anxiety or other disorders. For example, panic attacks may occur with **agoraphobia** (anxiety about being in a situation in which escape may be difficult or embarrassing). In severe cases of agoraphobia, a youth may remain at home or become terrified of leaving home. This agoraphobia is an attempt to avoid certain circumstances in which an uncontrollable or embarrassing anxiety or panic attacks may occur. The youth with agoraphobia may fear that in such situations escape may be difficult or help may not be available.

Panic Disorder

While panic attacks may occur in the context of a variety of disorders, these attacks are a central component of **panic disorder**.

FRANK Panic Attacks

While falling asleep, Frank often experienced discrete episodes of his heart beating quickly, shortness of breath, tingling in his hands, and extreme fearfulness. These episodes lasted only 15 to 20 minutes, but Frank could not fall asleep in his bedroom and began sleeping on the living room couch. His father brought him back to his bed once he was asleep, but Frank was tired during the day, and his schoolwork began to deteriorate.

Adapted from Rapoport & Ismond, 1996, pp. 240–241

Panic disorder involves recurrent unexpected panic attacks. To receive a DSM diagnosis of Panic Disorder, a month or more of one or both of the following must follow at least one of these attacks:

- persistent concern about having other panic attacks or worry about the implications of the attack ("going crazy," having a heart attack)
- a significant maladaptive change in behavior related to attacks (e.g., avoidance of situations).

Although there is an established literature regarding adults, it is only relatively recently that the occurrence of panic in children and adolescents has received attention. This discrepancy was, in part, due to controversy regarding the existence of panic attacks and panic disorder in youth (Kearney & Silverman, 1992; Kearney et al., 1997; Klein et al., 1992; Suveg et al., 2005). Much of the controversy revolved around two issues.

One issue is whether young people experience both the physiological and cognitive symptoms of panic. Adults who experience panic attacks report fear of losing control, going "crazy," or dying during the attack. They also worry about future attacks. Such cognitive symptoms may not occur in children or young adolescents.

The second issue arises based on the requirement that panic attacks be unexpected (uncued) in order to diagnose Panic Disorder. It may be difficult to determine whether panic experienced by a young person is truly uncued. Youth may think attacks are "out of the blue" because they may not be sufficiently aware of, or as likely to monitor, cues in their environment. Careful and detailed questioning may be needed to reveal precipitating cues. This problem is particularly acute in younger children.

Epidemiology

Although the diagnosis of panic may be difficult, it is suggested that panic attacks and panic disorder occur in adolescents and, to a lesser degree, in prepubertal children (Ollendick, Birmaher, & Mattis, 2004a; Suveg et al., 2005). For example, many adults who experience panic attacks or panic disorder report that onset occurred during adolescence or earlier.

Also, both community samples and clinic-based studies suggest that panic attacks may not be uncommon in adolescents. For example, 16% of young people between the ages of 12 and 17 in a community sample of Australian youth reported at least one full-blown panic attack in their lifetimes (King et al., 1997) and similar rates were reported in a sample of German adolescents (Essau et al., 1999). Regarding panic disorder, the condition is rarely diagnosed prior to mid- or late adolescence (Suveg et al., 2005). For example, Ford and colleagues (2003) found that while panic disorder was rarely diagnosed in younger British children,

about 0.5% of youth between the ages of 13 and 15 met the criteria for panic disorder. Similar or slightly higher rates have been reported in a community sample of Puerto Rican, German, and U.S. youth (Canino et al., 2004; Essau et al., 1999; Kessler et al., 2009). In clinical samples of adolescents, reported prevalence is higher—about 10 to 15% (e.g., Biederman et al., 1997; Last & Strauss, 1989). Panic attacks occur equally in boys and girls; however, panic disorder is typically reported more frequently in girls. Little information is available regarding ethnic differences (Suveg et al., 2005).

Description and Developmental Pattern

Adolescents who experience panic attacks experience considerable distress and impairment. Few, however, seem to seek treatment (Ollendick et al., 2004a). Studies of adolescents seen in clinics indicate that these youth evidence both the physiological and cognitive symptoms of panic. For example, Kearney and colleagues (1997) found that physiological symptoms of panic attacks were the most commonly reported symptoms, but the cognitive symptoms of fear of "going crazy" and fear of dying were also reported by 50% of young people.

Whether panic attacks are cued or spontaneous is less clear. Psychosocial stressors (e.g., family conflict, peer problems) were reported as possible precipitants by 26 of the 28 adolescents in this study. Some studies, however, report that for some youth, panic attacks are judged to be spontaneous. As we have mentioned, though, there is a problem in judging the spontaneous nature of panic attacks in young people.

Less is known regarding panic in younger children. Although both panic attacks and panic disorder are reported in clinical samples of children, their expression may differ somewhat from their presentation in adolescents and adults. Young children may report a general fear of becoming sick rather than describing specific physiological symptoms such as palpitations or breathlessness, or verbalizing fears of dying, going crazy, or losing control (Albano et al., 2003).

Youth with panic attacks or panic disorder who present at clinics are likely to have a family history of panic attacks or other severe anxiety symptoms. They are also likely to present with a variety of other symptoms, and the majority meet the criteria for additional diagnoses, particularly other anxiety disorders and depression (Kearney et al., 1997; Masi et al., 2000). Many of the youth with panic disorder seen in clinical settings also exhibit agoraphobia (Suveg et al., 2005). The high proportion of youth who report a history of separation anxiety led to the suggestion that SAD is a precursor to panic disorder. There are findings of neurophysiological signs of greater arousal among infants of mothers with panic disorder than among controls. This is consistent with the idea of an early vulnerability (Warren et al., 2003). However, it seems likely that SAD would be only one of many possible paths to the development of panic disorder (Hayward et al., 2004; Ollendick et al., 2004a).

Etiology of Anxiety Disorders

The development of anxiety disorders is influenced by multiple risk factors that, over time, interact with one another in complex ways (Bosquet & Egeland, 2006; Kendall et al., 2018; Weems & Silverman, 2017). A developmental perspective suggests that this ongoing interaction of influences interface with normal developmental challenges to influence how anxiety is expressed. For example, multiple anxiety risk factors may, for young children, interface with typical challenges such as separation concerns and developing autonomy and anxiety is expressed as separation anxiety disorder. Similarly, among adolescents, multiple anxiety risk factors may interface with typical social and evaluative concerns and anxiety is expressed as social anxiety. Our understanding of risk factors and causal mechanisms continues to evolve and be informed by ongoing research.

Biological Influences

There is evidence for a genetic contribution to anxiety disorders (Gregory & Eley, 2011; Smoller, Gardner-Schuster, & Misiaszek, 2008; Weems & Silverman, 2017). Aggregation of anxiety disorders in families is consistent with a genetic contribution. For example, family studies indicate that children whose parents have an anxiety disorder are at risk for developing an anxiety disorder, and parents whose children have anxiety disorders are, themselves, likely to have anxiety disorders (Lawrence, Murayama, & Creswell, 2019). In addition, more specific examinations of the influence of inheritance (e.g., twin studies, genome-wide association studies) indicate a genetic component that, along with environmental influences, contributes to the development of anxiety disorders (Franić et al., 2010; Gregory & Eley, 2011).

Estimates of the degree of heritability vary but moderate heritability is suggested. In the Virginia Twin Study of Adolescent Behavioral Development (Eaves et al., 1997), heritability estimates for anxiety tended to be lower than for other disorders; however, other findings suggest higher heritability estimates (Bolton et al., 2006). Heritability may depend on the nature of the anxiety presentation and is perhaps greatest for generalized anxiety and obsessive-compulsive disorder (OCD) (Eley et al., 2003a). Also, research suggests that the impact of heritability may change with development as genetic vulnerabilities unfold and interact with evolving environmental risks (Beauchaine et al., 2017a).

In sum, findings suggest that genetic factors likely play a role in the development of anxiety disorders. There may be different patterns of inheritance for different disorders. Also, what may be inherited, rather than a specific anxiety disorder, is a general tendency toward anxiety. For example, research suggests that youth with anxiety disorders experience heightened sympathetic nervous system reactivity to stimuli (e.g., increased heart rate and blood pressure). Genetic research indicates a substantial contribution of environment to anxiety disorders. Thus, there may be a general genetic risk and unique experiences then contribute to specific expressions of this vulnerability (Boomsma, van Beijsterveldt, & Hudziak, 2005; Gregory & Eley, 2011; Lawrence et al., 2019; Lichtenstein & Annas, 2000; Weems & Silverman, 2017).

Genetic influences may be expressed through differences in specific brain circuits and neurotransmitter systems. For example, neurotransmitters such as serotonin are thought to play a role in the development of anxiety and panic. The neurotransmitter gamma aminobutyric acid (GABA) also has received attention. GABA is known to inhibit anxiety. Anxious individuals have low levels of GABA in particular areas of the brain. Attention also has focused on corticotrophin-releasing hormone (CRH). CRH, when released in reaction to stress or a perceived threat, causes the release of cortisol and has effects on other hormones and areas of the brain implicated in anxiety. Findings regarding the role of these neurotransmitters in the etiology of anxiety disorders in children and adolescents have been inconsistent (Gregory & Eley, 2011; Pliszka, 2011).

Multiple brain structures are involved in the expression of anxiety. The limbic system—and the amygdala, in particular—is the portion of the brain that has received particular attention with regard to anxiety. Neuroscience research has examined processes such as attention, fear conditioning, and other emotional learning and has made use of neuroimaging techniques such as the fMRI. Findings suggest that the amygdala and portions of the prefrontal cortex play a central role in anxiety (Ollendick & Muris, 2015). Heightened activity in the amygdala is associated with amplification of arousal, whereas lesser activity in the prefrontal cortex is associated with less emotion regulation and coping activities. Anxious and non-anxious youth shown threatening stimuli have been found to exhibit different reactions in these regions of the brain (Pine, Guyer, & Leibenluft, 2008).

Temperament

The general vulnerability to anxiety discussed earlier, as well as the onset and persistence of anxiety disorders, may be associated with aspects of the child's temperament—biologically based, possibly inherited, individual differences in emotionality, attention, behavioral style, and the like (Bosquet & Egeland, 2006; Bufferd et al., 2018; Kagan, 2017; Kendall et al., 2018; Pérez-Edgar & Fox, 2005).

The work of Jerome Kagan and his colleagues (Kagan, 1997, 2017) describes an important contribution to an understanding of the relationship of temperament and anxiety disorders. Their findings are based on longitudinal research regarding the temperament quality known as **behavioral inhibition** (BI). Behaviorally inhibited children are identified as hypervigilant of their environment, particularly in novel or unfamiliar situations, and extremely likely to withdraw from unfamiliar people or events. It is suggested that about 15–20% of children would display heightened BI and that about half of these children will continue to display these characteristics across childhood (Degnan & Fox, 2007; Fox et al., 2005). Particular autonomic and brain activity patterns, including greater autonomic system reactivity, elevated morning cortisol levels, and heightened activation in the amygdala to novel or threatening stimuli have been reported (Degnan, Almas, & Fox, 2010; Fox & Pine, 2012; Pérez-Edgar et al., 2007).

Of particular interest is the development of internalizing problems in these inhibited children. At 5.5 years of age, children who were originally classified as inhibited had developed more fears than had uninhibited children. Furthermore, whereas fears in uninhibited children could usually be related to a prior trauma, this was not true for the inhibited children (Kagan, Reznick, & Snidman, 1990). Other research also suggests that inhibited children are at risk for developing anxiety disorders such as social anxiety, separation anxiety, and agoraphobia. Inhibited children, compared with non-inhibited children, also seem more likely to meet the criteria for multiple anxiety disorders. While there are conceptual and methodological issues with regard to the temperament–anxiety relationship, this and other evidence suggests that BI and similar temperament differences may, in the context of certain environmental influences such as parenting styles or peer relationships, be a vulnerability pathway toward the development of anxiety disorders during later childhood, adolescence, and young adulthood (Biederman et al., 1993; Chronis-Tuscano et al., 2009; Degnan et al., 2010; Hirshfeld-Becker, 2010; Kagan, 2017; Nigg, 2006).

Gray (1987) has described a functional brain system (described further in Chapter 9), part of which is a behavioral inhibition system (BIS), involving multiple areas of the brain. The BIS system is related to the emotions of fear and anxiety, and tends to inhibit action in novel or fearful situations or under conditions of punishment or nonreward. Gray's model of inhibition has also informed thinking about the contribution of temperament to the development of anxiety disorders (Chorpita, 2001; Lonigan et al., 2004).

Another approach to the contribution of temperament to anxiety disorders derives from Clark and Watson's (1991) model of emotion and the concept of **negative affectivity** (NA). NA is a temperament dimension characterized by a general and persistent negative (e.g., nervous, sad, angry) mood. Research supports the hypothesis that high levels of NA may contribute to the development of both anxiety and depression and that this may, in part, be responsible for high rates of co-occurrence of these disorders. Low levels of the separate temperament dimension of positive affectivity—pleasurable mood—are thought to be characteristic of depression but not anxiety (Chorpita, 2002; Gaylord-Harden et al., 2011; Lonigan et al., 2004).

Negative affectivity may also combine with low levels of the temperament factor of **effortful control** (EC), the ability to employ self-regulative processes (Lonigan et al., 2004). Children and adolescents with anxiety may show a bias toward attending to threatening stimuli. Anxious youth with high NA thus may attend to more negative stimuli and react more strongly to them. They would, therefore, have a need for greater EC. Thus, the combination of the temperament qualities of low EC and high NA may contribute to the development and maintenance of anxiety and anxiety disorders.

Psychosocial and Cognitive Influences

Psychosocial and cognitive influences are clearly a part of the complex interplay of risk factors that can lead to the development of anxiety disorders. Children and adolescents with a general vulnerability to anxiety may be exposed to a variety of experiences that alter their risk for anxiety disorders (Emerson, Ogielda, & Rowse, 2019).

One way of conceptualizing psychosocial influences is Rachman's three pathway theory. Rachman (1977, 1991) suggested three main ways in which fears and phobias might be learned: through the classical conditioning of fear, through modeling— observing another's fearful reaction to a situation, and through transmission of verbal threat information. There is research support for each of these pathways toward the development of fear (Askew & Field, 2008; Field, 2006; Mineka & Zinbarg, 2006; Muris & Field, 2010).

The first pathway, through classical conditioning, is illustrated by Watson & Rayner's case of Little Albert (see p. 48) and there is support for this model as one potential route to the development of fears. The child's development of fear or anxiety, thus, may begin with exposure to some traumatic or threatening event and subsequent avoidance is reinforced by reducing anxiety.

The second pathway, in which the child vicariously learns to fear some object or situation by observing another's fearful reactions, suggests that children may learn to be anxious from their parents who prompt, model, and reinforce anxious behavior. Parents, who are themselves anxious, in particular, express and model fearful behavior (Degnan et al., 2010). For example, infants of anxious mothers exhibited fearful behaviors and avoidance of a female stranger who had previously interacted with their mothers. Infants' avoidance was related to the anxiety they saw expressed by their mothers and their mothers' low levels of encouragement (Murray et al., 2008). That children can learn from observing their parents' reactions also is illustrated in a study of toddlers who were presented with a rubber snake or rubber spider (Gerull & Rapee, 2002). The toddlers' approach to or avoidance of these toys was measured. Toddlers whose mothers' expressions were negative toward a toy in an earlier trial were less likely to approach and more likely to show negative emotional reactions to the toy. Comparable findings were obtained in a study of 6–11-year-old children (Askew et al., 2013). Children were shown pictures of various objects. The pictures were presented alone or together with scared faces. Children's fear beliefs and avoidance preferences were greater for pictures they had seen with scared faces.

Rachman's third pathway suggests that fear may be acquired through the transmission of information. Thus, in addition to modeling anxious behaviors, parents may transmit information that a situation is threatening. A study by Field and Schorah (2007) illustrates the transmission of information pathway. Children 6 to 9 years of age were given information (threatening, positive, or no information) regarding unknown animals. The children were asked to approach and put their hand into a box that contained the novel animal. The children's heart rates were significantly higher when they approached the box that supposedly contained the animal for which they had received threatening information. Parallel findings supporting the transmission of fear-promoting information by parents to their older children has also been reported (Muris et al., 2010, 2013).

In addition to modeling anxious behavior or relating information of fearful and traumatic experiences, parents may influence the development of anxiety through other parenting styles or practices (Degnan et al., 2010; Emerson et al., 2019; Kendall et al., 2018). For example, Dadds and his colleagues (1996) demonstrated that anxious children and their parents are more likely to perceive threat and therefore choose avoidant solutions to ambiguous social problems. Videotaped discussions between children 7 to 14 years old and their families revealed that parents of anxious children listened less to their children, pointed out fewer positive consequences of adaptive behavior, and were more likely to respond to a child's solutions that were avoidant. In contrast, parents of nonclinic children were more likely to listen to their children and agree with their children's plans that were not avoidant. Following the family discussion, children from both groups were asked for their plan for the situation. Anxious children offered more avoidant solutions. Parenting practices may thus contribute to the development of certain cognitive styles often seen among children with anxiety disorders. These include the perception of situations as threatening, negative self-talk, and low levels of perceived control over threatening situations (Field & Lester, 2010; Kendall et al., 2018; Stuijfzand et al., 2018).

The impact of parenting to the development of anxiety disorders may begin early in the caregiving process (Main, 1996). The quality of early caregiving can contribute to the development

of anxious behavior, particularly among children with a fearful temperament (Fox, Hane, & Pine, 2007). For example, Hane and Fox (2006) investigated the impact of maternal care behaviors, defined by constructs such as sensitivity and intrusiveness. They found that infants receiving low-quality maternal care behaviors exhibited EEG and behavioral differences, including more fearful behavior, compared with infants who received high-quality maternal care behaviors.

It has been suggested that the psychosocial influences on the development of anxiety are related to the child's perception of control and the child's development of an avoidant coping style (Chorpita, 2001; Chorpita & Barlow, 1998; Rapee et al 2009). From birth, caregiving that is sensitive to the infant's needs helps to reduce/control arousal before it becomes overwhelming. It is thought that through such caregiving processes children learn to regulate their emotions. As children develop, what constitutes sensitive parenting changes with changes in the children's needs and in a way that fosters their developing abilities to self-regulate.

Parents of anxious children have often been described as overprotective or intrusive. Such **overprotective/intrusive parenting** is defined by parent–child interactions that anticipate threats, overly regulate and limit children's activities, and instruct children in how to think and feel (Rapee et al., 2009; Wood et al., 2003). Such parenting behavior may affect children's sense of control/effectiveness, and their development of adaptive problem-solving and coping styles. Mothers of anxious children have been observed to be more intrusive and more critical with their children than mothers of non-anxious children (Hudson & Rapee, 2002; Hudson, Comer, & Kendall, 2008). However, influences are likely bidirectional (van der Bruggen, Stams, & Bögels, 2008). An anxious child may evoke an overprotective and intrusive parental response (Drake & Ginsburg, 2012; Hudson, Doyle, & Gar, 2009).

Insecure mother–child attachments have also been shown to be a risk factor for the development of anxiety disorders (Bögels & Brechman-Toussaint, 2006; Brumariu & Kerns, 2010; Colonnesi et al., 2011). As described earlier (pp. 30–32), the attachment relationship is thought to contribute to the child's development in a number of important ways including emotion regulation and the nature of social relationships. It is not surprising, then, that an insecure attachment may be one of the factors that contributes to the development of anxiety disorders.

We have been discussing how families may contribute to the development of anxiety problems in children. We should also remember that families can protect children from developing these problems. Family support, for example, has been found to protect children who are exposed to traumatic circumstances (Donovan & Spence, 2000). Also, families may foster children's abilities to cope with potentially anxiety-provoking circumstances by modeling positive reactions and approach behaviors and by encouraging children to take risks and explore unfamiliar situations (Majdanzić et al., 2018). The potential of such positive influence is illustrated by the findings of Ollendick and colleagues (2012). Clinic-referred youth (ages 7–14) with specific (animal) phobias were asked to approach the feared object twice—alone and with the parent present. Children were less avoidant with their parent present particularly if the parent was more involved and displayed greater warmth.

Peer relationships are another aspect of socialization that can affect the development of anxiety in children and adolescents (Degnan et al., 2010; Kendall et al., 2018). There may be several ways in which peer relationships influence the development of anxiety. Withdrawn/inhibited youth may be rated as less popular by their peers and peer exclusion may occur because children's withdrawn and inhibited behavior is contrary to childhood peer interaction norms (Rubin, Bukowski, & Parker, 2006). Being withdrawn and rejected or excluded by one's peers has been found to be associated with internalizing difficulties including high levels of anxiety (Klima & Repetti, 2008). Similarly, withdrawn children may be viewed as easy targets for bullying and victimization by peers and this has been found to be related to high levels of anxiety. In contrast to the risk associated with being socially withdrawn, being part of a peer group may be a protective factor with regard to the development of anxiety even if one's "crowd" is not an "in group" (La Greca & Harrison, 2005). Similarly, having a close friend may protect a youth from the negative effects of rejection by the larger peer group. But the close friendships of withdrawn youth may also serve as risk factors. These close friends may themselves be withdrawn and less socially capable and these friendships may be of lower quality in terms of aspects such as communication and guidance. This, then, may serve to maintain the inhibited youths' behavior and make social relationships less satisfying. In these ways such friendships may contribute to the development of problematic levels of anxiety and to social anxiety in particular (La Greca & Harrison, 2005; Shanahan et al., 2008).

Assessment of Anxiety Disorders

A comprehensive assessment of a child or adolescent presenting with anxiety will likely involve a variety of assessment needs. Assessment strategies must be developmentally sensitive. The assessment process should be guided by how anxiety and anxiety disorders are conceptualized and differentiated from developmentally typical fears and worries. Assessment must address ongoing developmental changes and appreciate development-related differences in comprehension and expressive abilities (Byrne et al., 2018; Silverman & Ollendick, 2005).

Assessment also needs to be sensitive to the needs of culturally, ethnically diverse populations (Anderson & Mayes,

2010; Cooley & Boyce, 2004). For example, Wren and colleagues (2007) examined the properties of a widely used rating scale for anxiety disorders in a multi-ethnic population. They found ethnic differences in the factor structure—that is, items that comprised the different anxiety factors (e.g., somatic/panic, generalized) of the scale varied by ethnicity. The variation was greatest for Hispanic children and their parents. Ethnicity also may influence the reporting of particular anxiety symptoms. For example, Pina and Silverman (2004) found that ethnicity and language choice (Spanish or English) influenced the reporting of somatic symptoms. Thus, initial and ongoing assessment presents a considerable challenge.

The child or adolescent's anxiety is not the only thing that needs to be addressed. The young person's environment will need to be assessed as well. For example, it may be desirable to assess the specific environmental events that are associated with heightened anxiety, to evaluate patterns of family interactions and communication, to assess the reactions of adults or peers to the young person's behavior, and to assess the existence of problems in other family members. The assessment of multiple aspects of the problem and the use of multiple informants, including the child or adolescent, are likely to yield valuable information.

The tripartite model of anxiety often guides assessment of anxiety disorders. Thus, assessment methods address one or more of the three response systems (behavioral, cognitive, physiological). Various methods of assessment exist (Byrne et al., 2018; Kendall et al., 2018; Silverman & Ollendick, 2005).

Interviews and Self-Report Instruments

As is usually the case, a general clinical interview is likely to yield information that is valuable to the clinician in formulating an understanding of the case and in planning an intervention. The youth and at least one parent will typically be interviewed. Structured diagnostic interviews are available and may be employed to derive a clinical diagnosis. For example, the Anxiety Disorders Interview Schedule for Children (ADIS-C/P) is a semi-structured interview for the child and parent (Albano & Silverman, 2017) designed to determine DSM diagnoses.

The most widely used method for assessing child and adolescent anxiety is self-report instruments. These measures provide reports of the behavioral, cognitive, and physiological aspects of anxiety. It is clearly important to assess symptoms from the child's or adolescent's viewpoint because it may be difficult for adults reliably to identify the existence of such discomfort. However, particularly younger children may have difficulty in labeling and communicating their subjective feelings, creating a considerable assessment challenge. Parallel measures that allow parents, teachers, and clinicians to describe the youth's anxiety also are available.

Table 6.3 Examples of Anxiety Cognitions and Self-Talk

That dog looks dangerous.
If I am away from my parents something bad may happen to them.
People will think what I say is stupid.
I know that I will embarrass myself in front of the other kids.
I usually get very good grades, but I am going to fail this test.
I know that those other kids are talking about me.
I know that the new teacher is looking through the class list and will call on me.
This is going to go badly.
There is nothing I can do to make this situation better.

There are a number of different types of self-report measures. Some instruments allow children and adolescents to report how anxious they are in a specific situation. There are also self-report instruments that assess overall (across situations) subjective anxiety, such as the State-Trait Anxiety Inventory for Children (Spielberger, 1973) and the Revised Children's Manifest Anxiety Scale (Reynolds & Richmond, 2008), which contains items such as "I have trouble making up my mind" and "I am afraid of a lot of things." Also, the Multidimensional Anxiety Scale for Children, developed by March and his colleagues (March, 2013), is a self-report measure that addresses the multidimensional nature of anxiety.

In addition, there are self-report instruments specifically designed to address the cognitive component of anxiety. Youth with anxiety disorders frequently experience anxious/negative thoughts and self-talk (see Table 6.3). The Negative Affect Self-Statement Questionnaire (Ronan, Kendall, & Rowe, 1994) is used to assess the cognitive content associated with negative affect. A subscale for assessing anxious self-talk (e.g., "I am going to make a fool of myself") can discriminate between anxious and non-anxious children. The Coping Questionnaire-Child Version (Kendall et al., 1997a) assesses the child's ability to cope with anxiety in challenging situations. The Children's Automatic Thoughts Scale (Schniering & Rapee, 2002) assesses automatic thoughts about threats, failure, and hostility.

Some self-report instruments also exist to assess specific anxiety disorders and situations (Rowa et al., 2018); for example, the Fear Survey Schedule for Children (Ollendick, 1983; Muris et al., 2014) to assess specific fears, the Social Anxiety Scales for Children and Adolescents (La Greca, 1999), the Social Anxiety Questionnaire for Children (Ollendick et al., 2019), and the Generalized Anxiety Disorder Questionnaire (Newman et al., 2002). The Screen for Child Anxiety Related Emotional Disorders (SCARED; Birmaher et al., 1997, 1999) assesses for the symptoms of several anxiety disorders.

Given that children and adolescents with anxiety disorders often present with a variety of other problems as well, the assessment process should include a broader exploration of problem areas. Instruments, such as the Achenbach behavior checklists, can help in describing a range of behavior problems. These instruments also provide an examination of various perspectives (the young person, parents, teacher) on problems.

Direct Observations

Direct observation procedures are primarily employed for assessing the overt behavioral aspects of fears and anxieties, but may also be used to assess environmental influences that may be controlling anxiety (Byrne et al., 2018; Ollendick & Muris, 2015; Silverman & Ollendick, 2005). Behavioral approach tests require the child or adolescent to perform a series of tasks involving the feared object or situation. Thus, the young person might be asked to move closer and closer to a feared dog and then increasingly to interact with the dog. In addition, behavioral approach tests can provide information regarding the cognitive and physiological aspects of anxiety. For example, at each step the child can be asked about their level of anxiety and report on beliefs and expectancies regarding the feared object or situation. Physiological data (e.g., heart rate) can also be collected.

Observations can also be made by observers in the natural environment where the fear or anxiety occurs. Alternatively, self-monitoring procedures require the youth to observe and to systematically record his or her behavior. A daily diary of such observations may be part of an initial assessment and is also often part of treatment efforts.

Physiological Recordings

As noted earlier, the physiological aspects of anxiety are included in self-report instruments. However, measuring parameters such as heart rate, blood pressure, skin conductance, and cortisol levels can more directly assess this component of anxiety. Practical difficulties often inhibit clinicians from obtaining these measures. However, as methods become more accessible, these assessments might be conducted more frequently and be of appreciable value.

Interventions for Anxiety Disorders

Psychological Treatments

Much of the research on treatments for children and adolescents with anxiety disorders has supported the use of behavioral or cognitive-behavioral interventions (Comer et al., 2019; Higa-McMillan et al., 2016; Kendall et al., 2017; van Schalkwyk & Silverman, 2019; Weisz et al., 2017).

Cognitive-behavioral interventions contain multiple therapeutic components. We will provide a description of several of the components that are typically part of cognitive-behavioral treatments (CBT) before proceeding to a discussion of specific CBT programs.

Exposure to anxiety-provoking situations is a central element of successful fear-reduction and anxiety treatment programs (Chorpita & Southam-Gerow, 2006; Ollendick, Davis, & Muris, 2004; Silverman & Kurtines, 2005). Thus, many of the behavioral treatments for phobias and components of cognitive-behavioral treatments for other anxiety disorders can be conceptualized as various ways of facilitating the youth's exposure to the relevant anxiety object or situation.

Relaxation and Desensitization

Relaxation training teaches individuals to be aware of their physiological and muscular reactions to anxiety and provides them with skills to control these reactions. By tensing and relaxing various muscle groups, the person comes to sense early signs of bodily tension and to use these sensations as signals to relax. With practice, the person is able to relax muscle groups in real-life situations when initial signs of tension are detected. Cue-controlled relaxation can also be taught. During muscle relaxation training, the individual is taught to subvocalize a cue word such as "calm." The cue word can be used in actual situations when anxiety is anticipated or experienced to help induce a relaxed state. Relaxation procedures are often accompanied by the incorporation of imagery—the therapist encourages the client to create vivid positive mental images designed to produce relaxation.

When relaxation training is combined with exposure to feared situations, the procedure is known as **desensitization** or **systematic desensitization**. In imaginal desensitization, a hierarchy of fear-provoking situations is constructed, and the person is asked to visualize scenes, progressing from the least to the most fear producing. These visualizations are presented as the person is engaged in relaxation. This process is repeated until the most anxiety-provoking scene can be comfortably visualized. In in vivo desensitization, the actual feared object or situation is employed rather than using visualizations.

Modeling

A commonly employed behavioral procedure is **modeling**. The early work of Bandura and his colleagues (e.g., Bandura & Menlove, 1968) was the impetus for subsequent research. In all modeling therapies, the youth observes another person interacting adaptively with the feared situation. The model can be live or symbolic (e.g., on film). Participant modeling, in which following observation the fearful child joins the model in making gradual approaches to the feared object, is one of the most potent treatments (Ollendick et al., 2004b).

Contingency Management

Modeling and systematic desensitization and its variants are treatments that were developed as ways of reducing a young person's fear or anxiety. **Contingency management** procedures are based on operant principles and, instead, address the child or adolescent's avoidant/anxious behavior directly by altering the contingencies for such behavior—ensuring that positive consequences follow exposure to but not avoidance of the feared stimulus and that the young person is rewarded for improvement. These procedures are also sometimes described as reinforced practice. Contingency management or reinforced practice has been shown to be effective in treating fears and phobias and as part of the treatment for other anxiety disorders (Kendall & Suveg, 2006; Ollendick et al., 2004b). Contingency management is often combined with modeling, relaxation, or desensitization procedures.

Cognitive-Behavioral Treatments

There is considerable support for the efficacy of CBT programs for anxiety disorders in children and adolescents (Comer et al., 2019; Higa-McMillan et al., 2016; Kendall et al., 2017; van Schalkwyk & Silverman, 2019; Weisz et al., 2017). These treatment programs integrate a number of behavioral and cognitive-behavioral strategies. The overall goals of these interventions are to teach the young person to:

- recognize the signs of anxious arousal,
- identify the cognitive processes associated with anxious arousal, and
- employ strategies and skills for managing anxiety.

CBT programs employ a variety of therapeutic strategies to achieve these goals, as shown in Table 6.4.

CBT for children with anxiety disorders is illustrated by the work of Kendall and his colleagues (Kendall et al., 2017). They describe a 16-week program that makes use of a variety of behavioral and cognitive-behavioral procedures (see Table 6.4), and is divided into two segments. The first eight sessions are devoted to introducing basic concepts and a progressive building of skills. During the second eight sessions, these skills are practiced in situations that expose the child to increasing levels of anxiety. The behavioral strategies include modeling, in vivo exposure, role play, relaxation training, and contingency management. The cognitive strategies include recognizing the physiological symptoms of anxiety, challenging and modifying anxious talk, developing a plan to cope with the situation, evaluating the success of coping efforts, and utilizing self-reinforcement. Throughout treatment the therapist serves as a coping model, demonstrating each of the new skills in each new situation. The following preparation of a young person for an in vivo exposure—a visit to a mall—illustrates an exchange that

Table 6.4 Treatment Strategies Included in Cognitive-Behavioral Treatments for Anxiety Disorders in Children and Adolescents

Education about anxiety and emotions
Teaching awareness of bodily reactions and physical symptoms
Relaxation procedures
Recognition of anxious cognitions (self-talk) and shifting to coping-focused thinking
Role playing and contingent reward procedures
Teaching problem-solving models
Use of coping models
Exposure to anxiety-provoking situations
Practice in using newly acquired skills in increasingly anxiety-provoking situations
Homework assignments
Develop ways to generalize gains and prevent relapse

Sources: Adapted from Kendall & Suveg, 2006; Kendall et al., 2017.

might occur between a therapist and a child during Kendall's cognitive-behavioral treatment program.

> *Therapist: So are you feeling nervous now?*
> *Child: I don't know. Not really.*
> *Therapist: How would you know you were starting to get nervous?*
> *Child: My heart would start beating faster.*
> *Therapist: (recalling a common somatic complaint for this child) What about your breathing?*
> *Child: I might start breathing faster.*
> *Therapist: And what would you be thinking to yourself?*
> *Child: I might get lost or I don't know where I am.*
> *Therapist: And what are some things you could do if you start getting nervous?*
> *Child: I could take deep breaths and say everything is going to be okay.*
> *Therapist: That's good, but what if you were unsure where you were or got lost?*
> *Child: I could ask somebody.*
> *Therapist: Yes, you could ask somebody. Would it be a good idea to ask one of the guards or policemen? How are you feeling? Do you think you are ready to give it a try?*
> *Kendall & Suveg, 2006, p. 273*

The program, for children 7–13, makes use of the *Coping Cat Workbook* (Kendall, 1992; Kendall & Hedtke, 2006) and the acronym "FEAR" to highlight the four skills that the child learns in the program (Kendall et al., 2017).

F—Feeling frightened? (recognizing bodily symptoms of anxiety)
E—Expecting bad things to happen? (recognizing anxious cognition—see Figure 6.1)
A—Attitudes and actions that may help (developing a repertoire of coping strategies)
R—Results and rewards (contingency management)

Research supports the efficacy of this approach (Kendall et al., 2017). For example, children diagnosed with anxiety disorders randomly assigned to a treatment condition fared better by the end of treatment than control children on a number of anxiety measures. Treated children returned, on average, to the normal range on these measures. In addition, 64% of the children who were treated no longer met diagnostic criteria for an anxiety disorder, compared with 5% (1 case) of the control children. Follow-up assessments, over 7 to 19 years, of young people enrolled in this program indicated that these treatment gains were maintained (Benjamin et al., 2013; Kendall et al., 2004). Research also suggests the efficacy of delivering CBT in a group rather than in an individual format (Liber et al., 2008; Villabø et al., 2018). Kendall's program is a child-focused program, but the contextual influences on anxiety are appreciated. Thus, parents play a central role. They are educated regarding the problem and the treatment program. They also are involved as consultants and collaborators. They attend two sessions and actively participate in a supportive role. A teen program also is available (Kendall et al., 2002).

The Child-Adolescent Anxiety Multimodal Longitudinal Study compared Coping Cat (CBT), medication (sertraline; SRT), their combination (COMB), and pill placebo (PBO) treatments. Initial post-treatment findings suggested that the combined treatment was more effective than either CBT or SRT alone. Post-treatment improvements were comparable for the CBT and SRT conditions and were superior to the placebo condition. Follow-up assessments approximately 6.5 years post-treatment indicated no differences between the CBT, SRT, and COMB conditions in terms of remission status (no longer meeting criteria for an anxiety disorder). However, over the course of the follow-up period, youth treated with CBT demonstrated better outcomes with regard to aspects of functioning such as increased life satisfaction, decreased overall impairment, and lower academic impairment. In contrast, the follow-up adjustment trajectories of the SRT participants were not different from those who received placebo treatment (Ginsburg et al., 2018; Swan et al., 2018; Walkup et al., 2008).

A computer-assisted version of the program has been developed (Kendall et al., 2011; Storch et al., 2015). The first half of the program is completed independently by the child and the second half, primarily exposure sessions, is completed with the assistance of a therapist/coach.

An Australian adaptation of Kendall's program, referred to as the FRIENDS program, extended the role of family involvement

Figure 6.1 A therapist can use illustrations such as this to help elicit a child's anxiety-related cognitions or self-talk.

(Barrett, Dadds, & Rapee, 1996; Pahl & Barrett, 2010). The program has a child-focused component using the *Coping Koala Group Workbook*, an adaptation of Kendall's *Coping Cat Workbook* and program. In addition, in the family component, the child and parents are treated in small family groups. Thus, in addition to treating the child with cognitive-behavioral procedures, the program trains parents in, and allows them to practice, child management, anxiety management, and communication and problem-solving skills to build a supportive family environment.

Research evaluations of the program indicate that the vast majority of youth, in both a child-only or child-plus-family treatment, no longer meet criteria for an anxiety disorder by the end of treatment, or at follow-up several years later. Greater involvement of parents may be the treatment of choice for some young people. Although results are mixed, findings from this and other research suggest the possible value of parent participation and indicate that this may particularly be the case for younger children (Comer et al., 2019; Kendall et al., 2008; Kreuze et al., 2018). Barrett and colleagues have developed a successful extension of the FRIENDS program for younger children 4–7 years old (Barrett, Fisak, & Cooper, 2015).

Pharmacological Treatments

Psychotropic medications are often employed in treating children and adolescents with anxiety disorders. Although not approved by the Federal Drug Administration (FDA) for this purpose, selective serotonin reuptake inhibitors (SSRIs; e.g., fluvoxamine, fluoxetine, sertraline) are most commonly employed and have the most extensive evidence-base of medications used to treat anxiety disorders in children and adolescents. While side effects of SSRIs are typically described as mild and transitory, the FDA has issued a warning to carefully monitor young people on SSRIs for worsening depression or suicidality. Also, the benefit and risks of long-term use require continued investigation. Furthermore, SSRIs may reduce anxious arousal but may not address the anxiety coping skills that are also addressed by CBT. Thus, the use of pharmacological treatment for anxiety in youth may not be the treatment of first choice (Scahill & Rojas, 2019; Scharfstein et al., 2011; van Schalkwyk & Silverman, 2019). Clinicians may choose to use medications in certain circumstances, for example when the young person's anxiety symptoms are severe.

Prevention of Anxiety Disorders

Beyond the logic of early intervention, there are multiple reasons to think in terms of preventing anxiety disorders (Weissberg, Kumpfer, & Seligman, 2003; Werner-Seidler et al., 2017). Anxiety disorders are common in childhood and adolescence. Furthermore, anxiety disorders may increase the risk for other disorders and the impact of these conditions may extend throughout the child and adolescent period and into adulthood.

The content of prevention programs for anxiety is highly similar to that described in the discussion of CBT for anxiety disorders (Pahl & Barrett, 2010). Indicated prevention programs target individuals who already display some symptoms but do not meet diagnostic criteria or have a mild form of the targeted problem. For example, an intervention based on the FRIENDS program, described earlier, was offered to youth between the ages of 7 and 14 years of age and their parents. Youth ranged from those who did not have a disorder but showed mild anxious features to those who met the criteria for an anxiety disorder but were in the less severe range (Dadds et al., 1999). A two-year follow-up that compared these youth with a control group that did not receive the intervention suggested that the program was useful in preventing youth with mild to moderate anxiety problems from developing more serious anxiety disorders.

Barrett and colleagues (2006) have described a school-based universal prevention program provided to Grade 6 (ages 10 to 11 years) and Grade 9 (ages 13 to 14 years) youth in several schools. Again, the intervention was the FRIENDS program. At the end of the intervention, and at a 36-month follow-up, participants reported significantly lower anxiety scores and were less likely to be classified as high risk than those in the control condition who did not receive the intervention. Youth in Grade 6 appeared to benefit more than students in Grade 9, suggesting the value of earlier intervention.

A selected prevention program targets youth who may be at risk for a later anxiety disorder. Rapee and colleagues (2005, 2010) provided a brief (six 90-minute sessions) parent education program, Cool Little Kids, to parents of preschool children with high levels of withdrawn/inhibited behaviors—a risk factor for later anxiety disorders. The group sessions provided information on the nature and development of anxiety, parent management techniques (especially the role of overprotection in maintaining anxiety), principles of gradual exposure to anxiety-provoking situations, and cognitive restructuring of the parents' own worries. At 12-month and three-year follow-ups, children whose parents participated in the program exhibited lower levels of anxiety diagnoses than those whose parents received no intervention. An 11-year follow-up indicated that the benefits of the program were maintained for girls (Rapee, 2013). An online version of the Cool Little Kids program also proved to be effective (Morgan et al., 2017).

Obsessive-Compulsive Disorder

Diagnostic Criteria

Obsessive-compulsive disorder (OCD) was included among the anxiety disorders in earlier versions of the DSM. In DSM-5 OCD is part of a separate grouping of Obsessive-Compulsive and Related Disorders (OCRD). In addition to OCD, the OCRD chapter of the DSM describes several other disorders including hoarding disorder, trichotillomania (hair-pulling disorder), excoriation (skin-picking) disorder, and body dysmorphic disorder (preoccupation with perceived flaws in one's physical appearance that are not observable or are perceived as only slight to other individuals). These disorders are grouped together based on their shared phenomenology (e.g., repetitive behaviors, urges, and preoccupations) and neurobiology (Ricketts et al., 2017). We will concentrate our discussion on OCD.

Obsessions are unwanted, repetitive, intrusive thoughts that are not simply excessive real-life concerns and that, in most individuals, cause considerable distress or anxiety. **Compulsions** involve repetitive, stereotyped behaviors that the youth feels compelled to perform and that are meant to reduce anxiety or to prevent a dreaded event. **Obsessive-Compulsive Disorder** (OCD) involves either obsessions or compulsions or, in a majority of

young people, both (American Psychiatric Association, 2013). The DSM criteria for OCD also indicate that young children may not be able to articulate why they engage in these compulsions. However, even among very young children, odd repetitive acts may be seen as strange. Children, as we see in the case of Stanley, may even initially have their own explanations. The child may, over time, come to recognize that the ideas or behaviors involved are unreasonable yet still feel the need to repeat them.

Another criterion for the diagnosis of OCD is that the obsessions or compulsions are highly time-consuming. These obsessions and rituals interfere considerably with normal routines, academic functioning, and social relationships and have an appreciable effect on other family members and family functioning (Piacentini et al., 2003; Stewart et al. 2017). The impact on Sergei's life illustrates the nature and consequences of the disorder.

Description

Judith Rapoport and her colleagues at the National Institute for Mental Health (NIMH) conducted a series of studies that increased the attention given to obsessive-compulsive behavior in young people. Table 6.5 indicates common obsessions and compulsions among children and adolescents reported by this group and others (Henin & Kendall, 1997; Leonard et al., 2005; Rapoport, 1989).

Compulsive rituals are reported more frequently than obsessions; this finding is different from reports concerning adults, in which obsessions and compulsions are reported at fairly equivalent rates. There appear to be two broad themes to the excessive concerns and rituals: the first theme is a preoccupation with cleanliness, grooming, and averting danger, and the second theme is a pervasive doubting—not knowing when one is "right."

Childhood OCD is often recognized only when symptoms are very severe. If a youth reaches out for help, it is frequently only after years of suffering. Young people often admit having kept their problems a secret. Among those who do seek help, many indicate that their parents were unaware of their problem. For example, diagnostic interviews conducted with a community-based sample of youth ages 9 through 17 and their mothers found that of the 35 cases of OCD identified, four youths were diagnosed

STANLEY The Martian Rituals

[A]t age seven Stanley saw a television program in which friendly Martians contacted human beings by putting odd thoughts into their heads. On the basis of that program Stanley decided his compulsion to do everything in a sequence of four was a sign that the Martians had picked him as their "contact man" on earth. After two years of sterile counting rituals, no contact had been made and Stanley gave up this explanation. He did not, however, give up counting.

Rapoport, 1989, p. 84

SERGEI Impairment in Functioning

Sergei is a 17-year-old former high school student. Only a year or so ago Sergei seemed to be a normal adolescent with many talents and interests. Then, almost overnight he was transformed into a lonely outsider, excluded from social life by his psychological disabilities. Specifically, he was unable to stop washing. Haunted by the notion that he was dirty—in spite of the contrary evidence of his senses—he began to spend more and more of his time cleansing himself of imaginary dirt. At first his ritual ablutions were confined to weekends and evenings and he was able to stay in school while keeping them up, but soon they began to consume all his time, forcing him to drop out of school, a victim of his inability to feel clean enough.

Rapoport, 1989, p. 83

as having OCD on the basis of the parent's report, and 32 as the result of the youth's report, but in only one case did the youth and parent concur (Rapoport et al., 2000).

Epidemiology

Epidemiological studies suggest a prevalence rate for OCD of about 1–2.7% and a lifetime prevalence rate for OCD of between 1.8% and 5.5% in the general child and adolescent population. Most estimates also suggest that at younger ages, boys outnumber girls, but that by adolescence, the genders are equally represented. Research suggests an earlier average age of onset among boys (9–11 years old) than among girls (11–13 years old) (Flament et al., 1988; Johnco & Storch, 2018; Rapoport et al., 2000; Ricketts et al., 2017). OCD is reported in many Western and other countries with similarities regarding age of onset, sex distribution, and comorbidities. Cross-cultural differences in predominant type of obsessions and compulsions are, however, reported (Austin & Chorpita, 2004; Ricketts et al., 2017).

Most children and adolescents diagnosed with OCD meet the criteria for at least one other disorder. Multiple anxiety disorders, conduct and oppositional disorders, substance abuse, and depression are often reported (Geller 2006: Leonard et al.,

2005; Ricketts et al., 2017). OCD also often occurs with **Tourette's disorder**. Tourette's disorder is a chronic disorder with a genetic and neuroanatomical basis. It is characterized by motor and vocal tics and related urges or other tic disorders (Scharf et al., 2012; Swain et al., 2007). **Tics** are sudden, rapid, recurrent, stereotyped motor movements or vocalizations. Although it remains unclear, there is some thought that children and adolescents with tics represent a distinct subtype of OCD with regard to symptomatology, developmental course, family patterns, and response to treatment (American Psychiatric Association, 2013; Storch et al., 2008; Swain et al., 2007).

Developmental Course and Prognosis

Behavior with obsessive-compulsive qualities occurs in various stages of normal development and it is therefore important to distinguish between normal clinically non-adaptive behaviors (Evans & Leckman, 2006; Johnco & Storch, 2018). For example, very young children may have bedtime and eating rituals or may require things to be "just so." Disruption of these routines often leads to distress. Also, young children are often observed to engage in repetitive play and to show a distinct preference for sameness. In his widely read book for parents, Benjamin Spock noted that mild compulsions—such as stepping over cracks in the sidewalk or touching every third picket in a fence—are quite common in 8-, 9-, and 10-year-olds (Spock & Rothenberg, 1992). Many readers of this text likely recall engaging in such behaviors. Behaviors that are common to the youth's peer group are probably best viewed as games. Only when they dominate the young person's life and interfere with normal functioning is there cause for concern. In addition, the specific content of OCD rituals generally does not resemble common developmental rituals and OCD rituals have a later stage of onset.

There is heterogeneity regarding the course of OCD. The disorder commonly follows a course in which symptoms wax and wane (emerge and fade over time). Multiple obsessions and compulsions are usually present at any one time, and usually the symptoms change in content and intensity over time. Research also suggests that the disorder is likely to be chronic. Although

Table 6.5 Some Common Obsessions and Compulsions

Obsessions
Contamination concerns (e.g., dirt, germs, environmental toxins)
Harm to self or others (e.g., death, illness, kidnapping)
Symmetry, order, exactness
Doing the right thing (scrupulosity, religious obsessions)
Compulsions
Washing, grooming
Repeating (e.g., going in and out of a door)
Checking (e.g., doors, homework)
Ordering or arranging

Keeping things in certain specific locations and order is common. It is only when these kinds of behaviors interfere with a young person's normal functioning that they should cause concern for clinicians and other adults. (Courtesy of Kevin Haworth)

a majority of youth receiving treatment may show substantial improvement, problems persist for many (Johnco & Storch, 2018; Leonard et al., 2005; Rettew et al., 1992).

Etiology

The etiology of OCD is likely complex, however, most researchers and clinicians believe in a strong genetic and biological basis (Johnco & Storch, 2018; Ricketts et al., 2017). Twin and family studies suggest considerable heritability for OCD. For example, the disorder has been found to be more prevalent among youth with a first-degree relative with obsessive-compulsive behavior than among the general population, and many parents of youth with the disorder meet diagnostic criteria for OCD or exhibit obsessive-compulsive symptoms. Also, concordance rates for monozygotic twins more than double those for dizygotic twins are reported (Monzani et al., 2014). In addition, a number of studies have reported that both OCD and Tourette's disorder (or less severe tic disorders) occur in the same individuals at higher than expected rates, and these studies have found a familial association between the two disorders. It seems likely that OCD and Tourette's disorder have some shared genetic basis (Matthews & Grados, 2011; Yu et al., 2015). The genetic influence on OCD is likely to be complex, involving multiple genes, and research is ongoing to identify the network of genes involved in the development of OCD (Grados, 2010; Ricketts et al., 2017).

Neuroimaging studies have suggested that OCD is linked to neurobiological abnormalities of the basal ganglia, a group of brain structures lying under the cerebral cortex and several areas of the prefrontal cortex. Studies employing fMRI have also found disruptions in the communication between these regions of the brain. It is hypothesized that such disruption may underlie the ritualistic and inflexible behavior characteristic of OCD (Abramovitch et al., 2012; Bernstein et al., 2016; Johnco & Storch, 2018).

Research support for the role of environmental influences in the etiology of OCD is more limited. Reports of OCD triggered by stressful life events or trauma are often offered in clinical settings. However, research findings are mixed and much of this literature has appreciable methodological limitations (Ricketts et al., 2017). The potential role of infectious agents has received some attention. A subset of cases of OCD, known as **PANS** (pediatric acute-onset neuropsychiatric syndrome) and one subtype of PANS, **PANDAS** (pediatric autoimmune neuropsychiatric disorders associated with streptococcal infections), has been noted (Johnco & Storch, 2018; Leckman et al., 2011; Ricketts et al., 2017). This possible subset of OCD involves a sudden onset or exacerbation of OCD symptoms following infection and the youth also exhibits tics. The OCD symptoms in these cases are believed to result from an autoimmune reaction produced when antibodies formed by the body against the infection react with and cause inflammation in cells of the basal ganglia. Information regarding a potential subgroup of OCD caused by infectious agents and its treatment is, however, limited.

Although research support for environmental influences on the etiology of OCD is limited, this does not mean that such influences don't have an impact on the disorder. Indeed, family and other aspects of the youth's environment are likely to have an influence on the developmental course of the disorder (Johnco & Storch, 2018; Farrell, Mathieu, & Lavell, 2019).

Assessment of OCD

The assessment of a young person suspected of having an obsessive-compulsive disorder should be comprehensive and include multiple assessment measures and examine a broad range of aspects of the youth and her or his environment (Farrell et al., 2019; Johnco & Storch, 2018). The assessment is likely to include a general clinical interview of both the youth and parent(s) that can provide the clinician with a broad picture of the presenting problems, youth, and family. A structured diagnostic interview may also be part of the initial assessment, particularly in research settings, so as to provide a diagnosis of OCD and other potential co-occurring disorders. The Children's Yale-Brown Obsessive Compulsive Scale (CY-BOCS; Scahill et al., 1997; Storch et al., 2019) is a clinician-administered semi-structured interview that can readily be employed in a typical clinical setting. The first section of the CY-BOCS is a checklist to assess the presence of a wide range of obsessions and compulsions. The second section then assesses the severity (frequency, distress, interference, resistance, controllability) of the youth's obsessions and compulsions.

Parent- and self-report measures such as those of the ASEBA system (Achenbach) are helpful in assessing a broad range of potential presenting problems as reported by a variety of informants. Parent- and self-report measures that focus more narrowly on obsessive-compulsive symptoms are also available (Johnco & Storch, 2018). These include the Obsessive Compulsive Inventory–Child Version (Foa et al., 2010), the Children's Obsessional Compulsive Inventory–Revised (Uher et al., 2008), and the Children's Florida Obsessive Compulsive Inventory (Storch et al., 2009). In addition to measures of OCD symptoms, parent- and self-report measures of other aspects of the child and family's functioning are also available. For example, the Child Obsessive Compulsive Impact Scale–Revised (Piacentini et al., 2007) assesses the level of impairment in child and family functioning related to the child's OCD symptoms. The Family Accommodation Scale–Parent Report (Flessner et al., 2011) assesses family involvement in rituals (e.g., providing reassurance, providing items needed for rituals) and modifications in family functioning (e.g., changing family routines, facilitating avoidance of items/places) resulting from the child's OCD symptoms.

Treating OCD

Two kinds of intervention, alone or in combination seem to be frequently offered treatments for OCD (Farrell et al., 2019; Freeman et al., 2018; Johnco & Storch, 2018; Uhre et al., 2020). Cognitive-behavioral interventions are the first-line treatment of choice (Kemp & Freeman, 2019).

CBT typically involves educating the youth and family about OCD, training in modifying cognitions to resist obsessions and compulsions and to enhance change, and contingency management and self-reinforcement. The central aspect of cognitive-behavioral approaches, however, is **exposure** with **response prevention** (M. E. Franklin et al., 2017). The child or adolescent is gradually exposed to the situation that causes the obsessions and compulsions and is given help in resisting the urge to perform the ritual.

In imaginal exposure, the child is presented with a detailed and an embellished description of the feared situation for several minutes so as to create anxiety. At the same time, the child is not permitted to engage in any thoughts or behaviors to avoid the anxiety. The several-minute exposure is repeated until the anxiety is reduced to a predetermined level. The following is an example of imaginal exposure to anxiety-provoking germs.

You walk up to the school door and have to open the door with your hands. You forgot your gloves, so there is nothing to protect you from the germs. As you touch the handle, you feel some sticky and slimy wet stuff on your hand and your skin begins to tingle. Oh no! You've touched germs that were left there by someone and they're oozing into your skin and contaminating you with some sickness. You start to feel weak, and can feel the germs moving under your skin. You try to wipe your hands on your clothes, but it's too late. Already the germs are into your blood and moving all through your body. You feel weak and dizzy, and you can't even hold the door open. You start to feel like you're going to vomit, and you can taste some vomit coming up to your throat ...

Albano & DiBartolo, 1997

In addition to, or as an alternative to, imaginal exposure, the child may be exposed to the actual anxiety-provoking situations. Training to enhance generalization and prevent relapse is also included. The involvement of the family is characteristic of most CBT programs. Families affect and are affected by the young person's OCD. Also, it is typical that families have made accommodations to the young person's OCD symptoms. Inclusion of family in treatment is supported and, especially with younger children and those with complicated family dynamics, may be an important component of treatment (M. E. Franklin et al., 2017; Freeman et al., 2018; Peris et al., 2017).

Psychotropic medications are another treatment option (APA, 2006; Waslick, 2006). Various SSRIs (e.g., sertraline, fluoxetine, and fluvoxamine) and the tricyclic antidepressant clomipramine have often been prescribed, with SSRIs preferred because of their more tolerable side effects. More recently, DCS (D-Cycloserine) which partially interferes with the action of certain neurotransmitters and is hypothesized to facilitate the extinction of fear has received some attention (Hofmann, Wu, & Boettcher, 2013; Storch et al., 2016). There are a number of reasons that CBT remains the initial treatment of choice (Freeman et al., 2018; Johnco & Storch, 2018). The efficacy of pharmacological interventions is modest. For example, SSRIs appear to be superior to placebo conditions, but not more effective than CBT alone. Also, for most young people with OCD, the combination of SSRIs and CBT does not appear to be superior to CBT alone. In addition, scrutiny regarding the safety of SSRIs suggests caution in their use. It is possible that in some circumstances, such as very severe cases, augmenting CBT with use of a pharmacological agent (e.g., an SSRI) might be recommended. Whether, and under what circumstances, to combine medication with CBT remains a topic of ongoing investigation (Freeman et al., 2018).

Looking Back

An Introduction to Internalizing Disorders

- There is appreciable evidence of a broad category of child and adolescent internalizing problems. Conclusions regarding more specific disorders are less certain. One issue of particular concern is the high rate of co-occurrence of multiple internalizing disorders.

Defining and Classifying Anxiety Disorders

- Anxiety or fear is generally viewed as a complex pattern of three response systems: overt behavioral, cognitive, and physiological responses. Anxiety is part of normal developmental processes.
- Fears are quite common in children. There seem to be age- and gender-related variations in numbers and content of fears. The most common fears seem to be similar across cultures.
- The DSM-5 describes a number of anxiety disorders including Separation Anxiety Disorder, Specific Phobia, Social Anxiety Disorder, Panic Disorder, and Generalized Anxiety Disorder.
- The empirical approach to classification describes subcategories of internalizing behaviors. These subcategories do not, however, suggest separate anxiety disorders and suggest that anxiety and depression tend to co-occur.

Epidemiology of Anxiety Disorders

- Anxiety disorders are among the most common disorders experienced by children and adolescents. Young people are likely to meet the criteria for more than one anxiety disorder.

Specific Phobias

- Phobias, as distinguished from normal fears, are excessive, persistent, or non-adaptive. Specific phobias are among the most commonly diagnosed anxiety disorders in children and adolescents. They are likely to begin in childhood and, at least for some individuals, may persist over time. Young people with this diagnosis, as with other anxiety disorders, frequently have co-occurring disorders.

Social Anxiety Disorder (Social Phobia)

- Children and adolescents with social anxiety are likely to be concerned about being embarrassed or negatively evaluated.
- Young people with selective mutism do not talk in selected social situations. Selective mutism may be an extreme form of social anxiety.
- Prevalence of social anxiety probably increases with age. Social anxieties are quite common during adolescence, making the interpretations of prevalence and degree of disturbance difficult.
- Young people with social anxiety disorder are also likely to meet the criteria for one or more other disorders and depression is a common co-occurring problem among adolescents.

Separation Anxiety and School Refusal

- Separation anxiety is excessive anxiety regarding separation from a major attachment figure and/or home. It is a common problem among children but becomes less common by adolescence.
- School refusal is anxiety that keeps a child or adolescent from attending school. This term accommodates cases of both separation anxiety and phobias or anxieties related to aspects of the school situation. School refusal in adolescence is likely to be complex.
- Treatment of school refusal is most successful if it is begun early, and it probably needs to be tailored to the specific kinds of school refusal exhibited.

Generalized Anxiety Disorder

- Children and adolescents diagnosed with Generalized Anxiety Disorder (GAD) exhibit excessive worry and anxiety that is not focused on any particular object or situation. GAD is common among youth seen in clinical settings, and the disorder may persist. The issue of overlap with other diagnoses is of concern with regard to how GAD is conceptualized.

Panic Attacks and Panic Disorder

- Panic attacks may be expected (cued) or unexpected (uncued), and they may occur in the context of several anxiety disorders. Panic disorder is associated with recurrent unexpected panic attacks. The presence of panic in adolescents seems likely, but the existence, particularly of unexpected panic, in younger children is less clear. Family histories of panic and severe anxiety are commonly reported.

Etiology of Anxiety Disorders

- The development and maintenance of anxiety disorders are influenced by multiple factors that interact in complex ways.
- There is a familial aggregation for anxiety disorders. Genetic factors may play a role, but for many disorders, what may be inherited is a general tendency toward emotional reactivity.
- The role of various neurotransmitters and regions of the brain such as the amygdala and prefrontal cortex have received attention with regard to the development of anxiety disorders.
- A general vulnerability to anxiety may be associated with the child's temperament. The temperament characteristic of behavioral inhibition appears to be a risk factor for the development of anxiety disorders.
- Psychosocial and cognitive influences play a considerable role in the development of anxiety disorders. Direct exposure, imitation, information transmission, parenting practices, and peer relationships are some of the mechanisms of influence.

Assessment of Anxiety Disorders

- Assessments of anxiety should consider developmental issues and various perspectives on the young person's problem. Information about a full range of problems, and information about the child or adolescent's environment should be obtained.
- Assessment of anxiety is typically guided by the three response systems: behaviors, cognitions, and physiological responses.

- Self-report instruments provide subjective reports of the various aspects of anxiety. Direct observation and behavioral approach tests assess overt behavioral aspects. Physiological recordings of anxiety are conducted less frequently.

Interventions for Anxiety Disorders

- Appreciable support exists for the effectiveness of psychological treatments for youths' anxiety problems. Many treatments are, at least in part, based on exposure to the feared stimulus.
- Procedures such as modeling, desensitization, and contingency management contribute to successful treatment. Cognitive-behavioral treatments (CBTs) that include a number of therapeutic strategies have proven effective in treating anxiety disorders. Pharmacotherapy, if employed, is usually an adjunct to psychological treatments.
- Investigations of prevention programs, drawing on cognitive-behavioral procedures, suggest that they may be effective in preventing the development of anxiety disorders.

Obsessive-Compulsive Disorder

- Obsessive-compulsive disorder (OCD) is characterized by repetitive and intrusive thoughts and/or behaviors.
- The obsessions and rituals associated with OCD cause considerable interference in multiple aspects of the youth's and family's functioning.
- Unless treated, OCD often appears to follow a chronic course.
- Evidence seems strong for a genetic and biological basis for OCD.
- Multi-component CBTs involving exposure and response prevention and pharmacological treatment employing selective serotonin reuptake inhibitors have been shown to be effective in treating OCD. Cognitive-behavioral intervention is the first-line treatment of choice.

Key Terms

internalizing disorders *110*

anxiety *111*

fear *111*

worry *111*

phobia *113*

Specific Phobia *113*

Social Anxiety Disorder (Social Phobia) *115*

Selective Mutism *116*

Separation Anxiety Disorder *118*

school refusal *119*

functional analysis *119*

truancy *120*

Generalized Anxiety Disorder *120*

panic attack *122*

agoraphobia *122*

panic disorder *122*

behavioral inhibition *125*

negative affectivity *125*

effortful control *125*

overprotective/intrusive parenting *126*

exposure *129, 135*

relaxation training *129*

desensitization (systematic desensitization) *129*

modeling *129*

contingency management *129*

obsessions *132*

compulsions *132*

Obsessive-Compulsive Disorder *132*

Tourette's disorder *133*

tics *133*

PANS/PANDAS *134*

response prevention *135*

CHAPTER 7
Trauma- and Stressor-Related Disorders

Looking Forward

After reading this chapter, you should be able to discuss:

- The nature of trauma and the features of posttraumatic stress disorder (PTSD)
- Reactive attachment disorder and disinhibited social engagement disorder
- The epidemiology of reactions to trauma/PTSD

- The developmental course of reactions to trauma/PTSD
- The treatment of PTSD
- The nature and various forms of maltreatment
- Various factors contributing to maltreatment
- Consequences of maltreatment
- Approaches to treating and preventing maltreatment

The current version of the DSM introduced a separate chapter of trauma- and stressor-related disorders and these disorders are the focus of the current chapter. However, it is important to note that trauma and stressors are implicated in the development of multiple disorders, internalizing, externalizing, and others (psychoses, substance abuse) not just in the development of disorders included in this DSM grouping. Indeed, there is accumulating evidence that experience of early-life stress has considerable impact on multiple aspects of mental and physical health across the lifespan (Ehrlich, Miller, & Chen, 2016; Hostinar, Nusslock, & Miller, 2018; McLaughlin, 2016). Furthermore, individuals receiving one of the trauma- or stressor-related diagnoses often also meet the diagnostic criteria for one or more of these other disorders.

Reactions to Traumatic Events

How do young people react to experiencing devastating natural disasters, other disasters such as fires or major transportation accidents, to acts of violence and terrorism, or other potentially traumatic events?

Trauma is usually defined as an event outside everyday experience that would be distressing to almost anyone. Early descriptions of children's exposure to trauma suggested that reactions might be relatively mild and transient, and thus these experiences were not given a great deal of attention. However, reports began to emerge of more severe and long-lasting reactions. More recent literature indicates that exposure to traumatic events may lead to significant distress and psychological impairment (Bonanno et al., 2010; Carliner et al., 2017; Furr et al., 2010; Nader & Williams, 2018).

The investigation of 26 children kidnapped from their Chowchilla, California, school bus in 1976 is one study that influenced the understanding of children's posttraumatic responses. The children and their bus driver were held for 27 hours. At first they were driven around in darkened vans; then they were moved to a buried tractor trailer, where they remained until some of the victims dug themselves out. The child victims and at least one parent of each child were interviewed within five to 13 months of the kidnapping. All of the children were found to be symptomatic, with 73% showing moderately severe or severe reactions. Assessments two to five years after the kidnapping revealed that many symptoms had persisted (Terr, 1979, 1983).

DSM Classification

Systematic study of youths' reactions to trauma was also stimulated by the introduction, in the third version of the DSM, of a specific diagnosis—**Posttraumatic Stress Disorder (PTSD)**.

In DSM III, IV, and IVTR, PTSD was included among the anxiety disorders. In DSM-5, PTSD (as well as **Acute Stress Disorder— ASD**) is part of a separate grouping of Trauma- and Stressor- Related Disorders. However, these disorders continue to be viewed as related to the anxiety disorders.

Diagnostic Criteria

The diagnosis of **PTSD** is defined by the development of a characteristic set of symptoms following exposure to one or more traumatic events. Thus, to receive a diagnosis of PTSD the young person must experience exposure to a serious traumatic event(s). The child or adolescent is considered to have experienced exposure if she or he has directly experienced the traumatic event, or has witnessed a traumatic event occurring to others, or has learned that a traumatic event occurred to a close relative or friend. In addition, repeated or extreme exposure to aversive information about a traumatic event(s) may also be considered traumatic exposure, but not if such exposure is only through modes such as electronic media or television. The diagnosis of PTSD also requires that following exposure to the traumatic event(s) the person must experience symptoms from each of four different clusters:

- Reexperiencing
- Avoidance
- Negative alterations in cognitions and mood
- Arousal and reactivity

The **reexperiencing** cluster describes intrusive symptoms that begin after the traumatic event. This cluster of symptoms includes disturbing memories of the traumatic event, recurrent distressing trauma-related dreams, prolonged or intense psychological distress or physiological reactions in response to cues that are reminders of the event, or dissociative reactions. **Dissociation** refers to alterations in self-awareness. Dissociative reactions my include depersonalization (feeling cut off from one's feelings or environment) and derealization (a marked sense of unreality). Thus, the person experiencing a dissociative reaction may act or feel as if the traumatic event were recurring (e.g., flashbacks).

Avoidance symptoms may include persistent efforts to avoid trauma-related thoughts or feelings. This reaction may also include avoidance of external stimuli (e.g., people or situations) associated with the trauma.

Negative alterations in cognitions and mood may include cognitive symptoms such as difficulty in remembering important aspects of the traumatic event, distorted thoughts about the causes or consequences of the traumatic event, or exaggerated negative beliefs or expectations. Alterations in mood may include persistent negative emotional states (e.g., fear, anger, shame), persistent inability to experience positive emotions, diminished interest in significant activities, or feelings of detachment from others.

The fourth cluster of symptoms involves marked alteration in the young person's **arousal or reactivity** that begins or worsens after the occurrence of the traumatic event(s). These symptoms may include irritable behavior and angry outbursts, reckless behavior, heightened vigilance, exaggerated startle responses, concentration difficulties, or sleep disturbances.

The diagnostic criteria for ASD are similar to those for PTSD. The principal distinction is that ASD symptoms last for at least three days, but less than four weeks, whereas PTSD lasts for at least one month following the trauma or has a delayed onset.

The DSM acknowledges potential developmental differences in the expression of PTSD. For example, the description of reexperiencing symptoms indicates that children, rather than reporting memories, may engage in repetitive trauma-related play or that children who have experienced a trauma may have frightening dreams without recognizable trauma-related content. These developmental considerations were included in earlier versions of the DSM; however, there were still concerns that young children were under-diagnosed using existing criteria and that it was necessary to pay greater attention to developmental considerations in defining PTSD in children. Indeed, some suggested that existing criteria were not appropriate for infants or very young children and alternative criteria were proposed (De Young, Kenardy, & Cobham, 2011; Scheeringa, Zeanah, & Cohen, 2011). In response to such concerns DSM-5 includes a set of diagnostic criteria for adults and youth older than 6 years of age and a separate parallel set of criteria for children 6 years of age and younger. This "preschool" set of criteria reduces the number of symptoms required for diagnosis, provides examples of how the various symptoms of PTSD might present in this age group, and gives less emphasis to highly internalized and cognitively advanced symptoms. Also, in this "preschool" set of criteria symptoms are grouped into three (rather than four) clusters. The avoidance and cognitive/mood clusters are combined and only one symptom from this combined cluster is required for diagnosis. Although, developed for children 6 years and under, it has been suggested that using these criteria for older children may be appropriate (Danzi & La Greca, 2017).

In addition to the "preschool" diagnostic criteria for PTSD, the DSM-5 section on trauma- and stress-related disorder describes two other reactions of children 0–6 years of age—**Reactive Attachment Disorder (RAD)** and **Disinhibited Social Engagement Disorder (DSED)**. Both RAD and DSED are, in part, defined by the absence of adequate caregiving during childhood. Both these diagnoses are intended to apply only to children who should be developmentally ready and able to form appropriate selective attachments (Zeanah & Gleason, 2015). Thus, for both diagnoses, the child must have a developmental age of at least 9 months.

For both RAD and DSED it must be established that the child has experienced extremes of insufficient care. This level of social neglect is evidenced by one or more of the following:

- a persistent lack of having caregivers provide for basic needs such as affection, comfort, and stimulation,
- repeated changes of primary caregivers—thus limiting opportunities to form stable attachments,
- rearing in unusual situations (e.g., institutions with poor child–staff ratios) that severely limit opportunities to form attachments.

The two disorders are, thus, thought to share a common etiology, inadequate caregiving, but differ in how the child's difficulties are expressed.

The diagnosis of RAD describes children who display extremely underdeveloped attachments to their adult caregivers. A socially neglected child receiving this diagnosis displays persistent inhibited and withdrawn behavior toward adult caregivers. The child, when distressed, rarely seeks comfort and when comfort is offered the child rarely responds. In addition, the child displays a persistent social/emotional disturbance that is characterized by symptoms such as minimal social and emotional responsiveness, limited positive affect, and unexplained fearfulness, irritability, or sadness.

In contrast, a socially neglected child receiving a diagnosis of DSED displays socially disinhibited behaviors. A child receiving this diagnosis displays a pattern of culturally inappropriate, overly familiar behavior toward strangers. This child might show little or no reticence in approaching or interacting with unfamiliar adults, be overly familiar (verbally or physically) with unfamiliar adults, fail to check back with an adult caregiver when venturing away or when in unfamiliar settings, and/or be willing to go off with an unfamiliar adult with little or no hesitation.

Both RAD and DSED have been diagnosed in children who are currently or previously institutionalized. These disorders have also been noted in children who have not been institutionalized and not all children who have experienced institutionalized care exhibit signs of RAD or DSED. For children moved from institutions early enough and placed in foster care, symptoms of RAD have improved. For children with DSED, rotating caregivers and many different caregivers per infant (rather than fewer caregivers per infant) are associated with increased risk, regardless of other aspects of institutional care (Nader & Williams, 2019).

Description of Reactions to Traumatic Events

The reactions of young people to traumatic events may vary considerably (La Greca & Danzi, 2019). Fortunately, most youth are resilient. Following a traumatic event many youth experience posttraumatic stress symptoms (PTSS). Some of these young people, although not meeting diagnostic criteria for PTSD, still experience considerable distress and interference with functioning. Studies suggest that most youth who experience these subclinical levels of PTSS do recover. However, a significant number (20–30%) exhibit persistent symptoms and go on to meet the criteria for a diagnosis of PTSD.

In terms of their experiences, most youth become upset at reminders of the trauma, and they experience repetitive, intrusive thoughts about the event. Even children who experience mild levels of exposure to life-threatening disasters may have such thoughts. Preschool and school age children frequently reenact aspects of the disaster in drawings, stories, and play. Initially such behavior may be part of reexperiencing symptoms, but it may become a useful part of the recovery process as well. Saylor, Powell, and Swenson (1992), for example, report that after Hurricane Hugo occurred in South Carolina, children's play progressed from blowing houses down to acting out the role of roofers during rebuilding.

Young people may also exhibit increased frequency and intensity of specific fears directly related to or associated with the traumatic experience. Thus, adolescent British girls on a school trip who experienced the sinking of their cruise ship developed fears of swimming, of the dark, or of boats and other forms of transportation. These girls, however, did not show elevated levels of unrelated fears (Yule, Udwin, & Murdoch, 1990).

Separation difficulties and clingy, dependent behaviors are also common. These behaviors may be exhibited as reluctance to go to school or as a desire to sleep with parents. Other sleep problems, such as difficulty in getting to sleep, nightmares, and repeated dreams related to the traumatic event, are also common. A sense of vulnerability and loss of faith in the future have also been reported. In adolescents, this loss may interfere with planning for future education and careers; moreover, school performance is reported to suffer. Other commonly noted symptoms include depressed mood, loss of interest in previously enjoyed activities, irritability, anxiety, grief, and angry or aggressive outbursts. Guilt about surviving when others have died can also occur. Indeed, it is common for young people with PTSD to meet the criteria for additional and multiple diagnoses such as depression, anxiety, and substance use disorders (Bonanno et al., 2010; Kilpatrick et al., 2003; La Greca & Danzi, 2019).

Epidemiology

Natural disasters, terrorism, and accidents are catastrophic events that are unpredictable in nature, making it difficult to determine the number of children and adolescents who will be exposed to traumatic events each year (Fletcher, 2003). Estimates likely vary

A number of factors influence children's reactions to a traumatic event, including aspects of the experience and the reactions of their parents and other adults. (VStock/Alamy Stock Photo)

as a function of the type, severity, and duration of potentially traumatic experiences that are considered. Also, youth who are not directly exposed to a traumatic event may be exposed to the event through interactions with family and peers, television, the internet, and social media (Comer, DeSerisy, & Greif Green, 2016b). It seems likely that an appreciable number of young people experience a traumatic event. Estimates suggest that between one-quarter and two-thirds of children and adolescents are exposed to trauma during their youth (Costello et al., 2002; Nader & Williams, 2019).

A review of studies conducted in the 1990s (Fletcher, 2003) suggests that about one-third of youth exposed to traumatic events are diagnosed with PTSD—a rate slightly higher than for traumatized adults—and some findings suggest that half or more of exposed youth experience PTSD (De Bellis & Van Dillen, 2005). Most studies find a higher incidence of PTSD among girls.

The relationship between age and the development of PTSD is unclear. This is likely due, in part, to the reliance on parental reports because of young children's difficulty in reporting on their emotions and thoughts. Parental reports are thought to likely underestimate children's posttraumatic stress symptoms (Alisic et al., 2014; La Greca & Danzi, 2019).

On average, the incidence of particular PTSD symptoms appears to be above 20%. The PTSD cluster of symptoms (reexperiencing, avoidance, alterations in cognition/mood, and arousal) has been reported in youth from a variety of different cultures (Perrin, Smith, & Yule, 2000). The most frequently occurring category of symptom is probably reexperiencing (De Bellis & Van Dillen, 2005).

Not all children and adolescents experience the same pattern or intensity of symptoms, and not all youth who experience traumas meet the criteria for PTSD. The amount of time that symptoms persist may vary, and problems may fluctuate over time. A number of factors seem to influence youths' initial reactions and the duration and severity of symptoms (La Greca & Danzi, 2019; Trickey et al., 2012; Udwin et al., 2000).

The nature of the traumatic event may influence reactions. For example, stressors can be grouped into two categories: (1) acute, nonabusive stressors—nonabusive traumatic events that occur only once, such as floods or accidents, and (2) chronic or abusive stressors—ongoing stressors such as war or physical or sexual abuse (Fletcher, 2003). Some symptoms of PTSD appear likely to occur regardless of the type of traumatic event (e.g., trauma-related fears, difficulty sleeping). However, other symptoms vary depending on the type of trauma experienced. Also, while young people experiencing either kind of trauma appear equally likely to receive the diagnosis of PTSD, other diagnoses that they are likely to receive may vary. These differences are illustrated in Table 7.1. It may seem surprising that some symptoms or problems occur more often among young people exposed to acute, nonabusive trauma than among those exposed to chronic or abusive trauma. One possible explanation may be that children or adolescents exposed to chronic stressors come to some kind of accommodation over time with their traumas (Fletcher, 2003).

The degree of exposure to the traumatic event also appears to be an important influence. Pynoos and his colleagues (1987) studied 159 California schoolchildren who were exposed to a sniper attack on their school in which one child and a passerby were killed and 13 other children were injured. Children who were trapped on the playground showed much greater effects than those who had left the immediate vicinity of the shooting or who were not in school that day. At a 14-month follow-up among the most severely exposed children, 74% still reported moderate to severe PTSD symptoms, whereas 81% of the nonexposed children reported no PTSD (Nader et al., 1991). Although level of exposure to this life-threatening trauma was an important factor, reactions

Table 7.1 Rates of PTSD Symptoms and Associated Symptoms/Diagnoses in Response to Acute, Nonabusive Stressors and Chronic or Abusive Stressors

	Type of Stressor	
	Acute-Nonabusive	**Chronic or Abusive**
DSM Symptom Cluster		
Reexperiencing	92%	86%
Avoidance/cognitive-mood alterations	30%	54%
Overarousal	55%	71%
Associated Symptoms/Diagnoses		
PTSD	36%	36%
Generalized anxiety	55%	26%
Separation anxiety	45%	35%
Panic	35%	6%
Depression	10%	28%
ADHD	22%	11%

Source: Adapted from Fletcher, 2003.

did occur among children who did not experience a high degree of exposure. Less exposed children who had a subjective experience of threat and greater knowledge of the schoolmate who was killed were more likely to have PTSD symptoms.

A number of other individual and contextual factors may contribute to a youth's risk for developing PTSD (La Greca & Danzi, 2019). Individual differences that existed prior to a traumatic event (e.g., anxiety level, ethnicity) are also likely to influence the youth's reaction. So, for example, a child or adolescent's prior level of anxiety or depression may influence her or his reaction to the traumatic event. A young person's existing coping strategies are also a likely influence on reactions to traumatic events. Negative coping strategies (e.g., poor emotion-regulation skills, blaming others) are particularly likely to contribute to poor reactions to trauma. Multiple genes and their interactions likely play a role in reactions to traumatic events. Understanding of particular genetic influences on reactions to trauma is largely based on research with adults and additional research with youth samples is needed. Finally, aspects of the young person's post-trauma environment can have an appreciable influence on the child or adolescent's reactions. The availability and quality of the youth's social support systems are important influences on initial reactions, duration of symptoms, and recovery. Relatedly, parental and family functioning are important factors in the young person's post-trauma reactions. The reactions of parents and other family members to the traumatic event likely influence the youth's reaction. Parental depression, family conflict, and poor family functioning have all been associated with poorer child and adolescent reactions to trauma.

Developmental Course and Prognosis

In general, symptoms of PTSD decline over time, but substantial numbers of children and adolescents continue to report difficulties. For example, La Greca and her colleagues (1996) examined third- through fifth-grade children during the school year after Hurricane Andrew occurred in Florida. Symptoms of avoidance and alterations of cognition/mood were present in about 49% of the children at three months but only about 24% of the children at ten months. Similarly, the number of children with symptoms of arousal decreased from 67% to about 49% in the same time period. However, substantial numbers of children continued to report reexperiencing symptoms—approximately 90% at three months and 78% at ten months.

Children's initial attempts at coping may also affect the course of their reactions. Children who tend to use negative coping strategies (e.g., blaming others, screaming) may be more likely to experience persistent symptoms (La Greca et al., 1996). The reactions of children and adolescents to traumatic events are also related to the reactions of their parents and others in their environment. If the parents themselves suffer severe posttraumatic stress or for some other reason are unable to provide an atmosphere of support and communication, their children's reactions are likely to be more severe.

Larger social and cultural issues may also need to be considered in examining the impact of trauma on youth. For example, Taylor and colleagues (2018) examined the impact of exposure to community violence in a sample of low-income urban fifth- to ninth-grade youth. The youth were followed across a

ACCENT Reactions to Mass Violence

Unfortunately, incidents of mass violence occur all too frequently. What is the impact of such events on children and adolescents?

Reactions to mass violence seem similar in many ways to reactions to other traumatic events, but there may be unique aspects (Fremont, 2004). Terrorism presents an unpredictable threat and there is extensive media coverage. There is also a profound effect on the adults and communities that typically provide support for young people. Thus, there may be considerable impact on the young person's development (e.g., emotion regulation, coping, and social and political attitudes) as well as on longer-term post-disaster life disruptions (e.g., lost jobs, restricted travel) and economic hardship (Comer et al., 2010; Eisenberg & Silver, 2011).

On September 11, 2001, terrorists attacked New York City and Washington DC. Many people suffered the loss of a loved one in the attack or in rescue efforts and loss and health concerns continued well past the actual events. Nearly 3,000 persons were known to be or presumed dead as an immediate result of the attacks. Survivors, relatives, and many more were left with vivid images of planes crashing into buildings, buildings burning and falling, loss of human life, and terror and sadness on the faces of those involved. The impact on families was appreciable. In New York City, many children and adolescents knew someone who was killed, knew a teacher or coach who lost someone, or had a parent who was among the responders to the attacks. Often many hours passed between the attacks and the reunion of parent and child (Hoven et al., 2009; Stuber et al., 2002).

Most youth learned about the attacks indirectly. They may have watched the events on television in their classrooms, been informed by others or through subsequent media coverage. Indeed, widespread and frequent media coverage brought the trauma into many homes around the country (Noppe, Noppe, & Bartell, 2006; Saylor et al., 2003). Many youth, even children physically distant from the attacks, may have experienced stress-related symptoms and worry about safety (Hoven et al., 2009; Schuster et al., 2001; Whalen et al., 2004). Time watching TV significantly correlated with the number of reported stress symptoms (Otto et al., 2007; Saylor et al., 2003; Schuster et al., 2001).

Evidence suggests that for most young people, there was a modest effect of the attacks in terms of psychological symptoms. Among the youth who were more likely to experience significant PTSS were those who suffered a loss, who had a family member who was directly exposed but survived, or whose post-attack travel around the city was restricted (Comer et al., 2010, 2016a; Eisenberg & Silver, 2011). For some of these young people, increased risk for adjustment difficulties persisted for an appreciable number of years (Gargano, Welch, & Stillman, 2017; Gargano et al., 2018; Mullet et al., 2008).

Parents' trauma-related experiences play a role in their children's reactions. Parents' reactions to the events and their parenting behaviors likely interact with characteristics of the child (e.g., temperament), and her or his environment (e.g., school) to affect the risk of PTSS (Mijanovich & Weitzman, 2010; Wilson et al., 2010). In addition, disruptions in the parents' lives may impact their children's adjustment. For example, children who had a family member who lost a job due to the World Trade Center attacks were approximately twice as likely to suffer from PTSD and anxiety disorders as peers whose family members' jobs were not affected (Comer et al., 2010). Additionally, a parent being at risk due to the attack situation can impact the child's risk. For example, following the 2013 Boston Marathon bombing, there was a six times greater presence of signs of PTSD and other difficulties among children and adolescents who had a relative in law enforcement who participated in the hunt for the bombing suspects. This was the case even when controlling for the young person's own exposure to the bombing and manhunt (Comer et al., 2014, 2016b).

After the attacks of September 11, an extensive screening (CATS Consortium, 2007) in New York City indicated that as many as 75,000 young people experienced PTSS, and many reported other symptoms (e.g., depression, anxiety disorder symptoms). However, less than one-third of these youth sought help (Hoagwood et al., 2007). In the wake of these and other events of mass violence, attention continues to be focused on investigating and understanding the effects of such trauma and on developing successful and accessible interventions (Dorsey et al., 2017; Eisenberg & Silver, 2011; La Greca & Danzi, 2019).

The exposure of youth to school shootings and other instances of mass violence is a continuing concern. (MediaNews Group/Los Angeles Daily News via Getty Images/Contributor/Getty Images)

three-year period. Youth and parent reports of externalizing and internalizing symptoms were assessed. As illustrated in Figure 7.1, exposure to community violence was more strongly associated with externalizing symptoms than with internalizing symptoms. Youth experienced a decline in both types of symptoms over time. The decrease over time for *youth-reported* symptoms (particularly externalizing symptoms) was greater for those youth with higher levels of exposure to community violence. The authors suggest that desensitization to the emotional impact of community violence may occur over time, resulting in less distress, and that youth report may be more valid than parent report in the context of urban poverty.

Treatment of PTSD

A variety of interventions have been attempted to help youth with PTSD or subclinical levels of PTSS. Systematic reviews of the literature reveal that considerable evidence regarding psychosocial treatments has been generated in recent years. Evidence is strongest for cognitive-behavior therapy (CBT) approaches and especially CBT with parent involvement (Dorsey et al., 2017; La Greca & Danzi, 2019; Mavranezouli et al., 2020). Trauma-focused CBT, an example of this approach to treatment, has received considerable research attention and support (Cohen, Mannarino & Deblinger, 2017a, 2017b).

Trauma-focused cognitive-behavioral therapy (TF-CBT) is a multi-component treatment program delivered through a combination of parallel individual/separate sessions for child and parent and joint child–parent or family sessions. The program addresses trauma-related symptoms in youth 3–18 years of age and adaptations are made depending on the developmental level of the child. TF-CBT typically includes between 8 and 20 sessions. In cases of more complex trauma, treatment may extend between 16 and 25 sessions. The acronym PRACTICE describes the components of the TF-CBT model (J. A. Cohen et al., 2017a, 2017b).

Psychoeducation provides information to children and parents about the nature of traumatic experiences and common reactions of children and parents. Such information helps children and parents normalize their experiences and can, thus, be reassuring.

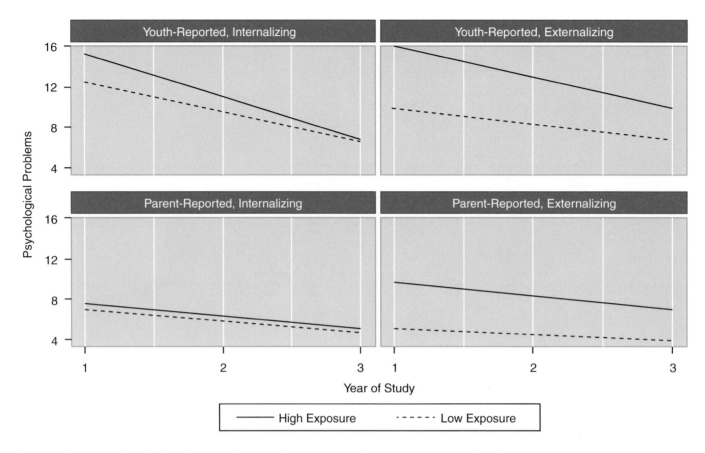

Figure 7.1 Trajectories of psychological problems for low and high community violence exposure groups. (From Taylor et al., 2018)

Parenting skills recognizes the central role that parents play in their children's reactions to and recovery from trauma. This component is itself multifaceted, promotes positive parenting, and provides parents with ability to apply interventions parallel to those that the children are receiving in treatment sessions.

Relaxation skills are intended to help reduce some of the trauma-related physiological dysregulation experienced following a trauma. These skills also can aid in distracting children and parents from upsetting thoughts or reminders of the trauma and encourage participants to learn how to self-soothe and focus on enjoyable activities.

Affective modulation involves a variety of interpersonal and cognitive techniques to encourage expression and management of feelings. Children learn to express and manage their feelings. Parents also are encouraged to express their feelings and also learn to assist their children with appropriate affective regulation skills.

Cognitive coping helps children and parents to understand the connections among thoughts, feelings, and behaviors. Through the use of examples from daily life the therapist helps participants learn to examine patterns of negative thinking and to change dysfunctional thoughts.

Trauma narration and cognitive processing provide an interactive therapeutic experience in which the therapist helps children to develop and process a detailed narrative of their traumatic experiences. During this phase the child typically develops a concrete product (e.g., a book) that is an ongoing part of the therapeutic process.

In vivo mastery of trauma reminders involves exposure to increasingly distressing reminders of the traumatic experiences. The therapist, child, and parent collaborate to assist the child in tolerating successive steps in this in vivo desensitization process and the child is encouraged to use skills acquired during the earlier steps described above. This desensitization process is employed only if the exposure situation is safe.

Conjoint child–parent sessions become an integral part of the TF-CBT program after the child has completed trauma narration and cognitive processing. It is expected that, at this point, children and parents are prepared to effectively communicate about the trauma and this is a key time in transferring responsibility for change from therapist to parent.

Enhancing safety and future developmental trajectory is a component of the treatment that facilitates planning for the child's safety and discussing prevention of future traumatic events.

Child Maltreatment

Child maltreatment is one form of trauma that has been viewed within the framework of PTSD. Indeed, many young people who experience maltreatment exhibit meaningful symptoms or meet the diagnostic criteria for PTSD (De Bellis & Van Dillen, 2005). However, maltreatment of youth can be viewed as a failure of the family and larger social system to protect the child and/or provide positive aspects of parenting. Such experiences might be expected to adversely affect a wide array of developmental processes and increase the risk for a variety of problematic outcomes.

Although child maltreatment has probably existed since the beginning of civilization, recent concern is usually dated to the early 1960s (Cicchetti & Olsen, 1990). Especially influential was an article by pediatrician C. Henry Kempe and his colleagues, in which the term *battered child syndrome* was coined (Kempe et al., 1962). Their efforts were stimulated by alarm at the large number of children at pediatric clinics with non-accidental injuries. By 1970, all 50 states had mandated the reporting of child abuse. In 1974, the U.S. Congress passed the Child Abuse Prevention and Treatment Act (Public Law 93–247) to give national focus to the problem and to prescribe actions that the states should take. Since the late 1970s, the problem has become both a major public concern and the focus of increased research and professional attention (Cicchetti & Manly, 2001).

Unfortunately, the magnitude of the problem is significant. According to a report issued by the U.S. Department of Health and Human Services (DHSS) (2019), in 2017 there were about 674,000 children who were victims of abuse and neglect. In addition, in that year an estimated 1,720 children died due to abuse or neglect.

Defining Maltreatment

When most people hear the widely used term **child abuse**, they assume that it refers to physical assault and serious injury. However, the general legal definition of child abuse or **child maltreatment** that has evolved over several decades includes both the commission of injuries and acts of omission, that is, failure to care for and protect (National Institute of Mental Health, 1977). The Keeping Children and Families Safe Act of 2003 defines child abuse and **neglect** as, at a minimum:

> *any recent act or failure to act on the part of a parent or caretaker which results in death, serious physical or emotional harm, sexual abuse or exploitation, or an act or failure to act which presents an imminent risk of serious harm.*
>
> *DHHS, 2010*

The term **maltreatment** thus refers to both abuse and neglect—acts of commission and omission. Four major types of maltreatment are typically described in the literature: physical abuse, sexual abuse, neglect, and emotional abuse (psychological maltreatment). The definitions provided by the Centers for Disease Control and Prevention (Leeb et al., 2008) are presented in Table 7.2.

Table 7.2 Definitions of the Major Forms of Maltreatment

Physical abuse: The intentional use of physical force against a child that results in, or has the potential to result in, physical injury. Examples include hitting, kicking, punching, beating, stabbing, biting, pushing, shoving, throwing, pulling, dragging, dropping, shaking, strangling/choking, smothering, burning, scalding, and poisoning. Physical abuse can result from discipline or physical punishment.

Sexual abuse: Any completed or attempted (non-completed) sexual act, sexual contact with, or exploitation (i.e., noncontact sexual interaction) of a child by a caregiver. Sexual acts can be performed by the caregiver on the child or by the child on the caregiver. A caregiver can also force or coerce a child to commit a sexual act on another individual (child or adult). Noncontact sexual abuse does not include physical contact of a sexual nature between the caregiver and the child. Noncontact sexual abuse can include the following: acts which expose a child to sexual activity (e.g., pornography), filming of a child in a sexual manner, sexual harassment of a child, prostitution of a child or sexual trafficking.

Psychological abuse: Intentional caregiver behavior (i.e., act of commission) that conveys to a child that he/she is worthless, flawed, unloved, unwanted, endangered, or valued only in meeting another's needs. Psychologically abusive behaviors may include blaming, belittling, degrading, intimidating, terrorizing, isolating, restraining, confining, corrupting, exploiting, spurning, or otherwise behaving in a manner that is harmful, potentially harmful, or insensitive to the child's developmental needs, or can potentially damage the child psychologically or emotionally.

Neglect: Failure by a caregiver to meet a child's basic physical, emotional, medical/dental, or educational needs—or combination thereof. *Physical neglect*: the caregiver fails to provide adequate nutrition, hygiene, or shelter; or, the caregiver fails to provide clothing that is adequately clean, an appropriate size, or adequate for the weather. *Emotional neglect*: the caregiver ignores the child, or denies emotional responsiveness or adequate access to mental health care (e.g., caregiver does not respond to infant cries or older child's attempt to interact). *Medical/dental neglect*: the caregiver fails to provide adequate access to medical, vision, or dental care for the child. *Educational neglect*: the caregiver fails to provide access to adequate education.

Source: Adapted from Leeb et al., 2008.

It is probably easier to detect **physical abuse** than other forms of maltreatment. However, the nature and severity of injuries can vary considerably. In some cases, injuries may be intentionally inflicted, but more often they result from extreme forms of discipline and physical punishment. Moreover, whereas we can define physical abuse as a separate category from other forms of maltreatment, children likely experience it in conjunction with emotional abuse and/or neglect.

In general, **sexual abuse** refers to sexual experiences that occur between youth and older persons or to the sexual exploitation of the young, such as in pornographic film. Sexual abuse of girls is more common than that of boys, and cases of sexual abuse can vary with factors such as age of onset of abuse, the identity of the primary perpetrator, the number of perpetrators, the severity of the abuse, and whether the abuse was accompanied by physical violence or threats (Finkelhor, 1994; Wolfe, 2006).

The definition of **psychological (or emotional) maltreatment** is probably the most difficult to agree on and the most controversial. Different standards for appropriate parenting practices and for desired outcomes are particularly at issue when **psychological/emotional maltreatment** is considered (Azar, Ferraro, & Breton, 1998; McGee & Wolfe, 1991). Emotional maltreatment is defined as persistent and extreme actions or neglect that thwart the child's basic emotional needs and that are damaging to the behavioral, cognitive, affective, or physical functioning of the child (Brassard, Hart, & Hardy, 2000; Cicchetti & Lynch, 1995). Emotional maltreatment can be seen both as a distinct entity and as part of all abuse and neglect (Binggeli, Hart, & Brassard, 2001).

Neglect, the most common form of maltreatment, refers to failure to provide for a child's basic needs. Defining a parent–child relationship as neglectful, especially in less extreme instances, clearly requires sensitivity to family and cultural values and to considerations of economic and social conditions.

Neglect refers to failure to provide for a child's basic needs and is the most common form of maltreatment. (Twin Design/Shutterstock.com)

Neglect can involve a failure to meet physical needs—such as the need for health care or physical shelter—or it can involve abandonment or inadequate supervision. Neglect may also take the form of not meeting the young person's educational needs by allowing repeated truancy or not attending to special education needs. The child's emotional needs may also be neglected. Emotional neglect is difficult to define, however. It may include failure to ensure adequate psychological care or failure to protect the youth from witnessing harmful situations involving violence or substance use.

Prevalence

Neglect is the most common form of maltreatment. Figure 7.2 shows the percentage of types of maltreatment in the United States in 2017 (DHHS, 2019). The 7.1% of "other" types of maltreatment indicated in Figure 7.2 includes events such as threatened abuse or neglect, drug/alcohol addiction, and lack of supervision.

In 2017, about 14% of U.S. child maltreatment victims experienced multiple forms of maltreatment. The most common combination was neglect and physical abuse.

Factors Contributing to Maltreatment

Conceptualizations of maltreatment recognize the influence of complex, multiple, and interrelated risk factors (Assink et al., 2019; Cicchetti & Toth, 2016; Doidge et al., 2017; Margolin et al., 2009; van IJzendoorn et al., 2020; Wolfe & Kelly, 2019). The

following general factors are often recognized as contributing to maltreatment:

- Characteristics of the abuser
- Characteristics of the child
- Parenting practices
- Parent–child interactional processes
- Social/cultural influences

The last category includes both the immediate social environment (e.g., family, employment, extended family, social networks) and the larger social/cultural context (e.g., poverty, societal tolerance for violence). It is recognized that maltreatment most often occurs in the context of family, social, and community deprivation and exposure to multiple sources of stress. Many influences have been examined for their contribution to maltreatment. Here we highlight only some of the findings.

Drawing on information for the 2017 calendar year, characteristics of perpetrators of maltreatment can be described (DHHS, 2019). Children may be maltreated by more than one perpetrator. Parents were the perpetrators of maltreatment in 81.6% of cases. Sixty-nine percent of perpetrators are mothers either acting alone (40.8%) or in combination with a father (28.2%). More than 13% of victims are maltreated by a non-parent. The largest categories on non-parent perpetrators are a relative (4.7%) or parent partner (2.9%). Maltreatment by parents may be understood, at least in part, within the context of parenting behavior (Alink, Cyr, & Madigan, 2019; Cicchetti & Toth, 2016; Savage et al., 2019). Maltreating parents exhibit a variety of problems in parenting and parent–child interactions. For example,

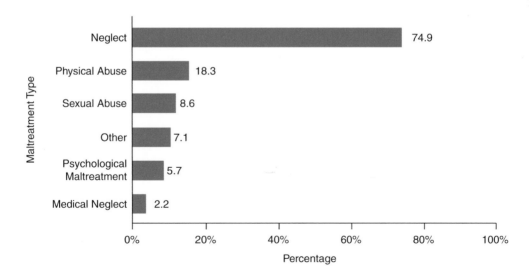

Figure 7.2 Child maltreatment cases 2017 by type. Note more than one type of maltreatment may be substantiated per child. Therefore, percentages total more than 100%. (From U.S. Department of Health and Human Services, Child Maltreatment 2017 Washington, DC, 2019; reprinted with permission)

they tend to engage in fewer positive interactions with their child and to use more coercive and negative discipline techniques. These parents also may exhibit negative attitudes toward parenting, limited child-rearing knowledge, and less sensitivity to and inappropriate expectations regarding developmentally appropriate infant and child behavior.

Several other characteristics of abusive parents have been noted, including difficulty in managing stress, difficulty in inhibiting their own impulsive behavior, social isolation from family and friends, more emotional symptoms and mood changes, and more physical health problems. High rates of substance abuse and partner violence in the home have also been reported (DHHS, 2019; Wekerle et al., 2007).

Maltreating parents are more likely to have experienced maltreatment as a child (Berlin, Appleyard, & Dodge, 2011; Kaufman & Zigler, 1987; Madigan et al., 2019; Widom, Czaja, & DuMont, 2015). However, it is generally agreed that the majority of maltreated children do not become maltreating parents. What, then, is the link between generations? This pathway is clearly the result of a complex interaction of risk and protective factors that include characteristics of the individual, family, and social environment. For example, Enlow, Englund, and Egeland (2018) found that mothers who themselves had been maltreated were more likely to have maltreated their own children during early childhood. These mothers also experienced greater stress and diminished social support. Thus, frequent and intense stress and poor quality and low levels of social support may be factors that help predict intergenerational maltreatment effects. In addition, by age 7, the children of these maltreated mothers also were at increased risk for significant emotional and behavioral problems. The influences of early childhood maltreatment, maternal stress exposure, and diminished maternal social support appear to be at least part of the pathway between maternal childhood maltreatment and emotional and behavioral problems in their offspring.

In addition to looking at characteristics of abusing parents, professionals have asked whether certain attributes of children increase the likelihood of their being the target of maltreatment. The likelihood of being a victim of maltreatment is similar for boys and girls. Youngest children are the most vulnerable. From birth to 1 year of age appears to be a period of high risk for maltreatment and more than one-quarter of victims are younger than 3 years of age (DHHS, 2019). In addition, research suggests that children and adolescents with disabilities (e.g., neurodevelopmental disorders, intellectual disability, physical disability, visual or hearing impairment) are at high risk (Jones et al., 2012; Maclean et al., 2017; McDonnell et al., 2019; Ohlsson et al., 2018).

Maltreatment also is influenced by the larger social context. A relationship between socioeconomic disadvantage and maltreatment, and particularly neglect, has been described (English, 1998). It is important to recognize, however, that the majority of families who experience disadvantage do not maltreat

their offspring. Although it is hard to isolate the specific causal factors, reduced resources, stress, and other problems associated with socioeconomic disadvantage put the family and child at increased risk. The relationship of poverty and maltreatment may be due to other factors as well (Azar & Bober, 1999). For example, poor interpersonal and problem-solving skills in parents may lead both to economic disadvantage and to problematic parenting, including maltreatment. Cultural factors, too, may play a role. Korbin and colleagues (1998), for instance, found that impoverishment had a lesser impact on maltreatment in African American neighborhoods than in European American neighborhoods. This difference seemed to be mediated by the perceived quality of social connectedness found in the two kinds of neighborhoods. A sense of community, resources, and extended family may serve as protective factors against maltreatment.

Consequences of Maltreatment

Maltreated children are at risk for a variety of adverse outcomes. Maltreated children can experience health-related difficulties such as physical injury and sexually transmitted diseases. Fatalities also are a particularly disturbing consequence of maltreatment for some children. During the 2017 calendar year an estimated 1,720 children died in the U.S. from abuse and neglect. This is a rate of 2.32 per 100,000 children in the population and an increase of 11% from the 2013 national estimate. Although the rate of fatalities is relatively low, this is an issue of grave concern. Approximately half of child fatalities due to abuse and neglect are younger than 1 year old and this is nearly four times the fatality rate for 1-year-olds in the general population (DHHS, 2019).

Some evidence suggests that early maltreatment may be associated with neurobiological outcomes, such as alterations of gene expression, dysregulation of the stress regulating system (the limbic-hypothalamic-pituitary-adrenocortical system), alteration of neurotransmitter systems, dysregulation of immune function, and alteration of brain structure and function (Gordis et al., 2010; Jaffee, 2017a; Margolin & Gordis, 2000; Wolfe & Kelly, 2019). The degree to which these neurobiological outcomes occur seems to be related to a number of factors (De Bellis, 2001; Jaffee, 2017a; McCrory, De Brito, & Viding, 2010), including individual genetic makeup, age of onset of abuse, duration of abuse, and the presence of trauma-related psychological symptoms. There may also be gender differences in adverse brain development outcomes, with both boys and girls being affected but males being more vulnerable.

The effects of maltreatment are a telling example of how adverse environments may alter basic biological functioning. The neurobiological outcomes may, in turn, contribute to cognitive and psychosocial difficulties. De Bellis's (2001) developmental traumatology model describes how neurobiological outcomes may underlie the variety of negative outcomes associated with abuse and neglect. In this model, maltreatment and its effects

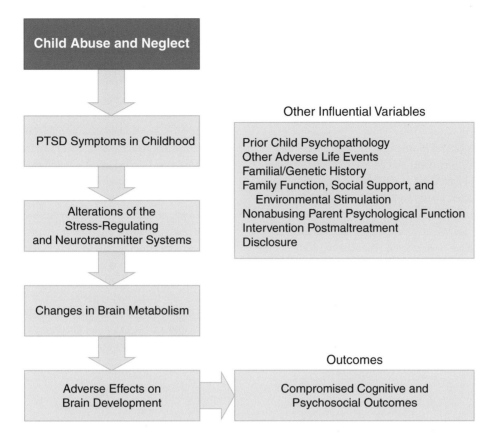

Figure 7.3 A developmental traumatology model of biological stress systems and brain maturation in maltreated children. In this model compromised neurocognitive and psychosocial outcomes are understood to be a result of adverse brain development. (Adapted from De Bellis, 2001. Copyright 2001 by Cambridge University Press; reprinted with permission)

are viewed within a broad ecological-transactional model that recognizes the effects of many other variables (Figure 7.3). For instance, subsequent supportive caregiving environments may positively modify the neurobiological changes resulting from the stress of maltreatment.

Given the neurobiological outcomes and the failure of parenting involved, it is unsurprising that maltreatment can result in a variety of undesirable outcomes. Outcomes of maltreatment are likely to be affected by many factors including the type and severity of maltreatment, developmental timing, aspects of the child's genotype, and characteristics of the young person's family, peer relationships, and neighborhood (Haskett et al., 2006; Jaffee, 2017a; Jaffee et al., 2007; Manly et al., 2001). These various factors likely interact in complex ways to influence the outcome of maltreatment.

Children can manifest health-related difficulties, appreciable impairments in all early developmental domains, and serious symptoms for a variety of psychological disorders (English, 1998; Jaffee, 2017b; Kearney et al., 2010; Thornberry et al., 2010).

For example, research suggests that physical abuse places children at risk for the development of externalizing and antisocial

behavior problems (Carliner et al., 2017; Cullerton-Sen et al., 2008; Jaffee et al., 2004; Lansford et al., 2002; Lau & Weisz, 2003). Physically maltreated youth often display high levels of hostility and aggression and have frequent angry outbursts. These young people have higher than expected rates of conduct and oppositional defiant disorders. Various mechanisms probably account for the association between maltreatment and conduct problems. As might be expected, persistent maltreatment may be particularly detrimental. For example, Bolger and Patterson (2001) found that chronically maltreated children were more likely to be aggressive and rejected by peers. A suggested mechanism for this maltreatment–aggression–peer rejection pattern is the coercive interactional style the child has learned in the family of origin. Physical maltreatment may also contribute to learning of problematic cognitive/social information-processing patterns. Indeed, the relationship between early maltreatment and later aggressive behavior is, in part, mediated by biased social information-processing patterns such as interpreting ambiguous social cues as threatening and responding to them with aggression (Cullerton-Sen et al., 2008; Dodge, 2003). Thus, physical maltreatment may, in part, contribute to conduct problems through the development of problematic peer relationships and cognitive processes.

However, not all youth who are maltreated exhibit aggression and conduct problems. There may be a variety of factors that influence the relationship between maltreatment and outcomes (Margolin & Gordis, 2004). Individual differences, for example, may moderate outcomes.

Gordis and colleagues (2010) examined individual differences in sympathetic nervous system (SNS) and parasympathetic nervous system (PNS) activity as moderators of the link between childhood maltreatment and adolescent aggression. Both SNS and PNS functioning have been linked to aggression (see pp. 213–214) and various mechanisms for the association between SNS and PNS activity and aggression have been offered (Beauchaine, 2001; Raine, 2005). Level of aggression was examined in adolescents who had experienced prior maltreatment and in a non-maltreated comparison group. Overall, levels of aggression were higher for the maltreated youth. However, individual differences moderated this relationship. As illustrated in Figure 7.4a, boys with a high baseline level of a measure of heart rate across the respiratory

cycle (RSA—respiratory sinus arrhythmia)—an indicator of PNS functioning—exhibited levels of aggression comparable to comparison boys. In contrast, maltreated boys with low baseline RSA exhibited higher levels of aggression. This protective effect of high baseline RSA also was observed for maltreated girls, but with one further qualification. The protective effect was found, but only for those girls who, in addition to high RSA levels, also exhibited low levels of skin conductance (SCL) reactivity—an indicator of SNS functioning (see Figures 7.4 b and c). This suggests that for girls the moderating effect of PNS differences was further moderated by SNS differences.

A number of studies have also indicated that this maltreatment/antisocial behavior relationship may be moderated by certain genotypes. For example, the monoamine oxidase A (MAOA) gene is involved in the breakdown of the neurotransmitters serotonin, epinephrine, norepinephrine, and dopamine. Boys who had experienced maltreatment and had a low-activity variant of the MAOA gene were found to be at increased risk for childhood conduct and adult antisocial problems. However, boys who had been maltreated and carried the high activity

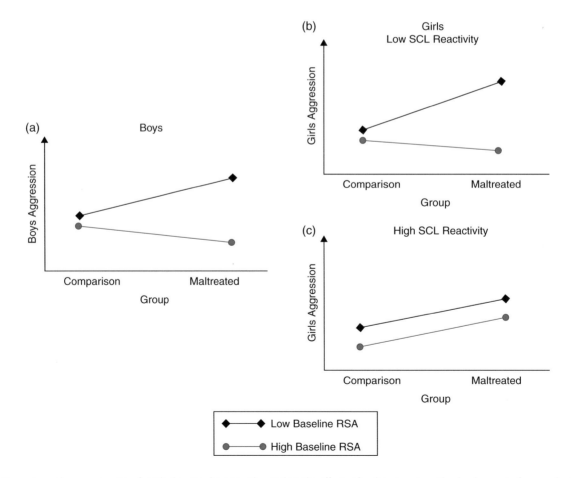

Figure 7.4 How autonomic nervous system functioning may be protective against the effects of maltreatment on the development of aggressive behaviors in boys and girls. (Adapted from Gordis et al., 2010)

variant of the MAOA gene were not at elevated risk for these externalizing outcomes (Byrd & Manuck, 2014; Jaffee, 2017a).

The impact of maltreatment may also be evident at different developmental stages from infancy through adolescence and into adulthood (Shaffer, Yates, & Egeland, 2009; Springer et al., 2007; Wolfe & Kelly, 2019). Although this is certainly a disheartening picture, it should be acknowledged that some maltreated children develop as competent individuals and that youth can be resilient even in the face of maltreatment (Cicchetti, 2010b; Haskett et al., 2006; Jaffee, 2017a).

In general, then, the impact of maltreatment is best viewed as disrupting basic developmental processes. The social and emotional support necessary for children's successful adaptations is diminished, affecting areas such as attachment, cognitive functioning, self-concept, social relationships, and emotional regulation (Azar & Bober, 1999; Haskett et al., 2006; Wolfe & Kelly, 2019). Furthermore, these young people may have fewer opportunities for positive experiences that might reduce the risk associated with maltreatment (Azar & Wolfe, 2006; Haskett et al., 2006; Salzinger et al., 2001; Toth et al., 2011).

Interventions for Maltreatment

Given the combination of factors that causes maltreatment, effective prevention and intervention need to address many contexts—individual, familial, community, cultural, and societal—and thus include multiple components. A variety of interventions have been attempted to help youth who have experienced maltreatment. The treatment research described earlier in our discussion of interventions for PTSD included youth who had experienced a variety of traumatic experiences including maltreatment. Reviews of this literature indicate that, with regard to treating youth exposed to maltreatment, evidence is strongest for CBT approaches, especially CBT with parent involvement (Dorsey et al., 2017; La Greca & Danzi, 2019) and for trauma-focused cognitive-behavioral therapy (TF-CBT) in particular (J. A. Cohen et al., 2017a, 2017b). The TF-CBT approach and program were described earlier. With TF-CBT and other cognitive-behavioral interventions, the treatment is adapted to the particular trauma experienced by the young person—in this case maltreatment and the particular nature of the youth's maltreatment experiences.

A focus on prevention has become an emphasis of professionals concerned about child maltreatment. As described above, research is ongoing to identify multiple risk factors. Thus, maltreatment, more so than most other traumatic experiences, is viewed as a potentially preventable experience. Progress has been made in identifying effective programs (Damashek et al., 2018). There are a number of promising programs. Here we briefly highlight some of the programs for which research evidence is strongest.

The Nurse-Family Partnership (NFP) and Safe Environment for Every Kid (SEEK) are programs that involve primary health care professionals. NFP is a program in which registered nurses, through home visits, provide education regarding child health and safety to low-income mothers (Olds et al., 2013). Mothers are enrolled in early pregnancy and can continue in the program until their child is 2 years old. Home visits are tailored to individual needs and address multiple domains such as personal health, child development, available services, and the social support of family and friends. The SEEK program is designed to take place in a pediatric primary care setting and provides services to at-risk families with children ages 0–5 (Dubowitz, 2014). Health care professionals are trained to identify and help families with major risk factors for child maltreatment. These providers help to educate parents, provide referrals to community resources, and work to engage parents in services.

The Incredible Years (IY) is a behavioral intervention originally designed to reduce behavior problems in young children (Webster-Stratton & Reid, 2017). We will describe the program further in the chapter on conduct problems (Chapter 9). The IY program is delivered through group sessions and includes curriculum for parents, teachers, and children. The intervention addresses domains such as child management skills, child–parent relationships, emotion regulation, and facilitating social support. The IY intervention has proven effective in addressing problems and skills relevant to the risk for child maltreatment and has been shown to be effective with populations likely to be at risk for child maltreatment (Domashek et al., 2018). As we gain more precise understanding of maltreatment, we are better able to shape preventive interventions that are most effective and that fit the specific needs of youth and families (van IJzendoorn et al., 2020).

Looking Back

Reactions to Traumatic Events

- Trauma is usually defined as an event outside of everyday experience that would be distressing to almost anyone.

- The DSM-5 grouping of trauma- and stressor-related disorders includes the diagnoses of Posttraumatic Stress Disorder, Acute Stress Disorder, Reactive Attachment Disorder, and Disinhibited Social Engagement Disorder.

- The diagnosis of Posttraumatic Stress Disorder requires reexperiencing of a traumatic event, avoidance of stimuli associated with the trauma, and symptoms of increased arousal.
- The diagnosis of Acute Stress Disorder may be given during the first month following the trauma. In general, symptoms decline over time, but substantial numbers of youth continue to report symptoms a long time after the trauma.
- There may be age-related differences in reactions to trauma. DSM-5 includes a set of criteria for children 6 years of age and younger. Reactions also may differ based on the nature of the traumatic event.
- The diagnoses of Reactive Attachment Disorder and Disinhibited Social Engagement Disorder are also intended for children 6 years of age and younger. Both disorders are defined by the absence of adequate caregiving, but differ in how the child's difficulties are expressed.
- The nature of the traumatic event, degree of exposure to the trauma, preexisting youth characteristics and coping abilities, and reactions of parents are among the influences that may determine a young person's reaction to a trauma.
- In general, symptoms of PTSD decline over time, but substantial numbers of youth continue to report difficulties.
- A variety of interventions have been attempted to help youth with PTSD or subclinical levels of symptoms. Evidence is strongest for cognitive-behavioral approaches, especially treatments with parent involvement.

Child Maltreatment

- Child maltreatment is one form of trauma that has been viewed within the framework of PTSD. However, such experiences adversely affect a wide array of developmental processes and increase the risk for a variety of problematic outcomes.
- The general legal definition of child maltreatment includes both the commission of injuries and acts of omission, that is, failure to care for and protect. The term maltreatment thus refers to both abuse and neglect.
- Four major types of maltreatment are typically described: physical abuse, sexual abuse, neglect, and psychological (emotional) abuse.
- Neglect is the most common form of maltreatment. Many youth experience multiple types of maltreatment.
- Conceptualizations of maltreatment recognize the influence of complex, multiple, and interrelated risk factors including characteristics of the abuser, characteristics of the youth, parenting practices, parent–child interactions, and larger social/cultural influences.
- Maltreated children face the risk for a variety of adverse outcomes including death, health-related difficulties, alteration of neurobiological systems, disruption of basic developmental processes, and PTSD and other psychological disorders.
- Given the combination of factors that causes maltreatment, effective prevention and intervention need to address many contexts—individual, familial, community, cultural, and societal—and thus include multiple components. Maltreatment, more so than most other traumatic experiences, is viewed as a potentially preventable experience and a number of promising prevention programs exist.

Key Terms

trauma *139*
Posttraumatic Stress Disorder *139, 140*
Acute Stress Disorder *140*
reexperiencing *140*
dissociation *140*
avoidance *140*
negative alterations in cognitions and mood *140*
arousal or reactivity *140*
Reactive Attachment Disorder *140*

Disinhibited Social Engagement Disorder *140*
posttraumatic stress symptoms (PTSS) *141*
child abuse *147*
child maltreatment *147*
neglect *147, 148*
physical abuse *148*
sexual abuse *148*
psychological (emotional) maltreatment *148*

CHAPTER 8
Mood Disorders

Looking Forward

After reading this chapter, you should be able to discuss:

- How depression has been conceptualized, defined, and classified
- The epidemiology and developmental course of depression
- Biological and psychosocial influences on the development of depression
- Assessment of depression

- Approaches to treating and preventing depression
- Mania and the classification of bipolar disorders in youth
- The epidemiology, developmental course, and etiology of bipolar disorders
- Treatment of bipolar disorders
- Suicidal behavior, nonsuicidal self-injury, suicidal risk, and suicide prevention

Problems of mood or affect are a major aspect of internalizing disorders. Children and adolescents can experience moods that are, on the one hand, unusually sad, or on the other hand, unusually elated. When these moods are particularly extreme or persistent or when they interfere with the individual's functioning, they may be labeled as "depression" and "mania," respectively.

For a long time, mood disorders in children and adolescents did not receive much attention. The increase in interest in affective problems can be traced to a number of influences. Promising developments in the identification and treatment of mood disorders in adults played a role. Also, the emergence of a number of assessment measures allowed researchers to examine the phenomenon in clinical and normal populations of youth. In addition, improvements in diagnostic practices facilitated the study of mood disorders in children and adolescents. However, finding that we can apply adult diagnostic criteria to youth should not lead us to prematurely conclude that these phenomena are the same in youth and adults.

When we attempt to place mood disorders in separate categories, we confront many of the same problems that we found in examining anxiety disorders. For example, children and adolescents who meet the criteria for a diagnosis of depression are often also given other diagnoses. Should we think of these problems as distinct entities or, for example, as part of a larger internalizing construct (Trosper et al., 2012)? Nonetheless, examining depression and mania makes sense in terms of how the research and treatment literature is organized.

A Historical Perspective

A brief look at history can aid our understanding of current views of childhood depression. The dominant view in child clinical work for many years was the orthodox psychoanalytic perspective. From this perspective, depression was viewed as a phenomenon of superego and mature ego functioning (Kessler, 1988). It was argued, for example, that in depression, the superego acts as a punisher of the ego. Because a child's superego is not sufficiently developed to play this role, it was believed to be impossible for a depressive disorder to occur in children. Therefore, it is not surprising that depression in children received little attention.

A second major perspective added to the controversy regarding the existence of a distinct disorder of childhood depression. The concept of **masked depression** held that there was indeed a disorder of childhood depression, but that the sad mood and other features usually considered essential to the diagnosis of depression frequently were not present. It was believed that an underlying depressive disorder did exist but that it was "masked" by other problems (depressive equivalents), such as hyperactivity or delinquency. The "underlying" depression itself was not directly displayed but could be inferred by the clinician. Some professionals, indeed, suggested that masked depression was quite common and that because it was masked, childhood depression was underdiagnosed (Cytryn & McKnew, 1974; Malmquist, 1977).

The notion of masked depression was clearly problematic. There was no operational way to decide whether a particular symptom was or was not a sign of depression. Were, for example, a child's angry outbursts a part of an aggressive style or a sign of depression? Indeed, the symptoms that were suggested as masking depression included virtually the full gamut of problem behaviors in youth. The concept of masked depression was, therefore, quite controversial.

This concept was important, however. It clearly recognized depression as an important and a prevalent childhood problem. And the central notions of masked depression—that depression in children does exist and may be displayed in a variety of age-related forms different from adult depression—are still widely held. The concept that depression is manifested differently in children and adults contributed, in part, to the evolution of a developmental psychopathology perspective.

Early in the evolution of this perspective, it was suggested that behaviors that led to the diagnosis of depression (e.g., insufficient appetite, excessive reserve) might be only transitory developmental phenomena that were common among children in certain age groups (Lefkowitz & Burton, 1978). This early position drew attention to the need to differentiate transient episodes of sadness and negative affect, which may be common reactions among children, from more long-lasting expressions of such emotions. Also, the distinction between depression as a *symptom* and depression as a *syndrome* is important to consider here. One or two depressive behaviors may be viewed as typical of that developmental stage. However, it is different to suggest that a cluster of such behaviors accompanied by other problems and impaired functioning is likely to occur in a large number of children (Kovacs, 1997). The developmental perspective has become an important aspect of the study of mood disorders (Cicchetti, 2010; Hinshaw, 2017; Luby & Whalen, 2019).

The DSM Approach to the Classification of Mood Disorders

Mood disorders are sometimes described as **unipolar** (one mood is experienced, typically depression) or **bipolar** (both moods are experienced, depression and mania). The DSM includes descriptions of both unipolar and bipolar mood disorders. In the DSM, depression and mania are described in two chapters titled "Depressive Disorders" and "Bipolar and Related Disorders."

However, despite these kinds of distinctions, the relatedness of these two groups of mood disorders is acknowledged in several ways. This includes providing a "specifier" for both depressive and bipolar disorders that allows the diagnostician to indicate the potential presence of mixed depressive and manic symptoms for both types of disorders.

We begin our examination of mood disorders with the problem of depression, then consider mania/bipolar disorder, and conclude with a discussion of suicide.

Definition and Classification of Depression

Defining Depression

Understanding depression in children and adolescents is a complex task. The phenomenon itself involves a complex interplay of influences and a complex clinical presentation. In addition, there have been a variety of perspectives on depression in young people and a variety of ways in which depression has been defined.

Research findings indicate that different groups of youth may or may not be designated as depressed, depending on how depression is defined and assessed (Carlson & Cantwell, 1980; Hammen & Rudolph, 2003; Kaslow & Racusin, 1990). Such variations can lead to different conclusions regarding the causes and correlates of depression.

A study by Kazdin (1989) illustrates how the source of information and the method employed can affect how depression is viewed. DSM diagnoses of 231 consecutive child admissions to an inpatient psychiatric facility were made on the basis of direct interviews with the children and their parents. This method of diagnosing depression was compared with diagnosis based on exceeding a cutoff score on the Children's Depression Inventory (CDI). Both the children and their parents completed the CDI. In addition, children and/or their parents completed other measures to assess attributes reported to be associated with depression. Different groups of children appeared to be designated as depressed depending on the method employed. For example, near but below one-third of the cases met the criteria for depression using two of the three definitions (DSM, child CDI, parent CDI) and 4.8% of the children met all three criteria for depression. In addition, characteristics associated with depression varied depending on the method used. Some of these results are illustrated in Table 8.1. When depression was defined as a high child-reported score on the CDI, depressed children differed from non-depressed children on the characteristics associated with depression. They were more hopeless; had lower self-esteem; made more internal (as opposed to external) attributions regarding negative events; and were more likely to believe that control was due to external factors rather than to

Table 8.1 Mean Characteristic Scores of Depressed and Non-Depressed Children as Designated by Different Criteria for Depression

	Criteria					
	Children's Depression Inventory (by child)		Children's Depression Inventory (by parent)		DSM diagnosis	
Measures	High	Low	High	Low	Depressed	Non-Depressed
Hopelessness	7.3	3.3	5.3	5.0	5.4	4.8
Self-esteem	22.7	38.9	28.2	30.8	29.2	30.9
Attributions	5.4	6.5	5.8	5.8	6.0	6.0
Locus of control	9.8	6.8	8.2	8.7	7.9	8.4
Total behavior problems (CBCL)	75.8	75.3	81.6	69.0	76.5	75.0

Source: Adapted from Kazdin, 1989. Copyright 1989 by Springer; reprinted with permission.

themselves (locus of control). Depressed and non-depressed children defined by the other two criteria (parent CDI and DSM) did not differ from each other on these "depression-related" characteristics. When the parent CDI score defined depression, children with high depression scores exhibited more problems across a wide range of symptoms (as measured by the Child Behavior Checklist—CBCL) than those with very low depression scores. Depression as designated by the other two criteria did not appear to be associated with this wide range of problems. Thus, the informant and method employed to designate youth as depressed may affect conclusions regarding correlates of depression.

It is not possible at this point to make definitive statements about the "correct" definition of depression. It is probably fair, however, to state that the dominant view is that child/adolescent depression is a syndrome, or disorder, and that the most often employed definition is that offered by the DSM.

Depressive Disorders: The DSM Approach

The DSM describes several types of depressive disorders. These disorders all have in common symptoms of sad, empty, or irritable mood accompanied by related somatic and cognitive changes.

Major Depressive Disorder (MDD) is the primary DSM category for defining depression. This disorder is described by the presence of one or more major depressive episodes. The symptoms required for the presence of a major depressive episode are listed below and are the same for children, adolescents, and adults (with one exception). The one exception is that in children or adolescents, irritable mood can be substituted for depressed mood. This is based on the finding that many depressed youth exhibit irritable mood.

1. Depressed or irritable mood
2. Loss of interest or pleasure
3. Change in weight or appetite

4. Sleep problems
5. Motor agitation or retardation
6. Fatigue or loss of energy
7. Feelings of worthlessness or guilt
8. Difficulty thinking, concentrating, or making decisions
9. Thoughts of death or suicidal thoughts/behavior

To diagnose a major depressive disorder, the DSM requires that five or more of the above symptoms listed above must be present. One of these symptoms must be either depressed (or irritable) mood or loss of interest or pleasure. In addition, the symptoms must be present for two weeks and the symptoms must cause clinically significant distress or impairment in important areas of the youth's functioning (e.g., social, school).

MDD is characterized by one or more depressive episodes (with remission of symptoms between episodes). In contrast, **Persistent Depressive Disorder** (**Dysthymia**) describes a more chronic form of depression. The term *Persistent Depressive Disorder* was introduced in DSM-5 as a substitute for the earlier diagnosis of dysthymic disorder. Persistent Depressive Disorder (Dysthymia) is essentially a disorder in which many of the symptoms of a major depressive episode are present, perhaps in less severe form, but are more chronic—that is, they persist for a longer period of time. Depressed mood (or in children and adolescents, irritable mood) is present for at least one year (two years in adults) along with two or more of the other symptoms listed below.

1. Depressed or irritable mood
2. Poor appetite or overeating
3. Sleep disturbance
4. Low energy or fatigue
5. Loss of self-esteem
6. Concentration or decision-making problems
7. Feelings of hopelessness

Again, the symptoms must cause clinically significant distress or impairment. The term **double depression** has sometimes been employed to describe instances in which both chronic and less severe depression (dysthymia) and major depressive episodes are present. Dysthymia is typically described as developing prior to the occurrence of a major depressive episode.

A new diagnosis, **Disruptive Mood Dysregulation Disorder (DMDD)**, is also included in the chapter on depressive disorders. This diagnosis was added in DSM-5, in part, in an attempt to address a problem we will turn to later in this chapter—potential confusion concerning, and overdiagnosis of, bipolar disorder in children. DMDD is described as symptoms of persistent irritability and frequent outbursts (e.g., extreme temper outbursts, physical aggression). (See Jennifer: Severe Mood Dysregulation.) The young person's angry or irritable mood is described as present even between the temper outbursts and as present most of the day and nearly every day. Age of onset for these symptoms is before 10 years of age and the diagnosis is not intended to be given before age 6 or after age 18. While this pattern of symptom presentation might be confused with a bipolar presentation, children with the DMDD symptom pattern are thought to be more likely to later develop unipolar depressive disorders or anxiety disorders rather than a bipolar disorder (American Psychiatric Association, 2013).

JENNIFER Severe Mood Dysregulation

Jennifer, a 13-year-old Caucasian female, resides in a middle-class home with two college-educated parents and a 16-year-old sister. Jennifer's parents describe her as "carefree" until the onset of irritability at age 11. With the transition to middle school and increased academic demands and more challenging peer relations, Jennifer's irritability worsened and she began having outbursts of aggression.

Jennifer's parents first sought treatment at age 12 for Jennifer's verbally and physically aggressive behaviors at home. The initial assessment indicated outbursts of physical aggression toward parents one or two times per month, verbally aggressive outbursts on average three times per week, and milder outbursts of yelling at her parents several times per day. Jennifer's sister felt resentful of the attention that Jennifer received and was critical of how Jennifer interacted with their parents. At times the sister tried to take on a parenting role, which led to verbal altercations between them. In addition to these difficulties at home, there was appreciable impairment in peer and school settings. The initial assessment also indicated that Jennifer met diagnostic criteria for Disruptive Mood Dysregulation Disorder (DMDD), Attention-Deficit/Hyperactivity Disorder, Generalized Anxiety Disorder, and past history of Major Depressive Disorder. In addition, neuropsychological testing indicated an average IQ, with specific weakness in visual–spatial reasoning abilities, and mild variability in measures of attention.

Initial treatments included weekly therapy sessions focused on behavioral management and the use of psychopharmacological agents. Jennifer's parents tried to maintain a unified approach, but struggled with how to manage her aggressive behavior at home—resulting in crisis agency home visits, emergency room visits, and hospitalizations in addition to outpatient treatment. During her course of outpatient treatment, Jennifer experienced four inpatient hospitalizations for physical aggression toward parents and suicidal ideation, and a day hospital admission following one of the inpatient admissions. An adaptation of an interpersonal psychotherapy for depressed adolescents (IPT-MBD) modified to address the verbal and physical outbursts and chronic irritability of DMDD was settled on as the approach to outpatient treatment. Jennifer began this treatment program on a stable dose of a selective serotonin reuptake inhibitor and an atypical antipsychotic—this pharmacological regimen was maintained throughout the course of this 20-week outpatient treatment.

During the 20-week treatment program Jennifer had no inpatient hospitalizations or emergency room visits. By the end of the treatment program there was an appreciable improvement in Jennifer's symptoms, an increase in positive interpersonal interactions, and Jennifer no longer met the diagnostic criteria for DMDD. Although Jennifer's symptoms were significantly improved, Jennifer, her parents, and the therapist agreed that it would be helpful to solidify Jennifer's gains and work toward continued improvement in a variety of areas. Jennifer continued in therapy that had an interpersonal focus and that addressed other areas of difficulty. Jennifer was also tapered off the atypical antipsychotic and in the six months following the completion of IPT-MBD Jennifer did not have any physical aggressive outbursts, outbursts continued to decrease in frequency, and she transitioned into a public school setting without accommodations.

Adapted from Miller et al., 2016

Depression: Empirical Approaches

Syndromes that involve depressive symptoms have also been identified by empirical approaches to taxonomy such as those identified by the Achenbach instruments (p. 90). The syndromes that include depressive symptoms also include symptoms characteristic of anxiety and withdrawn behavior. Thus, this research does not find a syndrome that includes symptoms of depression alone. A mixed presentation of depression and anxiety features has emerged consistently in research with children and adolescents.

How best to define and classify depression in children and adolescents remains a focus of ongoing research. One issue is determining developmentally sensitive criteria, as youth may experience depression differently at various points in development. A second issue is that depression in young people may best be conceptualized as dimensional rather than categorical (Hankin et al., 2005). Many professionals have chosen to concern themselves with children and adolescents who exhibit constellations of depressive symptoms whether or not they meet the DSM criteria for a mood disorder. This approach makes sense in that it is not clear that the cutoff set by the diagnostic criteria is the critical one. Many youth who fall short of meeting diagnostic criteria may still exhibit impairment in everyday functioning and be at risk for future difficulties (Georgiades et al., 2006; Klein et al., 2009; Lewinsohn et al., 2000).

Description of Depression

In everyday usage, the term *depression* refers to the experience of a pervasive unhappy mood. This subjective experience of sadness, or dysphoria, is also a central feature of the clinical definition of depression. Descriptions of children and adolescents viewed as depressed suggest that they experience a number of other problems as well. Concern may be expressed about a youth's irritability and temper tantrums—sudden outbursts, tears, throwing things, and yelling. Adults who know the child may describe changes in the young person such as loss of the experience of pleasure, social withdrawal, lowered self-esteem, inability to concentrate, and poor schoolwork. Alterations of biological functions (sleeping, eating, elimination) and somatic complaints are often noted as well. The young person may also express thoughts of wishing to die.

These children and adolescents frequently experience other psychological disorders. Anxiety disorders, such as separation anxiety disorder, are probably the most commonly noted. Conduct disorder and oppositional defiant disorder also occur among depressed youth. Among depressed adolescents, alcohol and substance abuse are also common additional problems.

The case of a 15-year-old boy, Nick, illustrates many of these features as well as some of the factors that contribute to the development and course of depression.

NICK The Problems of Depression

Nick lives with his mother. His father left before Nick was born. Nick was born with a curvature of the spine as a result of which he walks awkwardly and is limited in his physical abilities. The incident that resulted in Nick being brought to the clinic was his arrest for shoplifting. ... [His mother] reports that Nick is irritable and sullen much of the time, that they are constantly fighting and arguing. ... Nick's outbursts have escalated recently, including occasions when he has thrown things and punched holes in walls and doors. ...

Nick reveals that he is very unhappy, has few things in his life that give him pleasure, and feels hopeless about things improving for him. He is self-conscious about his appearance, his peers tease him and he feels that he is disliked, and he hates himself.

... Nick's typical day is described as: "He wakes up early in the morning after having stayed up late the night before watching television, but he lies in bed until 9:00 or 10:00 a.m. He then spends much of the day at home alone playing video games or watching television." Nick has gained considerable weight and he reports that he is having trouble controlling his appetite. ... Nick's mother returns home from work late in the afternoon. They often argue about his having missed another day of school. They eat dinner together silently while watching television. The rest of the evening is filled with arguments.

Adapted from Compas, 1997, pp. 197–198

Sad affect or dysphoria is the central characteristic of most definitions of depression. (Darren Baker/Shutterstock.com)

Epidemiology of Depression

Depression is often cited as a leading cause of disability in young people (World Health Organization, 2017). Major Depressive Disorder (MDD) is the most frequently diagnosed mood disorder among children and adolescents (Kessler et al., 2009; Lewinsohn, Rohde, & Seeley, 1998). Among youth with unipolar disorders, about 80% experience MDD, 10% dysthymia without MDD, and 10% "double depression." In community surveys, overall prevalence rates for MDD are estimated to be about 12%, with rates in children ranging between 0.4 and 2.8%, and in adolescents between 0.4 and 8.3%. Lifetime prevalence for any depressive disorder is frequently reported to be about 2.6%, but estimates range from 2.3 to 51%. Estimates of lifetime prevalence rates for MDD range from 4 to 25%, with rates of about 11 to 20% among adolescents and 1.5 to 2.5% among children (Avenevoli et al., 2015; Kessler et al., 2009; Lavigne et al., 2009; Merikangas & Hommer, 2019; Polanczyk et al., 2015). The epidemiology of dysthymia is less well studied. Prevalence rates between 0.5 and 1.5% for children and between about 1.5 and 8.0% among adolescents have been reported (Birmaher et al., 1996; Kessler et al., 2009; Lavigne et al., 2009).

Reported prevalence rates probably underestimate the scope of the problem. For example, lifetime prevalence rates, rather than prevalence rates at any one point in time, indicate that episodes of clinical depression may be quite common, particularly among adolescents. In the Oregon Adolescent Depression Project (OADP), a large prospective epidemiological study of a representative community sample of adolescents ages 14 to 18, Lewinsohn and his colleagues (1998) estimated that by age 19, approximately

28% of adolescents will have experienced an episode of MDD (35% of the females and 19% of the males). Other information suggests lifetime prevalence rates of diagnosable depressive disorders among the general population as high as 20 to 30% (Compas, Ey, & Grant, 1993; Lewinsohn et al., 1993). This finding means that about one out of four young people in the general population experiences a depressive disorder sometime during childhood or adolescence. Even higher estimates emerge when other definitions of clinical levels of depression are employed. For example, 40 to 50% of the OADP youth scored above the criteria for depression "caseness" on a standard self-report depression questionnaire. As a comparison, 16 to 20% of adults meet "caseness" criteria.

Finally, the extent of the problem is even clearer when one includes young people who exhibit depressive symptoms but who do not meet diagnostic criteria. These youth are not included in the prevalence estimates just cited. However, such youth often exhibit impairments in their academic, social, and cognitive functioning and also are at greater risk for future disorders than are youth not exhibiting depressive symptoms (Georgiades et al., 2006; Klein et al., 2009; Lewinsohn et al., 1998).

Age and Sex

Age and sex are clearly relevant to estimates of the prevalence of depression in young people (Salk, Hype, & Abramson, 2017; Zahn-Waxler, Shirtcliff, & Marceau, 2008). Depression is less prevalent in younger children than in adolescents (Ford, Goodman, & Meltzer, 2003; Lavigne et al., 2009). Usually no gender differences are reported for children less than 12 years of age (Angold & Rutter, 1992; Fleming, Offord, & Boyle, 1989; Lavigne et al., 2009). When differences are reported for this age group, depression is more prevalent in boys than in girls (Anderson et al., 1987; Twenge & Nolen-Hoeksema, 2002). Among adolescents, depression is more common among girls and begins to approach the 2:1 female-to-male ratio usually reported for adults. The age–gender pattern that is typically reported is illustrated in Figure 8.1. The OADP findings and other information (Hilt & Nolen-Hoeksema, 2014; Hyde, Mezulis, & Abramson, 2008) suggest that the sex difference in MDD prevalence probably emerges between the ages of 12 and 15. A recent review suggests that sex differences in prevalence of depression may emerge as early as age 12, peak between the ages of 13 and 15, and decrease somewhat into the 20s, and remain stable after that (Salk et al., 2017). It is worth noting that for *both* sexes, depression is more prevalent in adolescents than in younger children (Angold & Rutter, 1992; Cohen et al., 1993; Lewinsohn et al., 1993; Whitaker et al., 1990).

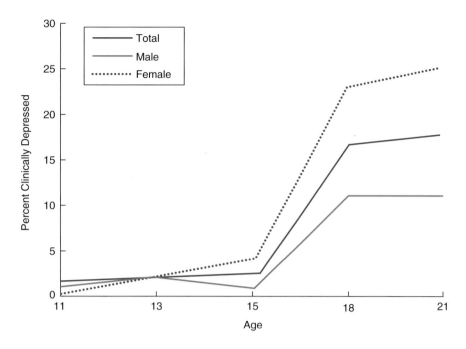

Figure 8.1 The development of clinical depression by age and sex. (From Hankin, Abramson, Moffitt, Silva, McGee, & Angell, 1998)

Socioeconomic, Ethnic, and Cultural Considerations

Lower socioeconomic status (SES) is reported to be associated with higher rates of depression. The link is probably through influences such as income, limited parental education, chronic stress, family disruption, environmental adversities, and racial/ethnic discrimination (Anderson & Mayes, 2010; Hammen & Rudolph, 2003; Wight, Sepúlveda, & Aneshensel, 2004). Although such SES differences may have a disproportionate impact on certain ethnic groups, there is not adequate information regarding racial and ethnic differences in the prevalence of depression. Comparable rates are often reported in various ethnic groups (Canino et al., 2004; Gibbs, 2003; Hammen & Rudolph, 2003). However, higher rates of depression have been reported among the population of Latinx youth (Anderson & Mayes, 2010; Organista, 2003). Ethnic minority youth may face a number of stressors that can contribute to the development of depression. Among these influences are discrimination and ethnic racial socialization practices (Park et al., 2020). Huq, Stein, & Gonzalez (2016) studied the relationship of discrimination and parent–adolescent acculturation conflict to depression in a sample of seventh-to tenth-grade Latinx adolescents. As illustrated in Table 8.2, discrimination and parent–child conflict regarding youth acculturation were both associated with higher levels of depression. Furthermore, further analysis revealed that

parent–child acculturation conflict predicted depression above and beyond the effects of general parent–child conflict.

Co-occurring Difficulties

Finally, children and adolescents who are depressed typically experience other problems as well (Avenevoli et al., 2015; Dietz, Silk, & Amole, 2019; Rawana et al., 2010). Indeed, reports suggest that about two-thirds of youth diagnosed with MDD also meet the criteria for at least one other disorder. Common additional non-mood disorders are anxiety disorders, disruptive behavior disorders, eating disorders, substance abuse disorders, and attention-deficit/hyperactivity disorder (ADHD).

Table 8.2 Relationship of General Conflict, Acculturation Conflict, and Discrimination with Depressive Symptoms

	1	2	3	4
1. General conflict			-	
2. Acculturation conflict	.19*		-	
3. Discrimination	.19*	.44**	-	
4. Depressive symptoms	.28**	.25**	.24**	-

*p<.05 **p<.10

Source: Adapted from Huq, Stein, & Gonzalez, 2016.

AMY Preschool Depression

Amy, 3 years, 6 months of age, presented to her pediatrician with stomachaches, associated with periodic vomiting, and regression in toilet training that had begun after the birth of a sibling. A medical work-up for gastrointestinal symptoms was negative and Amy and her family were referred to a mental health clinic. Amy's parents reported that she displayed a decreased interest in food and some sleep disturbance. In addition, they reported that Amy had become socially withdrawn at school and, at home, periods of extended sadness and episodes of irritability and social withdrawal occurred when her needs were not immediately met. The parents indicated that Amy was interested in her infant sibling and interacted with the baby in a positive way, but had displayed considerable anticipatory anxiety prior to the sibling's birth. They also reported that Amy had always been shy and slow to warm and that she was extremely fussy and difficult to

sooth as an infant. An extensive family history of depression was reported that included maternal depression during the pregnancy with Amy.

During her visit to the clinic Amy was slow to warm, displayed muted affect, and appeared shy. She did not appear to be persistently sad. Amy did, in fact, brighten at times during observational play and displayed age-appropriate play with her mother, who appeared positive, but fatigued and lacking in enthusiasm. During a brief separation from her mother, Amy became immediately withdrawn, stopped playing, appeared sad, and made no attempt to find her mother. Also, Amy became tearful and said she felt hurt and "left out" when the toys were put away while she was briefly out of the playroom.

Adapted from Luby, 2009, pp. 417–418

Depression and Development

It is interesting to examine how depression is manifested and how its prevalence changes over the course of development. Although the diagnostic criteria in the DSM are largely the same for children, adolescents, and adults, depression may be manifested differently in these groups.

A number of authors have described the phenomenology of depression at different developmental stages (Dietz et al., 2019; Fristad & Black, 2018; Schwartz, Gladstone, & Kaslow; 1998). Infants and toddlers lack the cognitive and verbal abilities necessary to self-reflect and report depressive thoughts and problems. It is difficult, therefore, to know what the equivalent to adult depressive symptoms may be in this age group. Given these differences in cognitive and language abilities, and other developmental differences, it is likely that depressive behavior in this age group may be quite different than in adults. Interestingly, the description of infants separated from their primary caregivers in many ways seems similar to that of depression (Bowlby, 1960; Spitz, 1946). These and other distressed infants, as well as infants of depressed mothers, have been observed to be less active and more withdrawn and to exhibit feeding and sleep problems, irritability, less positive affect, sad facial expression, excessive crying, and decreased responsiveness—behaviors often associated with depression (Luby & Whalen, 2019).

Depression in preschoolers is also difficult to assess. Many of the symptoms associated with later depression have been noted in

children in this age group (e.g., irritability, sad facial expression, changes of mood, feeding and sleep problems, lethargy, excessive crying) but the symptom picture may also present in different ways (see Amy: Preschool Depression). Again, differences in cognition and language, as well as limited information, make it a challenge to understand how these behaviors may be related to the experience of depression in older individuals and whether or not these represent stable patterns.

For the period of middle childhood (6 to 12 years), there is more evidence that a prolonged pattern of depressive symptoms may emerge. Younger children in this age group typically do not verbalize the hopelessness and self-deprecation associated with depression. However, 9- to 12-year-olds who exhibit other symptoms of depression may verbalize feelings of hopelessness and low self-esteem. Still, in children in this age group, depressive symptoms may not be a distinctive syndrome but may occur with a variety of symptoms usually associated with other disorders. So, for example, as mentioned before, mixed depressed/anxious syndromes rather than separate depressed syndromes emerge in empirical taxonomies (Achenbach & Rescorla, 2001).

During the early adolescent period, the manifestation of depression is in many ways similar to the way it appears in the childhood period. Over time, however, probably in relation to shifts in biological, social, and cognitive development, depression in older adolescents starts to resemble more closely the symptoms of adult depression. In their community sample of adolescents, Lewinsohn and his colleagues (1998) report a median age of onset for MDD at 15.5 years.

As part of their longitudinal research and their effort to examine the relationship of age of onset and familial contributions to depression, Harrington and his colleagues (1997) compared a group of prepubertal-onset depressed youth to a group whose onset of depression was postpubertal. Rates of depression in relatives of youth in the two groups did not differ. There were, however, other differences in the families of the two groups. Manic disorders tended to be more common among relatives of the postpubertal-onset group, whereas there were higher rates of criminality and family discord among relatives of the prepubertal depressed young people. This evidence supports the view that prepubertal-onset depressive disorders may be distinct from postpubertal-onset depression. In addition, continuity to major depression in adulthood was lower among prepubertal-onset youth than among those with postpubertal onset of depression. This finding is also consistent with viewing adolescent-onset depression as more similar to adult forms of the disorder and different from earlier onset depression (Klein, Goldstein, & Finsaas, 2017).

Adolescence thus appears to be a period when depressive syndromes similar to adult depression have their onset. What, then, is the clinical course of depression during adolescence and into adulthood? How long does an episode of major depression last? Are there future episodes?

Episodes of depression in adolescents may last for an appreciable period of time and for some individuals may present a recurring problem (Rohde et al., 2013; Swearer et al., 2011). The reported length of episodes tends to be shorter in community samples. In the OADP community sample (Klein et al., 2001; Lewinsohn et al., 1998), the median duration of an episode of MDD was eight weeks, with a range from two to 520 weeks. Earlier onset of depression (at or before the age of 15) was associated with longer episodes. The recurrent nature of depression is illustrated by the finding that among these adolescents, 26% had a history of recurrent major depressive episodes. Kovacs (1996), in her review of studies of clinically referred youth, found a median duration of MDD episodes of seven to nine months. It was found that about 70% of these clinically referred youth had recurrences of MDD episodes when followed for five or more years. Thus, the duration of episodes in clinical samples may be more than three times the duration in community samples, and recurrence of a major depressive episode more than twice as likely.

A sample of participants in the OADP project was interviewed after their 24th birthday. Those who prior to age 19 had met criteria for MDD or adjustment disorder with depressed mood were more likely to meet criteria for MDD during young adulthood than their peers with a nonaffective disorder or no disorder prior to age 19 (Lewinsohn et al., 1999). In addition, follow-up studies suggest that some adolescents with MDD later develop bipolar disorder. The questions of what percentage and which individuals exhibit this pattern continue to be a topic of investigation (Blader et al., 2017; Diler, Birmaher, & Miklowitz, 2010; Kovacs, 1996; Lewinsohn et al., 1999).

Etiology of Depression

Contemporary views of depression suggest a model that integrates multiple determinants, including biological, social-psychological, family, peer, and other environmental influences.

Biological Influences

Biological views of depression have focused on genetic and biochemical dysfunction. In addition, areas such as sleep patterns and structural and functional brain differences have received attention. Although there are some similarities regarding biological correlates of depression in adults and youth, developmental differences have also been noted (Klein et al., 2017).

Genetic Influences

Genetic influences are generally thought to play a role in depression in children and adolescents (Franić et al., 2010; Klein et al., 2017; Rice, Harold, & Thapar, 2002). Support for the role of genetics in depression derives from a number of findings. For example, the data based on twin, family, and adoption studies in adults suggest a heritability component (Kendler et al., 1992a; Weissman, Kidd, & Prusoff, 1982; Wender et al., 1986). Findings from twin, family, and adoption designs with child and adolescent samples also suggest a genetic component for depressive symptomatology (Franić et al., 2010; Glowinski et al., 2003; Weissman et al., 2005). The genetic contribution for adolescent depression may be greater than for depression in prepubertal children (Franić et al., 2010; Nivard et al., 2015; Scourfield et al., 2003).

Research that suggests heritability in depression also indicates the importance of environmental influences and the likely complex interaction of genes and environment (Klein et al., 2017). For example, Caspi and colleagues found that young adults who had a particular variant of the transporter gene (5-HTTLPR)—a gene suggested to be associated with depression—had an increased rate of depressive disorders, but only when exposed to stressful life events. Environments may interact with genetic influence in both positive and negative ways. Li, Berk, and Lee (2013) investigated adolescent boys who also had the variant of the transporter gene (5-HTTLPR) associated with depression. They found that, for these boys lower family support was associated with higher levels of depressive symptoms and higher levels of family support with a lower number of depressive symptoms.

There is also the issue of what is inherited. In a family genetic study by Rende and colleagues (1993), significant genetic influence was found when the depressive symptomatology of the full sample was examined. However, surprisingly, a significant genetic influence on depression was not found if only young people with high levels of depression were considered. These authors and others suggest that genetic influence operates through factors such as temperament, cognitive style, and stress reactivity to affect the full range of depressive symptomatology (Compas, Connor-Smith, & Jaser, 2004; Klein et al., 2017; Sullivan, Neale, & Kendler, 2000). It might then be that extreme depressive symptomatology may result, against this background of moderate genetic influence, under conditions of stressful life experiences.

The effort to identify specific genes involved in depression has proven difficult and has, to date, focused primarily on adults. It seems likely that multiple genes, each with small effects, are involved in the development of depression (Klein et al., 2017).

Neurochemistry and Brain Functioning

The roles of the dysregulation of the neurochemical and neuroendocrine systems and of abnormalities of brain structure and function in the etiology of depression have received considerable attention. The study of these processes in depression is complex and difficult. Research on several fronts that is increasingly sensitive to developmental considerations is ongoing (Colich et al., 2015 Klein et al., 2017; Zalsman et al., 2006).

The role of neurotransmitters, such as serotonin, norepinephrine, and acetylcholine, has been a central aspect of the study of the biochemistry of depression (Thase, 2009). The impetus to study these neurotransmitters came from findings that the effectiveness of certain antidepressant medications with adults was related to the individuals' levels of these neurotransmitters or receptivity to them. For example, low neurotransmitter levels may occur when too much neurotransmitter is reabsorbed by the neuron, or when enzymes break down the neurotransmitter too efficiently. This process is thought to result in too low a level of neurotransmitter at the synapse to fire the next neuron. Research continues to explore the role of neurotransmitters; however, the mechanisms of action are likely to be quite complicated, rather than simply the amount of neurotransmitters available.

Studies of the neuroendocrine systems (connections between the brain, hormones, and various organs) add to this etiological picture. Dysregulation of the neuroendocrine systems involving the hypothalamus, pituitary gland, and the adrenal and thyroid glands is considered a hallmark of depression. These neuroendocrine systems are also regulated by neurotransmitters. Thus, the picture regarding depression is likely to be a complex one and the rapid biological changes during childhood and adolescence create a particular challenge.

Our understanding of the neurobiology of child and adolescent depression remains an ongoing challenge. Research, however, suggests that during the earlier developmental periods of childhood and adolescence, the neuroregulatory system is not equivalent to that in adulthood. Later in development (in older adolescents), among those who are more severely depressed, or those at high risk for depression, biological indicators may be more similar to those for depressed adults (Rao, Hammen, & Poland, 2010; Yang et al., 2010; Zalsman et al., 2006). Thus, although many researchers still find evidence for a biological dysfunction in childhood depression, a simple translation of the adult findings is not sufficient.

Investigation of the role of **cortisol**, a stress hormone produced in the adrenal glands, is one example of research regarding the role of the neuroregulatory system. Depressed youth often exhibit dysregulation of the stress response including higher basal levels of cortisol and production of excessive levels of cortisol in response to stress (Lopez-Duran, Kovacs, & George, 2009). However, these patterns have not been observed consistently in investigations of cortisol functioning in young people. Cortisol responses similar to those for depressed adults may occur among older and more severely depressed adolescents and those at higher risk (Mazurka, Wynne-Edwards, & Harkness, 2016; Rao et al., 2010; Zalsman et al., 2006).

Neuroimaging studies, employing structural and functional MRI, have found evidence of anatomical and functional abnormalities in the prefrontal cortex, amygdala, and other areas of the brain in depressed adults. Such abnormalities may be more common among those with recurrent episodes of depression and with an earlier (before 21) onset of depression (Müller et al., 2017). While fewer studies have been conducted with children and adolescents, there is evidence that suggests structural and functional abnormalities of areas such as the amygdala and the prefrontal cortex of depressed youth and among youth with family histories of depression (Chen, Hamilton, & Gotlib, 2010; Hulvershorn, Cullen, & Anand, 2011; Miller et al., 2015; Yang et al., 2010; Zalsman et al., 2006).

How can we understand these various findings? In general, differences in biological markers of depression might suggest that the child, adolescent, and adult disorders are different. Alternatively, such differences in biological markers may represent developmental differences in the same disorder.

Temperament

Temperament is typically viewed as having a genetic or biological basis, but environmental influences are also thought to affect its development. Links between the development of depression and aspects of temperament have been suggested. Two aspects of temperament have received particular attention and various terms have been employed to describe these constructs. **Negative affectivity** (NA) or **negative emotionality** (NE) is thought of in terms of qualities such as a tendency to experience negative emotions, be sensitive to negative stimuli, and be wary and vigilant. **Positive affectivity** (PA) or **positive emotionality** (PE) is thought of in terms of qualities such as approach, energy, sociability, and sensitivity to reward cues. High levels of NE and low levels of PE have been associated with depression. For example, longitudinal research indicates that early high NE and low PE predict later depressive symptoms (Bould et al., 2014; Dougherty et al., 2010; Klein et al., 2012). The qualities of positive and negative emotionality may also interact with the temperament factor of effortful control in the development of depression (Van Beveren et al., 2019). **Effortful control** (EC) refers to the ability to employ self-regulation processes.

It seems clear, however, that the contribution of these temperament qualities to the development of depression occurs in interaction with other influences such as stressful life events, interpersonal relations, and cognitive processes. The link between temperament and depression may, for example, be greater for children whose parents employ harsh and inconsistent discipline than for those who experience parental warmth. And positive temperamental qualities may serve as a buffer against the contribution of parental rejection to depression. Thus, the relationship between child temperament and social-psychological influences such as parenting, peer relations, and stressful life events is likely bidirectional (Garber, 2010).

Social-Psychological Influences

The influences mentioned as interacting with temperament are illustrations of social-psychological influences thought to impact the development of depression. We will consider several of the social-psychological influences that have been examined with regard to depression in children and adolescents. While we describe "separate" influences, it is important to note that these influences overlap with each other. Furthermore, these various influences do not act separately, but, rather, interact with each other in the development of depression.

Separation and Loss

There is an appreciable history of viewing separation, loss, or rejection as contributing to the development of depression as well as other forms of psychopathology (Garber, 2010; Humphreys, 2019). For example, as mentioned earlier (p. 162), infants separated from their primary caregivers may exhibit behavioral and biological patterns similar to those seen in depression. Psychoanalytic explanations of depression, following from Freud, emphasize the notion of object loss. The loss may be real (parental death, divorce) or symbolic. Identification with and ambivalent

The theme of separation-loss is a central concept in many theories of depression. The loss may be real or imagined. (Twin Design/Shutterstock.com)

feelings toward the lost love object are thought to result in the person's directing hostile feelings concerning the love object toward the self. Some psychodynamic writers emphasize loss of self-esteem and feelings of helplessness that result from object loss, and they minimize the importance of aggression turned inward toward the self (Kessler, 1988).

Some behaviorally oriented explanations also involved the ideas of separation and loss by emphasizing the role of inadequate positive reinforcement in the development of depression (Ferster, 1974; Lewinsohn, 1974). Loss of or separation from a loved one is likely to result in a decrease in the child's sources of positive reinforcement. However, it is recognized that inadequate reinforcement may also result from factors such as not having adequate skills to obtain desired rewards.

Support for the theory that separation may play a role in the genesis of depression came from several different sources. For example, investigators have described a fairly typical sequence of reactions of young children to prolonged separation from their parents (e.g., Bowlby, 1960; Spitz, 1946). In this so-called anaclitic depression, the child initially goes through a period of "protest" characterized by crying, asking for the parents, and restlessness. This is followed shortly by a period of depression and withdrawal. Most children begin to recover after several weeks.

The connection between loss and depression also has been examined in adult depression. For a long time, the widely held view was that early loss puts one at high risk for later depression—especially women. More recent examinations question this view, in part because most studies were plagued with methodological problems (Finkelstein, 1988; Tennant, 1988). The current view is that early loss is not, in and of itself, pathogenic. The link between such loss and later depression is not direct. Rather, it is hypothesized that loss, as well as other circumstances, can set in motion a chain of adverse circumstances such as lack of care, changes in family structure, and socioeconomic difficulties that put the individual at risk for later disorder (Bifulco, Harris, & Brown, 1992; Saler & Skolnick, 1992).

Much of the research on the association between loss and depression has relied on the retrospective reports of adults. However, investigation of the impact of loss on children has received some attention (Dowdney, 2000; Tremblay & Israel, 1998). For example, Sandler and his colleagues found support for a model consistent with the indirect effects of loss (West et al., 1991). In a sample of 92 families who had lost a parent within the previous two years, depression in children (ages 8 to 15) was not directly linked to the loss. Rather, the level of demoralization of the surviving parent, family warmth, and stable positive events following the loss mediated the effects of parental death on depression in these young people. Indeed, children who experience the positive aspects of these family variables are likely to be resilient following the loss of a parent (Lin et al., 2004). Also, children who participated in a Family Bereavement Treatment that targeted these family and child risk variables exhibited less grief in general and fewer problematic grief reactions over a six-year period (Sandler et al., 2010). Also, at 15 years following treatment these individuals had lower mental health problems and lesser use of mental health services (Sandler et al., 2018).

Cognitive-Behavioral/Interpersonal Perspectives

Behavioral, cognitive, and cognitive-behavioral perspectives encompass many related and overlapping concepts. Influences such as interpersonal skills, cognitive distortions, views of self, control beliefs, self-regulation, and stress are the focus of these perspectives. The ways in which depressed individuals relate to others and are viewed by others, and the ways that these individuals view themselves and think, particularly in the context of acute stressful life events and chronic stressors, are believed to contribute to how depression develops and is maintained (Garber, 2010; Hammen, 2015; Michl et al., 2013).

Writers such as Ferster (1974) and Lewinsohn (1974) suggested that a combination of lowered activity level and inadequate interpersonal skills plays a role in the development and maintenance of depression. Depressed youth both contribute and react to problematic relationships. It is suggested that depressed individuals do not elicit positive interpersonal responses from others. Indeed, there is evidence that depressed youth may display deficits in social functioning, have negative interpersonal expectations and perceptions, and are viewed less positively by others (Klein et al., 2008; Parker et al., 2006; Vujeva & Furman, 2011).

A variety of cognitions may be related to depression. A **learned helplessness** explanation of depression (Seligman & Peterson, 1986) suggests that some individuals, as a result of their learning

histories, come to perceive themselves as having little control of their environment. This learned helplessness is, in turn, associated with the mood and behaviors characteristic of depression. Separation may be a special case of learned helplessness: the child's fruitless attempts to bring the parent back may result in the child's thinking that personal action and positive outcome are independent of each other.

Helplessness conceptualizations emphasize how the person thinks about activity and outcome—a person's **attributional** or **explanatory style**. Depressed individuals may have an explanatory style in which they blame themselves (internal) for negative events and view the causes of events as being stable over time (stable) and applicable across situations (global). The opposite style, external-unstable-specific attributions for positive events, may also be part of this depressed style. In revisions of this perspective, the interaction of stressful life events with cognitive style is given greater emphasis (Abramson, Metalsky, & Alloy, 1989). This revision is referred to as the **hopelessness** theory of depression. Attributional style (a vulnerability or diathesis) acts as a moderator between negative life events that the person sees as important (a stress) and hopelessness. Hopelessness, in turn, leads to depression. Figure 8.2 illustrates how the hopelessness theory of depression views the development of depression. The theory predicts that a young person with a diathesis of a negative attributional style who is also exposed to the stress of high levels of negative life events is more likely to develop depression. A number of studies have reported maladaptive attributional styles and hopelessness in depressed youth (Kaslow et al., 2000; Schwartz et al., 2000), and the vulnerability-stress notions of hopelessness theory have received support (Conley et al., 2001; Joiner, 2000). However, there is ongoing attention to inconsistencies in findings, developmental patterns, potential gender differences, and a clearer articulation

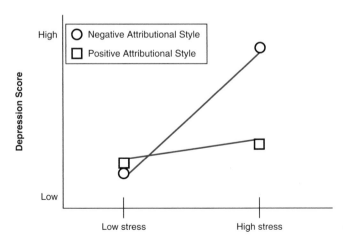

Figure 8.2 A schematic depiction of the interaction of attributional style and stress in the development of depression.

of the relationship of attributional style and life events (Abela & Hankin, 2008; Garber, 2010; Kaslow et al., 2000; Rueger & Malecki, 2011).

The role of cognitive factors in depression is also the major emphasis of some theorists. Beck (1967, 1976), for example, assumed that depression resulted from negative views of the self, others, and the future. Depressed individuals, Beck hypothesized, have developed certain errors in thinking that result in their distorting even mildly annoying events into opportunities for self-blame and failure. Although findings were mixed, some research studies found evidence in depressed youth of **cognitive distortions** such as those suggested by Beck's theory (Gencöz et al., 2001; Stark, Schmidt, & Joiner, 1996). Depressed youth exhibited a tendency to catastrophize, overgeneralize, personalize, and selectively attend to negative events. Other research suggested that depressed individuals, relative to non-depressed individuals, show negative information-processing styles (Gotlib & Joormann, 2010; Lau & Waters, 2017). This may be exhibited by increased elaboration of negative information, difficulty in disengaging from negative material, and deficits in cognitive control when processing negative information.

It is clear that there is an association between cognitive influences such as attributional style, hopelessness, or cognitive distortion and depression. The nature of the cognition–depression link, however, requires further clarification (Graber & Sontag, 2009; Hammen, 2018; Kaslow et al., 2000; Platt et al., 2017; Rudolph et al., 2006). It is unclear to what degree these cognitions play a causal role in depression as an underlying vulnerability or are associated with depression in some other way—perhaps co-occurring with depression, being a consequence of depression, or being part of an ongoing reciprocal interplay with depression. Nonetheless, challenging and changing problematic cognitions has become a central component of cognitive-behavioral treatments for depression. These procedures are often referred to as **cognitive restructuring.**

Earlier in our examination of the helplessness perspective we discussed the dimension of control. The roles of control and coping, along with emotion regulation, also have been the focus of research attention. Weisz and colleagues, for example, have found that low levels of perceived competence (the ability to perform relevant behavior) and perceived noncontingency (outcomes are not contingent on behavior) are both related to depression in children (Weisz et al., 1993). Similarly, researchers have examined style of coping with stress as a component of the development of depression. For example, lower levels of active coping (e.g., problem solving) and greater levels of rumination (repeatedly going over something in one's mind) and disengagement coping (e.g., avoidance) have been associated with young people's depression. Evolving models of stress and coping/emotion regulation are likely to contribute to a greater understanding of the development of depression (Abela et al., 2012; Compas et al., 2004; Garnefski & Kraaij, 2018; Joorman & Stanton, 2016). Given the suggestion of these difficulties in depressed youth, it may be worthwhile to examine the type of coping and self-regulatory behavior evoked or encouraged by parents of depressed youth (Goodman & Brand, 2009; Kaslow et al., 2000). With this observation in mind, we turn to the influences of parental depression on children and adolescents.

Impact of Parental Depression

A major area of research on childhood depression has been an examination of children of depressed parents. There are several reasons for the proliferation of such research. Because family aggregation of mood disorders in adults was known to exist, it was presumed that examining children of parents with mood disorders would reveal a population likely to experience childhood depression. Such a high-risk research strategy could be a more efficient means of investigating the problem than a random sampling of the population would be. In addition, such research might provide information on the continuity among child, adolescent, and adult mood disorders.

Numerous studies have found that children and adolescents with a depressed parent are at increased risk for developing a psychological disorder (Goodman et al., 2011; Murray, Halligan, & Cooper, 2019; Tichovolsky et al., 2018; Weissman et al., 2016). For example, Hammen and her colleagues (1990) compared the long-term effects of maternal depression and maternal chronic medical illness. Over the course of a three-year period, with evaluations at six-month intervals, children of both depressed mothers and medically ill mothers exhibited elevated rates of psychological disorder as compared with children of healthy mothers. Rates of disorder were higher for children of depressed mothers than for those with medically ill mothers.

Weissman and her colleagues (1997) followed the children of two groups of parents over a ten-year period. At the time of the follow-up, the offspring were in late adolescence or were adults. Parents and youth were assessed with a structured diagnostic interview. Youth for whom neither parent had a psychological disorder (low risk) were compared with those for whom one or both parents had a diagnosis of MDD (high risk). The youth with depressed parents had increased rates of MDD, particularly before puberty. The high-risk group also had increased rates of other disorders, including phobias and alcohol dependence. In addition, children of depressed parents experienced more serious depression than children of non-depressed parents. However, the depressed offspring of depressed parents were less likely to receive treatment than those of non-depressed parents; in fact, more than 30% never received any treatment.

Beardslee and his colleagues examined the impact of parental depression in a nonclinically referred population (Beardslee et al., 1996; Beardslee, Versage, & Gladstone, 1998). Families were recruited from a large health maintenance organization. Assessments, including a structured diagnostic interview, were conducted initially and four years later. Families were divided into three categories: parents with no diagnosis, parents with a non-mood disorder, and one or both parents with a mood disorder. Parental non-mood disorder, parental MDD, and the number of diagnosed disorders that the child experienced prior to the first assessment predicted whether the youth experienced a serious mood disorder during the time between assessments.

The findings presented here suggest that the risk associated with parental depressions may not be specific. Children with a depressed parent appear to be at risk for a variety of problems, not just depression. And children of parents with other diagnoses or with chronic medical conditions may also be at risk for depression. Perhaps various disorders that youth experience share common risk factors, whereas some risk factors are specific to depression. It is also possible that some disruptions to effective parenting are common to parents with various disorders, whereas other disruptions are more likely to occur among parents with a particular disorder such as depression.

There may be a variety of mechanisms whereby depressive mood states in parents are associated with dysfunction in their children (Goodman & Brand, 2009; Hammen, 2018; Murray et al., 2019). Shared heredity may play a role in the link between parental and child depression. Parental depression may also have an impact through a variety of non-biological pathways. For example, parents can influence their child through parent–child interactions, through coaching and teaching practices, and by arranging their child's social environment. Before we turn to a discussion of these mechanisms, it is important to remember that influences between parent and child are likely to be bidirectional (Elgar et al., 2004). A depressed youth may, for example, generate additional stress that lessens the adult's ability to parent effectively.

Mechanisms of Parental Influence

As we indicated before, both depression in adults and depression in young people are associated with certain characteristic ways of thinking and cognitive styles. Depressed parents may transmit these styles to their children. Garber and Flynn (2001), for example, assessed mothers and their children annually over three years, starting when the children were in sixth grade. A maternal history of depression was associated with lower perceived self-worth, a negative attributional style, and hopelessness among the children. Maladaptive ways of thinking may be modeled by parents and parents' maladaptive cognitions may also affect the manner in which depressed adults parent their offspring (Callender et al., 2012).

For example, depressed parents may exhibit negative affect such as anger or hostility and employ harsh styles of parenting. Also, depressed parents' absorption in their own difficulties may lead them to be withdrawn, less emotionally available, and to be perceived as less rewarding by their offspring. Depression may also make parents inattentive to their children and unaware of their children's behavior. Monitoring of a child's behavior is a key element in effective parenting. In addition, to being inattentive, depressed parents may also perceive behaviors to be problematic that other parents do not. This difference in perception is important, because being able to ignore or tolerate low levels of problematic behavior is likely to lead to less family disruption. Observations of families with a depressed parent or child reveal these relationship difficulties and indicate that interactional patterns in these families may serve to maintain the depression in the parent or child (Dadds et al., 1992; Ge et al., 1995; Hops et al., 1987; Koss et al., 2018; St. Clair et al., 2015). Depressed behavior by one family member may be maintained because it serves to avoid or reduce the high levels of aggression and discord that may be present in such families.

MARY Family Interactions and Depression

Mary is an adolescent with considerable problems with anxiety and depression. Mary's mother was diagnosed with major depression. Her parents fought often and frequently the topic was money or problems and stresses related to her father's job. Mary's mother dealt with these difficulties by self-medicating with alcohol and developed a serious drinking problem. The conflicts, alcohol abuse, and other stresses seemed to have contributed to the development of symptoms of depression in Mary's mother. For the good of all the family members and because of her concern for her mother, Mary felt that she had to serve as a mediator for her parents' disputes and that she was responsible for alleviating her mother's sadness. Over time these family conflicts and problems contributed to Mary developing psychological difficulties of her own.

Adapted from Cummings, Davies, & Campbell, 2000, pp. 305–306

JOE AND FRANK Different Outcomes

Joe's father was diagnosed with major depression and his paternal grandfather also experienced episodes of depression… but both his parents were attentive and responsive to him. Even when Joe's father's depressive symptoms were severe, he remained attentive and emotionally warm. Joe's mother was very supportive of his father and they had a secure marriage. … Joe also had a close and supportive relationship with his two sisters. Joe did well in school and was popular, although he tended to be shy in large groups. He attended an excellent university, studied medicine, and became a pediatrician. Joe married, and he and his wife were happy and were attentive and responsive parents. Joe experienced periods of anxiety and occasional mild to moderate symptoms of depression. The symptoms were rarely more than subclinical and Joe never felt the need to seek therapy.

Frank's mother was diagnosed with Major Depressive Disorder and her mother has also been depressed. His mother and father were divorced when Frank was 10. This followed many years of intense marital conflict. … Both parents had also been generally emotionally unresponsive toward the children … and they involved Frank and his sister in their marital conflicts. … Frank and his sister fought with each other and were never close to each other. In preschool Frank was highly aggressive and difficult. … By adolescence, Frank was habitually delinquent, and he dropped out of high school. As an adult, Frank was diagnosed with a depressive disorder and his interpersonal relationships were tumultuous and typically short-lived.

Adapted from Cummings, Davies, & Campbell, 2000, pp. 299–300

In addition to marital discord, families with a depressed parent may exist in adverse contexts (e.g., social disadvantage/ low standard of living) and may experience high levels of stressful life events (e.g., health and financial difficulties). These circumstances, in turn, are likely to exacerbate a parent's depressive episodes and contribute to disruptions in parenting. For example, high levels of parental stress may restrict the parent's ability to involve the child in activities outside the home and may limit the family's social networks. Thus, the child may have limited opportunity to interact with other adults outside the family or to have access to other sources of social support.

The link between parent and child depression also has been viewed in the context of attachment and parent–child interactions (Brumariu & Kerns, 2010; Cicchetti & Toth, 1998; Murray et al., 2019). The emotional unavailability and insensitivity that may be associated with parental depression have been shown to be strong and reliable predictors of insecure parent–child attachments. Attachment theory holds that children's internal working models or representations of the self and the social world are strongly influenced by early attachments. It is through these early relationships that the child also first experiences and learns to regulate intense emotions and arousal. In other words, working models that guide future experiences are thought to be first developed in these early attachment relationships. In children with insecure parent–child attachments, the cognitive and emotional contents of these working models have been described as remarkably similar to the cognitive and emotional patterns characteristic of depression (Cummings et al., 2000). Insecure attachments may interfere with the child's developing capacity to regulate affect and arousal and may be associated with poorer

self-concept and less trust in the availability and responsiveness of the social world.

The effects of parental depression on offspring probably vary with the age and gender of the child (Goodman et al., 2011; Lovejoy et al., 2000). Furthermore, although children of depressed parents are at increased risk for a number of difficulties, not all these children experience adverse outcomes (see the descriptions of Joe and Frank). Many of these children form secure attachments, experience good parenting, and are at decreased risk and may not develop disorders (Brennan, Le Brocque, & Hammen, 2003; Manczak, Donenberg, & Emerson, 2018; McMahon et al., 2006).

Indeed, there may be multiple ways in which family influences serve as protective factors against the potential adverse impact of parental depression. For example, Ivanova and Israel (2006) examined the influence of family stability (defined as the predictability and consistency of family activities and routines) on adjustment in a clinical sample of children. Children's reports of family stability as measured by the Stability of Activities in the Family Environment (SAFE; Israel, Roderick, & Ivanova, 2002) significantly attenuated the impact of parental depression on child internalizing, externalizing, and total problems. That is, parental depression was associated with problems in child adjustment when family stability was low, but not when family stability was high. Figure 8.3 illustrates this protective effect of family stability on parent-reported internalizing problems.

Peer Relations and Depression

Although problems with peers are common in the general population, these problems do distinguish youth referred to psychological services from non-referred youth (Achenbach

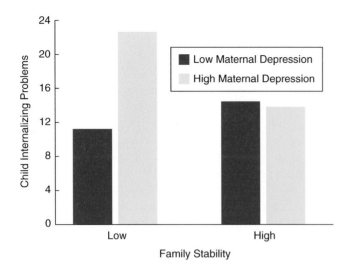

Figure 8.3 Family stability moderates the impact of parental depression on children's internalizing problems. (Adapted from Ivanova & Israel, 2006)

& Rescorla, 2001). Consistent with views that emphasize interpersonal aspects of depression, peer relation difficulties appear to contribute to the development and maintenance of depression (Boersma-van Dam et al., 2019; Epkins & Heckler, 2011; Stapinski et al., 2015).

Peer status, for example, has been found to be associated with adjustment difficulties, including depression. A study by Kupersmidt and Patterson (1991) illustrates the relationship between peer status and adjustment. The sociometric status of a sample of second, third, and fourth graders was assessed by asking the children to nominate their most liked and least liked peers. A peer status grouping was determined for each child. Two years later when the children were in the fourth through the sixth grade, several assessment instruments were completed, including a modified version of the Achenbach Youth Self-Report (YSR). As an index of a negative outcome, the authors examined whether a child had scores in the clinical range in one or more problem areas. Rejected boys and girls exhibited higher than expected rates of clinical-range difficulties. Girls with neglected peer status had even higher levels of clinical-range difficulties.

The authors also examined the relationship between peer status and each of the more specific problem areas defined by the various narrowband behavior problem scores. There was no relationship between peer status and any specific behavior problem area for boys. However, a finding of particular interest emerged for girls. Rejected girls were more than twice as likely to report high levels of depression than average, popular, and controversial girls. Furthermore, neglected girls were more than twice as likely as rejected girls and more than five times as likely as the other groups of girls to report depression problems.

Peer relation difficulties may both contribute to the development and be a consequence of depression. For example, research by Witvliet and colleagues (2010) illustrates how earlier peer relationships may predict later depression. The investigators prospectively studied a group of children from age 11 through age 14 years and measured various aspects of peer relationships and depressive symptoms through this time period. Peer rejection and friendlessness (having no reciprocal friendships) at age 11 years and not being a member of any clique of friends from age 11 to 13 years predicted depressive symptoms at age 14 years. On the other hand, depression may also contribute to peer relational difficulties (Oppenheimer & Hankin, 2011). Indeed, depression in young people has been found to be associated with a number of interpersonal characteristics important to peer relations and friendships. For example, depressed youth may perceive themselves as less interpersonally competent, have negative views of peers, have problematic social problem-solving styles, and exhibit distortions in processing of social information (Garber, 2010; Parker et al., 2006). Many of the problems in social relationships that accompany depression in young people may arise, in part, from the depressed youths' perceptions, including that others are rejecting and critical. This perception may then lead to behaviors by depressed youth that annoy peers, limit friendships, and result in isolation. Thus, as elsewhere, a reciprocal and transactional model of influences probably characterizes the contribution of peer and other social relationships to the development of depression.

As young people move into adolescence, peer relationships become more central and it becomes more likely that close friendships and intimate relationships will develop. Difficulties in such relationships have been found to be associated with increased risk for depression. These difficulties may be part of the developmental process that contributes to increases in

A withdrawn or socially isolated child may need assistance in developing appropriate social skills and in increasing peer interactions. (Eric Cote/Shutterstock)

depression during adolescence (Boersma-van Dam et al., 2019; Hammen, 2018).

Assessment of Depression

The assessment of depression is likely to involve a number of strategies, to sample a broad spectrum of attributes, and to include information from a variety of sources (Dougherty, Klein, & Olino, 2018). As we have seen, depression may manifest itself in a number of ways throughout development, and children and adolescents who experience depression are likely to exhibit other difficulties. A general clinical interview and the use of a broad assessment instrument such as the Child Behavior Checklist are common. Because a variety of influences may contribute to the development of depression, it is helpful to assess the parents, family, and social environments as well as the child or adolescent.

Structured and semi-structured interviews such as the Diagnostic Interview Schedule for Children (DISC; Costello et al., 1984) and the Schedule for Affective Disorders and Schizophrenia for School-Age Children (K-SADS; Ambrosini, 2000) may be employed to yield a DSM diagnosis. These interviews are more likely to be employed in research and specialty clinic settings than in typical clinical settings.

A variety of rating scales and inventories that focus on depression and related constructs have been developed to aid in various aspects of the assessment process (Dougherty et al., 2018; Reynolds, 1994). Of these, self-report instruments are among the most commonly employed. They are particularly important, given that many of the key problems that characterize depression, such as sadness and feelings of worthlessness, are subjective. The Children's Depression Inventory (CDI) (Kovacs, 2011) is probably the most frequently used measure of this type. It is an offshoot of the Beck Depression Inventory that is commonly used for adults. The CDI asks youth to choose which of three alternatives best characterizes them during the past two weeks. Items sample affective, behavioral, and cognitive aspects of depression. Research on the CDI suggest that it has good reliability, validity, and clinically meaningful cutoff scores (Kovacs, 2011; Reynolds, 1994). The Reynolds Child Depression Scale (Reynolds, 2010) and Reynolds Adolescent Depression Scale (Reynolds, 2002) also have been reported to have good psychometric properties (Dougherty et al., 2018; Reynolds, 1994). Despite the widespread use of self-report measures, some research suggests caution in assuming equivalent measurement of depression across various cultural and racial–ethnic groups (Crockett et al., 2005; Dere et al., 2015).

Many self-report measures are also rephrased so that they can be completed by significant others such as the child's parents. Measures completed by both the child and the parent often show only low levels of correlation, and agreement may vary with the age of the young person (Dougherty et al., 2018; Renouf & Kovacs, 1994). These results suggest that information provided by different sources may tap different aspects of the child's difficulties. Thus, assessment measures completed by teachers, clinicians, other adults, or peers can provide a unique perspective.

Measures of constructs related to depression have also been developed (Muris et al., 2016; Winters, Myers, & Proud, 2002). For example, attributes such as self-esteem (e.g., Harter, 1985) and perceived control over events (e.g., Connell, 1985) are likely candidates for evaluation. In addition, assessing various cognitive processes such as hopelessness (Kazdin, Rodgers, & Colbus, 1986), attributional style (Seligman & Peterson, 1986), and cognitive distortions (e.g., Leitenberg, Yost, & Carroll-Wilson, 1986) have been and are likely to be helpful for both clinical and research purposes.

Direct observation of the depressed youth interacting with others can provide information helpful to the clinician. A clinician may wish to assess, through observation, certain aspects of functioning such as parent–child communication, expression of affect, and level of criticism or praise. A number of observational measures can aid the assessment of depression in children and adolescents (Garber & Kaminski, 2000; Schroeder & Smith-Boydston, 2017). More systematic observations, involving formal coding, of depressed youth interacting with others in controlled settings can potentially provide an opportunity to observe the social behavior of these youth. Table 8.3 lists some of the categories of behaviors that can be observed using existing systems for coding social interactions relevant to depression. Systematic/formal observational measures may not be used as frequently as other assessment measures because they require considerable training, and coding itself is very labor intensive.

Table 8.3 Categories and Examples of Depression-Related Behaviors that Can Be Observed in Social Interaction Tasks

Emotions: smiling, frowning, crying, happiness, sadness, anger, fear
Affect Regulation: control or expression of affect
Problem Solving: identifying problems, proposing solutions
Nonverbal Behaviors: eye contact, posture
Conflict: noncompliance, ignoring, demanding, negotiating
Cognitive Content: criticism, praise, self-derogation
Speech: rate, volume, tone of voice, initiation
Engaged or Disengaged: enthusiasm, involvement, persistence
On or Off Task Behavior
Physical Contact: threatening, striking, affection
Symptoms: depression, irritability, psychomotor agitation or retardation, fatigue, concentration

Source: Adapted from Garber & Kaminski, 2000.

There is also concern regarding the ecological validity of these observations, that is, the extent to which a brief laboratory interaction reflects real-world social interactions.

Treatment of Depression

Making effective treatment of depression available to young people is challenging. Often young people and their families do not seek treatment and effective psychological treatments are not readily available in many communities. Our discussion of treatment emphasizes pharmacological, cognitive-behavioral, and interpersonal treatments, because these interventions, alone and in combination, have received the most research attention (Curry & Meyer, 2019; Eckshtain et al., 2020; Scahill & Rojas, 2019; Weersing et al., 2017).

Pharmacological Treatments

The practice of prescribing antidepressant medication for children and adolescents is widespread (Olfson, Druss, & Marcus, 2015). However, such treatment is controversial, because the effectiveness and safety of pharmacotherapy with depressed youth remains unclear (Bridge et al., 2007; Cipriani et al., 2016; Moreno, Roche, & Greenhill, 2006; Scahill & Rojas, 2019). Tricyclic antidepressants (TCAs) such as imipramine were once widely used to treat depression in young people. But TCAs have not been demonstrated to be effective in treating depressed youth and they have many side effects. **Selective serotonin reuptake inhibitors** (SSRIs) such as fluoxetine, escitalopram, and others (e.g., citalopram, paroxetine, vitazodone, and vortioxetine) also have been employed with depressed children and adolescents. SSRIs prevent the reabsorption of serotonin and, thus, more serotonin is available to the brain. SSRIs have fewer side effects than TCAs and are the medications most likely to be recommended.

The use of such medications is, however, based on limited research that does not clearly support the effectiveness of most antidepressant medications in either prepubertal children or adolescents (Cipriani et al., 2016; Gleason et al., 2007; Reyes et al., 2011). Also, little is known regarding long-term effectiveness. Fluoxetine (for youth ages 8 and older) and escitalopram (for youth ages 12 and older) are the only two FDA-approved medications for use with children and adolescents.

Medications may ultimately prove to be effective, alone or in combination with other treatments for certain youth. However, because antidepressant medications are developed and marketed principally for adults, there are less well-established guidelines for their administration and less systematic data on their safety. Issues of safety and side effects are of concern, in part, because little is known regarding the long-term impact of these medications on development, particularly in young children. Particular concern has been expressed about the possible association between SSRIs and increases in suicidal behavior (Cipriani et al., 2016; Curry & Meyer, 2019; Emslie et al., 2006; Moreno et al., 2006; Scahill & Rojas, 2019). As mentioned in our discussion of SSRIs in the treatment of anxiety disorders, such concerns led the FDA to issue a warning about their use with children and adolescents.

Since depression is itself associated with suicide, the issue of risk and benefit from the use of SSRIs is an important one. Families and clinicians may ask: Is the risk of not employing SSRIs to treat depression in certain youth who may be at risk for suicide greater than the suicide risk associated with the use of these medications? If antidepressants are employed in treatment, the FDA recommends that the youth return to the clinician's office for more frequent visits, particularly in the early stages of treatment or at times of dosage changes, and recommends that caregivers and clinicians be vigilant about unusual changes in behavior (U.S. Food and Drug Administration, 2007).

Combined Treatments

The Treatment of Adolescent Depressions Study (TADS Team, 2004, 2007, 2009) examined the combined use of fluoxetine (an SSRI) and a form of cognitive-behavior therapy (CBT). Adolescents (ages 12 to 17) with moderate to severe major depression were randomly assigned to treatment with fluoxetine alone, CBT alone, CBT combined with fluoxetine, or placebo (pill). The TADS Team has reported that at the end of treatment, the combined treatment produced the greatest improvement in symptoms of MDD and was superior to either treatment alone. However, by the end of an 18-week follow-up period (week 36) there were no differences between the three treatment conditions. Overall, treatment gains were maintained at a one-year follow-up (TADS Team, 2009). While the results of this study are important, aspects of the methodology and interpretation of results have been questioned (TADS Team, 2007; Hollon, Garber, & Shelton, 2005; Rohde, 2017). Also, rates of **remission** (no longer meeting diagnostic criteria or cutoff scores) were low, many youth continued to have significant symptoms, and some youth who had improved experienced **relapse**—a worsening of depression during the follow-up period (Brent, 2006; Kennard et al., 2006; TADS Team, 2009).

However, an additional potential benefit of the combined treatment is germane to concerns about SSRIs and suicide risk. During the treatment period, suicide-related events were greatest among youth treated with fluoxetine alone (9.2%)—nearly twice as many as in the other conditions (Emslie et al., 2006). Such events may be particularly likely for youth with severe depressive symptoms and following interpersonal stressors such as conflicts with family members (Vitiello et al., 2009).

The use of combined treatment with moderately to severely depressed youth was also investigated in the Treatment of

Resistant Depression in Adolescents (TORDIA) study (Weersing & Brent, 2010). The adolescents in the TORDIA study had been depressed an average of two years, had a diagnosis of MDD, and evidenced significant suicidality and comorbidity. The participants also had a previously failed trial of an SSRI. They were randomly assigned to either a medication (a switch to a medication different from their previous SSRI) alone or a medication plus CBT condition. The CBT offered was an individual treatment protocol and also involved the family in a CBT-based approach to family problem solving. After 12 weeks of the program, 55% of the CBT-plus-medication participants, as compared to 41% of the medication-switch-alone participants, showed a substantial clinical improvement. In this sample of seriously depressed youth, the results supported the value of the combination of CBT and medication switch. In addition, the superiority of the combined treatment approach was more evident among youth with a greater number of co-occurring diagnoses (Asarnow et al., 2009).

The potential of reducing relapse by adding CBT to treatment with an SSRI is suggested by the findings of Kennard and colleagues (2014). Youth, ages 8–17, diagnosed with MDD were treated for six weeks with fluoxetine and then assigned to a continuation of treatment with medications alone or to a combined medication with relapse-prevention CBT condition. During the 30-week continuation of treatment the two conditions did not differ with regard to time to remission. However, the rate of relapse was significantly lower for youth in the medication plus CBT condition.

Psychosocial Treatments

Most psychological interventions for depression in children and adolescents derive from a cognitive-behavioral perspective. Cognitive-behavioral treatments confront and modify the young person's maladaptive cognitions (e.g., problematic attributions, excessively high standards, negative self-monitoring), and focus on goals such as increasing pleasurable experiences; increasing social skills; and improving communication, conflict resolution, social problem solving, and coping skills. Two programs are described here to illustrate interventions derived from a cognitive-behavioral perspective.

Stark and colleagues (1987, 1991) conducted several investigations of a treatment for depressed youth that combined training of self-control skills, behavioral problem solving, and other cognitive strategies. This cognitive-behavioral treatment resulted in greater reduction in depressive symptoms than did control conditions. Drawing on this earlier work, Stark and colleagues (2010) developed a school-based group CBT program for 9–13-year-old girls named the ACTION Treatment Program. A brief description of the content of the 20-session program, that also illustrates components characteristic of many CBT interventions for depression, is provided in Table 8.4. The authors

suggest that the main goals and themes of the ACTION program are captured by three messages on a card given to the girls (Stark et al., 2010, p. 94).

1. If you feel bad and you don't know why, use coping skills.
2. If you feel bad and you can change the situation, use problem solving.
3. If you feel bad and it is due to the negative thoughts, change the thoughts.

The session contents address these three core skills (see Table 8.4) and a subgoal throughout is to target **behavioral activation**— activities that encourage the participants to be active and do pleasant things. A parent training (PT) component was intended to help parents model and reinforce the use of therapeutic skills, to change the affective tone and communication style of the family, and to create a supportive environment that sends the girls a positive message.

Participants were randomly assigned to a CBT, CBT+PT, or a minimal contact control condition. At posttreatment, girls in the two active treatment conditions reported significantly lower levels of depressive symptoms than girls in the control condition. Also, 80% of the treatment girls as compared to 45% of control girls no longer met criteria for a depressive disorder. While there were some differences, the two treatment conditions did not differ from each other on these central measures. Improvements in the treated girls were maintained at one year posttreatment.

A cognitive-behavioral intervention for adolescents known as the Adolescent Coping with Depression program, a skills-training, multi-component group intervention, grew out of the Oregon Adolescent Depression Project (p. 160) and the work of Lewinsohn, Clarke, and colleagues (Rohde, 2017). In an initial study (Lewinsohn et al., 1990), adolescents ages 14 to 18 who met diagnostic criteria for depression were randomly assigned to one of three conditions: adolescent-only, adolescent-and-parent, and wait-list control. Adolescents attended 16 two-hour sessions, twice a week, in a group or class-like setting, that focused on monitoring of mood and increasing pleasant events, identifying and controlling irrational and negative thoughts, teaching methods of relaxation, increasing social skills, and teaching conflict resolution (communication and problem-solving) skills. In the parent-involvement condition, parents met for nine weekly sessions. They were provided with information on the skills being taught to their teenagers and were taught problem solving and conflict resolution skills.

Relative to the youth in the control group, individuals in the treatment groups improved on depression measures. For example, at the end of treatment, the recovery rate for treated adolescents was 46% whereas only 5% of the control group no longer met diagnostic criteria. A second similar study (Clarke et al., 1999) yielded comparable findings. The adolescents in the

Table 8.4 Primary Child Components of the ACTION Treatment Program for Girls

Meeting Number	Primary Treatment Component
1	Introductions and discussion of basic aspects of program
2	Affective education and introduction to coping
Individual session 1	Review concepts and develop treatment goals
3	Affective education and coping skills
4	Extend group cohesion; review goals, application of coping skills
5	Extend coping skills, introduction to problem solving
6	Cognition and emotion, introduction to idea of cognitive restructuring
7–9	Apply problem solving
Individual session 2	Review concepts and individualize therapeutic activities
10	Prepare for and practice cognitive restructuring in session
11	Continue illustrating cognitive restructuring
12–19	Cognitive restructuring practice and self-maps (identifying individual strengths)
20	Bring it all together and treatment termination

Source: Adapted from Stark et al., 2010. Copyright 2010 by Guilford Press; reprinted with permission.

treatment conditions were followed for two years after the end of treatment, and their treatment gains were maintained. In both studies there were few or no significant advantages for parent involvement. This may have been due, in part, to relatively low rates of parental participation and to the limited nature of the parental participation component (Rohde, 2017). One way of improving treatment efforts is to gain further understanding of the potential role of parental involvement. This may involve clarifying the optimal level of and mechanism for parental involvement and appreciating individual differences in when parental involvement may or may not be helpful.

A second approach to treating depression in adolescents, interpersonal psychotherapy for adolescents (IPT-A), modified from interpersonal psychotherapy for depressed adults, has also been found to be effective (Jacobson, Mufson, & Young, 2017). IPT-A is based on the premise that whatever the causes, the onset and course of depression is influenced by the individual's interpersonal relationships with significant others. The therapist employs a variety of active strategies that address psychoeducation, affect identification, and building interpersonal problem solving and communication skills. The adolescent is helped to understand current interpersonal issues such as separation from parents, role transitions, romantic relationships, interpersonal deficits, peer pressure, grief, and single-parent family status. Mufson and colleagues (1999) found that adolescents diagnosed with MDD who received IPT-A showed improvement in depressive symptoms, social functioning, and problem-solving skills compared with control youth whose clinical condition was monitored. A second study by Mufson and colleagues, in a school setting, also reported a greater reduction in depressive symptoms for IPT-A compared

with a treatment control condition (Mufson et al., 2004). IPT-A was effective for adolescents with more severe depression, co-occurring anxiety, and high levels of parent–adolescent conflict (Jacobson et al., 2017).

Rosselló and Bernal (1999) compared IPT-A with CBT and a wait-list control in a sample of clinically depressed adolescents in Puerto Rico. Both treatment groups showed significant improvements in depressive symptoms (see Figure 8.4) and self-esteem compared with those in the control condition. An additional study by these investigators also suggested comparable effectiveness for IPT-A and CBT (Rosselló et al., 2008).

It is interesting to note that the studies by Mufson and colleagues included a large proportion of Latinx youth and that Rosselló and colleagues made efforts to incorporate interpersonal aspects of Latino culture into their treatment: *personalismo*— the preference for interpersonal contacts, and *familismo*—a strong identification with and attachment to family. This was accomplished through a variety of adaptations to the treatment, such as selection of examples, sayings, and images from the adolescents' culture and context; emphasis on the interpersonal nature of the therapeutic approach; and discussion of family dependence and independence (Rosselló & Bernal, 1999, 2005). Although adolescents in both treatment groups in the Rosselló and Bernal study had comparable improvements in depression, improvement for some other outcome measures was better in the IPT-A group. The authors suggest that this may be because of the consonance of IPT-A with Puerto Rican cultural values.

A related challenge remains with regard to the treatment of youth with depression, or indeed other disorders. Identifying evidence-based treatments that have been evaluated with various ethnic and

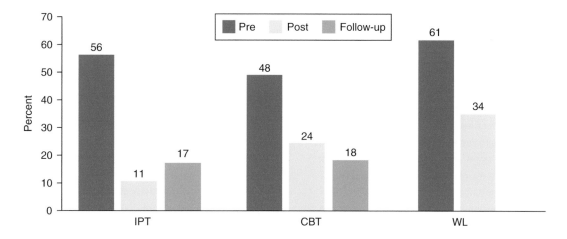

Figure 8.4 Percentage of severely depressed adolescents at pretreatment, posttreatment, and follow-up for each condition. IPT, interpersonal psychotherapy treatment; CBT, cognitive-behavioral treatment; WL, wait-list control; Pre, pretreatment; Post, posttreatment. (From Rosselló & Bernal, 1999)

cultural groups and/or have been adapted for use with these youth is a continuing effort and goal (Pina, Polo, & Huey, 2019).

Treatments that are derived from a cognitive-behavioral perspective and treatments that address interpersonal and family aspects of depression in adolescents are well established. Cognitive-behavioral treatments for children with depression are probably effective, however evidence is less strong than for adolescents. Furthermore, findings are modest, particularly with regard to severely depressed youth, those with co-occurring disorders, and with regard to long-term effectiveness (Curry & Meyer, 2019; Dietz, Silk, & Amole, 2019; Eckshtain et al., 2020; Rohde, 2017; Weersing et al., 2017). Efforts to identify key elements, refine treatment, determine optimal treatment length, enhance effectiveness in community/real-world settings, and generally improve treatment effectiveness are ongoing.

Prevention of Depression

A number of universal depression prevention programs have been implemented and evaluated (Spence & Shortt, 2007). Most of these programs have been school-based and have emphasized cognitive-behavioral procedures; a few have included components drawn from an interpersonal psychotherapy perspective. These programs are offered to all youth in a particular grade(s) at one or more schools.

For example, Spence and colleagues (Spence, Sheffield, & Donovan, 2003, 2005) evaluated a teacher-implemented, classroom-based universal intervention that taught Australian eighth graders a range of problem-solving and cognitive-coping skills to deal with challenging life circumstances. Sixteen schools were randomly assigned to the intervention or a control condition. Over the time of the program, students in the intervention condition did better than those in the control condition. The positive impact of the intervention (an increase in problem-solving skills and a decrease in depression symptoms) was most evident for those students with initial high levels of depressive symptoms. However, at one, two, three, and four-year follow-ups there were no differences in depressive symptoms (or for problem-solving skills) for the students in the two conditions. A separate large-scale evaluation for ninth graders (Sheffield et al., 2006) failed to find any differences between intervention and control conditions even at the end of the program.

In general, the findings for universal prevention programs for child and adolescent depression have been modest at best, and at long-term follow-ups effects have not been maintained. However, there is probably enough success to suggest that efforts should continue. As Spence and Shortt (2007) suggest, interventions may need to be longer and more intensive and, in keeping with ecological models of the etiology of depression, preventive approaches may need to place a greater emphasis on decreasing risk factors and increasing protective factors in the youth's environment.

Several of the universal programs reported greater impact for those young people with moderate to high initial levels of depressive symptoms. This may suggest the value of indicated prevention approaches. A number of such programs have been attempted, and, again, many of these programs are derived from a cognitive-behavioral approach (David-Ferdon & Kaslow, 2008; Evans & Commission on Adolescent Depression and Bipolar Disorder, 2005b; Rohde, 2017). The Adolescent Coping With Stress course (CWS-A) is an extension of the Adolescent Coping with Depression treatment program (p. 173) that emphasizes the cognitive restructuring component of the intervention. It is intended to prevent future depression in at-risk adolescents. Adolescents in the ninth grade at three high schools who had high scores on the Center for Epidemiologic Studies Depression Scale, but who were not currently depressed based on a structured diagnostic interview and/or had a depressed parent, were assigned to either a 15-session, after-school, cognitive-behavioral group intervention or a usual-care control condition (Clarke et al., 2001). At one-year follow-up there were significantly fewer MDD episodes among adolescents receiving the CWS-A intervention (8% versus 25%). This significant difference persisted at the two-year follow-up, but at a diminished level, suggesting that the prevention program effect had faded somewhat over time. A large four-site study (Beardslee et al., 2013) again supported the effectiveness of this prevention program. The rates of onset of an episode of depression over the course of a 33-month follow-up were significantly lower for the adolescents in the cognitive-behavioral prevention program than for those in the control condition (37% versus 48%). However, adolescents with a depressed parent did not experience comparable benefits of the prevention program.

Indicated prevention programs based on IPT-A also have shown some effectiveness (Benas et al., 2019; Young, Mufson, & Davies, 2006; Young et al., 2016). Adolescents receiving the Interpersonal Psychotherapy–Adolescent Skills Training (IPT-AST) had significantly fewer depressive symptoms and better overall functioning as compared to adolescents in the counseling control condition.

These and other indicated prevention programs suggest that this approach to intervention is promising and worthy of continued attention.

Bipolar Disorders

Does a 7-year-old child who demonstrates significant "rages," has clear evidence of ADHD and a family history positive for depression on the maternal side and bipolar disorder on the paternal side represent a safe candidate for stimulant treatment for his ADHD? What if he also has episodic daylong periods of being excessively giggly, needing little sleep, and appearing more active and talkative than usual? Does this represent a natural variant of childhood or is this a child who is showing early signs of a pediatric bipolar spectrum disorder ... and who will be at risk for future substance use, legal problems, incarceration, and suicide attempts?

Danner et al., 2009, p. 271

The description by Danner and colleagues of clinical and conceptual issues in many ways captures the challenges faced in considering the development of bipolar disorder and its presentation in children and adolescents. How might a youth with bipolar disorder present? Is there a pediatric bipolar disorder that is similar to the disorder seen in adults? How might the presentation be distinguished from other disorders? How might this be different from more typical developmental patterns? What

is the likely developmental course? These and other questions have become part of the substantial increase in attention to bipolar disorder in youth.

DSM Classification of Bipolar Disorders

The DSM category of **Bipolar and Related Disorders** describes disorders that involve the presence of mania as well as depressive symptoms. **Mania** is typically described as a period of abnormally, persistently elevated or irritable mood and increased energy or activity that is also persistent. The elevated mood that is experienced during mania is often described as **euphoric mood** and is characterized by features such as inflated self-esteem; high rates of activity, speech, and thinking; distractibility; and exaggerated feelings of physical and mental well-being. Children may exhibit happiness or "goofiness" that is excessive or inappropriate to the situation or the child's developmental level. Inflated self-esteem and grandiosity, in children, may take the form of overestimating one's abilities ("I'm the smartest person in the school") or attempting feats that are dangerous. These displays of euphoric mood represent changes that are clearly different from the child's typical behavior.

To meet the criteria for a manic episode, mania (lasting a week or more) and at least three (or four if the mood is only irritable) of the following additional symptoms must be present:

1. Inflated self-esteem
2. Decreased need for sleep
3. More talkative than usual
4. Racing thoughts
5. Distractibility
6. Increased goal-directed activity or motor agitation
7. Excessive activity that can lead to negative outcomes (e.g., excessive spending, sexual indiscretions)

Also, to receive a bipolar disorder diagnosis, the manic episode must result in a distinct impairment in social or academic functioning or require hospitalization to prevent youth from harming themselves or others.

The DSM includes a number of bipolar diagnoses that might be given to children and adolescents. The diagnosis of *Bipolar I Disorder* requires the presence of one or more manic episodes and typically also involves a history of major depression. *Bipolar II Disorder* includes a history of major depression and hypomania. **Hypomania** is defined as a euphoric mood that is of shorter duration (four consecutive days) and less severe than a manic episode. *Cyclothymic Disorder* involves chronic, but mild, fluctuations between distinct periods of hypomanic and depressive symptoms that do not meet the diagnostic criteria for major depressive or hypomanic episodes. In earlier versions of the DSM there was also a category of *Bipolar Disorder Not Otherwise Specified (NOS)*. This diagnosis was used for cases with symptoms characteristic of bipolar disorders but that did not meet full criteria for the other bipolar diagnoses. A large number of youth with bipolar symptoms received this NOS diagnosis (Birmaher & Axelson, 2005). The DSM-5 has, here and elsewhere, replaced the NOS terminology, but the general purpose of this designation remains the same. For bipolar presentations, the term *NOS* has been replaced with the diagnoses of Other Specified Bipolar and Related Disorder and Unspecified Bipolar and Related Disorder that, similar to NOS, are meant to be employed when symptoms of bipolar disorders are displayed, but the full criteria for other bipolar disorders are not met. In the first diagnosis, the clinician chooses to indicate the reasons that full criteria for another bipolar disorder are not met. In the "unspecified" diagnosis the clinician elects not to specify the reasons why the full criteria for another bipolar diagnosis are not met.

A major issue in the discussion of the diagnosis of bipolar disorders in young people is the question of the degree to which child-onset and adult-onset "versions" of bipolar disorders should be considered as the same or different disorders. Bipolar disorder epitomizes the challenges inherent in employing a disorder defined by symptom descriptions in one population (in this instance early to midlife adults) and applying it to another population (children) (Blader et al., 2017).

Historically, the DSM criteria have been primarily the same for adults, children, and adolescents. In the DSM-5 this largely continues to be the case; however, sensitivity to potential developmental issues has begun to be addressed. For example, in the text accompanying the diagnostic criteria, examples are provided of how symptoms such as euphoric mood and grandiosity might present in children. Also, earlier in the chapter (see p. 158), the introduction, in DSM-5, of a diagnosis of Disruptive Mood Dysregulation Disorder as a type of depressive disorder was described. This diagnosis was introduced because of concerns regarding over diagnosis of bipolar disorders in children.

A number of considerations have contributed to the ongoing concern with employing the same criteria to diagnose bipolar disorders in youth and adults (Blader et al., 2017). For example, juvenile mania is often characterized by symptom presentations and patterns that may differ from the typical descriptions of bipolar disorders in adults. Important developmental differences in presentation challenge clinicians to apply the existing criteria while being sensitive to developmental differences in expression (American Academy of Child and Adolescent Psychiatry (AACAP), 2007c; Blader et al., 2017; Danner et al., 2009; Meyer & Carlson, 2010). For example, in adults a typical clinical picture is of a cyclical disorder with acute onset of *distinct* episodes of mania or depression with periods of relatively good functioning between episodes. In contrast, some youth may not exhibit these distinct episodes. Instead, they may exhibit a chronic pattern (e.g., most days) of mood dysregulation without intervening periods of good functioning. Furthermore, young people are likely to exhibit very short mood episodes, very frequent mood shifts, and patterns of mixed moods rather than separate periods of depressed or manic mood.

This makes the usual "adult" distinctions a considerable challenge—defining what constitutes a manic or mood episode and describing how episodes cycle (Geller, Tillman, & Bolhofner, 2007). Should children who do not show episodic mood changes or who exhibit elevated symptoms of mania without meeting diagnostic criteria be considered a subtype of a group of juvenile bipolar disorders, or should they be classified in some other way (Brotman et al., 2006; Danner et al., 2009; Leibenluft & Rich, 2008)? For example, are children with a pattern of severe mood dysregulation (chronic irritability and hyperarousal)—a pattern that is persistent rather than occurring in distinct episodes—better classified as having a bipolar disorder, or as having disruptive mood dysregulation—a depressive disorder? (See Scott: Mixed Moods and Aggression.)

Also, euphoric mood is often considered the hallmark of adult mania/bipolar disorder. There are, however, a number of challenges to defining a comparable mood in youth. For one, in youth, irritable mood is commonly associated with bipolar disorder. Thus, there is the question of what is the predominant mood. Also, mania, particularly in prepubertal youth, if present, may look very different than in adult samples.

SCOTT Mixed Moods and Aggression

Scott, a 4-year-old boy was referred because of concerns about periods of extreme irritability associated with aggression that were interrupted by periods of sadness, guilt, and remorse. Scott's mother was unable to manage his intense tantrums that occurred multiple times daily and seemed to arise with little or no apparent provocation. But the greatest concern was aggression toward his younger sibling. Scott was hospitalized after pushing his younger sister down a flight of stairs and subsequently becoming inconsolably sad and crying for several hours.

Adapted from Luby, Belden, & Tandon, 2010, p. 116

In diagnosing bipolar disorder in children there is also the additional challenge of distinguishing symptoms of mania from typical behaviors (Blader et al., 2017; Stringaris et al., 2011). This can be a difficult task. One approach by Kowatch and colleagues (2005) describes the strategy of FIND (frequency, intensity, number, and duration of symptoms), and thresholds for each index. This is meant to assist clinicians in judging whether behavior is a symptom of bipolar disorder rather than a manifestation of developmentally more typical behavior. Similarly, Geller and her colleagues (2003) have attempted to describe how various mania criteria may present in children. Table 8.5 provides examples of what may be viewed as symptoms of mania in children and contrasting examples of typical child behavior. In making a diagnosis, clinicians must judge the child's behavior based on a number of considerations. For example, is the behavior appropriate for the child's age and developmental level? Are the behaviors, which might be appropriate in one context, displayed in contexts where they are clearly inappropriate or unexpected? What is the degree of impairment or interference with expected functioning?

Young people with bipolar disorder also are likely to present with high rates of co-occurring problems and disorders. For example, reported rates of comorbidity with ADHD are often quite high, ranging from 60% to 95% in children. Rates of comorbidity in adolescents are lower (Carlson & Klein, 2014; Geller et al., 2000). Also, patterns of co-occurrence may be different from those seen in adults. For example, manic episodes and bipolar disorders in older adolescents may in some ways be similar to adult presentations. However, manic episodes in adolescents are more likely to be associated with antisocial behaviors, school truancy, and academic failure. Manic episodes in adolescents are also likely to include psychotic features. Also, bipolar disorder may initially present as depression, with alterations of mood occurring only after some period of time.

Thus, diagnosing bipolar disorder in youth may be difficult because of confusion regarding definition, the symptom presentation, and overlap with co-occurring disorders. For a number of reasons, whether or how one should apply current DSM bipolar criteria to youth is part of ongoing debate and these concerns are likely to impact future diagnostic approaches (Black & Fristad, 2019; Blader et al., 2017; Jenkins & Youngstrom, 2016; Leibenluft & Rich, 2008). Part of this debate considers whether bipolar presentations may be better conceptualized as a collection of dimensional symptoms or as a spectrum of presentations rather than as distinct categorical disorders. It is suggested that this alternative dimensional approach may prove fruitful for understanding the presentations of both youth and adults and may help in conceptualizing these problems across the full developmental spectrum (Bebko et al., 2014; Black & Fristad, 2019; Cicchetti, 2010; Danner et al., 2009; Youngstrom, 2010).

Description of Bipolar Disorders

Descriptions of young people with bipolar disorder often refer to a variety of features. Kowatch & DelBello (2006) describe manic symptoms that may be displayed by children and adolescents with bipolar disorder. These are presented in Table 8.6 and we draw on their report for our description. Children with mania may irritate those around them by being extremely happy or silly when there seems to be no reason for this euphoric mood. Adolescents may also be extremely silly or unrealistically optimistic. Irritable

Table 8.5 Examples of Manifestations of Mania Symptoms in Children and Typical Child Behavior

Symptom	Child Mania	Typical Child
Elated mood	A 9-year-old girl continually danced around the house saying "I'm high, over the mountain high." A 7-year-old boy was repeatedly taken to the Principal for clowning and giggling in class (when no one else was).	A child was very excited when the family went to Disneyland on Christmas morning.
Grandiose behaviors	An 8-year-old girl set up a paper flower store in her classroom and was annoyed and refused to do class work when asked to by the teacher. A 7-year-old boy stole a go-cart. He knew it was wrong to steal but did not believe it was wrong for him. He thought that the police were arriving to play with him.	A 7-year-old boy pretended he was a fireman, directing others and rescuing victims. In his play, he did not call the firehouse. His play was age-appropriate and not impairing.
Hypersexual behavior	An 8-year-old boy imitated a rock star—gyrating his hips and rubbing his crotch during an interview. A 9-year-old boy drew pictures of naked ladies in public and said that they were his future wife.	A 7-year-old played doctor with a same-age friend.

Source: Adapted from Geller et al., 2003. Copyright 2003 by Guilford Press; reprinted with permission.

Table 8.6 Manic Symptoms that May Be Displayed by Youth with Bipolar Disorders

Euphoric mood
Irritable mood
Mood swings
Decreased need for sleep
Unusual energy
Hyperactivity
Increased goal-directed activity
Grandiosity
Accelerated, pressured, or increased amount of speech
Racing thoughts
Flight of ideas
Distractibility
Poor judgment
Hallucinations
Delusions

Source: Adapted from Kowatch & DelBello, 2006. Copyright 2006 by Elsevier; reprinted with permission.

mood also is common. A child may have many intense outbursts of anger. An adolescent may be extremely oppositional, curt, or hostile. Parents often report multiple intense mood swings daily (**labile mood**). Young people also report needing less sleep than usual and report having more energy than usual. Children and adolescents, when manic, may appear very restless or driven. Youth may do many things over a short period of time and, initially, be fairly productive. They may, however, become increasingly disorganized and unproductive as their mania progresses. Young people may exhibit **grandiosity**—an inflated opinion of one's worth or importance. Blader and colleagues (2017), for example, describe a girl who thought she was a pop star. She spent hours picking out items at a clothing boutique only to step aside and let others pay before her because she was waiting for her manager to arrive and complete the purchase. Young people may be loud, intrusive, and difficult to interrupt. Their speech may be rapid, pressured, unintelligible, or difficult to follow, and they may report that their thoughts are racing—they can't get their ideas out fast enough. The child or adolescent may also exhibit what is often termed "**flight of ideas**"—changing topics rapidly in a way that is confusing to others. Even adults who are familiar with them cannot easily follow their words. When manic, youth are easily distracted. Children and adolescents with mania also may show poor judgment, becoming involved in impulsive or high-risk pleasurable behaviors (e.g., frequent fighting, alcohol or drug use, reckless driving). Some youth with bipolar disorder also may experience hallucinations and delusions (see pp. 357–358).

Epidemiology of Bipolar Disorders

Definitional and methodological issues make accurate estimates of prevalence of manic symptoms and bipolar disorders difficult. Bipolar disorder is thought to be relatively rare in childhood and adolescence, but it seems that use of the diagnosis has become more common (Black & Fristad, 2019; Blader et al., 2017). Moreno and colleagues (2007) report on a national representative survey of visits to a physician's office by youth (ages 0–19 years). If one examines office visits in which the youth received a mental disorder diagnosis, one sees that the percentage of visits with a diagnosis of Bipolar Disorder increased from 0.42% in 1994–1995 to 6.67% in 2002–2003. This increase was larger than that among adults. Similarly, Blader and Carlson (2007) report an increase of Bipolar Disorder diagnoses among hospitalized youth. Between 1996 and 2004, the diagnosis rate increased from 1.4 to 7.3 per 10,000 for children and from 5.1 to 20.4 per 10,000 for adolescents.

Estimates of the prevalence of bipolar disorders among children and adolescents vary between 0 and 6.7% with a mean estimated prevalence of 1.8%. It is generally reported that females and males are equally represented and that bipolar disorder is much less prevalent in prepubertal youth than after puberty. There do not appear to be significant cultural/international differences in rates of child and adolescent bipolar disorders (Merikangas & Hommer, 2019; Van Meter, Moreira, & Youngstrom, 2011).

Similar to what we noted in our discussion of depression, in community samples of adolescents, manic-like symptoms of elevated, expansive, or irritable mood are present in adolescents who do not meet the criteria for a bipolar disorder. The youth with these subthreshold symptoms do experience substantial impairment in functioning (Vaudreuil et al., 2019). Indeed, as we have indicated, some evidence suggests a bipolar spectrum, that is, a continuum extending from normal emotion-regulation difficulties to subthreshold symptoms to mild and severe forms of the disorder rather than a categorical distinction (Alloy et al., 2010; Papolos, 2003; Youngstrom, 2010).

A number of other conditions commonly co-occur in youth diagnosed with Bipolar Disorder. ADHD, conduct disorder, oppositional defiant disorder, and substance abuse or dependence are among the problems commonly reported (Diler et al., 2010; Evans & Commission on Adolescent Depression and Bipolar Disorder, 2005a; Kowatch & DelBello, 2006; Papolos, 2003). These youth also experience significant impairment in cognitive, school, social, and family functioning (Alloy et al., 2010; Lewinsohn, Klein, & Seeley, 1995a; Lewinsohn, Seeley, & Klein, 2003; McClure-Tone, 2010; Pavuluri et al., 2009). Their families face a considerable challenge and require assistance and support that is sensitive to the child's difficulties and the family's needs (Fristad & Goldberg-Arnold, 2003; Miklowitz & Goldstein, 2010). The feelings of one mother who received support through an online support group illustrate this need (see Bipolar Disorders: Families Need Support).

BIPOLAR DISORDERS Families Need Support

One of the biggest stressors is the total isolation and lack of support. I *never* have a moment to myself. I have no friends, I have no life. I spend almost every day with a feeling of mortal terror that we will return to the horror before diagnosis and stabilization. No parent or child should ever have to experience what we and the many other parents I've met at CABF (Child and Adolescent Bipolar Foundation) have had

to go through. I am tired of this life. I grieve for the loss of what I thought motherhood would be. ... If I did not have the lifeline, I don't know what I would do some nights. I can log on after a bad day and get the support and strength to start the new day with a smile so that I can be there for my boys.

Adapted from Hellander, Sisson, & Fristad, 2003, p. 314

Developmental Course and Prognosis

Youth with bipolar disorders may experience relatively early onset of affective difficulties. They also may experience such difficulties for appreciable periods of time and follow a fluctuating course of high rates of recovery and recurrence (Diler et al., 2010).

Lewinsohn, Klein, and Seeley (1995a) examined the course of bipolar disorder in a large community sample of adolescents (ages 14 to 18). The median duration of the most recent manic episode for these young people was 10.8 months. Among the participants in the study, youth diagnosed with Bipolar Disorder had experienced their first affective episode earlier (mean age = 11.75 years) than had adolescents with a history of major depression with no periods of mania (mean age = 14.95 years). The total amount of time spent with an affective disorder was longer for the youth with bipolar disorder as well. The estimated mean duration of affective disorder for these youth with bipolar

disorder was 80.2 months compared with a mean duration of 15.7 months for youth in the OADP sample with MDD. This finding and others suggest that in some young people, a depressive disorder may be an early stage of bipolar disorder. There may be multiple risk factors predictive of a transition from MDD to bipolar disorder (Blader et al., 2017). For example, the switching from MDD to bipolar disorder may be more likely to occur in youth with an earlier and abrupt onset of depression and those with a family history of bipolar disorder (Luby et al., 2010).

Some of the adolescents in the OADP sample who met the criteria for bipolar disorder experienced a chronic/recurrent course. Twelve percent had not remitted by age 24 (that is, they continued to meet diagnostic criteria) and of those in remission at age 18, about one-quarter had another episode between the ages of 19 and 24 (Lewinsohn et al., 2003). Individuals with bipolar disorder during adolescence were far more likely to meet criteria for bipolar disorder during young adulthood than adolescents with

JOSEPH Early Bipolar Symptoms

Based on information gathered at his first hospital admission, Joseph suffered from childhood illnesses more than his eight siblings. By the time he started school at age 6 his parents described him as already having periods of being tired. Although Joseph was usually considered a "jolly boy who enjoyed himself," there were episodes of crying, irritability, and depressed moods. At school he was sometimes "extra good" and at others he "lost all interest."

By the time he was 13, the family said, "they could see it coming." Joseph began having alternating periods of "quietness and irritability." He would be at the playground ordering others around and being overly bossy at one moment and at the next he would be withdrawn, sitting quietly reading

the Bible. For periods of a week or so, Joseph would sit around, tired, not talking and sometimes crying. During these times he seemed "scared."

There were rapid and extreme changes when Joseph would destroy whatever his siblings were playing with. During these times Joseph was overactive, restless, overtalkative, bold, loud, demanding, and exhibited hostile behavior and angry outbursts. The brief spells of being "quiet versus irritable" persisted through ages 13 and 14. Joseph's symptoms and the cycling worsened dramatically at age 15, when he was first admitted to the hospital meeting the criteria for a bipolar disorder.

Adapted from Egeland et al., 2000, p. 1249

subthreshold bipolar symptoms. Adolescents with subthreshold bipolar symptoms did, however, experience high rates of MDD during young adulthood.

Geller and colleagues (2003) studied a group of prepubertal children and early adolescents with bipolar disorder. These youth were assessed in a research setting, but received care from community practitioners. During a two-year period about two-thirds of these young people experienced recovery (defined as at least eight consecutive weeks not meeting DSM criteria for mania or hypomania). A little over half of them relapsed after recovery and many continued to meet the criteria for another disorder during their recovery.

Prospective data are limited. However, the retrospective and prospective information that is available suggests that youth with bipolar disorders or symptoms might continue to display symptoms of affective disorders and experience considerable social and academic impairment, at least into the early adult period (Birmaher et al., 2014; Blader et al., 2017; Danner et al., 2009). Youth with co-occurring conditions are likely to experience a more adverse developmental course (Weintraub et al., 2019).

Risk Factors and Etiology

Discussions of the etiology of bipolar disorder have tended to emphasize biological influences and, indeed, genetic and neurobiological factors appear to be central to understanding the disorder. However, there also is growing consensus that bipolar disorder is a condition in which there is a genetic diathesis and for which, from the very beginnings of life, environmental experiences make a major contribution to the complex and dynamic interplay of influences that shape the expression of difficulties at each developmental level (Cicchetti, 2010; Meyer & Carlson, 2010; Youngstrom, 2010).

A family history of bipolar disorders is clearly a risk factor (Craddock & Sklar, 2013). Biological siblings and parents of youth diagnosed with Bipolar Disorder have appreciably higher than expected rates of bipolar disorder. Also, children of adult bipolar patients have an increased risk for bipolar disorder and mood disorders, in general. However, it is important to note that the majority of children of bipolar adults do not have a diagnosable bipolar disorder or other mood disorder (Evans & Commission on Adolescent Depression and Bipolar Disorder, 2005a).

Other research suggests a significant genetic influence (Blader et al., 2017; Willcutt & McQueen, 2010). Adult twin and adoption studies are consistent in showing a strong genetic component for bipolar disorders and indirect evidence from twin studies with children suggests significant heritability for bipolar disorder in children and adolescents. Heritability estimates of about 60–90% are reported in adult studies. Research employing candidate gene, linkage and association analysis, and genome-wide association studies are attempting to identify specific genes that may be involved. These molecular genetic studies, in combination with neuroimaging techniques, suggest that multiple genes, affecting areas of the brain such as the amygdala and hormonal and neurotransmitter processes, are involved in the development of bipolar disorder. Furthermore, research suggests that bipolar disorders and other disorders such as major depression and schizophrenia share a number of genetic risk loci (Arnold, Hanna, & Rosenberg, 2010; Blader et al., 2017; Liu et al., 2010).

Twin studies and other research also suggest that environmental influences play a role in the development of bipolar disorder (Black & Fristad, 2019; Blader et al., 2017; Willcutt & McQueen, 2010). Stressful life events, family relationships, and parenting styles have received considerable attention. Social difficulties with peers and poor social support are also noted as potential environmental influences that may interact with biological vulnerabilities over the course of development to impact the expression of bipolar symptoms and related difficulties. Additional research is needed to elucidate the timing and role of these and other environmental influences on the initial development, maintenance, and life-course of bipolar presentations.

Assessment of Bipolar Disorders

In the assessment of bipolar disorder in children and adolescents, a broad spectrum of information is, again, the assessment goal. The clinician should also be sure to obtain information about the developmental course of symptoms and of changes in the treatment, family, and environment over time (Black & Fristad, 2019; Johnson, Miller, & Eisner, 2018; Youngstrom, 2010).

In addition to the use of clinical unstructured interviews, structured diagnostic interviews such as versions of the K-SADS have been employed to make diagnostic decisions and to obtain additional information (Axelson et al., 2003; Black & Fristad, 2019; Geller et al., 2001). A number of mania rating scales have been adapted from adult scales and developed for use with clinicians, parents, and youth themselves. For example, the Young Mania Rating Scale (YMRS; Young et al., 1978) has been adapted for use with children and adolescents (PYMRS; Youngstrom, Findling, & Feeny, 2004). The General Behavior Inventory (GBI) is designed to assess symptoms of depression, hypomania, mania, and mixed mood states and to help inform diagnosis. The GBI has been adapted for use with children and adolescents and as a parent-report measure (Danielson et al., 2003; Youngstrom et al., 2001, 2008). Collecting information using these rating scales on large representative samples of children and adolescents is needed in order to provide comparison to information on normative development and to be sensitive to the possible range of mania/bipolar presentations (Johnson et al. 2018; Youngstrom, 2010).

Treatment of Bipolar Disorders

The treatment of bipolar disorder requires a multimodal approach to the disorder itself as well as attention to likely co-occurring difficulties and the considerable involvement of the family (AACAP, 2007c; Fristad & Roley-Roberts, 2019; Miklowitz & Goldstein, 2010). The young patient with mania may need to be admitted to a child or adolescent hospital unit so as to ensure the youth's safety and to provide an adequately controlled environment. The choice to use an inpatient setting would be guided by the level of disturbance displayed, the risk of harm or suicide, the level of support that the family is able to provide, and the need for medical supervision of medication.

The most common treatment for bipolar disorder is pharmacotherapy, and this is often considered the first-line treatment for the disorder (AACAP, 2007c; Black & Fristad, 2019). Pharmacotherapy for mania typically consists of mood stabilizers, such as lithium and divalproax sodium, and atypical antipsychotics (e.g., risperidone, aripiprazole, olanzapine) alone or in combination (Black & Fristad, 2019; Findling et al., 2019; Kowatch et al., 2005). However, there remains concern with regard to significant adverse side effects (Cohen et al., 2012; Liu et al., 2011; Tsai et al., 2011; Yee et al., 2019). Given these concerns regarding side effects, research has begun to investigate nutritional interventions. However, such research is limited and large-scale randomized trials are needed (Black & Fristad, 2019). Treatment of the depressive aspects of bipolar disorder may include the use of medications such as SSRIs. However, caution is suggested because antidepressants have been reported to destabilize the patient's mood or to incite a manic episode (Kowatch, Strawn, & DelBello, 2010; Tondo, Vázquez, & Baldessarini, 2010).

Although pharmacological treatment is typically employed in treating bipolar youth, the need to include other treatment components and the importance of incorporating family members is also recognized (see Table 8.7). A number of such programs designed for youth and their families, such as Psychoeducational psychotherapy (PEP; Fristad & MacPherson, 2014), Family-Focused Treatment (FFT; Miklowitz et al., 2013), and Child and Family-Focused CBT (CFF-CBT; West et al., 2014) have been developed and there is research support for their effectiveness. **Psychoeducation**, which seeks to educate the patient and family about the disorder, its likely course, and the nature of treatment, is an important component of these interventions. In addition to a psychoeducational component, these treatment programs include many of the skill-building elements described for the cognitive-behavioral treatment of depression such as problem solving, communication, and emotion-regulation strategies.

Interventions that employ **dialectical behavior therapy** (DBT) have also been developed (Goldstein et al., 2007). Originally

Table 8.7 Why Include the Family in Treatment?

- Children and adolescents diagnosed with Bipolar Disorder usually reside with their families.
- The family is likely to be instrumental in seeking and facilitating the treatment of their child.
- The disorder has significant impact on the family and family relationships, and family members are often affected by its societal stigma.
- The affective climate of the family environment can impact the course of the disorder and the success of medication treatments.
- Multiple members of the family are often affected by bipolar disorder.

Source: Adapted from Miklowitz & Goldstein, 2010.

developed for adults with borderline personality disorder, the DBT approach focuses on reducing emotional dysregulation. DBT interventions contain psychoeducation and cognitive-behavioral strategies. DBT also includes mindfulness techniques to help family members focus awareness and gain an increased sense of control over thoughts and emotions. Research support for the DBT approach with young people is more limited than for the other psychosocial programs mentioned.

In addition to other treatments, support groups and other forms of assistance for families, such as the website of the Child & Adolescent Bipolar Foundation (CABF) are likely to be needed (Hellander et al., 2003; Kowatch & DelBello, 2006).

Suicide

Suicide is often mentioned in discussions of mood disorders. This association probably occurs because depression, in particular, is an important risk factor for suicide, and the two problems share etiological and epidemiological patterns. However, although the two problems overlap, they are also distinct. Also, it is important to note that discussion of suicide includes not only concern with completed suicides, but also with attempted suicides and suicidal thoughts. There is reason to attend to this full range of suicidal behavior (Bridge, Goldstein, & Brent, 2006; Hawton & Fortune, 2008).

Prevalence of Completed Suicides

The rate of completed suicide is relatively low among young people compared with adults and lower for prepubertal children than for adolescents. Completed suicide by young people is nevertheless of concern. While the age ranges employed to group young people differs, reports are consistent in portraying a picture of youth suicide that is distressing (Glenn et al., 2020).

Rates of suicide deaths in the United States among youth ages 10 to 19 years increased sharply from 1975 through the early 1990s. From the early 1990s through 2007 there was a sharp decline, but from 2007 through 2016 there was, again, a sharp increase in the youth suicide death rate. The 2016 levels were at or higher than those reported in the early 1990s (Ruch et al., 2019). In the United States during the period from 2006 to 2016 suicide was the only leading cause of death among children 10–14 years of age to increase. Rates of completed suicides increased by an average of 9% a year during this period reaching 0.8 deaths per 100,000 in 2016. In 2016 there were 443 deaths by suicide among children 5–14 years of age. Among young persons 15–24 years of age, suicide replaced homicide as the second leading cause of death during the 2006–2016 period. Suicide rates in this age group increased by an average of 2.5% a year from 2006–2014 and increased at an average of 7% per year from 2014–2016, reaching 20.5 deaths per 100,000 in 2016. In 2016 there were 5,723 deaths by suicide among young people 15–24 years of age.

In 2016, rates per 100,000 of male deaths from suicides exceeded those for females in both the 5- to 14-year-old and 15- to 19-year-old age groups. Greater male rates of suicide death were characteristic of all racial/ethnic groups. Among young people in the 15–24 age range, 2016 rates of suicide were higher for white (non-Hispanic or Latino) youth than for other ethnic groups (Foster, Yeguez, & King, 2019; National Center for Health Statistics, 2018).

Suicidal Ideation and Attempts

If one considers the entire range of suicidal behavior, prevalence appears quite high, particularly among adolescents (Plemmons et al., 2018). Clearly, it is difficult to accurately assess the prevalence of suicidal behavior. Many attempts may go undetected and unreported, because not all cases seek medical or some therapeutic care. Also, methodological and definitional issues may limit interpretation of self-reports of suicidal ideation and attempts. Even some completed suicides may be mistakenly viewed as accidents. Although more young males die by suicide, females report more suicidal ideation and attempts.

A prospective longitudinal study of approximately 1,500 adolescents between 14 and 18 years of age by Lewinsohn and his colleagues (1996) also provides information about the prevalence of adolescent suicidal behavior. A total of 19.4% of these adolescents had a history of suicidal ideation. Such ideation was more prevalent in females (23.7%) than in males (14.8%). And although more frequent suicidal ideation predicted future suicide attempts, even mild and relatively infrequent suicidal thoughts increased the risk for an attempt.

Suicide attempts had occurred in 7.1% of this community sample. Females (10.1%) were more likely than males

PATTY A Suicide Attempt

Patty, a pretty 8-year-old, took an overdose of two of her mother's imipramine tablets just before going to sleep. Nobody knew about this until the next morning when Patty's mother had to wake her when she did not get up in time for school. Patty complained of a headache, dizziness, and tiredness. She was tearful and irritable and argued that her mother should "Leave me alone. I want to die." Alarmed, Patty's mother brought her to the pediatrician, who recommended that Patty be hospitalized for evaluation of suicidal behavior. ... He believed that Patty would not be safe at home. Patty insisted that the "best thing would be for me to die."

Patty's mother told the pediatrician that the last two months had been very stressful for the family. She and her husband had separated and were planning to divorce. The mother described feeling very depressed and anxious over the last year. Her husband often came home drunk and would be very hostile to her and threaten her ...

Patty is a fine student and has many friends. ... Patty's teacher had spoken to her mother about Patty's behavior over the previous two months. Patty was fidgety in class and unable to concentrate; she often day-dreamed. Her homework assignments were often not completed and her grades had dropped. Unlike her earlier behavior, Patty, in the last month, had preferred to be alone and had not joined her peers in after-school activities. She also had several arguments with her best friend.

Adapted from Pfeffer, 2000, p. 238

(3.8%) to attempt suicide. Suicide attempts before puberty were uncommon. The majority of attempts made by females consisted of either ingestion of harmful substances (55%) or cutting themselves (31%). Males employed a wider variety of methods—ingestion (20%), cutting (25%), gun use (15%), hanging (11%), and other methods, such as shooting air into their veins or running into traffic (22%). Some adolescents attempted suicide more than once. The first three months after an attempt were a period of particularly high risk for a repeated attempt. Approximately 27% of the boys and 21% of the girls made a repeated suicide attempt during this time. The likelihood of a suicidal attempt by these youth remained above the rates expected in the general population for at least two years. At 24 months, 39% of the boys and 33% of the girls had reattempted.

Young people are often thought to be vulnerable to suicide because their lesser problem-solving and self-regulatory skills and their abilities to cope with stressful circumstances may be limited. Some young people may be faced with circumstances that cause considerable stress that they view as beyond their control. These youth may also have limited understanding that undesirable situations can and often do change.

ACCENT Nonsuicidal Self-Injury

Nonsuicidal self-injury (NSSI) is typically defined as doing intentional harm to one's own body that is performed *without the intent to die*. The most common form of NSSI is cutting and behaviors such as burning, hitting, and biting are also common.

How might we understand NSSI? Some conceptualizations suggest the value of employing a broad framework of self-injurious thoughts and behaviors—a construct that includes both suicidal thoughts and behaviors and NSSI. In contrast, there also is some evidence of independent correlates and trajectories for NSSI and suicidal behaviors. Determining whether these behaviors exist on the same continuum or are separate phenomena is an ongoing challenge (Miller et al., 2019; Nock et al., 2019). Nonetheless, NSSI is associated with increased risk for suicide attempts (Horwitz, Czyz, & King, 2015; Ribeiro et al., 2016). Furthermore, the distinction between NSSI and suicidal behavior is not necessarily an easy one (Crowell, Beauchaine, & Lenzenweger, 2008; Goldston & Compton, 2007). Distinguishing NSSI from suicide attempts requires a discrimination of intent. One might carefully ask the young person whether "any part of them" wanted to die when engaging in the self-mutilating behavior. Often the distinction, however, is made based on the presumed lethality of the behavior (e.g., cutting or burning versus hanging or use of a gun).

Prevalence estimates of NSSI vary widely. NSSI is relatively rare early but increases during adolescence. An age of onset between 12 to 14 years is generally reported. Estimated lifetime prevalence among adolescents of about 17% is suggested. While findings are mixed, such behavior is more commonly observed in females than in males (Miller et al., 2019; Swannell et al., 2014). Sexual minority youth also appear to be at greater risk for NSSI (Batejan, Jarvi, & Swenson, 2015).

Since it is presumed that there is no suicidal intent, what might motivate the behavior? Several different reasons why youth may engage in NSSI have been suggested (Miller et al., 2019). All involve some form of psychological distress. Thus, for example, engaging in self-injury might be a way of escaping or avoiding negative feelings or relieving unbearable tension. NSSI may serve as a way of distracting oneself through physical pain from other highly negative feelings. Self-injury may serve interpersonal functions such as expressing anger or frustration or as a way to gain positive social attention. Alternatively, NSSI may serve as a way of avoiding or escaping aversive interpersonal situations. It is likely that NSSI may serve multiple functions for an individual.

In regard to etiology, NSSI is often hypothesized to develop in youth who have a biological vulnerability and/or who experience family and peer relationships that are high in conflict. These social environments fail to support a youth's attempts to regulate emotions and may, over time, place the youth at risk for NSSI (Adrian et al., 2011; Kaufman, Crowell, & Lenzenweger, 2017; Miller et al., 2019).

In adults, nonsuicidal self-mutilating behavior is part of the criteria for a diagnosis of Borderline Personality Disorder. Research suggests that among adolescents NSSI co-occurs with a variety of disorders including MDD, anxiety disorders, externalizing disorders, and substance abuse, and for some individuals may be an early aspect of a developmental trajectory with increased risk for the development of Borderline Personality Disorder (Jacobson et al., 2008; Kaufman et al., 2017).

Suicide and Psychopathology

Suicide is often thought of as a symptom of disorders such as depression. Indeed, depression is related to suicide among children and adolescents, and constructs such as hopelessness that are associated with depression have been found to predict suicidal behavior (Cha et al., 2018; Kovacs, Goldston, and Gatsonis, 1993). Also, there is a significant association between bipolar disorder and risk for suicide. Suicidal behavior, however, can be associated with a variety of disorders, and suicide risk increases with the number of diagnoses (Melhem et al., 2019). Conduct disorder and substance abuse diagnoses are common among completed suicides. Indeed, research suggests considerable diagnostic heterogeneity among youth who exhibit suicidal behavior. It is probably important to be aware that the presence of problems (e.g., aggression, impulsivity, substance use, in combination with or independent of depression) at levels below criteria for a diagnosis of disorder also may be associated with increased risk of suicidal behavior. However, even among individuals with a history of depression there are factors that may be protective with regard to the development of suicidal behavior (Zelazny et al., 2019). Therefore, although depression is an important risk factor, the presence of a depressive disorder is neither necessary nor sufficient for the occurrence of suicidal behavior.

Suicide Risk Factors

Although there has been an increase in research, recent reviews suggest that we know surprisingly little regarding the etiology of youth suicidal behavior (J. C. Franklin et al., 2017; Miller & Prinstein, 2019). Multiple characteristics of youth themselves and youths' social environments likely contribute to suicide risk (Foster et al., 2019; Glenn et al., 2018). The weeks following a psychiatric inpatient or emergency room visit are one of the highest risk times for youth. Also, a history of prior suicide attempts is a strong predictor of completed suicide. Although suicidal thinking is not uncommon, suicidal ideation that is frequent, severe (e.g., thoughts with a method and plan), and less controllable is predictive of future suicide attempts (Horwitz et al., 2015).

A family history of suicidal behavior increases risk. Family factors (such as abuse, low parental monitoring, and poor communication) and family disruption are also frequently cited as risk factors. Research suggests that young people who attempt suicide are likely to grow up in families characterized by high levels of negative affect and turmoil (Crowell et al., 2008; Wagner, Silverman, & Martin, 2003). However, high levels of involvement and support from family, as well as from schools or other institutions, may serve a protective function (Gould et al., 2003; King & Merchant, 2008).

Research has highlighted the relationship between bullying and suicide (Espelage & Hong, 2019; Koyanagi et al., 2019; Sigurdson et al., 2018) and indicates that certain groups may be at particular risk (see Accent: "Suicidality and Sexual Minority Youth"). Other factors such as high levels of stress, family and peer relations, and sociocultural influences—including the availability of firearms—are also thought to contribute to increased suicide risk and protection. Considerable discussion also exists regarding **contagion** ("imitation" or increased suicidal behavior) following media presentations of stories of youth suicide (Bridge et al., 2020; Niederkrotenthaler et al., 2019; Van Meter, Paksarian, & Merikangas, 2019).

As suggested above, psychological disorders such as mood disorders and substance abuse are associated with suicide. Problematic functioning characterized by attributes such as depression, hopelessness, impulsivity, and aggression contribute to suicide risk. In addition, research suggests that biological factors such as atypical responses to acute stress probably affect suicide risk (Kaufman et al., 2017; Miller & Prinstein, 2019). Risks for suicide such as depression and maltreatment also are associated with these atypical biological responses to stress.

ACCENT Suicidality and Sexual Minority Youth

It is frequently suggested that suicide risk is particularly high among sexual minority youth as compared to the general adolescent population (Aitken et al., 2016; Silenzio et al., 2007). This view is supported by research that suggests an appreciable increased risk for suicidal ideation and attempts. These young people also may be more likely to make suicide attempts that require medical attention (Marshal et al., 2011; Silenzio et al., 2007). Why might this be the case?

Research suggests that sexual minority youth are likely to report experiences that are known to be important risk factors. For example, they are more likely to be bullied and victimized at school. Many clinicians believe that the difficulties of dealing with stigma and interpersonal difficulties might lead to depression, and there are reports of high levels of depression in these youth.

Data from the National Study of Adolescent Health, a nationally representative study of U.S. adolescents, support the view that sexual orientation is a risk factor for suicidal ideation and suicide attempts (Russell & Joyner, 2001). About 12,000 adolescents completed the survey in their

(continued)

(continued)

homes, and information regarding the issues of sexuality and suicide was collected in a manner to minimize issues of privacy and confidentiality. Youth with a same-sex orientation (having a same-sex romantic attraction or relationship) were more likely to report suicidal thoughts and were more than twice as likely to attempt suicide as their same-sex peers. It is important to note, however, that the vast majority of youth with a same-sex sexual orientation reported no suicidal thoughts or attempts (about 85% of boys and 72% of girls). Young people with a same-sex orientation also scored higher on several important adolescent suicide risk factors: more alcohol abuse and

depression, higher rates of suicide attempts by family members and friends, and victimization experiences. These and other findings suggest that sexual orientation per se is not a risk factor for suicide attempts, but rather same-sex orientation interacts with known risk factors common to all adolescents (Savin-Williams & Ream, 2003). Awareness of social environments and other risk factors for suicidal ideation and attempts that may be of relatively greater importance to sexual minority youth may deserve particular attention (Silenzio et al., 2007). Also, awareness that supportive environments will likely decrease such risk should inform future efforts (Hatzenbuehler, 2011).

Suicide Prevention

Programmatic attempts to prevent youth suicide are widespread, however, evidence of their effectiveness is limited (Foster et al., 2019). The most common programs have taken a universal prevention approach—targeting all youth in a specific setting, such as schools, regardless of individual risk. Suicide awareness and education programs aim to increase students' awareness of and knowledge about suicidal behavior and to encourage them to seek help. These programs also seek to improve awareness by school staff and other adults in the community. Most awareness and education programs involve a limited number of brief sessions and are frequently part of a larger curriculum targeting high-risk behaviors. There is some support for the effectiveness of universal prevention programs, but additional research is needed (Asarnow & Mehlum, 2019; Godoy Garraza et al., 2019). Universal suicide prevention may also be viewed as including policies and laws that aim to reduce suicide by making access to lethal weapons, medications, or environments more difficult (Zalsman et al., 2016).

Selective or targeted suicide prevention may involve screening populations of youth for suicide and then providing additional support to those identified as at risk. Selective prevention

programs, in general, are directed at youth who may have not yet exhibited suicidal behavior, but who are thought to be particularly vulnerable to suicide. For example, such a program might target young people who have recently been exposed to the suicide of a family member or peer. The assumption of such programs is that exposed youth are at increased risk for depression, posttraumatic stress, and suicidal behavior. These programs are often implemented through schools, provide training and support to adults who have contact with these young people (e.g., school staff), and seek to identify and support those at risk, and to assist the community in returning to its normal functioning. These programs often do not collect longitudinal data on suicide outcomes for targeted youth and what data are available are limited and mixed with regard to outcome (Given & Apter, 2016; Zalsman et al., 2016).

In general, scientifically valid evaluations have lagged behind the development and implementation of suicide prevention programs. While a number of interventions seem promising, much remains to be learned about youth suicide and effective intervention (Foster et al., 2019; Given & Apter, 2016; Nock et al., 2019).

Looking Back

- Children and adolescents may experience moods that are unusually sad (depression) or unusually elated (mania).

A Historical Perspective

- The classical psychoanalytic theory of depression suggested that the problem did not exist in children.

- The concept of masked depression, although problematic, brought greater attention to the problem and highlighted developmental issues. A developmental perspective to understanding depression has continued to evolve.

The DSM Approach to the Classification of Mood Disorders

- Mood disorders are sometimes described as unipolar (one mood is experienced) or bipolar (both depression and mania are experienced).
- In the DSM, depression and mania are described in two chapters titled "Depressive Disorders" and "Bipolar and Related Disorders."

Definition and Classification of Depression

- The definition of depression is affected by how depression is measured and who provides information.
- Major Depressive Disorder, Persistent Depressive Disorder (Dysthymia), and Disruptive Mood Dysregulation Disorder are among the DSM diagnoses related to depression.
- Empirical approaches to classification suggest that children and adolescents experience syndromes that include a mixed presentation of depression and anxiety features.
- Developmental differences in presentation of depression challenge the use of the same diagnostic criteria in all age groups. Whether it is best to conceptualize depression as dimensional rather than categorical is an ongoing consideration.
- The subjective experience of sadness is a central feature of the clinical definition of depression. Descriptions of children and adolescents viewed as depressed suggest that they experience a number of other problems as well.

Epidemiology of Depression

- Major depressive disorder is the most frequently diagnosed mood disorder among children and adolescents.
- Episodes of clinical depression are quite common among adolescents. Depression is more prevalent among adolescents than children and among girls during adolescence.
- Higher rates of depression are reported among low SES groups. Although comparable rates of depression are typically reported for different ethnic groups, research suggests attention to possible differences.
- Youth who are depressed are likely to experience a number of other difficulties and to meet the diagnostic criteria for a variety of other disorders.

Depression and Development

- How depression is manifested varies over the course development.
- Episodes of depression may last for an appreciable period of time and for some young people may present a recurring problem.

Etiology of Depression

- Contemporary views of depression in children and adolescents suggest a model that integrates multiple determinants.
- Research suggests a genetic component to depression and also considerable environmental influence.
- Research on the biochemistry of depression emphasizes the role of neurotransmitters and the neuroendocrine system. Findings suggest that during childhood and early adolescence, the biological aspects of depression likely differ from adult cases. Anatomical and functional abnormalities in particular areas of the brain and differences in temperament have also received attention with regard to the etiology of depression.
- Separation/loss has been a major theme in many theories of depression. Cognitive and behavioral theories suggest additional contributions to the development of depression, including stress and interpersonal and cognitive aspects of functioning.
- A learned helplessness perspective suggests that a learned perception of lack of control leads to a cognitive style and behaviors characteristic of depression. Hopelessness theory emphasizes the interaction of stressful life events and cognitive style.
- Cognitive theories, such as Beck's, information processing, coping/emotion regulation, and self-control models of depression also have received attention.
- Parental depression appears to be related to childhood dysfunctions, but this relationship does not seem to be either specific to childhood depression or inevitable. Various mechanisms may link parental depression and child dysfunction.
- Interpersonal relationships with peers contribute to the development of depression, and a youth's depression affects peers' relationships with the depressed youth.

Assessment of Depression

- Assessment of depression is likely to sample a broad spectrum of attributes and to involve a number of strategies. It is important to obtain information from a variety of informants and through a variety of measures.
- A variety of assessment strategies are available. Self-report measures completed by the youth are among the most commonly employed and may be particularly important.
- Instruments available to assess attributes associated with depression (e.g., hopelessness) and observational measures add to our ability to conduct a thorough assessment.

Treatment of Depression

- The prescription of antidepressant medications to treat children and adolescents with depression is widespread and may be an important component of treatment for some youth. However, the use of medications continues to be controversial because there are concerns about efficacy and safety. Selective serotonin reuptake inhibitors are most commonly employed.
- Treatments derived from behavioral and cognitive-behavioral perspectives and treatments that address interpersonal and family aspects of depression in young people are promising. However, continued development of treatments that are sensitive to multiple aspects of psychological, social, and family influences and to cultural differences are a goal.

Prevention of Depression

- A number of universal depression prevention programs have been implemented. Most have employed cognitive-behavioral procedures and some have included interpersonal components. In general, the effectiveness of universal prevention programs has been modest and not maintained over the long term.
- Indicated prevention programs, derived from a cognitive-behavioral approach, have also been implemented and appear to be effective in preventing depression in at-risk youth.

Bipolar Disorders

- Bipolar disorders involve the presence of mania as well as depressive symptoms.

- The DSM describes a number of bipolar disorders including Bipolar I Disorder, Bipolar II Disorder, Cyclothymic Disorder, and Other Specified (or Unspecified) Bipolar and Related Disorders.
- There are a number of challenges in using "adult" bipolar disorder criteria to diagnose children and adolescents, and relevant behavior likely varies with development.
- Definitional issues make estimates of prevalence difficult. Bipolar disorders are thought to be rare, particularly in prepubertal youth. However, the diagnosis of bipolar disorders in young people has become more common.
- Youth with bipolar disorders are likely to experience co-occurring disorders and to exhibit considerable impairment in functioning.
- Young people who meet the criteria for bipolar disorders may experience a chronic and recurrent course of difficulties.
- A family history of bipolar disorders is clearly a risk factor. A strong genetic influence is suggested and environmental influences likely interact with this genetic diathesis to shape mood and related difficulties.
- Development of assessment approaches for bipolar disorders that are specific to children and adolescents is ongoing.
- Treatment of bipolar disorders requires a multimodal approach. The primary treatment involves the use of pharmacological agents, particularly mood stabilizers and atypical antipsychotics. Psychoeducation, incorporating family members into treatment, and the use of CBT and DBT strategies are likely to be components of treatment as well. Further research regarding all aspects of treatment for bipolar disorders in youth is needed.

Suicide

- Completed suicide is a serious concern. The range of suicidal behavior that includes suicidal thoughts and attempted suicide is more prevalent than actual, completed suicide. A larger category of self-injurious thoughts and behaviors includes both suicidal thoughts and behaviors and nonsuicidal self-injury (NSSI).
- NSSI is rare in children, but increases during adolescence. It is likely that NSSI may serve multiple functions for an individual.
- Suicidal behavior is related to depression but to other problems as well.
- Multiple complex factors contribute to suicidal behavior.
- Attempts to prevent youth suicide are widespread; however, evidence of success of such is limited.

Key Terms

masked depression *155*

unipolar mood disorder *156*

bipolar mood disorder *156*

Major Depressive Disorder *157*

Persistent Depressive Disorder (Dysthymia) *157*

double depression *158*

Disruptive Mood Dysregulation Disorder *158*

cortisol *164*

negative affectivity/emotionality *165*

positive affectivity/emotionality *165*

effortful control *165*

learned helplessness *166*

attributional (explanatory) style *166*

hopelessness *166*

cognitive distortions *167*

cognitive restructuring *167*

selective serotonin reuptake inhibitors *172*

remission *172*

relapse *172*

behavioral activation *173*

Bipolar and Related Disorders *176*

mania *176*

euphoric mood *176*

hypomania *176*

labile mood *179*

grandiosity *179*

flight of ideas *179*

psychoeducation *182*

dialectical behavior therapy *182*

nonsuicidal self-injury *184*

contagion *185*

CHAPTER 9
Conduct Problems

Looking Forward

After reading this chapter, you should be able to discuss:

- Various ways externalizing behaviors/conduct problems are described and classified
- Features of oppositional defiant disorder and conduct disorder
- The epidemiology of conduct problems
- Approaches to understanding the developmental course of conduct problems

- Psychosocial and biological influences on the development of conduct problems
- Substance use in youth, its epidemiology, risk factors, and developmental course
- Assessment strategies for youth with conduct problems
- Approaches to treating and preventing conduct problems

The term *externalizing* denotes problems that tend to place young people in conflict with others. These behaviors are in contrast to the seemingly more inner-directed problems discussed in previous chapters. Various other terms also are employed to describe these types of problems—disruptive, impulsive, undercontrolled, oppositional, antisocial, conduct-disordered, and delinquent.

Among disruptive behavior problems, a distinction has often been made between inattention, hyperactivity, and impulsivity on the one hand, and aggression, oppositional behaviors, and more serious conduct problems on the other. The behaviors in the first grouping are discussed in greater detail in the next chapter, which is devoted to attention-deficit/hyperactivity disorder (ADHD). The conduct problem behaviors of the second grouping are considered in this chapter. Young people with these problems have high rates of referral for mental health and other social and legal services, and some portion of these youth have contributed to broad societal concern with levels of violence and crime. Conduct problems are thus the focus of considerable societal and scientific concern.

A number of constructs exist to describe such youth. We use the term **conduct problems** to refer to this general group of disruptive/antisocial behavior problems. The terms *conduct disorder* and *disruptive behavior disorder* are used to refer to the particular diagnostic grouping that addresses these kinds of difficulties. The term **delinquency** is primarily a legal term used in the criminal justice system to describe youth who exhibit conduct problem/antisocial behavior. As a legal term, it refers to a juvenile (usually under age 18) who has committed an index crime or a status offense. An index crime is an act that would be illegal for adults as well as for juveniles (e.g., theft, aggravated assault, rape, or murder). A status offense is an act that is illegal only for juveniles (e.g., truancy, association with "immoral" persons, violation of curfews, or incorrigibility).

Classification and Description

Disruptive behaviors are common at various stages of development. Clinicians commonly hear complaints of

Table 9.1 Types of Conduct Problem Behaviors Viewed as Problematic from Early Childhood through Adolescence, and Related Disorders

Developmental Period	Problem Behaviors	Related Disorders
Early childhood	Noncompliance	
	Oppositional	Oppositional defiant disorder
	Temper tantrums	
Middle childhood	Overt/covert	Oppositional defiant disorder
	Antisocial behavior	Conduct disorder
	Relational aggression	
Adolescence	Delinquency	
	Substance use	Conduct disorder
	High-risk sexual behavior	

Source: Adapted from Dishion and Patterson, 2006.

noncompliant, aggressive, and antisocial behavior. Parents and teachers often describe young children and adolescents who do not follow directions, do not comply with requests, or seem irritable or angry. Preschool age children often hit, kick, or bite other children. From early school years through middle school, children may engage in various forms of aggression and bullying. Many adolescents engage in dangerous behaviors and use illegal substances. The fact that these problems are common and disruptive makes them a topic of concern for parents and for those who work with children and adolescents. They may cause considerable distress for parents and teachers, create discord among family members, or interfere with classroom functioning. Extreme and persistent forms of these behaviors cause a degree of disturbance and destruction well beyond the common experience. Thus, they are of particular concern not only for the family but also for institutions such as the school and for society at large. The seeming persistence of these behaviors over time for some individuals—perhaps from early childhood through adult life—also contributes to their importance. Table 9.1 provides an overview of types of conduct problem behaviors that adults often describe as problematic and aversive and the DSM disorders associated with them.

DSM Approach: Overview

The diagnoses of Oppositional Defiant Disorder (ODD) and Conduct Disorder (CD), which are discussed in the present chapter, fall within the larger DSM category of Disruptive, Impulse-Control, and Conduct Disorders. This DSM chapter, in addition to oppositional defiant disorder and conduct disorder, includes disorders such as intermittent explosive disorder, antisocial personality disorder,

pyromania (fire setting), kleptomania (stealing), and the diagnoses of other specified and unspecified disruptive, impulse-control, and conduct disorders.

Intermittent Explosive Disorder is characterized by recurring and frequent behavioral outbursts. The aggressive outbursts may be verbal (e.g., temper tantrums, tirades) and/or physical (e.g., physical aggression toward property or persons or animals). These outbursts are seen as representing the individual's failure to control impulsive aggressive behavior. Thus, the outbursts are generally impulsive or angry and not premeditated or committed so as to achieve a tangible objective. Outbursts are often rapid and brief and the response is grossly out of proportion to the perceived provocation. The diagnosis is not intended for children younger than 6 years of age or for youth whose aggressive behavior might better be explained by another disorder (e.g., bipolar disorder, disruptive mood dysregulation disorder, adjustment disorder).

The diagnosis of **Antisocial Personality Disorder** (APD) is included in this grouping of disorders, and also is included among the Personality Disorders. The diagnosis of APD may be applied to individuals who display a persistent pattern of aggressive and antisocial behavior after the age of 18. APD is characterized by "a pattern of disregard for, and violation of, the rights of others" (American Psychiatric Association, 2000). This pattern is often accompanied by multiple illegal and aggressive behaviors. The diagnosis of APD requires that the pattern be present since the age of 15 with evidence that the individual did meet, or would have met, the criteria for Conduct Disorder with an onset before 15 years of age.

We will concentrate our discussion on oppositional defiant disorder and conduct disorder.

HENRY Preschool Oppositional Behavior

Mrs. Sweet reported that her 3.5-year-old son, Henry, was causing problems. She viewed Henry as a normal, active, bright boy. However, she felt the need to talk with a professional because her friends and family had made some comments about Henry's escalating disruptive behavior.

Henry was the older of two children and had a 9-month-old sister. Mrs. Sweet's responses to initial questionnaires indicated that she perceived Henry as engaging in a significant amount of disruptive behavior but the behavior was not problematic to her. The mother's log of the past week contained descriptions of inappropriate behaviors such as: "Henry hit his grandfather on the shin with a baseball bat" and "Henry scraped a knife across the kitchen wall."

Mr. Sweet did not attend the initial interview because he saw the difficulty as primarily "my wife's problem." Mrs. Sweet indicated that Henry's developmental milestones were within normal limits but that from birth Henry had been a "difficult" child. Henry spent three mornings a week at a preschool and these were problem-free. The teachers initially reported, however, that they had to be rather "firm" in their expectations. When Henry was invited to spend time with friends in their homes things went well. Difficulties were reported when friends visited him—his behavior was described as very active, getting into things that were forbidden, and in general creating chaos. Henry's father often took Henry on full-day outings and thoroughly enjoyed this time. Mr. Sweet felt that his wife should be firmer with Henry. Mrs. Sweet described the major problems as "not listening," "refusing to do as requested," and "talking back." All of these occurred primarily with her, but were beginning to occur with other people in the family.

According to Mrs. Sweet, on a typical day Henry managed routine events such as eating and bathing easily. However, when any demands were placed on him, he would refuse to comply. To avoid confrontations, Mrs. Sweet spent much of her time rearranging her schedule, but this was becoming increasingly difficult as her 9-month-old demanded more of her attention.

Henry came to a clinic-observation session wearing an army camouflage outfit, cowboy hat, and boots, and carrying two six-shooters and a toy machine gun. He greeted the clinician with "I'm going to shoot your eyes out." The clinician responded with a firm "We don't talk like that in my office." Henry quickly responded in a contrite voice, "Oh, I'm sorry." Observation of parent–child interaction indicated that Mrs. Sweet gave Henry a high rate of noncontingent positive reinforcement, placed many demands on him, and tried to get compliance through reasoning. Henry placed many demands on his mother and rarely complied with her requests. Henry and his mother seemed to enjoy playing together. Henry refused to comply with his mother's requests to pick up the toys; however, he readily complied with the clinician's requests to clean up the toys.

A recommendation was made that both parents attend classes on child development and management. Both parents and Henry were also involved in treatment sessions to increase positive parent–child interactions, to set age-appropriate limits, to increase Henry's compliance, and to determine a consistent method of discipline. This parent training program was carried out over a six-week period with two follow-up appointments. After treatment, Henry was still described as "headstrong"; however, both parents felt that his behavior was acceptable and for the most part easily managed.

Adapted from Schroeder & Smith-Boydston, 2017, pp. 385–387

DSM Approach: Oppositional Defiant Disorder

Children and adolescents are often stubborn, do not comply with requests or directions, and in a variety of ways exhibit oppositional behavior. The case of Henry illustrates that not all such behavior is indicative or predictive of clinical problems. Indeed, perhaps particularly for older children and adolescents, appropriate and skilled assertions of autonomy may be desirable and may facilitate development (Johnston & Ohan, 1999). It is the less skilled and excessive oppositional and defiant behavior that may indicate present or future problems.

Oppositional Defiant Disorder (ODD) is described by a pattern of symptoms that the DSM groups into three clusters: angry/irritable mood, argumentative/defiant behavior, and vindictiveness.

In order to receive a diagnosis of ODD a young person must *frequently* (beyond what is normative for the youth's age, gender, and culture) display at least four of the symptoms listed below.

1. Loses temper
2. Easily annoyed/touchy
3. Angry and resentful
4. Argues with adults/authority figures
5. Refuses to comply with or defies adult's requests or does not follow rules
6. Deliberately annoys others
7. Blames others for own mistakes or bad behavior
8. Spiteful or vindictive

The symptoms must be present for a period of at least six months and the frequency of mood or behavioral symptom occurrence required for a diagnosis varies by developmental level. For children younger than 5 years of age these symptoms must occur on most days, whereas for youth 5 years or older the symptoms must occur at least once a week. A lesser frequency is required for the spiteful or vindictive behavior criteria—at least twice within the six-month period. Diagnosticians are also asked to specify the severity of ODD symptoms as mild (occur in only one setting—most frequently the home), moderate (some symptoms present in two settings), or severe (some symptoms present in three or more settings) (American Psychiatric Association, 2013).

By grouping the symptoms of ODD, the DSM highlights that the criteria for ODD contain both emotional/mood (e.g., angry) and behavioral (e.g., argues) indicators. It is suggested that youth often display the behavioral features of ODD without the problems of negative mood. However, young people diagnosed with ODD who do display the negative mood features typically exhibit the behavioral symptoms as well. There is some suggestion that both the emotional and behavioral symptoms of ODD contribute to the prediction of later disruptive/externalizing disorders. However, the emotional symptoms of ODD may also contribute uniquely to the prediction of later internalizing disorders (Evans et al., 2020; Stringaris & Goodman, 2009).

In considering a diagnosis of ODD it is important to distinguish problem-level behaviors and emotional reactions from expected levels of opposition and assertiveness. Diagnosis should therefore require high levels of such problems. Thus, a behavior or emotional reaction must be judged to occur more frequently than is typical for a young person of comparable age. Furthermore, in order to make a diagnosis of ODD the oppositional defiant behaviors and emotional reactions must cause distress for the youth or others or result in meaningful impairment in the young person's social, academic, or other important area of functioning.

Oppositional and noncompliant mood and behavior is clearly a common problem, particularly during preschool age and again during adolescence (Coie & Dodge, 1998; Loeber et al., 2000). Noncompliance represents a practical problem for parents, teachers, and clinicians. Also, high levels of noncompliant, stubborn, and oppositional behavior may represent, for some youth, the earliest steps on a developmental path of persistent antisocial behavior and other difficulties (Loeber, Burke, & Pardini, 2009b). The appropriateness of the ODD diagnosis thus rests on a balance between "overdiagnosing" common problems of children and adolescents as disorders versus ignoring potential serious problems that also may be early precursors of persistent antisocial behaviors or other problems.

DSM Approach: Conduct Disorder

The diagnosis of **Conduct Disorder** represents more seriously aggressive and antisocial behaviors. Indeed, the violence and property destruction characteristic of many of these behaviors may considerably impact individuals, families, and communities. Nonaggressive conduct-disordered behaviors (e.g., truancy, theft) also can result in considerable harm.

The essential feature of the diagnosis of Conduct Disorder (CD) is a repetitive and persistent pattern of behavior that violates both the basic rights of others and major age-appropriate societal norms. The 15 criteria used by the DSM to define the disorder are organized into the following four categories:

- Aggression to people and animals
- Destruction of property
- Deceitfulness or theft
- Serious violations of rules

The aggression category includes behaviors such as bullying, physical fights, use of a weapon, physical cruelty to people or animals, stealing while confronting a victim, and forced sexual activity. In the nonaggressive property destruction category a differentiation is made between destruction of property by setting fires versus some other means. The deceitfulness or theft grouping includes breaking into someone else's house, building, or car; lying to avoid obligations or obtain good or favors; and stealing without confronting the victim. The serious violation of rules grouping includes staying out at night despite parental prohibitions (beginning before age 13), running away from home, and school truancy (beginning before age 13). The diagnosis of Conduct Disorder requires that three or more of these behaviors be present during the past 12 months, with at least one of them present in the past six months. Also, the behavior must cause clinically meaningful impairment in social or academic functioning (American Psychiatric Association, 2013).

Subtypes of conduct disorder are described based on the age of onset. A diagnosis of Childhood-Onset or Adolescent-Onset is made based on whether one or more of the criterion behaviors had an onset prior to age 10. If there is insufficient information regarding age of onset, an "Unspecified Onset" may be indicated. The diagnostician may also specify the severity as mild, moderate, or severe based on the number of conduct problems and the degree of harm that they cause to others. In addition, the diagnostician may specify if the youth being diagnosed with a conduct disorder has what is termed *limited prosocial emotions*—lack of guilt, lack of empathy, lack of concern about poor school or other performance, shallow or deficient feelings or emotions (American Psychiatric Association, 2013). These qualities, which have also been described as "callous-unemotional traits," are described further in our discussion of the developmental course of conduct problems.

The symptoms included in the DSM criteria for Conduct Disorder include diverse behaviors. Because only three symptoms are required for a diagnosis, the diagnosis of Conduct Disorder may represent a heterogeneous group of youth with different subtypes of conduct problems. Such heterogeneity may be of particular concern for research investigations.

There are a number of concerns regarding the Conduct Disorder diagnosis both in terms of over-inclusiveness (See Accent: "Are Conduct Problems a Mental Disorder?") and the lack of breadth of its coverage (Lahey & Waldman, 2017; Moffitt et al., 2008). For example, most research regarding conduct disorder has focused on school-age children and adolescents. The DSM indicates that the onset of conduct disorders typically occurs during middle childhood and adolescence. Thus, current criteria may not be applicable to younger children. Yet research also suggests that such problem behavior begins early, and persistent problems might be prevented with early intervention. Some have suggested modification of the DSM criteria so that they become more applicable to preschool children (Wakschlag & Danis, 2009). One of the challenges in undertaking such an effort would be to be able to discriminate between conduct problem behaviors that are very common in this age group and more serious behaviors that might be predictive of longer-term and more persistent difficulties.

In a similar fashion, concerns have been raised as to whether current conduct disorder criteria are equally applicable to both sexes. As we will see, conduct disorder is diagnosed more frequently in boys (a ratio of 3:1 or 4:1). Some have questioned whether this represents a true sex difference in prevalence or is due to bias in the diagnostic criteria. Indeed, the DSM does not contain sex-specific criteria. The forms of aggression included in the DSM criteria may be more characteristic of boys, and girls may be more likely to display relational aggression (see pp. 195–197)

than physical aggression. Findings that girls with subclinical levels of conduct disorder symptoms go on to develop clinically significant problems also raise concerns about the adequacy with which criteria capture conduct disorder in females. Continuing to include girls in research on conduct disorder will help inform decisions regarding the development of diagnostic criteria.

Empirically Derived Syndromes

The DSM diagnoses represent a categorical approach to externalizing problems. As with other problems, there is considerable evidence suggesting the benefit of conceptualizing externalizing problems in a dimensional rather than categorical manner (Lahey & Waldman, 2017; Walton, Ormel, & Krueger, 2011). An alternative dimensional approach to disruptive behavior problems does exist. As we saw in Chapter 5, an empirically derived syndrome involving aggressive, oppositional, destructive, and antisocial behavior has been identified in numerous studies. This syndrome is frequently referred to as **externalizing**. It is robust in that it emerges employing a variety of measures, reporting agents, and settings. There have been efforts to distinguish narrower groupings within this broad externalizing syndrome.

Achenbach and Rescorla (2001), for example, have described two syndromes, **aggressive behavior syndrome** (e.g., argues a lot, destroys things, is disobedient, fights) and **rule-breaking behavior syndrome** (e.g., breaks rules, lies, steals, is truant), within the broader externalizing syndrome. The behaviors that are characteristic of these two syndromes are listed in Table 9.2. Youth may exhibit one or both types of problems. The validity

ACCENT Are Conduct Problems a Mental Disorder?

The diagnosis of Conduct Disorder is frequently part of the controversy over what constitutes psychopathology or mental disorder (Hinshaw & Lee, 2003; Richters & Cicchetti, 1993). Richters and Cicchetti addressed this question in part by asking if Mark Twain's characters of Tom Sawyer and Huckleberry Finn suffered from a mental disorder. As these authors point out, the two boys engaged in a sustained pattern of antisocial behavior that would warrant a diagnosis of Conduct Disorder—lying, stealing, aggression, truancy, running away, cruelty to animals. The boys were judged by the townspeople in social–moral terms and opinions were mixed as to whether, at heart, they were good or bad boys.

The question of what constitutes a conduct disorder is complex. One issue is whether it is appropriate to

place the locus of the deviant behavior entirely within the individual and ignore the social/cultural context. The DSM acknowledges this issue of context. For example, the DSM indicates that a Conduct Disorder diagnosis may be misapplied to individuals when contexts such as threatening, high-crime areas, or war zones make patterns of disruptive behavior near normative.

How to determine whether a youth's behavior is a reaction to a specific cultural environment or an indication of individual psychopathology is a considerable challenge. Clinicians and researchers must be sensitive and aware of both typical development and the real impact of poverty, stress, and violent communities on the development of antisocial behavior.

Table 9.2 Behaviors from the Aggressive and Rule-Breaking Syndromes

Aggressive Behavior	Rule-breaking Behavior
Argues a lot	Drinks alcohol
Defiant	Lacks guilt
Mean to others	Breaks rules
Demands attention	Bad friends
Destroys own things	Lies, cheats
Destroys others' things	Prefers older kids
Disobedient at home	Runs away
Disobedient at school	Sets fires
Gets in fights	Sex problems
Attacks people	Steals at home
Screams a lot	Swearing
Explosive	Thinks of sex too much
Easily frustrated	Tardy
Stubborn, sullen	Uses tobacco
Mood changes	Truant
Sulks	Uses drugs
Suspicious	Vandalism
Teases a lot	
Temper	
Threatens others	
Loud	

Note: Items listed are summaries of the actual content (wording) of items on the instruments. Most items are included in the Child Behavior Checklist (CBCL), Teacher Report Form (TRF), and Youth Self Report (YSR) versions of these syndromes, whereas others are specific to one or two of these instruments.

Adapted from Achenbach & Rescorla, 2001. Copyright 2001 by T. M. Achenbach; reprinted with permission.

of this distinction is supported by a variety of research findings (Achenbach & Rescorla, 2001; Lahey & Waldman, 2017). For example, research suggests a higher degree of heritability for the aggressive than for the rule-breaking syndrome (Burt, 2009; Kendler, Aggen, & Patrick, 2013). Developmental differences also exist between the two syndromes. In a longitudinal analysis, Stanger, Achenbach, and Verhulst (1997) found that the average scores of the two syndromes declined between ages 4 and 10. After age 10, however, the scores on the aggressive syndrome continued to decline, whereas scores on the rule-breaking syndrome (previously called delinquent) increased. These findings are illustrated in Figure 9.1. These same authors also found that the stability (the similarity of a particular individual's behavior at two points in time) was

higher for the aggressive than for the rule-breaking (delinquent) syndrome. These and other findings suggest that it is important to distinguish between types of externalizing/conduct disorder problems.

Empirical approaches to classifying conduct disorders also suggest other ways of grouping problem behaviors within this broad category. These approaches are not mutually exclusive and indeed do overlap with the aggressive/rule-breaking distinction and with each other. Some approaches suggest a distinction based on *age of onset*: a later-onset or adolescent-onset category consisting principally of nonaggressive and rule-breaking behaviors, and an early-onset category that includes these behaviors as well as aggressive behaviors. The *salient symptom* approach is based on the primary behavior problem being displayed. Distinguishing antisocial children whose primary problem is aggression from those whose primary problem is stealing is an example. It may be particularly important to single out aggressive behavior in this way as there is support for distinguishing aggression from other conduct-disordered behavior (Lahey & Waldman, 2017).

Expansion of the salient symptom distinction suggests a broader distinction (Dishion & Patterson, 2006; Loeber & Schmaling, 1985) between **overt**, confrontational antisocial behaviors (e.g., fighting, temper tantrums), and **covert**, or concealed, antisocial behaviors (e.g., fire setting, stealing, truancy). A further expansion suggests that in addition to the overt–covert distinction, one might also consider a distinction between destructive and nondestructive conduct behavior problems (Frick, 1998). Examples of antisocial behaviors that are overt and destructive include aggression, cruelty to animals, fighting, assault, and bullying. Some overt antisocial behaviors may be nondestructive, for example, stubborn, oppositional, or defiant behavior, temper tantrums, and arguing are overt, but nondestructive. Examples of antisocial behaviors that are covert and destructive include lying and property-damaging behaviors such as stealing, fire setting, and vandalism. And, finally, status offenses such as running away from home and truancy and substance use are examples of antisocial behaviors that are covert and nondestructive. The various ways of distinguishing among conduct-disordered behaviors continue to be explored in the context of an empirical and a developmental approach to understanding conduct problems.

Gender Differences: Relational Aggression

Gender differences exist in prevalence, developmental course, and the influences that contribute to the development of conduct problems (Crick & Zahn-Waxler, 2003; van Lier et al., 2007b). Perhaps the most basic aspect of gender differences is the way that conduct problems are expressed in boys and girls.

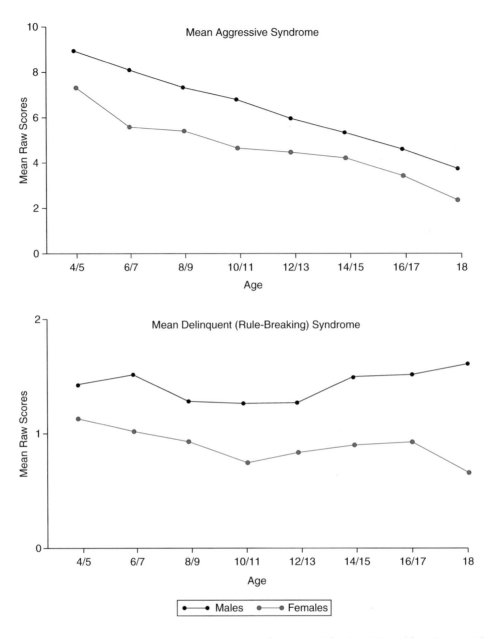

Figure 9.1 Mean aggressive and delinquent (rule-breaking) syndrome scores by age for males and females. (Adapted from Stanger, Achenbach, & Verhulst, 1997. Copyright 1997 by Cambridge University Press; reprinted with permission)

It is frequently reported that boys exhibit significantly higher levels of aggression than do girls. Is this because girls are less aggressive? Crick and colleagues (Crick & Grotpeter, 1995; Crick & Zahn-Waxler, 2003) started with a general definition of aggression as intent to hurt or harm others. They noted that during early and middle childhood, peer interactions tended to be segregated by gender. This suggested that children's aggression would focus on social issues most salient in same-gender peer groups. In studying externalizing behaviors, aggression has generally been defined in terms of overt physical or verbal behaviors intended to hurt or harm others (e.g., hitting or pushing, threatening to beat up others). It was reasoned that this is consistent with the characteristics of instrumentality and physical dominance typical of boys during childhood. Girls, in contrast, are focused on developing close, dyadic relationships. It was thus hypothesized that girls' attempts to harm others may focus on relational issues—behaviors intended to damage another individual's feelings or friendships. Examples of such **relational aggression** include the following:

Relational aggression can include behaviors intended to damage another individual's feelings or friendships. (SpeedKingz/Shutterstock.com)

- purposefully leaving a child out of some play or other activity
- getting mad at another person and excluding the person from a peer group
- telling a person you will not like him or her unless he or she does what you say
- saying mean things or lying about someone so that others will not like the person (Crick & Grotpeter, 1996).

Relational aggression may fit within the realm of covert antisocial behavior (Dishion & Patterson, 2006) and is found from preschool age through adolescence (Crick, Casas, & Ku,

1999; Prinstein, Boergers, & Vernberg, 2001). Moreover, relational aggression is associated with peer rejection, depression, anxiety, and feelings of loneliness and isolation (Crick & Grotpeter, 1995; Crick, Casas, & Mosher, 1997; Crick & Nelson, 2002).

Thus, it appears important to broadly define aggression. For one thing, a sole focus on physical aggression might fail to identify aggressive girls. Crick and Grotpeter (1995) found that over 80% of aggressive girls would not have been identified by a definition limited to physical aggression. The concept of relational aggression challenges the view that girls are nonaggressive and suggests caution in making non-gender-specific interpretations of findings (Javdani, Sadeh, & Verona, 2011).

ACCENT Fire Setting

Fire setting produces serious damage in terms of loss of life, injury, posttraumatic symptoms, and property damage. It is associated with serious difficulties for the youth, family, and community (Kolko, 2005; Peters & Freeman, 2016). Furthermore, early fire setting may be an indicator of future extreme antisocial behaviors.

Child and adolescent fire setters are a heterogeneous group of youth (MacKay et al., 2009). Therefore, there are attempts to subtype juvenile fire setters (Dalhuisen, Koenraadt, & Liem, 2017; Kolko, 2002; Lambie & Randell, 2011). For example,

youth might be viewed as differing in their motivation for fire setting. An early unusual interest in fire and involvement with fire seems to be an important predictor of fire setting. It is suggested that for other youth, fire setting is motivated by attention seeking—a "cry for help." For others, fire setting may be part of a larger picture of more general psychopathology.

It seems clear, however, that for a large proportion of juvenile fire setters, this behavior is part of a broader antisocial repertoire (Perks et al., 2019). Fire setting represents

(continued)

(continued)

a behavior that would be described as covert. Thus, fire setting may be seen as part of a cluster of covert antisocial behaviors that include destruction of property, stealing, lying, and truancy. In fact, among both community and clinically referred youth, level of covert antisocial behavior predicted later fire setting (Kolko et al., 2001).

Although only a relatively small proportion of youth with conduct problems engage in fire setting, these young people are likely to display more severe conduct problems (MacKay et al., 2006). Indeed, even among those youth with serious antisocial behavior, antisocial fire setters display more extreme antisocial behavior. Fire setters are at increased risk for later juvenile court referral and arrest for a violent crime beyond what would be predicted by the presence of conduct disorder (Becker et al., 2004).

The factors that may contribute to the development of fire setting in such youth appear similar to those that contribute to the development of conduct-disordered behavior in general. These factors include aspects of the youth (e.g., aggression, impulsivity), parents (e.g., lack of involvement, poor monitoring of the child, parental psychopathology), and family (e.g., conflict, stressful life events). Fire setters may be exposed to a greater number and a more extreme form of these risk factors (McCarty, McMahon, & Conduct Problems Prevention Research Group, 2005; Perks et al., 2019). For example, child fire setters were more likely to come from homes with marital violence and to have fathers who drank and abused pets (Becker et al., 2004). In general, fire setters are more likely to have experienced multiple adversities early in their lives including maltreatment (Perks et al., 2019).

Bullying

Bullying during childhood and adolescence has long been a problem that is familiar to many people. An appreciable increase in research and professional attention to this topic was generated by the work of Olweus (1978, 1993, 1994) in Scandinavia and by media attention following incidents of school violence in which bullying was implicated.

Bullying is characterized by an imbalance of power and involves intentionally and repeatedly causing fear, distress, or harm to someone who has difficulty defending him- or herself. Several different types of bullying have been identified including physical bullying, verbal bullying, relational bullying, and cyberbullying (Olweus, Limber, & Breivik, 2019).

"What'll it be, Tyler—your lunch money or heaps of verbal abuse?"

Danny Shanahan/The New Yorker Collection/Cartoon Bank/

Estimates of the incidence of bullying depend, in part, on definitions employed and other methodological issues (Hymel and Swearer, 2015). Bullying begins to emerge in the preschool years and is common among elementary school children (Hay, Payne, & Chadwick, 2004; Schwartz et al., 1997). Research findings across many countries suggest that between 9% and 54% of children are involved in bullying (Craig et al., 2009; Nansel et al., 2004). In a U.S, nationally representative survey of 12–18-year-olds (Musu-Gillette et al., 2018), about 21% of students reported being bullied at school (in school building, on school property, on school bus, going to and from school) during the 2015 school year. A higher percentage of girls (23%) than boys (19%) reported being bullied. Figure 9.2 presents these findings as well as results for various types of bullying. Frequency of bullying was higher for sixth graders than among students in grades eight through twelve. These rates are consistent with other findings (Ball et al., 2008). In general, there is a decrease with age in the percentage of youth who report being bullied (Craig et al., 2009; Kumpulainen,

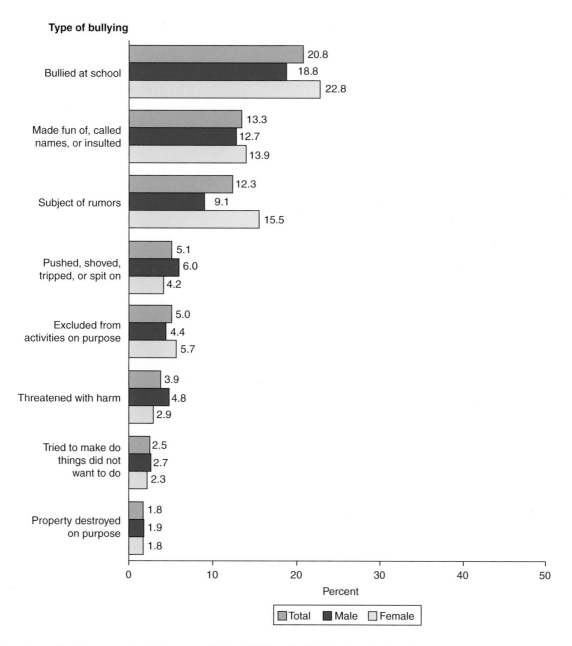

Type of bullying

Figure 9.2 Percentages of students ages 12–18 who reported being bullied at school during the school year, by type of bullying and sex: 2015.

Note: "At school" includes in the school building, on school property, on a school bus, and going to and from school. Students who reported experiencing more than one type of bullying at school were counted only once in the total for students bullied at school.

Source: U.S. Department of Justice Bureau of Justice Statistics, School Crime Supplement (SCS) to the National Crime Victimization Survey, 2015.

Räsänen, & Henttonen, 1999; Wolke et al., 2000). Information regarding cyberbullying was not collected in this study. However, the authors report that the most recent data available regarding cyberbullying indicated that 7% of the students had been the targets of one or more incidents of cyberbullying during the 2013 school year and, in general, cyberbullying is an important aspect of concern with the impact of social media on youth adjustment (Underwood & Ehrenreich, 2017).

An appreciable body of research has identified psychological, psychosocial and physical health impacts on the targets of bullying (Hawker & Boulton, 2000; Musu-Gillette et al., 2018; Olweus et al., 2019). Bullied youth often experience internalizing problems such as depression, poor self-esteem, and anxiety. In contrast, youth who bully more typically exhibit externalizing behaviors such as aggression, rule-breaking behavior, and delinquency.

The typical bully is described by Olweus (1994) as being highly aggressive to both peers and adults; having a more positive attitude toward violence than students in general; being impulsive; having a strong need to dominate others; having little empathy toward victims; and, if a boy, being physically stronger than average. Not all highly aggressive youth are bullies.

Differences between bullies and other aggressive young people and the processes that underlie bullying remain to be clarified.

The typical victim is more anxious and insecure than other students, and is cautious, sensitive, quiet, nonaggressive, and suffering from low self-esteem. If victims are boys, they are likely to be physically weaker. This so-called submissive, nonassertive style often seems to precede being selected as a victim (Schwartz, Dodge, & Coie, 1993). Also, victims often do not have a single good friend in their class. The protective importance of having a friend, especially a popular one, was illustrated in an interview with Eric Crouch, the 2001 Heisman Trophy winner as the outstanding college football player:

> *It was a source of pride to his mother ... that as a popular grade school kid, Eric often befriended students whom others teased. "I talk to them, become friends with them," he would tell his mother, "and they didn't get teased anymore."*
>
> *Murphy, 2001, p. 64*

In addition to warding off victimization, support from a close friend may buffer the effects of victimization (Prinstein et al.,

Bullying among boys is often characterized by physical aggression and intimidation. (Henry King/The Image Bank/Getty Images)

HENRY A Victim of Bullying

Henry was a quiet and sensitive 13-year-old. For several years he had been harassed and attacked occasionally by some of his classmates. ... During the past couple of months, the attacks had become more frequent and severe.

Henry's daily life was filled with unpleasant and humiliating events. His books were pushed from his desk, his tormentors broke his pencils and threw things at him, they laughed loudly and scornfully when he occasionally responded to the teacher's questions. Even in class, he was often called by his nickname, the "Worm."

As a rule, Henry did not respond; he just sat there expressionless at his desk, passively waiting for the next attack. The teacher usually looked in another direction when the harassment went on. Several of Henry's classmates felt

sorry for him but none of them made a serious attempt to defend him.

A month earlier, Henry had been coerced, with his clothes on, into a shower. His two tormentors had also threatened him several times to give them money and steal cigarettes for them. One afternoon, after having been forced to lie down in the drain of the school urinal, Henry quietly went home, found a box of sleeping pills, and swallowed a handful. Henry's parents found him unconscious but alive on the sofa in the living room. A note on his desk told them that he couldn't stand the bullying any more, he felt completely worthless, and believed the world would be a better place without him.

Adapted from Olweus, 1993, pp. 49–50

2001). Beyond the support of a close friend, other aspects of the peer group are of importance. Thus, efforts to encourage and support quality interactions by peers with victims and efforts to encourage and support the social attempts by chronic victims are likely to positively impact the lives of victims of bullying (Gregus, Craig, & Cavell, 2020).

The consequences for the victims of bullying also suggest the importance of intervening early. Repeated victimization is likely to be highly stressful and have appreciable negative consequences for some youth. For example, Sugden et al. (2010) found that some children may be particularly predisposed to experience the consequences of bullying. A particular variant of the serotonin transporter (5-HTT) gene is associated with greater risk of emotional disturbance after exposure to stressful events. Children who were bullied frequently and who had this particular variation of the 5-HTT genotype were more likely to exhibit emotional problems at age 12 than were frequently bullied children with other genotypes, even when controlling for pre-victimization emotional problems and other risk factors. The victims of bullying form a group of youth for whom school personnel and parents may be relatively unaware of the problem (Shakoor et al., 2011). One can imagine the effects of going through years of school in a state of fear, anxiety, and insecurity. Some of these young people may, indeed, be at increased risk for suicide (Winsper et al., 2012). A case described by Olweus (Henry) illustrates the pain that young people may suffer.

It is clearly important to address both sides of the bully–victim problem. Bullying may be part of a more general antisocial, conduct-disordered developmental pattern, and thus bullies, themselves, are at risk for continuing behavior problems. Indeed,

Olweus (1994) reports that 60% of boys classified as bullies in grades six through nine were convicted of at least one officially registered crime by age 24 and that 35–40% of former bullies had three or more convictions by this age, compared with only 10% of control boys.

Epidemiology

Conduct problems are one of the most frequently occurring child and adolescent difficulties. Exact prevalence is difficult to establish, due to a number of methodological and definitional factors (Essau, 2003; Loeber et al., 2000). Investigations employing DSM criteria suggest rates for ODD between about 1% and 15% with an average of 3.3%, and rates for CD between about 2% and 10% with a median of 4% (American Psychiatric Association, 2013; Canino et al., 2004; Fleitlich-Bilyk & Goodman, 2004; Ford, Goodman, & Meltzer, 2003; Kessler et al., 2009; Lavigne et al., 2009). Comparable rates are reported worldwide and do not appear to vary greatly across countries (Canino et al., 2010).

Gender, Age, and Context

Conduct disorders are more commonly diagnosed in boys than in girls (a ratio of about 3:1 or 4:1 is typically cited), however the sex ratio varies as a function of age and type of conduct problem (Lahey & Waldman, 2017). The DSM definition of CD may emphasize "male" expressions of aggression (e.g., physical aggression). Thus, CD may be underestimated in girls. Higher rates of ODD are also reported in boys. However, the degree of sex

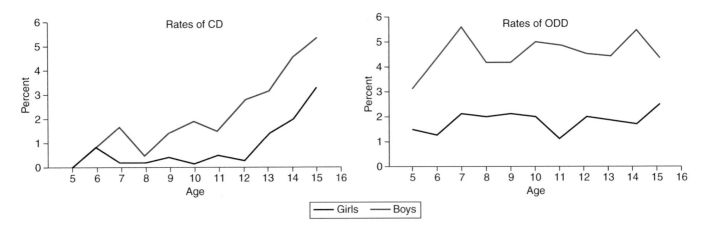

Figure 9.3 Rates of conduct disorder (CD) and oppositional defiant disorder (ODD) by age and sex. (Adapted from Maughan et al., 2004)

difference for ODD remains unclear and the applicability of the DSM criteria to girls has been questioned (Loeber et al., 2000; Maughan et al., 2004; Waschbusch & King, 2006). Sex and age differences in the prevalence of ODD and CD, based on a nationally representative sample in Great Britain (Maughan et al., 2004), are illustrated in Figure 9.3.

An increasing prevalence of CD with age is often reported for both boys and girls and there is some suggestion that, due to particular risk for girls in the period around puberty, the gender ratio narrows temporarily in the mid-teens (Maughan et al., 2004; Moffitt et al., 2001). Some reports suggest a decline in ODD with age, but findings are inconsistent and may be affected by existing diagnostic practices (Maughan et al., 2004; Weyandt, Verdi, & Swentosky, 2011).

Ethnic and socioeconomic differences are often reported. However, Roberts and colleagues (2006) examined the presence of a disruptive disorder or ADHD in African American, European American, and Mexican American youth, ages 11–17 years, and found no differences in prevalence for the combined problem category. Contextual factors such as poverty and the stress of high-crime neighborhoods are thought to increase the risk for conduct-disordered behavior. Greater prevalence is reported in urban than in rural environments (Canino et al., 2004; Fleitlich-Bilyk & Goodman, 2004). Also, official records often indicate greater delinquency among lower class and minority youth and in neighborhoods characterized by high crime rates. Such differences may be due to selection of certain groups for prosecution, suggesting that definitions other than official records should be considered. However, estimates based on alternative methods, such as self-report, present other methodological difficulties. Although further documentation is needed, real associations between conduct-disordered behavior/delinquency and social class and neighborhoods probably do exist; however, they are

probably more moderate than was once contended. The influence of these variables on child and adolescent conduct problem behavior is probably mediated by their impact on factors such as the ability of adults to parent effectively (Bendezú et al., 2018; Capaldi et al., 2002).

Patterns of Co-occurrence

Children and adolescents who receive one of the disruptive disorder diagnoses also frequently experience other difficulties and receive other diagnoses (American Academy of Child and Adolescent Psychiatry, 2007b; Lahey & Waldman, 2017). Most youth who receive the diagnosis of CD do meet the criteria for ODD. In the Developmental Trends Study of clinic-referred boys 7 to 12 years old, 96% of those who met criteria for CD also met criteria for ODD. The reported average age of onset was about 6 years for ODD and about 9 years for CD, suggesting that among boys with CD, this disorder is preceded by behaviors characteristic of ODD and that these behaviors are "retained" as additional antisocial behaviors emerge. On the other hand, ODD does not always result in CD. Of the boys with ODD (but no CD) at the initial assessment, 75% had not progressed to CD two years later. About half of the boys with ODD at Year 1 continued to meet the criteria for ODD at Year 3, and about one-quarter no longer met the criteria for ODD. Thus, although most cases of CD meet the criteria for ODD, most young people with oppositional defiant behaviors do not progress to a conduct disorder.

There is also considerable co-occurrence of ODD and CD with ADHD (Beauchaine, Zisner, & Sauder, 2017; Waschbusch, 2002). Among children diagnosed with ADHD, a substantial number develop ODD alone or ODD and CD. When these disorders co-occur, ADHD seems to precede the development of the other disorders.

It might be speculated that the impulsivity, inattention, and overactivity of ADHD present a particular parenting challenge. When parents' skills are limited, a pattern of noncompliant and aversive parent–child interactions may be set in motion (Patterson, DeGarmo, & Knutson, 2000). The challenges of parenting an ADHD child may thus play a role in the early onset of ODD behaviors and may continue over the course of development to maintain and exacerbate ODD/CD behaviors. Parent–child relationships are only one of the potential mechanisms whereby the presence of ADHD may increase the risk for ODD/CD. However, findings from a twin study suggest that although ADHD, ODD, and CD are each influenced by genetic and environmental factors, the covariation of the three disorders may be appreciably influenced by shared environmental factors (Burt et al., 2001). Such a finding is consistent with the potential contribution of parenting. Whatever factors contribute to the co-occurrence of these disorders, the co-occurrence of disruptive behavior disorders and ADHD may be one possible path toward more persistent and more severe conduct problems (Beauchaine & Neuhaus, 2008; Lahey, 2008).

In addition, youth with disruptive behavior disorders commonly experience a variety of other difficulties including substance use problems. Also, young aggressive children are frequently rejected by their peers (Parker et al., 2006). Youth with persistent conduct problems are also frequently described as having certain neurocognitive impairments and lower school achievement (Lahey, 2008; Maguin & Loeber, 1996). Verbal and language deficits, in particular, have been reported among community and clinical samples, as well as deficits in **executive functions** (higher-order cognitive functions that play a role in information processing and problem solving) (Gilmour et al., 2004; Moffitt et al., 2001). How such difficulties and conduct disorders relate to each other is a complex issue that suggests a number of questions. In what ways do cognitive and language difficulties contribute to the development of conduct disorders? What is the relationship among these deficits, CD, and poor academic performance? To what extent are some of these deficiencies related to ADHD—are they characteristic of only the subset of youth with conduct disorder who also have ADHD?

Internalizing disorders also occur at higher than expected rates among youth with disruptive behavior disorders (Loeber & Keenan, 1994; Loeber et al., 2000). There may be variations in rates of co-occurrence depending on the nature of a youth's conduct problems (McMahon & Frick, 2019). For example, patterns of co-occurrence may vary based on which cluster of ODD symptoms (angry/irritable mood or argumentative/defiant behavior) is present (Burke, 2012; Frick & Nigg, 2012).

Estimates of the rate of co-occurrence of conduct problems and anxiety disorders vary widely. Also, the literature on the nature of the association between anxiety and conduct problems is unclear and often contradictory (Ford et al., 2003; Hinshaw & Lee, 2003; Lahey, 2008). A central question is whether anxiety increases or decreases the risk for conduct-disordered behavior. In any event, the co-occurrence of anxiety and conduct problems is likely to be due to multiple influences (Gregory, Eley, & Plomin, 2004).

The co-occurrence of depression and CD is also clearly appreciable. Among a community sample of older adolescents, Lewinsohn, Rohde, and Seeley (1995b) found that a major depressive disorder co-occurred in 38% of youth with a externalizing behavior disorder (CD, ODD, or ADHD). In clinical samples, approximately 33% of children and adolescents have a co-occurrence of conduct and depressive disorders (Dishion, French, & Patterson, 1995). In community and clinic populations, boys show greater co-occurrence than girls (Dishion et al., 1995; Lewinsohn et al., 1995b). Numerous factors may help account for the frequent co-occurrence of conduct problems and depression. It may be that one disorder creates a risk for the other. For example, frequent failures and conflict experiences may contribute to depression in youth with conduct problems, the negative affect associated with oppositional behavior may predict later depression, or in some youth depression may be expressed as irritable, angry, antisocial behavior. Alternatively, the disorders may co-occur because of shared etiology including genetic and environmental influences.

Developmental Course

Stability of Conduct Problems

An important aspect of conduct problems is their reported stability over time for at least some individuals (Lahey, 2008; Loeber, Burke, & Pardini, 2009a). Considerable evidence exists that the presence of early conduct-disordered behavior is related to the development of later aggressive and antisocial behavior and to a range of adverse psychological and social-emotional outcomes (Burke et al., 2005; Fergusson, Horwood, & Ridder, 2005a, 2007; Hiatt & Dishion, 2008).

However, the question of the stability or continuity of antisocial/conduct-disordered behavior is a complex one. It appears that some but not all youth continue to exhibit aggressive and antisocial behavior (Loeber et al., 2009a; NICHD Early Child Care Research Network, 2004). The challenges are to describe patterns of both continuity and discontinuity, characterize shifts in the form that antisocial behaviors may take, and identify variables that influence the trajectory of antisocial behavior over time. Various ways of viewing developmental trajectories of conduct/antisocial problems have been proposed (Loeber et al., 2009a; Weyandt et al., 2011).

We will examine two of these to illustrate thinking about developmental trajectories.

Age of Onset and Developmental Paths

Many studies have found that early age of onset is related to more serious and persistent antisocial behavior (Babinski, Hartsough, & Lambert, 1999; Fairchild et al., 2013; Fergusson & Woodward, 2000; Silberg, Moore, & Rutter, 2015; Tolan & Thomas, 1995). A number of authors have proposed two developmental patterns leading toward antisocial behavior, one with a childhood onset and the other with a late/adolescent onset (Hinshaw et al., 1993; Moffitt, 1993, 2006).

Childhood Onset

The **childhood-onset developmental pattern** fits with the notion of the stability of conduct-disordered behavior. Indeed, Moffitt (1993, 2006) terms this pattern "life-course-persistent antisocial behavior." It must be remembered, however, that a substantial number of children with an early onset of antisocial behavior do not persist on this pathway. The early-onset pathway is less common than the adolescent-onset pattern (Hinshaw et al., 1993; Moffitt, 1993). Youth following this early-onset pattern are also more likely from preschool on to exhibit other problems, such as ADHD, neurobiological and neurocognitive deficits, and academic difficulties (Raine et al., 2005; van Goozen et al., 2007). These early difficulties may be the starting point for one developmental pathway characterized by early onset and by persistent disruptive and antisocial behavior during childhood and adolescence. For some this pathway may lead to antisocial personality disorder and other negative outcomes in adulthood (Fergusson, Horwood, & Ridder, 2005b; Maughan & Rutter, 1998; Moffitt et al., 2002).

Even though there is stability of problematic behavior for some young people with an early onset, antisocial behaviors exhibit qualitative change in the course of development. Hinshaw and colleagues (1993, p. 36) describe the features of this heterotypic continuity of antisocial behavior:

> The preschooler who throws temper tantrums and stubbornly refuses to follow adult instructions becomes the child who also initiates fights with other children and lies to the teacher. Later, the same youth begins to vandalize the school, torture animals, break into homes, steal costly items, and abuse alcohol. As a young adult, he or she forces sex on acquaintances, writes bad checks, and has a chaotic employment and marital history.

Callous-Unemotional Traits

As part of the effort to identify youth with early-onset conduct problems who are at particular risk for persistent and more severe difficulties, investigators have explored the notion of callous-unemotional traits (Ciucci et al., 2014; Kahn et al., 2012). Consistent with this literature, DSM-5 included "limited prosocial emotions" as a potential specification to the diagnosis of Conduct Disorder (see p. 193).

What is meant by **callous-unemotional traits**? A dimension of problematic affective experiences has been consistently identified to be part of the description of the notion of psychopathy in adults. This dimension has been labeled as "callous-unemotional traits" (CU) and consists of attributes such as a lack of guilt, lack of empathy, and callous use of others for one's own gain. This concept has been extended to youth and measures have been developed to assess such traits in children and adolescents. Research suggests that the behaviors that define CU are sufficiently stable to warrant considering the idea of an individual "trait" that is stable across development (Byrd, Loeber, & Pardini, 2012; Frick & White, 2008). It should be noted, however, that while CU traits are relatively stable, the level of these traits does decrease in some portion of youth who initially score high on these attributes.

Research studies of children and adolescents have demonstrated that CU traits are associated with conduct problems, aggression, and delinquency (Byrd et al., 2012; Frick et al., 2014). Of particular interest are findings that indicate that within samples of antisocial youth, CU traits are important in designating a group of such youth who are more aggressive, exhibit a more stable pattern of problem behavior, are more likely to have an early onset of delinquency, and are at increased risk for later antisocial and delinquent behavior. In addition, there is research consistent with the notion of different risk factors and different developmental processes than those described for other conduct problem/antisocial youth (McMahon & Frick, 2019; Pardini et al., 2012).

The idea of youth with stable CU traits being a distinct group of antisocial youth is supported by research indicating a substantial genetic influence on CU traits (Frick et al., 2014). Viding and colleagues (2005, 2008), for example, used participants from a large twin study to investigate the heritability of early-onset antisocial behavior in children at 7 and then again at 9 years of age. They found substantially greater heritability of early-onset antisocial behavior among children high on CU than among those antisocial children low on CU traits.

Other research also has supported the idea that CU traits are associated with characteristics that are distinguishable from general measures of conduct problems and antisocial behavior (Clark & Frick, 2018; Frick et al., 2014; McMahon & Frick, 2019). These distinct characteristics include deficits in how negative emotional stimuli are processed; less sensitivity to punishment cues; a greater likelihood of viewing aggression as more positive; blaming others for their behavior; and parenting practices (e.g., low parental warmth). Thus, such research suggests that there may be a subgroup of antisocial youth, described as having CU traits, who have a particular temperamental style that leads to the development of distinct personality traits and the development of more persistent and severe aggressive and antisocial behaviors.

Adolescent Onset

An **adolescent-onset developmental pattern** is illustrated in the Dunedin Multidisciplinary Health and Development Study (McGee et al., 1992). Prospective examination of a birth cohort of New Zealand youth revealed a large increase in the prevalence of nonaggressive conduct problems but no increase in aggressive behavior at age 15 compared with age 11. These young people were clearly exhibiting problem behavior; for example, they were as likely to be arrested for delinquent offenses as were childhood-onset delinquents. However, their offenses were less aggressive than those of childhood-onset delinquents. The majority of females were adolescent-onset cases, while males composed most of the conduct disorder cases at age 11. This rather common emergence during adolescence of nonaggressive antisocial behavior is contrasted to early-onset antisocial behavior.

The adolescent-onset pattern is the more common developmental pathway and is distinguished from the childhood-onset pathway in a number of ways (Fairchild et al., 2013; McMahon & Frick, 2019; Moffitt, 2006). Individuals who exhibit this pattern show little oppositional or antisocial behavior during childhood. During adolescence, they begin to engage in illegal activities, and although most exhibit only isolated antisocial acts, some engage in enough antisocial behavior to qualify for a diagnosis of Conduct Disorder. However, the antisocial behaviors are less likely to persist beyond adolescence and thus are sometimes termed *adolescent-limited* (Moffitt, 1993). In addition to being less likely than the childhood-onset individuals to continue antisocial behavior into adulthood, these youth are less likely to show neuropsychological deficits. They also have less severe levels of risk factors such as impulsivity, poor emotion regulation, and attention deficits. Some of the youth do continue to have difficulties later in life. Experiences such as incarceration or disruption in education may contribute to more negative outcomes. However, these difficulties may not be as severe as the outcomes for the life-course-persistent individuals. It is important to determine which individuals discontinue and which persist or escalate their antisocial behavior as they enter adulthood, and to identify what accounts for these differences over time.

Developmental Progression of Conduct Problems

In addition to groupings of individuals by age of onset, much attention also has been given to the conceptualization of developmental progressions of conduct problems (e.g., Dodge, 2000; Farrington, 1986; Loeber et al., 1993; Patterson,

DeBaryshe, & Ramsey, 1989). Loeber (1988) proposed a model that illustrates some of the attributes that might characterize the developmental course of conduct disorders within individuals. The model suggests that at each level, less serious behaviors precede more serious ones but that only some individuals progress to the next step. Progression on a developmental path is characterized by increasing diversification of antisocial behaviors. Children and adolescents who progress show new antisocial behaviors and may retain their previous behaviors rather than replacing them. Individuals may differ in their rate of progression.

Loeber's Three-Pathway Model

Loeber and colleagues (1993, 2009a) have suggested a model that conceptualizes antisocial behavior along multiple pathways. On the basis of a longitudinal study of inner-city youth, and following from distinctions between conduct problem behaviors described earlier, Loeber proposed a triple-pathway model (see Figure 9.4):

- an overt pathway starting with minor aggression, followed by physical fighting, followed by violence;
- a covert pathway starting with minor covert behaviors, followed by property damage, and then moderate to serious delinquency; and
- an authority conflict pathway prior to age 12, consisting of a sequence of stubborn behavior, defiance, and authority avoidance.

Individuals may progress along one or more of these pathways. As illustrated in Figure 9.4, entry into the authority conflict pathway typically begins earlier than entry into the other two pathways, and not all individuals who exhibit early behaviors on a particular pathway progress through the subsequent stages. The percentage of young people exhibiting behaviors characteristic of later stages of a pathway is less than those exhibiting earlier behaviors.

Investigators continue their efforts to describe the developmental pathways of antisocial, conduct-disordered behavior. At the same time, they also seek to identify the influences that first put young people on those pathways and that determine whether the antisocial behavior will continue or desist.

Etiology

The development of conduct problems is likely to involve the complex interplay of a variety of influences (Lahey & Waldman, 2017; Tremblay, 2010). In our description we present influences

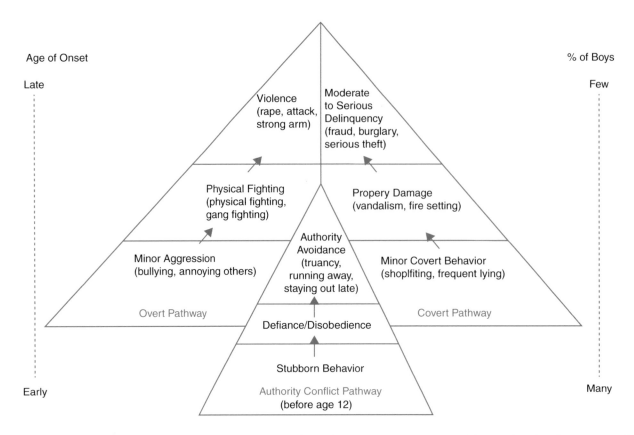

Figure 9.4 Three pathways to boys' problem behavior and delinquency. (Adapted from Loeber & Hay, 1994. Copyright 1994 by John Wiley & Sons; reprinted with permission)

in separate sections, but it is important to remember that causal explanations typically involve transactional influences and multiple variations in the association of influences (Burke, Pardini, & Loeber, 2008; Lahey & Waldman, 2017; Lee, 2011). While our emphasis will be on individual, relationship, and biological influences, the larger contexts in which these occur should not be ignored (Dishion & Patterson, 2006).

The Socioeconomic Context

Multiple findings suggest the importance of the larger social context. For example, poverty has an impact on a wide range of difficulties, including oppositional and conduct problems (Costello et al., 2003; Slopen et al., 2010; Wadsworth et al., 2018) (see Accent: "Moving Out of Poverty"). Other influences that are associated with poverty, such as neighborhood context, also have received attention (Burt et al., 2020; Jennings, Perez, & Reingle Gonzalez, 2018). Ingoldsby and Shaw (2002) consider the risk associated with residing in a disadvantaged community. A lack of economic and other resources, social disorganization, and racial division and tension define such neighborhoods. These factors are likely to increase the risk of exposure to neighborhood violence and involvement with neighborhood-based deviant peer groups,

and thus lead to increased risk for early-onset antisocial behavior. Perceived discrimination has also been found to amplify the effect of contextual risks for African American youth (Brody et al., 2006). Socioeconomic and other disadvantages likely reflect a process in which adverse individual, family, school, and peer factors combine to increase a young person's chance of developing conduct problems (Chung & Steinberg, 2006; Jennings et al., 2018; Wadsworth et al., 2018).

It is also likely that positive family, peer, and school influences can be protective and moderate the effects of disadvantage (Bendezú et al., 2018; Brody et al., 2006; Jennings & Perez, 2017). For example, Deane and colleagues (2018) studied the relationship of the impact of community violence, resulting posttraumatic stress, and aggression in a sample of African American seventh grade students from high-crime neighborhoods. Greater exposure to community violence was related to higher levels of posttraumatic stress symptoms (PTSS). Furthermore, higher levels of PTSS were related to higher levels of late aggression. However, the relationship between PTSS and later aggression existed only in families with low or very low levels of family cohesion and not if family cohesion was moderate, high, or very high. These finding are illustrated in Figure 9.5.

ACCENT Moving Out of Poverty

Costello and colleagues (2003) report on what might be described as a natural experiment (see p. 72 in this volume) that addresses the impact of poverty on conduct problems. The Great Smoky Mountains Study investigated the development of mental disorder and the need for mental health services for youth in North Carolina. Over several years data were collected from a sample of children, 25% of whom were Native American. In the middle of the eight-year study, a casino opened on the reservation that equally raised the income of all the Native American families. This allowed a comparison of children whose families moved out of poverty, remained poor, or were never poor. Young people whose families moved

out of poverty showed a significant decrease in symptoms, whereas no change occurred for the other children. The ex-poor children now exhibited nearly the same low rate of disorder as the never poor, which was lower than that of the persistently poor. The effect was quite specific to oppositional and conduct problems rather than anxiety and depression. Further analysis suggested that the lessening of problems could be attributed to the families having increased time to adequately supervise their offspring. An important aspect of this study is that the move out of poverty was not caused by characteristics of the families or the child—and so the findings could more clearly be attributed to the move from poverty itself.

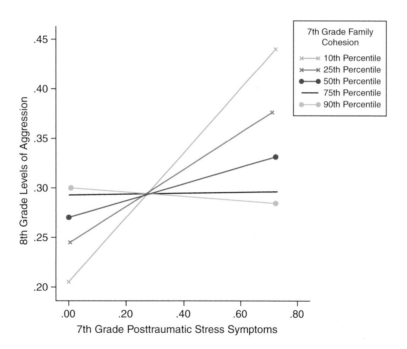

Figure 9.5 Moderation of the direct effect of posttraumatic stress in seventh grade on eighth-grade aggression by level of family cohesion. (From Deane, Richards, Mozley, Scott, Rice, & Garbarino, 2018)

Aggression as a Learned Behavior

Aggression is a central part of the definition of conduct-disordered behavior and a common difficulty among non-referred children. Children clearly may learn to be aggressive by being rewarded for such behavior (Patterson, 1976). Also, children may learn through imitation of aggressive models. They vicariously learn new and novel aggressive responses. Exposure to aggressive models also makes aggressive responses already in the child's repertoire more likely to occur—that is, disinhibition of aggression may occur. In addition, beyond learning-specific aggressive behaviors,

young people may acquire general "scripts" for aggressive/hostile interpersonal behavior.

Children and adolescents certainly have ample opportunity to observe aggressive models. Parents who engage in physical aggression toward their spouses or who physically punish their children serve as models for aggressive behavior. In fact, children exhibiting excessive aggressive or antisocial behaviors are likely to have siblings, parents, and even grandparents with histories of conduct problems and records of aggressive and criminal behavior (Farrington, 1995; Huesmann et al., 1984; Waschbusch, 2002) and to have observed especially high rates of aggressive behavior in their homes (Kashani et al., 1992; Margolin, 1998; Patterson et al., 1989). Aggression is also ubiquitous in television programs, games, and in other media, and although there remains reason for concern, the impact of such exposure is unclear (Anderson et al., 2003; Calvert et al., 2017; Mathur & VanderWeele, 2019; Prescott, Sargent, & Hull, 2018).

Family Influences

The family environment can play an important role in the development of conduct-disordered behaviors. As indicated before, a high incidence of deviant or criminal behavior has been reported in families of youth with conduct problems. Longitudinal studies, in fact, suggest that such behavior is stable across generations (D'Onofrio et al., 2007; Glueck & Glueck, 1968; Huesmann et al., 1984). It seems, then, that conduct-disordered children may be part of a deviant family system. Numerous family variables have been implicated, including low family socioeconomic status, large family size, marital disruption, poor-quality parenting, parental abuse and neglect, and parental psychopathology (Dishion & Patterson, 2016; Lahey & Waldman, 2017; Waschbusch, 2002). We highlight a few of these influences.

Parent–Child Interactions and Noncompliance

The manner in which parents interact with their children contributes to the development of conduct-disordered behavior. Defiant, stubborn, and noncompliant behaviors are often among the first problems to develop in children. Given that these occur in both clinic and nonclinic families, what factors might account for the greater rates in some families? One possible factor is suggested by evidence that parents differ in both the number and the types of commands that they give. Parents of clinic-referred children issue more commands, questions, and criticisms. Also, prohibitions and commands that are presented in an unclear, angry, humiliating, or nagging manner are less likely to result in child compliance (Dumas & Lechowicz, 1989; Forehand et al., 1975; Kuczynski & Kochanska, 1995). Consequences that parents deliver also affect the child's noncompliant behavior (Brinkmeyer & Eyberg, 2003; Forehand & McMahon, 1981). A combination of negative consequences (time-out) for noncompliant behavior and rewards and attention for appropriate behavior seems to be related to increased levels of compliance.

The Work of Patterson and His Colleagues

Gerald Patterson and his colleagues have created the Oregon Model—a developmental intervention model for families with aggressive antisocial children—based on a social interaction learning perspective (Dishion & Patterson, 2016; Patterson et al., 1975; Patterson, Reid, & Dishion, 1992). Although this approach

recognizes that characteristics of the child may play a role, the emphasis is on the social context.

> *If we are to change aggressive childhood behavior, we must change the environment in which the child lives. If we are to understand and predict future aggression, our primary measures will be of the social environment that is teaching and maintaining these deviant behaviors. The problem lies in the social environment. If you wish to change the child, you must systematically alter the environment in which he or she lives.*
> Patterson, Reid, & Eddy, 2002, p. 21

Patterson developed what he refers to as coercion theory to explain how a problematic pattern of behavior develops. Observations of referred families suggested that acts of physical aggression were not isolated behaviors. On the contrary, such acts tended to occur along with a wide range of noxious behaviors that were used to control family members in a process labeled as **coercion**. How and why does this process of coercion develop?

One factor is parents who lack adequate family management skills. According to Patterson (1976; Patterson et al., 1992), parental deficits in child management lead to increasingly coercive interactions within the family and to overt antisocial behavior. Central to this process are the notions of **negative reinforcement** and the **reinforcement trap**. Here is an example:

- A mother gives in to her child's tantrums in the supermarket and buys him a candy bar.
- The short-term consequence is that things are more pleasant for both parties:
  - The child has used an aversive event (tantrum) to achieve the desired goal (candy bar).
  - The mother's giving in has terminated an aversive event (tantrum and embarrassment) for her.
- Parents pay for short-term gains, however, with long-term consequences:
  - Although the mother received some immediate relief, she has increased the probability that her child will employ tantrums in the future.
  - The mother, too, has received negative reinforcement that increases the likelihood that she will give in to future tantrums.

In addition to this negative reinforcement trap, coercive behavior may also be increased by direct positive reinforcement. Aggressive behavior may meet with social approval.

The concept of reciprocity, in combination with the notion of reinforcement, adds to our understanding of how aggression and coercion may be learned and sustained. Children as young as nursery school age can learn in a short time that attacking

A child may engage in aversive behaviors in order to get something that he or she wants. If the parent repeatedly gives in, this capitulation may contribute to coercive patterns of interaction in the family. (Catchlight Visual Services/Alamy Stock Photo)

another person in response to some intrusion can terminate that intrusion. In addition, the victim of the attack may learn from the experience and may become more likely to initiate attacks in the future. But the eventual victim of escalating coercion also provides a negative reinforcer by giving in, thereby increasing the likelihood that the "winner" will start future coercions at higher levels of intensity and thus will get the victim to give in more quickly. In clinic families the coercive interactions are stable over time and across settings.

The description of a coercive process and ineffective parenting served as the basis for Patterson's intervention project and for his developmental model (Dishion & Patterson, 2016; Patterson et al., 1992; Patterson et al., 2002). In addition to describing the "training" of antisocial behavior in the home, the model describes a relationship between antisocial behavior and poor peer relationships and other adverse outcomes (Dishion & Patterson, 2006; Snyder, 2002). It is suggested that ineffective parenting produces the coercive, noncompliant core of antisocial behavior, which in turn leads to these other disruptions. Furthermore, it is hypothesized that each of these outcomes serves as a precursor to subsequent drift into deviant peer groups.

Later in the process, covert antisocial behaviors develop and are "added to" the overt/aggressive behaviors. Covert problem behaviors may develop as a way of avoiding harsh parenting practices and also may be reinforced by peers (Forgatch & Patterson, 2010).

The perspective of Patterson and his coworkers expanded to include a wide array of variables (e.g., poverty, stress, high-crime neighborhoods) that affect the family process and, thus, the problems known to be associated with antisocial behavior (Dishion & Patterson, 2006; Forgatch & Patterson, 2010). At the core of this complex theoretical model is the Parent Management Training—Oregon Model. Parenting training in this model seeks to both reduce coercive parenting practices and improve positive parenting practices.

To illustrate these parenting practices, consider parental discipline and parental monitoring, both of which contribute to, and are influenced by, the child's antisocial behavior. **Parental discipline** is defined by an interrelated set of skills: accurately tracking and classifying problem behaviors, ignoring trivial coercive events, and using effective consequences when necessary to back up demands and requests. Compared with other parents, parents of problem children have been found to be overinclusive in the behaviors that they classify as deviant. Thus, these parents differ in how they track and classify problem behavior. These parents also "natter" (nag, scold irritably) in response to low levels of coercive behavior or to behavior that other parents see as neutral and are able to ignore. Parents of antisocial children fail to back up their commands when the child does not comply, and they also fail to reward compliance when it does occur.

Parental monitoring of child behavior is also important to prevent the development and persistence over time of antisocial behavior. The amount of time a child spends unsupervised by parents increases with age. The amount of unsupervised time also is positively correlated with antisocial behavior. Patterson described treatment families as having little information about their children's whereabouts, whom the children were with, what they were doing, or when they would be home. This situation probably arises from a variety of considerations, including the repeated failures that these parents experienced in controlling their children even when difficulties occurred right in front of them. Also, requesting information would likely lead to a series of confrontations that the parents preferred to avoid. These parents did not expect to receive positive responses to their involvement either from their own children or from social agencies such as schools (Patterson et al., 1992).

It should be remembered that, within this model, parent and child behaviors are reciprocal in their influence. Thus, the parents' behaviors and parenting practices are also shaped by the child's behavior (Derella et al., 2020; Hails et al., 2018).

Extrafamilial Influences and Parental Psychopathology

The question of why some families and not others exhibit inept management practices has received some attention. Patterson (Patterson et al., 1992) posits that any number of variables may account for changes over time in family management skills. The handing down of faulty parenting practices from one generation to the next, in part, explains the problematic parenting characteristics of antisocial families. Also, Patterson's own findings and those of other investigators support the relationship between extrafamilial stressors (e.g., daily hassles, negative life events, financial problems, family health problems) and parenting practices (Capaldi et al., 2002; Dishion & Patterson, 2006; Wahler & Dumas, 1989). Social disadvantage and living in neighborhoods that require a very high level of parenting skills also place some families at risk (Bendezú et al., 2018; Burt et al., 2020).

Gerald R. Patterson founded the Oregon Social Learning Center. His work is widely considered as a major contribution to the understanding and treatment of conduct problems/antisocial behavior and to the entire field of psychology. (The estate of Gerald Patterson)

Finally, various forms of parental psychopathology are associated with poor parenting practices. Parents who themselves have antisocial difficulties may be particularly likely to have parenting practices (e.g., inconsistent discipline, low parental involvement) associated with the development of conduct-disordered behavior (Capaldi et al., 2002). Also, heavy drinking by parents may lower their threshold for reacting adversely to their child's behavior and also may be associated with inept monitoring of the child and less parental involvement (El-Sheikh & Flanagan, 2001; Lahey, Waldman, & McBurnett, 1999; West & Prinz, 1987). Figure 9.6 illustrates a model of how a variety of influences may disrupt effective parenting and lead to child antisocial behavior.

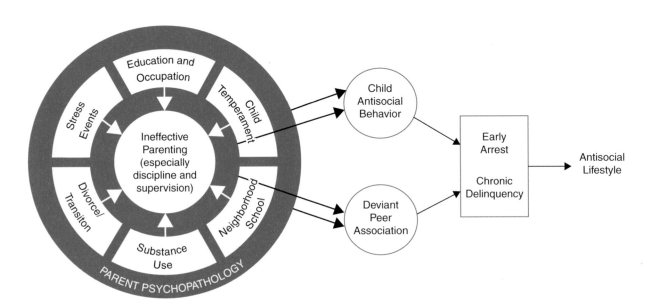

Figure 9.6 A mediational model for the association of family context and antisocial behavior. (Adapted from Capaldi et al., 2002)

Marital Discord

Parental conflict and divorce are common in homes of children and adolescents with conduct problems (Cummings, Davies, & Campbell, 2000; O'Leary & Emery, 1985). The conflict leading to and surrounding the divorce are principal influences in this relationship, and divorces characterized by less conflict and greater cooperation are associated with fewer problems in children (Amato & Keith, 1991; Hetherington, Bridges, & Insabella, 1998). If aggression between the parents is also present, childhood disorder seems even more likely than would be expected on the basis of marital discord alone (Cummings, Goeke-Morey, & Papp, 2004; Jaffee, Poisson, & Cunningham, 2001; Jouriles, Murphy, & O'Leary, 1989). The relationship between marital conflict and conduct disorders can be explained in a number of ways. Parents who engage in a great deal of marital conflict or aggression may serve as models for their children. The stress of marital discord may also interfere with parenting practices such as the ability to monitor the child's behavior. Hostility and anger may also affect the child's emotion-regulation development and thereby contribute to conduct problems. The relationship between discord and conduct problems may also operate in the opposite causal direction; that is, the child's disruptive behavior may contribute to marital discord.

Also, both child conduct problems and marital discord may be related to a "third variable," such as parental antisocial disorder. Indeed, there are high rates of antisocial personality disorder (APD) among parents of conduct-disordered youth, and APD is associated with high rates of marital instability and discord (Farrington, Ullrich, & Salekin, 2010).

The relationship between marital conflict and child adjustment is likely to be complex and change over time. It is important to remember that these problems exist in a larger context (Davies & Cummings, 2006). It may be that a high level of environmental risk (related to family and community/neighborhood factors such as socioeconomic difficulties and high-crime neighborhoods) directly affects the youth and is also experienced by the parents, contributing to both marital and parent–child difficulties (Farrington et al., 2010; Klahr et al., 2011; Richards et al., 2004; Wahler & Dumas, 1989).

Peer Relations

Peer relations are part of the complex interplay of influences that contribute to the development of conduct problems (Dishion, Kim, & Tein, 2016; Hay et al., 2004; Lahey & Waldman, 2017). Parents are often concerned that peers whose behaviors they view as "bad or dangerous" are influencing their children. Although, particularly in adolescence, affiliation with peers who engage in some form of conduct-disordered behavior may be somewhat normative, parents' concerns may be reasonable. Involvement with deviant peers may be one factor in the initiation, escalation, and maintenance of aggressive and antisocial behavior, particularly if such involvement begins early and if the involvement is with groups of peers with severe conduct problems and substance use (Fergusson & Horwood, 1998; Laird et al., 2001; Price, Drabick, & Ridenour, 2019; Snyder, 2002).

Beginning in childhood and accelerating in adolescence, conduct-disordered and delinquent youth may have friends who also engage in aggressive and antisocial behaviors. Research shows that the interactions and influences that characterize these deviant peer associations play a role in the initiation, maintenance, and acceleration of antisocial behavior (Dishion & Patterson, 2006). For example, Fergusson and Horwood (1998) reported on the linkages between early conduct problems and outcomes at age 18 in a group of New Zealand children studied longitudinally since birth. They found that conduct problems at age 8 were associated with poorer outcomes, such as leaving school by age 18 without appropriate educational qualifications and a period of three months or more of unemployment. One of the factors that mediated the relationship between early aggression and later poor outcomes was peer affiliations. Adolescents, who between the ages of 14 and 16 reported having friends who were delinquent, or who used illegal substances, were at greater risk for later negative outcomes.

Peer influences are not independent of other contextual factors (Dishion & Patterson, 2006). For example, in their longitudinal study of New Zealand youth, Fergusson and Horwood (1999) found that family variables such as parental conflict, parental history of drug abuse and criminal behavior, and problematic early mother–child interactions were predictive of affiliation with deviant peers at age 15. Cultural and community influences come into play as well. Brody and colleagues (2001) found, in a sample of African American children, that difficulty with deviant peers was less likely if parents were nurturing and involved, but more likely if parenting was harsh and inconsistent. Furthermore, affiliation with deviant peers was less likely in neighborhoods with collective socialization practices (e.g., adults who were willing to monitor and supervise youth from their own and other families). Community economic disadvantage also was associated with greater likelihood of deviant peer affiliation, and the benefits of nurturant/involved parenting and collective socialization were most pronounced for young people from the most disadvantaged neighborhoods.

There may be individual differences regarding the effect of deviant peer affiliation on youth. For example, Lee (2011) investigated genetic influences on the impact of deviant peers. The monoamine oxidase-A gene (MAOA) has been suggested to play a role in antisocial behavior since the enzyme associated with this gene plays a role in the efficient processing of relevant neurotransmitters. A large sample of adolescents was designated as belonging to either a high- (greater efficiency) or low-activity (lower efficiency) genotype group based on the number of repeats in a specific region of the MAOA gene. Greater affiliation with

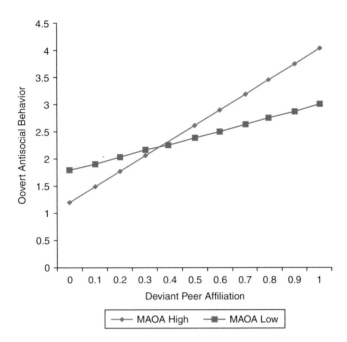

Figure 9.7 Overt antisocial behavior is influenced by the interaction of monoamine oxidase-A (MAOA) genotype and affiliation with deviant peers. (Adapted from Lee, 2011)

deviant peers was found to be associated with higher levels of both overt and covert antisocial behavior (ASB) across a six-year period. However, a gene–environment interaction was found for overt antisocial behavior. The influence of deviant peer affiliation was significantly stronger for youth with the high-activity MAOA genotype (see Figure 9.7). However, the MAOA genotype did not seem to play a similar role with regard to covert antisocial behavior. These findings illustrate, once again, the complex interaction of influences on the development of behavior.

Cognitive-Emotional Influences

Consider the adolescent boy who is walking down the street and is approached by a group of peers who begin to call him names, laugh, and tease him. Some boys respond to this situation by getting angry, escalating the conflict, and perhaps reacting violently, whereas other boys are able to deflect attention to another topic, ignore it, laugh, make light of the teasing, or firmly ask that the teasing stop. The cognitive and emotional processes that occur during this situation constitute proximal mechanisms for aggressive behavior.

Dodge, 2000, p. 448

Examining how children and adolescents think and feel about social situations is part of understanding the development of conduct problems. For example, a child may view another child's neutral actions as having a hostile intent; may fail to take another person's perspective; may fail to use social problem-solving skills;

may fail to think before they act; or, in general, fail to use self-regulation skills to control their emotions and behavior. These social-cognitive-emotional processes are part of the development and persistence of aggressive and antisocial behavior (Dodge, 2000; Lochman et al., 2000; Wells et al., 2020). In addition, youth with the callous/unemotional traits described earlier may display social-emotional information-processing patterns such as a focus on the positive aspects of aggression and a lack of responsiveness to emotional stimuli (McMahon & Frick, 2019; White & Frick, 2010).

The model articulated by Dodge and his colleagues illustrates how one might address social-emotional cognitions (Crick & Dodge, 1994; Dodge, 2003). The model suggests that cognitive processing begins with encoding (looking for and attending to) and then interpreting social and emotional cues. The next steps involve how to respond. These steps include searching for possible alternative responses, selecting a specific response, and finally enacting the selected response. Investigations reveal that youth with conduct problems have poorer social problem-solving skills and display cognitive deficits and distortions in various parts of this process (Fontaine, Burks, & Dodge, 2002). For example, during the earlier stages of the process, aggressive youth may use fewer social cues and misattribute hostile intent to their peers' neutral actions. Furthermore, they may be more likely to perceive and label the arousal they experience in conflict situations as anger rather than other emotions. These reactions to internal arousal may contribute to further distortion and restricted problem solving (Lochman et al., 2000). Thus, later in the process they may also generate fewer responses and ones that are less likely to be effectively assertive and are more likely to be aggressive solutions. They may also expect that aggressive responses will lead to positive outcomes. Problematic social-cognitive-emotional processes may start quite early in life and be part of the stability of early-onset conduct-disordered behavior (Coy et al., 2001).

Dodge and his colleagues (Dodge, 1991; D. Schwartz et al., 1998) distinguish between two types of aggressive behavior: reactive aggression and proactive aggression. **Reactive aggression** is an angry ("hot-blooded") retaliatory response to a perceived provocation or frustration. **Proactive aggression**, in contrast, is generally not associated with anger and is characterized by deliberate aversive behaviors (starting fights, bullying, teasing) that are oriented to specific goals or supported by positive environmental outcomes. Different social-cognitive deficiencies may be associated with these different types of aggression (Jambon & Smetana, 2018; Schippell et al., 2003). Reactively aggressive youth appear to display deficiencies in early stages of the social-cognitive process; for example, they underutilize social cues and attribute hostile intent to others. Proactively aggressive youth display deficiencies in later stages of the process; for example, they are likely to positively evaluate aggressive solutions and to expect that they will lead to positive outcomes. It is suggested that the two types of aggression also seem to be related to different outcomes.

A study by Brendgen and colleagues (2001), for example, illustrates different outcomes associated with the reactive–proactive distinction. This study also reminds us, once again, of the interrelatedness of influences. A sample of Caucasian, French-speaking boys from low socioeconomic neighborhoods in Montreal, Canada, were categorized at 13 years of age as either nonaggressive, proactive–aggressive, reactive–aggressive, or both proactive– and reactive–aggressive. The boys, at 16–17 years of age, were asked to report on their delinquency-related physical violence (e.g., beat up other boys, used a weapon in a fight) and on their physical violence against a dating partner. In general, proactive aggression was associated with greater delinquency-related violence, and reactive aggression with greater dating violence. However, the relationship between proactive aggression and delinquency-related violence was moderated by level of parental supervision. The relationship was strong for boys who had experienced low levels of parental supervision during their early adolescent years. However, the relationship between proactive aggression and delinquency-related violence was weak for boys who had experienced higher levels of parental supervision during this period. Similarly, the relationship between reactive aggression and dating violence was mediated by level of maternal warmth and caregiving. The relationship between reactive aggression and dating violence was strong for boys who had experienced low levels of maternal warmth and caregiving during their development. However, this relationship was weak among boys who had experienced higher levels of maternal warmth and caregiving. Thus, although development of proactive and reactive aggression may be influenced by social-cognitive style, the developmental course of such behavior may be affected by the parenting a young person receives.

Biological Influences

Discussions of the role of biological influences emphasize transactions among multiple biological and nonbiological influences (Beauchaine, Gatzke-Kopp, & Gizer, 2017; Tremblay, 2010; Viding & Larsson, 2010).

Genetics

That aggressive, antisocial, and other conduct-related behaviors run in families, within and across generations, is consistent with both environmental and genetic explanations of the development of such behavior. Despite considerable variation in estimates, which appears related to how conduct problem/antisocial behavior is measured and the source of information, there appears to be moderate genetic influence on such behavior (Farrington et al., 2001; Lahey & Waldman, 2017; Weyandt et al., 2011). However,

there may be greater heritability for problems in childhood than in adolescence (Young et al., 2009) and there is also the suggestion of a lesser genetic component for adolescent delinquency than for adult criminal behavior. How might this difference be explained? The childhood-onset versus adolescent-limited distinction discussed earlier may be germane. Conduct-disordered behavior and delinquent behavior are quite common during adolescence, and in many cases they do not persist into adulthood. It might, therefore, be reasonable to hypothesize an increased genetic component for antisocial behavior that persists from childhood into adult life (Eley, Lichtenstein, & Moffitt, 2003b; Moffitt, 2006).

Although genetic influences may play some role, they are likely to be indirect and interact in complex ways with environmental influences, such as social conditions, family variables, and certain social learning experiences in determining etiology (Rhee & Waldman, 2003; Weyandt et al., 2011). Various gene–environment correlations and interactions likely contribute to the development of conduct-disordered behavior (Lahey & Waldman, 2017). Gene–environment correlations may be manifested in a number of ways. For example, antisocial parents may both transmit genes that predispose their children to antisocial behavior and also affect their own parenting behavior. Also, young children genetically predisposed to oppositional defiant and conduct problems are likely to evoke coercive, hostile, and inconsistent parenting. Also, these same heritable characteristics may lead youth to form friendships with delinquent youth who encourage and maintain their antisocial behavior.

Gene–environment interactions also influence the development of conduct-disordered behavior. Earlier we described a finding by Lee (2011), regarding overt antisocial behavior, of an interaction between an MAOA genotype and affiliation with deviant peers. Similarly, a gene–environment interaction is suggested in the work of van Lier and colleagues (2007a). Their research, on a sample of 6-year-old twins, examined the contribution of affiliation with aggressive friends to level of aggression. Affiliation with aggressive peers was a risk factor for aggression. However, the contribution of having an aggressive friend was greatest for those children who were already at high genetic risk for aggression. In a similar vein, in a sample of 5-year-old twins and their families a gene–environment interaction was suggested regarding the contribution of maltreatment to the presence of CD (Jaffee et al., 2005). The presence of maltreatment increased the probability of a CD diagnosis by 2% among children at low genetic risk for CD and 24% among children at high genetic risk.

Neurobiological Influences

Psychophysiological variables have been frequently hypothesized to be related to antisocial behavior. Support for this notion comes from studies that find differences between delinquent or conduct-disordered youth and control youth on measures of autonomic arousal such as heart rate, electrodermal response (skin conductance), and cortisol levels (Beauchaine, Hong, & Marsh, 2008; Cappadocia et al., 2009; Latvala et al., 2015; Raine, 2015). Thus, a link between both the sympathetic and parasympathetic aspects of the autonomic nervous system functioning and conduct problem behavior has been suggested.

Quay (1993) hypothesized a biological foundation for aggressive, life-course-persistent conduct disorders. This hypothesis is based on Gray's (1987) theory of brain systems: a **behavioral inhibition system** (BIS) and a **behavioral activation (or approach) system** (BAS) that have distinct neuroanatomical and neurotransmitter systems. The BIS is related to the emotions of fear and anxiety, and tends to inhibit action in novel or fearful situations or under conditions of punishment or nonreward. The BAS tends to activate behavior in the presence of reinforcement; it is associated with reward seeking and pleasurable emotions. An imbalance between the two systems is hypothesized to create a predisposition that, in combination with adverse environmental circumstances, produces behavior problems. Quay (1993) suggested that an underactive BIS combined with an overactive reward system (BAS) may be implicated in the genesis of persistent aggressive conduct disorders.

There is an alternative model of how the two systems may operate. In this view, conduct-disordered, aggressive behavior results from an underactive BAS system in combination with an underactive BIS system (Beauchaine et al., 2001). Conduct-disordered and aggressive behavior represents a form of sensation seeking in response to chronic underarousal created by an underactive BAS system. Youth characterized as conduct-disordered also have low levels of inhibition (underactive BIS system) and engage in aggressive and other antisocial behaviors to achieve satisfactory reward states and positive arousal.

A third system, described by Gray (1987), might also be involved in conduct disorders. The **fight/flight system** (F/F) also involves distinct brain and autonomic nervous system functioning. It is proposed to mediate defensive reactions under conditions of frustration, punishment, or pain. Thus, stimuli that are viewed as threatening would activate the F/F system. Certain youth, such as those with conduct-disordered behavior, may have a reduced threshold for F/F responding, whereas youth with higher thresholds may possess characteristics such as social competence and empathy toward others in distress. In general, the BIS and BAS are viewed as motivational, whereas the F/F system is viewed as an emotion-regulation system (Beauchaine et al., 2001).

Structural and functional brain deficits have also been hypothesized to be associated with antisocial and disruptive behaviors. The frontal lobes, in particular, may play a role, through deficits in verbal and executive functions (e.g., inhibitory control, sustaining attention, abstract reasoning, goal formation, planning, emotion regulation) (Cappadocia et al., 2009; Rogers

& De Brito, 2016; Rubia et al., 2008; Sauder et al., 2012). Thus, neuroimaging studies have noted impaired patterns of frontal cortex functioning among youth with antisocial and aggressive behavior problems. Patterns of frontal cortex activity associated with lack of inhibitory control, problems in self-monitoring of task performance, and other cognitive abilities have been observed. However, findings are not always consistent across studies. Also, questions remain regarding sex differences and whether these findings are specific to conduct disorder. Frontal cortex activity functioning and related executive functioning deficits are not unique to CD; they have been found in youth with a variety of disorders. Thus, one goal is to clarify the unique roles of such deficits in CD/ODD versus co-occurring disorders such as ADHD (Weyandt et al., 2011). Furthermore, neurobiological conceptualizations of CD development such as these may not apply to all conduct-disordered youth, but only to certain subgroups such as those youth with co-occurring ADHD or to those with callous-unemotional traits.

Before turning to our discussion of assessment and intervention for conduct problems, we examine the problem of substance use.

Substance Use

Adolescent substance use is an important clinical and public health problem. The use of alcohol and other drugs is common among adolescents and preadolescents (Johnston et al., 2019b). Substance use and conduct problems are often considered as part of a larger externalizing behavior construct and there are probably both common (shared) and specific aspects of the two problems (Castellanos-Ryan & Conrod, 2011). The use of alcohol and other drugs can, thus, be part of the constellation of antisocial and rule-breaking behaviors exhibited by conduct-disordered youth. Indeed, the disruptive behavior disorders (CD and ODD) are the most likely disorders to be associated with youth substance use (Fergusson et al., 2007). Some youth engage in substance use, but do not display antisocial behavior.

There is widespread concern regarding illegal **(illicit) drugs** such as cocaine, MDMA (ecstasy, molly), hallucinogens (e.g., LSD), and heroin. Marijuana is the most commonly used illicit drug. It is classified as an illicit drug even though it is now legal in several states. There also is concern regarding use of **licit drugs** (drugs that are legal for adults or by prescription) and other substances. Alcohol, nicotine, psychoactive medications (e.g., stimulants, sedatives), over-the-counter medications (e.g., sleep aids and weight reduction aids), steroids, and inhalants (e.g., glue, paint thinner) are readily accessible and potentially harmful. Narcotics such as OxyContin and Vicodin also have become the focus of recent concern.

Classification and Description

Many adolescents experiment with substance use. One definition of a substance use problem views any use of alcohol or other substance by a minor as abuse since such use is illegal. However, those working with young people typically try to distinguish between time-limited patterns of experimentation or lesser use that are developmentally normative and patterns that may have serious short- and long-term consequences (Chassin et al., 2010).

The DSM substance-related and addictive disorders category describes pathological uses of ten classes of substances (e.g., alcohol, cannabis, hallucinogens, stimulants) and also includes gambling disorder. The excessive use of these classes of drugs and gambling are presumed to have in common the direct activation of brain reward systems. The substance-related disorders are divided into two groups: substance use disorders and substance-induced disorders. **Substance Use Disorders** involve a pattern of behavioral, cognitive, and physiological symptoms that indicate that the individual continues to use the substance despite appreciable substance-related problems. The diagnostic criteria used to describe this pattern of symptoms cluster into four groups:

- impaired control over substance use;
- social impairment (e.g., interpersonal, school);
- risky use;
- pharmacological criteria (tolerance, withdrawal).

Diagnosticians can also indicate the severity (mild, moderate, severe) based on the number of symptom criteria that are met. **Substance-Induced Disorders** include conditions of intoxication, withdrawal, and other mental disorders (e.g., depressive disorders, anxiety disorders, bipolar and related disorders) that are due to the recent use of a particular substance (American Psychiatric Association, 2013).

The DSM criteria for substance-related and addictive disorders are the same for youth and adults. However, the developmental appropriateness of these criteria for adolescents has been questioned (Brown, Tomlinson, & Winwood, 2017; Chassin et al., 2010; Chung & Bachrach, 2019). Adolescents, for example, often display symptoms that are just below diagnostic thresholds. Also, tolerance may be overestimated as youth "learn to use" substances. Withdrawal also may be overestimated based on short-term physiological reactions to "binge" pattern uses that are more common among adolescents. These developmental/diagnostic issues may explain why adolescents with lower levels of use are more likely than adults to be diagnosed with substance use disorders. The possibility that characteristics of typical neurobiological development may make youth more susceptible to substance use during the adolescent period of development, however, should not be ignored.

Epidemiology

According to the Monitoring the Future (MTF) study (Johnston et al., 2019b)—a long-term study of American adolescents that annually surveys large samples of eighth, tenth, and twelfth graders—there was a decline in substance use among young people from peak years in the late 1990s and, with some variation, an overall leveling off in use since about 2009. However, 2018 information indicates that approximately 19% of eighth graders, 36% of tenth graders, and 48% of twelfth graders have used an illicit substance in their lifetime. Marijuana is the most widely used illicit drug in this age group. Reports of daily use of marijuana increased in all three grades after about 2007, reaching peaks around 2011–2013, before declining since. Daily use prevalence rates for 2018 were about 1%, 3%, and 6% for eighth, tenth, and twelfth graders, respectively.

The use of legal drugs is also reason for concern. The long decline in cigarette smoking, for example, resulted in dramatic decreases in nicotine use in this age group. However, MTF 2018 reported a dramatic increase in vaping by adolescents. Vaping involves inhaling aerosols (sometimes containing substances such as nicotine) using devices such as e-cigarettes. Alcohol remains the most used substance among teenagers according to the MTF study. Juvenile alcohol use seems to have shown a steady decline in recent years. However, some concern remains. While this decline continued for twelfth graders, in 2018 the decline was halted for eighth and tenth graders. Also, despite the good news of long-term declines, approximately 18% of twelfth graders, 8% of tenth graders, and 2% of eighth graders still report having been drunk at least once in the previous month (Johnston et al., 2019b). There is also concern with the misuse of prescription drugs such as amphetamines and tranquilizers by young people in this age group.

In addition, as reports of use of some substances decline there is concern about the increased popularity of other drugs. It is suggested that increases and decreases in the use of particular drugs are due to shifts in the perceived benefits and perceived risks that young people come to associate with each drug. The concern is that rumor of the supposed benefits spreads faster than information about adverse consequences.

Gender Differences

Most findings suggest greater illicit drug use among males. However, there have been some changes (Johnston et al., 2019b). For example, long-standing gender differences in the use of marijuana have narrowed or closed. Males continue to have higher use rates for many drugs. The use of prescription drugs such as amphetamines and tranquilizers may be the primary exception where females tend to have higher rates, particularly in the lower grades. In general, however, gender differences in substance use tend to emerge as students grow older—prevalence rates increase for both genders but the increases are often sharper for males.

215

Racial/Ethnic Differences

The picture with regard to ethnic differences is a complex one. The MTF study report (Johnston et al., 2019b) on differences between the three largest racial/ethnic groups—whites, African Americans, and Hispanics—illustrates the complexity of findings. Comparisons of racial/ethnic differences have varied over time, depending on which age group was examined and which substances were considered. For example, white students for many years had higher rates of illicit drug use than African Americans. But in recent years this difference has narrowed as a result of increasing marijuana use among African American students and some decline among white students. Hispanic students have had rates of use of various drugs that place them between the other two groups for twelfth graders—usually closer to whites than African Americans. However, among eighth graders, Hispanics tended to report the highest rates of use for nearly all classes of illicit drugs. Examining the use of specific drugs, African Americans have tended to have lower levels of use of certain drugs such as hallucinogens and synthetic marijuana, but higher levels of use of other drugs such as heroin and bath salts. In twelfth grade, Hispanics have the highest use rates for a number of drugs such as synthetic marijuana and cocaine. White students generally have higher rates of misusing prescription drugs than the other two groups, particularly in the upper grades. These few examples only begin to illustrate the complexity of discussions of racial/ethnic differences in substance use (Johnston et al., 2019a).

Patterns of Co-occurrence

Adolescents with substance use problems typically display a number of other difficulties (Armstrong & Costello, 2002; Roberts, Roberts, & Xing, 2007; U.S. Department of Health and Human Services, 2016). Many use multiple drugs. Academic and family difficulties are common, as are delinquent behaviors. As indicated earlier, substance use is often conceptualized as a later-occurring part of a constellation of conduct problem behaviors. It is not surprising, therefore, that young people who use drugs often meet the criteria for externalizing/disruptive behavior disorders (ODD, CD). Mood disorders also are frequently associated with substance use problems (Ahrnsbrak et al., 2017; Felton et al., 2020; Groenman, Janssen, & Oosterlaan, 2017).

Risk Factors and Developmental Course

Peak risk for the onset of substance use occurs during adolescence and early onset of substance use is a strong risk factor for later substance use disorders (Chung & Bachrach, 2019). Researchers and clinicians agree that understanding the development of substance use and substance disorders requires appreciation of multiple risk factors and multiple potential pathways (Cavell, Ennett, & Meehan, 2001; Chassin et al., 2016; Chung & Bachrach, 2019; Gray & Squeglia, 2018; Meyers & Dick, 2010). These factors overlap considerably with the factors that influence the development of conduct problems in general.

RODNEY Alcohol and Nicotine Use

"It was so hard to start, I had no idea it would be harder to stop." Rodney, age 17, didn't recall much about the motorcycle accident that had put him in the hospital. It involved quite a few brandy Alexanders and too little about hanging onto the passenger bar of the motorcycle. He was clear-headed enough to realize that he badly needed a cigarette.

By the time Rodney was 12, he was already attending high school classes, had won several statewide scholastic contests, and had appeared twice on a popular TV quiz show. When he was 14, his parents reluctantly let him accept a scholarship to a small but prestigious liberal arts college. "Of course I was the smallest one there … I'm sure I started smoking and drinking to compensate for my size."

Six months into college, Rodney was smoking a pack and a half a day. When studying for exams (he often felt he wasn't "measuring up"), he found himself lighting one cigarette from another, going through several packs in a day this way—far more than he meant to. The following year, he read the Surgeon General's report on smoking and saw a video about lung cancer ("in living—no, dying—color"). He swore he would never smoke again, but he noticed that he became restless, depressed, and "so irritable my roommate begged me to light up again." Over the next year he had tried twice more to quit.

Rodney's parents were hardworking churchgoers who had never touched a drop of alcohol. Both had been appalled at what alcohol had done to their own fathers. Several times in the last few months, when he was so badly hung over he couldn't attend classes, Rodney had vaguely wondered whether he was about to follow in his grandfathers' unsteady footsteps.

When Rodney first awakened after the accident he had pins through his femur and a terrific hangover. Now, two days later, his vital signs were stable and normal except for a pulse of only 56. "I don't suppose you could smuggle in some nicotine gum?" Rodney asked.

Adapted from Morrison & Anders, 1999, pp. 286–287

Individual differences, such as exposure to trauma, temperament, self-regulation, and problem solving are often implicated in the onset and escalation of substance use (S. A. Brown et al., 2017). Cognitive-affective components—attitudes, expectations, intentions, and beliefs about control—are particularly prominent in conceptualizations of adolescent substance use. For instance, the expectancies of positive or negative consequences for drinking is an important influence on alcohol use (Smit et al., 2018). The importance of expectancy regarding the effects of alcohol is illustrated in a study of the development of drinking behavior (Smith & Goldman, 1994; Smith et al., 1995). Over a two-year period during which many of the youth first began to drink, expectations that drinking would facilitate social interactions predicted initiation into drinking. Those who expected social facilitation also drank more over the two-year period, and future expectations regarding the effects of drinking became more positive.

Families are an important influence on adolescent substance use patterns. Parental substance use is associated with the initiation and degree of adolescent substance use (Hussong, Bauer, & Chassin, 2008; Madras et al., 2019). Aspects of parent–child relationships such as less secure attachment, high level of family conflict, and ineffectiveness of parenting skills also have been linked to adolescent substance use (S. A. Brown et al., 2017). In addition, social learning theory explanations have drawn attention to the role of modeling of behavior and attitudes. Because parents and older siblings are potential models for such behavior, the child of a parent who uses or misuses alcohol or some other substance may be at particular risk. Research by Hops and his colleagues (2000), for example, indicates that when parents or older siblings use tobacco, alcohol, or marijuana, adolescents are more likely to initiate use of these substances. More than the adoption of the specific drug-use behavior observed is affected by modeling. The adolescent may also initiate the use of other substances that serve a similar function (e.g., escape, perceived facilitation of social interactions). Furthermore, the attitude displayed by the parent can affect the young person's behavior. Adolescents are more likely to use substances, for example, when they perceive less parental disapproval for use (Chassin et al., 1998).

Peer factors are considered among the strongest influences on adolescent substance use (S. A. Brown et al., 2017; Dishion & Owen, 2002). Perceived peer substance use and perceived peer approval have been shown to be important factors. Social learning theory explanations also suggest that adolescents who interact with substance-using peer models and who expect positive consequences from substance use will initiate and continue substance use. However, it is difficult to establish direct peer influence. To begin with, adolescent substance users tend to choose friends who use drugs. Also, research findings are based on adolescents' perceptions of their peers' behavior, and such perceptions may be affected by the bias to see one's own choices as common (Cavell et al., 2001).

School, neighborhood, community, and societal influences are likely to contribute to adolescent substance use. Poor academic performance and low involvement in school activities, for example, have been linked to substance use. In contrast, schools that foster a sense of commitment and community have lower rates of use. Although some information suggests that low-income and high-risk neighborhoods are associated with greater adolescent substance use, findings are mixed. Some studies suggest higher rates of initial experimentation in more affluent and suburban neighborhoods. Apart from difference in rate of use, the risks associated with substance experimentation may be greater for youth who reside in poorer neighborhoods, where there may be greater risk of trauma exposure (Carliner et al., 2017). Also, risk may be particularly high if other members of their family use or abuse substances (Chassin et al., 2010). Larger social and cultural influences, such as availability of drugs and social norms regarding drug use, also contribute to the likelihood and degree of youths' substance use. Clearly, continuing research on these influences is needed.

A variety of theories and conceptualizations that are not necessarily mutually exclusive have been suggested as ways of explaining how psychosocial risk and protective factors operate in the development of substance use. Social learning theory, as we have seen, emphasizes processes such as imitation, expectancy, and consequences. We will briefly examine two other theoretical and conceptual models.

One particular model views adolescence as a period of increasing freedom and exploration, and of a transition that is marked by attempts to engage in certain behaviors deemed appropriate for adults but not for adolescents (Bachman et al., 2002; Jessor & Jessor, 1977). Use of alcohol is an example of such a behavior. Individual differences and environmental variables are assumed to affect the rate at which an individual makes the transition to adulthood and thereby the age of onset of these behaviors. There also may be developmental changes in neurocircuitry during adolescence that make this a period of greater vulnerability for experimentation with substances and substance use disorders (Chambers, Taylor, & Potenza, 2003).

Adolescent substance use has also been viewed as developing within a negative affect, stress, and coping pathway (Colder et al., 2009). From this perspective, young people who are prone to experience high negative affect or who are facing greater negative life events and perceived stress, and/or those with elevated physiological responses to stress, may be more likely to use alcohol and other substances. Substance use may serve as a coping function for the adolescent, or at least it is perceived to do so. Whereas some young people employ a variety of adaptive-active coping mechanisms (e.g., seeking information, considering

Association with a peer group that supports the use of alcohol and other drugs may be a contributing influence to the development of substance use and abuse. (imageBROKER/Alamy Stock Photo)

alternatives, taking direct action), others may rely more heavily on the use of avoidant coping mechanisms (e.g., distraction, social withdrawal, wishful thinking) and use alcohol and other substances to deal with negative emotions and stress.

Neurobiological influences and adolescent brain development also are given frequent consideration (Chung & Bachrach, 2019; Rutherford, Mayes, & Potenza, 2010). Research has highlighted important developmental changes in brain systems regarding motivation/reward sensitivity on the one hand, and cognitive control on the other (O'Halloran et al., 2017; Squeglia et al., 2017). For example, changes occurring early in adolescence regarding dopaminergic systems, involving limbic and associated areas of the brain, are thought to produce changes in sensation seeking and increases in the salience of reward and, perhaps, adolescents' positive reactions to substances. In contrast, the changes in prefrontal regions and increases in white matter associated with development of cognitive control (executive function) systems are thought to develop more slowly and continue into the mid-20s. This developmental gap may place adolescents at increased risk for risky behaviors and substance use, in particular (Steinberg 2007, 2009).

There is support for genetic influences on substance use (Verhulst, Neale, & Kendler, 2015). Behavioral genetic studies have consistently linked parental substance abuse to risk for substance use and abuse in offspring (S. A. Brown et al., 2017). Thus, for example, youth with a parental history of alcoholism are more likely to demonstrate a number of vulnerabilities to problematic substance use such as greater impulsivity, poorer response inhibition, and physiological response to alcohol. Molecular genetic research has also identified a number of genes, each with relatively small effects, which likely interact with each other to influence the development of substance use and abuse. It is important to emphasize that considerable research indicates that the impact of these genetic influences on developmental substance use trajectories is through their interaction not only with each other, but also with multiple environmental risk factors (S. A. Brown et al., 2017; Gray & Squeglia, 2018).

Clearly, no single factor or theory can easily explain which youth start or persist in problematic substance use (S. A. Brown et al., 2017; Gray & Squeglia, 2018; Meyers & Dick, 2010). Explanations must include an array of variables—biological, psychological, and social—that interactively affect development over time. It seems clear, however, that conduct problems are associated with some appreciable percentage of adolescent substance use patterns (Fergusson et al., 2007; Groenman et al., 2017). We return now to our examination of the broader conduct problem domain.

Assessment

Assessment of conduct problems is likely to be a complex and multifaceted process. In the following sections we describe the primary procedures likely to be used by clinicians working to assess these children and adolescents. It should be recognized that the assessment process will likely need to address a variety of problems and is also likely to include evaluation of the problems of others in the youth's environment, and their attitudes and skills (e.g., parenting), as well as ongoing life stresses (De Los Reyes et al., 2015; Frick & McMahon, 2018).

Interviews

A general clinical interview with the parents and older children and adolescents themselves is typically part of the assessment process. An interview with younger children may not be as easily conducted or may not be a reliable source of information; however, the opportunity to interact with the young child may be helpful to the clinician. An interview with the entire family and with the teacher or school personnel may also provide valuable information. Structured interviews such as the Diagnostic Interview Schedule for Children (DICA; Reich, 2000) can help provide a comprehensive understanding of problems and their context, and can also help determine a diagnosis.

Behavior Rating Scales

Among general rating scales useful for assessing conduct problems are the Achenbach instruments (Achenbach & Rescorla, 2001) and the Behavior Assessment System for Children (BASC; Reynolds & Kamphaus, 2015). They allow evaluation of a broad array of problems through the reports of multiple informants. Also useful are behavior rating scales that focus specifically on conduct problems and disruptive behavior. The Conners' Parent and Teacher Rating Scales (Conners, 2008), the Eyberg Child Behavior Inventory (ECBI), and the Sutter-Eyberg Student Behavior Inventory (SESBI) are examples (Eyberg & Pincus, 1999).

The Self-Report Delinquency Scale (SRD; Elliot, Huizinga, & Ageton, 1985) is a youth self-report measure of conduct problems. Consisting of items derived from the Uniform Crime Reports and including index offenses (e.g., theft, aggravated assault), other delinquent behaviors, and drug use, it is intended for use with youth 11 to 19 years old. Self-report measures are less commonly used with younger children because these children may not be capable of reporting conduct problems accurately.

Behavioral Observations

There are a large number of behavioral observation systems designed for use in clinic, home, and school settings (Frick & McMahon, 2018). Behavioral observations are a desirable part of the assessment process because they avoid the potential bias of reports based on interviews and questionnaires and may measure aspects of conduct problem behaviors not captured by these other approaches (Weyandt et al., 2011).

The Behavioral Coding System (Forehand & McMahon, 1981) and the Dyadic Parent–Child Interaction Coding System (Eyberg et al., 2013) are two similar observational systems for assessing parent–child interactions in the clinic. Both observe the parent and the child in situations that vary from free-play and child-directed activities to adult-directed activities, and both focus on parental commands (antecedents) and consequences for child compliance or noncompliance. The Interpersonal Process Code (Rusby, Estes, & Dishion, 1991) is another observational system that is an outgrowth of observational systems developed by Patterson and his colleagues.

The observational systems just described have also been used in home settings, and these and other systems have been employed in schools (Nock & Kurtz, 2005; Reynolds & Kamphaus, 2015). Practicing clinicians seldom use these systems because they are complex and require extensive periods of training and trained observers. The observations themselves are lengthy, and it is challenging to coordinate with the times when relevant behaviors are occurring in homes or schools. An alternative to using trained observers in the home or other natural environments is to train adults in the child's environment to record and observe certain behaviors. An advantage of this approach is the opportunity to observe and record behaviors that occur at low rates (e.g., stealing or fire setting) and that would likely be missed by trained observers making occasional visits.

Intervention

Because of the challenges posed by children and adolescents with conduct problems and the impact they have on others, many different interventions have been attempted. Only a portion of these has received a careful empirical evaluation of their effectiveness. There is, however, appreciable evidence that psychosocial interventions for conduct problems are effective (McMahon & Frick, 2019; Weisz et al., 2017). Here we will briefly describe some of the interventions that have appreciable research support.

Family-Based Interventions

Family-based interventions for conduct problems, particularly those with a behavioral or cognitive-behavioral emphasis, have the strongest support for both children (Kaminski & Claussen, 2017) and adolescents (McCart & Sheidow, 2016). Successful approaches to reducing aggressive, noncompliant, and antisocial behaviors in children have typically been interventions employing social learning parent management training. These interventions focus on helping parents learn behavioral management strategies to encourage positive behaviors and reduce negative behaviors

Table 9.3 Common Features of Parent Training Programs

- Treatments are conducted primarily with the parents.
  - The therapist teaches the parents to alter interactions with their child so as to increase prosocial behavior and to decrease deviant behavior.
  - Young children may be brought into sessions to train both the parents and the child in how to interact. Older youth may participate in negotiating and developing behavior-change programs.
- New ways of identifying, defining, and observing behavior problems are taught.
- Social learning principles and procedures that follow from them are taught (e.g., social reinforcement, points for prosocial behavior, time out from reinforcement, loss of privileges).
- Treatment sessions are an opportunity to see how techniques are implemented and to practice using techniques. Behavior-change programs implemented in the home are reviewed.
- The child's functioning in school is usually incorporated into treatment.
  - Parent-managed reinforcement programs for school and school-related behavior are often part of the behavior-change program.
  - If possible, the teacher plays a role in monitoring behavior and providing consequences.

Source: Adapted from Kazdin, 1997. Copyright 1997 by John Wiley & Sons; reprinted with permission.

in their children. The pioneering work of Constance Hanf (1969) influenced many of these programs (Kaehler, Jacobs, & Jones, 2016; Reitman & McMahon, 2013). These **parent management training** programs have a number of features in common (see Table 9.3).

Some parent training programs have focused on reducing oppositional and defiant behavior. However, compliance is not always a positive behavior, and the child's ability to say "no" to certain requests may be desirable either to train or to retain (Dix et al., 2007). In this regard, it is important to assure that parents do not expect perfect compliance, which is neither the norm nor highly desirable in our society. A perfectly quiet, docile child should not be the treatment goal.

The program developed by Forehand and his colleagues illustrates successful parent training that focuses on noncompliant behavior (Forehand & McMahon, 1981; McMahon & Forehand, 2003). Parents of noncompliant children (ages 4–7 years) were taught to give direct, concise commands, allow the child sufficient time to comply, reward compliance with contingent attention, and apply negative consequences for noncompliance. Successful treatment of noncompliance also seems to reduce other problem behaviors, such as tantrums, aggression, and crying (Wells, Forehand, & Griest, 1980). Furthermore, at follow-up, treated children were not different from nonclinic community children across multiple areas such as academic performance, relationships with parents, and adjustment (Long et al., 1994). An additional benefit appeared to be that untreated siblings increased their compliance, and it seems likely that this outcome was due, at least in part, to the mother's use of her improved skills with the untreated child (Humphreys et al., 1978).

Attention to the effective use of parent commands to increase compliance and decrease inappropriate behavior is also part of the parent–child interaction therapy (PCIT) program developed by Eyberg and her colleagues (Zisser-Nathenson, Herschell, & Eyberg,

2017). This program seeks to enhance parent–child attachment and to improve the poor behavior-management skills of the parent. Here we highlight the portion of the program that teaches parents to use effective commands (Querido, Bearss, & Eyberg, 2002). The rules for effective use of commands that parents are taught (along with examples) are presented in Table 9.4.

As we have seen, Patterson's conceptualization of the development of antisocial behavior evolved in the context of treating conduct problem children and their families. The importance of parenting skills in Patterson's formulation led to the development of an evolving treatment program, currently known as Generation Parent Management Training-Oregon (Generation PMTO) that focuses on improving parenting skills (Forgatch & Gewirtz, 2017; Patterson et al., 1975, 1992; Reid et al., 2002). The program focuses on strengthening parenting practices. The core parenting practices taught are: teaching through encouragement (contingent positive reinforcement), positive involvement with children, effective family problem solving, monitoring and supervision, and effective limit setting. Each family attends clinic and home sessions and has regular phone contact with a therapist, who helps develop interventions for particular targeted behaviors and who models desired parenting skills. Problematic behaviors in the school and other community settings are also targeted, and interventions involve both the parents and relevant personnel.

Webster-Stratton and her colleagues (Webster-Stratton & Reid, 2017) have developed a multifaceted treatment program for young children (ages 2–8 years) with conduct problems, including ODD and CD, known as The Incredible Years Training Series. The initial program, designed for parents of children 2–8 years of age, now includes four separate programs: Baby (4 weeks to 9 months), Toddler (1–3 years), Preschool (2–5 years), and School-Age (6–12 years). One component of the basic program is a standard package of recorded programs of modeled parenting skills. These recordings, which contain a large number of vignettes of about

Table 9.4 Rules for Effective Commands from the PCIT Program

Rule	Example
Make commands *direct* rather than indirect.	Draw a circle. *Instead of* Will you draw a circle?
State command *positively*.	Come sit beside me. *Instead of* Stop running around!
Give commands *one at a time*.	Put your shoes in the closet. *Instead of* Clean your room.
Make commands *specific* rather than vague.	Get down off the table. *Instead of* Be careful.
Give *developmentally appropriate commands*.	Draw a square. *Instead of* Draw a cube.
Be *polite and respectful*. Give commands in a neutral tone of voice.	Please give me the block. *Instead of* Stop banging and give me the block now!
Explain commands *before* they are given or *after* they are obeyed.	Please wash your hands. *After the child obeys* Thank you. Clean hands keep germs away from your food so you won't get sick.
Use commands only when necessary or appropriate.	*(As child is running around)* Please sit in this chair. (Good time) *But not* Please give me a tissue. (Not good time and consider if command is necessary.)

Sources: Adapted from Zisser & Eyberg, 2010; Zisser-Nathenson, Herschell, & Eyberg, 2017.

two minutes each, include examples of parents interacting with their children in both appropriate and inappropriate ways. The videos are shown to groups of parents, and following each vignette, there is a therapist-led discussion of the relevant interactions. Parents are also given homework assignments that allow them to practice parenting skills at home with their children.

As with other parenting programs we have described, The Incredible Years treatment program has been evaluated in a number of studies in which it has been compared with various control conditions (Webster-Stratton & Reid, 2017). Parents completing the program have rated their children as having fewer problems than have control parents, and rated themselves as having better attitudes and more confidence regarding their parenting role. Observations in the home have also shown these parents to have better parenting skills and their children to have

greater reductions in problem behavior. These improvements were maintained at one- and three-year follow-up evaluations. Webster-Stratton (Webster-Stratton & Reid, 2017) has also expanded the program to include additional components that enhance parents' interpersonal skills and the social support that the family receives (ADVANCE), improve the child's social problem-solving skills (Dinosaur School), and train teachers in effective classroom management strategies (Teacher Classroom Management Intervention).

Cognitive Problem-Solving Skills Training

Parent training approaches focus on family aspects of conduct-disordered behavior. Other treatments focus more specifically on aspects of the youth's functioning. These interventions focus on the interpersonal and social-cognitive skill deficiencies and

Table 9.5 Anger Control Program Sessions

Session	Content/Focus
1	Introduction and group rules
2	Understanding and writing goals
3	Anger management: puppet self-control task
4	Using self-instruction
5	Perspective taking
6	Looking at anger
7	What does anger feel like?
8	Choices and consequences
9	Steps for problem solving
10	Problem solving in action
11	Student video productions – situations that illustrate lack of anger control and aggression – review situations using learned concepts and skills

Source: Adapted from Lochman et al., 2010. Copyright 2010 by Guilford Press; reprinted with permission.

dysfunctions associated with conduct-disordered behavior. The Coping Power and Anger Coping Programs of Lochman and colleagues (Lochman et al., 2010; Powell et al., 2017) are one example of skills training interventions. Table 9.5 describes the interventions that are part of the Anger Control Program.

Webster-Stratton and colleagues' cognitive-behavioral, social skills, problem solving, and anger management training program (Dinosaur School part of The Incredible Years series) is another example of interventions that address such deficits and skills (Webster-Stratton & Reid, 2017). Children ages 4–8 years with early-onset conduct problems receive the treatment in small groups. The program addresses interpersonal difficulties typically encountered by young children who have conduct problems. With therapist guidance, the children are taught to cope with such situations through a variety of techniques. Recorded vignettes of children in stressful situations are viewed and discussed, and acceptable solutions and coping skills are practiced. The intervention is made developmentally appropriate and includes the use of materials such as child-size puppets, coloring books, cartoons, stickers, and prizes to enhance learning. Strategies to ensure generalization to other settings are included in the children's sessions. Also, parents and teachers, who are involved through receiving regular letters, are asked to reinforce the targeted skills whenever they notice the child using them at home or at school and to complete weekly good-behavior charts. As compared with a waiting-list group of children, at posttreatment those in the treatment program exhibited significantly fewer aggressive, noncompliant, and other externalizing problems at home and school, more prosocial behavior with peers, and

more positive conflict-management strategies. Most of the posttreatment changes were maintained at a one-year follow-up. Combining this child-focused intervention with interventions targeting training of parents resulted in greater improvement (Webster-Stratton & Reid, 2017).

Combined Treatments

Kazdin and his colleagues (Kazdin, 2017) also have developed a successful parent management training intervention for children. However, they also have demonstrated the potential benefit of combining parent training and cognitive problem-solving skills training in treating children with conduct problems. A combination of cognitive problem-solving skills training (PSST) and parent management training (PMT) proved superior to either treatment alone for children 7–13 years of age and older (Kazdin, Siegel, & Bass, 1992). Treatment led to significant improvements in the youths' functioning at home, at school, and in the community, immediately after treatment and at a one-year follow-up, as well as to improvements in parental stress and functioning. In addition, adding a treatment component that addresses parent sources of stress improved outcomes for the child (Kazdin & Whitley, 2003). These findings, along with the multi-component programs described earlier, suggest the value of interventions that address the multiple influences operating in conduct-disordered youth and their families. Treatment components may be combined depending on the nature and pervasiveness of the youth and family's problems.

Community-Based Programs

Interventions described as successful with children, such as parent training, may be less successful under the more challenging circumstances presented by adolescents, children with more serious conduct problems, and chronic juvenile delinquents. Placing severely conduct-disordered or delinquent youth in institutions that are a part of the criminal justice system is a frequently considered alternative. Concerns exist regarding the effectiveness of such interventions and the impact of placement in institutions that expose young people to a subculture in which deviant behaviors may be learned and reinforced. These concerns and the success of some community-based programs have led to the search for less restrictive effective alternatives (McMahon & Frick, 2019). Day treatment programs and case management/ wrap around services (coordinating services necessary to meet the youth and family's needs) are two such approaches. The Teaching Family Model represents a third approach.

The Teaching Family Model (TFM), originally developed at the University of Kansas as Achievement Place, is an oft-cited example of a community-based program for delinquent youth and an example of behaviorally based interventions (Fixsen, Wolf, &

Phillips, 1973; James, 2011; Phillips, 1968). Adolescents who were declared delinquent or dependent neglect cases lived in a house with two trained teaching parents. The adolescents attended school during the day and also had regular work responsibilities. The academic problems, aggression, and other norm-violating behaviors exhibited by these adolescents were viewed as an expression of failures of past environments to teach appropriate behaviors. Accordingly, these deficits were corrected through modeling, practice, instruction, and feedback. The program centered on a **token economy** in which points and praise were gained for appropriate behaviors and were lost for inappropriate behaviors. Points could be used to purchase a variety of privileges that were otherwise unavailable. If a resident met a certain level of performance, the right to go on a merit system and thus avoid the point system could be purchased. This process was seen as providing a transition to usual sources of natural reinforcement and feedback, such as praise, status, and satisfaction. The goal was gradually to transfer a youth who was able to perform adequately on merit to his or her natural home. The teaching parents helped the natural parents or guardians to structure a program to maintain gains made at Achievement Place.

Both the program's developers and independent investigators evaluated the effectiveness of TFM (Kirigin, 1996; McMahon & Frick, 2019). These evaluations suggested that the TFM approach was more effective than comparison programs while the adolescents were involved in the group home setting. However, once they left this setting, differences disappeared.

Difficulties in transitions back to the youths' own families and failure to achieve long-term effectiveness are common in all interventions with delinquent populations. Given this consideration, the developers of TFM suggested a "long-term supportive family model" in which specially trained foster parents would provide care for a single adolescent into early adulthood (Wolf, Braukmann, & Ramp, 1987). In response, Treatment Foster Care Oregon (TFCO) (formerly Multidimensional Treatment Foster Care) was developed (Chamberlain & Smith, 2003). Like the TFM

approach, many of these programs are based on behavioral-social learning theory: the youth remains in the community, the youth is placed in family-like settings, and interventions occur in natural settings. However, one or perhaps two young people, rather than a group of youth, are placed in a specialized foster care home. This decision is consistent with literature suggesting possible negative effects of interventions that permit these youth to associate with peers with similar antisocial histories (Dishion & Dodge, 2005). Foster parents are trained in behavior-management skills and are provided with supervision and support by program staff. Explicit behavioral goals are set, and a systematic program including a point system is employed. The youth's school is also involved. Individual weekly sessions with a therapist that emphasize building skills are also provided for the youth. During the TFCO stay, staff members work with the youth's parents or other aftercare personnel to prepare them (and the young person) for reunification. Successful TFCO programs have been developed for both severely delinquent boys and girls and these programs have been found to be cost-effective. Research indicates that participants in the TFCO program were less likely to engage in delinquent activities, had fewer criminal referrals, had fewer arrests, and demonstrated decreased substance use. Girls in the TFCO program also had reduced depressive symptoms and fewer pregnancies (Buchanan, Chamberlain, & Smith, 2017; McCart & Sheidow, 2016).

Multisystemic Therapy

Interventions with antisocial youth are likely to require the cooperation of multiple human service agencies. Often it is difficult to coordinate services, and individualizing such efforts to fit the needs of youth and their families is even more challenging.

Multisystemic Therapy (MST; Henggeler & Schaeffer, 2017) is a family- and community-based approach. MST was designed to address the multiple risk factors associated with antisocial and delinquent behaviors. Bronfenbrenner's (1977) social ecological model provided a useful organizing framework. In this model the

MAGGIE The Need for Multiple Services

Maggie is a 13-year-old white seventh-grader who lives with her unemployed, crack-addicted mother, mother's live-in boyfriend, two sisters (ages 10 and 8), and a daughter of one of her mother's crack-addicted friends. Maggie was referred because she was physically violent at home (e.g., she was arrested several times for assaulting family members), at school (e.g., she beat a classmate with a stick and threatened to kill a teacher), and in the neighborhood (e.g., she was arrested twice for assaulting

residents of her housing development). Many of Maggie's aggressive actions followed all-night binges by her mother. Maggie, who primarily associates with delinquent peers, was placed in a special class, and was recommended for expulsion from school. The family resides in a high-crime neighborhood, and the only source of income is welfare benefits.

Adapted from Henggeler et al., 1998, p. 23

Table 9.6 Principles of Multisystemic Therapy

- The presenting **problem is assessed and defined from multiple perspectives** (e.g., youth, family members, teachers, juvenile justice personnel) and in multiple domains (e.g., youth, family, peers, school).
- Interventions are developed that **address problems in multiple domains** and do so in a **highly integrated manner**.
- Interventions are designed to be **intensive** (i.e., daily or weekly effort by family members).
- Interventions are **developmentally appropriate**.
- Interventions are **present-focused and action oriented**.
- Interventions are designed to **encourage responsible behavior** by all parties.
- Interventions are designed to, from the beginning, **promote generalization and maintenance** of therapeutic gains.
- Interventions make use of **strengths** in various ecological contexts as levers for change and an **optimistic perspective** is communicated.
- Intervention effectiveness is **evaluated continuously** from multiple perspectives, fed back into the system, and **needed modifications made** to the intervention.

Source: Adapted from Henggeler & Schaeffer, 2017.

young person is considered to exist within a number of systems, including family, peers, school, neighborhood, and community (see p. 51). MST focuses on enhancing the family's strengths and uses empirically supported treatments derived from cognitive-behavioral, parent training, and family-based interventions to treat adolescents and their families. Parents are viewed as the linchpin of this intervention and the approach seeks to preserve families and to maintain youth in their homes. MST addresses not only the family system but also skills of the youth and extrafamilial influences, such as peers, school, and neighborhood. Clinicians are available to the family 24/7. Family sessions are conducted in the home and community settings at times convenient for families and are flexible and individualized for each family. The basic principles of MST are summarized in Table 9.6.

The effectiveness of MST in treating serious antisocial behavior in adolescents has received considerable empirical support (Henggeler & Schaeffer, 2017; McCart & Sheidow, 2016). A report on a comparison of MST to the usual services offered to serious juvenile offenders and their families illustrates this approach (Henggeler, Melton, & Smith, 1992). These youth were at imminent risk for out-of-home placement. They averaged 3.5 previous arrests, 54% had at least one arrest for a violent crime, and 71% had been incarcerated previously for at least three weeks. The findings of this study indicate that MST was significantly more effective than the usual services. In addition, families receiving the MST intervention reported increased family cohesion, whereas reported cohesion decreased in the other families. Also, aggression with peers decreased for MST youth but remained the same for the youth receiving usual services. Multiple other reports indicate the usefulness of MST with a variety of populations, including violent and chronic juvenile offenders, adolescent sexual offenders, and substance abusing and dependent youth. These findings suggest the long-term effectiveness and the cost-effectiveness of this approach (Aos et al., 2006; Curtis, Ronan, & Borduin, 2004; Henggeler & Schaeffer, 2017; Johnides et al., 2017).

Pharmacological Intervention

Various types of psychoactive medications have been employed in the treatment of aggression and ODD and CD. These include mood stabilizers such as lithium and atypical antipsychotics such as risperidone. However, there is little research support for the effectiveness of such medications in treating disruptive behavior disorders (Gorman et al., 2015; McKinney & Renk, 2011; McMahon & Frick, 2019). Thus, psychosocial interventions, such as those described earlier, are considered the first line of treatment for conduct problems. Medications might be considered when other treatments have not been successful, or the presenting problems are extremely serious. Given lack of approval of medications for treating CD or ODD, issues regarding potential serious side effects, and a broad uneasiness regarding increased use of psychoactive medications with children, there is concern regarding the use of such medications to treat conduct-disordered behavior (Gorman et al., 2015; McKinney & Renk, 2011; McMahon & Frick, 2019; Scahill & Rojas, 2019).

It should be noted that some youth with conduct disorders also show symptoms of, or meet the diagnostic criteria for, ADHD. There is considerable support for pharmacological interventions for ADHD (American Academy of Child and Adolescent Psychiatry (AACAP), 2007a). Thus, children and adolescents who also present with this co-occurrence may benefit from the use of medications such as stimulants.

Prevention

The difficulties in treating adolescents with serious and persistent conduct disorders, the multidetermined nature of antisocial behavior, and the potential stability of conduct-disordered behavior certainly suggest that efforts should be directed at early, multifaceted, flexible, and ongoing interventions for some youth. Here we offer some examples of efforts at early intervention.

Interventions that provide treatment to families of young children with oppositional defiant behavior or early signs of aggression might be considered as prevention strategies. Successful treatment can reduce early aspects of the development of conduct-disordered behavior. Also, improvement of parenting skills and family interactions, for example, can reduce risk factors and provide protective influences associated with the developmental progression of conduct problems. Thus, interventions that target preschool and early elementary-age children and their families can be considered treatment for existing conduct problems and prevention of later conduct disorders.

Beyond this conceptual overlap, some of the treatment programs described earlier have been employed as prevention programs. For example, Webster-Stratton and her colleagues (Webster-Stratton, 1998; Reid, Webster-Stratton, & Beauchaine, 2001; Webster-Stratton, Reid, & Hammond, 2001) evaluated The Incredible Years program as a prevention program. The BASIC parent program was provided to Head Start families in some randomly selected centers as an addition to the regular Head Start program. Compared with control families at centers that received regular Head Start offerings, participating mothers improved their parenting skills. Their children exhibited significantly less misbehavior and more positive affect compared to control children, whose behavior remained unchanged. In addition, teachers reported increased involvement by program parents, whereas reports indicated that control parents' involvement remained the same. One year later, in kindergarten, improvements in parenting behavior and in child behavior and affect were maintained. Webster-Stratton has reported that the program is effective with socioeconomically disadvantaged families of multiple ethnicities (Webster-Stratton & Reid, 2017). Other independent investigators also have successfully employed the program as a preventive intervention (Hutchings et al., 2007; Perrin et al., 2014; Pidano & Allen, 2015; Posthumus et al., 2012).

There are also selective prevention trials focused on conduct problems that provide comprehensive intervention over a long period of time. For example, the Fast Track project (Conduct Problems Prevention Research Group, 1992, 2002b; McMahon & Frick, 2019) is a multisite collaborative project that is following a large high-risk sample of children identified as displaying high rates of conduct problems during kindergarten as well as a representative sample of children from the same schools. Half of the children in the high-risk sample participated in an intensive and long-term intervention that began in first grade and continued through tenth grade. This is consistent with the need to provide multiple interventions over an extended period of development for some early-onset conduct problem youth. The program targets the behaviors, skills, and other risk factors involved in the development of the early-onset pathway of conduct problems. Intervention components include parent training, social-cognitive skills training,

attention to peer affiliation, academic tutoring, home visits, and teacher-based classroom intervention. The adolescent portion of the intervention, starting in middle school, included increased emphasis on parent monitoring and positive involvement, peer affiliation and influence, academic achievement, and aspects of adolescent adjustment. Evaluations of the effects of the intervention have been encouraging throughout the intervention and beyond. By age 25, participants in the Fast Track intervention, as compared to controls, displayed fewer externalizing, internalizing, and substance use problems, fewer risky sexual behaviors, and fewer criminal convictions (Dodge et al., 2015a). In addition, the research has provided information regarding the variables that mediate change in conduct problems (Albert et al., 2015; Conduct Problems Prevention Research Group, 2002a; Erath et al., 2006; Milan et al., 2006; Pasalich et al., 2016; Sorenson, Dodge, & the Conduct Problems Prevention Research Group, 2016).

The Oregon group has adapted their clinical model to several prevention efforts. These interventions recognize that there is a need for programs that offer differing "levels" of intervention based upon the needs of the youth and family and that appreciate that youths' problems are embedded in multiple environments (Dishion & Stormshak, 2007). For example, the Adolescents Transition Program (Dishion & Kavanagh, 2002) is a family-based intervention that is embedded in the school setting and that has the goal of reducing adolescent problem behavior. It offers three levels of service to families. A Family Resource Center in the school facilitates parent–school collaboration and provides information and education to parents. This is a universal intervention. The Family Check-Up (FCU) was designed to support parents during developmental transitions. The transitions are periods of potential vulnerability for disruptions in parental management, child problem behavior, and emotional distress (Dishion et al., 2016). The FCU can, thus, be viewed as a selected intervention offered to families identified as having an at-risk youth (Dishion et al., 2008). This brief intervention provides an assessment, attempts to maintain current positive parenting, and seeks to enhance motivation to change problematic parenting practices. An indicated level of intervention is available to families of youth with ongoing conduct problems. A number of professional interventions, similar to those described in the discussion of treatment programs, are offered to these families. This intervention has been shown to be helpful in addressing conduct behaviors and other problems (Dishion & Stormshak, 2007; Dishion et al., 2016). For example, adolescents whose families engaged in the Family Check-Up during Grade 6 exhibited less substance use and other problem behavior between the ages of 11 and 17 and also had lower arrest records by age 18 relative to matched controls (Connell et al., 2007). The Family Check-Up was initially developed, and shown to be efficacious, for adolescents. It also has been successfully adapted for use with toddlers (Dishion et al., 2014; Gill et al., 2008; Shaw et al., 2006).

Looking Back

Classification and Description

- Aggression, oppositional behavior, and other antisocial behaviors are among the most common problems of referred youth, as well as in the general population.
- The DSM contains a group of disorders that includes Oppositional Defiant Disorder (ODD) and Conduct Disorder (CD), along with Intermittent Explosive Disorder, Antisocial Personality Disorder, and other disruptive, impulse-control, and conduct disorders.
- ODD is described as a pattern of anger/irritable mood, argumentative/defiant behavior and vindictiveness. CD is described as a repetitive and persistent pattern of behavior that violates both the basic rights of others and societal norms. Two subtypes, childhood-onset and adolescent-onset, are indicated.
- Empirical approaches have consistently identified a syndrome of aggressive, oppositional, antisocial behaviors. Two narrow syndromes within this broad externalizing syndrome have been designated as aggressive behavior and rule-breaking behavior.
- Other ways of distinguishing among groupings of conduct problems, such as age of onset, distinguishing aggression from other conduct-disordered behavior, an overt versus covert distinction, and a further destructive–nondestructive distinction, have also been suggested.
- There are gender differences in prevalence, developmental course, and etiological influences of conduct problems. In part, such differences may be related to how aggression is expressed. The concept of relational aggression has contributed to understanding gender differences.
- Fire setting is a covert behavior that may occur among youth with severe conduct problems.
- It is important to address bullying since bullying may be part of a more general antisocial developmental pattern. The victims of bullying also are at considerable risk.

Epidemiology

- Conduct problems are one of the most frequently occurring child and adolescent difficulties.
- CD and ODD are more commonly diagnosed in boys.
- An increasing prevalence of CD with age is often reported. The pattern for ODD is less clear.
- Contextual factors such as poverty and the stress of high-crime neighborhoods are thought to increase the risk for conduct problems.

- An important question is whether ODD is a precursor of CD.
- Youth who receive the diagnoses ODD or CD are likely to experience other difficulties. In particular, there is a high rate of co-occurrence of ODD and CD with ADHD. ADHD appears to be a risk factor for the other two disorders.

Developmental Course

- An important aspect of conduct problems is their reported stability over time for at least some individuals. The issue of stability is, however, a complex one.
- Age of onset is an important aspect of the development of conduct problems. A childhood-onset or life-course-persistent pathway is of great concern.
- Callous-unemotional traits have been suggested as an attribute that may be characteristic of a subgroup of youth who display early and stable aggressive and antisocial behavior.
- An adolescent-onset path is more common, and antisocial behavior among such youth may be less likely to persist beyond adolescence.
- Conduct-disordered behavior has been conceptualized in terms of developmental progressions or paths. Pathways characterized by overt, covert, and authority conflict behaviors have been described.

Etiology

- Conduct problems likely develop through a complex interaction of a variety of influences.
- Influences from the socioeconomic context, such as poverty, neighborhood disadvantage, and related stress, affect the development of conduct-disordered behavior.
- Parents, other family members, and media portrayals may serve as models for aggression and other conduct-disordered behavior.
- Family variables also are an important influence on the development of conduct-disordered behavior. Important mechanisms through which family influence occurs are parental involvement and parenting practices. The work of Patterson and his colleagues has contributed to our knowledge in this area.
- Stresses on the family, the parents' own psychological difficulties, and marital discord affect both the likelihood of a child developing conduct problems and the course of the behavior.

- Peer relations are part of the complex interplay of influences that contribute to the development of conduct problems. Affiliation with peers who engage in conduct-disordered behavior may be one factor in the initiation, escalation, and maintenance of aggressive and antisocial behavior.
- Cognitive-emotional characteristics of the youth, such as social information-processing skills and interpersonal problem-solving skills, also contribute to the development and persistence of conduct-disordered behavior.
- Biological influences, such as genetic and neurobiological influences, likely also play a role.

Substance Use

- The use of alcohol and other drugs may be a part of a pattern of antisocial and rule-breaking behavior. Substance use and substance-induced disorders are described in a group of DSM substance-related and addictive diagnoses. The high rate of substance use by young people is a widespread concern.
- Multiple risk factors including individual differences, and family, peer, and larger community and societal influences likely contribute to the development of substance use. A variety of theories and models have been suggested to help understand the development of substance use.

Assessment

- Assessment of conduct problems is likely to be complex and multifaceted. Interviews, behavior rating scales, and behavioral observations are employed.

Intervention

- Family-based interventions have the best support as treatments for children and adolescents with conduct problems. Parent training is central to efforts to improve parent management skills and, thereby, reduce noncompliant and other conduct problem behavior and increase appropriate and prosocial behaviors.
- Interventions employing cognitive problem-solving skills training focus on aspects of the youth's functioning. Research findings suggest the value of treatment programs that combine parent training and cognitive problem-solving approaches and address multiple influences.
- Community-based programs include the Teaching Family Model and Treatment Foster Care Oregon. Multisystemic Therapy is a systems-based intervention that attempts to keep the youth in their homes. It addresses the youths' functioning within various systems such as family, peers, school, neighborhood, and community.
- Various types of psychoactive medications have been employed in the treatment of conduct-disordered and antisocial behavior. Research support for the use of such medications is, however, limited.
- Interventions that provide treatment to families of young children with oppositional defiant behavior or early signs of aggression might be considered prevention strategies. Indeed, some treatment programs for young children have been adapted as prevention programs.
- Other selected prevention programs provide comprehensive interventions over long periods of time for at-risk youth. There are also programs that offer different "levels" of intervention based on the needs of the youth and family.

Key Terms

CHAPTER 10
Attention-Deficit/Hyperactivity Disorder

Looking Forward

After reading this chapter, you should be able to discuss:

- Evolving ideas about ADHD
- Classification and diagnosis of ADHD
- Features of ADHD and co-occurring disorders

- The epidemiology and developmental course of ADHD
- Neuropsychological theories of ADHD
- Neurobiological abnormalities of ADHD
- Etiology and a developmental schema of ADHD
- Assessment and intervention for ADHD

Elliot was extremely active as an infant and toddler. His mother discovered him at 12 months repeatedly climbing out of his crib onto a nearby dresser and jumping from the dresser to the crib. He was enrolled in preschool at age three because his mother was exhausted keeping up with him. Subsequently his teachers noted an inability to sit still and listen respectfully; "disruptive," "silly," and "loud and fast-moving" behavior; and eventually problems with social interactions.
Pennington, McGrath, & Peterson, 2019, pp. 243–247

Joan was referred for an evaluation in the eighth grade due to poor school performance. Concerns about academic progress started in early elementary school. By third grade she needed help in reading, and academic problems increased by fifth grade. Now an eighth-grader, Joan has difficulties in focusing and attending, organizing, keeping track of assignments, completing work on time, and reading and writing.
Pennington, McGrath, & Peterson, 2019, pp. 247–249

The heterogeneous manifestations of attention-deficit/hyperactivity disorder (ADHD), some of which are noted in the above case descriptions, are recognized in both dimensional and categorical classifications. Only a few disturbances of youth have garnered as much public interest and have been so surrounded by debate as ADHD. Controversy has focused on both the nature of ADHD and the pharmacological treatment that was widely introduced in the late 1960s.

Evolving Ideas about ADHD

ADHD is a neurodevelopmental disturbance that has lifelong implications. The disorder has traveled a winding path of descriptions and definitions (Barkley, 2015f). The history of ADHD in medical and scientific literature dates back more than two centuries (Barkley & Peters, 2012). One early account of the disorder was given by the English physician George Still, who described a group of boys with a "defect in moral control" as inattentive, impulsive, overactive, lawless, and aggressive, among other things. In the United States, epidemics of encephalitis in 1917–1918 aroused interest in patients who suffered this brain infection and who were left with some of these attributes. A comparable clinical picture also was noted in children who had suffered head injury, birth trauma, and exposure to infections and toxins.

By the late 1950s, emphasis was given to overactivity or motor restlessness in these children, and the terms *hyperkinesis*, *hyperkinetic syndrome*, and *hyperactive child syndrome* were variously applied. In time, hyperactivity was downgraded in importance, and attention deficits took center stage. The shift was reflected in the DSM-III (1980), which recognized attention deficit disorder (ADD) either *with* hyperactivity or *without* hyperactivity.

More change was yet to come. In the DSM-III-R (1987), the disorder was relabeled "Attention Deficit Hyperactivity Disorder." Children received the diagnosis if they showed eight or more of 14 items, which could be different mixes of inattention, hyperactivity, and impulsivity. That is, the disorder was viewed as unidimensional, so that any mix of symptoms met the criteria. Nevertheless, the relationship of these three primary features of ADHD was unsettled. Were they part of a single dimension? Or co-occurring but independent of each other? Were two of them alike but different from the third? In time, the unidimensional view fell by the wayside when factor analytic research designed to better understand the nature of ADHD suggested that the disorder consisted of two dimensions or factors: (1) inattention and (2) hyperactivity-impulsivity. Their association appears to be attributable to shared genetic influence, although each factor also has unique genetic influences (Barkley, 2015c). While there is now substantial cross-cultural agreement on the validity of these two factors (Barkley, 2015f), research continues to explore the possibility for other overlapping yet distinct forms of attention problems (Barkley, 2015a; Nichols et al., 2017).

Critical issues remain concerning the nature and treatment of ADHD, and the last decade or so has brought considerable change to the field. More recently, for example, increased emphasis has been given to understanding the roles poor self-regulation and sluggish cognitive tempo, a set of behaviors similar to inattention and discussed later in this chapter, may play in the disorder (Evans et al., 2018a; Musser & Nigg, 2019). Additionally, with increased recognition that ADHD is a chronic condition and does not disappear after childhood, adolescents and adults have been given more consideration. In addition, emerging research on the genetics of ADHD suggest overlap of the disorder with other psychiatric symptoms, including externalizing, internalizing, and neurodevelopmental disorders (Andersson et al., 2020; Thapar, 2018). Advances in genetics and brain science have created new challenges and understandings, and views regarding the nature of ADHD continue to evolve.

DSM Classification and Diagnosis

The current DSM-5 (American Psychiatric Association, 2013) classifies ADHD as a neurodevelopmental disorder characterized by an early onset in childhood and a persistent course. Because it is often accompanied by other subtle delays in language, motor, and social development and has been associated with enduring alterations in neural development, it is grouped with other disorders, such as autism spectrum disorder and specific learning disorder, that share these characteristics. The DSM-5 recognizes the two factors of inattention and hyperactivity-impulsivity, and uses the label "Attention-Deficit/Hyperactivity." Examples of symptoms of inattention are:

- makes careless mistakes in school or at work;
- seems to not listen when spoken to;

- fails to follow through on instructions, chores, etc.;
- has difficulty in organizing activities;
- is distracted by extraneous stimuli.

Hyperactivity and impulsivity are exemplified by:

- fidgets with hands or feet or squirms in seat;
- runs about inappropriately;
- talks excessively;
- has difficulty waiting one's turn;
- interrupts or intrudes on others.

Depending on the symptom presentation, a child is diagnosed with one of three presentations: **predominantly inattentive presentation** (ADHD-PI), **predominantly hyperactive/impulsive presentation** (ADHD-PHI), and **combined presentation** (ADHD-C) which shows both factors.

Diagnosis of ADHD demands the presence of several symptoms before age 12, and display of symptoms for at least six months. Because all the criterion behaviors are observed to some degree in normal children and may vary with developmental level, diagnosis is given only when symptoms are at odds with developmental expectations. The symptoms must be pervasive; that is, they must occur in at least two settings (e.g., home and school). There also must be evidence that the symptoms interfere with, or reduce the quality of, social, academic, or occupational functioning. In addition, the symptoms cannot be explained by another mental disorder.

Our discussion now turns to further description of the primary, or core, features of ADHD and to difficulties that are secondarily associated with the disorder. The general label "attention-deficit/hyperactivity disorder" (ADHD) is used to refer to youth diagnosed with the disorder.

Description: Primary Features

Inattention

Adults who come into contact with children with ADHD report various signs of inattention. These children do not listen to what is said to them, are easily distracted, jump rapidly from one activity to another rather than sticking to a task, lose things, and daydream. They may also have difficulties in planning, may seem disorganized, or have problems with time management and staying alert (Nigg & Barkley, 2014). One seemingly baffling aspect of the disorder is that the children appear unable to focus and concentrate at some times, while at other times they are able to sit for hours drawing or building with blocks. In fact, attention is situational; it can appear normal when the child is interested or otherwise motivated but problematic when the task is boring, repetitive, or effortful or when an adult is not present to supervise task performance (Nigg & Barkley, 2014).

Although the reports of adults provide good global descriptions of ADHD, formal observation and controlled research have been conducted to validate and elucidate attention deficits. Children and adolescents with ADHD do pay less attention to their work than children with learning disabilities or normal controls (Roberts, Milich, & Barkley, 2015). In the laboratory, children with ADHD do less well than control children on many tasks that demand attention, and specific deficits have been identified.

Among these is a deficit in *selective attention* (Brodeur & Pond, 2001; Huang-Pollock, Nigg, & Carr, 2005). Selective attention is the ability to focus on relevant stimuli and not be distracted by irrelevant stimuli. For children with ADHD, distraction appears more likely when tasks are boring or difficult or when irrelevant stimuli are novel or salient. Impairment also has been found in *attentional alerting*, that is, the ability to immediately focus on something of importance (Nigg & Nikolas, 2008). In addition, children with ADHD have difficulty in *sustained attention*—in continuing to focus on a task or stimulus over a period of time (Martel et al., 2016).

It is noteworthy that attention has many components and is conceptualized in different ways (Hinshaw, 2018). Different components, or abilities, develop over different periods and are linked to different brain structures or systems. There is much interest in the role that attention might play in the higher-order regulation of behavior and emotion. It is hypothesized that an executive attention network, involving the prefrontal cortex and anterior structures of the brain, modulates the activation of other brain networks (Nigg, 2016). Executive attention is thought to be important in tasks requiring the individual, for example, to monitor conflicting stimuli or to suppress a response. As such, executive attention is critical in ADHD because the regulation of behavior is considered central in the disorder.

Hyperactivity and Impulsivity

Hyperactivity

Children with ADHD are described as always on the run, driven by a motor, restless, fidgety, and unable to sit still (Nigg & Barkley, 2014). They may display gross bodily movements and talk excessively to themselves or others. In the classroom, they are out of their seats, moving their arms and legs, and engaging in things irrelevant to the task at hand.

Although much of the information about activity problems comes from parent and teacher reports, objective assessment can

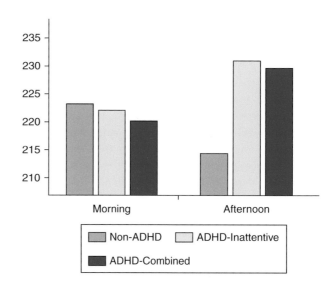

Figure 10.1 Mean activity level for morning and afternoon sessions. (Adapted from Dane, Schachar, & Tannock, 2000. Copyright 2000 by Elsevier; reprinted with permission)

be made with direct observations and with actigraphs (Wainer & Meltzer, 2018). The latter are small devices worn by the child to measure movement. Objective measures indicate the excessive movement of children with ADHD, as well as variation across young people and situations. In one study, actigraph recording showed no differences in the morning between children with or without ADHD, but in the afternoon non-ADHD youth became less active and ADHD youth became more active (Dane, Schachar, & Tannock, 2000) (see Figure 10.1). Another study that recorded movement continuously for one week showed that boys with hyperactivity were more active than controls during school reading and mathematics but not physical education and lunch/recess (Porrino et al., 1983). This heightened activity level seems to hold true even in sleep for some children. A recent study employing actigraphy methods demonstrated poorer sleep for adolescents with ADHD as compared to adolescents without the disorder (Becker et al., 2019a). In general, however, motor excess and restlessness are more likely to occur in highly structured situations that demand children to sit still and regulate their behavior in the face of little reinforcement.

Impulsivity

The essence of impulsivity is a deficiency in inhibiting behavior, holding back, or in controlling behavior, which appears as "acting without thinking." The child may interrupt others, cut in line in front of others, or heedlessly engage in dangerous behaviors (Nigg & Barkley, 2014). Activities that require patience or restraint are not well accomplished. Impulsivity often leads others to judge the youth as careless, irresponsible, immature, lazy, or rude.

In the laboratory, impulsivity has been assessed in different ways. Variations of the stop-signal task are widely used (Coghill et al., 2018). For example, stimuli—such as the letter X and the letter O—are presented on a screen, and the child is told to press one of two keys depending on which stimulus is presented. Key presses are to be withheld on a minority of trials when a special signal (a tone) comes on, so that the child must sometimes rapidly inhibit (stop) the response. Although there may be limits to how these types of tools are used, deficits on the stop-signal task have been shown in several studies with ADHD children (Molitor & Langberg, 2017). In conjunction with other research, these findings suggest problems with inhibition of motor responses are an important aspect of ADHD.

Description: Associated Features

In addition to the core problems of ADHD, youth with the disorder experience more than their share of difficulties in diverse areas of functioning. We note, however, that the findings are disproportionately based on school-age children displaying the combined presentation of ADHD, so caution must be taken in applying them to other youth with ADHD.

Motor Skills

Motor incoordination may affect about half of children with ADHD, a figure that exceeds that for typically developing children (Kaiser et al., 2015; Weyandt & Gudmundsdottir, 2015). The difficulties are shown in clumsiness, delay in motor milestones, poor performance in sports, and the like. The child may show neurological soft signs, and various tests indicate deficits in fine motor coordination and timing. In particular, tasks such as writing, drawing, and playing a musical instrument may be impaired. Children with ADHD appear especially affected when the task involves complex movement and sequencing, which suggests that higher-order control processes such as planning and regulation of behavior are affected (Kaiser et al., 2015).

Intelligence, Academic Achievement

As a group, children with ADHD perform lower on intelligence tests than normal control groups (Weyandt & Gudmundsdottir, 2015). However, just as is the case with the general population, intelligence levels vary individually, with a range of general intelligence reported for individuals with ADHD, including scores into the gifted range (Rommelse et al., 2017). Additionally, many children have specific learning disabilities in reading, mathematics, and other academic areas, which are not due to lowered intelligence (a topic discussed later in the chapter).

"My teacher said I don't pay enough attention in class. At least, that's what I think she said."

Dave Carpenter/Cartoon Collections

Reduced academic achievement is prominent among youth with ADHD (DuPaul & Langberg, 2015). In fact, between 50% and 80% of youth with ADHD are reported to have problems with learning and/or academic achievement (DuPaul & Stoner, 2014). Children and adolescents with ADHD may have lower school grades and achievement test scores, be held back in a grade, be placed in special education classes, or fail to graduate from secondary school (Fried et al., 2016). Notably, a study by Kent and colleagues (2011) found that adolescents with ADHD dropped out of school about eight times as often as those without ADHD. Teachers noted incomplete homework assignments, excessive absences from school, and failure to work up to potential. There is significant variability, however, in the factors that influence educational impairment. For example, for some youth, the core behavioral features associated with ADHD, including distractibility and disruptive behaviors, interfere with ability to complete academic tasks (DuPaul & Langberg, 2015). These behaviors may also impact the child–teacher relationship. In fact, distractible, disruptive school behaviors can be exhibited very early (Nigg & Barkley, 2014). Preschool teachers and parents rate young children with ADHD as having more problem behavior and executive function difficulties than typical children, although differences in ratings between parents and teachers have been noted in some domains (Schneider, Ryan, & Mahone, 2020). Deficits in aspects of executive function, discussed further below, may be particularly salient as children advance in school, as such deficits may impact their ability to plan and organize school materials or manage their time. As a result of these difficulties, many children and adolescents with ADHD need ongoing academic support and intervention.

Executive Functions

Most but not all children with ADHD exhibit deficits on numerous experimental and neuropsychological tasks that are interpreted as difficulties in **executive functions** (Krieger & Amador-Campos, 2018; Weyandt & Gudmundsdottir, 2015). Executive functions refer to several complex cognitive processes that are central in the regulation of goal-directed behavior. Executive functions are involved in planning and organizing actions; they include components such as working memory, verbal self-regulation, inhibition of behavior, and motor control. Central in these abilities is the brain's prefrontal cortex and its connections to other brain areas (Barkley, 2015d).

A recent study suggests nearly 90% of children with ADHD demonstrate executive functioning deficits, with variability in types of processes affected (Kofler et al., 2019). For children with ADHD, as well as typically developing youth, childhood executive functions have implications for concurrent functioning and they predict academic and social functioning in adolescence. Differences in executive function may help differentiate children with ADHD from those without as well as help explain the substantial heterogeneity within the disorder (Kofler et al., 2017).

Emotion Regulation

Children and adolescents with ADHD are also likely to display difficulties in emotion reactivity and regulation. For example, they may show low frustration tolerance, be impatient or quick to anger, or be easily excited to emotional reaction more generally (Barkley, 2015b). These difficulties in emotion regulation are thought to contribute to the social interaction problems (discussed further below) and impairments in other areas of functioning, such as academic difficulties, seen in ADHD (Ryckaert, Kuntsi, & Asherson, 2018). In general, more extreme levels of emotion-regulation problems have been associated with greater functional impairment in youth with ADHD (Biederman et al., 2012). Although difficulties in emotion regulation may be less observable than some of the essential features of ADHD, such as hyperactivity-impulsivity, there is increased recognition that emotion dysregulation may be a core component underlying ADHD (Barkley, 2015b; Musser & Nigg, 2019).

Adaptive Behavior

As children develop into adolescence and adulthood, they typically progress in their independence in everyday behaviors, such as self-care and communication skills. However, relative to their level of general intelligence, children with ADHD have been shown to have deficiencies in many domains of everyday adaptive behavior. The discrepancy appears larger than for typically developing children and for select other disorders (Weyandt & Gudmundsdottir, 2015). Deficits in self-care and independence are sometimes at the level that would be expected with much greater intellectual impairment (Hinshaw, 1998). Many of the children engage in behavior more immature than their abilities seem to warrant, and require greater monitoring by adults than might be anticipated. Although failure to learn everyday skills may occur, failure to *perform* known skills might well be more crucial (Barkley et al., 2002). Indeed, because ADHD involves deficits in sustained attention and in executive functions, which aid in implementing goal-directed behavior, ADHD is frequently viewed as a disorder of performance rather than a deficit in knowing what to do (Knouse, 2015).

Social Behavior and Relationships

Social difficulties are reported in a high proportion of cases of ADHD, and are an important reason for adults to seek professional help for youth with ADHD. Many children with ADHD demonstrate significant difficulties in social behavior, social information processing, and peer relationships (Ros & Graziano, 2018). In fact, it is estimated that between 50% and 70% of children with ADHD experience peer difficulties, and these difficulties often continue into adolescence (Gardner & Gerdes, 2015).

It is not difficult to see how the core features of ADHD (e.g., inattention, hyperactivity, impulsivity) may present challenges in social functioning. Restless and intrusive behaviors shown by excessive activity, inappropriate talkativeness, and interrupting others may be undesirable to peers (Willis et al., 2019). Similarly, the inattention shown in ADHD also may be linked to social difficulties. Not listening, being distracted, and having a slow behavioral style may get in the way of a child's ability to attend to peers effectively or to notice or respond to social cues appropriately (Nijmeijer et al., 2008). Children with ADHD may also demonstrate deficits in social problem-solving and perspective-taking skills, which may undermine their ability to understand and solve everyday social dilemmas (Gardner & Gerdes, 2015). Additionally, some children with ADHD may display an aggressive, negative style of social interaction, exemplified by physical and verbal aggression toward others, rule breaking, and hostile controlling behavior, which may contribute to heightened peer difficulties (McQuade & Hoza, 2015). This negative style likely reflects oppositional defiant disorder (ODD) or conduct disorder (CD) which frequently co-occur with ADHD.

Although roughhouse play is part of typical childhood activities, the child with ADHD often displays excessively energetic and undercontrolled behavior. (Celia Mannings/Alamy Stock Photo)

Not all children with ADHD have social problems, however, which raises the question: What underlies social difficulties? Various explanations have been offered. Children with ADHD may inadequately process social-emotional cues (Ferretti et al., 2019). Or they may know what is appropriate but be unable to enact the proper behavior, especially when excited or irritated (Aduen et al., 2018; McQuade & Hoza, 2015). Deficits in regulating emotions, planning and organizing, and working memory, all observed in ADHD, may mediate the relationship between the disorder and poor peer functioning (Kofler et al., 2018; Ryckaert et al., 2018). An interesting study, for example, brought together 233 elementary-aged children who were unfamiliar with one another and observed their interactions in small groups to help determine how ADHD symptoms and emotion regulation may affect first impressions among peers (Lee et al., 2018). During small playgroups, four to 11 unfamiliar, same-gender children participated in five tasks including structured (e.g., solving a puzzle) and unstructured play (e.g., free play) over the course of three hours. Approximately half the children in each group were diagnosed with ADHD. Overall, the study found that children with more severe ADHD experienced higher levels of emotion dysregulation, which was in turn associated with greater peer rejection. These findings aid in our understanding of the early precursors to the subsequent and often stable social problems seen in children with ADHD.

Additionally, some children with ADHD-C have a relatively stable **positive self-bias** or self-perception regarding their social competence, behavioral conduct, and academic competence (Hoza

et al., 2010; Owens et al., 2007). They may be unaware of their negative impact on others, rate their relationships as excessively positive, and overestimate the degree to which they are liked and accepted. Yet, not all children with ADHD display this bias. Recent research, for example, suggests gender differences in how young people with ADHD view their own impairments, with girls less likely to experience positive self-bias (Tu, Owens, & Hinshaw, 2019). Additionally, it would be mistaken not to recognize that some children with the disorder are aware of, and feel bad about, their social difficulties. In fact, some youth with ADHD may show a tendency toward anxiety, shyness, and withdrawal, and these factors may also impact social functioning.

Given all this, it is not surprising that children with ADHD are frequently disliked and rejected by peers (Gardner & Gerdes, 2015). As described earlier, after only a few social exchanges, peers may view the child with ADHD as disruptive and unpredictable and react with rejection and withdrawal (de Boo & Prins, 2007). An estimated 50% or more of school-age children with ADHD are peer rejected, compared to 10 to 15% of comparison youth (Mikami, 2010). Whereas negative reactions apply more strongly to children who are impulsive and hyperactive, young people with only attention problems tend to be neglected or ignored (McQuade & Hoza, 2015).

In addition to being rejected or neglected, children with ADHD have trouble making and keeping friends, since friendships require specific skills such as the ability to emotionally connect and express caring (Mikami, 2010). Children with ADHD report having no mutual friendships at much higher rates (56% to

76%) than typically developing peers (10% to 30%) (Gardner & Gerdes, 2015). Among other things, the lack of friends means less opportunity to acquire social competence and empathy, and to be protected from bullying. And as we have seen (p. 58), peer problems predict psychological and academic difficulties.

Family Relations

ADHD clearly takes a toll on family interaction. Negative exchanges may occur as early as the child's preschool years. In general, parents are less warm and rewarding and more negative and directive (Johnston & Chronis-Tuscano, 2015). Mother–child relations appear more difficult than father–child interactions, although the latter are affected. Evidence exists that mothers give more commands and rewards to sons than daughters, and that interactions are more emotional and rancorous. Parents and young people with ADHD seem to have more than the usual number of arguments, and conflict and negative interactions seem particularly high for families of adolescents with ADHD who have co-occurring symptoms of depression and aggressive behavior (Garcia, Medina, & Sibley, 2019). A negative family profile is especially associated with the child's oppositional behavior or display of conduct problems.

Broader family characteristics associated with ADHD (e.g., interparental conflict, parental depression, stress) play a role in child–parent relationships (Johnston & Chronis-Tuscano, 2015). Parents of youth with ADHD are themselves at genetic risk for a variety of problems, including the symptoms of ADHD. Additionally, parents of young people with ADHD report high levels of parenting stress (Biondic, Wiener, & Martinussen, 2019; Brown,

2005; Wiener et al., 2016). Importantly, research suggests the relationship between family and parent functioning and ADHD is likely bidirectional. A recent longitudinal study, for example, found maternal stress and overreactive parenting were predictive of child ADHD symptoms, and greater child ADHD symptoms predicted greater maternal stress and depressive symptoms as well as lower parental warmth (Breaux & Harvey, 2019). Although the extent and nature of influences varies with development, an awareness of the interrelated nature of family functioning and child adjustment informs our understanding of ADHD. The case example of Joey illustrates this point.

Health, Sleep, Accidents

There are many reports of general or specific health problems associated with ADHD, including allergies and asthma, but the data are inconsistent and do not allow clear conclusions (Barkley, 2015e).

It is not unusual for parents to report sleep difficulties in children with ADHD. The problems involve inability to fall asleep, night awakening, fewer hours of sleep, and involuntary movements during sleep (e.g., teeth grinding, leg restlessness). However, objective laboratory studies of overnight sleep are inconsistent regarding physiological differences in sleep (Barkley, 2015e; Wiggs, 2019). Nevertheless, compared to children with ADHD who do not have sleep difficulties, children with sleep problems tend to have poorer academic functioning and other impairments (Mulraney, Sciberras, & Lecendreaux, 2018). The relationship may be complex, and it is suggested that sleep difficulties may be

JOEY A Parent's Perspective

My eight-year-old, Joey, is not a bad kid; often he is charming and funny. But he really is a handful for everyday stuff! Every night, bedtime is a nightmare for at least an hour or two. Joey never feels tired and is always arguing to stay up. Even when he is really tired, it's tough to get him to quit whatever he is doing, to get him in pj's and into bed. He gets loud and stirs up the little ones. In the morning he gets up okay, but he is incredibly slow about getting himself dressed while I'm dressing myself and my two younger kids, so we can get out too. But if I don't stay on Joey constantly, talking him through every step of the morning routine, he'll never make his bus. His five-year-old brother is more independent!

Joey always gets involved in playing with his transformer toys and forgets what he is supposed to be doing. He'll still be sitting on the floor in just his underpants with one sock on when he needs to be walking out the door to catch his bus. Then when he finally hears me telling him it's too late, he gets upset, crying and blaming everyone else because he's going to miss his bus. It's the same routine every day! We've tried star charts and all kinds of rewards and punishments. He just hasn't learned how to be careful about time and getting things done so he won't make all of us late.

Doing this every morning and every night with him is exhausting, especially for a single parent like me. I never get any rest. And more than that, he's made me late to work so many times that I've gotten two warnings. I'm worried that I might get fired because of this. I can't afford to have that happen.

Adapted from Brown, 2005, pp. 94–95

ACCENT Autos, Adolescence, and ADHD

Most adolescents in the United States look forward to the time they can drive an automobile, whereas parents greet the advent with mixed emotions and worry. Parents appear to have good reason for concern (Barkley, 2015e; Centers for Disease Control and Prevention, 2018c). Several studies give evidence, through self-report and official records, that young people with ADHD are at heightened risk for:

- repeated traffic citations, especially for speeding;
- repeated and more severe vehicular crashes;
- suspension of driving licenses; and
- illegal driving prior to obtaining a license.

In young drivers with ADHD, there is some evidence of inattention, distractibility, impulsivity, and increased risk-taking (Barkley, 2015e). In a study of young adults who had scored high on ADHD symptoms during adolescence,

inattention was linked to serious motor accidents after other influential factors, such as conduct problems and relatively little driving experience, were accounted for (Woodward, Fergusson, & Horwood, 2000). A limited number of investigations have found differences in ratings of actual driving habits, that is, in safely maneuvering and otherwise managing the vehicle. However, individuals with ADHD may not view their driving performance as different from other, typical drivers and may therefore overestimate their abilities (Knouse et al., 2005). Additionally, texting on cell phones while driving is now widely understood as a source of distraction that adversely impacts the driving of both individuals with ADHD and those without (Narad et al., 2013). Driving while texting may place teens with ADHD at even greater risk for harm, especially since they may already experience driver inattention even without the distraction of their cell phone (Barkley, 2015e).

due to co-occurring symptoms, such as anxiety and depression. Treatment with stimulant medication may also interfere with sleep (Chen, Wardlaw, & Stein, 2019).

Relatively well documented is that children with ADHD suffer more accidental injury than those without ADHD (Amiri et al., 2017; Centers for Disease Control and Prevention, 2018c). A comprehensive review cited 57% of the children as "accident prone," and noted that 15% had at least four or more serious injuries such as broken bones, head lacerations, bruises, lost teeth, and poisonings (Barkley, 2015e). What accounts for these risks? Inattention and impulsivity have been related to unintentional injury (Rowe, Simonoff, & Silberg, 2007). According to parents, children with ADHD are inattentive in risky situations and unmindful of the consequences of their actions. Also noteworthy are motor incoordination, defiant and aggressive behavior associated with ADHD, and inadequate parental monitoring. Some of these factors are involved in the difficulties displayed by adolescents with ADHD regarding automobile-related behaviors. (See Accent: "Autos, Adolescence, and ADHD.")

DSM Presentations

As already noted, the DSM-5 recognizes three presentations of ADHD based on the individual's primary symptoms: Predominantly inattentive presentation (ADHD-PI), predominantly hyperactive-impulsive presentation (ADHD-PHI), and the combination of

these symptoms (ADHD-C). This conceptualization of different presentations of ADHD is based on research demonstrating the clustering of symptoms and other group differences. Although many investigations, including studies in different countries, have provided evidence to support different types of ADHD (e.g., Gadow et al., 2000; Graetz et al., 2001), the data are mixed and issues have arisen regarding these groupings (Gomez, Vance, & Gomez, 2013; Willcutt et al., 2012).

One of the concerns is the diagnosis of ADHD-PHI, which requires six or more symptoms of hyperactivity-impulsivity and fewer than six of inattention. The diagnosis is given to relatively few children, research on ADHD-PHI is scant, and the presentation type is minimally discussed in this chapter. It has been suggested that ADHD-PHI is an early developmental stage of ADHD-C rather than a unique presentation type (Roberts et al., 2015). In some cases, what seems to be ADHD-PHI in preschoolers might better be considered as oppositional defiant behaviors, which may or may not fade.

It is the combined presentation that is most prevalent in clinic samples and has most often been described and investigated. Diagnosis requires that the individual manifest at least six symptoms of hyperactivity-impulsivity and of inattention. The case description of Jimmy illustrates ADHD-C exhibited in a child of almost 7 years of age. The presence of inattention, hyperactivity, and impulsivity are obvious.

ADHD-PI appears to be the most prevalent presentation in population-based samples of children, although they are less often referred to clinics than children with ADHD-C (Willcutt, 2012).

JIMMY Combined Presentation of ADHD

Jimmy was not seen as a "bad" child by his parents; he was not oppositional, aggressive, stubborn, or ill-tempered. But he was in constant motion, and often wandered off, sometimes getting into dangerous situations such as running into the road without looking. Jimmy seemed eager to please his parents, but frequently did not follow through on their requests. It seemed that Jimmy was sidetracked by other things he found more interesting. His parents adopted an active style of dealing with him—monitoring him, reminding him, using immediate reinforcement and punishment.

When Jimmy was enrolled in preschool, his inattentive, overactive, and impulsive behaviors led his parents to withdraw him from one program and his being asked to leave a second program. Among the difficulties were talking during quiet times, lack of interest in group activities, distracting others, and engaging in too much imaginative play. Similar kinds of behaviors were reported in kindergarten, where he had

problems focusing attention, being too active, and being unable to work independently. An evaluation at that time showed Jimmy to have high average intelligence but achieving at somewhat lower levels.

By first grade, Jimmy's impulsivity began to interfere with his social relationships. He was described as immature and silly. His peers complained of his bothering them, grabbing them, and pulling them, and although Jimmy was friendly he was unable to maintain friendships. His behavior, more acceptable at early ages, was no longer accepted by peers. The coach noted an inability to participate in organized sports and off-task and silly behaviors. Teachers too had complaints: Jimmy did not follow directions or complete academic tasks on time, and he was disruptive due to excessive activity and noise making. He had fallen behind academically.

Adapted from Hathaway, Dooling-Litfin, & Edwards, 2006, pp. 390–391

Interest in an inattentive presentation has existed for many years, yet concern exists that the diagnostic category ADHD-PI may include more than one diagnostic subgroup (Diamond, 2005; Milich, Balentine, & Lynam, 2001). One group includes children with comparable, yet subclinical, symptoms of ADHD-C. Recall, if you will, that the DSM had once recognized a category of attention-deficit disorder without hyperactivity. ADHD-PI resembles this older category but the DSM-5 diagnosis, along with the requirement of at least six symptoms of inattention, permits up to five symptoms of hyperactivity-impulsivity. Thus, some cases of ADHD-PI do not look like "pure" inattention and rather share many "subthreshold" symptoms of hyperactivity-impulsivity with ADHD-C. Another group consists of children whose inattentive symptoms are linked to problems with arousal and a factor referred to as **sluggish cognitive tempo** (SCT) (Barkley, 2015a). Children displaying SCT tend to be lethargic, prone to daydreams, confused, and more socially withdrawn (Barkley, 2018b; Becker & Barkley, 2018). SCT behaviors do not appear on the DSM list of symptoms for ADHD and may represent a distinct group (Becker & Barkley, 2018; Becker et al., 2018). The portrayal of Tim shows SCT and attention deficits in childhood into adolescence. Tim's profile is notably different from the restless, on-the-go, and disruptive behaviors of a child with hyperactive and impulsive behaviors. (See Accent: "Sluggish Cognitive Tempo: Is There a Second Attention Disorder?")

For presentation types of a disorder to be valid, they must be different not only in symptoms but also in other important features. Children with ADHD-PI are thought to be distinct from

those with ADHD-C in several ways. Age of onset appears to be later, and girls with ADHD appear more likely to be diagnosed with the predominantly inattentive presentation than other presentations (Zalecki & Hinshaw, 2004). ADHD-PI children appear more passive and shy; they engage in less fighting and aggression. ADHD-PI also is less associated with externalizing disorders and perhaps more strongly linked with internalizing symptoms (Lahey & Willcutt, 2010). Unsurprising then, inattentive children are less rejected by their peers, although they may be isolated. Evidence also exists for differences in educational history, genetics, and biological brain functioning between the inattentive and combined presentations (Schmitz, Ludwig, & Rohde, 2010).

Although these differences are viewed as supporting ADHD-PI as a valid presentation type of ADHD, the matter is not settled. Differences between ADHD-PI and ADHD-C often have not been found on neuropsychological testing and laboratory studies of inattention and impulsivity (Hinshaw, 2001; Lahey, 2001; Nigg et al., 2002; Pelham, 2001). Such findings suggest to some that the presentation types are not distinct and that ADHD-PI may instead be a milder version of ADHD-C.

Additionally, a more general concern about DSM subtyping has to do with instability of diagnosis. Children diagnosed into a particular subtype at one point in time often are assigned to a different subtype at another time (Willcutt et al., 2012). While true change could occur, methodological factors appear to play a role. Valo and Tannock (2010) found that as many as 50% of cases in a clinic sample of children were reclassified depending on the assessment instruments

TIM Predominantly Inattentive Presentation of ADHD

Tim was a quiet, somewhat introverted child who was not noticeable in a crowd. His early development was unremarkable, and he was not a behavior problem.

In elementary school, Tim's behavior and academic performance were adequate. But he did not volunteer information, often appeared in a daze, and often did not catch what teachers said when they called upon him. He had no problem in reading words but had difficulty staying with a train of thought, which created comprehension problems. Approaching third grade, with new demands for independent schoolwork, Tim began to have increased difficulties, including completing his work on time. The school determined that he was not eligible for special services, but school personnel commented on his attention lapses, poor focusing, being "spacey," and getting lost in daydreams. His grades in middle school became less consistent, ranging from Bs to Ds, and

productivity declined further in seventh and eighth grades. Tim's attention problems and poor study habits took a larger toll in high school, and he was transferred to a vocational high school in eleventh grade.

Despite academic problems, Tim made and kept friends, although he was reserved and indifferent to organized recreational activities. His academic performance was a source of conflict with his mother, who reported that Tim was often irritable, talked back, and blamed others for his mistakes. He was, however, cooperative in other ways, for example, in completing home chores. Based on assessment when he was almost 18 years of age, Tim was described as presumably of average intelligence, with a chronic history of inattentiveness, distractibility, and underachievement.

Adapted from Hathaway et al., 2006, pp. 410–411

used, whether parents or teachers were the informants, and how the information from different sources was combined to reach a diagnosis. Such diagnostic instability challenges the usefulness of the presentation types for clinical and research purposes.

As noted previously, the transition from the DSM-IV to DSM-5 brought with it a move away from the "subtype" terminology in favor of a more flexible presentation system that acknowledges that symptoms may vary in the population and change over time (Roberts et al., 2015). Nevertheless, although the two dimensions of inattention and hyperactivity-impulsiveness are supported, considerable concern and controversy remain regarding the conceptualization of the structure of these dimensions and their utility (Nikolas & Nigg, 2013).

Co-occurring Disorders

A remarkable fact about ADHD, especially ADHD-C, is the degree to which it coexists with other disorders or symptoms, including learning disabilities, externalizing and internalizing disorders, and other neurodevelopmental disorders (Andersson et al., 2020; Pliszka, 2015). As with other psychopathologies, rates of co-occurrence depend on the samples, measures, the specific disorders, and the like. Comorbidity is higher in clinic than in community samples, with more of the referred youth likely than not to have another disorder (Reale et al., 2017) and a sizable number exhibiting two or more disorders. Indeed, "pure" ADHD may be the exception rather than the rule (Jarrett & Ollendick,

2008). Comorbidity generally is related to greater impairment and developmental risk.

Learning Disorders

Reports of the rates of learning disorders in youth with ADHD vary enormously, likely due to the various ways to define learning problems (Evans, Owens, & Power, 2019). For example, a review of 17 studies found learning disorder present in 8–76% of youth with ADHD with a median prevalence across studies of 47% (DuPaul, Gormley, & Laracy, 2013). When considering only those studies examining learning disorders with impairment in reading or math, and not problems of written expression, the rates appear somewhat lower at 24 to 38% (DuPaul, Gormley, & Laracy, 2013). Despite these differences, it is reasonable to estimate that approximately one in three children with ADHD also meet criteria for a learning disorder (DuPaul & Stoner, 2014).

The relationship between ADHD and learning problems is not completely understood, and the direction of the relationship remains unclear. In other words, it is unclear whether learning problems contribute to ADHD, whether the core symptoms of ADHD impact learning, or whether a common factor contributes to the development of both disorders. Nevertheless, the association between ADHD and learning problems is often viewed as one in which inattention is more crucially involved than hyperactivity/impulsivity (Greven et al., 2011; Paloyelis et al., 2010). Comorbid ADHD and reading problems also appear to reflect the combination of cognitive deficits found in each of the separate disorders—for example, the executive dysfunctions of ADHD and the phonological

ACCENT Sluggish Cognitive Tempo: Is There a Second Attention Disorder?

Primarily studied in the past as a feature of ADHD, recent years have seen increased interest in the study of the construct sluggish cognitive tempo (SCT), characterized by drowsiness, daydreaming, lethargy, mental confusion, poor motivation, and slowed thinking/behavior (Barkley, 2018b; Becker & Barkley, 2018). While the original research in this area grew out of that intended to distinguish subtypes of ADHD, more recent research has focused specifically on groups of children and adults with high levels of SCT behaviors. A body of research providing support for SCT as a construct separate from ADHD is quickly mounting.

For example, a meta-analysis by Becker and colleagues, which included findings of factor analytic studies amassing data from 19,000 children and adults, found strong support for 13 core behaviors that loaded consistently with the construct of SCT as opposed to loading on an ADHD factor (Becker et al., 2016). Related research has focused on the development of specific rating scales for SCT, which include items such as "I am slow at doing things," "I zone out or space out," and "My mind feels like it is in a fog" (Barkley, 2018b), which correspond with these core symptoms.

Fewer studies have examined SCT in relation to functioning and impairment, yet research does suggest SCT is related to poor adjustment in a variety of domains, even after controlling for ADHD (Becker & Barkley, 2018). Studies have documented, for example, an association between SCT and internalizing symptoms, such as depression and to a somewhat lesser extent anxiety (Becker, Webb, & Dvorsky, 2019b). Interestingly, SCT seems to predict a different pattern of impairment than the predominantly inattentive presentation of ADHD. Research demonstrates, for example, that children with predominantly inattentive ADHD and high levels of SCT are rated as having fewer externalizing behaviors and higher levels of internalizing problems and social impairment as compared to children with the inattentive presentation of ADHD who are not high in SCT symptoms (Carlson & Mann, 2002). While the findings with regard to academic functioning have been less consistent, SCT appears to be associated with a range of academic related difficulties (Becker & Barkley, 2018). Research exploring neuropsychological deficits associated with SCT are mixed and still emerging. However, generally this line of research suggests while SCT may be related to specific problems of neuropsychological functioning such as selective attention (Huang-Pollock et al., 2005), it is not associated with the pervasive neuropsychological impairments often seen in ADHD (Bauermeister et al., 2012).

Of note, as research in this area and discourse on SCT continue to emerge, debate also surrounds terminology of the construct. Some researchers have noted the term "sluggish cognitive tempo" is far from ideal and may, in fact, be pejorative in nature, proposing a change to concentration deficit disorder. Others have cautioned that it may be premature to use terminology of a "disorder" since it is not presently a recognized diagnostic category and may also detract from the notion of SCT as dimensional in nature (Becker & Barkley, 2018). Future research will likely inform this dialogue and our understanding of the construct.

(language sound) deficits of reading impairment (Gooch, Snowling, & Hulme, 2011). Neuroimaging studies have also identified a combination of shared and distinctive alterations in the brain that may contribute to comorbidity of ADHD and reading impairment (Langer et al., 2019). The co-occurrence of symptoms of ADHD with learning problems appears to be largely due to shared genetic influence that can persist over time (Willcutt et al., 2005). Notably, young people with ADHD and learning disorders are at greater risk for impairment than those with only ADHD (DuPaul et al., 2015).

Externalizing Disorders

Researchers once wondered whether ADHD and conduct disorders (ODD and CD) were actually only one common disorder. Epidemiological and clinic studies made it clear, however, that these disorders have distinct symptom clusters and other distinct features (Pliszka, 2015). For example, ADHD is more strongly associated with neurocognitive impairment than ODD (Luman et al., 2009), differences in brain abnormalities between ADHD and CD are reported (Rubia et al., 2009), and ODD and CD are more strongly related than ADHD to adverse family factors and psychosocial disadvantage (Waschbusch, 2002).

However, ADHD can lead to ODD that in turn can lead to CD, and the symptoms of ODD and CD frequently co-occur (Ahmad & Hinshaw, 2016). Indeed, substantial percentages of children and adolescents with ADHD develop ODD alone or with CD (Barkley, 2015b). The co-occurrence of the symptoms of these disorders in clinic and non-referred groups has been extensively investigated. Compared with children with only ADHD, those with the combination often appear more disturbed and impaired, both in ADHD symptoms and conduct problems (Pliszka, 2015). This finding holds for preschoolers as well (Gadow & Nolan, 2002). Importantly, behavioral difficulties appear earlier in children with the combined profile, problems are likely to persist, and outcome is more negative. Other differences are noteworthy. ADHD with co-occurring conduct problems is generally more strongly associated with coercive parent–child interactions, parental psychiatric symptoms and substance abuse, and adverse life events (Barkley, 2015b; Danforth, Connor, & Doerfler, 2014; Pliszka, 2015).

Internalizing Disorders

The estimated comorbidity rate of ADHD and anxiety is 25 to 50%, either in clinic or community samples (Bishop et al., 2019; Costello, Egger, & Angold, 2004). Some, but not all, data suggest that children with both disturbances are less hyperactive and impulsive than those with ADHD who do not have anxiety disorders, and they may display fewer conduct problems and higher levels of inattention. The presence of anxiety with ADHD also may be associated with some differences in performance on cognitive tasks (Jarrett et al., 2012), and limited research suggests that the comorbid condition is associated with maternal anxiety and overprotective families that discourage autonomy (Jarrett & Ollendick, 2008). Regardless of the etiology, the co-occurrence of ADHD and anxiety is an important consideration in treatment (Pliszka, 2019).

The co-occurrence of ADHD with mild depressive symptoms and major depression is found at varying rates in children and adolescents and in clinic and community samples. Perhaps somewhere between 12% and 50% of young people with ADHD also experience depression (Seymour & Miller, 2017). Interestingly, the positive self-bias exhibited by some children with ADHD

may serve as short-term protection against depression (Mikami, Calhoun, & Abikoff, 2010), but a proportion of youth will experience depressive symptoms. ADHD plus depression frequently results in poorer outcome than either disorder alone, including greater impairments in social functioning and higher rates of suicidality, especially in girls (Evans et al., 2019). The association of ADHD with depression is complex. For example, one study of clinic youth suggested that ADHD led to ODD and then to various paths to depression (Burke et al., 2005) (see Figure 10.2). More recent hypotheses emphasize the role poor emotion regulation, including poor frustration tolerance, may play in the association between ADHD and depression (Barkley, 2015b; Seymour & Miller, 2017). The co-occurrence of ADHD with depression in youth has been associated with greater family stress and pathology, as well as with an increased risk of family members having both disorders (Oxley & Stringaris, 2018; Pliszka, 2015).

The co-occurrence of ADHD and bipolar disorder has been reported in the range of 10 to 20%, but there is much controversy about this finding (Pliszka, 2015). The controversy stems in part from the similarity of the symptoms of ADHD and the mania of bipolar disorder—for example, high rates of activity, poor judgment, and talkativeness are observed in both ADHD and mania—and whether bipolar disorder in youth exists in the same episodic form it does in adults (Pliszka, 2015; Youngstrom & Algorta, 2014). It may be that a number of children and adolescents with ADHD experience a mix of severe emotion dysregulation, chronic irritability, and behavior problems characteristic of a new DSM-5 diagnosis of Disruptive Mood Dysregulation Disorder (see p. 158) (Mulraney et al., 2016; Mulraney, Stringaris, & Taylor, 2018). There is still much to learn about these and other co-occurring conditions.

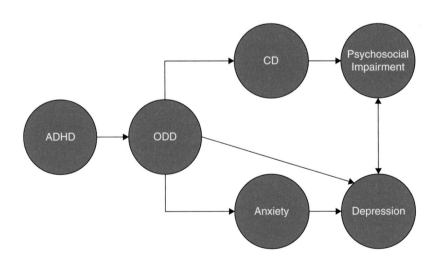

Figure 10.2 A developmental model suggested by a study of boys from age 7–12 to age 18. The relationship of ADHD to depression was complex. (Adapted from Burke et al., 2005. Copyright by John Wiley & Sons; reprinted with permission)

Epidemiology

The prevalence of ADHD has been the focus of considerable research. Significant variability in rates has been detected across research methodologies and geographic regions. Additionally, prevalence estimates of ADHD have trended upwards over the years, with marked increases in ADHD diagnoses (Danielson et al., 2018). Although the estimates appear to have leveled off in recent years, it remains unclear whether increased rates indicated a true change or reflect factors such as methodological differences or greater identification and diagnosis of ADHD (Collishaw, 2015; Roberts et al., 2015). Nevertheless, ADHD is widely acknowledged as a common condition, affecting millions of children throughout the world and of varying backgrounds, and it is a common reason for clinic referral.

Although the rates of ADHD can vary widely, the prevalence in school-age children in the United States is generally estimated around 5 to 9% (Centers for Disease Control and Prevention, 2018b). Systematic reviews estimate community prevalence globally between 2% and 7% with an average around 5% worldwide (Merikangas & Hommer, 2019; Polanczyk et al., 2015; Sayal et al., 2018), and similar rates are noted across most nations of the world (Hinshaw & Scheffler, 2018). In considering prevalence, the distinction must be made between clinically diagnosed ADHD and designations based on parent or teacher ratings of symptoms. Rates are typically higher in the latter kind of reports, and can reach over 20% (Polanczyk, 2018). In fact, higher rates might be expected because the method usually does not include criteria employed for clinical diagnosis such as age of onset, pervasiveness of symptoms, and functional impairment (McKeown et al., 2015; Roberts et al., 2015).

In general, less is known about prevalence during the preschool and adolescent years than during childhood. Nevertheless, follow-up studies of children diagnosed with ADHD show declines into adolescence. This finding may be confounded by the fact that diagnostic items for ADHD are suitable for children but have less adequately described how the disorder may be manifested in adolescence (Barkley, 2010; Nigg et al., 2006), or it may reflect informant-related effects, as adolescent self-report of symptoms may differ from parent-report (Roberts et al., 2015). Thus, adolescent ADHD has perhaps been underdiagnosed, although it appears that rates may be escalating (Hinshaw & Scheffler, 2018).

Gender

Although gender differences vary across studies, boys consistently outnumber girls. In the general population, the ratio of boys to girls is about 2 to 3:1 (American Psychiatric Association, 2013; Sayal et al., 2018). In clinic samples, this ratio is even higher, with estimates around 4:1 (Greven, Richards, & Buitelaar, 2018).

Gender differences in clinic samples probably reflect a referral bias due to boys' greater aggressive and antisocial behavior. In addition, the diagnostic criteria are biased toward behaviors observed more in males—such as excessive running, climbing, and leaving one's seat in the classroom. Moreover, when girls are identified it appears to be more on the basis of inattentive and disorganized behaviors, which, it can be argued, are less noticeable than hyperactivity and impulsiveness. These factors may help account for the finding that some girls display the symptoms of ADHD but at levels that do not meet the DSM criteria (Greven et al., 2018). Concern is expressed that girls are underdiagnosed, thereby missing out on preventive or ameliorative interventions (Mowlem et al., 2019).

In order to better understand the impairments of girls with ADHD, Hinshaw and colleagues compared a community sample of girls, ages 6 to 12, with a matched sample of girls without ADHD (Hinshaw, 2002). Among the findings for those with ADHD were executive function deficits, academic problems, negative peer evaluations, and high rates of anxiety, mood disorder, and conduct problems. A more recent longitudinal study examined the trajectories of executive functioning performance in a sample of girls with and without ADHD from childhood through emerging adulthood (Gordon & Hinshaw, 2019). Findings suggest women with ADHD consistently lagged behind women without ADHD on measures of executive function even if their ADHD symptoms had remitted by early adulthood. These studies indicate the need to address the impairments of girls with ADHD.

The question of gender differences has been studied more directly by comparing girls with boys. An early meta-analysis of the research showed that girls with ADHD were less hyperactive, displayed fewer externalizing symptoms, and had lower intelligence (Gaub & Carlson, 1997). No gender differences were found for a number of other behaviors and correlates. A recent large-scale study in Sweden examined sex difference in the severity and presentation of ADHD symptoms, conduct problems, and learning problems in boys and girls with and without clinically diagnosed ADHD (Mowlem et al., 2019). Findings suggest boys scored higher on all symptom domains compared to girls at the population level, but similar severity was found for boys and girls clinically diagnosed with ADHD. Moreover, while symptom severity was associated with diagnosis for both boys and girls, girls were more likely to be diagnosed and to receive treatment if they demonstrated more severe hyperactivity/impulsivity and conduct problems, again highlighting the concern that females may be misdiagnosed and undertreated unless they demonstrate considerable impairment. Research has suggested sex differences in the prevalence of ADHD may result from differing genetic and cognitive vulnerabilities between the sexes (Arnett et al., 2015), yet these differences are inconsistent across studies (Owens, Cardoos, & Hinshaw, 2015). Overall, the emerging picture suggests similarities across gender.

Social Class, Race/Ethnicity, and Culture

The symptoms of ADHD are reported worldwide with a clinical picture similar to that reported in the United States. That is, the disorder is diagnosed more in boys than girls, tends to decline in adolescence, and shows many of the same associated characteristics and comorbidities (Canino & Alegría, 2008). ADHD appears in all social classes, with higher rates sometimes associated with lower SES (Russell et al., 2016). In the United States, prevalence appears low but increasing among Hispanic youth relative to non-Hispanic youth, and higher in white children compared to African American youth (Collins & Cleary, 2016). Notably, research suggests racial and ethnic disparities may be related to underdiagnosis and undertreatment of African American and Hispanic/Latinx youth (Coker et al., 2016; Cummings et al., 2017).

An important study by Miller, Nigg, and Miller (2009) reviewed research published from 1990 to 2007 that compared African American youth, ages 3 to 18, to white youth. Two major findings of disparity emerged. First, as rated by their parents and teachers, African American youth had more ADHD symptoms than white youth, yet they were diagnosed with ADHD at two-thirds the rate of white youth. Other studies have also demonstrated that minority children are less likely to receive an ADHD diagnosis and treatment for ADHD. Morgan and colleagues (2013) examined disparities in diagnosis from kindergarten to eighth grade and found rates of diagnosis in minority children, including African American, Hispanic, and children of other races/ethnicities, was 69%, 50%, and 46% lower, respectively, as compared to white youth. Additionally, minority youth were less likely than white children to be taking prescription medication for the disorder.

What explains these seemingly paradoxical results? Disparities in access to information about the etiology and treatment of ADHD may differ by race. Minority youth and families may be less likely to receive accurate information, care, and diagnosis. In addition, various barriers to diagnosis and treatment, such as financial barriers or cultural factors, including language barriers for some youth, might make it more difficult for minority families to access treatment (Alvarado & Modesto-Lowe, 2016), which may lead to a lack of care and increased symptoms. Such group differences may also be influenced by broader societal factors, such as social disadvantage or the influence of education policy and practices on diagnosis (Danckaerts & Coghill, 2018; Hinshaw & Scheffler, 2018). Additional research is needed to inform a culturally sensitive understanding of the factors that might influence diagnosis and treatment.

Developmental Course

It is especially important to study ADHD across development. Because ADHD emerges early for many children, examination of the first years of life can be critical to understanding the origin of the disorder. At the same time, children do not necessarily "outgrow" ADHD, as was once believed, so the developmental course of ADHD can be understood only by observing the persistence of symptoms into adolescence and adulthood.

Infancy and the Preschool Years

At least some cases of ADHD might begin in infancy, but how would ADHD manifest itself so early in life? Behaviors symptomatic of ADHD are commonly reported by preschool age, but relatively little is known about ADHD in the early years (Gleason & Humphreys, 2016; M. Miller et al., 2018). Sanson and colleagues (1993) reported that a group of children who were hyperactive and aggressive at age 8 had displayed early difficult temperament, and by age 3 to 4 had been more active and less cooperative and manageable than typical children.

Campbell's (2002) study of hard-to-manage preschoolers indicates that problems often lessened, but that for some children symptoms persisted and could meet the criteria for ADHD in childhood. Investigation is ongoing to identify early behaviors that might predict later ADHD or conduct problems and to distinguish those behaviors from the misbehaviors that are typical of young children. Recent research in this area suggests the first signs of the disorder may emerge as motor or language delays or difficult temperamental tendencies (Athanasiadou et al., 2019; Frick et al., 2018).

Shaw, Lacourse, and Nagin (2005) contributed to our understanding of the early course of ADHD symptoms by following a community sample of boys from urban, low-income families from age 1.5 to 10 years. Based on multiple assessments of the core symptoms of ADHD, four developmental paths were suggested: Twenty percent of the children displayed a chronically high level of symptoms from age 2 into childhood, approximately 6% showed consistently low levels of symptoms, nearly 27% showed moderate levels of symptoms at age 2 that desisted by age 10, and 47% exhibited a relatively stable moderate level of symptoms. A growing number of studies support the notion of different developmental pathways with regard to ADHD symptoms, although patterns of pathways have differed somewhat, perhaps due in part to methodological differences. For example, Willoughby (Willoughby et al., 2012; Willoughby, 2017) describes the results of a study of children followed from age 2 months and assessed for ADHD symptomatology at ages 3 to 5 years. Again, four different developmental pathways were observed, but here 8% demonstrated a chronically high level of symptoms, 72% were characterized by persistently low symptoms, 16% showed initially elevated ADHD symptoms that desisted over time, and 4% of children had initially low ADHD symptoms that increased over time (Willoughby, 2017; Willoughby et al., 2012) (see Figure 10.3). Despite differences,

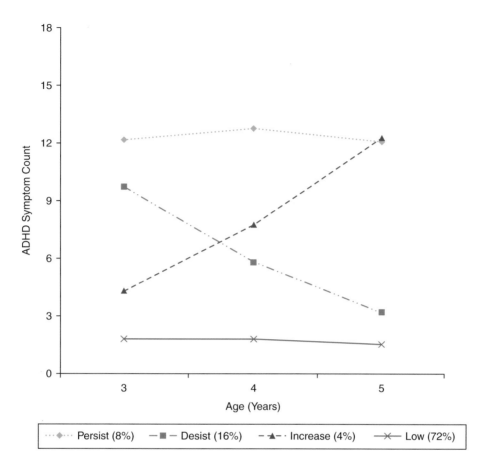

Figure 10.3 Trajectories of ADHD symptoms. (Adapted from Willoughby, 2017)

these studies suggest, while some children may "outgrow" their symptoms, a proportion of preschoolers will have symptoms that persist into childhood.

Childhood

Most cases of ADHD are referred between the ages of 6 and 12—probably in part due to school demands that children pay attention, follow rules, get along with others, and otherwise regulate their own behavior (Hinshaw, 2018; Spaniardi, Greenhill, & Hechtman, 2017). These are the years that have been well described and documented and are explored extensively throughout this chapter.

Childhood is generally a time during which deficits in inattention may become more obvious. Here too, heterogeneity in developmental pathways may be observed (Larsson et al., 2011; Sasser, Kalvin, & Bierman, 2016). For some children, particularly those with high levels of hyperactivity/impulsivity, these symptoms may decrease over the course of childhood while symptoms of inattention increase. Others may demonstrate inattention problems that continue to increase

over the course of childhood, or they may show declining or consistently low symptoms of ADHD throughout childhood. Multiple factors, including child characteristics and family risk factors among others, may predict the trajectory of ADHD (Sasser et al., 2016).

In addition to problems of inattention and hyperactivity/impulsivity, other problems may emerge in childhood. Self-regulation and self-organization are problematic, social relationships can be far from satisfactory, and poor academic achievement is observed. Clinical-level oppositional behaviors, conduct problems, and internalizing symptoms also can become apparent in some children.

Adolescence and Adulthood

In adolescence, the primary symptoms of ADHD—especially hyperactive/impulsive behaviors—decrease in a substantial number of cases, so that the diagnosis of ADHD may no longer apply. Still, the disorder persists in the vast majority of affected youth (Hinshaw, 2018). Two aspects of symptom manifestation are noteworthy. First, heterotypic continuity of symptoms is likely.

That is, the core symptoms may carry over in somewhat different forms; for example, overactive running about in childhood may later become manifest as inability to relax. Second, many adolescents who no longer meet diagnostic criteria nevertheless display high symptom levels compared to their non-ADHD peers (Barkley, 2010).

Longitudinal studies of ADHD leave no doubt that the disorder puts these children at risk for a variety of problems in adolescence. These include poor school achievement, reading problems, internalizing problems, conduct disorder, antisocial behavior, drug use or abuse, social problems, accidents, symptoms of eating disorder, and teenage pregnancy (Biederman et al., 2011; Oxley & Stringaris, 2018; Pliszka, 2015; Wadsworth et al., 2015; Wilens et al., 2011). Issues that often challenge family relationships in adolescence—noncompliance to rules and conflicts over curfews and schoolwork—may be particularly prominent (Johnston & Chronis-Tuscano, 2015). Although earlier work disproportionately focused on boys, more recent data confirm that ADHD places girls at similar risk (Hinshaw, 2018; Leopold et al., 2019). In a study that assessed adjustment in adolescent girls who had been identified in childhood either with or without ADHD, only 16% compared to 86%, respectively, were positively adjusted in several domains (Owens et al., 2009).

Based on studies that followed ADHD into the adult years, perhaps 60% of cases still display some core deficits and other problems (Spaniardi et al., 2017). Problems included impaired social relationships, depression, low self-concept, antisocial behavior and personality, drug use, and educational and occupational disadvantage (Asherson, Ramos-Quiroga, & Young, 2018; Merrill et al., 2019; Uchida et al., 2015). Research on girls with ADHD found that, in adulthood, 62% had some ADHD symptoms and significantly greater lifetime risks for mood, anxiety, and antisocial disorders relative to comparison girls. When these now-grown-up girls (mean age of 22 years) were compared to young men of the same age who had similarly been diagnosed with ADHD and similarly followed, risk for later problems was clear in both groups (Biederman et al., 2010). However, the profile of specific disorders was different, as illustrated in Figure 10.4. Recent research supports the notion that the persistence of ADHD into adulthood puts individuals at increased risk for a host of impairments (Hechtman et al., 2016; Owens et al., 2017).

Interest has increased in adults who for the first time are identified with the symptoms of ADHD and retrospectively report a history of childhood ADHD symptoms (Abrams et al., 2018). Although the question of reliability must be raised regarding retrospective reports, the prevalence of adult ADHD in the United States appears to be about 4%, with perhaps only 25% of the cases having been diagnosed in childhood or

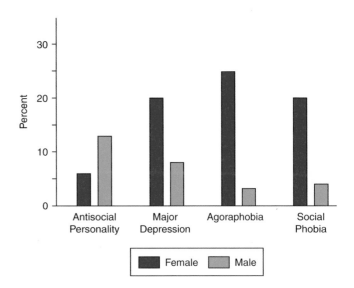

Figure 10.4 Percent of young adult females and males exhibiting specific disorders 11 years after being identified with ADHD in childhood/adolescence. (From Biederman et al., 2010. Copyright 2010 by the American Psychiatric Association; reprinted with permission)

adolescence. These cases of adult ADHD support the view of ADHD as a chronic, lifelong condition for many individuals. However, questions remain about whether adult-onset ADHD represents the late expression of ADHD or a distinct disorder (Shaw & Polanczyk, 2017).

Variation and Prediction of Outcome

In examining the developmental progression of ADHD, it is important to consider the overall picture. First, core symptoms, especially hyperactivity-impulsivity, appear to lessen over time. Second, many secondary problems develop and can exist into later years. Third, the course and outcome of ADHD vary. Some children overcome disorder; others continue to show different kinds and degrees of problems. This fact prompts the question, "What variables predict outcome?" Many predictors of adolescent and adult problems have been identified (Table 10.1). Genetic factors may have considerable influence on continuity, but the picture is complex. For example, risks may be different for different areas of functioning (Agnew-Blais et al., 2016; Cheung et al., 2015; Hinshaw, 2018; Ramos-Olazagasti et al., 2018). Poor educational outcome appears especially associated with early deficits in attention, intelligence, and academic skill, as well as with internalizing symptoms and some child-rearing practices. In contrast, the continuance of antisocial behavior is especially associated with family disturbance and the child's aggression and conduct problems.

Table 10.1 Some Variables that May Predict Adolescent and Adult Outcomes of Childhood ADHD

Age of onset
Severity of symptoms
Aggression; conduct problems
General intelligence
Academic ability and performance
Social functioning
Family adversities
Socioeconomic status
Parents' ADHD and psychiatric disorder
Parents' child-rearing practice; parent–child interaction
Genetic factors

Neuropsychological Theories of ADHD

Neuropsychological dysfunction in youth with ADHD has led to hypotheses to help account for the disorder. If one imagines a path leading from abnormal genes to ADHD, impaired neuropsychological functions are viewed as lying somewhere along the path. Several accounts of ADHD implicating such functions have been offered; they emphasize executive functions, inhibition, attention, arousal, response to reward, time perception, working memory, and/or self-regulation (Nigg, 2016; Shaw & Szekely, 2018; Willcutt, 2015). These accounts, which tend to be conceptually related, vary in how comprehensive they are, and frequently reference brain functioning. Our discussion highlights executive functions, reward sensitivity, and temporal processing.

Executive Functions and Inhibition

As we have already seen, children with ADHD exhibit deficits in executive functions, the higher-order skills required for planning, organizing, and implementing goal-directed behavior (Barkley, 2015d; Willcutt, 2015). One component of executive functions is the ability to inhibit responses. Impairments in executive functions and inhibition, which are well documented in ADHD, hold a central place in various explanations of the disorder.

Executive Functioning and Self-Regulation: Barkley's Evolving Model

As an example, we consider Barkley's multifaceted model, which centers on the interrelated constructs of executive function and self-regulation, both of which involve an individual's self-directed, goal-oriented actions (Barkley, 2014, 2015e). According to Barkley

(2015e), deficits in behavioral or **response inhibition** play a prominent role in the hyperactivity-impulsivity and difficulties in self-control seen in ADHD. Behavioral inhibition is viewed as consisting of three abilities. First is the ability to inhibit prepotent responses, that is, responses that are likely to be reinforced or have a history of reinforcement. Second is the ability to interrupt responses that are already under way and proving ineffective. The third ability then comes into play, which is the ability to inhibit competing stimuli—to protect the operation of the executive functions from interference. It can be thought of as freedom from distraction. By preventing prepotent responses, stopping ineffective responses, and hindering distraction, behavioral inhibition sets the occasion for self-regulation, which involves other executive functions. These are briefly described below.

- Nonverbal working memory is part of the memory system that allows the person to hold information in mind, or "on-line," that will be used to control a subsequent response. It involves memory of sensory-motor action.
- Internalization of speech can be thought of as verbal working memory. It allows the person to mentally reflect on rules and instructions that have been internalized to guide behavior.
- Self-regulation of affect, motivation, and arousal involves processes that allow the person to adapt emotion and motivation. It might involve, for example, a lessening of anger, which can affect motivation and arousal.
- Reconstitution allows the person to analyze and synthesize, that is, to break down and recombine nonverbal and verbal units. It allows the construction of novel, creative behaviors or sequences of behaviors.

These four executive functions provide the means for the individual to self-regulate their behavior.

Consider a hypothetical example of a child resisting the urge to taste a cake he encounters sitting on the kitchen counter on the morning of his birthday party. He knows eating the cake before his party and without permission will get him into trouble with his parents, yet inhibiting his behavior takes a great deal of self-regulatory behavior and mental effort. Figure 10.5 illustrates the mental activities involved in this hypothetical example. Although the illustration portrays a relatively linear process for ease of interpretation, it is important to keep in mind that a child's ability to engage in task-relevant, goal-directed, and flexible behavior is much more complex and is likely influenced by multiple, interrelated individual, biological, and contextual factors. When inhibition, executive function and self-regulation are intact, the result is often adaptive. In contrast, when these functions are disordered, behavior and adaptability are adversely affected.

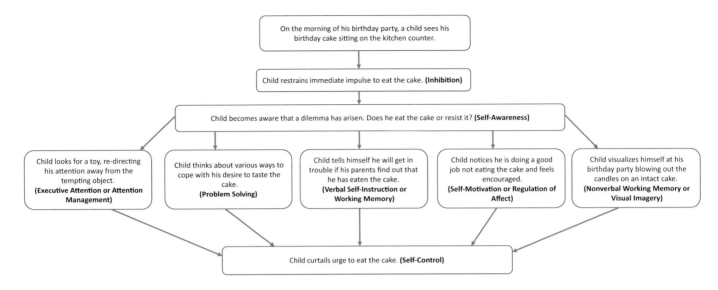

Figure 10.5 A hypothetical example of the role of executive functioning and self-regulation in behavior. (Based on Barkley, 2014)

Sensitivity to Reward

Unusual **sensitivity to reward** has been noted in children with ADHD (Furukawa et al., 2019; Nigg, 2017). This has been described as a motivational problem that is displayed as excessive reward-seeking behavior and decreased sensitivity to punishment. Children with ADHD have been shown to do poorly under partial schedules of reinforcement and otherwise low incentives (e.g., Slusarek et al., 2001). Particularly notable is an atypically high preference for immediate reward over delayed reward, even when the immediate reward is smaller (Sonuga-Barke et al., 2008). One study suggested that children with ADHD may have abnormal cardiac responses to reward and punishment (Luman et al., 2007). Another found evidence of differences in functioning of areas of the brain responsible for reward processing (van Hulst et al., 2017). These findings can be interpreted as abnormality in the brain's reward system, which may lead to differences in responding to the usual contingencies involved in paying attention, staying on task, following rules, and the like.

Temporal Processing and Aversion to Delay

The ability to process time is a multidimensional, fundamental skill that involves perceiving and organizing sequences of events and anticipating the occurrence of future events (Aguiar et al., 2010). Children with ADHD have a deficit in **temporal processing** that is exhibited in a variety of tasks; for example, they underestimate the passage of time. The processing of time is thought to be important in controlling and adapting behavior, and perhaps related to difficulties in impulsivity (e.g., waiting and planning) (Walg et al., 2017).

Sonuga-Barke and colleagues have proposed that one path to ADHD involves an aversion to the delay of time. In general, **delay aversion** would be manifested by attempts to avoid or escape delay (Sonuga-Barke et al., 2004). From this perspective, the preference that children with ADHD show for immediate over delayed reward may have more to do with avoiding delay than with the reward itself (Sonuga-Barke, 1994). It is argued that in situations where delay cannot be escaped or avoided, children will attend to aspects of the environment that help "speed up" the perception of time. Antrop and colleagues (2000) evaluated this idea by observing children with and without ADHD when they had to wait in a room with little available stimulation. On some measures, the children with ADHD engaged in more activity, presumably to lessen a subjective sense of delay. In another study, Sonuga-Barke and colleagues (2004) found support for the prediction that children with ADHD would be more sensitive to environmental cues for delay because delay has particular emotional or motivational significance for them. Recent research points to possible structural differences in the region of the brain responsible for processing negative emotions that may help explain these differences (Van Dessel et al., 2019).

A Move Toward Multiple-Deficit Models

Because many impairments in ADHD have been found, the early belief that a single neuropsychological or cognitive deficit would explain ADHD has given way to the hypothesis that multiple impairments more likely explain the disorder (Pauli-Pott et al., 2019; Willcutt, 2015). It is possible that a single deficit is central for some children while a different deficit defines others, and that different presentations based on neuropsychological impairments might exist. Yet, it is also possible that ADHD symptoms arise from multiple weaknesses that together cause the disorder but alone would not be sufficient to cause significant impairments. Perhaps ADHD is best viewed as a large umbrella that subsumes groups of individuals who exhibit different deficits and different etiological pathways (Taylor & Sonuga-Barke, 2008).

Multiple-Pathway Models

Simply put, independent pathway models of ADHD suggest some individuals exhibit symptoms due to one factor while others experience ADHD symptoms due to another factor. One of the first multiple pathways models was proposed by Sonuga-Barke and colleagues. The dual pathway model of ADHD proposes independent pathways in the development of the disorder, encompassing two alternative explanations (Sonuga-Barke, Dalen, & Remington, 2003). According to this model, one pathway is mediated by executive function deficits and the other by delay aversion. Somewhat different brain circuitry is thought to underlie these pathways. Sonuga-Barke, Bitsakou, and Thompson (2010) explored the possibility that temporal processing might constitute a third pathway. Children with ADHD and non-ADHD control children were given tasks that evaluated either inhibition, or delay aversion, or temporal processing. For those with ADHD, the co-occurrence of deficits on these three kinds of tasks was no greater than expected by chance. Moreover, deficits on only one type of task was observed in many children. The findings supported a triple pathway model and subtypes of neuropsychological impairment. While there is evidence for independent pathway models (Kerner auch Koerner, Gust, & Petermann, 2018), studies also suggest these pathways may not be entirely separate and that ADHD may be associated with weaknesses in multiple domains.

Multiple-Deficit Models

A shift has been made to considering ADHD as arising due to multiple neuropsychological deficits, which together cause the symptoms of ADHD but on their own are not necessary or sufficient to cause the disorder (Willcutt, 2015). This multiple-deficits model may help explain the heterogeneity within ADHD. For example, while executive functioning weaknesses may exist in many individuals with ADHD, those who also experience processing speed deficits may be more likely to display significant symptoms of inattention and learning difficulties, while those with disruptions in motivational processes may be more likely to display impulsive and disruptive behaviors (Willcutt, 2015). There is growing recognition that the etiology and presentation of ADHD is complex, and further research is needed to test and better understand these models.

Neurobiological Abnormalities

Brain damage or injury was once considered primary in ADHD. When it became evident that brain damage could not be identified in most children with the disorder, it was assumed that some undetectable "minimal brain dysfunction" existed. By the late 1950s and early 1960s, the need for better empirical evidence was recognized. Today, substantial evidence implicates brain dysfunction in ADHD (Hoogman et al., 2017).

Numerous brain structures are implicated, including the frontal lobe and underlying striatal regions, parietal lobe, temporal lobe, thalamus, corpus callosum, and cerebellum. For example, reduced brain volume has been revealed for several brain structures (Hoogman et al., 2017), with reductions in total volume estimated at 3 to 5% (Taylor, 2009). Also, an association between small brain volume and severity of ADHD symptoms has been reported (Hoogman et al., 2017). Research has also found an absence of the asymmetry observed in the frontal lobes in typical development in which the right lobe is usually larger than the left (Paclt et al., 2016).

Neurobiological findings have also helped to inform neuropsychological models of ADHD (Shaw & Szekely, 2018). Figure 10.6 illustrates the relationship between some current neurocognitive models of ADHD and brain level anomalies, and some related findings are discussed below. Interest has focused particularly on the prefrontal lobes and connections to the striatal region that lies deeper in the brain and to the cerebellum, and research findings are compelling. Smaller-than-average size of the prefrontal area and parts of the striatum and cerebellum has been associated with ADHD (Barkley, 2015c). Volume of the frontal, striatal, and temporal lobe region has been found to be directly related to inhibition (McAlonan et al., 2009). The prefrontal lobe and striatal area have been associated with the core symptoms of ADHD, as well as many of the neuropsychological deficits identified in ADHD—such as inhibition, working memory, and other executive functions—as well as reward and motivation (Casey et al., 1997; Semrud-Clikeman et al., 2000; Volkow et al., 2009). Recent research implicates differences in the amygdala, in particular, and hippocampus, which may contribute to difficulties in emotion regulation, motivation, and memory seen in ADHD, and provides neurobiological support for considering emotion dysregulation a core feature of the disorder (Hoogman et al., 2017). In addition, various brain scans and electrophysiological measures indicate that youth with ADHD have decreased blood flow, decreased glucose utilization, and slow brain waves—all signs of underactivity—in the frontal areas and pathways connected to the striatal areas and the cerebellum (Dickstein et al., 2006; McGrath & Peterson, 2009a). Deficits in connectivity

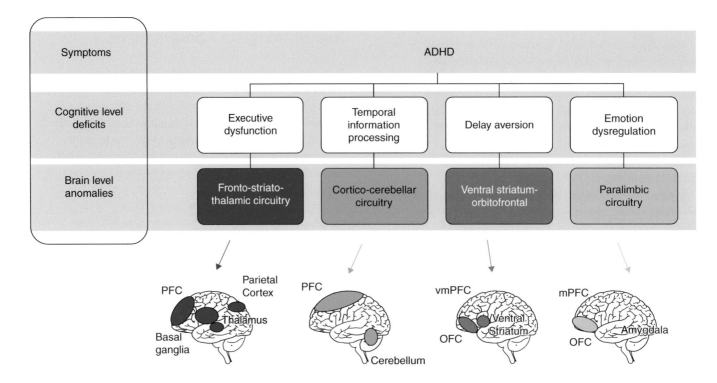

Figure 10.6 A sketch of some current neurocognitive models of ADHD and their potential relationship to neurobiological anomalies. m, medial; OFC, orbitofrontal cortex; PFC, prefrontal cortex; vm, ventromedial. (Adapted from Shaw & Szekely, 2018)

between the cerebellum and the prefrontal cortex, cingulate, and parietal regions may be implicated in deficits in temporal processing (Shaw & Szekely, 2018). Additionally, atypical neurophysiology and neuroanatomical correlates, including anomalies in white matter and prefrontal gray matter, may help explain variability in cognitive performance characteristic in ADHD (Shaw & Szekely, 2018).

A related focus of neurobiological research is the biochemistry of the brain. The best evidence implicates deficiencies in dopamine and norepinephrine. These neurotransmitter circuits have branches in the areas involving executive functions, reward, and motivation—all implicated in ADHD (Taylor & Sonuga-Barke, 2008; Volkow et al., 2009). Consistent with these findings, medications used to treat ADHD increase dopamine and norepinephrine by facilitating their release into the synapses or by blocking their reuptake by the presynaptic neurons (Aguiar et al., 2010). Nevertheless, it is likely that the interaction of several neurotransmitters is involved in ADHD, including serotonin and acetylcholine.

Several conclusions can be drawn from investigations of the brain. First, abnormalities in the frontal, striatal, and cerebellar structures and their networks appear to play an important role. Second, underarousal of the brain is implicated. Third, dopamine and norepinephrine deficiency are implicated. Fourth, other brain regions have been implicated. ADHD is undoubtedly a heterogeneous disorder with disturbances in various brain regions or networks involved. Progress has been made in understanding brain functioning but much is still to be learned.

A key issue regarding brain abnormalities in ADHD is whether they represent a deviation from typical development or a delay in maturation. The hypothesis of delayed brain maturation has received some support (Konrad, Di Martino, & Aoki, 2018). In typical development, the cortex of the brain thickens (increases in volume) throughout childhood, reaches a peak in late childhood, and thins out in adolescence. This progression occurs in primary sensory areas before higher-order association areas. A study by Shaw and colleagues (2007) has shown the same pattern in youth with ADHD, but with notable delay. In the typically developing comparison group, 50% of the cortical points reached peak thickness at the median age of 7.5 years; in the ADHD group this figure was 10.5 years. Delayed maturation was greatest in the prefrontal region. A more recent large-scale study confirms delayed brain maturation in ADHD (Hoogman et al., 2017). Research on the developmental thinning of the cortex and other alterations in brain structure in ADHD has addressed another crucial issue concerning ADHD: whether it is best viewed as categorical or dimensional (see Accent: "ADHD: Category or Dimension?").

ACCENT ADHD: Category or Dimension?

Although debate continues, the conceptualization of ADHD has shifted over the years, moving away from a categorical conceptualization to one in which ADHD is now largely considered a dimensional disorder (Mahone, 2016). While the DSM-5 criteria remain categorical in nature, much research suggests that the symptoms of ADHD, as well as the neuropsychological impairments associated with it, lie on a continuum of severity (Posner, Polancyzk, & Sonuga-Barke, 2020). In other words, rather than considering ADHD to be something an individual has or does not, the symptoms and cognitive impairments associated with ADHD are considered present in the general population with the clinical disorder lying at one extreme end of the spectrum.

Shaw and colleagues' (2011) research examining the neurobiological underpinnings of ADHD has contributed to this shift. They contrasted MRI brain images of youth, 8 years or older, diagnosed with ADHD with images from typically developing youth. All participants were evaluated for hyperactivity/impulsivity behaviors. The investigators then examined the rate of cortical thinning relative to the severity of these behaviors, or symptoms. The estimated rate of thinning was slowest for youth with ADHD, as would be expected from previous research. Tellingly, across all the participants, rate of thinning depended on the severity of symptoms, with greater severity associated with progressively

slower rates of thinning. The finding that non-diagnosed, typically developing youth exhibited brain changes similar to youth with the syndrome of ADHD lends neurobiological support to the dimensional view of ADHD.

More recent studies continue to explore categorical versus dimensional conceptualizations of ADHD by examining neurobiological alterations. For example, a recent study investigated white matter alterations in children with and without ADHD using both categorical and dimensional definitions of ADHD (Wu et al., 2017). Compared to healthy controls, children with ADHD showed a widespread pattern of altered white matter. Moreover, their findings suggest a complex picture in which alterations in brain structure were correlated with symptom severity, whereby a gradual shift in alteration was observed from healthy individuals to individuals with severe levels of inattention and hyperactivity/impulsivity. Although these studies address only aspects of the neurobiology of ADHD and do not fully resolve the debate, they present important findings and considerations. Patterns noted in these studies and others like them suggest that children diagnosed with ADHD are likely not categorically different from those who are not. Rather, subtle differences in the brain may contribute to differences in the frequency, duration, and severity of behaviors that characterize the disorder.

Etiology

Genetic Influences

Strong support for substantial genetic effects on ADHD comes from both behavioral and molecular genetic research. The families of children with ADHD have higher rates of psychopathology than would be expected, and between 10 to 35% of first-degree family members are likely to have ADHD (Barkley, 2015c). Children of parents with ADHD are also at high risk for the disorder. Family aggregation studies also suggest genetic influence on the co-occurrence of ADHD with some other disorders.

Twin studies provide clear evidence of genetic influence. Estimates of heritability are as high as .90, with heritability across studies suggested around .70 to .80 (Langley, 2018). Heritability has been documented with a variety of measures, informants, and populations. Individuals defined categorically with the diagnosis of ADHD or its subtypes have been studied, as well as individuals defined dimensionally (Goldstein, 2011). Overall, the research

suggests genetic influences on ADHD behavior operate on a continuum on which variation in heritability estimates are the same for normative populations as compared to those who meet criteria for diagnosis (Langley, 2018).

Molecular studies have increased our understanding of the etiology of ADHD. The DRD4 and the DAT1 genes—both involved with dopamine transmission—were the first to be associated with the disorder and other genes, including genes involving norepinephrine and serotonin, have been implicated (Taylor, 2009). Genome-wide association studies are being conducted and suggest that the genes identified each have only very small effects (Langley, 2018).

Genome-wide association studies have begun to compare copy number variations (CNVs) in ADHD samples and healthy controls with limited findings. One investigation showed a higher rate of rare missing or duplicated segments of DNA in children with the disorder, particularly those with lower IQ (Williams et al., 2010). (A CNV is considered rare when its population rate is less than 1%). Another study did not find increased rates, but the rare inherited CNVs that were identified involved genes important in CNS development, synaptic transmission, learning, and behavior (Elia et al., 2010). While genome-wide association studies of ADHD have been relatively limited to date, structural variations and candidate genes continue to be investigated and findings are emerging. A recent discovery, for example, from the largest internationally collaborative study of over 20,000 ADHD cases and 35,000 controls, identified 12 independent risk loci for ADHD (Demontis et al., 2019). Future research will hopefully shed more light on the molecular genetics underlying ADHD etiology.

Overall, it appears that the genetics of ADHD is far from simple. Perhaps there are no genes with large effects (Langley, 2018). Moreover, genetic heterogeneity is likely—that is, different genes or variations in a single gene, or different genetic mechanisms might contribute to the disorder. Genes may interact with each other and with other influences. In this regard, it is important to note that heritability estimates include the effects of gene–environment interaction (Franke & Buitelaar, 2018). Additionally, recent and novel research in the area of epigenetics, or the study of the influence of experience on the expression of genes, may lead to new understandings of ADHD in the coming years (Barkley, 2015c). The need for increased research in these areas is warranted.

Prenatal Influences and Birth Complications

Prenatal conditions are inconsistently associated with symptoms of ADHD or diagnosed ADHD. The discrepant findings may in part be due to methodological issues but may also be due to the complex relationship between prenatal influences and ADHD (Sciberras et al., 2017). Nonetheless, prenatal tobacco smoking, in particular, and alcohol consumption may represent important risk factors (Barkley, 2015c; Han et al., 2015; He et al., 2017). For example, a large population study conducted in Finland showed that maternal smoking was associated with hyperactivity after adjusting for several other variables (Kotimaa et al., 2003). Interestingly, mothers at high genetic risk for ADHD may also be at increased risk to engage in certain prenatal behaviors, including smoking, suggesting the association between maternal cigarette smoking during pregnancy and ADHD may be more complicated than the effect of nicotine exposure in utero alone (Barkley, 2015c; Gustavson et al., 2017; Leppert et al., 2019). Maternal alcohol use during pregnancy may also contribute to cognitive deficits and has been associated with later risk for ADHD (Eichler et al., 2018). In an extensive U.S. study that followed women from pregnancy to the time their offspring were 14 years old, prenatal alcohol use was linked to activity level, attention deficits, and difficulties in organizing tasks (Streissguth et al., 1995). Animal studies showing adverse effects of prenatal alcohol and nicotine exposure on the brains of offspring are consistent with the reduced size of brain networks reported for ADHD (Mick

et al., 2002). Neuroimaging studies in humans have also shown an association between fetal exposure to smoking and alcohol and reduced brain volume in children with ADHD (de Zeeuw et al., 2012). Research in this area is ongoing, and recent studies are expanding to better understand these complex relationships and to examine the role of paternal substance use in ADHD, as well (Biederman et al., 2017).

Some studies indicate a higher risk for ADHD among children who suffered injury at birth or were born preterm or with low birthweight (Getahun et al., 2013; Wagner et al., 2009). A study of a national cohort of children born in Sweden between 1987 and 2000 found that both moderate and especially extreme prematurity increased the risk of ADHD at school age (Lindström, Lindblad, & Hjern, 2011). The findings were not accounted for by genetic, perinatal, or socioeconomic variables, but low maternal education raised the effect of moderate prematurity. In addition, small body size and head circumference at birth were implicated in a study in which the effects appeared not accounted for by several other factors (Lahti et al., 2006). Low birthweight also is associated with risk of attention problems or ADHD. In fact, the evidence on the association between low birthweight and ADHD is striking, and research suggests it may be a strong risk factor for ADHD (Franz et al., 2018; Nigg & Song, 2018).

Diet and Lead

The possible etiological role of diet has been of interest for many years. One controversial idea was that foods containing artificial dyes, preservatives, and naturally occurring salicylates (e.g., in tomatoes and cucumbers) were related to hyperactivity. Subsequent research largely did not support the claim (Harley & Matthews, 1980; Spring, Chiodo, & Bowen, 1987). Similarly, meta-analysis of research showed that neither the behavior nor cognitive functioning of children with ADHD was affected by sugar intake (Wolraich, Wilson, & White, 1995). It is generally accepted that food does not play a strong, if any, role in causing ADHD. Nevertheless, there is some renewed interest in the hypothesis that hypersensitivity to select foods or additives may affect a subset of children with ADHD (Nigg et al., 2012; Pelsser et al., 2011).

That lead should be suspected of causing ADHD is not unreasonable because lead exposure has been linked to deficits in biological functioning, cognition, and behavior. Research has showed an association of lead exposure with diagnosed ADHD, as well as with deficits in several executive functions known to be impaired in children with ADHD (Eubig, Aguiar, & Schantz, 2010; Nigg et al., 2008). The overall influence of lead exposure on ADHD may be quite small, but it is still significant (Barkley, 2015c; Goodlad, Marcus, & Fulton, 2013; Ji et al., 2018). The toxic effects of lead, particularly its profound and permanent impact on the development of the brain and nervous system in young children, is cumulative. In other words, the range and severity of symptoms and effects on development increase with increased exposure (World Health Organization, 2018b). Prudence demands the continued protection of children from lead-based paints, toys, automobile emissions, leaded crystal and ceramic dishes, and solder on old copper pipes.

Psychosocial Influences

Few researchers and clinicians believe that psychosocial factors are a primary cause of ADHD. For one thing, genetic risk appears to account for a substantial portion of the variance of ADHD symptoms in the general population and in diagnosed ADHD (Langley, 2018). There is some evidence, however, that psychosocial factors are likely to affect the severity, continuity, and nature of the symptoms, as well as associated and co-occurring disturbances.

Family factors are among the psychosocial variables thought to be especially influential. Numerous family correlates of children's ADHD have been described, including economic disadvantage, stress, conflict and separation, and poor mental health and coping (Barkley, 2015c; Johnston & Chronis-Tuscano, 2015). In earlier studies, Nigg and Hinshaw (1998) observed that boys who had ADHD with or without antisocial behavior were more likely to have mothers with a history of depression and/or anxiety and fathers with a childhood history of ADHD. A more recent meta-analysis suggests parents of children with ADHD may be 2.85 times more likely than parents of children without ADHD to have a mental health disorder (Cheung & Theule, 2016). And, as noted earlier, research on families of children with ADHD consistently demonstrates disruptions in parent–child interactions (Johnston & Chronis-Tuscano, 2015; Theule et al., 2013). Tully and colleagues (2004), for example, examined ADHD symptoms displayed by 5-year-old twins who had been born with low birthweight; they found that maternal warmth had a moderating effect on ratings of symptoms. More recent longitudinal studies also demonstrate aspects of parenting, such as maternal sensitivity, may be predictive of ADHD (Choenni et al., 2019).

Overall, there is evidence that ADHD in children can affect parent behavior and that parent behavior can influence the nature and perhaps development of ADHD (Johnston & Chronis-Tuscano, 2015). For example, research suggests parenting practices, such as poor supervision and inconsistent discipline, may be related to greater ADHD symptomatology via their effect on child temperament (Ullsperger, Nigg, & Nikolas, 2016). It is important to note, however, that these relationships of influence are complex. Ineffective parenting styles in combination with or interaction with temperamental or behavioral aspects of the child may set the stage for more negative family processes and outcomes (Johnston & Chronis-Tuscano, 2015). Family influence, nevertheless, should be regarded cautiously, as findings have

been inconsistent, and more needs to be learned about the possible interactive influences of genetic and environmental influences. For example, a child and parent may share a genotype that readily leads to impulsive, disorganized behavior. The parent's behavior may affect the child's development of self-regulation, and the child's behavior may elicit ineffective parenting (Nigg, 2016). Moreover, the parent's and child's behavior may be influenced by other familial and social factors, such as interparental conflict, sibling interactions and relationships, and school/community factors (Johnston & Chronis-Tuscano, 2015).

Children's school behavior is important in the identification and diagnosis of ADHD. How teachers manage the behavior of their students might play a role in shaping classroom attentiveness and impulsivity (Leflot et al., 2010). In addition, classroom organization and how activities are structured can influence a child's behavior and academic achievement, perhaps especially a child predisposed to ADHD (Pfiffner & DuPaul, 2015). This does not imply that teacher behavior causes ADHD but that it may affect its manifestation and developmental course.

A Schema of the Development of ADHD

Overall, the research on ADHD has led to better understanding of genetic influences on ADHD, how brain functioning is related to the symptoms of the disorder, and how environmental influences may play some etiological role or shape and maintain the problem behaviors. It can be helpful to try to illustrate these influences in a model. Figure 10.7 presents a simple schematic representation of the development of ADHD. This schematic draws on the work of Taylor and Sonuga-Barke (2008) and is one potential way of understanding the development of ADHD. It indicates that various risk genes, possibly interacting with prenatal or perinatal influences, give rise to brain abnormalities and correlated neuropsychological impairments. As we have seen, different brain anomalies have been found in ADHD, as well as in different neuropsychological impairments. Thus, different pathways may lead to the diagnosis of ADHD. (The schema shows three hypothetical pathways.) Postnatal environmental influences play important roles in these pathways. Some secondary factors may directly affect brain processes (e.g., toxins). Other, tertiary, influences may mediate or moderate outcome by way of social interaction (e.g., negative parenting). This complex set of influences can lead not only to ADHD but also to the various disorders that commonly co-occur with ADHD.

This schema, does not, of course, include everything about the developmental course of ADHD. For example, it says nothing about the relative importance of genetic and environmental influences, nor is it very informative regarding some social, academic, and

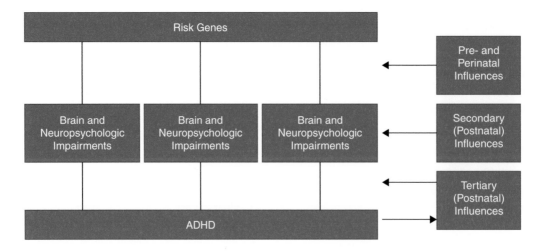

Figure 10.7 A complex interaction of genetic and environmental influences result in different pathways in the development of ADHD. (Based on Taylor & Sonuga-Barke, 2008. Copyright 2008 by John Wiley & Sons; reprinted with permission)

other functional problems that often characterize the disorder. Nevertheless, Figure 10.7 provides a basic framework for thinking about the development of ADHD.

Assessment

Whether the purpose of assessment is identification of ADHD, planning for treatment, or both, several aspects of the disorder serve as useful guidelines (Barkley, 2015g; DuPaul, Anastopoulos, & Kipperman, 2020; Hinshaw & Becker, 2020).

- Because ADHD is best conceptualized as a biopsychosocial disorder, assessment must be broad-based.
- Because ADHD is a developmental disorder, a developmental history is important and assessment will vary somewhat with developmental level.
- Because ADHD is pervasive and may manifest itself differently in different settings, information specific to the settings should be obtained.
- Because ADHD has high rates of co-occurrence with other psychological disorders, assessment requires careful distinction from other disorders.

The following discussion highlights a number of pertinent approaches to assessment.

Interviews

Perhaps the best approach to diagnosing ADHD relies on gathering comprehensive information from all available sources (DuPaul et al., 2020; Rohde et al., 2019). ADHD is most often assessed

early in life, so parents are critical in the interview process. Information needs to be obtained about the child's specific problems and impairments, strengths, developmental and medical history, academic achievement, and peer relationships (Barkley, 2015g). Questions about family stress and relationships are recommended because these are central in the child's social environment and have implications for treatment. A semi-structured interview combined with a standardized structured interview (e.g., The Diagnostic Interview for Children and Adolescents (DICA), The Schedule for Affective Disorders and Schizophrenia for School-age Children (K-SADS)) offers a reliable and efficient way to collect a wealth of information (Danckaerts & Coghill, 2018).

It is also important to assess specific parent–child interactions, not only for diagnosis but particularly for treatment planning (Barkley, 2015g; Rohde et al., 2019). It is useful to pose specific questions, directing attention to specific situations relevant to the child's problems and how they are managed. Questions may be asked about what the child does, how the parents respond, and how often problems occur in specific situations such as mealtimes, or when the child is asked to complete chores.

The youth being assessed should also be interviewed. With younger children, the interview may simply be a time for getting acquainted, establishing rapport, and observing the child's appearance, language, interpersonal skills, and the like (Barkley, 2015g). Observations must be interpreted cautiously, however, because children with ADHD may act more appropriately during office visits than they do in other settings (Danckaerts & Coghill, 2018). Discussion with older children and adolescents can include their views on their problems, school performance, peer relationships, the way they see their family functioning, and what they think would make life better, for example. Information can

Table 10.2 It Is Beneficial to Pose Interview Questions that Consider the Child's Perspective. These Examples Target the Child's School Experience

- "Do you ever find that you've been sitting in class, and all of a sudden you realize your teacher has been talking and you have no idea what she's [or he's] talking about?"
- "Does it ever seem to take you longer to get your work done compared to other kids?"
- "Do you think your work is messier than other kids' work?"
- "Do you have trouble keeping track of things you need for school?"
- "Do you have trouble finishing your homework?"
- "Does your teacher ever have to speak to you because you're talking when you're not supposed to be talking, or fooling around when you're supposed to be working?"

Source: From Barkley & Edwards, 2006. Copyright 2006 by Guilford Press; reprinted with permission.

also be gathered on other areas of functioning, including social functioning and sleep (DuPaul et al., 2020). Although the report of youth with ADHD may reflect a positive bias toward their symptoms, a private interview permits the reporting of problems or issues they may not want to discuss in the presence of parents (Pliszka et al., 2007). Interviews need to be adapted to the child's developmental status, of course, and with children it is beneficial to approach issues as they might see them (Table 10.2).

Teacher interviews can be invaluable to address difficulties in the school setting that may not be validly assessed by parents (Mitsis et al., 2000). Teachers can provide important information about learning, academic problems, and peer interaction. In addition, information can be obtained about parent–school interaction and cooperation, as well as school services. Teachers can also offer helpful information about the child's planning and organization skills and time management, important factors in their academic functioning (Danckaerts & Coghill, 2018). Some youth with ADHD have rights to special evaluation and educational services. Indeed, many of these children receive special education services under the Individuals with Disabilities Education Act, often under the categories of learning disabilities or behavior/emotional disturbance (see p. 293 for relevant discussion.) Archival information, including school and medical records, should be collected whenever possible as part of a comprehensive assessment (DuPaul et al., 2020).

Rating Scales

Parent and teacher rating scales and checklists, which are popular tools for assessing ADHD, can provide a great deal of information with relatively little time and effort. Many of the scales are reliable and valid, are consistent with the DSM conceptualization of ADHD, and can contribute to clinic and research efforts. Importantly, child behavior rating scales and checklists often permit comparison of the child's behavior to normative data (Barkley, 2015g). Some of these tools are broad in scope and identify not only ADHD but also its co-occurrence with other disorders, such as anxiety, depression, or conduct problems, or other aspects of adjustment, such as social functioning and emotion regulation (DuPaul et al., 2020). Scales with a narrower focus are useful in assessing specific aspects of ADHD.

An example of a widely employed instrument is the Conners rating scales. Based on elements of previous Conners scales, the Conners Third Edition offers parent, teacher, and self-report scales in long and abbreviated forms (Conners, 2008). The scales address both ADHD symptoms and associated disorders for ages 8 to 18 for the self-report version and 6 to 18 for the other two versions (Table 10.3). The ADHD Index is designed to rapidly identify those at risk for ADHD, and can be used to monitor the effectiveness of treatment. The Global Index, also sensitive to treatment effects, assesses general psychopathology.

Direct Observation

Direct observation in natural settings can be useful because the behavioral manifestations of ADHD are situational. Home and school observations can target behaviors for intervention and can be important for successful treatment (Jacob & Pelham, 2000). Signs of the primary features of ADHD are of utmost importance, of course, but so also are indications of noncompliance, aggression, attention-seeking, and other characteristics of social interactions and relationships. Structured classroom or home observations can be time-consuming and costly, however, and are not

Table 10.3 Conners Third Edition Scales

| Hyperactivity/impulsivity |
| Inattention |
| Learning problems |
| Executive functions |
| Aggression |
| Peer relations |
| Family relations |
| Oppositional defiant disorder |
| Conduct disorder |
| ADHD symptoms |
| ADHD index |
| Global index |

Source: From Conners, 2008.

always practical (Barkley, 2015g). Clinician observations during psychological testing procedures can provide another method of enhancing the quality of information gathered during the assessment process, and standardized observation coding systems may be useful (Achenbach, 2014; McConaughy et al., 2009).

Other Procedures

Additional assessment methods are often useful and/or necessary. Standardized tests of intelligence, academic achievement, executive functioning, and adaptive behavior can be helpful, particularly in clarifying issues pertaining to academic functioning (Danckaerts & Coghill, 2018; DuPaul et al., 2020).

Various kinds of procedures to specifically evaluate inattention and impulsivity have been developed (Gordon, Barkley, & Lovett, 2006). For example, the Conners' Continuous Performance Test III requires the client to press a computer key or click a mouse when any letter except X appears on a screen. Designed for children 8 years and over, the CPT III can be used in screening or as part of a comprehensive evaluation in the diagnosis of ADHD, as well as in monitoring treatment. The Connors' Kiddie Continuous Performance Test is an adaptation for 4- to 7-year-olds.

When medical factors are suspect, medical evaluation can provide potentially useful information for treatment or for understanding ADHD. Such assessment reasonably includes a neurological examination, but neurological tests such as the EEG and brain scans are not generally recommended for children because they do not validly distinguish ADHD and may present safety issues (Pliszka et al., 2007).

Intervention

Many treatment approaches exist for ADHD—for example, behavior-management interventions, parent training, education and training interventions, and cognitive-behavioral therapy (DuPaul et al., 2020; Evans et al., 2018b). Nevertheless, by far the most widely employed interventions—judged as evidence-based, short-term treatments—are stimulant medications, behaviorally oriented approaches, and a combination of these (American Psychological Association, 2006). Our discussion begins with pharmacological treatment.

Pharmacological Treatment

A report by Bradley in 1937 is usually cited as the first treatment of childhood behavioral disorders with **stimulant medication** (Swanson & Volkow, 2009). Many pharmacological agents have been used since then, but stimulants are the most frequently prescribed psychotropic medications for children, primarily for

ADHD. The stimulants increase dopamine and norepinephrine in the brain's neural networks. Among the most commonly used are methylphenidate and amphetamine (Table 10.4). The slow release, long-acting versions of these medications require only a daily dose and are more often used than the immediate release, short-acting versions that must be taken several times a day.

Although much controversy surrounds the use of stimulants, they are perhaps the best researched medication for ADHD (Evans et al., 2019). In the view of most professionals, stimulant medications help alleviate the primary deficits of ADHD. Approximately 65 to 75% of medicated children show improvements in core ADHD symptoms with stimulant medication (Pennington, McGrath, & Peterson, 2019). In addition, stimulants can reduce co-occurring aggressive, noncompliant, oppositional behaviors, and to a lesser extent, social problems. Perhaps not surprising, parents and teachers interact more positively with children who are benefitting from medication (Chronis et al., 2003). Some research also indicates benefits for academic performance, although the effects may be small and further investigation is needed (Kortekaas-Rijlaarsdam et al., 2019).

Most research on stimulants has been conducted with school-age children, but some studies have included preschoolers and adolescents. Although stimulant medication is generally effective in reducing ADHD symptoms in preschool children, the effects appear smaller than for school-age children and adverse side effects may be more common (American Academy of Pediatrics Subcommittee on Attention-Deficit/Hyperactivity Disorder, 2011).

Table 10.4 Some Commonly Used Medications to Treat ADHD

Stimulants (s)short acting, (l)long acting
Methlyphenidate
Ritalin (s)
Concerta (l)
Daytru (patch)
Amphetamines
Dexedrine (s)
Adderall (s)
Adderall XR (l)
Norephinephrine Reuptake Inhibitor
Atomoxetine (Strattera)
Other medications
Antidepressants
Bupropion
Tricyclics (Imipramine, Desipramine)
Antihypertensives
Clondine
Guanfacine (Intuniv)

ACCENT Medication Does Not Always Work

For a variety of reasons, medication is not a preferred or effective treatment for some youth and families, as the following indicates:

- For a small number of children, biological side effects are not tolerated (Briars & Todd, 2016; Johnson et al., 2020).
- Research shows that the primary symptoms of ADHD are not alleviated in 10 to 20% of children (Anastopoulos et al., 2006) and perhaps a larger percentage of preschoolers.
- Even when symptoms are alleviated, in only about 50% of cases is behavior improved so as to be comparable to that of typical children.

- Improvement dissipates when these drugs are no longer taken, and long-term effects have not been well documented (Posner et al., 2020).
- More than one-third of children do not adhere to treatment regimens (Kamimura-Nishimura, Brinkman, & Froelich, 2019); more than half of patients with ADHD discontinue treatment regardless of its efficacy (Pappadopulos et al., 2009). Parents may not always be aware of their child's non-adherence.
- Medication is simply rejected by some families (Vitiello et al., 2001). Limited data show that African American families especially may be unenthusiastic about pharmacological treatment (Miller et al., 2009).

Stimulants also benefit adolescents, although the response rate may be somewhat less than for children (Sibley et al., 2014). Overall, an impressive amount of data supports the claim for the effectiveness of stimulants across settings, measures, and ages. Nevertheless, stimulants do not work well for all youth and families, a fact that often goes unacknowledged. (See Accent: "Medication Does Not Always Work.") In addition, several concerns are expressed regarding pharmacological treatment of ADHD.

Concerns

An often-expressed concern is adverse biological side effects, which may affect preschoolers more than older children (Evans et al., 2019; Wolraich et al., 2019). Sleep problems, decreased appetite, stomach pain, headaches, irritability, and nervousness have all been reported (Coghill, Chen, & Silva, 2019). The effects are often mild to moderate and may diminish on their own or can be managed with dose adjustments or changes in the timing of medication intake (Connor, 2015). Nevertheless, side effects can lead to discontinuance of treatment. Also reported is a small suppression of growth in height and weight (Connor, 2015). A recent longitudinal analysis, for example, demonstrated that long-term consistent stimulant treatment in children with ADHD (i.e., 16 years of consistent use from childhood to adulthood) is associated with changes in height trajectory, reduction of adult height, and increase in weight and body mass index (Greenhill et al., 2020). An initiation or worsening of motor and vocal tics also has been reported but the finding has been challenged (Gadow et al., 2007; Pliszka et al., 2007).

There is also continuing concern that stimulant use in childhood is a risk factor for later substance use/abuse. Several investigations have confirmed that children with ADHD are at

significant risk for developing use/abuse for nicotine, alcohol, marijuana, cocaine, and other drugs (Charach et al., 2011; Lee et al., 2011). However, meta-analytic research suggests comparable substance use/abuse outcomes for children with ADHD treated with medication and those with ADHD not treated with stimulants (Humphreys, Eng, & Lee, 2013). Existing research suggests risk for substance abuse is related to ADHD itself and not to the treatment of the disorder (Connor, 2015). Numerous factors are likely involved. For example, shared genetic influence may underlie risk for both ADHD symptoms and substance abuse, and the comorbidity of ADHD and externalizing disorders may play a role (Brook et al., 2010; Wilens, 2011). Nonetheless, a related issue that warrants a watchful eye is the abuse of the stimulants themselves. In this regard, it is recommended that stimulants not be prescribed if there is any known or suspected drug use (Zuddas et al., 2018).

Despite the legitimate concerns about medication treatment, when stimulants are prescribed and used appropriately, they are considered relatively safe for most young people. This does not mean, of course, that the need for monitoring should be taken lightly. Individuals vary in their responses to different medications and to different dosages. Indeed, warnings exist, for example, about the use of Adderall XR in youth with underlying heart defects. Nonstimulant medications may be options for some children, but these also have side effects (Connor, 2015). Monitoring is always essential and reasonable caution always appropriate.

Even so, critics have argued that medication is too readily prescribed. This argument is supported by a rise in prescriptions from the 1980s through the 2000s, with a fourfold increase among children from 1987 to 1996 (Zuvekas, Vitiello, & Norquist, 2006).

Medication use leveled off between 2000 and 2007 among children 0–14 years of age, but increased in adolescents and young adults (Swanson & Volkow, 2009). Recent analyses suggest an overall upward trend in prevalence of ADHD medication use among young people (Girand, Litkowiec, & Sohn, 2020; Hales et al., 2018). Some critics argue that medication serves as a "quick fix" for some schools and parents. In this regard, it is interesting that some research shows differences in medication use across countries and greater use of stimulants in the United States, although increased ADHD medication use has been noted in several European countries as well (Bachmann et al., 2017). Several related factors are likely to explain such differences: cultural beliefs about behavioral disturbances and pharmacological intervention, government policies, advertising by pharmaceutical companies, and the like.

The issue of medication treatment is complex. For example, research suggests that combining even low-intensity behavioral treatment with stimulants may allow for lower dosage of medication—and thus fewer side effects (Fabiano et al., 2007). More general is the issue of inappropriate prescription practices. Reich and colleagues (2006) found that 59% of boys and 46% of girls who met the criteria for ADHD received medication, whereas 35% receiving stimulant medication did not meet the diagnostic criteria, although they had symptoms of ADHD. Yet another investigation, which showed increased use of anti-psychotic medications in 2- to 5-year-olds, found that almost one-fourth of the cases were of ADHD, and that most of the children had not received an assessment, a psychotherapy visit, or a visit with a psychiatrist during the year examined (Olfson et al., 2010).

Concern about the use and misuse of medication for ADHD has at times led to heated controversy, fed by media coverage in major magazines and on television. Media attention that serves to educate is beneficial, of course. Unfortunately, concerns about medications have sometimes been expressed in emotionally charged, exaggerated—and perhaps harmful—ways by parents, professionals, and organized groups (Barkley, 1998; Swanson et al., 1995). At the same time, professionals who recognize the benefits of stimulants also point to their limitations and warn against their misuse or overuse. Increased education for patients and their providers may help address issues of stimulant misuse (Colaneri, Keim, & Adesman, 2018). An additional consideration in the overall picture is the potential conflict of interest inherent in the participation of large pharmaceutical companies in clinical trials evaluating the effectiveness of medications, as well as the considerable marketing and advertising of medications, particularly to prescribing physicians (Parikh, Fleischman, & Agrawal, 2016).

Behaviorally Oriented Treatment

The substantial benefits of behaviorally oriented interventions for children and adolescents with ADHD have been shown in a variety of research designs (Caye et al. 2019; Evans et al., 2018b). The usual behavioral strategies are employed to target the primary symptoms of ADHD and to improve functional domains such as social relationships. Most interventions are conducted in the home or school, with parents or teachers working directly with the child. In addition, parent training programs are offered to optimize parents' management of their child with ADHD.

Parent Training (PT)

In general, parent involvement in treatment for youth disorders is beneficial (Dowell & Ogles, 2010). Parent training is an important aspect in treating ADHD. The disorder takes a toll on the parent–child relationship, parents tend to become overly directive, and some may view themselves as lacking the normal skills of parenting (Anastopoulos, Smith, & Wien, 1998). These facts coupled with the obvious influence that parents have on their offsprings' behavior make families a natural focus of intervention. Still, PT may not always be appropriate (Barkley, 2013). Although PT is considered an important treatment for a wide range of ages, it is most suitable for preschool- to school-age youth, and for families in which ADHD appears as a basis of family difficulty (Chacko et al., 2015). PT may not be suitable when parents are experiencing excessively high levels of stress due to interparental conflicts or other circumstances.

Although PT programs vary somewhat, they share the goal of teaching child management techniques (Chacko et al., 2015). As an example, we briefly examine an intervention that emphasizes the management of the noncompliant and defiant behavior that often accompanies ADHD in children between 2 and 12 years of age. This focus is consistent with the view that ADHD involves a deficit in behavioral inhibition and risk for conduct disturbances. Appropriate parental management of child behavior is viewed as bringing the child's behavior under increased parental control, facilitating the child's awareness of behavioral consequences, preventing the development of comorbid conditions, and alleviating parental stress.

The treatment program consists of ten core components that can be covered in weekly sessions with an individual family or groups of families. As Table 10.5 indicates, in addition to training in behavioral management, the sessions include information to increase understanding of child behavior, discussion of special and future problems, consideration of the child's school situation, and a booster session for review and troubleshooting.

In families in which a young child's behavior is oppositional and disruptive, PT can improve parenting skills and child behavior and, to a lesser extent, reduce ADHD symptoms (American Psychological Association, 2006). However, it may not be appropriate under circumstances of co-occurring ODD in adolescents or high levels of parent–youth conflict (Barkley, 2018a). Nevertheless, PT appears to be one of the most validated treatments for young children with ADHD (DuPaul et al., 2018).

Classroom Management

Teachers' behavioral management is an important aspect of student engagement and behavior (Gage et al., 2017; Spilt et al., 2016), and there is extensive support for the efficacy of school-based behavioral intervention in the treatment of ADHD (Evans et al., 2019). School-based intervention is effective in addressing inattention, disruptive behavior, and academic performance in children with ADHD, and recent research also shows a positive impact of school-based interventions on aspects of executive functioning, including organizational behavior (Pfiffner et al., 2018). Universal strategies often include teachers' use of praise and differential reinforcement, effective delivery of instructions, implementation of classroom rules, routines and structure, and

appropriate response to violation of classroom expectations (Evans et al., 2019). Targeted interventions commonly include teacher administration of contingency management interventions with training and consultation from a mental health specialist (Pfiffner & DuPaul, 2015). Functional assessment to carefully identify which problematic behaviors to target can be helpful. Procedures usually include token reinforcement, time out, and response cost. Contingency contracting, in which the child and the teacher sign a written agreement specifying how the child will behave and the contingencies that will accrue, can be helpful (Axelrod, 2017; Perkins & McLaughlin, 2015). Figure 10.8 provides an example. Often essential is a daily report card sent to parents that reflects the child's performance regarding targeted behaviors. The report card serves as feedback to the child, informs parents so that they can reward the child for progress, and promotes communication between the teacher and the parents. (See Accent: "The **Summer**

Table 10.5 Steps in a Parent Training Intervention as Described by Barkley

Step 1:	**Why Children Misbehave**
	Provides an overview of the typical causes of child misbehavior and what parents can do to begin identifying these causes in their own children and families.
Step 2:	**Pay Attention!**
	Provides parent training in methods of attending to and appreciating (e.g., praising) positive child behavior while differentially ignoring negative behavior.
Step 3:	**Increasing Compliance and Independent Play**
	Teaches parents effective ways to deliver commands to elicit child compliance and effective attending and monitoring skills to increase independent, nondisruptive child behavior.
Step 4:	**When Praise Is Not Enough: Poker Chips and Points**
	Establishes a formal system to reinforce child compliance and appropriate child behavior.
Step 5:	**Time Out and Other Disciplinary Methods**
	Introduces the use of effective time out methods and use of fines in the home token system as punishment for select child misbehavior.
Step 6:	**Extending Time Out to Other Misbehavior**
	Extends the use of time out to other select child misbehavior and troubleshoots and resolves problems parents are encountering in using these methods with their child.
Step 7:	**Anticipating Problems: Managing Children in Public Places**
	Trains parents in reducing misbehavior of children in public places, such as the grocery store or church.
Step 8:	**Improving School Behavior from Home: The Daily School Behavior Report Card (Optional)**
	Provides instruction on implementing a daily school behavior report card to increase opportunities to reinforce better child behavior in the classroom.
Step 9:	**Handling Future Behavior Problems**
	Encourages parents to think about how they might address possible future behavior problems and prepares parents for termination of therapy if appropriate.
Step 10:	**Booster Session and Follow-Up Meetings**
	Reviews methods learned and provides opportunity for problem solving and discussion of additional or adjunctive treatment, such as pharmacological intervention, if appropriate.

Source: Adapted from Barkley, 2013.

School Contract Between Mr. McQuade and Roger

When signed, this contract represents an agreement between Mr. McQuade, 4th grade teacher, and Roger, 4th grade student. This contract begins Monday October 1st and ends Friday October 5th.

The contract states:

Roger will:

- Turn in all math homework assignments during the week
- Turn in assignments by 8:25am each morning
- Attempt all assigned problems
- Complete all assignments with 90% accuracy

Mr. McQuade will:

- Record, on this contract, all completed assignments turned in on time and with 90% accuracy
- Reward Roger with 30 minutes of extra recess time Friday at 2:00pm if all boxes below are checked
- Allow Roger to choose two friends to join him in the extra recess time

Signatures

Roger: **Date:**

Mr. McQuade: **Date:**

Record of completed assignments:

Day	Monday	Tuesday	Wednesday	Thursday	Friday
Assignment completed					

Figure 10.8 A hypothetical child–teacher contingency contract. (From Axelrod, 2017. Reprinted with permission.)

Treatment Program (STP)" for an intervention using many of these behavioral techniques to strengthen functional outcomes.)

There is some evidence that children with different presentations of ADHD might profit from different kinds of teacher strategies tailored to meet specific needs (Pfiffner & DuPaul, 2015). For example, those with ADHD-PI might especially benefit from interventions that accommodate a slow work style. However, the targeting of behaviors on an individual basis is a key to success. Effective targeting should include the following considerations:

- Skills and behaviors that replace specific problems should be emphasized. A child with organizational problems needs to be taught how to manage desk and locker space, while a child with social deficits needs to learn appropriate interaction.
- Although on-task performance is important, broader academic performance goals need to be targeted. Amount of work completed is an important element for achievement. Young children need to strengthen basic skills (reading, writing, arithmetic) so they will not fall behind, while older students need help in additional academic areas.

- Behaviors occurring in situations that commonly cause difficulties need to be targeted—for example, behaviors required during recess and transitions between classes or activities.

Although behavioral interventions have typically focused on managing behavior through contingency-based principles, the structure and organization of both the classroom and learning tasks may be important to children with ADHD (Pfiffner & DuPaul, 2015). Classrooms that are well organized and predictable may be especially helpful for children with ADHD. Placing the child's desk away from other children and near the teacher can reduce peer reinforcement of inappropriate behavior and also facilitate teacher monitoring and feedback. Regarding learning tasks, there are several useful strategies. Among these are increasing stimulation within the task—for example, by the use of color, shape, or audio recordings—keeping the length of the task within the child's attention span, and varying the format and materials. There is evidence that allowing the child some task-related choice facilitates work productivity, and that computer-assisted instruction (which often includes clear rules, segmented tasks, and swift feedback) increases attention and work productivity. While many of these strategies are generally

ACCENT The Summer Treatment Program (STP)

Many professionals now view ADHD as a chronic disorder that usually requires comprehensive treatment over long periods of time. This view underlies the Summer Treatment Program developed by Pelham and colleagues (Fabiano, Schatz, & Pelham, 2014; Pelham et al., 2017). The program is an intensive social learning intervention that targets the functional impairments of ADHD rather than its primary symptoms. The reason for this focus is that functional behaviors are related to the outcome of ADHD. Available for youth ages 5 to 15, the program operates in a camp-like setting, typically for seven to eight weeks on weekdays. The goals are to improve (1) peer relationships (social skills, problem solving), (2) adult relationships (compliance), (3) academic performance, and (4) self-efficacy.

The participants are placed in small age-matched groups overseen by college student interns. The group serves as a natural backdrop for intensive work on peer and adult relationships. Social skills training is provided in brief daily sessions that include modeling and role playing, and there is opportunity for group problem solving. Appropriate social skills are continually prompted and reinforced with a point reward system.

Each day, the groups spend about three hours in classroom sessions conducted by teachers and aides. It is recognized not only that children with ADHD have academic problems but also that summer months without academic learning put even typically developing youth at risk for losing academic ground. About two hours of classroom time are devoted to individualized assignments in academic areas, cooperative reading with another student, and individualized computer-based skill building. The third hour is devoted to individual and group art projects. The latter provides the opportunity for cooperative peer interaction and the less structured activities can build skills for the transfer to regular school settings in which ADHD students often have difficulties.

The remainder of each day is given to leisure activities in group play and sports. Children with ADHD frequently have poor motor skills and fail to follow game rules, which can contribute to peer rejection and low self-esteem. The STP children receive intensive skill training and coaching. Although the skills are valued in themselves, sport competence also is valued because it is thought to enhance self-efficacy and behavior change.

The STP emphasizes behavioral approaches, and staff members are highly trained to record a child's behavior and respond appropriately. Parents have daily contact with staff members, participate in a daily report card component, and attend weekly training sessions designed to implement at home the behavioral techniques employed in the program. Opportunity also exists for evaluating the need and use of medication. When children return to school in the autumn, monthly parent training is offered, and teachers are aided in establishing a report card system.

Research on the nature and treatment of ADHD is an important component of the STP. The program has been manualized and adopted at many community and university sites. Evaluations at multiple sites document low dropout rates, high parent satisfaction, and improved participant behavior, primarily functional behavior.

Children in the STP receive skill training and coaching to enhance development. (FatCamera/iStock)

The well-being of children with ADHD is undoubtedly influenced by teachers' skills in organizing and managing classroom activities and behavior. (Radius Images/Alamy Stock Photo)

advantageous, they may be of critical help to students with ADHD. There is, however, a need for further research in this area.

Teachers are crucial, of course, in influencing the learning environment of the classroom and in implementing behavioral programs. A considerable amount of teachers' time and energy is required to effectively manage children with disabilities, as well as to collaborate with parents, administrators, and other professionals. Teachers generally appear to favor positive over negative contingencies, behavioral plus medication over medication-only approaches, and time-efficient (e.g., daily report cards) over time-consuming (e.g., response cost) techniques (Pfiffner & DuPaul, 2015; Pisecco, Huzinec & Curtis, 2001). In general, teacher knowledge, beliefs, attitudes, flexibility, tolerance for the disruptions common in ADHD, and interactional style may be important variables regarding the success of classroom-based programs (Merrell & Sayal, 2018).

Multimodal Treatment

As we have seen, the limitation and criticism of medication treatment has continued to raise questions about its use for ADHD. At the same time, behavioral methods often require much effort, time, and expense. This situation has resulted in the implementation and evaluation of multimodal treatments that combine the two approaches (Swanson et al., 2018).

The MTA Study
The **Multimodal Treatment Assessment Study (MTA)** is the largest long-term evaluation of treatment options. This six-center

investigation was initiated by the National Institutes of Mental Health. Close to 600 children with ADHD-C, ages 7 to 9 years, were randomly assigned to one of four treatment conditions lasting for 14 months (MTA Cooperative Group, 1999a). The treatments were as follows:

- *Medication Treatment.* Children received medication, mostly methylphenidate, with dosage carefully assigned, monitored, and adjusted at monthly sessions with the child and parents. Teacher input was available for these sessions, and medication was given for the entire time period.
- *Behavioral Treatment.* The intensive program consisted of PT sessions, school-based intervention, and a child-focused summer camp experience. Training gradually leveled off and by the end of the treatment period parents were seen monthly or not at all.
- *Combined Treatment.* The medication and behavioral treatments were integrated.
- *Community Care Treatment.* Children in this comparison group received various routine treatments in their communities. As it turned out, 67% were on medication, with dosage levels lower than for the medication treatment group. The children were seen only once or twice by a physician, and there was no teacher contact for feedback.

Initial evaluations of the MTA study were conducted before, during, and at the end of treatment. Numerous measures were taken of core ADHD symptoms, associated problems, and family factors. Core ADHD symptoms were reduced in all groups over the

14-month treatment, but the amount of improvement varied with the type of treatment (MTA Cooperative Group, 1999a, 1999b). Overall, the medication and combined treatments were superior to behavioral and community care treatments, and did not differ from each other. However, the findings were numerous and complex. For example, for several measures the combined treatment had the greatest effect, including parent ratings of externalizing and internalizing symptoms and measures of reading achievement (MTA Cooperative Group, 1999a). In addition, for children with comorbid ADHD and anxiety, behavioral treatment was as effective as the medication or the combined treatment. Moreover, social class moderated some of the outcomes (Rieppi et al., 2002). Families with more education benefitted the most from the combined treatment, but this was not so for families with less education.

Posttreatment Follow-Ups Several posttreatment evaluations have examined the persistence of effects of the four treatments on select measures. At 24 months after the initiation of intervention, children who had been in the medication or combined treatments still showed improvement compared with the other children regarding ADHD and oppositional defiant symptoms, but not some other problems (MTA Cooperative Group, 2004a, 2004b). But the positive effects were about 50% weaker than they had been at the end of treatment.

Subsequent follow-ups (at 36, 72, and 96 months) indicated no significant group differences on several ADHD symptom and functional scores (Jensen et al., 2007; Molina et al., 2009). Figure 10.9 shows the results for parent ratings of three symptom domains from the beginning of treatment. Included are ratings for a later-added comparison group of children. As can be seen, all of

the MTA groups showed some improvement over time. Nevertheless, at the 96-month evaluation, 30% were diagnosed with ADHD, most commonly with what would now be termed ADHD-PI. And the MTA participants performed relatively poorly compared to the normal comparison group on numerous measures. For example, they were doing less well in school, had relatively high rates of arrest and delinquency, and a greater number met the DSM criteria for ODD or CD (Molina et al., 2009). A 16-year follow-up study gives some insight into how those children who participated in the MTA study function as young adults in multiple domains, including educational, occupational, legal, emotional, substance use disorder, and sexual behavior outcomes (Hechtman et al., 2016). The results, in summary, suggest that impairments in functioning were generally worse when ADHD symptoms persisted, again highlighting the importance of early and sustained treatment.

It is perhaps unsurprising, however, that the early benefits of medication and combined treatments were not maintained for a longer period of time. Children and families were treated for a relatively short period, and at the termination of treatment had been on their own to make decisions about various intervention options. The effects of medication are not sustained when medication is discontinued, and previous research had suggested only short-term effects of behavioral and combined treatments. The MTA study clearly suggests that intervention for ADHD should be sustained over time.

While the MTA study led to substantial advances in our understanding of the trajectory and efficacy of ADHD intervention with children and adolescents, there is a need for continued development and evaluation of effective treatments. Attending

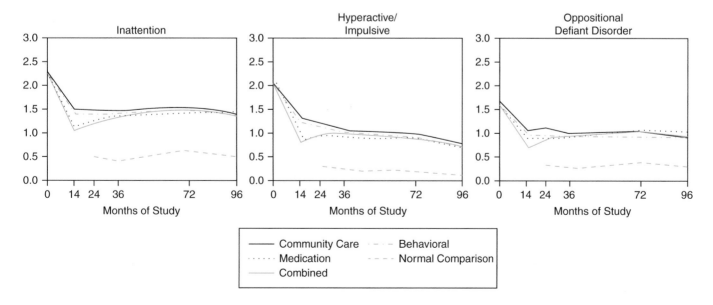

Figure 10.9 Mean scores (parent ratings) on three symptom domains across months, the MTA study. (From Molina et al., 2009. Copyright 2009 by Elsevier; reprinted with permission)

to barriers to intervention, cultural and contextual factors, and coordination across systems of care (e.g., mental health, schools, primary care) seems important (DuPaul et al., 2020; Evans et al., 2019). Primary care providers, for example, often play a role in providing services to children and adolescents with ADHD, and the American Academy of Pediatrics has issued treatment recommendations, which vary depending on the young person's age (American Academy of Pediatrics Subcommittee on Attention-Deficit/Hyperactivity Disorder, 2011). Overall, they recommend initiating treatment with behavioral interventions for preschool-age children (i.e., 4–5 years of age), using a combined or separate approach with school-age children (i.e., 6–11 years of age) that includes pharmacological treatment and/or behavior intervention, and pharmacological treatment and preferably behavior therapy for adolescents (i.e., ages 12–18 years). It is probably fair to say, however, that practitioners take various stances with regard to intervention. Medication is widely employed but is not given first preference by every professional and every family (Leslie et al., 2007). Many mental health professionals believe that a combination of medication and behaviorally oriented treatments is the best approach for a disorder that is as multidimensional as ADHD and carries considerable risk for comorbid disorders. Overall, progress has been made in treating ADHD. An increased number of medications provides options for the child or adolescent, behavioral intervention has been improved, and research results offer some guidance for treatment. At the same time, there is room for considerable improvement regarding medication prescription, sequencing of treatment, follow-up visits, discontinuance of

treatment, poor outcome, and youth transitioning to adulthood (Evans et al., 2019).

Prevention

It is reasonable to assume that prenatal care, avoidance of environmental toxins, and optimal family life might help prevent or minimize ADHD. Nevertheless, the most effective efforts are likely to be directed at both early treatment of symptoms and reduction of secondary problems that interfere with healthy development. As we have seen, the core symptoms of ADHD not only have immediate impact, but may also set into motion an array of functional problems that continue even after core symptoms lessen. It is important that these functional impairments be considered (Merrill et al., 2019).

For example, academic tutoring may avert the school problems many children with ADHD experience. Another example is training parents to manage their child with disruptive behaviors in order to prevent further development of noncompliant or oppositional child behaviors, which could put the child at risk for ODD and CD (Chacko et al., 2015). Efforts to facilitate appropriate social interaction might also be important because the negative social behaviors often observed in ADHD can be long lasting and affect other areas of functioning. In addition, monitoring the child's behavior for drug use/abuse and interventions aimed at interfering with this developmental path are important (Charach et al., 2011; Wilens, 2011). Early detection and intervention may help mitigate the risks of ADHD and its associated difficulties (Schoenfelder & Kollins, 2015).

Looking Back

Evolving Ideas about ADHD

- Accounts of ADHD have shifted over time regarding symptoms and their conceptualization. Two dimensions are now recognized as valid: inattention and hyperactivity-impulsivity.

DSM Classification and Diagnosis

- The DSM recognizes three presentations of ADHD: Predominantly Inattentive, Predominantly Hyperactive/Impulsive, and Combined.
- Diagnosis demands the presence of symptoms for at least six months by age 12 and impairment in at least two settings.

Description: Primary Features

- The core problems of inattention, hyperactivity, and impulsivity are described by parents and teachers and demonstrated with various laboratory instruments.

Description: Associated Features

- As a group, youth with ADHD display several secondary difficulties, among which are motor problems, somewhat lowered intelligence, academic failure, adaptive behavior deficits, social and conduct problems, and accident risk.

DSM Presentations

- Many differences and similarities exist between ADHD-PI and ADHD-C, and less is known about ADHD-PHI. Several dissatisfactions are voiced about these groupings.

Co-occurring Disorders

- ADHD co-occurs at high rates with learning disorders, externalizing disorders, and internalizing disorders.

Epidemiology

- About 5–9% of school-age children are estimated to have ADHD, with rates at the higher end more likely. Boys are diagnosed more frequently than girls, who display more inattention and less hyperactivity/impulsivity. Rates appear somewhat higher in children of lower social class, and ethnic/racial differences exist.

Developmental Course

- Hyperactivity and impulsivity are observed in preschoolers and a minority of these children continues to have problems into childhood.
- For some children, the primary features of childhood ADHD continue into adolescence and to a lesser degree into adulthood. Core features appear to weaken over time, but secondary difficulties are apparent. Continuity of problems is linked to several variables.

Neuropsychological Theories of ADHD

- Neuropsychological theories of ADHD emphasize various abnormalities, such as executive dysfunctions, unusual sensitivity to reinforcement, temporal processing deficits, and aversion to delay.
- Barkley's model proposes that deficits in behavioral inhibition interfere with other executive functions and self-regulatory abilities to produce impairment in the regulation of behavior. There is evidence for multiple pathways to ADHD.

Neurobiological Abnormalities

- Evidence exists for structural and functional abnormalities of the brain. Several regions are implicated, especially frontal-striatal-cerebellar networks. There is evidence for underactivity of the brain, and dopamine and norepinephrine are implicated. Delayed maturation of the brain may also underlie ADHD.

Etiology

- Substantial genetic transmission of ADHD is indicated by family and twin studies. Several genes have been identified. Genetic influence appears complex, probably involving many genes with small effects and genetic heterogeneity.
- There is some evidence for adverse effects of prenatal alcohol and tobacco use and low birthweight. Diet is unlikely to be an important causal factor. Exposure to lead is a small, but significant, factor in some cases.
- The psychosocial environment plays a role in shaping and maintaining ADHD behaviors. Both family factors and teacher behavior are important considerations.

A Schema of the Development of ADHD

- The development of ADHD can be depicted as following different pathways consisting of genetic risk, perhaps interacting with pre- or perinatal influences to produce brain and neuropsychological impairments that are influenced by additional postnatal factors.

Assessment

- The identification of ADHD requires broad-based assessment that takes into account developmental level, various settings, and co-occurrence with other disorders.
- A comprehensive assessment includes interviews with the youth, parents, and teachers; the administration of standardized rating scales; direct observation; intelligence and achievement testing; and consideration of medical and social factors.

Intervention

- Primary prevention of ADHD includes prenatal care and avoidance of environmental toxins. Important in prevention are early efforts to minimize core and secondary functional problems.
- There is substantial evidence that stimulant medication can relieve core and perhaps some secondary symptoms of ADHD for many youth. However, there are numerous concerns and limitations regarding medication use.
- Behaviorally oriented interventions, including parent training and school-based interventions, are evidence-based treatments for ADHD.
- The MTA study, the largest multimodal, long-term comparison of treatments, revealed initial but waning benefits for medication and medication plus behavioral treatments.
- Many researchers and professionals believe that multimodal treatment of the various aspects of ADHD is most appropriate.

Key Terms

CHAPTER 11
Communication and Learning Disorders

Looking Forward

After reading this chapter, you should be able to discuss:

- Historical definitions of communication and learning disorders
- Normal language development and communication disorders
- Specific impairments in reading, written expression, and mathematics

- Social and motivational problems concerning communication and learning disorders
- Brain abnormalities in communication and learning disorders
- Etiology of communication and learning disorders
- Assessment and intervention for communication and learning disorders
- Educational services

Specific problems that arise in the development of language and learning are discussed in this chapter. These disabilities can vary from subtle to severe, interfere with the innumerable daily needs and pleasures of communication, cast a shadow of failure and frustration over the school years, and adversely affect adult occupational life. Indeed, it can be argued that communication and learning disorders have had increasing impact on individual lives because of escalating demands for certain kinds of skills and learning in our industrial and technologically sophisticated world.

Child and adolescent difficulties in language and learning are associated with many known medical, genetic, and behavioral syndromes. Such conditions are not, however, the focus of this chapter. Rather, our primary interest is in young people who display specific impairments that are out of keeping with other aspects of their development. It is assumed that disturbance occurs relatively early and is not readily explained by social factors.

Professionals from diverse disciplines have been interested in communication and learning problems—notably educators, psychologists, physicians, and language specialists. Approaching their work from different perspectives, they have generated diverse, albeit often overlapping, terminology, definitions, emphases, causal theories, and treatments. This rich history is reflected throughout the present chapter.

A Bit of History: Unexpected Disabilities, Unmet Needs

Specific language and learning problems have been recognized for a long time. Two major themes have left a strong mark on the field (Fletcher et al., 2019). One is scientific and clinical interest in understanding individuals who display specific deficits that appear discrepant with their intelligence or other abilities. The other, more applied, theme is an emphasis on the need to improve services to young people exhibiting such deficits.

Curiosity about discrepant, or unexpected, lack of abilities within individuals can be traced to work in Europe in the 1800s. Consider as an early example the description of the 10-year-old boy, Thomas, that follows. Despite the boy's successes, it was reported that he was unable to learn to read. Many similarly puzzling cases were presented by physicians, and the field developed an early medical orientation that linked specific impairments with brain abnormalities (Decker, Bridges, & Vetter, 2018). For example, in the latter 1880s, Broca described the inability of his adult patients to express themselves verbally while maintaining the capacity to comprehend what others said. Soon after, Wernicke documented brain lesions in patients who had problems in understanding language but otherwise did not exhibit

THOMAS So Many Abilities

He was apparently a bright and in every respect an intelligent boy. He had been learning music for a year and had made good progress in it. ... In all departments of his studies where the instruction was oral he had made good progress, showing that his auditory memory was good. ... He performs simple sums quite correctly, and his progress in arithmetic has been regarded as quite satisfactory. He has no difficulty in learning to write. His visual acuity is good.

Hinshelwood, 1917, pp. 46–47

language and cognitive impairment. Each of these men traced the specific disability to an area in the brain that now carries his name. Over many years, behavioral symptoms such as specific speech problems, learning difficulties, and inattention were linked to brain damage in adults (Hammill, 1993). Such developmental problems in youth were similarly hypothesized to be caused by brain injury or brain dysfunction of some sort, perhaps too subtle to be identified.

Behavioral scientists in the United States, building on the European work, began to contribute a psychological orientation to the study of learning problems (Hallahan & Mock, 2003). Although brain dysfunction was often assumed, etiology was downplayed in favor of understanding the characteristics of learners and the educational remediation of learning deficits (Lyon et al., 2003). By the mid-1900s, several kinds of interventions were recommended. Nevertheless, concern was growing that a group of children had educational needs that were not being met by the schools.

In 1963, representatives from several organizations met at a symposium sponsored by the Fund for Perceptually Handicapped Children. In his address to the participants, Samuel Kirk, a well-respected psychologist, noted that the children of their concern exhibited a variety of deficiencies that were presumed to be related to neurological dysfunction—especially learning difficulties, perceptual problems, and hyperactivity. Kirk suggested and defined "learning disabilities" as a suitable term that he believed could encourage and guide the assessment and educational intervention so needed by these children. That evening the conferees organized into what is today called the Learning Disabilities Association of America (Pullen, 2016).

Kirk's presentation is recognized as a milestone in the emergence of the concept of learning disabilities (Alfonso & Flanagan, 2018). Parents and educators henceforth played an important role in an area previously dominated by physicians and psychologists (Lewandowski & Lovett, 2014). Parents were given hope that their children's problems were limited and treatable; teachers were relieved of the suspicion that they were to blame for student failure; concerned professionals were provided a term that could make children eligible for special services. It was recognized that youth labeled as "learning disabled" constituted a heterogeneous group.

By the late twentieth century, efforts were made to reach consensus on the definitions of learning disabilities, provide special education services, and conduct research into these disabilities. The last few decades have seen progress, and the number of youth categorized as having a learning disability has dramatically increased. Nonetheless, challenges remain regarding the definition and conceptualization of specific communication and learning disabilities, as well as related issues.

Definitional Concerns

To understand the problems of definition we turn to the **Education for All Handicapped Children Act of 1975** (Public Law 94–142), which has had enormous influence on the field of communication and learning disorders or disabilities. A sweeping educational mandate, it has been amended several times over the years and retitled the **Individuals with Disabilities Education Act (IDEA)**. Throughout the amendments, it has maintained its original intent to identify children with learning disabilities and ensure they receive free and appropriate public education (FAPE) (Grigorenko et al., 2020; Sotelo-Dynega, Flanagan, & Alfonso, 2018). Table 11.1 highlights the most important changes to this legislation. The IDEA's definition of learning disability has had a tremendous impact on the educational system, children and families, clinicians and researchers.

Specific learning disability means a disorder in one or more of the basic psychological processes involved in understanding or in using language, spoken or written, in which the disorder may manifest itself in an imperfect ability to listen, think, speak, read, write, spell, or to do mathematical calculations. The term includes such conditions as perceptual handicaps, brain injury, minimal brain dysfunction, dyslexia, and developmental aphasia. The term does not include children who have learning problems which are primarily the result of visual, hearing, or motor handicaps, or mental retardation, or emotional disturbance, or of environmental, cultural, or economic disadvantage.

U.S. Office of Education, 1977, p. 65083

Table 11.1 Important Changes in Special Education Law from 1975 to 2004

1975	Education for All Handicapped Children Act (EHA; P.L. 94–142)	Guaranteed school-age (5–21 years) children with disabilities the right to free and appropriate public education (FAPE).
1986	EHA (P.L. 99–457)	Extended the purpose of EHA to include children from birth to age 5 years. FAPE was mandated for children ages 3–21 years. States were encouraged to develop early-intervention programs for children with disabilities from birth to 2 years.
1990	EHA renamed the Individuals with Disabilities Act (IDEA; P.L. 101–476)	The term *child with a disability* replaced the term *handicapped child*, which had been used in previous legislation. Autism and traumatic brain injury classifications were added. Transition services for children with disabilities were mandated by age 16 years. Assistive technology devices were defined. It required that children with a disability be included in the general education environment to the maximum extent possible.
1997	IDEA (P.L. 105–17)	Extended the least restrictive environment to ensure that *all* students would have access to the general curriculum. Required schools to consider the inclusion of assistive technology devices and services in the individualized education plans of all students. Orientation and mobility services were added to the list of related services for children who need instruction in navigating within and to and from their school environment.
2004	IDEA renamed the Individuals with Disabilities Education Improvement Act (IDEIA; P.L. 108–446)*	Statute is aligned with the No Child Left Behind Act of 2001. Focus of statute is on doing what works and increasing achievement expectations for children with disabilities. Changes are made to the evaluation procedures used to identify specific learning disabilities.

Note: * Although the IDEA was renamed IDEIA in 2004, IDEA is used most often to refer to the 2004 reauthorization and, thus, will be the abbreviation used throughout this book.

Source: Based on Sotelo-Dynega, Flanagan, & Alfonso, 2018.

This is a general definition that refers to disorder in basic psychological processes but does not identify them. Although the definition points to several conditions, there are no specific criteria for identifying disabilities. In addition, the definition excludes children whose disabilities are due to several factors that could be expected to cause learning problems. The exclusionary criteria have been questioned, partly because it may be difficult to differentiate learning problems due to emotional disturbance, lack of motivation, or cultural or economic disadvantage. The presence of exclusionary criteria, in combination with the lack of specific criteria to define learning disabilities, has led to the notion that learning disabilities are defined more by what they are *not* than by what they are.

Definitional concerns have resulted in different, albeit overlapping, definitions and ways to identify disabilities (Pullen et al., 2017). Definitional problems have led to different prevalence rates, incomparability of groups chosen for research purposes, and varying standards to determine whether children will receive special education services. Here, we provide a snapshot of the definitional problem by considering how learning disabilities have often been identified and a newer approach that is both criticized and gaining acceptance.

Identifying Specific Disabilities

Similar to the problems in defining learning disabilities, a lack of agreed-upon methods and criteria to identify learning disabilities has been a continuing problem. What criteria and methods are to be used to decide that a child's language or learning skills are below expectations? Different guidelines have been offered and several methods generated.

Ability-Achievement Discrepancy

A common way once used exclusively to identify disabilities was by recognizing a discrepancy, or "gap," between the individual's intellectual ability and specific achievement level. In the IQ–achievement discrepancy model, it was assumed that if a specific disability exists, performance on measures of *general* ability (typically IQ tests) will exceed performance on achievement tests of the hypothesized *specific* impairment. A discrepancy of two or more standard deviations between intelligence test scores and achievement test scores was often employed. Although once widely used, the discrepancy model has been criticized for requiring severe discrepancies to meet eligibility criteria. In other words, children had to fall far below expected levels of performance in order to meet criteria for a learning disability. As a result of this and other criticisms discussed in more detail below, the discrepancy model is no longer a requirement in the identification of a learning disability (Pullen et al., 2017).

Another approach identifies disabilities by determining that the youth is performing below expected grade level or age in at least one academic area. Variations occur in the specific criterion, however. Thus, a sixth grader, for example, might be labeled with a learning disability when his or her achievement is on a fourth- *or* fifth-grade level. A general problem with this method of identification is that a large discrepancy is more serious for a younger than an older child: being two years behind is more serious for a third grader than for a sixth grader.

Poor achievement can also be identified by comparing the child's performance with those of peers of the same age on standardized tests of language, reading, writing, and arithmetic. The degree to which performance must fall below that of peers varies with school districts and researchers. The criterion is usually set in the range of one to two standard deviations below the mean on standardized tests.

The poor achievement and especially the IQ–achievement discrepancy approaches have been challenged in numerous ways (Alfonso & Flanagan, 2018). For example, it has been argued that the IQ–achievement discrepancy method is based on a flawed assumption that IQ accurately predicts achievement and represents a person's potential. Moreover, critics have argued that intelligence tests rely strongly on language abilities, so that overall intelligence may be underestimated in children with communication or learning disabilities—making a discrepancy less probable. Others have pointed out that when a discrepancy from a high IQ is identified, the "disability" might be quite different from that of a discrepancy from a much lower IQ. Additionally, the discrepancy model has been criticized for not being sensitive enough to pick up on early learning problems (i.e., before the student has experienced several years of academic failure) (Pullen et al., 2017). Still another criticism is that there is no way to discriminate between deficits of the child and of poor instruction. Serious questions also have been raised about the exclusion of children considered to be "slow learners," that is, for whom a discrepancy is not found (Fletcher et al., 2019). There is growing recognition that in several ways specific disabilities do not differ much from general learning problems that do not meet discrepancy formulations (Hulme & Snowling, 2009; Scruggs & Mastropieri, 2002). Overall, these arguments have weakened

the ability–achievement discrepancy approach. Nonetheless, intelligence often is considered by requiring that the child with low achievement also exhibit average intelligence or at least an IQ higher than the score that typically defines intellectual disability (about 70). By this practice, children who exhibit both low achievement and relatively low intelligence are not considered as having a learning disability.

Response to Intervention (RTI)

An innovative approach to defining and addressing learning disabilities, RTI depends on exposing children to intervention prior to diagnosing them with a disability (Grigorenko et al., 2020; Lewandowski & Lovett, 2014). The rationale is that children whose response to valid intervention is poorer than that of their peers can be identified as having a learning disability.

The RTI approach is a multitiered system of support (MTSS) that moves children through a series of interventions of increasing intensity, as represented in Figure 11.1 (Fletcher et al., 2019). Key components of the approach include school-wide instruction/intervention, monitoring of student progress, and identification of disability. The RTI model typically has three tiers or levels of support, including instruction provided in the general education classroom (Tier 1), prevention intervention offered to students who are not progressing in response to classroom instruction (Tier 2), and more intensive intervention (Tier 3) offered to students who do not respond adequately to the supports in the prior tiers (Gersten et al., 2017b). To illustrate, a group of children—say, kindergartners—is first exposed to a specific intervention—for example, a research-based reading program—and each child's reading skills are monitored. Children with deficits next receive special, more intensive intervention, perhaps in small groups, followed by another evaluation. At this point, or perhaps after an even more intensive additional intervention, the child who has not positively responded is recognized as having a disability and may be eligible for special education services. It is noteworthy that Tier 3 is most variable across programs.

The RTI approach was given impetus in the 2004 reauthorization of IDEA and is lauded by its proponents for identifying and intervening early when students show signs of difficulties (Gersten, Jayanthi, & Dimino, 2017a). It has gained momentum in schools, and there is growing evidence that the model may provide a valid method of identifying learning disabilities (Miciak, Fletcher, & Stuebing, 2015). Nonetheless, professionals hold differing views and attitudes regarding the approach, and there remain many unresolved issues. Some have described the implementation of RTI, for example, as "easier said than done" (Denckla, 2018). Implementation of RTI requires many decisions, including decisions about the selection of evidence-based intervention, criteria for determining deficits, and how RTI is conducted in classrooms. Overall, there is considerable variation in how states and schools implement RTI, and rigorous and

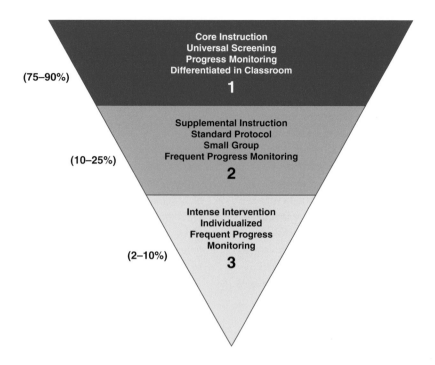

Figure 11.1 Three levels of Response to Intervention (RTI), a multitiered system of support (MTSS). Tier 1 generally addresses the learning needs of 75–90% of students, Tier 2 addresses 10–25%, and Tier 3, which involves intensive intervention, addresses 2–10%. (Adapted from Fletcher et al., 2019)

comprehensive evaluation of its effectiveness has been somewhat limited (Fuchs & Fuchs, 2017; Gersten et al., 2017b). More recently, hybrid approaches to identifying learning disabilities have been proposed, which utilize multiple criteria to determine disability and combine features of the discrepancy approaches with RTI (Bradley, Danielson, & Hallahan, 2002; Fletcher et al., 2019). In other words, both low achievement and difficulties responding to intervention are important considerations.

Despite the problems of definitional confusion and differing approaches to identifying disabilities, substantial progress has been made in understanding learning disabilities and there is general consensus that at the core of learning disorder is "unexpected underachievement." We begin the following discussion with the development of language because problems with language development are likely to be identified earlier and are often implicated in other disabilities, including learning disorders.

Language Development

An overview of normal language development serves as a framework for understanding disabilities. In fact, language development may be considered a marker of general cognitive development, and early language problems may be predictive of later communication and learning difficulties among other problems (P. A. Thompson et al., 2015).

Language, as we usually know it, is a system of communication based on sounds that are combined into words and sentences to represent experience and carry meaning. Speech, more narrowly, is the way we say the sounds and words of spoken language. While language can be spoken, it can also be written or expressed with gestures and body language. Table 11.2 defines the basic components of language that must be mastered by all users of oral and written language.

Phonology has to do with the basic sounds of a language. English has 42 basic sounds, or **phonemes.** As a written language, it has 26 alphabet letters, which singly or in combinations are called **graphemes.** There is a correspondence between phonemes and graphemes. Alphabet letters are, of course, combined to form words, which carry meaning. **Morphology** has to do with the

Table 11.2 Basic Components of Language

Phonology	Sounds of a language and rules for combining them
Morphology	Formation of words, including the use of prefixes and suffixes (e.g., un, ed, s) to give meaning
Syntax	Organization of words into phrases and sentences
Semantics	Meanings in language
Pragmatics	Use of language in specific contexts

formation of words, and **syntax** refers to the organization of words into phrases and sentences. Morphology and syntax are parts of **grammar**, the system of rules that organize a language. Thus, English speakers who follow the rules say, "He dances well," not "He well dance." The rules of language help facilitate meaning in communication, which is referred to as **semantics**. Finally, **pragmatics** is the use of language in context; in social situations it includes such aspects as taking turns when speaking with another person or judging when to initiate conversation.

Superimposed on the basic components of language are reception and expression. **Receptive language** has to do with the comprehension of messages sent by others. **Expressive language** concerns the production of language, that is, sending messages. Reception is developmentally acquired earlier than expression—as anyone who tries to learn a second language quickly discovers.

Infants come into the world geared for language; their amazing capacity progresses rapidly and in sequential milestones during the first few years of life (Table 11.3). During the first year, infants can distinguish and produce sounds that are not part of the native language that surrounds them, and then this ability contracts to the sounds of their language. Thus, it appears that an innate ability to process language sounds is shaped through experience. By their first birthday, most infants are saying a few words. Some speech sounds are more difficult than others, and individual differences in pronunciation, or articulation, become obvious. Even before this time, infants have begun to understand the communications of others.

By 2 years of age, most children have gone from saying single words, to two-word utterances, to longer strings of words set in meaningful phrases or sentences. Vocabulary increases dramatically, different parts of speech are acquired, and the ability to arrange words improves. Comprehension also grows, and parents of 3-year-olds perceive that they are talking with someone who is no longer an "infant." Indeed, infancy—a term derived from a Latin word that means "incapable of speech"—is often said to be over at age 2. Progress continues at a rapid rate and includes pragmatics. By age 7, many of the basics of language are acquired, although language development continues into adolescence and even into adulthood.

Communication Disorders

Not all children proceed through the milestones of language development as described above. Delays or differences may emerge. From even a brief review of language development, it is obvious that a variety of impairments might occur. Specific problems can exist in phonology, morphology, syntax, semantics, and so forth. Problems can exist in speech, language, or both, and it is possible to have both receptive and expressive language

problems. While not all differences are predictive of subsequent problems, children who fail to develop language or who show persistent or severe delays or difficulties in speech or language development may have a communication disorder.

DSM Classification and Diagnosis

Children with communication disorders have deficits in language, speech, and/or communication. In the DSM-5, the broad category of Communication Disorders includes the diagnoses of Language Disorder and Speech Sound Disorder, as well as Childhood-Onset Fluency Disorder (stuttering) and Social (Pragmatic) Communication Disorder, which are not discussed here (American Psychiatric Association, 2013). It is important to note the terminology used to describe impairments in communication have changed over time and may be different among disciplines (Alfonso & Flanagan, 2018; Bishop, 2017; Leonard, 2017). For example, terms such as *developmental dysphasia*, *specific language impairment (SLI)*, *developmental language disorder (DLD)*, and *language disorder (LD)* have all been used to explain similar conditions. The following discussion uses the terms defined in the DSM-5 and describes these difficulties as they are presented in the clinical and research literature. In both Speech Sound Disorder and Language Disorder, symptom onset must occur during early development, abilities must be below those expected for age, and limitations must interfere with communication, social participation, and academic or occupational achievement.

Description

Speech Sound Disorder (SSD)
Children with SSD exhibit impairments in speech sound production or in articulating speech sounds (Dockrell & Joye, 2018). To be diagnosed with this disorder, a child must fail to display developmentally appropriate and dialect-appropriate speech sounds that interferes with their ability to be understood by or communicate with others. The difficulties are not due to physical, neurological, or hearing problems (American Psychiatric Association, 2013).

Children with impaired speech make incorrect speech sounds, substitute easily made sounds for more difficult ones, or omit sounds (Hayiou-Thomas et al., 2017). The ability to articulate speech sounds is a skill that follows a typical pattern of development. For example, while most children can produce intelligible speech at or around the age of 3 years, more difficult sounds such as *l, r, s, z, th, ch, dzh,* and *zh* may take longer to acquire (American Speech-Language-Hearing Association (ASHA), n.d.; First et al., 2017). For example, a child may say "yook" instead of *look* or "wabbit" instead of *rabbit*, as will be illustrated in the upcoming case of André (First et al., 2017).

Table 11.3 Language Development and Communication in the Early Years

	Reception *Hearing and Understanding*	Expression *Talking*
Birth to 3 months	Reacts to sudden noise. Is quieted by a voice. Seems to recognize caregiver's voice.	Cries. Smiles at people. Makes cooing sounds.
4 to 6 months	Locates sound. Responds to changes in tone of voice. Notices and pays attention to music and sounds.	Coos, babbles, giggles, and laughs. Initiates vocal play. Makes speech-like babbling sounds, like *pa, ba,* and *mi.*
7 to 12 months	Follows when someone points. Understands words for common items, like *cup, truck, milk, daddy.* Begins to respond to simple words and phrases, like "No" or "Want more?". Obeys simple instructions, like "Come here." Listens to songs and stories for a short time.	Babbles long strings of sounds and combines vowel sounds. Uses sounds and gestures to get and keep attention. Points to objects and shows them to others. Uses gestures, like waving bye, reaching to be picked up, and shaking head no. Imitates different speech sounds. Says first words, like *hi, dog, dada, mama, or uh-oh.*
1 to 2 years	Points to a few body parts when asked. Carries out one-part directions, like "Roll the ball." Responds to simple questions, like "Who's that?" or "Where's your shoe?" Listens to simple stories, songs, and rhymes. Points to pictures in a book or objects when they are named.	Uses many new words. Uses *p, b, m, h,* and *w* in words. Starts to name pictures in books. Asks questions like "What's that?" and "Where's kitty?" Puts two words together, like "more apple," "no bed," and "mommy book."
3 to 4 years	Understands many words and is able to categorize them (e.g., understands some colors, shapes, and words for family, like *brother, grandmother,* and *aunt*).	Answers simple who, what, and where questions; asks when and how questions. Says rhyming words, like *hat-cat.* Uses pronouns, like *I, you, me, we,* and *they.* Uses some plural words, like *toys, birds,* and *buses.* Speech is understood by most people. Puts four words together; uses about four sentences. Talks about what happened during the day.
4 to 5 years	Understands words for order, like *first, next,* and *last.* Understands words for time, like *yesterday, today,* and *tomorrow.* Follows longer directions, like "Put your pajamas on, brush your teeth, and then pick out a book." Follows classroom instructions, like "Draw a circle on your paper around something you eat." Increasing understanding of what is said at home and in school.	Says all speech sounds in words. May make mistakes on sounds that are harder to say, like *l, s, r, v, z, sh,* and *th.* Responds to "What did you say?" Talks without repeating sounds or words most of the time. Names letters and numbers. Uses sentences that have more than one action word, like *jump, play,* and *get.* Tells a short story. Keeps a conversation going. Talks in different ways, depending on the context, including listener and place.

Source: Based on American Speech-Language-Hearing Association (ASHA), n.d.

In SSD, typical errors made by young children learning to speak may persist beyond normal developmental expectations (Unicomb et al., 2017). Only 50% of speech may be intelligible in typically developing 2-year-olds, whereas most speech is understandable at age 4 (American Psychiatric Association, 2013). Since most children display some misarticulation as they acquire the linguistic and motor skills necessary for speech, developmental norms are crucial in diagnosis.

ANDRÉ Speech Sound Disorder

André, a 6-year-old in first grade, came to the clinic with his mother, who reported that her son was humming and making odd noises, was having problems speaking properly, and was reversing letters when writing. André's teacher sent a report stating that André was a "very good" student in reading readiness, phonics, and sports; was average in art; and seeming to have problems only in speech.

On examination, this friendly boy conversed intelligently on a number of topics. Speech errors noted during the conversation included "wabbit" for *rabbit*, "bwown" for *brown*, "dis" for *this*, and "wewwow" for *yellow*. Psychological testing revealed that André's intelligence was above average, and he was performing academically slightly above grade level.

Adapted from First et al., 2017

NICK Problems in Language Expression

Nick is a nine-year old boy who can produce sounds clearly, but his language is impaired. He produces short, immature sentences that leave off word endings ("I have two shoe"; "Mommy help me at the store"), uses incorrect forms of words ("Me like ice cream"; "He goed home"), and has trouble finding

the words he wants to say ("For lunch I had, you know, that spiky thing, yellow inside"). Nick likes to play with other children and enjoys talking, but has limited means at his disposal for expressing and elaborating his intentions.

Adapted from Norbury & Paul, 2015, p. 683

The production of speech sound, or articulation, requires motor control of the lips, tongue, and jaws in coordination with breathing and vocalizing. But SSD may also involve difficulties in phonology, or in understanding the sound structure and rules of language (Dodd et al., 2018; Preston, Hull, & Edwards, 2013). Thus, a child with phonological difficulties may correctly produce a speech sound in one context but not in another. For example, the child may correctly pronounce /s/ in *bus*, but say "pun" for *spoon* or "ton" for *sun* (Dodd et al., 2018). Phonological problems involving the understanding of the sound structure of language and the rules for combining them can have serious developmental implications, particularly in the acquisition of reading and spelling skills.

Language Disorder

The DSM cites the primary diagnostic features of Language Disorder as difficulties in acquiring or using language due to impairments in comprehending or producing vocabulary, sentences, and discourse (American Psychiatric Association, 2013). Deficits are not due to sensory or motor problems, other medical or neurological conditions, nor to intellectual disability or global developmental delay. Diagnosis depends on the combination of the child's history, clinical observation, and performance on standardized tests of language ability. Both expression and reception of language are implicated.

Expressive problems involve the production of language with regard to vocabulary, grammar, and other aspects of language

output. Young people with expressive problems may have a limited amount of speech and may speak in extremely short, simple sentences. Vocabulary may be small; critical parts of sentences may be missing; unusual word order may be displayed. Especially problematic, children may exhibit undue errors in making word forms such as plurals or verb tense. In addition, phonological problems may be observed. However, children with expressive problems understand speech and age-level concepts, and thus they can appropriately respond to others' communications. Some of these characteristics are seen in the description of Nick, who is motivated to connect but whose language disorder disrupts his ability to effectively communicate with others, particularly given his age (Norbury & Paul, 2015).

Difficulties in language reception involve comprehending the communication of others. Single words, phrases, sentences, the multiple meanings of a word, word play, and changes in verb tense may all be problematic. The child may fail to respond to speech, seem deaf, respond inappropriately to others' speech, be uninterested in television, or fail to follow instructions.

When considering language disorder, it is helpful to keep in mind the considerable variation children experience in the kinds and severity of problems. Imagine, if you will, the difference between a child who has only minor articulation deficits and one whose speech can hardly be understood by others. Life is different too for the child with relatively simple speech impairments and a child unable to comprehend much of what is

TRANG Problems in Language Reception and Expression

Trang understood a limited number of words for objects, actions, and relations. He often failed to follow classroom instructions, particularly those that involved words for time (e.g., yesterday, after, week) and space (e.g., beneath, in front of, around). His conversation with other children often broke down because he did not understand fully what they were saying, nor could he express his own ideas clearly. As a result he was not a favored playmate, and most of the children in his class ignored him. His limited interactions further reduced Trang's opportunities for improving and practicing his already

weak language skills. Additional assessment, conducted with the assistance of a Vietnamese interpreter, revealed that Trang showed similar receptive and expressive language deficits in Vietnamese. His nonverbal skills, however, were generally appropriate for his age. He readily constructed intricate buildings and vehicles with small, plastic building blocks; he easily completed complex jigsaw puzzles; and he successfully solved numerical, conceptual, or analogical problems, as long as they were presented nonverbally.

Adapted from Johnson & Beitchman, 2005, p. 2642

being communicated by others. It is also helpful to recognize that speech sound, expressive, and reception difficulties often occur together. The description of a 5-year-old boy, Trang, illustrates this point. Trang lived with his parents and siblings, who were proficient in both English and Vietnamese. His development in both languages was much slower than that of his siblings, and kindergarten assessment revealed impairments in both reception and expression.

Epidemiology and Developmental Course

Epidemiological studies suggest overall rates of communication disorders in the range of 3 to 7% (Dockrell & Joye, 2018). Prevalence varies with age, type of disorder and severity. For example, it is estimated that approximately two in every 30 students experience a language disorder at school entry severe enough to impede their learning (Norbury et al., 2016). Boys are widely reported as having higher rates than girls. Although higher prevalence in clinic samples may reflect referral bias, this does not seem to completely account for the gender difference (Viding et al., 2004).

Higher rates also have been noted in children from low socioeconomic groups (Dockrell & Joye, 2018). What might explain this correlation? If hereditary factors play a role, family language disabilities might result in families attaining low educational and occupational status. It is also possible that poor children who use dialects different from standard English employed in standardized assessment instruments are overidentified.

Different patterns of development have been identified in children with language difficulties (Snowling et al., 2016). Language disorders usually appear by age 3 or 4, but mild difficulties may not be identified until later (American Psychiatric Association, 2013). Some impairments may first become apparent with the demands of schoolwork and greater complexity of language. It may be more difficult to ascertain what a child

understands than to observe impairments in the expression of speech.

Studies of children and adults of various ages, followed for various periods of time, indicate that improvement can occur over time and that language abilities can reach the normal range; however, problems can persist in both spoken language and reading, and difficulties can extend beyond language difficulties, as discussed further below (Leonard, 2017). A hierarchy of risk based on the type of disorder has been suggested. Children who display only articulation problems are at lowest risk, those with expressive problems are at middle risk, and those with receptive problems are at highest risk for later language impairments (Baker & Cantwell, 1989; Rutter, Mawhood, & Howlin, 1992; Whitehurst & Fischel, 1994). However, other factors, including stability of educational experience and a variety of other risk factors also impact outcome (Norbury & Paul, 2015; Sylvestre et al., 2018).

Speech sound problems, especially when they are mild or occur without other language difficulties, often remit over time, and frequently respond to intervention (American Psychiatric Association, 2013). A substantial number of children with early expressive difficulties continue to exhibit impairment. Some children, often referred to as "late talkers," eventually reach the normal range of language development but still fall somewhat short of most of their peers (Preston et al., 2010; Rescorla, 2009). Regarding receptive difficulties, many children may never develop completely normal language and their problems may increase over time. A study that followed boys with severe receptive–expressive impairments into their early twenties found that 20% had a level of comprehension below that of 10-year-old children and about 25% had equally poor expressive skills (Mawhood, Howlin, & Rutter, 2000). Little change occurred over the next decade for this group (Clegg et al., 2005). In general, when problems do not remit by 5 to 6 years of age, children are at risk for continued language difficulties and later problems in reading (Hulme & Snowling,

2009). It has also been reported that even when remittance occurs, reading difficulties may arise later.

Co-occurring Disorders

One of the burdens of communication disorders is its association with poor academic progress. School achievement is affected: more students are retained at grade level and fewer students attend high school. At least in part, this finding is due to the association of communication disorders with learning disorders (Hayiou-Thomas et al., 2017; Pennington & Bishop, 2009). This association is not surprising. Consider, for example, the important role language plays in skilled reading, which depends both on decoding skills and comprehension of language. One longitudinal study, for example, followed 136 children with language impairment who were enrolled in early childhood special education classrooms and found that a quarter of the children could be classified as poor readers by the end of kindergarten (Murphy et al., 2016). This figure is much lower than other studies which typically report co-occurrence rates of 50% or higher (e.g., McArthur et al., 2000). The role that language impairment plays in reading problems is complex. Some children may be identified early as having a language disorder, show problems with early reading development and may be diagnosed with a specific learning disability instead of or in addition to language disorder (Nelson & Wiig, 2018). Others may show mild or no weaknesses in early language comprehension and expression but are identified with a learning disability in elementary school when they display difficulties learning to read. For others, language comprehension difficulties do not become apparent until later grades, where the relationship between language difficulties and learning problems may be overlooked (Nelson & Wiig, 2018). Youth with the combination of communication and learning disorders also have a higher than average risk for other disturbances (McKean et al., 2017; Özcebe, Noyan Erbas, & Karahan Tiğrak, 2020).

Communication disorders have been associated with externalizing and internalizing problems in youth of various ages (Charman et al., 2015; Curtis et al., 2018; Lum, Ullman, & Conti-Ramsden, 2016). A study of 5-year-olds, for example, showed that 40% displayed withdrawn behavior, bodily symptoms, and aggressive behavior (van Daal, Verhoeven, & van Balkom, 2007). A study of 7- to 9-year-olds identified language impairment in more than 40% of children with ADHD (Helland et al., 2012). The continuity of behavioral disturbance is suggested by a longitudinal study of a community sample identified with language deficits at age 5 (Beitchman et al., 1996, 2001). Follow-up conducted at about age 19 indicated that the individuals had higher rates of anxiety disorder than a control group, and males were at risk for antisocial personality. Nevertheless, some investigations indicate relatively low risk and the need to consider type and severity of

communication disorders (Snowling et al., 2006). Children with only articulation problems, for example, appear to show the fewest and least severe psychological difficulties (van Daal et al., 2007). Importantly, evidence suggests communication disorders likely impact multiple areas of the child's functioning and development, including peer relationships and academic skills, which may compound risk for other problem behaviors, particularly as the child ages (Curtis et al., 2018).

Cognitive Deficits and Theories

Children with communication disorders commonly exhibit nonlinguistic cognitive deficits. Speed of information processing, auditory perception, memory, attention, and various executive functions are among the areas examined (Schwartz, 2017).

A general limitation in information-processing capacity is hypothesized to play a role in language disorder. The information-processing model assumes, among other things, that rapid handling of information facilitates processing. Limitation in speed of processing is notable in children with language impairments (Leonard et al., 2007). They appear to respond more slowly across a variety of tasks, which suggests that a processing limitation affects performance across domains. When a particular language operation requires especially rapid processing, detrimental effects would be expected. A difficulty with this hypothesis—that processing speed accounts for language disorder—is that processing speed is deficient in youth with general learning problems, leading one to wonder why would effects show up only in language (Hulme & Snowling, 2009).

A second hypothesis relates language impairments to various deficits in auditory processing (Corriveau, Pasquini, & Goswami, 2007; Leonard, 1998). Perception of brief, rapid sound is considered important in language, so a child who cannot catch rapidly flowing sound cues might well have language difficulties. Research has shown that children with language impairments do appear to have difficulty identifying very fast sounds embedded in speech (Guiraud et al., 2018). Moreover, infants at family risk for communication/learning impairments have been shown to exhibit longer processing times for auditory stimuli. Further support for the hypothesis comes from studies indicating that when sound cues in speech syllables are extended in experimental studies, speech discrimination improves. Moreover, emerging research suggests abnormal auditory neural activity patterns in children with language impairment (van Bijnen et al., 2019). In general, however, research findings appear inconsistent. Hulme and Snowling (2009) speculate on possible reasons for inconsistency. Perhaps the youth examined had different kinds of language impairments, or age played a role, or there is a maturational delay in auditory processing. It is also possible that different tasks employed in research make different demands on the youth, or that auditory processing contributes to language acquisition in the context of other risk factors. Moreover, different auditory processing deficits may be differently related to language, whereby no single deficit is likely to be solely the cause for a specific language impairment (Halliday, Tuomainen, & Rosen, 2017).

A third proposal implicating cognition in communication disorders focuses on verbal short-term and working memory (Gillam et al., 2017). A distinction can be made between these aspects of memory. Verbal short-term memory is specialized for the temporary storage of information pertaining to language. It is thought to be involved with the sound structure, or phonology, of language. Deficits in verbal short-term memory are apparent in a variety of tasks, including the immediate repetition of a string of nonwords (e.g., "mep," "shom"). Research, including meta-analysis, shows that children with language disabilities have deficits in nonword repetition and phonological memory (Bishop, 2002; Conti-Ramsden, 2003; Estes, Evans, & Else-Quest, 2007), although the question has arisen about whether performance on nonword repetition tasks may be influenced by dialect or familiarity with more than one language (Chiat, 2015; McDonald & Oetting, 2019). Additionally, questions have been raised as to whether the task of nonword repetition is simply a pure measure of **phonological processing** rather than an index of phonological memory (Hulme & Snowling, 2009). It is worth noting, nonetheless, that phonological memory is related to the acquisition of speech production, vocabulary, comprehension, and the processing of syntax, and a significant number of children with specific language disorder have phonological impairments (Schwartz, 2017).

With regard to verbal working memory, both the storage and the processing of verbal information are involved. Verbal working memory requires holding verbal information in mind, for example, while it is being used in following a sequence of directions. Children with language disorders do poorly on measures of complex verbal memory (Vugs et al., 2016). Such difficulty may not be an underlying cause of language problems, but it likely contributes to the reading and mathematics problems that are associated with language disorder.

Neuroimaging studies have also investigated the neural basis of communication disorders and have identified structural differences in individuals with communication disorders compared to those without, although there is much variability in findings (Lum et al., 2016). For example, anomalies have been identified in areas of the brain known to support language as well as non-language centers (Liégeois, Mayes, & Morgan, 2014; Mayes, Reilly, & Morgan, 2015). Although progress is being made in understanding cognitive and neurological deficits exhibited by children with language impairments, much is yet to be investigated. Given the heterogeneity of problems, multiple deficits are probably involved.

Specific Learning Disorders: Reading, Written Expression, Mathematics

The term *specific learning disorder* refers to a specific neurodevelopmental problem in reading, writing, or arithmetic—the "three Rs" essential to classroom learning and everyday functioning. Historically, these disorders, respectively, have been known as *dyslexia, dysgraphia,* and *dyscalculia.* Although these terms are still used by some, "specific learning disorder" has become the umbrella term for difficulties in learning and using academic skills. Additionally, these and other terms, such as *learning disorder* and *learning disabilities* are sometimes used interchangeably, although their meanings are not completely the same. While a full discussion of terminology is beyond the scope of this book, briefly, the term *disorder* is a medical term used for diagnosis, while *disability* is used by the education and legal systems. However, specific learning disorders are recognized by the educational system and by the DSM and ICD. Additionally, although learning disabilities are often described as if they are "pure," deficits frequently occur in combinations. Most children with learning disorders have reading problems, and many have additional learning difficulties.

DSM Classification and Diagnosis

The DSM-5 refers to learning disabilities as Specific Learning Disorders (SLD), defined as difficulties in learning and using academic skills that have persisted for at least six months regardless of appropriate interventions (American Psychiatric Association, 2013). The impaired skills include difficulties in the following: word reading, understanding what is read, spelling, written expression, understanding number, and mathematical reasoning. These can be specified in three domains—as impairments in reading, written expression, or mathematics, and more than one domain can be specified. Subskills in each affected domain also are to be specified, as described by the DSM (e.g., number sense, accurate arithmetic calculation).

The problems must begin during the school-age years, although they may become fully manifest only when demand for the skill exceeds the person's abilities. Diagnosis requires that a person's achievement in at least one domain be substantially lower than expected for age, and the difficulties must interfere with academic or occupational performance or daily living activities that require the skill. Such deficits must be confirmed by individually administered standardized measures and a clinical assessment. Further, the difficulties cannot be accounted for by intellectual disabilities, visual or auditory acuity, other mental or neurological disorders, psychosocial adversity, lack of proficiency in the language of academic instruction, or inadequate educational instruction.

We discuss topics for each of the specific areas of impairment before examining more general issues. Emphasis is placed predominantly on impairment in reading because of its high prevalence and because it has been most investigated.

SLD with Impairment in Reading

Description

Reading can be defined as "the process of extracting and constructing meaning from written text for some purpose" (Vellutino et al., 2004, p. 5). It requires the ability to readily identify words in running text in order to discern the meaning of the text. Among the many skills involved in this "on-line" process are language abilities, cognitive skills, understanding of the conventions of written text (e.g., reading from left to right on a page), and a store of knowledge about the world.

An enormously complex process, reading virtually always entails instruction. When it is not mastered, children may struggle to recognize single written words or to pronounce them correctly when reading aloud, read excessively slowly or haltingly, have limited vocabulary, lack understanding of what they have read, or not remember what they have read. Given these complexities, extensive efforts have been made to discover whether reading problems fall into subtypes based on reading skills or underlying cognitive deficits (Burgess et al., 2018). Efforts to validate distinct subtypes of reading difficulties persist and consider a variety of reading profiles and causes (Willems et al., 2016). An important distinction is often made between problems in word-level reading and text-level reading, or the comprehension of written text.

Word-Level Reading Problems (Dyslexia) Word-level reading problems involve problems in accurate or fluent word recognition, poor decoding (breaking a word into parts in order to read the whole word fluently) and poor spelling abilities (Fletcher et al., 2019). The term *dyslexia* is an alternate term often used to describe this pattern of impairment in word-level reading, or the acquisition of basic reading skills. Historically, various processes have been implicated in dyslexia (American Psychiatric Association, 2013). Theories of visual system abnormalities were the most influential throughout the twentieth century until the 1970s and 1980s (Vellutino et al., 2004). For example, Samuel Orton, a central figure in early research on reading, erroneously noted that among other difficulties visual–perceptual deficits caused dyslexic children to reverse letters (*d* for *b*; *saw* for *was*) and even to write in mirror images (Vellutino, 1979). Other theorists have suggested that dyslexia is caused by visual system defects that lead to impairments in scanning, tracking, or processing visual stimuli.

Currently, a critical role is given to **phonological processing**, that is, using the sound structure of language to process written material, as underlying the difficulties in word reading, decoding, and spelling inherent in dyslexia (Fletcher et al., 2019). Before they can learn to read, children must realize that spoken words can be segmented into sounds, an ability referred to as phonological awareness. For instance, they must recognize that the word *sad* contains three sounds, even though *sad* is said as one unit of sound. Also essential to reading is phonological decoding, that is, understanding that letters (graphemes) correspond to sounds (phonemes) and being able to map letters to sounds.

Much evidence supports the importance of phonological processing in learning to read and the role deficits in phonological awareness play in dyslexia (Kudo, Lussier, & Swanson, 2015). Young children who are aware of the sounds of their language and who can decode letters, syllables, and single words become better readers. In contrast, phonological processing deficits are associated with difficulty in naming single words, reading, and spelling. Moreover, interventions that target phonological processing deficits have been shown to improve single-word identification and reading (McGill & Ndip, 2019). Cross-cultural studies confirm the importance of phonological processing in the reading of alphabet-based languages other than English. However, while there is much agreement about the important role phonological processing plays in dyslexia, evidence suggests multiple deficits are at play (Pennington et al., 2012).

Text-Level Reading Problems (Problems of Comprehension) Word-level reading and reading comprehension problems often co-occur, with rates near 60% reported (Willcutt, 2014). This is not surprising given that one must be able to read the majority of the words of a passage to understand the text. Despite this overlap, however, a significant proportion of children who do not exhibit word-level reading problems nevertheless have difficulties in understanding what they read (Landi & Ryherd, 2017). These children can decode and recognize single words; indeed, they may accurately read aloud a passage of text, but fail to understand it. Notably, they may often go unidentified by teachers (Cartwright et al., 2017).

Comprehension of written material is complex and entails the coordination of many cognitive processes and component skills (Fletcher et al., 2019). Among these is language foundation skills, including vocabulary, or knowledge of word meanings, as well as knowledge of background information, important for putting text into context (Cromley, Snyder-Hogan, & Luciw-Dubas, 2010). Competency regarding the grammatical structure of language is also necessary. Recall that grammar consists of the formation of words (morphology) and the organization of words into phrases and sentences to give meaning (syntax). Competence in grammar would contribute, for example, to understanding who is happy in "Susan gave Jane an apple and she was happy" (Snowling, 2000).

Children with reading comprehension difficulties also often show deficits in other aspects of language and cognition. One of these is the ability to make inferences from the specific information provided by text. Executive functioning skills, particularly working memory and the ability to organize and make sense of incoming information, are also important in reading comprehension (Feifer, 2018). Another is metacognitive ability, which might include considering the purpose of the text, evaluating one's understanding of the text, and rereading and revising one's understanding if necessary. There is considerable need for further investigation of these and other processes that underlie deficits in comprehension, possible developmental paths, and interventions.

Epidemiology and Developmental Course

The reported prevalence of SLD with impairment in reading varies considerably, likely due in part to inconsistencies in defining the disorder as well as sampling differences. Estimates of reading disabilities generally fall between 5 to 15% depending on the criteria used to define the groups (Fletcher et al., 2019). Of note, among the specific learning disorder diagnoses, impairment in reading is the most common type. In fact, it is estimated that 70 to 80% of individuals with a learning disorder have primary deficits in reading (Ferrer et al., 2010).

Boys have been more often diagnosed with impairment in reading than girls. The degree to which this difference reflects genetic influences has been debated. Selection and referral biases have been proposed as partial explanations for this difference, with boys referred more often for treatment for reading impairment due to co-occurring externalizing problems (A. B. Arnett et al., 2017). As a result, girls with reading impairment may be underdiagnosed and less likely to be referred for intervention (Pennington, McGrath, & Peterson, 2019). Nevertheless, the male to female ratio is reported to be about three or four to one in clinic samples, and perhaps smaller in the general child population (Willcutt & Pennington, 2000).

A disproportionate number of children from low SES families experience impairment in reading (Peterson & Pennington, 2015). Evidence suggests, however, these differences may reflect, in part, the impact of environmental factors such as language exposure and quality of school instruction which adversely affect literacy development (Romeo et al., 2017). Additionally, reading disorders have been identified at varying rates in many countries (Grigorenko, 2001). Further research would be useful in clarifying the degree to which this might be explained by the differing structures of different languages, societal attitudes toward reading disabilities, or methodological factors.

Disorder tends to persist during the school years into adolescence and adulthood (Snowling, Muter, & Carroll, 2007). This trajectory of persistent impairment was demonstrated by Ferrer and colleagues (2015), using data from the Connecticut

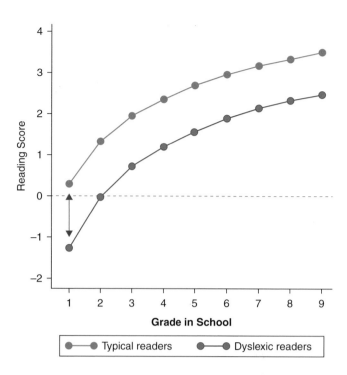

Figure 11.2 Achievement gap in reading demonstrated as early as first grade and persists through adolescence. (Adapted from Shaywitz & Shaywitz, 2020)

Longitudinal Study, a representative sample survey of children in Connecticut entering public kindergarten. The reading achievement, including measures of reading comprehension and word-level reading and decoding, of 414 children was examined annually from first through twelfth grade. The data, as illustrated in Figure 11.2, show that readers with dyslexia display substantially lower overall reading scores in first grade as compared to typical readers, and this discrepancy remained throughout the school years. In effect, the gap in achievement between typically developing children and children with dyslexia may be present early in development and persist through adolescence.

Reading disability can also worsen over time. The so-called **"Matthew Effect"** refers to the widening over time of the gap between strong and weak readers (McNamara, Scissons, Gutknecth, 2011). Although not always found, evidence exists for the effect regarding reading and other disabilities. Social class and behavior problems are among the possible predictors (Morgan, Farkas, & Wu, 2011). It is also thought that youth with initially severe problems in word reading are further disadvantaged by not being able to readily practice reading in text, which may impact their vocabulary development and comprehension (Duff, Tomblin, & Catts, 2015; Kempe, Eriksson-Gustavsson, & Samuelsson, 2011). It is important to note that reading impairment does not persist or worsen for all children, however, and some variation is seen in outcome. Some children with poor reading skills in early childhood

The classroom is often an unhappy place for a child with a learning disability. (Radius Images/Alamy Stock Photo)

have been reported to catch up with their peers by preadolescence or adolescence, and improvement can occur later, particularly with intensive intervention.

Although problems in the early acquisition of reading have been of great interest, it appears that reading difficulties—both in word-level reading and comprehension—can first emerge around the fourth or fifth grade when reading material becomes more complex, a phenomenon described as late-emerging reading disabilities (LERD) (Leach, Scarborough, & Rescorla, 2003). What accounts for this phenomenon? Lipka and colleagues (2006) conducted a study that addressed this issue. They identified a group of fourth graders with reading disability. The group had been drawn from a large representative sample of children who had been tested annually on several measures of reading, starting in kindergarten. The data showed that the children with reading disability in fourth grade had moved along three paths. One path involved consistently poor reading, a second path involved some fluctuation, and a third showed a more dramatic drop-off, with scores falling into the disability range only at fourth grade. On the basis of the various measures available over the years, the investigators suggested that children following this late-emerging path actually (1) had not mastered early phonological processing skills, but had masked the deficit by learning to sight read many words, or (2) had only inadequately mastered phonological processing skills, so that the increased demands of fourth-grade reading had taken their toll. Noteworthy is that this late-emerging group represented 36% of children with reading disabilities and that other studies have found somewhat larger rates of children whose reading problems appear to emerge

relatively late. Another study expanded upon the previous results by evaluating this same longitudinal cohort in Grade 7, following intervention (Etmanskie, Partanen, & Siegel, 2014). Among their findings, 33% of children with LERD had persistent reading comprehension problems, while the majority (67%) recovered by Grade 7. Together, these studies suggest the identification of early subtle deficits that may be indicators for reading difficulties is important and early intervention may help mitigate reading problems for some children, as discussed in more detail later in this chapter.

Co-occurring Disorders

We have already noted that reading impairment is associated with communication disorders and other learning disorders. In addition, reading impairment frequently co-occurs with an array of other problems, including ADHD, externalizing problems, autism spectrum disorder, anxiety, and depressive disorders, among others (McGill & Ndip, 2019). In fact, the co-occurrence of reading impairment and ADHD is well documented, with comorbidity estimates generally between 20 to 40% (Sciberras et al., 2014; Wadsworth et al., 2015). The relationship between the disorders is found most prominently in the inattentive presentation type of ADHD (Plourde et al., 2017). One potential explanation for the overlap of reading impairment and ADHD is that of shared genetic and neurocognitive risk factors (Mascheretti et al., 2017; Moura et al., 2017; Willcutt et al., 2010). A study investigating the neurocognitive functioning of children between the ages of 8 and 10, for example, found children with both dyslexia and ADHD exhibited weaknesses in nearly all neurocognitive

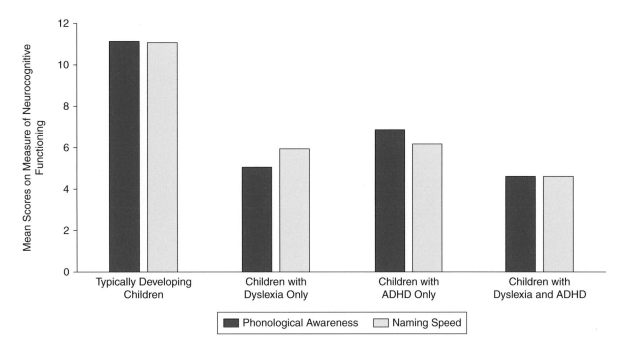

Figure 11.3 Neurocognitive deficits in children with dyslexia and ADHD. (Adapted from Moura et al., 2017)

abilities measured as compared to their typically developing peers. Particular weaknesses were noted in naming speed (the ability to quickly retrieve the name of a symbol) and phonological awareness, skills fundamental to reading (Moura et al., 2017). Figure 11.3 illustrates the major findings.

Reading impairment has also been linked to externalizing problems. For example, research utilizing a large longitudinal birth cohort identified children with specific word-reading difficulties and low reading attainment had elevated behavioral difficulties (Russell et al., 2015). The relationship between reading impairment and externalizing problems is complex, and while several causal connections are possible, longitudinal research has suggested an indirect path from reading disorder to later conduct problems (Hendren et al., 2018). In particular, one potential link between reading impairment and externalizing problems is the co-occurrence of both problems with ADHD (Hendren et al., 2018). As mentioned above, reading impairment and ADHD frequently co-occur, and ADHD and behavior disorders such as oppositional defiant disorder and conduct disorder frequently co-occur, with rates around 40% and 14%, respectively (Pliszka, 2015). While further research is needed to understand these relationships, the high rates of co-occurrence of these disorders again suggest potential shared risk factors.

SLD with Impairment in Written Expression

Children with disorders of written expression are typically the last to hand in classwork and may sit for hours over homework. Their writings may be rife with errors, be difficult to decipher, and contain disorganized content lacking in length and richness. Writing is multidimensional and implicates multiple language processes as well as visual–motor and other cognitive abilities (Berninger & Chanquoy, 2012; Fenwick et al., 2016). Although there is great complexity in the writing process, it has been useful to make a distinction between transcription and text generation—that is, composition.

Transcription is the mechanical act of writing and involves putting ideas into written form; it is fundamental in the early development of writing (Berninger & Chanquoy, 2012). Many deficiencies are observed in poor transcription—in punctuation, capitalization, word placement—but problems in handwriting and spelling are central. Disabilities can occur in one or both of these. In typical development, smooth, rapid, and clear handwriting develops gradually and entails effort. A child with transcription problems produces letters and words on paper slowly and laboriously, and sometimes is unsuccessful at writing (Figure 11.4). Good handwriting requires not only motor skill, but also that letters be stored in working and long-term memory, planned for, and retrieved from memory. Good spelling depends, among other abilities, on understanding the connections between sounds and conventional spelling, on word recognition, and on knowledge and retrieval of learned letters/words from memory (Berninger & Amtmann, 2003; Lyon et al., 2003). The case description of 11-year-old C.J. demonstrates some of the difficulties of deficient transcription and also the implication it has for text generation.

C.J. Writing, Writing, All Day Long

Fifth-grader C.J.'s problems had been increasing; he exhibited deteriorating grades, failure to complete assigned schoolwork, and some inattention and oppositional behaviors. C.J.'s identical twin had an early history of language and reading problems. C.J. participated in class discussions and had no problems with reading or math computation, but his written work was putting him at risk for failing his grade level. C.J. had an increasing dislike for school, sometimes skipped classes, found writing to be extremely tedious, and expressed a desire to talk rather than write about his many ideas. "It's writing, writing all day long—even in math and science." He reported that his teacher thought he was lazy and his writing atrocious. "He slings my work back at me to do over again, gives me detention, and when I try to explain he tells me I've got a bad attitude."

An assessment with the Wide Range Achievement Test-3 revealed average to high-average reading and math performance, but significant problems in spelling. C.J. also did poorly on a standardized test of written expression and an informal text generation task. On the latter, he produced three barely legible short sentences that lacked punctuation and capitalization and contained several spelling and grammar errors. C.J. attained average scores on a standardized oral language test but omitted sounds or syllables on a nonword test. The latter is sensitive to mild residual language impairments and written language impairments. The diagnosis of Disorder of Written Expression was formulated by the assessment team, with no other DSM disorder.

Adapted from Tannock, 2005a, pp. 3126–3127

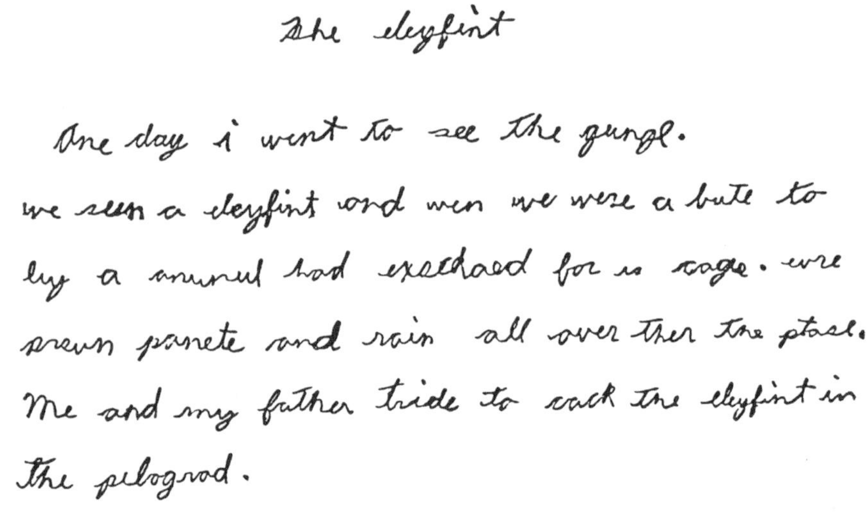

The Elephant
One day I went to see the jungle. We seen a elephant and when we were about to
leave an animal escaped from his cage. Every person panicked and ran all over the
place. Me and my father tried to catch the elephant in the playground.

Figure 11.4 The writing of an 11-year-old boy and the probable translation. The writing shows imagination, a rich vocabulary, and a basic grasp of storytelling. There also are misspellings of common and uncommon words, poorly formed letters, and retracing of letters that suggest difficulty in mechanics of writing. (Adapted from Taylor, 1988. Copyright 1988 by Guilford Press; reprinted with permission)

Text generation (or composition) can be viewed as the creation of meaning in written form. Among other requirements it demands that the child be able to retrieve from memory words, sentence structure, and stored information about the topic of interest. Also critical are higher-order executive functions and metacognitive skills, including planning, reviewing, and revising, which involve working memory, and the ability to maintain attention (Berninger & Chanquoy, 2012; Fletcher et al., 2019).

Hokey and basketball are two sports they both have comparesions they both sports, they contrast in many ways like in hokey you use a stick and a puck, but in basketball you use one ball and your hands. They also compare in that when you play them the goal is to get the puck or basketball into a goal or net. Another contrast is that hokey is played on ice and basketball is played on courts. When you play hokey or basketball you noticed that the puck and ball both touch the ground that is another way to compare.In hokey the goal.net is placed on the ground and in basketball the net is on a backboard in the air that is another contrast.If you have ever been to a hokey or basketball game there is always quaters or periods in a game so that the players can take a break,in that way they compare. Basketball has four quarters and Hockey has three periods to a game and they are different in that way.But the best comparisions in hokey and basketball is the fans,many people love hockey and basketball that's why they are one of most played and favored sports in the world.

Figure 11.5 A compare-and-contrast essay written by an adolescent with learning disabilities. (Adapted from Wong et al. 1997)

Individuals with impairment in written expression lack skills in understanding the goal of their writing, developing a plan, organizing the points to be made, linking ideas, and monitoring and revising their work. Many of these components apply to language and thinking more generally and are thus less specific to writing disorders than is transcription (Fletcher et al., 2019). Additionally, although transcription and text generation are considered separable components of writing, they are closely related and difficulty in one area can contribute to difficulty in the other (Mather & Wendling, 2018). Figure 11.5 provides an example of the work of an adolescent assigned to write a compare-and-contrast essay. The essay is comprehensible, but demonstrates weak sentence construction, awkward phrasing, lack of paragraphing, and deficits in organization. This student's writing greatly improved through an intervention program aimed at teaching cognitive and metacognitive skills.

Epidemiology and Developmental Course
Research on SLD with impairment in written expression is limited, and the prevalence is not definitively known. Perhaps 6 to 14% of school-age children have some form of writing impairment, depending on how the disorder is defined (O'Donnell & Colvin, 2019). Moreover, individuals with impairment in writing often have co-occurring learning difficulties or other disorders, such as ADHD (Mather & Wendling, 2018). Reliable standardized tests of a child's writing skills are limited, making it difficult to assess for impairments (Pennington et al., 2019). Developmental norms are important, of course, in judging the quality of a child's writing;

for example, before age 8 or so, motor skills may not be well developed and only simple narrative can be expected (Lipka & Siegel, 2006). Nevertheless, early signs of later difficulties in written expression have been observed in children's early writing development (Mather & Wendling, 2018). For example, problems in forming letters, segmenting words into syllables, or writing with ease may be suggestive of emerging difficulties. The disorder is usually apparent by second grade, and referral for problems sharply increases around the fourth grade, when school curricula demand increased writing (Berninger & Amtmann, 2003; Tannock, 2005b). Although longitudinal studies are limited, weaknesses in written expression can persist for some youth and, in turn, impact achievement across academic domains (O'Donnell & Colvin, 2019).

SLD with Impairment in Mathematics

Mathematics, or the science of numbers, is of course essential in the STEM (science, technology, engineering and math) fields, but it is also important in everyday activities, such as handling money, measuring time and distance, and understanding information necessary to make financial decisions (Soares, Evans, & Patel, 2018). Difficulties in mathematics are not uncommon, yet most students who experience difficulties in math at some point during their schooling do not have SLD (Mazzocco & Vukovic, 2018). SLD with impairment in mathematics is a diagnostic label that refers to problems in basic arithmetic skills or mathematical reasoning that are well below average for age and may include an array of difficulties including number sense, performing simple addition and subtraction, understanding arithmetic terms and symbols, memorizing mathematical facts, and demonstrating accurate math reasoning (American Psychiatric Association, 2013). While defining features of impairment in mathematics are not well established, the core deficits are thought to involve the understanding of number and more general cognitive abilities, such as memory and executive skills, which are emphasized in this discussion (Mazzocco & Vukovic, 2018).

Understanding of Number: Number Sense
It appears that primitive numerical abilities exist in some animals and in preverbal human infants (Snowling & Hulme, 2015). Chimps, for example, were taught to match a half-filled glass of water with another half-full, rather than three-quarters full, glass of water. When later expected to match the half-full glass with half an apple or three-quarters of an apple, they selected the half apple. This suggests some numerical appreciation or sense of quantity. Human 6-month-olds are able to distinguish between groups of 8 and 16 dots, or 16 and 32 dots, but they do not differentiate between 16 and 24. Such demonstrations indicate that prior to acquiring language, humans have a representation of magnitude upon which to build mathematics abilities.

Research on problems in mathematics has emphasized basic understanding of children's early counting and arithmetic abilities (Geary, 2003, 2004; Torbeyns, Verschaffel, & Ghesquière, 2004). Even the relatively simple calculations accomplished by very young children require some understanding of number and counting. By age 5, many typically developing children understand basic principles of counting (e.g., an object in an array of objects can be counted only once), although they may have difficulties with other principles (e.g., objects in an array can be counted in any order). As children take on simple calculations, there is a gradual transition to more advanced procedures. For example, *counting all* (e.g., 2 + 3 is added by counting 1-2-3-4-5) gradually gives way to *counting on* (e.g., the child starts with 2 and then adds on 3-4-5). Counting procedures are soon represented in memory and arithmetic facts can then be called up automatically. The addition of 2 + 3 thus no longer requires counting; rather, 5 is quite effortlessly and rapidly retrieved.

The trajectory for children with impairment in mathematics differs from that of typically developing children. Children with impairment in mathematics acquire many of these early counting and basic arithmetic procedures and strategies more slowly, employ them less frequently and with less speed and accuracy (Mazzocco & Vukovic, 2018). In addition, deficits or delays exist in memory-based retrieval processes, which persist through the elementary school years. Thus, children in third grade or above may exhibit errors in rapid retrieval of number facts (e.g., 7 × 9 = 63). It is possible, then, that the mathematics difficulties of older children hark back to difficulties in the acquisitions of basic procedures not mastered earlier in life (Snowling & Hulme, 2015). Problems occur in addition, subtraction, multiplication, and division for more complex problems; and in employing fractions and decimals (Tannock, 2005b). Youth with co-occurring reading problems are particularly susceptible to errors in arithmetic word problems and complex calculation (Cirino et al., 2007).

Cognitive Correlates

While impairment in mathematics involves deficits in numerical understanding and skills, these deficits do not occur apart from other cognitive abilities (Mazzocco & Vukovic, 2018). Though not specific to the domain of mathematics, growing emphasis is being given to the role deficits in visual–spatial skills, memory and attention, processing speed, and executive function play in mathematics impairment. Consider, for example, the cognitive tasks involved in solving a simple arithmetic problem. A student must attend to the problem at hand by ignoring classroom distractions (attention), carry out the steps necessary to solve the problem (executive function), and retrieve and apply previously learned math facts (working memory) in a timely manner (processing speed). Although this example oversimplifies the complexity of cognitive processes involved in mathematics, it highlights how difficulties in any one or more of these cognitive areas can impact learning and performance.

Working memory, in particular, has been identified as key in mathematics achievement, whereby children with higher working memory capacity tend to perform better in mathematics (Geary et al., 2017; Lee & Bull, 2016). Geary and colleagues (2017), for example, found a relatively stable effect for working memory on mathematics achievement from first through eighth grades. Moreover, students with impairment in mathematics tend to make more mistakes in math facts retrieval and work more slowly on overlearned arithmetic problems as compared to typically developing peers (Mazzocco & Vukovic, 2018). Further research is needed to better understand the underlying cognitive deficits involved in mathematics impairment (Snowling & Hulme, 2015).

Epidemiology and Developmental Course

There are relatively few studies of the prevalence of mathematics disabilities, and these studies vary in how they define and measure deficits. Given these limitations, it appears that approximately 7% of school-age children display impairment in mathematics, with rates ranging from approximately 3 to 14% across studies (Shalev, 2007). Early difficulties in the acquisition of mathematics skills (prior to Grade 3) likely account for differences seen in students with impairment in mathematics versus those without in later grades (Chu et al., 2019; Geary et al., 2013). However, most students are identified by eighth grade, suggesting a proportion of children with significant difficulties are not identified until later grades (Mazzocco & Vukovic, 2018). Failure to identify and intervene early may contribute to the persistence of difficulties seen in adolescence and adulthood (Morgan et al., 2016; Shalev, Manor, & Gross-Tsur, 2005). Fortunately, research-based child intervention has developed, focusing on basic skills (such as fact retrieval and procedures) and higher-order skills (such as word problems) (Lyon et al., 2006).

Social and Motivational Problems

Although many children and adolescents with communication and learning disorders do quite well socially, develop a positive sense of self, and maintain interest in learning, others find these areas problematic.

Social Relations and Competence

The social relations of at least some children with disabilities are less than satisfactory. Teachers associate learning disabilities with a variety of problematic behaviors (Mishna, 2003), and children with disabilities may experience social exclusion from peers (Nowicki, Brown, & Dare, 2018). Overall, children with disabilities

Social interaction and motivational factors play an important role in the development of communication and learning difficulties. (Syda Productions/ Shutterstock)

may have fewer friends, a lower quality of friendship, and higher levels of loneliness (Wiener & Tardif, 2004).

What underlies social difficulties? There is no definitive answer to this question. Behavioral problems associated with learning disabilities, such as ADHD, may adversely affect peers (DuPaul et al., 2016). In addition, children with learning disorders appear to have lower social competence and deficits in social cognition, or their ability to read social cues, than their typically developing peers, which might affect social relationships (Galway & Metsala, 2011). They may have difficulties identifying the emotional expression of others, understanding social situations, guessing how other young people feel in particular situations, and solving social problems.

Whatever the underlying causes, poor social relationships and poor social skills increase risk for school alienation and dropout, loneliness, and withdrawal (Deater-Deckard, 2001; Vaughn et al., 1999). Risk for being involved in bullying—both as the victim and the perpetrator—may also be increased (Mishna, 2003; Rose, Monda-Amaya, & Espelage, 2011). For example, one study found that over a third of students with reading difficulties were involved in bullying—either as victim, bully or both—as compared to less than a quarter of students without reading difficulties (Turunen, Poskiparta, & Salmivalli, 2017).

Academic Self-Concept and Motivation

Research with typically developing youth indicates that beliefs about achievement can influence effort and performance (Dweck &

Molden, 2017). In general, holding the belief that intelligence is malleable and that effort stimulates ability is adaptive. Moreover, responding to failure with a mastery orientation is more adaptive than responding with a helplessness orientation. Mastery is indicated by attributing failure to lack of effort or task difficulty, expecting future improvement, and maintaining problem solving and positive affect. In contrast, a helplessness orientation involves expecting failure, giving up, and demonstrating negative self-cognition and affect. Similarly, beliefs about one's abilities and about competence to carry out a task are related to outcome on that task (Bandura, 1997).

Research indicates that learning disorders are associated with a lowered sense of worth (Elbaum & Vaughn, 2003; Nowicki 2003). Some children with disabilities rate their general sense of self as relatively low and more consistently rate their academic abilities negatively (Lipka & Siegel, 2006). Compared with typical students, those with a learning disorder report more helplessness and lower self-efficacy even when their school grades are comparable (Lackaye et al., 2006; Núñez et al., 2005). In adolescence, confidence in the ability to manage learning has been shown to decline and also to be related to success in school (Klassen, 2010).

Given these considerations, it is easy to see that children with disabilities can enter a vicious cycle of academic failure and low motivation that works against them (Licht & Kistner, 1986). As a result of academic failure, they come to doubt their intellectual abilities and believe that their efforts to achieve are futile. Such learned helplessness exacerbates the situation as the children are

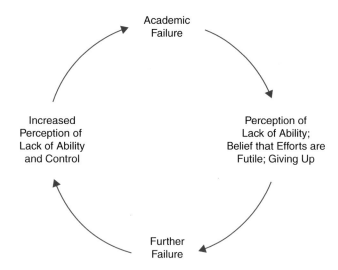

Figure 11.6 Children with learning disorders may experience a vicious cycle of academic failure and low motivation.

more likely to give up in the face of difficulty. In turn, further failure is experienced, which reinforces their belief in lack of ability and control (Figure 11.6).

While many students with learning difficulties show low levels of resilience (Panicker & Chelliah, 2016), not all youth with disabilities adopt negative perceptions and behaviors (Núñez et al., 2005). This was demonstrated in a study of the self-perceptions of middle school students with a learning disorder (Meltzer et al., 2004). Some of the students reported positive academic self-perceptions; others held negative self-perceptions. The former group reported expending greater effort on schoolwork than the latter group and employing learning strategies to bypass the effects of their impairments. Their teachers viewed them similarly, and also saw them as performing at a similar academic level as their peers without a learning disorder. This and related research suggest a need for further understanding of resilience factors regarding youth with a learning disorder.

Etiology of Communication and Learning Disorders

Determining the etiology of communication and learning disorders is complex. There is unlikely to be a single determinant or cause of the variety of difficulties seen in language and learning, and many factors that contribute to these difficulties remain unknown (Norbury & Paul, 2015; Pullen et al., 2017). Nevertheless, the development of cutting-edge technology and research has helped further our understanding of the multiple and complex factors that interact to contribute to difficulties in communication and

learning. Some major theoretical considerations and findings are discussed below.

Genetic Influences

Genetic effects on communication and learning disorders have been investigated with a gamut of genetic methods and are relatively well documented.

Communication

Communication disorders are highly heritable and aggregate in families (Norbury & Paul, 2015). Children with a family history of language impairments are at increased risk for language problems (Pennington et al., 2019). Although data vary across studies, a median rate of 35% compared to 11% in control families has been reported (Grigorenko, 2009). Twin comparisons show concordance in MZ pairs to be about 75% and about 45% in DZ pairs, suggesting genetic factors play an important role (Plomin, 2008). High heritability has been documented in twins for articulation problems, expressive language difficulties, and nonword repetition tasks that are considered an index of phonological memory (DeThorne et al., 2006; Grigorenko, 2009).

The study of the genetics of communication disorders has lagged somewhat compared to that of other developmental disorders but considerable advances are being made in understanding the genetic underpinnings of language development and disorders (Fisher, 2017). The identification of the FOXP2 gene in a family exhibiting a specific speech impairment represents a major genetic discovery and has laid the foundation for subsequent research (Scharff & Petri, 2011). (See Accent: "The FOXP2 Story.") Targeted and genome-wide linkage and association studies have identified regions on several candidate genes and chromosomes, such as 3p12–q13, 6p22, and 15q21, for example, that may be implicated in speech and language deficits, yet research is still emerging (Pennington et al., 2019).

Reading

Impairment in reading often runs in families. Parents of youth with reading impairment have high rates of reading problems and, conversely, about 30 to 50% of youth with a parent with impairment in reading will develop the disorder (Peterson & McGrath, 2009). Twin comparisons give evidence of genetic influence, with concordance in MZ twins being about 90% and in DZ about 40% (Snowling, 2019). Overall, heritability has been estimated at about 60 to 70% (Swagerman et al., 2017). Influence on several components of reading has been shown, including on phonological processing and single-word reading. For instance, several gene locations linked to reading impairment have been associated with phonological disorder (Smith et al., 2005). This is a particularly interesting finding given the importance of these processes in language and reading disorders. Some progress has

ACCENT The FOXP2 Story

The FOXP2 gene, the first gene implicated in communication disorders, was identified through the study of a large family known as the KE family (Newbury & Monaco, 2010). Many family members exhibited symptoms of a distinctive form of speech disorder called verbal dyspraxia. Multiple symptoms of verbal dyspraxia affect both oral and written language (Grigorenko, 2009). Problems exist in speech articulation and in expressive and receptive vocabulary, morphology, and syntax. Cognition is affected, and members of the KE family with the condition exhibit lower nonverbal IQ than family members without the condition.

Transmitted in a dominant pattern, the FOXP2 gene on chromosome 7 appears responsible for the malady. A mutation in the gene has been found in all affected but not unaffected family members. The gene codes for proteins that control the transcription of other genes and thus can have wide influence. FOXP2 is thought to be important in early prenatal development, especially at the time of brain development.

The discovery of FOXP2 stirred considerable interest: perhaps other communication disorders could be traced to FOXP2 or to other single genes. Investigators searched for but did not find FOXP2 to be related to other communication disorders, nor do single-gene abnormalities appear to play an important role in these problems. Nevertheless, the discovery of FOXP2 is a landmark because it precipitated an explosion of research to find other genes, like FOXP1, TBR1, and CNTNAP2 that are also linked to neurodevelopmental disorders including communication disorders, and has resulted in increased understanding of communication disorders (Fisher, 2017).

been made in identifying specific chromosomes and susceptibility genes that might contribute to impairment in reading. For example, evidence suggests DYX1C1 on chromosome 15 is likely involved in the migrations of neurons in brain development and may be linked to dyslexia (Tammimies et al., 2013).

The involvement of multiple genes in reading impairment is supported by evidence that reading skills in children and families appear to fall on a continuum (Bishop, 2015). Moreover, both general reading *ability* and *disability* are heritable and are genetically linked (Swagerman et al., 2017). While some single-gene and chromosome syndromes are associated with reading problems, they involve rare, severe forms of learning disabilities (Plomin, 2008). Rather, evidence suggests that a number of genes work together with other risk factors to produce susceptibility to reading disorders (Pennington et al., 2019).

Writing and Mathematics
Studies of the genetic influence on written expression are limited, but heritability and twin studies suggest spelling difficulties aggregate in families (Fletcher et al., 2019). In particular, chromosome 15 may be linked to impairment in spelling (Schulte-Körne, 2001). A more recent twin study evaluated broad writing abilities and demonstrated heritability for sentence composition and handwriting (Olson et al., 2013), but much is still to be understood about the influence of genetics on written expression.

Research also suggests heritability in mathematics impairment. Shalev and colleagues (2001) found that parents and siblings of probands with mathematics disabilities exhibited rates of impairment about ten times higher than would be expected in the general population. In addition, limited twin data indicate higher concordance for mathematics disability in identical than fraternal pairs (Lyon et al., 2003). A genome-wide association study of mathematics ability and disability has pointed to several locations of interest (Docherty et al., 2010). The findings from this and other research indicate that mathematics ability and disability are influenced by many genes of small effect.

Shared Genetic Influences and Generalist Genes
As we saw earlier in this chapter, communication and learning disorders in young people frequently occur together. Moreover, co-occurrence of these disorders tends to run in families—thus the question, "Do these disorders share a genetic predisposition?" Research has made it clear that the answer is "yes." For example, studies suggest about 50% of the correlation between impairment in reading and mathematics is the result of shared genetic effects (Davis et al., 2014).

Important research also indicates that the same set of genes—so-called generalist genes—that influence one disorder also influence another (Grigorenko et al., 2020). As noted by Plomin, Kovas, & Haworth (2007), this finding appears counterintuitive because some children have, say, a reading problem without a math problem, or vice versa. Such dissociation of the difficulties can be accounted for by the fact that only *some* genes are shared and that unshared environmental effects also play a role in making children different from one another. In any event, given the existence of generalist genes, the identification of a specific gene for one disability may be important for understanding another disability.

At the same time, communication and learning disorders are unlikely to be caused by a mutation in a single gene. Rather, these disorders are likely to involve the effects of multiple genes and other risk factors that interact to influence and shape brain development (Bishop, 2015; Pennington et al., 2019). We turn next to reviewing some of the major considerations in understanding the neurobiological basis of communication and learning disorders.

Neurobiological Influences

Our understanding of communication and learning disorders has been informed by advances in research in structural and functional brain development. Direct studies of the brain indicate an association between communication and learning problems with specific disabilities such as cerebral palsy, epilepsy, nervous system infections, head injury, prenatal alcohol use, very preterm/low birthweight, and neurological delays and soft signs (e.g., Aarnoudse-Moens et al., 2009; Snowling, 1991; Taylor, 1989; Vellutino et al., 2004). Many regions of the brain are likely to be involved in some way; for example, the cerebellum and certain visual and auditory pathways could play a role in perceptual processing in language or reading impairment (Heim & Benasich, 2006). The most consistent findings in neuroimaging research of reading impairment have pointed to the left hemisphere, long considered crucial to language functions (Hoeft & Wang, 2019).

Language and Reading: Brain Structure
Structures of the brain have been investigated through postmortem examination and neuroimaging research. Some of the earlier neurological findings pointed to differences in the planum temporale and surrounding region (Hynd, Marshall, & Gonzalez, 1991; Hynd & Semrud-Clikeman, 1989a, 1989b; Peterson, 1995). This area, which roughly corresponds with Wernicke's area and is

used in language, involves the upper surface of the temporal lobe extending to the lower surface of the parietal lobe. In most—but not all—adults in the general population the area is larger in the left hemisphere than the right. In persons with specific language and reading disorders, asymmetry often is absent. The right side has been found to be as large or even larger than the left, and the left temporal lobe to be smaller than normal (Adrián-Ventura et al., 2020; D'Mello & Gabrieli, 2018; Eckert et al., 2016). Moreover, reduced connectivity in brain regions important for reading have been identified (Tschentscher et al., 2019).

In addition, cell abnormalities in the brain have been observed to be more common in individuals with specific disabilities. However, as informative and interesting as these and other structural findings are, caution is needed in drawing conclusions. Differences in the brains of adults with disabilities may not be the same as in children, research samples are often small, and findings are not completely consistent (D'Mello & Gabrieli, 2018).

Language and Reading: Brain Function
Much attention has been given to evaluating brain activity with a variety of scanning methods as children and adults engage in language and reading tasks. Differences have been shown between impaired and nonimpaired readers in brain regions involved in language and reading (Figure 11.7). An area in the front of the brain (corresponding to Broca's area) aids in word analysis. A second area, the parietal-temporal area (including Wernicke's area), plays a central role in word analysis and phonological processing, that is, in integrating the visual and sound aspects of language. A third area at the junction of the occipital and temporal lobes is especially involved in rapid word recognition; it becomes increasingly important as readers come to rely more on automatic, almost instantaneous word form recognition rather

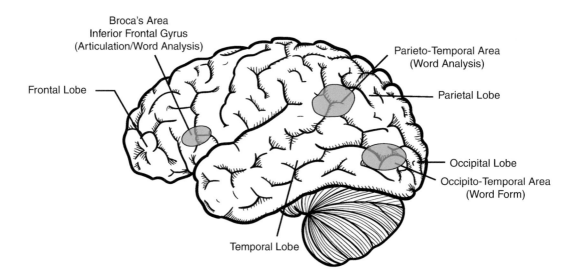

Figure 11.7 Approximate locations of the left hemisphere regions involved in language and reading. (Adapted from Shaywitz & Shaywitz, 2020)

than on basic phonological processes. In general, strong readers rely more on the back areas of the brain when reading, and most processing occurs on the left side.

It has been proposed that reading disorders involve faulty wiring of the system necessary for good language and reading. Several studies show that patterns of brain activation are different in children and adults with or without reading problems when they engage in various phonological and reading tasks. In individuals with reading impairment, the posterior left side appears underactive and the corresponding posterior right side may be overactive (D'Mello & Gabrieli, 2018). There is also some evidence that the front left area of the brain may be relatively overactive, and that as children with reading disabilities get older they may increasingly employ the frontal area of the brain (Shaywitz & Shaywitz, 2003).

In examining these findings, it is helpful to recall that the brain is a dynamic network: abnormalities in one area might affect another, perhaps as an effort to compensate for what is not working properly. Shaywitz and colleagues suggest that the use of alternative routes—greater reliance on the front brain area and the right hemisphere—allows some readers to achieve accurate, although not rapid and fluent, reading (Shaywitz, 2003; Shaywitz et al., 2003).

In an interesting recent study, Preston and colleagues (2010) examined elementary schoolchildren who had been early, on-time, or late talkers. Brain images were recorded while the children listened to and read words or pronounced nonwords. Children who had been late talkers showed lower activation in several cortical and sub-cortical areas previously implicated in speech and reading. This group of children also performed less well on the language and literary tasks.

Progress is being made in understanding brain functioning in language and reading disorders. Meanwhile, fascinating results have come from research that shows brain changes associated with interventions for reading and language deficits and suggest the brain can be plastic to change in response to intervention (D'Mello & Gabrieli, 2018). (See Accent: "Intervention and Brain Changes.")

Psychosocial Influences

While genes govern the general pathway of brain development, the environment plays an important role in influencing its outcome and function. Genetic behavior studies point to a role for both genetic and environmental influences on normal and impaired development relevant to specific disabilities. From other types of research, we know that several psychosocial variables are important in typical language development (Snow & Douglas, 2017). Early vocabulary growth is predicted by the number or sophistication of words the child hears from its mother. More rapid language development is predicted by, for example, the mother's elaborating on the child's speech and commenting on what the child is paying attention to. Additionally, research shows that

simply reading to a child is linked to vocabulary development (McQuillan, 2019). Although family variables may not be the root of language problems, they may play a role in maintaining deficits (Conti-Ramsden & Durkin, 2015).

Stevenson and Fredman (1990) found that large family size and certain aspects of mother–child interaction were linked to reading problems, and they noted that family involvement in the child's learning may be especially influential on early reading acquisition. However, family factors are not always found (Snowling et al., 2007). Lowered expectations of teachers and children themselves may be especially hazardous for those whose learning requires extraordinary effort.

It is also generally believed that factors such as overcrowded classrooms, math anxiety, and quality of instruction can affect the acquisition of mathematics skills (Shalev et al., 2001). Indeed, quality of teaching, class size, and interactive computer programs can markedly affect academic skills (Nisbett et al., 2012). Early learning especially may be facilitated by cognitive stimulation across home, preschool, and first-grade settings (Fowler, 2017).

Assessing Communication and Learning Disorders

Children's communication or learning problems are typically first noticed by parents or teachers, whose sensitivity to the difficulties is valuable for early intervention. (See Accent: "Clues for Identifying Reading Impairment.")

When communication disorders are suspected in preschoolers, parents seek assessment from a variety of professionals. Family and child history, speech and language evaluation, assessment of verbal and nonverbal intelligence, and screening for hearing, neurological, and medical problems are generally appropriate (Mohapatra, 2018). Detailed speech and language assessment usually are conducted by specialists who have broad knowledge of the language system, as well as intervention (Norbury & Paul, 2015). A multidisciplinary team including language specialists, preschool teachers, psychologists, and physicians, among others, may be formed to plan intervention (Kirk, Gallagher, & Anastasiow, 2000). Later occurring or more subtle communication problems and learning difficulties may be assessed in mental health settings, but are often evaluated in the educational system, following procedures recommended by government regulations for the assessment and education of youth with disabilities.

Best practice in identifying communication and learning disorders and understanding a child's particular deficits involves a holistic approach to identification that takes into consideration multiple domains of the child's functioning and uses information from multiple sources and methods of assessment to understand the full picture of the child's presenting difficulties (Pennington

ACCENT Intervention and Brain Changes

Simos and colleagues (2002) worked with 7- to 17-year-olds with average intelligence but severe disabilities in word recognition and phonological skills. Preintervention brain scans indicated an abnormal activation pattern for phonological tasks: little or no activation of the left posterior (parietal-temporal) region and increased activation of the corresponding region of the right brain. The youth received about 80 hours of phonological training over eight weeks. Not only did measures of word accuracy show improvement into the normal range, but brain scans also indicated increased activation in the left posterior hemisphere relative to the corresponding right side. No changes over time were shown in activation patterns for the normal control group. Figure 11.8 exemplifies the findings in one of the treated children. Simos and colleagues (2007) subsequently reported similarly positive results in 7- to 9-year-olds who received intervention focusing on phonological processing and reading fluency.

A more extensive investigation of 6- to 9-year-olds with reading disabilities examined the outcome of a phonologically based intervention delivered at school over eight months (Shaywitz et al., 2004). Daily 50-minute sessions progressively focused on letter-sound associations, phoneme analysis of words, timed reading of words, oral story reading, and word dictation. After intervention, the treated participants significantly improved in reading and brain activation was more in keeping with that of a nonimpaired control group. Follow-up of some of the children one year after intervention indicated continued improvement in the occipital-temporal region, known for its involvement with automatic word processing.

Research that documents both improvement in select language/reading skills and correlated neurobiological change suggests that psychosocial intervention can affect brain development. It holds promise of increased understanding of disabilities and of treatments for children who have difficulty in reading (Coyne et al., 2004; Hatcher et al., 2004).

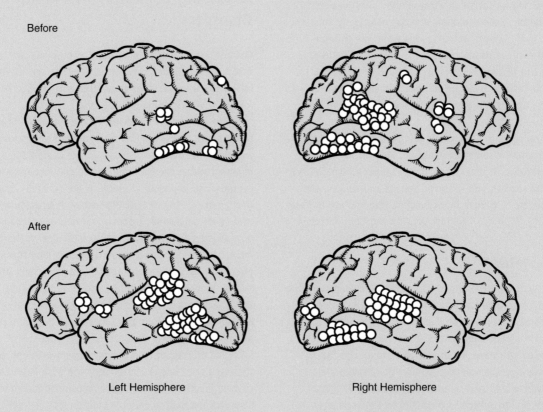

Figure 11.8 Changes in brain activation in a child after intervention. Most notable is increased activation in left posterior regions. (Based on Simos et al., 2002. Courtesy of J. M. Fletcher. Copyright 2002 by Lippincott Williams, and Wilkins; reprinted with permission)

ACCENT Clues for Identifying Reading Impairment

Sally Shaywitz, a neuroscientist and physician who has been in the forefront of reading disorder research, notes that parents can play an important role in identifying reading disorders (Shaywitz & Shaywitz, 2020). The identification requires the parents to carefully observe the child, know what to look for, and be willing to spend time listening to the child speak and read. With this in mind, Shaywitz has presented clues for recognizing that a child may need further assessment.

Clues During the Preschool Years

Delayed language
Difficulty in learning and appreciating common nursery rhymes
Mispronounced words; persistent baby talk
Difficulty in learning (and remembering) names of letters
Failure to know the letters in child's own name

Clues During Kindergarten and First Grade

Failure to understand that words can be segmented and sounded out
Inability to learn to associate letters with their appropriate sounds
Reading errors not connected to the sounds of the letters, for example, *big* is read as *goat*
Inability to read common one-syllable words or to sound out even simple words
Complaints about the difficulty of reading, or avoidance of reading
History of reading difficulties in parents or siblings

Clues from Second Grade and Beyond

Among the many clues in speaking:

mispronunciation of long, unfamiliar, or complicated words; influent speech (hesitations, pauses, use of

"ums"); inability to find the exact word; inability to reply rapidly when questioned; difficulty in remembering bits of verbal information such as dates and lists.

Among the many clues in reading:

slow reading progress; difficulty in reading unfamiliar words, function words such as *that* and *in*, or multisyllable words; omitting parts of words; oral reading that is choppy, labored, or slow; avoidance of reading; reading that improves in accuracy but not in fluency; family history of reading and spelling difficulties.

Sally Shaywitz, M.D. is a Professor of Pediatrics at Yale University School of Medicine and codirector of the Yale Center for Dyslexia & Creativity. (Courtesy of Sally Shaywitz)

et al., 2019). Standardized tests to evaluate language, intellectual functioning, and academic achievement are often utilized (Decker et al., 2018). Tests are available to assess specific components of these domains, for example, vocabulary, mathematics calculation, phonological awareness, or listening comprehension (Fletcher et al., 2019; Pennington et al., 2019).

Tests of general intelligence are also valuable in understanding the relationship of the child's cognitive functioning to their academic performance and may help to isolate underlying learning problems and determine particular strengths and weaknesses (Decker et al., 2018; Flanagan et al., 2018). Additional

psychological assessment, such as of executive functioning or motor skills, may be useful depending on the goals of assessment. When it is relevant, the evaluator should also discuss the child's study habits, motivations, self-esteem, and concerns.

Because communication and learning disorders are defined in terms of achievement, there may be a tendency to bypass the behavioral, social, and motivational contexts in which the child is operating. Yet, as mentioned above, a comprehensive approach that considers psychosocial factors is important in understanding the multiple and often interrelated factors that influence the child's functioning (Pennington et al., 2019).

Intervention for Communication and Learning Disorders

Prevention

As a general rule, prevention of developmental disorders is linked to early identification and treatment. Regarding communication disorders, with the exception of severe cases, it can be challenging to identify meaningful impairments in toddlers. Children 2 to 3 years old who are late talkers or exhibit other expressive problems can fall into the normal range of language development by early school age or they can continue to have difficulties (Rescorla, 2002). Thus, prevention requires the monitoring of early communication problems and appropriate referral when impairment is identified (Bishop et al., 2016).

There is considerable interest today in the prevention of learning problems. At the national level, much concern is expressed over the substantial number of youth who are not acquiring necessary academic skills. Some of these children have specific disabilities while others have more general achievement problems. We also know that untreated disabilities often continue, and that later treatment is not as successful as earlier intervention (Shaywitz & Shaywitz, 2020). Yet, too many reading problems go undetected, and referrals for learning problems too often occur only after several years of academic failure. Research is continuing into early risk factors for reading impairment and early identification (Snowling, 2013).

As we saw earlier in this chapter, the RTI approach is viewed by some as a method of prevention of reading impairment. The multiple instruction levels of RTI are intended to prevent or mitigate learning problems and disabilities in at-risk children (Fuchs et al., 2018). The initial exposure of all children to a carefully selected intervention (curriculum) is conceptualized as primary (universal) prevention. Students who do less well than their peers at this level are considered at risk and are provided with more intense educational efforts, or secondary (selective) prevention. Those who respond poorly to this second tier of intervention are viewed as demonstrating unexpected failure and they receive comprehensive evaluation to determine the appropriateness of special education services—that is, tertiary (indicated) prevention. RTI thus merges prevention and treatment. Regardless of how youth are identified with reading disability, early intervention tends to target basic skills, and reading programs predominate. Thus, many efforts focus on phonological processing and word-level reading.

Intervention for Communication Disorders

The history and literature on treatment for communication impairments differs somewhat from that for learning disorders, and our discussion only touches briefly on this area. Reviews and meta-analyses of interventions indicate that language development can be enhanced, although effects depend in part on the type of disorder and the measures employed, with greater support for interventions aimed at articulation and expressive language difficulties than receptive difficulties (Law, Garrett, & Nye, 2005; Leonard, 2017). There is some evidence that both clinician- and parent-directed therapy can be effective, and a suggestion that longer duration of treatment has the potential for better outcome.

Specific approaches to treating communication disorders, particularly expressive language difficulties, appear similar to the way that parents and other adults teach language to typically developing children (Leonard, 2017; Pennington et al., 2019). Operant procedures and modeling are widely used in treatment, and it is not unusual for toys and pictures to be a part of the training procedures. For example, the trainer presents language forms (e.g., plural nouns) and the child is encouraged to imitate the trainer, and/or reinforcers are given for the child's communication in natural settings. Treatment can result in some children, on some tasks, closing the gap between themselves and their typically developing peers (Leonard, 2017). There is limited evidence for the generalization of training; for instance, an acquired language form may be used in different sentences in spontaneous speech. In addition, follow-up evaluations show that the effects of training may endure over time.

Despite these findings, though, the picture is not all positive. Language often improves but does not reach adequate levels, so that many young people remain socially and academically disadvantaged. As mentioned, there is little evidence for the success of therapies for receptive deficits. Moreover, different treatments appear to work to about the same degree and may have common elements, but these elements have not been established (Law, Garrett, & Nye, 2004). Thus, both success and the need for empirically supported interventions are evident.

The treatments described above focus, for the most part, on the specific language deficits exhibited by the children. One intervention that has received considerable attention aims at improving the speed of auditory processing deficits hypothesized to underlie oral language. Fast ForWord consists of computer/internet programs of audiovisual games that contain acoustically modified speech, language training techniques similar to those used by speech and language therapists, as well as literacy training (Tallal & Jenkins, 2018). The language series is aimed at primary school-age children, and the literacy component is geared toward intermediate and high school-age students. The program is commercially produced, with claims of producing language and reading-related gains in a short period of time, and it is widely used in schools and clinics in numerous countries. There is evidence for and against the effectiveness of the program, and the efficacy is still to be determined (Dawson et al., 2015).

Emerging programs that systematically address prevention and early intervention in language development are receiving increased attention and empirical evaluation (Mahoney et al., 2020). These include population-level approaches aimed at promoting language- and literacy-rich activities beginning in infancy and continuing into school age, for example, with the notion that early intervention in language will set the foundation for optimal development and learning.

Intervention for Learning Disorders

Historically, interventions for learning disorders have reflected the multidisciplinary nature of the field. Psychologists, physicians, educators, optometrists, and communication therapists have all had a hand in treatment. In the late 1960s and 1970s, many different approaches were employed (Hammill, 1993; Lyon & Cutting, 1998). Conceptually these models, discussed briefly below, form the foundation for contemporary interventions for learning disorders (Figure 11.9).

The medically oriented approach viewed learning disabilities as stemming from biological pathology (Hallahan, Pullen, & Ward, 2013). Deficits in underlying neurological processes were hypothesized to hinder the development of language, visual and auditory perception, perceptual–motor functioning, and the like. For example, oral language problems might be viewed as the result of brain damage from anoxia, and treatment might entail exercise to stimulate the brain areas relevant to language. Historically, this approach was widely disseminated despite little evidence to support the model and related treatment methods (McGill & Ndip, 2019). Interestingly, with more recent advances in brain imaging technology, a revived emphasis is being placed on identifying the neurobiological underpinnings of learning disorders and related approaches for assessment, diagnosis, and intervention (De Smedt, Peters, & Ghesquière, 2019; Krishnan, Watkins, & Bishop, 2016).

The psychoeducational-remedial model also guided intervention in the field. This approach more specifically targeted various perceptual and cognitive processes assumed to underlie disabilities (McGill & Ndip, 2019). Training programs that involved practice in eye–hand coordination, spatial relationships, or language were offered by educational specialists. Unlike the medical approach, the teaching of academic and information-processing skills was advocated. Student strengths and weaknesses in visual, auditory, language, and motor modalities were taken into account and used to guide intervention. Despite the popularity of these efforts, many fell by the wayside due to lack of documented success (Dean & Burns, 2002; Hammill, 1993).

Cognitive-behavioral models of intervention move beyond attempting to identify underlying organic pathology or information-processing deficits and recognize the multiple variables—broader environmental contingencies and internal thoughts and feelings—that interact and influence learning (McGill & Ndip, 2019). Interventions involve direct skills

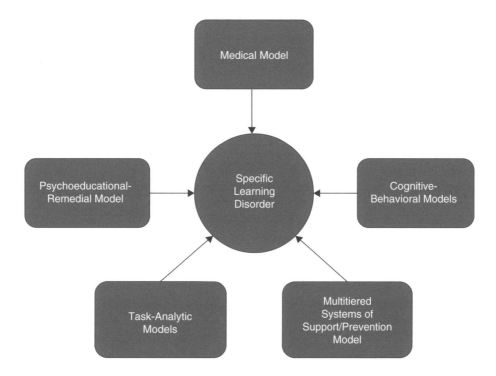

Figure 11.9 Conceptual foundations for learning disorder interventions. (Adapted from McGill & Ndip, 2019)

"I turned five. That's why I'm here. What are you in for?"

Jack Ziegler/Cartoon Collections

instruction, as well as the application of behavior modification techniques, modeling, and strategies that target self-regulation, problem solving, motivation, and metacognition. The cognitive-behavioral approach puts special emphasis on students directing their own learning. Students are taught to record their learning activities, assess their progress, self-reinforce their own behavior, and otherwise manage or regulate learning. The cognitive-behavioral technique is exemplified in intervention for writing skills deficits by, among other things, instructing students how to organize the writing task, employ different strategies, and evaluate their work (Graham & Harris, 2003). Cognitive-behaviorally informed interventions are generally shown to be effective and have been used to address a wide array of academic difficulties (Graham & Harris, 2017; Montague, Enders, & Dietz, 2011).

Similarly, the task-analytic models deemphasize underlying organic causes of learning problems and aim to improve academic or social skills through techniques based on learning principles, such as contingency management, feedback, and modeling. Interventions involve breaking down complex academic skills into a series of tasks or steps that are taught to the student in a sequential manner until the student achieves mastery (McGill & Ndip, 2019). For example, if a child has a disability in writing, exercises and practice are provided in writing sentences and then paragraphs. Among other things, the task-analytic model entails

selecting and stating goals, presenting new material in small steps and with clear and detailed explanations, incorporating student practice and student feedback, guiding students, and monitoring student progress (Gettinger & Koscik, 2001; Lyon & Cutting, 1998). The model has a long history in educational sciences, and its methods have demonstrated positive effects (Stockard et al., 2018).

As described earlier, the multitiered systems of support (MTSS)/prevention approach to intervention aims to identify and address learning difficulties early, before they emerge as learning disorders (McGill & Ndip, 2019). The model stems from cognitive-behavioral and task-analytic approaches and is influenced by public health models of prevention (Vaughn & Fletcher, 2012). As described earlier in the discussion of RTI, all students are monitored and screened for academic difficulties (Tier 1) and students identified as at risk for academic problems are provided with targeted interventions at varying intensity (Tiers 2 and 3), all while treatment progress is monitored systematically (Fletcher et al., 2019). This approach has seen a rise in influence in learning disorder intervention (Schulte, 2016).

While the models described above differ significantly, their approaches have each contributed to and/or form the basis of current interventions. Today's neurobiological models hark back to the early medical approach in their emphasis on underlying brain functioning, and they also incorporate the early psychoeducational approach by linking instruction to student strengths and weaknesses in cognitive processing. Cognitive-behavioral, task-analytic, and prevention methods are represented in today's direct instruction that pinpoint the acquisition of needed skills and teaches to them.

Overall, the possibility of substantial remediation of learning disabilities through thoughtfully designed and implemented interventions is indicated. This is not to say, of course, that the task is of equal challenge across disabilities, nor that equal progress has been made across disabilities. For example, there is significant understanding of dyslexia and evidence for the success of interventions that include training in phonological awareness, letter knowledge, and grapheme–phoneme correspondence within the context of reading and writing tasks (Duff & Clarke, 2011). On the other hand, treatments for difficulties in reading comprehension have been more challenging and have included metacognitive strategies, vocabulary, and spoken narrative. Finally, it is important to note that even when interventions are relatively ameliorative, a proportion of children are not helped. Further efforts are required to address the needs of these non-responders.

Special Education Services

In the United States, education services for individuals with various kinds of disabilities have evolved dramatically over the last decades. As touched upon earlier in this chapter, criticisms of services, legal decisions, and a growing social commitment to the rights of children with disabilities to appropriate education resulted in the Education for All Handicapped Children Act of 1975. Subsequent federal regulations extended opportunities and rights. Public Law 99–457 amended the Education for All Handicapped Children Act, extending provisions to developmentally delayed 3- to- 5-year-olds and creating voluntary intervention for infants. The Education for All Handicapped Children Act was expanded under the title the Individuals with Disabilities Education Act (IDEA) in 1990, and IDEA was reauthorized and amended in 1997 and in 2004.

IDEA encompasses several categories for serving youth with disabilities that include speech or language impairments, learning disabilities, intellectual disability, emotional disturbance, autism, and sensory and medical impairments such as blindness, deafness, and orthopedic problems. Increasing numbers of individuals have been served under IDEA. About 7 million individuals, ages 3 to 21 years, received services in 2017–2018 (McFarland et al., 2019). Thirty-four percent of these had specific learning disabilities, and 19% had speech or language impairments.

The four purposes of IDEA have remained essentially unchanged over the years (U.S. Department of Education, 2000):

- To ensure that all students with disabilities obtain an appropriate free public education that emphasizes special education and related services to meet their particular needs
- To ensure that the rights of these students and their parents are protected
- To assist states and localities in providing education to children with disabilities
- To assess and ensure the effectiveness of these educational efforts.

Appropriate education fundamentally means educational experiences tailored to each child's needs. An **individual education plan (IEP)** is constructed by a team of professionals, with parental participation, for each student receiving special education (U.S. Department of Education Office of Special Education and Rehabilitative Services, 2017). Table 11.4 provides a list of the members of the multidisciplinary team, as specified by the IDEA. Among other things, IEPs must consider the child's present functioning; annual educational goals; how and when the child's progress will be measured; special educational and other services to be provided; and, for older students, goals and services for the transition from school to postsecondary life (Building the Legacy: IDEA, 2004). The plans must be systematically reviewed by a committee and the child's parents.

Under IDEA, students with disabilities are to be educated in the **least restrictive environment**, that is, with their nondisabled peers to the maximum extent appropriate. Mainstreaming these students in regular classrooms became a central feature of educational placement. Then, in the late 1980s, through the Regular Education Initiative, a call went out for **inclusion** of students beyond mainstreaming. The premise of inclusion is that public schools should be restructured to be supportive, nurturing communities that meet the needs of all students (Mercer & Mercer,

Table 11.4 Members of the IEP Multidisciplinary Team

Parents of the child with a disability
Regular education teacher of the child (if the child is or may be participating in the regular education environment)
Special education teacher or provider of the child
Representative of the local public education agency
Educational professional who can interpret assessment results (can be a member of the team above)
Other individuals who may have knowledge or special expertise regarding the child
The child with a disability, when appropriate

Source: Based on U.S. Department of Education, Office of Special Education and Rehabilitative Services, 2017.

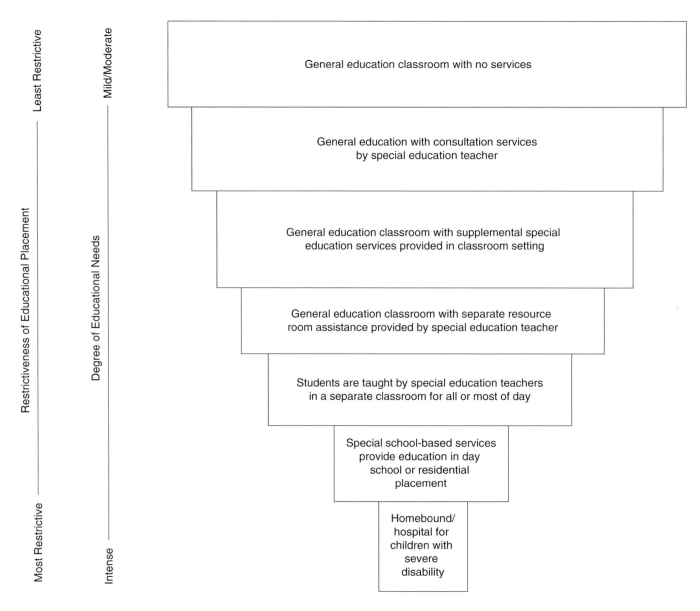

Figure 11.10 Alternative educational settings according to degree of restrictiveness. (Adapted from Lindstrom & Drolet, 2017)

2001), with the general education teacher assuming primary responsibility for included students (Beirne-Smith et al., 2006).

In practice, consistent with the concept of appropriate education in the least restrictive environment, several options should be available for students in need of special education services. The options range from the general education classroom, with or without supplemental services, to special classes in community schools, to special day and residential schools (Figure 11.10). These settings provide increasing levels of support, and appropriate education means matching the child with access to the curriculum within the most appropriate setting with the least amount of services and supports (Lindstrom & Drolet, 2017).

By 2017, 95% of students with disabilities ages 6 to 21 were served in the regular schools, 3% in separate public schools for youth with disabilities, and the small remainder in other settings (McFarland et al., 2019). Most students with learning or communication disorders are in general education classrooms with varying degrees of supplemental services, such as special instruction in the classroom or part-time instruction in resource rooms. In fact, in 2017, about 71% of youth with learning disabilities and 87% with speech or language impairments spend most of their school day inside the general classroom (McFarland et al., 2019).

Inclusion: Benefits and Concerns

The issue of how best to serve students with special needs has been controversial (Kauffman et al., 2018). This is not an easy matter to settle because research must address a variety of kinds and severity of disabilities, as well as many alternative programs. Given the complexity of the issue, a considerable amount of early research did not clearly support the once-anticipated academic and social benefits of contained special education classrooms (Detterman & Thompson, 1997).

With the policy of inclusion came both approval and criticism. Yet, research on the effectiveness of this policy and its implementation remains limited (Kauffman et al., 2017; Van Mieghem et al., 2020). Still, advocates have pointed to research showing benefits to academic achievement and social outcomes for the included students (Hobbs & Westling, 1998; Rea, McLaughlin, & Walther-Thomas, 2002; Waldron & McLeskey, 1998). Included students have been found to do better on standardized achievement tests and in relating to others, with no greater behavioral difficulties. Outcomes for nondisabled students in these classrooms have also been reported as favorable (Cole, Waldron, & Majd, 2004; Staub & Peck, 1994/1995). Advocates of inclusion believe that concern is best directed not toward *whether* inclusive education should be provided but toward *how* it should be implemented to maximize its effectiveness.

In contrast, critics of the movement argue that inclusion is not appropriate for every child, particularly those with severe impairments (Imray & Colley, 2017). Those who caution the sweeping practice of inclusion point to data that do not support it, including reports of little academic advantage and lower levels of self-esteem among students with disabilities (Cole et al., 2004). It is also argued that although the inclusion policy has helped reduce discrimination and segregation of students with disabilities, it has strengthened a false belief that no student requires special consideration and that placement in special education settings is a harmful discriminatory approach (Kauffman, McGee, & Brigham, 2004). Moreover, opponents see policies of inclusion as violating both children's rights and federal mandates for appropriate and individualized educational placement (Kauffman et al., 2018).

The policy of inclusion has brought benefits and concerns, and both "good" and "poor" programs likely are being implemented (Cole et al., 2004). In addition, it has also made demands on the educational system. The demands made on general education teachers, in particular, can be substantial, and teachers often lack specialized knowledge and have inadequate resources and time to implement special curricula and practices (Kauffman et al., 2017). Inclusion requires that those in the educational setting effectively work with students who require accommodation in curricula, instructional materials, teaching strategies, testing, and management (Polloway et al., 2010). For successful implementation, professional development for teachers on evidence-based inclusion practices is recommended (Van Mieghem et al., 2018). Moreover, it is argued that responsible and effective inclusion requires attention to the individual educational and instructional needs of students with disabilities (Kauffman et al., 2016). A continuum of educational settings may best serve the varying and individual needs of students and is fitting with the intents of IDEA.

Looking Back

A Bit of History: Unexpected Disabilities, Unmet Needs

- Today's field of communication and learning disorders can be traced to interest in individuals who exhibited discrepant abilities and to advocacy to improve services to them.
- Kirk's 1963 definition of learning disabilities was a milestone for the interdisciplinary field as we know it today.

Definitional Concerns

- The influential definition of specific learning disability offered by the federal government has been criticized and has led to variation in how specific disabilities are defined and identified.

- Specific disorders historically were identified by an IQ–achievement discrepancy or a discrepancy between a youth's achievement and what would be expected based on age or grade level. Criticism of the IQ–achievement discrepancy approach has led to reduced reliance on this model.
- Response to intervention has emerged as a widely used, multilevel approach to identifying disabilities and/or preventing them.

Communication Disorders

- As conceptualized by the DSM, communication disorders include Speech Sound Disorder and Language Disorder, among others.

- Epidemiological studies suggest a rate of 3 to 7%, but rates vary with age and type of disorder. Boys have higher rates than girls, and disability is linked to lower SES.
- Simple speech sound problems often remit; outcome is more variable for early expressive problems and poorest for receptive difficulties. Co-occurring problems include learning disabilities, academic difficulties, and internalizing and externalizing difficulties.
- Among the cognitive deficits proposed as contributing to communication disorders are slow general information processing, impaired auditory processing, and memory deficits.

Specific Learning Disorders: Reading, Written Expression, Mathematics

- Specific learning disorder with impairment in reading can be viewed in terms of word-level (dyslexia) and comprehension problems. Phonological processing deficits are considered critical in dyslexia. Impaired comprehension entails many language and cognitive processes.
- Specific learning disorder with impairment in reading, the most common learning disorder, may occur in 4 to 15% of school-age children, and rates are higher in boys. Reading problems can diminish but often tend to persist.
- Specific learning disorder with impairment in written expression entails deficits that affect transcription and text generation. Prevalence is estimated at about 6 to 14% of school-age children, and many children also display reading problems.
- The study of specific learning disorder with impairment in mathematics has focused on basic arithmetic skills. Basic deficits in understanding number, counting, calculation, and retrieval of arithmetic facts have been documented. Three to 14% of school-age children may be affected. Mathematics impairment can be identified during the early school years and can persist.

Social and Motivational Problems

- A disproportionate number of students with language and learning problems are at risk for poor social relations, self-concept, academic self-perceptions, self-efficacy, and a helplessness orientation.

Etiology of Communication and Learning Disorders

- Genetic transmission of various disabilities is documented in behavior genetic and quantitative genetic studies.

Progress is slowly being made in identifying specific genes. There is evidence for multiple gene effects, generalist genes, and shared genetic influence on co-occurring difficulties.
- Abnormalities of brain structure and brain activation are associated with specific disabilities. Most centrally involved in reading impairment and language are the temporal-parietal, temporal-occipital, and frontal lobes. Limited research suggests that intervention can lead to change in brain activation.
- Psychosocial factors, for example, family variables, poor instruction, and lowered expectations, may be implicated in etiology.

Assessing Communication and Learning Disorders

- Parents may call on a variety of professionals to assess early communication disorders. Evaluation of later occurring communication and learning problems is commonly conducted in educational settings.
- Standardized tests of language, reading, spelling, and arithmetic skills are critical in assessment. Intelligence tests can be helpful or necessary. Evaluation of cognitive and social functioning and the child's family context can provide a fuller assessment.

Intervention for Communication and Learning Disorders

- Early identification and intervention are critical to prevention efforts. Current emphasis is placed on the response to intervention (RTI) approach. Early intervention focuses on basic skills, and most are directed to reading disabilities.
- Intervention for communication disorders can be helpful, particularly for articulation and expressive language disorders, but there is a need for more effective and empirically supported treatments.
- Early treatment models of specific learning disorders can be conceptualized as medical and psychoeducational-remedial. Current evidence supports the effectiveness of task-analytic, cognitive-behavioral and prevention approaches.
- Well-implemented interventions can be effective, for both communication and learning disorders, although there is a continuing need to improve treatments.

Special Education Services

- The Individuals with Disabilities Education Act (IDEA) ensures a public education in the least restrictive environment possible to disabled students, and also safeguards the rights of families and ensures assistance in providing effective services.

- Of the children served by IDEA, about 34% are categorized as learning disabled and about 19% as language impaired.

Most attend general education classrooms with varying degrees of supplemental supports.

- Some disagreement continues over full inclusion of students with different impairments in regular classrooms.

Key Terms

Education for All Handicapped Children Act *266*
Individuals with Disabilities Education Act (IDEA) *266*
phonology *269*
phonemes *269*
graphemes *269*
morphology *269*
syntax *270*
grammar *270*
semantics *270*
pragmatics *270*

receptive language *270*
expressive language *270*
phonological processing *275, 276*
Matthew Effect *277*
transcription (written text) *279*
text generation *280*
individual education plan (IEP) *293*
least restrictive environment *293*
inclusion *293*

CHAPTER 12

Intellectual Disability (Intellectual Developmental Disorder)

Looking Forward

After reading this chapter, you should be able to discuss:

- AAIDD and DSM conceptualizations and classifications of Intellectual Disability (ID)
- The nature and measurement of intelligence and adaptive behavior
- Disabilities, characteristics, and co-occurring problems of youth with ID

- The epidemiology and developmental course of ID
- Organic, multigenic, psychosocial, and multifactor etiology
- Down, fragile X, Williams, and Prader–Willi syndromes
- Family accommodations and experiences
- Assessment of intelligence and adaptive behavior
- Approaches to prevention and intervention

Intellectual disability (ID), previously known as mental retardation, has long been recognized, but until about 1700 it was poorly understood and scarcely viewed as different from other disorders (Pennington, McGrath, & Peterson, 2019). By the early 1800s, the problem was understood to involve deficient intellectual functioning and deficits in the daily tasks of living. These two features remain central, although ideas about ID have transformed considerably and continue to evolve even today.

Perhaps more strongly than many other disturbances, ID had been seen as a trait of the individual. This perspective has largely been replaced by the view that ID is not "something you have, like blue eyes," nor "something you are, like being short or thin," nor a medical or mental disorder (Luckasson et al., 1992). Rather, it is a state of functioning that is best described as a problem of fit between the abilities of the individual and his or her personal and social environment. Biological causation is fully recognized, but increasing attention is given to the numerous ways in which the environment plays a role as well.

The labels applied to ID have also changed over time. The terms *idiot*, from the Greek meaning "ignorant person," *imbecile*, from the Latin meaning "weakness," and *moron*, meaning "foolish or having deficient judgment," were all once employed in the professional literature but are now considered pejorative (Potter, 1972; Scheerenberger, 1983). These terms had served as clinical descriptions, but because they also carried negative connotations,

terminology changed in an attempt to use more positive labels. The term *mental retardation*, employed for decades, was replaced by *intellectual disability* by the influential American Association on Mental Retardation and the organization itself took the name American Association on Intellectual and Developmental Disabilities (AAIDD). In 2010, President Obama signed Rosa's Law (S.2781), which adopted this change in terminology into federal law. Similarly, the fifth edition of the DSM replaced *mental retardation* with *intellectual disability* (American Psychiatric Association, 2013). The new designation is thought to more accurately describe individuals with general cognitive deficits while avoiding negative connotations. (See Accent: "Sticks, Stones, and Stigma.") In this chapter, the term *mental retardation* (MR) is used only the for the sake of clarity when it appears in the past clinical or research literature.

Definition and Classification

Although the words used to describe ID have changed over the years, the emphasis on three defining elements—intellectual limitations, deficits in adaptive functioning, and early onset—has remained virtually unchanged for more than the last half century (Pennington et al., 2019; Schalock, Luckasson, & Tassé, 2019).

Moreover, while ID has been defined by various diagnostic and classification criteria, current approaches are largely aligned and represent relative consensus on how ID is conceptualized (Farmer & Floyd, 2018). Nevertheless, updates and minor differences in their definitions and applications affect assessment and identification. Two major approaches to defining and classifying ID are discussed below.

The AAIDD Approach

The AAIDD, founded in 1876, has led efforts to understand and ameliorate intellectual impairment. This organization has long provided conceptualizations of ID that have often been adopted by other professional groups. In its latest manual, published in 2010, it offered the following definition:

> *Intellectual disability is characterized by significant limitations both in intellectual functioning and in adaptive behavior as expressed in conceptual, social, and practical adaptive skills. This disability originates before age 18.*
>
> *Schalock et al., 2010, p. 5*

As touched upon earlier, three criteria must be met before a person can be diagnosed with ID. The *age criterion*, before 18, signifies that ID is seen as a disturbance in development. This age serves as a criterion because 18 is approximately the age at which individuals in our society assume adult roles and when crucial psychosocial development and brain development have typically occurred. *Limitation in intellectual functioning* refers to functioning defined by performance on general tests of intelligence, that is, to scores that are approximately two or more standard deviations below the mean on tests such as the

Stanford–Binet and the Wechsler scales. Scores of 70 or below usually meet this criterion. *Limitation in adaptive skills* is defined as performance at least two standard deviations below the mean on standardized tests of conceptual, social, or practical skills. The requirement of *both* intellectual and adaptive behavior deficits means that individuals who fall into the range of deficiency on intelligence tests but otherwise get along adequately at home, school, or work do not meet the criteria for ID. Nor do those with deficits in adaptive behavior who perform adequately on intelligence tests warrant the diagnosis. In addition, assessment and judgments of functional limitation must consider the contexts of the individual's life: that is, the community, cultural diversity, and the like.

The AAIDD has presented a framework of human functioning to aid in understanding ID. As indicated in Figure 12.1, the model has two major components: five dimensions and a depiction of the role of supports in individual functioning. The manifestations of ID entail engagement between the five dimensions—intellectual abilities, adaptive behavior, physical and mental health, participation in daily life and social interaction/roles, characteristics of the environment and of the person—and supports the person receives. Consonant with this multidimensional framework, ID is not viewed as an absolute trait of the individual, and it is assumed that appropriate supports generally result in improved functioning. Moreover, children or adolescents with mental disability are viewed as complex individuals who have strengths as well as limitations.

Because great variability exists in the range of abilities of people with ID, it might seem reasonable to use subgroupings based on the severity of intellectual impairment in intervention and research. Following this line of reasoning, the AAIDD once employed four levels of impairment: mild, moderate, severe, and

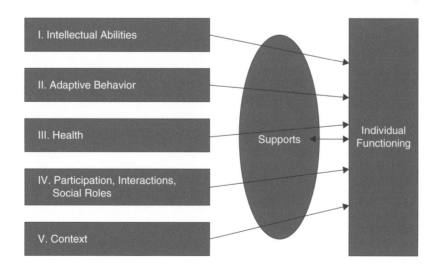

Figure 12.1 AAIDD's multidimensional model in which supports provided to the individual play a mediational role in the individual's functioning. (Adapted from Schalock et al., 2010)

ACCENT Sticks, Stones, and Stigma: What do Students do When they Hear the "r-word"?

The term *mental retardation*, once used as a clinical label to describe individuals with ID, has been corrupted into a shortened slang word, *retard* (i.e., the r-word), that carries negative connotations and is commonly used as an insult to demean and degrade others, with and without ID (Albert, Jacobs, & Siperstein, 2016). The term has been widely used in schools, with 92% of students in grades 3 through 12 reporting having used the word and approximately 84% having heard it used by their peers (Siperstein, Pociask, & Collins, 2010).

The use of the r-word expresses negative attitudes toward the person being called it and can have an adverse impact on that person. Yet, more broadly, the use of the r-word also has the potential to reinforce the devaluation and stigmatization of individuals with ID. To try to address and intervene in this process, advocates, educators, and community leaders have spearheaded efforts to educate youth about the negative impacts of using the r-word and encourage them to take action when they hear the word used. But, what is the likelihood that a student will take action in response to the use of the r-word toward individuals with and without ID?

A recent study examined the characteristics that contribute to whether a student takes an active or passive bystander role (Albert et al., 2016). A total of 2,297 students from 12 high schools throughout the U.S. participated in a survey assessing student behavior in response to the use of the word. Students completed questionnaires about their empathy and helping behavior, their perception of how socially accepting their school community is of students with ID, the frequency with which the r-word was used in their school, and their own behavior in response to use of the word (e.g., told others to stop using the word, did nothing).

Results of this study demonstrated the r-word continues to commonly be used in schools, with approximately four out of five students (82%) reporting they heard the r-word at school. In most cases, the r-word was directed at students without ID (94% of students who heard the r-word at school heard it directed toward students without ID). Less than half (41%) of students who heard the r-word at school heard it directed toward students with ID. When the r-word was directed toward a student without ID, only 33% of students reported taking some sort of action, such as telling others to stop, comforting the affected person, or telling a teacher. When the r-word was directed toward a student with ID, 65% of students reported taking action. In fact, students were nearly ten times more likely to take action when the use of the r-word was targeted at a student with ID. These findings suggest student reactions depend in part on who the term is directed toward.

Additionally, other factors also seemed to play an important role in whether students took action. Gender was one important factor. In fact, female students were more than twice as likely to intervene when they heard the r-word. Similarly, students who rated themselves as more prosocial, or tend to voluntarily behave in a way that benefits others, were more likely to take action as compared to students who were less prosocial. Other factors measured, such as students' age, race, and perceptions of the social inclusion of students with ID in their school did not seem to contribute to their likelihood to intervene.

Overall, the use of the r-word in schools remains prevalent and concerning. Although the word is reported more as general insult rather than being directed toward those with ID, its negative meaning and association with ID devalues and sets individuals with intellectual differences apart. Moreover, the findings that most students choose not to take action when the r-word is directed toward students without ID and are more likely to take action when it involves someone with ID reveals that students understand that using the r-word toward students with ID is wrong. Yet, importantly, they may not understand how using the word, in general, negatively impacts and contributes to the devaluation of people with ID. This study provides some insight into how schools and other programs can help to promote empathy and other methods for increasing prosocial behavior to help reduce the stigma of individuals with ID, yet there is still much work to be done.

profound. Individuals were assigned to a subgroup according to their intelligence test scores. This approach was widely adopted by other classification systems. Nonetheless, the AAIDD eliminated the approach in 1992. It noted that IQ subgroups might be appropriate for research purposes, but not for making decisions about the care of individuals with ID (Schalock et al., 2010). AAIDD recommended instead that each individual be assessed for levels of needed supports, that is, resources and strategies that will promote development and well-being. This approach recognizes that needs for supports might be different in one area of functioning than another and might change over time. It also highlights the view of ID as dynamically linked to the social environment rather than as a static quality of the individual.

Table 12.1 Classification of ID Severity

Severity category	Approximate percent distribution of cases by severity	DSM-IV criteria (severity levels were based on approximate IQ range)	DSM-5 criteria (severity classified on the basis of adaptive skills)
Mild	85%	50–69	Can live independently with minimal levels of support.
Moderate	10%	·36–49	Independent living may be achieved with moderate levels of support.
Severe	3.5%	20–35	Requires daily assistance with self-care activities and safety supervision.
Profound	1.5%	<20	Requires 24-hour care.

Source: Based on Committee to Evaluate the Supplemental Security Income Disability Program for Children with Mental Disorders, 2015.

The DSM and Past Approaches

The DSM-5 approach to diagnosis and classification is similar to the current AAIDD approach (American Psychiatric Association, 2013). The DSM-5 classifies ID, which it also terms intellectual developmental disorder, as a neurodevelopmental disorder that begins in childhood. Although no specific age of onset is noted, onset must occur during the developmental period. Concurrent intellectual and adaptive limitations are required for diagnosis. The DSM-5 notes that intellectual functioning is usually measured by appropriate, individually administered, standardized intelligence tests (e.g., a Wechsler scale), and that scores of 70±5 are usually attained by persons with ID. Adaptive behavior is assessed by clinical judgment and appropriate individually administered instruments, and includes difficulties in conceptual, social and practical areas of living; at least one domain of functioning must be impaired.

The DSM-5 specifies severity of ID based on adaptive functioning. Severity levels range from mild to profound. For example, with regard to personal self-care, the person may display age-appropriate skills but need some support for complex tasks (mild), require early extended teaching and time to reach independent self-care in adulthood (moderate), require support for all activities (severe), or rely on others for all aspects of care (profound).

Prior to 2013, the DSM assigned levels of severity of ID based on IQ scores. The shift from IQ to adaptive functioning increased the role of clinical judgment in determining severity level. While concerns have arisen that clinicians and researchers are left without a reliable and meaningful way to group individuals (Schalock & Luckasson, 2015), the change was intended to help better identify the level of environmental supports needed by considering adaptive skills rather than IQ alone (Pennington et al., 2019). Additionally, the new emphasis on adaptive functioning leaves open the possibility that severity level may change in response to development and

intervention (Matson et al., 2019). Nevertheless, variations in the basis of classification of severity persist (McNicholas et al., 2018), and many researchers and clinicians continue to rely on classification by IQ.

Table 12.1 shows the four levels of disability that have often been employed (Committee to Evaluate the Supplemental Security Income Disability Program for Children with Mental Disorders, 2015). About 85% of all cases are of mild disability. These are viewed as quite different in functioning and in other important ways from persons classified at the other three levels.

Changes in the diagnostic criteria for ID frequently have precipitated criticism. Many professionals criticized the AAIDD in 1992 when it recommended that 75 be considered the ceiling for the IQ criterion for diagnosis. The recommendation took into account the standard error of measurement of intelligence tests, which is about 5 points. However, the ceiling of 75 meant that the number of persons being diagnosed could be doubled (King, Hodapp, & Dykens, 2005), and especially affect persons from socially disadvantaged groups. Looking further back, there was concern in 1959 when the AAIDD employed a definition that allowed individuals to be diagnosed with ID when they scored one or more standard deviations below the mean on intelligence tests (Figure 12.2). Those who scored in the approximate range of 69 to 85 were labeled as retarded at the borderline level. By this definition, about 16% of the population could be diagnosed with ID. Critics argued that the criterion was unreasonable, given that the cutoff included many people who did not have problems in everyday life, and that it disproportionately labeled some disadvantaged groups as having intellectual limitations (Pennington et al., 2019). Subsequently, the AAIDD shifted the IQ criterion. Changes in and controversy about the definition of ID demonstrate the degree to which ID is a socially constructed category and how cutoffs on a continuum of ability are somewhat arbitrary. These issues have sometimes provoked heated debate.

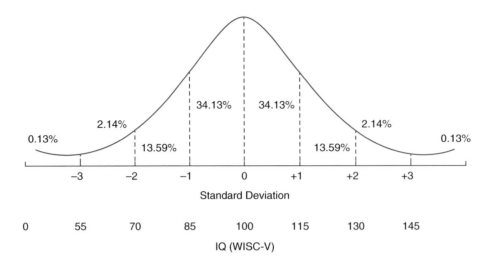

Figure 12.2 The distribution of scores on the WISC-V test of general intelligence fitted to the normal distribution. Standard deviation units indicate how far above or below a score is from the mean of 100. The standard deviation for the WISC-V is 15 points. When ID is defined by one or more standard deviations below the mean, approximately 16% of the population is disabled. When ID is defined by two or more standard deviations below the mean, 2 to 3% of the population is disabled.

Nature of Intelligence and Adaptive Behavior

Because measures of intelligence and assessment of adaptive behavior are central in defining ID, it is important to look more closely at their development and the concepts that underlie them.

Measured Intelligence

As simple as the concept of intelligence seems on the surface, its meaning has raised many questions. We might agree, as have theorists, that it involves the knowledge possessed by a person, the ability to learn or think, or the capacity to adapt to new situations. Beyond these general definitions, we might run into disagreements. Theorists themselves argue, at times passionately, about the precise nature of intelligence, and they hold various perspectives on it. Although we can hardly do justice to this topic, our goal is to address issues that are most relevant to understanding intellectual disabilities.

Modern intelligence testing goes back to the work of Alfred Binet and his colleagues at the beginning of the twentieth century. Their approach—the traditional psychometric approach—focused on individual differences and on the idea that distinct underlying abilities explained differences in intellectual functioning (Sternberg, 2019). Intelligence is often viewed as consisting of a general ability, called *g*, and numerous specific abilities, for example, motor and verbal abilities (Tan & Grigorenko, 2019). Intelligence is measured by the presentation of tasks that tap both general and specific abilities. This psychometric approach is sometimes described as examining the products of intellectual, or cognitive, abilities rather than the processes involved in the abilities.

In recent years, information-processing theories have come to the fore, focusing on the processes by which individuals perceive sensory stimuli, store information, manipulate information, and perhaps act on it. Different theorists have somewhat disparate ways of conceptualizing these processes, but in all cases, intelligence is measured according to how well a person performs on processing tasks. For example, the ability to attend to and simultaneously deal with several bits of information might be measured. Information-processing approaches contribute much to the understanding of ID and are increasingly integrated into the measurement of intelligence. However, it was the psychometric approach that largely shaped views of intelligence throughout most of the twentieth century.

Early Test Construction and Assumptions

When Binet and his colleague Simon were asked by school officials in Paris to find a way to identify children who needed special educational experiences, they tested students of different ages on brief tasks relevant to classroom learning. In 1905, their work resulted in the first intelligence scale, consisting of tasks that average students of various ages passed. When children were evaluated on the scale, they were assigned a **mental age** (MA), that is, the age corresponding to the chronological age (CA) of children whose performance they equaled. Thus a 7-year-old who passed the tests that average 7-year-olds passed was assigned

Table 12.2 Measures Relevant to Tests of Intelligence

CA	Chronological age.
MA	Mental age. The age score corresponding to the chronological age of children whose performance the examinee equals. For the average child, MA = CA.
IQ (ratio)	The ratio of mental age to chronological age multiplied by 100. IQ = MA/CA × 100.
IQ (deviation)	A standard score derived from statistical procedures that reflects the direction and degree to which an individual's performance deviates from the average score of the age group.

an MA of 7; a 7-year-old who only passed the tests that average 5-year-olds passed obtained an MA of 5.

Binet made several assumptions about intelligence (Siegler, 1992). He believed that intelligence encompassed many complex processes, was malleable within limits, and was influenced by the social environment. Binet argued that carefully constructed standardized tests were necessary to minimize inaccurate evaluations of children. Moreover, he and his colleagues devised methods to improve intellectual functioning, and they recommended that educational programs be fitted to each child's special needs.

Intelligence testing was brought to the United States when Henry Goddard translated and used the Binet scales with residents of the Vineland Training School in New Jersey. Then, in 1916, about five years after Binet's death, Lewis Terman, working at Stanford University, revised the early scales into the Stanford–Binet test. Terman adopted the idea of the **intelligence quotient** (IQ) as the ratio of an individual's mental age to chronological age, multiplied by 100 to avoid decimals. The ratio IQ enabled direct comparison between children of different ages. Today's major intelligence tests employ statistical comparison, so that what is often referred to as IQ is no longer a quotient, but a score that nevertheless denotes age comparison (Table 12.2).

Goddard and Terman made some notably different assumptions from those of Binet about the nature of intelligence. They assumed that the tests measured inherited intelligence that would remain stable over the life of the individual (e.g., Cravens, 1992). They also saw the need for eugenics, the improvement of the human species by control of inheritance. These beliefs had social implications that were to generate heated debate about the assumptions and uses of intelligence tests, as well as the treatment of persons with ID. (See Accent: "Measured Intelligence: A History of Abusive Ideas.")

Stability and Validity of Intelligence Tests

Intrinsic to the debates about intelligence is the issue of whether measured intelligence is stable over time. Stability can be examined by studying a group of people longitudinally and correlating earlier IQ scores with later IQ scores. When such test–retest measurements are made after preschool age, a median correlation of 0.77 has been found (King et al., 2005). Further, the IQ scores of persons with ID appear more stable than the IQ scores of persons with average or above scores, and the lower the score, the greater the stability. It is important to note, however, that such analyses examine groups of people and that individual scores can change, often in response to changing family situations or educational opportunities.

Another central issue about intelligence is what an IQ score tells us about a person. Fundamental to this question is the validity of intelligence tests—whether the test reveals what it is designed to reveal. For example, intelligence assessment has often been used for prediction—an IQ score may be used to try to predict a person's performance in the classroom, workplace, or in other life tasks (Ackerman, 2018). Generally, intelligence tests are reasonably good predictors of school grades (Nisbett et al., 2012), and measured intelligence is also related to later school completion, employment, and income (Fergusson, Horwood, & Ridder, 2005b). On the other hand, IQ tests tell us less about a variety of social behaviors (e.g., social adjustment). Nevertheless, it is relevant to note that IQ scores that fall below the average range are generally better predictors of academic and nonacademic performance than those in the normal range.

Overall, then, intelligence tests are an important tool, but caution is necessary in interpreting them. IQ scores are relatively stable, but they are not cast in stone. Serious questions have been raised about the cultural bias of the tests, and about their limitations as well; for example, IQ tests may not well reflect problem solving in the real world (Butler, Pentoney, & Bong, 2017). Consider also the uncertainty of intelligence tests due to the **Flynn effect**, the finding that IQ scores in populations systematically improve over time (Flynn, 2018). Periodic updating of the tests—that is, construction of new norms—results in resetting the mean score and the test becomes more difficult. Performance then drops several points on average for both typical children and those scoring in the disability range. Thus, as Kanaya, Scullin, and Ceci (2003) note, the diagnosis of ID can be affected by how old the test norms are when the child is assessed. In considering whether a child meets the IQ criterion for disability, "it may not be sufficient to simply look to see whether the IQ score is below some cutoff point," (p. 790) but rather to consider multiple criteria.

ACCENT Measured Intelligence: A History of Abusive Ideas

Not long after their introduction, intelligence tests became entwined with social and political issues in the United States and Europe (Dennis et al., 2009). In the United States, IQ tests played a role in establishing immigration quotas for people of southern European background and in introducing laws for the sterilization of people considered mentally deficient (Strickland, 2000). In fact, "unsexing" the "unfit," which had already begun, increased during the early 1900s (Wehmeyer, 2003). Many states passed sterilization laws, and such a law was upheld in 1927 by the Supreme Court in a Virginia case, *Buck v. Bell*. California law called for the sterilization of state hospital inmates and "feeble-minded" children residing in state-run homes. Forced sterilization affected over 50,000 persons before scientists and others overtly criticized the controversial practice.

Although not as overtly egregious, the use of intelligence tests in the schools has been controversial. After compulsory education laws were passed, the public schools employed intelligence tests to assess children's capacity for school learning (MacMillan & Reschly, 1997). Children of poor and some minority families generally performed relatively poorly on the tests. In more recent times, this group included children of African American, Hispanic, and Native American backgrounds, although the confounding of social class and racial/ethnic background should be recognized. Concern was—and still is—raised about test results disproportionately identifying minority and poor children as intellectually deficient—and their placement in special education classrooms (e.g., Schalock et al., 2010). Critics charged that standard English tests were used with bilingual students, the content of tests did not relate well to the students' subcultures, and the tests were not of good quality. Confrontations with the educational system ensued, some of which reached the courts (MacMillan, Keogh, & Jones, 1986). Legal outcomes often, but not always, favored plaintiffs from minority groups. The influential *Larry P. v. Riles* case, brought by black plaintiffs, resulted in restrictions on the use of intelligence tests for identifying and placing black children into special education programs in California. Overall, the educational system was required to stringently monitor the use and administration of intelligence tests.

Inherent in the early uses and abuses of tests was the assumption that measured intelligence is a stable, biologically programmed characteristic of individuals. The more accepted current view is that intelligence tests assess important aspects of functioning that result from the interaction of heredity and environment and that at least to some degree are modifiable by environmental factors (Fagan & Holland, 2002).

Adaptive Functioning

In addition to intellectual functioning, the failure to adapt socially to one's environment has been central to the concept of intellectual disability (Farmer & Floyd, 2018). Several decades ago, while working at the Vineland Training School, Edgar Doll focused on the importance of social and personal competence in the everyday lives of persons with ID (King et al., 2017). He published a scale to measure what, today, we call adaptive behavior. In 1959, the AAIDD first included deficits in adaptive functioning as a criterion for ID, and the most recent version of the AAIDD and DSM definitions emphasize adaptive functioning (AAIDD, 2010; American Psychiatric Association, 2013).

Adaptive behavior has generally been thought of as "what people do to take care of themselves and to relate to others in daily living" (Grossman, 1983, p. 42). Based on research as to what constitutes adaptive behavior, some consensus has emerged that it is multidimensional and includes the following domains (Matson et al., 2019):

- *Conceptual*: memory, language, reading and writing, reasoning, problem solving, time, number concepts.

- *Social*: awareness of others' thoughts and feelings, interpersonal skills, social responsibility, self-esteem, gullibility, rule following, avoidance of being victimized, social problem solving, friendship abilities.
- *Practical*: activities and personal care of daily living (e.g., bathing, cooking meals, dressing), use of money, safety, health care, travel, routines, use of telephone, occupational skills.

Adaptive behavior is viewed as overlapping with but not identical to intelligence. The conceptual domain, in particular, is closely related to intellectual functioning with memory, reasoning, and problem solving central to functioning. Research shows a positive correlation in the range of 0.3 to 0.6 between scores on adaptive behavior tests and intelligence tests (Kanaya et al., 2003; McGrath & Peterson, 2009b). Thus, as measured intelligence decreases, individuals are more likely to have difficulties in everyday functioning, and this appears especially true for individuals with lower levels of intelligence (Scherr, Kryszak, & Mulick, 2018).

When considering adaptive skills, developmental level obviously must be taken into account. Behaviors associated with sensorimotor, communication, self-help, and primary socialization

The ability to engage in routine activities and tasks substantially heightens the well-being of youth with intellectual disabilities. (Corbis/Getty Images)

skills are emphasized in early life, whereas during later childhood and adolescence, reasoning and judgments about the environment and social relationships increase in importance. When judgments of adaptation are made, consideration also should be given to expectations of the community and the sociocultural context in which the person is functioning. For example, a child may have social skill deficits in a school setting and yet meet the expectations of the neighborhood.

The importance of adaptive behavior has received increasing acceptance and empirical validation (Tassé, Luckasson, & Schalock, 2016a). Not all professionals have been in favor of adaptive behavior being as heavily weighed as intelligence in the definition of ID. In part, these concerns surrounded the correlation of intelligence and adaptive functioning as well as variability of clinical judgments of adaptive behavior. Yet, the concept of and instruments that measure adaptive behavior have evolved considerably over the years, giving support to the equal weight and joint consideration of intellectual functioning and adaptive behavior in the diagnosis of ID. Adaptive behavior, in particular, may be uniquely important in providing a framework for determining the resources necessary to support the functioning of individuals with ID (van Ool et al., 2019).

Description

ID is associated with many identified syndromes as well as with less understood conditions. In some cases, the deficits are mild, but in

others there are severe impairments in cognitive, sensory, motor, language, socioemotional, or behavioral systems. Differences in functioning can be illustrated in several ways. One way in which variation in functioning can be seen is by examining descriptions based on severity of disability. As detailed in our discussion of classification, Table 12.3 provides a description of mild, moderate, severe, and profound disability with a focus on expectations for the conceptual, social, and practical domains of adaptive functioning. Such a presentation provides a sense of the enormous differences in abilities. The case description of Annalise provides a brief account of some problems experienced by a child diagnosed with profound ID.

In looking at variation in functioning, a developmental perspective can also help inform our understanding of ID. This perspective considers biological, psychological, social, and developmental dimensions of functioning (Matson & Cervantes, 2019). *Biological* factors include genetic, neurological, or other medical disorders that impact functioning, including cognition and learning. Deficits in various abilities, including attention, perception, working memory, the use of effective strategies to mentally organize information, reasoning and evaluation, and other aspects of executive function have all been identified and impact functioning (Kirk, Gallagher, & Coleman, 2015). In addition, speech and language are variously and often significantly impaired. Additionally, the study of different syndromes of ID has demonstrated profiles of cognitive strengths and weaknesses, a topic to which we will return later (Goldstein & Reynolds, 2011). Until recently, cognitive functioning was the main consideration in determining ID, but an integrated approach can clarify

Table 12.3 Description of Functioning According to Severity of ID and Adaptive Functioning Domains

	Conceptual domain	Social domain	Practical domain
Mild	No obvious early conceptual differences Difficulties in learning core school subjects and managing time and money Difficulties in executive functioning skills (e.g., planning, setting priorities)	Develops social and communication skills but may be more concrete or immature than expected for age Difficulties in perceiving social cues and regulating emotions May be at risk for being manipulated by others (gullible)	May function age-appropriately in personal care but need guidance and assistance in daily living tasks May live successfully in the community with supports
Moderate	Delays in language and pre-academic skills Unlikely to progress beyond elementary-level mastery of academic skills Support required for tasks of daily life (e.g., managing money) and work	Usually develops communication skills but may be much less complex than that of peers May establish friendships and romantic relationships but be limited by communication or social deficits Can adapt to supervised community living with supports	Can care for age-appropriate personal needs with extended period of teaching and time Participation in adult household tasks can be achieved with supports Can benefit from occupational training and support to perform unskilled or semiskilled work
Severe	Limited conceptual skills Little understanding of written language or concepts involving numbers, quantity, time, and money Requires extensive supports for problem solving	Spoken language limited in vocabulary and grammar; may understand simple speech and gestures; communication aids may be helpful Communication focused on present moment and everyday events Relationships with family members and familiar others provides pleasure and assistance	Requires support for all activities of daily living (e.g., meals, dressing bathing, and elimination) Requires supervision and assistance at all times In most cases, can adapt to community living with family or in group homes Maladaptive behavior, including self-injury, may be present in significant minority
Profound	Conceptual skills limited to understanding objects and physical world Some skills (e.g., matching or sorting) may be acquired Co-occurring sensory and physical impairments likely present Likely neurological impairments	Very limited understanding and use of communication in speech or gesture Desires and emotions largely expressed through nonverbal communication Enjoys relationships with well-known family members, caretakers, and familiar others	Dependent on others for all aspects of daily physical care, health, and safety May do simple supervised tasks Requires structure and constant supervision for optimal development Maladaptive behavior, including self-injury, may be present

Sources: Based on American Psychiatric Association, 2013; Matson et al., 2019.

our understanding of an individual's functioning and inform interventions.

Indeed, the clinical picture can be further understood by considering other biological aspects of functioning, including physical/medical functioning. Most youth with ID, particularly those with mild impairments, show no unusual physical characteristics and blend into the general population. But a sizable number do show atypical appearance that ranges from minor to more obvious abnormalities. Disturbances in physical functions also occur, including problems such as seizures, motor difficulties, impaired vision, and deafness. Abnormalities of physical appearance and function are especially associated with the more severe levels of ID, as are many medical conditions, such as cerebral palsy, epilepsy, cardiac problems, and kidney disease. The lifespan of those with ID is below the average lifespan. Although the average lifespan has improved in recent decades, findings from a recent meta-analysis suggest the age of death of people with intellectual disabilities remains up to 20 years less than their peers in the general population (O'Leary, Cooper, & Hughes-McCormack, 2018).

ANNALISE Profound Intellectual Disability

Annalise was born after an unremarkable pregnancy. Her mother recalled significant feeding difficulties in the first few weeks of life, and Annalise's developmental milestones were delayed. She did not walk, for example, until approximately 4 years of age. Her progress was variable while she was enrolled in an early intervention program. She has essentially never been able to use spoken language.

The family reports that Annalise's medical history is extraordinarily complicated. It includes an episode of congestive heart failure, thyroid problems, diabetes, and an apparent allergy to milk. When she was 4 or 5 years of age, she became preoccupied with food, consuming everything in sight. Genetic testing for Prader–Willi syndrome was negative, but a deletion on chromosome 1 was later revealed.

Annalise has never been very sensitive to the thoughts or feelings of others, and she sometimes literally walked over other children. She has many circumscribed interests, and if allowed would watch small vignettes from Disney videos over and over again. She has been preoccupied with sorting and stacking objects, and at one time she would tantrum if not permitted to organize stones and pebbles as she passed them. Due to her preoccupation with food, the family has had to lock the refrigerator and food cabinets. They are hoping that medication will reduce Annalise's anxiety and obsessions that hinder her from fuller participation in activities.

Adapted from King et al., 2005, pp. 3084–3085

Variation also occurs within the *psychological* dimension of functioning, which includes psychosocial and emotional functioning of the individual. As discussed in more detail in the section below, co-occurrence of ID with other psychiatric problems is common, and the well-being and adaptation of individuals with ID are hindered by various behaviors and psychological diagnoses. The presence of psychiatric diagnoses in addition to ID (sometimes termed "dual diagnosis") poses challenges for adaptive functioning and intervention (Pennington et al., 2019), yet wide variation in and degree of co-occurring problems are observed.

Large heterogeneity is also observed in the domain of *social* functioning. While related to psychological functioning, social functioning more directly relates to a person's social skills and social understanding; in other words, the way they interact with those around them. These skills include behaviors as diverse as appropriate eye contact, facial expression, social greeting, reciprocal interaction, and expressing wants and needs (O'Handley et al., 2016). Research has identified a range of problems in peer relationships that frequently co-occur with ID. While youth with mild and moderate ID have many social competencies, they do exhibit impairments in understanding social cues, social situations, and others' perspectives.

It is reasonable to assume that some of the social problems of children with ID are attributable to the intellectual impairments, language deficits, and physical/medical problems characteristic of ID. It would be a mistake, however, not to recognize the influence of social experience. Youth with ID tend to experience greater social isolation despite today's heightened commitment to include them in social and educational activities. It is also likely that other people, perhaps due to discomfort, behave somewhat atypically during social interactions with these youth. Thus, individuals with ID likely have insufficient opportunity to practice social interaction and observe appropriate models and social relations. It appears, however, that social competence can gradually improve and that social skills can be facilitated. For example, research suggests that both emotional regulation in young children with developmental disability and maternal scaffolding—that is, maternal support and assistance that enables child success—predict social skills and could be important for increasing social functioning (Baker et al., 2007). Additionally, school-based social skills training has been effective in improving the social skills of young people with ID (O'Handley et al., 2016).

Finally, the *developmental* dimension emphasizes that functioning in each domain varies at each developmental level. For example, a child may lag behind typically developing peers in language, motor, academic, emotional, and social abilities at one time in development, whereas the developmental picture may look somewhat different at another point in time and with various supports in place. Additionally, a child with severe ID may demonstrate further deviation from typically developing peers in the various domains of functioning as compared to a child with mild ID. Skill levels in the various domains of functioning must be considered alongside age-appropriate expectations for behavior and in conjunction with the individual's level of functioning (Matson & Cervantes, 2019).

Co-occurring Disorders

As touched upon above, co-occurrence of ID with other psychiatric problems is common. About half the population of individuals with

ID display varying degrees of challenging behaviors, such as verbal and physical aggression, tantrums, self-injury, and an array of other disruptive behaviors, with more severe behaviors occurring in less than 10% of the ID population (Matson & Cervantes, 2019). Prevalence of diagnosed or significant psychological problems for children and adolescents with ID is in the range of 30 to 50%, with most research suggesting two to four times the rates found in the general population (Committee to Evaluate the Supplemental Security Income Disability Program for Children with Mental Disorders, 2015; Matson et al., 2019).

The kinds of disturbances exhibited are similar to those shown in the general population, with the rate of co-occurrence higher for some disorders than others. Among the most common are attention-deficit/hyperactivity disorder (ADHD), autism spectrum disorder, anxiety disorders, and oppositional/conduct problems (Matson et al., 2019). Co-occurrence rates of 50–70% have been reported for autism spectrum disorder, for example (Matson & Shoemaker, 2009), and symptoms of ADHD are common (King et al., 2017). Depression, aggression, obsessive-compulsive behavior, schizophrenia, and stereotypes have also all been reported. The developmental trajectories for many problems appear similar to those found for typical children (de Ruiter et al., 2007). Co-occurring problems are present in toddlers, tend to decline gradually into young adulthood, but still remain higher than in the general population (Einfeld & Emerson, 2008).

However, the kinds of problems may differ with level of disability. Individuals with mild ID display depressive feelings, anxiety, and antisocial problems observed in others of the same mental age. In addition to these kinds of problems, individuals with moderate or severe ID also may exhibit problems that are, by contrast, less common in the general population, such as autism, psychosis, and self-injurious behavior. Finally, particular problems are associated with specific syndromes of ID. For example, self-injury is associated with Lesch–Nyhan syndrome and insatiable eating with Prader–Willi syndrome.

While individuals with ID are more likely to experience psychological problems than their typically developing peers, they may be less likely to be diagnosed. It can be difficult to accurately identify or diagnose co-occurring problems in individuals with ID. One suggested cause is that professionals tend to view such difficulties as a part of ID rather than a separate disorder and thus may fail to recognize them (Jamieson & Mason, 2019). **Overshadowing**, as it has been called, has been documented among different professionals working in different settings. The cognitive and communication impairments of ID can also make it difficult to identify problems. Symptoms involving emotions and internal states are especially difficult to assess, particularly in individuals with severe ID (Adams & Oliver, 2011). The task of describing emotions may be complicated even for youth with mild disability. We would expect, for example, that depressive symptoms might be challenging to assess because the youth must

Table 12.4 Factors that May Contribute to Psychological Problems in ID

Underlying neurobiological processes
Underlying medical conditions
Side effects of medication
Communication deficits
Inadequate problem-solving and coping skills
Reduced opportunity for development of social skills
Reduced opportunity for development of supportive social relationships
Issues related to the physical environment
Stigma leading to low self-concept
Family stress
Significant life events or trauma
Vulnerability to exploitation and abuse

Sources: Based in part on King et al., 2017; Summers, Fletcher, & Bradley, 2017.

be able to identify and label sadness, hopelessness, and the like. Another factor that can hinder diagnosis of co-occurring problems is that, while standard diagnostic criteria apply quite well when IQ is about 50 or higher, they do not apply well at lower levels of disability (Einfeld & Emerson, 2008).

What accounts for high rates of problems or disorders in ID? Neurological factors no doubt explain some disturbances and probably play a stronger role in more severe disability. Indeed, biological causation is suggested by the association of specific genetic syndromes with specific problems (Hodapp, Thornton-Wells, & Dykens, 2009). But social-psychological variables enter into the picture as well. One study, for example, reported high prevalence of behavior problems in developmentally delayed 5-year-olds and showed that mothers' less sensitive teaching and family stress predicted the continuance of externalizing problems (Baker et al., 2010). The stigma of ID, low quality of living arrangements, and lack of developmental opportunities are among the factors that may underlie behavioral disturbances (Table 12.4). Some of these factors clearly can be modified. For example, social contacts can be broadened to facilitate learning the give-and-take of social interaction. Such efforts are worthwhile as co-occurring problems lower the quality of life and can affect family functioning, school placement, and community adjustment.

Epidemiology

Over the past decades, the number of children estimated with ID has fallen from about 3% to more current estimates of around 1% (McKenzie et al., 2016). Rates of course vary across studies and severity levels of ID, but the prevalence of ID is interesting in several aspects. First, the reduction in prevalence noted above does not necessarily mean that fewer children have disabilities as compared to decades past. Rather, the fluctuation in prevalence likely reflects other changes, such as shifts in diagnostic criteria, differential diagnosis, or services available to support the adaptive functioning of individuals with intellectual impairment.

To illustrate this impact of classification on prevalence, consider the changes in diagnostic criteria discussed earlier. When the diagnostic criteria focused on IQ, the prevalence rates were higher. Assuming a normal distribution of intelligence test scores and an IQ of about 70 as the criterion for ID, a rate of 2.3% would be expected (Simonoff, 2015) (Figure 12.2). However, the current definition of ID addresses both intelligence and adaptive behavior, meaning that both IQ and adaptive functioning are considered in making the diagnosis of ID. When adaptive functioning is considered jointly with IQ, only those individuals who are having significant problems in everyday life because of low intelligence are classified as having ID (Papazoglou et al., 2014).

Additionally, prevalence is especially interesting when age and severity of ID are inspected. Rates are lower prior to school age, and the children identified early in life tend to have moderate or lower IQ scores. It appears that the more severe cases attract more immediate attention, and also that professionals hesitate to diagnose so early, preferring to consider young children as developmentally delayed (Handen, 2007). A dramatic shift then occurs when children enter school. Prevalence increases as more mild cases are diagnosed, probably at least in part due to new demands and increased evaluations. Rates then fall in adolescence and decline further in adulthood. The latter may in part be due to the capacity of some adults to successfully work in unskilled jobs and otherwise function adequately, or perhaps adults become less available for evaluation. At the lower levels of ID, rates may drop because of the relatively short lifespan of these individuals.

Other variables are important when prevalence is examined. ID appears more in males than females—perhaps due to reporting bias, other environmental factors, and male vulnerability to biological influences (Pennington et al., 2019). In fact, males are at greater risk for genetic syndromes associated with ID, such as fragile X syndrome, as discussed in more detail below. In addition, children and adolescents from families of low socioeconomic circumstances account for a disproportionate number of cases, especially mild cases—an important finding also revisited later in the chapter. Interestingly, it has been noted that societal changes could impact future rates. In high-income countries, increased parental age, survival of very low birthweight infants, and assisted conception may increase incidence of the disorder. On the other hand, availability of prenatal screening for disorders associated with ID, as well as improved care of at-risk infants, could decrease incidence.

Developmental Course and Considerations

Very different life trajectories can be anticipated for children with ID. Stability of diagnosis is not inevitable and individuals with mild disability can, with appropriate training and opportunity, develop adequate intellectual or adaptive skills so that criteria for the disorder are no longer met (American Psychiatric Association, 2013). For most youth, though, ID is lifelong. Severity and cause of the disorder make a difference in course and outcome, as do various risk and protective factors such as associated medical problems, associated psychopathology, family variables, and education and support resources (Carr & O'Reilly, 2016).

Theorists and practitioners have been interested in developmental issues pertaining to cognition in children with ID relative to typical growth. Earlier research tended to focus on milder intellectual impairment for which there was no identified cause; later efforts included more severe impairment with known organic etiologies.

The *rate* of intellectual development has been of interest. Typical development is seen as occurring gradually over time throughout childhood and adolescence, with some spurts and regressions. In children with ID, development is slower than usual, but for many of these youth the rate of growth is fairly steady (King et al., 2017). Nonetheless, different patterns have been observed for specific syndromes, for example, a slowing after a few years of steady growth.

Another developmental consideration has to do with the *sequence*, or *ordering*, of intellectual growth. Intelligence normally develops in some orderly way, and a good deal of research has set out to examine whether children with ID follow a similar sequence. Early research in this area focused on whether young people with ID followed the four stages of cognitive growth that, according to Jean Piaget, all typically developing individuals display as they come to think in more complex ways. Research confirmed that children with ID generally do progress through the same Piagetian stages—and other cognitive sequences—as do non-ID children, but do so more slowly and ultimately do not progress as far (Hodapp & Dykens, 2003; Hodapp & Zigler, 1997).

These findings have practical implications for working with youth with ID. For example, the fact that the sequence of development in mild disability is often similar to that of typical development provides a guideline for teaching children with intellectual impairment.

Etiology

The etiology of ID is heterogeneous but is generally caused by abnormal brain development or injury to the brain resulting from

JOHNNY Unknown Cause of ID

Johnny is a 10-year-old boy with mild intellectual disability. Although from birth his parents considered him somewhat "slow," Johnny was not diagnosed ... until his early grade-school years. To this day, no clear [cause] has been provided for Johnny's mild [intellectual disability]. As measured by the Stanford–Binet IV, his IQ is 67, with no significant difference between his verbal and perceptual processing scores. Johnny does, however, show impulsivity and problems in attending. ... Johnny's [intellectual disability] first became apparent at

the end of the first grade. At that time, a student study team at his school worked with Johnny's classroom teacher and the resource room teacher to help Johnny improve his basic work organizational skills and increase his attention span. At his parents' request, Johnny was also evaluated for attention-deficit hyperactivity disorder by the local psychiatrist, who prescribed stimulant medication that seemed to help.

Adapted from King, Hodapp, & Dykens, 2000, p. 2599

genetic and/or environmental causes (King et al., 2017; Matson & Cervantes, 2019). These risk factors can be present before birth (prenatal), can occur at the time of birth (perinatal), or occur after birth (postnatal) (Bertelli, Salvador-Carulla, & Harris, 2016). Although intellectual disabilities are associated with hundreds of specific medical and genetic conditions, as well as with environmental circumstances, causation is not clearly identified in a substantial number of cases (Simpson, Mizen, & Cooper, 2016). A genetic or environment cause is known for nearly two-thirds of individuals with moderate to profound ID, but many causes remain unspecified (Hodapp, Dankner, & Dykens, 2016). For the majority of cases of mild ID, etiology is not understood, as noted in the case of Johnny.

Historically, individuals with intellectual disabilities were viewed as falling into two categories—an organic group and a cultural–familial group—that differed in several ways as outlined in Table 12.5 (Burack et al., 2016). This **two-group approach** has been influential in both theory and research. Biological etiology is clear for the organic group, and in the 1960s and 1970s causation for the cultural–familial group was attributed primarily to environmental deprivation. Current knowledge and theory indicate the wisdom of viewing causation as more complex and interactive and moving beyond the two-group approach (Burack

et al., 2016; Pennington et al., 2019). A multicausal model underlies our discussion, but it is informative to distinguish pathological organic, multigenic, and psychosocial etiology or risks.

Pathological Organic Influences

Attributing ID to pathological organic factors implies that some biological condition is crucial in accounting for disordered brain function and intellectual disability. There is considerable evidence for biological risk and causation. As already noted, IQ scores of persons with ID are normally distributed except for a "bump" at the low end (Burack, 1990; Zigler, Balla, & Hodapp, 1984). This excess of low scores, it is suggested, is accounted for by individuals who have suffered major biological impairment (Simonoff, 2015). In fact, evidence exists for a group of individuals with more severe disability that comes from all social classes and shows an excess of genetic abnormalities, multiple congenital anomalies, brain dysfunction such as in cerebral palsy, and reduced life expectancy. Underlying such cases may be genetic processes, prenatal or birth adversities, postnatal circumstances such as brain injury and disease, or some combination of these factors.

Table 12.5 The Two-Group Approach to ID

Organic	Cultural–familial
Individual shows a clear organic cause of intellectual disability	Individual shows no obvious cause of intellectual disability; sometimes another family member also has intellectual disability
More prevalent at moderate, severe, and profound levels of intellectual disability	More prevalent in mild intellectual disability
Equal or near-equal rates across all ethnic and SES levels	Higher rates within minority groups and low-SES groups
More often associated with other physical disabilities	Few associated physical or medical disabilities

Source: Adapted from Hodapp, & Dykens, 2003.

Multigenic Influences

Heredity has long been linked to ID. In early times, the link between inherited biological "defect" and ID was often based on flimsy or flawed "proof." For example, in his influential study of the Kallikak family, Goddard (1912) traced the quite distinct genealogical lines of Martin Kallikak. One line originated from Kallikak's liaison with a barmaid, the second from later marriage to a woman of "better stock." From information on several hundred of Kallikak's descendants, Goddard found a pronounced difference in the two families, namely, that the first liaison had resulted in more mental deficiency, criminality, alcoholism, and immorality. Obvious weaknesses existed in this study, most notably the questionable accuracy of the data. But the results were taken as evidence that ID was an inherited biological trait—although family environment could just as well have played a role.

Current understanding of hereditary influences on intelligence in the general population has a basis in behavior genetic research (Plomin & von Stumm, 2018). Intelligence test performance of identical twins is more similar than that of fraternal twins; when identical twins are reared apart, similarity decreases but is still high. Studies of families and adopted children lend support to the twin findings. It is estimated that about 50% of the variation in tested intelligence in the general population is due to genetic transmission of multiple genes, and the same appears to hold true for individuals with mild ID (Wadsworth et al., 2015). Interestingly, meta-analysis of longitudinal twin and adoption studies suggests the heritability of intelligence increases over development from infancy (20%) to childhood (40%) to adulthood (60%), highlighting the complexity of the multiple factors that influence heritability and intelligence (Briley & Tucker-Drob, 2013; Plomin & von Stumm, 2018).

Additionally, heritability appears lower for those with moderate and severe ID, with pathological organic factors more common in these groups (Pennington et al., 2019). This is not to say, of course, that pathological organic factors never cause mild ID. Indeed, we might anticipate that biological advances will reveal now-undetected organic abnormalities that contribute to mild impairments. Nevertheless, multiple factors are likely involved in the etiology of mild cases and these may include multiple genes as well as psychosocial influences (Pennington et al., 2019).

Psychosocial Influences

Interest in psychosocial causation of intellectual disabilities was historically tied to the conceptualization of cultural–familial retardation. The terms *garden variety* and *undifferentiated* also were used, reflecting the large number of cases that were not readily distinguished from one another (Crnic, 1988). These children appeared quite normal, possessed relatively good adaptive skills, were often first identified on entering school, and as adults

often blended into the general population. Their family members were frequently described in similar ways.

It has been observed for many years that mild ID occurs disproportionately in lower socioeconomic classes and in some minority groups, and could be caused by psychosocial disadvantage. Many psychosocial variables associated with lower SES put children at risk—such as low parental education, stressful life events, inadequate environmental stimulation, and increased risk for exposure to toxins, illness, and injury, for example (Maulik et al., 2011; Pennington et al., 2019). The adverse effects of psychosocial variables may operate through more than one pathway. Inadequate intellectual stimulation might hinder early brain development, especially the growth of synaptic pathways. Or there may be insufficient support of behavior and motivation conducive to success in the classroom or other learning environments.

Associations have been demonstrated among social class, home environment, and children's intellectual development. In general, parenting is a strong predictor of children's cognitive and academic performance (Burchinal et al., 2006; Pungello et al., 2010). For instance, child ability in preschool has been related to parental practices. One study, for example, found that parental interactions, including positive affect, sensitivity, engagement, and cognitive stimulation, are especially beneficial to children with developmental delays (Moody, Baker, & Blacher, 2018). As a group, educationally and economically deprived parents may lack the skills or otherwise be unable to stimulate children's language and cognitive growth. One team of investigators, which over many years engaged in an intervention and research program for disadvantaged preschool children, proposed a model for the development of ID that reaches across generations (Greenwood et al., 1992, 1994). In this model, due to limited parental interactions, young children begin to fall behind intellectually. When they reach school, the children's home situation combines with school practices that lead to low motivation, education exposure, and achievement, resulting in high rates of school dropout. In turn, when these children become parents, they are unable to contribute to the cognitive growth of their offspring.

It is nevertheless difficult to pinpoint any one cause of ID in disadvantaged children. These youth are also at risk for major inherited abnormalities, prenatal and birth adversities, postnatal malnutrition and disease, and unfavorable schools and neighborhoods. Variation due to multiple-gene inheritance is not ruled out. Given what is known about the intricacies of development, multifactor explanations might frequently apply.

Multifactor Causation

Although it is still easy to fall back on the historical tendency to view ID as a result of *either* biological *or* psychosocial factors, more complex explanations are now clearly recognized. The

Table 12.6 The Four AAIDD Categories of Risk and Etiology Pertaining to ID

Timing	Biomedical	Social	Behavioral	Educational
Prenatal	1. Chromosomal disorders 2. Single-gene disorders 3. Syndromes 4. Metabolic disorders 5. Cerebral dysgenesis 6. Maternal illnesses 7. Parental age	1. Poverty 2. Maternal malnutrition 3. Domestic violence 4. Lack of access to prenatal care	1. Parental drug use 2. Parental alcohol use 3. Parental smoking 4. Parental immaturity	1. Parental cognitive disability without supports 2. Lack of preparation for parenthood
Perinatal	1. Prematurity 2. Birth injury 3. Neonatal disorders	1. Lack of access to birth care	1. Parental rejection of caretaking 2. Parental abandonment of child	1. Lack of medical referral for intervention services at discharge
Postnatal	1. Traumatic brain injury 2. Malnutrition 3. Meningoencephalitis 4. Seizure disorders 5. Degenerative disorders	1. Impaired child–caregiver interaction 2. Lack of adequate stimulation 3. Family poverty 4. Chronic illness in the family 5. Institutionalization	1. Child abuse and neglect 2. Domestic violence 3. Inadequate safety measures 4. Social deprivation 5. Difficult child behaviors	1. Impaired parenting 2. Delayed diagnosis 3. Inadequate early intervention services 4. Inadequate special-educational services 5. Inadequate family support

Source: Adapted from Schalock et al., 2010. Copyright 2006 by Sage; reprinted with permission.

AAIDD suggests that multifactor explanations are not necessarily inconsistent with the two-group approach (Schalock et al., 2010). In some cases, biomedical factors may predominate, whereas in other cases, social, behavioral, or educational factors may be more important. But even when a known genetic syndrome is strongly associated with ID, the level of disability may be determined, within limits, by some mix of other biological and psychosocial factors. For example, intelligence, adaptive behavior, language development, and behavioral problems are influenced by the home and school environment in children with fragile X syndrome (Warren et al., 2010). The AAIDD views the development of disabilities within a multiple risk model that encompasses biomedical, social, behavioral, and educational factors that can operate at different times in life (Table 12.6).

Genetic Syndromes and Behavioral Phenotypes

Incredible advances in molecular genetics has led to increased focus on the investigation and diagnosis of genetic syndromes in individuals with ID. While there is still much to be understood about the etiology of ID, new genetic conditions that contribute to ID are identified each year, and information about the cause of ID can help inform prognosis, guide treatment, and help educate families about genetic risk (King et al., 2017).

In this discussion, we highlight four syndromes—Down, fragile X, Williams, Prader–Willi—associated with ID, noting the different genetic mechanisms underlying each and describing some of the cognitive features. As well, Table 12.7 briefly describes the physical appearance and behavior often reported for these syndromes. The association of specific syndromes and behavior has led to the notion of **behavioral phenotypes**, meaning that a specific disorder predisposes individuals to certain behaviors. Whereas this is clear in some instances (e.g., excessive eating in Prader–Willi syndrome), overlap of behavioral difficulties also is observed and there is individual variation within each disorder.

Down Syndrome

Down syndrome (DS), the most common single disorder of ID, occurs in 1–1.5 per 1,100 live births (Pennington et al., 2019). The condition was described in 1866 by John Langdon Down, who attributed it to maternal tuberculosis. In 1959, only three years after human chromosomes were first described, trisomy 21 was discovered in persons with DS. As shown in Figure 12.3 chromosome 21 appears in a triplet instead of a pair. About 95% of all cases are attributed to this abnormality, which is caused by failure of the chromosome pair to divide in meiosis, the process in which ova and sperm are formed. (The remaining cases involve other anomalies of chromosome 21.) Trisomy 21 seems to occur almost randomly, is not inherited, and is mostly traced to the mother. It is progressively related to advancing maternal age: the

Table 12.7 Some Physical, Behavioral, and Cognitive Attributes Associated with Four Syndromes of ID

	Physical	Behavioral/cognitive features
Down	Upward slant and folds at corner of eyes, flat facial features, fissured tongue, broad hands and feet, poor muscle tone, short stature	Wide IQ variation, mainly mild to moderate IQ, wide array of behavior problems (e.g., noncompliance, stubbornness, argumentativeness, inattention, social withdrawal, depression in adolescence), relative strength in social communication
Fragile X	Long face, large ears, soft skin, high-arched palate, double-jointed thumbs, oversized testicles in boys; these features less likely in females	Variable level of IQ, typically moderate to severe, variable behavioral difficulties, including inattention, hyperactivity, poor eye contact, shyness, anxiety, and autism-related features
Williams	"Elfinlike" face (e.g., small lower jaw, prominent cheeks), growth deficiency, often an aged appearance in late adolescence or early adulthood	Moderate ID, delays in language acquisition but subsequently relative strength in language, indiscriminate and overly friendly social interaction, poor social judgment, anxiety, perseverative thinking
Prader–Willi	Almond-shaped eyes, downturned mouth, short stature, small hands and feet, poor muscle tone, underdeveloped gonads, obesity	Mild ID, excessive eating and food-seeking/hoarding, excessive daytime sleepiness, delayed motor milestones and speech difficulties, obsessions and compulsions, stubbornness, tantrums, aggression, disobedience, anxiety, impulsivity

Sources: Based in part on Hagerman, 2011; Hazlett et al., 2011; King et al., 2017; Pennington et al., 2019; Simonoff, 2015.

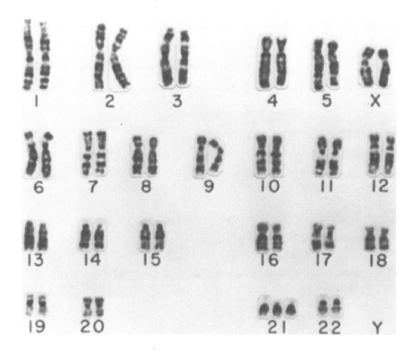

Figure 12.3 The chromosome complement of a female with trisomy 21. (Courtesy of the March of Dimes, copyright 2012; reproduced with permission)

risk for DS increases from about 1 per 1,000 live births for mothers less than 35 years old to about 20 per 1,000 for mothers 45 years of age or older (Loane et al., 2013).

Several parts of the brain are affected, with abnormalities that include reduced brain size, reduced number and density of neurons, and abnormal dendrites. Brain pathology very similar to the abnormal plaques and tangles found in the brains of Alzheimer's disease patients is observed in many persons with ID, and more than 80% of adults with DS may experience dementia by age 65 years (Hithersay et al., 2017). There is substantial risk of other health problems, such as heart defects, respiratory anomalies, gastrointestinal problems, and visual difficulties (Jackson, Wendland, & Ekvall, 2017). However, life expectancy has climbed considerably in recent decades, and is about 60 years.

Although children with DS show substantial intellectual growth during the first few years of life, disability is usually evident and the rate of development slows throughout childhood and adolescence (Hazlett et al., 2011). Disability typically ranges from moderate to severe, but learning can continue beyond adolescence. Evidence exists for deficits in verbal short-term memory and auditory processing (Pennington et al., 2019). Visual–spatial abilities are relatively good. Most children acquire speech but it is delayed, with expressive language more affected than comprehension. Unusually large declines in cognitive and adaptive functioning have inconsistently been reported in adults; these are perhaps related to the development of dementia (Hithersay et al., 2017).

Interestingly, although children with DS display a variety of social and emotional problems, they are thought to experience fewer psychiatric difficulties than found in other groups with ID (King et al., 2017). The phrase "Down syndrome advantage" is sometimes used to describe situations in which children with DS may be easier to rear relative to children with other syndromes. However, the picture remains complex. Increased understanding of the extent to which the "Down syndrome advantage" exists is worthwhile because it has implications for informing and supporting interventions for children with ID and their families. (See Accent: "The Down Syndrome Advantage.")

Fragile X Syndrome

First described in 1969, fragile X syndrome (FXS) is second to DS as a cause of ID and is the most common inherited form of ID. It affects an estimated 1 in 4,000 males and 1 in 8,000 females (National Institutes of Health, 2019), and it has been found in different countries and ethnicities/races (Sherman & Hunter, 2017).

FXS is caused by abnormal gene expression in a single gene, known as the FMR1 gene, and is inherited in an X-linked pattern in which males are more frequently affected by the disorder (Pennington et al., 2019). A male with an affected X chromosome will pass it to all daughters, but not to sons as they receive only the Y chromosome from fathers. A woman with an affected chromosome has a 50% chance of transmitting it to either sons or daughters. However, daughters are somewhat protected by the second X chromosome that they carry and may show less severe cognitive and emotional impairment. Males are more likely to experience more severe symptoms of the disorder. Although a single gene is responsible for FXS, the inheritance pattern is complex (Hagerman, 2011). The disorder is considered epigenetic because it involves a change in gene expression that results from an accumulation across generations of repeats of a triplet of DNA nucleotides (cytosine, guanine, guanine) on the FMR1 gene (Pennington et al., 2019). Normal persons carry

ACCENT The Down Syndrome Advantage

A popular notion exists that individuals with DS are easier to rear compared to children with other developmental disabilities (Corrice & Glidden, 2009). Two major questions have been raised about this "Down syndrome advantage." Is it true and, if so, what explains it? Several investigations have addressed the questions.

If rearing children with DS is actually relatively easy, it is reasonable to expect that their families would be comparably well adjusted and/or satisfied, optimistic, and so forth. Although not all results support this expectation, the weight of the evidence favors it (Esbensen & Seltzer, 2011). Mothers of young children with DS experience less stress, have more satisfying social support, and are less pessimistic about their children. The families are more cohesive and harmonious. Mothers of adolescents with the syndrome display better psychological adjustment, are less pessimistic, and report a reciprocated, closer relationship with their child. Further, there is similar evidence for mothers of adult children with the syndrome. In attempts to explain these findings, researchers have looked to both the (1) attributes of the individuals

with the syndrome and (2) factors peripherally related to the syndrome.

Regarding the syndrome itself, temperament, social behavior, and functional behavior have garnered considerable research interest. Evidence exists that individuals with DS, relative to those with other syndromes, are perceived by their parents as displaying more socially engaging behaviors, higher levels of adaptive behavior, and fewer behavioral problems (Corrice & Glidden, 2009). Moreover, these behaviors are associated with well-being in caretakers (Blacher & McIntyre, 2006; Esbensen & Seltzer, 2011).

Additional factors also seem to be involved. One of these is maternal age. Mothers of DS children often are older than mothers in comparison groups, and older age when the child is born correlates with some measures of well-being (e.g., less burden, greater satisfaction). Perhaps the greater maturity of mothers, and the financial stability that often comes with age, play a role. In addition, DS mothers may be less biologically vulnerable to poor functioning than mothers of some comparison groups—such as fragile X syndrome and autism.

SAMMIE An Example of Fragile X Syndrome

As a newborn, 51-month-old [Sammie] showed only minor problems. Developmental norms were slightly delayed: he sat at 10 months and walked at 15 months. In his first year, Sammie began to flap and bite his hands. He chews excessively on things, has poor eye contact, and displays tantrums. He is easily stimulated and exhibits high activity level, impulsivity, and distractibility. Among other physical features, Sammie

has prominent ears, a high-arched palate, and double-jointed thumbs. On the Bayley Scale of Infant Development, he performs as a child 23 to 25 months of age. On the Vineland Adaptive Behavior Scales, Sammie's performance is similar to that of a child 21 to 22 months.

Adapted from Hagerman, 2011, pp. 280–281

less than 50 repeats, but this number can increase in gamete production and be transmitted to offspring. Individuals with 55 to 200 repeats are carriers of the "premutation," which increases the risk of a still larger number of repeats in the next generation (King et al., 2017). In women, the premutation can occur in repeats that exceed 200 in cells that develop eggs, in which case, the FMR1 gene is not expressed and the full-blown FXS is manifest (National Institutes of Health, 2019). Thus, a variety of symptoms, or none at all, are seen in families with an affected X chromosome. The case of Sammie tells of a boy diagnosed with FXS by DNA testing.

The disorder involves disruption in the proteins involved in regulating the development of synapses and other processes important in early brain development (Pennington et al., 2019). Structural abnormalities have been found in several brain areas, and the brain may be affected prenatally and after birth (Hoeft et al., 2010). Several brain anomalies have been reported implicating, among other regions, the cerebellum and the frontal and parietal lobes. The large head circumference found in children with FXS indicates enlarged brain structures, which in turn suggests insufficient pruning of cells early in development.

Nearly all males with FXS have ID, usually mild to moderate, and about one-third of affected females experience intellectual impairment which tends to be mild (National Institutes of Health, 2019). There is a predictable slowing of cognitive growth as early as age 5, with development reaching a plateau by late childhood or early adolescence (Reiss & Dant, 2003). Weaknesses are notable in visual–spatial cognition, sequential information processing, motor coordination, arithmetic, and executive functions. Long-term memory and acquired information appear to be relative strengths. Learning disabilities, behavior problems, and social impairments are common in females with an affected X chromosome. While it was once reported that autism spectrum disorder occurs in a high percentage of boys with FXS, more recent research suggests that number may be closer to 5%, as many boys with FXS show a willingness to interact with others but experience social anxiety, shyness, gaze aversion, and social avoidance or withdrawal, which appear similar to some autism features but

may be better explained by an anxiety disorder (King et al., 2017; Neri, 2017).

Williams Syndrome

Williams syndrome (WS) is a rare disorder, occurring in an estimated 1 case in 7,500 individuals and results from a random mutation involving small deletions of several genes on chromosome 7 (King et al., 2017). Cardiac and kidney problems are among the reported medical difficulties. The syndrome is typically associated with mild to moderate intellectual disability, with IQs mostly in the range of 50 to 70. Both reduced and enlarged volumes are reported for several brain regions, as well as abnormal brain activation during tasks involving response inhibition, visual processing, and auditory processing of music and noise (Kesler et al., 2011).

Recent attention has been focused on a striking cognitive-linguistic profile of many children and adults with WS who display strengths in social aspects of cognitive functioning, such as language and face processing, but weaknesses in nonsocial aspects of cognitive ability, such as visual–spatial memory and skills, which are far below what would be expected in keeping with mental age (Campos, Martínez-Castilla, & Sotillo, 2017; King et al., 2017). Even at adolescence, there is an inability to perceive gross differences in spatial orientation and to copy simple stick figures. In contrast, short-term verbal memory is stronger and verbal IQ is typically significantly higher than performance IQ. Despite some weaknesses in aspects of language, individuals with the syndrome typically display strength in language as well as auditory processing and music (King et al., 2017).

Also notable, from an early age individuals with WS are excessively outgoing and friendly with both familiar individuals and strangers (Pennington et al., 2019). Key neuroimaging findings have helped to shed some light on the social disinhibition seen in individuals with WS. In particular, findings have demonstrated that individuals with WS experience reduced amygdala activation in response to angry and fearful faces and thus may not discriminate in relating to others (Pennington et al.,

315

ROBERT An Example of Williams Syndrome

Robert's mother was a music teacher, his father a science teacher. Born after an unremarkable pregnancy, Robert was extremely fussy as a newborn and later he was a picky eater. His parents thought him high-strung, and he often cringed or cried when his sisters played too loudly. Robert's milestones were slightly delayed, but a pediatrician reassured his parents that boys often showed slight delay and that Robert was a lively, social child who would catch up.

When Robert was 3 years of age, his parents insisted on an assessment. Modest delays were found in motor, linguistic, and cognitive functioning. He was described as friendly and engaging, a charming child with a cute, appealing face. Robert was enrolled in a special kindergarten and the remainder of his school years were spent in a combination of special and regular classrooms.

At age 7, Robert was assessed as having an IQ of 66, with near-normal short-term memory and expressive language and notable deficits in visual–spatial skills. He had difficulty with writing and arithmetic, loved science and music, and was amazingly conversant when he had the chance to talk with others. Indeed, his parents felt he was overly friendly and active.

During early adolescence, Robert became increasingly anxious. He developed fears of storm clouds and dogs, refused to ride on elevators, and worried about his sister. Despite having nightmares, occasionally pacing with worry, and complaining of stomachaches, Robert attended school, had a small group of friends from Special Olympics, sang in the high school choir, and was often selected to play the piano at school concerts. When Robert was 17 years of age, his parents happened to see a television program on Williams syndrome and were "jolted" to see the similarity between their son and the people being portrayed. Genetic testing confirmed the diagnosis. This led to Robert's meeting and engaging in activities with other youth with WS and feeling less alone. His parents found a social community with which to share their feelings and concerns.

Adapted from King et al., 2005, p. 3082

2019). Despite their unusual friendliness, individuals with WS often have trouble making or keeping friends and show increased rates of generalized anxiety, worry, and other nonsocial forms of anxiety (King et al., 2017). Many of the characteristic behaviors and abilities of the syndrome are evident in the case description of Robert.

Prader–Willi Syndrome

Prader–Willi syndrome (PWS), which was first described in 1956, occurs in an estimated 1 in 15,000 births (King et al., 2017). It is the first syndrome found to be caused by a microdeletion of chromosome material and also the first human disorder to demonstrate genomic imprinting, in which genes are expressed depending on whether they are inherited from the mother or father. Prader–Willi syndrome involves genes on the long arm of chromosome 15 that are normally expressed solely by the chromosome inherited from the father (King et al., 2017). In approximately 70% of cases, there is a deletion of these genes. In most remaining cases, both chromosomes 15 are inherited from the mother so that the relevant paternal genes are absent.

While the pattern of inheritance of PWS influences an individual's cognitive profile, individuals with PWS typically show mild to moderate ID (Dykens et al., 2019). Cases of paternal gene deletion may show lower intelligence, especially verbal, and more frequent or severe behavioral difficulties.

At the same time, the ability to solve jigsaw puzzles is high (King et al., 2017). Cases involving two maternal number 15 chromosomes may show decreased performance on visual–spatial tasks, fewer facial characteristics consistent with PWS, and a tendency for severe depressive symptoms and impairments in social interaction.

PWS is best known for its food-intake features, which follow a characteristic pattern over the course of development (Miller, McCune, & Driscoll, 2017). Infants with PWS typically display low muscle tone, lethargy, and difficulty feeding, while hyperphagia (excessive eating) and food-seeking and hoarding behaviors develop between ages 2 and 6 and are lifelong. Without intervention and dietary management, these behaviors lead to obesity and death (King et al., 2017). Additionally, although food-related preoccupation and obsessions are common among individuals with PWS, high rates of nonfood obsessions and compulsions are also observed (King et al., 2017). These include skin picking and hoarding, as well as concerns with exactness, order, cleanliness, and sameness in the environment and daily routine. Other disruptive behaviors, including temper tantrums, aggression, stubbornness and impulsivity, may also be present. Research has shown behavioral differences based on the inheritance pattern of PWS (Butler et al., 2019; King et al., 2017). Further investigation of the role of genetics in PWS is needed and holds promise—as does research of other syndromes—of advancing our understanding of intellectual disabilities.

Family Accommodations and Experiences

Children with ID and their families experience profound challenges and represent a unique risk group in a number of ways (Crnic et al., 2017). Parents of children with ID worry about the child, realize that expectations will never be fulfilled, and in some instances experience a stressful and frustrating diagnostic process (Bailey, Skinner, & Sparkman, 2003). An unusual amount of attention must be given to the intellectual and psychological needs of the youth, and often to physical needs as well. In addition, parents often experience stigmatization—directed at both their child and themselves (Mitter, Ali, & Scior, 2019). Behavioral difficulties are common in children with ID, and parents are likely to experience more parenting stress as a result (Crnic et al., 2017). Parents of children with ID often also must face decisions that are unique or uncommon in typical families concerning, for example, living and school arrangements, health, and future planning for lifetime care and supervision. At times, these decisions have involved especially difficult practical and ethical issues. (See Accent: "Deciding What's Best for Children with ID.")

How should we think about families who have a child with ID or other developmental disorders? Most of the literature on family well-being has emphasized adverse effects on family members and proposed, for example, that mothers of children with ID are more likely to experience stress, anxiety, depression, and other negative reactions (McIntyre, 2016). However, it is obvious that some families do not experience difficulties and a shift of perspective has occurred toward understanding those factors that contribute to resiliency (Hastings, 2016). Today, families are viewed in a more normative way—as coping with stress. Overall, families of children with ID show only slightly negative outcomes, and many parents report that having a child with ID has been positive for their family and has strengthened family relationships (McConnell & Savage, 2015).

Numerous factors can affect parent coping and satisfaction, including severity of the disability, child behavior problems, parent coping strategies and optimism, and social support, in particular (Adams et al., 2018; Halstead, Griffith, & Hastings, 2018; McIntyre, 2016; Peer & Hillman, 2014). The effects of having a child with disabilities also may vary with family ethnic/racial background. Racial and ethnic disparities in the quality of health care and the systems that provide services to individuals with disabilities have been identified (Magaña, Parish, & Son, 2015), and represent a unique stressor with the potential to impact parent stress and family functioning. These numerous factors—child characteristics, family characteristics, and social variables—create a complex picture.

ACCENT Deciding What's Best for Children with ID

Particularly difficult decisions can arise concerning the care and management of children with ID. Two quite different examples demonstrate this point.

Since the 1970s, an unknown, but probably small number of parents opted for reconstructive facial surgery for their children with Down syndrome (Goeke et al., 2003). The surgery most often involved multiple procedures that included tongue reduction and implants in the nose, chin, and other facial areas. The stated goals were improved physical functioning (e.g., speech, breathing) and appearance. The distinctive and commonly recognized facial features of DS presumably act to stigmatize the child, which entails the devaluation, prejudice, and discrimination that has long occurred with mental disorders (Hinshaw, 2005; Major & O'Brien, 2005). Thus, reconstructive surgery for DS can in part be an attempt to lessen stigmatization. Nevertheless, questions have been raised about whether this goal is met, particularly in light of the pain surgery causes and possible negative psychological effects. It has also been suggested that reconstructive surgery may actually decrease the acceptance of DS and provokes important ethical considerations (Suzedelis, 2006).

In a quite different instance, controversy arose in the wake of a medical intervention to cause growth attenuation in a 6-year-old girl through high doses of estrogen and removal of the uterus and breast buds (Gunther & Diekema, 2006). The child, who was severely disabled, was cared for at home by loving parents who feared that, as she grew, they would no longer be able to provide care for her. Improved quality of life for the child was the main consideration, and the intervention was approved by a review committee. However, strong criticism of the decision was voiced, including by the AAIDD, at the time of the initial controversy and again in subsequent reiterations of opposition (AAIDD Position Statement, 2020). The drastic treatment was criticized as having unknown medical risk with no guarantee of avoiding eventual out-of-home care. The AAIDD also argued that growth attenuation devalues a child, has the potential for future medical abuse, and should be rejected as a treatment option. The organization advocates instead for support and services to parents who care for youth with extraordinary needs (AAIDD Position Statement, 2020).

Young people with intellectual disability or other developmental disabilities require and benefit from extraordinary care and nurturing from their families. The extent to which these families experience stress, adjust to high demands, and are fulfilled depends on many factors. (Tomasz Markowski/Shutterstock)

Family members likely are affected in various ways and to varying degrees. The child's behavioral problems are correlated with parental reports of stress, depression, and anxiety, and mothers may be more affected than fathers (Hastings et al., 2005). When mothers are employed, they face greater than usual work-related stress, for example, in finding child care and services for a young person with unique needs (Parish, 2006). Moreover, marital partners affect each other, and mothers' distress and children's behavior problems have a bidirectional relationship (Hastings et al., 2006).

Siblings also are undoubtedly challenged by the need to accommodate the child with ID and the impact having a child with disability has on family functioning (Dyke, Mulroy, & Leonard, 2009). Siblings may provide more than usual custodial care and emotional support to the child with disabilities, and may have difficulties in knowing how to talk to others about their sister or brother with disabilities. Siblings are also often socialized to anticipate caring for the child with ID in the future, particularly as the lifespan of individuals with disabilities increases (Hodapp et al., 2017). The overall research findings are mixed regarding outcomes for siblings. There are no differences from other youth in self-concept and self-efficacy, but findings are mixed for behavior problems, depression, and loneliness (Meadan, Stoner, & Angell, 2010). As is true for child–parent relationships, numerous variables may influence sibling relationships.

Rewards and Satisfactions

Despite the challenges of rearing a youth with developmental disabilities, many families do well and report positive aspects of their experiences. Scorgie and Sobsey (2000) investigated transformations in the lives of parents of children with disabilities. Transformations were defined as significant positive changes set into motion by a traumatic or challenging event. The parents reported learning to speak out, becoming stronger, seeing life from a new perspective, and having greater compassion. These parents recognized negative aspects of rearing a child with special needs—for example, career limitations and reduced social participation—and they emphasized the importance of balancing the challenging and positive aspects.

Some siblings have reported positive consequences of their experiences—such as increased empathy, patience, acceptance of differences, ability to help others, and appreciation for health and family (Eisenberg, Baker, & Blacher, 1998; Flaton, 2006). One woman, looking back on her extraordinary commitment to her brother with ID noted:

I don't know who I would be if Danny wasn't born. He gave me from a very early age, a direction. He has taught me in his own somewhat unorthodox way about prioritizing and about what's important. ... And he's taught me compassion and a lot about diversity. ... Certainly, I have learned patience because he has his own time frame ... the only thing Danny does quickly is eat. ... I like to think that being Danny's sister has made me more empathetic.

Flaton, 2006, pp. 140–141

Fortunately, considerable recognition is now given to more complete portraits of family interaction and functioning. Family systems perspectives focus on understanding numerous family needs and facilitating family quality of life (Turnbull, 2004). In addition, federal mandates for services for very young children have led to early interventions that are sensitive to family resources and priorities (Hodapp et al., 2009). Helping families identify and obtain community resources and supports can be especially advantageous (McIntyre, 2016). Among other things, these resources can provide child and family therapy, child care, economic assistance, medical and dental care, and adult education.

Assessment

Assessment for ID may be conducted for several purposes. An initial diagnosis can guide parents and teachers, and allow the family to obtain school and community services. Beyond this, more specific information about the child's cognitive strengths and weaknesses can contribute to educational planning. Assessment of the youth's behavioral tendencies and problems, as well as family dynamics, may be necessary for ensuring psychological well-being. Medical evaluation can shed light on current or potential health problems, and the diagnosis of a specific syndrome can be valuable in understanding health, intellectual, and behavioral issues. Assessment of ID begins with a comprehensive history and includes standardized measures of intellectual and adaptive functioning (Matson & Cervantes, 2019). A large number of psychological instruments can be helpful to assess individuals for ID (for a more extended discussion see Bruce & Wilmhurst, 2016; Handen, 2007). Our discussion only briefly describes some of the widely used tests to assess intelligence and adaptive behavior; later in the chapter we look at functional assessment as part of an approach to treatment.

Developmental and Intelligence Tests

Standardized, individually given intelligence tests are central to diagnosing ID. For infants, toddlers, or children with severe deficiency, developmental tests substitute for intelligence tests.

Infant and Toddler Tests

Several standardized, individually given scales exist to assess infants and preschoolers. Among the most popular is the Bayley scales. The newest version, the Bayley Scales of Infant and Toddler Development-Third Edition, which covers age 1 month to 42 months, includes scales for cognition, language, and motor development (Bayley, 2005). These domains are tested by presenting the child with situations or tasks designed to elicit observable behavioral responses. In addition, the parent or caregiver completes a social-emotional and an adaptive behavior scale.

Performance on tests for young children is referred to as a developmental quotient (DQ), because somewhat different abilities are evaluated than for IQ of older children. These scales give greater emphasis to sensorimotor functioning and less emphasis to language and abstraction. This feature may partly explain why performance on early tests is not highly correlated with later IQ in the general population. Nevertheless, developmental tests may be better predictors of intellectual development in young children with severe disability as compared to those with mild impairment (Matson & Cervantes, 2019).

Stanford–Binet Intelligence Scales

This test (SB5) is now in its fifth edition (Roid & Barram, 2004). Five areas are assessed: Fluid Reasoning, Knowledge, Quantitative Reasoning, Visual–Spatial Processing, and Working Memory. The SB5 includes toys and objects helpful in assessing young children, and nonverbal evaluation is possible in each cognitive area. Scores can be obtained for each of the cognitive areas; in addition, a Nonverbal, Verbal, and Full-Scale IQ can be obtained. The standardization group for the SB5 is a representative U.S. sample, ages 2 to 85 years.

Wechsler Tests

Like the Stanford–Binet scales, these tests are immensely popular for assessing ID. The Wechsler Preschool and Primary Scale of Intelligence-IV (WPPSI-IV) is designed for ages 2 years 6 months to 7 years 7 months, and is divided into two age bands (Wechsler, 2012). For both age groups (those under 4 years and those over 4 years), the test provides a comprehensive cognitive measure, as well as more narrow measures of verbal comprehension, visual–spatial, and working memory abilities. For children 4 years and older, the test additionally provides measures of fluid reasoning and processing speed.

The Wechsler Intelligence Scale for Children–Fifth Edition (WISC-V) is one of the most widely used tests of intelligence and measures the cognitive ability of children ages 6 years to 16 years 11 months in five cognitive domains (Wechsler, 2014a, 2014b). The index scores, which represent the five domains, include verbal comprehension, visual–spatial, fluid reasoning, working memory, and processing speed. Examples of subtests are vocabulary, visual puzzles, figure weights, digit span, and coding. A Full-Scale IQ is derived from six core subtests included among 16 subtests that make up the entire battery.

Kaufman Battery

The Kaufman Assessment Battery for Children–Second Edition (KABC-II) recently underwent a normative update (KABC-II NU) to reflect changes in U.S. demographics and educational curriculum and practices (Kaufman & Kaufman, 2018). The test is designed for ages 3 to 18 years and offers five scales of cognitive and processing ability: sequential processing, simultaneous processing, planning, learning, knowledge. For example, the sequential processing/short-term memory scale requires step-by-step processing of content, whereas the simultaneous processing scale requires integrating several pieces of visual–spatial information at the same time. The subtests are designed to minimize verbal instructions and responses so that it can be used with children whose verbal skills are more limited. The KABC-II NU employs specific scales based on two different models relevant to the reason for referral or the child's background. One of the models is more applicable to the child from a mainstream language and cultural background, whereas the other may be more suitable for a child of different background. Both models result in a global intelligence score.

Assessing Adaptive Behavior

Adaptive behavior can be assessed through interviews with families or caretakers, direct observation, and self-report in some cases. Given the increased emphasis on adaptive functioning as a criterion for diagnosis of ID, standardized measurement of adaptive behavior in the assessment of ID is important (Floyd et al., 2015). Several standardized scales have been constructed, and attention has been given to reliability and validity (Tassé et al., 2016c).

Vineland Adaptive Behavior Scales

These scales, originated by Doll at the Vineland Training School and now in their third edition (Vineland-3), are widely employed (Sparrow, Cicchetti, & Saulnier, 2016). Information can be collected for individuals from birth to age 90 through semi-structured interviews or rating scales with parents or caregivers. Also available is a questionnaire for teachers to assess individuals ages 3 through 21 years. The scales cover communication, daily living skills, and socialization. In addition, the optional domains of motor skills and maladaptive behavior can be used (Table 12.8). Scores from the separate domains and an overall score can be compared with scores from a normal standard group and special groups with disabilities.

Adaptive Behavior Assessment System

The Adaptive Behavior Assessment System, in its third edition, measures adaptive skills across the lifespan from birth through age 89 years (Harrison & Oakland, 2015). Using behavior rating

Table 12.8 Domains Evaluated by the Vineland Adaptive Behavior Scales (Vineland-3)

Communication	Receptive Expressive Written
Daily living skills	Personal Domestic Community
Socialization	Interpersonal relationships Play and leisure Coping skills
Motor skills (optional)	Fine Gross
Maladaptive behavior (optional)	Internalizing Externalizing Critical items

scales typically completed by the individual's parent, caregiver, and/or teacher, it assesses 11 skill areas with three major adaptive domains. The domains include conceptual, social, and practical skills, which align with the AAIDD, DSM-5, and IDEA specifications in the classification of ID. The measure's items focus on practical activities that occur daily and are required to meet developmentally appropriate demands.

AAIDD's Assessment of Adaptive Functioning

The AAIDD's Diagnostic Adaptive Behavior Scale (DABS), is a relatively new measure designed for individuals age 4 to 21 years (Tassé et al., 2016b). The measure provides a comprehensive assessment of adaptive behavior, focusing on information relevant to determining significant limitations in adaptive behavior in the domains of conceptual, social, and practical skills, thereby aiding diagnosis. Consistent, of course, with the AAIDD definition on ID, the criteria also align with the DSM-5 and IDEA. The DABS focuses on identifying the critical "cutoff area" for the purpose of classifying a person as meeting criteria for diagnosis. Recent research suggests the measure has strong validity and reliability and converges with other measures such as the Vineland Adaptive Behavior Scale.

AAIDD's Assessment for Supports

The AAIDD has developed guidelines for assessing each person's needs for supports aligned with facilitating adaptive behavior (Schalock et al., 2010). Consistent with the AAIDD's philosophy, the aim is to provide services to improve the functional capabilities of those with ID. As detailed in Figure 12.4, supports are intended to address the mismatch between people and

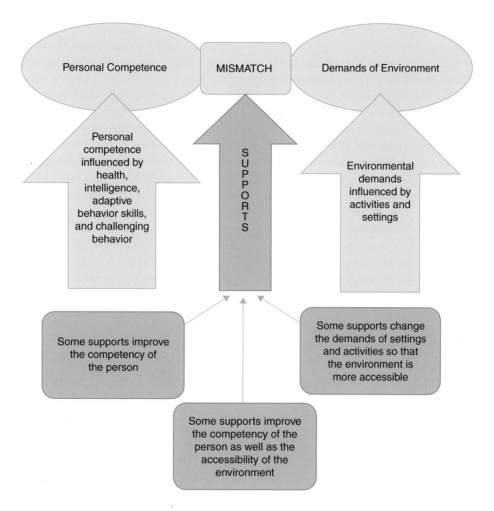

Figure 12.4 Supports address the mismatch between the individual with ID and their environment. (Adapted from Thompson et al., 2018)

their environment. The process involves identifying areas in which support is needed, appropriate support activities, and the level of support needed in each activity. Support could be provided through simple monitoring, teaching activities, or physical supports. For example, an adolescent may require aid in interacting with community members or in personal hygiene. The level of support judged necessary could range from minimal to substantial. To assess need, the AAIDD published the Supports Intensity Scales, with both adult (SIS-A) and child (SIS-C) versions now available (J. R. Thompson et al., 2015, 2016; Thompson, Schalock, & Tassé, 2018). The SIS-A is normed for individuals age 16 years and older, and the SIS-C is designed to assess the support needs of children ages 5 to 16 years. The SIS-C has two sections, which focus on exceptional medical and behavioral needs (Part I), as well activities for home living, community and neighborhood, school participation, school learning, health and safety, social activities, and advocacy (Part II).

Intervention

Evolving Understanding of Support Needs

Recognition of and attitudes toward intellectual disability have reflected the general beliefs of the times and have influenced how those with ID were treated by the societies in which they lived (King et al., 2017). Modern attitudes can be traced to the late 1700s and the case of the "Wild Boy of Aveyron," otherwise known as Victor. The boy, first seen running naked through the woods, was captured and assigned to a medical officer, Jean M. Itard, at the National Institute for the Deaf and Dumb in Paris. Victor's senses were underdeveloped; his memory, attention, and reasoning were deficient; and his ability to communicate was almost nil (Itard, as cited in Harrison & McDermott, 1972). Itard attributed the boy's deficits to lack of contact with civilized people, but the treatment he designed failed and Victor remained in custodial care until his death. Despite the disappointing outcome, Itard's effort stimulated interest in the "feeble-minded" or "retarded" (Rie, 1971).

The middle to late 1800s saw a favorable climate spread across the United States. Residential schools opened to educate children with ID and return them to the community (Brown, Radford, & Wehmeyer, 2017). Unfortunately, optimism waned. Increased interest in biological causation, the rise of psychoanalysis, and the misuse or misunderstanding of IQ tests strengthened the belief that persons with ID could hardly be helped and were a detriment, if not a danger, to society. Widespread institutionalization and custodial care ensued, with institutions growing in number and size throughout the first half of the twentieth century.

The last several decades have again witnessed more favorable attitudes, conditions, and interventions. In addition to increased knowledge and scientific advances, the 1960s brought commitment to the rights of poor, handicapped, and minority populations. Extensively adopted was the philosophy of **normalization**, which contends that each individual has the right to life experiences that are as normal and as least restrictive as possible. Normalization has influenced many aspects of life for people with ID, including living arrangements, educational services, work life, and treatments.

Regarding living arrangements, at one time families were encouraged to place their children with disability in out-of-home care. Substantial numbers resided in large institutions that provided questionable care (Noll, 2018). Although some individual circumstances may still warrant out-of-home arrangements, attitudes have shifted dramatically. In fact, a move toward "deinstitutionalization" arose in 1967, and over the course of the next 40 years (1967–2007), the number of individuals with intellectual and developmental disabilities residing in state institutions decreased more than 80% (Scott, Lakin, & Larson, 2008). Many large institutions have since been closed or downsized (King et al., 2017). In their place are small out-of-home community settings, which generally have improved the quality of life for residents (Felce, 2017). Moreover, most youth with ID live at home and, to varying degrees, are integrated into their neighborhoods. Because ID usually persists at some level, concern for these young people underscores the need for social and work opportunities in their adult years.

The concept of normalization applies to intervention, as well. Indeed, a general goal of intervention is to identify the mismatch between a person's skill level and the demands of their environment and provide the necessary supports to enable as normal a level of functioning as possible within the individual's daily life (Matson & Cervantes, 2019; Thompson et al., 2018). This applies to prevention, educational efforts, and treatment.

Prevention

In keeping with the multiple risks and causes of ID, prevention efforts vary substantially. Universal prevention includes prenatal care and diet, as well as the avoidance of alcohol and other teratogens during pregnancy. Efforts continue to identify and reduce environmental chemicals that adversely affect prenatal and postnatal cognitive development. Advances in genetics have contributed to prevention through prenatal screening or early postnatal detection. For example, Down syndrome can be recognized prenatally, and early postnatal identification of PKU enables immediate dietary adjustments to reduce ID.

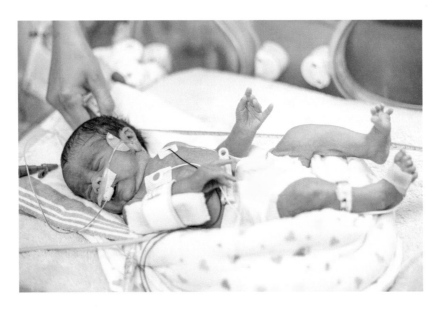

Medical advances have lowered the death rate of premature or low birthweight infants and investigations are under way in how best to optimize development and prevent problems. (Brocreative/Shutterstock)

The provision of early intervention programs that focus on at-risk infants and preschoolers is an important selective prevention effort for cognitive and other deficits. Federal policies have encouraged intervention during the first five years of life (Matson & Cervantes, 2019). Many of the programs emphasize child and family needs, include several elements, and entail an educational component. (See Accent: "Examples of Early Intervention Programs.")

As we turn to school services and treatments, it is important to recognize the multiple and individual needs of youth with ID. Intervention can be as varied as academic classes in reading or arithmetic, programs to teach self-help or social skills, interventions for communication problems, physical therapy, efforts to reduce maladaptive behaviors, medication to reduce seizures or hyperactivity, and psychotherapy. It is suggested that the approach to treatment begin with a comprehensive assessment and with the diagnostic process, as consideration of the underlying cause of ID can inform treatment (King et al., 2017). The following discussion examines, to varying degrees, educational services, behavioral intervention, pharmacological treatment, and psychotherapy.

Educational Supports

The most common intervention for individuals with ID is educational supports and services (Matson & Cervantes, 2019). Historically, special education was closely aligned to the needs of children with ID, especially mild disability (Polloway et al., 2010). These youth were central in much of the initial research and development of the field, as well as to the early criticism of educational practices that isolated them from other children. In the 1960s and 1970s, most children with ID were in self-contained classrooms, either for educable (mild) disability or trainable (moderate or lower) disability. As previously noted, the adoption of IDEA and subsequent federal policies gradually changed the face of education for exceptional students. For persons with ID, this meant increased individualized programming, parent and student participation in educational decision making, use of specialized technologies (e.g., tablets, augmented communication devices), and opportunity for alternative educational settings, if appropriate (Matson & Cervantes, 2019). Despite variation that exists across school districts and regions, more children with ID are attending local

ACCENT Examples of Early Intervention Programs

The goal of one type of early intervention for children at risk for ID is to prevent or reduce adverse outcomes of low birthweight or prematurity. Some programs are delivered in hospital neonatal care units. In one type of intervention, newborns receive systematic bodily massage or exercise (Field, Diego, & Hernandez-Reif, 2010). Stroking and/or flexion and extension of the upper and lower limbs are applied daily. Treated infants have been shown to achieve significantly greater weight gain—an important goal for these infants—and earlier hospital discharge. In the "PremieStart" hospital program, parents received several weeks of training aimed at buffering the effects of infant stress and enhancing brain development (Milgrom et al., 2010). The multiple components included training to recognize stress reactions in the newborns; to provide vocal and visual stimulation; and to engage in touch and movement interactions. Training has been associated with maturation and connectivity of white matter of the brain.

Other programs for low birthweight children provide support after hospital discharge. An example is the multisite Infant Health and Development Program, a comprehensive three-year randomized clinical trial that consists of home visits, family education and support, and educational day care for the children (Chaparro, Sojourner, & Huey, 2019). Evaluation of the at-risk children at age 3 showed several positive effects,

including benefits to cognitive development. At age 8, children of relatively high birthweight (2,100–2,500 grams), but not those weighing less, showed some cognitive and academic benefits (McCarton et al., 1997). At age 18, this group had better language skills and mathematics achievement, although there was no difference from controls in grade retention and special education placement (Olds, Sadler, & Kitzman, 2007).

Among the most significant early intervention efforts are multipurpose programs for preschoolers designed to reduce the risks of economic disadvantage. It is assumed that early experience is vital for cognitive and social growth. A major effort is Head Start, which was initiated by the federal government in 1965 (Mashburn & Yelverton, 2019). In addition to a child educational component, Head Start included child health care, parent education and involvement, and social services. It now serves children from birth to age 5, including those with disabilities. Over a 30-year period, the effectiveness of many preschool interventions, including that of Head Start, has been studied (Child Care & Early Education Research Connections, 2014). Among the conclusions is that (1) children in these programs receive cognitive and social benefits and (2) it is crucial to continue educational and other supports into childhood.

schools and joining their peers in general classrooms. Overall, students with ID can be integrated into community schools, and outcome is influenced more by instructional and other variables than by placement itself.

Inclusion of students with disabilities in general education classrooms has been increasingly accepted and practiced (Heward, 2013). Research, although still limited, points toward generally positive results, whereby inclusion, as compared to separate educational settings, seems to result in equal, or better, progress for students with ID (Dessemontet, Bless, & Morin, 2012). Importantly, supports and instruction that are modified to best meet the child's impairment and skill levels and considers the child's strengths and weaknesses are recommended (Matson & Cervantes, 2019). Under the regulations of the IDEA, decisions and accompanying procedures, accommodations, and educational goals are determined through collaboration of a multidisciplinary team and outlined in the student's individualized education program (IEP) (Causton & Tracy-Bronson, 2015; Matson & Cervantes, 2019), as introduced in the previous chapter on communication and learning disabilities. This could result, for example, in recommendations that the education of a child with mild ID take place mostly in a general education classroom with supports that emphasize acquisition and mastery of academic skills, while a student with moderate ID may require more supports in daily living and receive educational support services aimed at helping the child acquire basic academic skills. For a child with severe ID, it may be more appropriate to provide supports and educational services in an alternative setting. Again, consideration of the individual strengths and weaknesses of each child is important. The description of Jim provides a glimpse of how general education is possible, and may even be preferable, for a child with severe disability.

In addition to how best to deliver educational services to students with ID are the issues of the relatively low rate of high school graduation and of planning for transition to life after school. IDEA specifies that all children should have transitional services, which should be reflected in their IEPs (U.S. Department of Education Office of Special Education and Rehabilitative Services, 2017). Transitional services are activities to facilitate movement into postsecondary education, vocational education, employment, independent living, or community participation. Additionally, the Higher Education Opportunities Act of 2008 and related transition coordinating programs improved access to higher education for students with ID (Smith Lee, 2009). Youth who did not graduate high school or who would not otherwise meet entrance requirements are able to participate in postsecondary education with a focus on career education (Matson & Cervantes, 2019). Although increased progress is required in this area, it is promising that education and community integration across the lifespan is now an aspect of educational planning for youth with ID.

Increased numbers of children with intellectual disability attend community schools in which they are fully or partially integrated into general education classrooms. (BSIP SA/Alamy Stock Photo)

Behavioral Intervention and Supports

In the 1960s, advocates of behavior modification began to work in institutions that provided custodial care but little training or education (Whitman, Hantula, & Spence, 1990). Behavior modification gradually became dominant and was the subject of an enormous amount of research. A wide range of behaviors at all levels of disability was targeted. Operant procedures were used to enhance adaptive skills and reduce maladaptive behavior.

Over the years, behavioral techniques have progressed. Guidelines have been established for various methods, and precision in teaching and generalization of learned skills have been advanced (Handen, 1998). An important distinction has been made between **discrete trial learning** and **naturalistic, or incidental, learning**. In discrete trial learning, the clinician selects the task to be learned and provides clear directives, prompts, and consequences for appropriate behavior. Teaching is usually conducted in a quiet place, away from distractions. In naturalistic learning, the teaching situation is informal and less structured. It is more likely to be initiated by the child, amid everyday contexts; for example, the child's request for a toy is used as an opportunity for teaching. Both discrete trial learning

JIM Life in the Mainstream

At birth, Jim was identified as being developmentally at-risk. He was diagnosed with a cleft palate, failure to thrive, microcephaly, and possible cortical blindness. At 4 months, he began to receive at-home intervention services that focused on language and physical development. He was fed with a gastrointestinal tube until his cleft palate was repaired at age 2. Jim then attended preschool from age 3 to 5, spending part of the time in a general preschool and part in a self-contained special education program. Evaluations at ages 3 and 5 indicated an overall IQ score of 40.

Jim's mother's request that he be enrolled in a general kindergarten class was denied by the school district on the basis that he would not benefit from inclusion and that communication needs would not be met. Jim's parents refused to sign his Individualized Education Plan (IEP) and invoked due process complaints. Meanwhile, the school district moved Jim to a half-day, general kindergarten setting with supports. His parents' due process claim was decided in their favor, and Jim spent a second year in all-day, general kindergarten class, with various services somewhat more coordinated. He made notable progress in language development and reduction of anxiety.

Jim's subsequent school years were spent in general education. His disability label changed from "multiple disabilities" to "cognitive disability." Beginning in the third grade, his IEPs focused on academic content. Curricula for science, social studies, math, and reading were modified and emphasis was put on Jim's participation to the fullest extent possible. He continued to receive language, occupational, and physical therapies, with many of these services delivered in the general classroom.

This pattern generally was maintained in middle school. IEPs focused on functional academic skills, including keyboarding and the development of first-grade skills in reading, writing, and math. Progress was demonstrated, and no particular academic or behavioral concerns were reported. In the fifth grade, with parental encouragement, Jim began to participate in regularly scheduled extracurricular activities with special supports. He developed positive relationships with other students, although no close friendships beyond the school context.

During the three years of high school for which data were kept, Jim was in general classes with modified curricula, materials, instruction, and assessment. An exception occurred in his junior year, when he spent 1.5 hours a day in a special education classroom. Although this was discrepant with his IEP, the special education teacher who provided the instruction noted that she did not favor inclusive education. Jim performed academically at a K-2nd grade level, and his IQ was reported as 46. He continued to participate in marching band, track, and student clubs, including Students Against Driving Drunk. His experiences in high school focused on participating with age peers without disabilities. He "hung out" until the school bell rang for class; used his locker appropriately; prepared for and participated in class activities as others did; and exchanged smiles, brief verbal greetings, and "high-fives" with other students. In many ways, Jim blended into the social context of the school.

Adapted from Ryndak et al., 2010, pp. 43–49

and naturalistic learning have been shown to be effective, and naturalistic learning is believed to be especially effective for generalization of learning.

Efforts have also been made to train those who work with youth with ID—in the home, school, community programs, or residential placements. Courses and curricula have been developed to disseminate information to caregivers. Parent training has been shown to be effective, and parents can profit from ongoing contact with professionals (Matson et al., 2019). Overall, behavioral intervention has had considerable success in serving young people with ID.

Enhancing Adaptive Behavior

Operant techniques have been employed to enhance a variety of adaptive behaviors. These include self-help skills, imitation, language, social behavior, academic skills, and work behaviors. Here, we comment on two of these areas.

The acquisition of daily living skills is an important goal of intervention (Matson et al., 2019). For youth with more severe levels of disability, it may be a central component. Children and adolescents who cannot dress and feed themselves or otherwise cannot take care of their basic needs are often limited from participating in educational and social activities. Those who are unable to shop, order food in restaurants, wash their clothes, or catch a bus can hardly enjoy independence in community living. Thus, adaptive skills training targets a gamut of everyday living skills.

Given the impairments in social functioning common to individuals with ID, considerable attention also has been given to facilitating social skills (Matson et al., 2019). Social

Special Olympics is an example of community programs that attempt to normalize the lives of youth with disability and to provide opportunities to develop social skills as well as a sense of accomplishment and self-worth. (Xinhua/Alamy Stock Photo)

skills training is aimed at improving social functioning and teaching specific skills, such as eye contact and initiation of and appropriate response to social interactions. Training has been provided in various settings and has included behavioral and cognitive-behavioral techniques such as prompting, reinforcement, and modeling (Walton & Ingersoll, 2013). Combined behavioral skills training and video modeling has been shown to substantially improve social skills, including conversation and turn taking for example (O'Handley et al., 2016). In addition to these treatments, it is recognized that everyday activities can enhance social development. For example, participation in sports and Special Olympics by children and adults with ID has been linked with psychosocial benefits such as increased social skills, friendships, and self-worth (Tint, Thomson, & Weiss, 2017).

Reducing Challenging Behavior

Self-stimulation, bizarre speech, tantrums, aggression, and self-injury are among the behaviors that interfere with social relationships, learning, and community living—and sometimes directly harm individuals with ID. A variety of techniques have been employed to reduce these challenging behaviors, and success has been documented with single-subject research designs.

In this discussion, we emphasize self-injury because the behaviors themselves and the interventions aimed at addressing them have been especially problematic. **Self-injurious behavior** (SIB) appears more common at the lower levels of intellectual

functioning with prevalence estimates around 4 to 5% in individuals with severe ID (Oliver, Licence, & Richards, 2017), and it occurs in an unusually high frequency in particular genetic syndromes, such as fragile X and Prader–Willi, for example (Huisman et al., 2018). SIBs differ in form—head banging, biting, hitting the self, are common, among other behaviors—and intensity ranges from minor to life-threatening damage. The association of SIB with some genetic syndromes suggests an abnormal organic need for sensory stimulation that self-injurious behavior might provide. Even so, SIB is clearly influenced by environmental variables. Biological or environmental factors, or their combination, likely underlie the behavior.

The history of treating SIB shows that it can be relatively difficult to change (Bregman & Gerdtz, 1997). Medications are only somewhat successful, and early behavioral interventions often failed. When self-injury threatened the child and interventions were ineffective, punishments such as squirting lemon juice into the mouth and contingent electric shock were sometimes employed. Although aversive consequences were somewhat effective, they raised serious ethical questions and are dissonant with a respectful approach to treatment. Aversive procedures, such as electric shock, have been condemned by the AAIDD as they can cause substantial risk and harm (AAIDD, 2019). Effective and more acceptable procedures have evolved and are recommended.

Positive behavioral support (PBS) is an approach that aims to increase skills and alter environmental contingencies. It is considered the treatment framework of choice for children with ID at risk for challenging behaviors (Gore, McGill, & Hastings, 2019) and is promoted by the AAIDD (AAIDD, 2019). PBS has been adapted to various settings and employed with youth diagnosed with ID, autism, and other developmental disabilities. With origins in applied behavior analysis, PBS relies on behavioral principles and research-based **functional assessment**, or analysis (Condillac & Baker, 2017; Kincaid et al., 2016; Schmidt et al., 2016). Central to the approach are modification of the environment and behavioral consequences, with the teaching of new responses to substitute for maladaptive behaviors often incorporated.

The rationale for functional assessment is the assumption that understanding the variables that influence challenging behaviors can be helpful in preventing or alleviating them. Figure 12.5 presents a schema that conceptualizes such influences and can be applied to SIB (Newsom, 1998). It considers the environmental context in which the behavior occurs and the consequences that accrue to the behavior. *Setting events* are background variables that can affect the probability that the behavior will occur. For example, fatigue can make it more likely that the child will respond with SIB. *Antecedent stimuli* occur just prior to self-injury and precipitate the behavior. *Positive consequences* are contingencies that likely strengthen or maintain SIB.

Numerous studies have shown that SIB and other challenging behaviors are reinforced by consequences that commonly fall into four categories: attention seeking, tangible-item seeking, escape or avoidance, and nonsocial contingencies (Schmidt et al., 2016). As Figure 12.5 indicates, self-injury can be positively reinforced by attention from caretakers as they try to deter a child from the behavior and by tangibles such as food and activities. Self-injury

also can be negatively reinforced. For example, when unwanted demands are made, the child may engage in self-injury, with the result that caregivers may cease to make the demands—thereby allowing the child to escape the demands. In other cases, reinforcement appears nonsocial, and is often attributed to some unknown sensory consequence experienced by the child. Figure 12.5 also points to how challenging behaviors can be modified. Altering the setting events and antecedent stimuli—for example, by minimizing them—can prevent SIB from occurring at all. Altering reinforcement contingencies can reduce or eliminate self-injury.

Functional assessment examines how the child is behaving in what situations, with what consequences, and what variables maintain and influence the behavior (Matson et al., 2019). It can be conducted by acquiring information from detailed interviews with adults interacting with the child or observation of the child in the natural setting. Rating scales have been developed to aid in such assessment, such as the Questions About Behavioral Function scale. Assessment can also be accomplished by an analogue (or experimental) **functional analysis**, which entails a manipulation of variables to determine their influence on the behavior. Based on functional assessment, an individual treatment plan is constructed which might include modification of the environment, and/or the behavioral consequences operating, as well as the teaching of new responses. Interventions most often employed reinforcement, reinforcement with extinction, or Functional Communication Training with or without reinforcement (Matson, Shoemaker et al., 2011). For a demonstration of the latter approach, see Accent: "Functional Communication Training."

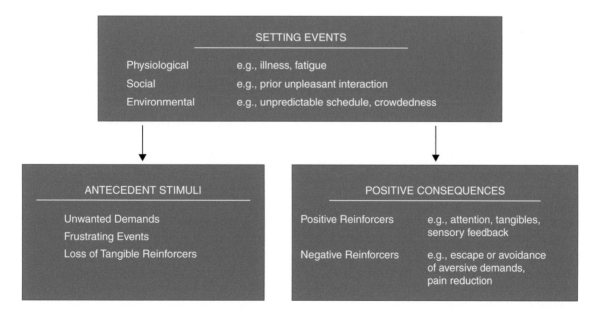

Figure 12.5 A schema of variables that can influence challenging behaviors. (Adapted from Newsom, 1998. Copyright 1998 by Guilford Press; reprinted with permission)

ACCENT Functional Communication Training

Functional Communication Training aims to reduce challenging behavior by encouraging the child to substitute in its place an adaptive behavior. It is assumed that maladaptive behaviors are often used as a way to communicate needs or desires. The first step in Functional Communication Training is functional analysis; the second is to select and train a more positive way to communicate.

The approach is exemplified in the case of Matt, a 5-year-old boy who was diagnosed with moderate ID and cerebral palsy (Durand, 1999). Matt lived with his parents and attended a school for students with developmental disabilities. He lacked verbal language, but he was able to point to express his desires. Matt frequently bit his hand and screamed—behaviors that had not succumbed to prior interventions. The treatment strategy had several components:

- Matt's teacher was trained to conduct the intervention in the classroom.
- The teacher determined the circumstances in which Matt most frequently engaged in self-biting and screaming. She assessed Matt's behavior by using a rating scale and also by systematically observing his behavior under four

conditions: low teacher attention during a task, low access to a preferred tangible object during a task, a more difficult task, and a control condition. This analysis showed that Matt's maladaptive behavior occurred when he was faced with a difficult task.
- Matt was trained to ask for help on difficult tasks by pressing a pad on a device, which activated a voice saying, "I need help."
- The effectiveness of the training was evaluated.

The entire intervention required several weeks. The results of the functional analysis (A) and the final evaluation of Matt's behavior (B) are shown in Figure 12.6. The positive outcome is consistent with similar studies showing the effectiveness of Functional Communication Training in which individuals are taught to communicate their desires through adaptive spoken language or with mechanical devices when needed. Of particular interest in the present study is that it included trips to a community store in which Matt had experienced difficulty and frustration handling money as he purchased candy. After intervention, Matt used the mechanical device to ask the shopkeeper for help in managing his money.

(continued)

Research findings support the effectiveness of PBS, and it has been applied within a multitiered framework in school contexts (Kincaid et al., 2016). Although extensive planning and training are important, there is continued sensitivity to maximizing the usefulness of PBS and expanding its utility in multiple settings and for children with and without ID (Keller-Bell & Short, 2019).

Psychopharmacology and Psychotherapy

Pharmacological Treatment

Medications are not known to strengthen intellectual functioning in cases of ID, but are aimed at alleviating medical and psychological symptoms. Although data are lacking with regard to the number of children or adolescents taking medication, it is likely to be substantial. Given the prevalence and variation of psychological problems associated with ID, all major categories of psychotropic medications have been prescribed. Nevertheless, limited evidence exists for the effectiveness of pharmacological treatment and the impact of side effects of psychotropic medications (Matson et al., 2019).

We comment here only on two classes of medications. The symptoms of ADHD, which affect perhaps 9 to 18% of children with ID, lessen with stimulant medication (King et al., 2017). However, response rates are lower than for typical cases of ADHD,

perhaps particularly for those with moderate and severe ID, and negative side effects may be greater (Matson et al., 2019). Antipsychotic medications are the most commonly prescribed psychotropic medications, often employed to treat challenging behaviors, such as aggressive behavior and SIB (Bowring et al., 2017; Deb, Unwin, & Deb, 2015; Matson et al., 2019). Evidence for the efficacy of antipsychotics is mixed, and possible side effects—for example, weight gain, sedation, movement disorder—require serious consideration. More recently, atypical antipsychotic medications have been used more often in children as opposed to traditional typical antipsychotics because they may have fewer side effects, however their use is cautioned (Unwin & Deb, 2011).

Overall, it appears that medication response is similar to that shown by other populations, but that fewer persons with ID benefit from medications and that negative side effects may be more frequent, requiring unique consideration and dosing for individuals with ID (King et al., 2017). Moreover, research on the efficacy of medications is inadequate both for youth and adults. Indeed, there is general concern over inappropriate practices, including inadequate evaluation of effects and side effects and questionable choice of medication and prescription dosage (Matson et al., 2019). It is clear, however, that the management of medication for youth with ID requires special consideration. The difficulty of diagnosing comorbid psychopathology raises the

(continued)

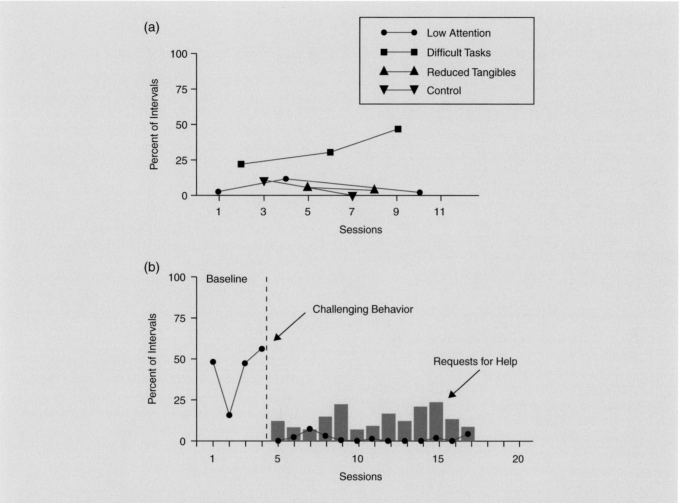

Figure 12.6 (A) Functional analysis showed that Matt's challenging behaviors occurred mostly during difficult tasks. (B) The training sessions indicated a drop in Matt's challenging behaviors and Matt's requests for help. (From Durand, 1999. Copyright 1999 by *Journal of Applied Behavior Analysis*; reprinted with permission)

issue of the appropriateness of any prescribed medication. Added to this, determining the effectiveness and side effects of drugs is especially challenging due to the limited ability of those with ID to describe what they are experiencing. Possible drug interactions also require a watchful eye, particularly in cases involving medical conditions (King et al., 2017).

Psychotherapy Approaches

Research into the use and effectiveness of psychotherapy for individuals with ID is scant (Matson et al., 2019). There is some indication that professionals recommend behavioral interventions over more traditional counseling or "talking" approaches. In addition, the literature indicates disagreement on the effectiveness and usefulness of psychotherapy. Some professionals argue that it has little or no place in treating youth with ID (Sturmey, 2005). Others argue that it should not be precluded in the presence of mild and moderate intellectual deficits (Hurley, 2005).

It is agreed that psychotherapy techniques must be adapted to the developmental level of the child or adolescent (King et al., 2017). Active, skills-based approaches, such as teaching brief relaxation techniques, may be helpful. Additionally, modification, such as using concrete and clear language and nonverbal techniques (e.g., using pictures, body language, play or other activities), may be necessary when expressive and receptive deficits exist (Summers, Fletcher, & Bradley, 2017). Short, frequent sessions also may be required.

Research on the effectiveness of psychotherapy for individuals with ID remains limited, and relatively little evidence exists to guide modifications for applying psychotherapy techniques with this special population (Unwin et al., 2016). There is an interest in encouraging high-quality investigation into what psychotherapy methods are effective for what kinds of problems and at what level of intellectual disability.

Looking Back

- Perspectives on ID have changed over the decades, as have the labels applied to the disorder.

Definition and Classification

- ID is defined by subaverage intellectual functioning with concurrent deficits in adaptive skills manifested before age 18 or during the developmental period.
- The AAIDD views ID as multidimensional, with environmental supports mediating outcome.
- The severity of ID historically has been recognized as mild, moderate, severe, and profound, based on IQ performance. More recently, severity is specified by levels of needed supports (AAIDD) or adaptive behavior (DSM).

Nature of Intelligence and Adaptive Behavior

- Binet and colleagues viewed intelligence as somewhat malleable and influenced by the social environment. The subsequent assumption of fixed inheritance and the misuse of intelligence tests resulted in controversies and legal battles.
- Measured intelligence is relatively reliable for most people and correlates reasonably well with academic-related achievements. IQ scores must be interpreted with care, however.
- Adaptive behavior refers to domains of everyday behavior, and includes conceptual, social, and practical skills.

Description

- The abilities of young people with ID show immense variation. Difficulties are manifest in intellectual and adaptive functioning, physical and medical attributes, learning and cognitive ability, communication, and social functioning.

Co-occurring Disorders

- Rates of psychological problems and disorders are high in youth with ID. The kinds of problems appear similar to those in the general population, but can be difficult to identify and diagnose.

Epidemiology

- The prevalence of ID in the general population is estimated around 1%. Rates are disproportionately high in school-age children, males, and individuals of lower social class.

Developmental Course and Considerations

- The developmental course and outcome of ID varies widely but most youth will require some degree of support throughout life.
- Compared with typically developing intelligence, the intellectual abilities of youth with ID tend to develop in the same sequences but at slower rates.

Etiology

- The historic two-group approach to etiology conceptualized ID as falling into an organic or a cultural–familial group.
- Pathological organic influences, which are associated with more severe ID, can originate in genetic, prenatal, birth, or postnatal adversities.
- Multiple-gene effects are considered especially important in mild ID of unknown etiology.
- Psychosocial influence, which may operate across generations of socially disadvantaged families, is also viewed as particularly relevant to milder levels of ID.
- AAIDD's multiple risk model reflects the current perspective of etiology as complex and interactive.

Genetic Syndromes and Behavioral Phenotypes

- Genetic syndromes—such as Down, fragile X, Williams, and Prader–Willi—are currently receiving much research attention. Each syndrome tends to be associated with a particular physical, cognitive, and behavioral phenotype.

Family Accommodations and Experiences

- Family adjustment to having a child with ID is influenced by child characteristics, family characteristics, and social variables.
- Family members likely are affected differently and experience both unique stress and rewards.

Assessment

- Comprehensive assessment for ID is best guided by its goals. Diagnosis typically entails assessment of intelligence and adaptive behavior with standardized tests.

Intervention

- Treatment for ID historically has varied in approach and quality. In recent decades, the philosophy of normalization has taken center stage.
- Universal and selective prevention for ID targets prenatal care, diet, genetic conditions, environmental risks, and the risks of low birthweight and economic disadvantage.
- IDEA and related policies have brought increased educational integration to students with ID, although complex issues remain about school inclusion.

- A range of behavioral techniques are effective in strengthening appropriate skills and weakening maladaptive behaviors. Positive behavioral support and functional assessment are effective approaches.
- Pharmacological treatment and psychotherapy are both in need of controlled outcome studies. The former is relatively common, but several concerns exist regarding medication use. Psychotherapy, with adaptations, arguably may be useful in mild or moderate ID.

Key Terms

mental age *302*
intelligence quotient *303*
Flynn effect *303*
overshadowing *308*
two-group approach *310*
behavioral phenotype *312*
normalization *322*

discrete trial learning *324*
naturalistic (incidental) learning *324*
self-injurious behavior *326*
positive behavioral support *326*
functional assessment *327*
functional analysis *327*

CHAPTER 13

Autism Spectrum Disorder and Schizophrenia

Looking Forward

After reading this chapter, you should be able to discuss:

- The historical association of schizophrenia and autism spectrum disorder
- The DSM approach to autism spectrum disorder
- Description, etiology, assessment, treatment, and other aspects of autism

- Assessment and intervention for autism spectrum disorder
- Classification, diagnosis, description, and other aspects of schizophrenia
- Etiology of schizophrenia
- Assessment and intervention for schizophrenia

The disorders discussed in this chapter are characterized by pervasive problems in social, emotional, and cognitive functioning that have a basis in neurobiological abnormality. Development may be qualitatively different from typical development in ways that have compelled an enormous amount of interest and investigation. Autism spectrum disorder and schizophrenia in youth are now considered distinct from each other, but they share a rich history.

A Bit of History

Although the disorders we are about to discuss have long been recognized, they are surrounded by confusion and debate. Historically, these disorders were associated with adult psychoses—that is, severely disruptive disturbances implying abnormal perceptions of reality. Psychotic disturbances were noted in early twentieth-century classifications of mental disorders based on Kraepelin's work. Bleuler applied the term "schizophrenias" to disorders that involve disturbances in reality, such as hearing voices and seeing images that do not exist. Investigators noted a small percentage of cases that had begun in childhood (Marenco & Weinberger, 2000).

Ideas about psychoses and other severe disturbances developed gradually over many years. Some investigators

described groups of children with early onset of schizophrenia, and others pointed to syndromes that appeared similar, but not identical, to schizophrenia. Various diagnostic terms were applied, including *disintegrative psychoses* and *childhood psychoses*. Beginning around 1930 and for several years afterward, *childhood schizophrenia* served as a general label for many severe early-occurring disturbances (Asarnow & Kernan, 2008).

In a landmark report in 1943, Leo Kanner described what he called "early infantile autism," arguing that it was different from other cases of severe disturbance, which generally had later onset. Shortly afterward, Hans Asperger, working in a different country, described a group of children whose symptoms overlapped with Kanner's cases. These men did not know each other—and apparently believed they were writing about different types of disturbances (Frith, 2004).

By the early 1970s, data from several countries showed that severe disturbances in youth were age related. A relatively large number of cases appeared before age 3, remarkably few first appeared during childhood, and prevalence increased in adolescence (Kolvin, 1971). This pattern suggested that different syndromes might underlie the earlier-occurring and later-occurring disturbances. Gradually, on the basis of symptoms and several other features, a distinction was made between schizophrenia and a group of nonpsychotic disturbances of youth. Schizophrenia affects a small number of children, rises in frequency in adolescence, and increases still more in early

PAUL Autistic Aloneness

Paul was a slender, well built, attractive child, whose face looked intelligent and animated. ... He rarely responded to any form of address, even to the calling of his name. ... He was obviously so remote that the remarks did not reach him. He was always vivaciously occupied with something and seemed to be highly satisfied. ... There was, on his side, no affective tie to people. He behaved as if people as such did not matter or even exist. It made no difference if one spoke to him in a friendly or harsh way. He never looked up at people's faces. When he had any dealings with persons at all, he treated them, or rather parts of them, as if they were objects.

Adapted from Kanner, 1943, reprinted, 1973, pp. 14–15

adulthood. The syndromes described by Kanner and Asperger, along with other similar disturbances, appear early in life, and it is now understood that while they share some overlapping symptoms and commonalities with schizophrenia (Hommer & Swedo, 2015), they are etiologically distinct with different developmental courses (Pennington, McGrath, & Peterson, 2019).

Kanner's early descriptions of autism noted communication deficits, good but atypical cognitive potential, and behavioral problems such as obsessiveness, repetitive actions, and unimaginative play. He emphasized, however, that the fundamental disturbance was an inability to relate to people and situations from the beginning of life. He quoted parents who referred to their disturbed children as "self-sufficient," "like in a shell," "happiest when left alone," and "acting as if people weren't there" (Kanner, 1973, p. 33). To this extreme disturbance in socioemotional contact with others, Kanner applied the term "autistic." The case description of Paul is a brief depiction of one of the cases presented by Kanner in his classic paper. Although not all of Kanner's observations proved accurate, most of the characteristics described were subsequently noted by others. Children displaying manifestations of these disorders are now widely diagnosed with Autism Spectrum Disorder. An enormous amount of research has increased our understanding of autism and is reflected in the current conceptualization of autism spectrum disorder in the DSM.

Autism Spectrum Disorder (ASD)

To understand the current approach to autism and related disturbances, it is helpful to take a historical perspective of DSM classification and diagnoses, in particular. The DSM-IV included, among disorders first evident in youth, the category of Pervasive Developmental Disorders. Specifically described were Autistic Disorder, Asperger's Disorder, Childhood Disintegrative Disorder, and Pervasive Developmental Disorder Not Otherwise Specified (PDD-NOS). (Also included was Rett's Disorder, which is now seen as categorically different and is therefore not included in

our discussion.) To varying degrees, these disorders displayed similar characteristics, but several issues were raised about their relationship to each other. For example, some investigators questioned whether Autistic Disorder and Asperger's Disorder were two distinct disturbances rather than a single disorder.

In the DSM-5 (American Psychiatric Association, 2013), the disorders named above are no longer recognized as distinct. Rather, Autism Spectrum Disorder (ASD) serves as the diagnosis for individuals who display an array or continuum of symptoms previously encompassed by the DSM-IV disorders.

According to the DSM-5, ASD is classified as a neurodevelopmental disorder consisting of primary symptoms that fall into two domains.

- Persistent deficits in social communication and interaction across multiple contexts. These are shown in social-emotional reciprocity, nonverbal communicative behaviors, and social relationships.
- Restricted, repetitive patterns of behaviors, interests, and activities. These must be displayed by two or more of the following:
  - stereotyped or repetitive motor movements, use of objects, or speech
  - insistence on sameness, inflexible adherence to routines, or ritualized behavior
  - restricted, fixated interests of abnormal intensity or focus
  - over- or undersensitivity to sensory input or unusual interest in sensory aspects of the environment.

Symptoms must occur during the early developmental period and significantly impair social, occupational, and other aspects of functioning. Moreover, the disorder cannot better be attributed to intellectual disability or global developmental delay.

It is noteworthy that when the DSM-5 adopted the category of ASD, this conceptualization already had been used by many workers in the field. However, some professionals in the field still question the wisdom of collapsing the previously recognized disorders into one broad category, and some labels—in particular Asperger's—continue to be utilized in community settings (Pennington et al., 2019). Nevertheless, advances in scientific knowledge lend support to the dimensional system of diagnosis in the current DSM (Lord & Bishop, 2015; Pennington et al., 2019).

In the following sections, we discuss many aspects of ASD and its wide spectrum of severity and variability in clinical presentation and potential etiology. We use the terms "autism spectrum disorder" and "autism" interchangeably to refer to this complex disorder and to reflect the transition from distinct disorder to an emphasis on a spectrum of autism and the changes in terminology that went with it.

Description: Primary Features

In examining the features of ASD, it is necessary to again emphasize that the diagnosis encompasses a wide spectrum of clinical presentation—not all children with the disorder necessarily display all features, nor are they identical in the severity of their symptoms. As outlined above, the core symptoms of ASD are conceptualized in the DSM-5 as falling into two domains—persistent impairments in social communication and interaction and the presence of restricted and repetitive behaviors. Symptoms severity is rated in the DSM-5 on a 3-point scale based on the level of support needed (Level 1, *requiring support*; Level 2, *requiring substantial support*; and Level 3, *requiring very substantial support*) (American Psychiatric Association, 2013).

Deficits in Social Communication and Interaction
The impairment in social communication and interaction seen in ASD impacts multiple domains of social functioning and varies depending on the developmental level of the child and severity of autism symptoms. Children with ASD typically show few symptoms at 6 months, but many show subtle differences from typically developing infants before 12 months (Pennington et al., 2019). While parents of children later diagnosed with ASD often report having concerns between their child's first and second birthday, recent advances in studies of infants with siblings with ASD (i.e., infants at high genetic risk for ASD diagnosis) have improved our understanding of the earliest signs of autism (Faja & Dawson, 2017). Table 13.1 provides an overview of some signs and symptoms of autism.

Very young children with autism may have decreased social interest, may be less likely to respond to their names, and more likely to show unusual responses to sensory stimuli, such as aversion to being touched by another person or high levels of sensory seeking behavior (Baranek et al., 2018; Faja & Dawson, 2017; Kadlaskar et al., 2019; M. Miller et al., 2017). They fail to track people visually, have decreased eye contact, exhibit an "empty" gaze, fail to respond to others with emotional expression and positive affect, and may show little interest in being held (Haroon, 2019b).

Table 13.1 Some Signs and Symptoms of ASD

In Preschool-Aged Children
• Delay or absence of spoken language
• Difficulty reading facial expressions
• Unusual eye contact, may appear to stare through or past people
• Social deficits, such as lack of interest in other people, difficulty turn taking, poor initiation of play
• Reduced or absent pretend play
• Unusual motor behaviors, such as rocking, spinning, or tip-toe walking
• Difficulties with change in routine
• Abnormal interests or play behavior
• Sensory interests or avoidance
In School-Aged Children
• Speech abnormalities, including delays, repetitive speech, echolalia, and other difficulties
• Limited, sometimes very literal understanding of language
• Impairments in nonverbal communication, such as limited use of eye contact, expression, and gestures
• Socialization difficulties, including problems initiating or joining in with others in play or difficulty understanding social norms (e.g., personal space)
• Difficulty with unexpected changes in routine
• Unusual interests or interests that are overly intense
• Sensory interests or avoidance

Source: Adapted from Haroon, 2019b.

Young children with ASD typically present with delayed or atypical early language acquisition—both verbal and nonverbal. Quite striking in autism are deficits in **joint attention** interactions, which usually develop after 6 months. These interactions involve preverbal gestures, such as pointing and eye contact that center the child's and caregiver's attention on an object or situation, in order to share an experience (Adamson et al., 2019). In addition, as compared to typical youth, young children with autism show other delays or declines in communication, including reduced babbling, unusual vocalizations, and reduced imitation of others (Faja & Dawson, 2017; Lobban-Shymko, Im-Bolter, & Freeman, 2017). They appear to miss out on the mutual connection between two people and the potential it holds for learning about themselves and others.

Because such behaviors interfere with social interaction, we might expect a lack of attachment to parents. A recent meta-analysis showed that children with ASD are capable of forming secure attachments, with nearly half of the children with autism showing secure attachment in the Strange Situation (Teague et al.,

2017). However, some of the symptoms of autism and attachment difficulties overlap, and children with ASD show higher levels of insecure attachment patterns than typically developing children and other clinical groups (McKenzie & Dallos, 2017). Secure attachment between parents and children with ASD is associated with improved outcome. Given the enormous variability of these children—and the stress that parents can experience in caring for an infant with autism symptoms—further understanding of attachment in these children could be helpful in facilitating and supporting parenting practices.

Abnormal processing of social stimuli, notably of the face, is another component of atypical social interaction. Facial processing is considered crucial to social development (Webb, Neuhaus, & Faja, 2017). Typically developing infants are attracted to the human face and rapidly recognize the faces of their mothers. Children with autism often show impairment in recognizing faces, matching emotional faces, and memorizing faces. They may also visually process faces in unusual ways, for example, by focusing on the mouth or eyes in ways different from what typically developing children do (Chawarska & Shic, 2009), and they may show specific deficits in facial expression processing (Van der Donck et al., 2020). Overall, by the toddler-preschool period, delayed or atypical social behaviors can be seen in at least five domains of social behavior: orienting to social stimuli, joint attention, emotion, imitation, and face processing (Faja & Dawson, 2017). Although there is some symptom change over time, many social impairments persist.

During childhood, a variety of social deficits, such as lack of understanding of social cues and inappropriate social actions, are evident. There is a certain aloofness, disinterest, and lack of social reciprocity and empathy. The child may ignore others or fail to participate in cooperative play or engage others in conversation (Klinger & Dudley, 2019). Even higher functioning adolescents and adults may seem "odd," have difficulty with the subtleties of social interaction, and have problems forming friendships as they move through life.

Persistent difficulties in communication—both nonverbal and verbal—is a widely observed aspect of autism. As described earlier, nonverbal communication involving gestures, visual gaze, and facial expression of emotion is atypical or deficient. In addition, perhaps 30% of children with autism remain minimally verbal (Rose, Trembath, Keen, & Paynter, 2016). In those who acquire language, development is delayed and often abnormal. Echolalia and pronoun reversal are commonly observed. In **echolalia** the person echoes back what another has said, a behavior also seen in dysfunctions such as language disorders, schizophrenia, and blindness. **Pronoun reversal** is more common in autism than in other disorders or typical development and may persist into adulthood. The child may refer to others as *I* or *me*, and to the self as *he, she, them,* or *you.*

Impairment in both understanding and use of language (i.e., in receptive and expressive language) vary in the ASD population, but are common (Kwok et al., 2015). Specific difficulties in syntax, comprehension, and other structural forms of language also exist; these may resemble, but are not identical to, specific language impairments (Williams, Botting, & Boucher, 2008). Notable is impairment in pragmatics, that is, the communicative and social use of language (Parsons et al., 2017). Conversation may be marked by irrelevant details, inappropriate shifts in topic, or disregard of normal give-and-take of conversation—or there may be an overall failure to develop conversation. The case example of Steven illustrates the multiple deficits in social-communication skills that may be present in ASD.

It is worth noting that within the wide range of symptoms of autism, some children function at a higher level. They may be able to communicate better when given prompts, tell stories, and read. Some exhibit hyperlexia, a little-understood feature in which single-word reading is extraordinary but comprehension of what is read is problematic (Ostrolenk et al., 2017). As will be discussed later in this chapter, interventions that target specific social and communication skill deficits may be helpful in enhancing the

STEVEN Early Social-Communication Deficits

Steven is a 30-month-old boy diagnosed with ASD at 24 months of age at a university-based autism clinic. He speaks in short (i.e., two- to three-word) phrases and consistently labels objects and pictures in books. However, Steven's words are not always directed toward other people and are not integrated with eye gaze or gestures. He shows an interest in a variety of toys but is not yet engaging in pretend play. While clearly excited by some materials, he is not using eye contact or showing or pointing gestures to share his interests with others (i.e., he is not using joint attention). Steven is not interested in playing with peers and prefers to play alone with blocks, puzzles, and toys with numbers. He enjoys some social games and songs with his parents; however, he is not imitating the movements in the game/song. Steven has strengths in his preacademic skills and can label colors, shapes, and numbers.

Adapted from Klinger & Dudley, 2019, p. 398

social communication and interactions of some individuals with ASD (Klinger & Dudley, 2019).

Restricted, Repetitive Patterns of Behavior, Interests, or Activities (RRBs)

Some repetitious behaviors—such as kicking and rocking in infancy and later preference for sameness—are features of typical development that mostly subside by school age (Klinger & Dudley, 2019). In contrast, both younger and older youth with autism display odd behaviors, interests, and activities that are described as restricted, repetitive, and occurring in high frequency.

Traditionally, these behaviors have been grouped into two widely recognized domains (Klinger & Dudley, 2019). One of these is characterized as lower-order "repetitive sensorimotor behaviors" such as hand flapping, rocking, twirling, and toe walking, repetitive use of objects, and some self-injurious behaviors. Although such peculiarities are seen in typically developing young children and in children with other disorders, they differ in autism, occurring in greater frequency and severity and persisting through late childhood (Berry, Russell, & Frost, 2018). They appear to be especially common in younger children with autism and those with lower intelligence.

The second category of RRBs is characterized as higher-order "insistence on sameness" (Mirenda et al., 2010; Turner, 1999). Here, children appear preoccupied with aspects of the environment. Children may seem obsessed with numbers, compulsively collect articles, or be overly absorbed in hobbies. They may adopt motor routines, such as rearranging objects, and insist on following rituals for eating and going to bed. Minor changes in the environment, such as rearrangement of furniture or schedules, can upset them. These obsessive behaviors may be more common in older children with ASD.

Why RRBs occur or how they are maintained is not understood (Factor et al., 2016). Perhaps excessive arousal or anxiety plays a role, or perhaps some of the behaviors serve as self-stimulation that results from the child's inability to engage the world in other ways. For whatever reasons, a study that examined RRBs from age 2 to 9 years in children with ASD found sizeable heterogeneity in patterns of change over time (Richler et al., 2010).

Description: Secondary Features

Several additional features are often observed in autism and are meaningful in understanding the disorder.

Sensory/Perceptual Impairments

While the sensory organs are typically intact in individuals with ASD, abnormal responses to stimuli suggest issues in sensory and perceptual processing. Both oversensitivity and undersensitivity occur significantly more in than in typical development, and these features have been given increased importance in the

Stereotyped movements commonly occur in youth with autism. (John Birdsall Social Issues Photo Library/Science Photo Library)

DSM-5 classification of ASD (American Psychiatric Association, 2013; Bogdashina, 2016). Youth who are oversensitive to stimuli may be disturbed by the sound of a vacuum cleaner, seams on their clothing, or a light embrace. Sensory input may thus be disliked, feared, or avoided. One adult with autism described her earlier experiences as "horrible oversensitivity" to sound and touch and as "an overwhelming, drowning wave of stimulation" in response to being touched by another person (Grandin, 1997). In contrast, undersensitivity, which may be the more common problem, is exemplified by children's failing to respond to voices or other sounds or walking into things. The clinical picture may be puzzling; for example, a child may seem unaware of a loud noise but fascinated by the quiet ticking of a watch (Volkmar & Klin, 2000). In some cases, a child's failure to respond to sound leads parents to think their child has a hearing impairment. Interestingly, indirect evidence that sensory perceptual issues may be at the core of ASD come from studies examining similar behaviors in individuals who have experienced severe sensory deprivation or visual and/or auditory impairments (Bogdashina, 2016).

Overselectivity is also common in autism. Here, the individual focuses on a select portion of a stimulus array while neglecting other components (Duarte & Baer, 2019). Overselectivity occurs in many populations, including typically developing children and those with specific and general learning problems or intellectual disability (Dube et al., 2016). It has been variously conceptualized (e.g., as sensory overload or a deficit in attention), and is recognized as interfering with normal development and functioning. Neglecting specific aspects of a learning task obviously can hinder performance on the task. Social interaction can also be affected and have social consequences. The child with ASD, for example, may pay attention to a toy held by another child but not to the accompanying verbalization (e.g., "Let's play with the truck" versus "Go away, this is my truck"), thus hindering their social functioning.

Intellectual Performance

Although there is a wide range of intelligence in ASD, including above average, intellectual impairment is common and includes severe and profound deficits. In past years, the prevalence of intellectual disability (ID) in individuals with ASD was often estimated at about 70%, but current estimates suggest 31% of individuals with ASD have co-occurring ID, 25% have borderline difficulties in intellectual functioning, and 44% have average to above-average intelligence (Baio et al., 2018). The lower estimates of ID may take into account the fact that autism symptoms affect measurement of intelligence. Additionally, lower estimates may also be due to increased diagnosis of the disorder in children who once would not have met diagnostic criteria, or it may reflect improved functioning due to early intervention (Klinger & Dudley, 2019).

A distinction based on intelligence has been made between individuals functioning at a higher or lower level, with an IQ of about 70 being the defining score. This distinction may be an important way in which persons with autism differ. Higher IQ is associated with less severe ASD symptoms, different educational needs, and greater chance of normal functioning in later life (Klinger et al., 2018). Additionally, the test profiles of persons with autism have generally indicated uneven cognitive development, with higher nonverbal than verbal IQ frequently identified. For example, individuals with ASD may show strengths on nonverbal visual–spatial tasks, such as those involving puzzles, patterns, or block design. These findings led to a belief that individuals with ASD show a specific cognitive profile (Klinger et al., 2018). However, group findings are not consistently identified when examining the cognitive profiles of individual children with ASD, and considerable variability in cognitive strengths and weaknesses has been identified. As a result, current research suggests there is not one cognitive profile of ASD, but rather it may be that the unpredictable, heterogeneous presentation of cognitive strengths and weaknesses across

individuals with ASD is characteristic of the disorder (Klinger et al., 2018; Mandy, Murin, & Skuse, 2015).

That ASD symptoms occur amid such wide variability in general intelligence is puzzling. To make matters more perplexing, a small minority of youth exhibit so-called **splinter skills**—abilities much higher than expected on the basis of their general intelligence—and **savant abilities**, which are skills that are strikingly better than those seen in normally developing youth. Savant abilities are not unique to autism, but they occur at high rates (J. E. A. Hughes et al., 2018). Spectacular feats are displayed—usually in memory, mathematical calculations, visuo-spatial abilities, drawing, and music (Happé, 2018). Although often associated with higher IQ levels, savant abilities have been reported in individuals with IQs as low as 55 and in children whose deficits preclude testing.

Adaptive Behavior

Autism is characterized by difficulties in dealing with the comings and goings of everyday life. Impairments in the social area of adaptive behavior, in particular, are considered by most to be a hallmark of ASD (Cronin & Freeman, 2017). Even at high-functioning levels, youth with ASD do less well on the Vineland Adaptive Behavior Scales (VABS) compared to typical developing peers matched on IQ, and less well than would be expected based on IQ scores (Mazefsky, Williams, & Minshew, 2008). Understanding the discrepancy between cognitive ability and performance in practical skills has been a focus of research.

Research suggests impairments in adaptive functioning tend to increase with age and, in general, the mismatch with intelligence is greater in high-functioning autism (Kanne et al., 2011). Family factors and co-occurring psychiatric conditions may also help explain the enormous variability shown in adaptive behavior; for example, in one study a history of family depression and shyness was related to VABS scores, especially in the social domain (Mazefsky et al., 2008). In addition, severity of autism symptoms, while not predictive of adaptive functioning on its own, may interact with age and cognitive skills to impact functioning (Cronin & Freeman, 2017). Executive functioning deficits may also play a role in adaptive behavior as well as other areas of adjustment (Pugliese et al., 2015; Wallace et al., 2016).

Cognitive Theories of ASD

Cognitive deficits have been theorized to underlie ASD, and three prominent cognitive theories in particular have been the focus of much of the research on autism. These theories have approached explaining autism from a single-deficit perspective. In other words, they each suggest a single cognitive limitation underlies the presentation of ASD. While these theories have had great influence on the field, they have been challenged to fully explain the two symptom dimensions (social communication and RRBs) of ASD. As a result, at present there exists no consensus on one cognitive theory that can fully explain the spectrum of symptoms associated with this complex disorder (Happé, Ronald, & Plomin, 2006; Pennington et al., 2019). Nevertheless, these theories have been highly influential in ASD research, and their strengths and limitations are described below.

Cognition: Theory of Mind One theory in particular has had long lasting influence on the field. **Theory of mind** (ToM) is the ability to infer mental states in others and in one's self. Having a theory of mind means that we understand that mental states exist—that humans have desires, intentions, beliefs, feelings, and so forth—and that these mental states are connected to action. ToM can be thought of as the ability to read others' minds, which guides our interaction with others. In typical development, by age 3 to 4 years children have first-order abilities, that is, some understanding of people's private mental states (Happé, 2015). A good example of this is pretend play. At about age 5 or 6, children acquire second-order abilities: They can think about another person's thinking about a third person's thoughts.

Aspects of ToM have been evaluated with various tasks. The Sally–Anne test is a classic test used to determine whether a child understands that another person can hold a false belief (Baron-Cohen, 1989). The child is told that after Sally placed a marble in a basket and left the room, Anne transferred the marble to another container and also exited. The child is asked where Sally will look for the marble when she returns. To demonstrate ToM, the child must understand that Sally falsely believes the marble is in the basket where she placed it. This first-order task can be modified to evaluate second-order ability. In this case, when Sally leaves the room, she peeks back and sees Anne transfer the marble. The child being tested is asked, "Where does Anne think Sally will look for the marble?" The child must "read" what Anne is thinking about Sally's thoughts. There is compelling evidence that the majority of children with autism fails first-order tests and that a greater number fails second-order tests (Baron-Cohen & Swettenham, 1997). Exactly what accounts for these failures is not completely understood, and the fact that not all children with ASD fail the test has challenged the theory (Rajendran & Mitchell, 2007). Language ability and executive functions do correlate with ToM (Miller, 2009), but false belief impairment in young toddlers has been demonstrated in a task not requiring verbal ability, as well (Senju et al., 2010).

Many measures of ToM have been developed. For example, the ToM Storybooks presents several tasks so as to gain a comprehensive understanding of ToM development in preschool children (Blijd-Hoogewys et al., 2008). It taps various aspects of ToM, such as emotions, desires, and beliefs. Figure 13.1 shows one of the tests, which evaluates the child's emotional understanding

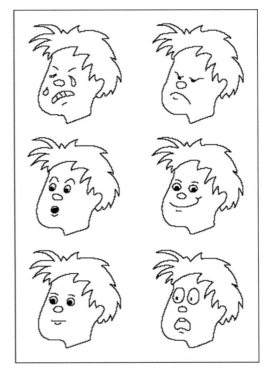

Figure 13.1 An example of an emotion recognition task from the Theory of Mind Storybooks. The child is told, "Sam has won shooting marbles. He has won the most beautiful marble." The child is asked to choose the appropriate face and provide the correct emotion label. Additional situations are depicted. (From Blijd-Hoogewys et al., 2008. Copyright 2008 by Springer; reprinted with permission)

and recognition. More challenging tasks have been developed for older children or children who are able to pass second-order tests. In the faux pas test, for example, the child is told stories in which character A commits a faux pas—that is, unintentionally says something that might negatively impact character B. The child being evaluated is asked to identify the faux pas. In order to succeed on this task, the child must understand that (1) the two characters in the stories have different knowledge and that (2) the statement of character A emotionally affects character B. On this test, children with autism or a related disorder who were able to pass second-order ToM tests did less well than typically developing children (Baron-Cohen et al., 1999). Related research utilizing different tests of ToM also support the notion that deficits in inferring other people's emotions and understanding their beliefs are present in individuals with ASD (Mazza et al., 2017).

Since ToM is considered critical in understanding the social world, it is hypothesized that such deficits—sometimes referred to as "mind blindness"—may underlie many of the social and communication deficits of autism. A limitation of ToM is that it does not address the defining symptoms of RRBs in ASD. Yet, overall the research evidence shows that ToM deficits in autism exist across different ages and can be present in higher functioning autism. Additionally, ToM deficits may alter the learning environment for children with ASD in ways that are still to be understood (Happé, 2015). More recent research suggests some individuals with ASD may be able to compensate for underlying difficulties in ToM, which

may help explain why some individuals with ASD are able to pass ToM tests (Livingston et al., 2019). Nevertheless, core cognitive deficits in ToM are still hypothesized to set individuals with ASD apart from their typically developing peers.

Cognition: Weak Central Coherence In normal cognition, individuals have a tendency to use context to weave together bits of information to make a whole, or get to the gist. This penchant, which is referred to as **central coherence**, is viewed as varying from strong to weak in the general population (Happé, Briskman, & Frith, 2001). On the basis of performance on specific visual–perceptual tasks, Happé and Frith (2006) proposed that individuals with autism are weak in central coherence (WCC); that is, they tend to focus on parts of stimuli rather than on integrating information into wholes. Simply put, they see the trees rather than the forest.

Performance on perceptual tasks illustrates deficits in central coherence. For example, children with autism generally perform better than controls on embedded figure tasks, which call for recognizing a stimulus figure that is embedded within a larger picture. In an important study, Shah and Frith (1993) investigated the quite striking superior performance that persons with autism showed on the block design task of the Wechsler intelligence test. They not only perform well compared with their achievement on other IQ tasks, but also outperform typically developing children and control children with ID. Ability to break the block design into segments helps on this task (Figure 13.2).

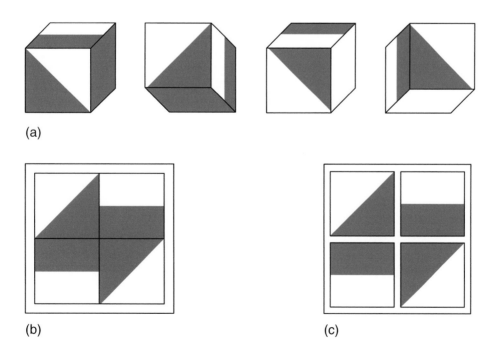

(a)

(b)   (c)

Figure 13.2 A block design task. Participants are asked to use four patterned blocks (a) to make a design (b). In some instances, they are first shown the design as segmented (c). Control groups benefit from observing (c); participants with autism perform as well with or without observing (c). This finding suggests that persons with autism have greater ability to "see" the parts of the design. (From Happé, Briskman, & Frith, 2001. Copyright 2000 by John Wiley & Sons; reprinted with permission)

Such findings suggest that youth with autism may have a bias to process information in a more analytic, less global and integrative way than do normal youth—which can lead to exceptional performance on some tasks and poor performance on others. One of the strengths cited for this theory is that it helps explain some of the social as well as nonsocial features of autism, such as sensory differences and the attention to acute detail seen in some RRBs (Happé & Frith, 2020; Rajendran & Mitchell, 2007). Further understanding of WCC has been sought, and the theory has changed over time. More recent research suggests the cognitive processes involved in ASD may be much more complex than once theorized, and individuals with a bias toward "seeing the trees" may exhibit slower global processing as opposed to reduced abilities (Booth & Happé, 2018) and may be able to shift their attention to process their environment more globally with effort (Stevenson et al., 2018). These findings suggest WCC may reflect a cognitive style as opposed to a dysfunction and may represent one part of the cognitive picture of ASD.

Cognition: Executive Function It has been proposed that executive dysfunction may underlie autism symptoms. Difficulties in initiating, sustaining, and shifting attention, planning, and impulse control are posited to contribute to the difficulties seen in ASD, such as the need for sameness, tendency to perseverate, and problems with cognitive flexibility and motor planning. Children, adolescents, and adults with autism perform more poorly than control groups on tests of executive functions (Corbett et al., 2009; McEvoy, Rogers, & Pennington, 1993; Ozonoff, 1997), but results are mixed and not all individuals with autism show executive functioning problems (Rajendran & Mitchell, 2007). Data have been accumulating that late preschool-age children with ASD do not differ in executive function from their typically developing peers. A study of toddlers (mean age 2.9 years), for example, showed almost no differences from the performance of age-matched typical children in executive functioning (Yerys et al., 2007). Additionally, executive dysfunction is not unique to ASD and is seen in other disorders, such as attention-deficit/hyperactivity disorder (ADHD). It thus seems that executive dysfunction is not a primary deficit but may develop secondarily in autism. Nevertheless, it may be a particularly important predictor of functional outcomes for individuals with ASD (Bertollo & Yerys, 2019).

Multiple-Deficit Framework The notion that a single deficit might explain the symptoms of autism was applied to several cognitive or perceptual deficits of autism, including impairments in ToM and WCC. However, no single impairment accounts for all ASD symptoms, all persons with autism do not display all deficits, nor are all deficits specific to autism. Although these impairments are still of importance, researchers are now turning to consider divergent ways of studying and understanding ASD and other neurodevelopmental disorders (McGrath, Peterson, & Pennington,

2020). Attention has been given to understanding the multiple possible factors involved in the affective social development that is so deviant in autism. To some extent, this interest harks back to a perspective that has persisted since Kanner's time—that is, to **intersubjectivity**, a special awareness that persons have of each other that motivates them, from the moment of birth, to communicate with the emotions and interests of others (Heasman & Gillespie, 2019). Additionally, more recent findings about the developmental trajectory of ASD—discussed in more detail later in this chapter—challenge the notion that there is a single developmental pathway in ASD (Ozonoff et al., 2010). Recent accounts describe a cascading development of ASD, in which early differences in sensory responsiveness and attention set in motion a series of effects that lead to the deficits involved in ASD symptomatology (Baranek et al., 2018; Klin, Shultz, & Jones, 2015). A multiple-deficit framework of ASD may help explain the variability in symptoms, onset, and severity of ASD, and longitudinal studies of high-risk infants and breakthroughs in genetic and neuropsychological understandings of ASD will likely help inform our understanding of the disorder (Pennington et al., 2019).

Physical and Other Features

Young children with autism are often described as physically attractive, but higher than normal physical abnormalities, including minor physical anomalies (MPAs), are associated with ASD (Ozgen et al., 2010, 2011) (Figure 13.3). Examples of MPAs are a prominent forehead, atypical head size, a high narrow palate, and low-set ears. MPAs are not medically or cosmetically of consequence, but they implicate genetic processes and disturbed prenatal development. The head/face, limbs, and brain develop from the same prenatal cell layers in early gestation, and MPAs in these bodily areas may point to abnormal neuron migration affecting brain development (Myers et al., 2017).

Some individuals with autism possess a certain gracefulness and bodily agility, but others exhibit impairments in motor development, including poor balance, uncoordinated gait, impaired fine and gross motor skills, and motor awkwardness from infancy into adulthood. Motor impairments may represent the earliest signs of abnormal development in ASD and may interfere with other aspects of development, such as social interaction and physical activity (Wilson, Enticott, & Rinehart, 2018). In addition, unusual eating preferences are observed, and rates of sleep problems, near 80% in some samples, are higher than for typical youth and youth with ID without autism (Valicenti-McDermott et al., 2019; Zickgraf & Mayes, 2019) and may be associated with more severe behavioral difficulties (Taylor & Siegel, 2019). Behaviorally, youth with ASD exhibit a variety of maladaptive behaviors, such as aggression, uncooperativeness, withdrawal, and self-injurious behaviors (Oliver & Richards, 2010).

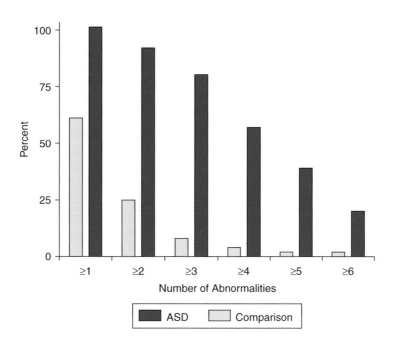

Figure 13.3 Percent of children with ASD and a matched group of typically developing children with minor physical abnormalities. Children with ASD did not have ID nor any known syndrome. (From Ozgen et al., 2011. Copyright 2011 by Springer; reprinted with permission)

Co-occurring Disorders

We have already seen that the coexistence of ID with ASD creates a varied clinical presentation of autism. Co-occurring emotional and behavioral problems engender even greater heterogeneity. Additionally, since the DSM-5 no longer excludes most additional diagnoses as it once did, the issue of co-occurring disorder in ASD is being given increased attention (Deprey & Ozonoff, 2018). Determining comorbidity can be especially challenging because language and cognitive problems hinder communication. In addition, some primary features of ASD and psychiatric disorders may be difficult to distinguish (Pennington et al., 2019). For example, the abnormal social interactions observed in youth with ASD may be difficult to differentiate from social phobia, and the repetitive behaviors of ASD may be hard to tell from obsessive-compulsive disorder. Due in part to such hindrances, as well as to differences in samples and methodology, the extent of co-occurrence is unclear—although it is thought to be high. In a population-based study, 71% of children with ASD met criteria for at least one co-occurring psychiatric disorder, 41% met criteria for two or more, and 24% had three or more diagnoses (Simonoff et al., 2008). In a community/clinic study of 9- to 16-year-olds, 74% comorbidity was found, and many youth had multiple co-occurring disorders (Mattila et al., 2010). Among the symptoms and disorders that co-occur with ASD are anxiety, depression, ADHD, and oppositional defiant behaviors.

As an example, we look briefly at comorbidity with anxiety, which includes specific phobias, social anxiety, and generalized anxiety among other anxiety disorders. Prevalence of anxiety disorders in children with ASD is estimated to be well above that in the general population, with estimates ranging from 49% to 79% (Deprey & Ozonoff, 2018; Kent & Simonoff, 2017). An array of unknown factors might underlie the association of ASD and anxiety. Excessive sensitivity to stimuli is found in about half of the children with ASD, raising the possibility that oversensitivity might lead to some forms of anxiety, such as fear of loud noises (Green & Ben-Sasson, 2010). Older children and adolescents with ASD appear to experience greater levels of anxiety, as do those functioning at higher cognitive levels. This suggests that perhaps children and adolescents at higher functioning levels may have greater awareness of their struggles with social deficits, which may generate anxiety and lead to worsening social interactions and social isolation and, in turn, increased anxiety. Thus, bidirectional effects may operate for ASD and anxiety.

Level of intellectual functioning may be related to the co-occurrence of other symptoms as well (Totsika et al., 2011). For example, lower functioning may be especially associated with irritability and hyperactivity, whereas higher functioning may be especially related to depression. More generally, although many youth with ASD have intellectual impairments, the effects of ID are often not separated from those of ASD. To address this issue, Totsika and colleagues (2011) drew on research that surveyed emotional and behavioral problems in representative samples of youth with ASD, age 5 to 16 years. They compared four groups: ASD only, ASD with ID, ID only, and a group with neither condition. Although both ASD and ID were associated with problems, difficulties were more likely with ASD, with or without

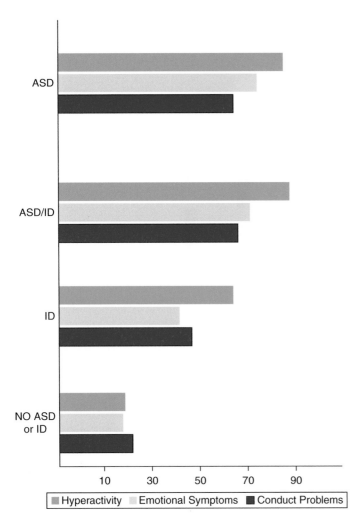

Figure 13.4 Percent of behavioral and emotional problems by child group. (Data from Totsika et al., 2011)

ID (Figure 13.4). In conjunction with other research, these results point to the need to address comorbidity, which impairs functioning in youth with ASD.

Epidemiology

Many epidemiological studies of ASD have been conducted over the years. The most recent report by the Centers for Disease Control and Prevention (CDC) estimates that the prevalence of ASD in the United States has risen in recent decades, from 1 in 150 8-year-olds in 2002 to 1 in 59 8-year-olds in 2014 (Baio et al., 2018). The CDC estimates represent a 154% increase in prevalence, a striking epidemiological finding (Klinger & Dudley, 2019). As might be expected, there is considerable concern about this phenomenon and debate about whether it represents a true increase in the number of children with ASD. (See Accent: "An Epidemic of Autism? Or an Illusion?")

One aspect of autism that has remained constant over time is sex difference. Boys display autism more often than girls, with boys four times more likely than girls to be diagnosed with ASD (Baio et al., 2018). Girls also tend to be older when they are first diagnosed (Bargiela, Steward, & Mandy, 2016), and they may be at risk for underdiagnosis—girls are less likely than boys to receive an autism diagnosis even when their symptoms are comparable to boys their age (Carpenter, Happé, & Egerton, 2019; Dworzynski et al., 2012). ID and severe symptoms are more likely in girls, so that the gender ratio is perhaps 2:1 in lower functioning ASD. It is worth noting that boys are at greater risk for several genetic disorders associated with autism, which could, at least in part, explain differences in gender prevalence. Several other hypotheses have been proposed, including a possible "female protective effect" in which girls may require a greater genetic load to display ASD behaviors than boys (Happé & Frith, 2020), or that the presentation of ASD symptoms in girls may look different (e.g., fewer RRBs, fewer externalizing behaviors, more internalizing problems) than it does in boys and may not fit current diagnostic criteria (Bargiela et al., 2016).

Epidemiological research has largely failed to support the once-held belief that autism and social class are related. Reports of high prevalence in the upper social classes probably result from nonrepresentative samples (Fombonne, 2003). There is evidence, however, of racial and ethnic disparities. In particular, ASD is diagnosed more in white children in the United States and may be underdiagnosed in black/African American and Hispanic children (Durkin et al., 2017).

Developmental Course

Understanding the onset and early development of ASD is provided by retrospective parental reports and videotapes of infants taken prior to diagnosis, and, as described previously, important advances in understanding have come from the prospective study of at-risk siblings of children with ASD, as well as emerging imaging research. Although most parents of children with autism become concerned about symptoms by the time their infants are 2 years of age, diagnosis usually occurs a few years later, with parents, teachers or other important caregivers noting language delays and social abnormalities as signs of autism (Haroon, 2019a).

Three patterns of onset have traditionally been described (Pennington et al., 2019). The first pattern has historically been thought to occur in most children and indicates that abnormalities become obvious in the first year of life or soon afterward. The second pattern involves regression, in which typical or near typical development is followed by arrested skill acquisition and loss of previously acquired language, social, and/or motor skills. The third pattern, known as "developmental plateau," is manifest by mild delays until about age 2 and then a gradual or abrupt developmental arrest and plateau.

ACCENT An Epidemic of Autism? Or an Illusion?

What accounts for the escalating rates of autism or ASD? Is there a true increase or are other factors at work? Many investigators emphasize changes in the conceptualization, understanding, and management of the disorders (Happé & Frith, 2020; Bennett et al., 2018). Consider the following:

- The criteria for ASD have broadened over several years. It appears that children at both higher and lower levels of functioning are more likely to be diagnosed.
- Children are being diagnosed at younger ages. In part, this is attributable to better understanding of neurodevelopmental disorders and the availability of early screening and diagnostic tests.
- Increased awareness has resulted in more cases being identified. Parents are more familiar with the symptoms of the disorders, physicians are receiving better training about developmental disorders, and media focus on autism has increased public awareness.
- Diagnosis of ASD has been encouraged by expansion of services. Medical clinics for developmental disorders

have increased, and diagnosis rose in the United States after changes occurred in insurance benefits and in the Individuals with Disabilities Education Act (IDEA).

- There is evidence of "diagnostic switching," in which youth who were once likely to be diagnosed as having ID, a learning disability, or other psychiatric diagnosis began to receive the diagnosis of ASD. Diagnostic switching appears related to changes in the availability of services.

The extent to which these factors influence the incidence of autism and related disorders is unclear. The possibility of a true increase in ASD is not entirely ruled out—a true increase in incidence would pose critical questions about etiology, especially whether changing environmental variables are putting children at increased risk. However, given the multiple influences that have likely contributed to the increase in incidence and prevalence of ASD, current theories and research suggest an "autism epidemic" is likely an illusion.

Regression may be far more common in ASD than was once thought (Pennington et al., 2019). While previous studies suggested the regression pattern of onset occurred in approximately 20% of children with ASD (Fombonne, 2001), more recent longitudinal studies suggests a much higher rate—in fact, one study identified that 86% of infants who went on to develop ASD by age 3 years experienced an unexpected decline in social-communication skills (Ozonoff et al., 2010). Retrospective studies, relying on parent report of their observations, may have underestimated the subtle and gradual regression in skills in this developmental pattern, while prospective studies of high-risk infants provide a more robust design for detecting regressive patterns, such as declines in the child's use of meaningful words, orienting to their names, or spontaneously imitating others, among other behaviors. There is evidence that regressed children, despite relatively good early development, show more severe autism symptoms and poorer outcome than children with other types of onset (Kalb et al., 2010).

Imaging research has also expanded our understanding of onset. Recent prospective neuroimaging research suggests that while behavioral symptoms may not emerge until later in childhood, ASD is present from early in development (Klinger & Dudley, 2019). A recent study, for example, identified that expansion of the cortical surface area of the brain was present between 6 and 12 months of age and predicted brain volume growth and the emergence of social-communication

impairments consistent with autism by age 2 years (Hazlett et al., 2017). Taken together, there appears to be heterogeneity in when behavioral symptoms emerge, and prospective studies, including neuroimaging research, will likely help inform our understanding of the developmental unfolding leading to the onset of ASD.

Research has also pointed to heterogeneous developmental pathways following diagnosis. Six common trajectories, from diagnosis to age 14, were described in a study of a large community population (Fountain, Winter, & Bearman, 2012). Regarding social and communication behaviors, most children improved over time. But some trajectories showed slower change and little improvement. Children whose symptoms were least severe at diagnosis tended to improve more rapidly. Interestingly, though, one group—identified as "bloomers"—began as low functioning and improved so rapidly that at adolescence it resembled a group whose functioning had been consistently high. In general, children of white, well-educated mothers showed higher functioning at outcome, perhaps due to access to resources and intervention.

Other investigations indicate that from childhood onward, modest improvement occurs in social, communication, and self-help skills (Piven et al., 1996; Sigman, 1998; Taylor & Seltzer, 2010). These findings were demonstrated in longitudinal research examining change from early childhood into adulthood (Shattuck et al., 2007). Many individuals showed decreases in the core symptoms of ASD and in associated maladaptive behaviors as well. Still, considerable variation occurred across individuals. Overall, individuals with ID improved less and lower family income also was related to less improvement, suggesting less availability of quality services. Interestingly, yet another study showed that improvement slowed after adolescents and young adults exited the secondary school system, especially for those without ID (Taylor & Seltzer, 2010). This was perhaps due to the lack of stimulating occupational and educational activities available for higher functioning individuals with ASD.

Despite modest improvement over time, symptoms generally persist into adulthood for most persons with ASD. Perhaps 20% achieve independence, with successful work placement and some social life (Haroon, 2019c). Research consistently shows that long-term outcome is relatively poor (Steinhausen, Mohr Jensen, & Lauritsen, 2016), particularly when early general intelligence and communicative language are impaired (Howlin et al., 2004; Shattuck et al., 2007; Volkmar & Klin, 2000). Individuals with childhood IQs 70 or above seem to do notably better, suggesting that this IQ level is a good predictor of adult independent living (Seltzer et al., 2003). For these individuals, although some difficulties may persist, life may include typical achievements and rewards. Temple Grandin, who has written extensively about her experiences as a person diagnosed with autism and whose personal and career achievements were depicted in an award-winning television film, wrote of the motivations and balances in her life in this way:

> Many people with autism become disillusioned and upset because they do not fit in socially and they do not have a girlfriend or boyfriend. I have just accepted that such a relationship will not be part of my life. ... I want to be appreciated for the work I do. I am happiest when I am doing something for fun, like designing an engineering project, or making something that makes a contribution to society.
> *Grandin, 1997, p. 1039*

On an optimistic note, as we see later in the chapter, progress in early intervention could be lessening the impact of ASD, particularly for higher functioning youth.

Neurobiological Abnormalities

Similar to the discussion in the previous sections, no one neurobiological anomaly has been identified in ASD (Pennington et al., 2019). Technological and methodological advances in research hold promise in advancing our understanding of the structural and functional brain abnormalities, and various brain structures and regions have been examined with postmortem examination, brain imaging, and other types of research. Nevertheless, there remain great diversity in findings

and difficulties with replication of results (Pua, Bowden, & Seal, 2017).

Despite these variations, a consistent finding in neurobiological research is altered brain growth. Overall, approximately 16% of individuals with ASD show significantly larger head size (i.e., macrocephaly) and approximately 9% show brain overgrowth (Sacco, Gabriele, & Persico, 2015). At birth, brain size is small to normal, but an atypical growth spurt occurs soon afterward— perhaps as early as 6 months—and soon levels off (Faja & Dawson, 2017). As noted earlier, cortical surface area overgrowth has been identified in infants at high risk of ASD and is predictive of diagnosis at age 2 years (Hazlett et al., 2017). Numerous other investigations of youth and adults with ASD indicate brain volume anomalies. Excessive volume of gray and white tissue has been found in the cerebrum and excessive white matter in the temporal lobe and cerebellum.

Research has also looked to identify region-specific differences in the brain structure of individuals with ASD, with particular focus on the limbic system and frontal-striatal circuitry, which have been associated with the social-communication deficits and RRBs characteristic of ASD (Ecker, 2017). Microscopic studies of the temporal lobe–limbic system, frontal lobes, and cerebellum indicate abnormalities in cell structure and organization (Filipek, 1999; Tanguay, 2000; van Engeland & Buitelaar, 2008). These include decreased number and size of cells, high cell density, less dendritic branching, and abnormal cell migration. Some of the microscopic cell studies suggest that brain anomalies may develop prenatally.

With regard to brain functioning, reduced activity has been shown in several regions, most notably the frontal lobes and limbic system, particularly the amygdala (Newsom & Hovanitz, 2006). Studies of brain function during visual or auditory tasks suggest both underactivation and overactivation of particular areas of the brain important for facial processing, namely the fusiform gyrus (Dichter, 2012). For example, a meta-analysis showed consistent findings of slowed electrical activity of the brain during face processing, as well as aberrant structural findings and connectivity responses (Nickl-Jockschat et al., 2015). Functional differences have also been identified in the front regions (e.g., prefrontal cortex) and frontal-striatal regions important in executive functioning tasks (Pennington et al., 2019).

Increased attention is being given to atypical brain connectivity patterns in ASD (Mohammad-Rezazadeh et al., 2016). Compromises in many white matter tracts that connect different regions of the brain to each other and connect the hemispheres have been identified (Pardo & Eberhart, 2007; Shukla, Keehn, & Müller, 2011), and inefficiencies have been identified in areas important for auditory and language processing (Pruett, Botteron, & McKinstry, 2017). While there are variations in results across studies, emerging research suggests a complex pattern of both underconnectivity and overconnectivity of functional brain networks and vulnerability of particular areas of structural connectivity.

Although interest exists in the biochemical systems, consistent findings are lacking. The most dependable, although not understood, biochemical finding is high levels of serotonin in blood platelets in 23% to 28% of cases (Gabriele, Sacco, & Persico, 2014). Very early in development, serotonin plays a role in the development of neurons, and brain serotonin and its synthesis are implicated in the expression of autism symptoms (Daly, Tricklebank, & Wichers, 2019). Among other neurotransmitters examined are dopamine, glutamate (important in excitation), and GABA (important in inhibition). In general, there are conflicting findings about their roles. Several additional biochemicals have been examined. Findings related to oxytocin and vasopressin, which are implicated in social behavior, have not provided a clear picture, whereas studies of secretin and melatonin give no support to their involvement. At times, the importance of some of these substances has received media attention that appeared to go beyond research results (Azar, 2011).

Understanding of the neurobiology of autism is progressing, although a definitive portrait has not yet emerged. Important in this work are efforts to connect brain structure and functioning to the clinical picture of ASD. For example, enlargement of the amygdala in toddlers has been associated with more severe course of development during the preschool period (Faja & Dawson, 2017), and, as just noted, abnormal brain activity may occur during tasks such as face processing. Research findings and the mix of symptoms of the disorder point to abnormalities of multiple brain regions and networks. Overall, ASD may result from early brain overgrowth and neuron anomalies leading to a cascade of biological aberrations, including atypical or decreased connections between brain regions (Pruett et al., 2017).

Etiology

Among early etiological proposals, a dominant idea was that parenting played a critical role in autism. Kanner described the typical parents of a child with autism as highly intelligent, professionally accomplished people who were preoccupied with scientific, literary, and artistic concerns, and who treated their offspring in a coldly mechanical way (Kanner, 1943; Kanner & Eisenberg, 1956). Inadequate "refrigerator" parenting became implicated in causing autism, even though Kanner hypothesized an innate social deficit. Bettelheim's (1967a, 1967b) psychoanalytic theory was an especially influential psychosocial explanation (Mesibov & Van Bourgondien, 1992). Accordingly, autism was thought to be caused by parental rejection or pathology that resulted in the young child's retreating into an autistic "empty fortress." Due to lack of evidence, this approach eventually went by the wayside, and the explanation currently is viewed as regrettable. Today's parents play important roles in advocacy and treatment for their children. Current interest in etiology emphasizes the continuum of presentation of ASD and the multiple and transactional nature of variables that might account for neurobiological abnormalities and emergence and severity of symptoms characteristic of ASD.

Genetic Influence

Twin and Family Studies Pioneering twin studies of autism documented higher concordance in monozygotic twins than in dizygotic twins (Bailey et al., 1995; Steffenburg et al., 1989). Although studies have been variable in the degree to which genetic versus shared environmental factors effect predisposition to ASD, recent twin studies continue to demonstrate a strong genetic etiology of ASD. For example, meta-analytic heritability estimates range between 64% to 91%, with shared environmental effects ranging between 7% and 35% (Tick et al., 2016).

Family studies of autism also point to genetic influence. The rate of autism in siblings of children with autism is generally reported in the range of 10% to 15% but may be underestimated due to a tendency for families to choose not to have additional children after receiving a diagnosis of ASD for one child (a phenomenon known as reproductive stoppage), and recurrence risk may be closer to 19% (Ozonoff et al., 2011; Pennington et al., 2019; Wood et al., 2015). Other interesting findings have also emerged. A higher than expected rate of autism-like developmental disorders is found in families, and first-degree relatives of individuals with ASD are more likely to exhibit impairments in social, communicative, and repetitive behaviors and cognitive processes that are similar to autism but not severe enough for diagnosis (Billeci et al., 2016; Lee et al., 2020). Family members also show characteristics that, although not diagnosable symptoms of ASD, are observed in those with autism, such as macrocephaly, elevated serotonin, and neuroanatomical abnormalities (Mosconi et al., 2010). Additionally, siblings of youth with ASD can show very early differences, for example, atypical pre-speech vocalizations in their first year of life (Paul et al., 2010). Some siblings with early manifestations (e.g., low rates of joint attention) go on to be diagnosed with ASD (Rozga et al., 2011). Moreover, recent cross-disorder genetic methods suggest family members of children with ASD may be more likely to be diagnosed with other psychiatric disorders, such as ADHD and schizophrenia (Demontis et al., 2019).

The combined research supports the view that genetic predisposition leads to autism, autism-like disorders, or other and sometimes milder related problems. Because what is transmitted in families is broader than the specific symptoms of the diagnostic category of ASD, autism might be best conceptualized as occurring along a continuum of severity (Woodbury-Smith & Scherer, 2018). Support for a dimensional approach to classification also comes from studies indicating that autism traits—such as social reciprocity and language skills—are continuously distributed in the general population (Robinson et al., 2016a).

Chromosomes and Genes What do we know more specifically about genetic influence? The picture is complex and, again, suggests heterogeneity in etiology. Genetic studies have implicated hundreds of different types of genetic variations in ASD (Vorstman et al., 2017). As of January 2020, there were more than 1,100 genes included in the Autism Database (AutDB), a resource for tracking genetic findings in autism research (Basu, Kollu, & Banerjee-Basu, 2020). These include both common and rare variants in the population, those that are inherited or *de novo* (i.e., detected for the first time in the individual with ASD and are not present in the parental genome), and those that range in size from a single mutation to duplication or deletion of millions of base pairs (Pennington et al., 2019). It is estimated that rare genetic variations that are either inherited or *de novo* are causal in approximately 10% to 30% of cases, with intellectual disability often present in these (Ivanov et al., 2015; Vorstman et al., 2017). Two genetic conditions notably associated with autism are fragile X syndrome (p. 314) and tuberose sclerosis, the latter caused by inherited or new gene mutations resulting in tumors of the brain and other organs. Approximately 15% to 50% of cases are thought to result from common polygenic variation, or from the combined effect of multiple genes (Vorstman et al., 2017).

While a full review of the genetic findings in ASD is beyond the scope of this book, several notable findings are described here in brief. For instance, in an estimated 1 to 3% of cases of autism, a duplication of genes in a particular region of chromosome 15 has been observed; of note, this chromosomal region also houses many genes with essential function in the brain, such as GABRA5 and GABRB3 (genes for GABA receptors) among others (Wiśniowiecka-Kowalnik & Nowakowska, 2019). This chromosomal region is also linked to other developmental disorders, suggesting common etiological factors.

In addition, genome-wide association studies have revealed copy number variations (CNV; i.e., large segments of DNA that are duplicated or deleted) associated with ASD. An interesting CNV finding is related to 7q11.23. Chromosome 7q11.23 deletion has long been implicated in Williams syndrome (p. 315), which is associated with relatively intact language skills in relation to other cognitive weaknesses and excessive social disinhibition, while a duplication of this same 7q11.23 region has more recently been associated with autism and other disorders involving impairment in language (Klein-Tasman & Mervis, 2018). This pattern in which deletion is associated with hypersocial behavior and duplication is associated with ASD symptomatology suggests a dosage-sensitive impact on the genome, but much is still to be understood about how this mutation functions (Pennington et al., 2019).

Progress has also made in identifying several susceptibility genes and their implications for brain functioning. For example,

the FOXP1, GRIN2B, SCN2A, KATNAL2, and CHD8 genes among others play important roles in early brain development and have been associated with ASD (Wiśniowiecka-Kowalnik & Nowakowska, 2019). In addition, each gene mutation has been associated with various clinical features of ASD. For example, animal studies of disruptions in CHD8, which is involved in embryonic central nervous systems development, indicate an association with macrocephaly consistent with findings in ASD (Bernier et al., 2014).

Some investigators favor the idea that many interacting genes best explain most cases of ASD. This possibility is suggested by the continuum of disorder, the varied clinical picture, and research findings. The fact that concordance in less than 100% in MZ twins with autism also suggests that gene–environment interactions and epigenetic processes may play some role in the development of autism, and there is evidence for both (Kubota, 2017).

Prenatal and Pregnancy Risk
Most environmental risk factors associated with ASD impact the very early—pre- or perinatal—stages of development. Numerous pregnancy and birth variables have been inconsistently associated with autism and related disorders. A comprehensive review of environmental influences on ASD suggests several key environmental risk factors for autism: advanced paternal and maternal age, maternal medication use, maternal exposure to toxic chemicals, maternal obesity/gestational diabetes, maternal metabolic factors, and maternal immune reactions during pregnancy (e.g., maternal infection/fever) (Mandy & Lai, 2016). Complications during childbirth, such as fetal distress, birth injury or trauma, multiple birth, low birthweight, maternal hemorrhage, and other complications, have also been associated with ASD, but it seems these factors are unlikely to be causal and instead may be associated with atypical fetal development and risk for ASD (Gardener, Spiegelman, & Buka, 2011).

Medical Conditions
In addition to the already-mentioned genetic syndromes, numerous medical conditions are associated with autism—cerebral palsy, infections such as meningitis, hearing impairment, and seizure disorders. About 6% of those with ASD have epilepsy with a range of prevalence from approximately 4% to 47% depending on the type of seizure disorder (Strasser et al., 2018). Gastrointestinal symptoms, such as abdominal pain, bloating, diarrhea, nausea and food allergy/intolerance are also common, occurring in an estimated 50% of children with ASD overall (Bresnahan et al., 2015; McElhanon et al., 2014). Children with ASD also frequently exhibit sleep disturbance, particularly insomnia, with rates estimated between 40% and 80%, depending on the type of sleep problem (Devnani & Hegde, 2015). Moreover, sleep disturbance in ASD is related to increases in both the core symptoms of the disorder, such as social impairment and RRBs, as well as other

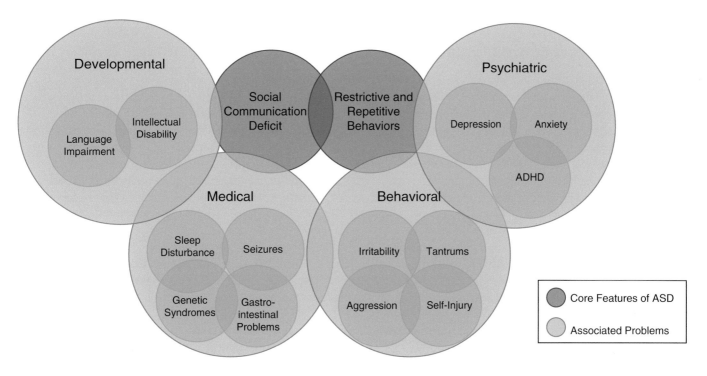

Figure 13.5 Overlap of co-occurring diagnoses and problems in ASD. (Adapted from Klinger & Dudley, 2019)

co-occurring problems, including cognitive functioning, irritability, and hyperactivity (Sannar et al., 2018; Veatch et al., 2017). Figure 13.5 provides a model of the ways in which the core clinical features of ASD overlap with medical conditions and other broad categories of co-occurring difficulties, including development, behavioral, and psychiatric diagnoses—discussed earlier in this chapter. Also related to medical conditions is the controversial issue of association between ASD and vaccines given to prevent other diseases otherwise unassociated with ASD. The issue has been scientifically discredited, yet continues to be widely debated despite strong scientific evidence that there is no association between vaccines and ASD (See Accent "Do Vaccines Cause Autism? The Scientific Consensus Is No.").

Environment and Social Interaction
The search for etiology has focused to a great extent on possible causes of early brain abnormalities to the relative neglect of possible later-occurring environmental and psychosocial influences. Noting that ASD is now recognized as involving a spectrum of presentations with etiologies involving different combinations of genetic and environmental risk, Faja and Dawson (2017) suggest the disorder may be best understood using a developmental model for autism that considers a more comprehensive perspective. Figure 13.6 presents a three-component formulation, including vulnerabilities, altered patterns of development, and outcomes. The model proposes that genetic and/or early environmental susceptibility factors lead to brain

abnormalities that influence interactions between the child and his or her environment. In turn, these altered interactions are hypothesized to disrupt input critical for further brain development, leading to additional brain anomalies and autism with varying symptom expression. Individual pathways of altered social interactions are proposed to mediate the connection between early risk factors and later outcome. These developmental pathways, which involve the context of the child's environment, can vary and change to a limited extent, but the longer the child travels a maladaptive pathway, the less probable is normal development. The Faja and Dawson model contributes to our thinking about ASD by focusing on child–environment interactions and the advisability of early intervention, topics to which we return later in the chapter.

Assessment of ASD

Because ASD encompasses many areas of functioning and implicates neurobiological deficits, it requires broad-based assessment that addresses a wide range of behaviors and areas of functioning, including social and emotional functioning, communication, cognitive ability, and adaptive behavior (Wilkerson, 2018). The clinician must include information from a variety of sources and involve the parents or caregivers in order to obtain a unique picture of the child's functioning and also to lay the groundwork for possible treatment. It is also important to take a history of prenatal, birth, developmental, familial, and medical

ACCENT Do Vaccines Cause Autism? The Scientific Consensus Is No

The question of whether vaccines cause ASD arose when parents in England associated their children's onset of neurodevelopmental disorders with the measles, mumps, and rubella vaccine (MMR) the children had received to prevent these diseases. The parents had sought advice from gastrointestinal experts after the children had developed intestinal problems. From this consultation with a very small, nonrepresentative sample of children, Wakefield and colleagues (1998) hypothesized that, through a complex route involving immune responses, the measles virus in the vaccine was responsible for both the intestinal illness and developmental disorder. However, numerous investigations in different countries have failed to find a connection between MMR and autism (Madsen et al., 2002; Taylor, Swerdfeger, & Eslick, 2014), and flaws in Wakefield's study were identified (Davidson, 2017). The original article by Wakefield and his colleagues was retracted by the journal in which it had been published and Wakefield, who lost his British professional credentials, became a controversial figure, as depicted in the *New York Times Magazine* (Dominus, 2011). Nevertheless, the paper contributed to widespread anxiety about the potential harmful effects of the MMR vaccine (Hotez, 2019; Mandy & Lai, 2016). Research continues to be conducted, providing remarkably sound and consistent evidence that there is no association between autism and the MMR vaccine. A recent nationwide cohort study in Denmark following 657,461 children, for example, provides strong evidence that the MMR vaccination does not increase risk for autism, even in susceptible children (Hviid et al., 2019).

Concern also has been expressed that vaccines with thimerosal, a mercury-containing preservative, put children at risk for neurodevelopmental disorders. The potential negative effects of mercury are well known, and among the arguments are that (1) some children may be especially susceptible, and (2) the amount of thimerosal received by children has increased due to an increase in recommended vaccinations. As with the MMR studies, the weight of the evidence does not support a relationship between ASD and thimerosal-containing vaccines (Costello, Foley, & Angold, 2006; Newsom & Hovanitz, 2006). In any event, mercury in vaccines has been eliminated or reduced in many countries (Kirby, 2005).

Despite the numerous large-scale epidemiological studies and reviews by major government and professional groups in the United States and abroad that do not support the role of vaccines as causative of ASD, the debate over vaccines and autism continues to be contentious even more than two decades after the original article by Wakefield and colleagues. Research suggests parents' beliefs in misinformation about vaccines persists despite efforts to counter it (Pluviano et al., 2019), and sentiments appear to have amplified on the internet and other media and political outlets (Hotez, 2019). Parents tell of the plight of their damaged children in court, advocacy groups call for more research, and some parents refuse vaccines that protect children from hazardous diseases. The antivaccine movement, as it has been termed, is thought to have contributed to declines in vaccination and increased incidence of measles outbreaks, causing considerable concern for public health.

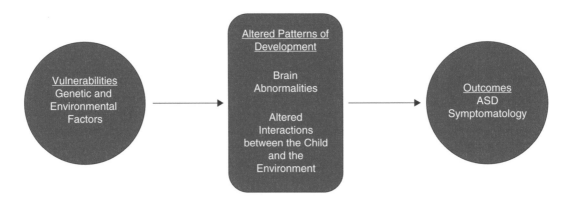

Figure 13.6 A developmental model of autism. (Adapted from Faja & Dawson, 2017)

factors, as well as of any past intervention. Medical examination and testing may be valuable in helping to identify ASD, investigate its causes, and treat associated conditions such as seizures.

Psychological and behavioral evaluations typically include interviews, direct observation of the child, and psychological tests. Tests of intelligence, adaptive behavior, and language are among the useful instruments, depending on the individual case. Several tools are based on observation of the child and/or reports of past or present behavior. The following briefly described instruments serve somewhat different purposes or employ somewhat different approaches and are examples of empirically validated instruments that may be selected and used as part of a comprehensive evaluation for ASD.

Evaluating ASD

As discussed earlier in the chapter, parents of children later diagnosed with ASD usually first notice concerns about their child's development before age 2, yet the median age of diagnosis of ASD in the United States is approximately 4 to 5 years old (Christensen et al., 2016). Given the importance of early intervention in ASD, early identification is crucial. The goal of early screening is to identify very young children who may or may not be showing obvious manifestations of disorder. Pediatricians are among the professionals who come into contact with very young children, and The Academy of Pediatrics has published guidelines for universal screening of children for ASD at 18 and 24 months, in addition to broad developmental screening at 9, 18, and 24 months (American Academy of Pediatrics, 2010; Johnson & Myers, 2007). Since some children may not show signs of ASD until later (e.g., 36 months), repeated screening has also been recommended (Ozonoff et al., 2015). Discussion with parents, direct observation of the child, and the use of screening tools are suggested. An example of an early screening instrument is the M-CHAT, the Modified Checklist for Autism in Toddlers, which was revised (M-CHAT-R/F) to add a follow-up component to assess children who obtain high scores on the initial screening (Robins et al., 2014). A brief set of questions is asked of parents or caregivers about the child's behavior, such as whether the child takes an interest in other children, seems oversensitive to noise, or responds to his/her name being called. It is recommended that a child suspected of developmental delay or risk immediately be referred for more extensive evaluation or for attendance in an early intervention program. A "wait and see" posture is to be avoided.

The Childhood Autism Rating Scale, 2nd Edition (CARS-2) is widely employed for screening children and older persons (Schopler et al., 2010). Two forms are available: (1) the standard form for children under age 6 or individuals with communication problems or below-average estimated IQ; and (2) a newer form for verbally fluent persons 6 years or older with IQ above 80. There is also a questionnaire to gather information from parents

or caregivers. Both assessment forms consist of 15 items rated by a professional after observation of the individual. The items cover many areas of functioning, including emotional response, imitation, social relations, communication, and perception. The CARS-2 distinguishes autism from other severe cognitive deficits and also indicates the severity of autism.

The Autism Diagnostic Interview–Revised (ADI-R) is a widely used 93-item semi-structured interview conducted with parents and caregivers (Rutter, LeCouteur, & Lord, 2006). It provides comprehensive assessment of individuals suspected of autism or ASD. It assesses communication, social interaction, and restricted, repetitive behavior and interests in youth and adults with a mental age above 2 years. The ADI-R is useful for diagnosis and treatment/educational planning, and it discriminates autism from other developmental disorders. It is considered a gold standard for assessment for ASD.

The Autism Diagnostic Observation Schedule, 2nd Edition (ADOS-2), also a gold standard instrument, was developed out of the need to assess children in direct interaction with a clinician (Lord et al., 2012). It consists of several modules of standardized activities that create the opportunity for the person to display behaviors relevant to ASD, for example, while engaging in standardized play activity or a construction task. One of the modules is selected as relevant to the age and language abilities of the person being evaluated. Modules are available to assess toddlers 12 months through adulthood. During the session, observations are recorded and later coded for a diagnosis. In addition, severity of symptoms can be compared to severity shown in a large sample of persons of similar age and expressive language.

Prevention of ASD

As with other early-onset developmental disorders with an apparent genetic and neurobiological etiology, universal prevention includes prenatal care and improvement in environmental quality. However, early identification and intervention are at the heart of prevention, an approach that merges with treatment.

Common settings for early intervention programs for young children are the home, public schools, preschool settings in universities, and classrooms originating from private educational organizations (Charman, 2011; Newsom & Hovanitz, 2006). Behavioral approaches are frequently employed. The curriculum often focuses on social skills such as joint attention and social engagement with others, imitation, and language. Research indicates that these programs can improve language acquisition, social communication, behavior regulation, and cognitive development, as well as decrease ASD symptoms in some children (Landa, 2018). However, many questions remain, including why only some children profit from the programs.

Outcome research on early programs—which vary in duration and intensity—has improved, and efforts continue to better establish efficacy as well as the programs themselves. One empirically validated early intervention program is the Early Start Denver Model for toddler and preschool-age children (see Accent: "The Early Start Denver Model (ESDM)").

Intervention for ASD

The mainstay approaches to treatment for ASD are behavioral, psychosocial, and educational, are often intensive and initiated early in development. Pharmacological intervention, discussed briefly below, has an ancillary role.

ACCENT The Early Start Denver Model (ESDM)

The ESDM is based on a broad, naturalistic developmental approach combined with the principles of applied behavior analysis (Devlantis, Dawson, & Rogers, 2017). The early intervention is designed for use with children ages 12 to 60 months who are diagnosed with ASD or at risk for the disorder and engages the child in positive interactions with another person to create naturalistic opportunities for learning and developing social and communication skills. Treatment goals are individualized and based on developmental domains (e.g., receptive and expressive language, imitation, joint attention) that are broken down into teaching steps. The child is taught the skills until mastery and generalization of the skill. Notably, ESDM is designed to be flexible—it can be delivered in a variety of settings (e.g., preschool/day care, at home, in the clinic, and in the community), by a trained therapist or parents—and to take place in naturalistic interactions, such as daily caretaking or play activities.

Numerous studies have evaluated the efficacy of ESDM. Overall, the intervention has been shown to have positive effects on children's social communication, language, cognition, adaptive behavior, and ASD symptoms, as well as benefits to parents, including enhanced interaction skills with their children, lower levels of stress, and better working relationships with their child's therapist. The efficacy of ESDM was evaluated in a randomized, controlled trial (Dawson et al., 2010). The trial included 48 toddlers, aged 22 months on average, with ASD. As reported by the authors, 72% were Caucasian; the remainder were Asian, Latino, and multiracial. The male–female ratio was 3.5:1.

The toddlers were assigned to either the ESDM or a comparison group (A/M) that was referred for intervention commonly provided in the community. ESDM intervention was conducted in the home and followed a detailed manual. Trained therapists worked with each child for 20 hours weekly for 2 years. Verbal and nonverbal communication were emphasized with developmentally appropriate strategies involving positive affect, real-life activities, and sensitivity to the child's cues.

Teaching techniques included operant conditioning, shaping, and the like. An individualized plan was followed for each child. In addition, parents were taught the principles and techniques of ESDM and were asked to use ESDM strategies with the child.

The intervention was evaluated by comparing measures taken prior to the program with outcome at 1 and 2 years later. The primary outcome measures were scores on the Vineland Adaptive Behavior Scales and on the Mullen Scales of Early Learning, a developmental test for children from birth to 68 months of age that evaluates motor, visual reception, and language performance. The ESDM toddlers improved in cognition at both year 1 and 2, as shown on the Mullen scales (Figure 13.7). At year 2, they had gained 17.6 points compared to 7.0 for the comparison groups, mostly due to increases in language performance. Adaptive behavior scores differed only on year 2 measures, with ESDM performance showing a steady rate of development and the control group

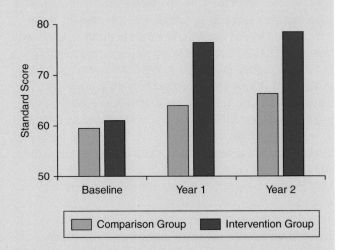

Figure 13.7 Mean scores on the Mullen Scales of Early Learning for children in the ESDM and the comparison groups at baseline, and 1 and 2 years after entering the program. (Adapted from Dawson et al., 2010)

(continued)

(continued)

children showing decline. Two years after the beginning of the intervention, the ESDM children were significantly more likely than the comparison children to have reduced severity of ASD symptoms. Two secondary measures indicated no group difference for ASD symptoms. This randomized, controlled demonstration of significant improvement in Mullen scales scores, language, adaptive behavior, and diagnosis holds promise for early efforts to modify or prevent the maladaptive and damaging pathways to ASD. Additionally, children who had received ESDM utilized fewer services at follow-up, suggesting the intervention may demonstrate both clinical and cost benefits (Cidav et al., 2017).

Pharmacological Treatment

While medication has been used to target problem behaviors associated with ASD, such as aggression, self-injury, agitation, and stereotypic behaviors, it has not been shown to address the core features of the disorder. The typical antipsychotic medications antagonistic to dopamine can help some youth by reducing problematic behaviors, but adverse side effects occur over time in a minority of cases (American Psychological Association, 2006). Of particular concern are side effects such as motor problems, including tremors and tardive dyskinesia (involuntary repetitive movements of the tongue, mouth, and jaw). Typical antipsychotic medications have thus been largely replaced by second-generation, or atypical, antipsychotic medications that are antagonistic both to dopamine and serotonin. Risperidone is an example: it is considered effective for irritability, aggression, self-injury, and temper tantrums that may accompany ASD (Maneeton et al., 2018).

Stimulant medication has been shown to lessen hyperactive behavior in children and adolescents with attention problems and ASD (Bratt, Masanyero-Bennie, & Kelley, 2017). However, methylphenidate appears to have negative side effects, including agitation, irritability, insomnia, and social withdrawal, for many of these children. In one study, 18% of children discontinued use of stimulant medication due to intolerable side effects (Jahromi et al., 2009).

Many other classes of medications are employed, and approximately half of youth with ASD are receiving at least one psychoactive medication (Madden et al., 2017). However, evidence for efficacy is weak or not established. Side effects may be relatively high. Although a substantial number of children with ASD receive medication, much is still unknown about the effects, including long-term effects.

Behavioral Interventions

Behaviorally based treatments are considered the most empirically supported interventions for ASD (Klinger & Dudley, 2019). They are based on the principles of learning and the notion that behavior can be changed by altering the events that influence behavior in order to decrease maladaptive behavior and increase adaptive behavior. The applied approach that stems from this theory is called applied behavior analysis (ABA). Many of the most effective interventions for ASD are based on ABA principles.

Behavioral interventions for ASD can also be viewed as falling into two approaches: targeted or comprehensive (Grigorenko et al., 2018). The first approach focuses on specific targets. These may involve deficits, such as in language or social skills, or specific maladaptive behaviors, such as stereotyped behaviors or self-injury. The second approach is intensive, comprehensive treatment over a relatively long period of time that aims to improve numerous primary and secondary problems of autism.

Early behavioral intervention consisted of simple demonstrations of behavior change in children with autism (Koegel, Koegel, & McNerney, 2001; Schreibman, 2000). Subsequent efforts were made to teach a variety of adaptive behaviors and to discourage undesirable behaviors. An outstanding example of this early work was the approach taken by Lovaas and his colleagues at the University of California at Los Angeles, who were among the first to utilize ABA to teach verbal communication to children with autism (Lovaas, Young, & Newsom, 1978; Newsom, 1998). In highly structured sessions, they used the tools of operant intervention, such as contingent reinforcement, prompts, shaping, modeling, and procedures to facilitate the generalization of learning.

Early behavioral efforts enjoyed success but were also challenged by failures. For instance, young people receiving language training often failed to initiate speech or to use speech in everyday activities (Koegel, 2000). Children who acquired responses often did not generalize the responses to different situations. Some maladaptive behaviors could only be modified by punishment, and other behaviors were hardly modifiable at all (Schreibman, 1997).

Improved behavioral procedures have brought increased success and substantial efforts to improve behaviors such as social skills, joint attention, and emotion regulation, and research has demonstrated the efficacy of such behavioral interventions (Pennington et al., 2019). Functional analysis of maladaptive behavior and Functional Communication Training (p. 328) have been used successfully with children with autism, including those with ID. These children can acquire adaptive behaviors through both discrete trial and naturalistic learning that is more likely to generalize to other settings. In addition, the acquisition of some skills may facilitate other positive behaviors; for example, teaching children to initiate social and academic interactions may help them learn language and social skills. Various behavioral approaches have been incorporated and are often combined in comprehensive behavioral interventions for ASD.

Discrete Trial Training (DTT) One of the most common ABA approaches, DTT is a structured intervention that aims to teach children with ASD complex skills by breaking them down into smaller "discrete" components or skills (Klinger & Dudley, 2019). These subskills are taught in multiple teaching trials, during which the DTT therapist uses prompts, such as requests that the child perform the targeted behavior, to help the child learn. If they do not engage in the behavior, the behavior is modeled and the child is offered multiple trials to learn the task. Once the child exhibits the behavior, they are reinforced with praise or in some other way (i.e., given access to something they want). Each discrete skill builds upon the next so that the child learns to perform more complex tasks.

A groundbreaking DTT intervention, The UCLA Young Autism Project, was developed in 1970 by Lovaas and his colleagues (Lovaas, 1987; Lovaas & Smith, 1988). A key assumption of the intervention is that intensive comprehensive programs that are implemented in the child's everyday environments are necessary to bring about substantial improvement in the lives of children with autism (Smith, Eikeseth, & Larsson, 2018).

The Young Autism Project employs discrete trial learning throughout, incidental learning after the first few months, and small group teaching in preschool during the final years (Table 13.2). Initially, it is usually necessary to reduce maladaptive behaviors that interfere with learning, such as tantrums; to teach imitation and compliance with verbal commands; and to train basic behaviors such as dressing and

playing with toys. Considerable effort is then given to language and communication skills, as well as to peer interaction and interactive play. During the last year or so, emphasis is placed on advanced communication and school adjustment. Parents are an integral part of the intervention. They attend all meetings regarding their child, work with therapists for the first three to four months implementing discrete trial learning, and subsequently use incidental learning to encourage appropriate behaviors in everyday settings.

Participants in the original outcome study of the Young Autism Project were children under age 4 who were free of major medical problems (Lovaas & Smith, 2003). Most received 40 hours per week of one-to-one intervention with experienced behavioral therapists, with sessions tapering off near the end of the program. An initial evaluation compared three groups. Group I had received behavioral treatment for more than 40 hours each week, Group II had received almost the same treatment but for fewer than 10 hours weekly, and Group III had received no training in the project. The groups were similar in characteristics and intervention lasted for two or more years. Group I children, who now averaged 7 years of age, had an increase of 30 points in IQ, and significantly higher educational placement than the other two groups, which did not differ from each other. A second evaluation when Group I children averaged 13 years of age showed that they had maintained improvements over Group II youth (McEachin, Smith, & Lovaas, 1993). Eight of the nine Group I children who had done well at the first evaluation were holding their own in regular classrooms and approached normal functioning.

This influential research led to dramatic increases in the use of ABA strategies, in particular DTT (Klinger & Dudley, 2019).

Table 13.2 Treatment Stages in the Young Autism Project

Stage	Length	Teaching methods	Goals (examples)
1. Establishing a teaching relationship	~2–4 weeks	Primarily discrete trial training (DTT)	Following directions such as "sit" or "come here," reducing interfering behaviors such as tantrums
2. Teaching foundational skills	~1–4 months	Primarily DTT	Imitating gross motor actions, identifying objects, dressing, beginning play with toys
3. Beginning communication	~6+ months	DTT, incidental teaching	Imitating speech sounds, expressively labeling objects, receptively identifying actions and pictures, expanding self-help and play skills
4. Expanding communication, beginning peer interaction	~12 months	DTT, incidental teaching, dyads with typical peers	Labeling colors and shapes, beginning language concepts such as big/little and yes/no, beginning sentences such as "I see —," beginning pretend play and peer interaction
5. Advanced communication, adjusting to school	~12 months	DTT, incidental teaching, small group, regular education preschool	Conversing with others, describing objects and events, comprehending stories, understanding perspective of others, working independently, helping with chores

Source: Adapted from Lovaas & Smith, 2003. Copyright 2003 by Guilford Press; reprinted with permission.

Although the original outcome study had a stronger scientific design than most treatment studies at that time (Rogers, 1998), it received some criticism (Mundy, 1993; Rogers, 1998; Schopler, Short, & Mesibov, 1989). Since then, numerous evaluations of behavioral programs similar to the Lovaas approach have described several benefits (Newsom & Hovanitz, 2006; Reichow & Wolery, 2009; Rogers & Vismara, 2008; Virués-Ortega, 2010), and a review of meta-analyses concluded that the UCLA Young Autism Project has the strongest support (Reichow, 2012). Overall, the research indicates some children "recover" in that they attain IQs in the normal range and placement in typical age-level classrooms. Improved language skills, social behavior, and adaptive functioning have also been found. Not all children benefit from treatment, however, suggesting that the approach does not fit all children (Smith, 2010). Nevertheless, the approach encouraged specialized interventions and research that continues to this day, and it has affected schools and other agencies involved in providing services to children with autism (Smith et al., 2018).

Pivotal Response Treatment Also building on the techniques of ABA, Pivotal Response Treatment (PRT) assumes that strengthening pivotal or foundational behaviors will improve other behaviors (Klinger & Dudley, 2019; Koegel et al., 2017). The overall goal is to provide comprehensive treatment in areas that will facilitate the child's independence. Intervention occurs in naturalistic settings with parents, teachers, and other service providers. Because impairments in autism tend to be extensive, and because targeting each problem is extremely time-consuming and expensive, pivotal response training holds promise for time-efficient and cost-effective intervention.

Table 13.3 shows some of the strategies employed in PRT. Motivation is seen as a key component: it is pivotal to almost all areas of functioning (Gengoux, 2018). Motivation may be particularly problematic in ASD because the child has experienced repeated failures, as well as noncontingent assistance and reinforcement from caretakers. Specific strategies are employed to mitigate this unfortunate history—strategies that include child selection of activities, liberal and contingent reinforcement, and opportunity for the practice of acquired responses. Areas of function that have been targeted for improvement include expressive language, social interaction, and motivation to self-initiate (e.g., to seek information, initiate joint attention). It is presumed that improved motivation and behaviors tend to spill over to other areas and strengthen independence and learning.

PRT has been evaluated with different research designs in varied research settings with manualized procedures (Koegel et al., 2017). These studies indicate treatment gains in both targeted behaviors and untargeted spill-over behaviors. Preliminary evidence exists for the effectiveness of PRT group training for parents (Minjarez et al., 2011) and for the sustainability of PRT in a community setting (Smith et al., 2010).

Table 13.3 Procedures Used in Pivotal Response Training to Strengthen the Child's Motivation and Other Pivotal Areas to Initiate and Respond to Environmental Stimuli

PIVOTAL AREA

Motivation

- Teaching occurs when the child is paying attention and clear prompts are provided.
- Child is permitted to select activities and objects.
- Tasks are varied.
- Reinforcement is given liberally to the child's attempts to respond.
- Natural reinforcers are employed.
- Opportunity is given to the child to use acquired responses as new ones are learned.

Responding to Multiple Cues

- Child is taught to simultaneously understand and respond to multiple aspects of a question or set of materials.

Self-Initiation

- Child is taught to start interactions by asking questions or independently making comments.

Self-Regulation

- Child is taught to track their own behavior to increase their capacity to set and achieve goals independently.

Source: Based on Gengoux, 2018.

Despite evidence in support of behavioral approaches, limitations and evaluations of applied behavior interventions have been variously noted. Some investigators cite a need for better controlled studies that compare behavioral programs with specified other interventions (rather than "eclectic" programs). Nevertheless, the overall findings have made the behavioral approach a leading option for treatment. Drawing on evaluations of behavioral approaches—and also of psychoeducational interventions such as TEACCH, which is discussed in the next section—Schreibman's (2000) summary of the following well-established facts is informative.

- Intensive treatments—that is, treatments given for many hours a day and/or in many of the child's daily environments—can be extremely effective.
- Intervention when children are very young has the potential for significant gains.
- Effective treatments are associated with carefully controlled learning situations.
- Effective interventions must use techniques to promote generalization and maintenance of acquired learning (e.g., naturalistic teaching).

- When parents are trained to be major treatment providers, children are more likely to generalize and maintain their learning.
- Variation exists in outcome and different children may benefit from different approaches.

Psychosocial Interventions

Psychosocial treatments for ASD focus on improving the social skills and emotional functioning of children and adolescents with ASD. Social skills training is aimed at addressing the difficulties initiating and sustaining reciprocal social interactions central in ASD. While research on comprehensive social skills training programs is limited, social skills training has been integrated into other approaches, and several specific practices have been shown to be effective in addressing skill deficits, including video and video self-modeling, peer-mediated instruction and intervention, scripting, social narratives and social skills training groups (Wong et al., 2015). Video-modeling, for example, allows children to learn new skills by observing others successfully perform the skill and has been associated with increased social-communication skills in children and adolescents with ASD (Bellini & Akullian, 2007; Watkins et al., 2017). Peer interventions involving typically developing peers in role plays, modeling of appropriate behaviors, and other interventions have also been shown to improve several aspects of social functioning, including social communication, social initiation, social response, and engagement with peers (Chang & Locke, 2016; Sterrett, Shire, & Kasari, 2017). Direct and explicit teaching of social skills have also been shown to improve social functioning for children and adolescents with ASD (Klinger & Dudley, 2019; Watkins et al., 2017). Scripting involves teaching individuals with ASD how to respond verbally and nonverbally to specific situations (e.g., how to initiate play with another child), while social narratives provide social stories that teach appropriate behavior (e.g., shaking hands when you meet a new person). More research is needed to assess the impact of these techniques on the social functioning of children and adolescents with ASD.

Psychosocial interventions are also aimed at addressing the co-occurring problems of anxiety and depression in ASD. Cognitive-behavioral therapy (CBT) is now considered an evidence-based practice for individuals with ASD (White et al., 2018), although it may need to be adapted to the needs and presentations of the individual (Klinger & Dudley, 2019). For example, individuals with cognitive impairment may have difficulty with the elements of CBT focused on cognition (e.g., those that require the ability to identify, monitor, and modify thoughts). Treatment modification, such as greater use of visual supports and increased parent involvement, may help support individuals with ASD in treatment. Nevertheless, improvements have been demonstrated in response to CBT both in affective symptoms and core ASD symptoms (Weston, Hodgekins, & Langdon, 2016). The case of Sarah provides an example of the use of psychosocial intervention with children with ASD.

Psychoeducational Treatment and Services

Structured educational approaches have been shown to have small to moderate effects for school-age children (Pennington et al., 2019). One structured teaching approach, TEACCH, which stands for Treatment and Education of Autistic and related Communication handicapped Children, is a university-based statewide program in North Carolina mandated by law to provide

SARAH Psychosocial Intervention for ASD

Sarah is an 8-year-old girl with a diagnosis of ASD and co-occurring anxiety who was referred to a CBT group therapy program targeting anxiety in children with ASD. Intellectual testing reveals that Sarah is of average intellectual ability. She attends third grade in a general education classroom and has an Individualized Education Plan (IEP). An assessment of Sarah's psychosocial functioning indicates that Sarah meets diagnostic criteria for co-occurring generalized anxiety disorder and has a specific phobia of making mistakes. In particular, Sarah is terrified of making mistakes, often erases and rewrites her answers on her classwork several times to make sure they are perfect or refuses to write an answer for fear it might be wrong. As a result, she is often unable to finish her assignments and sits at her desk crying. Sarah's grades are declining, and she believes that her teachers are angry with her performance.

Sarah and her mother participated in a 14-week, 80-minute group CBT program. The sessions included a large-group time (parents and children together), parent alone and children alone (occurring simultaneously in separate rooms), and work in parent–child pairs. Therapy techniques include support of the specific learning and social needs of children with ASD, including the use of a visual schedule, predictable routines (e.g., a beginning and ending routine for each session), explicit verbal scripts (e.g., "I can face this fear"), modeling of appropriate social skills by therapists, and video self-modeling to reinforce learning anxiety reduction techniques. All group sessions are interactive and use a combination of worksheets and group activities to teach and reinforce new skills.

Adapted from Klinger & Dudley, 2019, pp. 399–402

services, research, and training for autism and related disorders (Schopler, 1997). The approach has evolved over several decades as an alternative to a psychoanalytic-based approach used in the 1960s at the University of North Carolina. From the beginning, families played a critical role in developing TEACCH, and priority was given to three areas: home adjustment, education, and community adaptation. A clear philosophy and set of values emerged over the years, which included formal assessment for individualized treatment, teaching new skills through cognitive and behavior theory, parent–professional collaboration, and a holistic orientation. The TEACCH Autism Program operates regional centers that provide individual assessment, training for parents to serve as co-therapists for their children, family support, employment support for older persons with autism, consultation, professional training for teacher and therapists, and collaboration with other relevant agencies.

TEACCH is based on the notion that learning differences and unique cognitive challenges associated with ASD contribute to difficulties understanding behavioral expectations and managing uncertainty in daily life, which in turn contribute to the behavioral difficulties seen in ASD (Klinger et al., 2018). The approach includes structured teaching techniques, the use of visual supports (e.g., daily schedule), environmental structure (e.g., organizing the child's physical environment to clearly define boundaries) and predictable routines to reduce challenging behaviors and enhance learning.

The evidence-base for TEACCH is limited by relatively few extensive treatment studies, and those that have been conducted include a wide range of designs making it difficult to compare across studies (Klinger et al., 2018). Although there are weaknesses in outcome studies, including lack of control groups (Smith, 1999), evidence does support the use of visual support strategies in the classroom (Boyd et al., 2014). As a broad psychoeducational approach, TEACCH has been recognized for excellence across the United States and in Europe and is often utilized in educational settings (McLay, Hansen, & Carnett, 2019).

Educational Opportunities

ASD is among the disabilities included in the IDEA. School districts are obliged to identify children with ASD, provide services from birth, include families in evaluation and intervention, and deliver appropriate educational programs. Commitment to the least restrictive placements and school inclusion has diminished institutionalization and has increased educational opportunities for children with autism.

Full inclusion of students with ASD in the general classroom setting is an issue that has received a great deal of attention (de Boer & Pijl, 2016). It is argued that the marked differences in abilities in persons with ASD require alternative educational settings, including special classrooms with special services. More recently, concern has been expressed that inclusion in regular classrooms puts children with ASD at risk for peer rejection and unfavorable social and emotional outcomes (Jones & Frederickson, 2010). There is evidence that many mainstreamed children with high-functioning ASD have relatively fewer reciprocal friendships and poorer quality friendships (Kasari et al., 2011).

The successful teaching of children with autism usually requires special strategies and intensive interaction. (Angela Hampton Picture Library/Alamy Stock Photo)

On the other hand, it is argued that typically developing peers can be active participants in intervention and otherwise model socially appropriate behavior. It does appear that some children with ASD can benefit from interventions targeting peer relationships and social outcomes (Sterrett et al., 2017), and the benefits of settings that promote peer relationships between individuals with disability and those without can be bidirectional (Athamanah et al., 2019). However, critical questions require further examination: What factors predict successful integration into mainstream classrooms? And do some children benefit from alternative school settings and, if so, which settings best advantage which students?

In the broader scheme of things, there are multiple aspects of school life that can be challenging for individuals with ASD and their families, including morning routine, traveling to/from school, peer interactions, individual and group work, transitions, and extracurricular activities, for example (Haroon, 2019d). Support to families is essential as they experience many challenges making their way through the complexities of acquiring the best educational services for their child and otherwise rearing a child with disabilities (Schieve et al., 2007). Also important are postschool services that promote independent functioning and quality of life for youth with ASD. Transition planning that includes consideration of individual transition goals and education plans, provides opportunities to teach skills, and evaluates progress can help students with ASD experience greater successes in postsecondary environments, such as employment, continuing education, and independent living (Szidon, Ruppar, & Smith, 2015).

Given the diverse needs of children with ASD, a team-based approach involving a diversity of health disciplines (e.g., medical care, psychology, applied behavior analysis, speech-language pathology, occupational therapy, school-based support) is recommended (LaFrance et al., 2019). Availability of autism-related health services can be limited, however, and there is a need for greater investment in enhancing the services available to children with ASD (McBain et al., 2020). Similarly, much progress has been made in improving the lives of youth with ASD, due to both rigorous research and the commitment and advocacy of families and professionals alike, but sustained efforts are crucial.

Schizophrenia

As we noted at the beginning of this chapter, for many years the term *childhood schizophrenia* was applied to heterogeneous groups of children with certain severe impairments. Even after diagnostic confusion was reduced—for example, by defining autism as a distinct disorder—a fundamental question remained:

Did schizophrenia appearing in children differ from adult schizophrenia or was it the same basic disorder with different manifestations at different times of life? By 1980, some consensus was reached that the essential features of schizophrenia hold across age, and the same basic diagnostic criteria were applied to individuals of all ages.

Thus, although our primary interest in this chapter is schizophrenia of young people, we consider adult-onset schizophrenia when it bears on this topic. In keeping with the clinical and research literature, our discussion often distinguishes between childhood-onset schizophrenia (COS), with onset usually defined as before age 13, and adolescent schizophrenia, which is viewed as more similar to adult-onset schizophrenia.

DSM Classification and Diagnosis

The DSM-5 places schizophrenia in the broad category of Schizophrenia Spectrum and Other Psychotic Disorders (American Psychiatric Association, 2013). The essential features of schizophrenia are:

hallucinations
delusions
disorganized speech
disorganized or catatonic behavior
negative symptoms.

For diagnosis, at least two of these features are required for a significant part of the time during a one-month period, with the presence of at least one of the first three symptoms above. Continuous signs of disorder must persist for at least six months. When onset occurs in childhood or adolescence, there must be failure to reach expected levels of interpersonal, academic, or occupational achievement.

The first four of these features, referred to as **positive symptoms**, indicate distortion or excess in normal functioning. **Hallucinations**, or erroneous perceptions, and **delusions**, or erroneous beliefs, are viewed as hallmarks of the psychosis of schizophrenia. **Disorganized speech**, which reflects thought disorder, is another critical feature. **Disorganized behavior** is manifested in many ways: inappropriate silliness, unexpected agitation or aggression, lack of self-care, and the like. **Catatonic behaviors** are motor disturbances, such as decreased or excessive motor reactivity, and rigid and strange bodily postures.

Individuals with schizophrenia also may display **negative symptoms**, that is, a diminution or lack of normally occurring behaviors. Thus, they may exhibit little emotion (flat affect), their speech may consist of brief replies that do not seem to convey much information (alogia), or they may neither initiate nor maintain goal-directed actions (avolition).

The diagnosis of youth with schizophrenia is reasonably reliable, particularly in inpatient psychiatric settings (Vernal et al., 2018), but the strong emphasis on positive symptoms, such as hallucinations and delusions, has implications for very young children. Early developmental level may not lend itself to these psychotic manifestations, nor to such symptoms being reported by the child or being reliably assessed. Moreover, the symptoms of schizophrenia must be distinguished from typical development and in the context of the child's developmental level (Knorr, 2017). Diagnosis prior to age 13 is rare (Driver, Gogtay, & Rapoport, 2013).

Description: Primary and Secondary Features

Hallucinations

Hallucinations are false perceptions that occur in the absence of identifiable stimuli. Individuals experiencing hallucinations report hearing, seeing, or smelling things that others do not hear, see, or smell. Such perceptual abnormalities can vary in content and in complexity. For example, simple hallucinations are indistinct shapes or sounds, whereas complex hallucinations are more organized, such as identifiable figures or voices, or include multiple senses (Garralda, 2017).

As one might imagine, it is important to differentiate normative childhood experiences, such as having an imaginary friend, from hallucinations indicative of psychopathology (Haut et al., 2016). Children often hear or see things that frighten them, such as a noise or shadow on the wall at night, or engage in imaginative play, and these experiences are usually part of typical development (American Academy of Child & Adolescent Psychiatry, 2017). While the experience of hallucinations was previously

conceptualized as central to psychotic disorders, hallucinatory experiences are now increasingly considered as occurring on a continuum, with healthy children and adolescents at one end and those experiencing hallucinations of a clinical nature at the other (Maijer et al., 2019). The following examples of hallucinations were drawn from the accounts of a study with 9-year-olds who met diagnostic criteria for schizophrenia (Russell, Bott, & Sammons, 1989).

Auditory: The kitchen light said to do things and "shut up."
Visual: A ghost with a red, burned, scarred face was seen several times in different places.
Command: A man's voice said "murder your stepfather" and "go play outside."
Persecutory: Monsters said that the child is "stupid" and that they will hurt him.

Auditory hallucinations are the most commonly reported type of hallucinations for adults and children alike. Visual hallucinations are reported more frequently in COS as compared to cases with adult-onset schizophrenia (David et al., 2011). Figure 13.8 shows the types of hallucinations, broken down by sense (i.e., auditory, visual, somatic/tactile, olfactory) reported for 117 patients with COS who were evaluated as part of the large-scale National Institutes of Mental Health (NIMH) Childhood Onset Schizophrenia cohort. Auditory hallucinations were reported most frequently and were often the basis for psychiatric hospital referral, and nonauditory hallucinations were reported in higher rates than typically reported for adults. Moreover, there was considerable overlap between auditory, visual, and the other types

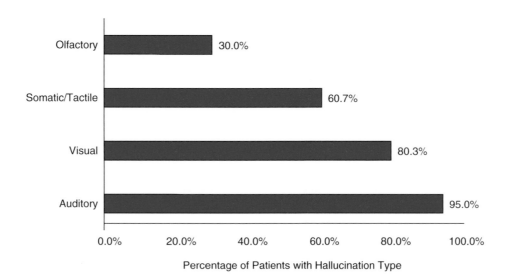

Figure 13.8 Types of hallucinations in the National Institute of Mental Health (NIMH) Childhood Onset Schizophrenia (COS) cohort. (Adapted from David et al., 2011)

of hallucinations, with most children experiencing more than one type.

Delusions

Delusions are false beliefs that are maintained even in the face of realistic contradiction. They vary in content. For example, delusions of persecution involve beliefs of impending harm from someone, whereas delusions of reference involve inaccurate beliefs that certain events or objects have particular significance. Delusions can also be simple or complex, and fragmented or organized and occur quite consistently in the majority of the children diagnosed with Schizophrenia. Delusions should also be considered within the developmental context of the child, as superstitions, fantasies, or magical thinking may be common in typically developing children. The following are examples of delusions experienced by children who met criteria for diagnosis of Schizophrenia (Russell et al., 1989).

Persecutory: A child believed his father had escaped jail and was coming to kill him.
Somatic: A child believed that a boy and a girl spirit lived inside his head.
Bizarre: A boy was convinced he was a dog and growing fur. One time he refused to leave a veterinarian's office unless he got a shot.
Grandiose: A boy had the firm belief that he was different and able to kill people. He believed that when God zoomed through him, he became strong.

Disorganized Symptoms

Delusions are a disturbance in the content of thought, but the form of thinking is also distorted in schizophrenia. Thought problems involve difficulties in organizing thoughts and behavior and are reflected in disorganized speech, bizarre behavior, and poor attention (Sharma & McClellan, 2019). There are several indications of disorganized symptoms. The person may display loose associations, that is, jump from topic to topic with no obvious connection between topics. Speech may be illogical, incoherent, and incomprehensible to others. It may also convey little information because it is vague, too abstract or concrete, or repetitive. It may include neologisms, made-up words that are meaningless to others. Again, it is important to distinguish these symptoms from those of typical child behavior or from other common diagnoses, such as ADHD or ASD (Knorr, 2017). Disorganized thinking is suggested in this excerpt from an interview with a 7-year-old boy:

> I used to have a Mexican dream. I was watching TV in the family room. I disappeared outside of this world and then I was in a closet. Sounds like a vacuum dream. It's a Mexican dream. When I was close to that dream earth I was turning upside down. I don't like to turn upside down. Sometimes I have Mexican dreams and vacuum dreams. It's real hard to scream in dreams.
>
> Russell et al., 1989, p. 404

Severe disruptions in thinking and behavior may be prominent during the acute phase of the disorder and can substantially impair a person's social and adaptive functioning (Sharma & McClellan, 2019).

Secondary Features

Among the secondary features associated with COS are social impairments, motor abnormalities, including delayed milestones and poor coordination, and language delays (Filatova et al., 2017; Petruzzelli et al., 2015). Although not always present, approximately 67% of children with COS show disturbances in social, motor, and language domains prior to the onset of the disorder, as well as learning problems and co-occurring mood and anxiety symptoms (Driver et al., 2013). In addition, minor physical abnormalities (MPAs)—irregularities of the face, head, hands, and feet—occur at elevated rates in schizophrenia (Weinberg et al., 2007).

Impaired social communication is common (St Pourcain et al., 2018). For example, when asked a question, children with schizophrenia may be less likely to reply, and when they do reply, they may be less likely to give information to supplement their simple answers (Abu-Akel et al., 2000). Children with schizophrenia speak less and show poorer discourse skills as compared to typically developing children (Asarnow & Forsyth, 2017). Atypical features such as echolalia and neologisms may be present. A portion of children with COS meet criteria for ASD prior to the onset of psychotic symptoms (Driver et al., 2013).

Cognitive impairment is also common in schizophrenia (Harvey & Isner, 2020; Remberk, Hintze, & Rybakowski, 2015). A general cognitive deficit is reflected in intelligence test scores. Many children with schizophrenia display intellectual deficits; perhaps 10 to 20% of cases show intellectual impairment ranging from mild to severe (Kodish & McClellan, 2016). A pattern of deterioration around the time of onset of psychosis, followed by stability, has been observed. One study found that test scores showed significant cognitive impairment present at the first episode of psychotic symptoms and that impairment remained stable over the first two years following diagnosis (Bombin et al., 2013). Consonant with general cognitive impairments, neuropsychological and other evaluations indicate specific deficits in COS and adolescent schizophrenia, for example, on tasks of attention, memory, and executive functions (Remberk et al., 2015). Many deficits are generally similar to those of adult schizophrenia (Reichenberg & Harvey, 2007), but are reported to be more severe (Frazier et al., 2007).

Emotional and social impairments are also evident in COS and impact functioning. Some reflect the flat affect and lack of social interest—the negative symptoms—that reportedly are more common in early-onset than adult-onset schizophrenia and are associated with poorer outcomes (Remberk et al., 2015). Social cognition may be impaired and social deficits, including shyness, withdrawal, isolation, social relatedness, may also be evident (Kodish & McClellan, 2016). Emotional problems, including anxiety and depression, have been reported (Riglin et al., 2018). These secondary features and impairments may strongly affect functional outcomes (Harvey & Isner, 2020).

Epidemiology

The prevalence of schizophrenia in children is considered rare, but precise prevalence rates are not known. Schizophrenia is estimated in less than 1% of the general population (Simeone et al., 2015). It is estimated to occur in 0.003% to 0.02% of children under 13 years of age, and 0.01% to 0.2% in adolescence (Woodberry, Kline, & Giuliano, 2019). Onset climbs dramatically during adolescence into early adulthood, and generally peaks from about age 15 to 30 with a median age of onset of 16 for both boys and girls. Childhood schizophrenia appears more common in boys, with the sex ratio nearly equal in adolescence (Asarnow & Kernan, 2008).

COS may occur at higher rates in families with lower socioeconomic status; however, the data are mixed and likely reflect shared mechanisms rather than causal processes (Gallagher & Jones, 2017; Kodish & McClellan, 2016). Similarly, urban living, minority ethnicity status, cultural migration and lack of social support are associated risk factors (Kodish & McClellan, 2016). Schizophrenia is observed in cultures all over the world, with similar symptom profiles.

Developmental Course

The onset of schizophrenia in childhood is likely to be **insidious**, or gradual, with only 5% of cases being acute (Asarnow & Forsyth, 2017). The course of the illness varies across individuals, but youth and adults typically progress through four phases of the disorder: prodromal, acute, recuperative/recovery, and residual (Sharma & McClellan, 2019). Nonpsychotic symptoms occur prior to psychotic symptoms and diagnosis. Early premorbid characteristics include delays and aberrations in language, motor, sensory, and cognitive functions—as well as social withdrawal, peer difficulties, school problems, mood disturbances, and "odd" preoccupations and behaviors (Asarnow & Forsyth, 2017; Sharma & McClellan, 2019). The case description of Tommy describes several significant prodromal symptoms, including social and behavior difficulties as well as learning problems, that were present prior to a dramatic decline in functioning and the emergence of psychotic features during the acute phase of the disorder.

As we might expect, schizophrenia in youth presents important developmental considerations. Symptom reports must be considered in the context of the young person's age, culture, and developmental and cognitive level (Sharma & McClellan, 2019). Developmental level also makes its way into children's symptoms (Volkmar, 2001). The negative symptoms of the disorder may be less common in young children. Early hallucinations are likely to include animals, toys, and monsters, and to be simple. Hallucinations may be accompanied by delusions (Garralda, 2017). When they first appear, delusions are quite simple (e.g., a monster wants to kill me), and then they gradually become more elaborate, complex, abstract, and systematized (e.g., children may say they are being poisoned or followed). These changes are in keeping with cognitive and socioemotional development (Volkmar, 2001).

Adolescent onset of schizophrenia seems not to be as insidious as child onset. Many diagnosed adolescents nonetheless have histories of attention, motor-perceptual, and other neurodevelopmental problems as well as worry, shyness, moodiness, and aggression. This picture is more similar to adult-onset schizophrenia, in which there is considerable variation in the timing, severity, and nature of early features (Asarnow & Forsyth, 2017). The psychotic symptoms exhibited by adolescents also are more similar to those seen in adults. For instance,

TOMMY Early Manifestations of Schizophrenia

Tommy is a 15-year-old adolescent boy brought to the emergency room by the police after he was found walking the streets at 2:30 in the morning. Tommy told the police that he was searching for the Illuminati. He hears them whispering, telling him that they are coming to get him. Tommy's parents report that he stopped going to school 2 weeks previously and spends most of the time in his room. They hear him yelling and talking to himself and describe odd changes in behavior, such as taking apart his laptop to remove the camera. He has always been shy, with only a few friends during elementary and middle school, and was diagnosed with a reading disorder in the third grade. In the months preceding the evaluation, he has become increasingly withdrawn and isolated. His parents worry that he is depressed or using drugs. They tried taking him to the family doctor, but he refused to go. They called the local crisis line, but were told that nothing could be done unless he was dangerous to himself or others.

Adapted from McClellan, 2018, p. 308

persecutory and grandiose delusions are more common than in child cases, and delusions are more complex and systematized (Volkmar, 2001).

In general, variation has been reported in the course of schizophrenia, that is, some individuals have a chronic condition, some experience episodes of difficulties that come and go, and still others partially or fully recover. In general, early onset is associated with poor outcomes—more severe and chronic symptoms, as well as cognitive and functional impairment (McClellan, 2018). In addition to age of onset, poor adjustment before onset, insidious onset, negative symptoms, and a longer time lapse before treatment are among the factors that predict poor outcome of schizophrenia (Díaz-Caneja et al., 2015). Table 13.4 lists some of the factors associated with poor outcomes in early-onset schizophrenia that were identified as part of a systematic review of 75 studies on the disorder. It appears that about one-fifth of children and adolescents has good outcome with mild impairments, and one-third remains severely impaired (Hollis, 2015).

Child and adolescent schizophrenia carry a higher than usual risk for premature death, as does adult-onset schizophrenia (Hollis, 2015; Sharma & McClellan, 2019). This outcome appears to be due to a mix of causes, such as undetected medical conditions, suicide, and other violent events. The case description of Mary depicts childhood-onset schizophrenia that terminated in tragedy.

Neurobiological Abnormalities

Neuroanatomical abnormalities have been revealed for schizophrenia and linked with several brain regions. Many findings come from adult cases and from children at high risk

Table 13.4 Some Factors Associated with Poor Outcomes in Schizophrenia

Premorbid adjustment difficulties
Greater symptom severity, especially negative symptoms
Lower age at onset
Insidious onset
Lower IQ
Attentional difficulties
Learning and memory difficulties
Greater developmental delays (e.g., motor impairment)
Longer time lapse before treatment
Poor treatment adherance

Source: Adapted from Díaz-Caneja et al., 2015.

who were diagnosed in adolescence or adulthood. Important studies also have been conducted with children diagnosed with the disorder. The findings are notably similar across age groups. Neurobiological dysfunction is suggested by general symptoms of children with schizophrenia, such as motor delay, coordination problems, and minor physical abnormalities. More direct evidence comes from brain imaging and postmortem studies which have contributed to a growing body of evidence in support of two central neurobiological hypotheses (Berman et al., 2015). First, as discussed in more detail later in this chapter, schizophrenia is increasingly being viewed as a neurodevelopmental disorder, in which alterations in brain development precede the characteristic symptoms of the disorder (Weinberger, 2017). The second hypothesis highlights brain connectivity, or abnormal synaptic processes and connections with and between brain regions, as a key feature of the disorder (Friston et al., 2016).

MARY A Tragic Course of Childhood Schizophrenia

Mary had always been a very shy child. She would become mute at times, had severe difficulties making friends, was frequently oppositional, and had occasional enuresis. By the time she reached roughly 10 years of age, Mary showed academic difficulties in addition to continuing social isolation. She became depressed, felt that the devil was trying to make her do bad things, believed that her teacher was trying to hurt her, and was preoccupied with germs. Her behavior became increasingly disorganized. She talked of killing herself, appeared disheveled, and ran in front of a moving car in an apparent suicide attempt.

This episode precipitated an inpatient psychiatric evaluation, during which Mary continued to show bizarre behavior. Although Mary's functioning improved during

hospitalization and she returned to her family, throughout her childhood and adolescent years she was tormented by fears, hallucinations, the belief that others were out to get her, and occasional bouts of depression often accompanied by suicide attempts. She continued to be socially isolated and withdrawn, and to perform poorly in school. At age 17 (after several brief inpatient hospitalizations), Mary was admitted to a state hospital, where she remained until the age of 19. During this period her affect was increasingly flat, and her psychotic symptoms persisted. One week after discharge from the hospital, Mary went into her room, locked the door, and overdosed on her medications. She was found dead the next morning.

Adapted from Asarnow & Asarnow, 2003, p. 455

Regarding the structure of the brain, neurons sometimes appear abnormal, to be in abnormal locations, and may be densely packed. Individuals with schizophrenia show a variety of changes in brain volume (Haut et al., 2016). A common finding is enlargement of the brain's fluid-filled lateral ventricles, which has been found across age groups, including children (Brennan & Walker, 2010). In contrast, extensive research suggests small volume of brain tissue and gray matter deficits in schizophrenia, most prominently in the prefrontal and temporal areas, hippocampus, amygdala, and thalamus, among other regions (Ganzola, Maziade, & Duchesne, 2014; Kodish & McClellan, 2016; Rapoport, Giedd, & Gogtay, 2012). Reduced brain volume and enlarged ventricles generally have been associated with negative symptoms, poor adjustment before diagnosis, and neuropsychological deficits (Buchanan & Carpenter, 2000; Davis et al., 2003; Gur et al., 1998), and the pattern of reduced brain volume and enlarged ventricles has been consistently demonstrated over numerous studies (Haijma et al., 2012; van Erp et al., 2016).

Brain abnormalities tend to be present early in the course of the disorder, and earlier age of onset of the disorder may be associated with greater neuroanatomical abnormalities (Rapoport et al., 2012). Longitudinal studies also show neuroanatomical integrity changes over the course of the illness. Of special interest to our discussion are brain imaging studies with youth enrolled in a comprehensive ongoing National Institute of Mental Health investigation of COS. Gray matter loss was shown to occur early in the parietal lobe and later in adolescence in the frontal and temporal lobes (Gogtay, 2007). Interestingly, the progression of loss mirrors the back-to-front pattern of brain development in healthy youth.

White matter deficits have also been identified in schizophrenia, which suggests deficits in multiple domains of brain functioning (Rapoport et al., 2012). In a study of white matter, comparison was made between 14-year-olds with COS and matched healthy youth. MRI images were obtained annually for 4.5 years (Gogtay et al., 2008). For those with COS, significantly slower growth was seen each year in the frontal, parietal, and occipital lobes, especially in the right hemisphere. This occurred in the same pattern as white tissue growth in typically developing youth—that is, front-to-back. This disturbance in maturation implicated myelination of fibers and connectivity of brain regions. Important in this and other studies was the finding that brain growth was correlated with measures of clinical functioning (Figure 13.9).

Brain anomalies have been demonstrated in other ways. Brain activity has been examined with various types of scans and widespread alterations in activation and connectivity have been identified in COS (Asarnow & Forsyth, 2017). Findings indicate a complex picture of under- and overactivity in different brain regions and on different tasks (Haut et al., 2016; Kronbichler et al., 2017).

Research conducted over many years indicates that dopamine dysregulation plays a role in schizophrenia (Howes et al., 2017). Dopamine is important in several cerebral pathways, including the frontal and temporal–limbic areas. This neurotransmitter is blocked by medications that relieve psychosis, and substances that increase dopamine worsen symptoms of schizophrenia. Nevertheless, other neurotransmitters are implicated. Second-generation antipsychotic medications strongly impede serotonin. The possible roles of genes associated both with schizophrenia

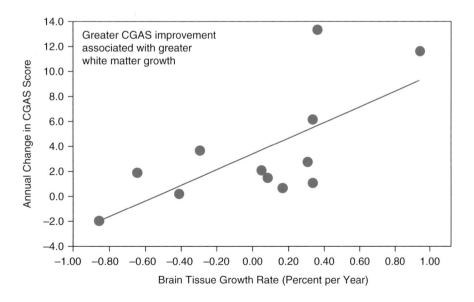

Figure 13.9 The relationship between a measure of clinical functioning (CGAS) and brain tissue growth. (From Gogtay et al., 2008. Copyright 2020 National Academy of Sciences, U.S.A.; reprinted with permission)

and encoding dopamine receptors and those involved in glutamate and GABA pathways, which are important in cerebral functioning, are being investigated. It appears that numerous complex transmitter dysfunctions might exist.

What is to be made of the various findings about the brain? Taken together, the evidence suggests that several brain areas and neurotransmitters, functioning in complex ways, are central in schizophrenia. Structural, functional, and biochemical studies suggest that the disorder involves abnormalities in the connections among parts of a distributed network, predominantly of frontal and temporal–limbic circuits (Kodish & McClellan, 2016).

Etiology

Given the evidence for brain abnormalities, etiological hypotheses and investigations have sought to explain both their origins and how they might account for schizophrenia. Again, there is a disproportionate amount of research for adult-onset, but the study of youth with schizophrenia is increasing. Overall, schizophrenia is considered the result of a combination of genetic predisposition and environmental influences, with potentially stronger influence of genetic factors in earlier onset cases (Anvari et al., 2018).

Genetic Factors

Extensive research conducted in several countries on adult-onset schizophrenia suggests heritability as high as 81% (Charney & Sklar, 2018). Twin data show greater concordance in identical than fraternal pairs—on average, about 56% versus 14% (Asarnow & Forsyth, 2017). Risk for the disorder increases as genetic relationship to an adult proband increases (Gottesman, 1993; Mortensen et al., 1999). For example, risk is about 12% for children of a schizophrenic parent but only 2% for first cousins. Genetic vulnerability in families is also expressed in disorders similar to but less severe than schizophrenia and in cognitive processing deficits associated with schizophrenia (Asarnow et al., 2001; Lui et al., 2018). This suggests that what is inherited may be a general vulnerability and quantitative traits rather than a category of disorder (Hollis, 2015). Finally, risk for schizophrenia-like disorders in the parents of COS patients has been found to be higher than for parents of adult-onset patients (Nicolson & Rapoport, 2000). This finding suggests greater family vulnerability in COS.

No single gene with substantial effect has been found, and it is generally believed that multiple genes with small to moderate effects are involved (Christensen & Børglum, 2019). Genetic deletions and duplications, such as 22q11.2, are associated with brain structure and function consistent with what is known about schizophrenia, yet may only be associated with a small percentage of cases (Knorr, 2017). Research of COS has replicated the presence of a few of the susceptibility genes found in

adult-onset schizophrenia and identified common variants that may implicate a greater genetic vulnerability in COS (Ahn et al., 2016). For example, the COMT gene (chromosome 22) is implicated in dopamine regulation, the DISC gene (chromosome 1) in reduced brain matter, and the NRD1 gene (chromosome 8) in neuron migration and connectivity, but their involvement in schizophrenia remains debated (Henriksen, Nordgaard, & Jansson, 2017).

In addition, genome-wide studies have demonstrated shared genetic risk between schizophrenia and other psychiatric disorders, including mood disorders, ASD, and ADHD (Purcell et al., 2009; Rees, O'Donovan, & Owen, 2015), although these common variants may only explain a small proportion of the heritability of schizophrenia (Henriksen et al., 2017). Rare, *de novo* (i.e., new, not inherited) and inherited copy number variations (i.e., deletions and duplications of gene sequences) have been shown to occur at rates much higher than in a comparison group (Chang et al., 2016; International Schizophrenia Consortium, 2008). Finally, there is evidence for epigenetic processes (Braff & Tamminga, 2016). Roth and Sweatt (2011) reported as many as 100 relevant gene locations showing epigenetic change, that is, altered methylation. As they speculate, epigenetic changes initiated in early prenatal or postnatal life could predispose the development of schizophrenia.

The involvement of several genes and several processes creates a complex etiological picture, but genetic influences may not tell the entire story. The fact that so many identical cotwins of adults with schizophrenia do not have schizophrenia suggests that non-genetic influences likely play some role. Twin studies indicate small but significant shared environmental influences, which could include early exposure to toxins, infections, and prenatal stress and other influences (Cattane, Richetto, & Cattaneo, 2018). Some environmental effects may operate independently of genetic influence; for example, perhaps some prenatal factors directly affect the brain. Other environmental effects likely act in conjunction with genes, such as in epigenetic effects and gene–environment interactions.

Prenatal Factors and Pregnancy Complications

Prenatal adversities have been associated with child and adult schizophrenia. Among these are prenatal malnutrition, maternal stress, and infections during pregnancy (Cattane et al., 2018). The association of prenatal malnutrition and schizophrenia has been demonstrated by ecological studies examining times of famine. Famines in Holland and China, for example, increased the risk of schizophrenia in individuals conceived or in early gestation during the times of extreme scarcity of food (Boks et al., 2018; Wang & Zhang, 2017). Epidemiological studies have demonstrated that exposure to bacterial, viral, or parasitic infection during fetal development is associated with increased risk for schizophrenia, as well as other neurodevelopmental disorders, such as ASD (Brown, 2012; Brown & Derkits, 2010; Fuglewicz, Piotrowski, & Stodolak, 2017). Interesting results came from a study of Finnish women who had been exposed in pregnancy to influenza virus during an epidemic (Mednick et al., 1988). Children whose mothers had been exposed during the second trimester of pregnancy had a greater risk for eventually developing schizophrenia. Some additional studies have replicated risk from influenza, whereas others have found insufficient evidence (Selten & Termorshuizen, 2017).

Numerous complications of pregnancy and birth have been associated with schizophrenia, for example, bleeding during pregnancy and emergency cesarean birth (Asarnow & Kernan, 2008; Brown et al., 2005). In fact, birth complications, particularly those in which the infant is deprived of oxygen (fetal hypoxia), have shown a stronger association with schizophrenia relative to other environmental factors (Cannon & Rosso, 2002). Moreover, fetal hypoxia has been associated with structural brain abnormalities consistent with schizophrenia, including reduced gray matter and enlarged ventricles (Jenkins, 2013). Nonetheless, it is difficult to draw firm conclusions from these findings. Obstetrical complications may cause schizophrenia, but complications could also result from fetuses already abnormal due to genetic or prenatal factors. The interaction of genetic and obstetric factors must also be considered. Indeed, evidence exists that serious prenatal adversities and obstetric complications may interact with neurobiological development and specific genes via epigenetic mechanisms to affect the risk of schizophrenia (Cattane et al., 2018).

Psychosocial Influences

There is reason to believe that psychosocial stress could contribute to schizophrenia in youth. For adult-onset schizophrenia, trauma and other adverse life events (stress) occurring during childhood or adulthood have been associated with schizophrenia (Beards et al., 2013; Belbasis et al., 2018; Stilo & Murray, 2019; Varese et al., 2012). Stress has been found to occur prior to symptom onset for some individuals with schizophrenia, particularly those of low socioeconomic status (Gallagher, Jones, & Pardes, 2016), and psychosocial stress also has been linked to worsening of symptoms (Docherty et al., 2008). Increased stress hormones, in particular cortisol, has been of interest in the study of schizophrenia and has been related to psychotic symptoms (Labad, 2019), affective symptoms (Corcoran et al., 2012), and cognitive impairment associated with schizophrenia (Aas et al., 2019; Cherian, Schatzberg, & Keller, 2019). In addition, in a study of at-risk adolescents, those who went on to develop schizophrenia had a more dramatic increase in cortisol compared to those who did not develop the disorder (Walker et al., 2010). Other studies have shown mixed findings with regard to the link between cortisol and schizophrenia (Bolhuis et al., 2019).

Family characteristics have long been suspected of causing schizophrenia. Indeed, the phrase "schizophrenogenic mothering" was once used to capture the idea that pathological parenting was the basic cause of the condition. Although that hypothesis currently is given no credence, there has been vacillating interest in the role of family interaction. Limited research with adoptees has implicated family processes. The possible influence of family climate has come from data collected as part of the Finnish Adoption Study, which examined adopted children of mothers with schizophrenia or related disorders and a comparison adopted group whose mothers had no such diagnoses (Tienari et al., 1990; Tienari, Wynne, & Wahlberg, 2006). Ratings of the functioning of the adoptive families permitted analysis of the rearing environment. The findings indicated that the genetically at-risk adoptees who later developed schizophrenia and related disorders had been reared in families with disturbed relationships. Also suggested was that low genetic risk served as protection against negative family climate, thereby implicating gene–environment interaction.

Neurodevelopmental Model

As noted previously, present knowledge about schizophrenia has led to the proposal that etiology involves multiple factors. A vulnerability-stress model is often invoked as a general framework. It assumes that an organismic vulnerability, probably genetic but possibly prenatal, interacts with environmental stress to produce somewhat different developmental paths and outcomes. Some individuals reach a threshold to exhibit diagnosable schizophrenic symptoms or similar but less severe symptoms, whereas others do not.

The last few decades have seen growing interest in and support for the neurodevelopmental model of schizophrenia (Haut et al., 2016; Rapoport et al., 2012; Weinberger, 2017). Indeed, much of the research we examined supports such a perspective. According to this model, schizophrenia is the result of abnormal neurodevelopmental processes that start well before the onset of the disorder (Figure 13.10). In effect, early development of the brain goes awry, affecting critical brain development and circuitry. In individuals later diagnosed with schizophrenia, early development is marked by premorbid difficulties, such as motor and language problems, and increased difficulties occur in cognitive, social, and psychological function. In most cases of schizophrenia, the core psychotic symptoms are manifested when the brain further matures in adolescence or early adulthood. Investigators have pointed to numerous changes occurring in the hormonal and brain systems during adolescence that could "enable" expression of the disorder (Haut et al., 2016; Woodberry et al., 2019). Of particular interest is that late adolescence is an important time for selective pruning of the synapses in the frontal lobes and association areas. It is hypothesized that excessive

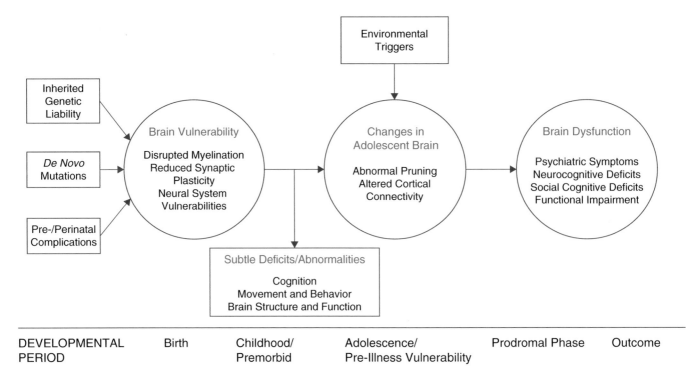

Figure 13.10 A neurodevelopmental model of schizophrenia. (Adapted from Haut et al., 2016)

pruning at this time is related to the appearance of symptoms, however neurodevelopmental processes are likely interrupted early in brain development (Birnbaum & Weinberger, 2017). Although brain changes are viewed as biological, it is well established that social environmental influences interact with biological factors to produce development.

The neurodevelopmental picture of schizophrenia is quite complex. The "normal" trajectory of development may be subtly altered by various genetic risk variants for schizophrenia that may be influenced by environmental risk factors and epigenetic processes resulting in the wide range of symptoms and associated features of the disorder (Birnbaum & Weinberger, 2017). The exact way or extent to which the neurodevelopmental model applies to childhood schizophrenia is unclear. As we have seen, numerous similarities between early-onset and late-onset schizophrenia strongly suggest that they are not different disorders. However, there is evidence that COS involves more severe symptoms, less favorable outcome, and greater family vulnerability. This suggests that greater genetic liability or greater biological vulnerability, perhaps combined with greater environmental adversity, may produce the disorder so early in life.

Assessment

The following categories can serve as a guide for comprehensive assessment for suspected child or adolescent schizophrenia (Driver et al., 2020; Hollis, 2015; Knorr, 2017; Woodberry et al., 2019).

- Historical information, including data on pregnancy complications, early development, age of onset, course of symptoms, and medical and family history.
- Assessment for the positive and negative symptoms of schizophrenia and associated features.
- Psychological assessment that includes evaluation of intelligence, communication, and adaptive skills.
- Physical examination, as well as EEGs, brain scans, and laboratory tests, as needed in some cases.
- Consultation with the school and social services as necessary.

Although early identification can facilitate appropriate treatment, it presents particular challenges for accurate diagnosis. The early-occurring nonpsychotic behavioral maladjustments of schizophrenia are observed in other disorders as well. In addition, hallucinations can present in children with various disorders and disturbances—such as bipolar disorder, major depression, posttraumatic responses, and sleep disturbance (Jardri et al., 2014; Sharma & McClellan, 2019). Indeed, children with schizophrenia may initially receive diagnoses of mood disorders, anxiety disorders, PTSD, and other neurodevelopmental disorders, such as ASD and ADHD, prior to the onset or diagnosis of schizophrenia or may experience co-occurring syndromes (Sharma & McClellan, 2019).

As previously noted, assessment is further challenged by difficulties identifying and distinguishing the positive symptoms of schizophrenia in children. Standardized rating scales and semi-structured interviews can be helpful. Nevertheless, children in nonclinic and clinic populations report seeing ghosts or shapes, hearing voices, and the like—and such hallucinations often do not indicate psychosis (Garralda, 2017). They may be the transient result of exhaustion, fever, or medications, for example. Similarly, it can be difficult to tell whether bizarre ideas, obsessions, and preoccupations reported by young people should be considered psychotic delusions. This is especially true in children younger than 5 or 6, who are still limited in thinking logically and in distinguishing reality from fantasy (Volkmar, 2001). In addition, assessment of thought disorder has been especially difficult. It can be affected by a child's language skills, which are crucial in evaluating thinking processes (Hollis, 2015). Moreover, what is considered abnormal thinking varies with developmental level.

Assessment of adolescents, especially older adolescents, is less problematic than that of children. Psychotic symptoms appear more similar to those of adult-onset schizophrenia, although they do not always indicate full-blown schizophrenia and a high rate of psychotic symptoms occur in adolescent-onset major depression and mania, making differential diagnosis complex (Hollis, 2015). Psychotic symptoms at this time of life can be associated with several other disorders, as well, including substance abuse, epilepsy, and endocrine disorders, for example (Woodberry et al., 2019). Thus, manifestations of psychosis must be interpreted within the broader clinical presentation.

Prevention

Although considerable interest exists in prevention, limited knowledge about etiology hinders progress. The association of schizophrenia with prenatal and birth complications suggests the advisability of special care during pregnancy, especially in high-risk families (Seidman & Nordentoft, 2015). Similarly, increased sensitivity to early developmental and cognitive deficits, poor social and emotional functioning, and behavior problems with the approach of adolescence may be helpful in early identification (Laurens & Cullen, 2016).

Early identification and treatment generally are associated with improved outcome for schizophrenia, and the insidious onset that occurs in many youth presents a window of opportunity for preventive efforts. Currently, there is considerable interest in recognizing a "risk syndrome" for individuals who appear to be at very high risk and are displaying attenuated symptoms (Yung et al., 2019). Persons so identified have been shown to develop the onset of psychosis at higher rates than the general population. Nonetheless, identifying young people, especially very young children, who are at risk for transition into psychosis has been criticized. Many of the early problems of youth who eventually are diagnosed with schizophrenia are evident in other young people. Further, even adolescents and adults whose symptoms put them

at very high risk often show remission and/or do not eventually progress to full-blown schizophrenia (McGorry, Killackey, & Yung, 2008; Ziermans et al., 2011). Despite this dilemma—and the peril of stigmatizing or medicating youth who are falsely identified—some investigations are committed to early intervention. In the words of McGorry and colleagues, "Withholding treatment until severe and less reversible symptomatic and functional impairment have become entrenched represents a failure of care" (McGorry et al., 2008, p. 148). Early intervention aims to delay, attenuate, or even prevent schizophrenia.

Intervention

As with other aspects of early-occurring schizophrenia, a great deal must be generalized from what is known about treatment of adults. Treatment can vary substantially, depending on the severity of the case, whether the case is in an acute or a chronic phase, available opportunities for intervention, and community/family support. Children and adolescents with the disorder may live at home and attend local schools, some with severe disturbance may remain at home and may attend special schools or may be placed in hospitals and other residential settings for periods of time. As a result, coordinated care across settings is important (Woodberry et al., 2019). It is believed that the best treatment strategy employs multiple methods, combining pharmacological treatment and psychosocial interventions, to alleviate the multiple problems frequently encountered by individuals with schizophrenia and their families (Sharma & McClellan, 2019).

Pharmacological Treatment

Traditional antipsychotic and second-generation antipsychotic agents are central in treating schizophrenia (McClellan & Stock, 2013). In adults and youth, they can alleviate hallucinations, delusions, thought disturbance, and other symptoms—although not all individuals respond to antipsychotic medications (Pagsberg et al., 2017; Sharma & McClellan, 2019). Second-generation antipsychotic medications (e.g., risperidone, clozapine, olanzapine) are widely used as they have fewer side effects. But these medications do have some adverse side effects, which may impact young people more than adults (Correll et al., 2009). Among these are weight gain, sedation, constipation, and elevated cholesterol and triglyceride levels. Clozapine, which appears especially effective for children and adolescents, carries greater risk for serious adverse side effects, including seizures and reduction in white blood cells important in immune function, and thus warrants cautious use (Gee & Taylor, 2018; Sharma & McClellan, 2019). In addition to some medications being somewhat risky in themselves, adverse side effects may lead young people to discontinue treatment (Stafford et al., 2015), which is associated with poorer outcomes. Moreover, the long-term impacts of pharmacological intervention on neurodevelopment and physical health remain uncertain. Thus, decisions with regard to pharmacological intervention must consider both potential short- and long-term risks and benefits as well as risks associated with untreated or undertreated psychiatric symptoms (Woodberry et al., 2019).

Psychosocial Intervention

Medications largely aim at reducing psychotic symptoms, whereas psychosocial treatment encompasses broader objectives. Among the approaches that are ameliorative or most promising are skills training, CBT, cognitive remediation and family approaches (McClellan & Stock, 2013; Woodberry et al., 2019).

The goal of skills training is to increase social and daily living skills through instruction, modeling, positive reinforcement, and other behavioral techniques. CBT recognizes that the symptoms of schizophrenia—particularly hallucinations and delusions—interfere with social functioning and aims to temper these symptoms or facilitate coping with them. Family therapy is an accepted strategy for adults that is likely to be critical for youth. Today's family interventions are fueled by a collaborative philosophy in which blame is not placed on families, as it sometimes was in the past. Family psychoeducation incorporates the individual with schizophrenia's family members and other caregivers into ongoing cognitive, behavioral, and supportive therapeutic and rehabilitative intervention and has been shown to be effective in reducing relapse rates and improving functioning and family well-being (McFarlane, 2016; Substance Abuse and Mental Health Services Administration, 2009). Table 13.5 indicates some of the major components of family psychoeducation.

Over the last two decades there has been an increase in approaches to treating cognitive deficits that commonly occur in schizophrenia, such as deficits in memory, attention, executive functioning, social cognition, reasoning, and problem solving (Revell et al., 2015). Computer-based programs are frequently employed to enhance cognition and are encouraging. Social cognition training, which seeks to improve the perception and understanding of the social world (e.g., of emotion and theory of mind), also shows promise as a supplement to computer-assisted cognitive remediation (Fisher et al., 2017; Lindenmayer et al., 2018).

Table 13.5 Major Components of Family Psychoeducation for Schizophrenia

Education about schizophrenia (e.g., symptoms, causal hypotheses, course, treatments)
Guidance and skills training to help manage stress and better cope with schizophrenia
Training in family communication emphasizing partnership in treatment process
Training in structured problem solving to better manage and address current issues
Social and emotion support to validate experience and facilitate problem solving
Crisis intervention and planning during severe stress and/or signs of relapse of the disorder

Sources: Based on Substance Abuse and Mental Health Services Administration, 2009; Woodberry, Kline, & Giuliano, 2019.

A comprehensive approach and a supportive environment are recommended for treating schizophrenia (McClellan & Stock, 2013; Sharma & McClellan, 2019). For young people, disruption of normal development must be addressed (Woodberry et al., 2019). Thus, treatment must include not only the reduction of specific symptoms but also the facilitation of psychological, social, educational, and occupational development. Since youth with schizophrenia may require relatively intensive home, community, and school-based services, early identification, intervention, and coordinated specialty care with intensive support and case management is beneficial (McFarlane et al., 2014).

And as with other aspects of early-onset schizophrenia, the importance of research in advancing knowledge about the effectiveness of intervention can hardly be overstated. Fortunately, more emphasis is being given to expanding early recognition and treatment of young people at risk for schizophrenia or to intervening during early stages of the disorder. Schizophrenia is now viewed as more similar to other chronic conditions, and evidence-based care and multimodal treatment have been promoted (Woodberry et al., 2019). The previous pessimistic focus on long-term disability has shifted to a more hopeful emphasis on recovery.

Looking Back

A Bit of History

- Today, autism spectrum disorder and schizophrenia of youth are viewed as distinct categories of disturbance but were historically associated with each other.
- Autism, Asperger's disorder, childhood disintegrative disorder, and pervasive developmental disorder not otherwise specified, once considered as distinct, are now viewed together as a continuum of symptoms comprising autism spectrum disorder.

Autism Spectrum Disorder (ASD)

- The core manifestations of ASD are persistent deficits in social communication and interaction and restricted, repetitive patterns of behaviors, interests, and activities. Secondary features involve perception, intelligence, adaptive behavior, cognition, MPAs, and motor skills.
- Considerable research has been devoted to ToM, central coherence, and executive functions.
- Co-occurrence of ASD, with or without intellectual disabilities, and other disorders is high and includes anxiety, depression, ADHD, and oppositional defiant behaviors.
- The prevalence of ASD has greatly increased in recent years. Methodological and social factors may at least partly account for increases. Prevalence is higher in boys and is unrelated to social class.
- ASD symptoms are often recognized by age 2. Different patterns of onset and developmental pathways have been reported. From childhood onward, symptoms can lessen, but perhaps only 20% of youth with autism achieve independent living.
- Neurobiological research suggests that ASD involves impairment in multiple brain areas or networks. Altered brain growth often is observed, and most implicated are the frontal lobe, temporal lobe–limbic system, and the cerebellum.
- The evidence for genetic influence is substantial and prenatal/birth complications may play some causal role. Faja and Dawson's developmental perspective gives importance to child–environment interactions. Research does not support a causal role for vaccines or thimerosal.

- Assessment for ASD must be broad based. Several valid instruments exist for the assessment of ASD symptoms.
- Early identification/intervention is critical in preventing maladaptive pathways to ASD. Behavioral and educational interventions are the mainstay of treatment and prevention, with medication as an adjunct. ASD falls under the mandates of the IDEA.

Schizophrenia

- The hallmarks of schizophrenia are hallucinations, delusions, disorganized symptoms, and negative symptoms. Secondary features include MPAs, impaired communication and cognition, motor abnormalities, and social dysfunction.
- The prevalence of schizophrenia is low in childhood and escalates in adolescence. Rates appear higher in males during childhood but the gender difference may flatten in adolescence.
- The onset of child schizophrenia often is insidious, with nonpsychotic symptoms appearing prior to psychotic symptoms. The course of schizophrenia can vary, but good outcome occurs only in 20% of cases of child- and adolescent-onset schizophrenia. Childhood schizophrenia is viewed as a severe form of the disorder.
- Neurobiological abnormalities in schizophrenia are evidenced in several ways. Frontal and temporal–limbic circuits and dopamine are especially implicated, and the disorder likely involves several regions, several neurotransmitters, and brain connectivity.
- Complex genetic influences, prenatal/birth variables, and psychosocial factors are causally implicated in schizophrenia. These multiple susceptibility factors are incorporated into neurodevelopmental models of the disorder.
- Comprehensive assessment is required for schizophrenia. It can be problematic to identify psychotic symptoms in children.
- Prevention is challenging and emphasis is on early intervention. A multimethod, supportive treatment approach is recommended, which includes pharmacological and psychosocial treatments such as CBT, social skills training, and family interventions.

Key Terms

joint attention *334*

echolalia *335*

pronoun reversal *335*

overselectivity *337*

splinter skills/savant abilities *337*

theory of mind *338*

central coherence *339*

intersubjectivity *340*

positive symptoms *356*

hallucinations *356*

delusions *356*

disorganized speech *356*

disorganized behavior *356*

catatonic behavior *356*

negative symptoms *356*

insidious onset *359*

CHAPTER 14
Disorders of Basic Physical Functions

Looking Forward

After reading this chapter, you should be able to discuss:

- Classification of the elimination disorders of enuresis and encopresis
- Etiology of elimination disorders and their treatment
- Common sleep problems and the description and classification of sleep disorders
- Treatment of sleep problems
- Early feeding and eating problems and disorders

- Influences on the development of and interventions for obesity
- The definition and classification of eating disorders
- The epidemiology and developmental course of eating disorders
- Biological, psychosocial, and cultural influences on the development of eating disorders
- Treatment and prevention of eating-disordered behavior

In this chapter and the next we discuss problems of physical functioning and health. Because in many ways these problems represent the interface between psychology and pediatrics, the term *pediatric psychology* is often applied to this field of research and practice. For many of the problems discussed (e.g., toilet training, sleep difficulties), parents first turn to their pediatrician for help. Some problems may require collaboration between psychologists and physicians. The life-threatening starvation of adolescents with anorexia nervosa and the problem of enlarged colons in children with encopresis are two examples.

It is common for children to exhibit some difficulty in acquiring appropriate habits of elimination, sleep, and eating. Both the child's ability to master these relevant tasks and the parents' ability to assist the child in developing skills are important to the immediate well-being of both. Parents may be judged, by themselves and others, based on how they manage these early child-rearing tasks. Also, how these tasks are handled can set the foundation for later interactions. Although parents solve many early difficulties themselves, they also frequently seek professional assistance. This chapter examines some commonly encountered difficulties that are part of normal development. The principal focus, however, is on problems that are serious enough to be of clinical concern.

Problems of Elimination

Typical Elimination Training

Toilet training is an important concern for parents of young children. Parents may view control of elimination as a developmental milestone for the child. Furthermore, entry into day care or another program may depend on achievement of appropriate toileting. For the child, pleasing the parent, a sense of mastery, and the feeling of no longer being a "baby" may all contribute to the importance of achieving toileting control.

The usual sequence of acquisition of control over elimination is nighttime bowel control, daytime bowel control, daytime bladder control, and finally, nighttime bladder control. Although there is considerable variation as to when children are developmentally ready to achieve control over elimination, bowel and daytime bladder training usually are completed between the ages of 18 and 36 months.

Parents differ on when they feel it is appropriate to begin daytime training. Much of this decision is related to cultural values, attitudes, and real-life pressures on the parent (e.g., day care requirements, other siblings). An example of how day-to-day considerations probably affect this decision is illustrated by the advent of the disposable diaper. Ready availability of disposable diapers reduced many parents' inclinations to start training early.

There are probably several factors that contribute to successful training. Being able to determine that the child is developmentally ready to begin training is certainly important. Among other factors that are likely to contribute to successful toilet training are the child's ability to cooperate and communicate with the parent. This is an important aspect of readiness. Adequate preparation, a stimulus-free environment (e.g., bathroom), and having a child-size potty seat available are also helpful. Finally, the common practice of providing praise and concrete positive reinforcers (e.g., stickers, raisins) for appropriate toileting behavior, and doing so in a relaxed manner, has been demonstrated to be an important component of effective toilet training (Schroeder & Smith-Boydston, 2017).

Enuresis

Description and Classification

The term **enuresis** comes from the Greek word meaning "I make water." It refers to the repeated voiding of urine during the day or night into the bed or clothes when such voiding is not due to a physical disorder (e.g., diabetes, urinary tract infection). A certain frequency of lack of control is required before the diagnosis of enuresis would be made, and the frequency employed typically varies with the age of the child. The DSM definition requires that wetting occur at least twice weekly for at least three consecutive months. The diagnosis of enuresis may also be made when wetting is less frequent if wetting is associated with clinically significant distress or impairment in important areas of functioning. A lack of urinary control is not usually diagnosed as enuresis prior to age 5 (or the equivalent developmental level). The age/developmental level of 5 years is selected, as this is when continence might be expected (American Psychiatric Association, 2013).

A distinction is typically made between the more common nighttime bedwetting and daytime wetting. Enuresis is also referred to as **primary** if the child has never demonstrated bladder control and as **secondary** when the problem is preceded by a period of urinary continence. About 85% of all cases of enuresis are of the nighttime wetting alone/primary type (Mellon & Houts, 2017).

Epidemiology

Estimates of prevalence indicate that about 10% of school-age children exhibit enuresis. Prevalence at 6 years of age is about 15%, declines steadily with age, and by age 18 prevalence decreases to 1% for males and less than 1% for females. The problem is at least twice as common among boys compared to girls (Mellon & Houts, 2017; Shepard & Cox, 2017).

Etiology

A number of factors have been proposed as causes of enuresis. At one time, enuresis was widely believed to be the result of emotional disturbance (Gerard, 1939). However, evidence does not support the view that enuresis is primarily a psychopathological disorder. When emotional difficulties are present in a child with enuresis, they most commonly are a consequence of enuresis rather than a cause (Shepard & Cox, 2017). Parents of children with combined nighttime and daytime wetting may be particularly likely to report psychological problems in their children (Van Hoecke et al., 2006). Children with enuresis, especially as they become older, are very likely to experience difficulties with peers and family members. Also, enuresis and emotional problems may occur together because similar factors (e.g., a chaotic home environment) contribute to the development of both.

A maturational delay in the ability to recognize the sensation of a full bladder while asleep is the most common explanation for the development of enuresis. Other explanations are also sometimes offered (Shepard & Cox, 2017).

It is sometimes suggested that sleep abnormalities contribute to the development of enuresis. Many adults, for example, assume that nocturnal enuresis occurs because the child is an unusually

JAY Enuresis and Its Consequences

Jay, a 7-year-old, had never achieved nighttime continence but had been continent during daytime for several years. He wets his bed an average of four days per week. No other significant behavior problems are present except for mild academic difficulties, and Jay's developmental history is unremarkable except for mild oxygen deprivation at birth and a delay in acquiring speech. Jay's biological father wet the bed until age 9.

Jay's mother and stepfather disagree on how they view his bedwetting. His mother feels he will grow out of it. His stepfather views Jay's bedwetting as laziness and removes privileges following episodes of enuresis. Both parents change the sheets when they are wet and attempt to restrict Jay's fluids prior to bedtime. They see the enuresis as a significant source of distress for the family and the conflict over how to handle it as exacerbating the problem.

Adapted from Ondersma & Walker, 1998, pp. 364–365

deep sleeper. Indeed, parents of children with enuresis often spontaneously report difficulty in arousing their child during the night. However, research regarding the role of sleep and arousal is inconsistent. Wetting can occur in any of the stages of sleep, not just in deep sleep. This and other evidence raises doubts about viewing all or most cases of enuresis as a disorder of sleep arousal. However, in some subgroups of youth, enuresis may, at least in part, be due to sleep arousal patterns.

Another biological pathway that has been suggested is reduced bladder capacity or higher production of urine due to a lack of normal nocturnal increases in antidiuretic hormone (ADH). Among evidence for this hypothesis is the fact that some children with enuresis respond well to an antidiuretic medication (desmopressin acetate, a hormone analog). However, evidence is not consistent and does not support low levels of ADH as the only or the primary cause of enuresis, although it may be a factor in some cases.

Family histories of youth with enuresis frequently reveal a number of relatives with the same problem. Higher rates of concordance for enuresis also have been reported among monozygotic than dizygotic twins, and multigenerational studies further support the notion of a significant genetic contribution to the disorder.

Overall, information regarding biological influences strongly suggests that at least some children with enuresis have an organic predisposition (Sethi, Bhargava, & Phil, 2005). This predisposition may or may not result in the development of enuresis, depending on various experiential factors, such as parental attitude and training procedures.

The central tenet of behavioral theories of enuresis is that wetting results from a failure to learn control over reflexive wetting. Failure can result from either faulty training or other environmental influences that interfere with learning (e.g., a chaotic or stressful home environment). Most behavioral theories incorporate some maturational delay/physical difficulty, such as bladder capacity or arousal deficit, into their explanation.

Treatment

Prior to beginning any treatment, the child should be evaluated by a physician to rule out any medical cause for the urinary difficulties. If a parent seeks treatment for a very young child, a discussion of developmental norms may be helpful. Finally, if treatment for enuresis is to be initiated, careful preparation and parental cooperation are necessary.

A variety of pharmacological agents have been used in the treatment of enuresis. Desmopressin acetate (DDAVP) has become the primary pharmacological treatment for enuresis, in part because it may have a lower risk of side effects than other pharmacological agents. Desmopressin was suggested as a treatment on the basis of its ability to control high urine output during sleep. Research findings suggest that DDAVP may reduce bedwetting even in cases that are difficult to treat. However,

relapse occurs; that is, wetting resumes if the drug is discontinued (Schroeder & Smith-Boydston, 2017; Shepard & Cox, 2017).

Behavioral treatments for nocturnal enuresis have received considerable research attention (Shepard, Poler, & Grabman, 2017). The most well-known method is the urine-alarm system. This procedure was originally introduced by the German pediatrician Pflaunder in 1904 and was adapted and systematically applied by Mowrer and Mowrer (1938). Since then, the device and the procedures have been refined by a number of investigators. The basic device consists of an absorbent sheet between two foil pads. When the sheet absorbs urine, an electric circuit is completed which activates an alarm that sounds until it is manually turned off (see Figure 14.1). The parents are instructed to awaken the child when the alarm sounds. The child is taught to turn off the alarm and to go to the bathroom to finish voiding. The bedding is then changed, and the child returns to sleep. Usually the family keeps records of dry and wet nights, and after 14 consecutive nights of dryness, the device is removed.

Research conducted on treatments using the urine-alarm system indicates that it is successful in a clear majority of cases. Indeed, research findings indicate that the urine-alarm is an essential component of successful enuresis treatment (Shepard

Figure 14.1 A urine alarm for treatment of enuresis. The child wears a urine sensor in the underclothes attached to an alarm worn on the nightclothes or wrist.

et al., 2017). However, relapse rates as high as 40% of cases were reported (Mellon & Houts, 2017).

Thus, modifications of the standard urine-alarm procedures have been introduced to reduce relapses. Full Spectrum Home Training was designed to build on initial treatment success, to reduce relapse, and to decrease the rate at which families dropped out of treatment (Mellon & Houts, 2017). The procedure, which is cost-effective, is a treatment manual-guided package that includes a urine-alarm system; cleanliness training (having the child change his or her own bed and night clothes); a procedure to increase bladder capacity, which is known as retention control training; and overlearning, a process of training children to a higher criterion of successive dry nights. The family is provided with material including a treatment manual to follow. With the guidance of a trainer, the parents and child contract to complete the training at home with regular support from the treatment staff. Typically, treatment is completed in a 16–20-week period. This is followed by an overlearning segment. During this segment, the child consumes increasing amounts of water prior to bedtime and treatment continues until an additional 14 dry nights are achieved.

A study by Houts, Peterson, and Whelan (1986) illustrated the program's success and examined the contribution of the components to reducing relapse. Participating families received one of three treatment combinations: Group 1 received the urine-alarm system plus cleanliness training (BP), Group 2 received these two components plus retention control training (BP-RCT), and Group 3 received these three components plus overlearning (BP-RCT-OL)—the full package. A control group of children was followed over an eight-week period. No spontaneous remission of wetting occurred in control children, and they were then randomly assigned to one of the three treatment conditions. The findings of this study indicate that the three conditions were equally effective in treating enuresis. However, at a three-month follow-up, relapse was significantly less in the BP-RCT-OL group than in the other two groups. These results and others suggest the importance of overlearning in preventing relapse. With overlearning included, relapse rates of only 10% are reported (Mellon & Houts, 2017).

While multi-component behavioral treatments for enuresis have proven highly successful, some challenges remain (Mellon & Houts, 2017; Shepard et al., 2017). Improvements are needed for working with families with additional challenges (e.g., single-parent families, high rates of marital discord, children with additional problems). Also, assuring better dissemination of these treatment approaches and increased use in primary care settings remain an ongoing goal.

Encopresis

Description and Classification
Functional **encopresis** refers to the passage of feces into the clothing or other unacceptable area when this is not due to physical disorder. The diagnosis is given when this event occurs at least once a month, for at least three months, in a child of at least 4 years of age or the equivalent developmental level (American Psychiatric Association, 2013). Two subtypes of encopresis are recognized on the basis of the presence or absence of constipation. The vast majority of children with encopresis are chronically constipated and are classified as having constipation with overflow incontinence (or retentive encopresis).

Epidemiology
Estimates of the prevalence of encopresis range between 1.5 and 7.5% of children. Percentages appear to decrease with age, and the condition is very rare by adolescence. The problem occurs more frequently in males (Mellon & Houts, 2017; Shepard & Cox, 2017).

Pediatricians, who are likely to see a broad population of children, argue that the majority of children with encopresis have no associated psychopathology, a position supported by other professionals. However, encopresis occurs during the day more often than at night and thus it is more socially evident than enuresis and also is more likely to carry a social stigma. Consequently, encopresis is likely to be a source of considerable

SUSAN Encopresis and Its Consequences

Susan, a 6-year-old, had been soiling at least once per day since birth. The frequency of soiling had not decreased despite nearly constant attempts to convince her to use the toilet. Following careful medical examination, Susan's physician was certain that all medical causes for her condition had been ruled out. Tests, however, did reveal a considerable amount of fecal matter in her colon. During the course of the assessment, Susan's mother indicated that both she and her daughter were becoming very frustrated. It was also revealed that Susan was experiencing significant anxiety and pain with toileting. It appeared that Susan had learned to retain feces and to fear toileting following early experiences with large and painful bowel movements. The toileting problems had begun to affect Susan's social functioning and self-esteem.

Adapted from Ondersma & Walker, 1998, pp. 371–372

distress to both parents and children, and may therefore be associated with more behavior problems (Shepard & Cox, 2017). For example, children with encopresis who had been referred to a pediatric gastroenterology clinic were reported to have more behavior problems and lower social competence scores than children without toileting problems (Young et al., 1996). Following treatment, these children had fewer problems and improved social skills. To the extent that associated psychological difficulties do exist, they may be a consequence, rather than an antecedent, of encopresis, or both may be related to common environmental factors (e.g., stressful family circumstances).

Etiology

Most theories acknowledge that encopresis may result from a variety of causative mechanisms (Butler, 2008; Mellon & Houts, 2017; Reiner, 2008; Shepard & Cox, 2017). Initial constipation and soiling may be influenced by factors such as diet, fluid intake, medications, environmental stresses, or inappropriate toilet training. Constipation may lead to painful defecation and stool withholding. The hard feces may distend the rectum and colon. The bowel then becomes incapable of responding with a normal defecation reflex to normal amounts of fecal matter.

Medical perspectives on the problem tend to stress a neurodevelopmental approach (Butler, 2008; Reiner, 2008). Encopresis is viewed as more likely to occur in the presence of developmental inadequacies in the structure and functioning of the physiological and anatomical mechanisms required for bowel control. These organic inadequacies are viewed as temporary.

A behavioral perspective on encopresis stresses faulty toilet training procedures. Poor dietary choices may combine with the failure to apply appropriate training methods consistently. Some cases of encopresis may also be accounted for by avoidance conditioning principles. Retention is reinforced by avoidance of pain or fear. Positive consequences may also maintain soiling, and inadequate reinforcement may be given for appropriate toileting. These various learning explanations are not incompatible with physiological explanations. For example, poor toilet training may compound insufficient physiological–neurological mechanisms.

Treatment

Most treatments for encopresis combine medical and behavioral management (Mellon & Houts, 2017; Shepard & Cox, 2017). After the parent and the child have been educated about encopresis, the first step usually consists of an initial cleanout phase using enemas or high fiber intake to eliminate fecal impactions. Next, parents are asked to schedule regular toilet times and to use suppositories if defecation does not occur. Modifications in fluid intake, diet, laxatives, and stool softeners are employed to facilitate defecation. Positive consequences, such as stickers and/or a shared activity chosen by the child, are used to reward progress (e.g., unassisted–no suppository bowel movements in the

toilet, clean pants). If soiling occurs, children may be instructed to clean themselves and their clothes. Later in the course of training, laxatives and suppositories are withdrawn. While interventions are not as well established as for enuresis, research suggests that such treatment is effective and that relapse rates are low (Mellon & Houts, 2017; Shepard & Cox, 2017). An internet version of one such program, Enhanced Toilet Training (ETT), has been developed so as to improve accessibility and reduce cost. This internet version of ETT has been shown to be effective (Ritterband et al., 2013).

Sleep Problems

Sleep is essential to human development and functioning. By the age of 18 years young people have spent about 40% of their lives sleeping (Mindell & Owens, 2015). Many typically developing children have sleep problems. Parents commonly complain of difficulties in getting their young children to go to sleep and to sleep through the night. Nightmares are another concern that parents often report. Insufficient sleep is common across development and particularly during adolescence (Owens & Adolescent Sleep Working Group, 2014). To understand these problems, as well as more serious sleep disorders, it is necessary to understand the variations in normal sleep for children.

Sleep Development

At all ages, there is considerable individual variability in a normal sleep pattern. Furthermore, patterns of sleep change with development (Alfano, Palmer, & Bower, 2018; Honaker, Meltzer, & Mindell, 2017). For example, the average newborn (ages 0–3 months) sleeps between 12 and 17 hours per day and the amount of time a child sleeps decreases over the course of development. The American Academy of Sleep Medicine has developed recommendations for the amount of sleep needed to promote optimal health for children and adolescents (Paruthi et al., 2016). These recommendations are presented in Table 14.1.

In addition to the number of hours of sleep, other aspects of sleep change with development as well. For example, newborns distribute their sleeping equally between day and night. Fortunately for parents, by about 3 months of age, infants have adopted the day–night pattern typical in adults, and by 18 months, sleep patterns are usually quite stable.

Within sleep periods there are two broad phases: **rapid eye movement (REM) sleep** and **nonrapid eye movement (NREM) sleep**. NREM sleep is divided into three stages (N1–N3). The third stage, the deepest part of sleep, is characterized by very slow waves in the EEG. Throughout the night, the brain cycles through

Table 14.1 Recommended Amount of Sleep per 24 Hours

Age Group	Recommended Amount of Sleep
Infants (4–12 months*)	12–16 hours (including naps)
Toddlers (1–2 years)	11–14 hours (including naps)
Preschoolers (3 to 5 years)	10–13 hours (including naps)
School-age children (6–12 years)	9–12 hours
Adolescents (13–18 years)	8–10 hours

* Recommendations for infants younger than 4 months are not made since there is a wide range of normal variations in sleep during this newborn period.

Source: Adapted from Paruthi et al., 2016.

these stages of sleep. The time spent in different stages of sleep varies and changes with development. In the first year of life, for example, active (REM) sleep changes from about eight hours to about half this amount, thus also reducing the proportion of time spent in REM relative to other phases of sleep. Thus, N3, slow-wave sleep, occupies about 25% to 30% of school-age children's sleep. The sequencing, or pattern in which the various stages of sleep occur, also changes. The phases of sleep are intermixed in an irregular pattern in infants. However, as the child develops, regular patterns of light NREM, deep NREM, and REM sleep are gradually established.

Common Sleep Problems

During the first year of life, parents' most frequent complaint is that the child does not sleep through the night. A reluctance to go to sleep and nightmares often occur during the second year, and 3- to 5-year-old children may present a variety of problems, including difficulty in going to sleep, nighttime awakenings, and nightmares. Sleep problems are common with 25–40% of typically developing children experiencing some type of sleep problem (Mindell & Owens, 2015). Differences in parents' expectations and tolerance levels may, in part, determine whether a "sleep problem" exists (Coulombe & Reid, 2012).

School-age children also experience a variety of sleep problems, including bedtime resistance, delayed sleep onset, and night waking (Blader et al., 1997; Sadeh, Raviv, & Gruber, 2000). Indeed, sleep problems in older children may be underestimated, because older children are less likely to alert their parents to their difficulties (Gregory, Rijsdijk, & Eley, 2006; Meltzer, 2017; Owens et al., 2000). Even in adolescence, complaints regarding sleep are common, particularly the need for more sleep and difficulty in falling asleep (Alfano et al., 2018; Dahl & Harvey, 2008). At this age, youth often experience decreasing amounts of sleep. This is likely the result of biological changes associated with this developmental period, but also due to cultural influences such as later bedtimes combined with earlier school start times. The greatest decrease in sleep duration appears to occur at the time

of transition into adolescence, and there is actually an increase in sleep time as adolescents transition out of high school. Insufficient sleep and night-to-night variability in sleep schedules may contribute to problems such as poor academic performance, anxiety, depression, and health difficulties (McMakin et al., 2019; Meltzer, 2017; Rigney et al., 2019).

Whether early sleep difficulties continue and/or develop into more serious sleep disorders is probably a function of a complex interplay of individual and environmental influences (Dauvilliers, Maret, & Tafti, 2005; El-Sheikh et al., 2006; Warren et al., 2006). Indeed, clear discrimination between common sleep difficulties and some sleep disorders is difficult. However, sleep problems that are frequent, persistent, and associated with other problems for the young person are considered sleep disorders. Sleep problems that do not cause the youth significant distress or do not result in impairment in important areas of functioning may not be considered a diagnosable disorder.

Sleep Disorders

There are many types of sleep disorders that are of concern to clinicians working with infants, children, and adolescents (Alfano et al., 2018; Honaker et al., 2017). DSM-5 includes multiple sleep disorders. The International Classification of Sleep Disorders (American Academy of Sleep Medicine (AASM), 2014) is the classification system more commonly employed by sleep researchers and professionals. The sleep disorders of primary concern are sometimes classified into two major groupings: difficulties in initiating and maintaining sleep or of excessive sleepiness and disorders of arousal, partial arousal, or sleep-stage transitions (**parasomnias**).

Difficulties Initiating or Maintaining Sleep

Problems of getting to sleep and sleeping through the night are common. If they are severe and chronic enough, they may fall into the category of an **insomnia disorder** (AASM, 2014). These sleep and waking problems are frequently viewed as manifestations of the child's neurophysiological development and therefore are

Insufficient sleep may contribute to poor academic performance and other problems. (Wavebreak Media ltd/Alamy Stock Photo)

expected eventually to resolve. However, child, parental, and environmental factors do play a role in a substantial number of cases. For example, when a parent rocks and soothes a young child to assist the child in falling asleep at night, the child may not learn to soothe her or himself or learn to return to sleep during a normal night waking. A comparison of poor sleepers and good sleepers between 12 and 36 months of age revealed some surprising findings (Minde et al., 1993). Mothers' sleep diaries indicated more night wakings for the poor sleepers. However, filmed recordings indicated no differences in the actual number of wakings for the two groups. The poor sleepers were unable or unwilling to go back to sleep and woke their parent. In contrast, good sleepers were able to return to sleep on their own either by looking around and falling asleep or by quieting themselves, for example, by hugging a toy animal or sucking their thumbs. Also, parental failure to provide bedtime routines and set limits may help maintain difficulties in falling asleep. Whatever the cause, these problems may persist over many years, and they can result in considerable distress to the children and families involved (Alfano et al., 2018; Chardon et al., 2018).

The presence of this type of sleep problem may be underestimated. Young children's reports of difficulty in getting to sleep or staying asleep may be mistaken for attention seeking or the young child's level of cognitive development may not allow them to recognize a sleep problem. Alternatively, a child may present with a variety of difficulties, and objective recording of sleep may reveal sleep problems that were not recognized by either the child or the parent (Sadeh et al., 2000). Sleep problems contribute to impairments in psychological, social, educational, or other areas of functioning. Yet the family may not be aware that sleep difficulties are contributing to these other problems and to parental distress.

Sleep problems may be related to other problems in a number of ways. One possible mechanism is that emotional difficulties lead to the development of sleep problems. For example, children's fear or worries may contribute to difficulties in falling and staying asleep. In older children, sleep problems may stem from worrisome cognitions—concerns about school or peers, ruminations about past or anticipated experiences, or fears. Alternatively, sleep problems may contribute to the development of emotional and behavioral difficulties (Bélanger et al., 2018; Mindell et al., 2017). Also, sleep difficulties are often described as part of the presentation of other disorders such as attention-deficit/hyperactivity disorder (ADHD), autism, depression, and anxiety (Alfano et al., 2018; Honaker et al., 2017). Medications prescribed for these various disorders may also contribute to sleep difficulties. Another reason that sleep difficulties and other problems may occur together is that they may share a common set of etiological mechanisms (e.g., difficult temperament, family discord, or parenting practices). Clearly the relationship between sleep and the development of psychopathology is likely to be complex and is, thus, the focus of ongoing investigation (Barrios et al., 2018; Marver & McGlinchey, 2020; Meltzer, 2017).

Sleep Arousal Disorders
Several of the childhood sleep disorders that cause concern for parents fall into the category of disorders of sleep arousal or parasomnias. This spectrum of related disorders includes

sleepwalking and sleep terrors and occur in about 3% of children (Mindell & Owens, 2015).

Sleepwalking An episode of **sleepwalking** (somnambulism) begins with the child's sitting upright in bed. The eyes are open but appear "unseeing." Usually the child leaves the bed and walks around, but the episode may end before the walking stage is reached. During the episode, the child may be non-responsive. For example, not answering or responding when her or his name is called. An episode may last for a few seconds or 30 minutes or longer. The child usually has no later memory of the episode. This failure to remember the sleepwalking episode may result in confusion or distress. The child may, for example, wake up in a different room of the house after going to sleep in his or her own room. Thus, children who are sleepwalkers may experience distress and concern about their sleep problem but be otherwise well adjusted—functioning well at school and with family and peers. It was once believed that the sleepwalking child was exceptionally well coordinated and safe. This belief has proven to be a myth, and physical injury is a danger of the disorder.

Approximately 15% or more of children have isolated experiences of walking in their sleep (Alfano et al., 2018; Mindell & Owens, 2015). Sleepwalking disorder, that is, persistent sleepwalking, is estimated to occur in 1 to 6% of the population. The problem may continue for a number of years but is likely to diminish in frequency with increasing age (American Psychiatric Association, 2013).

The vast majority of sleepwalking episodes occur in the first three hours following sleep onset. The fact that sleepwalking occurs during the later stages of NREM sleep (deep sleep) appears to invalidate the idea that sleepwalking is the acting out of a dream, because dreams occur in REM sleep. A characteristic EEG pattern has been found to precede each episode of sleepwalking. This EEG pattern exists in 85% of all children during the first year of life but is present in only 3% of 7- to 9-year-olds. Thus, it has been suggested that central nervous system immaturity is of significance in sleepwalking disorder, and knowledge that the disorder is usually outgrown is consistent with that conceptualization. This view does not, however, rule out psychological or environmental factors. Thus, reports indicate that the frequency of sleepwalking may be influenced by insufficient sleep, changes in sleep routines, the specific setting, and by stress and physical illness (Dahl & Harvey, 2008). There appears to be a strong genetic component to sleepwalking with many patients having a first degree relative with a history of parasomnias (Honaker et al., 2017).

Sleep Terrors Approximately 3% of children experience **sleep terrors**, which are also known as **night terrors**. Sleep terrors typically occur between the ages of 4 and 12 and most individuals outgrow the problem by adolescence (Mindell & Owens, 2015).

Sleep terrors occur during deep, slow-wave sleep and at a fairly constant time, usually about two hours into sleep. The event is quite striking in that the still-sleeping child suddenly sits upright in bed and screams. The face shows obvious distress, and there are signs of autonomic arousal, such as rapid breathing and dilated pupils. In addition, repetitive motor movements may occur, and the child appears disoriented and confused. Attempts to comfort the child are largely unsuccessful. The child usually returns to sleep without fully awakening and has little or no memory of this event the next morning. The conceptualization of the causes of sleep terrors is similar to that previously described for sleepwalking, and, indeed, they occur in the same part of the sleep cycle.

Nightmares Both sleep terrors and **nightmares** are fright reactions that occur during sleep. Nightmares and sleep terrors are often confused, but they differ in a number of ways. Differences include the phase of sleep during which nightmares (REM) and sleep terrors (NREM) occur. Nightmares are accompanied by only moderate physiological arousal whereas sleep terrors are associated with intense physiological arousal. Also, nightmares are often remembered whereas there is typically little or no memory of sleep terror episodes.

Occasional nightmares are common occurring in 60–75% of children. Frequent recurrent nightmares, however, occur in about 1–5% of children (Honaker et al., 2017). Children who meet diagnostic criteria for PTSD and anxiety disorders such as separation anxiety disorder and generalized anxiety disorder often report frequent nightmares (Alfano et al., 2018). Parents may underestimate their children's nighttime fears. The findings illustrated in Figure 14.2 suggest that this may be particularly true for older children (Muris et al., 2001). It is frequently thought that the dreams are a direct manifestation of anxieties that the child faces. It has been suggested that children typically extinguish their fears by gradually exposing themselves during daytime hours to the feared stimulus (Kellerman, 1980). Factors such as parental protectiveness or lack of awareness of their children's fears, however, might limit the child's ability to engage in such daytime exposure or coping. In the absence of exposure and coping, anxieties and associated nightmares may continue or be exacerbated.

No single theoretical framework has proven successful in explaining the development of nightmares, and explanations allowing for multiple causes (e.g., developmental, physiological, and environmental factors) are likely to have the greatest utility.

Treating Sleep Problems

Initiating and Maintaining Sleep

A number of different behavioral and environmental interventions have been demonstrated to be effective in dealing with the problems of bedtime refusal, difficulty in falling asleep, and nighttime wakings (de Bruin et al., 2018; Rigney et al.,

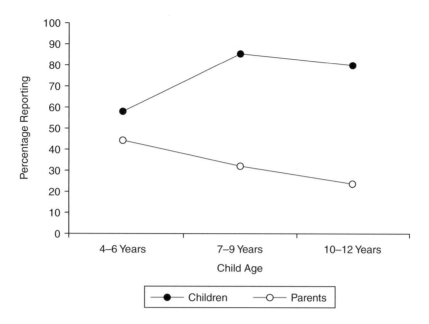

Figure 14.2 Percentage of children and their parents reporting that the children experience nighttime fears. (From Muris et al., 2001)

MATTHEW Recurrent Nightmares

The recurrent nightmares that 11-year-old Matthew experienced led his parents to seek help. Matthew was doing well in school, was involved in many activities, and had friends. His parents described him as sensitive and serious, but quite happy. A sleep diary indicated that nightmares had occurred on 11 of 14 nights. Matthew went to sleep in his own bed, but after the nightmare slept in his parents' or older brother's bedroom. Although his parents and brother did not mind, Matthew felt it was immature to have to sleep in their rooms. Recently, Matthew had been taking longer to fall asleep at night. Matthew complained of being tired during the day and upset about having another nightmare.

The parents indicated that Matthew had experienced occasional night terrors between the ages of 4 and 6. These had begun at the time of his maternal grandfather's death and after a difficult bout with the flu and high fever. During his preschool years Matthew had at least one nightmare a week, but since then only occasional nightmares until the past month. There were no health or other problems in the family except that the paternal grandfather had experienced a heart attack two months earlier, but he was home and recovering.

Matthew described his life as enjoyable and stimulating, but reported a number of situations that made him very sad or angry. Several bullies on the school bus repeatedly teased and pushed younger children including his younger brother. Matthew was also having difficulty completing a particular

Scout badge and he described his older brother as being particularly irritating to the entire family.

Matthew's parents were reassured and told that he was a child with many strengths and also sensitivity to injustices and others being hurt. It was suggested that his nightmares were related to these stresses at home and at school. A brief intervention was recommended. The treatment consisted of Matthew discussing the content of his nightmares with his parents and keeping a diary of the content. Matthew was also taught relaxation techniques. The clinician and Matthew reviewed the content of the nightmares and role played responses that resulted in a victory over the scary events. There was also a focus on the events that were creating stress. Matthew and the clinician took a problem-solving approach to the bullies on the bus and the parents had the school principal investigate and intervene in the bullying incidents. The family discussed sibling squabbles and the older brother was encouraged to spend more time with his own friends.

Matthew's nightmares decreased over the next month. This coincided with Matthew's having greater control over daily events and the resolution of the bullying problem. Matthew realized that he might have occasional nightmares and that if they became recurrent he would identify and cope with stressors in his environment.

Adapted from Schroeder & Smith-Boydston, 2017, pp. 210–212

Establishing a predictable bedtime routine is helpful in reducing children's sleep problems. (Courtesy of Daniel Israel)

2019). These interventions typically include education about sleep, teaching good sleep hygiene, and graduated extinction procedures. In addition to reducing sleep problems, such interventions may have positive effects on associated psychological difficulties.

As part of implementing good sleep hygiene, parents are taught to put the child to bed at a designated, consistent time and also are taught to develop a consistent bedtime routine at the regularly scheduled bedtime. The routine involves calm activities that the child enjoys. Once the routine is completed and the child is in bed, the parents are told to ignore the child until a set time the next morning. Extinction (ignoring) procedures are based on the assumption that attention to nighttime fussing maintains children's sleep problems. Some parents find it very stressful to ignore long periods of bedtime crying, so they may use a variant of the extinction procedure, graduated extinction, that has proven to be successful. First, parents ignore bedtime crying for an agreed-upon time for which they feel comfortable, and then over several nights, they increase the period before they check on the child.

There also is research to support the value of parent education in preventing the development and worsening of these kinds of sleep problems. Parents are provided information about sleep, the importance of routine, and the importance of putting the child to bed while partially awake so that the child can learn to go to sleep without an adult being present. Older children and adolescents also may benefit from the addition of relaxation training and other procedures that reduce bedtime arousal.

Pharmacological agents are often prescribed. However, there are no FDA-approved medications for the treatment of childhood insomnia and good support for the effectiveness and safety of medications is lacking. There also is concern regarding negative side effects and recurrences of sleep disturbances with discontinuation of treatment. Given such concerns, behavioral interventions are recommended as the first line of treatment (Alfano et al., 2018; Honaker et al., 2017; Rigney et al., 2019).

Parasomnias

In many cases of sleep terrors and sleepwalking, intensive treatment may not be indicated, because the episodes usually disappear spontaneously. Education and support along with procedures to ensure the child's safety may be sufficient. However, a number of treatments have been suggested. These include increasing sleep time, instructional procedures, and anxiety-reduction procedures (Dahl & Harvey, 2008; Meltzer & Mindell, 2009).

Nightmares

Consistent with the view of anxiety as the basis for nightmares, the majority of treatments for nighttime fears have involved cognitive-behavioral anxiety-reduction and coping/competence building techniques (Gordon et al., 2007; Schroeder & Smith-Boydston, 2017). These treatments have typically been effective, but the active components of the various treatments need to be clarified.

ACCENT Sleep Apnea

Young people may experience disrupted or inadequate sleep for a number of reasons. One of these is **obstructive sleep apnea** (OSA). OSA is a sleep-related breathing disorder characterized by repeated brief episodes of upper airway obstruction that disrupt normal breathing and normal sleep patterns. OSA is associated with a number of difficulties (Marcus et al., 2012; Mindell & Owens, 2015). OSA events result in fragmented and insufficient sleep and daytime fatigue. These sleep disruption events may also be associated with a number of other difficulties including cognitive and neurological deficits, hyperactivity and inattention, and a number of other behavioral problems.

Common nighttime symptoms of sleep apnea include loud snoring, pauses and difficulty in breathing, restless sleep, and sweating during sleep. In addition to fatigue, daytime symptoms may include mouth breathing, chronic nasal congestion or infection, and morning headaches.

Parents may be unaware of the symptoms that occur during sleep or otherwise fail to report them to their pediatricians. Instead, parents often initially complain of difficulties such as excessive sleepiness, behavior problems, depressed mood, hyperactivity, inattentiveness, and academic problems. OSA symptoms may become evident to parents only after they are directly questioned about their child's sleep. Information from interview and physical examination is important, but the best way to reliably and validly diagnose OSA is by a sleep study (nocturnal polysomnography; PSG), in which the youth sleeps overnight in a laboratory. EEG and other physiological measurements are taken and the youth's sleep is observed. Although the PSG is the "gold standard" for diagnosing OSA, there are a number of possible barriers to testing for families. These include cost and sleep laboratory accessibility. The use of a home sleep apnea test is being explored as a potential alternative (Kirk et al., 2017).

OSA is a common sleep disorder occurring in 1–5% of children. In young children enlarged tonsils and adenoids are the most common risk factors. OSA is also associated with childhood obesity and increased rates of childhood obesity make this a common risk factor.

Removal of the tonsils and adenoids is a common treatment in children, and symptom relief typically follows. Not all youth are candidates for such surgery, however. The use of a CPAP (continuous positive airway pressure) device can relieve apnea symptoms, but does not cure the problem. The youth wears a nasal/face mask during sleep and the device delivers pressure to keep the airways open. Some children and families have difficulties tolerating this device and adherence should be monitored. For young people who are obese, weight loss is recommended.

Problems of Feeding, Eating, and Nutrition

Establishing eating habits and food preferences is one of the primary aspects of early socialization. Mealtimes are often an occasion for family interactions and rituals, and other social interactions frequently revolve around food and eating. These and other considerations suggest the importance of food and eating-related behaviors.

Common Eating and Feeding Problems

A wide range of problems having to do with eating and feeding are commonly reported in typically developing young children and are even more common in children with chronic medical conditions or developmental disabilities (Silverman & Tarbell, 2017). These include undereating, finicky eating, overeating, chewing and swallowing problems, bizarre eating habits, annoying mealtime behaviors, and delays in self-feeding. Many of these problems can cause considerable concern for parents and appreciable disruption of family life. For example, Crist and Napier-Phillips (2001) indicated that over 50% of parents report one problem feeding behavior and more than 20% report multiple problems. Also, O'Brien (1996) found that approximately 30% of a sample of parents of infants and toddlers reported that their children refused to eat the foods presented to them. Adequate nutrition and growth are clearly a concern, but eating and feeding difficulties are also often accompanied by behavioral problems such as tantrums, spitting, and gagging. Severe cases of such difficulties may be associated with even more difficult social and psychological problems, and may result in medical complaints and malnourishment. Indeed, some cases of failure to thrive (life-threatening weight loss or failure to gain weight) can be conceptualized as a special case of eating and feeding difficulties (Benoit, 2009; Kelly & Heffer, 1990; Kerwin & Berkowitz, 1996). Thus, some feeding and eating problems may actually endanger the physical health of the child. The problems discussed in the following sections are disorders that appear in the DSM chapter Feeding and Eating Disorders or are problems that have attracted attention from researchers and clinicians.

Young children often exhibit feeding and eating problems. This difficulty may result in disruption and cause their parents considerable distress. (Antonio Guillem Fernández/Alamy Stock Photo)

Early Feeding and Eating Disorders

Rumination Disorder

Rumination disorder is characterized by the voluntary and repeated regurgitation of food or liquid in the absence of an organic cause. When infants ruminate, they appear deliberately to initiate regurgitation. The child throws his or her head back and makes chewing and swallowing movements until food is brought up. In many instances, the child initiates rumination by placing his or her fingers down the throat or by chewing on objects. The child exhibits little distress; rather, pleasure appears to result from the activity. If rumination continues, serious medical complications can result, with death being the outcome in extreme cases (American Psychiatric Association, 2013).

Rumination is most often observed in two groups, in infants and in persons with intellectual disabilities. Among children who are developmentally normal, rumination usually appears during the first year of life and is thought to be a form of self-stimulation. Sensory and/or emotional deprivation is associated with rumination. In individuals with intellectual disabilities, later onset is often observed, and the incidence of the disorder seems to increase with greater degrees of intellectual disability. In both groups, rumination appears to be more prevalent in males (Kerwin & Berkowitz, 1996; Mayes, 1992; Silverman & Tarbell, 2017).

Management of the problem will probably involve a multidisciplinary team. Behavioral treatments emphasizing the use of social attention contingent on appropriate behavior have been successful, and there is some suggestion that with infant ruminators, improving mothers' ability to provide a nurturing and responsive environment is effective (Mayes, 1992; Nicholls, 2004). These procedures have the advantage of being easily implemented by the parents in the home and of being acceptable to them. However, controlled evaluations of interventions are needed.

Pica

Pica is the Latin term for magpie, a bird known for the diversity of objects that it eats. **Pica** is characterized by the habitual eating of substances usually considered inedible, such as paint, dirt, paper, fabric, hair, and bugs.

During the first year of life, most infants put a variety of objects into their mouths, partly as a way of exploring the environment. Within the next year, they typically learn to explore in other ways and come to discriminate between edible and inedible materials. The diagnosis of pica is therefore usually made when there is persistent consumption of inedible objects beyond this age, and pica is most common in 2- and 3-year-olds.

Information regarding prevalence is limited, but pica is reported to be particularly high among individuals with intellectual disabilities (American Psychiatric Association, 2013; McAlpine & Singh, 1986; Nicholls, 2004). Pica can lead to a variety of damage, including parasitic infection and intestinal obstruction due to the accumulation of hair and other materials. The disorder also appears to be related to accidental lead poisoning (American Psychiatric Association, 2013; Halmi, 1985).

"I'm warning you—peas and carrots are gateway vegetables."

Tom Toro/Cartoon Collections

A number of causes for pica have been postulated including parental inattention, lack of supervision, and lack of adequate stimulation. Cultural influences such as superstitions regarding eating certain substances should also be considered (Millican & Lourie, 1970; Paniagua, 2000). The diagnosis of pica should be made only when the eating behavior is not part of a culturally supported or normative practice (American Psychiatric Association, 2013).

Educational approaches aimed at informing parents of the dangers of pica and at encouraging them to deter the behavior may be somewhat successful. However, it is necessary to supplement such interventions with more intensive therapeutic endeavors in some cases. Behavioral interventions such as noncontingent reinforcement and environmental enrichment have been found to be effective in reducing pica (Feldman, Runfola, & Lock, 2019). Noncontingent reinforcement provides access to preferred outcomes (e.g., attention, praise) that is scheduled, but is not contingent on the child's behavior. Environmental enrichment involves adding preferred items (e.g., toys, foods) to the child's environment. These non-restrictive procedures are the recommended first-line interventions. However, there is also evidence to support the use of more restrictive interventions such as overcorrection. Overcorrection involves responding to pica behavior with corrective tasks such as spitting out the nonfood item or brushing teeth.

Avoidant/Restrictive Food Intake Disorder

The essential feature of this disorder is a persistent failure to eat adequately. This may result in a number of serious difficulties. The child may fail to gain weight (or experience a significant weight loss), experience nutritional deficiency, experience appreciable interference with psychosocial functioning, and/or may become dependent on methods of directly supplying nutrition to the stomach or intestinal tract (e.g., tube feeding) or to the use of oral nutritional supplements. The DSM-5 diagnosis of **Avoidant/ Restrictive Food Intake Disorder** (ARFID) replaces the earlier term Feeding Disorder of Infancy or Early Childhood (American Psychiatric Association, 2013). However, the diagnostic boundaries and definition of ARFID remain unclear. Researchers and clinicians are defining what is probably a heterogeneous disorder differently across studies and thus clear understanding of ARFID and its treatment is an ongoing challenge (Eddy & Thomas, 2019; Strand, von Hausswolff-Juhlin, and Welch, 2019).

ARFID appears to be equally common in males and females and is more prevalent in infants and children with low birthweight and those with developmental disabilities or medical illness (Benoit, 2009). Severe feeding problems requiring medical attention are estimated to affect 3–20% of children. Approximately 1–5% of hospital admissions are the result of these severe feeding problems (Silverman & Tarbell, 2017).

That an infant or a young child would cease to eat adequately is puzzling and clearly troublesome. This problem and associated malnutrition can result in disruption in multiple areas of physical, cognitive, and social-emotional development at this critical time. The young child may be irritable and difficult to console or may appear apathetic and withdrawn—characteristics that may further contribute to feeding difficulties.

Multiple causes, including, physical illness, and physiological, behavioral, and environmental factors, most likely contribute to the development of food intake disorders (Benoit, 2009; Silverman & Tarbell, 2017). The particular influences that contribute are difficult to determine, in part because it is difficult to observe the child and family prior to the development of the problem. Feeding requires an effective interaction between the child and parent. Successful feeding relies on the parent's competence—defined as sensitivity to the child's developing repertoire and an ability to communicate with and involve the child in the feeding process (Drotar & Robinson, 2000; Silverman & Tarbell, 2017). A parent's competence may be influenced by a number of factors.

The parent's personal parenting resources likely play a role. These may include identification with the parental role, knowledge of effective parenting skills, and attachment to and relationships with one's child. Problems in these areas may, in part, be due to traumatic experiences in the parent's own childhood that disrupted the development of these parenting processes. Parental psychopathology may also contribute to diminished parental resources. Maternal eating disorders, for example, may lead to the mother experiencing anxiety and depression surrounding feeding and thereby increase the risk for food intake difficulties in her offspring (Micali et al., 2011).

A second set of factors includes characteristics of the infant or child that may contribute to a feeing problem by increasing the complexity of child rearing for parents with limited personal resources. Thus, child factors such as low birthweight, acute physical illnesses, various disabilities, and temperamental characteristics may contribute to the development of a feeding problem.

Finally, the family's social context is likely to interact with personal parental resources and child characteristics to affect parenting competence. Poverty or economic stress, serious parental or family conflict, the family's social networks and resources, and availability of community resources are among the contextual factors that may influence parenting competence.

The focus of intervention has been on treating the physical/nutritional symptoms to improve growth and developmental outcome. Multidisciplinary treatments that include behavioral, medical, nutritional, educational, and psychological components are typical. There is considerable evidence supporting the use of behavioral interventions as a central part of these treatments of problematic eating and feeding behaviors (Linscheid, 2006; Lukens & Silverman, 2014; Sharp et al., 2010). Several behavioral

procedures are typically included in interventions. These include modifications to the eating environment (e.g., a consistent and non-distracting feeding environment), modifications to the feeding schedule (e.g., timing when the child is hungry), use of behavior-management strategies (e.g., reinforcing eating new foods, ignoring negative behaviors), and parent training (Silverman & Tarbell, 2017).

Obesity

Although childhood obesity is not a feeding or eating disorder, it is a problem for which psychology has made an important contribution. **Obesity** is typically defined in terms of **body mass index (BMI**, weight in kilograms divided by square of height in meters). A BMI at or above the 85th percentile for age and gender is often defined as overweight, at or above the 95th percentile as obese, and at or above 120% of the 95th percentile as severely obese. Distinguishing between the terms overweight and obese is important for research purposes; however, the terms are often used interchangeably.

Obesity is an important health problem and is among the most prevalent nutritional diseases in children and adolescents. An estimated 18.5% of youth ages 2–19 years are obese. This includes 5.6% who are severely obese. Another 16.6% are overweight (Fryar, Carroll, & Ogden, 2018). Data from the National Health and Nutrition Examination Survey (NHANES) provides estimates of the prevalence of obesity (BMI ≥ 95th percentile) in the United States for 2015–2016 (Hales et al., 2017). An estimated 13.9% of preschoolers (2–5 years), 18.4% of school-aged children (6–11 years), and 20.6% of adolescents (12–19 years) were obese. Certain ethnic/racial groups appear to be at particular risk. For example, Hispanic males and females and non-Hispanic black females are more likely to be obese (Hales et al., 2017). In addition, reports over several decades indicate that rates of child and adolescent obesity have been increasing (Fryar et al., 2018). Data from the NHANES illustrate this increasing trend (Figure 14.3).

Obesity in childhood is associated with numerous physical, psychological, interpersonal, and educational difficulties (Kohut, Robbins, & Panganiban, 2019; McCullough et al., 2017; Schroeder & Smith-Boydston, 2017). Physical health problems associated with obesity include type 2 diabetes, heart disease, asthma, and sleep apnea. In addition, there are associations with educational, social, and psychological difficulties. For example, Geier and colleagues (2007) found that among a sample of inner city fourth to sixth graders, overweight children were absent from school significantly more than normal weight children even when controlling for age, gender, and race/ethnicity. In addition, some research does suggest higher rates of psychopathology among obese youth, particularly among adolescents (McCollough et al., 2017). In a study by Israel and Shapiro (1985), the behavior

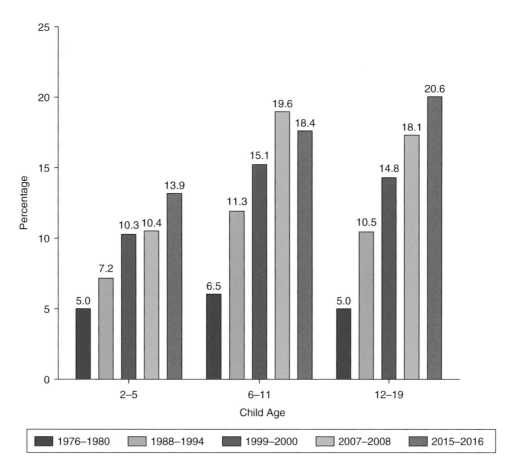

Figure 14.3 Percentage of obese children and adolescents. (Adapted from Fryar, Carroll, Ogden, 2018)

problem scores of children who were enrolled in a weight-loss program were significantly higher than the norms for the general population, but significantly lower than the norms for children referred to clinics for psychological services. This and other findings indicate that overweight youth are not necessarily at risk for significant psychological difficulties, but some youth seeking services and others may be at increased risk. Identifying the factors that help predict which youth are at risk is of potential importance (Russel-Mayhew et al., 2012).

The obese child is often exposed to stigmatizing behaviors and attitudes from peers, family, and in health care settings (Puhl, Peterson, & Luedicke, 2013). The child's social interactions may be adversely affected by these negative evaluations (Ciupitu-Plath, Wiegand, & Babitsch, 2018; McCullough et al., 2017). Because children hold negative views of obesity, children who are perceived as overweight are ranked as less liked (Latner & Stunkard, 2003; Skinner et al., 2017). Negative attitudes toward overweight peers have been found in children as young as age 3. Overweight youth may experience social isolation, teasing, rejection, and bullying (Griffiths et al., 2006; Jensen & Steele, 2012). In contrast, having a close friend may protect them from

negative social consequences (Reiter-Purtill et al., 2010). Effects of being overweight appear to continue throughout development. College acceptance rates are lower for obese adolescent girls than for non-obese girls with comparable academic credentials, and discrimination and lowered expectations may continue into college (Puhl & Latner, 2007). The obese youth's self-esteem may be adversely affected by such experiences (Nelson, Jensen, & Steele, 2011; Stern et al., 2007). For example, overweight and associated lower self-esteem have been found to contribute to smoking initiation among middle school youth (Murphy et al., 2019). Also, overweight adolescent girls have reported greater body dissatisfaction and made more negative attributions regarding their appearance than did their normal weight peers (Thompson et al., 2007). However, many obese youth do not have adjustment difficulties and they may maintain their general self-esteem despite reactions to their physical appearance (Israel & Ivanova, 2002).

Etiology

The causes of obesity are certainly multiple and complex. Any explanation must include biological, psychological, and social/

SEAN Obesity and Family Environment

Sean, a 10-year-old who was 50% overweight for his height and age, enrolled in a treatment program for obese children and their families. Sean's pediatrician described a history of steady, greater than expected weight gains with extreme increases in the last three years. Sean's father was normal weight, but his mother was about 40% overweight and had made numerous unsuccessful weight-loss attempts. Neither of Sean's two siblings was overweight. Sean snacked frequently on large amounts of high-calorie food, with most of his calories consumed after school while his parents were at work. His mother often found candy wrappers in Sean's room and pockets. Sean's parents reported that as Sean gained weight, his physical activity decreased and most of his leisure time

was spent watching television. They were concerned with his frequent shortness of breath. Sean had no close friends and was something of a loner. He was teased about his weight at school and by his siblings. Although the parents indicated that they were committed to Sean's losing weight, there were indications of some family "sabotage." Much of the family's activities revolved around food, and food was used as a reward. Sean's father described himself as a gourmet cook, and his high-calorie, high-fat meals were "family times." Sean spent considerable time visiting his grandmother, who took pleasure in providing him with food and snacks.

Adapted from Israel & Solotar, 1988

cultural influences (Cawley, 2006; Kohut et al., 2019; McCullough et al., 2017; Sallis & Glanz, 2006).

Biological influences include the metabolic effects of diet and exercise and genetic factors. Twin and adoption studies suggest a heritable component of body size and composition and for aspects of food intake. In addition, ongoing research suggests promise in locating specific genes that may be associated with obesity. Multiple genes are likely to be involved and genetic contributions are likely to be complex rather than simple. Of course, biological influences are not independent of environmental influences; rather, these influences interact (McCullough et al., 2017; Kral & Faith, 2009).

Psychosocial factors are also important in the development of obesity. Both logic and research suggest that the food intake and activity level of obese children are in need of change (Anderson & Butcher, 2006). Problematic food intake and inactivity are likely to be affected by family, peer, culture, and other environmental influences and to be learned in the same manner as any other behavior (Laessle, Uhl, & Lindel, 2001; McCullough et al., 2017; Olvera & Power, 2010; Salvy et al., 2012; Storch et al., 2007). For example, parents influence and support weight-related behaviors (Moens, Braet, & Soetens, 2007; Sato et al., 2011; van den Berg et al., 2010). And children also observe and imitate the eating behavior of their parents and others around them, and are reinforced for engaging in that style of eating (Klesges & Hanson, 1988). Eating and inactivity may also become strongly associated with physical and social stimuli, so that they become almost automatic in some circumstances. Moreover, people may learn to use food to overcome stress and negative mood states, such as boredom and anxiety. The treatment of obesity that has been developed from a social learning perspective seeks to break these learned patterns and to develop more adaptive ones.

Larger cultural influences are also germane. Television provides a striking example of how the larger society might contribute to the development of weight problems. American children and adolescents have easy access to high-caloric foods, have large amounts of screen time that includes watching a great deal of television, and in general lead a somewhat sedentary lifestyle. In addition to the negative effects of inactivity associated with television watching, the negative impact is probably also due to the influence of television viewing on food intake. The majority of food product advertisements viewed by children and adolescents are high in sugar and fat (Powell et al., 2007). There is similar concern about the marketing of unhealthy food choices to children via electronic media (White House Task Force on Childhood Obesity, 2011).

Interventions

Multifaceted programs that emphasize behavioral interventions and education and that specifically target both the child and family members are the most effective treatments for childhood obesity (Altman & Wilfley, 2015; Hayes et al., 2019). The work of Israel and his colleagues (Israel et al., 1994; Israel & Solotar, 1988) illustrates the general approach. Children and parents attend meetings during which the following four areas are regularly addressed: *intake*, which includes nutritional information, caloric restriction, and changes in actual eating and food preparation behaviors; *activity*, which includes both specific exercise programs and increasing the energy expended in daily activities—for example, walking to a friend's house rather than being driven; *cues*, which identify the external and internal stimuli associated with excessive eating or inactivity; and *rewards*, which provide positive consequences for progress by both the child and the parent. Homework assignments are employed to encourage the families to change their environments and to practice more appropriate behavior.

The role of parental involvement has been noted as an important treatment element (Hayes et al., 2019; Janicke et al., 2014; Kitzman-Ulrich et al., 2010). Israel, Stolmaker, and Andrian (1985), for example, provided parents with a brief course in the general principles of child management. The parents then participated with their children in a behavioral weight-reduction program that emphasized the application of the general parenting skills to weight reduction. Another group of parents and children received only the behavioral weight-reduction program. At the end of treatment, both groups achieved a significantly greater weight loss than the control children who were not receiving treatment. One year following treatment, children whose parents had received separate child management training had maintained their weight losses better than other treated children.

These results and others suggest the importance of changing family lifestyles and of providing parents with the skills necessary to maintain appropriate behavior once the treatment program has ended (Hayes et al., 2019; Israel, 1988; Kitzman-Ulrich et al., 2010). This is a particularly important issue in light of repeated evidence that individuals frequently regain the weight they have lost. In addition to parental involvement, the importance of increased activity, particularly when it is part of the family's lifestyle, and various other family factors have been shown to

be related to treatment outcome (Epstein et al., 1995; Israel, Silverman, & Solotar, 1986).

In addition to improving parental involvement, enhancing the child's self-regulatory skills may be valuable (Israel et al., 1994). Children receiving a multidimensional treatment program, comparable to the four-area program described before, were compared with children receiving a similar intervention plus enhanced training in comprehensive self-management skills. The results of this study are presented in Figure 14.4. In the three years prior to treatment, children in the two conditions had shown similar patterns of increasing percentage of overweight. Both treatment conditions resulted in comparable reductions in the percentage of overweight during treatment. However, whereas children in the standard condition appeared to return to pretreatment trends in the three years following intervention, children in the enhanced self-regulation condition did not.

Although research supports the effectiveness of the multifaceted/behavioral approach to children's weight reduction, there is a need for improved interventions that produce greater, more consistent, and more long-lasting weight loss, and for attention to issues of setting appropriate treatment goals and tailoring interventions to particular populations (Altman & Wilfley, 2015; Hayes et al., 2019; Israel, 1999; Jelalian et al., 2007).

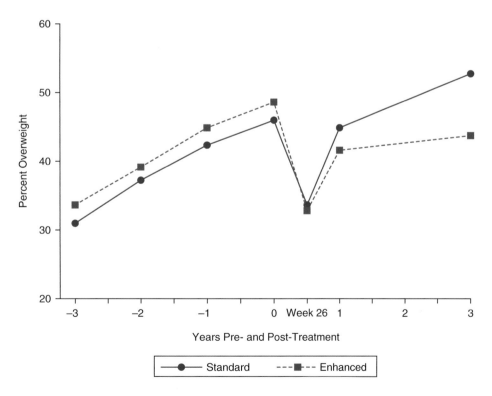

Figure 14.4 Mean percentage overweight from three years prior to treatment through three years following treatment. (Adapted from Israel et al., 1994. Copyright 1994 by the Oxford University Press; reprinted with permission)

Interventions that target obesity address both problematic food intake and inactivity. (Indiapicture/Alamy Stock Photo)

With increases in the prevalence of childhood obesity there have been calls for interventions that impact larger numbers of youth. Thus, broader societal interventions and prevention efforts are also needed (Andrews, Silk, & Eneli, 2010; Cradock et al., 2017; Stice, Shaw, & Marti, 2006). Programs targeting the general population that can be implemented on a national or statewide level are one approach. Targeting the nutritional content of diet and increasing physical activity also can be implemented at the school district level. School interventions may include improved availability of healthy food options (see Figure 14.5) and restricted accessibility of unhealthy food options along with increased time in physical education classes and increased physical activities during breaks and before and after school (Brown & Summerbell, 2009; De Bourdeaudhuij et al., 2011; Hoffman et al., 2010). These programs should seek, through the media and schools, to educate youth and their families and to actively change harmful nutritional and activity lifestyles.

Eating Disorders

Anorexia nervosa, bulimia nervosa, and binge eating disorder are eating disorders that involve maladaptive attempts to control body weight, significant disturbances in eating behavior, and abnormal attitudes about body shape and weight. These disorders typically begin during adolescence. However, the weight-control behaviors and attitudes toward body shape and weight that are characteristic of these disorders have also been noted in younger children.

Definition and Classification: An Overview

How might one best define and classify eating disorders (Walsh & Sysko, 2009; Wonderlich et al., 2007)? Several dimensions are involved in making distinctions between eating disorders or attempting to subcategorize a particular disorder. An individual's weight status is one such consideration. A person with an eating disorder may be underweight, within the normal weight range, or overweight.

A second consideration is whether the individual engages in binge eating. **Binge eating** is defined by the DSM as (1) eating a larger amount of food during a discrete period of time (e.g., a two-hour period) than most people would be expected to eat during that time and (2) feeling a lack of control of eating during this episode. However, there is some question as to whether the amount of food consumed is important in defining the episode as a binge. Some suggest that the feeling of loss of control, rather than the consuming of a large amount of food, is the central characteristic of a binge, particularly among youth (Lock & Osipov, 2019; Marcus & Kalarchian, 2003; Wolfe et al., 2009). Binge eating typically takes place in secret and the young person may go to great lengths to hide the behavior from family.

A third consideration is the method that the person uses to control her or his weight. A distinction is often made between restricting and purging strategies. The first strategy refers to severely **restricting** food intake and/or engaging in highly vigorous exercise. The second strategy involves **purging** oneself of unwanted calories through methods such as vomiting or the misuse of laxatives, diuretics, or enemas. As with bingeing, the

Figure 14.5 Providing healthy food options in the school setting may help prevent childhood obesity.

young person typically attempts to conceal these compensatory behaviors from family.

Weight status, the presence or absence of binge eating, and the method employed to control one's weight, therefore, are important considerations in thinking about eating disorders. We turn now to how these dimensions are involved in describing eating disorders.

Classification and Description: DSM Approach

The DSM describes three primary eating disorder diagnoses: Anorexia Nervosa and Bulimia Nervosa and Binge Eating Disorder. The DSM also includes a category of Other Feeding or Eating Disorder. This diagnosis may be applied to eating disorders that would not meet the criteria for one of the specific eating disorders.

Anorexia Nervosa

Individuals with eating disorders whose body weight is well below minimally normal or expected levels are likely to be given the diagnosis of **Anorexia Nervosa** (AN). The diagnosis of AN has three essential features. The first is a persistent restriction of energy intake that results in lower than expected body weight. In addition, the diagnosis of AN requires a fear of gaining weight or persistent behavior to avoid gaining weight. Finally, a disturbance in how the individual perceives their weight or shape is part of the criteria. These individuals may "feel fat" despite their low body weight, self-esteem may be unduly influenced by body weight and shape considerations, or there may be lack of adequate recognition of the seriousness of the medical implications of current low body weight. The DSM distinguishes between two subtypes of AN—restricting type and binge eating/purging type—on the basis of whether or not the person binges.

The seriousness of the extreme weight loss associated with AN is illustrated by Bruch's (1979) classic description of one of her clients, Alma.

Bulimia Nervosa

In contrast to AN, individuals with eating disorders whose body weight is not below expected levels are likely to be given the diagnosis of **Bulimia Nervosa** (BN). The diagnosis of BN requires the presence of three central features. First, individuals with a diagnosis of BN engage in recurrent episodes of binge eating.

ALMA Like a Walking Skeleton

When she came for consultation she looked like a walking skeleton, scantily dressed in shorts and a halter, with her legs sticking out like broomsticks, every rib showing, and her shoulder blades standing up like little wings. Her mother mentioned, "When I put my arms around her I feel nothing but bones, like a frightened little bird." Alma's arms and legs were covered with soft hair, her complexion had a yellowish tint, and her dry hair hung down in strings. Most striking was the face – hollow like that of a shriveled-up old woman with a wasting disease, sunken eyes, a sharply pointed nose on which the juncture between bone and cartilage was visible.

Bruch, 1979, p. 2

Again, **binge eating** is defined as consuming a larger than expected quantity of food in a discrete period of time and there is a feeling of a lack of control of eating during these episodes. Second, in order to prevent weight gain, the individual employs some inappropriate method of compensating for binge eating. Self-induced vomiting is probably the most common method employed; however, some individuals use multiple methods including both "purging"—vomiting and the use of laxatives or diuretics—and "restricting"—excessive exercise, or fasting—strategies. The third diagnostic criterion is that body shape and weight unduly influence the individual's self-evaluation.

To receive the diagnosis of BN, the binge eating and inappropriate compensatory behaviors must both occur at least once a week for three months. Also, the symptoms must not occur exclusively during episodes of AN—that is, a person who displays the symptoms as part of AN would not receive both diagnoses.

Binge Eating Disorder

The central feature of **Binge Eating Disorder** (BED) is recurrent episodes of binge eating. Again, **binge eating** is defined as consuming a larger than expected quantity of food in a discrete period of time and there is a feeling of a lack of control of eating during these episodes. To meet diagnostic criteria, binge eating must occur, on average, at least once per week for three months. Also, binge eating episodes must be associated with three or more of the following features: rapid eating, eating until uncomfortably full, eating large amounts of food when not physically hungry, eating alone because of embarrassment, feeling disgusted, guilty,

or depressed after overeating. In addition, the individual must exhibit marked distress regarding binge eating and there must be an absence of regular compensatory behaviors (e.g., vomiting). Finally, if the symptoms of binge eating occur exclusively during episodes of AN or BN these diagnoses take precedence.

Epidemiology

Eating disorders occur predominantly in young women. The lifetime prevalence of AN in adolescent U.S. females is about 0.3–0.7%. Prevalence in males is less clear. BN is more common, with lifetime prevalence in adolescent U.S. females of about 1–2% and 0.5% in adolescent U.S. males. The lifetime prevalence of BED is about 2.3% in adolescent U.S. females and about 0.8% in adolescent U.S. males (Feldman et al., 2019; Swanson et al., 2011).

These numbers may actually underestimate the prevalence of eating disorders, because individuals with these disorders may be overrepresented among those who do not cooperate with prevalence studies (Wilson, Becker, & Heffernan, 2003). Perhaps more importantly, the stated prevalence rates are based on individuals' meeting full diagnostic criteria for AN, BN, or BED. But many other young people exhibit various aspects of disordered eating and disturbances of body image (Ackard, Fulkerson, & Neumark-Sztainer, 2007). Of these youth, many may meet the criteria for Other Feeding or Eating Disorder (formerly Eating Disorder Not Otherwise Specified), Also, some youth do not meet diagnostic criteria but still exhibit eating-disordered behaviors and attitudes that are associated with symptoms of

Extreme concern with weight and body shape has become common among girls and young women. (Photographee.eu/Shutterstock.com)

depression, anxiety, and behavior problems (Lock & Osipov, 2019). These cases are also sometimes described as "subclinical" or "subthreshold."

Of particular interest is the finding that subclinical concerns with weight and shape and unusual eating behaviors are quite common among younger adolescents and even preadolescent girls. Thus, although eating disorders that meet full diagnostic criteria typically occur in late adolescence, dieting and disordered eating behaviors and attitudes appear in younger children (Rodgers et al., 2020; Stinton & Birch, 2005; Thompson & Smolak, 2001). These problems may be precursors of more serious eating disorders (Brewerton et al., 2014; Tanofsky-Kraff et al., 2011).

We have known for some time that by the fourth and fifth grade, many girls are worried about being or becoming overweight and desire to become thinner. Among middle school children, concerns about weight remain prevalent, and more extreme weight-control behaviors seem to be employed (Childress et al., 1993). Evidence suggests that extreme weight concern in these young girls is predictive of the emergence of later eating disorder symptoms and of depression, lowered self-esteem, and feelings of inadequacy and personal worthlessness (Killen et al., 1994a, 1994b; Lewinsohn et al., 1993; Stice & Bearman, 2001). Such feelings may, in turn, lead to increased concern with weight and shape among girls who already place great personal value on these physical attributes (Cohen-Tovee, 1993). Even at this young age concerns with weight and shape have been reported to be more prevalent among girls than boys (Shapiro, Newcomb, & Loeb, 1997; Thelen et al., 1992).

Ethnic and Cultural Differences

Early stereotypes described eating disorders as occurring predominantly in young white women from middle to upper class backgrounds. However, several large studies have found no racial or ethnic differences in the prevalence of eating disorder symptoms or risk factors for eating disorders. However, one consistent finding is of lesser body dissatisfaction among young African American females than among their white counterparts (Cheng et al., 2019; Kronenfeld et al., 2010; Stice & Linville, 2017).

It is suggested that eating disorders are culturally related phenomena, particularly for BN (Keel & Klump, 2003; Stice et al., 2017). This would suggest that the more "Westernized" young women from other cultures become, the more likely they are to develop eating disorders. Within Western culture, certain groups may be at particular risk. These include individuals involved in activities such as gymnastics, wrestling, ballet, and cheerleading in which weight-control behaviors and abnormal eating are used to enhance performance or appearance (Eddy et al., 2010; Jacobi et al., 2004; Smolak, Murnen, & Ruble, 2000; Thomas, Keel, & Heatherton, 2006).

Co-occurring Disorders

Eating disorders commonly co-occur with a number of other disorders (O'Brien & Vincent, 2003; Stice & Linville, 2017). Lewinsohn, Striegel-Moore, and Seeley (2000) report that in a community sample of adolescent girls, 90% of those with full syndrome eating disorders experienced one or more co-occurring disorders. Depression, anxiety disorders, and substance use disorders are commonly reported as co-occurring with eating- and weight-related difficulties and with AN and BN. Less information is available regarding co-occurrence with BED, but anxiety and depression appear to be associated with BED among adolescents (Fischer & Le Grange, 2007; Lock & Osipov, 2019; Rawana et al., 2010; Rancourt & Boepple, 2017).

Developmental Course and Prognosis

Anorexia Nervosa

The age of onset of AN is typically during adolescence, between 17 and 19 years of age (Eddy et al., 2010; Stice, Marti, & Rohde, 2013). Cases of earlier onset are rare but do exist (Gowers & Bryant-Waugh, 2004). The course of AN can vary. Some individuals may exhibit full recovery; others fluctuate between periods of restoration of normal weight and relapse; and for others AN follows a chronic course. Some individuals may gain weight and no longer meet the diagnostic criteria for AN, but continue to engage in eating-disordered behaviors and may meet the criteria for BN or another eating disorder diagnosis (American Psychiatric Association, 2013; Stice & Linville, 2017).

AN is a serious disorder, and a substantial proportion of young people with the disorder have poor outcomes (Katzman, 2005; Lock & Osipov, 2019; Steinhausen, 2002). Extreme weight loss can lead to significant medical complications (e.g., anemia, hormonal changes, cardiovascular problems, dental problems, loss of bone density), and the disorder may be life threatening. It has been reported that women with AN are 11–12% more likely to die than other women of a similar age, many of the deaths resulting from suicide (Birmingham et al., 2005; Stice & Linville, 2017).

Bulimia Nervosa

The onset of BN extends from adolescence into early adulthood with a peak period of onset between 16 and 20 years of age in females (Stice et al., 2013). Binge eating often begins during or after a period of restrictive dieting driven by extreme dissatisfaction with body shape and weight. The DSM describes the course of the disorder as either chronic or intermittent, with periods of remission alternating with recurrences of binge eating. However, over the long term, symptoms of BN diminish in many individuals (American Psychiatric Association, 2013). Although some individuals may no longer meet the diagnostic criteria for BN, problems may persist. They may, for example, continue to binge but no longer engage in inappropriate compensatory behaviors. Some of these individuals may meet the criteria for BED or Other Feeding or Eating Disorder, and many meet the criteria for other disorders such as major depressive disorder (Steinhausen & Weber, 2009; Stice & Linville, 2017).

Individuals engaging in bulimic behaviors are at appreciable risk for physical complications including cardiovascular and hormonal difficulties. The recurrent vomiting associated with BN can result in dental problems such as the loss of tooth enamel and gum disease. Other medical problems such as irritation of the esophagus, alterations of the colon, and fluid and electrolyte disturbances may also occur, particularly among those who employ purging compensatory behaviors (Lock & Osipov, 2019; Mehler, 2011).

Binge Eating Disorder

The peak age of onset for BED is between 18 and 20 years of age. Most individuals with either BED or subthreshold BED recover. However, some individuals with subthreshold levels of BED go on to meet the criteria for BED and some individuals

go on to meet the criteria for diagnostic or subthreshold levels of BN (Stice et al., 2013). There is limited information available regarding other outcomes, but some evidence suggests that binge eating is a risk factor for obesity (Fairburn et al., 2000). Individuals with BED and associated obesity are at increased risk for physical difficulties such as type 2 diabetes and hypertension (Lock & Osipov, 2019). They may also experience the social difficulties associated with obesity such as stigmatization, discrimination, bullying, and associated adverse psychological outcomes.

Etiology

A variety of risk factors and causal mechanisms have been proposed to explain the development of eating disorders. Indeed, it is likely that eating disorders are multiply determined and result from a variety of different patterns of influences (Rancourt & Boepple, 2017; Stice et al., 2017; Striegel-Moore & Bulik, 2007). Identifying risk factors for eating disorders is a challenge. Prospective research is needed to distinguish risk factors from

RILEY A Combination of Factors Leading to an Eating Disorder

Riley, a 17-year-old who had begun to talk about "feeling suicidal," began treatment at an eating disorders clinic. Riley's mother reported that Riley had always been healthy and performed well in school and in a variety of extracurricular activities. Indeed, during the past summer she had been selected for and attended an 8-week enrichment program for gifted and talented students. Riley had attended summer camps since the age of 10, but this was her longest period away from home, family, and friends. Riley had difficulty with this transition and reported that early in the summer program she had a hard time meeting people and making friends. She felt particularly insecure about interactions with boys and perceived that everyone, including her roommate, was pairing up into couples. To avoid feeling awkward, Riley used her free time to begin an intensive exercise program and reasoned that this would ensure that she was in particularly good shape for her school's fall soccer season. Initially, Riley was happy with this rigorous exercise program, but one day she overheard some boys making derogatory comments about her body. She entered the locker room, looked in the mirror, and thought that her thighs looked "pale and lumpy like cottage cheese" and reported realizing at that moment that she was "too fat." She began restricting her diet to small amounts of "healthy foods." Riley indicated that she developed her diet based on articles she had read in her mother's magazines on how to "lose 10 pounds in a week!" She reported that she and her mother had

gone on a diet together when she was 12 years old (around the age of puberty) and that she and her friends had previously gone on short-lived diets together. The summer experience was her first rigid program of diet and exercise. She reported that it made her feel "great," "strong," and "in control" and that she was frequently complimented by her roommate for how "good" she was.

When Riley returned home after the summer her mother was concerned with how much weight her daughter had lost. Riley refused to eat anything with her family, but her mother noticed that certain food items would disappear overnight. Riley reported that after 4 months of rigid adherence to her summer program she "lost control" and ate entire packages of cookies. She was distraught by her binge and ate nothing the next time and doubled her exercise routine. This was the beginning of a pattern of binges that became more frequent and increased during times of stress. Despite frantic efforts to fast and exercise, Riley regained all of the weight she had lost. By late fall she felt that she had lost control and was becoming increasingly anxious and depressed. Her mother was concerned about Riley's mood and also about the impact that Riley's eating disorder was having on the family. Riley's 10-year-old sister had begun to talk about "feeling fat" and "needing to lose weight."

Adapted from Eddy et al., 2010, pp. 440–441

ACCENT Infections, Medications, and Eating Disorders

A recent report suggests that girls who experience serious or multiple infections during childhood are at increased risk for developing an eating disorder (Breithaupt et al., 2019). Previous literature suggested an association between infections and psychopathology, and eating disorders in particular. However, the small number of studies and methodological limitations of existing research led the researchers to further explore this association in a large-scale population-based study.

Researchers followed all girls born in Denmark between 1989 and 2006, drawing data from nationwide longitudinal registers. Anonymous information, coded by an individual identification number, was available for all outpatient, hospital, and pharmacy contacts. From these national registers the investigators were able to record all prescriptions filled for antibiotics and other anti-infective medications, all hospitalizations for infection, and all diagnoses of eating disorders for this cohort.

Among the 525,643 adolescent girls, there were 4,240 female adolescents who had received an eating disorder diagnosis. Of these, 2,131 girls received a diagnosis of Anorexia Nervosa (median age 15.2 years), 711 received a diagnosis of Bulimia Nervosa (median age 17.9 years), and 1,398 received a diagnosis of an Eating Disorder Not Otherwise Specified (median age 15.6).

Compared to girls who had never been hospitalized for infection, girls who had been hospitalized for infections had a 22% increased risk for AN, a 35% increased risk for BN, and a 39% increased risk for Other Eating Disorders Not Otherwise Specified. Having filled three or more prescriptions for anti-infective agents was associated with a 23% increased risk of a subsequent diagnosis of AN, a 63% increased risk for a diagnosis of BN, and a 45% increased risk for a diagnosis of Eating Disorder Not Otherwise Specified.

Temporal and "dose-response" relationships between infections and eating disorders were also observed. The risk for an eating disorder onset was greatest in the first three months following hospitalization and the first three months after redemption of the last anti-infective prescription. In addition, the more infections and hospitalizations a girl had the greater was her likelihood of receiving an eating disorder diagnosis.

As the authors acknowledge, the study design does not allow one to make cause and effect conclusions regarding the relationship between infections and eating disorders. However, the authors see their findings as consistent with other evidence that suggests an involvement of the immune system in the development of eating disorders. Although their results do suggest a temporal pattern between infection and the diagnosis of an eating disorder, the authors acknowledge that mechanisms other than a direct infection–eating disorder link are possible. It is possible that individuals who are likely to develop an eating disorder also have an increased susceptibility to infections for reasons not measured in the current research. Other so-called "third variables" such as stress, anxiety, or particular genetic factors may increase the risk for both infection and eating disorders. Additional research is needed to clarify whether the relationship is causal and to clarify the mechanisms of the association between infections and eating disorders.

other factors observed once the disorder exists. Such other factors may be consequences of the disorder. Alternatively, these other factors may be associated with the disorder through influences that contribute to the development of both the eating-disordered behavior and these other factors.

Being female is probably the most reliable risk factor. Additional influences, however, are needed to help explain the mechanisms by which the gender difference in eating disorders occurs. Also, while there is probably some overlap, it would appear that it is worthwhile to distinguish factors influencing AN from those influencing BN and BED.

Biological Influences

Eating and the biological mechanisms behind it are complex; thus, numerous biological mechanisms have been studied. (See Accent:

"Infections, Medications, and Eating Disorders" regarding some intriguing recent research.)

A significant genetic contribution to eating disorders has been suggested although estimates vary across studies (Trace et al., 2013). There are higher than expected rates of eating disorders among family members of individuals with eating disorders. Twin studies also suggest a genetic component to eating disorders. It seems likely that multiple genetic influences contribute to the development of eating disorders and interact with other influences in complex ways (Bulik, Blake, & Austin, 2019). Klump and colleagues (2010), for example, examined genetic influences on disordered eating in a large female twin sample (10–41 years of age). They found that genetic influences were modest in preadolescents, but significant from early adolescence through middle adulthood. In a subsequent study of male and female twins, this age-related pattern was true for girls, but not for boys. Among girls, heritability was 0% pre puberty, but 51% during and beyond puberty. In contrast, heritability for boys was 51% during the prepubertal period, puberty, and adulthood (Klump et al., 2012).

Molecular genetic research attempting to identify particular genes and the manner in which genes contribute to eating disorders is under way. The serotonin transporter gene (5-HTTLPR), which is involved in appetite, weight regulation, and mood, is one of the genes that have received research attention. This research suggests that the 5-HTTLPR gene may be implicated in eating disorders as well as in other disorders such as depression and, thus, its influence may not be specific to eating disorders. Indeed, this gene may, in part, contribute to the co-occurrence of these disorders (Calati et al., 2011; Mata & Gotlib, 2011). Findings regarding the 5-HTTLPR gene are consistent with research suggesting that differences in neurotransmitter (e.g., serotonin, norepinephrine) activity are associated with eating disorders (Trace et al., 2013). For example, serotonin plays a major role in the inhibition of feeding, and decreased serotonin activity has been observed in individuals with anorexia and bulimia nervosa—both during the illness and after recovery.

Attention has also been given to neuroendocrine and neurohormonal influences. For example, it is hypothesized that prenatal hormonal exposure and hormonal changes during puberty may moderate genetic influences on eating-disordered behavior (Klump et al., 2012). There is some suggestion that prenatal sex hormone exposure (lower testosterone and higher estrogen) may be associated with eating-disordered behavior. It is hypothesized that increased prenatal testosterone exposure in males protects against binge eating, with possible additional protection provided by pubertal testosterone exposure. In contrast, for females the lack of prenatal testosterone exposure and pubertal activation of the ovarian hormones estrogen and progesterone are hypothesized to contribute to females' increased risk (Klump, Culbert, & Sisk, 2017).

Eating behavior can both be influenced by and effect changes in neurobiological and neuroendocrine systems, so determining causal relationships is not easy. It has been difficult to determine whether a particular biological difference found in young women with eating disorders placed them at initial risk for the disorder or has resulted from changes in the biological system due to disordered eating.

Behavioral/Environmental/Cultural Factors

A variety of behavioral, environmental, and cultural risk factors are assumed to transact with the biological risks described above in the development of eating disorders. Feeding difficulties in early childhood are suggested as one of the risk factors for later eating problems and disorders. Clinical reports mention early feeding difficulties in individuals with eating disorders, and there is some research support for this position. For example,

Kotler and colleagues (2001) found that maternal reports, during early childhood, of eating conflicts, struggles around meals, and unpleasant meals were predictive of later AN in adolescence or young adulthood. It may be that experiences that begin early in childhood, such as differentiating internal cues of hunger from other emotional reactions, food acceptance patterns, and the balance between external and self-control of eating, are among potential factors shaping later eating problems (Eddy et al., 2010).

Weight history is also frequently mentioned as a risk factor for the development of eating disorders. It has been suggested that the self-starvation that is characteristic of AN begins as an attempt to control genuine overweight, perhaps in response to comments that the young girl is "getting plump." Contrary to such thinking, prospective research findings indicate that low BMI in girls predicts onset of threshold or subthreshold AN several years later. These findings, in combination with the early feeding difficulties described above, suggest a contrasting description to the "attempt to control genuine overweight" theory of the development of AN. Perhaps youth who have conflicts or are ambivalent about food and therefore have lower BMIs and less need for dieting are at risk for the development of AN (Stice & Linville, 2017). With regard to the relationship of weight history to the development of BN and BED, findings from prospective research do not find BMI to be a risk factor for the development threshold or subthreshold levels of either disorder (Stice et al., 2017; Stice & Linville, 2017).

Characteristics of temperament and personality traits have also been suggested as risk factors in the development of eating disorders. An association between the temperament quality of negative affectivity and eating-disordered behaviors and attitudes has been reported. For example, there is support from prospective research for negative affectivity as a risk factor for subthreshold and clinical levels of BN and BED. This risk relationship for negative affectivity was not found for AN (Stice et al., 2017; Stice & Linville, 2017). It is worth noting that negative affectivity is also associated with other disorders, such as anxiety and depression, that frequently co-occur with eating disorders. Thus, this temperament quality may be a non-specific risk factor for eating disorders (Eddy et al., 2010).

The relationship between certain personality traits and eating disorders also has received considerable attention. For example, perfectionism (striving for unreasonably high standards and defining one's worth based on accomplishments) has been reported to be associated with eating disorders (Bardone-Cone et al., 2007; Dahlenburg, Gleaves, & Hutchinson, 2019). However, prospective research does not support viewing perfectionism and other personality traits such as obsessionality, impulsivity, restraint, and conformity as preexisting risk factors for BN and BED and suggest that there is only limited support with regard to AN (Stice & Linville, 2017). At best, the relationship between personality traits and eating disorders remains unclear. Alternatively, personality traits may be factors that affect the course of an eating disorder, or they may be consequences of an eating disorder (Walsh & Commission on Adolescent Eating Disorders, 2005; Wonderlich et al., 2005).

Impaired social functioning appears to be a risk factor for the development of eating disorders. There is support for impaired social functioning as a risk factor for AN, BN, and BED (Stice et al., 2017; Stice & Linville, 2017). Youth who have difficulty getting along with family, friends, and peers may be at increased risk for developing eating-disordered behavior.

Central to many models of the development of eating disorders are influences related to perception of one's body. And, indeed, factors such as body dissatisfaction, perceived pressure to be thin, internalization of a thin body as ideal, and dieting/fasting have emerged as risk factors for BN and BED in several prospective studies (Stice et al., 2017; Stice & Linville, 2017). To further understand the role of such influences, Stice and Van Ryzin (2019) employed data from an eight-year prospective study of nearly 500 adolescent girls to examine the potential sequence of such risk factors in the development of threshold or subthreshold BN and BED. A likely sequence of influences emerged in their analysis. Girls who ultimately showed onset of these eating disorders first showed emergence of high levels of pressure to be thin and/or thin-ideal internalization, before the onset of high levels of body dissatisfaction, before showing high levels of dieting and/or negative affect, before onset of eating disorder.

Influences such as perceived pressure to be thin, internalization of a thin ideal of beauty, body dissatisfaction, and dieting/fasting have regularly emerged as central risks factors for the development of eating-disordered behaviors and attitudes. Thus, any discussion of the development of eating disorders is likely to address the topics of cultural influences and gender roles for women.

Emphasis on and valuing of slim and young bodies, particularly for women, likely is part of the contribution of societal influences to the valuing of thinness, body dissatisfaction and, potentially, the development of eating disorders (Anderson-Fye, 2018; Mirkin, 1990; Striegel-Moore & Bulik, 2007). For example, Dittmar, Halliwell, and Ive (2006) asked the question, "Does Barbie make girls want to be thin?" Many young girls own at least one Barbie doll. Barbie is exceptionally thin and her body proportions are unattainable and unhealthy. In the study, girls ages 5 to 8 were exposed to picture-book images of either Barbie dolls, Emme dolls (body proportions of a dress size 16), or neutral stimuli without any descriptions of bodies. Girls exposed to Barbie reported lower body esteem and greater desire for a thinner body than girls in the other conditions. This was particularly true for younger girls. Girls exposed to Emme did not differ from those who viewed neutral images. Such findings raise concerns that at a very young age girls may internalize a thin ideal.

Media, peers, and families transmit these cultural messages of thinness (Dohnt & Tiggeman, 2006; Wertheim, Paxton, & Blaney, 2004). Clark and Tiggeman (2007), for example, found that, among girls in grades 4 to 7, greater exposure to television shows and magazines that emphasized appearance, along with involvement in appearance conversations with peers, were related to greater body dissatisfaction. These cultural influences appear to have contributed to the importance placed on appearance, which, in turn, contributed to body dissatisfaction. Additional research also points to the influence of the media and suggests that young women may unfavorably compare themselves to persons depicted in the media (Levine & Harrison, 2004; Wiseman, Sunday, & Becker, 2005). Similar concerns are increasing with regard to young men. (See Accent: "Weight and Shape Concerns in Young Men.") Beyond possible direct influences, body dissatisfaction also can contribute to lowered self-esteem and depressed mood (Paxton et al., 2006), which, in turn, may contribute to the development and/or maintenance of eating disorders (Measelle, Stice, & Hogansen, 2006).

Thus, one perspective on the development of eating disorders emphasizes social influences that place too great an emphasis on physical appearance, and may transmit a message that personal, social, and economic opportunity are associated with appearance and a particular body shape (Anderson-Fye & Becker, 2004; Eddy et al., 2010; Smith et al., 2007). In order to counteract their contribution to the development of eating-disordered behavior, it is important to understand both why and how this exposure and the social pressure to internalize this message impact only certain youth.

Some authors remind us that unusual eating styles are not recent phenomena, and that historical accounts can assist us in examining our conceptualization of eating disorders (Attie & Brooks-Gunn, 1995). There was, for example, a group of women living in the High Middle Ages (thirteenth through sixteenth centuries) who maintained extreme eating restrictions and what might be viewed as bizarre and pervasive behaviors and images regarding eating and food (Bell, 1985; Brumberg, 1986). Descriptions of the behavior of these women bear a remarkable similarity to contemporary eating disorders. The most interesting twist to this tale, however, is that these women were later canonized as saints. Bell (1985) chose the term "holy anorexia" to describe the condition of these women and to call attention to the cultural dimension in diagnostic efforts.

Intervention

As we have seen, eating disorders likely develop from and are maintained by a variety of influences, and there is considerable heterogeneity among individuals with eating disorders. Thus, interventions that address multiple influences are needed and we briefly highlight some approaches.

ACCENT Weight and Shape Concerns in Young Men

Much of the literature has focused on eating-disordered behavior and weight and body image concerns in young women. This is, at least in part, due to the high rates of such difficulties among females. More recently, attention has begun to turn to young men, and whether eating, weight, and body shape concerns are underestimated in the male population (Limbers, Cohen, & Gray, 2018). Part of what we should recognize here is a possible gender bias in how a disorder is defined. So, for example, drawing from the literature on young women, interest has largely focused on issues such as the desire for a smaller and thinner body and losing weight. Although losing weight may be a concern for some young men who are overweight, most young men do not desire a small, thin body. The ideal for many young men may be a larger or at least more muscular body. Perhaps defining body dissatisfaction and weight concerns in a different way would paint a different picture regarding body image concerns and disordered eating in young men. Research does suggest that there are gender differences regarding idealized bodies and that attention should be given to culturally influenced shifts in these ideals over time (Watson, Murnen, & College, 2019).

It has been acknowledged that the prevalence of male eating-disordered behavior and attitudes has likely been underestimated and that increased attention should be given to considerations of weight and shape concerns among males (Murray et al., 2017). McCabe and Ricciardelli (2004) highlighted some of the reasons for this trend. Male bodies featured in popular magazines have become more muscular.

Popular athletes, film stars, and many other male icons also have become increasingly muscular. Action figures, such as G.I. Joe, and Halloween costumes have followed the same trend and are likely to have physiques equal to or exceeding those of advanced body builders. Also, weight training has become more prevalent among young men and may be viewed as normative. Thus, similar to what young women have experienced, cultural pressures may be increasingly affecting young men.

What are the consequences of these trends? Appearance and weight have, for a long time, been considered overly important influences on young women's self-esteem. Similar concerns may be emerging as central to men's feelings of self-worth, mood, and overall adjustment (Allen et al., 2013; Paxton et al., 2006). Problematic eating styles may be increasing. In addition, excessive exercise and muscle-building strategies may be escalating among young males, including the use of steroids to achieve results.

The literature is not extensive regarding disordered eating and body dissatisfaction in young men. Nonetheless, there is information that suggests the presence of eating-disordered behavior in young men. In addition, both disordered eating and the pursuit of muscularity in adolescent males seem to be influenced by similar factors (Dryer et al., 2016). Furthermore, several factors consistently associated with disordered eating in young women (e.g., importance of appearance, BMI, negative affect, overall adjustment, self-esteem, perfectionism) also appear to be associated with problematic eating behaviors in young men (Allen et al., 2013; Ricciardelli & McCabe, 2004).

Anorexia Nervosa

A variety of interventions have been employed to treat AN including pharmacotherapy, hospitalization, and individual therapy. Support, however, is greatest for the effectiveness of family interventions with a behavioral focus in treating adolescents with AN (Hamadi & Holliday, 2020; Le Grange & Robin, 2017; Lock & Osipov, 2019).

Family therapy for AN derives from the observation by clinicians of varying persuasions that families are intimately involved in the maintenance of this behavior. Historically, many explanations emphasized the contribution of family variables to the development of eating disorders. Bruch's (1979) description of Ida is a classic example of suggested family influences. The girl is described as the object of much family attention and control, and as trapped by a need to please. AN, according to Bruch, is a desperate attempt by the child to express an individual identity.

The approaches to the treatment of AN for which evidence is strongest have their origin in the interventions originally developed at the Maudsley Hospital in London (Eisler et al., 2000). These approaches avoid viewing families as pathological and blaming them and the adolescent for the development of AN. The position taken is that the causes of the disorder are likely complex combinations of psychosocial and biological factors and the family is considered an important resource for the adolescent's recovery. Thus, the goal is to remobilize family resources to work with the professionals. Two versions of family treatment for AN have been adapted from the Maudsley program and are supported by well-controlled research (Le Grange & Robin, 2017). These two approaches are behavioral family systems therapy (BFST; Robin et al., 1999) and family-based treatment (FBT-AN; Lock & Le Grange, 2005). These two approaches are similar. Our description of this treatment approach is based on the FBT-AN program (Lock & Le Grange, 2013).

IDA A Sparrow in a Golden Cage

Even as a child Ida had considered herself not worthy of all the privileges and benefits that her family offered her, because she felt she was not brilliant enough. An image came to her, that she was like a sparrow in a golden cage, too plain and simple for the luxuries of her home, but also deprived of the freedom of doing what she truly wanted to do. Until then she had spoken only about the superior features of her background; now she began to speak about the ordeal, the restrictions, and obligations of growing up in a wealthy home.

Bruch, 1979, pp. 22–23

Treatment, which initially involves intense support of the family that is gradually faded over time, is broadly divided into three phases. The first phase, which includes a family meal session, is highly focused on restoring the adolescent's weight and also seeks to reinvigorate the parents in their role as agents of change. Families are encouraged, with therapist consultation, to work out for themselves the best way to restore good nutrition and their child's weight. Once the adolescent is gaining weight and eating takes place with minimal struggle, the second phase begins. Eating disorder symptoms are the main subject of sessions, but the goal is to assist the family in a supportive, but less directive manner, and to find ways to return control back to the adolescent. As this occurs, issues of adolescent development and the ways they have been affected by AN can begin to be reviewed. Once the adolescent achieves a healthy weight the final phase is undertaken and issues of adolescent development continue to be addressed. The goal is to assure that the adolescent is back on a normal developmental trajectory and that the family is prepared to manage typical developmental concerns. Relapse prevention strategies are also discussed.

As an example of the research conducted on the FBT-AN program, two modes of family involvement in FBT-AN have been compared: conjoint family therapy (CFT), in which the whole family is seen together, and separated family therapy (SFT), in which the same therapist sees the adolescent individually and the parents in separate sessions. Overall, CFT and SFT produced significant and comparable weight gain, improved menstrual functioning, and improved psychological functioning by the end of treatment and at a five-year follow-up (Eisler et al., 2000, 2007). For a subset of families in which mothers were highly critical, adolescents who received SFT achieved greater weight gain during follow-up than did those who received CFT. Family involvement may have to be tailored to the family and/or adjusted over the course of treatment.

Research has consistently supported FBT-AN as a treatment for anorexia nervosa and has shown that, in general, the inclusion of the family in treatment is effective in restoring the weight of adolescents and avoiding hospitalization. However, some adolescents with AN do not respond to FBT-AN and, therefore, adaptations or new treatments need to be explored (Le Grange & Robin, 2017; Lock & Osipov, 2019).

Bulimia Nervosa and Binge Eating Disorder

There are no well-established treatments for youth with BN or BED (Lock, 2015: Lock & Osipov, 2019). The limited number of well-controlled research studies restricts the ability to identify efficacious interventions. However, research does provide some suggestions as to treatment approaches that may be effective for adolescents with BN or BED. The majority of these studies have focused on family or cognitive-behavioral approaches.

A family-based treatment, with a behavioral focus, for adolescents with BN (FBT-BN) has been developed. The treatment program is an adaption of the FBT-AN program described above and the general approach of FBT-AN is also employed for FBT-BN (Le Grange & Locke, 2009; Locke & Osipov, 2019). In Phase 1 parents are helped to work with their child to identify strategies to stop binge eating and purging behaviors and to reestablish healthy eating patterns. The transition to Phase 2 occurs once weight is stabilized across sessions, there has been a significant reduction in binge eating and purging behaviors, and adolescents demonstrate the ability to eat in a healthy manner without much struggle. Phase 2 focuses on gradually reducing parental supervision and transferring greater control and responsibility to the adolescent. Problem solving regarding difficult situations and assisting the adolescent to return to a more typical adolescent life are central aspects of this second phase. Once there are minimal issues, Phase 3 includes discussion of typical challenges of adolescence. Relapse prevention strategies are discussed and the youth and family's growth and achievements are highlighted. Although initial findings are promising (Le Grange et al., 2007), there is still only limited research regarding the effectiveness of FBT-BN.

There is some limited research evidence that supports the use of adolescent adaptations of cognitive-behavior therapy (CBT) in treating BN and BED in youth (Lock, 2015; Lock & Osipov, 2019). However, most support for the use of CBT derives from the adult literature. Cognitive-behavioral treatment of BN and BED in adults has appreciable research support and is viewed by many as a treatment of choice (Brownley et al., 2017; Keel, 2018; Slade et al., 2018; Wilson, 2011). This treatment evidence is based largely on adult samples that do, however, sometimes include some older adolescents.

The treatment of BN illustrates the CBT approach to both disorders. Treatment involves a multifaceted program that is largely based on the rationale that a dysfunctional schema for self-evaluation—one that overvalues shape and weight and their control—is what maintains eating disorder pathology (Cooper & Fairburn, 2010; Fairburn, 1997). According to this view, these cognitions regarding shape and weight are the primary features of the disorder and other features—such as dieting and self-induced vomiting—are secondary expressions of these concerns. The "dietary slips" and binges that are part of the pattern of behavior among individuals with BN are most likely to occur in response to negative moods or adverse events.

In the initial stage of treatment, the patient is educated regarding BN and the cognitive view of the disorder is made clear. During this early stage, behavioral techniques are also employed to reduce bingeing and compensatory behaviors (e.g., vomiting) and to establish control over eating patterns. These techniques are supplemented with cognitive restructuring techniques, and as treatment progresses, there is an increasing focus on targeting inappropriate weight-gain concerns and on training self-control strategies for resisting binge eating. Next, additional cognitively oriented interventions address inappropriate beliefs concerning food, eating, weight, and body image. Finally, a maintenance strategy to sustain improvements and to prevent relapses is also included.

As discussed earlier, many adolescents do not meet the diagnostic criteria for a specific eating disorder. Thus, adolescents seeking treatment may present with a wide range of eating disorder problems. Fairburn and colleagues (Cooper & Fairburn, 2010; Fairburn, Cooper, & Shafran, 2003) have developed a cognitive-behavioral individualized treatment program based on a "transdiagnostic" model of eating disorders. This intervention is an "enhanced" version of CBT for Bulimia (CBT-E). The program matches specific therapeutic interventions to the particular eating disorder features of the individual, rather than providing treatment based on diagnosis. Fairburn and colleagues (2009) have evaluated CBT-E with a population of adults either meeting diagnostic criteria for BN or for those with symptoms that do not meet full diagnostic criteria. The treatment was comparably effective for both groups—about half of the treated individuals reached a level on eating disorder measures that was close to the mean of a community sample. The success of CBT-E for individuals who do not meet full diagnostic criteria further suggests that a cognitive-behavioral approach may also be appropriate for adolescents.

Interpersonal psychotherapy (IPT) focuses on interpersonal problems involved in the development and maintenance of a disorder. Research suggests that IPT also may be an effective treatment for BN and BED in adults (Keel, 2018; Karam et al., 2019) but research focused on youth is limited (Lock, 2015; Lock & Osipov, 2019). This therapeutic approach does not directly target eating disorder symptoms, but seeks to enhance interpersonal functioning and communication skills. The rationale for such an approach is based, in part, on research indicating poor interpersonal functioning in individuals with BN and BED and the role of interpersonal influences (e.g., actions of peers, friends, family; comparison with others) on the development of body image and self-esteem (Tanofsky-Kraff & Wilfley, 2010). An assessment of the individual's interpersonal history is obtained. One or more of four interpersonal problem areas are the focus of the intervention: interpersonal deficits, interpersonal role disputes, role transitions, and grief.

Pharmacological Treatment

Although a few small studies suggest that pharmacological treatments such as selective serotonin uptake inhibitors and atypical antipsychotics can be used to treat AN in adolescents, there is not strong evidence for their use (Lock & La Via, 2015; Lock & Osipov, 2019). The role of pharmacotherapy in treating BN and BED in children and adolescents remains unclear and research is limited (Broft et al., 2010; Lock & Osipov, 2019). Moreover, caution is indicated regarding side effects with individuals who are already psychologically and physiologically at risk.

Prevention

There is a considerable prevalence among adolescents of eating-disordered behavior that does not meet the criteria for AN, BN, or BED or is considered "subclinical." In addition, signs of eating-disordered behavior and attitudes in younger children are frequent. Thus, there is reason to think in terms of prevention (Wilfley et al., 2011).

Prevention programs attempt to address modifiable risk factors for eating disorders and/or promote factors that are protective against the development of eating disorders. A variety of programs employing universal, selected, and indicated prevention strategies have demonstrated moderate effectiveness in reducing eating disorder risk factors or symptoms (Chua, Tam, & Shorey, 2020; Le et al., 2017; Watson et al., 2016).

Universal prevention programs, which target entire/general populations, are primarily group-based and delivered in school classes. Also, media literacy programs are among the universal prevention approaches to eating disorders that have demonstrated some effectiveness. The potentially negative influence of messages in the media regarding thin body ideal and other maladaptive attitudes is the basis for this approach. Media literacy approaches seek to empower participants to critically evaluate and challenge media content regarding internalization of the thin ideal and other unhealthy messages and to generate alternatives to these stereotypical mass media messages (Wade et al., 2017).

It has been suggested that evidence is strongest for selective approaches to prevention of eating disorders (Watson et al., 2016). Selective prevention interventions are targeted at individuals who are at above average risk for eating disorders. These programs also are typically delivered in a group format in classes, face-to-face or online. Cognitive-behavioral programs are among the selective prevention programs that have demonstrated some effectiveness in reducing eating-disordered behaviors and risk factors. These programs are multi-component interventions that parallel the cognitive-behavioral treatment programs for eating disorders described above. Cognitive dissonance interventions, which are designed to reduce acceptance of the thin ideal, and media literacy programs are also selective prevention approaches that have demonstrated some effectiveness (Stice et al., 2011).

Indicated prevention programs target high-risk individuals who show minimal symptoms or other indications of the beginnings of an eating disorder. There is less evidence available regarding the effectiveness of indicated prevention programs for eating disorders as compared to other prevention approaches. Cognitive-behavioral intervention is the indicated prevention approach for which there is evidence of effectiveness.

Additional research regarding prevention programs for eating disorders is needed. For example, some limited research suggests the potential value of also targeting parents as part of prevention efforts (Hart et al., 2015). Further research with improved methodologies that improves effectiveness and also addresses the dissemination/accessibility of cost-effective programs can provide valuable information to clinicians and those responsible for providing health-related services (Le et al., 2017; Watson et al., 2016).

Looking Back

- It is common for children to exhibit some difficulty in acquiring habits of elimination, sleep, and eating. For some children, these problems are serious enough to be of clinical concern.

Problems of Elimination

- Toilet training is an important concern for parents of young children. Knowledge of the typical sequence of control over elimination and of appropriate parenting practices can contribute to successful training.
- Enuresis and encopresis are disorders of elimination that seem best explained by a combination of biological predisposition and failure to train and/or learn bodily control.
- Desmopressin is the best-supported medically oriented procedure for treating enuresis. Behavioral interventions that include a urine-alarm procedure have high success rates and low rates of remission, and they are the treatments of choice at present.
- Encopresis is probably best dealt with through a combination of medical and behavioral procedures.

Sleep Problems

- Sleep problems are common in infants, children, and adolescents. Sleep disorders are persistent sleep difficulties that cause the child distress or interfere with other functioning.
- Difficulties in initiating and maintaining sleep may be related to neurophysiological development, but are probably also affected by environmental influences such as bedtime routines and the appropriate cues for sleep. Sleep disorders such as sleepwalking and sleep terrors (parasomnias) are probably best conceptualized as resulting from a combination of nervous system immaturity and environmental factors.

Problems of Feeding, Eating, and Nutrition

- A wide range of problems having to do with eating and feeding are commonly reported in young children. Many of these problems cause considerable concern for parents and appreciable disruption of family life.
- Some eating and feeding problems are more serious and persistent, and may actually endanger the physical health of the young person.
- The DSM describes a number of early feeding and eating disorders including rumination disorder, pica, and avoidant/restrictive food intake disorder.
- Childhood obesity is quite prevalent. It is an important health problem that may be associated with a variety of physical, social, and psychological difficulties. The development of obesity is influenced by a complex interaction of biological, psychological, and sociocultural influences.
- The learning of adaptive eating and activity patterns is the basis of behavioral treatment programs for obesity. The treatments that include both the child and parent(s) are the most effective interventions for childhood obesity. However, greater weight loss and better maintenance still need to be achieved, and priority needs to be given to prevention and early intervention.

Eating Disorders

- Weight status, the presence or absence of binge eating, and the method employed to control one's weight are important considerations in thinking about eating disorders.
- The DSM describes three primary eating disorders: anorexia nervosa, bulimia nervosa and binge eating disorder. A category of other feeding or eating disorders is also described.
- Anorexia nervosa (AN) is a serious disorder characterized by extreme weight loss, an intense fear of gaining weight, persistent behaviors meant to avoid weight gain, and disturbance in the perception of body weight and shape. A number of other physical and psychological problems are present as well. A distinction is made between restricting and binge eating/purging anorexia.
- Bulimia nervosa (BN) refers to a repeated pattern of binge eating followed by some inappropriate compensatory behaviors. An undue influence of body shape and weight on self-esteem also is part of the criteria for a diagnosis of BN.
- Binge eating disorder (BED) is characterized by recurrent episodes of binge eating.
- Eating disorders occur predominantly in young women. Many young people may not meet full diagnostic criteria for AN, BN, or BED and they may be given a diagnosis of Other Feeding or Eating Disorder. Also, "subclinical" cases of eating disorders are quite common among younger adolescent and preadolescent girls. Indeed, increasing prevalence of eating-disordered behavior and attitudes among young girls has been noted. There is also increased concern regarding disordered eating and body dissatisfaction in young males.
- Ethnic and cultural differences deserve further consideration and certain groups, such as some athletes and dancers, may be at particular risk.
- Depression, anxiety disorders, and substance abuse commonly co-occur with eating disorders.
- Age of onset for AN is typically during adolescence. For many individuals the disorder, or other eating problems, persists over a considerable period of time. Significant medical complications may occur and for some, the disorder may be life threatening.
- The onset of BN extends from adolescence into early adulthood. Although symptoms diminish for many individuals, there is concern regarding persistent eating difficulties and depression. Also, various medical problems may occur, particularly among those who purge.
- The peak age of onset for BED is between 18 and 20 years of age. Most individuals with BED recover, but some may go on to meet the criteria for BN. BED may be associated with obesity and this poses increased medical and psychosocial risk.
- Explanations that incorporate multiple influences are needed to understand the development and maintenance of eating disorders. Although there is probably some overlap, it is worthwhile to distinguish factors influencing AN from those influencing BN and BED. Genetic and other biological influences, early feeding difficulties, temperament, social functioning, and cultural influences relating to body type ideal and gender roles are among the influences to consider.
- A variety of interventions have been employed to treat AN; however, support is greatest for family treatments with a behavioral focus. The Maudsley approach to treating AN is the best-studied family therapy.
- Treatments for BN and BED specific to adolescents have received limited attention, and current treatment recommendations are therefore based largely on downward extensions of studies with adults. Cognitive-behavioral treatment is the intervention for BN and BED in adults for which there is the best research support. A similar program for individuals who may fall in the subclinical category has been developed. Interpersonal psychotherapy has also proven to be effective with young adults with BN or BED.
- Controlled studies regarding the effectiveness of pharmacological treatments for eating disorders in adolescents are limited and findings unclear.
- Prevention programs attempt to address modifiable risk factors for eating disorders and/or promote factors that are protective against the development of eating disorders. A variety of prevention programs have demonstrated moderate effectiveness in reducing eating disorder risk factors or symptoms.

Key Terms

CHAPTER 15
Psychological Factors Affecting Medical Conditions

Looking Forward

After reading this chapter, you should be able to discuss:

- How the interface between psychology and medicine is conceptualized
- Psychological and family influences on the course of medical conditions such as asthma

- Psychological adjustment to chronic illnesses
- Challenges faced by youth and families in adapting to chronic illnesses such as cancer
- Psychological contributions to facilitating medical treatment
- Challenges in assisting a dying child and his or her family

In this chapter we examine how psychological factors contribute to our understanding of youth with chronic medical conditions. We also examine how psychological influences contribute to the delivery of effective medical treatment. In addressing these topics, we touch on issues such as the role of the family, the young person's adaptation and adjustment to chronic conditions, and the adherence of youth and families to regimens recommended by health care practitioners. In order to illustrate the interfaces between psychology and medicine, we describe the application of psychology to various medical conditions such as asthma, cancer, diabetes, and HIV/AIDS. We also discuss the history of such endeavors in order to understand how current thinking and practice has evolved.

Historical Context

In the past, the topics discussed in this chapter would have come under the heading of **psychosomatic disorders**. The focus of interest for such named disorders was on physical conditions, such as asthma, headaches, and ulcers, that were presumed to be affected by psychological factors. Terminology has undergone a number of changes in the last few decades. The term *Psychosomatic Disorders*, which appeared in previous versions of the DSM, was replaced in subsequent editions by the terms *Psychophysiological Disorders*, *Psychological Factors Affecting*

Physical Condition, and *Psychological Factors Affecting Medical Condition*. In the DSM-5 a new chapter—Somatic Symptoms and Related Disorders—includes the category *Psychological Factors Affecting Other Medical Conditions*.

The uncertainty over terminology reflects a long-standing controversy over the nature of the relationship between mind and body, the psyche and the soma. During the twentieth century, interest in the effects of psychological processes on the body resulted in the development of the field of **psychosomatic medicine**. Early investigators began to accumulate evidence and to develop theories of how psychological factors played a causative role in specific physical disorders (Alexander, 1950; Grace & Graham, 1952; Selye, 1956). As this field developed, several trends emerged. An increasing number of physical disorders were seen to be related to psychological factors. Even the common cold was thought to be affected by emotional factors. The question therefore arose as to whether it was fruitful to identify a specific group of psychosomatic disorders or whether psychological factors were operating in all physical conditions. In addition, the focus began to shift from psychogenesis, that is, psychological cause, to multicausality, the idea that biological, social, and psychological factors all contribute to both health and illness at multiple points. The latter view is holistic, assuming a continuous transaction among influences.

With this shift in thinking, the field began to expand considerably. The ongoing role of social and psychological factors in the development, consequences, and treatment of medical conditions and the role of those same factors in prevention and health maintenance all began to receive increased attention. When the focus of such interest is on children and adolescents, the field is typically referred to as **pediatric psychology**. The redefinition and expansion of the field is also reflected in the formation of professional societies and journals with a pediatric psychology focus, the development of training programs in pediatric psychology, and in the growth of integrated systems of health care (Aylward & Lee, 2017; Karazsia, Kazak, & Palermo, 2019).

Currently, pediatric psychology encompasses a multifaceted and integrated field of research and clinical practice that addresses a range of issues related to the physical and psychological health and development of children, adolescents, and their families. Specialized research, assessment, and intervention focus on the relationship between a young person's cognitive, social, and emotional functioning and their physical health, including the ways in which psychosocial, developmental, and contextual factors may be related to the etiology, course, and outcome of pediatric medical conditions (American Psychological Association, 2019). In this chapter, we will examine some of the specific medical problems that have received the attention of pediatric psychologists and look at some other selected topics of interest. Our examination will allow us to illustrate the changes that have occurred and the current status and diversity of this field.

Psychological and Family Influences on Medical Conditions

The experience of children with medical conditions is influenced by multiple and complex factors. For most children, illness and medical intervention make up a small part of their experience—a vaccine to ward off illness, an antibiotic to treat infection, or an X-ray to assess the impact of a fall while at play. Children with chronic and recurrent health conditions, however, regularly experience uncomfortable medical procedures and interventions, altered physiological experience, and variations in social interactions and experiences that impact their development, adjustment, and behavior (Slifer, 2014). The young person must not only cope with these unique stressors but also simultaneously encounters the same developmental tasks and challenges as their healthy peers (Brown & Kupst, 2016). While illnesses and treatments vary considerably, the developmental process may be affected by the interplay of medical illness and intervention with other influences of normative development, presenting unique challenges to the child and their caregivers as well as to their medical care (Kazak, Alderfer, & Reader, 2017a).

The family often plays a central role in management of the health condition. The ways in which a parent or caregiver responds to a child's illness can affect the behavioral and emotional response of the children for whom they are caring and can promote or impede the child's health outcomes. The young person's adaptation is both affected by and affects the family and is reciprocally related to their stress, coping, and psychological adjustment.

Asthma as an Example

In this section, we will look at information on asthma to illustrate how psychological and family variables may influence the symptoms of pediatric medical problems and management of the disease. This examination of asthma will allow us to see how thinking about the role of psychological variables in physical illness has changed and expanded.

Description and Prevalence

Defining and describing asthma is complex, as it is heterogeneous disease with variable symptoms (Global Initiative for Asthma, 2019; McQuaid & Fedele, 2017). Generally defined, asthma is a chronic disorder of the respiratory system that is characterized by hyperresponsiveness of the airways to a potentially wide range of stimuli. Hyperresponsiveness results in chronic inflammation and narrowing of air passages, and air exchange is impaired, particularly during expiration. Intermittent episodes of wheezing, shortness of breath, chest tightness and/or cough result. The course and intensity of symptoms and limitations in airflow vary. Severe attacks or exacerbations of asthma, known as status asthmaticus, which are life threatening may occur and require emergency medical treatment. The fear of not being able to breathe and the danger of severe exacerbations are likely to create appreciable anxiety in the young person and in family members.

Asthma is a common chronic illness in young people, and prevalence has increased over the years (Akinbami, Simon, & Rossen, 2016). Currently, approximately 9% of youth are estimated to be affected by asthma, and urban, minority, and poor children are overrepresented (Akinbami et al., 2016; McQuaid & Fedele, 2017). Asthma is a potentially reversible disorder, but the impact of the disease on the young person is considerable. It can include hospitalization, emergency room use, and many lost school days (Nunes, Pereira, & Morais-Almeida, 2017; Zahran et al., 2018).

Clearly, the greatest threat is loss of life, and all measures used to treat the physical symptoms of asthma—daily medication to prevent wheezing, environmental control of potential irritants, desensitization to allergens, avoidance of infection, and emergency treatment to stop wheezing—are geared to prevent death. Although much has been done to improve treatment, high prevalence rates, as well as increases in medical costs, hospitalization, and mortality rates, are reasons for continuing concern and, again, urban poor youth are at particular risk (Ferrante & La Grutta, 2018; McQuaid & Fedele, 2017).

LOREN Managing Asthma

Loren is a 12-year-old boy with moderate to severe asthma. For the fourth time in a year, he was hospitalized because of asthma. At hospital rounds, Loren's physician pointed out that his asthma could be controlled if he avoided triggers of his asthma, including exercise-induced attacks, and if he complied with his medication regimen. It was also pointed out that Loren did not use his nebulizer properly. Instead of alleviating his respiratory distress, most of the medication was wasted because of inappropriate inhaler use. Lack of quick relief frustrated Loren. As a result he tended to become angry, a behavior that only exacerbated his asthma. It was decided to
(1) teach Loren to identify and avoid triggers of his asthma,
(2) review his medication and adjust the regimen if possible,
(3) improve his compliance to his medical treatment regimen,
(4) teach him how to use his nebulizer correctly, and
(5) teach him skills to control his frustration.

Adapted from Creer, 1998, p. 411

Etiology

The causes of asthma are complex, and there is a considerable history of controversy concerning etiology. However, it is broadly acknowledged that genetic or other factors place some youth at risk for developing asthma. The onset and persistence of the condition is thought to be the result of the interaction of biological and environmental factors (Clawson et al., 2019; Global Initiative for Asthma, 2019). While these causes are not fully understood, they are thought to produce a hypersensitivity of the air passages that, once established, results in the young person's responding to various irritants more easily than would an individual without asthma.

Individuals with highly sensitive and labile respiratory tracts are potentially exposed to a set of factors that influence whether asthma attacks or exacerbations occur. These influences have come to be thought of as *trigger* mechanisms or *irritants*, rather than direct causes of asthma. Every child or adolescent has different triggers, and triggers can differ over time for the same youth (Janssens & Harver, 2015; McQuaid & Fedele, 2017).

Physical illness, specifically repeated respiratory infection, may play a role in the development of asthma, and some respiratory viral infections can set off or worsen the severity of an attack (Centers for Disease Control and Prevention, 2020; Papadopoulos et al., 2020). Allergies may also be related to the development and occurrence of asthma exacerbations. A young person may have allergies to inhaled substances (such as dust, the dander of a pet, or pollen) or to ingested substances (such as milk, wheat, or chocolate). Physical factors such as cold temperatures, tobacco smoke, pungent odors, exercise, and rapid breathing may also contribute to wheezing. Poor medical management and/or adherence can exacerbate the course of illness. Furthermore, psychological stimuli and emotional upset are often considered important triggers of asthma exacerbations (Bray et al., 2017; Clawson et al., 2019; McQuaid & Fedele, 2017).

Psychological and Family Influences

Although we have come to view the causes of asthma differently, in much of the early literature asthma was viewed primarily as a disease with psychological causes and, in fact, was at one time referred to as "asthma nervosa" (Alexander, 1950). Early investigations of treatment for asthma also focused on psychological bases for improvement in symptoms. Purcell and his colleagues (1969)—working at the Children's Asthma Research Institute and Hospital (CARIH) in Denver—for example, observed that some children became free of symptoms fairly soon after being sent away from their parents for treatment. These observations, and others like it, led investigators to view changes in the psychological atmosphere as a basis for improvement in asthma symptoms. Indeed, in the 1950s, "parentectomy" was suggested as the treatment of choice for some children (Peshkin, 1959). While the symptoms of some children did improve during their separation from parents, questions remained. Were these observed effects of separation due to changes in the emotional environment or in the physical environment? Could changes have been due to other factors, such as increased compliance with prescribed medical regimens while in specialized care?

Over time, research has begun to address these and other questions, and it has become clear that there is little evidence that psychological or family factors play a significant role as an original cause of the reduced respiratory capacity characteristic of asthma. Yet, this does not mean that psychological factors and family functioning play no role in asthma. In fact, there is evidence that these factors may play an important role both in precipitating or triggering asthma symptoms in at-risk youth and in influencing the course of illness (Clawson et al., 2019; Global Initiative for Asthma, 2019; McQuaid & Fedele, 2017). Home environment (e.g., dust, animal dander), activities of family members (e.g., smoking, outdoor activities), family stress (e.g., family fights, psychosocial problems), and individual emotional states (e.g., anxiety, embarrassment, laughter) are among the influences that may trigger the onset and/or exacerbation of asthma symptoms. In other words, while physiological factors may predispose asthma in young people, family functioning and psychological factors also play important roles.

The psychological factors that contribute to asthma have been further investigated in the field of psychoneuroimmunology (PNI), which examines the ways in which the central nervous, neuroendocrine, and immune systems interact with psychological variables and physical health in what is referred to as the "mind-body connection" (Bray et al., 2017). In asthma, emotional stress is theorized to affect the autonomic nervous system, which regulates bodily functions including lung function, contributing to the onset or exacerbation of respiratory symptoms when youth with asthma experience negative emotions. While stress and emotions may contribute to the onset or exacerbation of asthma symptoms in some individuals, the condition can also impact adjustment for some. For example, asthma may restrict or limit a young person's activities, such as their participation in sports, opportunities for outside play, and other physical activities, which may in turn impact their adjustment (Bhagat et al., 2019). Moreover, as already mentioned, the respiratory symptoms themselves and adverse implications of the disorder can be cause for emotional distress in children and their families.

Indeed, overall, children and adolescents with asthma experience psychosocial difficulties, in particular internalizing symptoms such as anxiety and depression, at higher rates than healthy peers (Dudeney et al., 2017; Lu et al., 2012; Shankar et al., 2019). Youth with asthma are also more likely to experience behavioral difficulties (McQuaid, Kopel, & Nassau, 2001) and other disruptions in functioning, such as disturbances in sleep (Koinis-Mitchell et al., 2017). Research also suggests that children with more severe asthma symptoms display greater emotional and behavioral difficulties, and youth with co-occurring psychiatric problems, notably anxiety and depression, are more likely to report greater asthma symptom severity (Booster, Oland, & Bender, 2016; McQuaid & Fedele, 2017). Moreover, psychological difficulties are also associated with poorer asthma control and outcomes (Baiardini et al., 2015). The relationship between psychological difficulties and asthma is complex and likely bidirectional. Having a chronic health condition, such as asthma, may increase stress and impairment which may contribute to the development of adjustment difficulties, or psychological difficulties may exacerbate the impact of asthma and confound management of the condition, resulting in greater distress and difficulties (Clawson et al., 2019; Goodwin et al., 2012).

The young person's asthma also may affect the family in many ways. Parents may experience increased anxiety, lose work days because of their child's illness, and suffer high medical costs (Easter, Sharpe, & Hunt, 2015; Nunes et al., 2017; Sullivan et al., 2018). Siblings may experience loss of attention and restrictions in choice of family activities. For example, Annett and colleagues (2010) investigated the relationships among the aspects of

the child's asthma condition, child and family psychological functioning, and child and parent quality of life. Their findings support the idea that family functioning affects the child's functioning and that the child's functioning and the control of the child's asthma condition affect both the child's and parents' quality of life (see Figure 15.1).

Psychological and family factors may also influence outcome in asthma via their effects on treatment adherence. The goal of treatment for pediatric asthma is to achieve well-controlled symptoms using pharmacological and non-pharmacological intervention (Clawson et al., 2019; Global Initiative for Asthma, 2019). Current treatments to improve asthma functioning focus on improving management and adherence. Family members likely have to assist in the management of the disease, especially for younger children. It is, therefore, not surprising that interventions have included basic medical management, pharmacological management, and psychological components that have focused on educating families about the triggers of asthma attacks, on the consequences of asthma, and on helping young people and their families manage the disease (Global Initiative for Asthma, 2019). Moreover, psychologically based mind–body interventions, such as relaxation and guided imagery, written emotional expression, yoga, and mindfulness therapy, have been shown to be effective in improving lung functioning and overall quality of life for children and adolescents with asthma (Bray et al., 2017).

Thus, the focus on psychological and family factors has shifted from the cause of a chronic illness such as asthma to an interest in the relationship between physical and psychological factors and how children, parents, family, and health care professionals may influence the frequency and severity of symptoms and the management of the disorder (Clawson et al., 2019; McQuaid & Fedele, 2017).

Consequences of Chronic Conditions

Major advances in early detection, diagnosis, and treatment of chronic illnesses, such as asthma, diabetes, and cancer, in children and adolescents has led to increased rates of survival from previously life-threatening diseases (Compas et al., 2012). Although the definition can vary, chronic illness may be defined as any condition that endures for an extended period of time—typically defined as three or more months—that creates **functional impairment**, such as difficulty attending school or participating in regular activities, and that necessitates medical needs greater than would be expected given the child's age (Brown & Kupst, 2016). Some examples of chronic illness include asthma, cancer, epilepsy, sickle cell disease, diabetes, and chronic pain. The estimated prevalence of childhood chronic illness varies considerably based on a number of factors, including the method

Figure 15.1 The relationship among asthma, child and parent functioning, and quality of life. (Adapted from Annett et at., 2010. Copyright 1994 by the Oxford University Press; reprinted with permission)

used to collect prevalence data, the definition of chronic illness, and type of condition. However, overall, approximately 10–35% of children and adolescents are estimated to be affected by chronic illness (Riccio et al., 2018). Of note, the prevalence of chronic conditions in children has been increasing over time, the result of numerous factors including advances in medicine that have increased survival rates for children with serious medical conditions (Brown & Kupst, 2016).

What are the consequences of chronic medical conditions for young people and their families? As introduced in our discussion of asthma, interest in the interplay of health and illness on the physical and psychological development of children, adolescents, and their families has become part of the interface between psychology and medicine. The effects of any chronic illness are likely to be pervasive, particularly if the illness is life threatening. The young person is likely to experience substantial

stress and anxiety. In addition, limitations due to illness often place obstacles in the way of normal development. Contact with peers may be limited, for example, or school attendance may be disrupted.

Of course, the family, too, needs to cope with the illness, its treatment, and its effects over long periods of time. Such long-term demands are bound to be difficult to handle, and the consistency required by treatment regimens is stressful in its own right. Thus, the entire family may experience considerable anxiety and have appreciable stress placed on its daily routines.

Adjustment and Chronic Illness

Research on chronic illness has become a priority for pediatric psychologists (Brown & Kupst, 2016; Roberts & Steele, 2017). One frequent question is whether chronic illness leads to poor

Parental concern over precipitating a symptomatic attack may lead children with chronic illnesses, such as asthma, to spend appreciable time isolated from their peers. (Picture Partners/Alamy Stock Photo)

adjustment. The answer would appear to be not necessarily, but these illnesses and related life experiences probably place the young person at increased risk for adjustment problems (Bennett et al., 2015; Drotar, 2006; Ferro & Boyle, 2015; Lemanek, Hahn, & McNaull, 2017; McGavock, Dart, & Wicklow, 2014; Quittner, Saez-Flores, & Barton, 2016; Reed-Knight, Mackner, & Crandall, 2017). Research findings suggest there is considerable variation in adjustment among chronically ill youth. Although the majority of young people with a chronic illness do not experience serious adjustment problems, subsets of more vulnerable patients do exist (Mullins & Chaney, 2019; Rapoff, Lindsley, & Karlson, 2017; Vannatta & Salley, 2017).

However, measuring adjustment at any one time is unlikely to provide a complete picture. Adjustment for the young person and family members is likely to be an ongoing process, beginning at diagnosis and continuing through treatment, treatment completion, perhaps relapse, and the long-term course that is inherent in a chronic illness (Kazak et al., 2017a). This has led some professionals to consider a traumatic stress framework to understand the initial reaction to diagnosis and treatment and to adjustment over time (Kazak, Price, & Kassam-Adams, 2017b; Price et al., 2015).

Adjustment to chronic illness is best thought of as a complex function of a number of variables (Kazak et al., 2017a; Mullins et al., 2015). Characteristics of the young person and family members probably contribute to the adjustment of both the young person and the family; for example, the youth's existing competencies and the types and variety of coping skills that

the young person possesses are likely to be important in this process. A second category of variables is disease factors, such as severity, degree of impairment, and the functional independence of the young person. In addition, the youth's environment (e.g., family, school, health care) is likely to be a factor in variations in adjustment. While several useful models have emerged to help understand risk and coping processes in children with chronic illness (Brown & Kupst, 2016), an appreciation of the complexity of the problem is well illustrated in the model offered by Wallander, Varni, and their colleagues (Wallander & Varni, 1998; see Figure 15.2).

In the following sections, we examine two of the influences on adjustment to chronic illness: illness parameters and family functioning.

Illness Parameters and Adjustment

In seeking to understand the adjustment among young people with chronic illnesses, it is reasonable to ask whether aspects of the illness itself contribute to differences in adjustment. In attempting to answer this question, the severity of the illness, predictability of the illness, visibility of the condition, stress related to the illness, perceptions regarding the illness, and the degree of functional impairment produced by the illness are among the variables that have been examined. Of course, analyzing these dimensions separately is not always possible. For example, a more severe illness is likely to be related to greater restrictions in normal functioning. However, each of the variables can be important.

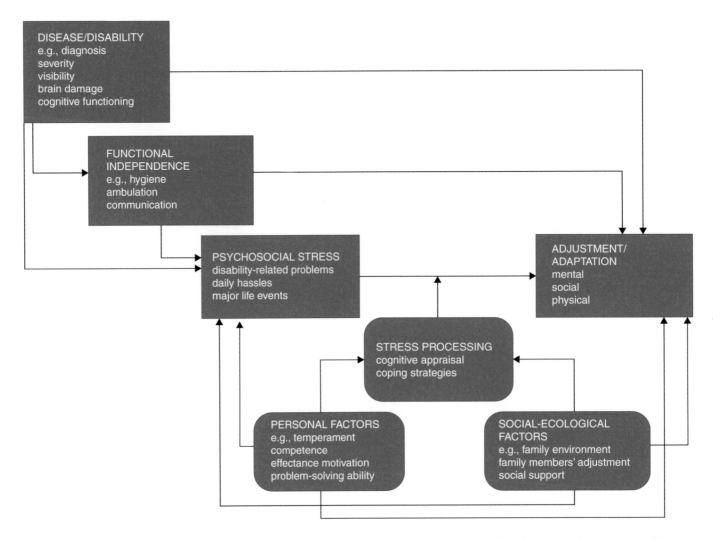

Figure 15.2 A conceptual model of child adjustment to chronic illness or disorder. Square-corner boxes indicate risk factors; round-corner boxes indicate resistance (protective) factors. (Adapted from Wallander & Varni, 1998. Copyright 1998 by John Wiley & Sons; reprinted with permission)

Certain conditions are more severe than others, but severity of illness also can vary among young people with the same condition. What, then, might be the impact of severity of the medical problem? Findings are conflicting (Kazak et al., 2017a; Rapoff et al., 2017); however, some research does suggest a relationship between illness severity and adjustment (Booster et al., 2016; Lamanek, Hahn, & McNaull, 2017; Shaw & DeMaso, 2020). For example, a recent systematic review summarized the findings of 13 studies examining the prevalence of depression among youth diagnosed with sickle cell disease (SCD), a common hematological disorder with variable disease severity. Youth with SCD may experience numerous complications, including vaso-occlusive crises (blood vessel blockage) and anemia (low hemoglobin levels), which result in frequent episodes of pain. A range of prevalence of depression (4–46%) was reported among studies assessing depression among children and adolescents

with SCD, and pain was identified as predicting higher occurrence of depressive symptoms (Moody, Mercer, & Glass, 2019). Illness severity, however, is not always associated with poorer adjustment, and the relationships are likely complex and may rely on the young person's and family's perceptions of the severity of the condition, among other factors (Chaney et al., 2016; Roberts et al., 2019).

The young person's attitude toward the illness and the degree of stress experienced by the youth and family also may impact adjustment. For example, LeBovidge, Lavigne, & Miller (2005) examined the adjustment of young people aged 8 to 18 with chronic arthritis. Greater illness-related and nonillness-related stresses were both associated with higher levels of anxiety and depressive symptomatology and parent reports of adjustment problems. A more positive attitude toward illness, in contrast, was associated with lower levels of anxiety and depressive

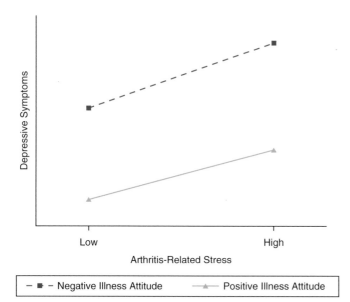

Figure 15.3 Arthritis-related stress, illness attitude, and depressive symptomatology. (Adapted from LeBovidge, Lavigne, & Miller, 2005. Copyright 2005 by Oxford University Press; reprinted with permission)

symptomatology. Figure 15.3 illustrates the relationship of arthritis-related stress and illness attitude to depressive symptomatology.

Adjustment also may be associated with the degree of functional limitation (how restricted the youth is) due to the chronic condition (Law et al., 2017; McQuaid & Fedele, 2017). Functional limitations may affect the number of absences from school, relationships with friends, or other aspects of the youth's functioning (Riccio et al., 2018; Rohrig & Puliafico, 2018). For example, inflammatory bowel disease (IBD) is a condition characterized by chronic inflammation of the gastrointestinal tract. Children with IBD experience frequent diarrhea, abdominal pain, weight loss, growth delay, delayed puberty, fatigue, and other symptoms. IBD is an unpredictable and potentially embarrassing disease. Youth may be embarrassed about their symptoms and frequent bathroom visits, and this may lead to their limiting social activities. Also, social activities may be cancelled due to disease flare-ups. Youth with IBD report poorer functioning across a number of domains (Schurman et al., 2017).

Interpreting the impact of aspects of illness is inevitably difficult. In research, we cannot ethically manipulate emotional conditions or illness severity, nor can we randomly assign young people to diseases. As a result, it can be difficult to distinguish causal risk factors from associated ones. Furthermore, although illness factors may help predict adjustment, predictive ability is not very strong. Integrating illness factors into a more normative approach—one that combines these factors with the stress, risk, and resilience factors included in etiological models for

young people without chronic medical disorder—is a useful approach and several models have been proposed and supported by research (Mullins et al., 2015). Such an approach would allow for identification of factors relatively specific to chronic illness, as well as those common to other young people and families. Among the variables that might be the focus of such a normative approach is family functioning.

Family Functioning and Adjustment

Just as family functioning plays a major role in typical child development, the family is an important consideration in child adjustment to chronic illness. The majority of research suggests no mean differences in family functioning between families of children with a chronic illness and normative data or control groups. However, it is not surprising that family functioning is related to the psychological adjustment of chronically ill children and adolescents (Kazak et al., 2017a; Van Schoors et al., 2016). Without denying the particular risks and stressors associated with chronic conditions, it is reasonable as a starting point to assume that some of the family influences that are related to adjustment of physically healthy children and adolescents, such as specific parenting behaviors, parental depression, disruptions in family life, and marital conflict, are also related to the adjustment of young people with chronic illness. Indeed, this seems to be the case (Kazak et al., 2017a; Mullins et al., 2016).

A variety of family influences known to be related to child and adolescent adjustment in general have also been investigated in populations of young people with a chronic condition (Brown & Kupst, 2016; Cousino & Hazen, 2013; Pinquart, 2013; Van Gampelaere et al., 2018). Overall, the research suggests the same family influences that serve as protective or risk factors for adjustment difficulties in healthy young people are also associated with psychological well-being or risk for children with chronic illness (Brown & Kupst, 2016; Watson et al., 2014). For example, parenting styles characterized by high levels of warmth and support, which are generally associated with positive child adjustment, are also related to better adjustment, including less depressive symptoms and fewer externalizing behavior problems, in children with chronic physical conditions (Crandell et al., 2018).

Yet, parents of children with chronic medical conditions invariably face parenting challenges that exceed those of parents of typically developing youth, and consideration of the interplay of family functioning and child illness is important. As described by Crandell and colleagues (2018), parenting a child with a chronic physical condition involves both ordinary parenting behaviors, such as supervising a child on a playground or managing school activities, and extraordinary parenting behaviors specific to the child's condition, such as monitoring the glucose level of a child with diabetes or managing the multiple medical appointments and distress of a child undergoing intensive cancer

ERIN Chronic Illness and School Refusal

Erin was a 14-year-old with an extensive medical history. At 14 months old, Erin was diagnosed with kidney failure and underwent bladder reconstructive surgery. Thereafter, Erin utilized a catheter and external reservoir to supplement her urinary function. Because of her compromised health, Erin experienced many medical complications (e.g., severe dehydration, infections) and multiple hospitalizations throughout her upbringing. This impacted her school attendance over many years and resulted in frequent absences. Medically justified absences quickly transitioned to school refusal in the spring of the seventh grade, however, after a severe infection required her to be hospitalized for three weeks. Upon her return to school in the spring of the seventh grade, Erin reported feeling ill in the morning and endorsed a fear of becoming sick in school. When she did attend school, Erin frequently visited the nurse's office and bathroom to avoid being in the classroom with her peers. She often requested for her mother to pick her up when she experienced any physical discomfort (e.g., stomachache) in school. Partial school attendance quickly escalated to absences; by the end of seventh grade, Erin had attended only 28 full days of school.

Upon intake [for cognitive-behavioral therapy to address school refusal], Erin endorsed anxiety regarding her medical issues. Specifically, she reported feeling apprehensive about attending school for fear that she would become ill (i.e., vomit) in front of her peers; she noted that this did in fact happen once during seventh grade. Erin also endorsed feeling nervous that others would make fun of her if they found out about her catheter and external urine reservoir. As a result, Erin often neglected to empty her catheter while at school, which contributed to infections and hospitalizations in the past. Last, both the parent interview and assessment with Erin revealed that she exhibited symptoms of depression, such as a loss of appetite and interest in things she previously enjoyed (e.g., going to a coffee shop with friends), sleeping for long periods of time (especially when staying home from school), feeling isolated, and experiencing self-blame and scrutinizing thoughts. Erin reported that she had experienced passive suicidal ideation (i.e., "I don't want to deal with this anymore") but denied any current plan or intent to harm herself.

Adapted from Rohrig & Puliafico, 2018, pp. 3–4

treatment. While many parents of children with medical conditions adapt well to their child's illness, some may be at increased risk for psychological distress, including symptoms of depression, anxiety, and posttraumatic stress (Shaw & DeMaso, 2020; Woolf et al., 2016). Research also indicates that parental distress and childhood illness are likely bidirectional in nature—childhood illness affects the developing child and the family, and in turn, the family influences the child's adaptation to illness (Kazak et al., 2017a; Palermo, Valrie, & Karlson, 2014). Moreover, illness-related parameters and family factors do not operate independently of each other and may moderate or mediate each other's relationship to adjustment.

Research has examined, for example, child and family adaptation to juvenile idiopathic arthritis (JIA), the most common rheumatic disease in childhood, which is characterized by chronic pain and functional limitations. Among other factors, research suggests parental distress is associated with child outcomes in JIA, including poorer quality of life and higher levels of functional disabilities (Hynes et al., 2019; Seid et al., 2014; Timko et al., 1993). Moreover, the significant demands on parents of youth with JIA and other juvenile rheumatic diseases, such as regimen management, frequent medical appointments, and financial strain, have been associated with parental distress and child depressive symptoms (Chaney et al., 2016).

Qualities of the parent–child relationship may also be important in understanding the link between parental functioning and youth adjustment. A recent study of adjustment in childhood cancer survivors, for example, examined the role of the parent–child relationship in the association between parental psychological functioning and adjustment outcomes (Schepers et al., 2018). The study included 206 childhood cancer survivors between the ages of 8 and 21 years and their primary caregivers. Youth reported on the quality of the parent–child relationship and on their adjustment. Parents reported on their own distress, quality of the parent–child relationship, and their child's adjustment, among other factors. Results indicated that parent distress was associated with higher youth-reported internalizing symptoms. Similarly, parents who reported more distress reported more internalizing problems in their child as compared to parents who were less distressed, and this relationship was mediated by parental perceptions of their relationship with their child. The more distressed parents were, the more likely they were to feel less attached to their child and more frustrated in the parent–child relationship. However, while a portion of parents and youth reported higher levels of distress and adjustment difficulties, overall, childhood cancer survivors and their parents were found to demonstrate considerable resilience with equal or lower levels of psychological distress as compared to healthy peers. These findings are in line with the literature on high rates of family resilience after pediatric cancer (Van Schoors et al., 2015; Vannatta & Salley, 2017).

The influence of the parent–child relationship on child adjustment has also been demonstrated in studies of other chronic conditions. Berg and colleagues (2011), for example, examined the role of parental involvement in young adolescents with diabetes. Better quality of both the mothers' and fathers' relationships with their child (acceptance, independence and encouragement, and communication) was associated with better diabetes outcomes (metabolic control and adherence). In addition, mothers' and fathers' monitoring of the young person's general daily activities and of the young person's diabetes care behaviors was associated with better diabetes outcomes. Many of the relationships between parental involvement and diabetes outcomes were mediated by the adolescents' perceptions of self-efficacy. That is, better parental involvement was associated with the adolescents' greater confidence in their ability to manage diabetes situations and this, in turn, was associated with better diabetes outcomes.

Another study, examining the role of family functioning on adolescent diabetes adherence and glycemic control, also demonstrated an association between parental involvement and family conflict with diabetes outcomes (Mackey et al., 2014). Findings suggest maternal depressive symptoms may lead to less parental monitoring and more conflict, which in turn are each associated with poorer adherence and glycemic control. Moreover, poor youth adherence was associated with more parent–child conflict which, in turn, was associated with maternal depressive symptoms. Families with a diabetic child have appreciable demands placed on them to organize daily routines involved in the management of the illness. Conceivably, these demands could impact the psychological functioning of the parent or, alternatively, may be more difficult to monitor given the fatigue, anhedonia, and other symptoms associated with existing parental depression. Additionally, poor adherence and glycemic control may be associated with greater family stress and conflict. These considerations highlight the powerful interplay between illness parameters, family functioning, and adjustment.

Also important is consideration of adjustment as a process over time. Attention to critical developmental transitions such as transition to school, to early adolescence, and the expanding responsibilities of disease management that come with entry into adulthood. The young person's condition may change, and the effect of the illness on the family may not be static. Furthermore, changes in the young person and in the illness may require changing styles of family involvement. Because young people with chronic illnesses have a greater chance of survival than ever before, these findings suggest the need for continued exploration of how time since treatment, current developmental level, age at

diagnosis, and other variables may be related to the association of family environment and the young person's psychological adjustment (Kazak et al., 2017a; Palermo et al., 2014).

As more children and adolescents survive chronic illnesses, the complexities of studying long-term adjustment become clear. Rather than asking about better disease adjustment, it may be more reasonable to ask how the experience of chronic illness affects individual development.

Cancer: Adapting to Chronic Illness

Childhood cancer is a life-threatening and serious disease, which presents considerable distress to children and their families. Long viewed as fatal, cancer remains the leading cause of death by disease for children (Kazak & Noll, 2015). Advances in cancer therapies, however, have led to dramatic treatment gains and improvements in rates of survival. For example, in 1960, the survival rate of acute lymphocytic leukemia, the most common form of childhood cancer, was 1% five years after diagnosis. By the mid-1970s, the survival rate had increased to about 49%, and by the early twenty-first century, to about 88%. Advances in treatment have improved the overall five-year survival rate for childhood cancers to about 80% (Vannatta & Salley, 2017).

With increasing survival rates, emphasis has shifted from "dying from" to "living with" cancer (Eiser, 1998). For many young people, it may now be more appropriate to view cancer as a chronic condition rather than a fatal disease. However, improvements in survival are the result of increasingly aggressive interventions, which are often lengthy, highly invasive, stressful, and accompanied by considerable pain. While treatments for childhood cancer vary in length and intensity, they typically have considerable health and psychological implications for at least one year following diagnosis and often longer (Kazak & Noll, 2015). Working with this population thus presents multiple and complex challenges.

The distinct phases in the course of cancer diagnosis and treatment are associated with different stressors for children and families (Vannatta & Salley, 2017). The initial hours, days, and weeks leading up to and after diagnosis, for example, are typically filled with urgency and upheaval of daily life. The time frame for diagnosis and treatment decisions is often compressed and involves multiple tests and evaluations. During this time, young people and their caregivers must take in extensive information about their diagnosis and make decisions about treatment options (Kazak & Noll, 2015). In addition to the initial task of helping the young person and family understand and come to accept the illness, it is important to assist them in coping with a long and stressful treatment regimen and the additional stressors that the illness and its treatment place on them. During

Families may require continuing assistance to help them in supporting their child with cancer. (E+/Getty Images)

treatment, children not only experience various physical side effects, including procedural pain, nausea, and other symptoms of treatment, but may experience hospitalizations and barriers to participation in normative activities, such as school and peer activities (Vannatta & Salley, 2017). Parents also experience considerable distress and burden. The eventual transition from active treatment to remission can also bring a mixture of positive emotions and worry regarding the uncertainty about disease recurrence or other complications.

Concerns regarding the longer-term psychosocial impact of the disease and its treatment are considerable (Vannatta & Salley, 2017). Potential effects are probably related to developmental period. For adolescents, the disease may interfere with the development of autonomy as a result of increased dependence on family and medical staff, and it may impose restrictions on social life and the development of close interpersonal relationships. Adolescence also is a developmental period during which some high-risk behaviors (substance use) may be somewhat normative. Even brief involvement in such behaviors can have significant consequences for young people with cancer. Problematic outcomes, however, are not inevitable. The provision of ongoing psychosocial services to families throughout this process may buffer the impact of the cancer experience and allow these young people to develop and function much like their peers. Such support and services may also assist siblings and other family members who are affected (Alderfer et al., 2010; Dolgin et al., 2007; Kazak, 2005; Lobato & Kao, 2005).

One must also be aware that the very treatments that have resulted in longer survival may contribute to other long-term challenges. Advances in treatments such as chemotherapy and radiation have contributed to increased life expectancy. However, young people who have completed these treatments are at increased risk for physical health difficulties such as growth and reproductive difficulties, cardiological, pulmonary, renal/urological, orthopedic, sensory motor, and neurological impairments, and secondary malignancies. Cosmetic impairments and functional limitations (e.g., diminished stamina) have also been frequently noted. Some of these effects may not be apparent immediately after treatment, but may occur later among survivors, and their impact may evolve over time (Armstrong et al., 2016; Landier, Armenian, & Bhatia, 2015; Vannatta & Salley, 2017). Follow-up care and interventions designed to help promote healthy behaviors and decrease high-risk behaviors can help prevent and control negative physical outcomes (Landier et al., 2015; Tyc & Klosky, 2015).

Challenges in psychological and cognitive domains may also be associated with medical treatments for cancer. For example, the immediate and long-term impacts on the central nervous system (CNS) of treatments such as craniospinal irradiation (CSI) and chemotherapy to prevent CNS occurrence of leukemia are of concern. Neurocognitive late effects—impairment in cognitive and academic functioning—appear to manifest during or following treatment completion and, thus, CSI may be reserved for children who relapse or who are at high risk for CNS involvement. Nonetheless, continued concern and attention to long-term neurocognitive impacts remain and require monitoring and intervention (Askins, Ann-Yi, & Moore, 2015; Vannatta & Salley, 2017).

The shift to coping, adjusting, and adapting to cancer is clearly a more optimistic approach than in years past when survival rates were very low. However, while we continue to attempt to understand this process and assist young people and families, we must also monitor long-term outcomes and side effects of treatment. In addition, relapse remains possible, and these individuals are at increased risk for secondary cancers. Maintaining vigilance without creating additional and undue anxiety, and at the same time promoting an optimistic and adaptive attitude, presents a considerable challenge.

A similar perspective on adaptation applies to other chronic illnesses such as SCD and HIV/AIDS (see Accent: "The Impact of HIV/AIDS on Children and Adolescents"). While the majority of children, adolescents, and their families cope and adapt to the considerable stressors associated with childhood cancer, the consequences of the illness or condition itself as well as the impact of intensive, demanding, and long-term treatments need to be addressed in understanding adaptation to these chronic conditions over time (Kupst & Patenaude, 2016; Vannatta & Salley, 2017).

ACCENT The Impact of HIV/AIDS on Children and Adolescents

With advances in HIV testing, more efficacious treatment, and more effective preventive measures, the global HIV epidemic has experienced an overall stabilization and reversal with fewer new infections and better health outcomes (Gillespie, 2016). However, an appreciable number of those infected with HIV and AIDS are women of childbearing age. The HIV-positive children born to women with HIV and AIDS are some of the saddest images of the AIDS story. These babies are often very sick and frequently are given away or taken from their mothers. Many of them are taken in by foster parents who are willing to take on the challenge of caring for such a child. Fortunately, with medical advances, the number of HIV babies born to HIV-positive women in the United States has dropped dramatically over time (Centers for Disease Control and Prevention, 2019b). However, this problem remains a considerable international concern (Joint United Nations Programme on HIV/AIDS (UNAIDS), 2019).

Although the majority (approximately 90%) of young people become infected through vertical transmission from their mothers, some, such as those with hemophilia, become infected through the blood supply. For older children and adolescents, there is also risk for transmission by drug use or sexual contact (Gillespie, 2016). With medical advances producing greater survival rates, attention has shifted from terminal care for affected youth to management of the condition, adherence to medication regimens, and improving quality of life (Deeks, Lewin, & Havlir, 2013; Dinaj-Koci et al., 2019; Raymond et al., 2017).

We have known for some time that children born infected with HIV are likely to have developmental and neurocognitive problems (Nichols, 2016; Phillips et al., 2016). Improved antiretroviral therapy, however, has improved the situation by slowing down the progression of central nervous system disease (Nichols, 2016). However, by school age if these neurological problems exist, they may result in significant learning, language, and attention difficulties, and emotional and social difficulties may also be evident. The impact may be greater for young people with greater compromise of their immune system (Eckard et al., 2017). Young people with HIV/AIDS are thus likely to have to continue to adapt to extraordinary circumstances and are also likely to present their caregivers with exceptional challenges.

It is important to remember that not all HIV-infected youth have clinically significant cognitive, emotional, and behavioral problems. However, among those who do, a complex set of influences is likely contributing to the difficulties. Clearly, some of the problems are direct outcomes of their disease. The medical treatments, stress of adhering to a long-term medical regimen and a chronic illness, and other contextual factors are probably factors as well (Benki-Nugent & Boivin, 2019; Hermetet-Lindsay et al., 2017).

Families also face difficult decisions regarding disclosure of the illness both to the child and others. In addition, many of these young people were born to mothers whose prenatal care was not optimal, who may have abused drugs when they were pregnant, or who had serious psychopathology themselves. Those youth who contract the disease from drug use or sexual contact are also likely to have been exposed to other risk factors (Outlaw et al., 2010). All of these powerful influences, as well as family and environmental risks that the young people may have faced after their births, make current problematic outcomes understandable. The adaptation challenges are considerable and call for a coordinated and intensive program of assistance for these young people and their families (Gillespie, 2016; Martinez, Chakraborty, & Committee on Pediatric AIDS, 2014).

Facilitating Medical Treatment

Attempts to provide psychological treatment that would improve a patient's medical condition have long been an aspect of the interface between psychology/psychiatry and medicine. The vast majority of early attempts sought to provide the patient with psychotherapy as a means of reducing physical symptoms or curing illness. Such direct assaults on illness through psychotherapy proved to be largely ineffective (Werry, 1986). Tremendous progress has been made in pediatric psychology, and more recent efforts are likely to integrate a psychological perspective into the clinically relevant, evidence-based treatment of medical problems, incorporating the best available research and clinical expertise (Nelson & Hankey, 2017). Pediatric psychologists have been influential in collaborating with medical care professionals in improving care and outcomes for children with chronic illnesses and their families (Kazak & Noll, 2015; Roberts, Johnson, & Amaro, 2020). Although a comprehensive review of these multiple efforts and strategies is beyond the scope of the present chapter, a few important illustrations follow.

Adherence to Medical Regimens

The terms **adherence** and **compliance**, which are often used interchangeably, describe how well a young person or family follows recommended medical treatments such as taking medications, following diets, or implementing lifestyle changes. Research has demonstrated that numerous factors influence adherence—individual, family, disease and medical regimen, and community and health care system factors all seem to play a role (McQuaid & Landier, 2018; Psihogios et al., 2018; Schwartz, Axelrad, & Hilliard, 2015; Shaw & DeMaso, 2020; Tanenbaum et al., 2017). The implications of nonadherence are numerous and can be considerable, including poorer treatment outcomes, treatment resistance, poorer quality of life, increased health care utilization and costs, and increased incidence of disease and death (Hommel et al., 2017). Diabetes provides an excellent illustration of the way psychologists have increasingly attempted to understand the complex tasks encountered by families managing chronic childhood disorders (La Greca & Spetter, 2018; Wysocki, Buckloh, & Pierce, 2017).

Diabetes: An Example of Disease Management

Diabetes is one of the most common chronic diseases in young people, affecting approximately 2.8 youth per 1,000 (Li et al., 2016). Type 1 diabetes (T1D), also known as insulin-dependent diabetes mellitus, is a lifelong disorder that results when the pancreas produces insufficient insulin. Daily replacement of insulin by injection is required. Because the onset of T1D typically occurs in childhood, this form of diabetes is often referred to as childhood or juvenile diabetes. In Type 2 diabetes (T2D), rather than insulin deficiency, insulin resistance occurs, impairing cellular uptake of insulin. T2D was previously viewed as an adult-onset disorder. However, along with increases in childhood obesity, there has been an increase in T2D such that approximately 20% of new cases of diabetes in youth are of this type. T2D is disproportionately high among black/African American, Indigenous, and Hispanic/Latinx populations. T2D may be managed by weight reduction, exercise, and careful diet. However, many young people with this form of diabetes need insulin injections (Centers for Disease Control and Prevention, 2018a; Wysocki et al., 2017).

Onset of T1D occurs most often around puberty, but can occur at any time from infancy to early adulthood. Genetic factors appear to be involved in the etiology of T1D. Both forms of diabetes increase the long-term risk for damage to the heart, kidneys, eyes, and nervous system. If the disorder is not controlled, a condition known as ketosis, or ketoacidosis, may occur. This is a very serious condition that can lead to neurocognitive effects, coma, and death.

The young person with diabetes and their family face a treatment regimen that includes dietary restrictions, daily injections of insulin, testing of blood glucose levels, and learning how to balance insulin needs with physical activity (see Table 15.1). On the basis of the daily tests for level of sugar—and factors such as timing of meals, diet, exercise, physical health, and emotional state—the daily dosages of insulin must be adjusted. Even under the best of circumstances, "insulin reactions" occur often. Thus, the young person must be sensitive to the signs and symptoms of both hyperglycemia (excessively high levels of blood glucose) and hypoglycemia (excessively low blood glucose). Adverse reactions involve irritability, headache, tremor/shaking, weakness, and—if not detected early enough—unconsciousness and seizures. The fact that symptoms are different for different individuals and are subjectively experienced makes the task of identifying them complicated. Parents and youth are therefore faced with a difficult, often unpredictable, and emotion-laden therapeutic program that requires careful integration into daily life and into their functioning in school and other settings (American Diabetes Association, 2019; Chiang et al., 2018; Wood & Peters, 2018; Wysocki et al., 2017).

The first task in treatment is for the team of professionals to gain and maintain control of the diabetic condition. As this task is achieved, insulin requirements often decrease, and the initial fears and concerns of the youth and family are often reduced. This has come to be known as the "honeymoon period" (Senior et al., 2018). This period of partial remission may terminate gradually and often ends about one to two years after initial diagnosis. In any case, beginning a diabetes self-management program with families during the first few months after diagnosis may avoid deterioration in metabolic function, and early intervention

Table 15.1 Some Activities Required of Youth with Diabetes and Their Families

Monitor blood glucose regularly
Inject insulin regularly or use continuous subcutaneous insulin pump (a device placed under the skin)
Monitor carbohydrate intake
Maintain a healthy diet
Eat meals regularly
Monitor weight gain
Adjust diet to physical activity
Eat a bedtime snack
Take care of injuries
Carry diabetes supplies everywhere
Engage in daily physical activity and exercise
Monitor for symptoms of complications (e.g., hypoglycemia, ketosis)
Inject insulin as directed
Change injection site
Manage the effects of illness and diet on glucose levels
Maintain proper hygiene
Take medications as prescribed
Watch for glucose patterns and make adjustments as appropriate
Manage stress

Source: Adapted from American Diabetes Association, 2019; Chiang et al., 2018; Wood & Peters, 2018.

with young children and their families may help to reduce adherence problems and problems in diabetic control during later periods (Davis et al., 2001; Delamater et al., 1990). Self-management education and support, medical nutrition therapy, and psychosocial support are considered essential (American Diabetes Association, 2019). Transferring control for management of the disease from the professional to the family and child or adolescent, as well as requiring maintenance of such control over long periods of time, is one of the challenges of working with chronic illness (Chiang et al., 2018).

Adherence to the Diabetes Regimen
The concept of adherence is multifaceted (Hommel et al., 2017). Appreciation of this complexity has led to the development of evidence-based intervention programs that combine strategies such as education, training in self-management skills, and facilitating family involvement and communication, as well as a new wave of technology and electronic health (eHealth) delivery, such as text-message reminders or phone applications for diabetes tasks and monitoring (Hilliard, Powell, & Anderson, 2016). Such programs appear to be promising (Wysocki et al., 2017). Medical

advances—such as implantable continuous glucose monitoring and insulin infusion systems, which are programmable devices inserted under the skin that automatically monitor glucose or infuse insulin, respectively—also have the potential to improve adherence and glycemic control although still require frequent monitoring and adjustments by the youth or caregiver (Chiang et al., 2018; Lal & Maahs, 2017).

Regardless of the treatment regimen, the initial step in most intervention programs is to educate the youth and family about the disease. Although such efforts are regularly made, it cannot be assumed that, following these efforts, the family's knowledge will be adequate. Therefore, it is helpful to regularly assess knowledge. Behavioral observation methods have been employed to assess whether the young person knows how to execute necessary skills such as urine and blood glucose testing. Questionnaires are frequently used to measure knowledge of the disease and the application of that knowledge to different situations (e.g., the role of insulin and adjusting diet based on blood sugar readings). However, adherence is not just a matter of accurate information and knowledge; it requires that the prescribed tasks be accurately and consistently carried out.

We will highlight several important variables that are involved in adherence. Developmental level is one important variable (Chiang et al., 2018; Shaw & DeMaso, 2020; Wysocki et al., 2017). In general, knowledge and skills seem to increase with age. For example, in young children, parents and school personnel are responsible for monitoring glucose levels and symptoms of hypo- and hyperglycemia and intervening with appropriate management strategies and treatment. As the child ages, they may start to share in the identification of symptoms of hypo- and hyperglycemia and gain more autonomy in managing their diabetes with planning and supervision from adults (Chiang et al., 2018). Children under 9 years may have difficulty accurately measuring and injecting insulin, but adolescents may be expected to monitor glucose levels, particularly when away from primary caregivers, and may experience increasing autonomy for many management tasks.

However, adolescence and emerging adulthood are periods during which management of diabetes often deteriorates (Clements et al., 2016). In fact, on average, young people between the ages of 16 and 25 years have the highest blood glucose levels of any group (Wood & Peters, 2018). There are several reasons why adolescents may have poorer adherence and glycemic control. The adolescent's knowledge of the disease and its management may be overestimated. Adolescents may, for instance, make errors in estimating their blood glucose levels, particularly when blood glucose levels are quite variable (Gurnani et al., 2018). Whereas increasing cognitive development potentially allows the adolescent to better understand the illness and the complex routine, there are other aspects of cognition that may affect management of the disease. For example, Berg and colleagues (2011) found that

AMIRAH Ten French Fries: A Lifetime of Disease Management

"The first doctor was wrong: I didn't have mono, a disease that would last a few weeks. I had type 1 diabetes, a disease that would last my lifetime.

 The doctor tried to explain to me how things would work now that I was a type 1 diabetic officially. She said, to an 80-pound 15-year-old, 'Everything will pretty much be the same.

Like, you can still eat French fries. You just have to count how many you eat, and you can't eat more than 10 fries, and you have to take medicine via syringe before you eat them.' 'No,' I thought, 'That's not the same.'"

Adapted from Wood & Peters, 2018, p. 6

greater adolescent perceived diabetes self-efficacy—confidence in the ability to manage difficult diabetes situations—was related to better adherence and a better level of metabolic control.

 During adolescence, control is often gradually transferred to the youth, and parental participation often ceases, but total withdrawal of adult involvement may not be advisable (Chiang et al., 2018; Wood & Peters, 2018). It may be important, for example, for the parent to continue to monitor the adolescent's diabetic care behaviors in a developmentally appropriate and supportive manner (Goethals et al., 2017). Also, individual judgments of a young person's developmental readiness, psychological functioning, and the balance of child and parent involvement must be made (Wood & Peters, 2018).

 For example, as youth begin to take more responsibility for their diabetes regimen it is important that they have the regulatory capacity and skills necessary to manage diabetes independently. A recent longitudinal study examined the relationship between cognitive and psychosocial maturity in the transition to adolescence and diabetes management (Silva & Miller, 2019). The study included young people between the ages of 8 and 16 years who had a diagnosis of T1D for at least one year and their parents. Youth and parents reported on adherence to the diabetes treatment regimen (e.g., glucose testing, administering and adjusting insulin, and eating regular snacks) and perceptions of who was responsible for various aspects of T1D care. Youth also completed tasks measuring verbal cognitive ability and self-reported on their impulse control abilities. Treatment regimen and glycemic control was assessed through medical chart review. Results of the study indicate that overall adherence declined as children aged from 8 to 18 years. Adherence was found to decline more slowly, however, in youth with higher levels of verbal ability. Moreover, when youth experienced an increase in responsibility and better impulse control, adherence and glycemic control was higher than would be expected based on age. It seems youth who are better able to manage their emotions and behavior may be better able to manage diabetes independently.

 Social and emotional concerns, such as peer acceptance and greater participation in activities, also are associated with decreased adherence (Wiebe, Helgeson, & Berg, 2016; Wysocki

et al., 2017). Young people with diabetes may wish to avoid appearing different. The unusual behaviors required for control of their condition (e.g., injections, glucose testing), the dietary demands of eating frequently (when others are not), and the need to avoid high-fat foods and sweets (when others are eating junk food), make conformity difficult. Moreover, managing diabetes requires problem solving, including analysis of the factors that might influence adherence with the diabetes regimen, generation of possible solutions to address any problems, and evaluation of the risks and benefits of behaviors and outcomes of management strategies (Wysocki et al., 2008). Some of these challenges are illustrated in Table 15.2. In addition, conflicts with parents over issues of independence are likely to be present. Such social and interpersonal issues most likely combine with actual physical changes, like those associated with puberty, to increase management and compliance difficulties for adolescents. Interventions should maintain parental involvement yet minimize parent–adolescent and peer conflict and improve communication and problem-solving skills (La Greca & Spetter, 2018; Wysocki et al., 2017).

 Many other problems regarding adherence are worthy of continued attention. For example, anticipating environmental obstacles to compliance is important. Creating interventions that help adolescents deal with peers concerning their diabetes and that facilitate appropriate peer support, for instance, are likely to facilitate compliance with recommendations (Wiebe et al., 2016). The realization that the immediate consequences of diabetes management are often negative, and therefore may reduce the individual's commitment to adherence, may also help to anticipate difficulties. For example, the immediate consequence of injections is discomfort, whereas the adverse effect of skipping injections is not immediate. Thus, interventions that reduce the immediate negative effects of compliance may be of value.

 Caregivers also may be impacted by the illness and the disease management process (Robinson et al., 2016b; Van Gampelaere et al., 2018). Attention to the needs of caregivers is likely to improve adherence. Attention to the role of the health care system and behavior of primary care providers (pediatrician, nurse) is another important aspect of the adherence process (Wysocki

Table 15.2 Examples of Vignettes and Questions to Assess Problem Solving in Youth with Diabetes

Correction of low blood sugar (hypoglycemia)
Tim played basketball before lunch at school. Later he was waiting in line for lunch. He started feeling dizzy, hot, and shaky.
Colin is at school and starts to feel shaky and weak in the middle of math class.
Correction of high blood sugar (hyperglycemia)
Emma was at dinner at her great aunt's house. Before dinner, she guessed that she would be eating 75 g of carbohydrates and she took her premeal insulin based on that guess. On the way home, she asked her parents about this and they thought she had eaten more like 100 g of carbs.
Mary Ann went to the pool with her friends. She thought she was going to be swimming, so she took less insulin than usual before her lunch. But, when she arrived at the pool, it was closed.

Questions to assess problem solving	
1. What is the diabetes problem here?	5. How would you fix this problem?
2. Why is this a problem?	6. How would that solution work?
3. What are all the ways this problem could be fixed?	7. How would you know if you really fixed the problem?
4. What would happen if he/she did nothing?	

Source: Adapted from Wysocki et al., 2008.

et al., 2017). Information provided by health care providers must be sufficient and presented in a manner that allows the family to carry out complex regimens (Beverly et al., 2016). Health care providers, too, must be sufficiently aware of the youth's level of cognitive development so as to not overestimate or underestimate the youth's understanding of the illness and treatment regimen. Providers also must assist the youth and family in achieving a developmentally appropriate balance of responsibilities for diabetes care (American Diabetes Association, 2019). These issues suggest the importance of training health care providers to be sensitive to the needs of individual families and youth and to improve professional–patient communication (Caccavale et al., 2019; Patel, Datye, & Jaser, 2018). Given the complexities involved in diabetes care and treatment adherence, pediatric psychologists are well-suited to support youth with diabetes and their families in promoting treatment adherence (Hilliard et al., 2016).

The Impact of Chronic Pain

Pain is a normal and common experience of childhood and adolescence. Typically, pain begins when the body experiences physical harm and serves as a warning sign to the body to prevent further injury and pain. The pain of a scraped knee, for example, may signal to a child to seek the comfort and help of a parent who, in turn, takes steps to care for the wound in an effort to reduce the child's immediate pain and prevent future infection (Slifer, 2014). When pain persists or recurs, typically for three months or more, it is no longer considered protective and instead is termed "chronic pain" (Law et al., 2017). Chronic pain in children and adolescents may be related to injury (e.g., burns, orthopedic trauma), to a chronic or underlying disease

(e.g., cancer, sickle cell disease), or it may be idiopathic, meaning the cause is unknown and the pain itself is the condition (e.g., headaches, recurrent abdominal pain) (Palermo et al., 2014; World Health Organization, 2012). Chronic pain has the potential to impede adherence with medical treatment for chronic illness and impact quality of life and may be associated with impairments in physical, emotional, and academic functioning (Blackwell & Quittner, 2015; Shaw & DeMaso, 2020).

Prevalence estimates vary considerably, but overall epidemiological studies suggest 11–38% of children and adolescents experience pain that is chronic or recurrent (King et al., 2011). Variability in prevalence appears to depend on multiple factors, including type of condition and age of the youth (Baldridge, Wallace, & Kadakia, 2018), with prevalence generally increasing with age from childhood to adolescence (Chan, Connelly, & Wallace, 2017; Palermo et al., 2014).

Individual differences in pain are likely the result of the interaction of a range of physiological and psychosocial factors (Gatchel et al., 2018; Turk & Monarch, 2018). These may include individual factors, such as emotional functioning and coping, physiological or biological factors, such as pubertal development and sleep quality, and broader social influences, such as family functioning and parental response to the child's experience of pain (Law et al., 2017; Palermo et al., 2014). The relationship between these factors and chronic pain is complex and likely bidirectional—difficulties in psychosocial functioning, for example, can both contribute to and result from chronic pain. Indeed, chronic pain in children and adolescents is associated with considerable physical, psychological, and psychosocial difficulties for children and their families (Coakley & Wihak, 2017). Young people with chronic pain may report persistent and recurrent problems including peer difficulties, poorer social functioning, elevated symptoms of anxiety and depression, sleep disturbance, changes in appetite, and family disruption (Chan et al., 2017; Clinch & Eccleston, 2009). Functional impairment, such as frequent school absences and reduced participation in social activities with peers, may be common among children and adolescents with chronic pain, and they may be at risk for co-occurring psychiatric problems and disability (Bettini & Steinhorn, 2018; Law et al., 2017). A recent study of children ages 6 to 17 years in the United States, for example, found that pain was associated with higher rates of chronic absences from school (missing more than 15 days of school), with nearly five times as many children with pain experiencing chronic absenteeism as compared to children without pain (Groenewald, Giles, & Palermo, 2019). Similarly, a study of individuals who experienced chronic pain in adolescence identified higher rates of lifetime anxiety (21.1% vs. 12.4%) and depressive disorders (24.5% vs. 14.1%) in adulthood as compared to individuals who did not have a history of chronic pain (Law et al., 2017). Figure 15.4 illustrates the widespread impact of chronic illness on the psychosocial adjustment of young people.

Psychological Modification of Chronic Pain

The shifting emphasis in understanding mind–body relationships has led to greater systematic and scientific study regarding how psychology can be used to treat physical symptoms such as pain. Treatment of chronic pain in children and adolescents has the potential to reduce young people's experience of pain and impairment. Typically, treatment of childhood chronic pain involves a multidisciplinary approach, which may include psychological intervention, pharmacological intervention, and specialized therapies (e.g., physical therapy, occupational therapy), as well as alternative and complementary approaches to medicine (e.g., acupuncture, yoga, massage) (Law et al., 2017). The use of relaxation and biofeedback to treat young people's headaches is one example of attempts to directly modify physical functioning through psychological interventions.

Headaches are usually classified as tension, migraine, or a combination of the two. The pain and suffering that can accompany intense headaches, and the desire to avoid potential negative aspects of drug treatment, led to the exploration of non-pharmacological approaches (Bougea, Spantideas, & Chrousos,

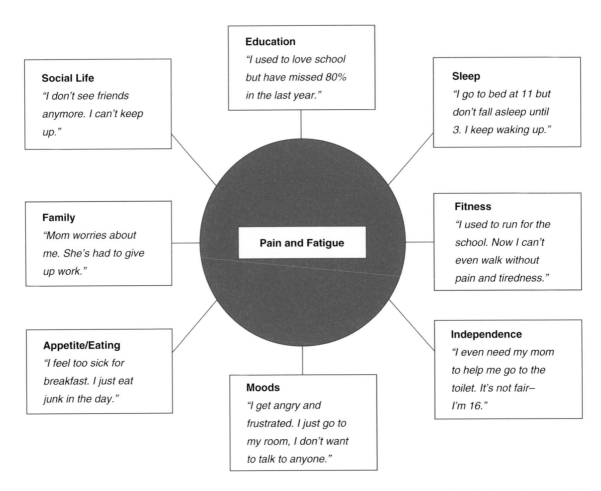

Figure 15.4 Examples of the widespread impact of chronic pain on child and adolescent functioning. (Adapted from Clinch & Eccleston, 2009)

CINDY Chronic Headache Pain

Cindy, 14 years old, attended a demanding private school. She reported that she had been experiencing daily headaches for 18 months. She described constant pain that varied in intensity but she never experienced total relief from the pain. She had carefully followed the medication and other recommendations of her neurologist, but experienced only minimal improvement. Cindy did not feel well enough to participate in social activities and had become isolated from her friends. She could not concentrate when the pain intensified and her grades had begun to suffer. Cindy also stopped participating in sports to avoid exacerbating the pain. She described experiencing fatigue and frustration and believed that she would never get rid of her headaches. Cindy received biofeedback-assisted

relaxation training that incorporated guided imagery, breathing exercises, and progressive muscle relaxation. Within three sessions Cindy was able to produce dramatic changes in the physiological indices targeted by the biofeedback and reported decreased pain and anxiety while practicing the cognitive-behavioral techniques. Cindy was encouraged to use these skills at school. After six sessions, Cindy reported marked decreases in the intensity of her headaches and feelings of efficacy in coping with pain. Her headaches rarely decreased to the level of being undetectable, but the pain levels dropped to the point where she was able to resume her previous activities, and her grades improved.

Adapted from Powers, Jones, & Jones, 2005, p. 72

2017; Faedda et al., 2016). **Biofeedback**, which refers to a procedure in which a device gives immediate feedback to the person about a particular biological function, has been used in the treatment of headache in children (Kacynski, 2019). The feedback, typically provided by a signal such as a light or tone or by some graphic display, helps the individual make subtle changes in their body, such as relaxing certain muscles or changing the pace or pattern of breathing, to regulate physiological functioning and reduce pain. Such feedback, alone or in combination with some form of relaxation training, seems effective in producing clinically meaningful levels of improvement in children's headaches (Dowell, Martin, & Waters, 2017; Esparham et al., 2018; Stubberud et al., 2016).

Relaxation procedures also have been employed as part of cognitive-behavioral packages for the treatment of chronic pain associated with headache and other conditions such as arthritis, SCD, and recurrent abdominal pain. These cognitive-behavioral treatments often include imagery training to reduce or control pain and teaching youth to modify unhelpful thoughts and behavioral patterns, such as replacing negative and catastrophizing thoughts with positive and encouraging self-statements, that may be influencing chronic pain (Coakley & Wihak, 2017; Dowell et al., 2017).

Innovations to increase accessibility of treatments have also been explored. Internet-based interventions for pediatric pain, for example, are emerging and show promise in reducing pain and functional impairment at least for some individuals and conditions (Coakley & Wihak, 2017; Dowell et al., 2017; Fisher et al., 2019; Voerman et al., 2015). For example, Voerman and colleagues (2015) examined the effects of a seven-week guided, interactive, internet-based CBT intervention called "Move It Now" in the treatment of adolescents with chronic pain in the Netherlands. The

intervention is intended to help adolescents improve their coping strategies for pain by providing education on strategies of self-regulation, such as distraction and relaxation. The intervention was delivered with minimal therapist contact via a combination of independently completed online modules for adolescents and their parents in addition to weekly email/telephone support from a therapist. Overall, adolescents who participated in the intervention had significant reductions in the intensity of their pain after treatment as well as improvements in quality of life, whereas adolescents in the wait-list control showed no significant changes in pain during the wait-list period. Parent behavior was also modified by the intervention with reductions in parent rewarding of adolescent pain. A subset of adolescents in the study, however, dropped out because they found the intervention to be too time-consuming or were not satisfied with it for other reasons. More research is needed to improve implementation of internet-based interventions and to better understand the conditions under which they may be most efficacious.

Reducing Procedure-Related Pain and Distress

Another important and growing area of interest is developing psychologically based procedures for enhancing the effectiveness of medical treatment. Procedures for dealing with pain and discomfort associated with medical treatment illustrate this potentially important contribution.

Pain and Distress
Despite its seeming simplicity, pain is a complex phenomenon that is difficult to assess and, as a result, may be underestimated and undertreated in children and adolescents (Beltramini, Milojevic, & Pateron, 2017). Numerous factors, including

the age and developmental level of the child, influence pain assessment. Additionally, it may be difficult to separate the pain or discomfort that the person is suffering from the anxiety that the person is experiencing while undergoing a painful medical procedure. This difficulty has led some to use the term *distress* to encompass pain, anxiety, and other negative affect (L. L. Cohen et al., 2017). Whatever term is chosen, multiple assessment methods have been employed to assess the cognitive-affective, behavioral, and physiological aspects of pain and include self-reports, observer reports, physiological indices, and observational measures (Beltramini et al., 2017; L. L. Cohen et al., 2017; Cowen et al., 2015).

Self-report measures of the cognitive-affective component of pain are the measures most frequently employed. Because pain is a subjective experience, assessing the youth's experience of pain is important. In addition, the greater accessibility of this component and the relative ease of measurement are certainly factors. However, measurement is not without its difficulties. For example, the young person's developmental level plays a large role in selecting a self-report measure. Because older children may be able to describe pain in semantic terms, they can be assessed by means of interviews and questionnaires. Visual methods may also be useful (see Figure 15.5). Visual analog scales (VASs) provide a visual gauge—typically a 100-millimeter vertical line with behavioral anchors for pain (e.g., "no pain" and "severe pain")—on which a child can indicate their level of pain (L. L. Cohen et al., 2017). Considered the gold standard and most validated self-assessment tool for older children and adolescents, VASs may be difficult for younger children to understand (Beltramini et al., 2017; L. L. Cohen et al., 2017). For younger children, professionals rely on more concrete methods, such as faces with expressions ranging from neutral or smiles to severe frowns. If photographs are employed, use of ethnically appropriate images may be important (Beyer & Knott, 1998; Hicks et al., 2001).

The behavioral component of children's distress (e.g., crying, screaming, verbalizations of pain or fear, facial indicators of pain, or need for physical restraint) can often interfere with effective medical treatment (L. L. Cohen et al., 2017). Observational methods are often used to assess children's distress behaviors. Structured behavioral observations employing a system of defined behaviors and trained observers have been employed in a variety of contexts. Such procedures can be expensive and time-consuming; an alternative is to use global observation ratings of the young person's distress behaviors by health care providers or parents, such as the Faces, Legs, Activity, Cry, and Consolability (FLACC) scale or the Postoperative Pain Measure for Parents, for example (Beltramini et al., 2017; Gordon, 2015).

Assessment of the physiological aspect of pain is far less common and concerns about reliability exist (L. L. Cohen et al., 2017). Melamed and Siegel's (1975) measurement of palmar sweat before and after young people underwent elective surgery, and Jay and colleagues' (1987) monitoring of pulse rate prior to bone marrow aspiration are examples of use of physiological measures. However, the equipment necessary and the difficulty involved in reliably obtaining measures such as heart rate, blood pressure, and skin conductance make such measures less likely to be employed.

Helping the Child Cope

Procedures have been developed to assist young people in coping with the pain associated with their disease or disorder, or with the treatments they receive (L. L. Cohen et al., 2017; Slifer, 2014). Many of the medical procedures used to assess and treat children with chronic disorders are aversive. Well-timed preparation of the young person that contains appropriate information that

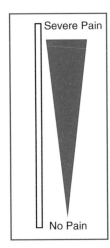

Figure 15.5 Visual methods have been used to assess pain in children. On the left is a visual analog scale (VAS) typically used with older children and adolescents. On the right are illustrated drawings that may suggest two ends of a range of choices—neutral (left) through very painful (right)—which may be used with young children. (Adapted in part from Beltramini, Milojevic, & Pateron, 2017)

It is common for young people to exhibit distress during medical procedures. Techniques that reduce or help control distress can facilitate good medical care. (Stígur Már Karlsson/Heimsmyndir/E+/Getty Images)

he or she can understand and remember is the first step in reducing distress and in helping the young person cope. The basic rationale for preparation is that unexpected stress is worse than predictable stress. Likewise, a variety of interventions, such as distraction, hypnosis, controlled breathing, and cognitive-behavioral interventions, have been identified as effective for reducing child pain and distress in response to medical procedures (Birnie et al., 2018; Flowers & Birnie, 2015). However, from the simple statement that preparation and support are good follows the complex question of how this is best achieved for varying situations and for different young people. Research provides some guidance and suggests certain procedures (L. L. Cohen et al., 2017; Gulur et al., 2019).

Numerous factors influence children's reactions to medical procedures. The behavior of parents is an important factor in children's distress and experiences of pain during medical procedures (L. L. Cohen et al., 2017). When parents use strategies to distract the child or to direct the child to use coping techniques, the child exhibits less distress. Parental focus on symptoms and parental anxiety may increase distress and reduce the effectiveness of distraction techniques (Campbell et al., 2017; L. L. Cohen et al., 2017; Hoehn et al., 2016; Racine et al., 2015). Also, when parents attempt to comfort the child using reassuring statements (e.g., "it'll be ok," "it'll be over soon") or apologies, distress may be greater (Blount, 2019; L. L. Cohen et al., 2017).

The behavior of the medical practitioner is also likely to affect the young person. Increased focus is now being given to training medical providers in behavioral interventions aimed at increasing medical provider interactions that promote children's coping and decreasing those that may increase distress. For example, research suggests the reinterpretation of medical experience and equipment as non-threatening by health care providers has the potential to increase children's coping under certain circumstances (Gulur et al., 2019; Martin et al., 2011). Additionally, the incorporation of procedures to mitigate children's physical experience of pain, such as the use of topical and local anesthetics, when appropriate is an important consideration for health care providers (L. L. Cohen et al., 2017; Slifer, 2014).

Young people themselves have made some recommendations regarding coping strategies (Ross, 1988). Many of these suggestions cluster around the perception of being in control (Carpenter, 1992), and many involve the young person's controlling the environment during the aversive treatment procedure. The following comment by a 10-year-old boy undergoing emergency room burn treatment illustrates this phenomenon:

I said, "How about a hurting break?" and he (intern) said, "Hey, man, are you serious?" And I said, "Sure. Even when ladies are having babies they get a little rest between the bad pains." And they (the pediatric emergency room personnel) all laughed and he said, "OK, you get a 60-second break whenever you need it," and then it was much, much better, like you wouldn't believe it.

Ross, 1988, p. 5

Although young people may be capable of generating their own strategies for coping with pain and distress, procedures for teaching effective stress management/coping skills are also needed. Most interventions consist of a variety of coping strategies derived from behavioral and cognitive-behavioral perspectives and these seem to be effective procedures (Birnie et al., 2018; L. L. Cohen et al., 2017).

Distraction techniques are frequently used to draw children's attention away from the stressful or painful stimuli associated with medical procedures (e.g., needles, medical equipment) and bring their attention to stimuli that are more appealing or relaxing for the child (L. L. Cohen et al., 2017; Reinfjell & Diseth, 2018). Distraction can take multiple forms: it can be internal (e.g., imagery) or external to the individual and can include various modalities, including audio (e.g., music), visual (e.g., book, bubbles), audiovisual (e.g., movies, iPad), or interactive (e.g., conversation, video games, virtual reality), and it can be introduced and coached by parents, health care professionals and psychologists (Birnie, Chambers, & Spellman, 2017; Reinfjell & Diseth, 2018; Slifer, 2014). Strong evidence exists for the efficacy of distraction in reducing pain and distress in children, however variability has also been noted (Birnie et al., 2014). To be most effective, it is recommended that distraction be tailored to the child's developmental level and interests (Reinfjell & Diseth, 2018). Relaxation techniques, including hypnosis and controlled breathing, have also been shown to be effective in helping reduce children's experience of pain and distress during medical procedures (Birnie et al., 2018).

Cognitive-behavioral interventions are also used to minimize pain and distress in children undergoing medical procedures, particularly for older children and adolescents who have had previous medical experiences (Birnie et al., 2018; Reinfjell & Diseth, 2018). These methods include preparation and education about the procedure, coping skills training, including breathing exercises, the use of coping statements (e.g., "I can do this," "I can control my anxiety with my breathing"), distraction techniques, visual imagery (e.g., imagining a day at the beach), and muscle relaxation, in addition to behavioral reinforcement (e.g., praise, small rewards) for engaging in coping strategies or cooperating with the procedure (Reinfjell & Diseth, 2018; Slifer, 2014). Exposure therapy, interventions that allow a child to practice coping by gradually exposing the youth to the anxiety-producing stimuli (e.g., a needle stick), have also been shown to be effective in reducing distress and increasing cooperation with medical procedures in children with a history of procedure-related anxiety or distress (Rachamim et al., 2015; Slifer et al., 2011).

Research on interventions for young people with cancer, who often endure repeated painful procedures such as bone marrow aspirations (BMAs), lumbar punctures, and biopsies, provides a good example of the ways in which psychological interventions can help mitigate the pain and distress of children undergoing medical procedures. BMAs are often conducted at regular intervals for children and adolescents with leukemia in order to examine the marrow for evidence of cancer cells. The procedure, in which a large needle is inserted into the hip bone and the marrow is suctioned out, is very painful. While highly invasive procedures such as these are often performed under sedation or general anesthesia, the child still may endure considerable postoperative pain, as well as undergo less invasive but still painful procedures in advance of the BMA, such as IV placement or local anesthesia injections (Zarnegar-Lumley et al., 2019).

An intervention developed by Jay and colleagues (Jay et al., 1987, 1991, 1995) is often cited in the literature on psychosocial interventions for youth undergoing painful medical procedures. The cognitive-behavioral intervention developed by this research group consisted of five major components—filmed modeling, breathing exercises, emotive imagery/distraction, positive incentive, and behavioral rehearsal—and was designed to be delivered in a brief intervention on the day of the scheduled BMA. The intervention has been found to significantly lower children's behavioral distress, pain ratings, and pulse rates (a physiological indicator of distress) (Jay et al., 1987).

More recent studies have also demonstrated the efficacy of psychological interventions on reducing the distress and anxiety of children with cancer undergoing invasive medical procedures. A study in Taiwan, for example, examined the impact of procedural preparation and cognitive-behavioral interventions on children ages 3 to 13 years old undergoing BMA and lumbar puncture (LP) (Hsiao et al., 2019). For children ages 3 to 6 years, a certified child life specialist (CCLS) provided a one-hour session with the child and family two days prior to their first scheduled BMA or LP to develop rapport and assess past medical experiences, behavioral patterns of the child and both the child's and parents' understanding of the procedure. Another one-hour session was held one day prior to the scheduled BMA or LP to prepare the child for the procedure. During this preparation session, the child was engaged in medical play as a way to help them understand and become familiar with the procedure and learn coping strategies they could utilize before sedation. The medical play involved materials such as tape, gauze, and syringes. Parents accompanied their child during the intervention session and were encouraged to coach their child in coping strategies during the medical procedure. On the day of the scheduled BMA or LP, the CCLS accompanied the child to the procedure room and used distraction strategies, such as counting, blowing bubbles, and reading stories, to help divert the child's attention away from the medical preparation that occurs in advance of sedation. On the day following the procedure, the CCLS visited the child and family to review how the child felt throughout the procedure and to provide emotional support to the child and family.

For older children, ages 7 to 13 years, the intervention was provided in two one-hour sessions three days before the first scheduled BMA or LP. Similar to the intervention with younger children, the focus of the first session was on building rapport

ACCENT Preventing Childhood Injury

Each year millions of children are injured. Indeed, injuries are the leading cause of death and medical visits for youth over the age of 1 in the United States (Centers for Disease Control and Prevention, 2019a) and for youth over the age of 5 worldwide (World Health Organization, 2018a). As Schwebel (2019) describes, the Global Burden of Diseases project estimates that 2 million children ages 0 to 19 died as a result of injury in 2017, amounting to a child death every 15 seconds of every day. Clearly, the loss of life and function is tragic, and the medical costs and psychological consequences can be considerable (Schwebel, 2019).

Injuries are the result of multiple events and risk factors involving personal characteristics of the child and caregivers (e.g., risk-taking behavior, caregiver supervision), environmental influences (e.g., playground hazards), and broader sociocultural factors, such as safety regulations (e.g., automobile restraint regulations, bicycle helmet laws) (Morrongiello & Schwebel, 2017; Schwebel, 2019). Research suggests that 91% of children's injuries could have been prevented if circumstances leading up to the injury had been different (Rimsza et al., 2002). Initiatives to understand and prevent childhood injury are an important public health focus (McClure et al., 2015) and an important aspect of pediatric psychology (Schwebel, 2019).

There are a number of challenges to injury prevention, and multiple factors must be considered in developing strategies for injury prevention (Morrongiello & Schwebel, 2017). One obstacle is that serious injuries are often mistakenly assumed to occur infrequently and to be chance events and, thus, unavoidable. Such assumptions do not encourage an active prevention effort. Professionals therefore suggest abandoning the common term *accent* in favor of ***unintentional injury***, a term that acknowledges that the event, though not deliberate, might have been avoided.

Another challenge to injury prevention is the variety of contributing factors and modes of injury and thus potential for intervention (Schwebel, 2019). As described by Tremblay and Peterson (1999), "A toddler mastering the operation of the gate blocking access to the swimming pool, a 7-year-old riding a bicycle without a helmet, and a 16-year-old driving with peers who ridicule him when he stays within the speed limit are all candidates for a variety of potential interventions." While there are multiple contributing factors in childhood injury, there are also multiple pathways in which to intervene.

Many efforts to prevent injury to children are inspired by the work of Lizette Peterson (DiLillo & Tremblay, 2005).

A basic contribution of psychology is the perspective that there are important behavioral antecedents to injury prevention. Behaviors of young people (e.g., impulsivity, risk taking), parents (e.g., supervision, protectiveness), and peers (e.g., persuasion, modeling), and environment-based variables (e.g., chaos, hazards), can contribute to child injury and likely interact with each other (Morrongiello & Schwebel, 2017; Schwebel, 2019). The risk, for example, of a child ingesting household poisons is increased when the child is old enough to explore his or her environment but still young enough to impulsively ingest a substance, and by a setting in which poisons are accessible and constant supervision is lacking.

Prevention efforts can be implemented at a variety of levels and involve tactics directed at the entire population (e.g., legislative action, consumer product safety, multimedia campaigns), particular subsets of the population (e.g., bicycle safety programs for families with young children), or at certain milestones (e.g., counseling at yearly visits to the pediatrician). Prevention efforts at only one level (e.g., a lock on a pool gate, child-resistant medicine closures) may not be sufficient, however, as they still require individual actions (e.g., an adult locking the gate or replacing the lid correctly) to ensure compliance (Morrongiello & Schwebel, 2017). Parents should not be lulled into a false sense of security. For example, a study of parents of young children taking swimming lessons found parents to judge their children as increasingly capable of keeping themselves safe from drowning and, in turn, in need of less active parental supervision (Morrongiello, Sandomierski, & Spence, 2014). Providing education about vulnerability and the seriousness and extent of childhood injuries as well as information regarding safety behaviors can be part of prevention efforts (American Academy of Pediatrics, 2019). For example, evidence-based behavioral interventions targeting parent knowledge, beliefs, and behavior relevant to keeping their children safe around water delivered alongside children's swimming education show promise in promoting closer adult supervision of children around water and preventing injury (Sandomierski, Morrongiello, & Colwell, 2019).

Multiple-component prevention programs aimed at modifying risk behaviors and that include modeling, and rewards and incentives for appropriate injury-prevention behavior are needed to supplement information (Schwebel, 2019).

with the child and family. The second session included preparation and assessment of the child's concerns, as well as interventions to develop coping strategies, such as breathing exercises, talking, and guided imagery. The CCLS accompanied the child to the treatment room on the day of the BMA or LP and coached the child to apply their coping strategies. Again, the CCLS visited the child and family on the day following the BMA or LP. Overall, as compared to children who did not receive the intervention, children who participated in the intervention exhibited less distress in anticipation of the procedure.

The findings of this study represent one example of interventions that can help young people and families cope with the distress associated with certain medical procedures. While the study did not evaluate the long-term impact of the intervention on the child's anxiety and distress during subsequent medical procedures, making the first procedure as comfortable as possible has the potential to positively impact the child's learned response and future coping. The incorporation of parents or other family members into such programs can improve the maintenance of child coping, reduce parent/family distress, and improve the cost-effectiveness of interventions that otherwise might require a great deal of professional time. Such interventions hold the promise of making delivery of effective medical treatment more likely (L. L. Cohen et al., 2017).

Preparation for Hospitalization

Young people suffering from chronic illness often require periodic hospitalization to stabilize their functioning. Other young people, too, may need to enter the hospital for scheduled surgery, for some other procedure, or in an emergency. Indeed, about one-third of all young people are hospitalized at least once. Siegel and Conte (2001), writing on the history and status of hospitalization for medical care, indicated that in the mid-1950s the importance of the child's psychological reaction to early hospitalization and surgery began to be recognized. Two films by James Robertson at the Tavistock Clinic are suggested to have been instrumental in changing attitudes and practices. One film portrayed a young child's intense distress at being separated from his parents for a week while undergoing minor surgery. The other film demonstrated the positive adjustment of a young person whose mother remained with him while he was hospitalized for surgery. Also, a substantial research literature documented the stressful effects of hospitalization (Siegel & Conte, 2001). Improvements have occurred since the 1950s and 1960s, when much of this research was conducted. For example, in 1954 most New York hospitals allowed parental contact only during two visiting hours per week. While the majority of general pediatric units in the United States and other countries now permit 24-hour parental visitation, there may still be limitations on the presence of family members, including more restrictive policies in intensive care units

or during emergencies in addition to other barriers (Foster et al., 2018; Institute for Patient- and Family-Centered Care, 2019). In addition to separation from family and from their familiar home environment, children who are hospitalized may undergo other disruptions and stressors, such as pain or discomfort associated with medical procedures, limited activities, impaired sleep, and exposure to frightening or unusual sights, sounds, or feelings (Linder & Seitz, 2016). Families of hospitalized children, too, face multiple challenges and stressors (Nabors et al., 2018; Rennick et al., 2018).

Nevertheless, pediatric care has made considerable strides toward improving the experiences and outcomes of children who are hospitalized. A variety of changes in hospital care have been observed, including, for example, increasing parental involvement, re-design of many pediatric care units to include sleeping areas for parents, efforts to facilitate opportunities for hospitalized children to play and participate in enjoyable activities, and integration of psychological and psychiatric services in pediatric inpatient settings (Dokken, Parent, & Ahmann, 2015; Institute for Patient- and Family-Centered Care, 2017; Ollendick & Schroeder, 2003; Shaw & DeMaso, 2020). Emphasis is now also placed on creating a medical environment that is quiet and calming, in an attempt to reduce the distress of children who are hospitalized (L. L. Cohen et al., 2017).

Prehospital preparation for both the child and the parents when admissions are planned is now common (Aranha, Sams, & Saldanha, 2017; Bray, Appleton, & Sharpe, 2019). Preparation programs might include orientation tours of the hospital or operating room, rehearsal with dolls or puppets, modeling, medical play, teaching of coping and relaxation skills, written or oral presentations, interactive computer programs, as well as instructional and educational videos (Aranha et al., 2017; L. L. Cohen et al., 2017). One well-supported method involves the use of audiovisual equipment to portray models who, although apprehensive, cope with the hospitalization stresses. The use of such methods to reduce anxiety and improve coping skills of children undergoing surgery dates back to interventions such as Melamed and Siegel's (1975) film, *Ethan Has an Operation*, which showed a 7-year-old boy prior to, during, and after surgery. The child narrated the story and showed realistic but adaptive reactions to the procedures. The film was shown to be an effective means of preparation for hospitalization and surgery (Melamed & Siegel, 1980; Peterson et al., 1984), and more recent studies and reviews continue to demonstrate the efficacy of using audiovisual intervention for reducing preoperative anxiety in children (Chow et al., 2015), as well as their parents (Chow et al., 2018). Interventions often combine methods such as education and modeling with explicit training of coping techniques and programs targeting preparation for surgery, as well as other anxiety-reduction procedures (L. L. Cohen et al., 2017). Current efforts are directed at preparation procedures that are well timed;

are matched to individual characteristics of the child, parent, and family; and are cost-effective. Other novel, technological interventions, such as virtual support groups, show promise in reducing distress and enhancing coping for some children who are hospitalized, although more research is needed (Aldiss et al., 2015; Canter et al., 2019).

Hospital-related anxiety and distress require attention and need to be more effectively anticipated, prevented, identified, and treated (Schlegelmilch et al., 2019). Improvement may enhance medical aspects of treatment and may be associated with shorter lengths of stay in the hospital (Bujoreanu et al., 2015; L. L. Cohen et al., 2017). Interventions also appear to enhance the mood state and adjustment of young people and this seems particularly important to those youth who are chronically ill and may require frequent hospitalizations.

The Dying Child

Clearly, one of the most distressing aspects of working with severely ill children and adolescents is the prospect of death. Even though much progress has been made at increasing survival rates, the numbers still fall appreciably short of 100% (UNICEF, 2019). Increased survival rates may make the death of a child even harder to bear when it does occur (Parshuram & Dryden-Palmer, 2018). Several important and difficult questions are raised by the prospect of a dying child:

- What is the child's understanding of death?
- How can we best prepare the young person and the family?
- How do we best include the young person in communication and decision making?
- How do we prepare people for death while sustaining their motivation for treatment?
- Can we help the family begin to accept the child's impending death but prevent the family from prematurely distancing from the child?
- What do we do after the young person dies?
- How is the helper affected by working with the dying child?

Children's ideas about death change during development and are influenced by experiences, family attitude, and cultural factors. Cognitive development plays a role in the evolving conceptualization of death (Bates & Kearney, 2015; Gerhardt et al., 2017). Young children may think of death as being less alive and assume it to be reversible. At about 5 years of age, an appreciation of the finality of death may be present, but death still does not seem inevitable. An understanding of death as final and inevitable and of personal mortality emerges at about age 9 or 10. Nevertheless, children may be aware of death and be

worried about their fatal illness even if they do not have a fully developed concept of death. Although adolescents' understanding of death may be similar to that of adults, attention to the particular aspects of this stage of development is needed (Leming & Dickinson, 2020).

Family members, too, must certainly be made aware of the seriousness of the young person's illness (Brackett & Baxter, 2015; Gerhardt et al., 2017; Kaye et al., 2018). However, an appropriate balance between acceptance of death and hope for life is probably adaptive. It is a genuine challenge to prepare parents for the death of their child, while also enabling them to help the child emotionally and to assist with the treatment regimen. This undertaking requires knowledgeable and sensitive mental health staff, and pediatric psychologists can play a key role in facilitating communication with the child, medical team, and family (L. L. Cohen et al., 2017). As our ability to lengthen survival—and perhaps to raise hopes of some future cure—increases, the problem becomes even more difficult. Integration of support services into the total treatment program and immediate availability and access are important in delivering needed help. Once a point is reached where the child's death is likely, the focus of intervention must shift. Information and support are still needed, but the focus must change to helping the child and family to be most comfortable and to make the best use of the remaining time. Moreover, the family should not be abandoned after the young person's death. Continued assistance is needed and such support should be a part of the total treatment (Gerhardt et al., 2017; Lövgren & Sveen, 2018).

Health care providers, too, are not immune to the effects of observing a dying child or adolescent. Efforts must be made to educate caregivers and to reduce the high cost of helping: the inevitable stress, the feelings of helplessness, and the likelihood of burnout (Roberts et al., 2020; Whitford, Nadel, & Fish, 2018). These are not trivial matters. The helpers' adjustment, their efficiency, and the potential impact of their behavior on the family and young person are of concern (Barnes, Jordan, & Broom, 2018). In "Who's Afraid of Death on a Leukemia Ward?" (1965), Vernick and Karon offered poignant anecdotes to this effect. One anecdote describes the impact of helpers' behavior on a 9-year-old patient who, after taking a turn for the worse, received some medical treatment and began to show improvement:

One day while she was having breakfast I commented that she seemed to have gotten her old appetite back. She smiled and agreed. ... I mentioned that it looked as if she had been through the worst of this particular siege. She nodded in agreement. I went on to say that it must have been very discouraging to feel so sick that all she could do was worry— worry about dying. She nodded affirmatively. I recognized that the whole episode must have been very frightening and that I knew it was a load off her mind to be feeling better. She let out a loud, "Whew," and went on to say that except for me, nobody really talked with her. "It was like they were getting ready for me to die."

Vernick & Karon, 1965, p. 395

Certainly, one of the most difficult decisions is what to tell the dying youth. A protective approach or "benign lying" was once advocated. The young person was not to be burdened, and a sense of normalcy and optimism was to be maintained. Most professionals now feel that this approach is not helpful and probably is doomed to failure anyway. The stress on the family of maintaining this deception is great, and the likelihood that the young person will believe the deception is questionable and may lead to increased fear and distress. Providing clear, empathic, and individualized information in an emotionally supportive and flexible manner is recommended (Kaye et al., 2018). In the decision about how best to communicate difficult news, and in other aspects of working with the child and family, some balance must be struck that takes into consideration the child's developmental level, past experiences, timing, and an understanding of the family's culture and belief system (Gerhardt

et al., 2017; Kaye et al., 2018). An example of such a balance is illustrated in the following excerpt:

A child with a life-threatening illness should be told the name of the condition, given an accurate explanation of the nature of the illness (up to the limit of his ability to comprehend), and told that it is a serious illness of which people sometimes die. At the same time, however, the child and family can be told about treatment options and enlisted as allies to fight the disease. An atmosphere must be established in which all concerned have the opportunity to ask questions, relate fantasies, and express concerns, no matter how scary or far-fetched they may seem. When the patient is feeling sick, weak, and dying, there is no need to [be reminded] of the prognosis. If a family and patient know a prognosis is poor but persist in clinging to hope, one has no right to wrest that from them. The truth, humanely tempered, is important, but we must be mindful of the patient and how [the patient's] needs are served. To tell the "whole truth" or a "white lie" for the benefit of the teller serves no one in the end.

Koocher & Sallan, 1978, p. 300

Looking Back

Historical Context

- The current view that psychological factors are relevant to physical disorders in a number of different ways represents a shift from the earlier, more limited view of psychosomatic diseases caused by emotional factors.

Psychological and Family Influences on Medical Conditions

- Current conceptualizations of the role of psychological and family factors in chronic illness are illustrated through the example of asthma. Psychological and family influences are among a variety of possible trigger mechanisms that can bring on an asthmatic episode. The child's asthma may impact other family members, and family assistance is needed in managing the medical condition.

Consequences of Chronic Conditions

- There is likely to be considerable individual variability in the adjustment of youth with chronic illnesses and in how youth and families cope with chronic conditions.

Adjustment is likely to be an ongoing process and is influenced by a number of variables.
- Researchers have sought to determine the impact of characteristics of the youth, parameters of the illness, such as severity, and of aspects of family functioning, such as parental distress, on the chronically ill youth's adjustment.
- With increasing survival rates for young people with chronic conditions, the adaptation over time of the young person and family to the illness and its treatment are of great interest. Adaptation to cancer and HIV/AIDS are two examples.

Facilitating Medical Treatment

- Psychology can contribute to effective treatment of medical conditions in a number of ways.
- Medical treatment may be rendered ineffective because of difficulties that the patient and family experience in trying to adhere to prescribed treatment regimens. Attempts to improve adherence require attention to multiple dimensions such as the young person's developmental level, peer and social influences, family patterns of interaction, and the role of the health care professional.

- Psychological treatments (e.g., relaxation and biofeedback) may modify physical functioning and the pain associated with chronic conditions. Treatment of headaches is an example of this kind of application.
- Psychologically based procedures may also facilitate the delivery of medical interventions. Treatment programs to reduce the pain and distress felt by young people who are undergoing medical procedures and preparation for hospitalization are examples of psychological influences enhancing medical interventions.
- Understanding the antecedents of unintentional injury and developing interventions to prevent such injuries is another example of ongoing efforts at the interface of psychology and medicine.

The Dying Child

- Despite increasingly high survival rates, the prospect of death is one of the most distressing aspects of working with some chronically ill youth. Psychological contributions to helping these children, their families, and the professionals who work with them can be an aid in effective and caring treatment.

Key Terms

psychosomatic disorders *400*
psychosomatic medicine *400*
pediatric psychology *401*
functional impairment *403*

adherence to (compliance with) medical regimens *412*
biofeedback *417*
unintentional injury *421*

EPILOGUE
Evolving Concerns for Youth

The lives of young people are affected by a multitude of factors, including what is happening in their lives and the lives of their parents, their relationship with peers, their experiences in school, and the characteristics of their communities. Their lives are also affected by less proximal aspects of their experience, such as the priorities given to health care and education, the value assigned to the young, and the climate of broader global and political influences. Although many of these and related issues are woven throughout the preceding chapters in our discussion of specific disorders of childhood and adolescence, this final discussion is intended to highlight some of the current and evolving concerns for children and adolescents.

Identity Development

Identity development is considered a critical psychosocial task with important implications for health and psychological well-being (Galliher, McLean, & Syed, 2017). Identity construction begins early in the developmental process and is influenced by those around the young person—most notably their families, peers, the media, school—as well as the young person themselves (Blakemore, Berenbaum, & Liben, 2013; Fivush & Zaman, 2015). In other words, individual identity is constructed within the broader sociocultural context. While the present discussion cannot capture the depth and complexity of identity development and content, we briefly touch upon several domains of identity, including gender identity, sexual identity, and racial/ethnic identity.

Gender is a complex identity construct, incorporating biological and culturally constructed ways of organizing the world, and it plays a role in the behavior and experiences of children and adolescents (Blakemore et al., 2013). Recall from our discussion of the disorders of childhood and adolescence that the study of behavior disorders often includes examining relationships between sex/gender and youth adjustment. Research has also linked the construct of gender identity with the psychosocial adjustment of young people. Feeling compatible with one's gender group, for example, has been associated with more positive adjustment, whereas feeling pressure for gender conformity has

been associated with poorer psychosocial outcomes (Carver, Yunger, & Perry, 2003; Egan & Perry, 2001). Gender, though, may be best conceptualized as a multidimensional construct, and novel conceptualizations of gender identity as a flexible paradigm rather than one with a single dimension (i.e., male–female) suggest the relationship between gender and psychosocial adjustment is more nuanced and likely involves multiple risk and protective factors (Endendijk et al., 2019). Increased awareness of the diverse medical and psychosocial challenges and mental health needs of transgender and gender expansive youth, for example, has led to increased focus on developing empirically based gender-affirmative interventions and care (Tabuenca & Basile, 2019). Interest and research in this area continues to emerge and inform our understanding of the relationship between gender identity and adjustment in young people.

It is also important to consider the intersection of gender with other aspects of identity, such as sexual identity, race, and ethnicity. For most young people, sexual identity is a continuous process with attitudes and preferences typically emerging before puberty and continuing to evolve through adolescence (Mills-Koonce, Rehder, & McCurdy, 2018). This period of identity development is often challenging for youth in general but may be particularly so for sexual and gender minority youth (i.e., youth often identified with the umbrella acronym LGBT—lesbian, gay, bisexual, and transgender) as their experience may be incongruent with the sexual and gender expectations of the society, community, and even family in which they belong. Many LGBT youth describe this period as one of the most stressful of their lives and, even though the social environments in some regions of the world are more accepting and inclusive of LGBT people than they were in the past, many LGBT youth experience continued prejudice, stigma, discrimination, and even violence (Meyer, 2016; Mills-Koonce et al., 2018). In turn, these stressors have been associated with adjustment difficulties (see Accent: "Suicidality and Sexual Minority Youth" on p. 185, for example); yet coping, social support, and family acceptance have also been shown to serve as protective factors, buffering the impact of stress on adjustment (Meyer, 2015; Ryan et al., 2010).

Young people of color face unique challenges and stressors, including but not limited to negative stereotypes, institutional racism and discrimination, socioeconomic inequality, and interpersonal prejudice (Wang et al., 2020). The negative association between race/ethnicity-related stress and young people's psychosocial adjustment is well documented (Cave et al., 2020), and some of these concerns are highlighted in this text (e.g., see the discussion of racial disparities in ADHD diagnosis and treatment on p. 242). Racial/ethnic disparities, stress, and other factors, such as discriminatory mistreatment, are associated with poorer youth adjustment across multiple domains, including socioemotional, academic, behavioral, and physical health outcomes (Benner et al., 2018; Johnson, 2020). Parents play an important role in their child's formation of racial/ethnic identity. A recent review and meta-analysis, for example, suggests parents' messages about race and ethnicity may, under certain circumstances, serve an important protective role for children of color, enhancing their identity, sense of self-worth, and connection with others, as well as providing tools for coping with discrimination (Wang et al., 2020). However, a great deal of what we know about the deleterious effects of racial/ethnic discrimination is based on adult populations, and much is still to be understood about how racial/ethnic socialization and identity relates to child development and adjustment (Benner et al., 2018). Identifying aspects of culture and identity that foster positive development will be an important focus of future research in child and adolescent psychology.

Indeed, domains of identity are dynamic and interact with each other and other influences to affect development in complex ways (Galliher et al., 2017). Significant gaps in our knowledge base remain. Increased attention and greater focus on the intersection of social identities, including gender, sexual identity, and racial/ethnic identity, in the years to come will likely inform our understanding of child development and adjustment and, importantly, bring about advances in methods for intervention and prevention of risk.

Technology

The impact of digital technology—such as computers, tablets, and mobile phones—on adjustment is another area of emerging interest in child development (Kardefelt-Winther, 2017; Odgers & Jensen, 2020). In all parts of the world, young people's engagement with technology is increasing, and the question has arisen: Under what circumstances is technology healthy, and when is it harmful?

The findings of current research appear to be inconclusive. Overall, it seems moderate use of technology may have generally positive benefits for young people's psychosocial adjustment,

while too much use or none at all seem to have a small negative impact (Kardefelt-Winther, 2017). In addition to the amount of time children and adolescents spend using digital technology, the content of young people's "screen time" may be an important consideration. Digital technology may offer potential benefits to youth, allowing them access to educational resources, entertainment, and connection with peers.

One particularly salient example is the unprecedented role technology has played in attempts to support the well-being of young people during the public health threat posed by the coronavirus disease 2019 (COVID-19) pandemic. Beginning in March 2020, widespread school closures were implemented by many nations and localities as part of comprehensive public health strategies to reduce transmission of the disease, affecting roughly half the student population worldwide (Viner et al., 2020). In the United States, school closures were reported to have affected approximately 124,000 schools and 55.1 million kindergarten through twelfth grade students during the initial public health response (Martin & Sorensen, 2020). Prolonged school closures have the potential to substantially disrupt the lives of young people and their families, increasing the risk for educational, psychological, and physical health consequences, particularly for the most vulnerable youth. For children and adolescents who typically receive health and mental health services and other supports in the school setting, school closure may present a particularly meaningful challenge (Lee, 2020). While the long-term impact of the COVID-19 pandemic on the health and well-being of young people is yet to be determined, technology has played a central role in facilitating access for many young people to home-based distance-learning and may offer alternative methods of access to health and mental health care (Golberstein, Wen, & Miller, 2020; Scharff et al., 2020). Although it will likely take many years to fully understand the ways in which the COVID-19 pandemic has affected young people, it is clear that technology proved essential during a time of social distancing and rapid change.

Nevertheless, important concerns remain with regard to the impact of technology on youth. Concerns include, for example, who young people interact with online, if they experience access to inappropriate or dangerous content, are at risk for cyber-bullying, whether they may miss out on important social experiences that affect development, and whether digital engagement may negatively impact cognitive performance, adjustment, and other important areas of functioning, such as sleep and physical activity (George & Odgers, 2015; Kardefelt-Winther, 2017; Odgers & Jensen, 2020). Emerging research in this area is amassing (e.g., Christodoulou et al., 2020; Jensen et al., 2019; Przybylski & Weinstein, 2019; Rodriguez-Ayllon et al., 2020) and will likely help us understand and address some of these concerns.

Youth in a Global Society

Children are increasingly growing up in a global society. Advances in technology and communication along with increased access to mass transportation are making the functional world smaller day by day. The lives of youth are already being strongly influenced by this phenomenon, and the impact will become even more pervasive throughout the twenty-first century given the rapid changes unfolding in today's global context (Petersen et al., 2017). Nevertheless, the experiences of children and adolescents throughout the world vary considerably and are influenced by local, national, and global policies, economies, political leadership, and social climates (United Nations, 2018).

Many challenges to the development of young people are evident worldwide, such as poverty, inequality, and lack of health and mental health services. Poverty can be conceptualized as arising as a consequence of inequalities between and within societies (Wilkinson & Pickett, 2020), and the link between poverty and developmental well-being is observed in various measures—prenatal care, nutrition, disease, access to screening and treatment, educational opportunity, housing, disability, and death. Despite progress in many of these domains, social, economic, and environmental inequalities continue to contribute to disparities in the physical and psychological well-being of youth. In a recent analysis of the economic and social determinants of child mortality across 43 countries, for example, unimproved sanitation contributed to greater child mortality inequalities than any other variables explored and the largest disparities in child mortality came from mothers who had the least education (Kayser, McElroy, & Benmarhnia, 2019). These findings and others like it highlight the importance of continued efforts to enhance our understanding of, and ability to intervene in, youth development at both the individual level and on a larger scale.

Social and political factors influence the development of young people in multiple ways. Millions of children and adolescents suffer loss and physical and psychological damage from armed and sociopolitical conflicts. Youth have experienced the horrors of "ethnic cleansing," have lived in areas in which the threat of war was chronic, and have been abducted into or otherwise become a part of the military. Moreover, millions have fled their homelands as refugees to live in refugee camps or to relocate to foreign countries. In addition to direct traumatic experiences and bodily threats to the self and loved ones, these situations are often characterized by uncertainty, temporary or permanent separation from family, loss of community, inadequate nutrition, lack of shelter, discrimination and hostility, and the like.

The global refugee population has reached an all-time high in recent years, with 25.4 million refugees estimated worldwide in 2017, more than half of those children (UNHCR The UN Refugee Agency, 2018). Although research on refugee youth mental health is limited, it is estimated that up to 80% of refugees ages 8 years and under experience psychological problems including depression, anxiety, PTSD, and behavioral difficulties, and adolescent refugees, particularly those who are unaccompanied minors, may be at even greater risk (Frounfelker et al., 2020).

Significant numbers of youth throughout the world are exposed to the risks of sociopolitical conflict and life in refugee camps. (Michael Honegger/Alamy Stock Photo)

The accumulation of traumatic and stressful experiences on both biological and psychosocial development is of particular interest to those attempting to understand and intervene in refugee youth mental health. Despite the multiple challenges of war-related trauma and stress, young people and their families may exhibit remarkable resilience in the face of considerable adversity (Denov et al., 2019), and there is a need to better understand the effects of war, displacement, and migration on young people and their families and the factors that contribute to their resilience. The case of David illustrates the effect of resilience in the face of war and displacement. There is a compelling need for interventions to alleviate and prevent trauma and war-related disorders.

An obvious implication of the shrinking world is the increased challenge to get along well with others of different appearance, color, dress, custom, behavior, and beliefs. The task of adapting to diversity, although not new by any means, is substantial and is heightened by the current massive relocation of people across the globe into foreign countries and cultures.

In the United States, the challenge of diversity has a long history. Prejudice and fears have had adverse effects on people of various groups—Indigenous People and individuals of African American, Irish, Polish, Asian, Arab, Mexican, Latin American, Jewish, and Catholic descent, as well as undocumented individuals, to name a few. Being of minority status remains a risk factor for quality of life, health, and opportunity (Miranda, Snowden, & Legha, 2020), even as the United States becomes increasingly multicultural.

As a discipline, psychology has participated in the study of issues related to diversity, although efforts have perhaps not always been as timely as could be hoped. A historic example is the work of Kenneth Clark and his colleagues that played a role in the 1954 Supreme Court decision *Brown v. Board of Education*, which overthrew the "separate but equal" doctrine that had permitted racial segregation in the public schools (Clark, Chein, & Cook, 2004). Clark, an African American, became president of the American Psychological Association in the late 1960s (Pickren & Tomes, 2002). At about that time, the American Psychological Association became more committed to addressing problems of race and related matters. Today, concerns exist about the problems and progress of diverse cultural and racial groups living in the United States.

The need also exists for increased study across cultures and the processes of international cooperation. In fact, an important outgrowth of closer communication among the peoples of the world is greater international effort to solve problems and to optimize living conditions. Over several decades, the United Nations has drawn world attention to promoting the healthy development of children and protecting, among other rights, basic rights to a family environment, an adequate standard of living, education, and freedom from harms such as abuse and exploitation and has sponsored world summits and conferences, numerous

DAVID The Power of Resilience

David was born in a small village in a war-torn country in Africa. His father was killed during the war when he was very young and he was raised by his mother. His mother worked on a farm to provide food. They lived in constant fear of David being recruited as a child soldier and having to hide when the armed groups were close by. At the age of 10, while he was hiding from an armed group, his mother was brutally murdered trying to protect him. After briefly living with a family member, he and other children were abducted by an armed group at school and put on a truck. He narrowly escaped with his life a few hours later by jumping off the truck and running away into the forest while being shot at. He was later smuggled to another African country by a man trying to help him. He was transported in a toolbox in a truck across two countries and eventually dropped off in a big city with only a few dollars when he was merely age 10. In a new country, David did not speak the language and had to fend for himself.

In an interview, David explained, "I had come from the real war, people killing each other, and now I faced a different kind of war: learning the language, and living on the street." David lived on the street in extreme poverty and was subjected to ongoing violence from gang groups. Six years later, when he was age 16 years and still living on the street, he boarded a docked ship while scavenging for food, which started moving before he could jump off. He hid in the ship's cargo area for nine days until he was discovered, at which point the ship members allowed him to remain onboard if he worked doing odd manual jobs. The ship eventually led him to a Canadian city where he had to navigate a complex immigration system. He had the good fortune of meeting a social worker who took him under his wing and helped him through the long immigration process, during which time he was terrified he might be sent back to Africa. David began to attend school shortly after he arrived in Canada and graduated high school in three years. He is now attending university, is involved in sports, and does volunteer work with youth.

Adapted from Denov et al., 2019, pp. 27–38

programs to benefit children, and the collection of data on youth to monitor progress and make recommendations. Countless other concerned organizations—both private and public—are addressing global issues such as poverty, education, infant mortality, medical and mental health needs, violence, and environmental pollution. The American Psychological Association, for example, recently highlighted the important role of psychologists in giving focus to and addressing issues such as access to mental health resources (Huff, 2020; Weir, 2020), gun violence (DeAngelis, 2020), climate change (Greenbaum, 2020), and racial and ethnic diversity (Bailey, 2020), among other pressing issues. Because such efforts can have a crucial influence on the development of children and adolescents, international cooperation holds the promise of optimizing the lives of young people.

Mental Health Services for Youth

International attention is being paid to psychological and behavioral problems of youth, in particular, with increasing worldwide focus on the study of positive youth development (Lerner & Chase, 2019; Petersen et al., 2017). However, it is widely agreed that children and adolescents are underserved by lacking or fragmented mental health services, and the mental health needs of many young people go unmet (Kazdin, 2019; Merikangas & Hommer, 2019). Children's mental health resources are subject to direct and indirect effects of policies that impact children, as well as their families and communities (Hoagwood et al., 2018). The economic resources of nations make a difference, so that even basic care and opportunity are problematic in developing countries. Very often, for example, countries and communities with the greatest stressors are also the ones with the fewest mental health services (Weir, 2020). Nevertheless, because the implementation of programs devoted to youth also depends on social attitudes, availability and quality of care can vary enormously even when resources are adequate. Efforts are under way to expand access and quality of mental health care through dissemination of evidence-based interventions (Chorpita, Becker, & Higa-McMillan, 2019; Okamura et al., 2020), developing new models of delivery (Weir, 2020), and integrating mental health services into primary care (Burkhart et al., 2019; Huff, 2020) and school settings (Eklund et al., 2020; Miller & O'Brien, 2019), for example. Related to availability and quality of mental health services are efforts to enhance early prevention. One issue that is getting increased attention worldwide is that of comprehensive solutions to childcare, including the availability and quality of care. Focus has increased, for example, on the impact of family friendly policies on paid parental leave, support for breastfeeding, and availability and accessibility of affordable, high-quality childcare and education (Chzhen, Gromada, & Rees, 2019). Sensitive and attentive adults are looking at these influences with an eye toward better comprehensive care for youth.

Progress in understanding human development is clearly stimulating efforts toward optimizing the potential of the young. Although knowledge about development is incomplete, we have come far from viewing children and adolescents simply as incomplete adults. Their unique needs are better known; the general course of physical, intellectual, and social growth is well on the way to being mapped; and developmental influences, including risk and protective factors, are increasingly understood. There is enthusiasm for using this knowledge to enhance development, even as we seek to better understand the experiences of young people.

Glossary

ABA (reversal) research design Single-case experimental design in which the behavior being examined is measured during a baseline period (A), a period of manipulation (B), and a period in which the manipulation is removed (A). The manipulation (B) is reintroduced when treatment is the goal.

Accelerated longitudinal research designs Various designs that combine the longitudinal and cross-sectional research strategies to maximize the strengths of those methods.

Acute onset The sudden (rather than gradual) onset of a disorder.

Adaptive behavior scales Psychological instruments that measure an individual's ability to perform in the everyday environment—for example, to wash one's hair, interact socially, and communicate.

Adoption studies In genetic research, the comparison of adopted children with their biological and their adoptive families to determine hereditary and environmental influences on characteristics.

Affect Emotion or mood. By extension, an affective disorder is a mood disorder such as depression or mania.

Agoraphobia Excessive anxiety about being in a situation in which escape might be difficult or embarrassing.

Anoxia Lack of oxygen.

Antisocial behavior A pattern of behavior that violates widely held social norms and brings harm to others (e.g., stealing, lying).

Aphasia Loss or impairment of language, caused by brain anomalies.

Attachment A strong socioemotional bond between individuals. Usually discussed in terms of the child–parent or child–caretaker relationship, attachment is generally viewed as having a strong influence on a child's development.

Attention The focusing or concentration of mental energy on an object or event. Attention has many components, which are linked to different brain regions. Attention deficits are manifested in problems such as distractibility and difficulty in sustaining effort.

Attribution (attributional style) The way an individual thinks about or explains actions and outcomes; for example, a child's attributing his or her school failure to lack of innate intelligence.

Authoritative parenting Style of parenting in which parents set rules and expectations for their children, follow through with consequences, and simultaneously are warm, accepting, and considerate of their children's needs. This style is thought to be associated with positive development in children.

Autoimmune disorder A condition in which the body's immune system attacks its own healthy tissue.

Autonomic nervous system A part of the nervous system that regulates functions usually considered involuntary, such as the operation of smooth muscles and glands. The system controls physiological changes associated with emotion. (*See* central nervous system.)

Baseline The measured rate of a behavior before an intervention is introduced. Baseline rates of a behavior being examined can then be compared with rates measured during and following an intervention.

Behavior therapy/behavior modification An approach to treatment that is based primarily on learning principles.

Behaviorally inhibited temperament A temperamental tendency in which the individual is highly reactive to and stressed by unfamiliar stimuli.

Binge A relatively brief episode of excessive consumption (e.g., of food) over which the individual feels no control.

Biofeedback Procedures by which an individual is provided immediate information (feedback) about his or her physiological functioning (e.g., muscle tension, skin temperature). It is assumed that the individual can come to control bodily functioning through such feedback.

Brain imaging Methods of studying the brain that depict brain structure or functioning. Examples are PET (positive emission tomography), MRI (magnetic resonance), and fMRI (functional magnetic resonance) scans.

Case study Method of research in which an individual case is described. The case study can be informative but cannot be generalized with confidence to other persons or situations.

Categorical approach Conceptualizing behavior into qualitatively different groupings. When applied to behavior disorder, persons are viewed as either displaying or not displaying the behavior; for example, as either displaying or not displaying anxiety. (*See* dimensional approach.)

Central coherence The tendency of individuals to weave bits of information together so as to create a whole, or global, meaning. Central coherence is contrasted with the (analytic) tendency to focus on parts of stimuli, rather than the whole.

Central nervous system In humans, the brain and spinal cord. (*See* autonomic nervous system.)

Chromosome A threadlike structure in the cell nucleus that contains the genetic code. Human cells possess 23 pairs of chromosomes, except for the ovum and sperm, which possess 23 single chromosomes.

Chromosome abnormalities Abnormalities in the number and/or structure of the chromosomes, which can lead to fetal death or anomalies in development.

Classical conditioning A form of learning, also referred to as Pavlovian conditioning. In classical conditioning, an individual comes to respond to a stimulus (conditioned stimulus or CS) that did not previously elicit a response. Classical conditioning occurs when a CS is paired with another stimulus (the unconditioned stimulus, or UCS) that does elicit the desired response (unconditioned response, or UCR). When this response is elicited by the conditioned stimulus alone, it is called a conditioned response (CR).

Clinical significance The degree to which research findings are meaningful regarding real-life applications.

Clinical utility The adequacy of a classification system, diagnosis, or assessment instrument; judged on the basis of how fully the observed phenomena are described and how useful the descriptions are.

Coercion A process in which a noxious or aversive behavior of one person (e.g., aggression by a child) is rewarded by another person (e.g., a parent). Often applied to the development of conduct-disordered behavior.

Cognitive-behavioral therapy An approach to treatment that is based on a theoretical perspective that considers behavioral events, cognitive processes, and their interactions.

Cognitive distortion Inaccurate thought processes that are dysfunctional. An example is a depressed person's believing that he or she is incompetent even though others do not hold this view.

Cognitive strategies Strategies related to information processing, memory, and the like; for example, rehearsing and categorizing information or addressing the interpretation of an experience or event.

Cohort A particular age group of individuals. A cohort may differ in life experiences and values from an age group born and raised during a different era.

Comorbidity A term used when an individual meets the criteria for more than one disorder (e.g., attention-deficit/ hyperactivity disorder and oppositional defiance disorder). (*See* co-occurrence.)

Compulsions Behaviors the individual feels compelled to repeat over and over again, even though they appear to have no rational basis.

Computerized tomography (CT) scan A procedure that assesses the density of brain tissue and produces a photographic image of the brain. A CT scan allows investigators to directly assess abnormalities of brain structures. Also sometimes referred to as a computerized axial tomography (CAT) scan.

Concordant In genetic research, refers to individuals who are similar in particular attributes; for example, individuals may be concordant in activity level or in meeting the diagnostic criteria for a disorder.

Conditioned stimulus (CS) A neutral stimulus, which through repeated pairings with a stimulus (unconditioned stimulus) that already elicits a particular response, comes to elicit a similar response (conditioned response).

Contingency management Use of procedures that seek to modify behavior by altering the causal relationship between stimulus and response events, for example, modifying a particular outcome or consequence of a behavior.

Control group In an experiment, a group of participants treated differently from the group of participants who receive the experimental manipulation. The two groups are later compared. The purpose of a control group is to ensure that the results of the experiment can be attributed to the manipulation rather than to other variables.

Co-occurrence A term used when individuals experience the problems (symptoms) associated with more than one disorder (e.g., anxiety and depression). (*See* comorbidity.)

Correlation coefficient A number, obtained through statistical analysis, that reflects the presence or absence of a correlation and the strength and direction (positive or negative) of a correlation. Pearson *r* is a commonly used coefficient. (*See* positive correlation; negative correlation.)

Correlational research A research method aimed at establishing whether two or more variables covary, or are associated. (*See* positive correlation; negative correlation.) The establishment of a correlation permits the prediction of one variable from the other, but does not automatically establish a causal relationship.

Cortisol A stress hormone produced by the adrenal gland.

Covert behaviors Behaviors that are not readily observable. When describing antisocial behaviors this term refers to behaviors that are concealed, such as lying, stealing, and truancy. (*See* overt behaviors.)

Cross-sectional research A research strategy aimed at observing and comparing different groups of participants at one point in time. Cross-sectional research is a highly practical way to gather certain kinds of information.

Defense mechanisms In psychoanalytic theory, psychological processes that distort or deny reality so as to control anxiety. Examples are repression, projection, and reaction formation.

Deinstitutionalization The movement to place or treat people with disorders at home or in various community settings rather than in institutions.

Delinquency A legal term that refers to an illegal behavior by a person under 18. Such behavior may be illegal for an adult as well (e.g., theft) or may be illegal only when committed by a juvenile (e.g., truancy).

Delusion An idea or belief that is contrary to reality and is not widely accepted in one's culture (e.g., delusions of grandeur or of persecution).

Dependent variable In the experimental method of research, the measure of behavior that may be influenced by the manipulation (the independent variable).

Development Change in structure and function that occurs over time in living organisms. Typically viewed as change from the simple to the complex, development is the result of transactions among several variables.

Developmental level The level at which an individual is functioning with regard to physical, intellectual, or socioemotional characteristics.

Developmental psychopathology The study of behavioral disorders within the context of developmental influences.

Developmental quotient (DQ) A measure of performance on infant tests of development, paralleling the intelligence quotient (IQ) derived from intelligence tests for older children.

Diathesis Vulnerability to a disease or disorder.

Differential reinforcement of other behaviors (DRO) In behavior modification, application of relatively more reinforcement to desirable behaviors that are incompatible with specific undesirable behaviors.

Difficult temperament Tendency of an individual to display negative mood, intense reactions to stimuli, irritability, and the like. A difficult temperament is a risk factor for behavior problems.

Dimensional approach Conceptualizing behavior as varying along a quantitative continuum, such as anxiety being manifested from very low, through moderate, to very high. When applied to behavior disorder, persons are evaluated along a continuum rather than being viewed as either displaying or not displaying anxiety. (*See* categorical approach.)

Discordant In genetic research, refers to individuals who are dissimilar in particular attributes; for example, two individuals may be discordant in activity level or clinical diagnosis.

Discrete trial learning Method of modifying behavior or teaching in which the clinician or teacher presents specific tasks or materials in small steps, provides clear directives or prompts,

and applies consequences. The setting is structured for learning. (*See* incidental learning.)

Dizygotic (fraternal) twins Twins resulting from two independent unions of ova and sperm that occur at approximately the same time. Dizygotic twins are genetically no more alike than are non-twin siblings.

DNA Deoxyribonucleic acid. The chemical carrier of the genetic code, found in the chromosomes and composed of sugar, phosphates, and nucleotides. The nucleotides carry the hereditary information.

Dyslexia General term referring to impairment in reading not due to general intellectual disability.

Echolalia The repetition of the speech of others, either immediately or delayed in time. A pathological speech pattern found in autism and other disorders.

Education for All Handicapped Children Act of 1975 Public Law 94–142, which set influential federal guidelines for the rights of handicapped children to an appropriate public education. Reauthorized and expanded, the law is now titled the Individuals with Disabilities Education Act (IDEA).

Electroencephalograph (EEG) A recording of the electrical activity of the brain.

Emotion dysregulation Refers to dysfunctional patterns of emotional regulation.

Emotion regulation Refers to behaviors, skills, or strategies that modulate, inhibit, or enhance emotional experiences and expression.

Empirical The process of verification or proof by accumulating information or data through observation or experiment (in contrast to reliance on impression or theory).

Epidemiology The study of the occurrence and distribution of a disorder within a population. Epidemiology seeks to understand the development and etiology of disorder.

Epigenetic Modification of the genome that helps regulate gene function without changing the genetic code. Such modification can occur in response to the environment, implicating environmental influence on gene expression. The term "epigenetics" often is used to refer to the study of epigenetic processes.

Equifinality The concept that different factors or paths can result in the same or similar developmental outcomes. For example, somewhat different paths can lead to conduct-disordered behavior.

Ethnicity Refers to common customs, values, language, or traits that are associated with national origin or geographic area.

Etiology The cause or origin of a disease or behavior disorder.

Eugenics Efforts to improve human characteristics through the systematic control of reproduction and thus genetics.

Evidence-based assessments and treatments Assessments and interventions for which there is empirical support for their effectiveness; procedures that have been deemed worthy through scientific evaluation.

Executive functions Higher-order mental abilities involved in goal-directed behavior. Included among executive function are planning and organizing behavior, using short-term or working memory, inhibiting responses, and evaluating and switching strategies.

Experimental research A research method that can establish causal relationships among variables. Participants are exposed to the independent variable in order to determine possible effects on the dependent variable. Comparison groups are included, and procedures are carefully controlled to help rule out effects of extraneous factors.

Expressive language The production and use of words, sentences, gestures, and writing to convey meaning and messages to others.

External validity In research, the degree to which findings of an investigation can be generalized to other populations and situations.

Externalizing disorders Behavioral disorders in which the problems exhibited seem directed at others (e.g., aggression and lying).

Extinction A weakening of a learned response, produced when reinforcement that followed the response no longer occurs.

Factor analysis A statistical procedure that suggests which behaviors or characteristics tend to occur together by correlating each item with every other item and then grouping correlated items into factors.

Fraternal twins *See* dizygotic twins.

Functional analysis Behavior analysis; that is, the assessment of variables that might be influencing the occurrence and maintenance of a behavior. Determining such antecedent variables and consequences for behavior can be crucial in modifying the behavior.

Functional impairment The loss or limitation of ability which substantially interferes with participation in family, school, or community activities.

Functional magnetic resonance imaging (fMRI) A noninvasive magnetic radiowave technology which produces images that indicate areas of brain activity by tracking subtle changes in oxygen in different parts of the brain. (*See* magnetic resonance imaging.)

Gene The unit of the chromosome that carries the genetic code.

Gene–environment correlation Correlation indicating the presence of genetic differences in exposure to environments. That is, genetic influences play a role in determining the experiences a person has. For example, a child who is genetically predisposed to be shy may be treated in certain ways by others or may elect to avoid highly social activities.

Gene–environment interaction Differential sensitivity to experience due to differences in genotype. For example,

children with recessive genes for PKU (phenylketonuria), but not other children, develop intellectual disabilities when they ingest certain kinds of foods.

Generalization of learning The process by which a response is made to a new stimulus that is different from, but similar to, the stimulus present during learning.

Genome All the biological information needed to construct and maintain life. In humans, the term often refers to genes and non-coding sequences of DNA in the cell nucleus. It may also include information not carried in the nucleus, such as in DNA found in the cell's mitochrondria of females that is transmitted to offspring.

Genome-wide association studies A promising method to help identify genes associated with a disorder or trait. The genome is searched for small variations in DNA (single nucleotide polymorphisms, SNPs) that occur more often in persons with a disorder than in those without the disorder. Large numbers of genomes must be searched, and the method is especially appropriate for complex disorders.

Genome-wide linkage studies A method to help identify genes associated with a disorder or trait that is found in families. The genomes of family members are searched for variations in DNA and comparison is made between members displaying or not displaying the disorder.

Genotype The complement of genes that a person carries; the genetic endowment.

Goodness-of-fit Degree to which an individual's attributes or behaviors match or fit the attributes or demands of the individual's environment.

Grammar A set of rules for organizing language.

Grapheme A unit of a writing system—a letter or a combination of letters—that represents the sounds of a language (the phonemes).

Hallucination A false perception (e.g., hearing a noise, seeing an object) that occurs in the absence of any apparent environmental stimulation.

Heritability The degree to which genetic influences account for variations in an attribute among individuals in a population.

Heterotypic continuity The continuity of a problem or disorder over time in which the form in which the problem is expressed changes over time. Contrasts with homotypic continuity.

High-risk prevention strategies (also called selective prevention strategies) Prevention strategies targeted at individuals who are at higher than average risk for disorder.

Homotypic continuity The continuity of a problem or disorder over time in which the form in which the problem is expressed remains relatively stable over time. Contrasts with heterotypic continuity.

Hypothesis In science, a proposition or "educated guess" put forth for evaluation by some scientific method.

Identical twins See monozygotic twins.

Impulsivity Acting without thinking; a failure to inhibit behavior. Some children with attention-deficit/hyperactivity disorder exhibit impulsivity.

Incidence Number or proportion of persons in a population newly diagnosed with a disorder during a specific time period.

Incidental learning Method of modifying behavior or teaching in informal, natural settings. Incidental learning takes advantage of the everyday context—for example, by teaching tasks relevant to what a child is engaging in at the moment. Learning procedures, such as contingency management, are typically employed.

Inclusion The idea that all children with disabilities can best be educated, and should be included, in regular classrooms.

Independent variable In the experimental method of research, the variable manipulated by the researcher.

Indicated prevention strategies Prevention strategies that are targeted at high-risk individuals who show minimal symptoms or early signs of a disorder, or who have biological markers for a disorder, but do not meet the criteria for the disorder.

Individual Education Plan (IEP) Detailed educational plan legally mandated for each person being served by the Individuals with Disabilities Education Act.

Individuals with Disabilities Education Act (IDEA) Current federal law ensuring the rights of handicapped persons from birth to age 21 to appropriate public education.

Information processing Complex mental processes by which the organism attends to, perceives, interprets, and stores information. (*See* attention, working memory, executive functions, cognitive strategies.)

Informed consent In research or treatment, the ethical and legal guideline that potential participants be reasonably informed about the research or treatment as a basis for their consent or willingness to participate.

Insidious onset Gradual, rather than sudden (acute), onset of a disorder.

Intelligence quotient (IQ), deviation A standard score, derived from statistical procedures, that reflects the direction and degree to which an individual's performance on an intelligence test deviates from the average score of the individual's age group.

Intelligence quotient (IQ), ratio The ratio of mental age (MA), derived from performance on tests of intelligence, to chronological age (CA), multiplied by 100. (IQ = MA/CA ×100.)

Interactional model of development The view that development is the result of the interplay of organismic and environmental variables. (*See* transactional model of development.)

Internal validity The degree to which research findings can be attributed to certain factors. Internal validity frequently concerns the degree to which the result of an experiment can be attributed to the experimental manipulation (the independent variable) rather than to extraneous factors.

Internalizing disorders The large category of disorders—many of which were traditionally referred to as neuroses—in which the problems exhibited seem directed more at the self than at others (e.g., fears, depression, and withdrawal).

Interrater reliability The extent to which different raters agree on a particular diagnosis or measurement.

In vivo A term referring to the natural context in which behavior occurs. For example, in vivo treatment is delivered in the setting in which the behavior problem occurs (e.g., the home rather than the clinic).

Joint attention interactions Behaviors, such as pointing and eye contact, that simultaneously focus the attention of two or more people on the same object or situation, presumably for sharing an experience.

Learned helplessness Passivity and a sense of lack of control over one's environment that is learned through experiences in which one's behavior was ineffective in controlling events.

Least restrictive environment Regarding education, refers to the idea that individuals with disabilities have the right to be educated with their typically developing peers to the extent that such education is maximally feasible.

Lifetime prevalence Number or proportion of persons in a population diagnosed with a disorder at any time during life.

Longitudinal research A research strategy in which the same participants are observed over a relatively long period of time, with their behavior measured at certain points in time. Longitudinal research is particularly helpful in tracing developmental change.

Magnetic resonance imaging (MRI) A noninvasive procedure that creates a magnetic field around the brain. Cells in the brain respond to the radio waves, and a three-dimensional image of the structures of the brain is created. (*See* functional magnetic resonance imaging.)

Mainstreaming The educational practice of placing individuals with disabilities into community schools and into the least restrictive settings appropriate to their needs. Most of the children who are mainstreamed spend the majority of their school time in classrooms with typically developing peers, with various degrees of special support.

Maltreatment Includes both the commission of injuries and acts of omission, that is, failure to care for and protect a child. Maltreatment (often referred to as child abuse) can include physical abuse, sexual abuse, neglect, and emotional abuse (psychological maltreatment) alone or in combination.

Maturation Changes that occur in individuals relatively independently of the environment, provided that basic conditions are satisfied. For example, most humans develop the ability to walk, given normal physical health and opportunity for movement.

Mediating influence The effect that a variable has to bring about or cause an outcome. For example, when variable A affects variable M, which, in turn, affects variable B, the impact of A on B is said to be mediated by M.

Mental age (MA) The score corresponding to the chronological age (CA) of persons whose intellectual test performance the examinee equals. For the average child, MA = CA.

Metacognition The understanding of one's own information-processing system.

Minimal brain dysfunction (MBD) The assumption that the central nervous system or brain is functioning in a pathological way to a degree that is not clearly detectable.

Moderating influence The effect that a variable has to reduce or strengthen an outcome. For example, when the relationship of variable A to variable B depends on the level of variable M, M is said to be the moderator of the relationship of A to B.

Monozygotic (identical) twins Twins resulting from one union of an ovum and a sperm. The single zygote divides early into two, with the new zygotes having identical genes (and thus being of the same sex).

Morphology Regarding language, refers to the forms of words or the study of word formation.

Multifinality The concept that a factor may lead to different developmental outcomes. For example, child abuse may result in different kinds of behavior problems.

Multigenic influence The influences of multiple genes that combine in some way to affect an attribute or behavior. Also referred to as multiple-gene or polygenic influence.

Multiple baseline research designs Single-case experimental designs in which a manipulation is made and multiple behaviors or multiple participants are measured over time.

Mutation Spontaneous change in the genes that can be transmitted to the next generation. One of the genetic mechanisms that accounts for variation in species and individuals.

Nature vs. nurture controversy The debate about the relative influence of innate and experiential factors on the shaping of the individual. Also known as the hereditary vs. environmental debate.

Negative (inverse) correlation Correlation in which two (or more) variables covary such that high scores on one variable are associated with low scores on the other and vice versa.

Negative reinforcement The process whereby the probability or strength of a response increases because the response was followed by the removal of an aversive stimulus.

Neuropsychological assessment The use of psychological tests and behavioral measures to indirectly evaluate the functioning of the nervous system. Performance on these measures is known or presumed to reflect specific aspects of the functioning of the brain.

Neurotransmitter A chemical that carries the nerve impulse from one neuron, across the synaptic space, to another neuron. Examples of neurotransmitters are serotonin, dopamine, and norepinephrine.

Nonnormative developmental influences The effects on development which stem from events that are not necessarily unusual in themselves, but that occur only to some individuals, perhaps at unpredictable times. Examples are serious injury in childhood and the premature death of a parent. (See normative developmental influences.)

Nonshared environmental influences Environmental influences on an attribute that are experienced by one family member, but not other members. (See shared environmental influences.)

Normal distribution (curve) The bell-shaped theoretical distribution or probability curve that describes the way in which many attributes (e.g., height, intelligence) occur or are assumed to occur in the population.

Normalization The philosophy that persons with disabilities have the right to experiences that are as normal as possible for the individual. (See mainstreaming; least restrictive environment.)

Normative developmental influences The effects on development which stem from events that happen to most individuals in some more or less predictable way. An example is puberty. (See nonnormative developmental influences.)

Norms Data based on information gathered from a segment of the population that represents the entire population. Norms serve as standards for evaluating individual development or functioning.

Nuclear family A family unit consisting of the father, mother, and children.

Observational learning Learning that occurs through viewing the behavior of others. Modeled behavior can be presented in live or symbolic form.

Obsessions Recurring and intrusive irrational thoughts over which the individual feels no control.

Operant learning Learning in which responses are acquired, maintained, or eliminated as the result of consequences (e.g., reinforcement, punishment) and other learning processes.

Operational criteria (definition) A specified set of observable operations that are measurable and that allow one to define some concept. For example, maternal deprivation might be defined by the amount of time the child is separated from its mother.

Overlearning The procedure whereby learning trials are continued beyond the point at which the child has satisfied the stated criteria. Overlearning is intended to increase the likelihood that the new behavior will be maintained.

Overt behaviors Behaviors that are readily observable. When describing antisocial behaviors, this term refers to behaviors that are confrontational such as physical aggression, temper tantrums, and defiance. (*See* covert behaviors.)

Panic attack A discrete period of intense apprehension, fear, or terror that has a sudden onset and reaches a peak quickly.

Paradigm A shared perspective or framework consisting of a set of assumptions and conceptions that guide the work of a group of scientists.

Partial correlation statistical procedure A statistical procedure that aids in the interpretation of a demonstrated correlation by removing the effects of one or more specific variables.

Pediatric psychology The integrated field of science and practice in which principles of psychology are applied within the context of pediatric health.

Perinatal The period at or around the time of birth.

Phenotype Observable attributes of an individual that result from the individual's genetic endowment, developmental processes, and the transactions of these.

Phobia Anxiety about, and avoidance of, some object or situation. This reaction is judged to be excessive, overly persistent, unadaptive, or inappropriate.

Phonological awareness The understanding that spoken words can be segmented into sounds (e.g., that "cat" has three sounds) and that sounds are represented by letters or combinations of letters of the alphabet.

Phonological decoding In alphabet-based languages, mapping letters to sounds.

Phonological processing Using the sound structure of a language to process written material. Deficits in such processing are central in reading disorders.

Phonology The sounds of a language or the study of speech sounds.

Placebo A treatment that alters a person's behavior because he or she expects that change will occur. Placebos are often employed as control conditions to evaluate whether a treatment being tested is effective for reasons other than the person's belief in it.

Positive (direct) correlation Correlation in which two (or more) variables covary with each other such that high scores on one variable are associated with high scores on the other variable and low scores on the one variable are associated with low scores on the other.

Positive reinforcement The process whereby the probability or strength of a response increases because the response is followed by a positive stimulus.

Positron emission tomography (PET scan) A procedure for directly assessing activity in different parts of the brain by assessing the use of oxygen and glucose that fuel brain activity.

Pragmatics (of language) The use of speech and gestures in a communicative way, considering the social context. Pragmatic skills include using appropriate gestures and language style.

Predictive validity The extent to which predictions about future behavior can be made (e.g., by knowing the individual's diagnosis or performance on some test).

Premorbid adjustment The psychological, social, or academic/vocational adjustment of a person prior to the onset of the symptoms of a disorder or its diagnosis.

Prenatal Having to do with the period of development that occurs during pregnancy or gestation.

Prevalence Number or proportion of persons in a population with a disorder at a given time.

Proband The designated individual whose relatives are assessed to determine whether an attribute occurs in other members of the individual's family. Also called an index case.

Prognosis A forecast or prediction of the probable course or outcome of a disorder.

Projective tests Psychological tests that present ambiguous stimuli to the person. The person's response is presumed to reflect unconscious thoughts and feelings that are unacceptable to the ego and therefore cannot be expressed directly.

Pronoun reversal Deviant speech pattern in which speakers refer to themselves as "you," "she," or "he" and refer to others as "I" or "me." Often found in autism.

Prospective research designs Designs that identify participants and then follow them over time. (*See* retrospective research designs.)

Protective or promotive factors Influences that contribute to the development of resilience. (*See* resilience.)

Psychoactive (psychotropic) drugs Chemical substances that influence psychological processes (e.g., behavior, thinking, emotions) by their effects on nervous system functioning. Examples are stimulants and antidepressants.

Psychopharmacological treatment An approach to treatment through the use of psychoactive medications that affect behavior, thinking, or the emotions. Examples are the use of stimulant medications for attention-deficit/hyperactivity disorder and selective serotonin reuptake inhibitors for depression.

Psychosis A general term for severe mental disorder that affects thinking, the emotions, and other psychological systems. The hallmark of a psychosis is disturbed contact with reality.

Punishment A process whereby a response is followed by either an unpleasant stimulus or the removal of a pleasant stimulus, thereby decreasing the frequency of the response.

Qualitative research A research approach which assumes that events are best understood when they are observed in context and from a personal frame of reference. The methods employed include in-depth interviews and intensive case studies. (*See* quantitative research.)

Quantitative research A research approach that places a high value on objective quantitative measurement in a highly controlled situation, as characterized by the experiment. (See qualitative research.)

Random assignment In research, the assignment of individuals to different groups so that each individual has an equal chance of being assigned to any group. Such chance assignment helps make the groups comparable on factors that might influence the findings.

Receptive language The ability to understand and comprehend spoken or written language.

Recidivism The return to a previous undesirable pattern. The juvenile delinquent who again commits a crime after completing a treatment program illustrates recidivism.

Reciprocal relationship The situation in which it is possible for two variables to mutually influence one another.

Reinforcement A process whereby a stimulus that occurs contingent on a particular behavior results in an increase in the likelihood of that behavior. (See positive reinforcement; negative reinforcement.)

Relapse The reoccurrence of a problem after it has been successfully treated.

Reliability The degree to which an observation is consistently made. The term can be applied to a test or other measurement or to a system of classification. (See test-retest reliability; interrater reliability.)

Remission As applied to disorder or disease, disappearance or reduced manifestation of symptoms.

Resilience A relatively positive outcome in the face of significantly adverse circumstances or traumatic experiences. Resilience may speak to differences in attributes of the individual and/or to characteristics of the environment that allow the young person to resist or overcome life's adversities.

Response prevention A behavioral treatment procedure in which the person is not allowed to engage in, or is discouraged from engaging in, a compulsive ritual or avoidant behavior.

Retrospective research designs Designs that utilize information about past events; follow-back designs. (See prospective research designs.)

Risk The degree to which variables (risk factors) operate to increase the chance of behavior problems.

Savant abilities Specific and remarkable cognitive abilities (e.g., in memory or arithmetic) of individuals who otherwise exhibit intellectual disability.

Scientific method An empirical approach to understanding phenomena. The scientific approach involves systematic formulation, observation, and measurement, and interpretation of findings.

Selective prevention strategies (See high-risk prevention strategies.)

Self-injurious behavior Repetitious action that damages the self physically, such as head banging or pulling one's own hair.

Self-injurious behavior is observed especially in autism and intellectual disability.

Self-monitoring A procedure in which the individual observes and records his or her own behaviors or thoughts and the circumstances under which they occur.

Self-stimulatory behavior Sensorimotor behavior that serves as stimulation for the person. Often refers to a pathological process, such as when an autistic child repetitiously flaps his or her hands.

Semantics The study of meanings in language.

Separation anxiety Childhood anxiety regarding separation from the mother or other major attachment figures.

Shared environmental influences Environmental influences on an attribute that are experienced by two or more family members. (See nonshared environmental influences.)

Single-case experiments Experimental research designs employed with a single participant (or a few participants) in which a manipulation is made and measurements are taken across periods of time. (See ABA; multiple baseline designs.)

Socioeconomic status (SES) Social class. Indices of SES include income, amount of education, and occupational level.

Spectrum disorder This term is applied to sets of disordered behavior or linked conditions that are thought to share certain psychological, behavioral, or biological characteristics and are viewed not as separate but as part of a larger spectrum. An example is autism spectrum disorder.

Stage theories of development Theories of development which postulate that growth occurs in a recognizable order of noncontinuous stages or steps that are qualitatively different from each other. Examples are Piaget's cognitive theory and Freud's psycho-sexual theory.

Statistical significance In research, the probability equal to or below which the findings are due merely to chance. By tradition, a finding is statistically significant when there is a 5% or lower probability that it occurred by chance.

Stereotypy A repetitive action or movement, such as hand flapping.

Stigmatization Refers to stereotyping, prejudice, discrimination, or self-degradation associated with membership in a socially devalued group.

Stop-signal task A method for evaluating behavioral inhibition. The individual must press a button when a target stimulus comes on a screen but must withhold this response when a special signal also comes on.

Stress A situation or event that brings strain to the individual. Stress is considered a risk factor for behavioral and physical illness.

Sympathetic nervous system A part of the autonomic nervous system that, among other things, accelerates the heart rate, increases blood glucose, inhibits intestinal activity, and, in general, seems to prepare the organism for stress or activity.

Syndrome A group of behaviors or symptoms likely to occur together.

Syntax The aspect of grammar that deals with the way words are put together to form phrases, clauses, and sentences.

Systematic desensitization A behavioral treatment for anxiety. In systematic desensitization, the client visualizes a hierarchy of scenes, each of which elicits more anxiety than the previous scene. The visualizations are paired with relaxation until they no longer produce anxiety.

Systematic direct observation Observation of specific behaviors of an individual or group of individuals in a particular setting, with the use of a specific observational code or instrument.

Temperament Individual differences in emotionality, social responsiveness, activity level, and self-control. One's temperament is a biologically based disposition that can be transformed by experience.

Teratogens Conditions or agents that are potentially harmful to the prenatal organism.

Test-retest reliability The degree to which a test or diagnostic system yields the same result when applied to the same individual(s) at different times.

Theory An integrated set of propositions that explains phenomena and guides research.

Theory of mind The ability to infer mental states (e.g., beliefs, knowledge) in others or the self.

Time-out Behavior modification technique in which an individual displaying an undesirable behavior is removed from the immediate environment, usually by placement in an isolated room. Time-out is viewed conceptually as the elimination of positive reinforcement or as punishment.

Token economy A behavioral treatment procedure developed from operant conditioning principles. A set of behaviors is established that earns or costs reward points, given in the form of some scrip, such as poker chips. These tokens can then be exchanged for prizes, activities, or privileges.

Transactional model of development The view that development is the result of the continuous interplay of organismic and environmental variables. The transactional model of development is conceptually similar to the interactional model of development, but emphasizes the ongoing, mutual influences of factors.

Transgender To have a gender identity that is incongruent with one's assigned sex at birth.

Translational research A term that in general refers to efforts to apply research findings to the "real world" of clinical practice and community programs.

Trauma An event outside of everyday experience that would be distressing to almost anyone.

Treatment foster care An effort to alleviate behavioral problems of children in foster care by working with foster parents and linking the child to the community mental health system.

Twin study In genetic research, the comparison of monozygotic twin pairs with dizygotic twin pairs to determine whether the former are more like each other than the latter. A type of research investigation frequently employed to examine the effects of hereditary and environmental variables.

Unconditioned stimulus (UCS) A stimulus that elicits a particular response prior to any conditioning trials. The loud noise that causes an infant to startle is an example of an unconditioned stimulus.

Universal prevention strategies Prevention strategies that are targeted at entire populations for which greater-than-average risk has not been identified.

Validity A term used in several different ways, all of which address issues of correctness, meaningfulness, and relevancy. (*See* internal validity; external validity; predictive validity.)

Wait-list (waiting-list) control group Group of participants in a research study who do not receive the treatment being investigated. A wait-list control group allows the investigators to compare changes in a group of individuals who received treatment with changes in a group of similar individuals who did not receive treatment. The term *wait-list* is derived from the fact that those in the control group are offered treatment once the comparison is completed.

Working memory Part of the memory system that briefly holds and actively manipulates, or works on, information that it receives from the sensory systems or calls up from long-term memory. Working memory is sometimes referred to as short-term memory.

Zygote The cell mass formed by the joining of an ovum and sperm; the fertilized egg.

References

AAIDD. (2010). *Intellectual disability: Definition, classification, and systems of support* (11th ed.). Washington, DC: Author.

AAIDD. (2019). Electric shock: Position statement of AAIDD. Retrieved from www.aaidd.org/news-policy/policy/position-statements/electric-shock

AAIDD Position Statement. (2020). Unjustifiable non-therapy: There is not objective evidence in support of growth attenuation therapy for young people with disabilities, as first descrbied by Gunther & Diekma (2006). A statement from the Board of Directors of the American Association on Intellectual and Developmental Disabilities. Retrieved from www.aamr.org/Policies/growth.shtml

Aarnoudse-Moens, C. S. H., Weisglas-Kuperus, N., van Goudoever, J. B., & Oosterlaan, J. (2009). Meta-analysis of neurobiological outcomes in very preterm and/or very low birth weight children. *Pediatrics, 124,* 717–728.

Aas, M., Pizzagalli, D. A., Laskemoen, J. F., Reponen, E. J., Ueland, T., Melle, I., et al. (2019). Elevated hair cortisol is associated with childhood maltreatment and cognitive impairment in schizophrenia and in bipolar disorders. *Schizophrenia Research, 213,* 65–71.

Abela, J. R. Z., & Hankin, B. L. (2008). Cognitive vulnerability to depression in children and adolescents: A developmental perspective. In J. R. Z. Abela & B. L. Hankin (Eds.), *Handbook of depression in children and adolescents.* New York: The Guilford Press.

Abela, J. R. Z., Hankin, B. L., Sheshko, D. M., Fishman, M. B., & Stolow, D. (2012). Multi-wave prospective examination of the stress-reactivity extension of response styles theory of depression in high-risk children and early adolescents. *Journal of Abnormal Child Psychology, 40,* 277–287.

Abidin, R. R. (2012). *Parenting Stress Index, Fourth Edition (PSI-4).* Lutz, FL: Psychological Assessment Resources, Inc.

Abramovitch, A., Mittelman, A., Henin, A., & Geller, D. (2012). Neuroimaging and neuropsychological findings in pediatric obsessive-compulsive disorder: A review and developmental considerations. *Neuropsychiatry, 2,* 313–329.

Abrams, J., Faraone, S. V., Woodworth, K. Y., Spencer, T. J., Biederman, I., & Biederman, J. (2018). Are adult ADHD patients good informants of their symptoms? A qualitative literature review of concordance between clinician and self-report ADHD symptoms. *The Journal of Nervous and Mental Disease, 206,* 739–743.

Abramson, L. Y., Metalsky, G. I., & Alloy, L. B. (1989). Hopelessness depression: A theory-based subtype of depression. *Psychological Bulletin, 96,* 358–372.

Abu-Akel, A., Caplan, R., Guthrie, D., & Komo, S. (2000). Childhood schizophrenia: Responsiveness to questions during conversation. *Journal of the American Academy of Child and Adolescent Psychiatry, 39,* 779–786.

Achenbach, T. M. (1982). *Developmental psychopathology.* New York: Wiley.

Achenbach, T. M. (1990). Conceptualizations of developmental psychopathology. In M. Lewis & S. M. Miller (Eds.), *Handbook of developmental psychopathology.* New York: Plenum.

Achenbach, T. M. (2000). Assessment of psychopathology. In A. J. Sameroff, M. Lewis, & S. M. Miller (Eds.), *Handbook of developmental psychopathology* (2nd ed.). New York: Kluwer Academic/Plenum Publishers.

Achenbach, T. M. (2013). *Child Behavior Checklist-Direct Observation Form (CBCL-DOF).* Burlington, VT: Achenbach System of Empirically Based Assessment.

Achenbach, T. M. (2014). *The Achenbach system of empirically based assessment (ASEBA).* Burlington, VT: Author.

Achenbach, T. M. (2017). Future directions for clinical research, services, and training: Evidence-based assessment across informants, cultures, and dimensional hierarchies. *Journal of Clinical Child and Adolescent Psychology, 46,* 159–169.

Achenbach, T. M., & Rescorla, L. A. (2000). *Manual for the ASEBA preschool forms & profiles.* Burlington, VT: University of Vermont Research Center for Children, Youth, and Families.

Achenbach, T. M., & Rescorla, L. A. (2001). *Manual for the ASEBA school-age forms & profiles.* Burlington, VT: University of Vermont, Research Center for Children, Youth, & Families.

Achenbach, T. M., & Rescorla, L. A. (2007). *Multicultural supplement to the manual for the ASEBA school-age forms & profiles.* Burlington, VT: University of Vermont, Research Center for Children, Youth and Families.

Achenbach, T. M., & Rescorla, L. A. (2015). *Multicultural supplement to the manual for the ASEBA adult forms &*

profiles. Burlington, VT: University of Vermont Research Center for Children, Youth, and Families.

Achenbach, T. M., Dumenci, L., & Rescorla, L. A. (2003). DSM-oriented and empirically based approaches to constructing scales from the same item pools. *Journal of Clinical Child and Adolescent Psychology, 32,* 328–340.

Achenbach, T. M., Ivanova, M. Y., Rescorla, L. A., Turner, L. V., & Althoff, R. R. (2016). Internalizing/externalizing problems: Review and recommendations for clinical research applications. *Journal of the American Academy of Child and Adolescent Psychiatry, 55,* 647–656.

Ackard, D. M., Fulkerson, J. A., & Neumark-Sztainer, D. (2007). Prevalence and utility of DSM-IV eating disorder diagnostic criteria among youth. *International Journal of Eating Disorders, 40,* 409–417.

Ackerman, P. L. (2018). Intelligence as potentiality and actuality. In R. J. Sternberg (Ed.), *The nature of human intelligence*. New York: Cambridge University Press.

Adams, D., & Oliver, C. (2011). The expression and assessment of emotions and internal states in individuals with severe or profound intellectual disabilities. *Clinical Psychology Review, 31,* 293–306.

Adams, D., Rose, J., Jackson, N., Karakatsani, E., & Oliver, C. (2018). Coping strategies in mothers of children with intellectual disabilities showing multiple forms of challenging behaviour: Associations with maternal mental health. *Behavioural and Cognitive Psychotherapy, 46,* 257–275.

Adamson, L. B., Bakeman, R., Suma, K., & Robins, D. L. (2019). An expanded view of joint attention: Skill, engagement, and language in typical development and autism. *Child Development, 90,* e1–e18.

Adelman, H. S. (1996). Appreciating the classification dilemma. In W. Stainback & S. Stainback (Eds.), *Controversial issues confronting special education: Divergent perspectives* (2nd ed.). Boston, MA: Allyn and Bacon.

Adrian, M., Zeman, J., Erdley, C., Lisa, L., & Sim, L. (2011). Emotional dysregulation and emotional difficulties as risk factors for nonsuicidal self-injury in adolescent girls. *Journal of Abnormal Child Psychology, 39,* 389–400.

Adrián-Ventura, J., Soriano-Ferrer, M., Fuentes-Claramonte, P., Morte-Soriano, M., Parcet, M. A., & Ávila, C. (2020). Grey matter reduction in the occipitotemporal cortex in Spanish children with dyslexia: A voxel-based morphometry study. *Journal of Neurolinguistics, 53,* 100873.

Aduen, P. A., Day, T. N., Kofler, M. J., Harmon, S. L., Wells, E. L., & Sarver, D. E. (2018). Social problems in ADHD: Is it a skills acquisition or performance problem? *Journal of Psychopathology and Behavioral Assessment, 40,* 440–451.

Agnew-Blais, J. C., Polanczyk, G. V., Danese, A., Wertz, J., Moffitt, T. E., & Arseneault, L. (2016). Evaluation of the persistence, remission, and emergence of Attention-Deficit/Hyperactivity Disorder in young adulthood. *JAMA Psychiatry, 73,* 713–720.

Aguiar, A., Eubig, P. A., & Schantz, S. L. (2010). Attention deficit/hyperactivity disorder: A focused overview for children's environmental health researchers. *Environmental Health Perspectives, 118,* 1646–1653.

Ahmad, S. I., & Hinshaw, S. P. (2016). Attention-deficit/hyperactivity disorder: Similarities to and differences from other externalizing disorders. In *The Oxford handbook of externalizing spectrum disorders*. New York: Oxford University Press.

Ahn, K., An, S. S., Shugart, Y. Y., & Rapoport, J. L. (2016). Common polygenic variation and risk for childhood-onset schizophrenia. *Molecular Psychiatry, 21,* 94–96.

Ahrnsbrak, R., Bose, J., Hedden, S., Lipari, R., & Park-Lee, E. (2017). *Key substance use and mental health indicators in the United States: Results from the 2016 National Survey on Drug Use and Health.* Center for Behavioral Health Statistics and Quality, Substance Abuse and Mental Health Services Administration: Rockville, MD, USA.

Ainbinder, J. G., Blanchard, L. W., Singer, G. H. S., Sullivan, M. E., Powers, L. K., Marquis, J. G., & Santelli, B. (1998). A qualitative study of parent to parent support for parents of children with special needs. *Journal of Pediatric Psychology, 23,* 99–109.

Aitken, M., VanderLaan, D. P., Wasserman, L., Stojanovski, S., & Zucker, K. J. (2016). Self-harm and suicidality in children referred for gender dysphoria. *Journal of the American Academy of Child & Adolescent Psychiatry, 55,* 513–520.

Akinbami, L. J., Simon, A. E., & Rossen, L. M. (2016). Changing trends in asthma prevalence among children. *Pediatrics, 137,* e20152354.

Aktar, E., Majdandžić, M., De Vente, W., & Bögels, S. M. (2018). Parental expressions of anxiety and child temperament in toddlerhood jointly predict preschoolers' avoidance of novelty. *Journal of Clinical Child & Adolescent Psychology, 47*(sup1), S421–S434.

Albano, A. M., & DiBartolo, P. M. (1997). Cognitive-behavioral treatment of obsessive-compulsive disorder and social phobia in children and adolescents. In L. VandeCreek (Ed.), *Innovations in clinical practice* (Vol. 15). Sarasota, FL: Professional Resource Exchange.

Albano, A. M., & Silverman, W. (2017). *Anxiety disorders interview schedule for the DSM-5.* New York: Oxford University Press.

Albano, A. M., Chorpita, B. F., & Barlow, D. H. (2003). Childhood anxiety disorders. In E. J. Mash & R. A. Barkley (Eds.), *Child psychopathology* (2nd ed.). New York: Guilford Press.

Albee, G. W. (1996). Revolutions and counterrevolutions in prevention. *American Psychologist, 51,* 1130–1133.

Albert, A. B., Jacobs, H. E., & Siperstein, G. N. (2016). Sticks, stones, and stigma: Student bystander behavior in response to hearing the word "retard." *Intellectual and Developmental Disabilities, 54,* 391–401.

References

Albert, D., Belsky, D. W., Crowley, D. M., Bates, J. E., Pettit, G. S., Lansford, J. E., et al. (2015). Developmental mediation of genetic variation in response to the Fast Track prevention program. *Development and psychopathology, 27*, 81–95.

Aldao, A., & De Los Reyes, A. (2015). A practical guide for translating basic research on affective science to implementing physiology in clinical child and adolescent assessments. *Journal of Clinical Child and Adolescent Psychology, 44*, 341–351.

Alderfer, M. A., Long, K. A., Lown, A., Marsland, A. L., Ostrowski, N. L., Hock, J. M., et al. (2010). Psychosocial adjustment of siblings of children with cancer: A systematic review. *Psycho-Oncology, 19*, 789–805.

Aldiss, S., Baggott, C., Gibson, F., Mobbs, S., & Taylor, R. M. (2015). A critical review of the use of technology to provide psychosocial support for children and young people with long-term conditions. *Journal of Pediatric Nursing, 30*, 87–101.

Alexander, F. (1950). *Psychosomatic medicine: Its principles and applications*. New York: W. W. Norton and Co.

Alfano, C. A., Palmer, C., & Bower, J. (2018). Sleep disorders in children and adolescents. In J. N. Butcher & P. C. Kendall (Eds.), *APA handbook of psychopathology* (Vol. 2). Washington, DC: American Psychological Association.

Alfonso, V. C., & Flanagan, D. P. (2018). *Essentials of specific learning disability identification*. Hoboken, NJ: John Wiley & Sons.

Algozzine, B. (1977). The emotionally disturbed child: Disturbed or disturbing? *Journal of Abnormal Child Psychology, 5*, 205–211.

Alink, L. R., Cyr, C., & Madigan, S. (2019). The effect of maltreatment experiences on maltreating and dysfunctional parenting: A search for mechanisms. *Development and Psychopathology, 31*, 1–7.

Alisic, E., Zalta, A. K., Van Wesel, F., Larsen, S. E., Hafstad, G. S., Hassanpour, K., & Smid, G. E. (2014). Rates of post-traumatic stress disorder in trauma-exposed children and adolescents: meta-analysis. *The British Journal of Psychiatry, 204*, 335–340.

Allen, K. L., Byrne, S. M., Oddy, W. H., & Crosby, R. D. (2013). DSM–IV–TR and DSM-5 eating disorders in adolescents: Prevalence, stability, and psychosocial correlates in a population-based sample of male and female adolescents. *Journal of Abnormal Psychology, 122*, 720–732.

Alloy, L. B., Abramson, L. Y., Walshaw, P. D., Keyser, J., & Gerstein, R. K. (2010). Adolescent onset bipolar spectrum disorders: A cognitive vulnerability-stress perspective. In D. J. Miklowitz & D. Cicchetti (Eds.), *Understanding bipolar disorder: A developmental psychopathology perspective*. New York: The Guilford Press.

Altman, M., & Wilfley, D. E. (2015). Evidence update on the treatment of overweight and obesity in children and adolescents. *Journal of Clinical Child & Adolescent Psychology, 44*, 521–537.

Alvarado, C., & Modesto-Lowe, V. (2016). Improving treatment in minority children with attention deficit/hyperactivity disorder. *Clinical Pediatrics, 56*, 171–176.

Amato, P. R. (2010). Research on divorce: Continuing trends and new developments. *Journal of Marriage and Family, 72*, 650–666.

Amato, P. R., & Keith, B. (1991). Parental divorce and the wellbeing of children: A meta-analysis. *Psychological Bulletin, 110*, 26–46.

Ambrosini, P. J. (2000). Historical development and present status of the Schedule for Affective Disorders and Schizophrenia for School-Age Children (K-SADS). *Journal of the American Academy of Child and Adolescent Psychiatry, 39*, 48–58.

American Academy of Child and Adolescent Psychiatry. (2007a). Practice parameter for the assessment and treatment of children and adolescents with attention-deficit/hyperactivity disorder. *Journal of the American Academy of Child and Adolescent Psychiatry, 46*, 894–921.

American Academy of Child and Adolescent Psychiatry. (2007b). Practice parameter for the assessment and treatment of children and adolescents with oppositional defiant disorder. *Journal of the American Academy of Child and Adolescent Psychiatry, 46*, 126–141.

American Academy of Child and Adolescent Psychiatry. (2007c). Practice parameters for the assessment and treatment of children and adolescents with bipolar disorder. *Journal of the American Academy of Child and Adolescent Psychiatry, 46*, 107–125.

American Academy of Child and Adolescent Psychiatry. (2017). Hearing voices and seeing things. Retrieved from www.aacap.org/AACAP/Families_and_Youth/Facts_for_Families/FFF-Guide/Hearing-Voices-and-Seeing-Things-102.aspx

American Academy of Pediatrics. (2000). Fetal alcohol syndrome and alcohol-related neurodevelopmental disorders. *Pediatrics, 106*, 358–361.

American Academy of Pediatrics. (2010). AAP Publications Retired and Reaffirmed. *Pediatrics, 126*, e1622.

American Academy of Pediatrics. (2019). *Safety and injury prevention program*. Retrieved from www.aap.org/en-us/advocacy-and-policy/aap-health-initiatives/healthy-child-care/Pages/Safety-and-Injury-Prevention.aspx

American Academy of Pediatrics Subcommittee on Attention-Deficit/Hyperactivity Disorder. (2011). ADHD: Clinical practice guideline for the diagnosis, evaluation, and treatment of attention-deficit/hyperactivity disorder in children and adolescents. *Pediatrics, 128*, 2011–2654.

American Academy of Sleep Medicine (2014). *The international classification of sleep disorders* (3rd ed.). Westchester, IL: Author.

American Diabetes Association. (2019). 13. Children and adolescents: Standards of medical care in diabetes—2019. *Diabetes Care, 42*(sup1), S148–S164.

American Psychiatric Association. (1952, 1968, 1980, 1987, 1994, 2000). *Diagnostic and statistical manual of mental disorders.* Washington, DC: American Psychiatric Association.

American Psychiatric Association. (2011). *DSM-5 development.* Retrieved July 2011 from www.dsm5.org

American Psychiatric Association. (2013). *Diagnostic and statistical manual of mental disorders* (5th ed.). Washington, DC: American Psychiatric Association.

American Psychological Association. (2006). *APA working group on psychoactive medications for children and adolescents.* Washington, DC: Author.

American Psychological Association. (2010). 2010 Amendments to the 2002 "Ethical Principles of Psychologists and Code of Conduct." *American Psychologist, 65,* 493.

American Psychological Association. (2016). Revision of ethical standard 3.04 of the "Ethical Principles of Psychologists and Code of Conduct" (2002, as amended 2010). *American Psychologist, 71,* 900.

American Psychological Association. (2017). *Ethical principles of psychologists and code of conduct* (2002, Amended June 1, 2010 and January 1, 2017). Retrieved from www.apa.org/ethics/code/index

American Psychological Association. (2019). Society of Pediatric Psychology. Retrieved from www.apa.org/about/division/div54

American Speech-Language-Hearing Association (ASHA). (n.d.). How does your child hear and talk? Retrieved from www.asha.org/public/speech/development/chart/

Amiri, S., Sadeghi-Bazargani, H., Nazari, S., Ranjbar, F., & Abdi, S. (2017). Attention deficit/hyperactivity disorder and risk of injuries: A systematic review and meta-analysis. *Journal of Injury & Violence Research, 9,* 95–105.

Anastasi, A., & Urbina, S. (1997). *Psychological testing.* Upper Saddle River, NJ: Prentice Hall.

Anastopoulos, A. D., Rhoads, L. H., & Farley, S. E. (2006). Counseling and training parents. In R. A. Barkley (Ed.), *Attention-deficit hyperactivity disorder. A handbook for diagnosis and treatment.* New York: The Guilford Press.

Anastopoulos, A. D., Smith, J. M., & Wien, E. E. (1998). Counseling and training parents. In R. A. Barkley (Ed.), *Attention-deficit hyperactivity disorder.* New York: Guilford Press.

Anderson, C. A., Berkowitz, L., Donnerstein, E., Huesmann, R., Johnson, J. D., Linz, D., et al. (2003). The influence of media violence on youth. *Psychological Science in the Public Interest, 4,* 81–110.

Anderson, C. A., Bushman, B. J., Bartholow, B. D., Cantor, J., Christakis, D., Coyne, S. M., et al. (2017). Screen violence and youth behavior. *Pediatrics, 140*(sup2), S142–S147.

Anderson, E. R., & Mayes, L. C. (2010). Race/ethnicity and internalizing disorders in youth: A review. *Clinical Psychology Review, 30,* 338–348.

Anderson, J. C., Williams, S., McGee, R., & Silva, P. A. (1987). DSM-III disorders in preadolescent children: Prevalence in a large sample from the general population. *Archives of General Psychiatry, 44,* 69–76.

Anderson, P. M., & Butcher, K. F. (2006). Childhood obesity trends and potential causes. *The Future of Children, 16,* 19–45.

Anderson, V., Northam, E., Hendy, J., & Wrennall, J. (2001). *Developmental neuropsychology. A clinical approach.* Philadelphia, PA: Taylor & Francis.

Anderson-Fye, E. P. (2018). Cultural influences on body image and eating disorders. In W. S. Agras & A. Robinson (Eds.), *The Oxford handbook of eating disorders* (2nd ed.). New York: Oxford University Press.

Anderson-Fye, E. P., & Becker, A. E. (2004). Sociocultural aspects of eating disorders. In J. K. Thompson (Ed.), *Handbook of eating disorders and obesity.* Hoboken, NJ: John Wiley.

Andersson, A., Tuvblad, C., Chen, Q., Du Rietz, E., Cortese, S., Kuja-Halkola, R., & Larsson, H. (2020). Research Review: The strength of the genetic overlap between ADHD and other psychiatric symptoms – a systematic review and meta-analysis. *Journal of Child Psychology and Psychiatry.*

Andrews, K. R., Silk, K. S., & Eneli, I. U. (2010). Parents as health promoters: A theory of planned behavior perspective on the prevention of childhood obesity. *Journal of Health Communication, 15,* 95–107.

Angold, A., & Costello, E. J. (2009). Nosology and measurement in child and adolescent psychiatry. *Journal of Child Psychology and Psychiatry, 50,* 9–15.

Angold, A., & Rutter, M. (1992). Effects of age and pubertal status on depression in a large clinical sample. *Development and Psychopathology, 4,* 5–28.

Angold, A., Costello, E. J., & Erkanli, A. (1999). Comorbidity. *Journal of Child Psychology and Psychiatry, 40,* 57–87.

Annett, R. D., Turner, C., Brody, J. L., Sedillo, D., & Dalen, J. (2010). Using structural equation modeling to understand child and parent perceptions of asthma quality of life. *Journal of Pediatric Psychology, 35,* 870–882.

Anthony, E. J. (1970). Behavior disorders. In P. H. Mussen (Ed.), *Carmichael's manual of child psychology* (Vol. II). New York: John Wiley.

Anthony, E. J. (1981). The psychiatric evaluation of the anxious child: Case record summarized from the clinic records. In E. J. Anthony & D. C. Gilpin (Eds.), *Three further clinical faces of childhood.* New York: S P Medical & Scientific Books.

References

Antrop, I., Roeyers, H., Van Oost, P., & Buysse, A. (2000). Stimulation seeking and hyperactivity in children with ADHD. *Journal of Child Psychology and Psychiatry, 41,* 225–231.

Anvari, A., Loeb, F., Rapoport, J. L., & Driver, D. I. (2018). Childhood-onset schizophrenia. In D. I. Driver & S. S. Thomas (Eds.), *Complex disorders in pediatric psychiatry: A clinician's guide.* St. Louis, MO: Elsevier.

Aos, S., Miller, M., & Drake, E. (2006). *Evidence-based public policy options to reduce future prison construction, criminal justice costs and crime rates.* Retrieved August 2007 from www.wsipp.wa.gov/rptfiles/06–10–1201.pdf

APA Working Group on Psychoactive Medications for Children and Adolescents. (2006). *Report of the working group on psychoactive medications for children and adolescents. Psychopharmacological, psychosocial, and combined interventions for childhood disorders: Evidence base, contextual factors, and future directions.* Washington, DC: American Psychological Association.

Aranha, P., Sams, L., & Saldanha, P. (2017). Preoperative preparation of children. *International Journal of Health & Allied Sciences, 6,* 1–4.

Arbel, R., Perrone, L., & Margolin, G. (2018). Adolescents' daily worries and risky behaviors: The buffering role of support seeking. *Journal of Clinical Child & Adolescent Psychology, 47,* 900–911.

Archambault, I., Vandenbossche-Makombo, J., & Fraser, S. L. (2017). Students' oppositional behaviors and engagement in school: The differential role of the student–teacher relationship. *Journal of Child and Family Studies, 26,* 1702–1712.

Ariés, P. (1962). *Centuries of childhood.* New York: Vintage Books.

Armstrong, G. T., Chen, Y., Yasui, Y., Leisenring, W., Gibson, T. M., Mertens, A. C., et al. (2016). Reduction in late mortality among 5-year survivors of childhood cancer. *New England Journal of Medicine, 374,* 833–842.

Armstrong, T. D., & Costello, E. J. (2002). Community studies of adolescent substance use, abuse, or dependence and psychiatric comorbidity. *Journal of Consulting and Clinical Psychology, 70,* 1224–1239.

Arnett, A. B., Pennington, B. F., Peterson, R. L., Willcutt, E. G., DeFries, J. C., & Olson, R. K. (2017). Explaining the sex difference in dyslexia. *Journal of Child Psychology and Psychiatry, 58,* 719–727.

Arnett, A. B., Pennington, B. F., Willcutt, E. G., DeFries, J. C., & Olson, R. K. (2015). Sex differences in ADHD symptom severity. *Journal of Child Psychology and Psychiatry, 56,* 632–639.

Arnett, P., Meyer, J. E., Merritt, V. C., Gatzke-Kopp, L., & Bowen, K. E. S. (2017). Brain injury and vulnerability to psychopathology. In T. P. Beauchaine & S. P. Hinshaw (Eds.), *Child and adolescent psychopathology* (3rd ed.). Hoboken, NJ: John Wiley & Sons Inc.

Arnold, P. D., Hanna, G. L., & Rosenberg, D. R. (2010). Imaging the amygdala: Changing the face of gene discovery in child psychiatry. *Journal of the American Academy of Child and Adolescent Psychiatry, 49,* 7–10.

Arsenio, W. F., & Lemerise, E. A. (2004). Aggression and moral development: Integrating social information processing and moral domain models. *Child Development, 75,* 987–1002.

Asarnow, J. R., & Asarnow, R. F. (2003). Childhood-onset schizophrenia. In E. J. Mash & R. A. Barkley (Eds.), *Child psychopathology.* New York: Guilford Press.

Asarnow, J. R., & Mehlum, L. (2019). Practitioner Review: Treatment for suicidal and self-harming adolescents–advances in suicide prevention care. *Journal of Child Psychology and Psychiatry, 60,* 1046–1054.

Asarnow, J. R., Emslie, G. J., Clarke, G., Wagner, K. D., Spirito, A., Vitiello, B., et al. (2009). Treatment of SSRI-resistant depression in adolescents (TORDIA): Predictors and moderators of treatment response. *Journal of the American Academy of Child and Adolescent Psychiatry, 48,* 330–339.

Asarnow, R. F., & Forsyth, J. K. (2017). Childhood-onset schizophrenia. In T. P. Beauchaine & S. P. Hinshaw (Eds.), *Child and adolescent psychopathology* (3rd ed.). Hoboken, NJ: John Wiley & Sons, Inc.

Asarnow, R. F., & Kernan, C. L. (2008). Childhood schizophrenia. In T. P. Beauchaine & S. P. Hinshaw (Eds.), *Child and adolescent psychopathology.* New York: John Wiley & Sons.

Asarnow, R. F., Nuechterlein, K. H., Fogelson, D., Subotnik, K. L., Payne, D. A., Russell, A. T., et al. (2001). Schizophrenia and schizophrenia-spectrum personality disorders in the first-degree relatives of children with schizophrenia: The UCLA family study. *Archives of General Psychiatry, 58,* 581–588.

Asherson, P., Ramos-Quiroga, J. A., & Young, S. (2018). Adult ADHD: Clinical presentation and assessment. In T. Banaschewski, D. Coghill, & A. Zuddas (Eds.), *Oxford textbook of attention deficit hyperactivity disorder.* Oxford: Oxford University Press.

Askew, C., & Field, A. P. (2008). The vicarious learning pathway to fear 40 years on. *Clinical Psychology Review, 28,* 1249–1265.

Askew, C., Dunne, G., Özdil, Z., Reynolds, G., & Field, A. P. (2013). Stimulus fear-relevance and the vicarious learning pathway to childhood fears. *Emotion, 13,* 915–925.

Askins, M. A., Ann-Yi, S., & Moore, B. D. (2015). Neurocognitive late effects in children treated for cancer: Psychological impact, identification, and prevention and remediation. In G. A. Mucci & L. R. Torno (Eds.), *Handbook of long term care of the childhood cancer survivor.* New York: Springer.

Assink, M., van der Put, C. E., Meeuwsen, M. W., de Jong, N. M., Oort, F. J., Stams, G. J. J., & Hoeve, M. (2019). Risk factors for child sexual abuse victimization: A meta-analytic review. *Psychological Bulletin, 145,* 459–489.

Astley, S. J., Aylward, E. H., Olson, H. C., Kerns, K., Brooks, A., Coggins, T. E., et al. (2009). Magnetic resonance imaging outcomes from a comprehensive magnetic resonance study of children with fetal alcohol spectrum disorders. *Alcoholism: Clinical and Experimental Research, 33,* 1–19.

Athamanah, L. S., Josol, C. K., Ayeh, D., Fisher, M. H., & Sung, C. (2019). Understanding friendships and promoting friendship development through peer mentoring for individuals with and without intellectual and developmental disabilities. In R. M. Hodapp & D. J. Fidler (Eds.), *International Review of Research in Developmental Disabilities*. Amsterdam: Academic Press.

Athanasiadou, A., Buitelaar, J., Brovedani, P., Chorna, O., Fulceri, F., Guzzetta, A., & Scattoni, M. L. (2019). Early motor signs of attention-deficit hyperactivity disorder: A systematic review. *European Child & Adolescent Psychiatry*, 1–14.

Atkins, M. S., Rusch, D., Mehta, T. G., & Lakind, D. (2016). Future direction for dissemination and implementation science: Aligning ecological theory and public health to close the research to practice gap. *Journal of Clinical Child & Adolescent Psychology, 45,* 215–226.

Attie, I., & Brooks-Gunn, J. (1995). The development of eating regulation across the life span. In D. Cicchetti & D. J. Cohen (Eds.), *Developmental psychopathology, Vol. 2: Risk, disorder, and adaptation*. New York: John Wiley.

Austin, A. A., & Chorpita, B. F. (2004). Temperament, anxiety, and depression: Comparisons across five ethnic groups of children. *Journal of Clinical Child & Adolescent Psychology, 33,* 216–226.

Auyeung, A., Wheelwright, S., Allison, C., Atkinson, M., Samarawickrema, N., & Baron-Cohen, S. (2009). The Children's Empathy Quotient and Systemizing Quotient: Sex differences in typical development and in autism spectrum conditions. *Journal of Autism and Developmental Disorders, 39,* 1509–1521.

Avenevoli, S., Swendsen, J., He, J.-P., Burstein, M., & Merikangas, K. R. (2015). Major depression in the national comorbidity survey–adolescent supplement: Prevalence, correlates, and treatment. *Journal of the American Academy of Child & Adolescent Psychiatry, 54,* 37–44.

Axelrod, M. I. (2017). *Behavior analysis for school psychologists.* New York: Routledge.

Axelson, D., Birmaher, B. J., Brent, D., Wassick, S., Hoover, C., Bridge, J., & Ryan, N. (2003). A preliminary study of the Kiddie Schedule for Affective Disorders and Schizophrenia for School-Age Children mania rating scale for children and adolescents. *Journal of Child and Adolescent Psychopharmacology, 13,* 463–470.

Axline, V. M. (1947). *Play therapy.* Boston, MA: Houghton Mifflin.

Aylward, B. S., & Lee, J. L. (2017). Historical developments and trends in pediatric psychology. In M. C. Roberts & R. G. Steele (Eds.), *Handbook of pediatric psychology* (5th ed.). New York: The Guilford Press.

Azar, B. (2011). Oxytocin's other side. *Monitor on Psychology, 42,* 40–42.

Azar, S. T., & Bober, S. L. (1999). Children of abusive parents. In W. K. Silverman & T. H. Ollendick (Eds.), *Development issues in the clinical treatment of children.* Boston, MA: Allyn & Bacon.

Azar, S. T., & Wolfe, D. A. (2006). Child physical abuse and neglect. In E. J. Mash & R. A. Barkley (Eds.), *Treatment of childhood disorders* (3rd ed.). New York: The Guilford Press.

Azar, S. T., Ferraro, M. H., & Breton, S. J. (1998). Intra-familial child maltreatment. In T. H. Ollendick & M. Hersen (Eds.), *Handbook of child psychopathology* (3rd ed.). New York: Plenum Press.

Azar, S. T., Goslin, M. C., & Patallo, B. J. (2019). Children of divorce and relationship dissolution. In T. H. Ollendick, S. W. White, & B. A. White (Eds.), *The Oxford handbook of clinical child and adolescent psychology.* New York: Oxford University Press.

Babinski, L. M., Hartsough, C. S., & Lambert, N. M. (1999). Childhood conduct problems, hyperactivity-impulsivity, and inattention as predictors of adult criminal activity. *Journal of Child Psychology and Psychiatry, 40,* 347–355.

Bachman, J. G., O'Malley, P. M., Schulenberg, J. E., Johnston, L. D., Bryant, A. L., & Merline, A. C. (2002). *The decline of substance use in young adulthood: Changes in social activities, roles, and beliefs.* Mahwah, NJ: Erlbaum.

Bachmann, C. J., Wijlaars, L. P., Kalverdijk, L. J., Burcu, M., Glaeske, G., Schuiling-Veninga, C. C. M., et al. (2017). Trends in ADHD medication use in children and adolescents in five western countries, 2005–2012. *European Neuropsychopharmacology, 27,* 484–493.

Baiardini, I., Sicuro, F., Balbi, F., Canonica, G. W., & Braido, F. (2015). Psychological aspects in asthma: Do psychological factors affect asthma management? *Asthma Research and Practice, 1,* 7.

Bailey, A., Le Couteur, A., Gottesman, I., Bolton, P., Simonoff, E., Yuzda, E., & Rutter, M. (1995). Autism as a strongly genetic disorder: Evidence from a British twin study. *Psychological Medicine, 25,* 63–78.

Bailey, D. (2020). Answering the demand for services. *Monitor on Psychology, 51,* 68–71.

Bailey, D. B., Skinner, D., & Sparkman, K. L. (2003). Discovering fragile X syndrome: Family experiences and perceptions. *Pediatrics, 111,* 407–416.

Baio, J., Wiggins, L., Christensen, D. L., Maenner, M. J., Daniels, J., Warren, Z., et al. (2018). Prevalence of autism spectrum disorder among children aged 8 years: Autism and

References

developmental disabilities monitoring network, 11 sites, United States, 2014. *MMWR Surveillance Summaries, 67,* 1–23.

Baker, B. L., Neece, C. L., Fenning, R. M., Crnic, K. A., & Blacher, J. (2010). Mental disorders in five year old children with or without developmental delay: Focus on ADHD. *Journal of Clinical Child and Adolescent Psychology, 39,* 492–505.

Baker, J. K., Fenning, R. M., Crnic, K. A., Baker, B. L., & Blacher, J. (2007). Prediction of social skills in 6-year-old children with and without developmental delays: Contributions of early regulation and maternal scaffolding. *American Journal on Mental Retardation, 112,* 375–391.

Baker, L., & Cantwell, D. P. (1989). Specific language and learning disorders. In T. H. Ollendick & M. Hersen (Eds.), *Handbook of child psychopathology.* New York: Plenum.

Bakermans-Kranenburg, M. J., & van IJzendoorn, M. H. (2006). Gene-environment interaction of the dopamine D4 receptor (DRD4) and observed maternal insensitivity predicting externalizing behavior in preschoolers. *Developmental Psychobiology, 48,* 406–409.

Bakermans-Kranenburg, M. J., & van IJzendoorn, M. H. (2011). Differential susceptibility to rearing environment depending on dopamine-related genes: New evidence and a meta-analysis. *Development and Psychopathology, 23,* 39–52.

Bakermans-Kranenburg, M. J., & van IJzendoorn, M. H. (2015). The hidden efficacy of interventions: Gene × environment experiments from a differential susceptibility perspective. *Annual Review of Psychology, 66,* 381–409.

Baldridge, S., Wallace, L., & Kadakia, A. (2018). The epidemiology of outpatient pain treatment in pediatrics. *Journal of Pain Research, 11,* 913–921.

Ball, H. A., Arseneault, L., Taylor, A., Maughan, B., Caspi, A., & Moffitt, T. E. (2008). Genetic and environmental influences victims, bullies, and bully-victims in childhood. *Journal of Child Psychology and Psychiatry, 49,* 104–112.

Bandura, A. (1977). *Social learning theory.* Englewood Cliffs, NJ: Prentice Hall.

Bandura, A. (1997). *Self-efficacy: The exercise of control.* New York: Freeman.

Bandura, A., & Menlove, F. L. (1968). Factors determining vicarious extinction of avoidance behavior through symbolic modeling. *Journal of Personality and Social Psychology, 8,* 99–108.

Baranek, G. T., Woynaroski, T. G., Nowell, S., Turner-Brown, L., DuBay, M., Crais, E. R., & Watson, L. R. (2018). Cascading effects of attention disengagement and sensory seeking on social symptoms in a community sample of infants at-risk for a future diagnosis of autism spectrum disorder. *Developmental Cognitive Neuroscience, 29,* 30–40.

Bardone-Cone, A. M., Wonderlich, S. A., Frost, R. O., Bulik, C. M., Mitchell, J. E., Uppala, S., & Simonich, H. (2007).

Perfectionism and eating disorders: Current status and future directions. *Clinical Psychology Review, 27,* 384–405.

Bargiela, S., Steward, R., & Mandy, W. (2016). The experiences of late-diagnosed women with autism spectrum conditions: An investigation of the female autism phenotype. *Journal of Autism and Developmental Disorders, 46,* 3281–3294.

Barker, E. D., Walton, E., & Cecil, C. A. (2018). Annual research review: DNA methylation as a mediator in the association between risk exposure and child and adolescent psychopathology. *Journal of Child Psychology and Psychiatry, 59,* 303–322.

Barker, K. M., Subramanian, S. V., Berkman, L., Austin, S. B., & Evans, C. R. (2019). Adolescent sexual initiation: A cross-classified multilevel analysis of peer group-, school-, and neighborhood-level influences. *Journal of Adolescent Health, 65,* 390–396.

Barkley, R. A. (1998). *Attention-deficit/hyperactivity disorder.* New York: Guilford Press.

Barkley, R. A. (2010). Against the status quo: Revising the diagnostic criteria for ADHD. *Journal of the American Academy of Child and Adolescent Psychiatry, 49,* 205–207.

Barkley, R. A. (2013). *Defiant children: A clinician's manual for assessment and parent training* (3rd ed.). New York: The Guilford Press.

Barkley, R. A. (2014). The important role of executive functioning and self-regulation. Retrieved from www.russellbarkley.org/factsheets/ADHD_EF_and_SR.pdf

Barkley, R. A. (2015a). Concentration deficit disorder (sluggish cognitive tempo). In R. A. Barkley (Ed.), *Attention-deficit hyperactivity disorder: A handbook for diagnosis and treatment* (4th ed.). New York: The Guilford Press.

Barkley, R. A. (2015b). Emotion dysregulation is a core component of ADHD. In R. A. Barkley (Ed.), *Attention-deficit hyperactivity disorder: A handbook for diagnosis and treatment.* New York: The Guilford Press.

Barkley, R. A. (2015c). Etiologies of ADHD. In *Attention-deficit hyperactivity disorder: A handbook for diagnosis and treatment* (4th ed.). New York: The Guilford Press.

Barkley, R. A. (2015d). Executive function and self-regulation viewed as an extended phenotype: Implications of the theory for ADHD and its treatment. In R. A. Barkley (Ed.), *Attention-deficit hyperactivity disorder: A handbook for diagnosis and treatment* (4th ed.). New York: The Guilford Press.

Barkley, R. A. (2015e). Health problems and related impairments in children and adults with ADHD. In R. A. Barkley (Ed.), *Attention-deficit hyperactivity disorder: A handbook for diagnosis and treatment* (4th ed.). New York: The Guilford Press.

Barkley, R. A. (2015f). History of ADHD. In R. A. Barkley (Ed.), *Attention-deficit hyperactivity disorder: A handbook for diagnosis and treatment* (4th ed.). New York: The Guilford Press.

Barkley, R. A. (2015g). Psychological assessment of children with ADHD. In R. A. Barkley (Ed.), *Attention-deficit hyperactivity disorder: A handbook for diagnosis and treatment* (4th ed.). New York: The Guilford Press.

Barkley, R. A. (2018a). Adverse events associated with behavior management training for families experiencing parent–ADHD teen conflict. *The ADHD Report, 26,* 1–5.

Barkley, R. A. (2018b). *Barkley Sluggish Cognitive Tempo Scale-Children and Adolescents (BSCTS-CA)*. New York: The Guilford Press.

Barkley, R. A., & Edwards, G. (2006). Diagnostic interview, behavior rating scales, and the medical examination. In R. A. Barkley (Ed.), *Behavioral and emotional disorders in adolescents: Nature, assessment, and treatment*. New York: The Guilford Press.

Barkley, R. A., & Peters, H. (2012). The earliest reference to ADHD in the medical literature? Melchior Adam Weikard's description in 1775 of "attention deficit." *Journal of Attention Disorders, 16,* 623–630.

Barkley, R. A., Shelton, T. L., Crosswait, C., Moorehouse, M., Fletcher, K., Barrett, S., et al. (2002). Preschool children with disruptive behavior: Three-year outcome as a function of adaptive disability. *Development and Psychopathology, 14,* 45–67.

Barlow, D. H. (2002). *Anxiety and its disorders: The nature and treatment of anxiety and panic* (2nd ed.). New York: Guilford Press.

Barnes, S., Jordan, Z., & Broom, M. (2018). Health professionals' experiences of grief associated with the death of pediatric patients: A qualitative systematic review protocol. *JBI Database of Systematic Reviews and Implementation Reports, 16,* 2085–2091.

Baron-Cohen, S. (1989). The autistic child's theory of mind: A case of specific developmental delay. *Journal of Child Psychology and Psychiatry, 30,* 285–297.

Baron-Cohen, S., & Swettenham, J. (1997). Theory of mind in autism: Its relationship to executive functions and central coherence. In D. J. Cohen & F. R. Volkmar (Eds.), *Handbook of autism and pervasive developmental disorders*. New York: John Wiley.

Baron-Cohen, S., O'Riordan, M., Stone, V., Jones, R., & Plaisted, K. (1999). Recognition of faux pas by normally developing children and children with Asperger syndrome or high-functioning autism. *Journal of Autism and Developmental Disabilities, 29,* 407–418.

Barrett, P. M., Dadds, M. R., & Rapee, R. M. (1996). Family treatment of childhood anxiety: A controlled trial. *Journal of Consulting and Clinical Psychology, 64,* 333–342.

Barrett, P. M., Farrell, L. J., Ollendick, T. H., & Dadds, M. (2006). Long-term outcomes of an Australian universal prevention trial of anxiety and depression symptoms in children and youth: An evaluation of the Friends Program. *Journal of Clinical Child and Adolescent Psychology, 35,* 403–411.

Barrett, P., Fisak, B., & Cooper, M. (2015). The treatment of anxiety in young children: Results of an open trial of the Fun FRIENDS Program. *Behaviour Change, 32,* 231–242.

Barrios, B. A., & O'Dell, S. L. (1998). Fears and anxieties. In E. J. Mash & R. A. Barkley (Eds.), *Treatment of childhood disorders* (2nd ed.). New York: Guilford Press.

Barrios, C. S., Jay, S. Y., Smith, V. C., Alfano, C. A., & Dougherty, L. R. (2018). Stability and predictive validity of the Parent–Child Sleep Interactions Scale: A longitudinal study among preschoolers. *Journal of Clinical Child & Adolescent Psychology, 47,* 382–396.

Basu, S. N., Kollu, R., & Banerjee-Basu, S. (2020). *Nucleic acids research*. Retrieved from http://autism.mindspec.org/autdb/Welcome.do

Batalle, D., Edwards, A. D., & O'Muircheartaigh, J. (2018). Not just a small adult brain: Understanding later neurodevelopment through imaging the neonatal brain. *Journal of Child Psychology and Psychiatry, 59,* 350–371.

Batejan, K. L., Jarvi, S. M., & Swenson, L. P. (2015). Sexual orientation and non-suicidal self-injury: A meta-analytic review. *Archives of Suicide Research, 19,* 131–150.

Bates, A. T., & Kearney, J. A. (2015). Understanding death with limited experience in life: Dying children's and adolescents' understanding of their own terminal illness and death. *Current Opinion in Supportive and Palliative Care, 9,* 40–45.

Bauermeister, J. J., Barkley, R. A., Bauermeister, J. A., Martínez, J. V., & McBurnett, K. (2012). Validity of the sluggish cognitive tempo, inattention, and hyperactivity symptom dimensions: Neuropsychological and psychosocial correlates. *Journal of Abnormal Child Psychology, 40,* 683–697.

Bayley, N. (2005). *Bayley Scales of Infant and Toddler Development, Third Edition (Bayley-III)*. San Antonio, TX: Harcourt Assessment.

Bearden, C. E., Meyer, S. E., Loewy, R. L., Niendam, T. A., & Cannon, T. D. (2006). The neurodevelopmental model of schizophrenia: Updated. In D. Cicchetti & D. J. Cohen (Eds.), *Developmental psychopathology* (Vol. 3). Hoboken, NJ: John Wiley & Sons.

Beards, S., Gayer-Anderson, C., Borges, S., Dewey, M. E., Fisher, H. L., & Morgan, C. (2013). Life events and psychosis: A review and meta-analysis. *Schizophrenia Bulletin, 39,* 740–747.

Beardslee, W. R., Brent, D. A., Weersing, V. R., Clarke, G. N., Porta, G., Hollon, S. D., et al. (2013). Prevention of depression in at-risk adolescents: Longer-term effects. *JAMA Psychiatry, 70,* 1161–1170.

References

Beardslee, W. R., Keller, M. B., Seifer, R., Lavorie, P. W., Staley, J., Podorefsky, D., & Shera, D. (1996). Prediction of adolescent affective disorder: Effects of prior parental affective disorders and child psychopathology. *Journal of the American Academy of Child and Adolescent Psychiatry, 35,* 279–288.

Beardslee, W. R., Versage, E. M., & Gladstone, T. R. G. (1998). Children of affectively ill parents: A review of the past 10 years. *Journal of the American Academy of Child and Adolescent Psychiatry, 37,* 1134–1141.

Beauchaine, T. P., & Hinshaw, S. P. (2020). RDoC and psychopathology among youth: Misplaced assumptions and an agenda for future research, *Journal of Clinical Child & Adolescent Psychology, 49,* 322–340.

Beauchaine, T. P. (2001). Vagal tone, development, and Gray's motivational theory: Toward an integrated model of autonomic nervous system functioning in psychopathology. *Development and Psychopathology, 13,* 183–214.

Beauchaine, T. P., & Cicchetti, D. (2016). A new generation of comorbidity research in the era of neuroscience and Research Domain Criteria. *Development and Psychopathology, 28,* 891–894.

Beauchaine, T. P., & Cicchetti, D. (2019). Emotion dysregulation and emerging psychopathology: A transdiagnostic, transdisciplinary perspective. *Development and Psychopathology, 31,* 799–804.

Beauchaine, T. P., & Klein, D. N. (2017). Classifying psychopathology: The DSM, empirically based taxonomies, and the Research Domain Criteria. In T. P. Beauchaine & S. P. Hinshaw (Eds.), *Child and adolescent psychopathology* (3rd ed). Hoboken, NJ: John Wiley & Sons.

Beauchaine, T. P., & Neuhaus, E. (2008). Impulsivity and vulnerability to psychopathology. In T. P. Beauchaine & S. P Hinshaw (Eds.), *Child and adolescent psychopathology.* Hoboken, NJ: John Wiley & Sons.

Beauchaine, T. P., Gatzke-Kopp, L., & Gizer, A. R. (2017a). Genetic, environmental, and epigenetic influences on behavior. In T. P. Beauchaine & S. P. Hinshaw (Eds.), *Child and adolescent psychopathology* (3rd ed). Hoboken, NJ: John Wiley & Sons.

Beauchaine, T. P., Hong, J., & Marsh, P. (2008). Sex differences in autonomic correlates of conduct problems and aggression. *Journal of the American Academy of Child and Adolescent Psychiatry, 47,* 788–796.

Beauchaine, T. P., Katkin, E. S., Strassberg, Z., & Snarr, J. (2001). Disinhibitory psychopathology in male adolescents: Discriminating conduct disorder from attention-deficit/hyper-activity disorder through concurrent assessment of multiple autonomic states. *Journal of Abnormal Psychology, 110,* 610–624.

Beauchaine, T. P., Zisner, A. R., & Sauder, C. L. (2017b). Trait impulsivity and the externalizing spectrum. *Annual Review of Clinical Psychology, 13,* 343–368.

Beauchaine, T. P., Zisner, A., & Hayden, E. P. (2019). Neurobiological mechanisms of psychopathology and treatment action. In T. H. Ollendick, S. W. White, & B. A. White (Eds.), *The Oxford handbook of clinical child and adolescent psychology.* New York: Oxford University Press.

Bebko, G., Bertocci, M. A., Fournier, J. C., Hinze, A. K., Bonar, L., Almeida, J. R., et al. (2014). Parsing dimensional vs diagnostic category-related patterns of reward circuitry function in behaviorally and emotionally dysregulated youth in the longitudinal assessment of manic symptoms study. *JAMA Psychiatry, 71,* 71–80.

Beck, A. N., Cooper, C. E., McLanahan, S., & Brooks-Gunn, J. (2010). Partnership transitions and maternal parenting. *Journal of Marriage and Family, 72,* 219–233.

Beck, A. T. (1967). *Depression: Clinical, experimental, and theoretical aspects.* New York: Harper & Row.

Beck, A. T. (1976). *Cognitive theory and emotional disorders.* New York: International Universities Press.

Beck, H. P., Levinson, S., & Irons, G. (2009). Finding Little Albert: A journey to John B. Watson's infant laboratory. *American Psychologist, 64,* 605–614.

Becker, K. D., Stuewig, J., Herrera, V. M., & McCloskey, L. A. (2004). A study of firesetting and animal cruelty in children: Family influences and adolescent outcomes. *Journal of the American Academy of Child and Adolescent Psychiatry, 43,* 905–912.

Becker, S. P., & Barkley, R. A. (2018). Sluggish cognitive tempo. In T. Banaschewski, D. Coghill, & A. Zuddas (Eds.), *Oxford textbook of attention deficit hyperactivity disorder.* Oxford: Oxford University Press.

Becker, S. P., Burns, G. L., Leopold, D. R., Olson, R. K., & Willcutt, E. G. (2018). Differential impact of trait sluggish cognitive tempo and ADHD inattention in early childhood on adolescent functioning. *Journal of Child Psychology and Psychiatry, 59,* 1094–1104.

Becker, S. P., Langberg, J. M., Eadeh, H.-M., Isaacson, P. A., & Bourchtein, E. (2019a). Sleep and daytime sleepiness in adolescents with and without ADHD: Differences across ratings, daily diary, and actigraphy. *Journal of Child Psychology and Psychiatry, 60,* 1021–1031.

Becker, S. P., Leopold, D. R., Burns, G. L., Jarrett, M. A., Langberg, J. M., Marshall, S. A., et al. (2016). The internal, external, and diagnostic validity of sluggish cognitive tempo: A meta-analysis and critical review. *Journal of the American Academy of Child & Adolescent Psychiatry, 55,* 163–178.

Becker, S. P., Webb, K. L., & Dvorsky, M. R. (2019b). Initial examination of the bidirectional associations between sluggish cognitive tempo and internalizing symptoms in children. *Journal of Clinical Child & Adolescent Psychology,* 1–9.

Beidel, D. C., Silverman, W. K., & Hammond-Laurence, K. (1996). Overanxious disorder: Subsyndromal state or specific disorder?

A comparison of clinic and community samples. *Journal of Clinical Child Psychology, 25,* 25–32.

Beidel, D. C., Turner, S. M., & Morris, T. L. (1999). Psychopathology of childhood social phobia. *Journal of the American Academy of Child and Adolescent Psychiatry, 38,* 630–646.

Beitchman, J. H., Wilson, B., Brownlie, E. B., Walters, H., Inglis, A., & Lancee, W. (1996). Long-term consistency in speech/language profiles: II. Behavioral, emotional, and social outcomes. *Journal of the American Academy of Child and Adolescent Psychiatry, 35,* 815–825.

Beitchman, J. H., Wilson, B., Johnson, C. J., Atkinson, L., Young, A., Adlaf, E., et al. (2001). Fourteen-year follow-up of speech/language-impaired and control children: Psychiatric outcome. *Journal of the American Academy of Child and Adolescent Psychiatry, 40,* 75–82.

Bélanger, M.-È., Bernier, A., Simard, V., Desrosiers, K., & Carrier, J. (2018). Sleeping toward behavioral regulation: Relations between sleep and externalizing symptoms in toddlers and preschoolers. *Journal of Clinical Child & Adolescent Psychology, 47,* 366–373.

Belbasis, L., Köhler, C. A., Stefanis, N., Stubbs, B., van Os, J., Vieta, E., et al. (2018). Risk factors and peripheral biomarkers for schizophrenia spectrum disorders: An umbrella review of meta-analyses. *Acta Psychiatrica Scandinavica, 137,* 88–97.

Belitz, J. (2018). Ethics in assessing and treating children and adolescents. In J. N. Butcher & P. C. Kendall (Eds.), *APA handbook of psychopathology: Child and adolescent psychopathology* (Vol. 2). Washington, DC: American Psychological Association.

Bell, R. (1985). *Holy anorexia.* Chicago, IL: University of Chicago Press.

Bellak, L., & Abrams, D. M. (1997). *The T.A.T., C.A.T., and S.A.T. in clinical use* (6th ed.). Needham Heights, MA: Allyn and Bacon.

Bellak, L., & Bellak, S. (1982). *Children's Apperception Test (CAT).* Lutz, FL: Psychological Assessment Resources, Inc.

Bellini, S., & Akullian, J. (2007). A meta-analysis of video modeling and video self-modeling interventions for children and adolescents with autism spectrum disorders. *Exceptional Children, 73,* 264–287.

Belsky, J. (1980). Child maltreatment: An ecological integration. *American Psychologist, 15,* 320–335.

Belsky, J., & Pluess, M. (2009). The nature (and nurture?) of plasticity in early human development. *Perspectives on Psychological Science, 4,* 345–351.

Belsky, J., & Pluess, M. (2016). Differential susceptibility to environmental influences. In D. Cicchetti (Ed.), *Developmental psychopathology: Risk, resilience, and intervention* (Vol. 2). Hoboken, NJ: John Wiley & Sons.

Belsky, J., & van IJzendoorn, M. H. (2017). Genetic differential susceptibility to the effects of parenting. *Current Opinion in Psychology, 15,* 125–130.

Belsky, J., Bakermans-Kranenburg, M. J., & van IJzendoorn, M. H. (2007). For better and for worse: Differential susceptibility to environmental influences. *Current Directions in Psychological Science, 16,* 300–304.

Beltramini, A., Milojevic, K., & Pateron, D. (2017). Pain assessment in newborns, infants, and children. *Pediatric Annals, 46,* e387–e395.

Benas, J. S., McCarthy, A. E., Haimm, C. A., Huang, M., Gallop, R., & Young, J. F. (2019). The Depression Prevention Initiative: Impact on adolescent internalizing and externalizing symptoms in a randomized trial. *Journal of Clinical Child & Adolescent Psychology, 48*(sup1), S57–S71.

Bendezú, J. J., Pinderhughes, E. E., Hurley, S. M., McMahon, R. J., & Racz, S. J. (2018). Longitudinal relations among parental monitoring strategies, knowledge, and adolescent delinquency in a racially diverse at-risk sample. *Journal of Clinical Child & Adolescent Psychology, 47*(sup1), S21–S34.

Benjamin, C. L., Beidas, R. S., Comer, J. S., Puliafico, A. C., & Kendall, P. C. (2011). Generalized anxiety disorder in youth: Diagnostic considerations. *Depression and Anxiety, 28,* 173–182.

Benjamin, C. L., Harrison, J. P., Settipani, C. A., Brodman, D. M., & Kendall, P. C. (2013). Anxiety and related outcomes in young adults 7 to 19 years after receiving treatment for child anxiety. *Journal of Consulting and Clinical Psychology, 81,* 865–876.

Benki-Nugent, S., & Boivin, M. J. (2019). Neurocognitive complications of pediatric HIV infections. In M. A. Geyer, B. A. Ellenbroek, C. A. Marsden, T. R. E. Barnes, & S. L. Andersen (Eds.), *Current topics in behavioral neurosciences.* Berlin, Heidelberg: Springer.

Benner, A. D., Wang, Y., Shen, Y., Boyle, A. E., Polk, R., & Cheng, Y.-P. (2018). Racial/ethnic discrimination and well-being during adolescence: A meta-analytic review. *The American Psychologist, 73,* 855–883.

Bennett, M., Webster, A. A., Goodall, E., & Rowland, S. (2018). *Exploring the identity of autistic individuals: Reconstructing the autism epidemic myth.* Singapore: Springer.

Bennett, S., Shafran, R., Coughtrey, A., Walker, S., & Heyman, I. (2015). Psychological interventions for mental health disorders in children with chronic physical illness: A systematic review. *Archives of Disease in Childhood, 100,* 308–316.

Benoit, D. (2009). Feeding disorders, failure to thrive, and obesity. In C. H. Zeanah, Jr. (Ed.), *Handbook of infant mental health* (3rd ed.). New York: The Guilford Press.

Berg, C. A., King, P. S., Butler, J. M., Pham, P., Palmer, D., & Wiebe, D. J. (2011). Parental involvement and adolescents' diabetes management: The mediating role of self-efficacy and externalizing and internalizing behavior. *Journal of Pediatric Psychology, 36,* 329–339.

References

Bergman, P., Chetty, R., DeLuca, S., Hendren, N., Katz, L. F., & Palmer, C. (2019). *Creating moves to opportunity: Experimental evidence on barriers to neighborhood choice* (Working paper no. w26164). National Bureau of Economic Research.

Berlin, L. J., Appleyard, K., & Dodge, K. A. (2011). Intergenerational continuity in child maltreatment: Mediating mechanisms and implications for prevention. *Child Development, 82,* 162–176.

Berman, R. A., Gotts, S. J., McAdams, H. M., Greenstein, D., Lalonde, F., Clasen, L., et al. (2015). Disrupted sensorimotor and social–cognitive networks underlie symptoms in childhood-onset schizophrenia. *Brain, 139,* 276–291.

Bernier, R., Golzio, C., Xiong, B., Stessman, Holly A., Coe, Bradley P., Penn, O., et al. (2014). Disruptive CHD8 mutations define a subtype of autism early in development. *Cell, 158,* 263–276.

Berninger, V. W., & Amtmann, D. (2003). Preventing written expression disabilities through early and continuing assessment and intervention for handwriting and/or spelling problems: Research into practice. In H. L. Swanson, K. R. Harris, & S. Graham (Eds.), *Handbook of learning disabilities.* New York: Guilford Press.

Berninger, V. W., & Chanquoy, L. (2012). What writing is and how it changes across early and middle childhood development. In E. L. Grigorenko, E. Mambrino, & D. D. Preiss (Eds.), *Writing: A mosaic of new perspectives.* New York: Psychology Press.

Bernstein, D. M. (1996). The discovery of the child: A historical perspective on child and adolescent psychiatry. In M. Lewis (Ed.), *Child and adolescent psychiatry: A comprehensive textbook.* Baltimore, MD: Williams & Wilkins.

Bernstein, G. A., Bernat, D. H., Davis, A. A., & Layne, A. E. (2008). Symptom presentation and classroom functioning in a nonclinical sample of children with social phobia. *Depression and Anxiety, 25,* 752–760.

Bernstein, G. A., Hektner, J. M., Borchardt, C. M., & McMillan, M. H. (2001). Treatment of school refusal: One-year followup. *Journal of the American Academy of Child and Adolescent Psychiatry, 40,* 206–213.

Bernstein, G. A., Mueller, B. A., Schreiner, M. W., Campbell, S. M., Regan, E. K., Nelson, P. M., et al. (2016). Abnormal striatal resting-state functional connectivity in adolescents with obsessive–compulsive disorder. *Psychiatry Research: Neuroimaging, 247,* 49–56.

Berry, K., Russell, K., & Frost, K. (2018). Restricted and repetitive behaviors in autism spectrum disorder: A review of associated features and presentation across clinical populations. *Current Developmental Disorders Reports, 5,* 108–115.

Bertelli, M. O., Salvador-Carulla, L., & Harris, J. (2016). Classification and diagnosis. In C. Hemmings & N. Bouras (Eds.), *Psychiatric and behavioral disorders in intellectual and developmental disabilities.* Cambridge: Cambridge University Press.

Bertollo, J. R., & Yerys, B. E. (2019). More than IQ: Executive function explains adaptive behavior above and beyond nonverbal IQ in youth with autism and lower IQ. *American Journal on Intellectual and Developmental Disabilities, 124,* 191–205.

Berzenski, S. R., & Yates, T. M. (2013). Preschoolers' emotion knowledge and the differential effects of harsh punishment. *Journal of Family Psychology, 27,* 463–472.

Bettelheim, B. (1967a). *The empty fortress.* New York: Free Press.

Bettelheim, B. (1967b, February 12). Where self begins. *New York Times.*

Bettini, E., & Steinhorn, D. M. (2018). Pediatric chronic pain. In R. J. Moore (Ed.), *Handbook of pain and palliative care: Biopsychosocial and environmental approaches for the life course* (2nd ed.). Cham, Switzerland: Springer.

Beverly, E. A., Worley, M., Prokopakis, K., & Ivanov, N. (2016). Patient-physician communication and diabetes self-care. *Journal of Clinical Outcomes Management, 23,* 509–518.

Beyer, J. E., & Knott, C. (1998). Construct validity estimation for the African-American and Hispanic Oucher Scale. *Journal of Pediatric Nursing, 13,* 20–31.

Bhagat, D., Fagnano, M., Halterman, J. S., & Reznik, M. (2019). Asthma symptoms, interactive physical play and behavioral and academic outcomes in urban children with persistent asthma. *Journal of Asthma, 56,* 711–718.

Biederman, J., Faraone, S. V., Marrs, A., Moore, P., Garcia, J., Ablon, S., et al. (1997). Panic disorder and agoraphobia in consecutively referred children and adolescents. *Journal of the American Academy of Child and Adolescent Psychiatry, 36,* 214–223.

Biederman, J., Fitzgerald, M., Spencer, T. J., Bhide, P. G., McCarthy, D. M., Woodworth, K. Y., et al. (2017). Is paternal smoking at conception a risk for ADHD? A controlled study in youth with and without ADHD. *Journal of Attention Disorders,* 1087054717690809.

Biederman, J., Petty, C. R., Clarke, A., Lomedico, A., & Faraone, S. V. (2011). Predictors of persistent ADHD: An 11-year follow-up study. *Journal of Psychiatric Research, 45,* 150–155.

Biederman, J., Petty, C. R., Day, H., Goldin, R. L., Spencer, T., Faraone, S. V., et al. (2012). Severity of the aggression/anxiety-depression/attention (AAA) CBCL profile discriminates between different levels of deficits in emotional regulation in youth with ADHD. *Journal of Developmental and Behavioral Pediatrics, 33,* 236.

Biederman, J., Petty, C. R., Monuteaux, M. C., Fried, R., Byrne, D., Mirto, T., et al. (2010). Adult psychiatric outcomes of girls with attention deficit hyperactivity disorder: 11-year follow-up in a longitudinal case-control study. *American Journal of Psychiatry, 167,* 409–417.

Biederman, J., Rosenbaum, J. F., Bolduc-Murphy, E. A., Faraone, S. V., Chaloff, J., Hirshfeld, D. R., & Kagan, J. (1993). A 3-year follow-up of children with and without behavioral inhibition. *Journal of the American Academy of Child and Adolescent Psychiatry, 32,* 814–821.

Bierman, K. L., & Schwartz, L. A. (1986). Clinical child interviews: Approaches and developmental considerations. *Journal of Child and Adolescent Psychotherapy, 3,* 267–278.

Bifulco, A., Harris, T., & Brown, G. (1992). Mourning or early inadequate care? Reexamining the relationship of maternal loss in childhood with adult depression and anxiety. *Development and Psychopathology, 4,* 433–449.

Bijou, S. W., Peterson, R. F., Harris, F. R., Allen, K. E., & Johnston, M. S. (1969). Methodology for experimental studies of young children in natural settings. *The Psychological Record, 19,* 177–210.

Billeci, L., Calderoni, S., Conti, E., Gesi, C., Carmassi, C., Dell'Osso, L., et al. (2016). The broad autism (endo)phenotype: Neurostructural and neurofunctional correlates in parents of individuals with autism spectrum disorders. *Frontiers in Neuroscience, 10.*

Binggeli, N. J., Hart, S. N., & Brassard, M. R. (2001). *Psychological maltreatment of children.* Thousand Oaks, CA: Sage Publications.

Biondic, D., Wiener, J., & Martinussen, R. (2019). Parental psychopathology and parenting stress in parents of adolescents with attention-deficit hyperactivity disorder. *Journal of Child and Family Studies, 28,* 2107–2119.

Birmaher, B., & Axelson, D. (2005). Bipolar disorder in children and adolescents. In A. Marneros & F. Goodwin (Eds.), *Bipolar disorders: Mixed states, rapid cycling, and atypical forms.* Cambridge, UK: Cambridge University Press.

Birmaher, B., Brent, D., Chiapetta, L., Bridge, J., Monga, S., & Bauger, M. (1999). Psychometric properties for the Screen for Child Anxiety Related Emotional Disorders (SCARED): A replication study. *Journal of the American Academy of Child and Adolescent Psychiatry, 38,* 1230–1236.

Birmaher, B., Gill, M. K., Axelson, D. A., Goldstein, B. I., Goldstein, T. R., Yu, H., et al. (2014). Longitudinal trajectories and associated baseline predictors in youths with bipolar spectrum disorders. *American Journal of Psychiatry, 171,* 990–999.

Birmaher, B., Khetarpal, S., Brent, D., Cully, M., Balach, L., Kaufman, J., & McKenzie Neer, S. (1997). The Screen for Child Anxiety Related Emotional Disorders (SCARED): Scale construction and psychometric characteristics. *Journal of the American Academy of Child and Adolescent Psychiatry, 36,* 545–553.

Birmaher, B., Ryan, N. D., Williamson, D. E., Brent, D. A., Kaufman, J., Dahl, R. E., et al. (1996). Childhood and adolescent depression: A review of the past 10 years. Part I. *Journal of the American Academy of Child and Adolescent Psychiatry, 35,* 1427–1439.

Birmingham, C. L., Su, J., Hlynsky, J. A., Goldner, E. M., & Gao, M. (2005). The mortality rate from anorexia nervosa. *International Journal of Eating Disorders, 38,* 143–146.

Birnbaum, R., & Weinberger, D. R. (2017). Genetic insights into the neurodevelopmental origins of schizophrenia. *Nature Reviews Neuroscience, 18,* 727–740.

Birnie, K. A., Chambers, C. T., & Spellman, C. M. (2017). Mechanisms of distraction in acute pain perception and modulation. *Pain, 158,* 1012–1013.

Birnie, K. A., Noel, M., Chambers, C. T., Uman, L. S., & Parker, J. A. (2018). Psychological interventions for needle-related procedural pain and distress in children and adolescents. *Cochrane Database of Systematic Reviews, 10.* Retrieved from www.cochranelibrary.com/cdsr/doi/10.1002/14651858. CD005179.pub4/full

Birnie, K. A., Noel, M., Parker, J. A., Chambers, C. T., Uman, L. S., Kisely, S. R., & McGrath, P. J. (2014). Systematic review and meta-analysis of distraction and hypnosis for needle-related pain and distress in children and adolescents. *Journal of Pediatric Psychology, 39,* 783–808.

Bishop, C., Mulraney, M., Rinehart, N., & Sciberras, E. (2019). An examination of the association between anxiety and social functioning in youth with ADHD: A systematic review. *Psychiatry Research, 273,* 402–421.

Bishop, D. V. M. (2002). Speech and language difficulties. In M. Rutter & E. Taylor (Eds.), *Child and adolescent psychiatry.* Oxford: Blackwell Publishing.

Bishop, D. V. M. (2015). The interface between genetics and psychology: Lessons from developmental dyslexia. *Proceedings of the Royal Society B: Biological Sciences, 282,* 20143139.

Bishop, D. V. M. (2017). Why is it so hard to reach agreement on terminology? The case of developmental language disorder (DLD). *International Journal of Language & Communication Disorders, 52,* 671–680.

Bishop, D. V. M., Snowling, M. J., Thompson, P. A., Greenhalgh, T., & CATALISE Consortium. (2016). CATALISE: A multinational and multidisciplinary Delphi consensus study: Identifying language impairments in children. *PLoS One, 11,* e0158753.

Björkqvist, K. (2018). Gender differences in aggression. *Current Opinion in Psychology, 19,* 39–42.

Blacher, J., & McIntyre, L. L. (2006). Syndrome specificity and behavioural disorders in young adults with intellectual disability: Cultural differences in family impact. *Journal of Intellectual Disabilities Research, 50,* 184–198.

Black, B., & Uhde, T. W. (1995). Psychiatric characteristics of children with selective mutism: A pilot study. *Journal of the American Academy of Child and Adolescent Psychiatry, 34,* 847–856.

Black, S. R., & Fristad, M. A. (2019). Bipolar and related disorders. In T. H. Ollendick, S. W. White, & B. A. White (Eds.), *The*

Oxford handbook of clinical child and adolescent psychology. New York: Oxford University Press.

Blackwell, L. S., & Quittner, A. L. (2015). Daily pain in adolescents with CF: Effects on adherence, psychological symptoms, and health-related quality of life. *Pediatric Pulmonology, 50,* 244–251.

Blader, J. C., & Carlson, G. A. (2007). Increased rates of bipolar disorder diagnoses among U.S. child, adolescent, and adult inpatients, 1996–2004. *Biological Psychiatry, 62,* 107–114.

Blader, J. C., Koplewicz, H. C., Abikoff, H., & Foley, C. (1997). Sleep problems of elementary school children: A community survey. *Archives of Pediatrics and Adolescent Medicine, 151,* 473–480.

Blader, J. C., Roybal, D. J., Sauder, C. L., & Carlson, G. A. (2017). Bipolar disorder. In T. P. Beauchaine & S. P. Hinshaw (Eds.), *Child and adolescent psychopathology* (3rd ed.). Hoboken, NJ: John Wiley & Sons Inc.

Blagg, N., & Yule, W. (1994). School refusal. In T. H. Ollendick, N. J. King, & W. Yule (Eds.), *International handbook of phobic and anxiety disorders in children and adolescents*. New York: Plenum Press.

Blakemore, J. E. O., Berenbaum, S. A., & Liben, L. S. (2013). *Gender development*. New York: Psychology Press.

Blijd-Hoogewys, E. M. A., van Geert, P. L. C., Serra, M., & Minderaa, R. B. (2008). Measuring theory of mind in children: Psychometric properties for the ToM Storybooks. *Journal of Autism and Developmental Disorders, 38,* 1907–1930.

Blount, R. L. (2019). Commentary: Acute pediatric procedural pain, distress, and coping. *Journal of Pediatric Psychology, 44,* 798–802.

Boersma-van Dam, E., Hale, B., Koot, H., Meeus, W., & Branje, S. (2019). Adolescents' and best friend's depressive symptoms and conflict management: Intraindividual and interpersonal processes over time. *Journal of Clinical Child & Adolescent Psychology, 48,* 203–217.

Bogdashina, O. (2016). *Sensory perceptual issues in autism and Asperger syndrome: Different sensory experiences – different perceptual worlds*. London: Jessica Kingsley Publishers.

Bogels, S. M., & Brechman-Toussaint, M. L. (2006). Family issues in child anxiety: Attachment, family functioning, parental rearing and beliefs. *Clinical Psychology Review, 26,* 834–856.

Boks, M., Houtepen, L., Xu, Z., He, Y., Ursini, G., Maihofer, A., et al. (2018). Genetic vulnerability to DUSP22 promoter hypermethylation is involved in the relation between in utero famine exposure and schizophrenia. *NPJ Schizophrenia, 4,* 16.

Bolger, K. E., & Patterson, C. J. (2001). Developmental pathways from child maltreatment to peer rejection. *Child Development, 72,* 549–568.

Bolhuis, K., Tiemeier, H., Jansen, P. R., Muetzel, R. L., Neumann, A., Hillegers, M. H. J., et al. (2019). Interaction of schizophrenia polygenic risk and cortisol level on pre-adolescent brain structure. *Psychoneuroendocrinology, 101,* 295–303.

Bolton, D., Eley, T. C., O'Connor, T. G., Perrin, S., Rabe-Hesketh, S., Fijsdilk, F., & Smith, P. (2006). Prevalence and genetic and environmental influences on anxiety disorders in 6-year-old twins. *Psychological Medicine, 36,* 335–344.

Bombin, I., Mayoral, M., Castro-Fornieles, J., Gonzalez-Pinto, A., de la Serna, E., Rapado-Castro, M., et al. (2013). Neuropsychological evidence for abnormal neurodevelopment associated with early-onset psychoses. *Psychological Medicine, 43,* 757–768.

Bonanno, G. A., Brewin, C. R., Kaniasty, K., & La Greca, A. M. (2010). Weighing the costs of disaster: Consequences, risks, and resilience in individuals, families, and communities. *Psychological Science in the Public Interest, 11,* 1–49.

Bongers, I. L., Koot, H. M., Van der Ende, J., & Verhulst, F. C. (2003). The normative development of child and adolescent problem behavior. *Journal of Abnormal Psychology, 112,* 179–192.

Boomsma, D. I., van Beijsterveldt, C. E. M., & Hudziak, J. J. (2005). Genetic and environmental influences on anxious/ depression during childhood: A study from the Netherlands twin register. *Genes, Brain, and Behavior, 48,* 466–481.

Booster, G. D., Oland, A. A., & Bender, B. G. (2016). Psychosocial factors in severe pediatric asthma. *Immunology and Allergy Clinics, 36,* 449–460.

Booth, R. D. L., & Happé, F. G. E. (2018). Evidence of reduced global processing in autism spectrum disorder. *Journal of Autism & Developmental Disorders, 48,* 1397–1408.

Booth-LaForce, C., & Groh, A. M. (2018). *Parent–child attachment and peer relations*. In W. M. Bukowski, B. Laursen, & K. H. Rubin (Eds.), *Handbook of peer interactions, relationships, and groups*. New York: The Guilford Press.

Boris, N. W., Renk, K., Lowell, A., & Kolomeyer, E. (2019). Parental substance abuse. In C. H. Zeanah (Ed.), *Handbook of infant mental health* (4th ed.). New York: The Guilford Press.

Bornstein, M. H. (2016). Determinants of parenting. In D. Cicchetti (Ed.), *Developmental psychopathology: Risk, resilience, and intervention* (Vol. 4). Hoboken, NJ: John Wiley & Sons.

Bosquet, M., & Egeland, B. (2006). The development and maintenance of anxiety symptoms from infancy through adolescence in a longitudinal sample. *Development and Psychopathology, 18,* 517–550.

Bougea, A., Spantideas, N., & Chrousos, G. P. (2017). Stress management for headaches in children and adolescents: A review and practical recommendations for health promotion programs and well-being. *Journal of Child Health Care, 22,* 19–33.

Bould, H., Araya, R., Pearson, R. M., Stapinski, L., Carnegie, R., & Joinson, C. (2014). Association between early temperament and depression at 18 years. *Depression and Anxiety, 31,* 729–736.

Bowlby, J. (1960). Grief and mourning in infancy and early childhood. *Psychoanalytic Study of the Child, 15,* 9–52.

Bowlby, J. (1969). *Attachment and loss* (Vol. 1). New York: Basic Books.

Bowring, D. L., Totsika, V., Hastings, R. P., Toogood, S., & McMahon, M. (2017). Prevalence of psychotropic medication use and association with challenging behaviour in adults with an intellectual disability. A total population study. *Journal of Intellectual Disability Research, 61,* 604–617.

Boyce, W. T. (2016). Differential susceptibility of the developing brain to contextual adversity and stress. *Neuropsychopharmacology, 41,* 142–162.

Boyd, B. A., Hume, K., McBee, M. T., Alessandri, M., Gutierrez, A., Johnson, L., et al. (2014). Comparative efficacy of LEAP, TEACCH and non-model-specific special education programs for preschoolers with autism spectrum disorders. *Journal of Autism and Developmental Disorders, 44,* 366–380.

Brackett, J., & Baxter, P. (2015). When the death of a child is anticipated and imminent. In D. L. Palazzi, M. I. Lorin, T. L. Turner, M. A. Ward, & A. G. Cabrera (Eds.), *Communicating with pediatric patients and their families: The Texas Children's Hospital guide for physicians, nurses and other healthcare professionals.* Baylor College of Medicine.

Bradley, R. B., & Corwyn, R. F. (2008). Infant temperament, parenting, and externalizing behavior in first grade: A test of the differential susceptibility hypothesis. *Journal of Child Psychology and Psychiatry, 49,* 124–131.

Bradley, R., Danielson, L., & Hallahan, D. P. (2002). *Identification of learning disabilities: Research to practice.* New York: Routledge.

Braff, D. L., & Tamminga, C. A. (2016). Endophenotypes, epigenetics, polygenicity and more: Irv Gottesman's dynamic legacy. *Schizophrenia Bulletin, 43,* 10–16.

Brassard, M. R., Hart, S. N., & Hardy, D. B. (2000). Psychological and emotional abuse of children. In R. T. Ammerman & M. Hersen (Eds.), *Case studies in family violence* (2nd ed.). New York: Kluwer Academic/Plenum Publishers.

Bratt, A. M., Masanyero-Bennie, B., & Kelley, S. P. (2017). A meta-analytical assessment of the efficacy of immediate release methylphenidate to reduce hyperactivity in children with autistic spectrum disorder (ASD). *Journal of Pharmaceutical Sciences & Experimental Pharmacology, 1,* 10–18.

Braver, S. L., Ellman, I. M., & Fabricius, W. V. (2003). Relocation of children after divorce and children's best interests: New evidence and legal considerations. *Journal of Family Psychology, 17,* 206–219.

Bray, L., Appleton, V., & Sharpe, A. (2019). The information needs of children having clinical procedures in hospital: Will it hurt? Will I feel scared? What can I do to stay calm? *Child: Care, Health and Development, 45,* 737–743.

Bray, M. A., Kehle, T. J., Root, M. M., Sassu, K. A., Theodore, L. A., & Bracken, B. A. (2017). Evidence-based interventions for asthma in children and adolescents. In L. A. Theodore (Ed.), *Handbook of evidence-based interventions for children and adolescents.* New York: Springer Publishing Company.

Breaux, R. P., & Harvey, E. A. (2019). A longitudinal study of the relation between family functioning and preschool ADHD symptoms. *Journal of Clinical Child & Adolescent Psychology, 48,* 749–764.

Bregman, J. D., & Gerdtz, J. (1997). Behavioral interventions. In D. J. Cohen & F. R. Volkmar (Eds.), *Handbook of autism and pervasive developmental disorders.* New York: John Wiley.

Breithaupt, L., Köhler-Forsberg, O., Larsen, J. T., Benros, M. E., Thornton, L. M., Bulik, C. M., & Petersen, L. (2019). Association of exposure to infections in childhood with risk of eating disorders in adolescent girls. *JAMA Psychiatry, 76,* 800–809.

Brendgen, M., Vitaro, F., Tremblay, R. E., & Lavoie, F. (2001). Reactive and proactive aggression: Predictions to physical violence in different contexts and moderating effects of parental monitoring and caregiving behavior. *Journal of Abnormal Child Psychology, 29,* 293–304.

Brennan, P. A., & Walker, E. F. (2010). Vulnerability to schizophrenia in childhood and adolescence. In R. E. Ingram & J. M. Price (Eds.), *Vulnerability to psychopathology across the lifespan.* New York: Guilford Press.

Brennan, P. A., Le Brocque, R., & Hammen, C. (2003). Maternal depression, parent-child relationships, and resilient outcomes in adolescence. *Journal of the American Academy of Child and Adolescent Psychiatry, 42,* 1469–1477.

Brent, D. A. (2006). Commentary: Glad for what TADS adds, but many TADS grads still sad. *Journal of the American Academy of Child and Adolescent Psychiatry, 45,* 1461–1464.

Bresnahan, M., Hornig, M., Schultz, A. F., Gunnes, N., Hirtz, D., Lie, K. K., et al. (2015). Association of maternal report of infant and toddler gastrointestinal symptoms with autism: Evidence from a prospective birth cohort. *JAMA Psychiatry, 72,* 466–474.

Bress, J. N., Meyer, A., & Hajcak, G. (2015). Differentiating anxiety and depression in children and adolescents: Evidence from event-related brain potentials. *Journal of Clinical Child and Adolescent Psychology, 44,* 238–249.

Brewerton, T. D., Rance, S. J., Dansky, B. S., O'Neil, P. M., & Kilpatrick, D. G. (2014). A comparison of women with child-adolescent versus adult onset binge eating: Results from the National Women's Study. *International Journal of Eating Disorders, 47,* 836–843.

Briars, L., & Todd, T. (2016). A review of pharmacological management of attention-deficit/hyperactivity disorder.

References

The Journal of Pediatric Pharmacology and Therapeutics, 21, 192–206.

Bridge, J. A., Goldstein, T. R., & Brent, D. A. (2006). Adolescent suicide and suicidal behavior. *Journal of Child Psychology and Psychiatry, 47,* 372–394.

Bridge, J. A., Greenhouse, J. B., Ruch, D., Stevens, J., Ackerman, J., Sheftall, A. H., et al. (2020). Association between the release of Netflix's 13 Reasons Why and suicide rates in the United States: An interrupted times series analysis. *Journal of the American Academy of Child & Adolescent Psychiatry, 59,* 236–243.

Bridge, J. A., Iyengar, S., Salary, C. B., Barbe, R. P., Birmaher, B., Pincus, H. A., et al. (2007). Clinical response and risk for reported suicidal ideation and suicide attempts in pediatric antidepressant treatment: A meta-analysis of randomized controlled trials. *JAMA, 297,* 1683–1696.

Briggs, K., Hubbs-Tait, L., Culp, R. E., & Morse, A. S. (1994). Sexual abuse label: Adults' expectations for children. *The American Journal of Family Therapy, 22,* 304–314.

Briggs-Gowan, M. J., Horwitz, S. M., Schwab-Stone, M. E., Leventhal, J. M., & Leaf, P. J. (2000). Mental health in pediatric settings: Distribution of disorders and factors related to service use. *Journal of the American Academy of Child & Adolescent Psychiatry, 39,* 841–849.

Briley, D. A., & Tucker-Drob, E. M. (2013). Explaining the increasing heritability of cognitive ability across development: A meta-analysis of longitudinal twin and adoption studies. *Psychological Science, 24,* 1704–1713.

Brinkmeyer, M. Y., & Eyberg, S. M. (2003). Parent-child interaction therapy for oppositional children. In A. E. Kazdin & J. R. Weisz (Eds.), *Evidence-based psychotherapies for children and adolescents.* New York: Guilford Press.

Brockie, T. N., Dana-Sacco, G., Wallen, G. R., Wilcox, H. C., & Campbell, J. C. (2015). The relationship of adverse childhood experiences to PTSD, depression, poly-drug use and suicide attempt in reservation-based Native American adolescents and young adults. *American Journal of Community Psychology, 55,* 411–421.

Brodeur, D. A., & Pond, M. (2001). The development of selective attention in children with attention deficit hyperactivity disorder. *Journal of Abnormal Child Psychology, 29,* 229–239.

Brody, G. H., Chen, Y. F., Murry, V. M., Ge, X., Simons, R. L., Gibbons, F. X., et al. (2006). Perceived discrimination and the adjustment of African American youths: A five-year longitudinal analysis with contextual moderation effects. *Child Development, 77,* 1170–1189.

Brody, G. H., Ge, X., Conger, R., Gibbons, F. X., Murry, V. M., Gerrard, M., & Simons, R. L. (2001). The influence of neighborhood disadvantage, collective socialization, and parenting on African-American children's affiliation with deviant peers. *Child Development, 72,* 1231–1246.

Broft, A., Berner, L. A., & Walsh, T. (2010). Pharmacotherapy for bulimia nervosa. In C. M. Grilo & J. E. Mitchell (Eds.), *The treatment of eating disorders: A clinical handbook.* New York: The Guilford Press.

Bronfenbrenner, U. (1977). Toward an experimental ecology of human development. *American Psychologist, 32,* 320–335.

Brook, D. W., Brook, J. S., Zhang, C., & Koppel, J. (2010). Association between attention-deficit/hyperactivity disorder in adolescence and substance use disorders in adulthood. *Archives of Pediatrics and Adolescent Medicine, 164,* 930–934.

Brotman, M. A., Schmajuk, M., Rich, B. A., Dickstein, D. P., Guyer, A. E., Costello, E. J., et al. (2006). Prevalence, clinical correlates, and longitudinal course of severe mood dysregulation in children. *Biological Psychiatry, 60,* 991–997.

Brouillard, C., Brendgen, M., Vitaro, F., Dionne, G., & Boivin, M. (2018). Links between the mother–adolescent and father–adolescent relationships and adolescent depression: A genetically informed study. *Journal of Clinical Child & Adolescent Psychology, 47*(sup1), S397–S408.

Brown, A. S. (2012). Epidemiologic studies of exposure to prenatal infection and risk of schizophrenia and autism. *Developmental Neurobiology, 72,* 1272–1276.

Brown, A. S., & Derkits, E. J. (2010). Prenatal infection and schizophrenia: A review of epidemiologic and translational studies. *American Journal of Psychiatry, 167,* 261–280.

Brown, A. S., Bresnahan, M., & Susser, E. S. (2005). Schizophrenia: Environmental epidemiology. In B. J. Sadock & V. A. Sadock (Eds.), *Kaplan & Sadock's comprehensive textbook of psychiatry* (Vol. I). Philadelphia, PA: Lippincott Williams & Wilkins.

Brown, C. S., & Chu, H. (2012). Discrimination, ethnic identity, and academic outcomes of Mexican immigrant children: The importance of school context. *Child Development, 83,* 1477–1485.

Brown, I., Radford, J. P., & Wehmeyer, M. L. (2017). Historical overview of intellectual and developmental disabilities. In M. L. Wehmeyer, I. Brown, M. Percy, K. A. Shogren, & W. L. A. Fung (Eds.), *A comprehensive guide to intellectual and developmental disabilities.* Baltimore, MD: Paul H. Brookes Publishing Co.

Brown, J. V., Bakeman, R., Coles, C. D., Platzman, K. A., & Lynch, M. E. (2004). Prenatal cocaine exposure: A comparison of 2-year-old children in parental and nonparental care. *Child Development, 75,* 1282–1295.

Brown, R. T. (2017). Pediatric pharmacology and psychopharmacology. In M. C. Roberts & R. G. Steele (Eds.), *Handbook of pediatric psychology* (5th ed.). New York: The Guilford Press.

Brown, R. T., & Kupst, M. J. (2016). Coping with chronic illness in children and their families. In C. DeMichelis & M. Ferrari (Eds.), *Child and adolescent resilience within medical contexts: Integrating research and practice.* Switzerland: Springer.

Brown, S. A., Tomlinson, K. L., & Winward, J. (2017). Substance use disorders. In T. P. Beauchaine & S. P. Hinshaw (Eds.), *Child and adolescent psychopathology* (3rd ed.). Hoboken, NJ: John Wiley & Sons.

Brown, T. E. (2005). *Attention deficit disorder: The unfocused mind in children and adults*. New Haven, CT: Yale University Press.

Brown, T., & Summerbell, C. (2009). Systematic review of school-based interventions that focus on changing dietary intake and physical activity levels to prevent childhood obesity: An update to the obesity guidance produced by the National Institute for Health and Clinical Excellence. *Obesity Reviews, 10,* 110–141.

Brownley, K. A., Berkman, N. D., Peat, C. M., Lohr, K. N., & Bulik, C. M. (2017). Binge-eating disorder in adults. *Annals of Internal Medicine, 166,* 231–232.

Bruce, A., & Wilmhurst, L. (2016). *Essentials of intellectual disability assessment and identification*. Hoboken, NJ: John Wiley & Sons, Inc.

Bruch, H. (1979). *The golden cage: The enigma of anorexia nervosa*. New York: Vintage Books.

Brumariu, L. E., & Kerns, K. A. (2010). Parent-child attachment and internalizing symptoms in childhood and adolescence: A review of empirical findings and future directions. *Development and Psychopathology, 22,* 177–203.

Brumberg, J. J. (1986). "Fasting girls": Reflections on writing the history of anorexia nervosa. In A. B. Smuts & J. W. Hagen (Eds.), *History and research in child development: Monographs of the Society for Research in Child Development, 50* (4–5, Serial No. 211).

Buchanan, R. W., & Carpenter, W. T. (2000). Schizophrenia: Introduction and overview. In B. J. Sadock & V. A. Sadock (Eds.), *Kaplan & Sadock's comprehensive textbook of psychiatry* (Vol. II). Philadelphia, PA: Lippincott Williams & Wilkins.

Buchanan, R., Chamberlain, P., & Smith, D. K. (2017). Treatment Foster Care Oregon for adolescents: Research and implementation. In J. R. Weisz & A. E. Kazdin (Eds.), *Evidence-based psychotherapies for children and adolescents* (3rd ed.). New York: The Guilford Press.

Bufferd, S. J., Dougherty, L. R., & Olino, T. M. (2019). Mapping the frequency and severity of anxiety behaviors in preschool-aged children. *Journal of Anxiety Disorders, 63,* 9–17.

Bufferd, S. J., Dougherty, L. R., Olino, T. M., Dyson, M. W., Carlson, G. A., & Klein, D. N. (2018). Temperament distinguishes persistent/recurrent from remitting anxiety disorders across early childhood. *Journal of Clinical Child & Adolescent Psychology, 47,* 1004–1013.

Bufford, S. J., Dyson, M. W., Hernandez, I. G., & Wakschlag, L. S. (2016). Explicating the "developmental" in preschool psychopathology. In D. Cicchetti (Ed.), *Developmental psychopathology; Vol. 3. Maladaption and psychopathology* (3rd ed.). Hoboken, NJ: Wiley.

Bujoreanu, S., White, M. T., Gerber, B., & Ibeziako, P. (2015). Effect of timing of psychiatry consultation on length of pediatric hospitalization and hospital charges. *Hospital Pediatrics, 5,* 269–275.

Bukowski, W. M., & Adams, R. (2005). Peer relationships and psychopathology: Markers, moderators, mediators, mechanisms, and meanings. *Journal of Clinical Child and Adolescent Psychology, 34,* 3–10.

Bukowski, W. M., Laursen, B., & Hoza, B. (2010). The snowball effect: Friendship moderates escalations in depressed affect among avoidant and excluded children. *Development and Psychopathology, 22,* 749–757.

Bukowski, W. M., Laursen, B., & Rubin, K. H. (2018). *Handbook of peer interactions, relationships, and groups* (2nd ed.). New York: Guilford Publications.

Bulik, C. M., Blake, L., & Austin, J. (2019). Genetics of eating disorders: What the clinician needs to know. *Psychiatric Clinics of North America, 42,* 59–73.

Burack, J. A. (1990). Differentiating mental retardation: The two-group approach and beyond. In R. M. Hodapp, J. A. Burack, & D. Zigler (Eds.), *Issues in the developmental approach to mental retardation*. New York: Cambridge University Press.

Burack, J. A., Russo, N., Green, C. G., Landry, O., & Iarocci, G. (2016). Developments in the developmental approach to intellectual disability. In D. Cicchetti (Ed.), *Developmental psychopathology: Maladaptation and psychopathology* (3rd ed., Vol. 3). Hoboken, NJ: John Wiley & Sons.

Burchinal, M., Roberts, J. E., Zeisel, S. A., Hennon, E. A., & Hooper, S. (2006). Social risk and protective child, parenting, and child care factors in early elementary school years. *Parenting: Science and Practice, 6,* 79–113.

Burgess, A. P., Witton, C., Shapiro, L., & Talcott, J. B. (2018). From subtypes to taxons: Identifying distinctive profiles of reading development in children. In *Reading and Dyslexia*. Cham, Switzerland: Springer.

Burke, J. D. (2012). An affective dimension within oppositional defiant disorder symptoms among boys: Personality and psychopathology outcomes into early adulthood. *Journal of Child Psychology and Psychiatry, 53,* 1176–1183.

Burke, J. D., Loeber, R., Lahey, B. B., & Rathouz, P. J. (2005). Developmental transitions among affective and behavioral disorders in adolescent boys. *Journal of Child Psychology and Psychiatry, 46,* 1200–1210.

Burke, J. D., Pardini, D. A., & Loeber, R. (2008). Reciprocal relationships between parenting behavior and disruptive psychopathology from childhood through adolescence. *Journal of Abnormal Child Psychology, 36,* 679–692.

Burkhart, K., Asogwa, K., Muzaffar, N., & Gabriel, M. (2019). Pediatric integrated care models: A systematic review. *Clinical Pediatrics, 59,* 148–153.

References

Burt, S. A. (2009). Are there meaningful etiological differences within antisocial behavior? Results of a meta-analysis. *Clinical Psychology Review, 29,* 163–178.

Burt, S. A., Krueger, R. F., McGue, M., & Iacono, W. G. (2001). Sources of covariation among attention-deficit/hyperactivity disorder, oppositional defiant disorder, and conduct disorder: The importance of shared environment. *Journal of Abnormal Psychology, 110,* 516–525.

Burt, S. A., Pearson, A. L., Carroll, S., Klump, K. L., & Neiderhiser, J. M. (2020). Child antisocial behavior is more environmental in origin in disadvantaged neighborhoods: Evidence across residents' perceptions and geographic scales in two samples. *Journal of Abnormal Child Psychology, 48,* 265–276.

Bushman, B. J., & Anderson, C. A. (2001). Media violence and the American public: Scientific facts versus media misinformation. *American Psychologist, 56,* 477–489.

Bushman, B. J., & Anderson, C. A. (2015). Understanding causality in the effects of media violence. *American Behavioral Scientist, 59,* 1807–1821.

Butler, H. A., Pentoney, C., & Bong, M. P. (2017). Predicting real-world outcomes: Critical thinking ability is a better predictor of life decisions than intelligence. *Thinking Skills and Creativity, 25,* 38–46.

Butler, M. G., Hartin, S. N., Hossain, W. A., Manzardo, A. M., Kimonis, V., Dykens, E., et al. (2019). Molecular genetic classification in Prader-Willi syndrome: A multisite cohort study. *Journal of Medical Genetics, 56,* 149–153.

Butler, R. J. (2008). Wetting and soiling. In M. Rutter et al. (Eds.), *Rutter's child and adolescent psychiatry* (5th ed.). Malden, MA: Blackwell Publishing.

Byrd, A. L., & Manuck, S. B. (2014). MAOA, childhood maltreatment, and antisocial behavior: Meta-analysis of a gene-environment interaction. *Biological Psychiatry, 75,* 9–17.

Byrd, A. L., Loeber, R., & Pardini, D. A. (2012). Understanding desisting and persisting forms of delinquency: The unique contributions of disruptive behavior disorders and interpersonal callousness. *Journal of Child Psychology and Psychiatry, 53,* 371–380.

Byrne, S. P., Lebowitz, E. R., Ollendick, T. H., & Silverman, W. K. (2018). Anxiety disorders in children and adolescents. In J. Hunsley & E. J. Mash (Eds.), *A guide to assessments that work* (2nd ed.). New York: Oxford University Press.

Caccavale, L. J., Corona, R., LaRose, J. G., Mazzeo, S. E., Sova, A. R., & Bean, M. K. (2019). Exploring the role of motivational interviewing in adolescent patient-provider communication about type 1 diabetes. *Pediatric Diabetes, 20,* 217–225.

Calati, R., De Ronchi, D., Bellini, M., & Serretti, A. (2011). The 5-HTTLPR polymorphism and eating disorders: A meta-analysis. *International Journal of Eating Disorders, 44,* 191–199.

Callender, K. A., Olson, S. L., Choe, D. E., & Sameroff, A. J. (2012). The effects of parental depressive symptoms, appraisals, and physical punishment on later child externalizing behavior. *Journal of Abnormal Child Psychology, 40,* 471–483.

Calvert, S. L., Appelbaum, M., Dodge, K. A., Graham, S., Nagayama Hall, G. C., Hamby, S., et al. (2017). The American Psychological Association Task Force assessment of violent video games: Science in the service of public interest. *American Psychologist, 72,* 126–143.

Cambron, C., Kosterman, R., Catalano, R. F., Guttmannova, K., & Hawkins, J. D. (2018). Neighborhood, family, and peer factors associated with early adolescent smoking and alcohol use. *Journal of Youth and Adolescence, 47,* 369–382.

Campbell, F. A., & Ramey, C. T. (1994). Effects of early intervention on intellectual and academic achievement: A follow-up study of children from low-income families. *Child Development, 65,* 684–698.

Campbell, F. A., Ramey, C. T., Pungello, E. P., Miller-Johnson, S., & Burchinal, M. (2001). The development of cognitive and academic abilities: Growth curves from an early childhood educational experiment. *Developmental Psychology, 37,* 231–242.

Campbell, F., Conti, G., Heckman, J. J., Moon, S. H., Pinto, R., Pungello, E., & Pan, Y. (2014). Early childhood investments substantially boost adult health. *Science, 343*(6178), 1478–1485.

Campbell, L., DiLorenzo, M., Atkinson, N., & Riddell, R. P. (2017). Systematic review: A systematic review of the interrelationships among children's coping responses, children's coping outcomes, and parent cognitive-affective, behavioral, and contextual variables in the needle-related procedures context. *Journal of Pediatric Psychology, 42,* 611–621.

Campbell, S. B. (2002). *Behavior problems in preschool children.* New York: The Guilford Press.

Campos, R., Martínez-Castilla, P., & Sotillo, M. (2017). False belief attribution in children with Williams syndrome: The answer is in the emotion. *Journal of Intellectual Disability Research, 61,* 1003–1010.

Canino, G., & Alegría, M. (2008). Psychiatric diagnosis: Is it universal or relative to culture? *Journal of Child Psychology and Psychiatry, 49,* 237–250.

Canino, G., Polanczyk, G., Bauermeister, J. J., Rohde, L. A., & Frick, P. J. (2010). Does the prevalence of CD and ODD vary across cultures? *Social Psychiatry and Psychiatric Epidemiology, 45,* 695–704.

Canino, G., Shrout, P. E., Rugio-Stipic, M., Bird, H. R., Bravo, M., Ramirez, R., et al. (2004). The DSM-IV rates of child and adolescent disorders in Puerto Rico. *Archives of General Psychiatry, 61,* 85–93.

Cannon, T. D., & Rosso, I. M. (2002). Levels of analysis in etiological research on schizophrenia. *Development and Psychopathology, 14,* 653–666.

Canter, K. S., Christofferson, J., Scialla, M. A., & Kazak, A. E. (2019). Technology-focused family interventions in pediatric chronic illness: A systematic review. *Journal of Clinical Psychology in Medical Settings, 26,* 68–87.

Cantwell, D. P. (1980). The diagnostic process and diagnostic classification in child psychiatry: DSM-III. *Journal of the American Academy of Child Psychiatry, 19,* 345–355.

Capaldi, D., DeGarmo, D., Patterson, G. R., & Forgatch, M. (2002). Contextual risk across the early life span and association with antisocial behavior. In J. B. Reid, G. R. Patterson, & J. Snyder (Eds.), *Antisocial behavior in children and adolescents: A developmental analysis and model for intervention.* Washington, DC: American Psychological Association.

Caplan, G. (1964). *The principles of preventive psychiatry.* New York: Basic Books.

Cappadocia, M. C., Desrocher, M., Pepler, D., & Schroeder, J. H. (2009). Conceptualizing the neurobiology of conduct disorder in an emotion dysregulation framework. *Clinical Psychology Review, 29,* 506–518.

Carliner, H., Gary, D., McLaughlin, K. A., & Keyes, K. M. (2017). Trauma exposure and externalizing disorders in adolescents: Results from the National Comorbidity Survey Adolescent Supplement. *Journal of the American Academy of Child & Adolescent Psychiatry, 56,* 755–764.

Carlson, C. L., & Mann, M. (2002). Sluggish cognitive tempo predicts a different pattern of impairment in the attention deficit hyperactivity disorder, predominantly inattentive type. *Journal of Clinical Child & Adolescent Psychology, 31,* 123–129.

Carlson, G. A. (2020). Presidential address: Emotion dysregulation in children and adolescents. *Journal of the American Academy of Child & Adolescent Psychiatry, 59,* 15–19.

Carlson, G. A., & Cantwell, D. P. (1980). Unmasking masked depression in children and adolescents. *American Journal of Psychiatry, 137,* 445–449.

Carlson, G. A., & Klein, D. N. (2014). How to understand divergent views on bipolar disorder in youth. *Annual Review of Clinical Psychology, 10,* 529–551.

Carpenter, B., Happé, F., & Egerton, J. (2019). Where are all the autistic girls? In B. Carpenter, F. Happé, & J. Egerton (Eds.), *Girls and autism.* London: Routledge.

Carpenter, P. J. (1992). Perceived control as a predictor of distress in children undergoing invasive medical procedures. *Journal of Pediatric Psychology, 17,* 757–773.

Carr, A., & O'Reilly, G. (2016). Lifespan development and the family lifecycle. In A. Carr, C. Linehan, G. O'Reilly, P. N. Walsh, & J. McEvoy (Eds.), *The handbook of intellectual disability and clinical psychology practice.* Abingdon, Oxon: Routledge.

Carrey, N., & Ungar, M. (2007). Resilience theory and the diagnostic and statistical manual: Incompatible bed fellows?

Child and Adolescent Psychiatric Clinics of North America, 16, 497–513.

Carson, C., & Rutter, M. (1991). Comorbidity in child psychopathology: Concepts, issues and research strategies. *Journal of Child Psychology and Psychiatry, 32,* 1063–1080.

Cartwright, K. B., Coppage, E. A., Lane, A. B., Singleton, T., Marshall, T. R., & Bentivegna, C. (2017). Cognitive flexibility deficits in children with specific reading comprehension difficulties. *Contemporary Educational Psychology, 50,* 33–44.

Carver, P. R., Yunger, J. L., & Perry, D. G. (2003). Gender identity and adjustment in middle childhood. *Sex Roles, 49,* 95–109.

Casey, B. J., Castellanos, F. X., Giedd, J. N., Marsh, W. L., Hamburger, S. D., Schubert, A. B., et al. (1997). Implication of right frontostriatal circuity in response inhibition and attention-deficit/hyperactivity disorder. *Journal of the American Academy of Child and Adolescent Psychiatry, 36,* 374–383.

Caspi, A., Elder, G. H., Jr., & Bem, D. J. (1987). Moving against the world: Life-course patterns of explosive children. *Developmental Psychology, 23,* 308–313.

Caspi, A., Houts, R. M., Belsky, D. W., Goldman-Mellor, S. J., Harrington, H., Israel, S., et al. (2014). The p factor: One general psychopathology factor in the structure of psychiatric disorders? *Clinical Psychological Science, 2,* 119–137.

Caspi, A., Sudgen, K., Moffitt, T. E., Taylor, A., Craig, I. W., Harrington, H., et al. (2003). Influence of life stress on depression: Moderation by a polymorphism in the 5-HTT gene. *Science, 301,* 386–389.

Cassano, M., Adrian, M., Veits, G., & Zeman, J. (2006). The inclusion of fathers in the empirical investigation of child psychopathology: An update. *Journal of Clinical Child and Adolescent Psychology, 35,* 583–589.

Castellanos-Ryan, N., & Conrod, P. J. (2011). Personality correlates of the common and unique variance across conduct disorder and substance misuse symptoms. *Journal of Abnormal Child Psychology, 39,* 563–576.

Cattane, N., Richetto, J., & Cattaneo, A. (2018). Prenatal exposure to environmental insults and enhanced risk of developing schizophrenia and autism spectrum disorder: Focus on biological pathways and epigenetic mechanisms. *Neuroscience & Biobehavioral Reviews.* Retrieved from https://doi.org/10.1016/j.neubiorev.2018.07.001

Causton, J., & Tracy-Bronson, C. P. (2015). *The educator's handbook for inclusive school practices.* Baltimore, MD: Paul H. Brookes Publishing Co.

Cave, L., Cooper, M. N., Zubrick, S. R., & Shepherd, C. C. J. (2020). Racial discrimination and child and adolescent health in longitudinal studies: A systematic review. *Social Science & Medicine, 250,* 112864.

Cavell, T. A., Ennett, S. T., & Meehan, B. T. (2001). Preventing alcohol and substance abuse. In J. N. Hughes, A. M. La Greca,

References

& J. C. Conoley (Eds.), *Handbook of psychological services for children and adolescents*. New York: Oxford University Press.

Cawley, J. (2006). Markets and childhood obesity policy. *The Future of Children, 16,* 69–88.

Caye, A., Swanson, J. M., Coghill, D., & Rohde, L. A. (2019). Treatment strategies for ADHD: An evidence-based guide to select optimal treatment. *Molecular Psychiatry, 24,* 390–408.

Centers for Disease Control and Prevention. (2018a). *Diabetes Report Card 2017*. Retrieved from www.cdc.gov/diabetes/pdfs/library/diabetesreportcard2017-508.pdf

Centers for Disease Control and Prevention. (2018b). Data and statistics about ADHD. Retrieved from www.cdc.gov/ncbddd/adhd/data.html

Centers for Disease Control and Prevention. (2018c). Other concerns and conditions with ADHD. Retreived from www.cdc.gov/ncbddd/adhd/conditions.html

Centers for Disease Control and Prevention. (2019a). *Fatal injury data*. Retrieved from www.cdc.gov/injury/wisqars/fatal.html

Centers for Disease Control and Prevention. (2019b). *HIV and Pregnant Women, Infants, and Children*. Retrieved from www.cdc.gov/hiv/pdf/group/gender/pregnantwomen/cdc-hiv-pregnant-women.pdf

Centers for Disease Control and Prevention. (2020). *People with moderate to severe asthma*. Retrieved from www.cdc.gov/coronavirus/2019-ncov/need-extra-precautions/asthma.html

Cha, C. B., Franz, P. J., Guzmán, E. M., Glenn, C. R., Kleiman, E. M., & Nock, M. K. (2018). Annual Research Review: Suicide among youth: epidemiology, (potential) etiology, and treatment. *Journal of Child Psychology and Psychiatry, 59,* 460–482.

Chacko, A., Allan, C., Uderman, J., Cornwell, M., Anderson, L., & Chimiklis, A. (2015). Training parents of youth with ADHD. In R. A. Barkley (Ed.), *Attention-deficit hyperactivity disorder: A handbook for diagnosis and treatment*. New York: The Guilford Press.

Chamberlain, P., & Smith, D. K. (2003). Antisocial behavior in children and adolescents: The Oregon multidimensional treatment foster care model. In A. E. Kazdin & J. R. Weisz (Eds.), *Evidence-based psychotherapies for children and adolescents*. New York: Guilford Press.

Chambers, R. A., Taylor, J. R., & Potenza, M. N. (2003). Developmental neurocircuitry of motivation in adolescence: A critical period of addiction vulnerability. *American Journal of Psychiatry, 160,* 1041–1052.

Chan, S. F., Connelly, M., & Wallace, D. P. (2017). The relationship between pain characteristics, peer difficulties, and emotional functioning among adolescents seeking treatment for chronic pain: A test of mediational models. *Journal of Pediatric Psychology, 42,* 941–951.

Chandler, L. A. (2003). The projective hypothesis and the development of projective techniques for children. In C. R.

Reynolds & R. W. Kamphaus (Eds.), *Handbook of psychological & educational assessment of children: Personality, behavior, and context* (2nd ed.). New York: Guilford Press.

Chaney, J. M., Gamwell, K. L., Baraldi, A. N., Ramsey, R. R., Cushing, C. C., Mullins, A. J., et al. (2016). Parent perceptions of illness uncertainty and child depressive symptoms in juvenile rheumatic diseases: Examining caregiver demand and parent distress as mediators. *Journal of Pediatric Psychology, 41,* 941–951.

Chang, H., Li, L., Peng, T., Li, M., Gao, L., & Xiao, X. (2016). Replication analyses of four chromosomal deletions with schizophrenia via independent large-scale meta-analyses. *American Journal of Medical Genetics Part B: Neuropsychiatric Genetics, 171,* 1161–1169.

Chang, Y., & Locke, J. (2016). A systematic review of peer-mediated interventions for children with autism spectrum disorder. *Research in Autism Spectrum Disorders, 27,* 1–10.

Chaparro, J. C., Sojourner, A., & Huey, N. (2019). 13 differential effects of high-quality early care: Lessons from the infant health and development program. In A. J. Reynolds & J. A. Temple (Eds.), *Sustaining early childhood learning gains: Program, school, and family influences*. New York: Cambridge University Press.

Charach, A., Yeung, E., Climans, T., & Lillie, E. (2011). Childhood attention-deficit/hyperactivity disorder and future substance use disorders: Comparative meta-analysis. *Journal of the American Academy of Child and Adolescent Psychiatry, 50,* 9–21.

Chardon, M. L., Stromberg, S. E., Lawless, C., Fedele, D. A., Carmody, J. K., Dumont-Driscoll, M. C., & Janicke, D. M. (2018). The role of child and adolescent adjustment problems and sleep disturbance in parent psychological distress. *Journal of Clinical Child & Adolescent Psychology, 47,* 374–381.

Charman, T. (2011). Commentary: Glass half full or half empty? Testing social communication interventions for young children with autism: Reflections on Landa, Holman, O'Neill, and Stuart (2011). *Journal of Child Psychology and Psychiatry, 52,* 22–23.

Charman, T., Ricketts, J., Dockrell, J. E., Lindsay, G., & Palikara, O. (2015). Emotional and behavioural problems in children with language impairments and children with autism spectrum disorders. *International Journal of Language & Communication Disorders, 50,* 84–93.

Charney, A., & Sklar, P. (2018). Genetics of schizophrenia and bipolar disorder In D. S. Charney, E. J. Nestler, P. Sklar, & J. D. Buxbaum (Eds.), *Charney & Nestler's Neurobiology of Mental Illness* (5th ed.). New York: Oxford University Press.

Chasnoff, I. J., Wells, A. M., Telford, E., Schmidt, C., & Messer, D. (2010). Neurodevelopmental functioning in children with FAS, pFAS, and ARND. *Journal of Developmental and Behavioral Pediatrics, 31,* 192–201.

Chassin, L., Beltran, I., Lee, M., Haller, M., & Villalta, I. (2010). Vulnerability to substance use disorders in childhood and adolescence. In R. E. Ingram & J. M. Price (Eds.), *Vulnerability to psychopathology: Risk across the lifespan* (2nd ed.). New York: The Guilford Press.

Chassin, L., Colder, C. R., Hussong, A., & Sher, K. J. (2016). Substance use and substance use disorders. In D. Cicchetti (Ed.), *Developmental psychopathology* (3rd ed., Vol. 3). Hoboken, NJ: John Wiley & Sons.

Chassin, L., Presson, C. C., Todd, M., Rose, J., & Sherman, S. J. (1998). Maternal socialization of adolescent smoking: The intergenerational transmission of parenting and smoking. *Developmental Psychology, 34,* 1189–1201.

Chavira, D. A., & Stein, M. B. (2005). Childhood social anxiety disorder: From understanding to treatment. *Child and Adolescent Psychiatric Clinics of North America, 14,* 797–818.

Chavira, D. A., Shipon-Blum, E., Hitchcock, C., Cohan, S., & Stein, M. B. (2007). Selective mutism and social anxiety disorder: All in the family? *Journal of the American Academy of Child and Adolescent Psychiatry, 46,* 1464–1472.

Chawarska, K., & Shic, F. (2009). Looking but not seeing: A typical visual scanning and recognition of faces in 2- and 4-year-old children with autism spectrum disorder. *Journal of Autism and Developmental Disorders, 39,* 1663–1672.

Chen, M. C., Hamilton, J. P., & Gotlib, I. H. (2010). Decreased hippocampal volume in healthy girls at risk of depression. *Archives of General Psychiatry, 67,* 270–276.

Chen, M., Wardlaw, M., & Stein, M. A. (2019). ADHD medications and sleep. In H. Hiscock & E. Sciberras (Eds.), *Sleep and ADHD.* London: Academic Press.

Chen, X., & Liu, C. H. (2016). Culture, peer relationships, and developmental psychopathology. In D. Cicchetti (Ed.), *Developmental psychopathology: Risk, resilience, and intervention* (Vol. 4). Hoboken, NJ: John Wiley & Sons.

Cheng, Z. H., Perko, V. L., Fuller-Marashi, L., Gau, J. M., & Stice, E. (2019). Ethnic differences in eating disorder prevalence, risk factors, and predictive effects of risk factors among young women. *Eating Behaviors, 32,* 23–30.

Cherian, K., Schatzberg, A. F., & Keller, J. (2019). HPA axis in psychotic major depression and schizophrenia spectrum disorders: Cortisol, clinical symptomatology, and cognition. *Schizophrenia Research, 213,* 72–79.

Chess, S., & Thomas, A. (1972). Differences in outcome with early intervention in children with behavior disorders. In M. Roff, L. Robins, & M. Pollack (Eds.), *Life history research in psychopathology* (Vol. 2). Minneapolis: University of Minnesota Press.

Chess, S., & Thomas, A. (1977). Temperamental individuality from childhood to adolescence. *Journal of the American Academy of Child Psychiatry, 16,* 218–226.

Chetty, R., Hendren, N., & Katz, L. F. (2016). The effects of exposure to better neighborhoods on children: New evidence from the Moving to Opportunity experiment. *American Economic Review, American Economic Association, 106,* 855–902,

Cheung, C. H. M., Rijdijk, F., McLoughlin, G., Faraone, S. V., Asherson, P., & Kuntsi, J. (2015). Childhood predictors of adolescent and young adult outcome in ADHD. *Journal of Psychiatric Research, 62,* 92–100.

Cheung, K., & Theule, J. (2016). Parental psychopathology in families of children with ADHD: A meta-analysis. *Journal of Child and Family Studies, 25,* 3451–3461.

Chiang, J. L., Maahs, D. M., Garvey, K. C., Hood, K. K., Laffel, L. M., Weinzimer, S. A., et al. (2018). Type 1 diabetes in children and adolescents: A position statement by the American Diabetes Association. *Diabetes Care, 41,* 2026.

Chiat, S. (2015). Nonword repetition. In S. Armon-Lotem, J. de Jong, & N. Meir (Eds.), *Methods for assessing multilingual children: Disentangling bilingualism from language impairment.* Bristol: Multilingual Matters.

Child Care & Early Education Research Connections. (2014). *Head start impact study (HSIS) bibliography.* Retrieved from www.researchconnections.org/childcare/resources/28706/pdf

Child Welfare Information Gateway. (2019a). Foster care statistics 2017. Washington, DC: U.S. Department of Health and Human Services, Children's Bureau.

Child Welfare Information Gateway. (2019b). Working with the courts for permanency. Washington, DC: U.S. Department of Health and Human Services, Children's Bureau.

Childress, A. C., Brewerton, T. D., Hodges, E. L., & Jarrell, M. P. (1993). The Kids' Eating Disorders Survey (KEDS): A study of middle school students. *Journal of the American Academy of Child and Adolescent Psychiatry, 32,* 843–850.

Choenni, V., Lambregtse-van den Berg, M. P., Verhulst, F. C., Tiemeier, H., & Kok, R. (2019). The longitudinal relation between observed maternal parenting in the preschool period and the occurrence of child ADHD symptoms in middle childhood. *Journal of Abnormal Child Psychology, 47,* 755–764.

Chorpita, B. F. (2001). Control and the development of negative emotions. In M. W. Vasey & M. R. Dadds (Eds.), *The developmental psychopathology of anxiety.* New York: Oxford University Press.

Chorpita, B. F. (2002). The tripartite model and dimensions of anxiety and depression: An examination of structure in a large school sample. *Journal of Abnormal Child Psychology, 30,* 177–190.

Chorpita, B. F. (2019). Metaknowledge is power: Envisioning models to address unmet mental health needs: reflections on Kazdin (2019). *Journal of Child Psychology and Psychiatry, 60,* 473–476.

References

Chorpita, B. F., & Barlow, D. H. (1998). The development of anxiety: The role of control in the early environment. *Psychological Bulletin, 124,* 3–21.

Chorpita, B. F., & Southam-Gerow, M. A. (2006). Fears and anxieties. In E. J. Mash & R. A. Barkley (Eds.), *Treatment of childhood disorders* (3rd ed.). New York: The Guilford Press.

Chorpita, B. F., Becker, K. D., & Higa-McMillan, C. K. (2019). The new frontier: Dissemination of EBTs and beyond. In T. H. Ollendick, S. W. White, & B. A. White (Eds.), *The Oxford handbook of clinical child and adolescent psychology.* New York: Oxford University Press.

Chow, C. H. T., Van Lieshout, R. J., Schmidt, L. A., Dobson, K. G., & Buckley, N. (2015). Systematic review: Audiovisual interventions for reducing preoperative anxiety in children undergoing elective surgery. *Journal of Pediatric Psychology, 41,* 182–203.

Chow, C. H. T., Wan, S., Pope, E., Meng, Z., Schmidt, L. A., Buckley, N., & Van Lieshout, R. J. (2018). Audiovisual interventions for parental preoperative anxiety: A systematic review and meta-analysis. *Health Psychology, 37,* 746–758.

Christensen, D. L., Baio, J., Braun, K. V. N., Bilder, D., Charles, J., Constantino, J. N., et al. (2016). Prevalence and characteristics of autism spectrum disorder among children aged 8 years: Autism and developmental disabilities monitoring network, 11 sites, United States, 2012. *MMWR Surveillance Summaries, 65*(SS-3), 1–23.

Christensen, J. H., & Børglum, A. D. (2019). Modeling the cooperativity of schizophrenia risk genes. *Nature Genetics, 51,* 1434–1436.

Christodoulou, G., Majmundar, A., Chou, C.-P., & Pentz, M. A. (2020). Anhedonia, screen time, and substance use in early adolescents: A longitudinal mediation analysis. *Journal of Adolescence, 78,* 24–32.

Chronis, A. M., Pelham, W. E., Gnagy, E. M., Roberts, J. E., & Aronoff, H. R. (2003). The impact of late-afternoon stimulant dosing for children with ADHD on parent and parent-child domains. *Journal of Clinical Child and Adolescent Psychology, 32,* 118–126.

Chronis-Tuscano, A., Degnan, K. A., Pine, D. S., Pérez-Edgar, K., Henderson, H. A., Diaz, Y., et al. (2009). Stable early maternal report of behavioral inhibition predicts lifetime social anxiety disorder in adolescence. *Journal of the American Academy of Child and Adolescent Psychiatry, 48,* 928–935.

Chu, F. W., vanMarle, K., Hoard, M. K., Nugent, L., Scofield, J. E., & Geary, D. C. (2019). Preschool deficits in cardinal knowledge and executive function contribute to longer-term mathematical learning disability. *Journal of Experimental Child Psychology, 188,* 104668.

Chu, J., & Leino, A. (2017). Advancement in the maturing science of cultural adaptations of evidence-based interventions. *Journal of Consulting and Clinical Psychology, 85,* 45–57.

Chua, J. Y. X., Tam, W., & Shorey, S. (2020). Research Review: Effectiveness of universal eating disorder prevention interventions in improving body image among children: A systematic review and meta-analysis. *Journal of Child Psychology and Psychiatry, 61,* 522–535.

Chung, H. L., & Steinberg, L. (2006). Relations between neighborhood factors, parenting behaviors, peer deviance, and delinquency among serious juvenile offenders. *Developmental Psychology, 42,* 319–331.

Chung, T., & Bachrach, R. L. (2019). Substance use problems. In M. J. Prinstein, E. A. Youngstrom, E. J. Mash, & R. A. Barkley (Eds.), *Treatment of disorders in childhood and adolescence* (4th ed.). New York: Guilford Press.

Chzhen, Y., Gromada, A., & Rees, G. (2019). *Are the world's richest countries family friendly? Policy in the OECD and EU.* Florence, Italy: UNICEF.

Cicchetti, D. (1984). The emergence of developmental psychopathology. *Child Development, 55,* 1–7.

Cicchetti, D. (1989). Developmental psychology: Some thoughts on its evolution. *Development and Psychopathology, 1,* 1–3.

Cicchetti, D. (2006). Development and psychopathology. In D. Cicchetti & D. J. Cohen (Eds.), *Developmental psychopathology, Vol. 1: Theory and method.* Hoboken, NJ: John Wiley & Sons.

Cicchetti, D. (2010a). A developmental psychopathology perspective on bipolar disorder. In D. J. Miklowitz & D. Cicchetti (Eds.), *Understanding bipolar disorder: A developmental psychopathology perspective.* New York: Guilford Press.

Cicchetti, D. (2010b). Resilience under conditions of extreme stress: A multilevel perspective. *World Psychiatry, 9,* 145–154.

Cicchetti, D., & Lynch, M. (1995). Failures in the expectable environment and their impact on individual development: The case of child maltreatment. In D. Cicchetti & D. J. Cohen (Eds.), *Developmental psychopathology: Risk, disorder, and adaptation* (Vol. 2). New York: John Wiley & Sons.

Cicchetti, D., & Manly, J. T. (2001). Operationalizing child maltreatment: Developmental processes and outcomes. *Development and Psychopathology, 13,* 755–757.

Cicchetti, D., & Olsen, K. (1990). The developmental psychopathology of child maltreatment. In M. Lewis & S. M. Miller (Eds.), *Handbook of developmental psychopathology.* New York: Plenum Press.

Cicchetti, D., & Rogosch, F. A. (2002). A developmental psychopathology perspective on adolescence. *Journal of Consulting and Clinical Psychology, 70,* 6–20.

Cicchetti, D., & Sroufe, L. A. (2000). Editorial: The past as prologue to the future: The times, they've been a-changin'. *Development and Psychopathology, 12,* 255–264.

Cicchetti, D., & Toth, S. L. (1998). The development of depression in children and adolescents. *American Psychologist, 53,* 221–241.

Cicchetti, D., & Toth, S. L. (2009). The past achievements and future promises of developmental psychopathology: The coming of age of a discipline. *Journal of Child Psychology and Psychiatry, 50,* 16–25.

Cicchetti, D., & Toth, S. L. (2016). Child maltreatment and developmental psychopathology: A multilevel perspective. In D. Cicchetti (Ed.), *Developmental psychopathology* (3rd ed., Vol. 3). Hoboken, NJ: John Wiley & Sons.

Cicchetti, D., & Toth, S. L. (2017). Using the science of developmental psychopathology to inform child and adolescent psychotherapy. In J. R. Weisz & A. E. Kazdin (Eds.), *Evidence-based psychotherapies for children and adolescents* (3rd ed.). New York: The Guilford Press.

Cidav, Z., Munson, J., Estes, A., Dawson, G., Rogers, S., & Mandell, D. (2017). Cost offset associated with Early Start Denver Model for children with autism. *Journal of the American Academy of Child & Adolescent Psychiatry, 56,* 777–783.

Cipriani, A., Zhou, X., Del Giovane, C., Hetrick, S. E., Qin, B., Whittington, C., et al. (2016). Comparative efficacy and tolerability of antidepressants for major depressive disorder in children and adolescents: A network meta-analysis. *The Lancet, 388*(10047), 881–890.

Cirino, P. T., Fletcher, J. M., Ewing-Cobbs, L., Barnes, M. A., & Fuchs, L. S. (2007). Cognitive arithmetic differences in learning difficulty groups and the role of behavioral inattention. *Learning Disabilities Research & Practice, 22,* 25–35.

Ciucci, E., Baroncelli, A., Franchi, M., Golmaryami, F. N., & Frick, P. J. (2014). The association between callous-unemotional traits and behavioral and academic adjustment in children: Further validation of the Inventory of Callous-Unemotional Traits. *Journal of Psychopathology and Behavioral Assessment, 36,* 189–200.

Ciupitu-Plath, C., Wiegand, S., & Babitsch, B. (2018). The Weight Bias Internalization Scale for Youth: Validation of a specific tool for assessing internalized weight bias among treatment-seeking German adolescents with overweight. *Journal of Pediatric Psychology, 43,* 40–51.

Clark, D. B., Smith, M. G., Neighbors, B. D., Skerlec, L. M., & Randall, J. (1994). Anxiety disorders in adolescence: Characteristics, prevalence, and comorbidities. *Clinical Psychology Review, 14,* 113–137.

Clark, J. E., & Frick, P. J. (2018). Positive parenting and callous-unemotional traits: Their association with school behavior problems in young children. *Journal of Clinical Child & Adolescent Psychology, 47*(sup1), S242–S254.

Clark, K. B., Chein, I., & Cook, S. W. (2004). The effects of segregation and the consequences of desegregation: A (September 1952) Social Science Statement in the *Brown v. Board of Education of Topeka* Supreme Court Case. *American Psychologist, 59,* 495–501.

Clark, L. A., & Watson, D. (1991). Tripartite model of anxiety and depression: Psychometric evidence and taxonomic implications. *Journal of Abnormal Psychology, 100,* 316–336.

Clark, L., & Tiggemann, M. (2007). Sociocultural influences and body image in 9- to 12-year-old girls: The role of appearance schemas. *Journal of Clinical Child and Adolescent Psychology, 36,* 76–86.

Clarke, G. N., Hornbrook, M., Lynch, F., Polen, M., Gale, J., Beardslee, W., et al. (2001). A randomized trial of a group cognitive intervention for preventing depression in adolescent offspring of depressed parents. *Archives of General Psychiatry, 58,* 1127–1134.

Clarke, G. N., Rohde, P., Lewinsohn, P. M., Hops, H., & Seeley, J. R. (1999). Cognitive-behavioral treatment for adolescent depression: Efficacy of acute group treatment and booster sessions. *Journal of the American Academy of Child and Adolescent Psychiatry, 38,* 272–279.

Clauss-Ehlers, C. S., Chiriboga, D. A., Hunter, S. J., Roysircar, G., & Tummala-Narra, P. (2019). APA Multicultural Guidelines executive summary: Ecological approach to context, identity, and intersectionality. *American Psychologist, 74,* 232–244.

Clawson, A. H., Ruppe, N., Nwankwo, C., Blair, A., Baudino, M., & Mehdi, N. (2019). Cognitive behavioral therapy for youth with asthma: Anxiety as an example. In R. D. Friedberg & J. K. Paternostro (Eds.), *Handbook of cognitive behavioral therapy for pediatric medical conditions*. Cham, Switzerland: Springer.

Clegg, J., Hollis, C., Mawhood, L., & Rutter, M. (2005). Developmental language disorders—a follow-up in later adult life: Cognitive, language, and psychosocial outcomes. *Journal of Child Psychology and Psychiatry, 46,* 128–149.

Clements, M. A., Foster, N. C., Maahs, D. M., Schatz, D. A., Olson, B. A., Tsalikian, E., et al. (2016). Hemoglobin A1c (HbA1c) changes over time among adolescent and young adult participants in the T1D exchange clinic registry. *Pediatric Diabetes, 17,* 327–336.

Clinch, J., & Eccleston, C. (2009). Chronic musculoskeletal pain in children: Assessment and management. *Rheumatology, 48,* 466–474.

Coakley, R., & Wihak, T. (2017). Evidence-based psychological interventions for the management of pediatric chronic pain: New directions in research and clinical practice. *Children, 4,* 9. Retrieved from www.mdpi.com/2227-9067/4/2/9

Coghill, D., Chen, W., & Silva, D. (2019). Organizing and delivering treatment for ADHD. In L. A. Rohde, J. K. Buitelaar, M. Gerlach, & S. V. Faraone (Eds.), *The world federation of ADHD guide*. Porto Alegre: World Federation of ADHD.

Coghill, D., Toplak, M., Rhodes, S., & Adamo, N. (2018). Cognitive functioning in ADHD. In T. Banaschewski, D. Coghill, & A.

References

Zuddas (Eds.), *Oxford textbook of attention deficit hyperactivity disorder* (1st ed.). Oxford: Oxford University Press.

Cohan, S. L., Chavira, D. A., Shipon-Blum, E., Hitchcock, C., Roesch, S. C., & Stein, M. (2008). Refining the classification of children with selective mutism: A latent profile analysis. *Journal of Clinical Child and Adolescent Psychology, 37,* 770–784.

Cohen, D., Bonnot, O., Bodeau, N., Consoli, A., & Laurent, C. (2012). Adverse effects of second-generation antipsychotics in children and adolescents: A Bayesian meta-analysis. *Journal of Clinical Psychopharmacology, 32,* 309–316.

Cohen, G. L., Garcia, J., Purdie-Vaughns, V., Apfel, N., & Brzustoski, P. (2009). Recursive processes in self-affirmation: Intervening to close the minority gap. *Science, 324,* 400–403.

Cohen, J. A., Mannarino, A. P., & Deblinger, E. (2017a). *Treating trauma and traumatic grief in children and adolescents* (2nd ed.). New York: The Guilford Press.

Cohen, J. A., Mannarino, A. P., & Deblinger, E. (2017b). Trauma-focused cognitive-behavioral therapy for traumatized children. In J. R. Weisz & A. E. Kazdin (Eds.), *Evidence-based psychotherapies for children and adolescents* (3rd ed.). New York: The Guilford Press.

Cohen, L. L., Blount, R. L., Chorney, J., Zempsky, W., Rodrgues, N., & Cousins, L. A. (2017). Management of pediatric pain distress due to medical procedures. In M. C. Roberts & R. G. Steele (Eds.), *Handbook of pediatric psychology* (5th ed.). New York: Springer.

Cohen, P., Cohen, J., & Brook, J. (1993a). An epidemiological study of disorders in late childhood and adolescence-II. Persistence of disorders. *Journal of Child Psychology and Psychiatry, 34,* 869–877.

Cohen, P., Cohen, J., Kasen, S., Velez, C. N., Hartmark, C., Johnson, J., et al. (1993b). An epidemiological study of disorders in late childhood and adolescence: I. Age- and gender-specific prevalence. *Journal of Child Psychology and Psychiatry, 34,* 851–867.

Cohen-Tovee, E. M. (1993). Depressed mood and concern with weight and shape in normal young women. *International Journal of Eating Disorders, 14,* 223–227.

Coie, J. D., & Dodge, K. A. (1998). Aggression and antisocial behavior. In W. Damon (Series Ed.) & N. Eisenberg (Vol. Ed.), *Handbook of child psychology: Vol. 3. Social, emotional, and personality development* (5th ed.). New York: John Wiley.

Coie, J. D., Miller-Johnson, S., & Bagwell, C. (2000). Prevention science. In A. J. Sameroff, M. Lewis, & S. M. Miller (Eds.), *Handbook of developmental psychopathology.* New York: Kluwer Academic/Plenum.

Coie, J. D., Watt, N. F., West, S. G., Hawkins, J. D., Asarnow, J. R., Markman, H. J., et al. (1993). The science of prevention: A conceptual framework and some directions for a national research program. *American Psychologist, 48,* 1013–1022.

Coker, T. R., Elliott, M. N., Toomey, S. L., Schwebel, D. C., Cuccaro, P., Tortolero Emery, S., et al. (2016). Racial and ethnic disparities in ADHD diagnosis and treatment. *Pediatrics, 138,* e20160407.

Colaneri, N., Keim, S. A., & Adesman, A. (2018). Physician training and qualification to educate patients on attention-deficit/hyperactivity disorder stimulant diversion and misuse. *Journal of Child and Adolescent Psychopharmacology, 28,* 554–561.

Colder, C., Chassin, L., Villalta, I., & Lee, M. (2009). Affect regulation and substance use: A developmental perspective. In J. Kassel (Ed.), *Substance use and emotion.* Washington, DC: American Psychological Association.

Cole, C. M., Waldron, N., & Majd, M. (2004). Academic progress of students across inclusive and traditional settings. *Mental Retardation, 42,* 136–144.

Cole, P. (2016). Emotion and the development of psychopathology. In D. Cicchetti (Ed.), *Developmental psychopathology: Risk, resilience, and intervention* (3rd ed., Vol. 1). Hoboken, NJ: John Wiley & Sons.

Cole, P. M., Hall, S. E., & Hajal, N. J. (2017). Emotion dysregulation as a vulnerability to psychopathology. In T. P. Beauchaine & S. P. Hinshaw (Eds.), *Child and adolescent psychopathology* (3rd ed.). Hoboken, NJ: John Wiley & Sons Inc.

Colich, N. L., Kircanski, K., Foland-Ross, L. C., & Gotlib, I. H. (2015). HPA-axis reactivity interacts with stage of pubertal development to predict the onset of depression. *Psychoneuroendocrinology, 55,* 94–101.

Collins, K. P., & Cleary, S. D. (2016). Racial and ethnic disparities in parent-reported diagnosis of ADHD: National survey of children's health (2003, 2007, and 2011). *The Journal of Clinical Psychiatry, 77,* 52–59.

Collishaw, S. (2015). Annual research review: Secular trends in child and adolescent mental health. *Journal of Child Psychology and Psychiatry, 56,* 370–393.

Collishaw, S., Maughan, B., Goodman, R., & Pickles, A. (2004). Time trends in adolescent health. *Journal of Child Psychology and Psychiatry, 45,* 1350–1362.

Collishaw, S., Maughan, B., Natarajan, L., & Pickles, A. (2010). Trends in adolescent emotional problems in England: A comparison of two national cohorts twenty years apart. *Journal of Child Psychology and Psychiatry, 51,* 885–894.

Colonnesi, C., Draijer, E. M., Stams, G. J. J. M., Van der Bruggen, C. O., & Bögels, S. M. (2011). The relation between insecure attachment and child anxiety: A meta-analytic review. *Journal of Clinical Child and Adolescent Psychology, 40,* 630–645.

Comer, J. S., Bry, L. J., Poznanski, B., & Golik, A. M. (2016a). Children's mental health in the context of terrorist attacks, ongoing threats, and possibilities of future terrorism. *Current Psychiatry Reports, 18,* 79.

Comer, J. S., DeSerisy, M., & Greif Green, J. (2016b). Caregiver-reports of internet exposure and posttraumatic stress among Boston-area youth following the 2013 Marathon bombing. *Evidence-Based Practice in Child and Adolescent Mental Health, 1,* 86–102.

Comer, J. S., Fan, B., Duarte, C. S., Wu, P., Musa, G. J., Mandell, D. J., et al. (2010). Attack-related life disruption and child psychopathology in New York City public schoolchildren 6-months post-9/11. *Journal of Clinical Child & Adolescent Psychology, 39,* 460–469.

Comer, J. S., Furr, J. M., Miguel, E. M., Cooper-Vince, C. E., Carpenter, A. L., Elkins, R. M., et al. (2017). Remotely delivering real-time parent training to the home: An initial randomized trial of internet-delivered Parent–Child Interaction Therapy (I-PCIT). *Journal of Consulting and Clinical Psychology, 85,* 909–917.

Comer, J. S., Hong, N., Poznanski, B., Silva, K., & Wilson, M. (2019). Evidence base update on the treatment of early childhood anxiety and related problems. *Journal of Clinical Child and Adolescent Psychology, 48,* 1–15.

Comer, J. S., Kerns, C. E., Elkins, R. M., Edson, A. L., Chou, T., Dantowitz, A., et al. (2014). Adjustment among children with relatives who participated in the manhunt following the Boston Marathon attack. *Depression and Anxiety, 31,* 542–550.

Committee to Evaluate the Supplemental Security Income Disability Program for Children with Mental Disorders. (2015). Clinical characteristics of intellectual disabilities. In T. F. Boat & J. T. Wu (Eds.), *Mental disorders and disabilities among low-income children*. Washington, DC: National Academies Press.

Compas, B. E. (1997). Depression in children and adolescents. In E. J. Mash & L. G. Terdal (Eds.), *Assessment of childhood disorders* (3rd ed.). New York: Guilford Press.

Compas, B. E., Connor-Smith, J., & Jaser, S. S. (2004). Temperament, stress reactivity, and coping: Implications for depression in childhood and adolescence. *Journal of Clinical Child and Adolescent Psychology, 33,* 21–31.

Compas, B. E., Ey, S., & Grant, K. E. (1993). Taxonomy, assessment, and diagnosis of depression during adolescence. *Psychological Bulletin, 14,* 323–344.

Compas, B. E., Gruhn, M., & Bettis, A. H. (2017). Risk and resilience in child and adolescent psychopathology. In T. P. Beauchaine & S. P. Hinshaw (Eds.), *Child and adolescent psychopathology* (3rd ed.). Hoboken, NJ: John Wiley & Sons Inc.

Compas, B. E., Hinden, B. R., & Gerhardt, C. (1995). Adolescent development: Pathways and processes of risk and resilience. *Annual Review of Psychology, 46,* 265–293.

Compas, B. E., Jaser, S. S., Dunn, M. J., & Rodriguez, E. M. (2012). Coping with chronic illness in childhood and adolescence. *Annual Review of Clinical Psychology, 8,* 455–480.

Condillac, R. A., & Baker, D. (2017). Behavioral intervention. In M. L. Wehmeyer, I. Brown, M. Percy, K. A. Shogren, & W. L. A. Fung (Eds.), *A comprehensive guide to intellectual and developmental disabilities*. Baltimore, MD: Paul H. Brookes Publishing Co.

Conduct Problems Prevention Research Group. (1992). A developmental and clinical model for the prevention of conduct disorder: The fast track program. *Development and Psychopathology, 4,* 509–527.

Conduct Problems Prevention Research Group. (2002a). Evaluation of the first 3 years of the fast track prevention trial with children at high risk for adolescent conduct problems. *Journal of Abnormal Child Psychology, 30,* 19–36.

Conduct Problems Prevention Research Group. (2002b). The implementation of the fast track program: An example of large-scale prevention science efficacy trial. *Journal of Abnormal Child Psychology, 30,* 1–18.

Conley, C. S., Haines, B. A., Hilt, L. M., & Metalsky, G. I. (2001). The children's attributional style interview: Developmental tests of cognitive diathesis-stress theories of depression. *Journal of Abnormal Child Psychology, 29,* 445–463.

Connell, A. M., Dishion, T. J., Yasui, M., & Kavanagh, K. (2007). An adaptive approach to family intervention: Linking engagement in family-centered intervention to reductions in adolescent problem behavior. *Journal of Consulting and Clinical Psychology, 75,* 568–579.

Connell, J. P. (1985). A new multidimensional measure of children's perceptions of control. *Child Development, 56,* 1018–1041.

Conners, C. K. (2008). *Conners' Rating Scales-3rd Edition: Conners 3 manual*. North Tonawanda, NY: Multi-Health Systems, Inc.

Connor, D. F. (2015). Stimulant and nonstimulant medications for childhood ADHD. In R. A. Barkley (Ed.), *Attention-deficit/hyperactivity disorder: A handbook for diagnosis and treatment*. New York: The Guilford Press.

Conti-Ramsden, G. (2003). Processing and linguistic markers in young children with specific language impairment (SLI). *Journal of Speech, Language, and Hearing Research, 46,* 1029–1037.

Conti-Ramsden, G., & Durkin, K. (2015). What factors influence language impairment considering resilience as well as risk. *Folia Phoniatrica et Logopaedica, 67,* 293–299.

Cooley, M. R., & Boyce, C. A. (2004). An introduction to assessing anxiety in child and adolescent multiethnic populations: Challenges and opportunities for enhancing knowledge and practice. *Journal of Clinical Child and Adolescent Psychology, 33,* 210–215.

Cooper, Z., & Fairburn, C. G. (2010). Cognitive behavior therapy for bulimia nervosa. In C. M. Grilo & J. E. Mitchell (Eds.), *The treatment of eating disorders: A clinical handbook*. New York: The Guilford Press.

References

Copeland, W. E., Shanahan, L., Costello, E. J., & Angold, A. (2009). Childhood and adolescent psychiatric disorders as predictors of young adult disorders. *Archives of General Psychiatry, 66,* 764–772.

Corbett, B. A., Constantine, L. J., Hendren, R., Rocke, D., & Ozonoff, S. (2009). Examining executive functioning in children with autism spectrum disorder, attention deficit hyperactivity disorder and typical development. *Psychiatry Research, 166,* 210–222.

Corcoran, C. M., Smith, C., McLaughlin, D., Auther, A., Malaspina, D., & Cornblatt, B. (2012). HPA axis function and symptoms in adolescents at clinical high risk for schizophrenia. *Schizophrenia Research, 135,* 170–174.

Correll, C. U., Manu, P., Olshanskiy, V., Napolitano, B., Kane, J. M., & Malhotra, A. K. (2009). Cardiometabolic risk of second-generation antipsychotic medications during first-time use in children and adolescents. *Journal of the American Medical Association, 302,* 1765–1773.

Corrice, A. M., & Glidden, L. M. (2009). The down syndrome advantage: Fact or fiction? *American Journal on Intellectual and Developmental Disabilities, 114,* 254–268.

Corrigan, P. W., & Nieweglowski, K. (2019). How does familiarity impact the stigma of mental illness? *Clinical Psychology Review, 70,* 40–50.

Corriveau, K., Pasquini, E., & Goswami, U. (2007). Basic auditory processing skills and specific language impairment: A new look at an old hypothesis. *Journal of Speech, Language, and Hearing Research, 50,* 647–666.

Costello, A. J., Edelbrock, C., Dulcan, M. K., Kalas, R., & Klaric, S. H. (1984). *Report of the NIMH Diagnostic Interview Schedule for Children (DISC).* Washington, DC: National Institute of Mental Health.

Costello, E. J. (2016). Early detection and prevention of mental health problems: Developmental epidemiology and systems of support. *Journal of Clinical Child and Adolescent Psychology, 45,* 710–717.

Costello, E. J., & Angold, A. (2001). Bad behaviour: An historic perspective on disorders of conduct. In J. Hill & B. Maughan (Eds.), *Conduct disorders in childhood and adolescence.* New York: Cambridge University Press.

Costello, E. J., & Angold, A. (2016). Developmental epidemiology. In D. Cicchetti (Ed.), *Developmental psychopathology.* Hoboken, NJ: John Wiley & Sons.

Costello, E. J., Compton, S. N., Keeler, G., & Angold, A. (2003). Relationships between poverty and psychopathology. *Journal of the American Medical Association, 290,* 2023–2029.

Costello, E. J., Egger, H. L., & Angold, A. (2004). Developmental epidemiology of anxiety disorders. In T. H. Ollendick & J. March (Eds.), *Phobic and anxiety disorders in children and adolescents: A clinician's guide to effective psychosocial and pharmacological interventions.* New York: Oxford University Press.

Costello, E. J., Egger, H. L., & Angold, A. (2005b). The developmental epidemiology of anxiety disorders: Phenomenology, prevalence, and comorbidity. *Child and Adolescent Psychiatric Clinics of North America, 14,* 631–648.

Costello, E. J., Egger, H., & Angold, A. (2005a). 10-year research update review: The epidemiology of child and adolescent psychiatric disorders: I. Methods and public health burden. *Journal of the American Academy of Child and Adolescent Psychiatry, 44,* 972–986.

Costello, E. J., Erkanli, A., Fairbank, J. A., & Angold, A. (2002). The prevalence of potentially traumatic events in childhood and adolescence. *Journal of Traumatic Stress, 15,* 99–112.

Costello, E. J., Foley, D. L., & Angold, A. (2006). 10-year research update review: The epidemiology of child and adolescent psychiatric disorders: II. Developmental epidemiology. *Journal of the American Academy of Child and Adolescent Psychiatry, 45,* 8–25.

Coulombe, J. A., & Reid, G. J. (2012). Agreement with night-waking strategies among community mothers of preschool-aged children. *Journal of Pediatric Psychology, 37,* 319–328.

Cousino, M. K., & Hazen, R. A. (2013). Parenting stress among caregivers of children with chronic illness: A systematic review. *Journal of Pediatric Psychology, 38,* 809–828.

Cowen, E. L. (1994). The enhancement of psychological wellness: Challenges and opportunities. *American Journal of Community Psychology, 22,* 149–179.

Cowen, R., Stasiowska, M. K., Laycock, H., & Bantel, C. (2015). Assessing pain objectively: The use of physiological markers. *Anaesthesia, 70,* 828–847.

Coy, K., Speltz, M. L., DeKlyen, M., & Jones, K. (2001). Social-cognitive processes in preschool boys with and without oppositional defiant disorder. *Journal of Abnormal Child Psychology, 29,* 107–119.

Coyne, M. D., Kame'enui, E. J., Simmons, D. C., & Harn, B. A. (2004). Beginning reading intervention as inoculation or insulin: First-grade reading performance of strong responders to kindergarten intervention. *Journal of Learning Disabilities, 37,* 90–104.

Cradock, A. L., Barrett, J. L., Kenney, E. L., Giles, C. M., Ward, Z. J., Long, M. W., et al. (2017). Using cost-effectiveness analysis to prioritize policy and programmatic approaches to physical activity promotion and obesity prevention in childhood. *Preventive Medicine, 95,* S17–S27.

Craddock, N., & Sklar, P. (2013). Genetics of bipolar disorder. *The Lancet, 381,* 1654–1662.

Craig, W., Harel-Fisch, Y., Fogel-Grinvald, H., Dostaler, S., Hetland, J., Simons-Morton, B., et al. (2009). A cross-national profile of bullying and victimization among adolescents in 40 countries. *International Journal of Public Health, 54,* S216–S224.

Crandell, J. L., Sandelowski, M., Leeman, J., Havill, N. L., & Knafl, K. (2018). Parenting behaviors and the well-being of children with a chronic physical condition. *Families, Systems, & Health, 36,* 45–61.

Craske, M. G. (2012). The R-DOC initiative: Science and practice. *Depression and Anxiety, 29,* 253–256.

Cravens, H. (1992). A scientific project locked in time: The Terman genetic studies of genius, 1920s–1950s. *American Psychologist, 47,* 183–189.

Cravens, H. (1993). *Before head start: The Iowa station and America's children.* Chapel Hill: University of North Carolina Press.

Creer, T. L. (1998). Childhood asthma. In T. H. Ollendick & M. Hersen (Eds.), *Handbook of child psychopathology* (3rd ed.). New York: Plenum Press.

Crick, N. R., & Dodge, K. A. (1994). A review and reformulation of social information-processing mechanisms in children's social adjustment. *Psychological Bulletin, 115,* 74–101.

Crick, N. R., & Grotpeter, J. K. (1995). Relational aggression, gender, and social-psychological adjustment. *Child Development, 66,* 710–722.

Crick, N. R., & Grotpeter, J. K. (1996). Children's treatment by peers: Victims of relational and overt aggression. *Development and Psychopathology, 8,* 367–380.

Crick, N. R., & Nelson, D. A. (2002). Victimization within peer relationships and friendships: Nobody told me there'd be friends like these. *Journal of Abnormal Child Psychology, 30,* 599–607.

Crick, N. R., & Zahn-Waxler, C. (2003). The development of psychopathology in females and males: Current progress and future challenges. *Development and Psychopathology, 15,* 719–742.

Crick, N. R., Casas, J. F., & Ku, H. C. (1999). Relational and physical forms of peer victimization in preschool. *Developmental Psychology, 35,* 376–385.

Crick, N. R., Casas, J. F., & Mosher, M. (1997). Relational and overt aggression in preschool. *Developmental Psychology, 33,* 579–588.

Criss, M. M., Smith, A. M., Morris, A. S., Liu, C., & Hubbard, R. L. (2017). Parents and peers as protective factors among adolescents exposed to neighborhood risk. *Journal of Applied Developmental Psychology, 53,* 127–138.

Crist, W., & Napier-Phillips, A. (2001). Mealtime behaviors of young children: A comparison of normative and clinical data. *Journal of Developmental and Behavioral Pediatrics, 22,* 279–286.

Crnic, K. A. (1988). Mental retardation. In E. J. Mash & L. G. Terdal (Eds.), *Behavioral assessment of childhood disorders: Selected core problems.* New York: Guilford.

Crnic, K. A., Neece, C. L., McIntyre, L. L., Blacher, J., & Baker, B. L. (2017). Intellectual disability and developmental risk: Promoting intervention to improve child and family well-being. *Child Development, 88,* 436–445.

Crockett, L. J., Randall, B. A., Shen, Y. L., Russell, S. T., & Driscoll, A. K. (2005). Measurement equivalence of the center for epidemiological studies depression scale for Latino and Anglo adolescents: A national study. *Journal of Consulting and Clinical Psychology, 73,* 47–58.

Cromley, J. G., Snyder-Hogan, L. E., & Luciw-Dubas, U. A. (2010). Reading comprehension of scientific text: A domain-specific test of the direct and inferential mediation model of reading comprehension. *Journal of Educational Psychology, 102,* 687–700.

Cronin, P., & Freeman, B. J. (2017). Assessment of adaptive behavior and autism spectrum disorder. In J. B. Leaf (Ed.), *Handbook of social skills and autism spectrum disorder: Assessment, curricula, and intervention.* Cham, Switzerland: Springer International Publishing AG.

Crosnoe, R., Morrison, F., Burchinal, M., Pianta, R., Keating, D., Friedman, S. L., et al. (2010). Instruction, teacher-student relations, and math achievement trajectories in elementary school. *Journal of Educational Psychology, 102,* 407–417.

Crowell, S. E., Beauchaine, T. P., & Lenzenweger, M. F. (2008). The development of borderline personality disorder and selfinjurious behavior. In T. P. Beauchaine & S. P Hinshaw (Eds.), *Child and adolescent psychopathology.* Hoboken, NJ: John Wiley & Sons.

Crowell, S. E., Beauchaine, T. P., McCauley, E., Smith, C. J., Vasilev, C. A., & Stevens, A. L. (2008). Parent-child interactions, peripheral serotonin, and self-inflicted injury in adolescents. *Journal of Consulting and Clinical Psychology, 76,* 15–21.

Cuijpers, P., Ebert, D. D., Reijnders, M., & Stikkelbroek, Y. (2017). Technology-assisted treatments for mental health problems in children and adolescents. In J. R. Weisz & A. E. Kazdin (Eds.), *Evidence-based psychotherapies for children and adolescents* (3rd ed.). New York: The Guilford Press.

Cullen, D. (2009). *Columbine.* New York: Twelve (Hachette Book Group).

Cullerton-Sen, C., Cassidy, A. R., Murray-Close, D., Cicchetti, D., Crick, N. R., & Rogosch, F. A. (2008). Childhood maltreatment and the development of relational and physical aggression: The importance of a gender-informed approach. *Child Development, 79,* 1736–1751.

Cummings, E. M., & Davies, P. T. (2010). *Marital conflict and children: An emotional security perspective.* New York: Guilford Press.

Cummings, E. M., Davies, P. T., & Campbell, S. B. (2000). *Developmental psychopathology and family process: Theory, research, and clinical implications.* New York: The Guilford Press.

Cummings, E. M., Goeke-Morey, M. C., & Papp, L. M. (2004). Everyday marital conflict and child aggression. *Journal of Abnormal Child Psychology, 32,* 191–202.

Cummings, J. R., Ji, X., Allen, L., Lally, C., & Druss, B. G. (2017). Racial and ethnic differences in ADHD treatment quality among Medicaid-enrolled youth. *Pediatrics, 139,* e20162444.

References

Curry, J. F., & Meyer, A. E. (2019). Depressive disorders. In M. J. Prinstein, E. A. Youngstrom, E. J. Mash, & R. A. Barkley (Eds.), *Treatment of disorders in childhood and adolescence* (4th ed.). New York: The Guilford Press.

Curtis, N. M., Ronan, K. R., & Borduin, C. M. (2004). Multisystemic treatment: A meta-analysis of outcome studies. *Journal of Family Psychology, 18,* 411–419.

Curtis, P. R., Frey, J. R., Watson, C. D., Hampton, L. H., & Roberts, M. Y. (2018). Language disorders and problem behaviors: A meta-analysis. *Pediatrics, 142,* e20173551.

Cuthbert, B. N. (2014). The RDoC framework: Facilitating transition from ICD/DSM to dimensional approaches that integrate neuroscience and psychopathology. *World Psychiatry, 13,* 28–35.

Cytryn, L., & McKnew, D. (1974). Factors influencing the changing clinical expression of the depressive process in children. *American Journal of Psychiatry, 131,* 879–881.

D'Mello, A. M., & Gabrieli, J. D. E. (2018). Cognitive neuroscience of dyslexia. *Language, Speech, and Hearing Services in Schools, 49,* 798–809.

D'Onofrio, B. M., Slutske, W. S., Turkheimer, E., Emery, R. E., Harden, P., Heath, A. C., et al. (2007). Intergenerational transmission of childhood conduct problems: A children of twins study. *Archives of General Psychiatry, 64,* 820–829.

Dadds, M. R., Barrett, P. M., Rapee, R. M., & Ryan, S. (1996). Family process and child anxiety and aggression: An observational analysis. *Journal of Abnormal Child Psychology, 24,* 715–734.

Dadds, M. R., Holland, D. E., Laurens, K. R., Mullins, M., Barrett, P M., & Spence, S. H. (1999). Early intervention and prevention of anxiety disorders in children: Results at 2-year follow-up. *Journal of Consulting and Clinical Psychology, 67,* 145–150.

Dadds, M. R., Sanders, M. R., Morrison, M., & Rebgetz, M. (1992). Childhood depression and conduct disorder: II. An analysis of family interaction patterns in the home. *Journal of Abnormal Psychology, 101,* 505–513.

Dahl, R. E., & Harvey, A. G. (2008). Sleep disorders. In M. Rutter et al. (Eds.), *Rutter's child and adolescent psychiatry* (5th ed.). Malden, MA: Blackwell Publishing.

Dahlenburg, S. C., Gleaves, D. H., & Hutchinson, A. D. (2019). Anorexia nervosa and perfectionism: A meta-analysis. *International Journal of Eating Disorders, 52,* 219–229.

Dalhuisen, L., Koenraadt, F., & Liem, M. (2017). Subtypes of firesetters. *Criminal Behaviour and Mental Health, 27,* 59–75.

Daly, E., Tricklebank, M. D., & Wichers, R. (2019). Neurodevelopmental roles and the serotonin hypothesis of autism spectrum disorder. In M. D. Tricklebank & E. Daly (Eds.), *The serotonin system.* London: Academic Press.

Damashek, A., Morgan, E. C., Corlis, M., & Richardson, H. (2018). Primary and secondary prevention of child maltreatment. In J. N. Butcher & P. C. Kendall (Eds.), *APA handbook of psychopathology* (Vol. 2). Washington, DC: American Psychological Association.

Danckaerts, M., & Coghill, D. (2018). Children and adolescents: Assessment in everyday clinical practice. In T. Banaschewski, D. Coghill, & A. Zuddas (Eds.), *Oxford textbook of attention deficit hyperactivity disorder.* Oxford: Oxford University Press.

Dane, A. V., Schachar, R. J., & Tannock, R. (2000). Does actigraphy differentiate ADHD subtypes in a clinical research setting? *Journal of the American Academy of Child & Adolescent Psychiatry, 39,* 752–760.

Danforth, J. S., Connor, D. F., & Doerfler, L. A. (2014). The development of comorbid conduct problems in children with ADHD: An example of an integrative developmental psychopathology perspective. *Journal of Attention Disorders, 20,* 214–229.

Danielson, C. K., Youngstrom, E. A., Findling, R. L., & Calabrese, J. R. (2003). Discriminative validity of the General Behavior Inventory using youth report. *Journal of Abnormal Child Psychology, 31,* 29–39.

Danielson, M. L., Bitsko, R. H., Ghandour, R. M., Holbrook, J. R., Kogan, M. D., & Blumberg, S. J. (2018). Prevalence of parent-reported ADHD diagnosis and associated treatment among U.S. children and adolescents, 2016. *Journal of Clinical Child & Adolescent Psychology, 47,* 199–212.

Danner, S., Fristad, M. A., Arnold, L. E., Youngstrom, E. A., Birhamer, B., Horwitz, S. M., et al., & The LAMS Group (2009). Early-onset bipolar spectrum disorders: Diagnostic issues. *Clinical Child and Family Psychology Review, 12,* 271–293.

Danzi, B. A., & La Greca, A. M. (2017). Optimizing clinical thresholds for PTSD: Extending the DSM-5 preschool criteria to school-age children. *International Journal of Clinical and Health Psychology, 17,* 234–241.

Dauvilliers, Y., Maret, S., & Tafti, M. (2005). Genetics of normal and pathological sleep in humans. *Sleep Medicine Review, 9,* 91–100.

David, C. N., Greenstein, D., Clasen, L., Gochman, P., Miller, R., Tossell, J. W., et al. (2011). Childhood onset schizophrenia: High rate of visual hallucinations. *Journal of the American Academy of Child & Adolescent Psychiatry, 50,* 681–686. e683.

David-Ferdon, C., & Kaslow, N. J. (2008). Evidence-based psychosocial treatments for child and adolescent depression. *Journal of Clinical Child and Adolescent Psychology, 37,* 62–104.

Davidson, M. (2017). Vaccination as a cause of autism-myths and controversies. *Dialogues in Clinical Neuroscience, 19,* 403–407.

Davies, P. T., & Cummings, E. M. (2006). Interparental discord, family process, and developmental psychopathology. In D. Cicchetti & D. J. Cohen (Eds.), *Developmental psychopathology, Vol. 3: Risk, disorder, and adaptation* (2nd ed.). Hoboken, NJ: John Wiley & Sons, Inc.

Davis, C. L., Delamater, A. M., Shaw, K. H., La Greca, A. M., Edison, M. S., Perez-Rodriguez, J. E., & Nemery, R. (2001). Parenting styles, regimen adherence, and glycemic control in 4- to 10-year-old children with diabetes. *Journal of Pediatric Psychology, 26,* 123–129.

Davis, K. L., Stewart, D. G., Friedman, J. I., Buchsman, M., Harvey, P. D., Hof, P. R., et al. (2003). White matter changes in schizophrenia. *Archives of General Psychiatry, 60,* 443–456.

Davis, O. S., Band, G., Pirinen, M., Haworth, C. M., Meaburn, E. L., Kovas, Y., et al. (2014). The correlation between reading and mathematics ability at age twelve has a substantial genetic component. *Nature Communications, 5,* 4204.

Dawson, G., D'Souza, S., Moreau, D., & Waldie, K. (2015). Behavioral interventions to remediate learning disorders: A technical report. The University of Aukland. Retrieved from https://nzla. org.nz/wp-content/uploads/2018/06/Report.pdf#page=46

Dawson, G., Rogers, S., Munson, J., Smith, M., Winter, J., Greenson, J., et al. (2010). Randomized, controlled trial of an intervention for toddlers with autism: The Early Start Denver Model. *Pediatrics, 125,* e17–e23.

De Bellis, M. D. (2001). Developmental traumatology: The psychobiological development of maltreated children and its implications for research, treatment, and policy. *Development and Psychopathology, 13,* 539–564.

De Bellis, M. D., & Van Dillen, T. (2005). Childhood posttraumatic stress disorder: An overview. *Child and Adolescent Psychiatric Clinics of North America, 14,* 745–772.

de Boer, A., & Pijl, S. J. (2016). The acceptance and rejection of peers with ADHD and ASD in general secondary education. *The Journal of Educational Research, 109,* 325–332.

de Boo, G. M., & Prins, P. J. M. (2007). Social incompetence in children with ADHD: Possible moderators and mediators in social-skills training. *Clinical Psychology Review, 27,* 78–97.

De Bourdeaudhuij, I., Van Cauwenberghe, E., Spittaels, H., Oppert, J. M., Rostami, C., Brug, J., et al. (2011). School-based interventions promoting both physical activity and healthy eating in Europe: A systematic review within the HOPE project. *Obesity Reviews, 12,* 205–216.

de Bruin, E. J., Bögels, S. M., Oort, F. J., & Meijer, A. M. (2018). Improvements of adolescent psychopathology after insomnia treatment: Results from a randomized controlled trial over 1 year. *Journal of Child Psychology and Psychiatry, 59,* 509–522.

de Castro, B., Slot, N. W., Bosch, J. D., Koops, W., & Weerman, J. W. (2003). Negative feelings exacerbate hostile attributions of intent in highly aggressive boys. *Journal of Clinical Child and Adolescent Psychology, 32,* 56–65.

De Los Reyes, A., & Langer, D. A. (2018). Assessment and the *Journal of Clinical Child and Adolescent Psychology*'s evidence base updates series: Evaluating tools for gathering evidence. *Journal of Clinical Child and Adolescent Psychology, 47,* 357–365.

De Los Reyes, A., Augenstein, T. M., & Lipton, M. F. (2019). Developmental issues in assessment and treatment. In T. H. Ollendick, S. W. White, & B. A. White (Eds.), *The Oxford handbook of clinical child and adolescent psychology.* New York: Oxford University Press.

De Los Reyes, A., Augenstein, T. M., Wang, M., Thomas, S. A., Drabick, D. A., Burgers, D. E., & Rabinowitz, J. (2015). The validity of the multi-informant approach to assessing child and adolescent mental health. *Psychological Bulletin, 141,* 858–900.

De Los Reyes, A., Drabick, D. A. G., Makol, B. A., & Jakubovic, R. J. (2020). Introduction to the special section: The Research Domain Criteria's units of analysis and cross-unit correspondence in youth mental health research, *Journal of Clinical Child & Adolescent Psychology, 49,* 279–296.

De Meyer, H., Beckers, T., Tripp, G., & van der Oord, S. (2019). Reinforcement contingency learning in children with ADHD: Back to the basics of behavior therapy. *Journal of Abnormal Child Psychology, 47,* 1889–1902.

de Ruiter, K. P., Dekker, M. C., Verhulse, F. C., & Koot, H. M. (2007). Developmental course of psychopathology in youths with and without intellectual disabilities. *Journal of Child Psychology and Psychiatry, 48,* 498–507.

De Smedt, B., Peters, L., & Ghesquière, P. (2019). Neurobiological origins of mathematical learning disabilities or dyscalculia: A review of brain imaging data. In A. Fritz, V. G. Haase, & P. Rasanen (Eds.), *International handbook of mathematical learning difficulties.* Cham, Switzerland: Springer.

De Young, A. C., Kenardy, J. A., & Cobham, V. E. (2011). Diagnosis of posttraumatic stress disorder in preschool children. *Journal of Clinical Child and Adolescent Psychology, 40,* 375–384.

de Zeeuw, P., Zwart, F., Schrama, R., van Engeland, H., & Durston, S. (2012). Prenatal exposure to cigarette smoke or alcohol and cerebellum volume in attention-deficit/hyperactivity disorder and typical development. *Translational Psychiatry, 2,* e84.

Dean, V. J., & Burns, M. K. (2002). Inclusion of intrinsic processing difficulties in LD diagnostic models: A critical review. *Learning Disability Quarterly, 25,* 170–176.

Deane, K., Richards, M., Mozley, M., Scott, D., Rice, C., & Garbarino, J. (2018). Posttraumatic stress, family functioning, and externalizing in adolescents exposed to violence: A moderated mediation model. *Journal of Clinical Child & Adolescent Psychology, 47*(sup1), S176–S189.

DeAngelis, T. (2020). Raising our voices on gun violence. *Monitor on Psychology, 51,* 40–43.

Deater-Deckard, K. (2001). Recent research examining the role of peer relationships in the development of psychopathology. *Journal of Child Psychology and Psychiatry, 42,* 565–579.

Deater-Deckard, K., Dodge, K. A., & Sorbring, E. (2005). Cultural differences in the effects of physical punishment. In M.

Rutter & M. Tienda (Eds.), *Ethnicity and causal mechanisms*. New York: Cambridge University Press.

Deb, S., Unwin, G., & Deb, T. (2015). Characteristics and the trajectory of psychotropic medication use in general and antipsychotics in particular among adults with an intellectual disability who exhibit aggressive behaviour. *Journal of Intellectual Disability Research, 59*, 11–25.

Decker, S. L., Bridges, R. M., & Vetter, T. (2018). Cognitive neuroscientific contributions to theoretical understanding of SLD. In V. C. Alfonso & D. P. Flanagan (Eds.), *Essentials of specific learning disability identification*. Hoboken, NJ: John Wiley & Sons.

Deeks, S. G., Lewin, S. R., & Havlir, D. V. (2013). The end of AIDS: HIV infection as a chronic disease. *The Lancet, 382*(9903), 1525–1533.

Degnan, K., & Fox, N. (2007). Behavioral inhibition and anxiety disorders: Multiple levels of resilience process. *Development and Psychopathology, 19*, 729–746.

Degnan, K. A., Almas, A. N., & Fox, N. A. (2010). Temperament and the environment in the etiology of childhood anxiety. *Journal of Child Psychology and Psychiatry, 51*, 497–517.

Dekovic, M., & Janssens, A. M. (1992). Parents' child-rearing style and child's sociometric status. *Developmental Psychology, 28*, 925–932.

Delamater, A. M., Bubb, J., Davis, S. G., Smith, J. A., Schmidt, L., White, N. H., & Santiago, J. V. (1990). Randomized prospective study of self-management training with newly diagnosed diabetic children. *Diabetes Care, 13*, 492–498.

Demontis, D., Walters, R. K., Martin, J., Mattheisen, M., Als, T. D., Agerbo, E., et al. (2019). Discovery of the first genome-wide significant risk loci for attention deficit/hyperactivity disorder. *Nature Genetics, 51*, 63–75.

Demos, J., & Demos, V. (1972). Adolescence in historical perspective. In D. Rogers (Ed.), *Issues in adolescent psychology*. Englewood Cliffs, NJ: Prentice-Hall.

Denckla, M. B. (2018). *Understanding learning and related disabilities: Inconvenient brains*. New York: Routledge.

Denham, S. A., Caverly, S., Schmidt, M., Blair, K., DeMulder, E., Caal, S., et al. (2002). Preschool understanding of emotions: Contributions to classroom anger and aggression. *Journal of Child Psychology and Psychiatry, 43*, 901–916.

Dennis, M., Francis, D. J., Cirino, P. T., Schachar, R., Barnes, M. A., & Fletcher, J. M. (2009). Why IQ is not a covariate in cognitive studies of neurodevelopmental disorders. *Journal of International Neuropsychology Society, 15*, 331–343.

Denov, M., Fennig, M., Rabiau, M. A., & Shevell, M. C. (2019). Intergenerational resilience in families affected by war, displacement, and migration: "It runs in the family". *Journal of Family Social Work, 22*, 17–45.

Deprey, L., & Ozonoff, S. (2018). Assessment of comorbid psychiatric conditions in autism spectrum disorder. In S.

Goldstein & S. Ozonoff (Eds.), *Assessment of autism spectrum disorder* (2nd ed.). New York: Guilford Press.

Dere, J., Watters, C. A., Yu, S. C.-M., Bagby, R. M., Ryder, A. G., & Harkness, K. L. (2015). Cross-cultural examination of measurement invariance of the Beck Depression Inventory–II. *Psychological Assessment, 27*, 68–81.

Derella, O. J., Burke, J. D., Stepp, S. D., & Hipwell, A. E. (2020). Reciprocity in undesirable parent–child behavior? Verbal aggression, corporal punishment, and girls' oppositional defiant symptoms. *Journal of Clinical Child & Adolescent Psychology, 49*, 420–433.

Dessemontet, R. S., Bless, G., & Morin, D. (2012). Effects of inclusion on the academic achievement and adaptive behaviour of children with intellectual disabilities. *Journal of Intellectual Disability Research, 56*, 579–587.

DeThorne, L. S., Hart, S. A., Deater-Deckard, K., Thompson, L. A., Schatschneider, C., & Davison, M. D. (2006). Children's history of speech-language difficulties: Genetic influences and associations with reading-related measures. *Journal of Speech, Language, and Hearing Research, 49*, 1280–1293.

Detterman, D. K., & Thompson, L. A. (1997). What is so special about special education? *American Psychologist, 52*, 1082–1090.

Deutsch, A. R., Crockett, L. J., Wolff, J. M., & Russell, S. T. (2012). Parent and peer pathways to adolescent delinquency: Variations by ethnicity and neighborhood context. *Journal of Youth and Adolescence, 41*, 1078–1094.

Devlantis, K. S., Dawson, G., & Rogers, S. (2017). Treating autism spectrum disorder with the Early Start Denver Model. In J. R. Weisz & A. E. Kazdin (Eds.), *Evidence-based psychotherapies for children and adolescents*. New York: The Guilford Press.

Devnani, P. A., & Hegde, A. U. (2015). Autism and sleep disorders. *Journal of Pediatric Neurosciences, 10*, 304–307.

Di Maggio, R., Zappulla, C., & Pace, U. (2016). The relationship between emotion knowledge, emotion regulation and adjustment in preschoolers: A mediation model. *Journal of Child and Family Studies, 25*, 2626–2635.

Diamond, A. (2005). Attention-deficit disorder (attention-deficit/hyperactivity disorder without hyperactivity): A neurobiologically and behaviorally distinct disorder from attention-deficit/hyperactivity disorder (with hyperactivity). *Development and Psychopathology, 17*, 807–825.

Díaz-Caneja, C. M., Pina-Camacho, L., Rodríguez-Quiroga, A., Fraguas, D., Parellada, M., & Arango, C. (2015). Predictors of outcome in early-onset psychosis: A systematic review. *NPJ Schizophrenia, 1*, 14005.

DiBartolo, P. M., Albano, A. M., Barlow, D. H., & Heimberg, R. G. (1998). Cross-informant agreement in the assessment of social phobia in youth. *Journal of Abnormal Child Psychology, 26*, 213–220.

Dichter, G. S. (2012). Functional magnetic resonance imaging of autism spectrum disorders. *Dialogues in Clinical Neuroscience, 14,* 319–351.

Dickstein, S. G., Bannon, K., Castellanos, F. X., & Milham, M. P. (2006). The neural correlates of attention deficit hyperactivity disorder: An ALE meta-analysis. *Journal of Child Psychology and Psychiatry, 47,* 1051–1062.

Dietz, L. J., Silk, J., & Amole, M. (2019). Depressive disorders. In T. H. Ollendick, S. W. White, & B. A. White (Eds.), *The Oxford handbook of clinical child and adolescent psychology.* New York: Oxford University Press.

Diler, R. S., Birmaher, B., & Miklowitz, D. J. (2010). Clinical presentation and longitudinal course of bipolar spectrum disorders in children and adolescents. In D. J. Miklowitz & D. Cicchetti (Eds.), *Understanding bipolar disorder: A developmental psychopathology perspective.* New York: The Guilford Press.

DiLillo, D., & Tremblay, G. C. (2005). Lizette Peterson: A collaboration of passion and science. *Journal of Pediatric Psychology, 30,* 533–535.

Dinaj-Koci, V., Wang, B., Naar-King, S., & MacDonell, K. K. (2019). A multi-site study of social cognitive factors related to adherence among youth living with HIV in the new era of antiretroviral medication. *Journal of Pediatric Psychology, 44,* 98–109.

Dishion, T. J., & Dodge, K. A. (2005). Peer contagion in interventions for children and adolescents: Moving towards an understanding of the ecology and dynamics of change. *Journal of Abnormal Child Psychology, 33,* 395–400.

Dishion, T. J., & Kavanagh, K. A. (2002). The adolescent transitions program: A family-centered prevention strategy for schools. In J. B. Reid, G. R. Patterson, & J. Snyder (Eds.), *Antisocial behavior in children and adolescents: A developmental analysis and model for intervention.* Washington, DC: American Psychological Association.

Dishion, T. J., & Owen, L. D. (2002). A longitudinal analysis of friendships and substance use: Bidirectional influence from adolescence into adulthood. *Developmental Psychology, 28,* 480–491.

Dishion, T. J., & Patterson, G. R. (2006). The development and ecology of antisocial behavior in children and adolescents. In D. Cicchetti & D. J. Cohen (Eds.), *Developmental psychopathology, Vol. 3: Risk, disorder, and adaptation* (2nd ed.). Hoboken, NJ: John Wiley & Sons.

Dishion, T. J., & Patterson, G. R. (2016). The development and ecology of antisocial behavior: Linking etiology, prevention, and treatment. In D. Cicchetti (Ed.), *Developmental psychopathology: Risk, resilience, and intervention* (3rd ed., Vol. 3). Hoboken, NJ: John Wiley & Sons.

Dishion, T. J., & Stormshak, E. A. (2007). *Intervening in children's lives: An ecological, family-centered approach to mental health care.* Washington, DC: American Psychological Association.

Dishion, T. J., Brennan, L. M., Shaw, D. S., McEachern, A. D., Wilson, M. N., & Jo, B. (2014). Prevention of problem behavior through annual family check-ups in early childhood: Intervention effects from home to early elementary school. *Journal of Abnormal Child Psychology, 42,* 343–354.

Dishion, T. J., French, D. C., & Patterson, G. R. (1995). The development and ecology of antisocial behavior. In D. Cicchetti & D. J. Cohen (Eds.), *Developmental psychopathology, Vol. 2: Risk, disorder and adaptation.* New York: John Wiley & Sons.

Dishion, T. J., Kim, H., & Tein, J.-Y. (2016). Friendship and adolescent problem behavior: Deviancy training and coercive joining as dynamic mediators. In T. P. Beauchaine & S. P. Hinshaw (Eds.), *The Oxford handbook of externalizing spectrum disorders.* New York: Oxford University Press.

Dishion, T. J., Shaw, D., Connell, A., Gardner, F., Weaver, C., & Wilson, M. (2008). The family check-up with high-risk indigent families: Preventing problem behavior by increasing parents' positive behavior support in early childhood. *Child Development, 79,* 1395–1414.

Dishion, T., Forgatch, M., Chamberlain, P., & Pelham III, W. E. (2016). The Oregon model of behavior family therapy: From intervention design to promoting large-scale system change. *Behavior Therapy, 47,* 812–837.

Dittmar, H., Halliwell, E., & Ive, S. (2006). Does Barbie make girls want to be thin? The effect of experimental exposure to images of dolls on the body image of 5- to 8-year-old girls. *Developmental Psychology, 42,* 283–292.

Dix, T., Stewart, A. D., Gershoff, E. T., & Day, W. H. (2007). Autonomy and children's reactions to being controlled: Evidence that both compliance and defiance may be positive markers in early development. *Child Development, 78,* 1204–1221.

Docherty, N. M., St-Hilaire, A., Aakre, J. M., & Seghers, J. P. (2008). Life events and high-trait reactivity together predict psychotic symptom increase in schizophrenia. *Schizophrenia Bulletin, 35,* 638–645.

Docherty, S. J., Davis, O. S. P., Kovas, Y., Meaburn, E. L., Dale, P. S., Petrill, S. A., et al. (2010). A genome-wide association study identifies multiple loci associated with mathematics ability and disability. *Genes, Brain and Behavior, 9,* 234–247.

Dockrell, J., & Joye, N. (2018). Communication disorders: Neurodevelopmental considerations. In T. H. Ollendick, S. W. White, B. A. White, J. Dockrell, & N. Joye (Eds.), *The Oxford handbook of clinical child and adolescent psychology.* Oxford: Oxford University Press.

Dodd, B., Reilly, S., Ttofari Eecen, K., & Morgan, A. T. (2018). Articulation or phonology? Evidence from longitudinal error data. *Clinical Linguistics & Phonetics, 32,* 1027–1041.

Dodge, K. A. (1991). The structure and function of reactive and proactive aggression. In D. Pepler & K. Rubin (Eds.), *The*

References

development and treatment of childhood aggression. Hillsdale, NJ: Erlbaum.

Dodge, K. A. (2000). Conduct disorder. In A. J. Sameroff, M. Lewis, & S. M. Miller (Eds.), *Handbook of developmental psychopathology* (2nd ed.). New York: Kluwer Academic/Plenum Publishers.

Dodge, K. A. (2003). Do social information-processing patterns mediate aggressive behavior? In B. B. Lahey, T. E. Moffitt, & A. Caspi (Eds.), *Causes of conduct disorder and juvenile delinquency.* New York: Guilford Press.

Dodge, K. A. (2020). Universal and targeted strategies for assigning interventions to achieve population impact. *Journal of Child Psychology and Psychiatry, 61,* 255–267.

Dodge, K. A., & Rabiner, D. L. (2004). Returning to roots: On social information processing and moral development. *Child Development, 75,* 1003–1008.

Dodge, K. A., Bierman, K. L., Coie, J. D., Greenberg, M. T., Lochman, J. E., McMahon, R. J., et al. (2015a). Impact of early intervention on psychopathology, crime, and well-being at age 25. *American Journal of Psychiatry, 172,* 59–70.

Dodge, K. A., Malone, P. S., Lansford, J. E., Sorbring, E., Skinner, A. T., Tapanya, S., et al. (2015b). Hostile attributional bias and aggressive behavior in global context. *Proceedings of the National Academy of Sciences, 112,* 9310–9315.

Dohnt, H., & Tiggemann, M. (2006). The contribution of peer and media influences on the development of body satisfaction and self-esteem in young girls: A prospective study. *Developmental Psychology, 42,* 929–936.

Doidge, J. C., Higgins, D. J., Delfabbro, P., & Segal, L. (2017). Risk factors for child maltreatment in an Australian population-based birth cohort. *Child Abuse & Neglect, 64,* 47–60.

Dokken, D., Parent, K., & Ahmann, E. (2015). Family presence and participation: Pediatrics leading the way ... and still evolving. *Pediatric Nursing, 41,* 204–206.

Dolgin, M. J., Phipps, S., Fairclough, D. L., Sahler, O. J. Z., Askins, M., Noll, R. B., et al. (2007). Trajectories of adjustment in mothers of children with newly diagnosed cancer: A natural history investigation. *Journal of Pediatric Psychology, 32,* 771–782.

Dollar, J. M., & Calkins, S. D. (2019). Developmental psychology. In T. H. Ollendick, S. W. White, & B. A. White (Eds.), *The Oxford handbook of clinical child and adolescent psychology.* New York: Oxford University Press.

Dominus, S. (2011). The denunciation of Dr. Wakefield. *New York Times Magazine,* April 24, pp. 36–39, 50–52.

Donnelly, L., McLanahan, S., Brooks-Gunn, J., Garfinkel, I., Wagner, B. G., Jacobsen, W. C., et al. (2016). Cohesive neighborhoods where social expectations are shared may have positive impact on adolescent mental health. *Health Affairs, 35,* 2083–2091.

Donovan, C. L., & Spence, S. H. (2000). Prevention of childhood anxiety disorders. *Clinical Psychology Review, 20,* 509–531.

Dore, M. M., & Mullin, D. (2006). Treatment foster care: Its history and current role in the foster care continuum. *Families in Society, 87,* 475–482.

Dorsey, S., McLaughlin, K. A., Kerns, S. E., Harrison, J. P., Lambert, H. K., Briggs, E. C., et al. (2017). Evidence base update for psychosocial treatments for children and adolescents exposed to traumatic events. *Journal of Clinical Child & Adolescent Psychology, 46,* 303–330.

Dougherty, L. R., Klein, D. N., & Olino, T. M. (2018). Depression in children and adolescents. In J. Hunsley & E. J. Mash (Eds.), *A guide to assessments that work* (2nd ed.). New York: Oxford University Press.

Dougherty, L. R., Klein, D. N., Durbin, C. E., Hayden, E. P., & Olino, T. M. (2010). Temperamental positive and negative emotionality and children's depressive symptoms: A longitudinal prospective study from age three to age ten. *Journal of Social and Clinical Psychology, 29,* 462–488.

Dowdney, L. (2000). Childhood bereavement following parental death. *Journal of Child Psychology and Psychiatry, 41,* 819–830.

Dowell, K. A., & Ogles, B. M. (2010). The effects of parent participation on child psychotherapy outcomes: A meta-analytic review. *Journal of Child and Adolescent Psychology, 39,* 151–162.

Dowell, T., Martin, P. R., & Waters, A. M. (2017). Headache and migraine. In J. L. Matson (Ed.), *Handbook of childhood psychopathology and developmental disabilities treatment.* Cham, Switzerland: Springer.

Doyle, K. W., Wolchik, S. A., Dawson-McClure, S. R., & Sandler, I. N. (2003). Positive events as a stress buffer for children and adolescents in families in transition. *Journal of Clinical Child and Adolescent Psychology, 32,* 536–545.

Doyle, L. R., & Mattson, S. N. (2019). Behavioral teratogenic effects of alcohol: Focus on neurobehavioral disorder associated with prenatal alcohol exposure. In T. H. Ollendick, S. W. White, & B. A. White (Eds.), *The Oxford handbook of clinical child and adolescent psychology.* New York: Oxford University Press.

Doyle, L. R., Crocker, N. A., Fryer, S. L., & Mattson, S. N. (2017). Exposure to teratogens as a risk factor for psychopathology. In T. P. Beauchaine & S. P. Hinshaw (Eds.), *Child and adolescent psychopathology* (3rd ed.). Hoboken, NJ: John Wiley & Sons Inc.

Drake, K. L., & Ginsburg, G. S. (2012). Family factors in the development, treatment, and prevention of childhood anxiety disorders. *Clinical Child and Family Psychology Review, 15,* 144–162.

Driver, D. I., Gogtay, N., & Rapoport, J. L. (2013). Childhood onset schizophrenia and early onset schizophrenia spectrum disorders. *Child and Adolescent Psychiatric Clinics, 22,* 539–555.

Driver, D. I., Thomas, S., Gogtay, N., & Rapoport, J. L. (2020). Childhood-onset schizophrenia and early-onset schizophrenia spectrum disorders: An update. *Child and Adolescent Psychiatric Clinics, 29,* 71–90.

Drotar, D. (2006). *Psychological interventions in childhood chronic illness.* Washington, DC: American Psychological Association.

Drotar, D., & Robinson, J. (2000). Developmental psychopathology of failure to thrive. In A. J. Sameroff, M. Lewis, & S. M. Miller (Eds.), *Handbook of developmental psychopathology* (2nd ed.). New York: Kluwer Academic/Plenum Publishers.

Dryer, R., Farr, M., Hiramatsu, I., & Quinton, S. (2016). The role of sociocultural influences on symptoms of muscle dysmorphia and eating disorders in men, and the mediating effects of perfectionism. *Behavioral Medicine, 42,* 174–182.

Duarte, A. M., & Baer, D. M. (2019). Overselectivity in the naming of suddenly and gradually constructed faces. In D. M. Baer & E. M. Pinkston (Eds.), *Environment and Behavior.* New York: Routledge.

Dube, W. V., Farber, R. S., Mueller, M. R., Grant, E., Lorin, L., & Deutsch, C. K. (2016). Stimulus overselectivity in autism, Down syndrome, and typical development. *American Journal on Intellectual and Developmental Disabilities, 121,* 219–235.

Dubowitz, H. (2014). The Safe Environment for Every Kid (SEEK) model: Helping promote children's health, development, and safety:. *Child Abuse and Neglect, 38,* 1725–1733.

Dudeney, J., Sharpe, L., Jaffe, A., Jones, E. B., & Hunt, C. (2017). Anxiety in youth with asthma: A meta-analysis. *Pediatric Pulmonology, 52,* 1121–1129.

Duff, D., Tomblin, J. B., & Catts, H. (2015). The influence of reading on vocabulary growth: A case for a Matthew effect. *Journal of Speech, Language, and Hearing Research, 58,* 853–864.

Duff, F. J., & Clarke, P. J. (2011). Practitioner review: Reading disorders: What are the effective interventions and how should they be implemented and evaluated? *Journal of Child Psychology and Psychiatry, 52,* 3–12.

Dumas, J. E., & Lechowicz, J. G. (1989). When do noncompliant children comply? Implications for family behavior therapy. *Child and Family Behavior Therapy, 11,* 21–38.

Duncan, G. J., & Brooks-Gunn, J. (2000). Family poverty, welfare reform, and child development. *Child Development, 71,* 188–196.

Duncan, L., Comeau, J., Wang, L., Vitoroulis, I., Boyle, M. H., & Bennett, K. (2019). Test–retest reliability of standardized diagnostic interviews to assess child and adolescent psychiatric disorders: A systematic review and meta-analysis. *Journal of Child Psychology and Psychiatry, 60,* 16–29.

DuPaul, G. J., & Langberg, J. M. (2015). Educational impairments in children with ADHD. In R. A. Barkley (Ed.), *Attention-deficit hyperactivity disorder: A handbook for diagnosis and treatment* (4th ed.). New York: Guilford Press.

DuPaul, G. J., & Stoner, G. (2014). *ADHD in the schools: Assessment and intervention strategies* (3rd ed.). New York: The Guilford Press.

DuPaul, G. J., Anastopoulos, A. D., & Kipperman, K. (2020). Assessing and diagnosing ADHD in adolescence. In S. P. Becker (Ed.), *ADHD in adolescents: Developmental, assessment, and treatment.* New York: The Guilford Press.

DuPaul, G. J., Evans, S. W., Mautone, J. A., Owens, J. S., & Power, T. J. (2020). Future directions for psychosocial interventions for children and adolescents with ADHD. *Journal of Clinical Child & Adolescent Psychology, 49,* 134–145.

DuPaul, G. J., Gormley, M. J., & Laracy, S. D. (2013). Comorbidity of LD and ADHD: Implications of DSM-5 for assessment and treatment. *Journal of Learning Disabilities, 46,* 43–51.

DuPaul, G. J., Kern, L., Belk, G., Custer, B., Hatfield, A., Daffner, M., & Peek, D. (2018). Promoting parent engagement in behavioral intervention for young children with ADHD: Iterative treatment development. *Topics in Early Childhood Special Education, 38,* 42–53.

DuPaul, G. J., Morgan, P. L., Farkas, G., Hillemeier, M. M., & Maczuga, S. (2016). Academic and social functioning associated with attention-deficit/hyperactivity disorder: Latent class analyses of trajectories from kindergarten to fifth grade. *Journal of Abnormal Child Psychology, 44,* 1425–1438.

DuPaul, G. J., Pinho, T. D., Pollack, B. L., Gormley, M. J., & Laracy, S. D. (2015). First-year college students with ADHD and/or LD: differences in engagement, positive core self-evaluation, school preparation, and college expectations. *Journal of Learning Disabilities, 50,* 238–251.

Durand, V. M. (1999). Functional communication training using assistive devices: Recruiting natural communities of reinforcement. *Journal of Applied Behavior Analysis, 32,* 247–267.

Durkin, M. S., Maenner, M. J., Baio, J., Christensen, D. L., Daniels, J., Fitzgerald, R., et al. (2017). Autism spectrum disorder among US children (2002–2010): Socioeconomic, racial, and ethnic disparities. *American Journal of Public Health, 107,* 1818–1826.

Durlak, J. A., & Wells, A. M. (1997). Primary prevention mental health programs for children and adolescents: A metaanalytic review. *American Journal of Community Psychology, 25,* 115–152.

Durlak, J. A., Weissberg, R. P., Dymnicki, A. B., Taylor, R. D., & Schellinger, K. B. (2011). The impact of enhancing students' social and emotional learning: A meta-analysis of school-based universal intervention. *Child Development, 821,* 405–432.

Dweck, C. S., & Molden, D. C. (2017). Their impact on competence motivation and acquisition. In A. J. Elliot, C. S. Dweck, & D.

References

S. Yeager (Eds.), *Handbook of competence and motivation: Theory and application*. New York: The Guilford Press.

Dworzynski, K., Ronald, A., Bolton, P., & Happé, F. (2012). How different are girls and boys above and below the diagnostic threshold for autism spectrum disorders? *Journal of the American Academy of Child & Adolescent Psychiatry, 51,* 788–797.

Dyke, P., Mulroy, S., & Leonard, H. (2009). Siblings of children with disabilities: Challenges and opportunities. *Acta Paediatrica, 98,* 23–24.

Dykens, E. M., Roof, E., Hunt-Hawkins, H., Daniell, C., & Jurgensmeyer, S. (2019). Profiles and trajectories of impaired social cognition in people with Prader-Willi syndrome. *PLoS One, 14,* e0223162.

Easter, G., Sharpe, L., & Hunt, C. J. (2015). Systematic review and meta-analysis of anxious and depressive symptoms in caregivers of children with asthma. *Journal of Pediatric Psychology, 40,* 623–632.

Eaves, L. J., Silberg, J. L., Meyer, J. M., Maes, H. H., Simonoff, E., Pickles, A., et al. (1997). Genetics and developmental psychopathology: 2. The main effects of genes and environment on behavioral problems in the Virginia Twin Study of Adolescent Behavioral Development. *Journal of Child Psychology and Psychiatry, 38,* 965–980.

Eckard, A. R., Rosebush, J. C., O'Riordan, M. A., Graves, C. C., Alexander, A., Grover, A. K., et al. (2017). Neurocognitive dysfunction in HIV-infected youth: Investigating the relationship with immune activation. *Antiviral Therapy, 22,* 669–680.

Ecker, C. (2017). The neuroanatomy of autism spectrum disorder: An overview of structural neuroimaging findings and their translatability to the clinical setting. *Autism, 21,* 18–28.

Eckert, M. A., Berninger, V. W., Vaden, K. I., Jr., Gebregziabher, M., & Tsu, L. (2016). Gray matter features of reading disability: A combined meta-analytic and direct analysis approach. *eNeuro, 3.*

Eckshtain, D., Kuppens, S., Ugueto, A., Ng, M. Y., Vaughn-Coaxum, R., Corteselli, K., & Weisz, J. R. (2020). Meta-analysis: 13-year follow-up of psychotherapy effects on youth depression. *Journal of the American Academy of Child & Adolescent Psychiatry, 59,* 45–63.

Eddy, K. T., & Thomas, J. J. (2019). Introduction to a special issue on child and adolescent feeding and eating disorders and avoidant/restrictive food intake disorder. *International Journal of Eating Disorders, 52,* 327–330.

Eddy, K. T., Keel, P. K., & Leon, G. R. (2010). Vulnerability to eating disorders in childhood and adolescence. In R. E. Ingram & J. M. Price (Eds.), *Vulnerability to psychopathology: Risk across the lifespan* (2nd ed.). New York: The Guilford Press.

Egan, S. K., & Perry, D. G. (2001). Gender identity: A multidimensional analysis with implications for psychosocial adjustment. *Developmental Psychology, 37,* 451–463.

Egeland, J. A., Hostetter, A. M., Pauls, D. L., & Sussex, J. N. (2000). Prodromal symptoms before onset of manic-depressive disorder suggested by first hospital admission histories. *Journal of the American Academy of Child and Adolescent Psychiatry, 39,* 1245–1252.

Egger, H. L., & Emde, R. N. (2011). Developmentally sensitive diagnostic criteria for mental health disorders in early childhood: The diagnostic and statistical manual of mental disorders-IV, the research diagnostic criteria—preschool age, and the Diagnostic Classification of Mental Health and Mental Disorders of Infancy and Early Childhood-Revised. *American Psychologist, 66,* 95–106.

Ehrlich, K. B., Miller, G. E., & Chen, E. (2016). Childhood adversity and adult physical health. In D. Cicchetti (Ed.), *Developmental psychopathology: Risk, resilience, and intervention* (Vol. 4). Hoboken, NJ: John Wiley & Sons.

Eichelsheim, V. I., Buist, K. L., Dekovic, M., Wissink, I. B., Frijns, T., van Lier, P. A. C., et al. (2010). Associations among the parent-adolescent relationship, aggression and delinquency in different ethnic groups: A replication across two Dutch samples. *Social Psychiatry and Psychiatric Epidemiology, 45,* 293–300.

Eichler, A., Hudler, L., Grunitz, J., Grimm, J., Raabe, E., Goecke, T. W., et al. (2018). Effects of prenatal alcohol consumption on cognitive development and ADHD-related behaviour in primary-school age: A multilevel study based on meconium ethyl glucuronide. *Journal of Child Psychology and Psychiatry, 59,* 110–118.

Einfeld, S., & Emerson, E. (2008). Intellectual disability. In M. Rutter, D. Bishop, D. Pine, S. Scott, J. Stevenson, E. Taylor, & A. Thapar (Eds.), *Rutter's child and adolescent psychiatry* (5th ed.). Malden, MA: Blackwell Publishing.

Eisenberg, L. (2001). The past 50 years of child and adolescent psychiatry: A personal memoir. *Journal of the American Academy of Child and Adolescent Psychiatry, 40,* 743–748.

Eisenberg, L., Baker, B. L., & Blacher, J. (1998). Siblings with children with mental retardation living at home or in residential placement. *Journal of Child Psychology and Psychiatry, 39,* 355–363.

Eisenberg, N., & Silver, R. C. (2011). Growing up in the shadow of terrorism: Youth in America after 9/11. *American Psychologist, 66,* 468–481.

Eisenberg, N., Spinard, T. L., & Eggum, N. D. (2010a). Emotion-related self-regulation and its relation to children's maladjustment. *Annual Review of Clinical Psychology, 6,* 495–525.

Eisenberg, N., Vidmar, M., Spinrad, T. L., Eggum, N. D., Edwards, A., Gaertner, B., et al. (2010b). Mothers' teaching strategies and children's effortful control: A longitudinal study. *Developmental Psychology, 46,* 1294–1308.

Eiser, C. (1998). Long-term consequences of childhood cancer. *Journal of Child Psychology and Psychiatry, 39,* 621–633.

Eiser, C., Eiser, J. R., Mayhew, A. G., & Gibson, A. T. (2005). Parenting the premature infant: Balancing vulnerability and quality of life. *Journal of Child Psychology and Psychiatry, 46,* 1169–1177.

Eisler, I., Dare, C., Hodes, M., Russell, G., Dodge, E., & Le Grange, D. (2000). Family therapy for adolescent anorexia nervosa: The results of a controlled comparison of two family interventions. *Journal of Child Psychology and Psychiatry, 41,* 727–736.

Eisler, I., Simic, M., Russell, G. F. M., & Dare, C. (2007). A randomised controlled treatment trial of two forms of family therapy in adolescent anorexia nervosa: A five-year follow-up. *Journal of Child Psychology and Psychiatry, 48,* 552–560.

Eisner, E. W. (2003). On the art and science of qualitative research in psychology. In P. M. Camic, J. E. Rhodes, & L. Yardley (Eds.), *Qualitative research in psychology.* Washington, DC: American Psychological Association.

Eklund, K., Meyer, L., Splett, J., & Weist, M. (2020). Policies and Practices to Support School Mental Health. In B. Levin & A. Hanson (Eds.), *Foundations of behavioral health.* Cham, Switzerland: Springer.

Elbau, I. G., Cruceanu, C., & Binder, E. B. (2019). Genetics of resilience: Gene-by-environment interaction studies as a tool to dissect mechanisms of resilience. *Biological Psychiatry, 86,* 433–442.

Elbaum, B., & Vaughn, S. (2003). Self-concept and students with learning disabilities. In H. L. Swanson, K. R. Harris, & S. Graham (Eds.), *Handbook of learning disabilities.* New York: Guilford Press.

Eley, T. C., Bolton, D., O'Connor, T. G., Perrin, S., Smith, P., & Plomin, R. (2003a). A twin study of anxiety-related behaviours in pre-school children. *Journal of Child Psychology and Psychiatry, 44,* 945–960.

Eley, T. C., Lichtenstein, P., & Moffitt, T. E. (2003b). A longitudinal behavioral genetic analysis of the etiology of aggressive and nonaggressive antisocial behavior. *Development and Psychopathology, 15,* 383–402.

Elgar, F. J., McGrath, P. J., Waschbusch, D. A., Stewart, S. H., & Curtis, L. J. (2004). Mutual influences on maternal depression and child adjustment problems. *Clinical Psychology Review, 24,* 441–459.

Elia, J., Gai, X., Xie, H. M., Perin, J. C., Geiger, E., Glessner, J. T., et al. (2010). Rare structural variants found in attention-deficit hyperactivity disorder are preferentially associated with neurodevelopmental genes. *Molecular Psychiatry, 15,* 637–646.

Elliot, D. S., Huizinga, D., & Ageton, S. S. (1985). *Explaining delinquency and drug use.* Beverly Hills, CA: Sage.

Elliott, J. G., & Place, M. (2019). School refusal: Developments in conceptualisation and treatment since 2000. *Journal of Child Psychology and Psychiatry, 60,* 4–15.

Ellis, B. J., Boyce, W. T., Belsky, J., Bakermans-Kranenburg, M. J., & van IJzendoorn, M. H. (2011). Differential susceptibility to the environment: An evolutionary-developmental theory. *Development and Psychopathology, 23,* 7–28.

Ellis, D. M., & Hudson, J. L. (2010). The metacognitive model of generalized anxiety disorder in children and adolescents. *Clinical Psychology Review, 13,* 151–163.

El-Sheikh, M., & Flanagan, E. (2001). Parental problem drinking and children's adjustment: Family conflict and parental depression as mediators and moderators of risk. *Journal of Abnormal Child Psychology, 29,* 417–432.

El-Sheikh, M., Buckhalt, J. A., Acebo, C., & Mize, J. (2006). Marital conflict and disruption of children's sleep. *Child Development, 77,* 31–43.

Emerson, L.-M., Ogielda, C., & Rowse, G. (2019). A systematic review of the role of parents in the development of anxious cognitions in children. *Journal of Anxiety Disorders, 62,* 15–25.

Emery, R. E., & Kitzmann, K. M. (1995). The child in the family: Disruptions in family functions. In D. Cicchetti & D. J. Cohen (Eds.), *Developmental psychopathology: Risk, disorder, and adaptation* (Vol. 2). New York: John Wiley & Sons.

Emslie, G., Kratochvil, C., Vitiello, B., Silva, S., Mayes, T., McNutty, S., et al., & the TADS Team. (2006). Treatment for Adolescents with Depression Study (TADS): Safety results. *Journal of the American Academy of Child and Adolescent Psychiatry, 45,* 1440–1455.

Endendijk, J. J., Andrews, N. C. Z., England, D. E., & Martin, C. L. (2019). Gender-identity typologies are related to gender-typing, friendships, and social-emotional adjustment in Dutch emerging adults. *International Journal of Behavioral Development, 43,* 322–333.

English, D. J. (1998). The extent and consequences of child maltreatment. *The Future of Children, 8,* 39–53.

English, D., Lambert, S. F., & Ialongo, N. S. (2016). Adding to the education debt: Depressive symptoms mediate the association between racial discrimination and academic performance in African Americans. *Journal of School Psychology, 57,* 29–40.

Enlow, M. B., Englund, M. M., & Egeland, B. (2018). Maternal childhood maltreatment history and child mental health: Mechanisms in intergenerational effects. *Journal of Clinical Child & Adolescent Psychology, 47*(sup1), S47–S62.

Enzer, N. B., & Heard, S. L. (2000). Psychiatric prevention in children and adolescents. In B. J. Sadock & V. A. Sadock (Eds.), *Kaplan & Sadock's comprehensive textbook of psychiatry* (Vol. II). Philadelphia, PA: Lippincott Williams & Wilkins.

References

Epkins, C. C., & Heckler, D. R. (2011). Integrating etiological models of social anxiety and depression in youth: Evidence for a cumulative interpersonal risk model. *Clinical Child and Family Psychology Review, 14,* 329–376.

Epstein, L. H., Valoski, A. M., Vara, L. S., McCurley, J., Wisniewski, L., Kalarchian, M. A., et al. (1995). Effects of decreasing sedentary behavior and increasing activity on weight change in obese children. *Health Psychology, 14,* 109–115.

Erath, S. A., Bierman, K. L., & the Conduct Problems Prevention Research Group. (2006). Aggressive marital conflict, maternal harsh punishment, and child aggressive-disruptive behavior: Evidence for direct and indirect relations. *Journal of Family Psychology, 20,* 217–226.

Erickson, S. K., Lilienfeld, S. O., & Vitacco, M. J. (2007). A critical examination of the suitability and limitations of psychological tests in family court. *Family Court Review, 45,* 157–174.

Ernst, M., Torrisi, S., Balderston, N., Grillon, C., & Hale, E. A. (2015). fMRI functional connectivity applied to adolescent neurodevelopment. *Annual Review of Clinical Psychology, 11,* 361–377.

Esbensen, A. J., & Seltzer, M. M. (2011). Accounting for the "Down syndrome advantage." *American Journal on Intellectual and Developmental Disabilities, 116,* 3–15.

Esparham, A., Herbert, A., Pierzchalski, E., Tran, C., Dilts, J., Boorigie, M., et al. (2018). Pediatric headache clinic model: Implementation of integrative therapies in practice. *Children, 5,* 74.

Espelage, D. L., & Hong, J. S. (2019). Children who bully or are bullied. In T. H. Ollendick, S. W. White, & B. A. White (Eds.), *The Oxford handbook of clinical child and adolescent psychology.* New York: Oxford University Press.

Essau, C. A. (2003). Epidemiology and comorbidity. In C. A. Essau (Ed.), *Conduct and oppositional defiant disorders: Epidemiology, risk factors, and treatment.* Mahwah, NJ: Erlbaum.

Essau, C. A., Conradt, J., & Petermann, F. (1999). Frequency of panic attacks and panic disorder in adolescents. *Depression and Anxiety, 9,* 19–26.

Essau, C. A., Conradt, J., & Petermann, F. (2000). Frequency, comorbidity, and psychosocial impairment of specific phobia in adolescents. *Journal of Clinical Child Psychology, 29,* 221–231.

Essex, M. J., Armstrong, J. M., Burk, L. R., Goldsmith, H. H., & Boyce, W. T. (2011). Biological sensitivity to context moderates the effects of the early teacher-child relationship on the development of mental health by adolescence. *Development and Psychopathology, 23,* 149–161.

Estes, K. G., Evans, J. L., & Else-Quest, N. M. (2007). Differences in the nonword repetition performance of children with and without specific language impairment: A meta-analysis.

Journal of Speech, Language, and Hearing Research, 50, 177–195.

Etmanskie, J. M., Partanen, M., & Siegel, L. S. (2014). A longitudinal examination of the persistence of late emerging reading disabilities. *Journal of Learning Disabilities, 49,* 21–35.

Eubig, P. A., Aguiar, A., & Schantz, S. L. (2010). Lead and PBCs as risk factors for attention deficit/hyperactivity disorder. *Environmental Health Perspective, 118,* 1654–1667.

Evans, D. L., & the Commission on Adolescent Depression and Bipolar Disorder. (2005a). Defining depression and bipolar disorder. In D. L. Evans, E. B. Foa, R. E. Gur, H. Hendin, C. P. O'Brien, M. E. P. Seligman, & B. T. Walsh (Eds.), *Treating and preventing adolescent mental health disorders. What we know and what we don't know: A research agenda for improving mental health of our youth.* New York: Oxford University Press.

Evans, D. L., & the Commission on Adolescent Depression and Bipolar Disorder. (2005b). Prevention of depression and bipolar disorder. In D. L. Evans, E. B. Foa, R. E. Gur, H. Hendin, C. P. O'Brien, M. E. P. Seligman, & B. T. Walsh (Eds.), *Treating and preventing adolescent mental health disorders. What we know and what we don't know: A research agenda for improving mental health of our youth.* New York: Oxford University Press.

Evans, D. W., & Leckman, J. F. (2006). Origins of obsessive compulsive disorder: Developmental and evolutionary perspectives. In D. Cicchetti & D. J. Cohen (Eds.), *Developmental psychopathology* (2nd ed., Vol. 1). Hoboken, NJ: John Wiley & Sons.

Evans, G. W. (2004). The environment of childhood poverty. *American Psychologist, 59,* 77–92.

Evans, R. B., & Koelsch, W. A. (1985). Psychoanalysis arrives in America. *American Psychologist, 40,* 942–948.

Evans, S. C., Bonadio, F. T., Bearman, S. K., Ugueto, A. M., Chorpita, B. F., & Weisz, J. R. (2020). Assessing the irritable and defiant dimensions of youth oppositional behavior using CBCL and YSR items. *Journal of Clinical Child & Adolescent Psychology.* doi:10.1080/15374416.2019.1622119.

Evans, S. W., Owens, J. S., & Power, T. J. (2019). Attention-deficit/hyperactivity disorder. In M. J. Prinstein, E. A. Youngstrom, E. J. Mash, & R. A. Barkley (Eds.), *Treatment of disorders in childhood and adolescence* (4th ed.). New York: The Guilford Press.

Evans, S. W., Owens, J. S., Monopoli, W. J., & Benson, K. (2018a). Attention deficit hyperactivity disorder. In T. H. Ollendick, S. W. White, & B. A. White (Eds.), *The Oxford handbook of clinical child and adolescent psychology.* Oxford: Oxford Library of Psychology.

Evans, S. W., Owens, J. S., Wymbs, B. T., & Ray, A. R. (2018b). Evidence-based psychosocial treatments for children and adolescents with attention deficit/hyperactivity disorder. *Journal of Clinical Child & Adolescent Psychology, 47,* 157–198.

Exner, J. E., Jr., & Weiner, I. B. (1995). *The Rorschach: A comprehensive system, Vol. 3: Assessment of children and adolescents* (2nd ed.). New York: Wiley.

Eyberg, S. M., Nelson, M. M., Ginn, N. C. Bhuiyan, N., & Boggs, S. R. (2013). *Dyadic Parent-Child Interaction Coding System, Fourth Edition (DPICS-4)*. Gainesville, FL: PCIT International.

Eyberg, S., & Pincus, D. (1999). *Eyberg Child Behavior Inventory & Sutter-Eyberg Student Behavior Inventory-Revised*. Lutz, FL: Psychological Assessment Resources.

Fabiano, G. A., & Caserta, A. (2018). Future directions in father inclusion, engagement, retention, and positive outcomes in child and adolescent research. *Journal of Clinical Child & Adolescent Psychology, 47*, 847–862.

Fabiano, G. A., Pelham, W. E., Gnagy, E. M., Burrows-MacLean, L., Coles, E. K., Chacko, A., et al. (2007). The single and combined effects of multiple intensities of behavior modification and methylphenidate for children with attention deficit hyperactivity disorder in a classroom setting. *School Psychology Review, 36*, 195–216.

Fabiano, G. A., Schatz, N. K., & Pelham, W. E., Jr. (2014). Summer treatment programs for youth with ADHD. *Child and Adolescent Psychiatric Clinics, 23*, 757–773.

Factor, R. S., Condy, E. E., Farley, J. P., & Scarpa, A. (2016). Brief report: Insistence on sameness, anxiety, and social motivation in children with autism spectrum disorder. *Journal of Autism and Developmental Disorders, 46*, 2548–2554.

Faedda, N., Cerutti, R., Verdecchia, P., Migliorini, D., Arruda, M., & Guidetti, V. (2016). Behavioral management of headache in children and adolescents. *The Journal of Headache and Pain, 17*, 80.

Fagan, J. F., & Holland, C. R. (2002). Equal opportunity and racial differences in IQ. *Intelligence, 30*, 361–387.

Fairburn, C. G. (1997). Eating disorders. In D. M. Clark & C. G. Fairburn (Eds.), *Science and practice of cognitive behaviour therapy*. Oxford: Oxford University Press.

Fairburn, C. G., Cooper, Z., & Shafran, R. (2003). Cognitive behaviour therapy for eating disorders: A "transdiagnostic" theory and treatment. *Behaviour Research and Therapy, 43*, 509–529.

Fairburn, C. G., Cooper, Z., Doll, H. A., Norman, P., & O'Connor, M. (2000). The natural course of bulimia nervosa and binge eating disorder in young women. *Archives of General Psychiatry, 57*, 659–665.

Fairburn, C. G., Cooper, Z., Doll, H. A., O'Connor, M. E., Bohn, K., Hawker, D. M., et al. (2009). Transdiagnostic cognitive behavior therapy for patients with eating disorders: A two-site trial with 60-week follow-up. *American Journal of Psychiatry, 166*, 311–319.

Fairchild, G., Van Goozen, S. H., Calder, A. J., & Goodyer, I. M. (2013). Research review: Evaluating and reformulating the developmental taxonomic theory of antisocial behaviour. *Journal of Child Psychology and Psychiatry, 54*, 924–940.

Faja, S., & Dawson, G. (2017). Autism spectrum disorder. In T. P. Beauchaine & S. P. Hinshaw (Eds.), *Child and adolescent psychopathology* (3rd ed.). Hoboken, NJ: John Wiley & Sons.

Farmer, R. L., & Floyd, R. G. (2018). Use of intelligence tests in the identification of children and adolescents with intellectual disability. In D. P. Flanagan, E. M. McDonough, & A. S. Kaufman (Eds.), *Contemporary intellectual assessment: Theories, tests, and issues* (4th ed.). New York: Guilford Publications.

Farrell, L. J., Mathieu, S. L., & Lavell, C. H. (2019). Obsessive-compulsive and related disorders. In T. H. Ollendick, S. W. White, & B. A. White (Eds.), *The Oxford handbook of clinical child and adolescent psychology*. New York: Oxford University Press.

Farrington, D. P. (1986). Stepping stones to adult criminal careers. In D. Olweus, J. Block, & M. R. Yarrow (Eds.), *Development of antisocial behavior and prosocial behavior*. New York: Academic Press.

Farrington, D. P. (1995). The development of offending and antisocial behaviour from childhood: Key findings from the Cambridge Study in Delinquent Development. *Journal of Child Psychology and Psychiatry, 36*, 929–964.

Farrington, D. P., Jolliffe, D., Loeber, R., Stouthamer-Loeber, M., & Kalb, L. M. (2001). The concentration of offenders in families, and family criminality in the prediction of boys' delinquency. *Journal of Adolescence, 24*, 579–596.

Farrington, D. P., Ullrich, S., & Salekin, R. T. (2010). Environmental influences on child and adolescent psychopathy. In R. T. Salekin & D. R. Lyman (Eds.), *Handbook of child and adolescent psychopathy*. New York: The Guilford Press.

Fearon, R. P., Bakermans-Kranenburg, M. J., van IJzendoorn, M. H., Lapsley, A. M., & Roisman, G. I. (2010). The significance of insecure attachment and disorganization in the development of children's externalizing behavior: A meta-analytic study. *Child Development, 81*, 435–456.

Fearon, R. P., Groh, A. M., Bakermans-Kranenburg, M. J., van IJzendoorn, M. H., & Roisman, G. I. (2016). Attachment and developmental psychopathology. In D. Cicchetti (Ed.), *Developmental psychopathology: Risk, resilience, and intervention* (3rd ed., Vol. 1). Hoboken, NJ: John Wiley & Sons.

Feder, A., Nestler, E. J., & Charney, D. S. (2009). Psychobiology and molecular genetics of resilience. *Nature Reviews Neuroscience, 10*, 446–457.

Federal Interagency Forum on Child and Family Statistics. (2011). *America's children: Key national indicators of wellbeing, 2011*. Washington, DC: U.S. Government Printing Office.

Federal Interagency Forum on Child and Family Statistics. (2019). *America's children: Key national indicators of well-being,*

References

2019. Retrieved December 2019 from www.childstats.gov/americaschildren/tables.asp

Feifer, S. G. (2018). The neuropsychology of reading disorders: How SLD manifests in reading. In V. C. Alfonso & D. P. Flanagan (Eds.), *Essentials of specific learning disability identification*. Hoboken, NJ: John Wiley & Sons.

Felce, D. (2017). Community living for adults with intellectual disabilities: Unravelling the cost effectiveness discourse. *Journal of Policy and Practice in Intellectual Disabilities, 14,* 187–197.

Feldman, T., Runfola, C. D., & Lock, J. (2019). Feeding and eating disorders. In T. H. Ollendick, S. W. White, & B. A. White (Eds.), *The Oxford handbook of clinical child and adolescent psychology*. New York: Oxford University Press.

Felton, J. W., Shadur, J. M., Havewala, M., Gonçalves, S., & Lejuez, C. W. (2020). Impulsivity moderates the relation between depressive symptoms and substance use across adolescence. *Journal of Clinical Child & Adolescent Psychology, 49,* 365–377.

Fenwick, M. E., Kubas, H. A., Witzke, J. W., Fitzer, K. R., Miller, D. C., Maricle, D. E., et al. (2016). Neuropsychological profiles of written expression learning disabilities determined by concordance-discordance model criteria. *Applied Neuropsychology: Child, 5,* 83–96.

Fergusson, D. M., & Horwood, L. J. (1998). Early conduct problems and later life opportunities. *Journal of Child Psychology and Psychiatry, 39,* 1097–1108.

Fergusson, D. M., & Horwood, L. J. (1999). Prospective childhood predictors of deviant peer affiliations in adolescence. *Journal of Child Psychology and Psychiatry, 40,* 581–592.

Fergusson, D. M., & Woodward, L. J. (2000). Educational, psychological, and sexual outcomes of girls with conduct problems in early adolescence. *Journal of Child Psychology and Psychiatry, 41,* 779–792.

Fergusson, D. M., Horwood, L. J., & Ridder, E. M. (2005a). Show me the child at seven: The consequences of conduct problems in childhood for psychosocial functioning in adulthood. *Journal of Child Psychology and Psychiatry, 46,* 837–849.

Fergusson, D. M., Horwood, L. J., & Ridder, E. M. (2005b). Show me the child at seven II: Childhood intelligence and later outcomes in adolescence and young adulthood. *Journal of Child Psychology and Psychiatry, 46,* 850–858.

Fergusson, D. M., Horwood, L. J., & Ridder, E. M. (2007). Conduct and attentional problems in childhood and adolescence and later substance use, abuse and dependence: Results of a 25-year longitudinal study. *Drug and Alcohol Dependence, 88,* S14–S26.

Ferrante, G., & La Grutta, S. (2018). The burden of pediatric asthma. *Frontiers in Pediatrics, 6.*

Ferrer, E., Shaywitz, B. A., Holahan, J. M., Marchione, K. E., Michaels, R., & Shaywitz, S. E. (2015). Achievement gap in reading is present as early as first grade and persists through adolescence. *The Journal of Pediatrics, 167,* 1121–1125.

Ferrer, E., Shaywitz, B. A., Holahan, J. M., Marchione, K., & Shaywitz, S. E. (2010). Uncoupling of reading and IQ over time: Empirical evidence for a definition of dyslexia. *Psychological Science, 21,* 93–101.

Ferretti, N. M., King, S. L., Hilton, D. C., Rondon, A. T., & Jarrett, M. A. (2019). Social functioning in youth with attention-deficit/hyperactivity disorder and sluggish cognitive tempo. *The Yale Journal of Biology and Medicine, 92,* 29–35.

Ferro, M. A., & Boyle, M. H. (2015). The impact of chronic physical illness, maternal depressive symptoms, family functioning, and self-esteem on symptoms of anxiety and depression in children. *Journal of Abnormal Child Psychology, 43,* 177–187.

Ferster, C. B. (1974). Behavioral approaches to depression. In R. J. Friedman & M. M. Katz (Eds.), *The psychology of depression: Contemporary theory and research*. Washington, DC: Winston.

Field, A. P. (2006). Is conditioning a useful framework for understanding the development and treatment of phobias? *Clinical Psychology Review, 26,* 857–875.

Field, A. P., & Lester, K. J. (2010). Is there room for "development" in the developmental models of information processing biases to threat in children and adolescents? *Clinical Child and Family Psychology Review, 13,* 315–332.

Field, A. P., & Schorah, H. (2007). The verbal information pathway to fear and heart rate changes in children. *Journal of Child Psychology and Psychiatry, 48,* 1088–1093.

Field, T., Diego, M., & Hernandez-Reif, M. (2010). Preterm infant massage therapy research: A review. *Infant Behavior and Development, 33,* 115–124.

Fiese, B. H., & Bickman, N. L. (1998). Qualitative inquiry: An overview for pediatric psychology. *Journal of Pediatric Psychology, 23,* 79–86.

Filatova, S., Koivumaa-Honkanen, H., Hirvonen, N., Freeman, A., Ivandic, I., Hurtig, T., et al. (2017). Early motor developmental milestones and schizophrenia: A systematic review and meta-analysis. *Schizophrenia Research, 188,* 13–20.

Filipek, P. A. (1999). Neuroimaging in the developmental disorders: The state of the science. *Journal of Child Psychology and Psychiatry, 40,* 113–128.

Findling, R. L., McNamara, N. K., Pavuluri, M., Frazier, J. A., Rynn, M., Scheffer, R., et al. (2019). Lithium for the maintenance treatment of bipolar I disorder: A double-blind, placebo-controlled discontinuation study. *Journal of the American Academy of Child & Adolescent Psychiatry, 58,* 287–296.

Fine, S. E., Izard, C. E., Mostow, A. J., Trentacosta, C. J., & Ackerman, B. P. (2003). First grade emotion knowledge as a predictor of fifth grade self-reported internalizing behaviors in children from economically disadvantaged families. *Development and Psychopathology, 15,* 331–342.

Finkelhor, D. (1994). The international epidemiology of child sexual abuse. *Child Abuse & Neglect, 18,* 409–417.

Finkelstein, H. (1988). The long term effects of early parent death: A review. *Journal of Clinical Psychology, 44,* 3–9.

First, M. B., Skodol, A. E., Williams, J. B., & Spitzer, R. L. (2017). *Learning DSM-5® by case example.* Arlington, VA: American Psychiatric Association Publishing.

Fischer, S., & Le Grange, D. (2007). Co-morbidity and high-risk behaviors in treatment seeking adolescents with bulimia nervosa. *International Journal of Eating Disorders, 40,* 751–753.

Fisher, E., Law, E., Dudeney, J., Eccleston, C., & Palermo, T. M. (2019). Psychological therapies (remotely delivered) for the management of chronic and recurrent pain in children and adolescents. *Cochrane Database of Systematic Reviews, 4.*

Fisher, M., Nahum, M., Howard, E., Rowlands, A., Brandrett, B., Kermott, A., et al. (2017). Supplementing intensive targeted computerized cognitive training with social cognitive exercises for people with schizophrenia: An interim report. *Psychiatric Rehabilitation Journal, 40,* 21–32.

Fisher, P. A., Leve, L. D., Delker, B., Roos, L. E., & Cooper, B. (2016). A developmental psychopathology perspective on foster care research. In D. Cicchetti (Ed.), *Developmental psychopathology: Risk, resilience, and intervention* (3rd ed., Vol. 3). Hoboken, NJ: John Wiley & Sons.

Fisher, S. E. (2017). Evolution of language: Lessons from the genome. *Psychonomic Bulletin & Review, 24,* 34–40.

Fivush, R., & Zaman, W. (2015). Gendered narrative voices: Sociocultural and feminist approaches to emerging identity in childhood and adolescence. In K. C. McLean & M. Syed (Eds.), *The Oxford handbook of identity development.* New York: Oxford University Press.

Fixsen, D. L., Wolf, M. M., & Phillips, E. L. (1973). Achievement place: A teaching-family model of community-based group homes for youth in trouble. In L. Hammerlynck, L. Handy, and E. Mash (Eds.), *Behavior change: Methodology, concepts and practice.* Champaign, IL: Research Press.

Flament, M. F., Whitaker, A., Rapoport, J. L., Davies, M., Berg, C. Z., Kalikow, K., et al. (1988). Obsessive compulsive disorder in adolescence: An epidemiological study. *Journal of the American Academy of Child and Adolescent Psychiatry, 27,* 764–771.

Flanagan, D. P., & McDonough, E. M. (Eds.) (2018). *Contemporary intellectual assessment: Theories, tests, and issues* (4th ed.). New York: The Guilford Press.

Flanagan, D., Alfonso, V., Sy, M., Mascolo, J., McDonough, E., & Ortiz, S. (2018). Dual discrepancy/consistency operational definition of SLD: Integrating multiple data sources and multiple data-gathering methods. In V. Alfonso & D. P. Flanagan (Eds.), *Essentials of specific learning disability identification* (2nd ed.). Hoboken, NJ: John Wiley and Sons.

Flannery-Schroeder, E. C. (2004). Generalized anxiety disorder. In T. L. Morris & J. S. March (Eds.), *Anxiety disorders in children and adolescents.* New York: Guilford Press.

Flaton, R. A. (2006). "Who would I be without Danny?" Phenomenological case study of an adult sibling. *Mental Retardation, 44,* 135–144.

Fleck, D. E., Cerullo, M. A., Nandagopal, J., Adler, C. M., Patel, N. C., Strakowski, S. M., & DelBello, M. P. (2010). Neurodevelopment in bipolar disorder: A neuroimaging perspective. In D. J. Miklowitz & D. Cicchetti (Eds), *Understanding bipolar disorder: A developmental psychopathology perspective.* New York: The Guilford Press.

Fleitlich-Bilyk, B., & Goodman, R. (2004). Prevalence of child and adolescent psychiatric disorders in southeast Brazil. *Journal of the American Academy of Child and Adolescent Psychiatry, 43,* 727–734.

Fleming, J. E., Offord, D. R., & Boyle, M. H. (1989). Prevalence of childhood and adolescent depression in the community: Ontario Child Health Study. *British Journal of Psychiatry, 155,* 647–654.

Flessner, C. A., Sapyta, J., Garcia, A., Freeman, J. B., Franklin, M. E., Foa, E., & March, J. (2011). Examining the psychometric properties of the Family Accommodation Scale-Parent-Report (FAS-PR). *Journal of Psychopathology and Behavioral Assessment, 33,* 38–46.

Fletcher, J. M., Lyon, G. R., Fuchs, L. S., & Barnes, M. A. (2019). *Learning disabilities: From identification to intervention* (2nd ed.). New York: The Guilford Press.

Fletcher, K. E. (2003). Childhood posttraumatic stress disorder. In E. J. Mash & R. A. Barkley (Eds.), *Child psychopathology* (2nd ed.). New York: Guilford Press.

Flick, U. (2018). *The Sage handbook of qualitative data collection.* Los Angeles, CA: Sage Reference.

Flouri, E. (2010). Fathers' behaviors and children's psychopathology. *Clinical Psychology Review, 30,* 363–369.

Flowers, S. R., & Birnie, K. A. (2015). Procedural preparation and support as a standard of care in pediatric oncology. *Pediatric Blood & Cancer, 62*(S5), S694–S723.

Floyd, R. G., Shands, E. I., Alfonso, V. C., Phillips, J. F., Autry, B. K., Mosteller, J. A., et al. (2015). A systematic review and psychometric evaluation of adaptive behavior scales and recommendations for practice. *Journal of Applied School Psychology, 31,* 83–113.

Flynn, J. R. (2018). Intelligence, society, and human autonomy. In R. J. Sternberg (Ed.), *The nature of human intelligence.* New York: Cambridge University Press.

Foa, E. B., Coles, M., Huppert, J. D., Pasupuleti, R. V., Franklin, M. E., & March, J. (2010). Development and validation of a child version of the Obsessive Compulsive Inventory. *Behavior Therapy, 41,* 121–132.

References

Follette, W. C., & Houts, A. C. (1996). Models of scientific progress and the role of theory in taxonomy development: A case study of DSM. *Journal of Consulting and Clinical Psychology, 64*, 1120–1132.

Fombonne, E. (2001). Is there an epidemic of autism? *Pediatrics, 107*, 411–412.

Fombonne, E. (2003). Epidemiological surveys of autism and pervasive developmental disorders: An update. *Journal of Autism and Developmental Disorders, 33*, 365–382.

Fonagy, P., & Target, M. (2003). *Psychoanalytic theories. Perspectives from developmental psychopathology*. New York: Brunner-Routledge.

Fonseca, A. C., Yule, W., & Erol, N. (1994). Cross-cultural issues. In T. H. Ollendick, N. J. King, & W. Yule (Eds.), *International handbook of phobic and anxiety disorders in children and adolescents*. New York: Plenum Press.

Fontaine, R. G., Burks, V. S., & Dodge, K. A. (2002). Response decision processes and externalizing behavior problems in adolescents. *Development and Psychopathology, 14*, 107–122.

Ford, M. A., Sladeczek, I. E., Carlson, J., & Kratochwill, T. R. (1998). Selective mutism: Phenomenological characteristics. *School Psychology Quarterly, 13*, 192–227.

Ford, T., Goodman, R., & Meltzer, H. (2003). The British child and adolescent mental health survey 1999: The prevalence of DSM-IV disorders. *Journal of the American Academy of Child and Adolescent Psychiatry, 42*, 1203–1211.

Ford, T., Goodman, R., & Meltzer, H. (2003). The British child and adolescent mental health survey 1999: The prevalence of DSM-IV disorders. *Journal of the American Academy of Child and Adolescent Psychiatry, 42*, 1203–1211.

Forehand, R., & McMahon, R. J. (1981). *Helping the noncompliant child: A clinician's guide to parent training*. New York: Guilford.

Forehand, R., King, H. E., Peed, S., & Yoder, P. (1975). Mother-child interactions: Comparisons of a noncompliant clinic group and a non-clinic group. *Behaviour Research and Therapy, 13*, 79–84.

Forgatch, M. S., & Gewirtz, A. H. (2017). The evolution of the Oregon model of parent management training: An intervention for antisocial behavior in children and adolescents. In J. R. Weisz & A. E. Kazdin (Eds.), *Evidence-based psychotherapies for children and adolescents* (3rd ed.). New York: The Guilford Press.

Forgatch, M. S., & Patterson, G. R. (2010). Parent management training-Oregon Model: An intervention for antisocial behavior in children and adolescents. In J. R. Weisz & A. E. Kazdin (Eds.), *Evidence-based psychotherapies for children and adolescents* (2nd ed.). New York: The Guilford Press.

Fosco, G. M., & Grych, J. H. (2007). Emotional expression in the family as a context for children's appraisals of interparental conflict. *Journal of Family Psychology, 21*, 248–258.

Foster, C. E., Yeguez, C. E., & King, C. A. (2019). Children and adolescents with suicidal thoughts and behaviors. In T. H. Ollendick, S. W. White, & B. A. White (Eds.), *The Oxford handbook of clinical child and adolescent psychology*. New York: Oxford University Press.

Foster, J. R., AlOthmani, F. I., Seabrook, J. A., AlOfisan, T., AlGarni, Y. M., & Sarpal, A. (2018). Parental presence at the bedside of critically ill children in a unit with unrestricted visitation. *Pediatric Critical Care Medicine, 19*, e387–e393.

Fountain, C., Winter, A. S., & Bearman, P. S. (2012). Six developmental trajectories characterize children with autism. *Pediatrics, 129*, e1112–e1120.

Fowler, W. (2017). The effect of early stimulation in the emergence of cognitive processes. In R. Hess (Ed.), *Early formal education: Current theory, research and practice*. New York: Routledge.

Fox, N. A., & Pine, D. S. (2012). Temperament and the emergence of anxiety disorders. *Journal of the American Academy of Child and Adolescent Psychiatry, 51*, 125–128.

Fox, N. A., Hane, A. A., & Pine, D. S. (2007). Plasticity for human neurocircuitry: How the environment affects gene expression. *Current Directions in Psychological Science, 16*, 1–5.

Fox, N. A., Henderson, H. A., Marshall, P. J., Nichols, K. E., & Ghera, M. M. (2005). Behavioral inhibition: Linking biology and behavior within a developmental framework. *Annual Review of Psychology, 56*, 235–262.

Fraley, R. C., & Spieker, S. J. (2003). Are infant attachment patterns continuously or categorically distributed? A taxometric analysis of strange situation behavior. *Developmental Psychology, 39*, 387–404.

Frances, A., & Ross, R. (2001). *DSM-IV-TR case studies: A clinical guide to differential diagnosis*. Washington, DC: American Psychiatric Association.

Franić, S., Middeldorp, C. M., Dolan, C. V., Ligthart, L., & Boomsma, D. I. (2010). Childhood and adolescent anxiety and depression: Beyond heritability. *Journal of the American Academy of Child and Adolescent Psychiatry, 49*, 820–829.

Franke, B., & Buitelaar, J. K. (2018). Gene–environment interactions. In T. Banaschewski, D. Coghill, & A. Zuddas (Eds.), *Oxford textbook of attention deficit hyperactivity disorder*. Oxford: Oxford University Press.

Franklin, J. C., Ribeiro, J. D., Fox, K. R., Bentley, K. H., Kleiman, E. M., Huang, X., et al. (2017). Risk factors for suicidal thoughts and behaviors: A meta-analysis of 50 years of research. *Psychological Bulletin, 143*, 187–232.

Franklin, M. E., Morris, S. H., Freeman, J. B., & March, J. S. (2017). Treating pediatric obsessive-compulsive disorder in children: Using exposure-based cognitive-behavioral therapy. In J. R. Weisz & A. E. Kazdin (Eds.), *Evidence-based psychotherapies for children and adolescents* (3rd ed.). New York: The Guilford Press.

Franz, A. P., Bolat, G. U., Bolat, H., Matijasevich, A., Santos, I. S., Silveira, R. C., et al. (2018). Attention-deficit/hyperactivity disorder and very preterm/very low birth weight: A meta-analysis. *Pediatrics, 141*, e20171645.

Frazier, J. A., McClellan, J., Findling, R. L.,Vitiello, B., Anderson, R., Zablotsky, B., et al. (2007). Treatment of early-onset schizophrenia spectrum disorders (TEOSS): Demographic and clinical characteristics. *Journal of the American Academy of Child and Adolescent Psychiatry, 46*, 979–988.

Freeman, J., Benito, K., Herren, J., Kemp, J., Sung, J., Georgiadis, C., et al. (2018). Evidence base update of psychosocial treatments for pediatric obsessive-compulsive disorder: Evaluating, improving, and transporting what works. *Journal of Clinical Child & Adolescent Psychology, 47*, 669–698.

Fremont, W. P. (2004). Childhood reactions to terrorism-induced trauma: A review of the past 10 years. *Journal of the American Academy of Child and Adolescent Psychiatry, 43*, 381–392.

Freud, A. (1946). *The psycho-analytical treatment of children.* London: Imago.

Freud, S. (1953). *Analysis of a phobia in a five-year-old boy (1909).* Standard Edition. Vol. 10. Ed. and trans. James Strachey. London: The Hogarth Press.

Frick, M. A., Bohlin, G., Hedqvist, M., & Brocki, K. C. (2018). Temperament and cognitive regulation during the first 3 years of life as predictors of inattention and hyperactivity/impulsivity at 6 years. *Journal of Attention Disorders, 23*, 1291–1302.

Frick, P. J. (1998). Conduct disorders. In T. H. Ollendick & M. Hersen (Eds.), *Handbook of child psychopathology* (3rd ed.). New York: Plenum Press.

Frick, P. J., & McMahon, R. J. (2018). Child and adolescent conduct problems. In J. Hunsley & E. J. Mash (Eds.), *A guide to assessments that work* (2nd ed.). New York: Oxford University Press.

Frick, P. J., & Nigg, J. T. (2012). Current issues in the diagnosis of attention deficit hyperactivity disorder, oppositional defiant disorder, and conduct disorder. *Annual Review of Clinical Psychology, 8*, 77–107.

Frick, P. J., & White, S. F. (2008). The importance of callous-unemotional traits for developmental models of aggressive and antisocial behavior. *Journal of Child Psychology and Psychiatry, 49*, 359–375.

Frick, P. J., Ray, J. V., Thornton, L. C., & Kahn, R. E. (2014). Can callous-unemotional traits enhance the understanding, diagnosis, and treatment of serious conduct problems in children and adolescents? A comprehensive review. *Psychological Bulletin, 140*, 1–57.

Fried, A. L., & Fisher, C. B. (2019). Emerging ethical and legal issues in clinical child and adolescent psychology. In T. H. Ollendick, S. W. White, & B. A. White (Eds.), *The Oxford handbook of clinical child and adolescent psychology.* New York: Oxford University Press.

Fried, A., & Fisher, C. B. (2017). Ethical issues in child and adolescent psychotherapy research. In J. R. Weisz & A. E. Kazdin (Eds.), *Evidence-based psychotherapies for children and adolescents* (3rd ed.). New York: The Guilford Press.

Fried, R., Petty, C., Faraone, S. V., Hyder, L. L., Day, H., & Biederman, J. (2016). Is ADHD a risk factor for high school dropout? A controlled study. *Journal of Attention Disorders, 20*, 383–389.

Fristad, M. A., & Black, S. R. (2018). Mood disorders in childhood and adolescence. In J. N. Butcher & P. C. Kendall (Eds.), *APA handbook of psychopathology* (Vol. 2). Washington, DC: American Psychological Association.

Fristad, M. A., & Goldberg-Arnold, J. S. (2003). Family interventions for early-onset bipolar disorder. In B. Geller & M. P. DelBello (Eds.), *Bipolar disorder in childhood and early adolescence.* New York: Guilford Press.

Fristad, M. A., & MacPherson, H. A. (2014). Evidence-based psychosocial treatments for child and adolescent bipolar spectrum disorders. *Journal of Clinical Child & Adolescent Psychology, 43*, 339–355.

Fristad, M. A., & Roley-Roberts, M. E. (2019). Bipolar disorders. In M. J. Prinstein, E. A. Youngstrom, E. J. Mash, & R. A. Barkley (Eds.), *Treatment of disorders in childhood and adolescence* (4th ed.). New York: The Guilford Press.

Friston, K., Brown, H. R., Siemerkus, J., & Stephan, K. E. (2016). The dysconnection hypothesis. *Schizophrenia Research, 176*, 83–94.

Frith, U. (2004). Emmanuel Miller lecture: Confusions and controversies about Asperger syndrome. *Journal of Child Psychology and Psychiatry, 45*, 672–686.

From Discovery to Cure. Accelerating the Development of New and Personalized Interventions for Mental Illness. (2010). Report of the National Advisory Mental Health Council's Workgroup. Retrieved from www.nimh.nih.gov/.../namhc/reports

Frounfelker, R. L., Miconi, D., Farrar, J., Brooks, M. A., Rousseau, C., & Betancourt, T. S. (2020). Mental health of refugee children and youth: Epidemiology, interventions, and future directions. *Annual Review of Public Health, 41*, 159–176.

Fryar, C., Carroll, M., & Ogden, C. (2018). *Prevalence of overweight, obesity, and severe obesity among children and adolescents aged 2–19 years: United States. 1963–1965 thru 2015–16.* Retrieved January 2020 from www.cdc.gov/nchs/data/hestat/obesity_child_15_16/obesity_child_15_16.htm

Fuchs, D., & Fuchs, L. S. (2017). Critique of the national evaluation of response to intervention: A case for simpler frameworks. *Exceptional Children, 83*, 255–268.

Fuchs, D., Patton III, S., Fuchs, L. S., Gilbert, J., Walsh, M., Lute, N., et al. (2018). RTI purposes and outcomes. In P.

C. Pullen & M. J. Kennedy (Eds.), *Handbook of response to intervention and multi-tiered systems of support*. New York: Routledge.

Fuglewicz, A. J., Piotrowski, P., & Stodolak, A. (2017). Relationship between toxoplasmosis and schizophrenia: A review. *Advances in Clinical and Experimental Medicine, 26,* 1031–1036.

Furr, J. M., Comer, J. S., Edmunds, J. M., & Kendall, P. C. (2010). Disasters and youth: A meta-analytic examination of posttraumatic stress. *Journal of Consulting and Clinical Psychology, 78,* 765–780.

Furukawa, E., Alsop, B., Caparelli-Dáquer, E. M., Casella, E. B., da Costa, R. Q. M., de Moura Queiroz, P., et al. (2019). Behavioral adjustment to asymmetric reward availability among children with and without ADHD: Effects of past and current reinforcement contingencies. *ADHD Attention Deficit and Hyperactivity Disorders, 11,* 149–158.

Gabbard, G. O. (2000). Psychoanalysis and psychoanalytic psychotherapy. In B. J. Sadock & V. A. Sadock (Eds.), *Kaplan & Sadock's comprehensive textbook of psychiatry* (Vol. II). Philadelphia, PA: Lippincott Williams & Wilkins.

Gabriele, S., Sacco, R., & Persico, A. M. (2014). Blood serotonin levels in autism spectrum disorder: A systematic review and meta-analysis. *European Neuropsychopharmacology, 24,* 919–929.

Gadow, K. D., & Nolan, E. E. (2002). Differences between preschool children with ODD, ADHD, and ODD+ADHD symptoms. *Journal of Child Psychology and Psychiatry, 43,* 191–201.

Gadow, K. D., Nolan, E. E., Litcher, L., Carlson, G. A., Panina, N., Golovakha, E., et al. (2000). Comparison of attention-deficit/hyperactivity disorder symptom subtypes in Ukrainian schoolchildren. *Journal of the American Academy of Child and Adolescent Psychiatry, 39,* 1520–1527.

Gadow, K. D., Sverd, J., Nolan, E. E., Sprafkin, J., & Schneider, J. (2007). Immediate-release methylphenidate for ADHD in children with comorbid chronic multiple tic disorder. *Journal of the American Academy of Child and Adolescent Psychiatry, 46,* 840–847.

Gage, N. A., Scott, T., Hirn, R., & MacSuga-Gage, A. S. (2017). The relationship between teachers' implementation of classroom management practices and student behavior in elementary school. *Behavioral Disorders, 43,* 302–315.

Gallagher, B. J., & Jones, B. J. (2017). Early-onset schizophrenia: Symptoms and social class of origin. *International Journal of Social Psychiatry, 63,* 492–497.

Gallagher, B. J., Jones, B. J., & Pardes, M. (2016). Stressful life events, social class and symptoms of schizophrenia. *Clinical Schizophrenia & Related Psychoses, 10,* 101–108.

Galliher, R. V., McLean, K. C., & Syed, M. (2017). An integrated developmental model for studying identity content in context. *Developmental Psychology, 53,* 2011–2022.

Galway, T. M., & Metsala, J. L. (2011). Social cognition and its relation to psychosocial adjustment in children with nonverbal learning disabilities. *Journal of Learning Disabilities, 44,* 33–49.

Ganzola, R., Maziade, M., & Duchesne, S. (2014). Hippocampus and amygdala volumes in children and young adults at high-risk of schizophrenia: Research synthesis. *Schizophrenia Research, 156,* 76–86.

Garber, J. (2010). Vulnerability to depression in childhood and adolescence. In R. E. Ingram & J. M. Price (Eds.), *Vulnerability to psychopathology: Risk across the lifespan* (2nd ed.). New York: The Guilford Press.

Garber, J., & Bradshaw, C. P. (2020). Developmental psychopathology and the Research Domain Criteria: Friend or foe? *Journal of Clinical Child & Adolescent Psychology, 49,* 341–352.

Garber, J., & Flynn, C. (2001). Predictors of depressive cognitions in young adolescents. *Cognitive Therapy and Research, 25,* 353–376.

Garber, J., & Kaminski, K. M. (2000). Laboratory and performance-based measures of depression in children and adolescents. *Journal of Clinical Child Psychology, 29,* 509–525.

Garcia, A. M., Medina, D., & Sibley, M. H. (2019). Conflict between parents and adolescents with ADHD: Situational triggers and the role of comorbidity. *Journal of Child and Family Studies, 28,* 3338–3345.

Garcia, G., Logan, G. E., & Gonzalez-Heydrich, J. (2012). Management of psychotropic medication side effects in children and adolescents. *Child and Adolescent Psychiatric Clinics of North America, 21,* 713–738.

Gardener, H., Spiegelman, D., & Buka, S. L. (2009). Prenatal risk factors for autism: Comprehensive meta-analysis. *British Journal of Psychiatry, 195,* 7–14.

Gardener, H., Spiegelman, D., & Buka, S. L. (2011). Perinatal and neonatal risk factors for autism: A comprehensive meta-analysis. *Pediatrics, 128,* 344–355.

Gardner, D. M., & Gerdes, A. C. (2015). A review of peer relationships and friendships in youth with ADHD. *Journal of Attention Disorders, 19,* 844–855.

Gargano, L. M., Locke, S., Li, J., & Farfel, M. R. (2018). Behavior problems in adolescence and subsequent mental health in early adulthood: Results from the World Trade Center Health Registry Cohort. *Pediatric Research, 84,* 205–209.

Gargano, L. M., Welch, A. E., & Stellman, S. D. (2017). Substance use in adolescents 10 years after the World Trade Center attacks in New York City. *Journal of Child & Adolescent Substance Abuse, 26,* 66–74.

Garnefski, N., & Kraaij, V. (2018). Specificity of relations between adolescents' cognitive emotion regulation strategies and symptoms of depression and anxiety. *Cognition and Emotion, 32,* 1401–1408.

Garralda, M. E. (2017). Hallucinations and mental health in children. *Oruen–The CNS Journal, 2,* 574–575.

Gast, D. L., Blair, P., & Ledford, J. R. (2018). Multiple baseline and multiple probe designs. In J. R. Ledford & D. L. Gast (Eds.), *Single case research methodology: Applications in special education and behavioral sciences* (3rd ed.). New York: Routledge, Taylor & Francis Group.

Gatchel, R. J., Haggard, R., Thomas, C., & Howard, K. J. (2018). Biopsychosocial approaches to understanding chronic pain and disability. In R. J. Moore (Ed.), *Handbook of pain and palliative care: Biopsychosocial and environmental approaches for the life course* (2nd ed.). Cham, Switzerland: Springer.

Gaub, M., & Carlson, C. L. (1997). Gender difference in ADHD: A meta-analysis and critical review. *Journal of the American Academy of Child and Adolescent Psychiatry, 36,* 1035–1045.

Gaylord-Harden, N. K., Elmore, C. A., Campbell, C. L., & Wethington, A. (2011). An examination of the tripartite mode of depressive and anxiety symptoms in African American youth: Stressors and coping strategies as common and specific correlates. *Journal of Clinical Child and Adolescent Psychology, 40,* 360–374.

Gazelle, H. (2010). Anxious solitude/withdrawal and anxiety disorders: Conceptualization, co-occurrence, and peer processes leading toward and away from disorder in childhood. In H. Gazelle & K. H. Rubin (Eds.), *Social anxiety in childhood: Bridging developmental and clinical perspectives. New directions for child and adolescent* (Vol. 127, pp. 67–78). San Francisco, CA: Jossey-Bass.

Ge, X., Conger, R. D., Lorenz, F. O., Shanahan, M., & Elder, G. H. (1995). Mutual influences in parent and adolescent psychological distress. *Developmental Psychology, 31,* 406–419.

Geary, D. C. (2003). Learning disabilities in arithmetic: Problem-solving differences and cognitive deficits. In H. L. Swanson, K. R. Harris, & S. Graham (Eds.), *Handbook of learning disabilities.* New York: Guilford Press.

Geary, D. C. (2004). Mathematics and learning disabilities. *Journal of Learning Disabilities, 37,* 4–15.

Geary, D. C., Hoard, M. K., Nugent, L., & Bailey, D. H. (2013). Adolescents' functional numeracy is predicted by their school entry number system knowledge. *PLoS One, 8,* e54651.

Geary, D. C., Nicholas, A., Li, Y., & Sun, J. (2017). Developmental change in the influence of domain-general abilities and domain-specific knowledge on mathematics achievement: An eight-year longitudinal study. *Journal of Educational Psychology, 109,* 680–693.

Gee, S., & Taylor, D. (2018). Pharmacological management of treatment-resistant schizophrenia: Advanced use of clozapine. In O. Howes (Ed.), *Treatment Response and Resistance in Schizophrenia.* Oxford: Oxford University Press.

Geier, A. B., Foster, G. D., Womble, L. G., McLaughlin, J., Borradaile, K. E., Nachmani, J., et al. (2007). The relationship between relative weight and school attendance among elementary schoolchildren. *Obesity, 15,* 2157–2161.

Geller, B. (2019). Antipsychotics, excess deaths and paradoxes of child psychiatry. *JAMA Psychiatry, 76,* 111–112.

Geller, B., Craney, J. L., Bolhofner, K., DelBello, M. P., Axelson, D., Luby, J., et al. (2003). Phenomenology and longitudinal course of children with prepubertal and early adolescent bipolar disorder phenotype. In B. Geller & M. P. DelBello (Eds.), *Bipolar disorder in childhood and early adolescence.* New York: Guilford Press.

Geller, B., Tillman, R., & Bolhofner, K. (2007). Proposed definitions of bipolar I disorder episodes and daily rapid cycling phenomena in preschoolers, school-aged children, adolescents, and adults. *Journal of Child and Adolescent Psychopharmacology, 17,* 217–222.

Geller, B., Zimerman, B., Williams, M., Bolhofner, K., & Craney, J. L. (2001). Bipolar disorder at prospective follow-up of adults who had prepubertal major depressive disorder. *American Journal of Psychiatry, 158,* 125–127.

Geller, B., Zimerman, B., Williams, M., Bolhofner, K., Craney, J. L., DelBello, M. P., & Soutullo, C. A. (2000). Diagnostic characteristics of 93 cases of prepubertal and early adolescent bipolar disorder phenotype by gender, puberty and comorbid attention deficit hyperactivity disorder. *Journal of Child and Adolescent Psychopharmacology, 10,* 157–164.

Geller, D. A. (2006). Obsessive-compulsive and spectrum disorders in children and adolescents. *Psychiatric Clinics, 29,* 353–370.

Gencöz, T., Voelz, A. R., Gencöz, F., Pettit, J. W., & Joiner, T. E. (2001). Specificity of information processing styles to depressive symptoms in youth psychiatric inpatients. *Journal of Abnormal Child Psychology, 29,* 255–262.

Gengoux, G. W. (2018). Pivotal response therapy. In E. Braaten (Ed.), *The SAGE encyclopedia of intellectual and developmental disorders.* Thousand Oaks, CA: SAGE Publications, Inc.

George, M. J., & Odgers, C. L. (2015). Seven fears and the science of how mobile technologies may be influencing adolescents in the digital age. *Perspectives on Psychological Science, 10,* 832–851.

Georgiades, K., Lewinsohn, P. M., Monroe, S. M., & Seeley, J. R. (2006). Major depressive disorder in adolescence: The role of subthreshold symptoms. *Journal of the American Academy of Child and Adolescent Psychiatry, 45,* 936–944.

Gerard, M. W. (1939). Enuresis: A study in etiology. *American Journal of Orthopsychiatry, 9,* 48–58.

Gerhardt, C. A., Baughcum, A. E., Fortney, C., & Lichtenthal, W. G. (2017). Palliative care, end of life, and bereavement. In M. C. Roberts & R. G. Steele (Eds.), *Handbook of pediatric psychology* (5th ed.). New York: The Guilford Press.

References

Gersten, R., Jayanthi, M., & Dimino, J. (2017a). Too much, too soon? Unanswered questions from national response to intervention evaluation. *Exceptional Children, 83,* 244–254.

Gersten, R., Newman-Gonchar, R., Haymond, K. S., & Dimino, J. (2017b). *What is the evidence base to support reading interventions for improving student outcomes in grades 1–3?* Retrieved from https://files.eric.ed.gov/fulltext/ED573686.pdf

Gerull, F. C., & Rapee, R. M. (2002). Mother knows best: The effects of maternal modeling on the acquisition of fear and avoidance behaviour in toddlers. *Behaviour Research and Therapy, 40,* 279–287.

Getahun, D., Rhoads, G. G., Demissie, K., Lu, S.-E., Quinn, V. P., Fassett, M. J., et al. (2013). In utero exposure to ischemic-hypoxic conditions and attention-deficit/hyperactivity disorder. *Pediatrics, 131,* e53–e61.

Gettinger, M., & Koscik, R. (2001). Psychological services for children with learning disabilities. In J. N. Hughes, A. M. La Greca, & J. C. Conoley (Eds.), *Handbook of psychological services for children and adolescents.* New York: Oxford University Press.

Ghandour, R. M., Sherman, L. J., Vladutiu, C. J., Ali, M. M., Lynch, S. E., Bitsko, R. H., & Blumberg, S. J. (2019). Prevalence and treatment of depression, anxiety, and conduct problems in US children. *The Journal of Pediatrics, 206,* 256–267.

Gibbs, J. T. (2003). African American children and adolescents. In J. T. Gibbs, L. N. Huang, and Associates (Eds.), *Children of color: Psychological interventions with culturally diverse youth.* San Francisco, CA: Jossey-Bass.

Gill, A. M., Hyde, L. W., Shaw, D. S., Dishion, T. J., & Wilson, M. N. (2008). The family check-up in early childhood: A case study of intervention process and change. *Journal of Clinical Child & Adolescent Psychology, 37,* 893–904.

Gillam, R. B., Montgomery, J. W., Gillam, S. L., & Evans, J. L. (2017). Working memory in child language disorders. In R. G. Schwartz (Ed.), *Handbook of child language disorders.* New York: Routledge.

Gillespie, S. L. (2016). Epidemiology of pediatric HIV infection. In T. Chenneville (Ed.), *A clinical guide to pediatric HIV.* Cham, Switzerland: Springer.

Gilmour, J., Hill, B., Place, M., & Skuse, D. H. (2004). Social communication deficits in conduct disorder: A clinical and community survey. *Journal of Child Psychology and Psychiatry, 45,* 967–978.

Ginsburg, G. S., & Silverman, W. K. (1996). Phobic and anxiety disorders in Hispanic and Caucasian youth. *Journal of Anxiety Disorders, 10,* 517–528.

Ginsburg, G. S., & Silverman, W. K. (2000). Gender role orientation and fearfulness in children with anxiety disorders. *Journal of Anxiety Disorders, 14,* 57–67.

Ginsburg, G. S., Becker-Haimes, E. M., Keeton, C., Kendall, P. C., Iyengar, S., Sakolsky, D., et al. (2018). Results from the Child/Adolescent Anxiety Multimodal Extended Long-Term Study (CAMELS): Primary anxiety outcomes. *Journal of the American Academy of Child & Adolescent Psychiatry, 57,* 471–480.

Ginsburg, G. S., LaGreca, A. M., & Silverman, W. K. (1998). Social anxiety in children with anxiety disorders: Relation with social and emotional functioning. *Journal of Abnormal Psychology, 26,* 175–185.

Ginsburg, G. S., Riddle, M. A., & Davies, M. (2006). Somatic symptoms in children and adolescents with anxiety disorders. *Journal of the American Academy of Child and Adolescent Psychiatry, 45,* 1179–1187.

Girand, H. L., Litkowiec, S., & Sohn, M. (2020). Attention-deficit/hyperactivity disorder and psychotropic polypharmacy prescribing trends. *Pediatrics,* e20192832.

Given, Y., & Apter, A. (2016). Evidence-based prevention and treatment of suicidal behavior in children and adolescents. In R. C. O'Connor & J. Pirkis (Eds.), *The international handbook of suicide prevention.* West Sussex, UK: John Wiley & Sons.

Glantz, L. H. (1996). Conducting research with children: Legal and ethical issues. *Journal of the American Academy of Child and Adolescent Psychiatry, 35,* 1283–1291.

Gleason, M. M. (2019). Infant mental health in primary care. In C. H. Zeanah (Ed.), *Handbook of infant mental health* (4th ed.). New York: The Guilford Press.

Gleason, M. M., & Humphreys, K. L. (2016). Categorical diagnosis of extreme hyperactivity, impulsivity, and inattention in very young children. *Infant Mental Health Journal, 37,* 476–485.

Gleason, M. M., & Humphreys, K. L. (2018). Hyperactivity, impulsivity, and inattention in young children. In C. H. Zeanah, Jr. (Ed.), *Handbook of infant mental health* (4th ed.). New York: Guilford Press.

Gleason, M. M., Egger, H. L., Emslie, G. J., Greenhill, L. L., Kowatch, R. A., Lieberaman, A. F., et al. (2007). Pharmacological treatment for very young children: Contexts and guidelines. *Journal of the American Academy of Child and Adolescent Psychiatry, 46,* 1532–1572.

Glenn, C. R., Kleiman, E. M., Cha, C. B., Deming, C. A., Franklin, J. C., & Nock, M. K. (2018). Understanding suicide risk within the Research Domain Criteria (RDoC) framework: A meta-analytic review. *Depression and Anxiety, 35,* 65–88.

Glenn, C. R., Kleiman, E. M., Kellerman, J., Pollak, O., Cha, C. B., Esposito, E. C., et al. (2020). A meta-analytic review of worldwide suicide rates in adolescents. *Journal of Child Psychology and Psychiatry, 61,* 294–308.

Global Initiative for Asthma. (2019). *Global strategy for asthma management and prevention, updated 2019.* Retrieved from https://ginasthma.org/wp-content/uploads/2019/06/GINA-2019-main-report-June-2019-wms.pdf

Glowinski, A. L., Madden, P. A. F., Bucholz, K. K., Lynskey, M. T., & Heath, A. C. (2003). Genetic epidemiology of self-reported lifetime DSM-IV major depressive disorder in a population-based twin sample of female adolescents. *Journal of Child Psychology and Psychiatry, 44,* 988–996.

Glueck, S., & Glueck, E. T. (1968). *Delinquents and nondelinquents in perspective.* Cambridge, MA: Harvard University Press.

Goddard, H. H. (1912). *The Kallikak family.* New York: Macmillan.

Godoy Garraza, L., Kuiper, N., Goldston, D., McKeon, R., & Walrath, C. (2019). Long-term impact of the Garrett Lee Smith Youth Suicide Prevention Program on youth suicide mortality, 2006–2015. *Journal of Child Psychology and Psychiatry, 60,* 1142–1147.

Goeke, J., Kassow, D., May, D., & Kundert, D. (2003). Parental opinions about plastic surgery for individuals with Down syndrome. *Mental Retardation, 41,* 29–34.

Goethals, E. R., Oris, L., Soenens, B., Berg, C. A., Prikken, S., Van Broeck, N., et al. (2017). Parenting and treatment adherence in type 1 diabetes throughout adolescence and emerging adulthood. *Journal of Pediatric Psychology, 42,* 922–932.

Gogtay, N. (2007). Cortical brain development in schizophrenia: Insights from neuroimaging studies in childhood-onset schizophrenia. *Schizophrenia Bulletin, 34,* 30–36.

Gogtay, N., Lu, A., Leow, A. D., Klunder, A. D., Lee, A. D., Chavez, A., et al. (2008). Three-dimensional brain growth abnormalities in childhood-onset schizophrenia visualized by using tensor-based morphometry. *Proceedings of the National Academy of Science, 105,* 15979–15984.

Golberstein, E., Wen, H., & Miller, B. F. (2020). Coronavirus disease 2019 (COVID-19) and mental health for children and adolescents. *JAMA Pediatrics.* doi:10.1001/jamapediatrics.2020.1456

Golden, C. J. (1997). The Nebraska neuropsychological children's battery. In C. R. Reynolds & E. Fletcher-Janzen (Eds.), *Handbook of clinical child neuropsychology* (2nd ed.). New York: Plenum Press.

Golds, L., de Kruiff, K., & MacBeth, A. (2020). Disentangling genes, attachment, and environment: A systematic review of the developmental psychopathology literature on gene–environment interactions and attachment. *Development and Psychopathology, 32,* 357–381.

Goldstein, S. (2011). Attention-deficit/hyperactivity disorder. In S. Goldstein & C. R. Reynolds (Eds.), *Handbook of neurodevelopmental and genetic disorders in children.* New York: Guilford Press.

Goldstein, S., & Reynolds, C. R. (Eds.) (2011). *Handbook of neurodevelopmental and genetic disorders in children.* New York: Guilford Press.

Goldstein, T. R., Axelson, D. A., Birmaher, B., & Brent, D. A. (2007). Dialectical behavior therapy for adolescents with bipolar disorder: A 1-year open trial. *Journal of the American Academy of Child & Adolescent Psychiatry, 46,* 820–830.

Goldston, D. B., & Compton, J. S. (2007). Adolescent suicidal and nonsuicidal self-harm behaviors and risk. In E. J. Mash & R. A. Barkley (Eds.), *Assessment of childhood disorders* (4th ed.). New York: The Guilford Press.

Gomez, R., Gomez, A., DeMello, L., & Tallent, R. (2001). Perceived maternal control and support: Effects on hostile biased social information processing and aggression among clinic-referred children with high aggression. *Journal of Child Psychology and Psychiatry, 42,* 513–522.

Gomez, R., Vance, A., & Gomez, R. M. (2013). Maternal ratings of the ADHD symptoms: Subtypes versus severity in clinic-referred children and adolescents. *Journal of Attention Disorders, 20,* 414–423.

Gooch, D., Snowling, M., & Hulme, C. (2011). Time perception, phonological skills and executive function in children with dyslexia and/or ADHD symptoms. *Journal of Child Psychology and Psychiatry, 52,* 195–203.

Goodlad, J. K., Marcus, D. K., & Fulton, J. J. (2013). Lead and attention-deficit/hyperactivity disorder (ADHD) symptoms: A meta-analysis. *Clinical Psychology Review, 33,* 417–425.

Goodman, S. H., & Brand, S. R. (2009). Infants of depressed mothers. In C. H. Zeanah, Jr. (Ed.), *Handbook of infant mental health* (3rd ed.). New York: The Guilford Press.

Goodman, S. H., Rouse, M. H., Connell, A. M., Broth, M. R., Hall, C. M., & Heyward, D. (2011). Maternal depression and child psychopathology: A meta-analytic review. *Clinical Child and Family Psychology Review, 14,* 1–27.

Goodwin, R. D., Bandiera, F. C., Steinberg, D., Ortega, A. N., & Feldman, J. M. (2012). Asthma and mental health among youth: Etiology, current knowledge and future directions. *Expert Review of Respiratory Medicine, 6,* 397–406.

Gordis, E. B., Feres, N., Olezeski, C. L., Rabkin, A. N., & Trickett, P. K. (2010). Skin conductance reactivity and respiratory sinus arrhythmia among maltreated and comparison youth: Relations with aggressive behavior. *Journal of Pediatric Psychology, 35,* 547–558.

Gordon, C. T., & Hinshaw, S. P. (2019). Executive functions in girls with and without childhood ADHD followed through emerging adulthood: Developmental trajectories. *Journal of Clinical Child & Adolescent Psychology,* 1–15.

Gordon, D. B. (2015). Acute pain assessment tools: Let us move beyond simple pain ratings. *Current Opinion in Anesthesiology, 28,* 565–569.

Gordon, J., King, N. J., Bullone, E., Muris, P., & Ollendick, T. H. (2007). Treatment of children's nighttime fears: The need for a modern randomized controlled trial. *Clinical Psychology Review, 27,* 98–113.

Gordon, M., Barkley, R. A., & Lovett, B. J. (2006). Tests and observational measures. In R. A. Barkley (Ed.),

References

Attention-deficit hyperactivity disorder. A handbook for diagnosis and treatment. New York: The Guilford Press.

Gore, N. J., McGill, P., & Hastings, R. P. (2019). Making it meaningful: Caregiver goal selection in positive behavioral support. *Journal of Child and Family Studies, 28,* 1703–1712.

Gorman, D. A., Gardner, D. M., Murphy, A. L., Feldman, M., Bélanger, S. A., Steele, M. M., et al. (2015). Canadian guidelines on pharmacotherapy for disruptive and aggressive behaviour in children and adolescents with attention-deficit hyperactivity disorder, oppositional defiant disorder, or conduct disorder. *The Canadian Journal of Psychiatry, 60,* 62–76.

Gotlib, I. H., & Joormann, J. (2010). Cognition and depression: Current status and future directions. *Annual Review of Clinical Psychology, 6,* 285–312.

Gottesman, I. I. (1993). Origins of schizophrenia: Past as prologue. In R. Plomin & G. E. McClearn (Eds.), *Nature and nurture & psychology.* Washington, DC: American Psychological Association.

Gould, M. S., Greenberg, T., Velting, D. M., & Shaffer, D. (2003). Youth suicide risk and preventive interventions: A review of the past 10 years. *Journal of the American Academy of Child and Adolescent Psychiatry, 42,* 386–405.

Gowers, S., & Bryant-Waugh, R. (2004). Management of child and adolescent eating disorders: The current evidence base and future directions. *Journal of Child Psychology and Psychiatry, 45,* 63–83.

Graber, J., & Sontag, L. M. (2009). Internalizing problems during adolescence. In R. M. Lerner & L. Steinberg (Eds.), *Handbook of adolescent psychology, Vol. 2: Contextual influences on adolescent development* (3rd ed.). Hoboken, NJ: John Wiley & Sons.

Grace, W. J., & Graham, D. T. (1952). Relationship of specific attitudes and emotions to certain bodily diseases. *Psychosomatic Medicine, 14,* 243–251.

Grados, M. A. (2010). The genetics of obsessive-compulsive disorder and Tourette Syndrome: An epidemiological and pathway-based approach to gene discovery. *Journal of the American Academy of Child and Adolescent Psychiatry, 49,* 810–819.

Graetz, B. W., Sawyer, M. G., Hazell, P. L., Arney, F., & Baghurst, P. (2001). Validity of DSM-IV ADHD subtypes in a nationally representative sample of Australian children and adolescents. *Journal of the American Academy of Child and Adolescent Psychiatry, 40,* 410–417.

Graham, S., & Harris, K. R. (2003). Students with learning disabilities and the process of writing: A meta-analysis of SRSD studies. In H. L. Swanson, K. R. Harris, & S. Graham (Eds.), *Handbook of learning disabilities.* New York: Guilford Press.

Graham, S., & Harris, K. R. (2017). Evidence-based writing practices: A meta-analysis of existing meta-analyses. In R. Fidalgo, K. R. Harris, & M. Braaksma (Eds.), *Design principles for teaching effective writing: Theoretical and empirical grounded principles.* Leiden: Brill.

Grandin, T. (1997). A personal perspective on autism. In D. J. Cohen & F. R. Volkmar (Eds.), *Handbook of autism and pervasive developmental disorders.* New York: John Wiley.

Grant, K. E., Compas, B. E., Stuhlmacher, A. F., Thurm, A. E., McMahon, S. D., & Halpert, J. A. (2003). Stressors and child and adolescent psychopathology: Moving from markers to mechanisms of risk. *Psychological Bulletin, 129,* 447–466.

Gray, J. A. (1987). *The psychology of fear and stress.* New York: Cambridge University Press.

Gray, K. M., & Squeglia, L. M. (2018). Research review: What have we learned about adolescent substance use? *Journal of Child Psychology and Psychiatry, 59,* 618–627.

Gregus, S. J., Craig, J. T., & Cavell, T. A. (2020). Toward evidence-based interventions for chronically bullied children: Candidate mechanisms and potential strategies. *Evidence-Based Practice in Child and Adolescent Mental Health, 5,* 83–101.

Green, J. (2006). Annotation: The therapeutic alliance—a significant but neglected variable in child mental health treatment studies. *Journal of Child Psychology and Psychiatry, 47,* 425–435.

Green, J., & Goldwyn, R. (2002). Annotation: Attachment disorganization and psychopathology: New findings in attachment research and their potential implications for developmental psychopathology in childhood. *Journal of Child Psychology and Psychiatry, 43,* 835–846.

Green, S. A., & Ben-Sasson, A. (2010). Anxiety disorders and sensory over-responsivity in children with autism spectrum disorders: Is there a causal relationship? *Journal of Autism and Developmental Disorders, 40,* 1495–1504.

Greenbaum, Z. (2020). Increasing action on climate change. *Monitor on Psychology, 51,* 68–71.

Greenhill, L. L., Swanson, J. M., Hechtman, L., Waxmonsky, J., Arnold, L. E., Molina, B. S. G., et al. (2020). Trajectories of growth associated with long-term stimulant medication in the multimodal treatment study of attention-deficit/hyperactivity disorder. *Journal of the American Academy of Child & Adolescent Psychiatry, 59,* 978–989.

Greenwood, C. R., Carta, J. J., Hart, B., Kamps, D., Terry, B., Arreaga-Mayer, C., et al. (1992). Out of the laboratory and into the community: 26 years of applied behavior analysis at the Juniper Gardens Children's Project. *American Psychologist, 47,* 1464–1474.

Greenwood, C. R., Hart, B., Walker, D., & Risley, T. (1994). The opportunity to respond and academic performance revisited: A behavioral theory of developmental retardation and its prevention. In R. Gardner et al. (Eds.), *Behavior analysis in education: Focus on measurably superior instruction.* Pacific Grove, CA: Brooks/Cole.

Gregory, A. M., & Eley, T. C. (2011). The genetic basis of child and adolescent anxiety. In W. K. Silverman & A. Field (Eds.), *Anxiety disorders in children and adolescents*. New York: Cambridge University Press.

Gregory, A. M., Eley, T. C., & Plomin, R. (2004). Exploring the association between anxiety and conduct problems in a large sample of twins aged 2–4. *Journal of Abnormal Child Psychology, 32,* 111–122.

Gregory, A. M., Rijsdijk, F. V., & Eley, T. C. (2006). A twin-study of sleep difficulties in school-aged children. *Child Development, 77,* 1668–1679.

Greven, C. U., Richards, J. S., & Buitelaar, J. K. (2018). Sex differences in ADHD. In T. Banaschewski, D. Coghill, & A. Zuddas (Eds.), *Oxford textbook of Attention Deficit Hyperactivity Disorder.* New York: Oxford University Press.

Greven, C. U., Rijsdijk, F. V., Asherson, P., & Plomin, R. (2011). A longitudinal twin study on the association between ADHD symptoms and reading. *Journal of Child Psychology and Psychiatry, 53,* 234–242.

Griffiths, L. J., Wolke, D., Page, A. S., & Horwood, J. P. (2006). Obesity and bullying: Different effects for boys and girls. *Archives of Disease in Childhood, 91,* 121–125.

Grigorenko, E. L. (2009). Speaking genes or genes for speaking? Deciphering the genetics of speech and language. *Journal of Child Psychology and Psychiatry, 50,* 116–125.

Grigorenko, E. L., Compton, D. L., Fuchs, L. S., Wagner, R. K., Willcutt, E. G., & Fletcher, J. M. (2020). Understanding, educating, and supporting children with specific learning disabilities: 50 years of science and practice. *American Psychologist, 75,* 37–51.

Grigorenko, E., Torres, S., Lebedeva, E., & Bondar, Y. (2018). Evidence-based interventions for ASD: A focus on applied behavior analysis (ABA) interventions. *Psychology. Journal of Higher School of Economics, 15,* 711–727.

Groenewald, C. B., Giles, M., & Palermo, T. M. (2019). School absence associated with childhood pain in the United States. *The Clinical Journal of Pain, 35,* 525–531.

Groenman, A. P., Janssen, T. W., & Oosterlaan, J. (2017). Childhood psychiatric disorders as risk factor for subsequent substance abuse: A meta-analysis. *Journal of the American Academy of Child & Adolescent Psychiatry, 56,* 556–569.

Groh, A. M., Fearon, R. P., Bakermans-Kranenburg, M. J., van IJzendoorn, M. H., Steele, R. D., & Roisman, G. I. (2014). The significance of attachment security for children's social competence with peers: A meta-analytic study. *Attachment & Human Development, 16,* 103–136.

Groh, A. M., Roisman, G. I., van IJzendoorn, M. H., Bakermans-Kranenburg, M. J., & Fearon, R. P. (2012). The significance of insecure and disorganized attachment for children's

internalizing symptoms: A meta-analytic study. *Child Development, 83,* 591–610.

Grossman, A. W., Churchill, J. D., McKinney, B. C., Kodish, I. M., Otte, S. L., & Greenough, W. T. (2003). Experience effects on brain development: Possible contributions to psychopathology. *Journal of Child Psychology and Psychiatry, 44,* 33–63.

Grossman, H. J. (1983). *Classification in mental retardation.* Washington, DC: American Association on Mental Deficiency.

Grusec, J. E. (1992). Social learning theory and developmental psychology: The legacies of Robert Sears and Albert Bandura. *Developmental Psychology, 28,* 776–786.

Guerra, N. G., Graham, S., & Tolan, P. H. (2011). Raising healthy children: Translating child development research into practice. *Child Development, 82,* 7–16.

Guiraud, H., Bedoin, N., Krifi-Papoz, S., Herbillon, V., Caillot-Bascoul, A., Gonzalez-Monge, S., & Boulenger, V. (2018). Don't speak too fast! Processing of fast rate speech in children with specific language impairment. *PLoS One, 13,* e0191808.

Gullone, E. (2000). The development of normal fear: A century of research. *Clinical Psychology Review, 20,* 429–451.

Gulur, P., Fortier, M. A., Mayes, L. C., & Kain, Z. N. (2019). Perioperative behavioral stress in children. In C. J. Coté, J. Lerman, & B. J. Anderson (Eds.), *A practice of anesthesia for infants and children* (6th ed.). Philadelphia, PA: Elsevier.

Gunther, D., & Diekema, D. (2006). Attenuating growth in children with developmental disability: A new approach to an old dilemma. *Archives of Pediatric and Adolescent Medicine, 160,* 1013–1017.

Gur, R. E., Cowell, P., Turetsky, B. I., Gallacher, F., Cannon, T., Bilker, W., & Gur, R. C. (1998). A follow-up magnetic resonance imaging study of schizophrenia. *Archives of General Psychiatry, 55,* 145–152.

Gurnani, M., Pais, V., Cordeiro, K., Steele, S., Chen, S., & Hamilton, J. K. (2018). One potato, two potato, … assessing carbohydrate counting accuracy in adolescents with type 1 diabetes. *Pediatric Diabetes, 19,* 1302–1308.

Gustavson, K., Ystrom, E., Stoltenberg, C., Susser, E., Surén, P., Magnus, P., et al. (2017). Smoking in pregnancy and child ADHD. *Pediatrics, 139,* e20162509.

Hagerman, R. J. (2011). Fragile X syndrome and fragile X-associated disorders. In S. Goldstein & C. R. Reynolds (Eds.), *Handbook of neurodevelopmental disorders in children.* New York: Guilford Press.

Haijma, S. V., Van Haren, N., Cahn, W., Koolschijn, P. C. M. P., Hulshoff Pol, H. E., & Kahn, R. S. (2012). Brain volumes in schizophrenia: A meta-analysis in over 18,000 subjects. *Schizophrenia Bulletin, 39,* 1129–1138.

Hails, K. A., Reuben, J. D., Shaw, D. S., Dishion, T. J., & Wilson, M. N. (2018). Transactional associations among maternal

References

depression, parent–child coercion, and child conduct problems during early childhood. *Journal of Clinical Child & Adolescent Psychology, 47*(sup1), S291–S305.

Hair, N. L., Hanson, J. L., Wolfe, B. L., & Pollak, S. D. (2015). Association of child poverty, brain development, and academic achievement. *JAMA Pediatrics, 169,* 822–829.

Hakvoort, E. M., Bos, H. M. W., Van Balen, F., & Hermanns, J. M. A. (2011). Postdivorce relationships in families and children's psychosocial adjustment. *Journal of Divorce and Remarriage, 52,* 125–146.

Hales, C. M., Carroll, M. D., Fryar, C. D., & Ogden, C. L. (2017). *Prevalence of obesity among adults and youth: United States, 2015–2016.* NCHS data brief, no. 288. Hyattsville, MD: National Center for Health Statistics.

Hales, C. M., Kit, B. K., Gu, Q., & Ogden, C. L. (2018). Trends in prescription medication use among children and adolescents. *JAMA, 319,* 2009–2020.

Hallahan, D. P., & Mock, D. R. (2003). A brief history of the field of learning disabilities. In H. L. Swanson, K. R. Harris, & S. Graham (Eds.), *Handbook of learning disabilities.* New York: Guilford Press.

Hallahan, D. P., Pullen, P. C., & Ward, D. (2013). A brief history of the field of learning disabilities. In H. L. Swanson, K. R. Harris, & S. Graham (Eds.), *Handbook of learning disabilities.* New York: Guilford Press.

Halliday, L. F., Tuomainen, O., & Rosen, S. (2017). Auditory processing deficits are sometimes necessary and sometimes sufficient for language difficulties in children: Evidence from mild to moderate sensorineural hearing loss. *Cognition, 166,* 139–151.

Halmi, K. A. (1985). Eating disorders. In H. I. Kaplan & B. J. Sadock (Eds.), *Comprehensive textbook of psychiatry* (4th ed.). Baltimore, MD: Williams & Wilkins.

Halstead, E. J., Griffith, G. M., & Hastings, R. P. (2018). Social support, coping, and positive perceptions as potential protective factors for the well-being of mothers of children with intellectual and developmental disabilities. *International Journal of Developmental Disabilities, 64,* 288–296.

Hamadi, L., & Holliday, J. (2020). Moderators and mediators of outcome in treatments for anorexia nervosa and bulimia nervosa in adolescents: A systematic review of randomized controlled trials. *International Journal of Eating Disorders, 53,* 3–19.

Hammen, C. (2018). Risk factors for depression: An autobiographical review. *Annual Review of Clinical Psychology, 14,* 1–28.

Hammen, C. L. (2015). Stress and depression: Old questions, new approaches. *Current Opinion in Psychology, 4,* 80–85.

Hammen, C., & Rudolph, K. D. (2003). Childhood mood disorders. In E. J. Mash & R. A. Barkley (Eds.), *Child psychopathology* (2nd ed.). New York: Guilford Press.

Hammen, C., Burge, D., Burney, E., & Adrian, C. (1990). Longitudinal study of diagnosis in children of women with unipolar and bipolar affective disorders. *Archives of General Psychiatry, 47,* 1112–1117.

Hammill, D. D. (1993). A brief look at the learning disabilities movement in the United States. *Journal of Learning Disabilities, 26,* 295–310.

Han, J.-Y., Kwon, H.-J., Ha, M., Paik, K.-C., Lim, M.-H., Gyu Lee, S., et al. (2015). The effects of prenatal exposure to alcohol and environmental tobacco smoke on risk for ADHD: A large population-based study. *Psychiatry Research, 225,* 164–168.

Handen, B. L. (1998). Mental retardation. In E. J. Mash & L. G. Terdal (Eds.), *Treatment of childhood disorders.* New York: Guilford Press.

Handen, B. L. (2007). Intellectual disability (mental retardation). In E. J. Mash & R. A. Barkley (Eds.), *Assessment of childhood disorders* (4th ed.). New York: Guilford Press.

Hane, A. A., & Fox, N. A. (2006). Ordinary variations in maternal caregiving influence human infants' stress reactivity. *Psychological Science, 17,* 550–556.

Hanf, C. (1969, June). *A two-stage program for modifying maternal controlling behaviors during mother-child interaction.* Paper presented at the meeting of the Western Psychological Association, Vancouver, BC, Canada.

Hanish, L. D., & Guerra, N. G. (2002). A longitudinal analysis of patterns of adjustment following peer victimization. *Development and Psychopathology, 14,* 69–89.

Hankin, B. L., Abramson, L. Y., Moffitt, T. E., Silva, P. A., McGee, R., & Angell, K. E. (1998). Development of depression from preadolescence to young adulthood: Emerging gender differences in a 10-year longitudinal study. *Journal of Abnormal Psychology, 107,* 128–140.

Hankin, B. L., Fraley, R. C., Lahey, B. B., & Waldman, I. D. (2005). Is depression best viewed as a continuum or discrete category? A taxometric analysis of childhood and adolescent depression in a population-based sample. *Journal of Abnormal Psychology, 114,* 96–110.

Happé, F. (2015). Autism as a neurodevelopmental disorder of mind-reading. *Journal of the British Academy, 3,* 197–209.

Happé, F. (2018). Why are savant skills and special talents associated with autism? *World Psychiatry: Official Journal of the World Psychiatric Association (WPA), 17,* 280–281.

Happé, F., & Frith, U. (2006). The weak coherence account: Detail-focused cognitive style in autism spectrum disorders. *Journal of Autism and Developmental Disorders, 36,* 5–25.

Happé, F., & Frith, U. (2020). Annual Research Review: Looking back to look forward—changes in the concept of autism and implications for future research. *Journal of Child Psychology and Psychiatry, 61,* 218–232.

Happé, F., Briskman, J., & Frith, U. (2001). Exploring the cognitive phenotype of autism: Weak "central coherence" in parents and siblings of children with autism: I. Experimental tests. *Journal of Child Psychology and Psychiatry, 42,* 299–307.

Happé, F., Ronald, A., & Plomin, R. (2006). Time to give up on a single explanation for autism. *Nature Neuroscience, 9,* 1218–1220.

Hardee, J. E., Benson, B. E., Bar-Haim, Y., Mogg, K., Bradley, B. P., Chen, G., et al. (2013). Patterns of neural connectivity during an attention bias task moderate associations between early childhood temperament and internalizing symptoms in young adulthood. *Biological Psychiatry, 74,* 273–279.

Harley, J. P., & Matthews, C. G. (1980). Food additives and hyperactivity in children: Experimental investigations. In R. M. Knights and D. J. Bakker (Eds.), *Treatment of hyperactive and learning disordered children.* Baltimore, MD: University Park Press.

Haroon, M. (2019a). The assessment and diagnosis of autism in children. In M. Haroon (Ed.), *ABC of autism.* Newark, NJ: John Wiley & Sons, Inc.

Haroon, M. (2019b). The features of autism in childhood. In M. Haroon (Ed.), *ABC of autism.* Newark, NJ: John Wiley & Sons, Inc.

Haroon, M. (2019c). An introduction to autism. In M. Haroon (Ed.), *ABC of autism.* Newark, NJ: John Wiley & Sons, Inc.

Haroon, M. (2019d). School and autism. In M. Haroon (Ed.), *ABC of autism.* Hoboken, NJ: John Wiley & Sons, Inc.

Harrington, R., Rutter, M., Weissman, M., Fudge, H., Groothues, C., Bredenkamp, D., et al. (1997). Psychiatric disorders in the relatives of depressed probands: I. Comparison of prepubertal, adolescent and early adult onset cases. *Journal of Affective Disorders, 42,* 9–22.

Harrison, P., & Oakland, T. (2015). *Adaptive Behavior Assessment System—Third Edition (ABAS-3).* Torrance, CA: Western Psychological Services.

Harrison, S. I., & McDermott, J. K. (1972). *Childhood psychopathology.* New York: International University Press.

Hart, L. M., Cornell, C., Damiano, S. R., & Paxton, S. J. (2015). Parents and prevention: A systematic review of interventions involving parents that aim to prevent body dissatisfaction or eating disorders. *International Journal of Eating Disorders, 48,* 157–169.

Harter, S. (1985). *Manual for the self-perception profile for children.* Denver, CO: University of Denver.

Hartung, C. M., & Widiger, T. A. (1998). Gender differences in the diagnosis of mental disorders: Conclusions and controversies of the DSM-IV. *Psychological Bulletin, 123,* 260–278.

Harvey, P. D., & Isner, E. C. (2020). Cognition, social cognition, and functional capacity in early-onset schizophrenia. *Child and Adolescent Psychiatric Clinics, 29,* 171–182.

Haskett, M. E., Nears, K., Ward, C. S., & McPherson, A. V. (2006). Diversity in adjustment of maltreated children: Factors associated with resilient functioning. *Clinical Psychology Review, 26,* 796–812.

Hastings, R. P. (2016). Do children with intellectual and developmental disabilities have a negative impact on other family members? The case for rejecting a negative narrative. In R. M. Hodapp & D. J. Fidler (Eds.), *International review of research in developmental disabilities* (Vol. 50). Waltham, MA: Academic Press.

Hastings, R. P., Daley, D., Burns, C., & Beck, A. (2006). Maternal distress and expressed emotion: Cross-sectional and longitudinal relationships with behavior problems of children with intellectual disabilities. *American Journal on Mental Retardation, 111,* 48–61.

Hastings, R. P., Kovshoff, H., Ward, N. J., degli Espinosa, F., Brown, T., & Remington, B. (2005). Systems analysis of stress and positive perceptions in mothers and fathers of preschool children with autism. *Journal of Autism and Developmental Disorders, 35,* 635–644.

Hatcher, P. J., Hulme, C., & Snowling, M. J. (2004). Explicit phoneme training combined with phonic reading instruction helps young children at risk of reading failure. *Journal of Child Psychology and Psychiatry, 45,* 338–359.

Hathaway, W. L., Dooling-Litfin, J. K., & Edwards, G. (2006). Integrating the results of an evaluation. In R. A. Barkley (Ed.), *Attention-deficit hyperactivity disorder: A handbook for diagnosis and treatment.* New York: The Guilford Press.

Hatzenbuehler, M. L. (2011). The social environment and suicide attempts in lesbian, gay, and bisexual youth. *Pediatrics, 127,* 896–903.

Haut, K. M., Schvarcz, A., Cannon, T. D., & Bearden, C. E. (2016). Neurodevelopmental theories of schizophrenia: Twenty-first century perspectives. In D. Cicchetti (Ed.), *Developmental psychopathology* (3rd ed.). Hoboken, NJ: John Wiley & Sons, Inc.

Hautala, D., & Sittner, K. (2019). Longitudinal mechanisms linking perceived racial discrimination to aggressive delinquency among North American indigenous youth. *Journal of Research in Crime and Delinquency, 56,* 694–735.

Hawker, D. S. J., & Boulton, M. J. (2000). Twenty years' research on peer victimization and psychosocial maladjustment: A meta-analytic review of cross-sectional studies. *Journal of Child Psychology and Psychiatry, 41,* 441–455.

Hawkins, E. H., Cummins, L. H., & Marlatt, G. A. (2004). Preventing substance abuse in American Indians and Alaska Native youths: Promising strategies for healthier communities. *Psychological Bulletin, 130,* 304–323.

Hawton, K., & Fortune, S. (2008). Suicidal behavior and deliberate self-harm. In M. Rutter et al. (Eds.), *Rutter's child and adolescent psychiatry* (5th ed.). Malden, MA: Blackwell Publishing.

Hay, D. F., Payne, A., & Chadwick, A. (2004). Peer relations in childhood. *Journal of Child Psychology and Psychiatry, 45,* 84–108.

References

Hayden, E. P., & Durbin, C. E. (2019). Development and psychopathology. In T. H. Ollendick, S. W. White, & B. A. White (Eds.), *The Oxford handbook of clinical child and adolescent psychology*. New York: Oxford University Press.

Hayes, G. J. (2003). Institutional review boards: Balancing conflicting values in research. In W. O'Donohue & K. Ferguson (Eds.), *Handbook of professional ethics for psychologists*. Thousand Oaks, CA: Sage Publications.

Hayes, J. F., Balantekin, K. N., Brown, M. L., & Wilfley, D. E. (2019). Obesity. In M. J. Prinstein, E. A. Youngstrom, E. J. Mash, & R. A. Barkley (Eds.), *Treatment of disorders in childhood and adolescence* (4th ed.). New York: The Guilford Press.

Hayiou-Thomas, M. E., Carroll, J. M., Leavett, R., Hulme, C., & Snowling, M. J. (2017). When does speech sound disorder matter for literacy? The role of disordered speech errors, co-occurring language impairment and family risk of dyslexia. *Journal of Child Psychology and Psychiatry, 58,* 197–205.

Hayward, C., Wilson, K. A., Lagle, K., Killen, J. D., & Taylor, B. B. (2004). Parent-reported predictors of adolescent panic attacks. *Journal of the American Academy of Child and Adolescent Psychiatry, 43,* 613–620.

Hayward, C., Wilson, K. A., Lagle, K., Kraemer, H. C., Killen, J. D., & Barr Taylor, C. (2008). The developmental psychopathology of social anxiety in adolescents. *Depression and Anxiety, 25,* 200–206.

Hazlett, H. C., Gu, H., Munsell, B. C., Kim, S. H., Styner, M., Wolff, J. J., et al. (2017). Early brain development in infants at high risk for autism spectrum disorder. *Nature, 542*(7641), 348–351.

Hazlett, H. C., Hammer, J., Hooper, S. R., & Kamphaus, R. W. (2011). Down syndrome. In S. Goldstein & C. R. Reynolds (Eds.), *Handbook of neurodevelopmental and genetic disorders in children*. New York: Guilford Press.

He, Y., Chen, J., Zhu, L.-H., Hua, L.-L., & Ke, F.-F. (2017). Maternal smoking during pregnancy and ADHD: Results from a systematic review and meta-analysis of prospective cohort studies. *Journal of Attention Disorders*. doi:10.1177/1087054717696766

Heasman, B., & Gillespie, A. (2019). Neurodivergent intersubjectivity: Distinctive features of how autistic people create shared understanding. *Autism, 23,* 910–921.

Hechtman, L., Swanson, J. M., Sibley, M. H., Stehli, A., Owens, E. B., Mitchell, J. T., et al. (2016). Functional adult outcomes 16 years after childhood diagnosis of attention-deficit/hyperactivity disorder: MTA results. *Journal of the American Academy of Child & Adolescent Psychiatry, 55,* 945–952.

Heim, S., & Benasich, A. A. (2006). Developmental disorders of language. In D. Cicchetti & D. J. Cohen (Eds.), *Developmental psychopathology: Vol. III. Risk, disorder, and adaptation*. Hoboken, NJ: John Wiley & Sons.

Helland, W. A., Posserud, M.-B., Helland, T., Heimann, M., & Lundervold, A. J. (2012). Language impairments in children with ADHD and in children with Reading Disorder. *Journal of Attention Disorders, 20,* 581–589.

Hellander, M., Sisson, D. P., & Fristad, M. A. (2003). Internet support for parents of children with early-onset bipolar disorder. In B. Geller & M. P. DelBello (Eds.), *Bipolar disorder in childhood and early adolescence*. New York: Guilford Press.

Heller, K. (1996). Coming of age of prevention science: Comments on the 1994 National Institute of Mental Health-Institute of medicine prevention reports. *American Psychologist, 51,* 1123–1127.

Hendren, R. L., Haft, S. L., Black, J. M., White, N. C., & Hoeft, F. (2018). Recognizing psychiatric comorbidity with reading disorders. *Frontiers in Psychiatry, 9.*

Henggeler, S. W., & Schaeffer, C. M. (2017). Treating serious antisocial behavior using Multisystemic Therapy. In J. R. Weisz & A. E. Kazdin (Eds.), *Evidence-based psychotherapies for children and adolescents* (3rd ed.). New York: The Guilford Press.

Henggeler, S. W., Melton, G. B., & Smith, L. A. (1992). Family preservation using multisystemic therapy: An effective alternative to incarcerating serious juvenile offenders. *Journal of Consulting and Clinical Psychology, 60,* 953–961.

Henggeler, S. W., Schoenwald, S. K., Borduin, C. M., Rowland, M. D., & Cunningham, P. B. (1998). *Multisystemic treatment of antisocial behavior in children and adolescents*. New York: Guilford Press.

Henin, A., & Kendall, P. C. (1997). Obsessive-compulsive disorder in childhood and adolescence. In T. H. Ollendick & R. J. Prinz (Eds.), *Advances in clinical child psychology* (Vol. 19). New York: Plenum Press.

Henriksen, M. G., Nordgaard, J., & Jansson, L. B. (2017). Genetics of schizophrenia: Overview of methods, findings and limitations. *Frontiers in Human Neuroscience, 11.*

Hermetet-Lindsay, K. D., Correia, K. F., Williams, P. L., Smith, R., Malee, K. M., Mellins, C. A., & Rutstein, R. M. (2017). Contributions of disease severity, psychosocial factors, and cognition to behavioral functioning in US youth perinatally exposed to HIV. *AIDS and Behavior, 21,* 2703–2715.

Hetherington, E. M., & Kelly, J. (2002). *For better or worse: Divorce reconsidered*. New York: W. W. Norton & Company.

Hetherington, E. M., & Stanley-Hagan, M. (1999). The adjustment of children with divorced parents: A risk and resiliency perspective. *Journal of Child Psychology and Psychiatry, 40,* 129–140.

Hetherington, E. M., Bridges, M., & Insabella, G. (1998). What matters? What does not? Five perspectives on the association between marital transitions and children's adjustment. *American Psychologist, 53,* 167–184.

Heward, W. (2013). *Exceptional children: An introduction to special education.* Upper Saddle River, NJ: Pearson.

Hiatt, K. D., & Dishion, T. J. (2008). Antisocial personality development. In T. P Beauchaine & S. P Hinshaw (Eds.), *Child and adolescent psychopathology.* Hoboken, NJ: John Wiley & Sons.

Hicks, C. L., von Baeyer, C. L., Spafford, P. A., van Korlaar, I., & Goodenough, B. (2001). The Faces Pain Scale-Revised: Toward a common metric in pediatric pain measurement. *Pain, 93,* 173–183.

Higa-McMillan, C. K., Francis, S. E., Rith-Najarian, L., & Chorpita, B. F. (2016). Evidence base update: 50 years of research on treatment for child and adolescent anxiety. *Journal of Clinical Child & Adolescent Psychology, 45,* 91–113.

Hill, K., & Roth, T. L. (2016). Epigenetic mechanisms in the development of behavior. In D. Cicchetti (Ed.), *Developmental psychopathology: Risk, resilience, and intervention* (Vol. 2). Hoboken, NJ: John Wiley & Sons.

Hilliard, M. E., Powell, P. W., & Anderson, B. J. (2016). Evidence-based behavioral interventions to promote diabetes management in children, adolescents, and families. *American Psychologist, 71,* 590–601.

Hilt, L. M., & Nolen-Hoeksema, S. (2014). Gender differences in depression. In I. H. Gotlib & C. L. Hammen (Eds.), *Handbook of depression* (3rd. ed.). New York: The Guilford Press.

Hinshaw, S. P. (2001, Winter). Is the inattentive type of ADHD a separate disorder? *Clinical Psychology: Science and Practice, 8,* 498–501.

Hinshaw, S. P. (2002). Preadolescent girls with attention-deficit/hyperactivity disorder: I. Background characteristics, comorbidity, cognitive and social functioning, and parenting practices. *Journal of Consulting and Clinical Psychology, 70,* 1086–1098.

Hinshaw, S. P. (2005). The stigmatization of mental illness in children and parents: Developmental issues, family concerns, and research needs. *Journal of Child Psychology and Psychiatry, 46,* 714–734.

Hinshaw, S. P. (2010). Growing up in a family with bipolar disorder: Personal experience, developmental lessons, and overcoming stigma. In D. J. Miklowitz & D. Cicchetti (Eds.), *Understanding bipolar disorder: A developmental psychopathology perspective.* New York: The Guilford Press.

Hinshaw, S. P. (2017). Developmental psychopathology as a scientific discipline: A 21st century perspective. In T. P. Beauchaine & S. P. Hinshaw (Eds.), *Child and adolescent psychopathology* (3rd ed.). Hoboken, NJ: John Wiley & Sons.

Hinshaw, S. P. (2018). Attention deficit hyperactivity disorder (ADHD): Controversy, developmental mechanisms, and multiple levels of analysis. *Annual Review of Clinical Psychology, 14,* 291–316.

Hinshaw, S. P., & Becker, S. P. (2020). Toward a developmental psychopathology approach for understanding, assessing, and treating ADHD in adolescents. In S. P. Becker (Ed.), *ADHD in adolescents: Development, assessment, and treatment.* New York: The Guilford Press.

Hinshaw, S. P., & Lee, S. S. (2003). Conduct and oppositional defiant disorders. In E. J. Mash & R. A. Barkley (Eds.), *Child psychopathology* (2nd ed.). New York: Guilford Press.

Hinshaw, S. P., & Scheffler, R. M. (2018). ADHD in the twenty-first century: Biology, context, policy, and the need for integrative perspective. In T. Banaschewski, D. Coghill, & A. Zuddas (Eds.), *Oxford textbook of attention deficit hyperactivity disorder.* Oxford: Oxford University Press.

Hinshaw, S. P., Lahey, B. B., & Hart, E. L. (1993). Issues of taxonomy and comorbidity in the development of conduct disorder. *Development and Psychopathology, 5,* 31–49.

Hinshelwood, J. (1917). *Congenital word-blindness.* London: H. K. Lewis.

Hirshfeld-Becker, D. R. (2010). Familial and temperamental risk factors for social anxiety disorder. In H. Gazelle & K. H. Rubin (Eds.), *Social anxiety in childhood: Bridging developmental and clinical perspectives. New directions for child and adolescent, 127,* 51–65. San Francisco, CA: Jossey-Bass.

Hithersay, R., Hamburg, S., Knight, B., & Strydom, A. (2017). Cognitive decline and dementia in Down syndrome. *Current Opinion in Psychiatry, 30,* 102–107.

Hoagwood, K. E. (2005). Family-based services in children's mental health: A research review and synthesis. *Journal of Child Psychology and Psychiatry, 46,* 690–713.

Hoagwood, K. E., & Cavaleri, M. A. (2010). Ethical issues in child and adolescent psychosocial treatment research. In J. R. Weisz & A. E. Kazdin (Eds.), *Evidence-based psychotherapies for children and adolescents.* New York: Guilford Press.

Hoagwood, K. E., Atkins, M., Horwitz, S., Kutash, K., Olin, S. S., Burns, B., et al. (2018). The threat to children's mental health from proposed federal budget cuts: A commentary on protecting policies and programs that promote collective efficacy. *Psychiatric Services (Washington, DC), 69,* 268–273.

Hoagwood, K. E., Peth-Pierce, R., Glaeser, E., Whitmyre, E., Shorter, P., & Vardanian, M. M. (2017). Implementing evidence-based psychotherapies for children and adolescents within complex mental health systems. In J. R. Weisz & A. E. Kazdin (Eds.), *Evidence-based psychotherapies for children and adolescents* (3rd ed.). New York: The Guilford Press.

Hoagwood, K. E., Vogel, J. M., Levitt, J. M., D'Amico, P. J., Paisner, W. I., & Kaplan, S. J. (2007). Implementing an evidence-based trauma treatment in a state system after September 11: The CATS Project. *Journal of the American Academy of Child and Adolescent Psychiatry, 46,* 773–779.

References

Hobbs, T., & Westling, D. L. (1998). Promoting successful inclusion through collaborative problem-solving. *Teaching Exceptional Children, 31,* 12–19.

Hodapp, R. M., & Dykens, E. M. (2003). Mental retardation (intellectual disabilities). In E. J. Mash & R. A. Barkley (Eds.), *Child psychopathology*. New York: Guilford Press.

Hodapp, R. M., & Dykens, E. M. (2019). Intellectual disabilities. In C. H. Zeanah, Jr. (Ed.), *Handbook of infant mental health* (4th ed.). New York: Guilford Press.

Hodapp, R. M., & Zigler, E. (1997). New issues in the developmental approach to mental retardation. In W. E. MacLean (Ed.), *Ellis' handbook of mental deficiency, psychological theory and research*. Mahwah, NJ: Lawrence Erlbaum.

Hodapp, R. M., Dankner, N. A., & Dykens, E. M. (2016). Behavioural phenotypes/genetic syndromes. In C. Hemmings & N. Bouras (Eds.), *Psychiatric and behavioural disorders in intellectual and developmental disabilities* (3rd ed.). Cambridge: Cambridge University Press.

Hodapp, R. M., Sanderson, K. A., Meskis, S. A., & Casale, E. G. (2017). Adult siblings of persons with intellectual disabilities: Past, present, and future. In R. M. Hodapp & D. J. Fidler (Eds.), *International review of research in developmental disabilities* (Vol. 53, pp. 163–202). Amsterdam: Academic Press.

Hodapp, R. M., Thornton-Wells, T. A., & Dykens, E. M. (2009). Intellectual disabilities. In C. H. Zeanah, Jr. (Ed.), *Handbook of infant mental health*. New York: Guilford Press.

Hoeft, F., & Wang, C. (2019). Intergenerational transmission in developmental dyslexia. In L. Verhoeven, C. Perfetti, & K. Pugh (Eds.), *Developmental Dyslexia across Languages and Writing Systems*. Cambridge: Cambridge University Press.

Hoeft, F., Carter, J. C., Lightbody, A. A., Hazlett, H. C., Piven, J., & Reiss, A. L. (2010). Region-specific alterations in brain development in one-to-three-year-old boys with fragile X syndrome. *Proceedings of the National Academy of Science, 107,* 9335–9339.

Hoehn, J., Foxen-Craft, E., Pinder, W., & Dahlquist, L. M. (2016). The role of parents in promoting children's adjustment to chronic illness. In C. DeMichelis & M. Ferrari (Eds.), *Child and adolescent resilience within medical contexts: Integrating research and practice*. Cham, Switzerland: Springer.

Hoffman, J. A., Franko, D. L., Thompson, D. R., Power, D. J., & Stallings, V. A. (2010). Longitudinal behavioral effects of a school-based fruit and vegetable promotion program. *Journal of Pediatric Psychology, 35,* 61–71.

Hofmann, S. G., Wu, J. Q., & Boettcher, H. (2013). D-Cycloserine as an augmentation strategy for cognitive behavioral therapy of anxiety disorders. *Biology of Mood & Anxiety Disorders, 3,* 1–10.

Hollis, C. (2015). Schizophrenia in children and adolescents. *BJPsych Advances, 21,* 333–341.

Hollon, S. D., Garber, J., & Shelton, R. C. (2005). Treatment of depression in adolescents with cognitive behavior therapy and medications: A commentary on the TADS project. *Cognitive and Behavioral Practice, 12,* 149–155.

Holt, M. K., Green, J. G., & Guzman, J. (2019). School settings. In T. H. Ollendick, S. W. White, & B. A. White (Eds.), *The Oxford handbook of clinical child and adolescent psychology*. New York: Oxford University Press.

Hommel, K. A., Ramsey, R. R., Rich, K. L., & Ryan, J. L. (2017). Adherence to pediatric treatment regimens. In M. C. Roberts & R. G. Steele (Eds.), *Handbook of pediatric psychology*. New York The Guilford Press.

Hommer, R. E., & Swedo, S. E. (2015). Schizophrenia and autism: Related disorders. *Schizophrenia Bulletin, 41,* 313–314.

Honaker, S. M., Meltzer, L. J., & Mindell, J. A. (2017). Pediatric sleep. In M. C. Roberts & R. G. Steele (Eds.), *Handbook of pediatric psychology* (5th ed.). New York: The Guilford Press.

Hoogman, M., Bralten, J., Hibar, D. P., Mennes, M., Zwiers, M. P., Schweren, L. S. J., et al. (2017). Subcortical brain volume differences in participants with attention deficit hyperactivity disorder in children and adults: A cross-sectional mega-analysis. *The Lancet Psychiatry, 4,* 310–319.

Hope, E. C., Hoggard, L. S., & Thomas, A. (2015). Emerging into adulthood in the face of racial discrimination: Physiological, psychological, and sociopolitical consequences for African American youth. *Translational Issues in Psychological Science, 1,* 342–351.

Hoppen, T. H., & Chalder, T. (2018). Childhood adversity as a transdiagnostic risk factor for affective disorders in adulthood: A systematic review focusing on biopsychosocial moderating and mediating variables. *Clinical Psychology Review, 65,* 81–151.

Hops, H., Andrews, J. A., Duncan, S. C., Duncan, T. E., & Tildesley, E. (2000). Adolescent drug use development: A social interactional and contextual perspective. In A. J. Sameroff, M. Lewis, & S. M. Miller (Eds.), *Handbook of developmental psychopathology* (2nd ed.). New York: Kluwer Academic/Plenum Publishers.

Hops, H., Biglan, A., Sherman, L., Arthur, J., Friedman, L., & Osteen, V. (1987). Home observations of family interactions of depressed women. *Journal of Consulting and Clinical Psychology, 55,* 341–346.

Horowitz, F. D. (1992). John B. Watson's legacy: Learning and environment. *Developmental Psychology, 28,* 360–367.

Horwitz, A. G., Czyz, E. K., & King, C. A. (2015). Predicting future suicide attempts among adolescent and emerging adult psychiatric emergency patients. *Journal of Clinical Child & Adolescent Psychology, 44,* 751–761.

Hostinar, C. E., Nusslock, R., & Miller, G. E. (2018). Future directions in the study of early-life stress and physical and emotional health: Implications of the neuroimmune network hypothesis. *Journal of Clinical Child and Adolescent Psychology, 47,* 142–156.

Hotez, P. (2019). The physician-scientist: Defending vaccines and combating antiscience. *The Journal of Clinical Investigation, 129,* 2169–2171.

Houts, A. C. (2002). Discovery, invention, and the expansion of the modern Diagnostic and Statistical Manual of mental disorders. In L. E. Beutler & M. L. Malik (Eds.), *Rethinking the DSM*. Washington, DC: American Psychological Association.

Houts, A. C., Peterson, J. K., & Whelan, J. P. (1986). Prevention of relapse in full-spectrum home training for primary enuresis: A component analysis. *Behavior Therapy, 17,* 462–469.

Hoven, C. W., Duarte, C. S., Wu, P., Doan, T., Singh, N., Mandell, D. J., et al. (2009). Parental exposure to mass violence and child mental health: The first responder and WTC evacuee study. *Clinical Child and Family Psychology Review, 12,* 95–112.

Howard, J., & Berzin, S. (2011). *Never too late: Achieving permanency and sustaining connections for older youth in foster care*. New York: Evan B. Donaldson Adoption Institute.

Howes, O. D., McCutcheon, R., Owen, M. J., & Murray, R. M. (2017). The role of genes, stress, and dopamine in the development of schizophrenia. *Biological Psychiatry, 81,* 9–20.

Howlin, P., Goode, S., Hutton, J., & Rutter, M. (2004). Adult outcome for children with autism. *Journal of Child Psychology and Psychiatry, 45,* 212–229.

Hoza, B., Murray-Close, D., Arnold, L. E., Hinshaw, S. P., Hechtman, L., & the MTA Cooperative Group. (2010). Time-dependent changes in positively biased self-perceptions of children with attention-deficit/hyperactivity disorder: A developmental psychopathology perspective. *Development and Psychopathology, 22,* 375–390.

Hsiao, H.-J., Chen, S.-H., Jaing, T.-H., Yang, C.-P., Chang, T.-Y., Li, M.-Y., et al. (2019). Psychosocial interventions for reduction of distress in children with leukemia during bone marrow aspiration and lumbar puncture. *Pediatrics & Neonatology, 60,* 278–284.

Huang-Pollock, C. L., Nigg, J. T., & Carr, T. H. (2005). Deficient attention is hard to find: Applying the perceptual load model of selective attention to attention deficit hyperactivity disorder. *Journal of Child Psychology and Psychiatry, 46,* 1211–1218.

Hudson, J. L., & Rapee, M. (2002). Parent-child interactions in clinically anxious children and their siblings. *Journal of Clinical Child and Adolescent Psychology, 31,* 548–555.

Hudson, J. L., Comer, J. S., & Kendall, P. C. (2008). Parental responses to positive and negative emotions in anxious and non anxious children. *Journal of Clinical Child and Adolescent Psychology, 37,* 303–313.

Hudson, J. L., Doyle, A. M., & Gar, N. (2009). Child and maternal influence on parenting behavior in clinically anxious children. *Journal of Clinical Child and Adolescent Psychology, 38,* 256–262.

Hudziak, J. J., Achenback, T. M., Althoff, R. R., & Pine, D. (2007). A dimensional approach to developmental psychopathology. *International Journal of Methods in Psychiatric Research, 16*(sup1), S16–S23.

Hudziak, J. J., Derks, E. M., Althoff, R. R., Rettew, D. C., & Boomsma, D. I. (2005). The genetic and environmental contributions to attention deficit-hyperactivity disorder as measured by the Conners' Rating Scales—Revised. *American Journal of Psychiatry, 162,* 1614–1620.

Hudziak, J. J., Heath, A. C., Madden, P. F., Reich, W., Bucholz, K. K., Slutske, W., et al. (1998). Latent class and factor analysis of DSM-IV ADHD: A twin study of female adolescents. *Journal of the American Academy of Child and Adolescent Psychiatry, 37,* 848–857.

Huesmann, L. R., Eron, L. D., Lefkowitz, M. M., & Walder, L. O. (1984). Stability of aggression over time and generations. *Developmental Psychology, 20,* 1120–1134.

Huey, S. J., & Polo, A. J. (2017). Evidence-based psychotherapies with ethnic minority children and adolescents. In J. R. Weisz & A. E. Kazdin (Eds.), *Evidence-based psychotherapies for children and adolescents* (3rd ed.). New York: The Guilford Press.

Huff, C. (2020). Improving care while saving money. *Monitor on Psychology, 51,* 64–67.

Hughes, E. K., Burton, C., Le Grange, D., & Sawyer, S. M. (2018). The participation of mothers, fathers, and siblings in family-based treatment for adolescent anorexia nervosa. *Journal of Clinical Child & Adolescent Psychology, 47*(sup1), S456–S466.

Hughes, J. E. A., Ward, J., Gruffydd, E., Baron-Cohen, S., Smith, P., Allison, C., & Simner, J. (2018). Savant syndrome has a distinct psychological profile in autism. *Molecular Autism, 9,* 53.

Huisman, S., Mulder, P., Kuijk, J., Kersholt, M., van Eeghen, A., Leenders, A., et al. (2018). Self-injurious behavior. *Neuroscience & Biobehavioral Reviews, 84,* 483–491.

Hulme, C., & Snowling, M. J. (2009). *Developmental disorders of language learning and cognition*. Malden, MA: Wiley-Blackwell.

Hulvershorn, L. A., Cullen, K., & Anand, A. (2011). Toward dysfunctional connectivity: A review of neuroimaging findings in pediatric major depressive disorder. *Brain Imaging and Behavior, 5,* 307–328.

References

Humphreys, K. L. (2019). Future directions in the study and treatment of parent–child separation. *Journal of Clinical Child & Adolescent Psychology, 48*, 166–178.

Humphreys, K. L., Eng, T., & Lee, S. S. (2013). Stimulant medication and substance use outcomes: A meta-analysis. *JAMA Psychiatry, 70*, 740–749.

Humphreys, K. L., King, L. S., & Gotlib, I. H. (2019). Neglect. In C. H. Zeanah (Ed.), *Handbook of infant mental health* (4th ed.). New York: The Guilford Press.

Humphreys, L., Forehand, R., McMahon, R., & Roberts, M. (1978). Parent behavioral training to modify child noncompliance: Effects on untreated siblings. *Journal of Behavior Therapy and Experimental Psychiatry, 9*, 235–238.

Hunsley, J., & Mash, E. J. (2018). Developing criteria for evidence-based assessment: An introduction to assessments that work. In J. Hunsley & E. J. Mash (Eds.), *A guide to assessments that work* (2nd ed.). New York: Oxford University Press.

Huq, N., Stein, G. L., & Gonzalez, L. M. (2016). Acculturation conflict among Latino youth: Discrimination, ethnic identity, and depressive symptoms. *Cultural Diversity and Ethnic Minority Psychology, 22*, 377–385.

Hurley, A. D. (2005). Psychotherapy is an essential tool in the treatment of psychiatric disorders for people with mental retardation. *Mental Retardation, 43*, 445–448.

Hussong, A. M., Bauer, D. J., & Chassin, L. (2008). Telescoped trajectories from alcohol initiation to disorder in children of alcoholic parents. *Journal of Abnormal Psychology, 117*, 63–78.

Hutchings, J., Gardner, F., Bywater, T., Daley, D., Whitaker, C., Jones, K., et al. (2007). Parenting intervention in Sure Start services for children at risk of developing conduct disorder: Pragmatic randomized control trial. *British Medical Journal, 334*, 1–7.

Hviid, A., Hansen, J. V., Frisch, M., & Melbye, M. (2019). Measles, mumps, rubella vaccination and autism: A nationwide cohort study. *Annals of Internal Medicine, 170*, 513–520.

Hyde, J. S., Mezulis, A. H., & Abramson, L. Y. (2008). The ABCs of depression: Integrating affective, biological, and cognitive models to explain the emergence of the gender difference in depression. *Psychological Review, 115*, 291–313.

Hymel, S., & Swearer, S. M. (2015). Four decades of research on school bullying: An introduction. *American Psychologist, 70*, 293–299.

Hynd, G. W., & Semrud-Clikeman, M. (1989a). Dyslexia and brain morphology. *Psychological Bulletin, 106*, 447–482.

Hynd, G. W., & Semrud-Clikeman, M. (1989b). Dyslexia and neurodevelopmental pathology: Relationships to cognition, intelligence, and reading skill acquisition. *Journal of Learning Disabilities, 22*, 205–218.

Hynd, G. W., Marshall, R., & Gonzalez, J. (1991). Learning disabilities and presumed central nervous system dysfunction. *Learning Disability Quarterly, 14*, 283–296.

Hynes, L., Saetes, S., McGuire, B., & Caes, L. (2019). Child and family adaptation to juvenile idiopathic arthritis: A systematic review of the role of resilience resources and mechanisms. *Frontiers in Psychology, 10*.

Imray, P., & Colley, A. (2017). *Inclusion is dead: Long live inclusion*. London: Routledge.

Ingoldsby, E., & Shaw, D. S. (2002). Neighborhood contextual factors and the onset and progression of early-starting antisocial pathways. *Clinical Child and Family Psychology Review, 5*, 21–55.

Ingram, R. E., & Price, J. M. (2010). Understanding psychopathology. The role of vulnerability. In R. E. Ingram & J. M. Price (Eds.), *Vulnerability to psychopathology: Risk across the lifespan*. New York: Guilford Press.

Insel, T., Cuthbert, B., Garvey, M., Heinssen, R., Pine, D. S., Quinn, K., et al. (2010). Research domain criteria (RDoC): Toward a new classification framework for research on mental disorders. *American Journal of Psychiatry, 167*, 748–751.

Institute for Patient- and Family-Centered Care. (2017). *Advancing the practice of patient- and family-centered care in hospitals: How to get started*. Retrieved from www.ipfcc.org/resources/getting_started.pdf

Institute for Patient- and Family-Centered Care. (2019). *Understanding the historical context for visiting policies*. Retrieved from www.ipfcc.org/bestpractices/Understanding-Historical-Context.pdf

International Schizophrenia Consortium. (2008). Rare chromosomal deletions and duplications increase risk of schizophrenia. *Nature, 455*(7210), 237–241.

Israel, A. C. (1988). Parental and family influences in the etiology and treatment of childhood obesity. In N. A. Krasnegor, G. D. Grave, & N. Kretchmer (Eds.), *Childhood obesity: A biobehavioral perspective*. Caldwell, NJ: The Telford Press.

Israel, A. C. (1999). Commentary: Empirically supported treatments for pediatric obesity: Goals, outcome criteria, and the societal context. *Journal of Pediatric Psychology, 24*, 249–250.

Israel, A. C., & Ivanova, M. Y. (2002). Global and dimensional self-esteem in preadolescent and early adolescent children who are overweight: Age and gender differences. *International Journal of Eating Disorders, 31*, 424–429.

Israel, A. C., & Shapiro, L. S. (1985). Behavior problems of obese children enrolling in a weight reduction program. *Journal of Pediatric Psychology, 10*, 449–460.

Israel, A. C., & Solotar, L. C. (1988). Obesity. In M. Hersen & C. G. Last (Eds.), *Child behavior therapy casebook*. New York: Plenum.

Israel, A. C., Guile, C. A., Baker, J. E., & Silverman, W. K. (1994). An evaluation of enhanced self-regulation training in the treatment of childhood obesity. *Journal of Pediatric Psychology, 19*, 737–749.

Israel, A. C., Pravder, M. D., & Knights, S. (1980). A peer administered program for changing the classroom behavior of disruptive children. *Behavioural Analysis and Modification, 4,* 224–238.

Israel, A. C., Roderick, H. A., & Ivanova, M. Y. (2002). A measure of the stability of family activities in a family environment. *Journal of Psychopathology and Behavioral Assessment, 24,* 85–95.

Israel, A. C., Silverman, W. K., & Solotar, L. C. (1986). An investigation of family influences on initial weight status, attrition, and treatment outcome in a childhood obesity program. *Behavior Therapy, 17,* 131–143.

Israel, A. C., Stolmaker, L., & Andrian, C. A. G. (1985). The effects of training parents in general child management skills in a behavioral weight loss program for children. *Behavior Therapy, 16,* 169–180.

Ivanov, H. Y., Stoyanova, V. K., Popov, N. T., & Vachev, T. I. (2015). Autism spectrum disorder: A complex genetic disorder. *Folia Medica, 57,* 19–28.

Ivanova, M. Y., & Israel, A. C. (2006). Family stability as a protective factor against psychopathology for urban children receiving psychological services. *Journal of Clinical Child and Adolescent Psychology, 35,* 564–570.

Ivanova, M. Y., Achenbach, T. M., Rescorla, L. A., Guo, J., Althoff, R. R., Kan, K.-J., et al. (2019). Testing syndromes of psychopathology in parent and youth ratings across societies. *Journal of Clinical Child & Adolescent Psychology, 48,* 596–609.

Izard, C. E., Fine, S., Mostow, A., Trentacosta, C., & Campbell, J. (2002). Emotion processes in normal and abnormal development and prevention intervention. *Development and Psychopathology, 14,* 761–787.

Jackson, P. D., Wendland, M., & Ekvall, S. W. (2017). Down syndrome. In S. W. Ekvall & V. K. Ekvall (Eds.), *Pediatric and adult nutrition in chronic diseases, developmental disabilities, and hereditary metabolic disorders: Prevention assessment and treatment.* New York: Oxford University Press.

Jacob, R. G., & Pelham, W. H. (2000). Behavior therapy. In A. J. Sadock & V. A. Sadock (Eds.), *Kaplan & Sadock's comprehensive textbook of psychiatry* (Vol. II). Philadelphia, PA: Lippincott Williams & Wilkins.

Jacobi, C., Hayward, C., de Zwaan, M., Kraemer, H. C., & Agras, W. S. (2004). Coming to terms with risk factors for eating disorders: Application of risk terminology and suggestions for a general taxonomy. *Psychological Bulletin, 130,* 19–65.

Jacobson, C. M., Muehlenkamp, J. J., Miller, A. L., & Turner, E. B. (2008). Psychiatric impairment among adolescents engaging in different types of deliberate self-harm. *Journal of Clinical Child and Adolescent Psychology, 37,* 363–375.

Jacobson, C. M., Mufson, L. H., & Young, J. F. (2017). Treating adolescent depression using interpersonal psychotherapy. In J. R. Weisz & A. E. Kazdin (Eds.), *Evidence-based psychotherapies for children and adolescents* (3rd ed.). New York: The Guilford Press.

Jaffee, P. G., Poisson, S. E., & Cunningham, A. (2001). Domestic violence and high-conflict divorce: Developing a new generation of research for children. In S. A. Graham-Bermann & J. L. Edleson (Eds.), *Domestic violence in the lives of children: The future of research, intervention, and social policy.* Washington, DC: American Psychological Association.

Jaffee, S. R. (2016). Quantitative and molecular behavioral genetic studies of gene-environment correlation. In D. Cicchetti (Ed.), *Developmental psychopathology: Risk, resilience, and intervention* (Vol. 2). Hoboken, NJ: John Wiley & Sons.

Jaffee, S. R. (2017a). Child maltreatment and risk for psychopathology. In T. P. Beauchaine & S. P. Hinshaw (Eds.), *Child and adolescent psychopathology* (3rd ed.). Hoboken, NJ: John Wiley & Sons Inc.

Jaffee, S. R. (2017b). Child maltreatment and risk for psychopathology in childhood and adulthood. *Annual Review of Clinical Psychology, 13,* 525–551.

Jaffee, S. R., Caspi, A., Moffitt, T. E., & Taylor, A. (2004). Physical maltreatment victim to antisocial child: Evidence of an environmentally mediated process. *Journal of Abnormal Psychology, 113,* 44–55.

Jaffee, S. R., Caspi, A., Moffitt, T. E., Dodge, K., Rutter, M., Taylor, A., et al. (2005). Nature × nurture: Genetic vulnerabilities interact with physical maltreatment to promote conduct problems. *Development and Psychopathology, 17,* 67–84.

Jaffee, S. R., Caspi, A., Moffitt, T. E., Polo-Tomás, M., & Taylor, A. (2007). Individual, family, and neighborhood factors distinguish resilient from non-resilient maltreated children: A cumulative stressors model. *Child Abuse & Neglect, 31,* 231–253.

Jaffee, S. R., Moffitt, T. E., Caspi, A., & Taylor, A. (2003). Life with (or without) father: The benefits of living with two biological parents depend on the father's antisocial behavior. *Child Development, 74,* 109–126.

Jahromi, L. B., Kasari, C. L., McCracken, J. T., Lee, L. S. Y., Aman, M. G., McDougle, C. J., et al. (2009). Positive effects of methylphenidate on social communication and self-regulation in children with pervasive developmental disorders and hyperactivity. *Journal of Autism and Developmental Disorders, 39,* 395–404.

Jambon, M., & Smetana, J. G. (2018). Individual differences in prototypical moral and conventional judgments and children's proactive and reactive aggression. *Child Development, 89,* 1343–1359.

James, S. (2011). What works in group care? A structured review of treatment models for group homes and residential care. *Children and Youth Services Review, 33,* 308–321.

References

James, S., Donnelly, L., Brooks-Gunn, J., & McLanahan, S. (2018). Links between childhood exposure to violent contexts and risky adolescent health behaviors. *Journal of Adolescent Health, 63,* 94–101.

Jamieson, D., & Mason, J. (2019). Investigating the existence of the diagnostic overshadowing bias in Australia. *Journal of Mental Health Research in Intellectual Disabilities, 12,* 58–70.

Janicke, D. M., Steele, R. G., Gayes, L. A., Lim, C. S., Clifford, L. M., Schneider, E. M., et al. (2014). Systematic review and meta-analysis of comprehensive behavioral family lifestyle interventions addressing pediatric obesity. *Journal of Pediatric Psychology, 39,* 809–825.

Janssens, T., & Harver, A. (2015). Effects of symptom perception interventions on trigger identification and quality of life in children with asthma. *Pulmonary Medicine,* 1–8.

Jardri, R., Bartels-Velthuis, A. A., Debbané, M., Jenner, J. A., Kelleher, I., Dauvilliers, Y., et al. (2014). From phenomenology to neurophysiological understanding of hallucinations in children and adolescents. *Schizophrenia Bulletin, 40*(sup4), S221–S232.

Jarrett, M. A., & Ollendick, T. H. (2008). A conceptual review of the comorbidity of attention-deficit/hyperactivity disorder and anxiety: Implications for future research and practice. *Clinical Psychology Review, 28,* 1266–1280.

Jarrett, M. A., Wolff, J. C., Davis, T. E., Cowart, M. J., & Ollendick, T. H. (2012). Characteristics of children with ADHD and comorbid anxiety. *Journal of Attention Disorders, 20,* 636–644.

Javdani, S., Sadeh, N., & Verona, E. (2011). Expanding our lens: Female pathways to antisocial behavior in adolescence and adulthood. *Clinical Psychology Review, 31,* 1324–1348.

Jay, S. M., Elliot, C. H., Katz, E., & Siegel, S. E. (1987). Cognitive behavioral and pharmacologic intervention for children's distress during painful medical procedures. *Journal of Consulting and Clinical Psychology, 55,* 860–865.

Jay, S. M., Elliot, C. H., Woody, P. D., & Siegel, S. (1991). An investigation of cognitive-behavioral therapy combined with oral valium for children undergoing painful medical procedures. *Health Psychology, 10,* 317–322.

Jay, S. M., Elliott, C. H., Fitzgibbons, I., Woody, P., & Siegel, S. (1995). A comparative study of cognitive behavioral therapy versus general anesthesia for painful medical procedures in children. *Pain, 62,* 3–9.

Jelalian, E., Wember, Y. M., Bungeroth, H., & Birmaher, V. (2007). Bridging the gap between research and clinical practice in pediatric obesity. *Journal of Child Psychology and Psychiatry, 48,* 115–127.

Jenkins, M. M., & Youngstrom, E. A. (2016). A randomized controlled trial of cognitive debiasing improves assessment and treatment selection for pediatric bipolar disorder. *Journal of Consulting and Clinical Psychology, 84,* 323–333.

Jenkins, T. A. (2013). Perinatal complications and schizophrenia: Involvement of the immune system. *Frontiers in Neuroscience, 7,* 110.

Jennings, W. G., & Perez, N. M. (2017). Neighborhood effects on the development of delinquency. In T. P. Beauchaine & S. P. Hinshaw (Eds.), *Child and adolescent psychopathology* (3rd ed.). Hoboken, NJ: John Wiley & Sons Inc.

Jennings, W. G., Maldonado-Molina, M. M., Reingle, J. M., & Komro, K. A. (2011). A multi-level approach to investigating neighborhood effects on physical aggression among urban Chicago youth. *American Journal of Criminal Justice, 36,* 392–407.

Jennings, W. G., Perez, N. M., & Reingle Gonzalez, J. M. (2018). Conduct disorder and neighborhood effects. *Annual Review of Clinical Psychology, 14,* 317–341.

Jensen, C. D., & Steele, R. G. (2012). Longitudinal associations between teasing and health-related quality of life among treatment-seeking overweight and obese youth. *Journal of Pediatric Psychology, 37,* 438–447.

Jensen, M., George, M. J., Russell, M. R., & Odgers, C. L. (2019). Young adolescents' digital technology use and mental health symptoms: Little evidence of longitudinal or daily linkages. *Clinical Psychological Science, 7,* 1416–1433.

Jensen, P. S., & Mrazek, D. A. (2006). Research and clinical perspectives in defining and assessing mental disorders in children and adolescents. In P. S. Jensen, P. Knapp, & D. A. Mrazek (Eds.), *Toward a new diagnostic system for child psychopathology: Moving beyond the DSM*. New York: The Guilford Press.

Jensen, P. S., Arnold, L. E., Swanson, J. M., Vitiello, B., Abikoff, H. B., Greenhill, L. L., et al. (2007). 3-year follow-up of the NIMH MTA study. *Journal of the American Academy of Child and Adolescent Psychiatry, 46,* 989–1002.

Jensen-Doss, A., Walsh, L. M., & Ringle, V. M. (2018). Dissemination and implementation of evidence-based assessment. In J. Hunsley & E. J. Mash (Eds.), *A guide to assessments that work* (2nd ed.). New York: Oxford University Press.

Jersild, A. T., & Holmes, F. B. (1935). Children's fears. Child Development Monograph, No. 20.

Jessor, R., & Jessor, S. L. (1977). *Problem behavior and psychosocial development*. New York: Academic Press.

Ji, Y., Hong, X., Wang, G., Chatterjee, N., Riley, A. W., Lee, L.-C., et al. (2018). A prospective birth cohort study on early childhood lead levels and attention deficit hyperactivity disorder: New insight on sex differences. *The Journal of Pediatrics, 199,* 124–131.

Johnco, C., & Storch, E. A. (2018). Understanding and managing obsessive-compulsive disorder in children and adolescents. In J. N. Butcher & P. C. Kendall (Eds.), *APA handbook of psychopathology* (Vol. 2). Washington, DC: American Psychological Association.

Johnides, B. D., Borduin, C. M., Wagner, D. V., & Dopp, A. R. (2017). Effects of multisystemic therapy on caregivers of serious juvenile offenders: A 20-year follow-up to a randomized clinical trial. *Journal of Consulting and Clinical Psychology, 85,* 323–334.

Johnson, C. J., & Beitchman, J. H. (2005). Mixed receptive-expressive disorder. In B. J. Sadock & V. A. Sadock (eds.), *Kaplan & Sadock's comprehensive textbook of psychiatry* (Vol. II). Philadelphia: Lippincott Williams and Wilkens.

Johnson, C. P., & Myers, S. M. (2007). Identification and evaluation of children with autism spectrum disorders. *Pediatrics, 120,* 1183–1215.

Johnson, J. K., Liranso, T., Saylor, K., Tulloch, G., Adewole, T., Schwabe, S., et al. (2020). A Phase II double-blind, placebo-controlled, efficacy and safety study of SPN-812 (extended-release viloxazine) in children with ADHD. *Journal of Attention Disorders, 24,* 348–358.

Johnson, S., Hollis, C., Kochhar, P., Hennessy, E., Wolke, D., & Marlow, N. (2011). Psychiatric disorders in extremely preterm infants: Longitudinal finding at age 11 years in the EPICure Study. *Journal of the American Academy of Child and Adolescent Psychiatry, 49,* 453–463.

Johnson, S. L., Miller, C., & Eisner, L. (2018). Bipolar disorder. In J. Hunsley & E. J. Mash (Eds.), *A guide to assessments that work* (2nd ed.). New York: Oxford University Press.

Johnson, T. J. (2020). Racial bias and its impact on children and adolescents. *Pediatric Clinics, 67,* 425–436.

Johnston, C., & Chronis-Tuscano, A. (2015). Families and ADHD. In R. A. Barkley (Ed.), *Attention-deficit hyperactivity disorder: A handbook for diagnosis and treatment.* New York: The Guilford Press.

Johnston, C., & Ohan, J. L. (1999). Externalizing disorders. In W. K. Silverman & T. H. Ollendick (Eds.), *Developmental issues in the clinical treatment of children.* Boston, MA: Allyn and Bacon.

Johnston, L. D., Miech, R. A., O'Malley, P. M., Bachman, J. G., Schulenberg, J. E., & Patrick, M. E. (2019a). *Demographic subgroup trends among adolescents in the use of various licit and illicit drugs, 1975–2018. Monitoring the Future Occasional Paper Series. Paper 92.* Ann Arbor, MI: Institute for Social Research, The University of Michigan.

Johnston, L. D., Miech, R. A., O'Malley, P. M., Bachman, J. G., Schulenberg, J. E., & Patrick, M. E. (2019b). *Monitoring the Future national survey results on drug use, 1975–2018: Overview, key findings on adolescent drug use.* Ann Arbor, MI: Institute for Social Research, University of Michigan.

Joiner, T. E. (2000). A test of hopelessness theory of depression in youth psychiatric inpatients. *Journal of Clinical Child Psychology, 29,* 167–176.

Joint United Nations Programme on HIV/AIDS (UNAIDS). (2019). *UNAIDS Data 2019.* Retrieved from www.unaids.org/sites/default/files/media_asset/2019-UNAIDS-data_en.pdf

Jones, A. P., & Frederickson, N. (2010). Multi-informant predictors of social inclusion for students with autism spectrum disorders attending mainstream school. *Journal of Autism and Developmental Disorders, 40,* 1094–1103.

Jones, L., Bellis, M. A., Wood, S., Hughes, K., McCoy, E., Eckley, L., et al. (2012). Prevalence and risk of violence against children with disabilities: A systematic review and meta-analysis of observational studies. *The Lancet, 380,* 899–907.

Jones, M. C. (1924). A laboratory study of fear: The case of Peter. *Pedagogical Seminary, 31,* 308–315.

Jones, S. C., & Neblett, E. W. (2017). Future directions in research on racism-related stress and racial-ethnic protective factors for Black youth. *Journal of Clinical Child & Adolescent Psychology, 46,* 754–766.

Joormann, J., & Stanton, C. H. (2016). Examining emotion regulation in depression: A review and future directions. *Behaviour Research and Therapy, 86,* 35–49.

Jouriles, E. N., Murphy, C. M., & O'Leary, K. D. (1989). Interspousal aggression, marital discord, and child problems. *Journal of Consulting and Clinical Psychology, 57,* 453–455.

Juffer, F., Bakermans-Kranenburg, M. J., & van IJzendoorn, M. H. (2005). The importance of parenting in the development of disorganized attachment: Evidence from a preventive intervention study in adoptive families. *Journal of Child and Adolescent Psychology, 46,* 263–274.

Juster, R. P., Seeman, T., McEwen, B. S., Picard, M., Mahar, I., Mechawar, N., et al. (2016). Social inequalities and the road to allostatic load: From vulnerability to resilience. In D. Cicchetti (Ed.), *Developmental psychopathology* (3rd ed., Vol. 4). Hoboken, NJ: John Wiley & Sons.

Kacynski, K. (2019). Cognitive-behavioral therapy for chronic headache disorders in children and adolescents. In R. D. Friedberg & J. K. Paternostro (Eds.), *Handbook of cognitive behavioral thearpy for pediatric medical conditions.* Cham, Switzerland: Springer.

Kadlaskar, G., Seidl, A., Tager-Flusberg, H., Nelson, C. A., & Keehn, B. (2019). Atypical response to caregiver touch in infants at high risk for autism spectrum disorder. *Journal of Autism and Developmental Disorders, 49,* 1946–2955.

Kaehler, L. A., Jacobs, M., & Jones, D. J. (2016). Distilling common history and practice elements to inform dissemination: Hanf-model BPT programs as an example. *Clinical Child and Family Psychology Review, 19,* 236–258.

Kagan, J. (1997). Temperament and the reactions to unfamiliarity. *Child Development, 68,* 139–143.

Kagan, J. (2017). High-reactive temperament, behavioral inhibition, and vulnerability to psychopathology. In T. P. Beauchaine & S. P. Hinshaw (Eds.), *Child and adolescent psychopathology* (3rd ed.). Hoboken, NJ: John Wiley & Sons Inc.

References

Kagan, J., Reznick, J. S., & Snidman, N. (1990). The temperamental qualities of inhibition and lack of inhibition. In M. Lewis & S. M. Miller (Eds.), *Handbook of developmental psychopathology*. New York: Plenum Press.

Kahn, R. E., Frick, P. J., Youngstrom, E., Findling, R. L., & Youngstrom, J. K. (2012). The effects of including a callous-unemotional specifier for the diagnosis of conduct disorder. *Journal of Child Psychology and Psychiatry, 53,* 271–282.

Kaiser, M. L., Schoemaker, M. M., Albaret, J. M., & Geuze, R. H. (2015). What is the evidence of impaired motor skills and motor control among children with attention deficit hyperactivity disorder (ADHD)? Systematic review of the literature. *Research in Developmental Disabilities, 36,* 338–357.

Kalb, L. G., Law, J. K., Landa, R., & Law, P. A. (2010). Onset patterns prior to 36 months in autism spectrum disorders. *Journal of Autism and Developmental Disorders, 40,* 1389–1402.

Kamimura-Nishimura, K. I., Brinkman, W. B., & Froehlich, T. E. (2019). Strategies for improving ADHD medication adherence. *Current Psychiatry, 18,* 25–38.

Kaminski, J. W., & Claussen, A. H. (2017). Evidence base update for psychosocial treatments for disruptive behaviors in children. *Journal of Clinical Child & Adolescent Psychology, 46,* 477–499.

Kamphaus, R. W., & Frick, P. J. (1996). *Clinical assessment of child and adolescent personality and behavior.* Boston, MA: Allyn and Bacon.

Kanaya, T., Scullin, M. H., & Ceci, S. J. (2003). The Flynn effect and U.S. policies. *American Psychologist, 58,* 778–790.

Kanne, S. M., Gerber, A. J., Quirmbach, L. M., Sparrow, S. S., Cicchetti, D. V., & Saulnier, C. A. (2011). The role of adaptive behavior in autism spectrum disorders: Implications for functional outcome. *Journal of Autism and Developmental Disorders, 41,* 1007–1018.

Kanner, L. (1943). Autistic disturbances of affective contact. *Nervous Child, 2,* 217–250.

Kanner, L. (1973). *Childhood psychoses: Initial studies and new insights.* Washington, DC: V. H. Winston & Sons.

Kanner, L., & Eisenberg, L. (1956). Early infantile autism, 1943–1955. *American Journal of Orthopsychiatry, 26,* 55–65.

Karam, A. M., Fitzsimmons-Craft, E. E., Tanofsky-Kraff, M., & Wilfley, D. E. (2019). Interpersonal psychotherapy and the treatment of eating disorders. *Psychiatric Clinics, 42,* 205–218.

Karazsia, B. T., Kazak, A. E., & Palermo, T. M. (2019). Introduction to the special issue: Historical developments in pediatric psychology: Influence on contemporary research and practice. *Journal of Pediatric Psychology, 44,* 749–753.

Kardefelt-Winther, D. (2017). *How does the time children spend using digital technology impact their mental well-being, social relationships and physical activity? An evidence-focused literature review.* Florence, Italy: UNICEF Office of Research-Innocenti.

Kasari, C., Locke, J., Gulsrud, A., & Rotheram-Fuller, E. (2011). Social networks and friendships at school: Comparing children with and without ASD. *Journal of Autism and Developmental Disorders, 41,* 533–544.

Kashani, J. H., Daniel, A. E., Dandoy, A. C., & Holcomb, W. R. (1992). Family violence: Impact on children. *Journal of the American Academy of Child and Adolescent Psychiatry, 31,* 181–189.

Kaslow, N. J., & Racusin, G. R. (1990). Childhood depression: Current status and future directions. In A. S. Bellack, M. Hersen, & A. E. Kazdin (Eds.), *International handbook of behavior modification and therapy* (2nd ed.). New York: Plenum.

Kaslow, N. J., Adamson, L. B., & Collins, M. H. (2000). A developmental psychopathology perspective on the cognitive components of child and adolescent depression. In A. J. Sameroff, M. Lewis, & S. M. Miller (Eds.), *Handbook of developmental psychopathology* (2nd ed.). New York: Kluwer Academic/Plenum Publishers.

Katz, L. J., & Brown, F. C. (2019). Aptitude and achievement testing. In G. Goldstein, D. W. Allen, & J. DeLuca (Eds.), *Handbook of psychological assessment* (4th ed.). London, UK: Academic Press.

Katzman, D. K. (2005). Medical complications in adolescents with anorexia nervosa: A review of the literature. *International Journal of Eating Disorders, 37*(sup1), 52–59.

Kauffman, J. M., Anastasiou, D., Badar, J., Travers, J. C., & Wiley, A. L. (2016). Inclusive education moving forward. In J. P. Bakken & F. E. Obiakor (Eds.), *General and special education inclusion in an age of change: Roles of professionals involved.* Bingley, UK: Emerald Group Publishing Limited.

Kauffman, J. M., Hallahan, D. P., Pullen, P. C., & Badar, J. (2018). Frequent criticisms and responses to them. In J. M. Kauffman, D. P. Hallahan, P. C. Pullen, & J. Badar (Eds.), *Special education: What it is and why we need it* (2nd ed.). New York: Routledge.

Kauffman, J. M., McGee, K., & Brigham, M. (2004). Enabling or disabling? Observations on changes in special education. *Phi Delta Kappan, 85,* 613–620.

Kauffman, J. M., Nelson, M. C., Simpson, R. L., & Ward, D. M. (2017). Contemporary issues. In J. M. Kauffman, D. P. Hallahan, & P. C. Pullen (Eds.), *Handbook of special education* (2nd ed.). New York: Routledge.

Kaufman, A. S., & Kaufman, N. L. (2004). *Administration and scoring material for the Kaufman assessment battery for children, second edition (KABC-II).* Circle Pines, MN: American Guidance Service.

Kaufman, A. S., & Kaufman, N. L. (2018). *Kaufman Assessment Battery for Children—Second edition normative update.* Circle Pines, MN: American Guidance Services.

Kaufman, E. A., Crowell, S. E., & Lenzenweger, M. F. (2017). The development of bordrerline personality and self-inflicted injury. In T. P. Beauchaine & S. P. Hinshaw (Eds.), *Child and adolescent psychopathology* (3rd ed.). Hoboken, NJ: John Wiley & Sons Inc.

Kaufman, J., & Zigler, E. (1987). Do abused children become abusive parents? *American Journal of Orthopsychiatry, 57,* 186–192.

Kaugars, A. S., Zebracki, K., Kichler, J. C., Fitzgerald, C. J., Greenley, R. N., Alemzadeh, R., & Holmbeck, G. N. (2011). Use of the family interaction macro-coding system with families of adolescents: Psychometric properties among pediatric and healthy populations. *Journal of Pediatric Psychology, 36,* 539–551.

Kaye, E. C., Snaman, J. M., Johnson, L., Levine, D., Powell, B., Love, A., et al. (2018). Communication with children and their families throughout the illness journey and at the end of life. In J. Wolfe, B. L. Jones, U. Kreicbergs, & M. Jankovic (Eds.), *Palliative care in pediatric oncology.* Cham, Switzerland: Springer.

Kayser, G., McElroy, S., & Benmarhnia, T. (2019). The role of inadequate water and sanitation on economic and social determinants of child mortality: A global analysis across 43 countries. Retrieved from https://ssrn.com/abstract=3311853

Kazak, A. E. (2005). Evidence-based interventions for survivors of childhood cancer and their families. *Journal of Pediatric Psychology, 30,* 29–39.

Kazak, A. E., & Noll, R. B. (2015). The integration of psychology in pediatric oncology research and practice: Collaboration to improve care and outcomes for children and families. *American Psychologist, 70,* 146–158.

Kazak, A. E., Alderfer, M. A., & Reader, S. K. (2017a). Families and other systems in pediatric psychology. In M. C. Roberts & R. G. Steele (Eds.), *Handbook of pediatric psychology* (5th ed.). New York: The Guilford Press.

Kazak, A. E., Price, J., & Kassam-Adams, N. (2017b). Pediatric medical traumatic stress. In M. C. Roberts & R. G. Steele (Eds.), *Handbook of pediatric psychology* (5th ed.). New York: The Guilford Press.

Kazdin, A. E. (1989). Identifying depression in children: A comparison of alternative selection criteria. *Journal of Abnormal Child Psychology, 17,* 437–454.

Kazdin, A. E. (2011). *Single-case research designs: Methods for clinical and applied settings* (2nd ed.). New York: Oxford University Press.

Kazdin, A. E. (2016). Single case experimental research designs. In A. E. Kazdin (Ed.), *Methodological issues and strategies in clinical research* (4th ed.). Washington, DC: American Psychological Association.

Kazdin, A. E. (2017). Parent management training and problem-solving skills training for child and adolescent conduct problems. In J. R. Weisz & A. E. Kazdin (Eds.), *Evidence-based psychotherapies for children and adolescents* (3rd ed.). New York: The Guilford Press.

Kazdin, A. E. (2019). Expanding mental health services through novel models of intervention delivery. *Journal of Child Psychology and Psychiatry, 60,* 455–472.

Kazdin, A. E., & Weisz, J. R. (2017). Introduction: Context, background, and goals. In J. R. Weisz & A. E. Kazdin (Eds.), *Evidence-based psychotherapies for children and adolescents* (3rd ed.). New York: The Guilford Press.

Kazdin, A. E., & Whitley, M. K. (2003). Treatment of parental stress to enhance therapeutic change among children referred for aggressive and antisocial behavior. *Journal of Consulting and Clinical Psychology, 71,* 504–515.

Kazdin, A. E., Rodgers, A., & Colbus, D. (1986). The hopelessness scale for children: Psychometric characteristics and concurrent validity. *Journal of Consulting and Clinical Psychology, 54,* 241–245.

Kazdin, A. E., Siegel, T. C., & Bass, D. (1992). Cognitive problem-solving skills training and parent management training in the treatment of antisocial behavior in children. *Journal of Consulting and Clinical Psychology, 60,* 733–747.

Kearney, C. A. (2018). *Helping school refusing children and their parents* (2nd ed.). New York: Oxford University Press.

Kearney, C. A., & Silverman, W. K. (1992). Let's not push the "panic button": A critical analysis of panic and panic disorder in adolescents. *Clinical Psychology Review, 12,* 293–305.

Kearney, C. A., Albano, A. M., Eisen, A. R., Allan, W. D., & Barlow, D. H. (1997). The phenomenology of panic disorder in youngsters: An empirical study of a clinical sample. *Journal of Anxiety Disorders, 11,* 49–62.

Kearney, C. A., Eisen, A., & Silverman, W. K. (1995). The legend and myth of school phobia. *School Psychology Quarterly, 10,* 65–85.

Kearney, C. A., Wechsler, A., Kaur, H., & Lemos-Miller, A. (2010). Posttraumatic stress disorder in maltreated youth: A review of contemporary research and thought. *Clinical Child and Family Psychology Review, 13,* 46–76.

Kearney, M. S., & Haskins, R. (2020). How cultural factors shape economic outcomes: Introducing the issue. *The Future of Children, 30,* 3–8.

Keel, P. K. (2018). Eating disorders. In J. N. Butcher & J. M. Hooley (Eds.), *APA handbook of psychopathology* (Vol. 1). Washington, DC: American Psychological Association.

Keel, P. K., & Klump, K. (2003). Are eating disorders culture-bound syndromes? Implications for conceptualizing their etiology. *Psychological Bulletin, 129,* 747–769.

Keller, M. B., Lavori, P. W., Wunder, J., Beardslee, W. R., Schwartz, C. E., & Roth, J. (1992). Chronic course of anxiety disorders in children and adolescents. *Journal of the American Academy of Child and Adolescent Psychiatry, 31,* 595–599.

References

Keller, P. S., Cummings, E. M., & Davies, P. T. (2005). The role of marital discord and parenting in relations between parental problem drinking and child adjustment. *Journal of Child Psychology and Psychiatry, 46,* 943–951.

Keller-Bell, Y., & Short, M. (2019). Positive behavioral interventions and supports in schools: A tutorial. *Language, Speech, and Hearing Services in Schools, 50,* 1–15.

Kellerman, J. (1980). Rapid treatment of nocturnal anxiety in children. *Journal of Behavior Therapy and Experimental Psychiatry, 11,* 9–11.

Kelly, J. B. (2000). Children's adjustment in conflicted marriage and divorce: A decade review of research. *Journal of the American Academy of Child and Adolescent Psychiatry, 39,* 963–973.

Kelly, M. L., & Heffer, R. W. (1990). Eating disorders: Food refusal and failure to thrive. In A. M. Gross & R. S. Drabman (Eds.), *Handbook of clinical behavioral pediatrics.* New York: Plenum.

Kemp, J., & Freeman, J. B. (2019). Obsessive-compulsive disorder. In M. J. Prinstein, E. A. Youngstrom, E. J. Mash, & R. A. Barkley (Eds.), *Treatment of disorders in childhood and adolescence* (4th ed.). New York: The Guilford Press.

Kempe, C. H., Silverman, F. N., Steele, B. B., Droegemueller, W., & Silver, H. K. (1962). The battered child syndrome. *Journal of the American Medical Association, 181,* 17–24.

Kempe, C., Eriksson-Gustavsson, A. L., & Samuelsson, S. (2011). Are there any Matthew effects in literacy and cognitive development? *Scandinavian Journal of Educational Research, 55,* 181–196.

Kendall, P. C. (1992). *Coping cat workbook.* Ardmore, PA: Workbook Publishing.

Kendall, P. C. (2006). Guiding theory for therapy with children and adolescents. In P. C. Kendall (Ed.), *Child and adolescent therapy: Cognitive-behavioral procedures.* New York: The Guilford Press.

Kendall, P. C., & Frank, H. E. (2018). Implementing evidence-based treatment protocols: Flexibility within fidelity. *Clinical Psychology: Science & Practice, 25*(4).

Kendall, P. C., & Hedtke, K. (2006). *Coping cat workbook* (2nd ed.). Ardmore, PA: Workbook Publishing.

Kendall, P. C., & Suveg, C. (2006). Treating anxiety disorders in youth. In P. C. Kendall (Ed.), *Child and adolescent therapy: Cognitive-behavioral procedures* (3rd ed.). New York: The Guilford Press.

Kendall, P. C., Choudhury, M. S., Hudson, J. L., & Webb, A. (2002). *The C.A.T. Project.* Ardmore, PA: Workbook.

Kendall, P. C., Compton, S. N., Walkup, J. T., Birmaher, B., Albano, A. M., Sherrill, J., et al. (2010). Clinical characteristics of anxiety disordered youth. *Journal of Anxiety Disorders, 24,* 360–365.

Kendall, P. C., Crawford, E. A., Kagan, E. R., Furr, J. M., & Podell, J. L. (2017). Child-focused treatment for anxiety. In J. R. Weisz & A. E. Kazdin (Eds.), *Evidence-based psychotherapies for children and adolescents* (3rd ed.). New York: The Guilford Press.

Kendall, P. C., Flannery-Schroeder, E., Panichelli-Mindel, S., Southam-Gerow, M., Henin, A., & Warman, M. (1997a). Therapy for youth with anxiety disorders: A second randomized clinical trial. *Journal of Consulting and Clinical Psychology, 65,* 366–380.

Kendall, P. C., Hedtke, K. A., & Aschenbrand, S. G. (2006). Anxiety disorders. In D. A. Wolfe & E. J. Mash (Eds.), *Behavioral and emotional disorders in adolescents: Nature, assessment, and treatment.* New York: The Guilford Press.

Kendall, P. C., Hudson, J., Gosch, E., Flannery-Schroeder, E., & Suveg, C. (2008). Cognitive-behavioral therapy for anxiety disordered youth: A randomized clinical trial evaluating child and family modalities. *Journal of Consulting and Clinical Psychology, 76,* 282–297.

Kendall, P. C., Khanna, M. S., Edson, A., Cummings, C., & Harris, M. S. (2011). Computers and psychosocial treatments for child anxiety: Recent advances and ongoing efforts. *Depression and Anxiety, 28,* 58–66.

Kendall, P. C., Panichelli-Mindel, S. M., Sugarman, A., & Callahan, S. A. (1997b). Exposure to child anxiety: Theory, research, and practice. *Clinical Psychology: Science and Practice, 4,* 29–39.

Kendall, P. C., Safford, S., Flannery-Schroeder, E., & Webb, A. (2004). Child anxiety treatment: Outcomes in adolescence and impact on substance use and depression at 7.4-year follow-up. *Journal of Consulting and Clinical Psychology, 72,* 276–287.

Kendall, P. C., Swan, A. J., Carper, M. M., & Hoff, A. L. (2018). Anxiety disorders among children and adolescents. In J. N. Butcher & P. C. Kendall (Eds.), *APA handbook of psychopathology* (Vol. 2). Washington, DC: American Psychological Association.

Kendler, K. S., Aggen, S. H., & Patrick, C. J. (2013). Familial influences on conduct disorder reflect 2 genetic factors and 1 shared environmental factor. *JAMA Psychiatry, 70,* 78–86.

Kendler, K. S., Neale, M. C., Kessler, R. C., Heath, A. C., & Eaves, L. J. (1992a). A population-based twin study of major depression in women: The impact of varying definitions of illness. *Archives of General Psychiatry, 49,* 257–266.

Kendler, K. S., Neale, M. C., Kessler, R. C., Heath, A. C., & Eaves, L. J. (1992b). The genetic epidemiology of phobias in women: The interrelationship of agoraphobia, social phobia, situational phobia, and simple phobia. *Archives of General Psychiatry, 49,* 273–281.

Kennard, B. D., Emslie, G. J., Mayes, T. L., Nakonezny, P. A., Jones, J. M., Foxwell, A. A., & King, J. (2014). Sequential treatment with fluoxetine and relapse-prevention CBT to improve outcomes in pediatric depression. *American Journal of Psychiatry, 171,* 1083–1090.

Kennard, B., Silva, S., Vitiello, B., Curry, J., Kratochvil, C., Simons, A., et al. & the TADS Team. (2006). Remission and residual symptoms after short-term treatment in the Treatment of Adolescents with Depression Study (TADS). *Journal of the American Academy of Child and Adolescent Psychiatry, 45,* 1404–1411.

Kent, K. M., Pelham, W. E., Molina, B. S. G., Sibley, M. H., Waschbusch, D. A., Yu, J., et al. (2011). The academic experience of male high school students with ADHD. *Journal of Abnormal Child Psychology, 39,* 451–462.

Kent, R., & Simonoff, E. (2017). Prevalence of anxiety in autism spectrum disorders. In C. M. Kerns, P. Renno, E. A. Storch, P. C. Kendall, & J. J. Wood (Eds.), *Anxiety in children and adolescents with autism spectrum disorder.* London: Academic Press.

Kerner auch Koerner, J., Gust, N., & Petermann, F. (2018). Developing ADHD in preschool: Testing the dual pathway model of temperament. *Applied Neuropsychology: Child, 7,* 366–373.

Kertz, S. J., Sylvester, C., Tillman, R., & Luby, J. L. (2019). Latent class profiles of anxiety symptom trajectories from preschool through school age. *Journal of Clinical Child & Adolescent Psychology, 48,* 316–331.

Kerwin, M. E., & Berkowitz, R. I. (1996). Feeding and eating disorders: Ingestive problems of infancy, childhood, and adolescence. *School Psychology Review, 25,* 316–328.

Kesler, S. R., Wilde, E., Bruno, J. L., & Bigler, E. D. (2011). Neuroimaging and genetic disorders. In S. Goldstein & C. R. Reynolds (Eds.), *Handbook of neurodevelopmental and genetic disorders in children* (2nd ed.). New York: The Guilford Press.

Kessler, J. W. (1988). *Psychopathology of childhood.* Englewood Cliffs, NJ: Prentice Hall.

Kessler, R. C., Avenevoli, S., Green, J., Gruber, M. J., Guyer, M., He, Y., et al. (2009). National comorbidity survey replication adolescent supplement (NCS-A): III. Concordance of DSM-IV/CIDI diagnoses with clinical reassessments. *Journal of the American Academy of Child and Adolescent Psychiatry, 48,* 386–399.

Killen, J. D., Hayward, C., Wilson, D. M., Taylor, C. B., Hammer, L. D., Litt, I., et al. (1994a). Factors associated with eating disorder symptoms in a community sample of 6th and 7th grade girls. *International Journal of Eating Disorders, 15,* 357–367.

Killen, J. D., Taylor, C. B., Hayward, C., Wilson, D. M., Haydel, K. F., Hammer, L. D., et al. (1994b). Pursuit of thinness and onset of eating disorder symptoms in a community sample of adolescent girls: A three-year prospective analysis. *International Journal of Eating Disorders, 16,* 227–238.

Kilpatrick, D. G., Ruggiero, K. J., Acierno, R., Saunders, B. E., Resnick, H. S., & Best, C. L. (2003). Violence and risk of PTSD, major depression, substance abuse/dependence, and comorbidity: Results from the National Survey of Adolescents. *Journal of Consulting and Clinical Psychology, 71,* 692–700.

Kim, S.-J., Kim, B.-N., Cho, S.-C., Kim, J.-W., Shin, M.-S., Yoo, H.-J., & Kim, H. W. (2010). The prevalence of specific phobia and associated co-morbid features in children and adolescents. *Journal of Anxiety Disorders, 24,* 629–634.

Kim, Y., & Steiner, P. (2016). Quasi-experimental designs for causal inference. *Educational Psychologist, 51*(3/4), 395–405.

Kincaid, D., Dunlap, G., Kern, L., Lane, K. L., Bambara, L. M., Brown, F., et al. (2016). Positive behavior support: A proposal for updating and refining the definition. *Journal of Positive Behavior Interventions, 18,* 69–73.

King, B. H., Hodapp, R. M., & Dykens, E. M. (2000). Mental retardation. In B. J. Sadock & V. A. Sadock (Eds.), *Kaplan & Sadock's comprehensive textbook of psychiatry* (Vol. II). Philadelphia, PA: Lippincott Williams & Wilkins.

King, B. H., Hodapp, R. M., & Dykens, E. M. (2005). Mental retardation. In B. J. Sadock & V. A. Sadock (Eds.), *Kaplan and Sadock's comprehensive textbook of psychiatry.* New York: Lippincott Williams & Wilkins.

King, B. H., Toth, K. E., De Lacy, N., & Doherty, D. (2017). Intellectual disability. In B. J. Sadock, V. A. Sadock, & P. Ruiz (Eds.), *Kaplan & Sadock's comprehensive textbook of psychiatry* (10th ed., Vol. 1). Rijn, Netherlands: Wolters Kluwer Health.

King, C. A., & Merchant, C. R. (2008). Social and interpersonal factors relating to adolescent suicidality: A review of the literature. *Archives of Suicide Research, 12,* 181–196.

King, N. J., & Bernstein, G. A. (2001). School refusal in children and adolescents: A review of the past 10 years. *Journal of the American Academy of Child and Adolescent Psychiatry, 40,* 197–205.

King, N. J., Ollendick, T. H., & Gullone, E. (1990). School-related fears of children and adolescents. *Australian Journal of Education, 34,* 99–112.

King, N. J., Ollendick, T. H., Mattis, S. G., Yang, B., & Tonge, B. (1997). Nonclinical panic attacks in adolescents: Prevalence, symptomatology, and associated features. *Behaviour Change, 13,* 171–183.

King, S., Chambers, C. T., Huguet, A., MacNevin, R. C., McGrath, P. J., Parker, L., & MacDonald, A. J. (2011). The epidemiology of chronic pain in children and adolescents revisited: A systematic review. *Pain, 152,* 2729–2738.

King, V. (2009). Stepfamily formation: Implications for adolescent ties to mothers, nonresident fathers, and stepfathers. *Journal of Marriage and Family, 71,* 954–968.

Kirby, D. (2005). *Evidence of harm.* New York: St Martin's Press.

Kirigin, K. A. (1996). Teaching-family model of group home treatment of children with severe behavior problems. In M. C. Roberts (Ed.), *Model programs in child and family mental health.* Mahwah, NJ: Erlbaum.

References

Kirk, S. A., Gallagher, J. J., & Anastasiow, N. J. (2000). *Educating exceptional children*. Boston, MA: Houghton Mifflin Company.

Kirk, S., Gallagher, J., & Coleman, M. R. (2015). *Educating exceptional children* (14th ed.). Stamford, CT: Cengage Learning.

Kirk, V., Baughn, J., D'Andrea, L., Friedman, N., Galion, A., Garetz, S., et al. (2017). American Academy of Sleep Medicine position paper for the use of a home sleep apnea test for the diagnosis of OSA in children. *Journal of Clinical Sleep Medicine, 13,* 1199–1203.

Kitzman-Ulrich, H., Wilson, D. K., St. George, S. M., Lawman, H., Segal, M., & Fairchild, A. (2010). The integration of a family systems approach for understanding youth obesity, physical activity, and dietary programs. *Clinical Child and Family Review, 13,* 231–253.

Klahr, A. M., Rueter, M. A., McGue, M., Iacono, W. G., & Burt, S. A. (2011). The relationship between parent-child conflict and adolescent antisocial behavior: Confirming shared environment mediation. *Journal of Abnormal Child Psychology, 39,* 683–694.

Klassen, R. (2010). Confidence to manage learning: The self-efficacy for self-regulated learning of early adolescents with learning disabilities. *Learning Disability Quarterly, 33,* 19–30.

Kleiger, J. H. (2001). Projective testing with children and adolescents. In C. E. Walker & M. C. Roberts (Eds.), *Handbook of clinical child psychology* (3rd ed.). New York: John Wiley & Sons.

Klein, D. F., Mannuzza, S., Chapman, T., & Fyer, A. (1992). Child panic revised. *Journal of the American Academy of Child and Adolescent Psychiatry, 31,* 112–113.

Klein, D. N., Dyson, M. W., Kujawa, A. J., & Kotov, R. (2012). Temperament and internalizing disorders. In M. Zentner & R. Shiner (Eds.), *Handbook of temperament*. New York: Guilford Press.

Klein, D. N., Goldstein, B. L., & Finsaas, M. (2017). Depressive disorders. In T. P. Beauchaine & S. P. Hinshaw (Eds.), *Child and adolescent psychopathology* (3rd ed.). Hoboken, NJ: John Wiley & Sons Inc.

Klein, D. N., Lewinsohn, P. M., Seeley, J. R., & Rohde, P. (2001). A family study of major depressive disorder in a community sample of adolescents. *Archives of General Psychiatry, 58,* 13–20.

Klein, D. N., Shankman, S. A., Lewinsohn, P. M., & Seeley, J. R. (2009). Subthreshold depressive disorder in adolescents: Predictors of escalation to full-syndrome depressive disorders. *Journal of the American Academy of Child & Adolescent Psychiatry, 48,* 703–710.

Klein, D. N., Torpey, D. C., & Bufferd, S. J. (2008). Depressive disorders. In T. P Beauchaine & S. P Hinshaw (Eds.), *Child and adolescent psychopathology*. Hoboken, NJ: John Wiley & Sons.

Klein, M. (1932). *The psycho-analysis of children.* London: Hogarth Press.

Klein-Tasman, B. P., & Mervis, C. B. (2018). Autism spectrum symptomatology among children with duplication 7q11. 23 syndrome. *Journal of Autism and Developmental Disorders, 48,* 1982–1994.

Klesges, R. C., & Hanson, C. L. (1988). Determining the environmental causes and correlates of childhood obesity: Methodological issues and future research directions. In N. A. Krasnegor, G. D. Grave, & N. Kretchmer (Eds.), *Childhood obesity: A biobehavioral perspective.* Caldwell, NJ: The Telford Press.

Klima, T., & Repetti, R. L. (2008). Children's peer relations and their psychological adjustment: Differences between close friendships and the larger peer group. *Merrill-Palmer Quarterly, 54,* 151–178.

Klin, A., Shultz, S., & Jones, W. (2015). Social visual engagement in infants and toddlers with autism: Early developmental transitions and a model of pathogenesis. *Neuroscience & Biobehavioral Reviews, 50,* 189–203.

Klinger, L. G., & Dudley, K. M. (2019). Autism spectrum disorder. In M. J. Prinstein, E. A. Youngstrom, E. J. Mash, & R. A. Barkley (Eds.), *Treatment of disorders in childhood and adolescence.* New York: The Guilford Press.

Klinger, L. G., Mussey, J. L., & O'Kelley, S. (2018). Assessment of intellectual functioning in autism spectrum disorder. In S. Goldstein & S. Ozonoff (Eds.), *Assessment of autism spectrum disorder* (2nd ed.). New York: Guilford Press.

Klump, K. L., Burt, S. A., Spanos, A., McGue, M., Iacono, W. G., & Wade, T. D. (2010). Age differences in genetic and environmental influences on weight and shape concerns. *International Journal of Eating Disorders, 43,* 679–688.

Klump, K. L., Culbert, K. M., & Sisk, C. L. (2017). Sex differences in binge eating: Gonadal hormone effects across development. *Annual Review of Clinical Psychology, 13,* 183–207.

Klump, K. L., Culbert, K. M., Slane, J. D., Burt, S. A., Sisk, C. L., & Nigg, J. T. (2012). The effects of puberty on genetic risk for disordered eating: Evidence for a sex difference. *Psychological Medicine, 42,* 627–637.

Knapp, P., & Jensen, P. S. (2006). Recommendations for DSM-V. In P. S. Jensen, P. Knapp, & D. A. Mrazek (Eds.), *Toward a new diagnostic system for child psychopathology. Moving beyond the DSM.* New York: The Guilford Press.

Knorr, J. (2017). Childhood-onset schizophrenia spectrum disorders. In S. Goldstein & M. DeVries (Eds.), *Handbook of DSM-5 disorders in children and adolescents.* Cham, Switzerland: Springer.

Knouse, L. E. (2015). Cognitive-behavioral therapies for ADHD. In R. A. Barkley (Ed.), *Attention-deficit hyperactivity disorder: A handbook for diagnosis & treatment* (4th ed.). New York: The Guilford Press.

Knouse, L. E., Bagwell, C. L., Barkley, R. A., & Murphy, K. R. (2005). Accuracy of self-evaluation in adults with ADHD: Evidence from a driving study. *Journal of Attention Disorders, 8,* 221–234.

Kodish, I., & McClellan, J. M. (2016). Early onset schizophrenia. In M. K. Dulcan (Ed.), *Dulcan's textbook of child and adolescent psychiatry* (2nd ed.). Arlington, VA: American Psychiatric Association Publishing.

Koegel, L. K. (2000). Interventions to facilitate communication in autism. *Journal of Autism and Developmental Disorders, 30,* 383–391.

Koegel, R. L., Koegel, L. K., & McNerney, E. K. (2001). Pivotal areas in intervention for autism. *Journal of Clinical Child Psychology, 30,* 19–32.

Koegel, R., Koegel, L. K., Vernon, T. W., & Brookman-Frazee, L. I. (2017). Pivotal response training for individuals with autism spectrum disorder. In J. R. Weisz & A. E. Kazdin (Eds.), *Evidence-based psychotherapies for children and adolescents* (3rd ed.). New York: The Guilford Press.

Kofler, M. J., Harmon, S. L., Aduen, P. A., Day, T. N., Austin, K. E., Spiegel, J. A., et al. (2018). Neurocognitive and behavioral predictors of social problems in ADHD: A Bayesian framework. *Neuropsychology, 32,* 344–355.

Kofler, M. J., Irwin, L. N., Soto, E. F., Groves, N. B., Harmon, S. L., & Sarver, D. E. (2019). Executive functioning heterogeneity in pediatric ADHD. *Journal of Abnormal Child Psychology, 47,* 273–286.

Kofler, M. J., Sarver, D. E., Spiegel, J. A., Day, T. N., Harmon, S. L., & Wells, E. L. (2017). Heterogeneity in ADHD: Neurocognitive predictors of peer, family, and academic functioning. *Child Neuropsychology, 23,* 733–759.

Kohut, T., Robbins, J., & Panganiban, J. (2019). Update on childhood/adolescent obesity and its sequela. *Current Opinion in Pediatrics, 31,* 645–653.

Koinis-Mitchell, D., Kopel, S. J., Seifer, R., LeBourgeois, M., McQuaid, E. L., Esteban, C. A., et al. (2017). Asthma-related lung function, sleep quality, and sleep duration in urban children. *Sleep Health, 3,* 148–156.

Kolko, D. J. (2005). Treatment and education for childhood firesetting: Description, outcomes, and implications. In E. D. Hibbs & P. S. Jensen (Eds.), *Psychosocial treatments for child and adolescent disorders: Empirically based strategies for clinical practice* (2nd ed.). Washington, DC: American Psychological Association.

Kolko, D. J. (Ed.) (2002). *Handbook of firesetting in children and youth.* San Diego, CA: Academic Press.

Kolko, D. J., Day, B. T., Bridge, J. A., & Kazdin, A. E. (2001). Two-year prediction of children's firesetting in clinically referred and nonreferred samples. *Journal of Child Psychology and Psychiatry, 42,* 371–380.

Kolvin, I. (1971). Psychoses in childhood: A comparative study. In M. Rutter (Ed.), *Infantile autism: Concepts, characteristics, and treatments.* London: Churchill-Livingstone.

Konrad, K., Di Martino, A., & Aoki, Y. (2018). Brain volumes and intrinsic brain connectivity in ADHD. In *Oxford textbook of attention deficit hyperactivity disorder.* Oxford: Oxford University Press.

Koocher, G. P., & Sallan, S. E. (1978). Pediatric oncology. In P. R. Magrab (Ed.), *Psychological management of pediatric problems* (Vol. 1). Baltimore, MD: University Park Press.

Koppitz, E. M. (1984). *Psychological evaluation of human figure drawings by middle school pupils.* Orlando, FL: Grune & Stratton.

Korbin, J. E., Coulton, C. J., Chard, S., Platt-Houston, C., & Su, M. (1998). Impoverishment and child maltreatment in African American and European American neighborhoods. *Development and Psychopathology, 10,* 215–233.

Korkman, M., Kirk, U., & Kemp, S. (2007). *NEPSY-II: Clinical and interpretive manual.* San Antonio, TX: The Psychological Corporation.

Kornilov, S. A., & Grigorenko, E. L. (2016). Molecular genetic methods for developmental scientists. In D. Cicchetti (Ed.), *Developmental psychopathology: Risk, resilience, and intervention* (Vol. 2). Hoboken, NJ: John Wiley & Sons.

Kortekaas-Rijlaarsdam, A. F., Luman, M., Sonuga-Barke, E., & Oosterlaan, J. (2019). Does methylphenidate improve academic performance? A systematic review and meta-analysis. *European Child & Adolescent Psychiatry, 28,* 155–164.

Koss, K. J., Cummings, E. M., Davies, P. T., Hetzel, S., & Cicchetti, D. (2018). Harsh parenting and serotonin transporter and BDNF Val66Met polymorphisms as predictors of adolescent depressive symptoms. *Journal of Clinical Child & Adolescent Psychology, 47*(sup1), S205–S218.

Kotimaa, A. J., Moilanen, I., Taanila, A., Ebeling, H., Smalley, S. L., McGough, J. J., et al. (2003). Maternal smoking and hyperactivity in 8-year-old children. *Journal of the American Academy of Child and Adolescent Psychiatry, 42,* 826–833.

Kotler, L. A., Cohen, P., Davies, M., Pine, D. S., & Walsh, B. T. (2001). Longitudinal relationships between childhood, adolescent, and adult eating disorders. *Journal of the American Academy of Child and Adolescent Psychiatry, 40,* 1434–1440.

Kovacs, M. (1992). *Children's Depression Inventory (CDI): Technical manual update.* North Tonawanda, NY: Multi-Health Systems, Inc.

Kovacs, M. (1996). Presentation and course of major depressive disorder during childhood and later years of the life span.

References

Journal of the American Academy of Child and Adolescent Psychiatry, 35, 705–715.

Kovacs, M. (1997). Depressive disorders in childhood: An impressionistic landscape. *Journal of Child Psychology and Psychiatry, 38,* 287–298.

Kovacs, M. (2011). *Children's Depression Inventory, Second Edition (CDI-2).* North Tonawanda, NY: Multi-Health Systems.

Kovacs, M., Goldston, D., & Gatsonis, C. (1993). Suicidal behaviors and childhood-onset depressive disorders: A longitudinal investigation. *Journal of the American Academy of Child and Adolescent Psychiatry, 32,* 8–20.

Kowatch, R. A., & DelBello, M. P. (2006). Pediatric bipolar disorder: Emerging diagnostic and treatment approaches. *Child and Adolescent Psychiatric Clinics of North America, 15,* 73–108.

Kowatch, R. A., Fristad, M., Birmaher, B., Wagner, K. D., Findling, R. L., & Hellander, M. (2005). Treatment guidelines for children and adolescents with bipolar disorder. *Journal of the American Academy of Child and Adolescent Psychiatry, 44,* 213–235.

Kowatch, R. A., Strawn, J. R., & DelBello, M. P. (2010). Developmental considerations in the pharmacological treatment of youth with bipolar disorder. In D. J. Miklowitz & D. Cicchetti (Eds.), *Understanding bipolar disorder: A developmental psychopathology perspective.* New York: The Guilford Press.

Koyanagi, A., Oh, H., Carvalho, A. F., Smith, L., Haro, J. M., Vancampfort, D., et al. (2019). Bullying victimization and suicide attempt among adolescents aged 12–15 years from 48 countries. *Journal of the American Academy of Child & Adolescent Psychiatry, 58,* 907–918.

Krahé, B. (2012). Report of the Media Violence Commission. *Aggressive Behavior, 38,* 335–341.

Krahn, G. L., Hohn, M. F., & Kime, C. (1995). Incorporating qualitative approaches into clinical child psychology research. *Journal of Clinical Child Psychology, 24,* 204–213.

Kral, T. V., & Faith, M. S. (2009). Influences on child eating and weight development from a behavioral genetics perspective. *Journal of Pediatric Psychology, 34,* 596–605.

Kreuze, L. J., Pijnenborg, G. H. M., de Jonge, Y. B., & Nauta, M. H. (2018). Cognitive-behavior therapy for children and adolescents with anxiety disorders: A meta-analysis of secondary outcomes. *Journal of Anxiety Disorders, 60,* 43–57.

Krieger, V., & Amador-Campos, J. A. (2018). Assessment of executive function in ADHD adolescents: Contribution of performance tests and rating scales. *Child Neuropsychology, 24,* 1063–1087.

Krishnan, S., Watkins, K. E., & Bishop, D. V. M. (2016). Neurobiological basis of language learning difficulties. *Trends in Cognitive Sciences, 20,* 701–714.

Kronbichler, L., Tschernegg, M., Martin, A. I., Schurz, M., & Kronbichler, M. (2017). Abnormal brain activation during theory of mind tasks in schizophrenia: A meta-analysis. *Schizophrenia Bulletin, 43,* 1240–1250.

Kronenfeld, L. W., Reba-Harrelson, L., Von Holle, A., Reyes, M. L., & Bulik, C. M. (2010). Ethnic and racial differences in body size perception and satisfaction. *Body Image, 7,* 131–136.

Kubota, T. (2017). Epigenetic understanding of gene-environment interaction in autism spectrum disorder. *Journal of Pediatric Neurology, 15,* 099–104.

Kuczynski, L., & Kochanska, G. (1995). Function and contexts of maternal demands: Developmental significance of early demands for competent action. *Child Development, 66,* 616–628.

Kudo, M. F., Lussier, C. M., & Swanson, H. L. (2015). Reading disabilities in children: A selective meta-analysis of the cognitive literature. *Research in Developmental Disabilities, 40,* 51–62.

Kuhn, T. S. (1962). *The structure of scientific revolutions.* Chicago, IL: University of Chicago Press.

Kumpulainen, K., Räsänen, E., & Henttonen, I. (1999). Children involved in bullying: Psychological disturbance and the persistence of the involvement. *Child Abuse and Neglect, 23,* 1253–1262.

Kupersmidt, J. B., & Patterson, C. J. (1991). Childhood peer rejection, aggression, withdrawal, and perceived competence as predictors of self-reported behavior problems in preadolescence. *Journal of Abnormal Child Psychology, 19,* 427–449.

Kupst, M. J., & Patenaude, A. F. (2016). Coping and adaptation in pediatric cancer: Current perspectives. In A. N. Abrams, A. C. Muriel, & L. Wiener (Eds.), *Pediatric psychosocial oncology: Textbook for multidisciplinary care.* Cham, Switzerland: Springer.

Kwok, E. Y. L., Brown, H. M., Smyth, R. E., & Oram Cardy, J. (2015). Meta-analysis of receptive and expressive language skills in autism spectrum disorder. *Research in Autism Spectrum Disorders, 9,* 202–222.

La Greca, A. M. (1999). *Manual and instructions for the SASC, SASC-R, SAS-A (Adolescents) and parent versions of the scales.* Miami, FL: University of Miami.

La Greca, A. M., & Danzi, B. A. (2019). Posttraumatic stress disorder. In M. J. Prinstein, E. A. Youngstrom, E. J. Mash, & R. A. Barkley (Eds.), *Treatment of disorders in childhood and adolescence* (4th ed.). New York: The Guilford Press.

La Greca, A. M., & Harrison, H. M. (2005). Adolescent peer relations, friendships, and romantic relationships: Do they predict social anxiety and depression? *Journal of Clinical Child and Adolescent Psychology, 34,* 49–61.

La Greca, A. M., & Spetter, D. S. (2018). Psychosocial aspects of childhood diabetes: A multivariate framework. In N.

Schneiderman, P. McCabe, & A. Baum (Eds.), *Stress and disease processes: Perspectives in behavioral medicine.* Abingdon, Oxon: Routledge.

La Greca, A. M., Silverman, W. K., Vernberg, E. M., & Prinstein, M. J. (1996). Symptoms of posttraumatic stress in children after Hurricane Andrew: A prospective study. *Journal of Consulting and Clinical Psychology, 64,* 712–723.

Labad, J. (2019). The role of cortisol and prolactin in the pathogenesis and clinical expression of psychotic disorders. *Psychoneuroendocrinology, 102,* 24–36.

Lackaye, T., Margalit, M., Ziv, O., & Ziman, T. (2006). Comparisons of self-efficacy, mood, effort, and hope between students with learning disabilities and their non-LD-matched peers. *Learning Disability Research & Practice, 21,* 111–121.

Laessle, R. G., Uhl, H., & Lindel, B. (2001). Parental influences on eating behavior in obese and nonobese preadolescents. *International Journal of Eating Disorders, 30,* 447–453.

LaFrance, D. L., Weiss, M. J., Kazemi, E., Gerenser, J., & Dobres, J. (2019). Multidisciplinary teaming: Enhancing collaboration through increased understanding. *Behavior Analysis in Practice, 12,* 709–726.

Lahey, B. B. (2001, Winter). Should the combined and predominantly inattentive types of ADHD be considered distinct and unrelated disorders? *Clinical Psychology: Science and Practice, 8,* 494–497.

Lahey, B. B. (2008). Oppositional defiant disorder, conduct disorder, and juvenile delinquency. In T. P. Beauchaine & S. P. Hinshaw (Eds.), *Child and adolescent psychopathology.* Hoboken, NJ: John Wiley & Sons.

Lahey, B. B., & Waldman, I. D. (2017). Oppositional defiant disorder, conduct disorder, and juvenile delinquency. In T. P. Beauchaine & S. P. Hinshaw (Eds.), *Child and adolescent psychopathology* (3rd ed.). Hoboken, NJ: John Wiley & Sons Inc.

Lahey, B. B., & Willcutt, E. G. (2010). Predictive validity of a continuous alternative to nominal subtypes of attention-deficit/hyperactivity disorder for DSM-V *Journal of Clinical Child and Adolescent Psychology, 39,* 761–775.

Lahey, B. B., D'Onofrio, B. M., & Waldman, I. D. (2009). Using epidemiological methods to test hypotheses regarding causal influences on child and adolescent mental disorders. *Journal of Child Psychology and Psychiatry, 50,* 53–62.

Lahey, B. B., Van Hulle, C. A., Singh, A. L., Waldman, I. D., & Rathouz, P. J. (2011). Higher-order genetic and environmental structure of prevalent forms of child and adolescent psychopathology. *Archives of General Psychiatry, 68,* 181–189.

Lahey, B. B., Waldman, I. D., & McBurnett, K. (1999). The development of antisocial behavior: An integrative causal model. *Journal of Child Psychology and Psychiatry, 40,* 669–682.

Lahti, J., Räikkönen, K., Kajantie, E., Heinonen, K., Pesonen, A.-K., Järvenpää, A.-L., & Stranberg, T. (2006). Small body size at birth and behavioural symptoms of ADHD in children aged five to six years. *Journal of Child Psychology and Psychiatry, 47,* 1167–1174.

Laird, R. D., Jordan, K. Y., Dodge, K. A., Petit, G. S., & Bates, J. E. (2001). Peer rejection in childhood, involvement with antisocial peers in early adolescence and the development of externalizing behavior problems. *Development and Psychopathology, 13,* 337–354.

Lal, R. A., & Maahs, D. M. (2017). Clinical use of continuous glucose monitoring in pediatrics. *Diabetes Technology & Therapeutics, 19*(sup2), S37–S43.

Lamanek, K. L., Hahn, A., & McNaull, M. (2017). Sickle cell disease. In M. C. Roberts & R. G. Steele (Eds.), *Handbook of pediatric psychology.* New York: The Guilford Press.

Lamb, M. E. (2010). *The role of the father in child development* (5th ed.). New York: John Wiley.

Lambie, I., & Randell, I. (2011). Creating a firestorm: A review of children who deliberately light fires. *Clinical Psychology Review, 31,* 307–327.

Landa, R. J. (2018). Efficacy of early interventions for infants and young children with, and at risk for, autism spectrum disorders. *International Review of Psychiatry, 30,* 25–39.

Landi, N., & Ryherd, K. (2017). Understanding specific reading comprehension deficit: A review. *Language and Linguistics Compass, 11,* e12234.

Landier, W., Armenian, S., & Bhatia, S. (2015). Late effects of childhood cancer and its treatment. *Pediatric Clinics, 62,* 275–300.

Lang, P. J. (1984). Cognition in emotion: Concept and action. In C. E. Izard, J. Kagan, & R. B. Zajonc (Eds.), *Emotions, cognition, and behavior.* New York: Cambridge University Press.

Langer, N., Benjamin, C., Becker, B. L. C., & Gaab, N. (2019). Comorbidity of reading disabilities and ADHD: Structural and functional brain characteristics. *Human Brain Mapping, 40,* 2677–2698.

Langley, K. (2018). ADHD genetics. In T. P. Beauchaine, D. Coghill, & A. Zuddas (Eds.), *Oxford textbook of attention deficit hyperactivity disorder.* Oxford: Oxford University Press.

Lansford, J. E., Chang, L., Dodge, K. A., Malone, P. S., Oburu, P., Palmérus, K., et al. (2005). Physical discipline and children's adjustment: Cultural normativeness as a moderator. *Child Development, 76,* 1234–1246.

Lansford, J. E., Deater-Deckard, K., Dodge, K. A., Bates, J. E., & Pettit, G. S. (2004). Ethnic differences in the link between physical discipline and later adolescent externalizing behaviors. *Journal of Child Psychology and Psychiatry, 45,* 801–812.

Lansford, J. E., Dodge, K. A., Pettit, G. S., Bates, J. E., Crozier, J., & Kaplow, J. (2002). A 12-year prospective study of the longterm effects of early childhood physical maltreatment on psychological, behavioral, and academic problems in adolescence. *Archives of Pediatrics and Adolescent Medicine, 156,* 824–830.

Lapouse, R., & Monk, M. A. (1959). Fears and worries in a representative sample of children. *American Journal of Orthopsychiatry, 29,* 803–818.

Larkin, R. W. (2007). *Comprehending Columbine.* Philadelphia, PA: Temple University Press.

Larsson, H., Dilshad, R., Lichtenstein, P., & Barker, E. D. (2011). Developmental trajectories of DSM-IV symptoms of attention-deficit/hyperactivity disorder: Genetic effects, family risk and associated psychopathology. *Journal of Child Psychology and Psychiatry, 52,* 954–963.

Last, C. G. (1988). Separation anxiety. In M. Hersen & C. G. Last (Eds.), *Child behavior therapy casebook.* New York: Plenum Press.

Last, C. G., & Strauss, C. C. (1989). Panic disorder in children and adolescents. *Journal of Anxiety Disorders, 3,* 87–95.

Last, C. G., & Strauss, C. C. (1990). School refusal in anxiety-disordered children and adolescents. *Journal of the American Academy of Child and Adolescent Psychiatry, 29,* 31–35.

Last, C. G., Perrin, S., Hersen, M., & Kazdin, A. E. (1992). DSMIII-R anxiety disorders in children: Sociodemographic and clinical characteristics. *Journal of the American Academy of Child and Adolescent Psychiatry, 31,* 1070–1076.

Last, C. G., Perrin, S., Hersen, M., & Kazdin, A. E. (1996). A prospective study of childhood anxiety disorders. *Journal of the American Academy of Child and Adolescent Psychiatry, 35,* 1502–1510.

Last, C. G., Strauss, C. C., & Francis, G. (1987). Comorbidity among childhood anxiety disorders. *Journal of Nervous and Mental Disease, 175,* 726–730.

Latner, J. D., & Stunkard, A. J. (2003). Getting worse: The stigmatization of obese children. *Obesity Research, 11,* 452–456.

Latvala, A., Kuja-Halkola, R., Almqvist, C., Larsson, H., & Lichtenstein, P. (2015). A longitudinal study of resting heart rate and violent criminality in more than 700 000 men. *JAMA Psychiatry, 72,* 971–978.

Lau, A. S., & Weisz, J. R. (2003). Reported maltreatment among clinic-referred children: Implications for presenting problems, treatment attrition, and long-term outcomes. *Journal of the American Academy of Child and Adolescent Psychiatry, 42,* 1327–1334.

Lau, J. Y. F., & Waters, A. M. (2017). Annual Research Review: An expanded account of information-processing mechanisms in risk for child and adolescent anxiety and depression. *Journal of Child Psychology and Psychiatry, 58,* 387–407.

Laurens, K. R., & Cullen, A. E. (2016). Toward earlier identification and preventative intervention in schizophrenia: Evidence from the London Child Health and Development Study. *Social Psychiatry and Psychiatric Epidemiology, 51,* 475–491.

Lavigne, J. V., Hopkins, J., Gouze, K. R., Bryant, F. B., LeBailley, S. A., Binns, H. J., et al. (2010). Is smoking during pregnancy a risk factor for psychopathology in young children? A methodological caveat and report on preschoolers. *Journal of Pediatric Psychology, 36,* 10–24.

Lavigne, J. V., LeBailly, S. A., Hopkins, J., Gouze, K. R., & Binns, H. J. (2009). The prevalence of ADHD, ODD, depression, and anxiety in a community sample of 4-year-olds. *Journal of Clinical Child and Adolescent Psychology, 38,* 315–328.

Law, E. F., Noel, M., Nagel, M. S., & Dahlquist, L. M. (2017). Chronic and recurrent pain. In M. C. Roberts & R. G. Steele (Eds.), *Handbook of pediatric psychology* (5th ed.). New York: The Guilford Press.

Law, J., Garrett, Z., & Nye, C. (2004). The efficacy of treatment for children with developmental speech and language delay/disorder. *Journal of Speech, Language, and Hearing Research, 47,* 924–943.

Law, J., Garrett, Z., & Nye, C. (2005). Speech and language therapy interventions for children with primary speech and language delay or disorder. *Campbell Systematic Reviews, 1,* 1–85.

Lawrence, P. J., Murayama, K., & Creswell, C. (2019). Systematic review and meta-analysis: Anxiety and depressive disorders in offspring of parents with anxiety disorders. *Journal of the American Academy of Child & Adolescent Psychiatry, 58,* 46–60.

Le, L. K. D., Barendregt, J. J., Hay, P., & Mihalopoulos, C. (2017). Prevention of eating disorders: A systematic review and meta-analysis. *Clinical Psychology Review, 53,* 46–58.

Le Grange, D., & Eisler, I. (2017). Family therapy for eating disorders. In K. D. Brownell & B. T. Walsh (Eds.), *Eating disorders and obesity: A comprehensive handbook* (3rd ed.). New York: The Guilford Press.

Le Grange, D., & Lock, J. (2009). *Treating bulimia in adolescents: A family-based approach.* New York: Guilford Press.

Le Grange, D., & Robin, A. L. (2017). Family-based treatment and behavioral family systems therapy for adolescent eating disorders. In J. R. Weisz & A. E. Kazdin (Eds.), *Evidence-based psychotherapies for children and adolescents* (3rd ed.). New York: The Guilford Press.

Le Grange, D., Crosby, R., Rathouz, P., & Leventhal, B. (2007). A controlled comparison of family-based treatment and supportive psychotherapy for adolescent bulimia nervosa. *Archives of General Psychiatry, 64,* 1049–1056.

Leach, J. M., Scarborough, H. S., & Rescorla, L. (2003). Late-emerging reading disabilities. *Journal of Educational Psychology, 95,* 211–224.

Lebel, C., Roussotte, F., & Sowell, E. R. (2011). Imaging the impact of prenatal alcohol exposure on the structure of the developing brain. *Neuropsychology Review, 21,* 102–118.

LeBovidge, J. S., Lavigne, J. V., & Miller, M. L. (2005). Adjustment to chronic arthritis of childhood: The roles of illness-related stress and attitude toward illness. *Journal of Pediatric Psychology, 30,* 273–286.

Leckman, J. F., King, R. A., Gilbert, D. L., Coffey, B. J., Singer, H. S., Dure, L. S., et al. (2011). Streptococcal upper respiratory tract infections and exacerbations of tic and obsessive-compulsive symptoms: A prospective longitudinal study. *Journal of the American Academy of Child and Adolescent Psychiatry, 50,* 108–118.

Lee, C. A., Milich, R., Lorch, E. P., Flory, K., Owens, J. S., Lamont, A. E., & Evans, S. W. (2018). Forming first impressions of children: The role of attention-deficit/hyperactivity disorder symptoms and emotion dysregulation. *Journal of Child Psychology and Psychiatry, 59,* 556–564.

Lee, J. (2020). Mental health effects of school closures during COVID-19. *The Lancet Child & Adolescent Health, 4,* 421.

Lee, K., & Bull, R. (2016). Developmental changes in working memory, updating, and math achievement. *Journal of Educational Psychology, 108,* 869–882.

Lee, M., Nayar, K., Maltman, N., Hamburger, D., Martin, G. E., Gordon, P. C., & Losh, M. (2020). Understanding social communication differences in autism spectrum disorder and first-degree relatives: A study of looking and speaking. *Journal of Autism and Developmental Disorders, 50,* 2128–2141.

Lee, S. S. (2011). Deviant peer affiliation and antisocial behavior: Interaction with monoamine oxidase A (MAOA) genotype. *Journal of Abnormal Child Psychology, 39,* 321–332.

Lee, S. S. (2018). Perspectives on parenting behavior: Origins, mechanisms, and future opportunities. *Journal of Clinical Child & Adolescent Psychology, 47*(sup1), S1–S4.

Lee, S. S., Humphreys, K. L., Flory, K., Liu, R., & Glass, K. (2011). Prospective association of childhood attention-deficit/hyperactivity disorder (ADHD) and substance use and abuse/dependence: A meta-analytic review. *Clinical Psychology Review, 31,* 328–341.

Leeb, R., Paulozzi, L., Melanson, C., Simon, T., & Arias, I. (2008). *Child maltreatment surveillance: Uniform definitions for public health and recommended data elements.* Atlanta, GA: Centers for Disease Control and Prevention, National Center for Injury Prevention and Control.

Lefkowitz, M., & Burton, N. (1978). Childhood depression: A critique of the concept. *Psychological Bulletin, 85,* 716–726.

Leflot, G., van Lier, P. A., Onghena, P., & Colpin, H. (2010). The role of teacher behavior management in the development of disruptive behaviors: An intervention study with the good behavior game. *Journal of Abnormal Child Psychology, 38,* 869–882.

Leibenluft, E., & Rich, B. A. (2008). Pediatric bipolar disorder. *Annual Review of Clinical Psychology, 4,* 163–187.

Leinonen, J. A., Solantaus, T. S., & Punamäki, R.-L. (2003). Parental mental health and children's adjustment: The quality of marital interaction and parenting as mediating factors. *Journal of Child Psychology and Psychiatry, 44,* 227–241.

Leitenberg, H., Yost, L. W., & Carroll-Wilson, M. (1986). Negative cognitive errors in children: Questionnaire development, normative data, and comparisons between children with and without self-reported symptoms of depression, low self-esteem, and evaluation anxiety. *Journal of Consulting and Clinical Psychology, 54,* 528–536.

Lemanek, K. L., Hahn, A., & McNaull, M. (2017). Sickle cell disease. In M. C. Roberts & R. G. Steele (Eds.), *Handbook of pediatric psychology* (5th ed.). New York: The Guilford Press.

Lemerise, E. A., & Arsenio, W. F. (2000). An integrated model of emotion processes and cognition in social information processing. *Child Development, 71,* 107–118.

Leming, M. R., & Dickinson, G. E. (2020). *Understanding dying, death, and bereavement* (8th ed.). Stanford, CT: Cengage Learning.

Leonard, H. L., Ale, C. M., Freeman, J. B., Garcia, A. M., & Ng, J. S. (2005). Obsessive-compulsive disorder. *Child and Adolescent Psychiatric Clinics of North America, 14,* 727–743.

Leonard, L. B. (1998). *Children with specific language impairment.* Cambridge, MA: The MIT Press.

Leonard, L. B. (2017). Specific language impairment. In *Oxford Research Encyclopedia of Psychology.* Oxford: Oxford University Press.

Leonard, L. B., Weismer, S. E., Miller, C. A., Francis, D. J., Tomblin, J. B., & Kail, R. V. (2007). Speed of processing, working memory, and language impairment in children. *Journal of Speech, Language, and Hearing Research, 50,* 408–428.

Leopold, D. R., Christopher, M. E., Olson, R. K., Petrill, S. A., & Willcutt, E. G. (2019). Invariance of ADHD symptoms across sex and age: A latent analysis of ADHD and impairment ratings from early childhood into adolescence. *Journal of Abnormal Child Psychology, 47,* 21–34.

Leppert, B., Havdahl, A., Riglin, L., Jones, H. J., Zheng, J., Smith, G. D., et al. (2019). Association of maternal neurodevelopmental risk alleles with early-life exposures. *JAMA Psychiatry, 76,* 834–842.

Lerner, R. M., & Chase, P. A. (2019). Enhancing theory and methodology in the international study of positive youth development: A commentary. *Child & Youth Care Forum, 48,* 269–277.

Leslie, L. K., Plemmons, D., Monn, A. R., & Palinkas, L. A. (2007). Investigating ADHD treatment trajectories: Listening to families' stories about medication use. *Journal of Developmental and Behavioral Pediatrics, 28,* 179–188.

Leslie, L. K., Weckerly, J., Landsverk, J., Hough, R. L., Hurlbut, M. S., & Wood, P. A. (2003). Racial/ethnic differences in the use of psychotropic medication in high-risk children and

References

adolescents. *Journal of the American Academy of Child and Adolescent Psychiatry, 42,* 1433–1442.

Leventhal, T., & Brooks-Gunn, J. (2000). The neighborhoods they live in: The effects of neighborhood residence on child and adolescent outcomes. *Psychological Bulletin, 126,* 309–337.

Levine, M. P., & Harrison, K. (2004). Media's role in the perpetuation and prevention of negative body image and disordered eating. In J. K. Thompson (Ed.), *Handbook of eating disorders and obesity.* Hoboken, NJ: John Wiley.

Levitt, H. M., Bamberg, M., Creswell, J. W., Frost, D. M., Josselson, R., & Suárez-Orozco, C. (2018). Journal article reporting standards for qualitative primary, qualitative meta-analytic, and mixed methods research in psychology: The APA Publications and Communications Board task force report. *American Psychologist, 73,* 26–46.

Levy, A. J. (2011). Psychoanalytic approaches to play therapy. In C. E. Schaefer (Ed.), *Foundations of play therapy.* Hoboken, NJ: John Wiley & Sons.

Lewandowski, L. J., & Lovett, B. J. (2014). Learning disabilities. In E. J. Mash & R. A. Barkley (Eds.), *Child psychopathology.* New York: The Guilford Press.

Lewinsohn, P. (1974). A behavioral approach to depression. In R. J. Friedman & M. M. Katz (Eds.), *The psychology of depression: Contemporary theory and research.* Washington, DC: Winston.

Lewinsohn, P. M., Clarke, G. N., Hops, H., & Andrews, J. (1990). Cognitive behavioral treatment for depressed adolescents. *Behavior Therapy, 21,* 385–402.

Lewinsohn, P. M., Hops, H., Roberts, R. E., Seeley, J. R., & Andrews, J. A. (1993). Adolescent psychopathology: I. Prevalence and incidence of depression and other DSM-III-R disorders in high school students. *Journal of Abnormal Psychology, 102,* 133–144.

Lewinsohn, P. M., Klein, D. N., & Seeley, J. R. (1995a). Bipolar disorders in a community sample of older adolescents: Prevalence, phenomenology, comorbidity, and course. *Journal of the American Academy of Child and Adolescent Psychiatry, 34,* 454–463.

Lewinsohn, P. M., Rohde, P., & Seeley, J. R. (1995b). Adolescent psychopathology: III. The clinical consequences of comorbidity. *Journal of the American Academy of Child and Adolescent Psychiatry, 34,* 510–519.

Lewinsohn, P. M., Rohde, P., & Seeley, J. R. (1996). Adolescent suicidal ideation and attempts: Prevalence, risk factors, and clinical implications. *Clinical Psychology: Science and Practice, 3,* 25–46.

Lewinsohn, P. M., Rohde, P., & Seeley, J. R. (1998). Major depressive disorder in older adolescents: Prevalence, risk factors, and clinical implications. *Clinical Psychology Review, 18,* 765–794.

Lewinsohn, P. M., Rohde, P., Klein, D. N., & Seeley, J. R. (1999). Natural course of adolescent Major Depressive Disorder: I.

Continuity into young adulthood. *Journal of the American Academy of Child and Adolescent Psychiatry, 38,* 56–63.

Lewinsohn, P. M., Seeley, J. R., & Klein, D. N. (2003). Bipolar disorder in adolescents: Epidemiology and suicidal behavior. In B. Geller & M. P DelBello (Eds.), *Bipolar disorder in childhood and early adolescence.* New York: Guilford Press.

Lewinsohn, P. M., Striegel-Moore, R. H., & Seeley, J. R. (2000). Epidemiology and natural course of eating disorders in young women from adolescence to young adulthood. *Journal of the American Academy of Child and Adolescent Psychiatry, 39,* 1284–1292.

Lewis-Fernández, R., Hinton, D. E., Laria, A. J., Patterson, E. H., Hofmann, S. G., Craske, M. G., et al. (2010). Culture and the anxiety disorders: Recommendations for DSM-V. *Depression and Anxiety, 27,* 212–229.

Leyfer, O., & Brown, T. A. (2011). The anxiety-depression spectrum. In D. H. Barlow (Ed.), *The Oxford handbook of clinical psychology.* New York: Oxford University Press.

Li, J. J., Berk, M. S., & Lee, S. S. (2013). Differential susceptibility in longitudinal models of gene–environment interaction for adolescent depression. *Development and Psychopathology, 25,* 991–1003.

Li, L., Jick, S., Breitenstein, S., & Michel, A. (2016). Prevalence of diabetes and diabetic nephropathy in a large U.S. commercially insured pediatric population, 2002–2013. *Diabetes Care, 39,* 278–284.

Li, M., Johnson, S. B., Musci, R. J., & Riley, A. W. (2017). Perceived neighborhood quality, family processes, and trajectories of child and adolescent externalizing behaviors in the United States. *Social Science & Medicine, 192,* 152–161.

Liaw, F., & Brooks-Gunn, J. (1994). Cumulative familial risk and low-birthweight children's cognitive and behavioral development. *Journal of Clinical Child Psychology, 23,* 360–372.

Liber, J. M., Van Widenfelt, B. M., Utens, E. M., Ferdinand, R. F., Van der Leeden, A. J., Van Gastel, W., et al. (2008). No differences between group and individual treatment of childhood anxiety disorders in a randomized clinical trial. *Journal of Child Psychology and Psychiatry, 49,* 886–893.

Licht, B. G., & Kistner, J. A. (1986). Motivational problems of learning-disabled children: Individual differences and their implications for treatment. In J. K. Torgesen & B. Y. L. Wong (Eds.), *Psychological and educational perspectives on learning disabilities.* New York: Academic Press.

Lichtenstein, P., & Annas, P. (2000). Heritability and prevalence of specific fears and phobias in childhood. *Journal of Child Psychology and Psychiatry, 41,* 927–937.

Liégeois, F., Mayes, A., & Morgan, A. (2014). Neural correlates of developmental speech and language disorders: Evidence from neuroimaging. *Current Developmental Disorders Reports, 1,* 215–227.

Lilienfeld, S. O., & Treadway, M. T. (2016). Clashing diagnostic approaches: DSM-ICD versus RDoC. *Annual Review of Clinical Psychology, 12,* 435–463.

Lilienfeld, S. O., Waldman, I. D., & Israel, A. C. (1994). A critical examination of the use of the term and concept of comorbidity in psychopathology research. *Clinical Psychology: Science and Practice, 1,* 71–83.

Lilienfeld, S. O., Wood, J. M., & Garb, H. N. (2000). The scientific status of projective techniques. *Psychological Science in the Public Interest, 1,* 27–66.

Lilly, M. S. (1979). Special education: Emerging issues. In M. S. Lilly (Ed.), *Children with exceptional needs.* New York: Holt, Rinehart and Winston.

Limbers, C. A., Cohen, L. A., & Gray, B. A. (2018). Eating disorders in adolescent and young adult males: Prevalence, diagnosis, and treatment strategies. *Adolescent Health, Medicine and Therapeutics, 9,* 111–116.

Lin, K. K., Sandler, I. N., Ayers, T. S., Wolchik, S. A., & Luecken, L. J. (2004). Resilience in parentally bereaved children and adolescents seeking preventive services. *Journal of Clinical Child and Adolescent Psychology, 33,* 673–683.

Linares, L. O., Montalto, D., Li, M. M., & Oza, V. S. (2006). A promising parenting intervention in foster care. *Journal of Consulting and Clinical Psychology, 74,* 32–41.

Lindenmayer, J.-P., Khan, A., McGurk, S. R., Kulsa, M. K. C., Ljuri, I., Ozog, V., et al. (2018). Does social cognition training augment response to computer-assisted cognitive remediation for schizophrenia? *Schizophrenia Research, 201,* 180–186.

Linder, L. A., & Seitz, M. (2016). Through their words: Sources of bother for hospitalized children and adolescents with cancer. *Journal of Pediatric Oncology Nursing, 34,* 51–64.

Lindstrom, C., & Drolet, B. M. (2017). *What's missing: Best practices for teaching students with disabilities.* Lanham, MD: Rowman & Littlefield.

Lindström, K., Lindblad, F., & Hjern, A. (2011). Preterm birth and attention-deficit/hyperactivity disorder. *Pediatrics, 127,* 858–865.

Linscheid, T. J. (2006). Behavioral treatments for pediatric feeding disorders. *Behavior Modification, 30,* 6–23.

Lipka, O., & Siegel, L. S. (2006). Learning disabilities. In D. A. Wolfe & E. J. Mash (Eds.), *Behavioral and emotional disorders in adolescents: Nature, assessment, and treatment.* New York: The Guilford Press.

Lipka, O., Lesaux, N. K., & Siegel, L. S. (2006). Retrospective analyses of the reading development of grade 4 students with reading disabilities. *Journal of Learning Disabilities, 39,* 364–378.

Liu, H. Y., Potter, M. P., Woodworth, K. Y., Yorks, D. M., Petty, C. R., Wozniak, J. R., et al. (2011). Pharmacologic treatments for pediatric bipolar disorder: A review and meta-analysis.

Journal of the American Academy of Child and Adolescent Psychiatry, 50, 749–762.

Liu, X., Akula, N., Skup, M., Brotman, M. A., Leibenluft, E., & McMahon, F. J. (2010). Amygdala activation in youth with and without bipolar disorder. *Journal of the American Academy of Child and Adolescent Psychiatry, 49,* 33–41.

Livingston, G., & Parker, K. (2019). 8 facts about American dads. *Pew Research Center.* Retrieved December 2019 from www.pewresearch.org/fact-tank/2019/06/12/fathers-day-facts/

Livingston, L. A., Colvert, E., Social Relationships Study Team, Bolton, P., & Happé, F. (2019). Good social skills despite poor theory of mind: Exploring compensation in autism spectrum disorder. *Journal of Child Psychology and Psychiatry, 60,* 102–110.

Loane, M., Morris, J. K., Addor, M.-C., Arriola, L., Budd, J., Doray, B., et al. (2013). Twenty-year trends in the prevalence of Down syndrome and other trisomies in Europe: Impact of maternal age and prenatal screening. *European Journal of Human Genetics, 21,* 27–33.

Lobato, D. J., & Kao, B. T. (2005). Family-based group intervention for young siblings of children with chronic illness and developmental disability. *Journal of Pediatric Psychology, 30,* 678–682.

Lobban-Shymko, J., Im-Bolter, N., & Freeman, N. (2017). Early social communicative skills as predictors of symptom severity in autism spectrum disorder. *Autism & Developmental Language Impairments, 2.* doi:10.2396941517743418

Lochman, J. E., Boxmeyer, C. L., Powell, N. P., Barry, T. D., & Pardini, D. A. (2010). Anger control training for aggressive youths. In J. R. Weisz & A. E. Kazdin (Eds.), *Evidence-based psychotherapies for children and adolescents* (2nd ed.). New York: The Guilford Press.

Lochman, J. E., Whidby, J. M., & FitzGerald, D. P. (2000). Cognitive-behavioral assessment and treatment with aggressive children. In P. C. Kendall (Ed.), *Child and adolescent therapy: Cognitive-behavioral procedures* (2nd ed.). New York: Guilford.

Lock, J. (2015). An update on evidence-based psychosocial treatments for eating disorders in children and adolescents. *Journal of Clinical Child & Adolescent Psychology, 44,* 707–721.

Lock, J., & La Via, M. C. (2015). Practice parameter for the assessment and treatment of children and adolescents with eating disorders. *Journal of the American Academy of Child & Adolescent Psychiatry, 54,* 412–425.

Lock, J., & Le Grange, D. (2005). Family-based treatment of eating disorders. *International Journal of Eating Disorders, 37*(sup1), 64–67.

Lock, J., & Le Grange, D. (2013). *Treatment manual for anorexia nervosa: A family-based approach* (2nd ed.). New York: The Guilford Press.

References

Lock, J., & Osipov, L. (2019). Eating disorders. In M. J. Prinstein, E. A. Youngstrom, E. J. Mash, & R. A. Barkley (Eds.), *Treatment of disorders in childhood and adolescence* (4th ed.). New York: The Guilford Press.

Loeber, R. (1988). Natural histories of conduct problems, delinquency, and associated substance use: Evidence for developmental progressions. In B. B. Lahey & A. E. Kazdin (Eds.), *Advances in clinical child psychology* (Vol. 11). New York: Plenum.

Loeber, R., & Keenan, K. (1994). Interaction between conduct disorder and its comorbid conditions: Effects of age and gender. *Clinical Psychology Review, 14,* 497–523.

Loeber, R., & Schmaling, K. B. (1985). Empirical evidence for overt and covert patterns of antisocial conduct problems: A metaanalysis. *Journal of Abnormal Child Psychology, 13,* 337–354.

Loeber, R., Burke, J. D., & Pardini, D. A. (2009a). Development and etiology of disruptive and delinquent behavior. *Annual Review of Clinical Psychology, 5,* 291–310.

Loeber, R., Burke, J. D., & Pardini, D. A. (2009b). Perspective on oppositional defiant disorder, conduct disorder, and psychopathic features. *Journal of Child Psychology & Psychiatry, 50,* 133–142.

Loeber, R., Burke, J. D., Lahey, B. B., Winters, A., & Zera, M. (2000). Oppositional defiant and conduct disorder: A review of the past 10 years, Part I. *Journal of the American Academy of Child and Adolescent Psychiatry, 39,* 1468–1484.

Loeber, R., Wung, P., Keenan, K., Giroux, B., Stouthamer-Loeber, M., Van Kammen, W. B., & Maughan, B. (1993). Developmental pathways in disruptive child behavior. *Development and Psychopathology, 5,* 103–133.

Long, P., Forehand, R., Wierson, M., & Morgan, A. (1994). Does parent training with young noncompliant children have long term effects? *Behaviour Research and Therapy, 32,* 101–107.

Lonigan, C. J., Vasey, M. W., Phillips, B. M., & Hazen, R. A. (2004). Temperament, anxiety, and the processing of threat-relevant stimuli. *Journal of Clinical Child and Adolescent Psychology, 33,* 8–20.

Lopez-Duran, N. L., Kovacs, M., & George, C. J. (2009). Hypothalamic–pituitary–adrenal axis dysregulation in depressed children and adolescents: A meta-analysis. *Psychoneuroendocrinology, 34,* 1272–1283.

Lord, C., & Bishop, S. L. (2015). Recent advances in autism research as reflected in DSM-5 criteria for autism spectrum disorder. *Annual Review of Clinical Psychology, 11,* 53–70.

Lord, C., Rutter, M., DiLavore, P. C., Risi, S., Gotham, K., & Bishop, S. (2012). *Autism Diagnostic Observation Schedule, second edition (ADOS-2)* Torrance, CA: Western Psychological Services.

Lorian, R. P. (2000). Community, prevention, and wellness. In M. Hersen & R. T. Ammerman (Eds.), *Advanced abnormal child psychology.* Mahwah, NJ: Lawrence Erlbaum Associates.

Lovaas, O. I. (1987). Behavioral treatment and normal educational and intellectual functioning in young autistic children. *Journal of Consulting and Clinical Psychology, 55,* 3–9.

Lovaas, O. I., & Smith, T. (1988). Intensive behavioral treatment for young autistic children. In B. B. Lahey & A. E. Kazdin (Eds.), *Advances in clinical child psychology* (Vol. 2). New York: Plenum.

Lovaas, O. I., & Smith, T. (2003). Early and intensive behavioral intervention in autism. In A. E. Kazdin & J. R. Weisz (Eds.), *Evidence-based psychotherapies for children and adolescents.* New York: Guilford Press.

Lovaas, O. I., Young, D. B., & Newsom, C. D. (1978). Childhood psychosis: Behavioral treatment. In B. B. Wolman (Ed.), *Handbook of treatment of mental disorders in childhood and adolescence.* Englewood Cliffs, NJ: Prentice Hall.

Lovejoy, M. C., Graczyk, P. A., O'Hare, E., & Newman, G. (2000). Maternal depression and parenting behavior: A meta-analytic review. *Clinical Psychology Review, 20,* 561–592.

Lövgren, M., & Sveen, J. (2018). Family bereavement care in pediatric oncology. In J. Wolfe, B. L. Jones, U. Kreicbergs, & M. Jankovic (Eds.), *Palliative care in pediatric oncology.* Cham, Switzerland: Springer.

Lu, Y., Mak, K.-K., van Bever, H. P. S., Ng, T. P., Mak, A., & Ho, R. C.-M. (2012). Prevalence of anxiety and depressive symptoms in adolescents with asthma: A meta-analysis and meta-regression. *Pediatric Allergy and Immunology, 23,* 707–715.

Luby, J. L. (2009). Depression. In C. H. Zeanah, Jr. (Ed.), *Handbook of infant mental health* (3rd ed.). New York: The Guilford Press.

Luby, J. L., & Whalen, D. (2019). Depression in early childhood. In C. H. Zeanah (Ed.), *Handbook of infant mental health* (4th ed.). New York: The Guilford Press.

Luby, J. L., Belden, A. C., & Tandon, M. (2010). Bipolar disorder in the preschool period. In D. J. Miklowitz & D. Cicchetti (Eds.), *Understanding bipolar disorder: A developmental psychopathology perspective.* New York: The Guilford Press.

Luciana, M. (2013). Adolescent brain development in normality and psychopathology. *Development and Psychopathology, 25,* 1325–1345.

Luckasson, R., Coulter, D. L., Polloway, E. A., Reese, S., Schalock, R. L., Snell, M. E., et al. (1992). *Mental retardation: Definition, classification, and systems of supports.* Washington, DC: American Association on Mental Retardation.

Lui, S. S. Y., Hung, K. S. Y., Wang, Y., Ho, K. K. Y., Yeung, H. K. H., Wang, Y., et al. (2018). Clustering of schizotypal features in unaffected first-degree relatives of schizophrenia patients. *Schizophrenia Bulletin, 44*(sup2), S536–S546.

Lukens, C. T., & Silverman, A. H. (2014). Systematic review of psychological interventions for pediatric feeding problems. *Journal of Pediatric Psychology, 39,* 903–917.

Lum, J. A., Ullman, M. T., & Conti-Ramsden, G. (2016). Language disorder. In N. Rinehart, J. L. Bradshaw, & P. G. Enticott (Eds.), *Developmental disorders of the brain.* New York: Routledge.

Luman, M., Oosterlaan, J., Hyde, C., van Meel, C. S., & Sergeant, J. A. (2007). Heart rate and reinforcement sensitivity in ADHD. *Journal of Child Psychology and Psychiatry, 48,* 890–898.

Luman, M., van Noesel, S. J. P., Papanikolau, A., van Oostenbruggen-Scheffer, J., Veugelers, D., Sergeant, J. A., et al. (2009). Inhibition, reinforcement sensitivity and temporal information processing in ADHD and ADHD+ODD: Evidence of a separate entity? *Journal of Abnormal Child Psychology, 37,* 1123–1135.

Luthar, S. S., Kumar, N. L., & Zillmer, N. (2020). High-achieving schools connote risks for adolescents: Problems documented, processes implicated, and directions for interventions. *American Psychologist.* Retrieved from https://doi.org/10.1037/amp0000556

Ly, T. M. (2008). Asian American parents' attributions of children with Down syndrome: Connections with child characteristics and culture. *Intellectual and Developmental Disabilities, 46,* 129–140.

Lynch, F. L., & Dickerson, J. F. (2019). Social costs of child and adolescent mental health disorders. In T. H. Ollendick, S. W. White, & B. A. White (Eds.), *The Oxford handbook of clinical child and adolescent psychology.* New York: Oxford University Press.

Lynch, M., & Cicchetti, D. (1998). An ecological–interactional analysis of children and contexts: The longitudinal interplay among child treatment, community violence, and children's symptomatology. *Development and Psychopathology, 10,* 235–257.

Lyon, G. R., & Cutting, L. E. (1998). Learning disabilities. In E. J. Mash & R. A. Barkley (Eds.), *Treatment of childhood disorders.* New York: Guilford Press.

Lyon, G. R., Fletcher, J. M., & Barnes, M. C. (2003). Learning disabilities. In E. J. Mash & R. A. Barkley (Eds.), *Child psychopathology.* New York: Guilford Press.

Lyon, G. R., Fletcher, J. M., Fuchs, L. S., & Chhabra, V. (2006). Learning disabilities. In E. J. Mash & R. A. Barkley (Eds.), *Treatment of childhood disorders.* New York: The Guilford Press.

Lyons-Ruth, K., Zeanah, C. H., & Benoit, D. (2003). Disorder and risk for disorder during infancy and toddlerhood. In E. J. Mash & R. A. Barkley (Eds.), *Child psychopathology.* New York: Guilford Press.

Maccoby, E. E. (1992). The role of parents in the socialization of children: An historic overview. *Developmental Psychology, 28,* 1006–1017.

Maccoby, E. E., & Martin, J. A. (1983). Socialization in the context of the family: Parent-child interaction. In P. H. Mussen (Ed.), *Handbook of child psychology* (Vol. IV). New York: John Wiley.

MacFarlane, J. W., Allen, L., & Honzik, M. P. (1954). *A developmental study of the behavior problems of normal children between 21 months and 14 years.* Berkeley: University of California Press.

MacKay, S., Henderson, J., Del Bove, G., Marton, P., Warling, D., & Root, C. (2006). Fire interest and antisociality as risk factors in the severity and persistence of juvenile firesetting. *Journal of the American Academy of Child and Adolescent Psychiatry, 45,* 1077–1084.

MacKay, S., Paglia-Boak, A., Henderson, J., Marton, P., & Adlaf, E. (2009). Epidemiology of firesetting in adolescents: Mental health and substance use correlates. *Journal of Child Psychology and Psychiatry, 50,* 1282–1290.

Mackey, E. R., Struemph, K., Powell, P. W., Chen, R., Streisand, R., & Holmes, C. S. (2014). Maternal depressive symptoms and disease care status in youth with type 1 diabetes. *Health Psychology, 33,* 783–791.

Maclean, M. J., Sims, S., Bower, C., Leonard, H., Stanley, F. J., & O'Donnell, M. (2017). Maltreatment risk among children with disabilities. *Pediatrics, 139,* e20161817.

MacMillan, D. L., & Reschly, D. J. (1997). Issues of definition and classification. In W. E. MacLean, Jr. (Ed.), *Ellis' handbook of mental deficiency, psychological theory and research.* Mahwah, NJ: Lawrence Erlbaum.

MacMillan, D. L., Keogh, B. K., & Jones, R. L. (1986). Special educational research on mildly handicapped learners. In M. C. Wittrock (Ed.), *Handbook of research on teaching.* New York: Macmillan.

Madden, J. M., Lakoma, M. D., Lynch, F. L., Rusinak, D., Owen-Smith, A. A., Coleman, K. J., et al. (2017). Psychotropic medication use among insured children with autism spectrum disorder. *Journal of Autism and Developmental Disorders, 47,* 144–154.

Madigan, S., Atkinson, L., Laurin, K., & Benoit, D. (2013). Attachment and internalizing behavior in early childhood: A meta-analysis. *Developmental Psychology, 49,* 672–689.

Madigan, S., Cyr, C., Eirich, R., Fearon, R. P., Ly, A., Rash, C., et al. (2019). Testing the cycle of maltreatment hypothesis: Meta-analytic evidence of the intergenerational transmission of child maltreatment. *Development and Psychopathology, 31,* 23–51.

Madras, B. K., Han, B., Compton, W. M., Jones, C. M., Lopez, E. I., & McCance-Katz, E. F. (2019). Associations of parental marijuana use with offspring marijuana, tobacco, and alcohol use and opioid misuse. *JAMA Network Open, 2,* e1916015–e1916015. Retrieved from https://doi.org/10.1001/jamanetworkopen.2019.16015

References

Madsen, K. M., Hviid, A., Vestergaard, M., Schendel, D., Wohlfahrt, J., Thorsen, P., et al. (2002). A population-based study of measles, mumps, and rubella vaccination and autism. *New England Journal of Medicine, 347*, 1477–1482.

Magaña, S., Parish, S. L., & Son, E. (2015). Have racial and ethnic disparities in the quality of health care relationships changed for children with developmental disabilities and ASD? *American Journal on Intellectual and Developmental Disabilities, 120*, 504–513.

Maguin, E., & Loeber, R. (1996). Academic performance and delinquency. In M. Tonry (Ed.), *Crime and justice* (Vol. 20). Chicago, IL: University of Chicago Press.

Mahone, M. E. (2016, August). ADHD as a dimensional disorder. *Attention, 24–27.*

Mahoney, A. D., McConnell, S. R., Larson, A. L., Becklenberg, A., & Stapel-Wax, J. L. (2020). Where do we go from here? Examining pediatric and population-level interventions to improve child outcomes. *Early Childhood Research Quarterly, 50*, 205–220.

Maijer, K., Hayward, M., Fernyhough, C., Calkins, M. E., Debbané, M., Jardri, R., et al. (2019). Hallucinations in children and adolescents: An updated review and practical recommendations for clinicians. *Schizophrenia Bulletin, 45*(sup1), S5–S23.

Main, M. (1996). Introduction to the special section on attachment and psychopathology: 2. Overview of the field of attachment. *Journal of Consulting and Clinical Psychology, 64*, 237–243.

Majdandžić, M., Lazarus, R. S., Oort, F. J., van der Sluis, C., Dodd, H. F., Morris, T. M., et al. (2018). The structure of challenging parenting behavior and associations with anxiety in Dutch and Australian children. *Journal of Clinical Child & Adolescent Psychology, 47*, 282–295.

Major, B., & O'Brien, L. T. (2005). The social psychology of stigma. *Annual Review of Psychology, 56*, 393–421.

Malmquist, C. P. (1977). Childhood depression: A clinical and behavioral perspective. In J. G. Schulterbrandt & A. Raskin (Eds.), *Depression in childhood: Diagnosis, treatment, and conceptual models.* New York: Raven Press.

Manassis, K., Fung, D., Tannock, R., Sloman, L., Fiksenbaum, L., & McInnes, A. (2003). Characterizing selective mutism: Is it more than social anxiety? *Depression and Anxiety, 18*, 153–161.

Manczak, E. M., Donenberg, G. R., & Emerson, E. (2018). Can mother–daughter communication buffer adolescent risk for mental health problems associated with maternal depressive symptoms? *Journal of Clinical Child & Adolescent Psychology, 47*(sup1), S509–S519.

Mandy, W., & Lai, M.-C. (2016). Annual research review: The role of the environment in the developmental psychopathology of autism spectrum condition. *Journal of Child Psychology and Psychiatry, 57*, 271–292.

Mandy, W., Murin, M., & Skuse, D. (2015). The cognitive profile in autism spectrum disorders. In M. Leboyer & P. Chaste (Eds.), *Autism spectrum disorders: Phenotypes, mechanisms and treatments* (Vol. 180). Basel: Karger Publishers.

Maneeton, N., Maneeton, B., Putthisri, S., Woottiluk, P., Narkpongphun, A., & Srisurapanont, M. (2018). Risperidone for children and adolescents with autism spectrum disorder: A systematic review. *Neuropsychiatric Disease and Treatment, 14*, 1811–1820.

Manly, J. T., Kim, J. E., Rogosch, F. A., & Cicchetti, D. (2001). Dimensions of child maltreatment and children's adjustment: Contributions of developmental timing and subtype. *Development and Psychopathology, 13*, 759–782.

March, J. S. (2013). *Multidimensional Anxiety Scale for Children, Second Edition (MASC-2): Technical manual.* North Tonawanda, NY: Multi-Health Systems.

Marchette, L. K., & Weisz, J. R. (2017). Empirical evolution of youth psychotherapy toward transdiagnostic approaches. *Journal of Child Psychology and Psychiatry, 58*, 970–984.

Marcus, C. L., Brooks, L. J., Ward, S. D., Draper, K. A., Gozal, D., Halbower, A. C., et al. (2012). Diagnosis and management of childhood obstructive sleep apnea syndrome. *Pediatrics, 130*, e714–e755.

Marcus, D. K., Fulton, J. J., & Clarke, E. J. (2010). Lead and conduct problems: A meta-analysis. *Journal of Clinical Child and Adolescent Psychology, 39*, 234–241.

Marcus, M. D., & Kalarchian, M. A. (2003). Binge eating in children and adolescents. *International Journal of Eating Disorders, 34*, S47–S57.

Marenco, S., & Weinberger, D. R. (2000). The neurodevelopmental hypothesis of schizophrenia: Following a trail of evidence from cradle to grave. *Development and Psychopathology, 12*, 501–527.

Margolin, G. (1998). Effects of domestic violence on children. In P. K. Trickett & C. J. Schellenbach (Eds.), *Violence against children in the family and the community.* Washington, DC: American Psychological Association.

Margolin, G., & Gordis, E. B. (2000). The effects of family and community violence on children. *Annual Review of Psychology, 51*, 445–479.

Margolin, G., & Gordis, E. B. (2004). Children's exposure to violence in the family and community. *Current Directions in Psychological Science, 13*, 152–155.

Margolin, G., Vickerman, K. A., Ramos, M. C., Serrano, S. D., Gordis, E. B., Iturralde, E., et al. (2009). Youth exposed to violence: Stability, co-occurrence, and context. *Clinical Child and Family Psychology Review, 12*, 39–54.

Markovic, A., & Bowker, J. C. (2017). Friends also matter: Examining friendship adjustment indices as moderators of anxious-withdrawal and trajectories of change in psychological maladjustment. *Developmental Psychology, 53*, 1462–1473.

Marshal, M. P., Dietz, L. J., Friedman, M. S., Stall, R., Smith, H. A., McGinley, J., et al. (2011). Suicidality and depression disparities between sexual minority and heterosexual youth: A meta-analytic review. *Journal of Adolescent Health, 49,* 115–123.

Martel, M. M., Levinson, C. A., Langer, J. K., & Nigg, J. T. (2016). A network analysis of developmental change in ADHD symptom structure from preschool to adulthood. *Clinical Psychological Science, 4,* 988–1001.

Martin, E. G., & Sorensen, L. C. (2020). Protecting the health of vulnerable children and adolescents during COVID-19-related K-12 school closures in the US. *JAMA Health Forum, June 16, 2020.* Retrieved from https://jamanetwork.com/channels/health-forum/fullarticle/2767411

Martin, J. A., Hamilton, B. E., Osterman, M. J. K., Driscoll, A. K., & Drake, P. (2018). Births: Final data for 2017. National Vital Statistics Reports; vol. 67 no. 8. Hyattsville, MD: National Center for Health Statistics.

Martin, S. R., Chorney, J. M., Tan, E. T., Fortier, M. A., Blount, R. L., Wald, S. H., et al. (2011). Changing healthcare providers' behavior during pediatric inductions with an empirically based intervention. *Anesthesiology: The Journal of the American Society of Anesthesiologists, 115,* 18–27.

Martinelli, A., Ackermann, K., Bernhard, A., Freitag, C., & Schwenck, C. (2018). Hostile attribution bias and aggression in children and adolescents: A systematic literature review on the influence of aggression subtype and gender. *Aggression and Violent Behavior, 39,* 25–32.

Martinez, A. G., & Hinshaw, S. P. (2016). Mental health stigma: Theory, developmental issues, and research priorities. In D. Cicchetti (Ed.), *Developmental psychopathology* (3rd ed., Vol. 4). Hoboken, NJ: John Wiley & Sons, Inc.

Martinez, C. R., Jr., & Eddy, J. M. (2005). Effects of culturally adapted parent management training on Latino youth behavioral health outcomes. *Journal of Consulting and Clinical Psychology, 73,* 841–851.

Martinez, J., Chakraborty, R., & Committee on Pediatric AIDS. (2014). Psychosocial support for youth living with HIV. *Pediatrics, 133,* 558–562.

Marver, J. E., & McGlinchey, E. A. (2020). Sex differences in insomnia and risk for psychopathology in adolescence. *Current Opinion in Psychology, 34,* 63–67.

Mascheretti, S., Trezzi, V., Giorda, R., Boivin, M., Plourde, V., Vitaro, F., et al. (2017). Complex effects of dyslexia risk factors account for ADHD traits: Evidence from two independent samples. *Journal of Child Psychology and Psychiatry, 58,* 75–82.

Mashburn, A. F., & Yelverton, R. (2019). Patterns of experiences across Head Start and kindergarten classrooms that promote children's development. In A. J. Reynolds & J. A. Temple (Eds.), *Sustaining early childhood learning gains:*

Program, school, and family influences. New York: Cambridge University Press.

Masi, G., Favilla, L., Mucci, M., & Millepiedi, S. (2000). Panic disorder in clinically referred children and adolescents. *Child Psychiatry and Human Development, 31,* 139–151.

Masi, G., Millepiedi, S., Mucci, M., Poli, P., Bertini, N., & Milantoni, L. (2004). Generalized anxiety disorder in referred children and adolescents. *Journal of the American Academy of Child and Adolescent Psychiatry, 43,* 752–760.

Masten, A. S. (2015). *Ordinary magic: Resilience in development.* New York: Guilford Publications.

Masten, A. S., & Cicchetti, D. (2016). Resilience in development: Progress and transformation. In D. Cicchetti (Ed.), *Developmental psychopathology: Risk, resilience, and intervention* (Vol. 4). Hoboken, NJ: John Wiley & Sons.

Mata, J., & Gotlib, I. H. (2011). 5-HTTLPR moderates the relation between changes in depressive and bulimic symptoms in adolescent girls: A longitudinal study. *International Journal of Eating Disorders, 44,* 383–388.

Mather, N., & Wendling, B. J. (2018). How SLD manifests in writing. In V. C. Alfonso & D. P. Flanagan (Eds.), *Essentials of specific learning disability identification.* Hoboken, NJ: John Wiley & Sons.

Mathur, M. B., & VanderWeele, T. J. (2019). Finding common ground in meta-analysis "wars" on violent video games. *Perspectives on Psychological Science, 14,* 705–708.

Matson, J. L., & Cervantes, P. E. (2019). Intellectual disabilities. In T. H. Ollendick, S. W. White, & B. A. White (Eds.), *The Oxford handbook of clinical child and adolescent psychology.* New York: Oxford University Press.

Matson, J. L., & Shoemaker, M. (2009). Intellectual disability and its relationship to autism spectrum disorders. *Research in Developmental Disabilities, 30,* 1107–1114.

Matson, J. L., Matheis, M., Estabillo, J. A., Burns, C. O., Issarraras, A., Peters, W. J., & Jiang, X. (2019). Intellectual disability. In M. J. Prinstein, E. A. Youngstrom, E. J. Mash, & R. A. Barkley (Eds.), *Treatment of disorders in childhood and adolescence.* New York: The Guilford Press.

Matson, J. L., Shoemaker, M. E., Sipes, M., Horovitz, M., Worley, J. A., & Kozlowski, A. M. (2011). Replacement behaviors for identified functions of challenging behaviors. *Research in Developmental Disabilities, 32,* 681–684.

Matthews, C. A., & Grados, M. A. (2011). Familiarity of Tourette syndrome, obsessive-compulsive disorder, and attention-deficit/hyperactivity disorder: Heritability analysis in a large sib-pair sample. *Journal of the American Academy of Child and Adolescent Psychiatry, 50,* 46–54.

Mattila, M.-L., Hurtig, T., Haapsamo, H., Jussila, K., Kuusikko-Gauffin, S., Kielinen, M., et al. (2010). Comorbid psychiatric disorders associated with Asperger syndrome/high-functioning autism: A community and clinic-based

References

study. *Journal of Autism and Developmental Disorders, 40,* 1080–1093.

Mattison, R. E. (2000). School consultation: A review of research on issues unique to the school environment. *Journal of the American Academy of Child and Adolescent Psychiatry, 39,* 402–413.

Maughan, B., & Rutter, M. (1998). Continuities and discontinuities in antisocial behavior from childhood to adult life. In T. H. Ollendick & R. J. Prinz (Eds.), *Advances in clinical child psychology* (Vol. 20). New York: Plenum Press.

Maughan, B., Rowe, R., Messer, J., Goodman, R., & Meltzer, H. (2004). Conduct disorder and oppositional defiant disorder in a national sample: Developmental epidemiology. *Journal of Child Psychology and Psychiatry, 45,* 609–621.

Maulik, P., Mascarenhas, M., Mathers, C., Dua, T., & Saxena, S. (2011). Prevalence of intellectual disability: A meta-analysis of population-based studies. *Research in Developmental Disabilities, 32,* 419–436.

Mavranezouli, I., Megnin-Viggars, O., Daly, C., Dias, S., Stockton, S., Meiser-Stedman, R., et al. (2020). Research review: Psychological and psychosocial treatments for children and young people with post-traumatic stress disorder: A network meta-analysis. *Journal of Child Psychology and Psychiatry, 61,* 18–29.

Mawhood, L., Howlin, P., & Rutter, M. (2000). Autism and developmental receptive language disorder—a comparative followup in early adult life I: Cognitive and language outcomes. *Journal of Child Psychology and Psychiatry, 41,* 547–559.

Mayes, A. K., Reilly, S., & Morgan, A. T. (2015). Neural correlates of childhood language disorder: A systematic review. *Developmental Medicine & Child Neurology, 57,* 706–717.

Mayes, S. D. (1992). Rumination disorder: Diagnosis, complications, mediating variables, and treatment. In B. B. Lahey & A. E. Kazdin (Eds.), *Advances in clinical child psychology* (Vol. 14). New York: Plenum.

Mazefsky, C. A., Williams, D. L., & Minshew, N. J. (2008). Variability in adaptive behavior in autism: Evidence for the importance of family history. *Journal of Abnormal Child Psychology, 36,* 591–599.

Mazurka, R., Wynne-Edwards, K., & Harkness, K. (2016). Stressful life events prior to depression onset and the cortisol response to stress in youth with first onset versus recurrent depression. *Journal of Abnormal Child Psychology, 44,* 1173–1184.

Mazza, M., Mariano, M., Peretti, S., Masedu, F., Pino, M. C., & Valenti, M. (2017). The role of theory of mind on social information processing in children with autism spectrum disorders: A mediation analysis. *Journal of Autism and Developmental Disorders, 47,* 1369–1379.

Mazzocco, M. M. M., & Vukovic, R. (2018). How SLD manifests in mathematics. In V. C. Alfonso & D. P. Flanagan (Eds.), *Essentials of specific learning disability identification.* Hoboken, NJ: John Wiley & Sons.

McAlonan, G. M., Cheung, V., Chua, S. E., Oosterlaan, J., Hung, S., Tang, C., et al. (2009). Age-related grey matter volume correlates of response inhibition and shifting in attention-deficit hyperactivity disorder. *British Journal of Psychiatry, 194,* 123–129.

McAlpine, C., & Singh, N. N. (1986). Pica in institutionalized mentally retarded persons. *Journal of Mental Deficiency Research, 30,* 171–178.

McArthur, G. M., Hogben, J. H., Edwards, V. T., Heath, S. M., & Mengler, E. D. (2000). On the "specifics" of specific reading disability and specific language impairment. *Journal of Child Psychology and Psychiatry, 41,* 869–874.

McBain, R. K., Kareddy, V., Cantor, J. H., Stein, B. D., & Yu, H. (2020). Systematic review: United States workforce for autism-related child healthcare services. *Journal of the American Academy of Child & Adolescent Psychiatry, 59,* 113–139.

McCabe, M. P., & Ricciardelli, L. A. (2004). Weight and shape concerns of boys and men. In J. K. Thompson (Ed.), *Handbook of eating disorders and obesity.* Hoboken, NJ: John Wiley.

McCaffrey, R. J., Lynch, J. K., & Westervelt, H. J. (2011). Clinical neuropsychology. In D. H. Barlow (Ed.), *The Oxford handbook of clinical psychology.* New York: Oxford University Press.

McCall, R. B., & Groark, C. J. (2015). Research on institutionalized children: Implications for international child welfare practitioners and policymakers. *International Perspectives in Psychology: Research, Practice, Consultation, 4,* 142–159.

McCart, M. R., & Sheidow, A. J. (2016). Evidence-based psychosocial treatments for adolescents with disruptive behavior. *Journal of Clinical Child & Adolescent Psychology, 45,* 529–563.

McCarton, C. M., Brooks-Gunn, J., Wallace, I. F., & Bauer, C. R. (1997). Results at age 8 years of early intervention for lowbirth-weight premature infants: The infant health and development program. *Journal of the American Medical Association, 277,* 126–132.

McCarty, C. A., McMahon, R. J., & Conduct Problems Prevention Research Group. (2005). Domains of risk to the developmental continuity of firesetting. *Behavior Therapy, 36,* 185–195.

McClellan, J. (2018). Psychosis in children and adolescents. *Journal of the American Academy of Child & Adolescent Psychiatry, 57,* 308–312.

McClellan, J. M., & Werry, J. S. (2000). Research psychiatric diagnostic interviews for children and adolescents: Introduction. *Journal of the American Academy of Child and Adolescent Psychiatry, 39,* 19–27.

McClellan, J., & Stock, S. (2013). Practice parameter for the assessment and treatment of children and adolescents with schizophrenia. *Journal of the American Academy of Child & Adolescent Psychiatry, 52,* 976–990.

McClure, R., Kegler, S., Davey, T., & Clay, F. (2015). Contextual determinants of childhood injury: A systematic review of studies with multilevel analytic methods. *American Journal of Public Health, 105,* e37–e43.

McClure-Tone, E. B. (2010). Social cognition and cognitive flexibility in bipolar disorder. In D. J. Miklowitz & D. Cicchetti (Eds.), *Understanding bipolar disorder: A developmental psychopathology perspective.* New York: The Guilford Press.

McConaughy, S. H. (2005). *Clinical interviews for children and adolescents: Assessment to intervention.* New York: The Guilford Press.

McConaughy, S. H., Ivanova, M. Y., Antshel, K., & Eiraldi, R. B. (2009). Standardized observational assessment of attention deficit hyperactivity disorder combined and predominantly inattentive subtypes. *School Psychology Review, 38,* 45–66.

McConnell, D., & Savage, A. (2015). Stress and resilience among families caring for children with intellectual disability: Expanding the research agenda. *Current Developmental Disorders Reports, 2,* 100–109.

McCrory, E., De Brito, S. A., & Viding, E. (2010). The neurobiology and genetics of maltreatment and adversity. *Journal of Child Psychology and Psychiatry, 51,* 1079–1095.

McCullough, M. B., Ranzenhofer, L., Evans, E. W., & Jeiian, E. (2017). Pediatric obesity. In M. C. Roberts & R. G. Steele (Eds.), *Handbook of pediatric psychology* (5th ed.). New York: The Guilford Press.

McDonald, J. L., & Oetting, J. B. (2019). Nonword repetition across two dialects of English: Effects of specific language impairment and nonmainstream form density. *Journal of Speech, Language, and Hearing Research, 62,* 1381–1391.

McDonnell, C. G., Boan, A. D., Bradley, C. C., Seay, K. D., Charles, J. M., & Carpenter, L. A. (2019). Child maltreatment in autism spectrum disorder and intellectual disability: Results from a population-based sample. *Journal of Child Psychology and Psychiatry, 60,* 576–584.

McEachin, J. J., Smith, T., & Lovaas, O. I. (1993). Longterm outcome for children with autism who received early intensive behavioral treatment. *American Journal on Mental Retardation, 97,* 359–372.

McElhanon, B. O., McCracken, C., Karpen, S., & Sharp, W. G. (2014). Gastrointestinal symptoms in autism spectrum disorder: A meta-analysis. *Pediatrics, 133,* 872–883.

McEvoy, R. E., Rogers, S. J., & Pennington, B. F. (1993). Executive functions and social communication deficits in young autistic children. *Journal of Child Psychology and Psychiatry, 34,* 563–578.

McFarland, J., Hussar, B., Zhang, J., Wang, X., Wang, K., Hein, S., et al. (2019). *The condition of education 2019.* Retrieved from https://nces.ed.gov/pubsearch/pubsinfo.asp?pubid=2019144

McFarlane, W. R. (2016). Family interventions for schizophrenia and the psychoses: A review. *Family Process, 55,* 460–482.

McFarlane, W. R., Susser, E., McCleary, R., Verdi, M., Lynch, S., Williams, D., & McKeague, I. W. (2014). Reduction in incidence of hospitalizations for psychotic episodes through early identification and intervention. *Psychiatric Services, 65,* 1194–1200.

McGavock, J., Dart, A., & Wicklow, B. (2014). Lifestyle therapy for the treatment of youth with type 2 diabetes. *Current Diabetes Reports, 15,* 568.

McGee, R. A., & Wolfe, D. A. (1991). Psychological maltreatment: Toward an operational definition. *Development and Psychopathology, 3,* 3–18.

McGee, R., Feehan, M., Williams, S., & Anderson, J. (1992). DSMIII disorders from age 11 to age 15 years. *Journal of the American Academy of Child and Adolescent Psychiatry, 31,* 50–59.

McGill, R. J., & Ndip, N. (2019). Learning disabilities. In M. J. Prinstein, E. A. Youngstrom, E. J. Mash, & R. A. Barkley (Eds.), *Treatment of disorders in childhood and adolescence.* New York: The Guilford Press.

McGorry, P. D., Killackey, E., & Yung, A. (2008). Early intervention in psychosis: Concepts, evidence and future directions. *World Psychiatry, 7,* 148–156.

McGorry, P. D., Purcell, R., Goldstone, S., & Amminger, G. P. (2010). Age of onset and timing of treatment for mental and substance use disorders: Implications for preventive intervention strategies and models of care. *Current Opinion in Psychiatry, 24,* 301–306.

McGrath, L. M., & Peterson, R. L. (2009a). Attention-deficit/ hyperactivity disorder. In B. F. Pennington (Ed.), *Diagnosing learning disorders.* New York: Guilford Press.

McGrath, L. M., & Peterson, R. L. (2009b). Intellectual disability. In B. F. Pennington (Ed.), *Diagnosing learning disorders.* New York: Guilford Press.

McGrath, L. M., Peterson, R. L., & Pennington, B. F. (2020). The multiple deficit model: Progress, problems, and prospects. *Scientific Studies of Reading, 24,* 7–13.

McGrath, R. E., & Carroll, E. J. (2012). The current status of "projective" tests. In H. Cooper, P. M. Camic, D. L. Long, A. T. Panter, D. Rindskopf, & K. J. Sher (Eds.), *APA handbook of research methods in psychology, Vol. 1: Foundations, planning, measures, and psychometrics.* Washington, DC: American Psychological Association.

McIntyre, L. L. (2016). Promoting well-being in families with children with intellectual and developmental disabilities. *Spotlight on Disability Newsletter.* Retrieved from www.apa.org/pi/disability/resources/publications/newsletter/2016/09/family-developmental-disabilities

McKean, C., Reilly, S., Bavin, E. L., Bretherton, L., Cini, E., Conway, L., et al. (2017). Language outcomes at 7 years:

References

Early predictors and co-occurring difficulties. *Pediatrics, 139,* e20161684.

McKenzie, K., Milton, M., Smith, G., & Ouellette-Kuntz, H. (2016). Systematic review of the prevalence and incidence of intellectual disabilities: Current trends and issues. *Current Developmental Disorders Reports, 3,* 104–115.

McKenzie, R., & Dallos, R. (2017). Autism and attachment difficulties: Overlap of symptoms, implications and innovative solutions. *Clinical Child Psychology and Psychiatry, 22,* 632–648.

McKeown, R. E., Holbrook, J. R., Danielson, M. L., Cuffe, S. P., Wolraich, M. L., & Visser, S. N. (2015). The impact of case definition on attention-deficit/hyperactivity disorder prevalence estimates in community-based samples of school-aged children. *Journal of the American Academy of Child & Adolescent Psychiatry, 54,* 53–61.

McKinney, C., & Renk, K. (2011). Atypical antipsychotic medications in the management of disruptive behaviors in children: Safety guidelines and recommendations. *Clinical Psychology Review, 31,* 465–471.

McLaughlin, K. A. (2016). Future directions in childhood adversity and youth psychopathology. *Journal of Clinical Child & Adolescent Psychology, 45,* 361–382.

McLay, L., Hansen, S., & Carnett, A. (2019). TEACCH and other structured approaches to teaching. In S. G. Little & A. Akin-Little (Eds.), *Behavioral interventions in schools: Evidence-based positive strategies* (2nd ed.). Washington, DC: American Psychological Association.

McLean, S. A., Paxton, S. J., & Wertheim, E. H. (2016). The role of media literacy in body dissatisfaction and disordered eating: A systematic review. *Body Image, 19,* 9–23.

McLeod, B. D., Cox, J. R., Martinez, R. G., & Christon, L. M. (2019). Assessment and case conceptualization. In T. H. Ollendick, S. W. White, & B. A. White (Eds.), *The Oxford handbook of clinical child and adolescent psychology.* New York: Oxford University Press.

McMahon, C. A., Barnett, B., Kowalenko, N. M., & Tennant, C. C. (2006). Maternal attachment state of mind moderates the impact of postnatal depression on infant attachment. *Journal of Child Psychology and Psychiatry, 47,* 660–669.

McMahon, R. J., & Forehand, R. L. (2003). *Helping the noncompliant child: Family-based treatment for oppositional behavior* (2nd ed.). New York: The Guilford Press.

McMahon, R. J., & Frick, P. J. (2019). Conduct and oppositional disorders. In M. J. Prinstein, E. A. Youngstrom, E. J. Mash, & R. A. Barkley (Eds.), *Treatment of disorders in childhood and adolescence* (4th ed.). New York: The Guilford Press.

McMakin, D. L., Ricketts, E. J., Forbes, E. E., Silk, J. S., Ladouceur, C. D., Siegle, G. J., et al. (2019). Anxiety treatment and targeted sleep enhancement to address sleep disturbance in pre/early adolescents with anxiety. *Journal of Clinical Child & Adolescent Psychology, 48,* S284–S297.

McNamara, J. K., Scissons, M., & Gutknecht, N. B. (2011). A longitudinal study of kindergarten children at risk for reading disabilities: The poor really are getting poorer. *Journal of Learning Disabilities, 44,* 421–430.

McNicholas, P. J., Floyd, R. G., Woods, I. L., Jr., Singh, L. J., Manguno, M. S., & Maki, K. E. (2018). State special education criteria for identifying intellectual disability: A review following revised diagnostic criteria and Rosa's Law. *School Psychology Quarterly, 33,* 75–82.

McNulty, M. A. (2003). Dyslexia and the life course. *Journal of Learning Disabilities, 36,* 363–381.

McQuade, J. D., & Hoza, B. (2015). Peer relationships of children with ADHD. In R. A. Barkley (Ed.), *Attention-deficit hyperactivity disorder: A handbook for diagnosis and treatment.* New York: The Guilford Press.

McQuaid, E. L., & Fedele, D. A. (2017). Pediatric asthma. In M. C. Roberts & R. G. Steele (Eds.), *Handbook of pediatric psychology* (5th ed.). New York: The Guilford Press.

McQuaid, E. L., & Landier, W. (2018). Cultural issues in medication adherence: Disparities and directions. *Journal of General Internal Medicine, 33,* 200–206.

McQuaid, E. L., Kopel, S. J., & Nassau, J. H. (2001). Behavioral adjustment in children with asthma: A meta-analysis. *Journal of Developmental and Behavioral Pediatrics, 22,* 430–439.

McQuillan, J. (2019). We don't need no stinkin' exercises: The impact of extended instruction and storybook reading on vocabulary acquisition. *Language and Language Teaching, 8,* 22–34.

McReynolds, P. (1987). Lightner Witmer: Little-known founder of clinical psychology. *American Psychologist, 42,* 849–858.

Meadan, H., Stoner, J. B., & Angell, M. E. (2010). Review of literature related to the social, emotional, and behavioral adjustment of siblings with autism spectrum disorder. *Journal of Developmental and Physical Disabilities, 22,* 83–100.

Measelle, J. R., Stice, E., & Hogansen, J. M. (2006). Developmental trajectories of co-occurring depressive, eating, antisocial, and substance abuse problems in female adolescents. *Journal of Abnormal Psychology, 115,* 524–538.

Mednick, S. A., Machon, R. A., Huttunen, M. O., & Bonnett, D. (1988). Fetal viral infection and adult schizophrenia. *Archives of General Psychiatry, 45,* 189–192.

Mehler, P. S. (2011). Medical complications of bulimia nervosa and their treatments. *International Journal of Eating Disorders, 44,* 95–104.

Meins, E., Fernyhough, C., Fradley, E., & Tuckey, M. (2001). Rethinking maternal sensitivity: Mothers' comments on infants' mental processes predict security of attachment at 12 months. *Journal of Child Psychology and Psychiatry, 42,* 637–648.

Melamed, B. G., & Siegel, L. J. (1975). Reduction of anxiety in children facing hospitalization and surgery by use of filmed modeling. *Journal of Consulting and Clinical Psychology, 43,* 511–521.

Melamed, B. G., & Siegel, L. J. (1980). *Behavioral medicine: Practical applications in health care.* New York: Springer.

Melhem, N. M., Porta, G., Oquendo, M. A., Zelazny, J., Keilp, J. G., Iyengar, S., et al. (2019). Severity and variability of depression symptoms predicting suicide attempt in high-risk individuals. *JAMA Psychiatry, 76,* 603–613.

Mellon, M., & Houts, A. (2017). Behavioural treatment for enuresis and encopresis. In J. R. Weisz & A. E. Kazdin (Eds.), *Evidence-based psychotherapies for children and adolescents* (3rd ed.). New York: The Guilford Press.

Meltzer, L. J. (2017). Future directions in sleep and developmental psychopathology. *Journal of Clinical Child & Adolescent Psychology, 46,* 295–301.

Meltzer, L. J., & Mindell, J. A. (2009). Pediatric sleep. In M. C. Roberts & R. G. Steele (Eds.), *Handbook of pediatric psychology* (4th ed.). New York: The Guilford Press.

Meltzer, L., Reddy, R., Pollica, L. S., Roditi, B., Sayer, J., & Theokas, C. (2004). Positive and negative self-perceptions: Is there a cyclical relationship between teachers' and students' perceptions of effort, strategy use, and academic performance? *Learning Disabilities Research & Practice, 19,* 33–44.

Merikangas, K. R. (2018). Time trends in the global prevalence of mental disorders in children and adolescents: Gap in data on US youth. *Journal of the American Academy of Child & Adolescent Psychiatry, 57,* 306–307.

Merikangas, K. R., & Hommer, R. (2019). Psychiatric epidemiology: Concepts and findings. In T. H. Ollendick, S. W. White, & B. A. White (Eds.), *The Oxford handbook of clinical child and adolescent psychology.* New York: Oxford University Press.

Merikangas, K. R., He, J.-P., Burstein, M., Swendsen, J., Avenevoli, S., Case, B., et al. (2011). Service utilization for lifetime mental disorders in U.S. adolescents: Results of the National Comorbidity Survey-Adolescent Supplement (NCSA). *Journal of the American Academy of Child and Adolescent Psychiatry, 50,* 32–45.

Merikangas, K. R., Nakamura, E. F., & Kessler, R. C. (2009). Epidemiology of mental disorders in children and adolescents. *Dialogues in Clinical Neuroscience, 11,* 7–20.

Merrell, C., & Sayal, K. (2018). ADHD and school. In T. Banaschewski, D. Coghill, & A. Zuddas (Eds.), *Oxford textbook of attention deficit hyperactivity disorder.* Oxford: Oxford University Press.

Merrill, B. M., Molina, B. S. G., Coxe, S., Gnagy, E. M., Altszuler, A. R., Macphee, F. L., et al. (2019). Functional outcomes of young adults with childhood ADHD: A latent profile analysis. *Journal of Clinical Child & Adolescent Psychology, 49,* 215–228.

Merz, E. C., Harlé, K. M., Noble, K. G., & McCall, R. B. (2016). Executive function in previously institutionalized children. *Child Development Perspectives, 10,* 105–110.

Mesibov, G. B., & Van Bourgondien, M. E. (1992). Autism. In S. R. Hooper, G. W. Hynd, & R. E. Mattison (Eds.), *Developmental disorders: Diagnostic criteria and clinical assessment.* Hillsdale, NJ: Erlbaum.

Meyer, I. H. (2015). Resilience in the study of minority stress and health of sexual and gender minorities. *Psychology of Sexual Orientation and Gender Diversity, 2,* 209–213.

Meyer, I. H. (2016). Does an improved social environment for sexual and gender minorities have implications for a new minority stress research agenda? *Psychology of Sexualities Review, 7,* 81–90.

Meyer, S. E., & Carlson, G. A. (2010). Development, age of onset, and phenomenology in bipolar disorder. In D. J. Miklowitz & D. Cicchetti (Eds.), *Understanding bipolar disorder: A developmental psychopathology perspective.* New York: The Guilford Press.

Meyers, J. L., & Dick, D. M. (2010). Genetic and environmental risk factors for adolescent-onset substance use disorders. *Child and Adolescent Psychiatric Clinics of North America, 19,* 465–477.

Micali, N., Simonoff, E., Stahl, D., & Treasure, J. (2011). Maternal eating disorders and infant feeding difficulties: Maternal and child mediators in a longitudinal general population study. *Journal of Child Psychology and Psychiatry, 52,* 800–807.

Michl, L. C., McLaughlin, K. A., Shepherd, K., & Nolen-Hoeksema, S. (2013). Rumination as a mechanism linking stressful life events to symptoms of depression and anxiety: Longitudinal evidence in early adolescents and adults. *Journal of Abnormal Psychology, 122,* 339–352.

Miciak, J., Fletcher, J. M., & Stuebing, K. K. (2015). Accuracy and validity of methods for identifying learning disabilities in a response-to-intervention service delivery framework. In S. R. Jimerson, M. K. Burns, & A. M. VanDerHeyden (Eds.), *Handbook of response to intervention: The science and practice of multi-tiered systems of support.* New York: Springer.

Mick, E., Biederman, J., Faraone, S. V., Sayer, J., & Kleinman, S. (2002). Case-control study of attention-deficit hyperactivity disorder and maternal smoking, alcohol use, and drug use during pregnancy. *Journal of the American Academy of Child and Adolescent Psychiatry, 41,* 378–385.

Mijanovich, T., & Weitzman, B. C. (2010). Disaster in context: The effects of 9/11 on youth distant from the attacks. *Community Mental Health Journal, 46,* 601–611.

Mikami, A. Y. (2010). The importance of friendship for youth with attention-deficit/hyperactivity disorder. *Clinical Child and Family Psychology Review, 13,* 181–198.

Mikami, A. Y., Calhoun, C. D., & Abikoff, H. B. (2010). Positive illusory bias and response to behavioral treatment among children with attention-deficit/hyperactivity disorder. *Journal of Clinical Child and Adolescent Psychology, 39,* 373–385.

References

Mikami, A. Y., Miller, M., & Lerner, M. D. (2019). Social functioning in youth with attention-deficit/hyperactivity disorder and autism spectrum disorder: Transdiagnostic commonalities and differences. *Clinical Psychology Review, 68,* 54–70.

Miklowitz, D. J., & Goldstein, T. R. (2010). Family-based approaches to treating bipolar disorder in adolescents: Family-focused therapy and dialectical behavior therapy. In D. J. Miklowitz & D. Cicchetti (Eds.), *Understanding bipolar disorder: A developmental psychopathology perspective.* New York: The Guilford Press.

Miklowitz, D. J., Schneck, C. D., Singh, M. K., Taylor, D. O., George, E. L., Cosgrove, V. E., et al. (2013). Early intervention for symptomatic youth at risk for bipolar disorder: A randomized trial of family-focused therapy. *Journal of the American Academy of Child & Adolescent Psychiatry, 52,* 121–131.

Milan, S., Pinderhughes, E. E., & the Conduct Problems Prevention Research Group. (2006). Family instability and child maladjustment trajectories during elementary school. *Journal of Abnormal Child Psychology, 34,* 43–56.

Milgrom, J., Newnhan, C., Anderson, P. J., Doyle, L. W., Gemmill, A. W., Lee, K., et al. (2010). Early sensitivity training for parents of preterm infants: Impact on the developing brain. *Pediatric Research, 67,* 330–335.

Milich, R., Balentine, A. C., & Lynam, D. R. (2001, Winter). ADHD combined type and ADHD predominantly inattentive type are distinct and unrelated disorders. *Clinical Psychology: Science and Practice, 8,* 463–488.

Miller, A. B., & Prinstein, M. J. (2019). Adolescent suicide as a failure of acute stress-response systems. *Annual Review of Clinical Psychology, 15,* 425–450.

Miller, A. B., Massing-Schaffer, M., Owens, S., & Prinstein, M. J. (2019). Nonsuicidal self-injury among youth. In T. H. Ollendick, S. W. White, & B. A. White (Eds.), *The Oxford handbook of clinical child and adolescent psychology.* New York: Oxford University Press.

Miller, A. B., Sheridan, M. A., Hanson, J. L., McLaughlin, K. A., Bates, J. E., Lansford, J. E., et al. (2018). Dimensions of deprivation and threat, psychopathology, and potential mediators: A multi-year longitudinal analysis. *Journal of Abnormal Psychology, 127,* 160–170.

Miller, A. L., & O'Brien, C. T. (2019). DBT for multi-problem adolescents. In R. D. Friedberg & J. K. Paternostro (Eds.), *Handbook of cognitive behavioral therapy for pediatric medical conditions.* Cham, Switzerland: Springer.

Miller, C. H., Hamilton, J. P., Sacchet, M. D., & Gotlib, I. H. (2015). Meta-analysis of functional neuroimaging of major depressive disorder in youth. *JAMA Psychiatry, 72,* 1045–1053.

Miller, D. C., & Maricle, D. E. (2018). The emergence of neuropsychological constructs into tests of intelligence and cognitive abilities. In D. P. Flanagan & E. M. McDonough (Eds.), *Contemporary intellectual assessment: Theories, tests, and issues* (4th ed.). New York: The Guilford Press.

Miller, J., McCune, H., & Driscoll, D. (2017). Prader-Willi syndrome. In S. W. Ekvall & V. K. Ekvall (Eds.), *Pediatric and adult nutrition in chronic diseases, developmental disabilities, and hereditary metabolic disorders.* New York: Oxford University Press.

Miller, L. C., Barrett, C. L., & Hampe, E. (1974). Phobias of childhood in a prescientific era. In A. Davids (Ed.), *Child personality and psychopathology: Current topics* (Vol. 1). New York: John Wiley.

Miller, L., Hlastala, S. A., Mufson, L., Leibenluft, E., & Riddle, M. (2016). Interpersonal psychotherapy for adolescents with mood and behavior dysregulation: Evidence-based case study. *Evidence-Based Practice in Child and Adolescent Mental Health, 1,* 159–175.

Miller, M., Iosif, A.-M., Hill, M., Young, G. S., Schwichtenberg, A. J., & Ozonoff, S. (2017). Response to name in infants developing autism spectrum disorder: A prospective study. *The Journal of Pediatrics, 183,* 141–146. e141.

Miller, M., Iosif, A.-M., Young, G. S., Hill, M. M., & Ozonoff, S. (2018). Early detection of ADHD: Insights from infant siblings of children with autism. *Journal of Clinical Child & Adolescent Psychology, 47,* 737–744.

Miller, S. A. (1998). *Developmental research methods.* Upper Saddle River, NJ: Prentice-Hall.

Miller, S. A. (2009). Children's understanding of second-order mental states. *Psychological Bulletin, 135,* 749–773.

Miller, T. W., Nigg, J. T., & Miller, R. L. (2009). Attention deficit hyperactivity disorder in African American children: What can be concluded from the past ten years. *Clinical Psychology Review, 29,* 77–86.

Millican, F. K., & Lourie, R. S. (1970). The child with pica and his family. In E. J. Anthony & C. Koupernik (Eds.), *The child in his family* (Vol. 1). New York: Wiley-Interscience.

Mills-Koonce, W. R., Rehder, P. D., & McCurdy, A. L. (2018). The significance of parenting and parent–child relationships for sexual and gender minority adolescents. *Journal of Research on Adolescence, 28,* 637–649.

Minde, K., Popiel, K., Leos, N., Falkner, S., Parker, K., & Handley-Derry, M. (1993). The evaluation and treatment of sleep disturbances in young children. *Journal of Child Psychology and Psychiatry, 34,* 521–533.

Mindell, J. A., & Owens, J. A. (2015). *A clinical guide to pediatric sleep: Diagnosis and management of sleep problems* (3rd ed.). Philadelphia, PA: Wolters Kluwer/Lippincott Williams & Wilkins.

Mindell, J. A., Leichman, E. S., DuMond, C., & Sadeh, A. (2017). Sleep and social-emotional development in infants and toddlers. *Journal of Clinical Child & Adolescent Psychology, 46,* 236–246.

Mineka, S., & Zinbarg, R. (2006). A contemporary learning theory perspective on the etiology of anxiety disorders: It's not what you thought it was. *American Psychologist, 61,* 10–26.

Minjarez, M. B., Williams, S. E., Mercier, E. M., & Hardan, A. Y. (2010). Pivotal response group treatment program for parents of children with autism. *Journal of Autism and Developmental Disabilities, 41,* 92–101.

Miranda, J., Snowden, L. R., & Legha, R. K. (2020). Policy effects on mental health status and mental health care disparities. In H. H. Goldman, R. G. Frank, & J. P. Morrissey (Eds.), *The Palgrave handbook of American mental health policy*. Cham, Switzerland: Springer.

Mirenda, P., Smith, I. M., Vaillancourt, T., Georgiades, S., Duku, E., Szatmari, P., et al. (2010). Validating the Repetitive Behavior Scale-R in young children with autism spectrum behavior. *Journal of Autism and Developmental Disorders, 40,* 1521–1530.

Mirkin, M. P. (1990). Eating disorders: A feminist family therapy perspective. In M. P. Mirkin (Ed.), *The social and political contexts of family therapy*. Boston, MA: Allyn & Bacon.

Mishna, F. (2003). Learning disabilities and bullying: Double jeopardy. *Journal of Learning Disabilities, 36,* 336–347.

Mitsis, E. M., McKay, K. E., Schulz, K. P., Newcorn, J. H., & Halperin, J. M. (2000). Parent-teacher concordance for DSM-IV attention-deficit/hyperactivity disorder in a clinic-referred sample. *Journal of the American Academy of Child and Adolescent Psychiatry, 39,* 308–313.

Mitter, N., Ali, A., & Scior, K. (2019). Stigma experienced by families of individuals with intellectual disabilities and autism: A systematic review. *Research in Developmental Disabilities, 89,* 10–21.

Moens, E., Braet, C., & Soetens, B. (2007). Observation of family functioning at mealtime: A comparison between families of children with and without overweight. *Journal of Pediatric Psychology, 32,* 52–63.

Moffitt, T. E. (1993). Adolescence-limited and life-course-persistent antisocial behavior: A developmental taxonomy. *Psychological Review, 100,* 674–701.

Moffitt, T. E. (2006). Life-course-persistent versus adolescence-limited antisocial behavior. In D. Cicchetti & D. J. Cohen (Eds.), *Developmental psychopathology, Vol. 3: Risk, disorder, and adaptation* (2nd ed.). Hoboken, NJ: John Wiley & Sons.

Moffitt, T. E., Arseneault, L., Jaffee, S. R., Kim-Cohen, J., Koenen, K. C., Odgers, C. L., et al. (2008). DSM-V conduct disorder: Research needs for an evidence base. *Journal of Child Psychology and Psychiatry, 49,* 3–33.

Moffitt, T. E., Caspi, A., Harrington, H., & Milne, B. J. (2002). Males on the life-course-persistent and adolescence-limited antisocial pathways: Follow-up at age 26 years. *Development and Psychopathology, 14,* 179–207.

Moffitt, T. E., Caspi, A., Rutter, M., & Silva, P. (2001). *Sex differences in antisocial behaviour: Conduct disorder, delinquency, and violence in the Dunedin longitudinal study.* Cambridge, UK: Cambridge University Press.

Mohammad-Rezazadeh, I., Frohlich, J., Loo, S. K., & Jeste, S. S. (2016). Brain connectivity in autism spectrum disorder. *Current Opinion in Neurology, 29,* 137.

Mohapatra, L. (2018). Language disorders. In E. Braaten (Ed.), *The SAGE encyclopedia of intellectual and developmental disorders*. Thousand Oaks, CA: SAGE Publications.

Molina, B. S. G., Hinshaw, S. P., Swanson, J. M., Arnold, L. E., Vitiello, B., Jensen, P. S., et al. (2009). The MTA at 8 years: Prospective follow-up of children treated for combined-type ADHD in a multisite study. *Journal of the American Academy of Child and Adolescent Psychiatry, 48,* 484–500.

Molitor, S. J., & Langberg, J. M. (2017). Using task performance to inform treatment planning for youth with ADHD: A systematic review. *Clinical Psychology Review, 58,* 157–173.

Montague, M., Enders, C., & Dietz, S. (2011). Effects of cognitive strategy instruction on math problem solving of middle school students with learning disabilities. *Learning Disability Quarterly, 34,* 262–272.

Monzani, B., Rijsdijk, F., Harris, J., & Mataix-Cols, D. (2014). The structure of genetic and environmental risk factors for dimensional representations of DSM-5 Obsessive-Compulsive Spectrum Disorders. *JAMA Psychiatry, 71,* 182–189.

Moody, C. T., Baker, B. L., & Blacher, J. (2018). Contribution of parenting to complex syntax development in preschool children with developmental delays or typical development. *Journal of Intellectual Disability Research, 62,* 604–616.

Moody, K. L., Mercer, K., & Glass, M. (2019). An integrative review of the prevalence of depression among pediatric patients with sickle cell disease. *Social Work in Public Health, 34,* 343–352.

Moos, B. S., & Moos, R. H. (1994). *Family Environment Scale* (3rd ed.). Menlo, CA: Mind Garden, Inc.

Moreno, C., Laje, G., Blanco, C., Jiang, H., Schmidt, A. B., & Olfson, M. (2007). National trends in the outpatient diagnosis and treatment of bipolar disorder in youth. *Archives of General Psychiatry, 64,* 1032–1039.

Moreno, C., Roche, A. M., & Greenhill, L. L. (2006). Pharmacotherapy of child and adolescent depression. *Child and Adolescent Psychiatric Clinics of North America, 15,* 977–998.

Morgan, A. J., Rapee, R. M., Salim, A., Goharpey, N., Tamir, E., McLellan, L. F., & Bayer, J. K. (2017). Internet-delivered parenting program for prevention and early intervention of anxiety problems in young children: Randomized controlled trial. *Journal of the American Academy of Child & Adolescent Psychiatry, 56,* 417–425.

Morgan, D. L., & Morgan, R. K. (2001). Single-participant research design. *American Psychologist, 56,* 119–127.

References

Morgan, P. L., Farkas, G., & Wu, Q. (2011). Kindergarten children's growth trajectories in reading and mathematics: Who falls increasingly behind? *Journal of Learning Disabilities, 44,* 472–488.

Morgan, P. L., Farkas, G., Hillemeier, M. M., & Maczuga, S. (2016). Who is at risk for persistent mathematics difficulties in the United States? *Journal of Learning Disabilities, 49,* 305–319.

Morgan, P. L., Staff, J., Hillemeier, M. M., Farkas, G., & Maczuga, S. (2013). Racial and ethnic disparities in ADHD diagnosis from kindergarten to eighth grade. *Pediatrics, 132,* 85–93.

Morgan, R. K. (1999). *Case studies in child and adolescent psychopathology.* Upper Saddle River, NJ: Prentice-Hall.

Morrison, J., & Anders, T. F. (1999). *Interviewing children and adolescents: Skills and strategies for effective DSM-diagnosis.* New York: The Guilford Press.

Morrongiello, B. A., & Schwebel, D. C. (2017). Understanding and preventing pediatric unintentional injury. In M. C. Roberts & R. G. Steele (Eds.), *Handbook of pediatric psychology* (5th ed.). New York: The Guilford Press.

Morrongiello, B. A., Sandomierski, M., & Spence, J. R. (2014). Changes over swim lessons in parents' perceptions of children's supervision needs in drowning risk situations: "His swimming has improved so now he can keep himself safe." *Health Psychology, 33,* 608–615.

Mortensen, P. B., Pedersen, C. B., Westergaard, M. D., Wohlfahrt, J., Ewald, H., Mors, O., et al. (1999). Effects of family history and place and season of birth on the risk of schizophrenia. *New England Journal of Medicine, 340,* 603–608.

Mosconi, M. W., Kay, M., D'Cruz, A.-M., Guter, S., Kapur, K., Macmillan, C., et al. (2010). Neurobehavioral abnormalities in first-degree relatives of individuals with autism. *Archives of General Psychiatry, 67,* 830–840.

Moser, J. S., Durbin, C. E., Patrick, C. J., & Schmidt, N. B. (2015). Combining neural and behavioral indicators in the assessment of internalizing psychopathology in children and adolescents. *Journal of Clinical Child and Adolescent Psychology, 44,* 329–340.

Moura, O., Pereira, M., Alfaiate, C., Fernandes, E., Fernandes, B., Nogueira, S., et al. (2017). Neurocognitive functioning in children with developmental dyslexia and attention-deficit/hyperactivity disorder: Multiple deficits and diagnostic accuracy. *Journal of Clinical and Experimental Neuropsychology, 39,* 296–312.

Mowlem, F. D., Rosenqvist, M. A., Martin, J., Lichtenstein, P., Asherson, P., & Larsson, H. (2019). Sex differences in predicting ADHD clinical diagnosis and pharmacological treatment. *European Child & Adolescent Psychiatry, 28,* 481–489.

Mowrer, O. H., & Mowrer, W. M. (1938). Enuresis: A method for its study and treatment. *American Journal of Orthopsychiatry, 8,* 436–459.

MTA Cooperative Group. (1999a). A 14-month randomized clinical trial of treatment strategies for attention-deficit/hyperactivity disorder. *Archives of General Psychiatry, 56,* 1073–1086.

MTA Cooperative Group. (1999b). Moderators and mediators of treatment response for children with attention-deficit/hyperactivity disorder. *Archives of Psychiatry, 56,* 1088–1096.

MTA Cooperative Group. (2004a). National Institute of Mental Health Multimodal Treatment Study of ADHD follow-up: Changes in effectiveness and growth after the end treatment. *Pediatrics, 113,* 762–769.

MTA Cooperative Group. (2004b). National Institute of Mental Health Multimodal Treatment Study of ADHD follow-up: 24-month outcomes of treatment strategies for attention-deficit/hyperactivity disorder. *Pediatrics, 113,* 754–761.

Mufson, L., Pollack Dorta, K., Wickramaratne, P., Nomura, Y., Olfson, M., & Weissman, M. M. (2004). The effectiveness of interpersonal psychotherapy for depressed adolescents. *Archives of General Psychiatry, 45,* 742–747.

Mufson, L., Weissman, M. M., Moreau, D., & Garfindel, R. (1999). Efficacy of interpersonal therapy for depressed adolescents. *Archives of General Psychiatry, 56,* 573–579.

Mukolo, A., Heflinger, C. A., & Wallston, K. A. (2010). The stigma of childhood mental disorders: A conceptual framework. *Journal of the American Academy of Child and Adolescent Psychiatry, 49,* 92–103.

Müller, V. I., Cieslik, E. C., Serbanescu, I., Laird, A. R., Fox, P. T., & Eickhoff, S. B. (2017). Altered brain activity in unipolar depression revisited: Meta-analyses of neuroimaging studies. *JAMA Psychiatry, 74,* 47–55.

Mullett-Hume, E., Anshel, D., Guevara, V., & Cloitre, M. (2008). Cumulative trauma and posttraumatic stress disorder among children exposed to the 9/11 World Trade Center attack. *American Journal of Orthopsychiatry, 78,* 103–108.

Mullins, L. L., & Chaney, J. M. (2019). Commentary: Lavigne and Faier-Routman (1992): Psychological adjustment to pediatric physical disorders: A meta-analytic review. *Journal of Pediatric Psychology, 44,* 846–848.

Mullins, L. L., Cushing, C. C., Suorsa, K. I., Tackett, A. P., Molzon, E. S., Mayes, S., et al. (2016). Parent illness appraisals, parent adjustment, and parent-reported child quality of life in pediatric cancer. *Pediatric Hematology and Oncology, 33,* 314–326.

Mullins, L. L., Molzon, E. S., Suorsa, K. I., Tackett, A. P., Pai, A. L. H., & Chaney, J. M. (2015). Models of resilience: Developing psychosocial interventions for parents of children with chronic health conditions. *Family Relations, 64,* 176–189.

Mulraney, M., Schilpzand, E. J., Hazell, P., Nicholson, J. M., Anderson, V., Efron, D., et al. (2016). Comorbidity and correlates of disruptive mood dysregulation disorder in

6–8-year-old children with ADHD. *European Child & Adolescent Psychiatry, 25,* 321–330.

Mulraney, M., Sciberras, E., & Lecendreaux, M. (2018). ADHD and sleep. In T. Banaschewski, D. Coghill, & A. Zuddas (Eds.), *Oxford textbook of attention deficit hyperactivity disorder.* Oxford: Oxford University Press.

Mulraney, M., Stringaris, A., & Taylor, E. (2018). Irritability, disruptive mood, and ADHD. In T. Banaschewski, D. Coghill, & A. Zuddas (Eds.), *Oxford textbook of attention deficit hyperactivity disorder* (1st ed.). Oxford: Oxford University Press.

Mundy, P. (1993). Normal versus high functioning status in children with autism. *American Journal on Mental Retardation, 97,* 381–384.

Munoz, R. F., Mrazek, P. J., & Haggerty, R. J. (1996). Institute of Medicine report on prevention of mental disorders: Summary and commentary. *American Psychologist, 51,* 1116–1122.

Muris, P., & Field, A. P. (2010). The role of verbal threat information in the development of childhood fear: "Beware the Jabberwock!" *Clinical Child and Family Psychology Review, 13,* 129–150.

Muris, P., Mayer, B., Borth, M., & Vos, M. (2013). Nonverbal and verbal transmission of disgust from mothers to offspring: Effects on children's evaluation of a novel animal. *Behavior Therapy, 44,* 293–301.

Muris, P., Meesters, C., Pierik, A., & de Kock, B. (2016). Good for the self: Self-compassion and other self-related constructs in relation to symptoms of anxiety and depression in non-clinical youths. *Journal of Child and Family Studies, 25,* 607–617.

Muris, P., Merckelbach, H., Ollendick, T. H., King, N. J., & Bogie, N. (2001). Children's nighttime fears: Parent-child ratings of frequency, content, origins, coping behaviors and severity. *Behaviour Research and Therapy, 39,* 13–28.

Muris, P., Ollendick, T. H., Roelofs, J., & Austin, K. (2014). The Short Form of the Fear Survey Schedule for Children-Revised (FSSC-R-SF): An efficient, reliable, and valid scale for measuring fear in children and adolescents. *Journal of Anxiety Disorders, 28,* 957–965.

Muris, P., van Zwol, L., Huijding, J., & Mayer, B. (2010). Mom told me scary things about this animal: Parents installing fear beliefs in their children via the verbal information pathway. *Behaviour Research and Therapy, 48,* 341–346.

Murphy, A. (2001). Front-runner. *Sports Illustrated, 95,* 62–66.

Murphy, C. M., Janssen, T., Colby, S. M., & Jackson, K. M. (2019). Low self-esteem for physical appearance mediates the effect of body mass index on smoking initiation among adolescents. *Journal of Pediatric Psychology, 44,* 197–207.

Murphy, K. A., Justice, L. M., O'Connell, A. A., Pentimonti, J. M., & Kaderavek, J. N. (2016). Understanding risk for reading difficulties in children with language impairment. *Journal of Speech, Language, and Hearing Research, 59,* 1436–1447.

Murray, L., de Rosnay, M., Pearson, J., Bergeron, C., Schofield, E., Royal-Lawson, M., & Cooper, P. J. (2008). Intergenerational transmission of social anxiety: The role of social referencing processes in infancy. *Child Development, 79,* 1049–1064.

Murray, L., Halligan, S., & Cooper, P. (2019). Postnatal depression and young children's development. In C. H. Zeanah (Ed.), *Handbook of infant mental health* (4th ed.). New York: The Guilford Press.

Murray, S. B., Nagata, J. M., Griffiths, S., Calzo, J. P., Brown, T. A., Mitchison, D., et al. (2017). The enigma of male eating disorders: A critical review and synthesis. *Clinical Psychology Review, 57,* 1–11.

Musci, R. J., Masyn, K. E., Benke, K., Maher, B., Uhl, G., & Ialongo, N. S. (2016). The effects of the interplay of genetics and early environmental risk on the course of internalizing symptoms from late childhood through adolescence. *Development and Psychopathology, 28,* 225–237.

Musser, E. D., & Nigg, J. T. (2019). Emotion dysregulation across emotion systems in attention deficit/hyperactivity disorder. *Journal of Clinical Child & Adolescent Psychology, 48,* 153–165.

Musu-Gillette, L., Zhang, A., Wang, K., Zhang, J., Kemp, J., Diliberti, M., & Oudekerk, B. (2018). *Indicators of school crime and safety: 2017* (NCES 2018–036/NCJ 251413). National Center for Education Statistics, U.S. Department of Education, and Bureau of Justice Statistics, Office of Justice Programs, U.S. Department of Justice. Washington, DC.

Myers, L., Anderlid, B.-M., Nordgren, A., Willfors, C., Kuja-Halkola, R., Tammimies, K., & Bölte, S. (2017). Minor physical anomalies in neurodevelopmental disorders: A twin study. *Child and Adolescent Psychiatry and Mental Health, 11,* 57.

Nabors, L., Cunningham, J. F., Lang, M., Wood, K., Southwick, S., & Stough, C. O. (2018). Family coping during hospitalization of children with chronic illnesses. *Journal of Child and Family Studies, 27,* 1482–1491.

Nader, K., & Williams, M. B. (2019). Trauma- and stressor-related disorders. In T. H. Ollendick, S. W. White, & B. A. White (Eds.), *The Oxford handbook of clinical child and adolescent psychology.* New York: Oxford University Press.

Nader, K., Pynoos, R. S., Fairbanks, L., & Frederick, C. (1991). Childhood PTSD reactions one year after a sniper attack. *American Journal of Psychiatry, 147,* 1526–1530.

Nagle, G. A. (2019). Investing in early childhood development and infant mental health. In C. H. Zeanah (Ed.), *Handbook of infant mental health* (4th ed.). New York: The Guilford Press.

Nagy, Z., Lagercrantz, H., & Hutton, C. (2011). Effects of preterm birth on cortical thickness measured in adolescence. *Cerebral Cortex, 21,* 300–306.

Nansel, T. R., Craig, W., Overpeck, M. D., Saluja, G., & Ruan, W. J. (2004). Cross-national consistency in the relationship between bullying behaviors and psychosocial adjustment. *Archives of Pediatric & Adolescent Medicine, 158,* 730–736.

Narad, M., Garner, A. A., Brassell, A. A., Saxby, D., Antonini, T. N., O'Brien, K. M., et al. (2013). Impact of distraction on the driving performance of adolescents with and without attention-deficit/hyperactivity disorder. *JAMA pediatrics, 167,* 933–938.

Nash, J. B., & Schaefer, C. E. (2011). Play therapy. Basic concepts and practices. In C. E. Schaefer (Ed.), *Foundations of play therapy.* Hoboken, NJ: John Wiley & Sons.

Nathan, P. E., & Langenbucher, J. W. (1999). Psychopathology: Description and classification. *Annual Review of Psychology, 50,* 79–107.

National Center for Health Statistics. (2018). Health, United States, 2017: With special feature on mortality. Hyattsville, MD.

National Commission for the Protection of Human Subjects of Biomedical and Behavioral Research. (1979). *The Belmont Report: Ethical principles and guidelines for the protection of human subjects of research.* Washington, DC: U.S. Government Printing Office.

National Institute of Mental Health. (1977). *Child abuse and neglect programs: Practice and theory.* Washington, DC: U.S. Government Printing Office.

National Institute of Mental Health. (2019a). Research Domain Criteria (RDoC). Retrieved from www.nimh.nih.gov/research-priorities/rdoc/index.shtml

National Institutes of Health. (2019b). Fragile X syndrome. *Genetics Home Reference.* Retrieved from https://ghr.nlm.nih.gov/condition/fragile-x-syndrome#

National Survey of Children's Health. (2019). *NSCH fact sheet: October 2019.* Rockville, MD: Health Resources and Services Administration/Maternal and Child Health Bureau.

Neal, J. A., & Edelmann, R. J. (2003). The etiology of social phobia: Toward a developmental profile. *Clinical Psychology Review, 23,* 761–786.

Nelson, F., & Mann, T. (2010). Opportunities in public policy to support infant and early childhood mental health. *American Psychologist, 66,* 129–139.

Nelson, N. W., & Wiig, E. H. (2018). How SLD manifests in oral expression and listening comprehension. In V. C. Alfonso & D. P. Flanagan (Eds.), *Essentials of specific learning disability identification* (2nd ed.). Hoboken, NJ: John Wiley & Sons.

Nelson, T. D., & Hankey, M. (2017). Evidence-based practice in pediatric psychology. In M. C. Roberts & R. G. Steele (Eds.), *Handbook of pediatric psychology.* New York: The Guilford Press.

Nelson, T. D., Jensen, C. D., & Steele, R. G. (2011). Weight-related criticism and self-perceptions among preadolescents. *Journal of Pediatric Psychology, 36,* 106–115.

Neri, G. (2017). The clinical phenotype of the fragile X syndrome and related disorders. In R. Willemsen & F. R. Kooy (Eds.), *Fragile X syndrome: From genetics to targeted treatment.* London: Academic Press.

Nestor, P., & Schutt, R. K. (2019). *Research methods in psychology: Investigating human behavior* (3rd ed.). Los Angeles, CA: SAGE.

Neuhaus, E., & Beauchaine, T. P. (2017). Impulsivity and vulnerability to psychopathology. In T. P. Beauchaine & S. P. Hinshaw (Eds.), *Child and adolescent psychopathology* (3rd ed.). Hoboken, NJ: John Wiley & Sons Inc.

Newbury, D. F., & Monaco, A. P. (2010). Genetic advances in the study of speech and language disorders. *Neuron, 68,* 309–320.

Newman, M. G., Zuellig, A. R., Kachin, K. E., Constantino, M. J., Przeworski, A., Erickson, T., & Cashman-McGrath, L. (2002). Preliminary reliability and validity of the Generalized Anxiety Disorder Questionnaire-IV: A revised self-report diagnostic measure of generalized anxiety disorder. *Behavior Therapy, 33,* 215–233.

Newsom, C. (1998). Autistic disorder. In E. J. Mash & R. A. Barkley (Eds.), *Treatment of childhood disorders.* New York: Guilford Press.

Newsom, C., & Hovanitz, C. A. (2006). Autistic spectrum disorders. In E. J. Mash & R. A. Barkley (Eds.), *Treatment of childhood disorders.* New York: The Guilford Press.

NICHD Early Child Care Research Network. (2004). Trajectories of physical aggression from toddlerhood to middle childhood: Predictors, correlates, and outcomes. *Monographs of the Society for Research in Child Development, 69* (4, serial no. 278).

Nicholls, D. (2004). Eating problems in childhood. In J. K. Thompson (Ed.), *Handbook of eating disorders and obesity.* Hoboken, NJ: John Wiley.

Nichols, J. Q. V., Shoulberg, E. K., Garner, A. A., Hoza, B., Burt, K. B., Murray-Close, D., & Arnold, L. E. (2017). Exploration of the factor structure of ADHD in adolescence through self, parent, and teacher reports of symptomatology. *Journal of Abnormal Child Psychology, 45,* 625–641.

Nichols, S. (2016). Developmental considerations for children and youth with HIV. In T. Chenneville (Ed.), *A clinical guide to pediatric HIV.* Cham, Switzerland: Springer.

Nickl-Jockschat, T., Rottschy, C., Thommes, J., Schneider, F., Laird, A. R., Fox, P. T., & Eickhoff, S. B. (2015). Neural networks related to dysfunctional face processing in autism spectrum disorder. *Brain Structure and Function, 220,* 2355–2371.

Nicolson, R., & Rapoport, J. L. (2000). Childhood-onset schizophrenia: What can it teach us? In J. L. Rapoport (Ed.), *Childhood onset of "adult" psychopathology.* Washington, DC: American Psychiatric Press.

Niederkrotenthaler, T., Stack, S., Till, B., Sinyor, M., Pirkis, J., Garcia, D., et al. (2019). Association of increased youth suicides in the United States with the release of 13 Reasons Why. *JAMA Psychiatry, 76,* 933–940.

Nigg, J. T. (2006). Temperament and developmental psychopathology. *Journal of Child Psychology and Psychiatry, 47,* 395–422.

Nigg, J. T. (2016). Attention and impulsivity. In D. Cicchetti (Ed.), *Developmental psychopathology* (Vol. 3). Hoboken, NJ: John Wiley & Sons, Inc.

Nigg, J. T. (2017). Attention-deficit/hyperactivity disorder. In T. P. Beauchaine & S. P. Hinshaw (Eds.), *Child and adolescent psychopathology* (3rd ed.). Hoboken, NJ: John Wiley & Sons.

Nigg, J. T., & Barkley, R. A. (2014). Attention-deficit/hyperactivity disorder. In E. J. Mash & R. A. Barkley (Eds.), *Child psychopathology* (3rd ed.). New York: The Guilford Press.

Nigg, J. T., & Hinshaw, S. P. (1998). Parent personality traits and psychopathology associated with antisocial behaviors in childhood attention-deficit hyperactive disorder. *Journal of Child Psychology and Psychiatry, 39,* 145–159.

Nigg, J., & Nikolas, M. (2008). Attention-deficit/hyperactivity disorder. In T. P. Beauchaine & S. P. Hinshaw (Eds.), *Child and adolescent psychopathology.* New York: John Wiley & Sons.

Nigg, J. T., & Song, M. (2018). ADHD and early experience: Revisiting the case of low birth weight. *Pediatrics, 141,* e20173488.

Nigg, J. T., Blaskey, L. G., Huang-Pollock, C. L., & Rappley, M. D. (2002). Neuropsychological executive functions and DSM-IV ADHD subtypes. *Journal of the American Academy of Child and Adolescent Psychiatry, 41,* 59–66.

Nigg, J. T., Hinshaw, S. P., & Huang-Pollock, C. (2006). Disorders of attention and impulse regulation. In D. Cicchetti & D. J. Cohen (Eds.), *Developmental psychopathology. Vol. III. Risk, disorder, and adaptation.* Hoboken, NJ: John Wiley & Sons.

Nigg, J. T., Knotterus, G. M., Martel, M. M., Nikolas, M., Cavanagh, K., Karmaus, W., et al. (2008). Low blood lead levels associated with clinically diagnosed attention-deficit/hyperactivity disorder and mediated by weak cognitive control. *Biological Psychiatry, 63,* 325–331.

Nigg, J. T., Lewis, K., Edinger, T., & Falk, M. (2012). Meta-analysis of attention-deficit/hyperactivity disorder or attention-deficit/hyperactivity disorder symptoms, restriction diet, and synthetic food color additives. *Journal of the American Academy of Child and Adolescent Psychiatry, 51,* 86–97.

Nijmeijer, J. S., Mindera, R. B., Buitelaar, J. K., Mulligan, A., Hartman, C. A., & Hoekstra, P. J. (2008). Attention-deficit/hyperactivity disorder and social dysfunctioning. *Clinical Psychology Review, 28,* 692–708.

Nikolas, M. A., & Nigg, J. T. (2013). Neuropsychological performance and attention-deficit hyperactivity disorder subtypes and symptom dimensions. *Neuropsychology, 27,* 107–120.

Nisbett, R. E., Aronson, J., Blair, C., Dickens, W., Flynn, J., Halpern, D. F., et al. (2012). Intelligence: New findings and theoretical developments. *American Psychologist, 67,* 130–159.

Nivard, M., Dolan, C., Kendler, K., Kan, K.-J., Willemsen, G., Van Beijsterveldt, C., et al. (2015). Stability in symptoms of anxiety and depression as a function of genotype and environment: A longitudinal twin study from ages 3 to 63 years. *Psychological Medicine, 45,* 1039–1049.

Nock, M. K., & Kurtz, S. M. S. (2005). Direct behavioral observation in school settings: Bringing science to practice. *Cognitive and Behavioral Practice, 12,* 359–370.

Nock, M. K., Boccagno, C. E., Kleiman, E. M., Ramirez, F., & Wang, S. B. (2019). Suicidal and nonsuicidal self-injury. In M. J. Prinstein, E. A. Youngstrom, E. J. Mash, & R. A. Barkley (Eds.), *Treatment of disorders in childhood and adolescence* (4th ed.). New York: The Guilford Press.

Noll, S. (2018). Institutions for people with disabilities in North America. In M. Rembis, C. Kudlick, & K. E. Nielsen (Eds.), *The Oxford handbook of disability history.* New York: Oxford University Press.

Noppe, I. C., Noppe, L. D., & Bartell, D. (2006). Terrorism and resilience: Adolescents' and teachers' responses to September 11, 2001. *Death Studies, 30,* 41–60.

Norbury, C. F., & Paul, R. (2015). Disorders of speech, language and communication. In A. Thapar (Ed.), *Rutter's Child and Adolescent Psychiatry* (6th ed.). Chichester, UK: John Wiley & Sons.

Norbury, C. F., Gooch, D., Wray, C., Baird, G., Charman, T., Simonoff, E., et al. (2016). The impact of nonverbal ability on prevalence and clinical presentation of language disorder: Evidence from a population study. *Journal of Child Psychology and Psychiatry, 57,* 1247–1257.

Noroña, A. N., Tung, I., Lee, S. S., Blacher, J., Crnic, K. A., & Baker, B. L. (2018). Developmental patterns of child emotion dysregulation as predicted by serotonin transporter genotype and parenting. *Journal of Clinical Child & Adolescent Psychology, 47*(sup1), S354–S368.

Nowicki, E. A. (2003). A meta-analysis of the social competence of children with learning disabilities compared to classmates of low and average to high achievement. *Learning Disability Quarterly, 26,* 171–188.

Nowicki, E. A., Brown, J. D., & Dare, L. (2018). Educators' evaluations of children's ideas on the social exclusion of classmates with intellectual and learning disabilities. *Journal of Applied Research in Intellectual Disabilities, 31,* e154–e163.

Nunes, C., Pereira, A. M., & Morais-Almeida, M. (2017). Asthma costs and social impact. *Asthma Research and Practice, 3,* 1.

Núñez, J. C., González-Pienda, J. A., González-Pumariega, S., Roces, G., Alvarez, L., & González, P. (2005). Subgroups of attributional profiles in students with learning disabilities and their relation to self-concept and academic goal. *Learning Disabilities Research & Practice, 20,* 86–97.

Nyborg, V. M., & Curry, J. F. (2003). The impact of perceived racism: Psychological symptoms among African American boys. *Journal of Clinical Child and Adolescent Psychology, 32,* 258–266.

O'Brien, K. M., & Vincent, N. K. (2003). Psychiatric comorbidity in anorexia and bulimia nervosa: Nature, prevalence, and causal relationships. *Clinical Psychology Review, 23,* 57–74.

O'Brien, M. (1996). Child-rearing difficulties reported by parents of infants and toddlers. *Journal of Pediatric Psychology, 21,* 433–446.

O'Connor, E. E., Dearing, E., & Collins, B. A. (2011). Teacher-child relationship and behavior problem trajectories in elementary school. *American Educational Research Journal, 48,* 120–162.

O'Connor, T. G. (2003). Natural experiments to study the effects of early experience: Progress and limitations. *Development and Psychopathology, 15,* 837–852.

O'Connor, T. G., & Parfitt, D. B. (2009). Applying research findings on early experience to infant mental health. In C. H. Zeanah, Jr. (Ed.), *Handbook of infant mental health.* New York: Guilford Press.

O'Connor, T. G., Dunn, J., Jenkins, J. M., & Rasbash, J. (2006). Predictors of between-family and within-family variation in parent-child relationships. *Journal of Child Psychology and Psychiatry, 47,* 498–510.

O'Connor, T. G., Monk, C., & Fitelson, E. M. (2014). Practitioner review: Maternal mood in pregnancy and child development—implications for child psychology and psychiatry. *Journal of Child Psychology and Psychiatry, 55,* 99–111.

O'Donnell, E. H., & Colvin, M. K. (2019). Disorders of written expression. In H. K. Wilson & E. B. Braaten (Eds.), *The Massachusetts General Hospital guide to learning disabilities: Assessing learning needs of children and adolescents.* Cham, Switzerland: Springer International Publishing.

O'Halloran, L., Nymberg, C., Jollans, L., Garavan, H., & Whelan, R. (2017). The potential of neuroimaging for identifying predictors of adolescent alcohol use initiation and misuse. *Addiction, 112,* 719–726.

O'Handley, R. D., Ford, W. B., Radley, K. C., Helbig, K. A., & Wimberly, J. K. (2016). Social skills training for adolescents with intellectual disabilities: A school-based evaluation. *Behavior Modification, 40,* 541–567.

O'Hara, K. L., Sandler, I. N., Wolchik, S. A., & Tein, J.-Y. (2019). Coping in context: The effects of long-term relations between interparental conflict and coping on the development of child psychopathology following parental divorce. *Development and Psychopathology, 31,* 1695–1713.

O'Leary, K. D., & Emery, R. E. (1985). Marital discord and child behavior problems. In M. D. Levine & P. Satz (Eds.), *Developmental variation and dysfunction.* New York: Academic Press.

O'Leary, L., Cooper, S. A., & Hughes-McCormack, L. (2018). Early death and causes of death of people with intellectual disabilities: A systematic review. *Journal of Applied Research in Intellectual Disabilities, 31,* 325–342.

Obradovic, J., Bush, N. R., Stamperdahl, J., Adler, N. E., & Boyce, W. T. (2010). Biological sensitivity to context: The interactive effects of stress reactivity and family adversity on socioemotional behavior and school readiness. *Child Development, 81,* 270–289.

Odgers, C. L., & Jensen, M. R. (2020). Annual Research Review: Adolescent mental health in the digital age: Facts, fears, and future directions. *Journal of Child Psychology and Psychiatry, 61,* 336–348.

Ohlsson Gotby, V., Lichtenstein, P., Långström, N., & Pettersson, E. (2018). Childhood neurodevelopmental disorders and risk of coercive sexual victimization in childhood and adolescence: A population-based prospective twin study. *Journal of Child Psychology and Psychiatry, 59,* 957–965.

Okamura, K. H., Orimoto, T. E., Nakamura, B. J., Chang, B., Chorpita, B. F., & Beidas, R. S. (2020). A history of child and adolescent treatment through a distillation lens: Looking back to move forward. *The Journal of Behavioral Health Services & Research, 47,* 70–85.

Olds, D., Donelan-McCall, N., O'Brien, R., MacMillan, H., Jack, S., Jenkins, T., et al. (2013). Improving the nurse–family partnership in community practice. *Pediatrics, 132*(sup2), S110–S117.

Olds, D. L., Sadler, D., & Kitzman, H. (2007). Programs for parents of infants and toddlers: Recent evidence from randomized trials. *Journal of Child Psychology and Psychiatry, 48,* 355–391.

Olfson, M., Crystal, S., Huang, C., & Gerhardt, T. (2010). Trends in antipsychotic drug use by very young, privately insured children. *Journal of the American Academy of Child and Adolescent Psychiatry, 49,* 13–23.

Olfson, M., Druss, B. G., & Marcus, S. C. (2015). Trends in mental health care among children and adolescents. *New England Journal of Medicine, 372,* 2029–2038.

Oliver, C., & Richards, C. (2010). Self-injurious behaviour in people with intellectual disability. *Current Opinion in Psychiatry, 23,* 412–416.

Oliver, C., Licence, L., & Richards, C. (2017). Self-injurious behaviour in people with intellectual disability and autism spectrum disorder. *Current Opinion in Psychiatry, 30,* 97–101.

Ollendick, T. H. (1983). Reliability and validity of the Revised Fear Survey Schedule for Children (FSSC-R). *Behaviour Research and Therapy, 21,* 685–692.

Ollendick, T. H., & King, N. J. (1998). Empirically supported treatments for children with phobic and anxiety disorders:

Current status. *Journal of Clinical Child Psychology, 27,* 156–167.

Ollendick, T. H., & Muris, P. (2015). The scientific legacy of Little Hans and Little Albert: Future directions for research on specific phobias in youth. *Journal of Clinical Child & Adolescent Psychology, 44,* 689–706.

Ollendick, T. H., & Schroeder, C. S. (2003). *Encyclopedia of clinical child and pediatric psychology.* New York: Springer Science & Business Media.

Ollendick, T. H., Birmaher, B., & Mattis, S. G. (2004a). Panic disorder. In T. L. Morris & J. S. March (Eds.), *Anxiety disorders in children and adolescents.* New York: Guilford Press.

Ollendick, T. H., Davis, T. E., & Muris, P. (2004b). Treatment of specific phobia in children and adolescents. In P. M. Barrett & T. H. Ollendick (Eds.), *Handbook of interventions that work with children and adolescents: Prevention and treatment.* Hoboken, NJ: John Wiley & Sons.

Ollendick, T. H., Lewis, K. M., Cowart, M. J. W., & Davis, T. (2012). Prediction of child performance on a parent–child behavioral approach test with animal phobic children. *Behavior Modification, 36,* 509–524.

Ollendick, T. H., Ryan, S. M., Capriola-Hall, N. N., Salazar, I. C., & Caballo, V. E. (2019). Evaluation of the reliability and validity of the Social Anxiety Questionnaire for Children in adolescents with social anxiety disorder. *Journal of Psychopathology and Behavioral Assessment, 41,* 16–24.

Olson, R. K., Hulslander, J., Christopher, M., Keenan, J. M., Wadsworth, S. J., Willcutt, E. G., et al. (2013). Genetic and environmental influences on writing and their relations to language and reading. *Annals of Dyslexia, 63,* 25–43.

Olvera, N., & Power, T. G. (2010). Parenting styles and obesity in Mexican American children: A longitudinal study. *Journal of Pediatric Psychology, 35,* 243–249.

Olweus, D. (1978). *Aggression in the schools: Bullies and whipping boys.* Washington, DC: Hemisphere Press.

Olweus, D. (1993). *Bullying at school: What we know and what we can do.* Cambridge, MA: Blackwell.

Olweus, D. (1994). Bullying at school: Basic facts and effects of a school based intervention program. *Journal of Child Psychology and Psychiatry, 35,* 1171–1190.

Olweus, D., Limber, S. P., & Breivik, K. (2019). Addressing specific forms of bullying: A large-scale evaluation of the Olweus Bullying Prevention Program. *International Journal of Bullying Prevention, 1,* 70–84.

Ondersma, S. J., & Walker, E. (1998). Elimination disorders. In T. H. Ollendick & M. Hersen (Eds.), *Handbook of child psychopathology* (3rd ed.). New York: Plenum Press.

Oppenheimer, C. W., & Hankin, B. L. (2011). Relationship quality and depressive symptoms among adolescents: A short-term multiwave investigation of longitudinal, reciprocal associations. *Journal of Clinical Child & Adolescent Psychology, 40,* 486–493.

Organista, K. C. (2003). Mexican American children and adolescents. In J. T. Gibbs, L. N. Huang, & Associates (Eds.), *Children of color: Psychological interventions with culturally diverse youth.* San Francisco, CA: Jossey-Bass.

Ortiz, S. O., Piazza, N., Ochoa, S. H., & Dynda, A. M. (2018). Testing with culturally and linguistically diverse populations. In D. P. Flanagan & E. M. McDonough (Eds.), *Contemporary intellectual assessment: Theories, tests, and issues* (4th ed.). New York: The Guilford Press.

Öst, L. (1987). Age of onset in different phobias. *Journal of Abnormal Psychology, 96,* 123–145.

Ostrolenk, A., Forgeot d'Arc, B., Jelenic, P., Samson, F., & Mottron, L. (2017). Hyperlexia: Systematic review, neurocognitive modelling, and outcome. *Neuroscience & Biobehavioral Reviews, 79,* 134–149.

Otto, M., Henin, A., Hirshfeld-Becker, D. R., Pollack, M. H., Biederman, J., & Rosenbaum, J. (2007). Posttraumatic stress disorder symptoms following media exposure to tragic events: Impact of 9/11 on children at risk for anxiety disorders. *Journal of Anxiety Disorders, 21,* 888–902.

Outlaw, A., Naar-King, S., Green-Jones, M., Wright, K., Condon, K., Sherry, L., & Janisse, H. (2010). Predictors of optimal HIV appointment adherence in minority youth: A prospective study. *Journal of Pediatric Psychology, 35,* 1011–1015.

Owens, E. B., Cardoos, S. L., & Hinshaw, S. P. (2015). Developmental progression and gender differences among individuals with ADHD. In R. A. Barkley (Ed.), *Attention-deficit hyperactivity disorder: A handbook for diagnosis and treatment.* New York: The Guilford Press.

Owens, E. B., Hinshaw, S. P., Lee, S. S., & Lahey, B. B. (2009). Few girls with childhood attention-deficit/hyperactivity disorder show positive adjustment during adolescence. *Journal of Clinical Child & Adolescent Psychology, 38,* 132–143.

Owens, E. B., Zalecki, C., Gillette, P., & Hinshaw, S. P. (2017). Girls with childhood ADHD as adults: Cross-domain outcomes by diagnostic persistence. *Journal of Consulting and Clinical Psychology, 85,* 723–736.

Owens, J. A., Spirito, A., McGuinn, M., & Nobile, C. (2000). Sleep habits and sleep disturbance in elementary school-aged children. *Developmental and Behavioral Pediatrics, 21,* 27–36.

Owens, J. S., Goldfine, M. E., Evangelista, N. M., Hoza, B., & Kaiser, N. M. (2007). A critical review of self-perceptions and the positive illusory bias in children with ADHD. *Clinical Child and Family Psychology Review, 10,* 335–351.

Owens, J., & Adolescent Sleep Working Group (2014). Insufficient sleep in adolescents and young adults: An update on causes and consequences. *Pediatrics, 134,* e921–e932.

Oxley, C., & Stringaris, A. (2018). Comorbidity: Depression and anxiety. In T. Banaschewski, D. Coghill, & A. Zuddas (Eds.),

References

Oxford textbook of attention deficit hyperactivity disorder. Oxford: Oxford University Press.

Özcebe, E., Noyan Erbas, A., & Karahan Tiğrak, T. (2020). Analysis of behavioural characteristics of children with developmental language disorders. *International Journal of Speech-Language Pathology, 22,* 30–36.

Ozgen, H. M., Hop, J. W., Hox, J. J., Beemer, F. A., & van Engeland, H. (2010). Minor physical anomalies in autism: A meta-analysis. *Molecular Psychiatry, 15,* 300–307.

Ozgen, H., Hellemann, G. S., Stellato, R. K., Lahuis, B., van Daalen, E., Staal, W. G., et al. (2011). Morphological features in children with autism spectrum disorders: A matched case-control study. *Journal of Autism and Developmental Disorders, 41,* 23–31.

Ozonoff, S. (1997). Casual mechanisms of autism: Unifying perspectives from an information-processing framework. In D. J. Cohen & F. R. Volkmar (Eds.), *Handbook of autism and pervasive developmental disorders.* New York: John Wiley.

Ozonoff, S., Iosif, A.-M., Baguio, F., Cook, I. C., Hill, M. M., Hutman, T., et al. (2010). A prospective study of the emergence of early behavioral signs of autism. *Journal of the American Academy of Child & Adolescent Psychiatry, 49,* 256–266. e252.

Ozonoff, S., Young, G. S., Carter, A., Messinger, D., Yirmiya, N., Zwaigenbaum, L., et al. (2011). Recurrence risk for autism spectrum disorders: A baby siblings research consortium study. *Pediatrics, 128,* e488.

Ozonoff, S., Young, G. S., Landa, R. J., Brian, J., Bryson, S., Charman, T., et al. (2015). Diagnostic stability in young children at risk for autism spectrum disorder: A baby siblings research consortium study. *Journal of Child Psychology and Psychiatry, and Allied Disciplines, 56,* 988–998.

Paclt, I., Přibilová, N., Kollárová, P., Kohoutová, M., Dezortová, M., Hájek, M., & Csemy, L. (2016). Reverse asymmetry and changes in brain structural volume of the basal ganglia in ADHD, developmental changes and the impact of stimulant medications. *Neuroendocrinology Letters, 37,* 29–32.

Pagsberg, A. K., Tarp, S., Glintborg, D., Stenstrøm, A. D., Fink-Jensen, A., Correll, C. U., & Christensen, R. (2017). Acute antipsychotic treatment of children and adolescents with schizophrenia-spectrum disorders: A systematic review and network meta-analysis. *Journal of the American Academy of Child & Adolescent Psychiatry, 56,* 191–202.

Pahl, K. M., & Barrett, P. M. (2010). Interventions for anxiety disorders in children using group cognitive-behavioral therapy with family involvement. In J. R. Weisz & A. E. Kazdin (Eds.), *Evidence-based psychotherapies for children and adolescents* (2nd ed.). New York: The Guilford Press.

Palermo, T. M., Valrie, C. R., & Karlson, C. W. (2014). Family and parent influences on pediatric chronic pain: A developmental perspective. *American Psychologist, 69,* 142–152.

Palinkas, L. A. (2018). *Achieving implementation and exchange: The science of delivering evidence based practices to at-risk youth.* Bristol: Policy Press.

Palitz, S. A., Davis, J. P., & Kendall, P. C. (2019). Anxiety disorders. In M. J. Prinstein, E. A. Youngstrom, E. J. Mash, & R. A. Barkley (Eds.), *Treatment of disorders in childhood and adolescence* (4th ed.). New York: The Guilford Press.

Paloyelis, Y., Rijsdijk, F., Wood, A. C., Asherson, P., & Kuntsi, J. (2010). The genetic association between ADHD symptoms and reading difficulties: The role of inattentiveness and IQ. *Journal of Abnormal Child Psychology, 38,* 1083–1095.

Paniagua, F. A. (2000). Culture-bound syndromes, cultural variations, and psychopathology. In I. Cuellar & F. A. Paniagua (Eds.), *Handbook of multicultural mental health.* San Diego, CA: Academic Press.

Panicker, A. S., & Chelliah, A. (2016). Resilience and stress in children and adolescents with specific learning disability. *Journal of the Canadian Academy of Child and Adolescent Psychiatry, 25,* 17–23.

Papazoglou, A., Jacobson, L. A., McCabe, M., Kaufmann, W., & Andrew Zabel, T. (2014). To ID or not to ID? Changes in classification rates of intellectual disability using DSM-5. *Intellectual and Developmental Disabilities, 52,* 165–174.

Papolos, D. F. (2003). Bipolar disorder and comorbid disorders: The case for a dimensional nosology. In B. Geller & M. P. DelBello (Eds.), *Bipolar disorder in childhood and early adolescence.* New York: Guilford Press.

Papadopoulos, N. G., Custovic, A., Deschildre, A., Mathioudakis, A. G., Phipatanakul, W., Wong, G., et al. (2020). Impact of COVID-19 on pediatric asthma: Practice adjustments and disease burden. *The Journal of Allergy and Clinical Immunology: In Practice.* doi:https://doi.org/10.1016/j.jaip.2020.06.001

Pappadopulos, E., Jensen, P. S., Chait, A. R., Arnold, L. E., Swanson, J. M., Greenhill, L. L., et al. (2009). Medication adherence in the MTA: Saliva methylphenidate samples versus parent report and mediating effect of concomitant behavioral treatment. *Journal of the Academy of Child and Adolescent Psychiatry, 48,* 501–510.

Pardini, D., Stepp, S., Hipwell, A., Stouthamer-Loeber, M., & Loeber, R. (2012). The clinical utility of the proposed DSM-5 callous-unemotional subtype of conduct disorder in young girls. *Journal of the American Academy of Child and Adolescent Psychiatry, 51,* 62–73.

Pardo, C. A., & Eberhart, C. G. (2007). The neurobiology of autism. *Brain Pathology, 17,* 434–447.

Parikh, K., Fleischman, W., & Agrawal, S. (2016). Industry relationships with pediatricians: Findings from the open payments sunshine act. *Pediatrics, 137,* e20154440.

Parish, S. L. (2006). Juggling and struggling: A preliminary worklife study of mothers with adolescents who have developmental disabilities. *Mental Retardation, 44,* 393–404.

Park, I. J. K., Du, H., Wang, L., Williams, D. R., & Alegría, M. (2020). The role of parents' ethnic-racial socialization practices in the discrimination–depression link among Mexican-origin adolescents. *Journal of Clinical Child & Adolescent Psychology, 49,* 391–404.

Parker, J. G., Rubin, K. H., Erath, S. A., Wojslawowicz, J. C., & Buskirk, A. A. (2006). Peer relationships, child development, and adjustment: A developmental psychopathology perspective. In D. Cicchetti & D. J. Cohen (Eds.), *Developmental psychopathology: Vol. 1. Theory and method.* Hoboken, NJ: John Wiley & Sons.

Parshuram, C., & Dryden-Palmer, K. (2018). Practice in pediatric intensive care: Death and dying. *Pediatric Critical Care Medicine, 19*(8S), S1–S3.

Parsons, L., Cordier, R., Munro, N., Joosten, A., & Speyer, R. (2017). A systematic review of pragmatic language interventions for children with autism spectrum disorder. *PLoS One, 12,* e0172242.

Paruthi, S., Brooks, L. J., D'Ambrosio, C., Hall, W. A., Kotagal, S., Lloyd, R. M., et al. (2016). Recommended amount of sleep for pediatric populations: A consensus statement of the American Academy of Sleep Medicine. *Journal of Clinical Sleep Medicine, 12,* 785–786.

Pasalich, D. S., Witkiewitz, K., McMahon, R. J., Pinderhughes, E. E., & the Conduct Problems Prevention Research Group. (2016). Indirect effects of the Fast Track intervention on conduct disorder symptoms and callous-unemotional traits: Distinct pathways involving discipline and warmth. *Journal of Abnormal Child Psychology, 44,* 587–597.

Patel, N. J., Datye, K. A., & Jaser, S. S. (2018). Importance of patient–provider communication to adherence in adolescents with type 1 diabetes. *Healthcare, 6,* 30.

Patterson, G. R. (1976). The aggressive child: Victim and architect of a coercive system. In L. A. Hamerlynck, L. C. Handy, & E. J. Mash (Eds.), *Behavior modification and families.* New York: Brunner/Mazel.

Patterson, G. R., DeBaryshe, B. D., & Ramsey, E. (1989). A developmental perspective on antisocial behavior. *American Psychologist, 44,* 329–335.

Patterson, G. R., DeGarmo, D. S., & Knutson, N. (2000). Hyperactive and antisocial behaviors: Comorbid or two points in the same process? *Development and Psychopathology, 12,* 91–106.

Patterson, G. R., Reid, J. B., & Dishion, T. J. (1992). *Antisocial boys.* Eugene, OR: Castalia Publishing Company.

Patterson, G. R., Reid, J. B., & Eddy, J. M. (2002). A brief history of the Oregon Model. In J. B. Reid, G. R. Patterson, & J. Snyder (Eds.), *Antisocial behavior in children and adolescents:*

A developmental analysis and model for intervention. Washington, DC: American Psychological Association.

Patterson, G. R., Reid, J. B., Jones, R. R., & Conger, R. E. (1975). *A social learning approach to family intervention* (Vol. 1). Eugene, OR: Castalia.

Paul, R., Fuerst, Y., Ramsey, G., Chawarska, K., & Klin, A. (2010). Out of the mouth of babes: Vocal production in infant siblings of children with ASD. *Journal of Child Psychology and Psychiatry, 52,* 588–598.

Pauli-Pott, U., Schloß, S., Heinzel-Gutenbrunner, M., & Becker, K. (2019). Multiple causal pathways in attention-deficit/hyperactivity disorder: Do emerging executive and motivational deviations precede symptom development? *Child Neuropsychology, 25,* 179–197.

Pavuluri, M. N., & Sweeney, J. A. (2008). Integrating functional brain neuroimaging and developmental cognitive neuroscience in child psychiatry research. *Journal of the American Academy of Child and Adolescent Psychiatry, 47,* 1273–1288.

Pavuluri, M. N., West, A., Hill, S. K., Jindal, K., & Sweeney, J. A. (2009). Neurocognitive function in pediatric bipolar disorder: 3-year follow-up shows cognitive development lagging behind healthy youths. *Journal of the American Academy of Child and Adolescent Psychiatry, 48,* 299–307.

Paxton, S. J., Neumark-Sztainer, D., Hannan, P. J., & Eisenberg, M. E. (2006). Body dissatisfaction prospectively predicts depressive mood and low self-esteem in adolescent girls and boys. *Journal of Clinical Child and Adolescent Psychology, 35,* 539–549.

Peer, J. W., & Hillman, S. B. (2014). Stress and resilience for parents of children with intellectual and developmental disabilities: A review of key factors and recommendations for practitioners. *Journal of Policy & Practice in Intellectual Disabilities, 11,* 92–98.

Pelham, W. E. (2001, Winter). Are ADHD/I and ADHD/C the same or different? Does it matter? *Clinical Psychology: Science and Practice, 8,* 502–506.

Pelham, W. E., Gnagy, E. M., Greiner, A. R., Fabiano, G. A., Waschbush, D. A., & Coles, E. K. (2017). Summer treatment programs for attention/deficit/hyperactivity disorder. In J. R. Weisz & A. E. Kazdin (Eds.), *Evidence-based psychotherapies for children and adolescents* (3rd ed.). New York: The Guilford Press.

Pelsch, V., Breslend, N. L., Jones, D. J., MacFarland, M., & Forehand, R. (2017). Young children with behavior disorders in low-income families: The role of clinic observations in the assessment of parenting. *Evidence-Based Practice in Child and Adolescent Mental Health, 2,* 201–211.

Pelsser, L. M., Frankena, K., Toorman, J., Savelkoul, H. F., Dubois, A. E., Pereira, R. R., et al. (2011). Effects of a restricted elimination diet on the behaviour of children

References

with attention-deficit hyperactivity disorder (INCA study): A randomized controlled trial. *The Lancet, 377,* 494–503.

Pennington, B. F., & Bishop, D. V. M. (2009). Relations among speech, language, and reading disorders. *Annual Review of Psychology, 60,* 283–306.

Pennington, B. F., McGrath, L. M., & Peterson, R. L. (2019). *Diagnosing learning disorders: From science to practice* (3rd ed.). New York: The Guilford Press.

Pennington, B. F., Santerre-Lemmon, L., Rosenberg, J., MacDonald, B., Boada, R., Friend, A., et al. (2012). Individual prediction of dyslexia by single versus multiple deficit models. *Journal of Abnormal Psychology, 121,* 212–224.

Perera, F. P., Wang, S., Vishnevetsky, J., Zhang, B., Cole, K. J., Tang, D., et al. (2011). Polycyclic aromatic hydrocarbons–aromatic DNA adducts in cord blood and behavior scores in New York City children. *Environmental Health Perspective, 119,* 1176–1181.

Pérez-Edgar, K., & Fox, N. A. (2005). Temperament and anxiety disorders. *Child and Adolescent Psychiatric Clinics of North America, 14,* 681–706.

Pérez-Edgar, K., Roberson-Nay, R., Hardin, M. G., Poeth, K., Guyer, A. E., Nelson, E. E., et al. (2007). Attention alters neural responses to evocative faces in behaviorally inhibited adolescents. *Neuroimage, 35,* 1538–1546.

Peris, T. S., Rozenman, M. S., Sugar, C. A., McCracken, J. T., & Piacentini, J. (2017). Targeted family intervention for complex cases of pediatric obsessive-compulsive disorder: A randomized controlled trial. *Journal of the American Academy of Child & Adolescent Psychiatry, 56,* 1034–1042.

Perkins, H., & McLaughlin, T. (2015). Classroom interventions for elementary school children with EBD: A brief review. *International Journal of Applied Research, 1,* 24–29.

Perks, D. L., Watt, B. D., Fritzon, K., & Doley, R. (2019). Juvenile firesetters as multiple problem youth with particular interests in fire: A meta-analysis. *Aggression and Violent Behavior, 47,* 189–203.

Perrin, E. C., Sheldrick, R. C., McMenamy, J. M., Henson, B. S., & Carter, A. S. (2014). Improving parenting skills for families of young children in pediatric settings: A randomized clinical trial. *JAMA Pediatrics, 168,* 16–24.

Perrin, S., Smith, P., & Yule, W. (2000). The assessment and treatment of post-traumatic stress disorder in children and adolescents. *Journal of Child Psychology and Psychiatry, 41,* 277–289.

Perry, B. D. (2017). Trauma- and stressor-related disorders in infants, children, and adolescents. In T. P. Beauchaine & S. P. Hinshaw (Eds.), *Child and adolescent psychopathology* (3rd ed.). Hoboken, NJ: John Wiley & Sons Inc.

Pescosolido, B. A., Jensen, P. S., Martin, J. K., Perry, B. L., Olafsdottir, S., & Fettes, D. (2008). Public knowledge and assessment of child mental health problems: Findings from the National Stigma Study-Children. *Journal of the American Academy of Child and Adolescent Psychiatry, 47,* 339–349.

Peshkin, M. M. (1959). Intractable asthma of childhood: Rehabilitation at the institutional level with a follow-up of 150 cases. *International Archives of Allergy, 15,* 91–101.

Peters, B., & Freeman, B. (2016). Juvenile firesetting. *Child and Adolescent Psychiatric Clinics, 25,* 99–106.

Petersen, A. C., Verma, S., Koller, S. H., & Motti-Stefanidi, F. (2017). Global positive youth development: Framing the issues. In A. C. Petersen, S. H. Koller, F. Motti-Stefandi, & S. Verma (Eds.), *Positive youth development in global contexts of social and economic change.* New York: Routledge, Taylor & Francis Group.

Peterson, B. S. (1995). Neuroimaging in child and adolescent neuropsychiatric disorders. *Journal of the American Academy of Child and Adolescent Psychiatry, 34,* 1560–1576.

Peterson, L., Schultheis, K., Ridley-Johnson, R., Miller, D. J., & Tracy, K. (1984). Comparison of three modeling procedures on the presurgical and postsurgical reactions of children. *Behavior Therapy, 15,* 197–203.

Peterson, R. L., & McGrath, L. M. (2009). Dyslexia. In B. F. Pennington (Ed.), *Diagnosing learning disorders.* New York: Guilford Press.

Peterson, R. L., & Pennington, B. F. (2015). Developmental dyslexia. *Annual Review of Clinical Psychology, 11,* 283–307.

Petruzzelli, M. G., Margari, L., Craig, F., Campa, M. G., Martinelli, D., Pastore, A., et al. (2015). Markers of neurodevelopmental impairments in early-onset psychosis. *Neuropsychiatric Disease and Treatment, 11,* 1793–1798.

Pfeffer, C. R. (2000). Suicidal behaviour in children: An emphasis on developmental influences. In K. Hawton & K. van Heeringen (Eds.), *The international handbook of suicide and attempted suicide.* Chichester, UK: John Wiley & Sons, Ltd.

Pfiffner, L. J., & DuPaul, G. J. (2015). Treatment of ADHD in school settings. In R. A. Barkley (Ed.), *Attention-deficit hyperactivity disorder: A handbook for diagnosis and treatment* (4th ed.). New York: The Guilford Press.

Pfiffner, L. J., Rooney, M. E., Jiang, Y., Haack, L. M., Beaulieu, A., & McBurnett, K. (2018). Sustained effects of collaborative school-home intervention for attention-deficit/hyperactivity disorder symptoms and impairment. *Journal of the American Academy of Child & Adolescent Psychiatry, 57,* 245–251.

Phillips, E. L. (1968). Achievement Place: Token reinforcement procedures in a home-style rehabilitation setting for "pre-delinquent" boys. *Journal of Applied Behavior Analysis, 1,* 213–223.

Phillips, N., Amos, T., Kuo, C., Hoare, J., Ipser, J., Thomas, K. G. F., & Stein, D. J. (2016). HIV-associated cognitive impairment in perinatally infected children: A meta-analysis. *Pediatrics, 138,* e20160893.

Piacentini, J., Bergman, L., Keller, M., & McCracken, J. (2003). Functional impairment in children and adolescents with obsessive-compulsive disorder. *Journal of Child and Adolescent Psychopharmacology, 13,* S61–S69.

Piacentini, J., Peris, T. S., Bergman, R. L., Chang, S., & Jaffer, M. (2007). Functional impairment in childhood OCD: Development and psychometrics properties of the Child Obsessive-Compulsive Impact Scale-Revised (COIS-R). *Journal of Clinical Child & Adolescent Psychology, 36,* 645–653.

Pianta, R. C. (2006). School, schooling, and developmental psychopathology. In D. Cicchetti & D. J. Cohen (Eds.), *Developmental psychopathology. Vol. 1. Theory and method.* Hoboken, NJ: John Wiley & Sons.

Pianta, R. C. (2016). Classroom processes and teacher-student interaction: Integrations with a developmental psychopathology perspective. In D. Cicchetti (Ed.), *Developmental psychopathology: Risk, resilience, and intervention* (Vol. 4). Hoboken, NJ: John Wiley & Sons.

Picci, G., Gotts, S. J., & Scherf, K. S. (2016). A theoretical rut: Revisiting and critically evaluating the generalized under-/ over-connectivity hypothesis of autism. *Developmental Science, 19,* 524–549.

Piccolo, L. R., & Noble, A. G. (2019). Poverty, early experience and brain development. In C. H. Zeanah (Ed.), *Handbook of infant mental health* (4th ed.). New York: The Guilford Press.

Pickren, W. E., & Tomes, H. (2002). The legacy of Kenneth B. Clark to APA. *American Psychologist, 57,* 51–59.

Pidano, A. E., & Allen, A. R. (2015). The Incredible Years series: A review of the independent research base. *Journal of Child and Family Studies, 24,* 1898–1916.

Pike, K. M., & Dunne, P. E. (2015). The rise of eating disorders in Asia: A review. *Journal of Eating Disorders, 3,* 1–14.

Pina, A. A., & Silverman, W. K. (2004). Clinical phenomenology, somatic symptoms, and distress in Hispanic/Latino and European American youths with anxiety disorders. *Journal of Clinical Child and Adolescent Psychology, 33,* 227–236.

Pina, A. A., Polo, A. J., & Huey, S. J. (2019). Evidence-based psychosocial interventions for ethnic minority youth: The 10-year update. *Journal of Clinical Child & Adolescent Psychology, 48,* 179–202.

Pine, D. S., Guyer, A. E., & Leibenluft, E. (2008). Functional magnetic resonance imaging and pediatric anxiety. *Journal of the American Academy of Child and Adolescent Psychiatry, 47,* 1217–1221.

Pinquart, M. (2013). Do the parent–child relationship and parenting behaviors differ between families with a child with and without chronic illness? A meta-analysis. *Journal of Pediatric Psychology, 38,* 708–721.

Pinquart, M. (2017a). Associations of parenting dimensions and styles with externalizing problems of children and adolescents: An updated meta-analysis. *Developmental Psychology, 53,* 873–932.

Pinquart, M. (2017b). Associations of parenting dimensions and styles with internalizing symptoms in children and adolescents: A meta-analysis. *Marriage & Family Review, 53,* 613–640.

Pisecco, S., Huzinec, C., & Curtis, D. (2001). The effect of child characteristics on teachers' acceptability of classroom-based behavioral strategies and psychostimulant medication for the treatment of ADHD. *Journal of Clinical Child Psychology, 30,* 413–421.

Piven, J., Harper, J., Palmer, P., & Arndt, S. (1996). Course of behavioral change in autism: A retrospective study of high-IQ adolescents and adults. *Journal of the American Academy of Child and Adolescent Psychiatry, 35,* 523–529.

Planalp, E. M., & Goldsmith, H. H. (2020). Observed profiles of infant temperament: Stability, heritability, and associations with parenting. *Child Development, 91,* e563–e580.

Platt, B., Waters, A. M., Schulte-Koerne, G., Engelmann, L., & Salemink, E. (2017). A review of cognitive biases in youth depression: Attention, interpretation and memory. *Cognition and Emotion, 31,* 462–483.

Plemmons, G., Hall, M., Doupnik, S., Gay, J., Brown, C., Browning, W., et al. (2018). Hospitalization for suicide ideation or attempt: 2008–2015. *Pediatrics, 141,* e20172426.

Pliszka, S. R. (2011). Anxiety disorders. In S. Goldstein & C. R. Reynolds (Eds.), *Handbook of neurodevelopmental and genetic disorders in children* (2nd ed.). New York: The Guilford Press.

Pliszka, S. R. (2015). Comorbid psychiatric disorders in children with ADHD. In R. A. Barkley (Ed.), *Attention-deficit hyperactivity disorder: A handbook for diagnosis and treatment* (4th ed.). New York: The Guilford Press.

Pliszka, S. R. (2019). ADHD and anxiety: Clinical implications. *Journal of Attention Disorders, 23,* 203–205.

Pliszka, S. and the AACAP Work Group on Quality Issues. (2007). Practice parameter for the assessment of children and adolescents with attention-deficit/hyperactivity disorder. *Journal of the Academy of Child and Adolescent Psychiatry, 46,* 894–921.

Plomin, R. (1994). *Genetics and experience: The interplay between nature and nurture.* Thousand Oaks, CA: Sage Publications.

Plomin, R. (2005). Finding genes in child psychology and psychiatry: When are we going to be there? *Journal of Child Psychology and Psychiatry, 46,* 1030–1038.

Plomin, R. (2008). Genetics and the future diagnosis of learning disabilities. *Mental capital and wellbeing: Making the most of ourselves in the 21st century.* Retrieved from www.foresight.gov.uk

Plomin, R., & Crabbe, J. (2000). DNA. *Psychological Bulletin, 126,* 806–828.

References

Plomin, R., & Davis, O. S. P. (2009). The future of genetics in psychology and psychiatry: Microarrays, genome-wide association, and non-coding RNA. *Journal of Child Psychology and Psychiatry, 50*, 63–71.

Plomin, R., & von Stumm, S. (2018). The new genetics of intelligence. *Nature Reviews Genetics, 19*, 148–159.

Plomin, R., Kovacs, Y., & Haworth, C. M. A. (2007). Generalist genes: Genetic links between brain, mind, and education. *Mind, Brain, and Education, 1*, 11–19.

Plourde, V., Boivin, M., Brendgen, M., Vitaro, F., & Dionne, G. (2017). Phenotypic and genetic associations between reading and attention-deficit/hyperactivity disorder dimensions in adolescence. *Development and Psychopathology, 29*, 1215–1226.

Pluviano, S., Watt, C., Ragazzini, G., & Della Sala, S. (2019). Parents' beliefs in misinformation about vaccines are strengthened by pro-vaccine campaigns. *Cognitive Processing, 20*, 325–331.

Poehlmann-Tynan, J., Cuthrell, H. R., Weymouth, L. A., & Burnson, C. F. (2019). Children with incarcerated parents. In T. H. Ollendick, S. W. White, & B. A. White (Eds.), *The Oxford handbook of clinical child and adolescent psychology*. New York: Oxford University Press.

Polanczyk, G. V. (2018). Epidemiology. In T. Banaschewski, D. Coghill, & A. Zuddas (Eds.), *Oxford textbook of attention deficit hyperactivity disorder*. Oxford: Oxford University Press.

Polanczyk, G. V., Salum, G. A., Sugaya, L. S., Caye, A., & Rohde, L. A. (2015). Annual Research Review: A meta-analysis of the worldwide prevalence of mental disorders in children and adolescents. *Journal of Child Psychology and Psychiatry, 56*, 345–365.

Pollock, L. A. (2001). Parent-child relations. In D. I. Kertzer & M. Barbagoli (Eds.), *The history of the European family. Vol. One. Family life in early modern times, 1500–1789*. New Haven, CT: Yale University Press.

Polloway, E. A., Lubin, J., Smith, J. D., & Patton, J. R. (2010). Mild intellectual disabilities: Legacies and trends in concepts and educational practices. *Education and Training in Autism and Developmental Disabilities, 45*, 54–68.

Porrino, L., Rapoport, J. L., Behar, D., Sceery, W., Ismond, D. R., & Bunney, W. E. (1983). A naturalistic assessment of the motor activity of hyperactive boys: I. Comparison with normal controls. *Archives of General Psychiatry, 40*, 681–687.

Posner, J., Polanczyk, G. V., & Sonuga-Barke, E. (2020). Attention-deficit hyperactivity disorder. *The Lancet, 395*, 450–462.

Posthumus, J. A., Raaijmakers, M A. J., Maassen, G. H., van Engeland, H., & Matthys, W. (2012). Sustained effects of Incredible Years as a preventive intervention in preschool children with conduct problems. *Journal of Abnormal Child Psychology, 40*, 487–500.

Potter, H. W. (1972). Mental retardation in historical perspective. In S. I. Harrison & J. F. McDermott (Eds.), *Childhood psychopathology*. New York: International Universities Press.

Pottick, K. J., Kirk, S. A., Hsieh, D. K., & Tian, X. (2007). Judging mental disorder in youths: Effects of client, clinician, and contextual differences. *Journal of Consulting and Clinical Psychology, 75*, 1–8.

Powell, L. M., Szczypka, G., Chaloupka, F. J., & Braunschweig, C. L. (2007). Nutritional content of television food advertisements seen by children and adolescents in the United States. *Pediatrics, 120*, 576–583.

Powell, N. P., Lochman, J. E., Boxmeyer, C. L., Barry, T. D., & Pardini, D. A. (2017). The Coping power program for aggressive behavior in children. In *Evidence-based psychotherapies for children and adolescents* (3rd ed.). New York: The Guilford Press.

Powers, A., & Casey, B. (2015). The adolescent brain and the emergence and peak of psychopathology. *Journal of Infant, Child, and Adolescent Psychotherapy, 14*, 3–15.

Powers, S. W., Jones, J. S., & Jones, B. A. (2005). Behavioral and cognitive-behavioral interventions with pediatric populations. *Clinical Child Psychology and Psychiatry, 10*, 65–77.

Prescott, A. T., Sargent, J. D., & Hull, J. G. (2018). Metaanalysis of the relationship between violent video game play and physical aggression over time. *Proceedings of the National Academy of Sciences of the United States of America, 115*, 9882–9888.

Preston, J. L., Frost, S. J., Mencl, W. E., Fulbright, R. K., Landi, N., Grigorenko, E., et al. (2010). Early and late talkers: School-age language, literacy, and neurolinguistic differences. *Brain, 133*, 2185–2195.

Preston, J. L., Hull, M., & Edwards, M. L. (2013). Preschool speech error patterns predict articulation and phonological awareness outcomes in children with histories of speech sound disorders. *American Journal of Speech-Language Pathology, 22*, 173–184.

Price, J. M., & Zwolinski, J. (2010). The nature of child and adolescent vulnerability. In R. E. Ingram & J. M. Price (Eds.), *Vulnerability to psychopathology: Risk across the lifespan*. New York: Guilford Press.

Price, J., Drabick, D. A., & Ridenour, T. A. (2019). Association with deviant peers across adolescence: Subtypes, developmental patterns, and long-term outcomes. *Journal of Clinical Child & Adolescent Psychology, 48*, 238–249.

Price, J., Kassam-Adams, N., Alderfer, M. A., Christofferson, J., & Kazak, A. E. (2015). Systematic review: A reevaluation and update of the integrative (trajectory) model of pediatric medical traumatic stress. *Journal of Pediatric Psychology, 41*, 86–97.

Priest, N., Paradies, Y., Trenerry, B., Truong, M., Karlsen, S., & Kelly, Y. (2013). A systematic review of studies examining the relationship between reported racism and health and wellbeing for children and young people. *Social Science & Medicine, 95,* 115–127.

Prinstein, M. J., & Giletta, M. (2016). Peer relations and developmental psychopathology. In D. Cicchetti (Ed.), *Developmental psychopathology: Risk, resilience, and intervention* (3rd ed., Vol. 1). Hoboken, NJ: John Wiley & Sons.

Prinstein, M. J., Boergers, J., & Vernberg, E. M. (2001). Overt and relational aggression in adolescents: Social-psychological adjustment of aggressors and victims. *Journal of Clinical Child Psychology, 30,* 479–491.

Prinstein, M. J., Youngstrom, E. A., Mash, E. J., & Barkley, R. A. (2019). *Treatment of disorders in childhood and adolescence.* New York: The Guilford Press.

Pruett, J. R., Jr., Botteron, K. N., & McKinstry, R. C. (2017). The emergence of network inefficiencies in infants with autism spectrum disorder. *Biological Psychiatry, 82,* 176–185.

Przybylski, A. K., & Weinstein, N. (2019). Digital screen time limits and young children's psychological well-being: Evidence from a population-based study. *Child Development, 90,* e56–e65.

Psihogios, A. M., Fellmeth, H., Schwartz, L. A., & Barakat, L. P. (2018). Family functioning and medical adherence across children and adolescents with chronic health conditions: A meta-analysis. *Journal of Pediatric Psychology, 44,* 84–97.

Pua, E. P. K., Bowden, S. C., & Seal, M. L. (2017). Autism spectrum disorders: Neuroimaging findings from systematic reviews. *Research in Autism Spectrum Disorders, 34,* 28–33.

Pugliese, C. E., Anthony, L., Strang, J. F., Dudley, K., Wallace, G. L., & Kenworthy, L. (2015). Increasing adaptive behavior skill deficits from childhood to adolescence in autism spectrum disorder: Role of executive function. *Journal of Autism and Developmental Disorders, 45,* 1579–1587.

Puhl, R. M., & Latner, J. D. (2007). Stigma, obesity, and the health of the nation's children. *Psychological Bulletin, 133,* 557–580.

Puhl, R. M., Peterson, J. L., & Luedicke, J. (2013). Weight-based victimization: Bullying experiences of weight loss treatment-seeking youth. *Pediatrics, 131,* e1–e9.

Pullen, P. C. (2016). Historical and current perspectives on learning disabilities in the United States. *Learning Disabilities: A Contemporary Journal, 14,* 25–37.

Pullen, P. C., Lane, H. B., Ashworth, K. E., & Lovelace, S. P. (2017). Specific learning disabilities. In J. M. Kauffman, D. P. Hallahan, & P. C. Pullen (Eds.), *Handbook of special education.* New York: Routledge.

Pungello, E. P., Kainz, K., Burchinal, M., Wasik, B. H., Sparling, J. J., Ramey, C. T., et al. (2010). Early educational intervention, early cumulative risk, and the early home environment as predictors of young adult outcomes within a high-risk sample. *Child Development, 81,* 410–426.

Purcell, K., Brady, K., Chai, H., Muser, J., Molk, L., Gordon, N., & Means, J. (1969). The effect on asthma in children of experimental separation from the family. *Psychosomatic Medicine, 31,* 144–164.

Purcell, S. M., Wray, N. R., Stone, J. L., Visscher, P. M., O'Donovan, M. C., Sullivan, P. F., & Sklar, P. (2009). Common polygenic variation contributes to risk of schizophrenia and bipolar disorder. *Nature, 460*(7256), 748–752.

Pynoos, R. S., Frederick, C., Nader, K., Arroyo, W., Steinberg, A., Eth, S., et al. (1987). Life threat and posttraumatic stress in school-age children. *Archives of General Psychiatry, 44,* 1057–1063.

Quay, H. C. (1993). The psychobiology of undersocialized aggressive conduct disorder: A theoretical perspective. *Development and Psychopathology, 5,* 165–180.

Querido, J. G., Bearss, K., & Eyberg, S. M. (2002). Theory, research, and practice of parent-child interaction therapy. In F. W. Kaslow & T. Patterson (Eds.), *Comprehensive handbook of psychotherapy: Vol. 2. Cognitive/behavioral/functional approaches.* New York: John Wiley.

Quittner, A. L., Saez-Flores, E., & Barton, J. D. (2016). The psychological burden of cystic fibrosis. *Current Opinion in Pulmonary Medicine, 22,* 187–191.

Rachamim, L., Mirochnik, I., Helpman, L., Nacasch, N., & Yadin, E. (2015). Prolonged exposure therapy for toddlers with traumas following medical procedures. *Cognitive and Behavioral Practice, 22,* 240–252.

Rachman, S. J. (1977). The conditioning theory of fear acquisition: A critical examination. *Behaviour Research and Therapy, 15,* 372–387.

Rachman, S. J. (1991). Neo-conditioning and the classic theory of fear acquisition. *Clinical Psychology Review, 11,* 155–173.

Racine, N. M., Pillai Riddell, R. R., Khan, M., Calic, M., Taddio, A., & Tablon, P. (2015). Systematic review: Predisposing, precipitating, perpetuating, and present factors predicting anticipatory distress to painful medical procedures in children. *Journal of Pediatric Psychology, 41,* 159–181.

Raine, A. (2005). The interaction of biological and social measures in the explanation of antisocial and violent behavior. In D. M. Stoff & E. J. Sussman (Eds.), *Developmental psychobiology of aggression.* New York: Cambridge University Press.

Raine, A. (2015). Low resting heart rate as an unequivocal risk factor for both the perpetration of and exposure to violence. *JAMA Psychiatry, 72,* 962–964.

Raine, A., Moffitt, T. E., Caspi, A., Loeber, R., Stouthamer-Loeber, M., & Lynam, D. (2005). Neurocognitive impairments in boys on the life-course persistent antisocial path. *Journal of Abnormal Psychology, 114,* 38–49.

Rajendran, G., & Mitchell, P. (2007). Cognitive theories of autism. *Developmental Review, 27,* 224–260.

References

Ramey, C. T., & Campbell, F. A. (1984). Preventive education for high-risk children: Cognitive consequences of the Carolina Abecedarian Project. *American Journal of Mental Deficiency, 88,* 515–523.

Ramos-Olazagasti, M. A., Castellanos, F. X., Mannuzza, S., & Klein, R. G. (2018). Predicting the adult functional outcomes of boys with ADHD 33 years later. *Journal of the American Academy of Child & Adolescent Psychiatry, 57,* 571–582.

Ramsey, M. (2010). Genetic and epigenetic insights into fetal alcohol spectrum disorders. *Genome Medicine, 2:*27. Retrieved from http://genomemedicine.com/content/2/4/27

Rancourt, D., & Boepple, L. (2017). Eating disorders. In M. C. Roberts & R. G. Steele (Eds.), *Handbook of pediatric psychology* (5th ed.). New York: The Guilford Press.

Rao, U., Hammen, C. L., & Poland, R. E. (2010). Longitudinal course of adolescent depression: Neuroendocrine and psychosocial predictors. *Journal of the American Academy of Child & Adolescent Psychiatry, 49,* 141–151.

Rapee, R. M. (2013). The preventative effects of a brief, early intervention for preschool-aged children at risk for internalising: Follow-up into middle adolescence. *Journal of Child Psychology and Psychiatry, 54,* 780–788.

Rapee, R. M., & Coplan, R. J. (2010). Conceptual relations between anxiety disorder and fearful temperament. In H. Gazelle & K. H. Rubin (Eds.), *Social anxiety in childhood: Bridging developmental and clinical perspectives.* Special issue of *New Directions for Child and Adolescent Development, 127,* 17–31.

Rapee, R. M., Kennedy, S. J., Ingram, M., Edwards, S. L., & Sweeney, L. (2010). Altering the trajectory of anxiety in at-risk young children. *American Journal of Psychiatry, 167,* 1518–1525.

Rapee, R. M., Kennedy, S., Ingram, M., Edwards, S., & Sweeney, L. (2005). Prevention and early intervention of anxiety disorders in inhibited preschool children. *Journal of Consulting and Clinical Psychology, 73,* 488–497.

Rapee, R. M., Schniering, C. A., & Hudson, J. L. (2009). Anxiety disorders during childhood and adolescence: Origins and treatment. *Annual Review of Clinical Psychology, 5,* 311–341.

Rapoff, M. A., Lindsley, C. B., & Karlson, C. W. (2017). Medical and psychosocial aspects of juvenile idiopathic arthritis. In M. C. Roberts & R. G. Steele (Eds.), *Handbook of pediatric psychology* (5th ed.). New York: The Guilford Press.

Rapoport, J. L. (1989). The biology of obsessions and compulsions. *Scientific American, 260,* 83–89.

Rapoport, J. L., & Gogtay, N. (2008). Brain neuroplasticity in healthy, hyperactive, and psychotic children: Insights from neuroimaging. *Neuropsychopharmacology, 33,* 181–197.

Rapoport, J. L., & Ismond, D. R. (1996). *DSM-IV training guide for diagnosis of childhood disorders.* New York: Brunner/Mazel.

Rapoport, J. L., Giedd, J. N., & Gogtay, N. (2012). Neurodevelopmental model of schizophrenia: Update 2012. *Molecular Psychiatry, 17,* 1228–1238.

Rapoport, J. L., Inhoff-Germain, G., Weissman, M. M., Greenwald, S., Narrow, W. E., Jensen, P. S., Lahey, B. B., & Canino, G. (2000). Childhood obsessive-compulsive disorder in the NIMH MECA study: Parent versus child identification of cases. *Journal of Anxiety Disorders, 14,* 535–548.

Rawana, J. S., Morgan, A. S., Nguyen, H., & Craig, S. G. (2010). The relation between eating- and weight-related disturbances and depression in adolescence: A review. *Clinical Child and Family Psychology Review, 13,* 213–230.

Ray, W. A., Stein, C. M., Murray, K. T., Fuchs, C., Patrick, S. W., Daugherty, J., et al. (2019). Association of antipsychotic treatment with risk of unexpected death among children and youths. *JAMA Psychiatry, 76,* 162–171.

Raymond, J. F., Bucek, A., Dolezal, C., Warne, P., Benson, S., Abrams, E. J., et al. (2017). Use of unannounced telephone pill counts to measure medication adherence among adolescents and young adults living with perinatal HIV infection. *Journal of Pediatric Psychology, 42,* 1006–1015.

Rea, P. J., McLaughlin, V. L., & Walther-Thomas, C. (2002). Outcome for students with learning disabilities in inclusive and pullout programs. *Exceptional Children, 68,* 203–222.

Reale, L., Bartoli, B., Cartabia, M., Zanetti, M., Costantino, M. A., Canevini, M. P., et al. (2017). Comorbidity prevalence and treatment outcome in children and adolescents with ADHD. *European Child & Adolescent Psychiatry, 26,* 1443–1457.

Reed-Knight, B., Mackner, L. M., & Crandall, W. V. (2017). Psychological aspects of inflammatory bowel disease in children and adolescents. In P. Mamula, A. Grossman, R. Baldassano, J. Kelsen, & J. Markowitz (Eds.), *Pediatric inflammatory bowel disease.* Cham, Switzerland: Springer.

Rees, E., O'Donovan, M. C., & Owen, M. J. (2015). Genetics of schizophrenia. *Current Opinion in Behavioral Sciences, 2,* 8–14.

Regier, D. A., Narrow, W. E., Kuhl, E. A., & Kupfer, D. J. (2009). The conceptual development of DSM-V. *American Journal of Psychiatry, 166,* 645–650.

Reich, W. (2000). Diagnostic Interview for Children and Adolescents (DICA). *Journal of the American Academy of Child and Adolescent Psychiatry, 39,* 59–66.

Reich, W., Huang, H., & Todd, R. D. (2006). ADHD medication use in a population-based sample of twins. *Journal of the Academy of Child and Adolescent Psychiatry, 45,* 801–807.

Reichenberg, A., & Harvey, P. D. (2007). Neuropsychological impairments in schizophrenia: Integration of performance-based and brain imaging findings. *Psychological Bulletin, 133,* 833–858.

Reichow, B. (2012). Overview of meta-analyses on early intensive behavioral intervention for young children with autism spectrum disorders. *Journal of Autism and Developmental Disorders, 42,* 512–520.

Reichow, B., & Wolery, M. (2009). Comprehensive synthesis of early intensive behavioral intervention for young children with autism based on the UCLA Young Autism Project Model. *Journal of Autism and Developmental Disorders, 39,* 23–41.

Reid, J. B. (Ed.) (1978). *A social learning approach to family intervention* (Vol. 2: *Observations in home settings*). Eugene, OR: Castalia.

Reid, J. B., Patterson, G. R., & Snyder, J. (Eds.) (2002). *Antisocial behavior in children and adolescents: A developmental analysis and model for intervention.* Washington, DC: American Psychological Association.

Reid, M. J., Webster-Stratton, C., & Beauchaine, T. P. (2001). Parent training in Head Start: A comparison of program response among African American, Asian American, Caucasian, and Hispanic mothers. *Prevention Science, 2,* 209–227.

Reiner, W. G. (2008). Pharmacotherapy in the management of voiding and storage disorders, including enuresis and encopresis. *Journal of the American Academy of Child and Adolescent Psychiatry, 47,* 491–498.

Reinfjell, T., & Diseth, T. H. (2018). Pre-procedure evaluation and psychological screening of children and adolescents in pediatric clinics. In A. P. S. Guerrero & P. C. Lee (Eds.), *Pediatric consultation-liaison psychiatry: A global, healthcare systems-focused and problem-based approach.* Cham, Switzerland: Springer.

Reiss, A. L., & Dant, C. C. (2003). The behavioral neurogenetics of fragile X syndrome: Analyzing gene-brain-behavior relationships in child developmental psychopathologies. *Development and Psychopathology, 15,* 927–968.

Reitan, R. M., & Wolfson, D. (1993). *The Halstead-Reitan Neuropsychological Test Battery: Theory and clinical interpretation* (2nd ed.). Tucson, AZ: Neuropsychology Press.

Reiter-Purtill, J., Ridel, S., Jordan, R., & Zeller, M. H. (2010). The benefits of reciprocal friendships for treatment-seeking obese youth. *Journal of Pediatric Psychology, 35,* 905–914.

Reitman, D., & McMahon, R. J. (2013). Constance "Connie" Hanf (1917–2002): The mentor and the model. *Cognitive and Behavioral Practice, 20,* 106–116.

Remberk, B., Hintze, B., & Rybakowski, F. (2015). Executive functioning improves after remission of psychosis and may not deteriorate at short follow-up in early-onset schizophrenia. *Neuroendocrinology Letters, 36,* 153–160.

Rende, R. D., Plomin, R., Reiss, D., & Hetherington, E. M. (1993). Genetic and environmental influences on depressive symptomatology in adolescence: Individual differences and extreme scores. *Journal of Child Psychology and Psychiatry, 34,* 1387–1398.

Rennick, J., St.-Sauveur, I., Ruddy, M., & Knox, A. (2018). Experiences of parent caregivers of children with medical complexity during pediatric intensive care unit hospitalization. *Pediatric Critical Care Medicine, 19*(6S), 12.

Renouf, A. G., & Kovacs, M. (1994). Concordance between mothers' reports and children's self-reports of depressive symptoms: A longitudinal study. *Journal of the American Academy of Child & Adolescent Psychiatry, 33,* 208–216.

Rescorla, L. (2002). Language and reading outcomes to age 9 in late-talking toddlers. *Journal of Speech, Language, and Hearing Research, 45,* 360–371.

Rescorla, L. (2009). Age 17 language and reading outcomes in late-talking toddlers: Support for a dimensional perspective on language delay. *Journal of Speech, Language, and Hearing Research, 52,* 16–30.

Rescorla, L. A., Achenbach, T. M., Ivanova, M. Y., Harder, V. S., Otten, L., Bilenberg, N., et al. (2011). International comparisons of behavioral and emotional problems in preschool children: Parents' reports from 24 societies. *Journal of Clinical Child and Adolescent Psychology, 40,* 456–467.

Rescorla, L., Achenbach, T., Ivanova, M. Y., Dumenci, L., Almqvist, D., Bilenberg, N., et al. (2007). Behavioral and emotional problems reported by parents of children ages 6 to 16 in 31 societies. *Journal of Emotional and Behavioral Disorders, 15,* 130–142.

Rettew, D. C., Swedo, S. E., Leonard, H. L., Lenane, M. C., & Rapoport, J. L. (1992). Obsessions and compulsions across time in 79 children and adolescents with obsessive compulsive disorder. *Journal of the American Academy of Child and Adolescent Psychology, 31,* 1050–1056.

Reuther, E. T., Davis, T. E., Moree, B. N., & Matson, J. L. (2011). Treating selective mutism using modular CBT for child anxiety: A case study. *Journal of Clinical Child and Adolescent Psychology, 40,* 156–163.

Revell, E. R., Neill, J. C., Harte, M., Khan, Z., & Drake, R. J. (2015). A systematic review and meta-analysis of cognitive remediation in early schizophrenia. *Schizophrenia Research, 168,* 213–222.

Reyes, M. M., Panza, K. E., Martin, A., & Bloch, M. H. (2011). Time-lag bias in trials of pediatric antidepressants: A systematic review and meta-analysis. *Journal of the American Academy of Child and Adolescent Psychiatry, 50,* 63–72.

Reynolds, C. R., & Kamphaus, R. W. (2015). *Behavior Assessment System for Children, Third Edition (BASC-3).* San Antonio, TX: Pearson.

Reynolds, C. R., & Mayfield, J. W. (2011). Neuropsychological assessment in genetically linked neurodevelopmental disorders. In S. Goldstein & C. R. Reynolds (Eds.), *Handbook of neurodevelopmental and genetic disorders in children* (2nd ed.). New York: The Guilford Press.

Reynolds, C. R., & Richmond, B. O. (2008). *Revised Children's Manifest Anxiety Scale: Second edition (RCMAS-2).* Los Angeles, CA: Western Psychological Services.

References

Reynolds, W. M. (2002). *RADS-2, Reynolds Adolescent Depression Scale: Professional manual*. Lutz, FL: Psychological Resources, Inc.

Reynolds, W. M. (1994). Assessment of depression in children and adolescents by self-report questionnaires. In W. M. Reynolds and H. F. Johnston (Eds.), *Handbook of depression in children and adolescents*. New York: Plenum Press.

Reynolds, W. M. (2010). *Reynolds Child Depression Scale-2nd Edition (RCDS-2)*. Lutz, FL: Psychological Assessment Resources.

Rhee, S. H., & Waldman, I. D. (2003). Testing alternative hypotheses regarding the role of development on genetic and environmental influences underlying antisocial behavior. In B. B. Lahey, T. E. Moffitt, & A. Caspi (Eds.), *Causes of conduct disorder and juvenile delinquency*. New York: Guilford Press.

Ribeiro, J., Franklin, J., Fox, K. R., Bentley, K., Kleiman, E. M., Chang, B., & Nock, M. K. (2016). Self-injurious thoughts and behaviors as risk factors for future suicide ideation, attempts, and death: A meta-analysis of longitudinal studies. *Psychological Medicine, 46*, 225–236.

Riccio, C. A., Maykel, C., Howell, M., & Bray, M. A. (2018). Coping with chronic illness and medical stress. In S. G. Forman & J. D. Shahidullah (Eds.), *Handbook of pediatric behavioral healthcare*. Cham, Switzerland: Springer.

Rice, F., Harold, G., & Thapar, A. (2002). The genetic aetiology of childhood depression: A review. *Journal of Child Psychology and Psychiatry, 43*, 65–79.

Richards, M. H., Larson, R., Miller, B. V., Luo, Z., Sims, B., Parrella, D. P., & McCauley, C. (2004). Risky and protective contexts and exposure to violence in urban African American young adolescents. *Journal of Clinical Child and Adolescent Psychology, 33*, 138–148.

Richler, J., Huerta, M., Bishop, S. L., & Lord, C. (2010). Developmental trajectories of restricted and repetitive behaviors and interests in children with autism spectrum disorders. *Development and Psychopathology, 22*, 55–69.

Richters, J. E., & Cicchetti, D. (1993). Mark Twain meets DSMIIIR: Conduct disorder, development, and the concept of harmful dysfunction. *Development and Psychopathology, 5*, 5–29.

Ricketts, E., Bose, D., & Piacentini, J. (2017). Obsessive-compulsive and related disorders. In T. P. Beauchaine & S. P. Hinshaw (Eds.), *Child and adolescent psychopathology* (3rd ed.). Hoboken, NJ: John Wiley & Sons Inc.

Rie, H. E. (1971). Historical perspectives of concepts of child psychopathology. In H. E. Rie (Ed.), *Perspectives in child psychopathology*. New York: Aldine-Atherton.

Rieppi, R., et al. (2002). Socioeconomic status as a moderator of ADHD treatment outcomes. *Journal of the American Academy of Child and Adolescent Psychiatry, 41*, 269–277.

Riglin, L., Collishaw, S., Richards, A., Thapar, A. K., Rice, F., Maughan, B., et al. (2018). The impact of schizophrenia and mood disorder risk alleles on emotional problems: Investigating change from childhood to middle age. *Psychological Medicine, 48*, 2153–2158.

Rigney, G., Isaacs, J., Weiss, S., Shea, S., & Corkum, P. (2019). Sleep–wake disorders. In T. H. Ollendick, S. W. Weiss, & B. A. Weiss (Eds.), *The Oxford handbook of clinical child and adolescent psychology*. New York: Oxford University Press.

Rimsza, M. E., Schackner, R. A., Bowen, K. A., & Marshall, W. (2002). Can child deaths be prevented? The Arizona Child Fatality Review Program experience. *Pediatrics, 110*, e11.

Ritterband, L. M., Thorndike, F. P., Lord, H. R., Borowitz, S. M., Walker, L. S., Ingersoll, K. S., et al. (2013). An RCT of an internet intervention for pediatric encopresis with one-year follow-up. *Clinical Practice in Pediatric Psychology, 1*, 68–80.

Roberts, C. M., Gamwell, K. L., Baudino, M. N., Perez, M. N., Delozier, A. M., Sharkey, C. M., et al. (2019). Youth and parent illness appraisals and adjustment in pediatric inflammatory bowel disease. *Journal of Developmental and Physical Disabilities, 31*, 777–790.

Roberts, G. E. (2005). *Roberts Apperception Test for Children 2*. Los Angeles, CA: Western Psychological Services.

Roberts, M. C., & Steele, R. G. (2017). *Handbook of pediatric psychology* (5th ed.). New York: The Guilford Press.

Roberts, M. C., Blossom, J. B., Evans, S. C., Amaro, C. M., & Kanine, R. M. (2017). Advancing the scientific foundation for evidence-based practice in clinical child and adolescent psychology. *Journal of Clinical Child and Adolescent Psychology, 46*, 915–928.

Roberts, M. C., Johnson, R. J., & Amaro, C. M. (2020). Pediatric consultation. In C. A. Falender & E. P. Shafranske (Eds.), *Consultation in psychology: A competency-based approach*. Washington, DC: American Psychological Association.

Roberts, R. E., Ramsay Roberts, C., & Xing, Y. (2006). Prevalence of youth-reported DSM-IV psychiatric disorders among African, European, and Mexican American adolescents. *Journal of the American Academy of Child and Adolescent Psychiatry, 45*, 1329–1337.

Roberts, R. E., Ramsey Roberts, C., & Xing, Y. (2007). Comorbidity of substance use disorders and other psychiatric disorders among adolescents: Evidence from an epidemiological survey. *Drug and Alcohol Dependence, 88S*, S4–S13.

Roberts, W., Milich, R., & Barkley, R. A. (2015). Primary symptoms, diagnostic criteria, subtyping, and prevalence of ADHD. In R. A. Barkley (Ed.), *Attention-deficit hyperactivity disorder: A handbook for diagnosis and treatment* (4th ed.). New York: The Guilford Press.

Robin, A. L., Koepke, T., & Moye, A. (1990). Multidimensional assessment of parent-adolescent relations. *Psychological Assessment, 2*, 451–459.

Robin, A. L., Siegel, P. T., & Moye, A. (1995). Family versus individual therapy for anorexia: Impact on family conflict. *International Journal of Eating Disorders, 17*, 313–322.

Robin, A. L., Siegel, P. T., Moye, A. W., Gilroy, M., Dennis, A. B., & Sikand, A. (1999). A controlled comparison of family versus individual therapy for adolescents with anorexia nervosa. *Journal of the American Academy of Child & Adolescent Psychiatry, 38,* 1482–1489.

Robins, D. L., Casagrande, K., Barton, M., Chen, C.-M. A., Dumont-Mathieu, T., & Fein, D. (2014). Validation of the modified checklist for Autism in toddlers, revised with follow-up (M-CHAT-R/F). *Pediatrics, 133,* 37–45.

Robinson, E. B., St. Pourcain, B., Anttila, V., Kosmicki, J. A., Bulik-Sullivan, B., Grove, J., et al. (2016a). Genetic risk for autism spectrum disorders and neuropsychiatric variation in the general population. *Nature Genetics, 48,* 552–555.

Robinson, E. M., Weaver, P., Chen, R., Streisand, R., & Holmes, C. S. (2016b). A model of parental distress and factors that mediate its link with parental monitoring of youth diabetes care, adherence, and glycemic control. *Health Psychology, 35,* 1373–1382.

Rodgers, R. F., Wertheim, E. H., Damiano, S. R., & Paxton, S. J. (2020). Maternal influences on body image and eating concerns among 7- and 8-year-old boys and girls: Cross-sectional and prospective relations. *International Journal of Eating Disorders, 53,* 79–84.

Rodriguez-Ayllon, M., Derks, I. P. M., van den Dries, M. A., Esteban-Cornejo, I., Labrecque, J. A., Yang-Huang, J., et al. (2020). Associations of physical activity and screen time with white matter microstructure in children from the general population. *NeuroImage, 205,* 116258.

Rogers, J. C., & De Brito, S. A. (2016). Cortical and subcortical gray matter volume in youths with conduct problems: A meta-analysis. *JAMA Psychiatry, 73,* 64–72.

Rogers, S. (1998). Empirically supported comprehensive treatments for young children with autism. *Journal of Clinical Child Psychology, 27,* 168–179.

Rogers, S. J., & Vismara, L. A. (2008). Evidence-based comprehensive treatments for early autism. *Journal of Clinical Child and Adolescent Psychology, 37,* 8–38.

Rohde, L. A., Coghill, D., Asherson, P., & Banaschewski, T. (2019). ADHD assessment across the life span. In L. A. Rohde, J. K. Buitelaar, M. Gerlach, & S. V. Faraone (Eds.), *The world federation of ADHD guide.* Porto Alegre: World Federation of ADHD.

Rohde, P. (2017). Cognitive-behavioral treatment for adolescent depression. In J. R. Weisz & A. E. Kazdin (Eds.), *Evidence-based psychotherapies for children and adolescents* (3rd ed.). New York: The Guilford Press.

Rohde, P., Lewinsohn, P. M., Klein, D. N., Seeley, J. R., & Gau, J. M. (2013). Key characteristics of major depressive disorder occurring in childhood, adolescence, emerging adulthood, and adulthood. *Clinical Psychological Science, 1,* 41–53.

Rohrig, S. N., & Puliafico, A. C. (2018). Treatment of school refusal in an adolescent with comorbid anxiety and chronic medical illness. *Evidence-Based Practice in Child and Adolescent Mental Health, 3,* 129–141.

Roid, G. H., & Barram, R. A. (2004). *Essentials of Stanford-Binet Intelligence Scales (SB5).* Hoboken, NJ: John Wiley & Sons.

Romeo, R. R., Christodoulou, J. A., Halverson, K. K., Murtagh, J., Cyr, A. B., Schimmel, C., et al. (2017). Socioeconomic status and reading disability: Neuroanatomy and plasticity in response to intervention. *Cerebral Cortex, 28,* 2297–2312.

Rommelse, N., Antshel, K., Smeets, S., Greven, C., Hoogeveen, L., Faraone, S. V., & Hartman, C. A. (2017). High intelligence and the risk of ADHD and other psychopathology. *British Journal of Psychiatry, 211,* 359–364.

Ronan, K., Kendall, P. C., & Rowe, M. (1994). Negative affectivity in children: Development and validation of a self-statement questionnaire. *Cognitive Therapy and Research, 18,* 509–528.

Ros, R., & Graziano, P. A. (2018). Social functioning in children with or at risk for attention deficit/hyperactivity disorder: A meta-analytic review. *Journal of Clinical Child & Adolescent Psychology, 47,* 213–235.

Rose, C. A., Monda-Amaya, L. E., & Espelage, D. L. (2011). Bullying perpetration and victimization in special education: A review of the literature. *Remedial and Special Education, 32,* 114–130.

Rose, V., Trembath, D., Keen, D., & Paynter, J. (2016). The proportion of minimally verbal children with autism spectrum disorder in a community-based early intervention programme. *Journal of Intellectual Disability Research, 60,* 464–477.

Rosenblum, K. L., Dayton, C. J., & Muzik, M. (2019). Infant social and emotional development: Emerging competence in a relational context. In C. H. Zeanah (Ed.), *Handbook of infant mental health* (4th ed.). New York: The Guilford Press.

Ross, A. O. (1972). The clinical child psychologist. In B. J. Wolman (Ed.), *Manual of child psychopathology.* New York: McGraw-Hill.

Ross, D. M. (1988). Aversive treatment procedures: The schoolage child's view. *Newsletter of the Society of Pediatric Psychology, 12,* 3–6.

Rosselló, J., & Bernal, G. (1999). The efficacy of cognitive-behavioral and interpersonal treatments for depression in Puerto Rican adolescents. *Journal of Consulting and Clinical Psychology, 67,* 734–745.

Rosselló, J., & Bernal, G. (2005). New developments in cognitive-behavioral and interpersonal treatments for depressed Puerto Rican adolescents. In E. D. Hibbs & P. S. Jensen (Eds.), *Psychosocial treatments for child and adolescent disorders: Empirically based strategies for clinical practice* (2nd ed.). Washington, DC: American Psychological Association.

Rosselló, J., Bernal, G., & Rivera-Medina, C. (2008). Individual and group CBT and IPT for Puerto Rican adolescents with depressive symptoms. *Cultural Diversity and Ethnic Minority Psychology, 14,* 234–245.

Roth, T. L. (2013). Epigenetic mechanisms in the development of behavior: Advances, challenges, and future promises of a new field. *Development and Psychopathology, 25*(4pt2), 1279–1291.

Roth, T. L., & Sweatt, J. D. (2011). Annual research review: Epigenetic mechanisms and environmental shaping of the brain during sensitive periods of development. *Journal of Child Psychology and Psychiatry, 52,* 398–408.

Rothenberger, A. (2009). Brain oscillations forever: Neuro-physiology in future research of child psychiatric problems. *Journal of Child Psychology and Psychiatry, 50,* 79–86.

Rowa, K., McCabe, R. E., & Antony, M. M. (2018). Specific phobia and social anxiety disorder. In J. Hunsley & E. J. Mash (Eds.), *A guide to assessments that work* (2nd ed.). New York: Oxford University Press.

Rowe, R., Simonoff, E., & Silberg, J. L. (2007). Psychopathology, temperament, and unintentional injury: Cross-sectional and longitudinal relationships. *Journal of Child Psychology and Psychiatry, 48,* 71–79.

Rozga, A., Hutman, T., Young, G. S., Rogers, S. J., Ozonoff, S., Dapretto, M., et al. (2011). Behavioral profiles of affected and unaffected siblings of children with autism: Contribution of measures of mother-infant interaction and nonverbal communication. *Journal of Autism and Developmental Disorders, 41,* 287–301.

Rubia, K., Halari, R., Smith, A. B., Mohammed, M., Scott, S., Giampietro, V., et al. (2008). Dissociated functional brain abnormalities of inhibition in boys with pure conduct disorder and in boys with pure attention deficit hyperactivity disorder. *American Journal of Psychiatry, 165,* 889–897.

Rubia, K., Smith, A. B., Halari, R., Matsukura, F., Mohammad, M., Taylor, E., et al. (2009). Disorder-specific dissociation of orbitofrontal dysfunction in boys with pure conduct disorder during reward and ventrolateral prefrontal dysfunction in boys with pure ADHD during sustained attention. *American Journal of Psychiatry, 166,* 83–94.

Rubin, K., Bukowski, W., & Parker, J. (2006). Peer interaction and social competence. In W. Damon & R. L. Lerner (Eds.), *Handbook of child psychology. Vol. 3* (6th ed.). New York: John Wiley & Sons.

Ruch, D. A., Sheftall, A. H., Schlagbaum, P., Rausch, J., Campo, J. V., & Bridge, J. A. (2019). Trends in suicide among youth aged 10 to 19 years in the United States, 1975 to 2016. *JAMA Network Open, 2,* e193886.

Rucker, J. M., Neblett, E. W., Jr., & Anyiwo, N. (2014). Racial identity, perpetrator race, racial composition of primary community, and mood responses to discrimination. *Journal of Black Psychology, 40,* 539–562.

Rudolph, K. D., Hammen, C., & Daley, S. E. (2006). Mood disorders. In D. A. Wolfe & E. J. Mash (Eds.), *Behavioral and emotional disorders in adolescents: Nature, assessment, and treatment.* New York: The Guilford Press.

Rueger, S. Y., & Malecki, C. K. (2011). Effects of stress, attributional style and perceived parental support on depressive symptoms in early adolescence: A prospective analysis. *Journal of Clinical Child and Adolescent Psychology, 40,* 347–359.

Rusby, J. C., Estes, A., & Dishion, T. (1991). *The Interpersonal Process Code (IPC).* Unpublished manuscript. Oregon Social Learning Center, Eugene.

Russell, A. E., Ford, T., Williams, R., & Russell, G. (2016). The association between socioeconomic disadvantage and attention deficit/hyperactivity disorder (ADHD): A systematic review. *Child Psychiatry & Human Development, 47,* 440–458.

Russell, A. T., Bott, L., & Sammons, C. (1989). The phenomenology of schizophrenia occurring in childhood. *Journal of the American Academy of Child and Adolescent Psychiatry, 28,* 399–407.

Russell, G., Ryder, D., Norwich, B., & Ford, T. (2015). Behavioural difficulties that co-occur with specific word reading difficulties: A UK population-based cohort study. *Dyslexia, 21,* 123–141.

Russell, S. T., & Joyner, K. (2001). Adolescent sexual orientation and suicide risk: Evidence from a national study. *American Journal of Public Health, 91,* 1276–1281.

Russell-Mayhew, S., McVey, G., Bardick, A., & Ireland, A. (2012). Mental health, wellness, and childhood overweight/obesity. *Journal of Obesity, 2012,* 1–9.

Rutherford, H. J. V., Mayes, L. C., & Potenza, M. N. (2010). Neurobiology of adolescent substance use disorders: Implications for prevention and treatment. *Child and Adolescent Psychiatric Clinics of North America, 19,* 479–492.

Rutter, M. (1989). Pathways from childhood to adult life. *Journal of Child Psychology and Psychiatry, 30,* 23–51.

Rutter, M. (2006). The promotion of resilience in the face of adversity. In A. Clarke-Stewart & J. Dunn (Eds.), *Families count: Effects on child and adolescent development.* New York: Cambridge University Press.

Rutter, M. (2011). Research review: Child psychiatric diagnosis and classification: Concept, findings, challenges, and potential. *Journal of Child Psychology and Psychiatry, 52,* 647–660.

Rutter, M., & Sroufe, L. A. (2000). Developmental psychopathology: Concepts and challenges. *Development and Psychopathology, 12,* 265–296.

Rutter, M., Caspi, A., & Moffitt, T. E. (2003). Using sex differences in psychopathology to study causal mechanisms: Unifying issues and research strategies. *Journal of Child Psychology and Psychiatry, 44,* 1092–1115.

Rutter, M., Kreppner, J., & Sonuga-Barke, E. (2009). Attachment insecurity, disinhibited attachment, and attachment disorders: Where do research findings leave the concept? *Journal of Child Psychology and Psychiatry, 50,* 529–543.

Rutter, M., LeCouteur, A., & Lord, C. (2006). Autism Diagnostic Interview, R (ADI-R). Torrance, CA: Western Psychological Services.

Rutter, M., Mawhood, L., & Howlin, P. (1992). Language delay and social development. In P. Fletcher & D. Hall (Eds.), *Specific speech and language disorders in children*. San Diego, CA: Singular Publishing Group.

Ryan, A. M., & Shin, H. (2018). Peers, academics and teachers. In W. M. Bukowski, B. Laursen, & K. H. Rubin (Eds.), *Handbook of peer interactions, relationships, and groups* (2nd ed.). New York: Guilford Press.

Ryan, C., Russell, S., Huebner, D., Diaz, R., & Sanchez, J. (2010). Family acceptance in adolescence and the health of LGBT young adults. *Journal of Child and Adolescent Psychiatric Nursing, 23,* 205–213.

Ryckaert, C., Kuntsi, J., & Asherson, P. (2018). Emotional dysregulation and ADHD. In T. Banaschewski, D. Coghill, & A. Zuddas (Eds.), *Oxford textbook of attention deficit hyperactivity disorder*. Oxford: Oxford University Press.

Ryndak, D., Ward, T., Alper, S., Storch, J. F., & Montgomery, J. W. (2010). Long-term outcomes in inclusive and self-contained settings for siblings with comparable significant disabilities. *Education and Training in Autism and Developmental Disabilities, 45,* 38–53.

Sacco, R., Gabriele, S., & Persico, A. M. (2015). Head circumference and brain size in autism spectrum disorder: A systematic review and meta-analysis. *Psychiatry Research: Neuroimaging, 234,* 239–251.

Sadeh, A., Raviv, A., & Gruber, R. (2000). Sleep patterns and sleep disruptions in school-age children. *Developmental Psychology, 36,* 291–301.

Saler, L., & Skolnick, N. (1992). Childhood parental death and depression in adulthood: Roles of surviving parent and family environment. *American Journal of Orthopsychiatry, 62,* 504–516.

Salk, R. H., Hyde, J. S., & Abramson, L. Y. (2017). Gender differences in depression in representative national samples: Meta-analyses of diagnoses and symptoms. *Psychological Bulletin, 143,* 783–822.

Sallis, J. F., & Glanz, K. (2006). The role of built environments in physical activity, eating, and obesity in childhood. *The Future of Children, 16,* 89–108.

Salvatore, J. E., Larsson Lönn, S., Sundquist, J., Lichtenstein, P., Sundquist, K., & Kendler, K. S. (2017). Alcohol use disorder and divorce: Evidence for a genetic correlation in a population-based Swedish sample. *Addiction, 112,* 586–593.

Salvy, S. J., Bowker, J. C., Nitecki, L. A., Kluczynski, M. A., Germeroth, L. J., & Roemmich, J. N. (2012). Effects of ostracism and social connection-related activities on adolescents' motivation to eat and energy intake. *Journal of Pediatric Psychology, 37,* 25–32.

Salzinger, S., Feldman, R. S., Ng-Mak, D. S., Mojica, E., & Stockhammer, T. F. (2001). The effect of physical abuse on children's social and affective status: A model of cognitive and behavioral processes explaining the association. *Development and Psychopathology, 13,* 805–825.

SAMHSA (Substance Abuse and Mental Health Services Administration). (2013). *Results from the 2012 National Survey on Drug Use and Health: Summary of National Findings*. NSDUH Series H-46, HHS Publication No. (SMA) 13–4795. Rockville, MD: Substance Abuse and Mental Health Services Administration.

Sanders, M. R., & Turner, K. M. (2017). The international dissemination of the Triple P – Positive Parenting Program. In J. R. Weisz & A. E. Kazdin (Eds.), *Evidence-based psychotherapies for children and adolescents* (3rd ed.). New York: The Guilford Press.

Sandler, I. N., Ma, Y., Tein, J. Y., Ayers, T. S., Wolchik, S., Kennedy, C., & Milsap, R. (2010). Long-term effects of the Family Bereavement Program on multiple indicators of grief in parentally bereaved children and adolescents. *Journal of Consulting and Clinical Psychology, 78,* 131–143.

Sandler, I., Gunn, H., Mazza, G., Tein, J.-Y., Wolchik, S., Kim, H., et al. (2018). Three perspectives on mental health problems of young adults and their parents at a 15-year follow-up of the family bereavement program. *Journal of Consulting and Clinical Psychology, 86,* 845–855.

Sandler, I., Wolchick, S., Mazza, G., Gunn, H., Tein, J. Y., Berkel, C., et al. (2020). Randomized effectiveness trial of the New Beginnings Program for divorced families with children and adolescents. *Journal of Clinical Child & Adolescent Psychology, 49,* 60–78.

Sandler, I., Wolchik, S. A., Cruden, G., Mahrer, N. E., Ahn, S., Brincks, A., & Brown, C. H. (2014). Overview of meta-analyses of the prevention of mental, substance abuse, and conduct problems. *Annual Review of Clinical Psychology, 10,* 243–273.

Sandomierski, M. C., Morrongiello, B. A., & Colwell, S. R. (2019). S.A.F.E.R. near water: An intervention targeting parent beliefs about children's water safety. *Journal of Pediatric Psychology, 44,* 1034–1045.

Sanislow, C. A., Pine, D. S., Quinn, K. J., Kozak, M. J., Garvey, M. A., Heinssen, R. K., et al. (2010). Developing constructs for psychopathology research: Research domain criteria. *Journal of Abnormal Psychology, 119,* 631–639.

Sannar, E. M., Palka, T., Beresford, C., Peura, C., Kaplan, D., Verdi, M., et al. (2018). Sleep problems and their relationship to

References

maladaptive behavior severity in psychiatrically hospitalized children with autism spectrum disorder (ASD). *Journal of Autism and Developmental Disorders, 48,* 3720–3726.

Sanson, A., Smart, D., Prior, M., & Oberklaid, F. (1993). Precursors of hyperactivity and aggression. *Journal of the American Academy of Child and Adolescent Psychiatry, 32,* 1207–1216.

Santostefano, S. (1978). *A biodevelopmental approach to clinical child psychology.* New York: Wiley-Interscience.

Sapienza, J. K., & Masten, A. S. (2011). Understanding and promotion resilience in children and youth. *Current Opinion in Psychiatry, 24,* 267–273.

Sargent, K. S., Jouriles, E. N., Chmielewski, M., & McDonald, R. (2020). Using virtual reality to create an observational assessment of adolescent resistance to antisocial peer pressure. *Journal of Clinical Child & Adolescent Psychology, 49,* 178–189.

Sasser, T. R., Kalvin, C. B., & Bierman, K. L. (2016). Developmental trajectories of clinically significant attention-deficit/ hyperactivity disorder (ADHD) symptoms from grade 3 through 12 in a high-risk sample: Predictors and outcomes. *Journal of Abnormal Psychology, 125,* 207–219.

Sato, A. F., Jelalian, E., Hart, C. N., Lloyd-Richardson, E. E., Mehlenbeck, R. S., Neill, M., & Wing, R. R. (2011). Associations between parent behavior and adolescent weight control. *Journal of Pediatric Psychology, 36,* 451–460.

Sattler, J. M. (2014). Broad measures of behavioral, social, and emotional functioning and of parenting and family variables. In J. M. Sattler, *Foundations of behavioral, social, and clinical assessment of children* (6th ed.). La Mesa, CA: Jerome M. Sattler Publisher.

Sattler, J. M., & Garro, A. (2014a). General interviewing techniques. In J. M. Sattler, *Foundations of behavioral, social, and clinical assessment of children* (6th ed.). La Mesa, CA: Jerome M. Sattler Publisher.

Sattler, J. M., & Garro, A. (2014b). Interviewing children, parents, teachers, and families. In J. M. Sattler, *Foundations of behavioral, social, and clinical assessment of children* (6th ed.). La Mesa, CA: Jerome M. Sattler Publisher.

Sattler, J. M., & Mrazik, M. (2014). Brain injuries: Assessment. In J. M. Sattler, *Foundations of behavioral, social, and clinical assessment of children* (6th ed.). La Mesa, CA: Jerome M. Sattler Publisher.

Sattler, J. M., & Pillai Riddell, R. (2014a). Observational methods, Part I. In J. M. Sattler, *Foundations of behavioral, social, and clinical assessment of children* (6th ed.). La Mesa, CA: Jerome M. Sattler Publisher.

Sattler, J. M., & Pillai Riddell, R. (2014b). Observational methods, Part II. In J. M. Sattler, *Foundations of behavioral, social, and clinical assessment of children* (6th ed.). La Mesa, CA: Jerome M. Sattler Publisher.

Sattler, J. M., Dumont, R., & Coalson, D. L. (2016). *Assessment of children WISC-V and WPPSI-IV.* La Mesa, CA: Jerome M. Sattler Publishers, Inc.

Sattler, J. M., Willis, J. O., Renk, K., & Kilanowski, L. A. (2014). Specific learning disabilities: Assessment and intervention. In J. M. Sattler, *Foundations of behavioral, social, and clinical assessment of children* (6th ed.). La Mesa, CA: Jerome M. Sattler Publisher.

Sauder, C. L., Beauchaine, T. P., Gatzke-Kopp, L. M., Shannon, K. E., & Aylward, E. (2012). Neuroanatomical correlates of heterotypic comorbidity in externalizing male adolescents. *Journal of Clinical Child & Adolescent Psychology, 41,* 346–352.

Savage, L.-É., Tarabulsy, G. M., Pearson, J., Collin-Vézina, D., & Gagné, L.-M. (2019). Maternal history of childhood maltreatment and later parenting behavior: A meta-analysis. *Development and Psychopathology, 31,* 9–21.

Savin-Williams, R. C., & Ream, G. L. (2003). Suicide attempts among sexual-minority male youth. *Journal of Clinical Child and Adolescent Psychology, 32,* 509–522.

Sawyer, M. G., Reece, C. E., Sawyer, A. C., Johnson, S. E., & Lawrence, D. (2018). Has the prevalence of child and adolescent mental disorders in Australia changed between 1998 and 2013 to 2014? *Journal of the American Academy of Child & Adolescent Psychiatry, 57,* 343–350.

Sayal, K., Prasad, V., Daley, D., Ford, T., & Coghill, D. (2018). ADHD in children and young people: Prevalence, care pathways, and service provision. *The Lancet Psychiatry, 5,* 175–186.

Saylor, C. F., Cowart, B. L., Lipovsky, J. A., Jackson, C., & Finch, A. J., Jr. (2003). Media exposure to September 11: Elementary school students' experiences and posttraumatic symptoms. *American Behavioral Scientist, 46,* 1622–1642.

Saylor, C. F., Powell, P., & Swenson, C. (1992). Hurricane Hugo blows down the broccoli: Preschoolers' post-disaster play and adjustment. *Child Psychiatry and Human Development, 22,* 139–149.

Scahill, L., & Rojas, J. (2019). Pediatric psychopharmacology: Commonly used medications in children. In T. H. Ollendick, S. W. White, & B. A. White (Eds.), *The Oxford handbook of clinical child and adolescent psychology.* New York: Oxford Library of Psychology.

Scahill, L., Riddle, M. A., McSwiggin-Hardin, M., Ort, S. I., King, R. A., Goodman, W. K., et al. (1997). Children's Yale-Brown Obsessive Compulsive Scale: Reliability and validity. *Journal of the American Academy of Child & Adolescent Psychiatry, 36,* 844–852.

Schaefer, C. E., & Drewes, A. A. (2011). The therapeutic power of play and play therapy. In C. E. Schaefer (Ed.), *Foundations of play therapy.* Hoboken, NJ: John Wiley & Sons.

Schalock, R. L., & Luckasson, R. (2015). A systematic approach to subgroup classification in intellectual disability. *Intellectual and Developmental Disabilities, 53,* 358–366.

Schalock, R. L., Borthwick-Duffy, S. A., Bradley, V. J., Buntinx, W. H. E., Coulter, D. L., Craig, E. M., et al. (2010). *Intellectual disability: Definition, classification, and systems of support.* Washington, DC: American Association on Intellectual and Developmental Disabilities.

Schalock, R. L., Luckasson, R., & Tassé, M. J. (2019). The contemporary view of intellectual and developmental disabilities: Implications for psychologists. *Psicothema, 31,* 223–228.

Scharf, J. M., Miller, L. L., Mathews, C. A., & Ben-Shlomo, Y. (2012). Prevalence of Tourette syndrome and chronic tics in the population-based Avon Longitudinal Study of Parents and Children cohort. *Journal of the American Academy of Child and Adolescent Psychiatry, 51,* 192–201.

Scharff, A., Breiner, C. E., Ueno, L. F., Underwood, S. B., Merritt, E. C., Welch, L. M., et al. (2020). Shifting a training clinic to teletherapy during the COVID-19 pandemic: A trainee perspective. *Counselling Psychology Quarterly,* 1–11.

Scharff, C., & Petri, J. (2011). Evo-devo, deep homology and FoxP2: Implications for the evolution of speech and language. *Philosophical Transactions of the Royal Society B: Biological Sciences, 366,* 2124–2140.

Scharfstein, L. A., Beidel, D. C., Finnell, L. R., Distier, A., & Carter, N. T. (2011). Do pharmacological and behavioral interventions differentially affect treatment outcome for children with social phobia? *Behavior Modification, 35,* 451–467.

Scheerenberger, R. C. (1983, 1987). *A history of mental retardation.* Baltimore, MD: Brookes Publishing Co.

Scheeringa, M. S., Zeanah, C. H., & Cohen, J. A. (2011). PTSD in children and adolescents: Toward an empirically based algorithma. *Depression and Anxiety, 28,* 770–782.

Schepers, S. A., Okado, Y., Russell, K., Long, A. M., & Phipps, S. (2018). Adjustment in childhood cancer survivors, healthy peers, and their parents: The mediating tole of the parent–child relationship. *Journal of Pediatric Psychology, 44,* 186–196.

Scherr, J. F., Kryszak, E. M., & Mulick, J. A. (2018). Intellectual and adaptive functioning. In S. Hupp (Ed.), *Child and adolescent psychotherapy: Components of evidence-based treatments for youth and their parents.* Cambridge: Cambridge University Press.

Schetky, D. H. (2000). Ethical issues in child and adolescent psychiatry. In B. J. Sadock & V. A. Sadock (Eds.), *Kaplan & Sadock's comprehensive textbook of psychiatry* (Vol. II). Philadelphia, PA: Lippincott Williams & Wilkins.

Schieve, L. A., Blumberg, S. J., Rice, C., Visser, S. N., & Boyle, C. (2007). The relationship between autism and parenting stress. *Pediatrics, 119*(sup1), S114–S121.

Schiff, B. (2019). *Situating qualitative methods in psychological science.* New York: Routledge.

Schippell, P. L., Vasey, M. W., Cravens-Brown, L. M., & Bretveld, R. A. (2003). Suppressed attention to rejection, ridicule, and failure cues: A unique correlate of reactive but not proactive aggression. *Journal of Clinical Child and Adolescent Psychology, 32,* 40–55.

Schlegelmilch, M., Punja, S., Jou, H., Mackie, S. A., Conway, J., Wilson, B., et al. (2019). Observational study of pediatric inpatient pain, nausea/vomiting and anxiety. *Children, 6,* 65.

Schmidt, J. D., Rooker, G. W., Fodstad, J. C., Orchowitz, P., Goetzel, A., Kurtz, P. F., & Hagopian, L. P. (2016). On the relation between adaptive functioning and the reinforcement function of challenging behavior. *International Journal of Developmental Disabilities, 62,* 174–182.

Schmitz, M., Ludwig, H., & Rohde, L. A. (2010). Do hyperactive symptoms matter in ADHD-I restricted phenotype? *Journal of Clinical Child and Adolescent Psychology, 39,* 741–748.

Schneider, H., Ryan, M., & Mahone, M. E. (2020). Parent versus teacher ratings on the BRIEF-preschool version in children with and without ADHD. *Child Neuropsychology, 26,* 113–128.

Schniering, C. A., & Rapee, R. M. (2002). Development and validation of a measure of children's automatic thoughts: The Children's Automatic Thoughts Scale. *Behaviour Research and Therapy, 40,* 1091–1109.

Schoenfelder, E. N., & Kollins, S. H. (2015). Topical review: ADHD and health-risk behaviors: Toward prevention and health promotion. *Journal of Pediatric Psychology, 41,* 735–740.

Schopler, E. (1997). Implementation of TEACCH philosophy. In D. J. Cohen & F. R. Volkmar (Eds.), *Handbook of autism and pervasive developmental disorders.* New York: John Wiley.

Schopler, E., Short, A., & Mesibov, G. (1989). Relation of behavioral treatment to "normal functioning": Comment on Lovaas. *Journal of Consulting and Clinical Psychology, 57,* 162–164.

Schopler, E., Van Bourgondien, M., Wellman, G. J., & Love, S. R. (2010). *Childhood Autism Rating Scale, Second Edition (CARS).* Los Angeles, CA: Western Psychological Services.

Schrank, F. A., Mather, N., & McGraw, K. S. (2014). *Woodcock Johnson IV Tests of Achievement.* Rolling Meadows, IL: Riverside.

Schreibman, L. (1997). Theoretical perspectives on behavioral intervention for individuals with autism. In D. J. Cohen & F. R. Volkmar (Eds.), *Handbook of autism and pervasive developmental disorders.* New York: John Wiley.

Schreibman, L. (2000). Intensive behavioral/psychoeducational treatments for autism: Research needs and future directions. *Journal of Autism and Developmental Disorders, 30,* 373–378.

Schroeder, A., Slopen, N., & Mittal, M. (2020). Accumulation, timing, and duration of early childhood adversity and behavior problems at age 9. *Journal of Clinical Child & Adolescent Psychology, 49,* 36–49.

Schroeder, C. S., & Smith-Boydston, J. M. (2017). *Assessment and treatment of childhood problems: A clinician's guide* (3rd ed.). New York: The Guilford Press.

Schulte, A. C. (2016). Prevention and response to intervention: Past, present, and future. In S. R. Jimerson, M. K. Burns, & A. M. VanDerHeyden (Eds.), *Handbook of Response to Intervention*. New York: Springer.

Schulte-Körne, G. (2001). Annotation: Genetics of reading and spelling disorder. *Journal of Child Psychology and Psychiatry, 42,* 985–997.

Schultz, D., Izard, C. E., Ackerman, B. P., & Youngstrom, E. A. (2001). Emotion knowledge in economically disadvantaged children: Self-regulatory antecedents and relations to social difficulties and withdrawal. *Development and Psychopathology, 13,* 53–67.

Schurman, J. V., Maddux, M. H., Blossom, J. B., & Friesen, C. A. (2017). Abdominal pain-related gastrointestinal disorders: Irritable bowel syndrome and inflammatory bowel disease. In M. C. Roberts & R. G. Steele (Eds.), *Handbook of pediatric psychology* (5th ed.). New York: The Guilford Press.

Schuster, M. A., Stein, B. D., Jaycox, L. H., Collins, R. L., Marshall, G. N., Elliott, M. N., et al. (2001). A national survey of stress reactions after the September 11, 2001 terrorist attacks. *New England Journal of Medicine, 345,* 1507–1512.

Schwartz, D. D., Axelrad, M. E., & Hilliard, M. E. (2015). Barriers and facilitators of adherence. In D. D. Schwartz & M. E. Axelrad (Eds.), *Healthcare partnerships for pediatric adherence.* Cham, Switzerland: Springer.

Schwartz, D., Dodge, K. A., & Coie, J. D. (1993). The emergence of chronic peer victimization in boys' play groups. *Child Development, 64,* 1755–1772.

Schwartz, D., Dodge, K. A., Coie, J. D., Hubbard, J. A., Cillessen, A. H. N., Lemerise, E. A., & Bateman, H. (1998). Social-cognitive and behavioral correlates of aggression and victimization in boys' play groups. *Journal of Abnormal Child Psychology, 26,* 431–440.

Schwartz, D., Dodge, K. A., Pettit, G. S., & Bates, J. E. (1997). The early socialization of aggressive victims of bullying. *Child Development, 68,* 665–675.

Schwartz, J. A. J., Gladstone, T. R. G., & Kaslow, N. J. (1998). Depressive disorders. In T. H. Ollendick & M. Hersen (Eds.), *Handbook of child psychopathology* (3rd ed.). New York: Plenum Press.

Schwartz, J. A. J., Kaslow, N. J., Seeley, J., & Lewinsohn, P. (2000). Psychological, cognitive, and interpersonal correlates of attributional changes in adolescents. *Journal of Clinical Child Psychology, 29,* 188–198.

Schwartz, R. G. (2017). Specific language impairment. In R. G. Schwartz (Ed.), *Handbook of child language disorders.* New York: Routledge.

Schwebel, D. C. (2019). Why "accidents" are not accidental: Using psychological science to understand and prevent unintentional child injuries. *American Psychologist, 74,* 1137–1147.

Sciberras, E., Mueller, K. L., Efron, D., Bisset, M., Anderson, V., Schilpzand, E. J., et al. (2014). Language problems in children with ADHD: A community-based study. *Pediatrics, 133,* 793–800.

Sciberras, E., Mulraney, M., Silva, D., & Coghill, D. (2017). Prenatal risk factors and the etiology of ADHD: Review of existing evidence. *Current Psychiatry Reports, 19,* 1.

Scorgie, K., & Sobsey, D. (2000). Transformational outcomes associated with parenting children who have disabilities. *Mental Retardation, 38,* 195–206.

Scorza, P., Duarte, C. S., Hipwell, A. E., Posner, J., Ortin, A., Canino, G., et al. (2019). Research review: Intergenerational transmission of disadvantage: Epigenetics and parents' childhoods as the first exposure. *Journal of Child Psychology and Psychiatry, 60,* 119–132.

Scott, K. M., de Jonge, P., Stein, D. J., & Kessler, R. C. (2018). *Mental disorders around the world: Facts and figures from the WHO World Mental Health surveys.* Cambridge: Cambridge University Press.

Scott, N., Lakin, C. K., & Larson, S. A. (2008). The 40th anniversary of deinstitutionalization in the United States: Decreasing state institutional populations, 1967–2007. *Intellectual and Developmental Disabilities, 46,* 402–405.

Scourfield, J., Rice, F., Thapar, A., Harold, G. T., Martin, N., & McGuffin, P. (2003). Depressive symptoms in children and adolescents: Changing aetiological influences with development. *Journal of Child Psychology and Psychiatry, 44,* 968–976.

Scruggs, T. E., & Mastropieri, M. A. (2002). On babies and bathwater: Addressing the problems of identification of learning disabilities. *Learning Disability Quarterly, 25,* 155–168.

Sears, R. R. (1975). *Your ancients revisited: A history of child development.* Chicago, IL: University of Chicago Press.

Seedat, S., Scott, K. M., Angermeyer, M. C., Berglund, P., Bromet, E. J., Brugha, T. S., et al. (2009). Cross-national associations between gender and mental disorders in the World Health Organization World Health Surveys. *Archives of General Psychiatry, 66,* 785–795.

Seid, M., Huang, B., Niehaus, S., Brunner, H. I., & Lovell, D. J. (2014). Determinants of health-related quality of life in children newly diagnosed with juvenile idiopathic arthritis. *Arthritis Care & Research, 66,* 263–269.

Seidman, L. J., & Nordentoft, M. (2015). New targets for prevention of schizophrenia: Is it time for interventions in the premorbid phase? *Schizophrenia Bulletin, 41,* 795–800.

Seligman, M. P., & Peterson, C. (1986). A learned helplessness perspective on childhood depression: Theory and research. In M. Rutter, C. E. Izard, & P. B. Read (Eds.), *Depression in young people: Developmental and clinical perspectives.* New York: Guilford.

Sellers, R., Warne, N., Pickles, A., Maughan, B., Thapar, A., & Collishaw, S. (2019). Cross-cohort change in adolescent outcomes for children with mental health problems. *Journal of Child Psychology and Psychiatry, 60,* 813–821.

Selten, J.-P., & Termorshuizen, F. (2017). The serological evidence for maternal influenza as risk factor for psychosis in offspring is insufficient: Critical review and meta-analysis. *Schizophrenia Research, 183,* 2–9.

Seltzer, M. M., Krauss, M. W., Shattuck, P. T., Orsmond, G., Swe, A., & Lord, C. (2003). The symptoms of autism spectrum disorders in adolescence and adulthood. *Journal of Autism and Developmental Disorders, 33,* 565–581.

Selye, H. (1956). *The stress of life.* New York: McGraw-Hill.

Semrud-Clikeman, M., Steingard, R. J., Filipek, P., Biederman, J., Bekken, K., & Renshaw, P. F. (2000). Using MRI to examine brain-behavior relationships in males with attention deficit disorder with hyperactivity. *Journal of the American Academy of Child and Adolescent Psychiatry, 39,* 477–484.

Senior, E., Fong, R., Christian, A., Markowitz, J. T., Strzok, S., Schmidt, T. I. M., et al. (2018). Impacts of type 1 diabetes on patients during the first two years: A qualitative research study. *Diabetes, 67*(sup1), 2338-PUB.

Senju, A., Southgate, V., Miura, Y., Matsui, T., Hasegawa, T., Tojo, Y., et al. (2010). Absence of spontaneous action anticipation by false belief attribution in children with autism spectrum disorder. *Development and Psychopathology, 22,* 353–360.

Serafica, F. C., & Vargas, L. A. (2006). Cultural diversity in the development of child psychopathology. In D. Cicchetti & D. J. Cohen (Eds.), *Developmental psychopathology. Vol. I. Theory and method.* Hoboken, NJ: John Wiley & Sons.

Sethi, S., Bhargava, S., & Phil, S. M. (2005). Nocturnal enuresis: A review. *Journal of Pediatric Neurology, 31,* 11–18.

Seymour, K. E., & Miller, L. (2017). ADHD and depression: The role of poor frustration tolerance. *Current Developmental Disorders Reports, 4,* 14–18.

Shadish, W. R., Cook, T. D., & Campbell, D. T. (2002). *Experimental and quasi-experimental designs for generalized causal inference.* Boston, MA: Houghton Mifflin.

Shaffer, A., Yates, T. M., & Egeland, B. R. (2009). The relation of emotional maltreatment to early adolescent competence: Developmental processes in a prospective study. *Child Abuse and Neglect, 33,* 36–44.

Shah, A., & Frith, U. (1993). Why do autistic individuals show superior performance on the block design task? *Journal of Child Psychology and Psychiatry, 34,* 1351–1364.

Shah, P. E., Browne, J., & Poehlmann-Tynan, J. (2019). Prematurity: Identifying risks and promoting resilience. In C. H. Zeanah (Ed.), *Handbook of infant mental health* (4th ed.). New York: The Guilford Press.

Shakoor, S., Jaffee, S. R., Andreou, P., Bowes, L., Amber, A. P., Caspi, A., et al. (2011). Mothers and children as informants of bullying victimization: Results from an epidemiological cohort of children. *Journal of Abnormal Child Psychology, 39,* 379–387.

Shalev, R. S. (2007). Prevalence of developmental dyscalculia. In D. B. Berch & M. M. M. Mazzocco (Eds.), *Why is math so hard for some children? The nature and origins of mathematical learning difficulties and disabilities.* Baltimore, MD: Paul H Brookes Publishing.

Shalev, R. S., Manor, O., & Gross-Tsur, V. (2005). Developmental dyscalculia: A prospective six-year follow-up. *Developmental Medicine & Child Neurology, 47,* 121–125.

Shalev, R. S., Manor, O., Kerem, B., Ayali, M., Badichi, N., Friedlander, Y., et al. (2001). Developmental dyscalculia is a familial learning disability. *Journal of Learning Disabilities, 34,* 59–65.

Shanahan, L., Copeland, W., Costello, E. J., & Angold, A. (2008). Specificity of putative psychosocial risk factors for psychiatric disorders in children and adolescents. *Journal of Child Psychology and Psychiatry, 49,* 34–42.

Shankar, M., Fagnano, M., Blaakman, S. W., Rhee, H., & Halterman, J. S. (2019). Depressive symptoms among urban adolescents with asthma: A focus for providers. *Academic Pediatrics, 19,* 608–614.

Shapiro, S., Newcomb, M., & Loeb, T. B. (1997). Fear of fat, disregulated-restrained eating, and body-esteem: Prevalence and gender differences among eight- to ten-year-old children. *Journal of Clinical Psychology, 26,* 358–365.

Sharma, A., & McClellan, J. (2019). Early-onset schizophrenia. In M. J. Prinstein, E. A. Youngstrom, E. J. Mash, & R. A. Barkley (Eds.), *Treatment of disorders in childhood and adolescence.* New York: The Guilford Press.

Sharma, A. N., Arango, C., Coghill, D., Gringras, P., Nutt, D. J., et al. (2016). BAP position statement: Off-label prescribing of psychotropic medications for children and adolescents. *Journal of Pharmacology, 30,* 416–421.

Sharp, W. G., Jaquess, D. L., Morton, J. F., & Herzinger, C. V. (2010). Pediatric feeding disorders: A quantitative synthesis of treatment outcomes. *Clinical Child and Family Review, 13,* 348–365.

Shattuck, P. T., Seltzer, M. M., Greenberg, J. S., Orsmond, G. I., Bolt, D., Kring, S., et al. (2007). Change in autism symptoms and maladaptive behaviors in adolescents and adults with an autism spectrum disorder. *Journal of Autism and Developmental Disorders, 37,* 1735–1747.

Shaw, D. S., Dishion, T. J., Supplee, L., Gardner, F., & Arnds, K. (2006). Randomized trial of a family-centered approach to the prevention of early conduct problems: 2-year effects of the family check-up in early childhood. *Journal of Consulting and Clinical Psychology, 74,* 1–9.

Shaw, D. S., Lacourse, E., & Nagin, D. S. (2005). Developmental trajectories of conduct problems and hyperactivity from ages 2 to 10. *Journal of Child Psychology and Psychiatry, 46,* 932–942.

Shaw, P., & Polanczyk, G. V. (2017). Combining epidemiological and neurobiological perspectives to characterize the lifetime trajectories of ADHD. *European Child & Adolescent Psychiatry, 26,* 139–141.

Shaw, P., & Szekely, E. (2018). Insights from neuroanatomical imaging into ADHD throughout the lifespan. In T. Banaschewski, D. Coghill, & A. Zuddas (Eds.), *Oxford textbook of attention deficit hyperactivity disorder.* Oxford: Oxford University Press.

Shaw, P., Eckstrand, K., Sharp, W., Blumenthal, J., Lerch, J. P., Greenstein, D., et al. (2007). Attention-deficit/hyperactivity disorder is characterized by a delay in cortical maturation. *Proceedings of the National Academy of Sciences, 104,* 19649–19654.

Shaw, P., Gilliam, M., Liverpool, M., Weddle, C., Malek, M., Sharp, W., et al. (2011). Cortical development in typically developing children with symptoms of hyperactivity and impulsivity: Support for a dimensional view of attention deficit hyperactivity disorder. *American Journal of Psychiatry, 168,* 143–151.

Shaw, R. J., & DeMaso, D. R. (2020). *Clinical manual of pediatric consultation-liaison psychiatry: Mental health consultation with physically ill children and adolescents.* Washington, DC: American Psychiatric Association Publishing.

Shaywitz, B. A., Shaywitz, S. E., Blachman, B. A., Pugh, K. R., Fulbright, R. K., Skudlarski, P., et al. (2004). Development of left occipitotemporal systems for skilled reading in children after a phonologically-based intervention. *Biological Psychiatry, 55,* 926–933.

Shaywitz, S. (2003). *Overcoming dyslexia.* New York: Knopf.

Shaywitz, S., & Shaywitz, J. (2020). *Overcoming dyslexia* (2nd ed.). New York: Knopf.

Shaywitz, S. E., & Shaywitz, B. A. (2003). Neurobiological indices of dyslexia. In H. L. Swanson, K. R. Harris, & S. Graham (Eds.), *Handbook of learning disabilities.* New York: The Guilford Press.

Shaywitz, S. E., Fletcher, J. M., & Shaywitz, B. A. (1996). A conceptual model and definition of dyslexia: Findings emerging from the Connecticut Longitudinal Study. In J. H.

Beitchman, N. J. Cohen, M. M. Konstantareas, & R. Tannock (Eds.), *Language, learning, and behavior disorders.* New York: Cambridge University Press.

Shedler, J. (2010). The efficacy of psychodynamic psychotherapy. *American Psychologist, 65,* 98–109.

Sheffield, J. K., Spence, S. H., Rapee, R. M., Kowalenko, N., Wignall, A., Davis, A., et al. (2006). Evaluation of universal, indicated, and combined cognitive-behavioral approaches to the prevention of depression among adolescents. *Journal of Consulting and Clinical Psychology, 74,* 66–79.

Shepard, J. A., & Cox, D. J. (2017). Elimination disorders: Enuresis and encopresis. In M. C. Roberts & R. G. Steele (Eds.), *Handbook of pediatric psychology* (5th ed.). New York: The Guilford Press.

Shepard, J. A., Poler, J. E., & Grabman, J. H. (2017). Evidence-based psychosocial treatments for pediatric elimination disorders. *Journal of Clinical Child & Adolescent Psychology, 46,* 767–797.

Sheppard, S. C., Malatras, J. W., & Israel, A. C. (2010). The impact of deployment on U.S. military families. *American Psychologist, 65,* 599–609.

Sherman, S. L., & Hunter, J. E. (2017). Epidemiology of fragile X syndrome. In R. Willemsen & F. Kooy (Eds.), *Fragile X syndrome: From genetics to targeted treatment.* London: Academic Press.

Shirk, S. R., Stiles, A. A., & Leonard, S. (2018). Psychological treatment of adolescents. In J. N. Butcher & P. C. Kendall (Eds.), *APA handbook of psychopathology: Child and adolescent psychopathology* (Vol. 2). Washington, DC: American Psychological Association.

Shukla, D. K., Keehn, B., & Müller, R.-A. (2011). Tract-specific analyses of diffusion tensor imaging show widespread white matter compromise in autism spectrum disorder. *Journal of Child Psychology and Psychiatry, 52,* 286–295.

Shulha, H. P., Cheung, I., Whittle, C., Wang, J., Virgil, D., Lin, C. L., et al. (2012). Epigenetic signatures of autism: Trimethylated H3K4 landscapes in prefrontal neurons. *Archives of General Psychiatry, 69,* 314–324.

Shumaker, D. M., Deutsch, R. M., & Brenninkmeyer, L. (2009). How do I connect? Attachment issues in adolescence. *Journal of Child Custody, 6,* 91–112.

Sibley, M. H., Kuriyan, A. B., Evans, S. W., Waxmonsky, J. G., & Smith, B. H. (2014). Pharmacological and psychosocial treatments for adolescents with ADHD: An updated systematic review of the literature. *Clinical Psychology Review, 34,* 218–232.

Siegel, L. J., & Conte, P. (2001). Hospitalization and medical care of children. In C. E. Walker & M. C. Roberts (Eds.), *Handbook of clinical child psychology* (3rd ed.). New York: John Wiley & Sons, Inc.

Siegler, R. S. (1992). The other Alfred Binet. *Developmental Psychology, 28,* 179–190.

Sigman, M. (1998). Change and continuity in the development of children with autism. *Journal of Child Psychology and Psychiatry, 39,* 817–828.

Sigurdson, J. F., Undheim, A. M., Wallander, J. L., Lydersen, S., & Sund, A. M. (2018). The longitudinal association of being bullied and gender with suicide ideations, self-harm, and suicide attempts from adolescence to young adulthood: A cohort study. *Suicide and Life-Threatening Behavior, 48,* 169–182.

Silberg, J., Moore, A. A., & Rutter, M. (2015). Age of onset and the subclassification of conduct/dissocial disorder. *Journal of Child Psychology and Psychiatry, 56,* 826–833.

Silenzio, V. M., Pena, J. B., Duberstein, P. R., Cerel, J., & Know, K. L. (2007). Sexual orientation and risk factors for suicidal ideation and suicide attempts among adolescents and young adults. *American Journal of Public Health, 97,* 2017–2019.

Silk, J. S., Nath, S. R., Siegel, L. R., & Kendall, P. (2000). Conceptualizing mental disorders in children: Where have we been going and where are we going? *Development and Psychopathology, 12,* 713–735.

Silva, K., & Miller, V. A. (2019). The role of cognitive and psychosocial maturity in type 1 diabetes management. *Journal of Adolescent Health, 64,* 622–630.

Silverman, A. H., & Tarbell, S. E. (2017). Feeding and vomiting problems in pediatric populations. In M. C. Roberts & R. G. Steele (Eds.), *Handbook of pediatric psychology* (5th ed.). New York: The Guilford Press.

Silverman, W. K., & Ginsburg, G. S. (1998). Anxiety disorders. In T. H. Ollendick & M. Hersen (Eds.), *Handbook of child psychopathology* (3rd ed.). New York: Plenum.

Silverman, W. K., & Kurtines, W. M. (2005). Progress in developing an exposure-based transfer-of-control approach to treating internalizing disorders in youth. In E. D. Hibbs & P. S. Jensen (Eds.), *Psychosocial treatments for child and adolescent disorders: Empirically based strategies for clinical practice* (2nd ed.). Washington, DC: American Psychological Association.

Silverman, W. K., & Mayes, L. C. (2018). Introduction to the Special Section: Applications/implications of the National Institute of Mental Health Research Domain Criteria for conceptualizing, assessing, and treating mental disorders in youth. *Clinical Psychology Review, 64,* 39–40.

Silverman, W. K., & Moreno, J. (2005). Specific phobia. *Child and Adolescent Psychiatric Clinics of North America, 14,* 819–843.

Silverman, W. K., & Ollendick, T. H. (2005). Evidence-based assessment of anxiety and its disorders in children and adolescents. *Journal of Clinical Child and Adolescent Psychology, 34,* 380–411.

Silverman, W. K., La Greca, A. M., & Wasserstein, S. (1995). What do children worry about? Worries and their relation to anxiety. *Child Development, 66,* 671–686.

Simeone, J. C., Ward, A. J., Rotella, P., Collins, J., & Windisch, R. (2015). An evaluation of variation in published estimates of schizophrenia prevalence from 1990–2013: A systematic literature review. *BMC Psychiatry, 15,* 193.

Simonoff, E. (2015). Intellectual disability. In A. Thapar, D. S. Pine, J. F. Leckman, S. Scott, M. J. Snowling, & E. Taylor (Eds.), *Rutter's child and adolescent psychiatry.* Chichester, UK: John Wiley & Sons.

Simonoff, E., Pickles, A., Charman, T., Chandler, S., Loucas, T., & Baird, G. (2008). Psychiatric disorders in children with autism spectrum disorders: Prevalence, comorbidity, and associated factors in a population-derived sample. *Journal of the American Academy of Child & Adolescent Psychiatry, 47,* 921–929.

Simos, P. G., Fletcher, J. M., Bergman, E., Breier, J. I., Foorman, B. R., Castillo, E. M., et al. (2002). Dyslexia-specific brain activation profile becomes normal following successful remedial training. *Neurology, 58,* 1203–1213.

Simos, P. G., Fletcher, J. M., Sarkari, S., Billingsley-Marshall, R., Denton, C. A., & Papanicolaou, A. C. (2007). Intensive instruction affects brain magnetic activity associated with oral word reading in children with reading disabilities. *Journal of Learning Disabilities, 40,* 37–48.

Simpson, N., Mizen, L., & Cooper, S.-A. (2016). Intellectual disabilities. *Medicine, 44,* 679–682.

Siperstein, G. N., Pociask, S. E., & Collins, M. A. (2010). Sticks, stones, and stigma: A study of students' use of the derogatory term "retard." *Intellectual and Developmental Disabilities, 48,* 126–134.

Skinner, A. C., Payne, K., Perrin, A. J., Panter, A. T., Howard, J. B., Bardone-Cone, A., et al. (2017). Implicit weight bias in children age 9 to 11 years. *Pediatrics, 140,* e20163936.

Skinner, B. F. (1948). *Walden two.* London: Macmillan.

Skinner, B. F. (1953). *Science and human behavior.* New York: Macmillan.

Skinner, B. F. (1968). *The technology of teaching.* New York: Appleton-Century-Crofts.

Slade, A., & Sadler, L. S. (2019). Pregnancy and infant mental health. In C. H. Zeanah (Ed.), *Handbook of infant mental health* (4th ed.). New York: The Guilford Press.

Slade, E., Keeney, E., Mavranezouli, I., Dias, S., Fou, L., Stockton, S., et al. (2018). Treatments for bulimia nervosa: A network meta-analysis. *Psychological Medicine, 48,* 2629–2636.

Slifer, K. J. (2014). *A clinician's guide to helping children cope and cooperate with medical care: An applied behavioral approach.* Baltimore, MD: The Johns Hopkins University Press.

Slifer, K. J., Hankinson, J. C., Zettler, M. A., Frutchey, R. A., Hendricks, M. C., Ward, C. M., & Reesman, J. (2011). Distraction, exposure therapy, counterconditioning, and topical anesthetic for acute pain management during needle

References

sticks in children with intellectual and developmental disabilities. *Clinical Pediatrics, 50,* 688–697.

Slopen, N., Fitzmaurice, G., Williams, D. R., & Gilman, S. E. (2010). Poverty, food insecurity, and the behavior for childhood internalizing and externalizing disorders. *Journal of the American Academy of Child & Adolescent Psychiatry, 49,* 444–452.

Slusarek, M., Velling, S., Bunk, D., & Eggers, C. (2001). Motivational effects on inhibitory control in children with ADHD. *Journal of the American Academy of Child and Adolescent Psychiatry, 40,* 355–363.

Smit, K., Voogt, C., Hiemstra, M., Kleinjan, M., Otten, R., & Kuntsche, E. (2018). Development of alcohol expectancies and early alcohol use in children and adolescents: A systematic review. *Clinical Psychology Review, 60,* 136–146.

Smith Lee, S. (2009). *Overview of the Federal Higher Education Opportunity Act Reauthorization.* Think College Insight Brief, Issue No. 1. Boston, MA: Institute for Community Inclusion, University of Massachusetts Boston.

Smith, E. P., Faulk, M., & Sizer, M. A. (2016). Exploring the meso-system: The roles of community, family, and peers in adolescent delinquency and positive youth development. *Youth & Society, 48,* 318–343.

Smith, G. T., & Goldman, M. S. (1994). Alcohol expectancy theory and the identification of high-risk adolescents. *Journal of Research on Adolescence, 4,* 229–248.

Smith, G. T., Goldman, M. S., Greenbaum, P. E., & Christiansen, B. A. (1995). Expectancy for social facilitation from drinking: The divergent paths of high-expectancy and low-expectancy adolescents. *Journal of Abnormal Psychology, 104,* 32–40.

Smith, G. T., Simmons, J. R., Flory, K., Annus, A. M., & Hill, K. K. (2007). Thinness and eating expectancies predict subsequent binge-eating and purging behavior among adolescent girls. *Journal of Abnormal Psychology, 116,* 188–197.

Smith, I. M., Koegel, R. L., Koegel, L. K., Openden, D. A., Fossum, K. L., & Bryson, S, E. (2010). Effectiveness of a novel community-based intervention model for children with autistic spectrum disorder. *American Journal on Intellectual and Developmental Disabilities, 115,* 504–523.

Smith, S. D., Pennington, B. F., Boada, R., & Shriberg, L. D. (2005). Linkage of speech sound to reading disability loci. *Journal of Child Psychology and Psychiatry, 46,* 1057–1066.

Smith, T. (1999, Spring). Outcome of early intervention for children with autism. *Clinical Psychology: Science and Practice, 6,* 33–49.

Smith, T. (2010). Early and intensive behavioral intervention in autism. In R. J. Weisz & A. E. Kazdin (Eds.), *Evidence-based psychotherapies for children and adolescents.* New York: Guilford Press.

Smith, T., Eikeseth, S., & Larsson, E. V. (2018). UCLA young autism project. In E. Braaten (Ed.), *The SAGE encyclopedia of intellectual and developmental disorders.* Thousand Oaks, CA: SAGE Publications, Inc.

Smolak, L., Murnen, S. K., & Ruble, A. E. (2000). Female athletes and eating problems: A meta-analysis. *International Journal of Eating Disorders, 27,* 371–380.

Smoller, J. W., Gardner-Schuster, E., & Misiaszek, M. (2008). Genetics of anxiety: Would the genome recognize the DSM? *Depression and Anxiety, 25,* 368–377.

Smuts, A. B. (2006). *Science in the service of children, 1893–1935.* New Haven, CT: Yale University Press.

Snedker, K. A., & Herting, J. R. (2016). Adolescent mental health: Neighborhood stress and emotional distress. *Youth & Society, 48,* 695–719.

Snow, P., & Douglas, J. (2017). Psychosocial aspects of pragmatic disorders. In L. Cummings (Ed.), *Research in clinical pragmatics.* New York: Springer.

Snowling, M. J. (1991). Developmental reading disorders. *Journal of Child Psychology and Psychiatry, 32,* 49–77.

Snowling, M. J. (2000). Language and literacy skills: Who is at risk and why? In D. V. M. Bishop & L. B. Leonard (Eds.), *Speech and language impairments in children: Causes, characteristics, intervention and outcome.* Philadelphia, PA: Taylor & Francis.

Snowling, M. J. (2013). Early identification and interventions for dyslexia: A contemporary view. *Journal of Research in Special Educational Needs, 13,* 7–14.

Snowling, M. J. (2019). *Dyslexia: A very short introduction.* Oxford: Oxford University Press.

Snowling, M. J., & Hulme, C. (2015). Disorders of reading, mathematical and motor development. In A. Thapar, D. S. Pine, J. F. Leckman, S. Scott, M. J. Snowling, & E. Taylor (Eds.), *Rutter's child and adolescent psychiatry* (6th ed.). Chichester, UK: John Wiley & Sons.

Snowling, M. J., Bishop, D. V. M., Stothard, S. E., Chipchase, B., & Kaplan, C. (2006). Psychosocial outcomes at 15 years of children with a preschool history of speech-language impairment. *Journal of Child Psychology and Psychiatry, 47,* 759–765.

Snowling, M. J., Duff, F. J., Nash, H. M., & Hulme, C. (2016). Language profiles and literacy outcomes of children with resolving, emerging, or persisting language impairments. *Journal of Child Psychology and Psychiatry, 57,* 1360–1369.

Snowling, M. J., Muter, V., & Carroll, J. (2007). Children at family risk of dyslexia: A follow-up in early adolescence. *Journal of Child Psychology and Psychiatry, 48,* 609–618.

Snyder, J. (2002). Reinforcement and coercion mechanisms in the development of antisocial behavior: Peer relationships. In J. B. Reid, G. R. Patterson, & J. Snyder (Eds.), *Antisocial behavior in children and adolescents: A developmental analysis and model for intervention.* Washington, DC: American Psychological Association.

Soares, N., Evans, T., & Patel, D. R. (2018). Specific learning disability in mathematics: A comprehensive review. *Translational Pediatrics, 7,* 48–62.

Sointu, E. T., Savolainen, H., Lappalainen, K., & Lambert, M. C. (2017). Longitudinal associations of student–teacher relationships and behavioural and emotional strengths on academic achievement. *Educational Psychology, 37,* 457–467.

Sokolowski, K. L., & Israel, A. C. (2008). Perceived anxiety control as a mediator of the relationship between family stability and adjustment. *Journal of Anxiety Disorders, 22,* 1454–1461.

Sonuga-Barke, E. J. S. (1994). On dysfunction and function in psychological theories of childhood disorder. *Journal of Child Psychology and Psychiatry, 35,* 801–815.

Sonuga-Barke, E. J. S. (2020). Editorial: "People get ready": Are mental disorder diagnostics ripe for a Kuhnian revolution? *Journal of Child Psychology and Psychiatry, 61,* 1–3.

Sonuga-Barke, E. J. S., Dalen, L., & Remington, B. (2003). Do executive deficits and delay aversion make independent contributions to preschool attention-deficit/hyperactivity disorder? *Journal of the American Academy of Child and Adolescent Psychiatry, 42,* 1335–1342.

Sonuga-Barke, E. J. S., De Houwer, J., De Ruiter, K., Ajzenstzen, M., & Hollands, S. (2004). AD/HD and the capture of attention by briefly exposed delay-related cues: Evidence from a conditioning paradigm. *Journal of Child Psychology and Psychiatry, 45,* 274–283.

Sonuga-Barke, E. J., Sergeant, J. A., Nigg, J., & Willcutt, E. (2008). Executive dysfunction and delay aversion in attention deficit hyperactivity disorder: Nosologic and diagnostic implications. *Child and Adolescent Psychiatric Clinics of North America, 17,* 367–384.

Sonuga-Barke, E., Bitsakou, P., & Thompson, M. (2010). Beyond the dual pathway model: Evidence for the dissociation of timing, inhibitory, and delay-related impairments in attention-deficit/hyperactivity disorder. *American Journal of the Academy of Child and Adolescent Psychiatry, 49,* 345–355.

Sorensen, L. C., Dodge, K. A., & the Conduct Problems Prevention Research Group (2016). How does the fast track intervention prevent adverse outcomes in young adulthood? *Child Development, 87,* 429–445.

Sotelo-Dynega, M., Flanagan, D. P., & Alfonso, V. C. (2018). Overview of specific learning disabilities. In V. C. Alfonso & D. P. Flanagan (Eds.), *Essentials of specific learning disability identification* (2nd ed.). Hoboken, NJ: John Wiley & Sons, Inc.

Southam-Gerow, M., & Prinstein, M. (2014). Evidence base updates: The evolution of the evaluation of psychological treatments for children and adolescents. *Journal of Clinical Child and Adolescent Psychology, 43,* 1–6.

Spaniardi, A. M., Greenhill, L. L., & Hechtman, L. I. (2017). Attention-deficit/hyperactivity disorder. In B. J. Sadock, V. A. Sadock, & P. Ruiz (Eds.), *Kaplan & Sadock's comprehensive textbook of psychiatry* (10th ed.). Philadelphia, PA: Wolters Kluwer.

Sparrow, S. S., Cicchetti, D. V., & Saulnier, C. A. (2016). *Vineland Adaptive Behavior Scales—Third Edition (Vineland-3).* Minneapolis, MN: Pearson Assessments.

Spence, S. H., & Shortt, A. L. (2007). Research review: Can we justify the widespread dissemination of universal, school-based interventions for the prevention of depression among children and adolescents? *Journal of Child Psychology and Psychiatry, 48,* 526–542.

Spence, S. H., Sheffield, J., & Donovan, C. L. (2003). Preventing adolescent depression: An evaluation of the problem solving for life program. *Journal of Consulting and Clinical Psychology, 71,* 3–13.

Spence, S. H., Sheffield, J., & Donovan, C. L. (2005). Long-term outcome of a school-based universal approach to prevention of depression in adolescents. *Journal of Consulting and Clinical Psychology, 73,* 160–167.

Spielberger, C. D. (1973). *Manual for the state-trait anxiety inventory for children.* Lutz, FL: Psychological Assessment Resources, Inc.

Spilt, J. L., Leflot, G., Onghena, P., & Colpin, H. (2016). Use of praise and reprimands as critical ingredients of teacher behavior management: Effects on children's development in the context of a teacher-mediated classroom intervention. *Prevention Science, 17,* 732–742.

Spitz, R. A. (1946). Anaclitic depression. In *The psychoanalytic study of the child* (Vol. 2). New York: International Universities Press.

Spock, B. M., & Rothenberg, M. (1992). *Dr. Spock's baby and child care.* New York: Pocket Books.

Spring, B., Chiodo, J., & Bowen, D. J. (1987). Carbohydrates, tryptophan, and behavior: A methodological review. *Psychological Bulletin, 102,* 234–256.

Springer, K. W., Sheridan, J., Kuo, D., & Carnes, M. (2007). Longterm physical and mental health consequences of childhood physical abuse: Results from a large population-based sample of men and women. *Child Abuse & Neglect, 31,* 517–530.

Squeglia, L. M., Ball, T. M., Jacobus, J., Brumback, T., McKenna, B. S., Nguyen-Louie, T. T., et al. (2017). Neural predictors of initiating alcohol use during adolescence. *American Journal of Psychiatry, 174,* 172–185.

Sroufe, L. A. (1997). Psychopathology as an outcome of development. *Development and Psychopathology, 9,* 251–268.

Sroufe, L. A. (2009). The concept of development in developmental psychopathology. *Child Development Perspectives, 3,* 178–183.

Sroufe, L. A., Coffino, B., & Carlson, E. A. (2010). Conceptualizing the role of early experience: Lessons from the Minnesota Longitudinal Study. *Developmental Review, 30,* 36–51.

References

Sroufe, L. A., Egeland, B., Carlson, E. A., & Collins, W. A. (2005). *The development of the person.* New York: The Guilford Press.

St. Clair, M. C., Croudace, T., Dunn, V. J., Jones, P. B., Herbert, J., & Goodyer, I. M. (2015). Childhood adversity subtypes and depressive symptoms in early and late adolescence. *Development and Psychopathology, 27,* 885–899.

St. Pourcain, B., Robinson, E. B., Anttila, V., Sullivan, B. B., Maller, J., Golding, J., et al. (2018). ASD and schizophrenia show distinct developmental profiles in common genetic overlap with population-based social communication difficulties. *Molecular Psychiatry, 23,* 263–270.

Stafford, M. R., Mayo-Wilson, E., Loucas, C. E., James, A., Hollis, C., Birchwood, M., & Kendall, T. (2015). Efficacy and safety of pharmacological and psychological interventions for the treatment of psychosis and schizophrenia in children, adolescents and young adults: A systematic review and meta-analysis. *PLoS One, 10,* e0117166.

Standart, S., & Le Couteur, A. (2003). The quiet child: A literature review of selective mutism. *Child and Adolescent Mental Health, 8,* 154–160.

Stanger, C., Achenbach, T. M., & Verhulst, F. C. (1997). Accelerated longitudinal comparisons of aggressive versus delinquent syndromes. *Development and Psychopathology, 9,* 43–58.

Stapinski, L. A., Araya, R., Heron, J., Montgomery, A. A., & Stallard, P. (2015). Peer victimization during adolescence: Concurrent and prospective impact on symptoms of depression and anxiety. *Anxiety, Stress, & Coping, 28,* 105–120.

Stark, K. D., Reynolds, W. M., & Kaslow, N. J. (1987). A comparison of the relative efficacy of self-control therapy and a behavioral problem-solving therapy for depression in children. *Journal of Abnormal Child Psychology, 15,* 91–113.

Stark, K. D., Rouse, L., & Livingston, R. (1991). Treatment of depression during childhood and adolescence: Cognitive behavioral procedures for the individual and family. In P. Kendall (Ed.), *Child and adolescent therapy.* New York: The Guilford Press.

Stark, K. D., Schmidt, K. L., & Joiner, T. E. (1996). Cognitive triad: Relationship to depressive symptoms, parents' cognitive triad, and perceived parental messages. *Journal of Abnormal Child Psychology, 24,* 615–631.

Stark, K. D., Streusand, W., Krumholz, L. S., & Patel, P. (2010). Cognitive-behavioral therapy for depression. The ACTION Treatment Program for Girls. In J. R. Weisz & A. E. Kazdin (Eds.), *Evidence-based psychotherapies for children and adolescents* (2nd ed.). New York: The Guilford Press.

Starr, L. R., Hammen, C., Conway, C. C., Raposa, E., & Brennan, P. A. (2014). Sensitizing effect of early adversity on depressive reactions to later proximal stress: Moderation by polymorphisms in serotonin transporter and corticotropin releasing hormone receptor genes in a 20-year longitudinal study. *Development and Psychopathology, 26,* 1241–1254.

Staub, D., & Peck, C. A. (January 1994/December 1995). What are the outcomes for nondisabled students? *Educational Leadership, 52,* 36–40.

Steffenburg, S., Gillberg, C., Hellgren, L., Andersson, L., Gillberg, I. C., Jakobsson, G., & Bohman, M. (1989). A twin study of autism in Denmark, Finland, Iceland, Norway and Sweden. *Journal of Child Psychology and Psychiatry, 30,* 405–416.

Steinberg, L. (2007). Risk taking in adolescence. *Current Directions in Psychological Science, 16,* 55–59.

Steinberg, L. (2009). Should the science of adolescent brain development inform public policy? *American Psychologist, 64,* 739–750.

Steinberg, L., Lamborn, S. D., Darling, N., Mounts, N. S., & Dornbusch, S. M. (1994). Over-time changes in adjustment and competence among adolescents from authoritative, authoritarian, indulgent, and neglectful families. *Child Development, 65,* 754–770.

Steinhausen, H. C. (1997). Outcome of anorexia nervosa in the younger patient. *Journal of Child Psychology and Psychiatry, 38,* 271–276.

Steinhausen, H. C. (2002). The outcome of anorexia nervosa in the 20th century. *American Journal of Psychiatry, 159,* 1284–1293.

Steinhausen, H. C., & Weber, S. (2009). The outcome of bulimia nervosa: Findings from one-quarter century of research. *American Journal of Psychiatry, 166,* 1331–1341.

Steinhausen, H.-C., Mohr Jensen, C., & Lauritsen, M. B. (2016). A systematic review and meta-analysis of the long-term overall outcome of autism spectrum disorders in adolescence and adulthood. *Acta Psychiatrica Scandinavica, 133,* 445–452.

Sterba, S. K., Prinstein, M. J., & Cox, M. J. (2007). Trajectories of internalizing problems across childhood: Heterogeneity, external validity, and gender differences. *Development and Psychopathology, 19,* 345–366.

Stern, M., Mazzeo, S. E., Gerke, C. K., Porter, J. S., Bean, M. K., & Laver, J. H. (2007). Gender, ethnicity, psychological factors, and quality of life among severely overweight, treatment-seeking adolescents. *Journal of Pediatric Psychology, 32,* 90–94.

Sternberg, R. J. (2019). Early history of theory and research on intelligence. In R. J. Sternberg (Ed.), *Human intelligence: An introduction.* Cambridge: Cambridge University Press.

Sterrett, K., Shire, S., & Kasari, C. (2017). Peer relationships among children with ASD: Interventions targeting social acceptance, friendships, and peer networks. In M. H. Fisher (Ed.), *International review of research in developmental disabilities* (Vol. 52). Amsterdam: Academic Press.

Stevenson, J., & Fredman, G. (1990). The social environmental correlates of reading ability. *Journal of Child Psychology and Psychiatry, 31,* 681–698.

Stevenson, R. A., Sun, S. Z., Hazlett, N., Cant, J. S., Barense, M. D., & Ferber, S. (2018). Seeing the forest and the trees: Default local processing in individuals with high autistic traits does not come at the expense of global attention. *Journal of Autism & Developmental Disorders, 48,* 1382–1396.

Stewart, S. E., Hu, Y.-P., Leung, A., Chan, E., Hezel, D. M., Lin, S. Y., et al. (2017). A multisite study of family functioning impairment in pediatric obsessive-compulsive disorder. *Journal of the American Academy of Child & Adolescent Psychiatry, 56,* 241–249.

Stice, E., & Bearman, S. K. (2001). Body image and eating disturbances prospectively predict increases in depressive symptoms in adolescent girls: A growth curve analysis. *Developmental Psychology, 37,* 1–11.

Stice, E., & Linville, D. (2017). Eating disorders. In T. P. Beauchaine & S. P. Hinshaw (Eds.), *Child and adolescent psychopathology* (3rd ed.). Hoboken, NJ: John Wiley & Sons.

Stice, E., & Van Ryzin, M. J. (2019). A prospective test of the temporal sequencing of risk factor emergence in the dual pathway model of eating disorders. *Journal of Abnormal Psychology, 128,* 119–128.

Stice, E., Gau, J. M., Rohde, P., & Shaw, H. (2017). Risk factors that predict future onset of each DSM–5 eating disorder: Predictive specificity in high-risk adolescent females. *Journal of Abnormal Psychology, 126,* 38–51.

Stice, E., Marti, C. N., & Rohde, P. (2013). Prevalence, incidence, impairment, and course of the proposed DSM-5 eating disorder diagnoses in an 8-year prospective community study of young women. *Journal of Abnormal Psychology, 122,* 445–457.

Stice, E., Rohde, P., Shaw, H., & Gau, J. (2011). An effectiveness trial of a selected dissonance-based eating disorder prevention program for female high school students: Long-term effects. *Journal of Consulting and Clinical Psychology, 79,* 500–508.

Stice, E., Shaw, H., & Marti, C. N. (2006). A meta-analytic review of obesity prevention programs for children and adolescents: The skinny on interventions that work. *Psychological Bulletin, 132,* 667–691.

Stiffman, A. R., Alexander-Eitzman, B., Silmere, H., Osborne, V., & Brown, E. (2007). From early to late adolescence: American Indian youths' behavioral trajectories and their major influences. *Journal of the American Academy of Child and Adolescent Psychiatry, 46,* 849–859.

Stifter, C., & Dollar, J. (2016). Temperament and developmental psychopathology. In D. Cicchetti (Ed.), *Developmental psychopathology: Risk, resilience, and intervention* (Vol. 4). Hoboken, NJ: John Wiley & Sons.

Stilo, S. A., & Murray, R. M. (2019). Non-genetic factors in schizophrenia. *Current Psychiatry Reports, 21,* 100.

Stinton, M. M., & Birch, L. L. (2005). Weight status and psychosocial factors predict the emergence of dieting in preadolescent girls. *International Journal of Eating Disorders, 38,* 346–354.

Stockard, J., Wood, T. W., Coughlin, C., & Rasplica Khoury, C. (2018). The effectiveness of direct instruction curricula: A meta-analysis of a half century of research. *Review of Educational Research, 88,* 479–507.

Stokes, J. O., Scudder, A., Costello, A. H., & McNeil, C. B. (2017). Parent–child interaction therapy with an eight-year-old child: A case study. *Evidence-Based Practice in Child and Adolescent Mental Health, 2,* 1–11.

Storch, E. A., Khanna, M., Merlo, L. J., Loew, B. A., Franklin, M., Reid, J. M., et al. (2009). Children's Florida Obsessive Compulsive Inventory: Psychometric properties and feasibility of a self-report measure of obsessive–compulsive symptoms in youth. *Child Psychiatry and Human Development, 40,* 467–483.

Storch, E. A., McGuire, J. F., Wu, M. S., Hamblin, R., McIngvale, E., Cepeda, S. L., et al. (2019). Development and psychometric evaluation of the Children's Yale-Brown Obsessive-Compulsive Scale Second Edition. *Journal of the American Academy of Child & Adolescent Psychiatry, 58,* 92–98.

Storch, E. A., Milsom, V. A., DeBraganza, N., Lewin, A. B., Geffken, G. R., & Silverstein, J. H. (2007). Peer victimization, psychosocial adjustment, and physical activity in overweight and at-risk-for-overweight youth. *Journal of Pediatric Psychology, 32,* 80–89.

Storch, E. A., Salloum, A., King, M. A., Crawford, E. A., Andel, R., McBride, N. M., & Lewin, A. B. (2015). A randomized controlled trial in community mental health centers of computer-assisted cognitive behavioral therapy versus treatment as usual for children with anxiety. *Depression and Anxiety, 32,* 843–852.

Storch, E. A., Stigge-Kaufman, D., Marien, W. E., Sajid, M., Jacob, M. L., Geffken, G. R., et al. (2008). Obsessive-compulsive disorder in youth with and without a chronic tic disorder. *Depression and Anxiety, 25,* 761–767.

Storch, E. A., Wilhelm, S., Sprich, S., Henin, A., Micco, J., Small, B. J., et al. (2016). Efficacy of augmentation of cognitive behavior therapy with weight-adjusted d-cycloserine vs placebo in pediatric obsessive-compulsive disorder: A randomized clinical trial. *JAMA Psychiatry, 73,* 779–788.

Storck, M., Beal, T., Bacon, J. G., & Olsen, P. (2009). Behavioral and mental challenges for indigenous youth: Research and clinical perspectives. In A. B. Chang & R. Singleton (Eds.), *Pediatric Clinics of North America, 56.* Philadelphia, PA: W. B. Saunders.

Stormshak, E. A., Connell, A. M., Veronneau, M. H., Meyers, M. W., Dishion, T. J., Kavanagh, K., & Caruthers, A. S. (2011). An

References

ecological approach to promoting early adolescent mental health and social adaptation: Family-centered intervention in public middle schools. *Child Development, 82,* 209–225.

Strand, M., von Hausswolff-Juhlin, Y., & Welch, E. (2019). A systematic scoping review of diagnostic validity in avoidant/restrictive food intake disorder. *International Journal of Eating Disorders, 52,* 331–360.

Strasser, L., Downes, M., Kung, J., Cross, J. H., & De Haan, M. (2018). Prevalence and risk factors for autism spectrum disorder in epilepsy: A systematic review and meta-analysis. *Developmental Medicine & Child Neurology, 60,* 19–29.

Strauss, C. C. (1994). Overanxious disorder. In T. H. Ollendick, N. J. King, & W Yule (Eds.), *International handbook of phobic and anxiety disorders in children and adolescents.* New York: Plenum Press.

Strauss, C. C., & Last, C. G. (1993). Social and simple phobias in children. *Journal of Anxiety Disorders, 7,* 141–152.

Strauss, C. C., Lease, C. A., Last, C. G., & Francis, G. (1988). Overanxious disorder: An examination of developmental differences. *Journal of Abnormal Child Psychology, 16,* 433–443.

Streissguth, A. P., Bookstein, F. L., Sampson, P. D., & Barr, H. M. (1995). Attention: Prenatal alcohol and continuities of vigilance and attentional problems from 4 through 14 years. *Development and Psychopathology, 7,* 419–446.

Strickland, B. R. (2000). Misassumptions, misadventures, and the misuse of psychology. *American Psychologist, 55,* 331–338.

Striegel-Moore, R. H., & Bulik, C. M. (2007). Risk factors for eating disorders. *American Psychologist, 62,* 181–198.

Stringaris, A., & Goodman, R. (2009). Longitudinal outcome of youth oppositionality: Irritable, headstrong, and hurtful behaviors have distinctive predictions. *Journal of the American Academy of Child and Adolescent Psychiatry, 48,* 404–412.

Stringaris, A., Stahl, D., Santosh, P., & Goodman, R. (2011). Dimensions and latent classes of episodic mania-like symptoms in youth: An empirical enquiry. *Journal of Abnormal Child Psychology, 39,* 925–937.

Stubberud, A., Varkey, E., McCrory, D. C., Pedersen, S. A., & Linde, M. (2016). Biofeedback as prophylaxis for pediatric migraine: A meta-analysis. *Pediatrics, 138,* e20160675.

Stuber, J., Fairbrother, G., Galea, S., Pfefferbaum, B., Wilson-Genderson, M., & Vlahov, D. (2002). Determinants of counseling for children in Manhattan after the September 11 attacks. *Psychiatric Services, 53,* 815–822.

Stuijfzand, S., Creswell, C., Field, A. P., Pearcey, S., & Dodd, H. (2018). Is anxiety associated with negative interpretations of ambiguity in children and adolescents? A systematic review and meta-analysis. *Journal of Child Psychology and Psychiatry, 59,* 1127–1142.

Sturmey, P. (2005). Against psychotherapy with people who have mental retardation. *Mental Retardation, 43,* 55–57.

Suades-Gonzalez, E., Gascon, M., Guxens, M., & Sunyer, J. (2015). Air pollution and neuropsychological development: A review of the latest evidence. *Endocrinology, 156,* 3473–3482.

Substance Abuse and Mental Health Services Administration. (2009). *Family psychoeducation: Building your program.* Rockville, MD: Center for Mental Health Services, Substance Abuse and Mental Health Services Administration, U.S. Department of Health and Human Services.

Sugden, K., Arseneault, L., Harrington, H., Moffitt, T. E., Williams, B., & Caspi, A. (2010). Serotonin transporter gene moderates the development of emotional problems among children following bullying victimization. *Journal of the American Academy of Child and Adolescent Psychiatry, 49,* 830–840.

Sullivan, P. F., Neale, M. C., & Kendler, K. S. (2000). Genetic epidemiology of major depression: Review and meta-analysis. *American Journal of Psychiatry, 157,* 1552–1562.

Sullivan, P. W., Ghushchyan, V., Navaratnam, P., Friedman, H. S., Kavati, A., Ortiz, B., & Lanier, B. (2018). The national burden of poorly controlled asthma, school absence and parental work loss among school-aged children in the United States. *Journal of Asthma, 55,* 659–667.

Summers, J., Fletcher, R., & Bradley, E. (2017). People with intellectual and developmental disabilities and mental health needs. In M. L. Wehmeyer, I. Brown, M. Percy, K. A. Shogren, & W. L. A. Fung (Eds.), *A comprehensive guide to intellectual and developmental disabilities.* Baltimore, MD: Paul H. Brookes Publishing Co.

Sun, Y., & Li, Y. (2011). Effects of family structure type and stability on children's academic performance trajectories. *Journal of Marriage and Family, 73,* 541–556.

Suveg, C., Aschenbrand, S. G., & Kendall, P. C. (2005). Separation anxiety disorder, panic disorder, and school refusal. *Child and Adolescent Psychiatric Clinics of North America, 14,* 773–795.

Suzedelis, A. K. (2006). Adding burden to burden: Cosmetic surgery for children with Down syndrome. *AMA Journal of Ethics, 8,* 538–540.

Swagerman, S. C., van Bergen, E., Dolan, C., de Geus, E. J. C., Koenis, M. M. G., Hulshoff Pol, H. E., & Boomsma, D. I. (2017). Genetic transmission of reading ability. *Brain and Language, 172,* 3–8.

Swain, J. E., Scahill, L., Lombroso, P. J., King, R. A., & Leckman, J. F. (2007). Tourette disorder and tic disorders: A decade of progress. *Journal of the American Academy of Child and Adolescent Psychiatry, 46,* 947–968.

Swan, A. J., Kendall, P. C., Olino, T., Ginsburg, G., Keeton, C., Compton, S., et al. (2018). Results from the Child/Adolescent Anxiety Multimodal Longitudinal Study (CAMELS): Functional outcomes. *Journal of Consulting and Clinical Psychology, 86,* 738–750.

Swannell, S. V., Martin, G. E., Page, A., Hasking, P., & St. John, N. J. (2014). Prevalence of nonsuicidal self-injury in nonclinical samples: Systematic review, meta-analysis and meta-regression. *Suicide and Life-Threatening Behavior, 44,* 273–303.

Swanson, J. M., & Volkow, N. D. (2009). Psychopharmacology: Concepts and opinions about the use of stimulant medications. *Journal of Child Psychology and Psychiatry, 50,* 180–193.

Swanson, J. M., Arnold, L. E., Jensen, P. S., Hinshaw, S. P., Hechtman, L. T., Pelham, W. E., et al. (2018). Long-term outcomes in the Multimodal Treatment Study of children with ADHD (the MTA). In T. Banaschewski, D. Coghill, & A. Zuddas (Eds.), *Oxford textbook of attention deficit hyperactivity disorder.* Oxford: Oxford University Press.

Swanson, J. M., McBurnett, K., Christian, D. L., & Wigal, T. (1995). Stimulant medications and the treatment of children with ADHD. In T. H. Ollendick & R. J. Prinz (Eds.), *Advances in clinical child psychology.* New York: Plenum Press.

Swanson, S. A., Crow, S. J., Le Grange, D., Swendsen, J., & Merikangas, K. R. (2011). Prevalence and correlates of eating disorders in adolescents: Results from the National Comorbidity Survey Replication Adolescent Supplement. *Archives of General Psychiatry, 68,* 714–723.

Swearer, S. M., Wang, C., Givens, J., Berry, B., & Reinemann, D. (2011). Mood disorders. In S. Goldstein & C. R. Reynolds (Eds.), *Handbook of neurodevelopmental and genetic disorders in children* (2nd ed.). New York: The Guilford Press.

Sweeney, D. S., & Landreth, G. L. (2011). Child-centered play therapy. In C. E. Schaefer (Ed.), *Foundations of play therapy.* Hoboken, NJ: John Wiley & Sons.

Sylvestre, A., Desmarais, C., Meyer, F., Bairati, I., & Leblond, J. (2018). Prediction of the outcome of children who had a language delay at age 2 when they are aged 4: Still a challenge. *International Journal of Speech-Language Pathology, 20,* 731–744.

Szidon, K., Ruppar, A., & Smith, L. (2015). Five steps for developing effective transition plans for high school students with autism spectrum disorder. *Teaching Exceptional Children, 47,* 147–152.

Tabuenca, A. C., & Basile, K. H. (2019). Working with transgender and gender expansive youth. In R. D. Friedberg & J. K. Paternostro (Eds.), *Handbook of cognitive behavioral therapy for pediatric medical conditions.* Cham, Switzerland: Springer.

Talge, N. M., Neal, C., & Glover, V. (2007). Antenatal maternal stress and long-term effects on child neurodevelopment: How and why? *Journal of Child Psychology and Psychiatry, 48,* 245–261.

Tallal, P., & Jenkins, W. (2018). The birth of neuroplasticity interventions: A twenty year perspective. In T. Lachman & T. Weis (Eds.), *Reading and dyslexia.* New York: Springer.

Tammimies, K., Vitezic, M., Matsson, H., Le Guyader, S., Bürglin, T. R., Öhman, T., et al. (2013). Molecular networks of DYX1C1

gene show connection to neuronal migration genes and cytoskeletal proteins. *Biological Psychiatry, 73,* 583–590.

Tan, M., & Grigorenko, E. L. (2019). Genetics/genomics and intelligence. In R. J. Sternberg (Ed.), *Human intelligence: An introduction.* Cambridge: Cambridge University Press.

Tanenbaum, M. L., Adams, R. N., Hanes, S. J., Barley, R. C., Miller, K. M., Mulvaney, S. A., & Hood, K. K. (2017). Optimal use of diabetes devices: Clinician perspectives on barriers and adherence to device use. *Journal of Diabetes Science and Technology, 11,* 484–492.

Tanguay, P. E. (2000). Pervasive developmental disorders: A 10-year review. *Journal of the American Academy of Child and Adolescent Psychiatry, 39,* 1079–1095.

Tannock, R. (2005a). Disorders of written expression and learning disorders not otherwise specified. In B. J. Sadock & V. A. Sadock (Eds.), *Kaplan & Sadock's comprehensive textbook of psychiatry.* Philadelphia, PA: Lippincott Williams and Wilkens.

Tannock, R. (2005b). Mathematics disorder. In B. J. Sadock & V. A. Sadock (Eds.), *Kaplan & Sadock's comprehensive textbook of psychiatry.* Philadelphia, PA: Lippincott Williams and Wilkens.

Tanofsky-Kraff, M., & Wilfley, D. E. (2010). Interpersonal psychotherapy for bulimia nervosa and binge-eating disorder. In C. M. Grilo & J. E. Mitchell (Eds.), *The treatment of eating disorders: A clinical handbook.* New York: The Guilford Press.

Tanofsky-Kraff, M., Shomaker, L. B., Olsen, C., Roza, C. A., Wolkoff, L. E., Columbo, K. M., et al. (2011). A prospective study of pediatric loss of control eating and psychological outcomes. *Journal of Abnormal Psychology, 120,* 108–118.

Tassé, M. J., Luckasson, R., & Schalock, R. L. (2016a). The relation between intellectual functioning and adaptive behavior in the diagnosis of intellectual disability. *Intellectual and Developmental Disabilities, 54,* 381–390.

Tassé, M. J., Schalock, R. L., Balboni, G., Spreat, S., & Navas, P. (2016b). Validity and reliability of the Diagnostic Adaptive Behaviour Scale. *Journal of Intellectual Disability Research, 60,* 80–88.

Tassé, M. J., Schalock, R. L., Thissen, D., Balboni, G., Bersani, H., Borthwick-Duffy, S. A., et al. (2016c). Development and standardization of the diagnostic adaptive behavior scale: Application of item response theory to the assessment of adaptive behavior. *American Journal on Intellectual and Developmental Disabilities, 121,* 79–94.

Tate, R. L., & Perdices, M. (2019). *Single-case experimental designs for clinical research and neurorehabilitation settings: Planning, conduct, analysis and reporting.* Oxon: Routledge.

Taylor, B. J., & Siegel, M. (2019). Characterization of Sleep Disturbance Profiles in Hospitalized Children with Autism Spectrum Disorder. *Sleep, 42*(sup1), A314–A315.

Taylor, E. (2009). Developing ADHD. *Journal of Child Psychology and Psychiatry, 50,* 126–132.

References

Taylor, E., & Sonuga-Barke, E. (2008). Disorders of attention and activity. In M. Rutter et al. (Eds.), *Rutter's child and adolescent psychiatry* (5th ed.). Malden, MA: Blackwell Publishing.

Taylor, H. G. (1989). Learning disabilities. In E. J. Mash & R. A. Barkley (Eds.), *Treatment of childhood disorders.* New York: Guilford.

Taylor, J. J., Grant, K. E., Zulauf, C. A., Fowler, P. J., Meyerson, D. A., & Irsheid, S. (2018). Exposure to community violence and the trajectory of internalizing and externalizing symptoms in a sample of low-income urban youth. *Journal of Clinical Child & Adolescent Psychology, 47,* 421–435.

Taylor, J. L., & Seltzer, M. M. (2010). Changes in the autism behavioral phenotype during the transition to adulthood. *Journal of Autism and Developmental Disorders, 40,* 1431–1446.

Taylor, L. E., Swerdfeger, A. L., & Eslick, G. D. (2014). Vaccines are not associated with autism: An evidence-based meta-analysis of case-control and cohort studies. *Vaccine, 32,* 3623–3629.

Teague, S. J., Gray, K. M., Tonge, B. J., & Newman, L. K. (2017). Attachment in children with autism spectrum disorder: A systematic review. *Research in Autism Spectrum Disorders, 35,* 35–50.

Tennant, C. (1988). Parental loss in childhood: Its effects in adult life. *Archives of General Psychiatry, 45,* 1045–1050.

Terr, L. (1979). Children of Chowchilla. *The Psychoanalytic Study of the Child, 34,* 522–563.

Terr, L. (1983). Chowchilla revisited: The effects of psychic trauma four years after a school-bus kidnapping. *American Journal of Psychiatry, 140,* 1543–1550.

Thapar, A. (2018). Discoveries on the genetics of ADHD in the 21st century: New findings and their implications. *American Journal of Psychiatry, 175,* 943–950.

Thapar, A., & Rutter, M. (2019). Do natural experiments have an important future in the study of mental disorders? *Psychological Medicine, 49,* 1079–1088.

Thase, M. (2009). Neurobiological aspects of depression. In I. H. Gotlib & C. L. Hammen (Eds.), *Handbook of depression.* New York: The Guilford Press.

The Carolina Abecedarian Project—FPG Child Development. (2008). www.fpg.unc.edu/-abc

Thelen, E., & Adolph, K. E. (1992). Arnold L. Gessell: The paradox of nature and nurture. *Developmental Psychology, 28,* 368–380.

Thelen, M. H., Powell, A. L., Lawrence, C., & Kuhnert, M. E. (1992). Eating and body image concerns among children. *Journal of Consulting and Clinical Psychology, 21,* 41–46.

Them, M. A., Israel, A. C., Ivanova, M. Y., & Chalmers, S. M. (2003). *An investigation of the assessment of and relationships between various aspects of family stability.*

Boston, MA: Association for the Advancement of Behavior Therapy.

Theule, J., Wiener, J., Tannock, R., & Jenkins, J. M. (2013). Parenting stress in families of children with ADHD: A meta-analysis. *Journal of Emotional and Behavioral Disorders, 21,* 3–17.

Thomas, J. J., Keel, P. K., & Heatherton, T. F. (2006). Disordered eating attitudes and behaviors in ballet students: Examination of environmental and individual risk factors. *International Journal of Eating Disorders, 38,* 263–258.

Thompson, J. K., & Smolak, L. (2001). Body image, eating disorders, and obesity in youth: The future is now. In J. K. Thompson & L. Smolak (Eds.), *Body image, eating disorders, and obesity in youth: Assessment, prevention, and treatment.* Washington, DC: American Psychological Association.

Thompson, J. K., Shroff, H., Herbozo, S., Cafri, G., Rodriguez, J., & Rodriguez, M. (2007). Relations among multiple peer influences, body dissatisfaction, eating disturbance, and self-esteem: A comparison of average weight, at risk of overweight, and overweight adolescent girls. *Journal of Pediatric Psychology, 32,* 24–29.

Thompson, J. R., Bryant, B. R., Schalock, R. L., Shogren, K. A., Tassé, M. J., Wehmeyer, M. L., et al. (2015). *Supports Intensity Scale—Adult Version (SIS-A) user's manual.* Silver Springs, MD: American Association on Intellectual and Developmental Disabilities.

Thompson, J. R., Schalock, R. L., & Tassé, M. J. (2018). *Evidence for the reliability and validity of the Supports Intensity Scales.* Retrieved from www.aaidd.org/docs/default-source/sis-docs/evidence-for-the-reliabilityandvalidity-of-the-sis.pdf?sfvrsn=7ed3021_0

Thompson, J. R., Wehmeyer, M. L., Hughes, C., Shogren, K. A., Seo, H., Little, T. D., et al. (2016). *The Supports Intensity Scale—Children's Version (SIS-C) user's manual.* Silver Spring, MD: American Association on Intellectual and Developmental Disabilities.

Thompson, P. A., Hulme, C., Nash, H. M., Gooch, D., Hayiou-Thomas, E., & Snowling, M. J. (2015). Developmental dyslexia: Predicting individual risk. *Journal of Child Psychology and Psychiatry, 56,* 976–987.

Thompson-Schill, S. L., Ramscar, M., & Chrysikou, E. G. (2009). Cognition without control. *Current Directions in Psychological Science, 18,* 259–263.

Thornberry, T. P., Henry, K. L., Ireland, T. O., & Smith, C. A. (2010). The causal impact of childhood-limited maltreatment and adolescent maltreatment on early adult adjustment. *Journal of Adolescent Health, 46,* 359–365.

Thorndike, E. L. (1905). *The elements of psychology.* New York: Seiler.

Tichovolsky, M. H., Griffith, S. F., Rolon-Arroyo, B., Arnold, D. H., & Harvey, E. A. (2018). A longitudinal study of fathers' and young children's depressive symptoms. *Journal of Clinical Child & Adolescent Psychology, 47*(sup1), S190–S204.

Tick, B., Bolton, P., Happé, F., Rutter, M., & Rijsdijk, F. (2016). Heritability of autism spectrum disorders: A meta-analysis of twin studies. *Journal of Child Psychology and Psychiatry, 57,* 585–595.

Tick, N. T., van der Ende, J., & Verhulst, F. C. (2008). Ten-year trends in self-reported emotional and behavioral problems of Dutch adolescents. *Social Psychiatry and Psychiatric Epidemiology, 43,* 349–355.

Tienari, P., Lahti, I., Sorri, A., Naarala, M., Moring, J., Kaleva, M., Wahlberg, K.-E., & Wynne, L. C. (1990). Adopted-away offspring of schizophrenics and controls: The Finnish adoptive family study of schizophrenia. In L. N. Robins & M. Rutter (Eds.), *Straight and devious pathways from childhood to adulthood.* New York: Cambridge University Press.

Tienari, P., Wynne, L. C., & Wahlberg, K. E. (2006). Genetics and family relationships in schizophrenia and the schizophrenia spectrum disorders. In S. M. Miller, S. H. McDaniel, J. S. Rolland, & S. L. Feetham (Eds.), *Individuals, families, and the new era of genetics.* New York: W W. Norton & Co.

Timko, C., Baumgartner, M., Moos, R. H., & Miller, J. J. (1993). Parental risk and resistance factors among children with juvenile rheumatic disease: A four-year predictive study. *Journal of Behavioral Medicine, 16,* 571–588.

Tint, A., Thomson, K., & Weiss, J. A. (2017). A systematic literature review of the physical and psychosocial correlates of Special Olympics participation among individuals with intellectual disability. *Journal of Intellectual Disability Research, 61,* 301–324.

Tolan, P. (2014). Future directions for positive development intervention research. *Journal of Clinical Child and Adolescent Psychology, 43,* 686–694.

Tolan, P. H., & Thomas, P. (1995). The implications of age of onset for delinquency risk II: Longitudinal data. *Journal of Abnormal Child Psychology, 23,* 157–181.

Tondo, L., Vázquez, G., & Baldessarini, R. (2010). Mania associated with antidepressant treatment: Comprehensive meta-analytic review. *Acta Psychiatrica Scandinavica, 121,* 404–414.

Tonge, B. (1994). Separation anxiety disorder. In T. H. Ollendick, N. J. King, & W. Yule (Eds.), *International handbook of phobic and anxiety disorders in children and adolescents.* New York: Plenum Press.

Torbeyns, J., Verschaffel, L., & Ghesquière, P. (2004). Strategy development in children with mathematical disabilities: Insights from the choice/no-choice method and the chronological-age/ability-level-match design. *Journal of Learning Disabilities, 37,* 119–131.

Torney-Purta, J. V. (2009). International research that matters for policy and practice. *American Psychologist, 64,* 825–837.

Toth, S. L., Stronach, E. P., Rogosch, F. A., Caplan, R., & Cicchetti, D. (2011). Illogical thinking and thought disorder in maltreated children. *Journal of the American Academy of Child and Adolescent Psychiatry, 50,* 659–668.

Totsika, V., Hastings, R. P., Emerson, E., Lancaster, G. A., & Berridge, D. M. (2011). A population-based investigation of behavioural and emotional problems and maternal mental health: Associations with autism spectrum disorder and intellectual disability. *Journal of Child Psychology and Psychiatry, 52,* 91–99.

Trace, S. E., Baker, J. H., Peñas-Lledó, E., & Bulik, C. M. (2013). The genetics of eating disorders. *Annual Review of Clinical Psychology, 9,* 589–620.

Treatment for Adolescents with Depression Study Team. (2004). Fluoxetine, cognitive-behavioral therapy, and their combination for adolescents with depression: Treatment for Adolescents with Depression Study (TADS) randomized controlled trial. *Journal of the American Medical Association, 292,* 807–820.

Treatment for Adolescents with Depression Study Team. (2007). The Treatment for Adolescents with Depression Study (TADS): Long-term effectiveness and safety outcomes. *Archives of General Psychiatry, 64,* 1132–1143.

Treatment for Adolescents with Depression Study Team. (2009). The Treatment for Adolescents with Depression Study (TADS): Outcome over one year of naturalistic follow-up. *American Journal of Psychiatry, 166,* 1141–1149.

Tremblay, G. C., & Israel, A. C. (1998). Children's adjustment to parental death. *Clinical Psychology: Science and Practice, 5,* 424–438.

Tremblay, G. C., & Peterson, L. (1999). Prevention of childhood injury: Clinical and public policy issues. *Clinical Psychology Review, 19,* 415–434.

Tremblay, R. E. (2010). Developmental origins of disruptive behaviour problems: The "original sin" hypothesis, epigenetics and their consequences for prevention. *Journal of Child Psychology and Psychiatry, 51,* 341–367.

Trentacosta, C. J., & Fine, S. E. (2010). Emotion knowledge, social competence, and behavior problems in childhood and adolescence: A meta-analytic review. *Social Development, 19,* 1–29.

Trickey, D., Siddaway, A. P., Meiser-Stedman, R., Serpell, L., & Field, A. P. (2012). A meta-analysis of risk factors for posttraumatic stress disorder in children and adolescents. *Clinical Psychology Review, 32,* 122–138.

Tronick, E., & Beeghly, M. (2011). Infants' meaning-making and the development of mental health problems. *American Psychologist, 66,* 107–119.

Trosper, S. E., Whitton, S. W., Brown, T. A., & Pincus, D. B. (2012). Understanding the latent structure of the emotional disorders in children and adolescents. *Journal of Abnormal Child Psychology, 40,* 621–632.

References

Tsai, A. C., Rosenlicht, N. Z., Jureidini, J. N., Parry, P. I., Spielmans, G. I., & Healy, D. (2011). Aripiprazole in the maintenance treatment of bipolar disorder: A critical review of the evidence and its dissemination into the scientific literature. *PLOS Medicine, 8*(5): e1000434.

Tschentscher, N., Ruisinger, A., Blank, H., Díaz, B., & von Kriegstein, K. (2019). Reduced structural connectivity between left auditory thalamus and the motion-sensitive planum temporale in developmental dyslexia. *The Journal of Neuroscience, 39,* 1720–1732.

Tu, J. W., Owens, E. B., & Hinshaw, S. P. (2019). Positive illusory bias still illusory? Investigating discrepant self-perceptions in girls with ADHD. *Journal of Pediatric Psychology, 44,* 576–588.

Tully, L. A., Arseneault, L., Caspi, A., Moffit, T. E., & Morgan, J. (2004). Does maternal warmth moderate the effects of birth-weight on twins' attention-deficit/hyperactivity disorder (ADHD) symptoms and low IQ? *Journal of Consulting and Clinical Psychology, 72,* 218–226.

Turk, D. C., & Monarch, E. S. (2018). Biopsychosocial perspective on chronic pain. In D. C. Turk & R. J. Gatchel (Eds.), *Psychological approaches to pain management: A practitioner's handbook* (3rd ed.). New York: Guilford Press.

Turnbull, A. P. (2004). President's address 2004: "Wearing two hats": Morphed perspectives on family quality of life. *Mental Retardation, 42,* 383–399.

Turner, M. (1999). Annotation: Repetitive behaviour in autism: A review of psychological research. *Journal of Child Psychology and Psychiatry, 40,* 839–849.

Turney, K. (2017). The unequal consequences of mass incarceration for children. *Demography, 54,* 361–389.

Turunen, T., Poskiparta, E., & Salmivalli, C. (2017). Are reading difficulties associated with bullying involvement? *Learning and Instruction, 52,* 130–138.

Twenge, J. M., & Nolen-Hoeksema, S. (2002). Age, gender, race, socioeconomic status, and birth cohort difference on the children's depression inventory: A meta-analysis. *Journal of Abnormal Psychology, 111,* 578–588.

Twenge, J. M., Gentile, B., DeWall, C. N., Ma, D., Lacefield, K., Schurtz, D. R. (2010). Birth cohort increases in psychopathology among Americans, 1938–2007: A cross-temporal meta-analysis of the MMPI. *Clinical Child Review, 30,* 145–154.

Tyc, V. L., & Klosky, J. L. (2015). Lifestyle factors and health risk behaviors. In G. A. Mucci & L. R. Torno (Eds.), *Handbook of long term care of the childhood cancer survivor.* New York: Springer.

Uchida, M., Spencer, T. J., Faraone, S. V., & Biederman, J. (2015). Adult outcome of ADHD: An overview of results from the MGH longitudinal family studies of pediatrically and psychiatrically referred youth with and without ADHD of both sexes. *Journal of Attention Disorders, 22,* 523–534.

Uddin, L. Q., & Karlsgodt, K. H. (2018). Future directions for examination of brain networks in neurodevelopmental disorders. *Journal of Clinical Child and Adolescent Psychology, 47,* 483–497.

Udwin, O., Boyle, S., Yule, W., Bolton, D., & O'Ryan, D. (2000). Risk factors for long-term psychological effects of a disaster experienced in adolescence: Predictors of Post Traumatic Stress Disorder. *Journal of Child Psychology and Psychiatry, 41,* 969–979.

Uher, R., Heyman, I., Turner, C. M., & Shafran, R. (2008). Self-, parent-report and interview measures of obsessive-compulsive disorder in children and adolescents. *Journal of Anxiety Disorders, 22,* 979–990.

Uhre, C. F., Uhre, V. F., Lønfeldt, N. N., Pretzmann, L., Vangkilde, S., Plessen, K. J., et al. (2020). Systematic review and meta-analysis: Cognitive-behavioral therapy for Obsessive-Compulsive Disorder in children and adolescents. *Journal of the American Academy of Child & Adolescent Psychiatry, 59,* 64–77.

Ullsperger, J. M., Nigg, J. T., & Nikolas, M. A. (2016). Does child temperament play a role in the association between parenting practices and child attention deficit/hyperactivity disorder? *Journal of Abnormal Child Psychology, 44,* 167–178.

Underwood, M. K., & Ehrenreich, S. E. (2017). The power and the pain of adolescents' digital communication: Cyber victimization and the perils of lurking. *American Psychologist, 72,* 144–158.

UNHCR The UN Refugee Agency. (2018). *Global trends: Forced displacement in 2017.* Geneva, Switzerland: UNHCR. Retrieved from www.unhcr.org/dach/wp-content/uploads/sites/27/2018/06/GlobalTrends2017.pdf

UNICEF. (2019). *Levels & trends in child mortality: Report 2019.* Retrieved from www.unicef.org/sites/default/files/2019-10/UN-IGME-child-mortality-report-2019.pdf

Unicomb, R., Hewat, S., Spencer, E., & Harrison, E. (2017). Evidence for the treatment of co-occurring stuttering and speech sound disorder: A clinical case series. *International Journal of Speech-Language Pathology, 19,* 251–264.

United Nations. (2018). *World youth report.* New York: United Nations.

Unwin, G., & Deb, S. (2011). Efficacy of atypical antipsychotic medication in the management of behaviour problems in children with intellectual disabilities and borderline intelligence: A systematic review. *Research in Developmental Disabilities, 32,* 2121–2133.

Unwin, G., Tsimopoulou, I., Kroese, B. S., & Azmi, S. (2016). Effectiveness of cognitive behavioural therapy (CBT) programmes for anxiety or depression in adults with intellectual disabilities: A review of the literature. *Research in Developmental Disabilities, 51–52,* 60–75.

U.S. Census Bureau. (2018a). *America's families and living arrangements: 2018*. Current Population Survey, 2018 Annual Social and Economic Supplement.

U.S. Census Bureau. (2018b). *American Community Survey: Poverty status in the past 12 months*. Retrieved December 2019 from https://data.census.gov/cedsci/table?q=S1701%3A POVE

U.S. Census Bureau. (2018c). *American Community Survey: Poverty status in the past 12 months of families*. Retrieved December 2019 from https://data.census.gov/cedsci/table?q=S1702%3A POVE

U.S. Census Bureau. (2019). *Living arrangements of children under 18 years old: 1960 to present*. Current Population Survey, March and Annual Social and Economic Supplements. Retrieved December 2019 from www.census.gov/data/tables/time-series/demo/families/children.html

U.S. Department of Education Office of Special Education and Rehabilitative Services. (2017). *A transition guide to postsecondary education and employment for students and youth with disabilities*. Washington, DC: Author.

U.S. Department of Health and Human Services. (2016). *Facing addiction in America: The Surgeon General's report on alcohol, drugs, and health*. Washington, DC: Author.

U.S. Department of Health and Human Services. (2018). Institutional Review Board (IRB) Written Procedures: Guidance for Institutions and IRBS (2018). Retrieved from www.hhs.gov/ohrp/regulations-and-policy/guidance/institutional-issues/institutional-review-board-written-procedures/index.html

U.S. Department of Health & Human Services, Administration for Children and Families, Administration on Children, Youth and Families, Children's Bureau. (2019). Child Maltreatment 2017. Retrieved from www.acf.hhs.gov/cb/research-data-technology/statistics-research/child-maltreatment

U.S. Food and Drug Administration. (2007). *Revisions to product labeling*. Retrieved July 11, 2007 from www.fda.gov/cder/drug/antidepressants/antidepressants_label_change_2007.pdf

U.S. Office of Education. (1977). Definition and criteria for defining students as learning disabled. Federal Register, 42:250, p. 65083. Washington, DC: U.S. Government Printing Office.

Vaidyanathan, U., Patrick, C. J., & Cuthbert, B. N. (2009). Linking dimensional models of internalizing psychopathology to neurobiological systems: Affect-modulated startle as an indicator of fear and distress disorders and affiliated traits. *Psychological Bulletin, 135*, 909–942.

Valicenti-McDermott, M., Lawson, K., Hottinger, K., Seijo, R., Schechtman, M., Shulman, L., & Shinnar, S. (2019). Sleep problems in children with autism and other developmental disabilities: A brief report. *Journal of Child Neurology, 34*, 387–393.

Valo, S., & Tannock, R. (2010). Diagnostic instability of DSM-IV ADHD subtypes: Effects of informant source, instrumentation, and methods for combining symptom reports. *Journal of Clinical Child and Adolescent Psychology, 39*, S749–S760.

Van Beveren, M.-L., Mezulis, A., Wante, L., & Braet, C. (2019). Joint contributions of negative emotionality, positive emotionality, and effortful control on depressive symptoms in youth. *Journal of Clinical Child & Adolescent Psychology, 48*, 131–142.

van Bijnen, S., Kärkkäinen, S., Helenius, P., & Parviainen, T. (2019). Left hemisphere enhancement of auditory activation in language impaired children. *Scientific Reports, 9*, 9087.

van Daal, J., Verhoeven, L., & van Balkom, H. (2007). Behaviour problems in children with language impairment. *Journal of Child Psychology and Psychiatry, 48*, 1139–1147.

van den Akker, A. L., Dekovic, M., Prinzie, P., & Asscher, J. J. (2010). Toddlers' temperament profile: Stability and relations to negative and positive parenting. *Journal of Abnormal Child Psychology, 38*, 485–495.

van den Berg, P. A., Keery, H., Eisenberg, M., & Neumark-Sztainer, D. (2010). Maternal and adolescent report of mothers' weight-related concerns and behaviors: Longitudinal associations with adolescent body dissatisfaction and weight control practices. *Journal of Pediatric Psychology, 35*, 1093–1102.

van der Bruggen, C. O., Stams, G. J. J. M., & Bogels, S. M. (2008). The relation between child and parent anxiety and parental control: A meta-analytic review. *Journal of Child Psychology and Psychiatry, 49*, 1257–1269.

Van der Donck, S., Dzhelyova, M., Vettori, S., Mahdi, S. S., Claes, P., Steyaert, J., & Boets, B. (2020). Rapid neural categorization of angry and fearful faces is specifically impaired in boys with autism spectrum disorder. *Journal of Child Psychology and Psychiatry*. doi:10.1111/jcpp.13201

van der Wal, R. C., Finkenauer, C., & Visser, M. M. (2019). Reconciling mixed findings on children's adjustment following high-conflict divorce. *Journal of Child and Family Studies, 28*, 468–478.

Van Dessel, J., Sonuga-Barke, E., Moerkerke, M., Van der Oord, S., Lemiere, J., Morsink, S., & Danckaerts, M. (2019). The amygdala in adolescents with attention-deficit/hyperactivity disorder: Structural and functional correlates of delay aversion. *The World Journal of Biological Psychiatry*, 1–12.

van Engeland, H., & Buitelaar, J. K. (2008). Autism spectrum disorder. In M. Rutter, D. Bishop, D. Pine, S. Scott, J. S. Stevenson, E. Taylor, & A. Thapar (Eds.), *Rutter's child and adolescent psychiatry* (5th ed.). Malden, MA: Blackwell Publishing.

van Erp, T. G. M., Hibar, D. P., Rasmussen, J. M., Glahn, D. C., Pearlson, G. D., Andreassen, O. A., et al. (2016). Subcortical brain volume abnormalities in 2028 individuals with schizophrenia and 2540 healthy controls via the ENIGMA consortium. *Molecular Psychiatry, 21*, 547–553.

References

Van Gampelaere, C., Luyckx, K., Van Ryckeghem, D. M. L., van der Straaten, S., Laridaen, J., Goethals, E. R., et al. (2018). Mindfulness, worries, and parenting in parents of children with type 1 diabetes. *Journal of Pediatric Psychology, 44,* 499–508.

van Goozen, S. H. M., Fairchild, G., Snoek, H., & Harold, G. T. (2007). The evidence for a neurobiological model of childhood antisocial behavior. *Psychological Bulletin, 133,* 149–182.

Van Hoecke, E., De Fruyt, F., De Clercq, B., Hoebeke, P., & Vande Walle, J. (2006). Internalizing and externalizing problem behavior in children with nocturnal and diurnal enuresis: A five-factor model perspective. *Journal of Pediatric Psychology, 31,* 460–468.

van Hulst, B. M., de Zeeuw, P., Bos, D. J., Rijks, Y., Neggers, S. F. W., & Durston, S. (2017). Children with ADHD symptoms show decreased activity in ventral striatum during the anticipation of reward, irrespective of ADHD diagnosis. *Journal of Child Psychology and Psychiatry, 58,* 206–214.

van IJzendoorn, M. H., & Bakermans-Kranenburg, M. J. (2015). Genetic differential susceptibility on trial: Meta-analytic support from randomized controlled experiments. *Development and Psychopathology, 27,* 151–162.

van IJzendoorn, M. H., Bakermans-Kranenburg, M. J., Coughlan, B., & Reijman, S. (2020). Annual research review: Umbrella synthesis of meta-analyses on child maltreatment antecedents and interventions: Differential susceptibility perspective on risk and resilience. *Journal of Child Psychology and Psychiatry, 61,* 272–290.

van Lier, P. A., & Koot, H. M. (2010). Developmental cascades of peer relations and symptoms of externalizing and internalizing problems from kindergarten to fourth-grade elementary school. *Development and Psychopathology, 22,* 569–582.

van Lier, P., Boivin M., Dionne, G., Vitaro, F., Brendgen, M., Koot, H., et al. (2007a). Kindergarten children's genetic vulnerabilities interact with friends' aggression to promote children's own aggression. *Journal of the American Academy of Child and Adolescent Psychiatry, 46,* 1080–1087.

van Lier, P. A. C., van der Ende, J., Koot, H. M., & Verhulst, F. C. (2007b). Which better predicts conduct problems? The relationship of trajectories of conduct problems with ODD and ADHD symptoms from childhood into adolescence. *Journal of Child Psychology and Psychiatry, 48,* 601–608.

Van Meter, A. R., Moreira, A. L. R., & Youngstrom, E. A. (2011). Meta-analysis of epidemiologic studies of pediatric bipolar disorder. *Journal of Clinical Psychiatry, 72,* 1250–1256.

Van Meter, A. R., Paksarian, D., & Merikangas, K. R. (2019). Social functioning and suicide risk in a community sample of adolescents. *Journal of Clinical Child & Adolescent Psychology, 48,* 273–287.

Van Mieghem, A., Verschueren, K., Petry, K., & Struyf, E. (2020). An analysis of research on inclusive education: A systematic search and meta review. *International Journal of Inclusive Education, 24,* 675–689.

van Ool, J. S., Snoeijen-Schouwenaars, F. M., Tan, I. Y., Schelhaas, H. J., Aldenkamp, A. P., & Hendriksen, J. G. M. (2019). Classification of intellectual disability according to domains of adaptive functioning and between-domains discrepancy in adults with epilepsy. *Journal of Intellectual Disability Research, 63,* 40–48.

van Oort, F. V. A., van der Ende, J., Wadsworth, M. E., Verhulst, F. C., & Achenbach, T. M. (2011). Cross-national comparison of the link between socioeconomic status and emotional and behavioral problems in youths. *Social Psychiatry and Psychiatric Epidemiology, 46,* 167–172.

van Schalkwyk, G. I., & Silverman, W. K. (2019). Anxiety disorders. In T. H. Ollendick, S. W. White, & B. A. White (Eds.), *The Oxford handbook of clinical child and adolescent psychology*. New York: Oxford University Press.

Van Schoors, M., Caes, L., Knoble, N. B., Goubert, L., Verhofstadt, L. L., Alderfer, M. A., et al. (2016). Systematic review: Associations between family functioning and child adjustment after pediatric cancer diagnosis: A meta-analysis. *Journal of Pediatric Psychology, 42,* 6–18.

Van Schoors, M., Caes, L., Verhofstadt, L. L., Goubert, L., & Alderfer, M. A. (2015). Systematic review: Family resilience after pediatric cancer diagnosis. *Journal of Pediatric Psychology, 40,* 856–868.

Vannatta, K., & Salley, C. G. (2017). Pediatric cancer. In M. C. Roberts & R. G. Steele (Eds.), *Handbook of pediatric psychology* (5th ed.). New York: The Guilford Press.

Varela, R. E., Vernberg, E. M., Sanchez-Sosa, J. J., Riveros, A., Mitchell, M., & Mashunkashey, J. (2004). Anxiety reporting and culturally associated interpretation biases and cognitive schema: A comparison of Mexican, Mexican American, and European American families. *Journal of Clinical Child and Adolescent Psychology, 33,* 237–247.

Varese, F., Smeets, F., Drukker, M., Lieverse, R., Lataster, T., Viechtbauer, W., et al. (2012). Childhood adversities increase the risk of psychosis: A meta-analysis of patient-control, prospective- and cross-sectional cohort studies. *Schizophrenia Bulletin, 38,* 661–671.

Vasey, M. W., & Daleiden, E. L. (1994). Worry in children. In G. C. L. Davey & F. Tallis (Eds.), *Worrying: Perspectives on theory, assessment and treatment*. Chichester, UK: Wiley.

Vaudreuil, C. A. H., Faraone, S. V., Di Salvo, M., Wozniak, J. R., Wolenski, R. A., Carrellas, N. W., & Biederman, J. (2019). The morbidity of subthreshold pediatric bipolar disorder: A systematic literature review and meta-analysis. *Bipolar Disorders, 21,* 16–27.

Vaughn, S., & Fletcher, J. M. (2012). Response to intervention with secondary school students with reading difficulties. *Journal of Learning Disabilities, 45,* 244–256.

Vaughn, S., La Greca, A. M., & Kuttler, A. (1999). The why, who, and how of social skills. In W. N. Bender (Ed.), *Professional issues in learning disabilities.* Austin, TX: PRO-ED.

Veatch, O. J., Sutcliffe, J. S., Warren, Z. E., Keenan, B. T., Potter, M. H., & Malow, B. A. (2017). Shorter sleep duration is associated with social impairment and comorbidities in ASD. *Autism Research, 10,* 1221–1238.

Vellutino, F. R. (1979). *Dyslexia: Theory and research.* Cambridge, MA: MIT Press.

Vellutino, F. R., Fletcher, J. M., Snowling, M. J., & Scanlon, D. M. (2004). Specific reading disability (dyslexia): What have we learned in the past four decades? *Journal of Child Psychology and Psychiatry, 45,* 2–40.

Velting, O. N., & Albano, A. M. (2001). Current trends in the understanding and treatment of social phobia in youth. *Journal of Child Psychology and Psychiatry, 42,* 127–140.

Verduin, T. L., & Kendall, P. C. (2003). Differential occurrence of comorbidity within childhood anxiety disorders. *Journal of Clinical Child and Adolescent Psychology, 32,* 290–295.

Verhulst, B., Neale, M. C., & Kendler, K. S. (2015). The heritability of alcohol use disorders: A meta-analysis of twin and adoption studies. *Psychological Medicine, 45,* 1061–1072.

Verhulst, F. C., & van der Ende, J. (1997). Factors associated with mental health service use in the community. *Journal of the American Academy of Child and Adolescent Psychiatry, 36,* 901–909.

Vernal, D. L., Stenstrøm, A. D., Staal, N., Christensen, A. M. R., Ebbesen, C., Pagsberg, A. K., et al. (2018). Validation study of the early onset schizophrenia diagnosis in the Danish Psychiatric Central Research Register. *European Child & Adolescent Psychiatry, 27,* 965–975.

Vernick, J., & Karon, M. (1965). Who's afraid of death on a leukemia ward? *American Journal of Diseases of Children, 109,* 393–397.

Viana, G. A., Beidel, D. C., & Rabian, B. (2009). Selective mutism: A review and integration of the last 15 years. *Clinical Psychology Review, 29,* 57–67.

Viding, E., & Larsson, H. (2010). Genetics and child and adolescent psychopathy. In R. T. Salekin & D. R. Lyman (Eds.), *Handbook of child and adolescent psychopathy.* New York: The Guilford Press.

Viding, E., Blair, R. J. R., Moffitt, T. E., & Plomin, R. (2005). Evidence for substantial genetic risk for psychopathy in 7-year-olds. *Journal of Child Psychology and Psychiatry, 46,* 592–597.

Viding, E., Jones, A. P., Frick, P. J., Moffitt, T. E., & Plomin, R. (2008). Heritability of antisocial behaviour at 9: Do callous-unemotional traits matter? *Developmental Science, 11,* 17–22.

Viding, E., Spinath, F. M., Price, T. S., Bishop, D. V. M., Dale, P. S., & Plomin, R. (2004). Genetic and environmental influences on language impairment in 4-year-old same-sex and opposite-sex twins. *Journal of Child Psychology and Psychiatry, 45,* 315–325.

Villabø, M. A., Narayanan, M., Compton, S. N., Kendall, P. C., & Neumer, S.-P. (2018). Cognitive–behavioral therapy for youth anxiety: An effectiveness evaluation in community practice. *Journal of Consulting and Clinical Psychology, 86,* 751–764.

Viner, R. M., Russell, S. J., Croker, H., Packer, J., Ward, J., Stansfield, C., et al. (2020). School closure and management practices during coronavirus outbreaks including COVID-19: A rapid systematic review. *The Lancet Child & Adolescent Health, 4,* 397–404.

Virués-Ortega, J. (2010). Applied behavior analytic intervention for autism in early childhood: Meta-analysis, meta-regression and dose-response meta-analysis of multiple outcomes. *Clinical Psychology Review, 30,* 387–399.

Vitiello, B., Severe, J. B., Greenhill, L. L., Arnold, L. E., Abikoff, H. B., Bukstein, O. G., et al. (2001). Methylphenidate dosage for children with ADHD over time under controlled conditions: Lessons from the MTA. *Journal of the American Academy of Child and Adolescent Psychiatry, 40,* 188–196.

Vitiello, B., Silva, S., Rohde, P., Kratochvil, C., Kennard, B., Reinecke, M., et al. (2009). Suicidal events in the Treatment for Adolescents with Depression Study (TADS). *Journal of Clinical Psychiatry, 70,* 741–747.

Voerman, J. S., Remerie, S., Westendorp, T., Timman, R., Busschbach, J. J. V., Passchier, J., & de Klerk, C. (2015). Effects of a guided internet-delivered self-help intervention for adolescents with chronic pain. *The Journal of Pain, 16,* 1115–1126.

Volkmar, F. R. (2001). Childhood schizophrenia: Developmental aspects. In H. Remschmidt (Ed.), *Schizophrenia in children and adolescents.* Cambridge, UK: Cambridge University Press.

Volkmar, F. R., & Klin, A. (2000). Pervasive developmental disorders. In B. J. Sadock & V. A. Sadock (Eds.), *Kaplan & Sadock's comprehensive textbook of psychiatry* (Vol. II). Philadelphia, PA: Lippincott Williams & Wilkins.

Volkow, N. D., Wang, G.-J., Kollins, S. H., Wigal, T. L., Newcorn, J. H., Telang, R., et al. (2009). Evaluating dopamine reward pathway in ADHD: Clinical implications. *Journal of the American Medical Association, 302,* 1084–1091.

Vollet, J. W., Kindermann, T. A., & Skinner, E. A. (2017). In peer matters, teachers matter: Peer group influences on students' engagement depend on teacher involvement. *Journal of Educational Psychology, 109,* 635–652.

Vorstman, J. A. S., Parr, J. R., Moreno-De-Luca, D., Anney, R. J. L., Nurnberger, J. I., Jr, & Hallmayer, J. F. (2017). Autism genetics: Opportunities and challenges for clinical translation. *Nature Reviews Genetics, 18,* 362–376.

References

Vugs, B., Knoors, H., Cuperus, J., Hendriks, M., & Verhoeven, L. (2016). Interactions between working memory and language in young children with specific language impairment (SLI). *Child Neuropsychology, 22,* 955–978.

Vujeva, H. M., & Furman, W. (2011). Depressive symptoms and romantic relationship qualities from adolescence through emerging adulthood: A longitudinal examination of influences. *Journal of Clinical Child and Adolescent Psychology, 40,* 123–135.

Wade, T. D., Wilksch, S. M., Paxton, S. J., Byrne, S. M., & Austin, S. B. (2017). Do universal media literacy programs have an effect on weight and shape concern by influencing media internalization? *International Journal of Eating Disorders, 50,* 731–738.

Wadsworth, M. E., Ahlkvist, J. A., McDonald, A., & Tilghman-Osborne, E. M. (2018). Future directions in research and intervention with youths in poverty. *Journal of Clinical Child & Adolescent Psychology, 47,* 1023–1038.

Wadsworth, M. E., Evans, G. W., Grant, K., Carter, J. S., & Duffy, S. (2016). Poverty and the development of psychopathology. In D. Cicchetti (Ed.), *Developmental psychopathology: Risk, resilience, and intervention* (Vol. 4). Hoboken, NJ: John Wiley & Sons.

Wadsworth, S. J., DeFries, J. C., Willcutt, E. G., Pennington, B. F., & Olson, R. K. (2015). The Colorado longitudinal twin study of reading difficulties and ADHD: Etiologies of comorbidity and stability. *Twin Research and Human Genetics, 18,* 755–761.

Wagner, A. I., Schmidt, N. L., Lemery-Chalfant, K., Leavitt, L. A., & Goldsmith, H. H. (2009). The limited effects of obstetrical and neonatal complications on conduct and ADHD symptoms in middle childhood. *Journal of Developmental and Behavioral Pediatrics: JDBP, 30,* 217–225.

Wagner, B. M., Silverman, M. A., & Martin, C. E. (2003). Family factors in youth suicidal behaviors. *American Behavioral Scientist, 46,* 1171–1191.

Wahler, R. G., & Dumas, J. E. (1989). Attentional problems in dysfunctional mother-child interactions: An interbehavioral model. *Psychological Bulletin, 105,* 116–130.

Wainer, A. L., & Meltzer, L. J. (2018). Actigraphy. In J. A. Accardo (Ed.), *Sleep in children with neurodevelopmental disabilities: An evidence-based guide* (1st ed.). New York: Springer Berlin Heidelberg.

Wakefield, A. J., Murch, S. H., Anthony, A., Linnell, J., Casson, D. M., Malik, M., et al. (1998). Ileal-lymphoid-nodular hyperplasia, non-specific colitis, and pervasive developmental disorder in children. *Lancet, 351,* 637–641.

Wakefield, J. C. (2016). Diagnostic issues and controversies in DSM-5: Return of the false positive problem. *Annual Review of Clinical Psychology, 12,* 105–132.

Wakschlag, L. S., & Danis, B. (2009). Characterizing early childhood disruptive behavior: Enhancing developmental sensitivity. In C. H. Zeanah, Jr. (Ed.), *Handbook of infant mental health* (3rd ed.). New York: The Guilford Press.

Wakschlag, L. S., Roberts, M. Y., Flynn, R. M., Smith, J. D., Krogh-Jespersen, S., Kaat, A. J., et al. (2019). Future directions for early childhood prevention of mental disorders: A road map to mental health, earlier. *Journal of Clinical Child & Adolescent Psychology, 48,* 539–554.

Waldron, H. B., Brody, J. L., & Hops, H. (2017). Functional Family Therapy for adolescent substance use disorders. In J. R. Weisz & A. E. Kazdin (Eds.), *Evidence-based psychotherapies for children and adolescents* (3rd ed.). New York: The Guilford Press.

Waldron, N. L., & McLeskey, J. (1998). The effects of an inclusive school program on students with mild and severe learning disabilities. *Exceptional Children, 64,* 395–405.

Walg, M., Hapfelmeier, G., El-Wahsch, D., & Prior, H. (2017). The faster internal clock in ADHD is related to lower processing speed: WISC-IV profile analyses and time estimation tasks facilitate the distinction between real ADHD and pseudo-ADHD. *European Child & Adolescent Psychiatry, 26,* 1177–1186.

Walker, E. F., Brennan, P. A., Esterberg, M., Brasfield, J., Pearce, B., & Compton, M. T. (2010). Longitudinal changes in cortisol secretion and conversion to psychosis in at-risk youth. *Journal of Abnormal Psychology, 119,* 401–408.

Walker, J. S., Coleman, D., Lee, J., Squire, P. N., & Friesen, B. J. (2008). Children's stigmatization of childhood depression and ADHD: Magnitude and demographic variation in a national sample. *Journal of the American Academy of Child and Adolescent Psychiatry, 47,* 912–920.

Walkup, J. T., Albano, A. M., Piacentini, J., Birmaher, B., Compton, S. N., Sherrill, J. T., et al. (2008). Cognitive-behavioral therapy, sertraline, or a combination in childhood anxiety. *New England Journal of Medicine, 359,* 2753–2766.

Wallace, G. L., Kenworthy, L., Pugliese, C. E., Popal, H. S., White, E. I., Brodsky, E., & Martin, A. (2016). Real-world executive functions in adults with autism spectrum disorder: Profiles of impairment and associations with adaptive functioning and co-morbid anxiety and depression. *Journal of Autism and Developmental Disorders, 46,* 1071–1083.

Wallander, J. L., & Varni, J. W. (1998). Effects of pediatric chronic physical disorders on child and family adjustment. *Journal of Child Psychology and Psychiatry, 39,* 29–46.

Waller, M. R. (2010). Viewing low-income fathers' ties to families through a cultural lens: Insights for research and policy. *Annals of the American Academy of Political and Social Science, 629,* 102–124.

Walsh, B. T., & Sysko, R. (2009). Broad categories for the diagnosis of eating disorders (BCD-ED): An alternative system for classification. *International Journal of Eating Disorders, 42,* 754–764.

Walsh, B. T., & the Commission on Adolescent Eating Disorders. (2005). Prevention of eating disorders. In D. L. Evans, E. B. Foa, R. E. Gur, H. Hendin, C. P. O'Brien, M. E. P. Seligman, & B. T. Walsh (Eds.), *Treating and preventing adolescent mental health disorders. What we know and what we don't know: A research agenda for improving mental health of our youth.* New York: Oxford University Press.

Walton, K. E., Ormel, J., & Krueger, R. F. (2011). The dimensional nature of externalizing behaviors in adolescence: Evidence from a direct comparison of categorical, dimensional, and hybrid models. *Journal of Abnormal Child Psychology, 39,* 553–561.

Walton, K. M., & Ingersoll, B. R. (2013). Improving social skills in adolescents and adults with autism and severe to profound intellectual disability: A review of the literature. *Journal of Autism and Developmental Disorders, 43,* 594–615.

Wang, C., & Zhang, Y. (2017). Schizophrenia in mid-adulthood after prenatal exposure to the Chinese Famine of 1959–1961. *Schizophrenia Research, 184,* 21–25.

Wang, M. T., & Huguley, J. P. (2012). Parental racial socialization as a moderator of the effects of racial discrimination on educational success among African American adolescents. *Child Development, 83,* 1716–1731.

Wang, M.-T., Henry, D. A., Smith, L. V., Huguley, J. P., & Guo, J. (2020). Parental ethnic-racial socialization practices and children of color's psychosocial and behavioral adjustment: A systematic review and meta-analysis. *American Psychologist, 75,* 1–22.

Warner, T. D., & Settersten, R. A., Jr. (2017). Why neighborhoods (and how we study them) matter for adolescent development. In *Advances in child development and behavior* (Vol. 52). Cambridge, MA: Elsevier.

Warren, S. F., Brady, N., Sterling, A., Fleming, K., & Marquis, J. (2010). Maternal responsivity predicts language development in young children with fragile X syndrome. *American Journal on Intellectual and Developmental Disabilities, 115,* 54–75.

Warren, S. L., Gunnar, M. R., Kagan, J., Anders, T. F., Simmens, S. J., Rones, M., et al. (2003). Maternal panic disorder: Infant temperament, neurophysiology, and parenting behaviors. *Journal of the American Academy of Child and Adolescent Psychiatry, 42,* 814–825.

Warren, S. L., Howe, G., Simmens, S. J., & Dahl, R. E. (2006). Maternal depressive symptoms and child sleep: Models of mutual influence over time. *Development and Psychopathology, 18,* 1–16.

Waschbusch, D. A. (2002). A meta-analytic examination of comorbid hyperactive-impulsive-attention problems and conduct problems. *Psychological Bulletin, 128,* 118–150.

Waschbusch, D. A., & King, S. (2006). Should sex-specific norms be used to assess attention-deficit/hyperactivity disorder or oppositional defiant disorder? *Journal of Consulting and Clinical Psychology, 74,* 179–185.

Waslick, B. (2006). Psychopharmacology interventions for pediatric anxiety disorders: A research update. *Child and Adolescent Psychiatric Clinics of North America, 15,* 51–71.

Wasserman, J. D. (2018). A history of intelligence assessment: The unfinished tapestry. In D. P. Flanagan & E. M. McDonough (Eds.), *Contemporary intellectual assessment: Theories, tests, and issues* (4th ed.). New York: The Guilford Press.

Watkins, C. E., Campbell, V. L., Nieberding, R., & Hallmark, R. (1995). Contemporary practice of psychological assessment by clinical psychologists. *Professional Psychology: Research and Practice, 26,* 54–60.

Watkins, L., Kuhn, M., Ledbetter-Cho, K., Gevarter, C., & O'Reilly, M. (2017). Evidence-based social communication interventions for children with autism spectrum disorder. *The Indian Journal of Pediatrics, 84,* 68–75.

Watson, A. R., Murnen, S. K., & College, K. (2019). Gender differences in responses to thin, athletic, and hyper-muscular idealized bodies. *Body Image, 30,* 1–9.

Watson, D., O'Hara, M. W., & Stuart, S. (2008). Hierarchical structures of affect and psychopathology and their implications for the classification of emotional disorders. *Depression and Anxiety, 25,* 282–288.

Watson, H. J., Joyce, T., French, E., Willan, V., Kane, R. T., Tanner-Smith, E. E., et al. (2016). Prevention of eating disorders: A systematic review of randomized, controlled trials. *International Journal of Eating Disorders, 49,* 833–862.

Watson, J. B. (1930). *Behaviorism.* New York: Norton.

Watson, J. B., & Rayner, R. (1920). Conditioned emotional reactions. *Journal of Experimental Psychology, 3,* 1–14.

Watson, K. H., Dunbar, J. P., Thigpen, J., Reising, M. M., Hudson, K., McKee, L., et al. (2014). Observed parental responsiveness/warmth and children's coping: Cross-sectional and prospective relations in a family depression preventive intervention. *Journal of Family Psychology, 28,* 278–286.

Webb, S. J., Neuhaus, E., & Faja, S. (2017). Face perception and learning in autism spectrum disorders. *The Quarterly Journal of Experimental Psychology, 70,* 970–986.

Webster-Stratton, C. (1998). Preventing conduct problems in Head Start children: Strengthening parenting competencies. *Journal of Consulting and Clinical Psychology, 66,* 715–730.

Webster-Stratton, C., & Reid, M. J. (2017). The Incredible Years Parents, Teachers, and Children Training Series: A multifaceted treatment approach for young children with conduct problems. In J. R. Weisz & A. E. Kazdin (Eds.), *Evidence-based psychotherapies for children and adolescents* (3rd ed.). New York: The Guilford Press.

Webster-Stratton, C., Reid, M. J., & Hammond, M. (2001). Preventing conduct problems, promoting social competence:

References

A parent and teacher training partnership in Head Start. *Journal of Clinical Child Psychology, 30,* 283–302.

Wechsler, D. (2009). *Wechsler Individual Achievement Test* (3rd ed.). San Antonio, TX: Pearson.

Wechsler, D. (2012). *Wechsler Preschool and Primary Scale of Intelligence—Fourth Edition (WPPSI-IV)*. San Antonio, TX: The Psychological Corporation.

Wechsler, D. (2014a). *Technical Manual for the Wechsler Intelligence Scale for Children* (5th ed.). San Antonio, TX: Pearson.

Wechsler, D. (2014b). *Wechsler Intelligence Scale for Children—Fifth Edition (WISC-V)*. San Antonio, TX: The Psychological Corporation.

Weems, C. F. S., & Silverman, W. K. (2017). Anxiety disorders. In T. P. Beauchaine & S. P. Hinshaw (Eds.), *Child and adolescent psychopathology* (3rd ed.). Hoboken, NJ: John Wiley & Sons Inc.

Weersing, V. R., & Brent, D. A. (2010). Treating depression in adolescents using individual cognitive-behavioral therapy. In J. R. Weisz & A. E. Kazdin (Eds.), *Evidence-based psychotherapies for children and adolescents* (2nd ed.). New York: The Guilford Press.

Weersing, V. R., Jeffreys, M., Do, M.-C. T., Schwartz, K. T., & Bolano, C. (2017). Evidence base update of psychosocial treatments for child and adolescent depression. *Journal of Clinical Child & Adolescent Psychology, 46,* 11–43.

Wehmeyer, M. L. (2003). Eugenics and sterilization in the heartland. *Mental Retardation, 41,* 57–60.

Weinberg, S. M., Jenkins, E. A., Marazita, M. L., & Maher, B. S. (2007). Minor physical anomalies in schizophrenia: A meta-analysis. *Schizophrenia Research, 89,* 72–85.

Weinberger, D. R. (2017). Future of days past: Neurodevelopment and schizophrenia. *Schizophrenia Bulletin, 43,* 1164–1168.

Weintraub, M. J., Axelson, D. A., Kowatch, R. A., Schneck, C. D., & Miklowitz, D. J. (2019). Comorbid disorders as moderators of response to family interventions among adolescents with bipolar disorder. *Journal of Affective Disorders, 246,* 754–762.

Weir, K. (2020). Elevating mental health on the world stage. *Monitor on Psychology, 51,* 44–47.

Weissberg, R. P., Kumpfer, K. L., & Seligman, M. E. P. (2003). Prevention that works for children: An introduction. *American Psychologist, 58,* 425–432.

Weissman, M. M., Kidd, K. K., & Prusoff, B. A. (1982). Variability in rates of affective disorders in relatives of depressed and normal probands. *Archives of General Psychiatry, 39,* 1397–1403.

Weissman, M. M., Warner, V., Wickramaratne, P., Moreau, D., & Olfson, M. (1997). Offspring of depressed parents: 10 years later. *Archives of General Psychiatry, 54,* 932–940.

Weissman, M. M., Wickramaratne, P., Gameroff, M. J., Warner, V., Pilowsky, D., Kohad, R. G., et al. (2016). Offspring of depressed parents: 30 years later. *American Journal of Psychiatry, 173,* 1024–1032.

Weissman, M. M., Wickramaratne, P., Nomura, Y., Warner, V., Verdeli, H., Pilowsky, D. J., Grillon, C., & Bruder, G. (2005). Families at high and low risk for depression: A 3-generation study. *Archives of General Psychiatry, 62,* 29–36.

Weisz, J. R., & Kazdin, A. E. (2017). The present and future of evidence-based psychotherapies for children and adolescents. In J. R. Weisz & A. E. Kazdin (Eds.), *Evidence-based psychotherapies for children and adolescents* (3rd ed.). New York: The Guilford Press.

Weisz, J. R., Chaiyasit, W., Weiss, B., Eastman, K. L., & Jackson, E. W. (1995). A multimethod study of problem behavior among Thai and American children in school: Teacher reports versus direct observations. *Child Development, 66,* 402–415.

Weisz, J. R., Kuppens, S., Ng, M. Y., Eckshtain, D., Ugueto, A. M., Vaughn-Coaxum, R., et al. (2017). What five decades of research tells us about the effects of youth psychological therapy: A multilevel meta-analysis and implications for science and practice. *American Psychologist, 72,* 79–117.

Weisz, J. R., Sandler, I. N., Durlak, J. A., & Anton, B. S. (2005). Promoting and protecting youth mental health through evidence-based prevention and treatment. *American Psychologist, 60,* 628–648.

Weisz, J. R., Sweeney, L., Proffitt, V., & Carr, T. (1993). Control-related beliefs and self-reported depressive symptoms in late childhood. *Journal of Abnormal Psychology, 102,* 411–418.

Wekerle, C., Wall, A. M., Leung, E., & Trocme, N. (2007). Cumulative stress and substantiated maltreatment: The importance of caregiver vulnerability and adult partner violence. *Child Abuse & Neglect, 31,* 427–443.

Wells, A. E., Hunnikin, L. M., Ash, D. P., & van Goozen, S. H. M. (2020). Children with behavioural problems misinterpret the emotions and intentions of others. *Journal of Abnormal Child Psychology, 48,* 213–221.

Wells, K. C., Forehand, R., & Griest, D. L. (1980). Generality of treatment effects from treated to untreated behaviors resulting from a parent training program. *Journal of Clinical Child Psychology, 9,* 217–219.

Wender, P. H., Kety, S. S., Rosenthal, D., Schulsinger, F., Ortmann, J., & Lunde, I. (1986). Psychiatric disorders in the biological and adoptive families of adopted individuals with affective disorders. *Archives of General Psychiatry, 43,* 923–929.

Werner, E. E. (1995). Resilience in development. *Current Directions in Psychological Science, 4,* 81–84.

Werner, E. E., & Smith, R. S. (1982). *Vulnerable but invincible.* New York: McGraw-Hill.

Werner, E. E., & Smith, R. S. (2001). *Journeys from childhood to midlife.* Ithaca, NY: Cornell University Press.

Werner-Seidler, A., Perry, Y., Calear, A. L., Newby, J. M., & Christensen, H. (2017). School-based depression and anxiety prevention programs for young people: A systematic review and meta-analysis. *Clinical Psychology Review, 51,* 30–47.

Werry, J. S. (1986). Physical illness, symptoms and allied disorders. In H. C. Quay & J. S.Werry (Eds.), *Psychopathological disorders of childhood* (3rd ed.). New York: Wiley.

Wertheim, E. H., Paxton, S. J., & Blaney, S. (2004). Risk factors for the development of body image disturbances. In J. K. Thompson (Ed.), *Handbook of eating disorders and obesity.* Hoboken, NJ: John Wiley.

West, A. E., Weinstein, S. M., Peters, A. T., Katz, A. C., Henry, D. B., Cruz, R. A., & Pavuluri, M. N. (2014). Child-and family-focused cognitive-behavioral therapy for pediatric bipolar disorder: A randomized clinical trial. *Journal of the American Academy of Child & Adolescent Psychiatry, 53,* 1168–1178.

West, M. O., & Prinz, R. J. (1987). Parental alcoholism and childhood psychopathology. *Psychological Bulletin, 102,* 204–218.

West, S. G., Sandler, I., Pillow, D. R., Baca, L., & Gersten, J. C. (1991). The use of structural equation modeling in generative research: Toward the design of a preventative intervention for bereaved children. *American Journal of Community Psychology, 19,* 459–480.

Westenberg, P. M., Drewes, M. J., Goedhart, A. W., Siebelink, B. M., & Treffers, P. D. A. (2004). A developmental analysis of self-reported fears in late childhood through mid-adolescence: Social-evaluative fears on the rise? *Journal of Child Psychology and Psychiatry, 45,* 481–495.

Weston, L., Hodgekins, J., & Langdon, P. E. (2016). Effectiveness of cognitive behavioural therapy with people who have autistic spectrum disorders: A systematic review and meta-analysis. *Clinical Psychology Review, 49,* 41–54.

Weyandt, L. L., & Gudmundsdottir, B. G. (2015). Developmental and neuropsychological deficits in children with ADHD. In R. A. Barkley (Ed.), *Attention-deficit hyperactivity disorder: A handbook for diagnosis and treatment* (4th ed.). New York: The Guilford Press.

Weyandt, L. L., Verdi, G., & Swentosky, A. (2011). Oppositional, conduct, and aggressive disorders. In S. Goldstein & C. R. Reynolds (Eds.), *Handbook of neurodevelopmental and genetic disorders in children* (2nd ed.). New York: The Guilford Press.

Whalen, C. K., Henker, B., King, P. S., Jamner, L. D., & Levine, L. (2004). Adolescents react to the events of September 11, 2001: Focused versus ambient impact. *Journal of Abnormal Child Psychology, 32,* 1–11.

Whitaker, A., Johnson, J., Shaffer, D., Rappoport, J., Kalikow, K., Walsh, B. T., Davies, M., Braiman, S., & Dolinsky, A. (1990). Uncommon troubles in young people: Prevalence estimates of selected psychiatric disorders in a nonreferred adolescent population. *Archives of General Psychiatry, 47,* 487–496.

White House Task Force on Childhood Obesity. (2011). *One year progress report.* Retrieved July 2011 from www.letsmove. gov/white-house-task-force-childhood-obesity-report-president

White, S. F., & Frick, P. J. (2010). Callous-unemotional traits and their importance to causal models of severe antisocial behavior in youth. In R. T. Salekin & D. R. Lyman (Eds.), *Handbook of child and adolescent psychopathy.* New York: The Guilford Press.

White, S. H. (1992). G. Stanley Hall: From philosophy to developmental psychology. *Developmental Psychology, 28,* 25–34.

White, S. W., Simmons, G. L., Gotham, K. O., Conner, C. M., Smith, I. C., Beck, K. B., & Mazefsky, C. A. (2018). Psychosocial treatments targeting anxiety and depression in adolescents and adults on the autism spectrum: Review of the latest research and recommended future directions. *Current Psychiatry Reports, 20,* 82.

Whitehurst, G. J., & Fischel, J. E. (1994). Early developmental language delay: What, if anything, should the clinician do about it? *Journal of Child Psychology and Psychiatry, 35,* 613–648.

Whitford, B., Nadel, A. L., & Fish, J. D. (2018). Burnout in pediatric hematology/oncology: Time to address the elephant by name. *Pediatric Blood & Cancer, 65,* e27244.

Whitman, T. L., Hantula, D. A., & Spence, B. H. (1990). Current issues in behavior modification with mentally retarded persons. In J. L. Matson (Ed.), *Handbook of behavior modification with the mentally retarded.* New York: Plenum.

Widiger, T. A., & Clark, L. A. (2000). Toward DSM-V and the classification of psychopathology. *Psychological Bulletin, 126,* 946–961.

Widiger, T. A., Frances, A. J., Pincus, H. A., Davis, W. W., & First, M. B. (1991). Toward an empirical classification for DSM-IV. *Journal of Abnormal Psychology, 100,* 280–288.

Widom, C. S., Czaja, S. J., & DuMont, K. A. (2015). Intergenerational transmission of child abuse and neglect: Real or detection bias? *Science, 347,* 1480–1485.

Wiebe, D. J., Helgeson, V., & Berg, C. A. (2016). The social context of managing diabetes across the life span. *American Psychologist, 71,* 526–538.

Wiener, J., & Tardif, C. Y. (2004). Social and emotional functioning of children with learning disabilities: Does special education placement make a difference? *Learning Disabilities Research & Practice, 19,* 20–32.

Wiener, J., Biondic, D., Grimbos, T., & Herbert, M. (2016). Parenting stress of parents of adolescents with attention-deficit hyperactivity disorder. *Journal of Abnormal Child Psychology, 44,* 561–574.

Wiggs, L. D. (2019). Epidemiology and etiology of behavioral insomnias, circadian rhythm disorders, and parasomnias in

References

ADHD. In H. Hiscock & E. Sciberras (Eds.), *Sleep and ADHD*. London: Academic Press.

Wight, R. G., Sepúlveda, J. E., & Aneshensel, C. S. (2004). Depressive symptoms: How do adolescents compare with adults? *Journal of Adolescent Health, 34,* 314–323.

Wilens, T. E. (2011). A sobering fact: ADHD leads to substance abuse. *Journal of the American Academy of Child and Adolescent Psychiatry, 50,* 6–8.

Wilens, T. E., Martelon, M., Joshi, G., Bateman, C., Fried, R., Petty, C., & Biederman, J. (2011). Does ADHD predict substance-use disorders? A 10-year follow-up study of young adults with ADHD. *Journal of the American Academy of Child & Adolescent Psychiatry, 50,* 543–553.

Wilfley, D. E., Kolko, R. P., & Kass, A. E. (2011). Cognitive-behavioral therapy for weight management and eating disorders in children and adolescents. *Child and Adolescent Psychiatric Clinics of North America, 20,* 271–285.

Wilkerson, T. T. (2018). Understanding the comprehensive assessment of autism spectrum disorder through case studies. In S. Goldstein & S. Ozonoff (Eds.), *Assessment of autism spectrum disorder* (2nd ed.). New York: The Guilford Press.

Wilkinson, G. S., & Robertson, G. J. (2017). *Wide Range Achievement Test (5th ed.) (WRAT-5)*. San Antonio, TX: Pearson.

Wilkinson, R., & Pickett, K. (2020). *The inner level: How more unequal societies reduce stress, restore sanity and improve everyone's well-being*. New York: Penguin Books.

Willcutt, E. G. (2012). The prevalence of DSM-IV attention-deficit/hyperactivity disorder: A meta-analytic review. *Neurotherapeutics, 9,* 490–499.

Willcutt, E. G. (2014). Behavioral genetic approaches to understand the etiology of comorbidity. In S. H. Rhee & A. Ronald (Eds.), *Behavior genetics of psychopathology*. New York: Springer.

Willcutt, E. G. (2015). Theories of ADHD. In R. A. Barkley (Ed.), *Attention-deficit hyperactivity disorder: A handbook for diagnosis and treatment* (4th ed.). New York: The Guilford Press.

Willcutt, E., & McQueen, M. (2010). Genetic and environmental vulnerability to bipolar spectrum disorders. In D. J. Miklowitz & D. Cicchetti (Eds.), *Understanding bipolar disorder: A developmental psychopathology perspective*. New York: The Guilford Press.

Willcutt, E. G., & Pennington, B. F. (2000). Psychiatric comorbidity in children and adolescents with reading disability. *Journal of Child Psychology and Psychiatry, 41,* 1039–1048.

Willcutt, E. G., Betjemann, R. S., McGrath, L. M., Chhabildas, N. A., Olson, R. K., DeFries, J. C., & Pennington, B. F. (2010). Etiology and neuropsychology of comorbidity between RD and ADHD: The case for multiple-deficit models. *Cortex, 46,* 1345–1361.

Willcutt, E. G., Nigg, J. T., Pennington, B. F., Solanto, M. V., Rohde, L. A., Tannock, R., et al. (2012). Validity of DSM-IV attention deficit/hyperactivity disorder symptom dimensions and subtypes. *Journal of Abnormal Psychology, 121,* 991–1010.

Willcutt, E. G., Pennington, B. F., Olson, R. K., Chhabildas, N., & Hulslander, J. (2005). Neuropsychological analyses of comorbidity between reading disability and attention deficit hyperactivity disorder: In search of the common deficit. *Developmental Neuropsychology, 27,* 35–78.

Willems, G., Jansma, B., Blomert, L., & Vaessen, A. (2016). Cognitive and familial risk evidence converged: A data-driven identification of distinct and homogeneous subtypes within the heterogeneous sample of reading disabled children. *Research in Developmental Disabilities, 53–54,* 213–231.

Williams, B., & Pow, J. (2007). Gender differences and mental health: An exploratory study of knowledge and attitudes to mental health among Scottish teenagers. *Child and Adolescent Mental Health, 12,* 6–12.

Williams, D., Botting, N., & Boucher, J. (2008). Language in autism and specific language impairment: Where are the links? *Psychological Bulletin, 134,* 944–963.

Williams, N. J., & Beidas, R. S. (2019). The state of implementation science in child psychology and psychiatry: A review and suggestions to advance the field. *Journal of Child Psychology and Psychiatry, 60,* 430–450.

Williams, N. M., Zaharieva, I., Martin, A., Langley, K., Mantripragada, K., Fossdal, R., et al. (2010). Rare chromosomal deletions and duplications in attention-deficit hyperactivity disorder: A genome-wide analysis. *The Lancet, 376,* 1401–1408.

Williamson, D. E., Forbes, E. E., Dahl, R. E., & Ryan, N. D. (2005). A genetic epidemiologic perspective on comorbidity of depression and anxiety. *Child and Adolescent Psychiatric Clinics of North America, 14,* 707–726.

Willis, D., Siceloff, E. R., Morse, M., Neger, E., & Flory, K. (2019). Stand-alone social skills training for youth with ADHD: A systematic review. *Clinical Child and Family Psychology Review, 22,* 348–366.

Willoughby, M. T. (2017). Developmental changes in ADHD symptoms across early childhood. *Child and Adolescent Psychopharmacology News, 22,* 1–6.

Willoughby, M. T., Pek, J., Greenberg, M. T.; Family Life Project Investigators. (2012). Parent-reported attention deficit/hyperactivity symptomatology in preschool-aged children: Factor structure, developmental change, and early risk factors. *Journal of Abnormal Child Psychology, 40,* 1301–1312.

Wills, T. A., & Dishion, T. J. (2004). Temperament and adolescent substance abuse: A transactional analysis of emerging self-control. *Journal of Clinical and Child and Adolescent Psychology, 33,* 69–81.

Wilson, A. C., Lengua, L. J., Metzoff, A. N., & Smith, K. A. (2010). Parenting and temperament prior to September 11, 2001 and parenting specific to 9/11 as predictors of children's posttraumatic stress symptoms following 9/11. *Journal of Clinical Child and Adolescent Psychology, 39,* 445–459.

Wilson, G. T. (2011). Treatment of binge eating disorder. *Psychiatric Clinics, 34,* 773–783.

Wilson, G. T., Becker, C. B., & Heffernan, K. (2003). Eating disorders. In E. J. Mash & R. A. Barkley (Eds.), *Child psychopathology* (2nd ed.). New York: Guilford Press.

Wilson, R. B., Enticott, P. G., & Rinehart, N. J. (2018). Motor development and delay: Advances in assessment of motor skills in autism spectrum disorders. *Current Opinion in Neurology, 31,* 134–139.

Winsper, C., Lereya, T., Zanarini, M., & Wolke, D. (2012). Involvement in bullying and suicide-related behavior at 11 years: A prospective birth cohort study. *Journal of the American Academy of Child and Adolescent Psychiatry, 51,* 271–282.

Winter, A. S., & Sampson, R. J. (2017). From lead exposure in early childhood to adolescent health: A Chicago birth cohort. *American Journal of Public Health, 107,* 1496–1501.

Winters, N. C., Myers, K., & Proud, L. (2002). Ten-year review of rating scales. III: Scales assessing suicidality, cognitive style, and self-esteem. *Journal of the American Academy of Child & Adolescent Psychiatry, 41,* 1150–1181.

Wiseman, C. V., Sunday, S. R., & Becker, A. E. (2005). Impact of the media on adolescent body image. *Child and Adolescent Psychiatric Clinics of North America, 14,* 453–471.

Wiśniowiecka-Kowalnik, B., & Nowakowska, B. A. (2019). Genetics and epigenetics of autism spectrum disorder: Current evidence in the field. *Journal of Applied Genetics, 60,* 37–47.

Witvliet, M., Brendgen, M., Van Lier, P. A., Koot, H. M., & Vitaro, F. (2010). Early adolescent depressive symptoms: Prediction from clique isolation, loneliness, and perceived social acceptance. *Journal of Abnormal Child Psychology, 38,* 1045–1056.

Wolf, M. M., Braukmann, C. J., & Ramp, K. A. (1987). Serious delinquent behavior as part of a significantly handicapping condition: Cures and supportive environments. *Journal of Applied Behavior Analysis, 20,* 347–359.

Wolfe, B. E., Baker, C. W., Smith, A. T., & Kelly-Weeder, S. (2009). Validity and utility of the current definition of binge eating. *International Journal of Eating Disorders, 42,* 674–686.

Wolfe, V. V. (2006). Child sexual abuse. In E. J. Mash & R. A. Barkley (Eds.), *Treatment of childhood disorders* (3rd ed.). New York: The Guilford Press.

Wolfe, V. V., & Kelly, B. M. (2019). Child maltreatment. In M. J. Prinstein, E. A. Youngstrom, E. J. Mash, & R. A. Barkley (Eds.), *Treatment of disorders in childhood and adolescence* (4th ed.). New York: The Guilford Press.

Wolke, D., Woods, S., Bloomfield, L., & Karstadt, L. (2000). The association between direct and relational bullying and behaviour problems among primary school children. *Journal of Child Psychology and Psychiatry, 41,* 989–1002.

Wolraich, M. L., Hagan, J. F., Allan, C., Chan, E., Davison, D., Earls, M., et al. (2019). Clinical practice guideline for the diagnosis, evaluation, and treatment of attention-deficit/hyperactivity disorder in children and adolescents. *Pediatrics, 144,* e20192528.

Wolraich, M., Wilson, D. B., & White, J. W. (1995). The effect of sugar on behavior or cognition in children. *Journal of the American Medical Association, 274,* 1617–1621.

Wonderlich, S. A., Joiner, T. E., Keel, P. K., Williamson, D. A., & Crosby, R. D. (2007). Eating disorder diagnoses. *American Psychologist, 62,* 167–180.

Wonderlich, S. A., Lilenfeld, L. R., Riso, L. P., Engel, S., & Mitchell, J. E. (2005). Personality and anorexia nervosa. *International Journal of Eating Disorders, 37,* S68–S71.

Wong, B. Y. L., Butler, D. L., Ficzere, S. A., & Kuperis, S. (1997). Teaching adolescents with learning disabilities and low achievers to plan, write, and revise compare-and-contrast essays. *Learning Disabilities Research & Practice, 12,* 2–15.

Wong, C., Odom, S. L., Hume, K. A., Cox, A. W., Fettig, A., Kucharczyk, S., et al. (2015). Evidence-based practices for children, youth, and young adults with autism spectrum disorder: A comprehensive review. *Journal of Autism and Developmental Disorders, 45,* 1951–1966.

Wood, C. L., Warnell, F., Johnson, M., Hames, A., Pearce, M. S., McConachie, H., & Parr, J. R. (2015). Evidence for ASD recurrence rates and reproductive stoppage from large UK ASD research family databases. *Autism Research, 8,* 73–81.

Wood, J. J., McLeod, B. D., Sigman, M., Hwang, W. C., & Chu, B. C. (2003). Parenting and childhood anxiety: Theory, empirical findings, and future directions. *Journal of Child Psychology and Psychiatry, 44,* 134–151.

Wood, J., & Peters, A. (2018). *The type 1 diabetes self-care manual.* Arlington, VA: American Diabetes Association.

Wood, M., & Valdez-Menchaca, M. C. (1996). The effect of a diagnostic label of language delay on adults' perceptions of preschool children. *Journal of Learning Disabilities, 29,* 582–588.

Woodberry, K. A., Kline, E., & Giuliano, A. J. (2019). Schizophrenia spectrum disorders. In T. H. Ollendick, S. W. White, & B. A. White (Eds.), *The Oxford handbook of clinical child and adolescent psychology.* New York: Oxford University Press.

Woodbury-Smith, M., & Scherer, S. W. (2018). Progress in the genetics of autism spectrum disorder. *Developmental Medicine & Child Neurology, 60,* 445–451.

Woodhouse, S., Miah, A., & Rutter, M. (2018). A new look at the supposed risks of early institutional rearing. *Psychological Medicine, 48,* 1–10.

References

Woodward, L. J., Fergusson, D. M., & Horwood, L. J. (2000). Driving outcomes of young people with attentional difficulties in adolescence. *Journal of the American Academy of Child and Adolescent Psychiatry, 39,* 627–634.

Woolf, C., Muscara, F., Anderson, V., & McCarthy, M. (2016). Early traumatic stress responses in parents following a serious illness in their child: A systematic review. *Journal of Clinical Psychology in Medical Settings, 23,* 53–66.

World Health Organization. (2012). *WHO guidelines on the pharmacological treatment of persisting pain in children with medical illnesses.* Geneva, Switzerland: World Health Organization.

World Health Organization. (2017). *Depression and other common mental disorders: Global health estimates* (No. WHO/MSD/MER/2017.2). World Health Organization.

World Health Organization. (2018a). *Global status report on road safety.* Geneva, Switzerland: World Health Organization. Retrieved from www.who.int/violence_injury_prevention/road_safety_status/2018/en/

World Health Organization. (2018b). Lead poisoning and health. Retrieved from www.who.int/news-room/fact-sheets/detail/lead-poisoning-and-health

World Health Organization. (2019). ICD-11: International Classification of Diseases 11th Revision. Retrieved from https://icd.who.int/en

Wren, F. J., Berg, E. A., Heiden, L. A., Kinnamon, C. J., Ohlson, L. A., Bridge, J. A., et al. (2007). Childhood anxiety in a diverse primary care population: Parent-child reports, ethnicity, and SCARED factor structure. *Journal of the American Academy of Child and Adolescent Psychiatry, 46,* 332–340.

Wright, H. F. (1960). Observational child study. In P. H. Mussen (Ed.), *Handbook of research methods in child development.* New York: John Wiley.

Wu, Z.-M., Bralten, J., Cao, Q.-J., Hoogman, M., Zwiers, M. P., An, L., et al. (2017). White matter microstructural alterations in children with ADHD: Categorical and dimensional perspectives. *Neuropsychopharmacology, 42,* 572–580.

Wysocki, T., Buckloh, L. M., & Pierce, J. (2017). The psychological context of diabetes mellitus in youth. In M. C. Roberts & R. G. Steele (Eds.), *Handbook of pediatric psychology.* New York: The Guilford Press.

Wysocki, T., Iannotti, R., Weissberg-Benchell, J., Laffel, L., Hood, K., Anderson, B., et al. (2008). Diabetes problem solving by youths with type 1 diabetes and their caregivers: Measurement, validation, and longitudinal associations with glycemic control. *Journal of Pediatric Psychology, 33,* 875–884.

Xerxa, Y., Rescorla, L. A., Serdarevic, F., Van IJzendoorn, M. H., Jaddoe, V. W., Verhulst, F. C., et al. (2020). The complex role of parental separation in the association between family conflict and child problem behavior. *Journal of Clinical Child & Adolescent Psychology, 49,* 79–93.

Yang, T. T., Simmons, A. N., Matthews, S. C., Tapert, S. F., Frank, G. K., Max, J. E., et al. (2010). Adolescents with major depression demonstrate increased amygdala activation. *Journal of the American Academy of Child and Adolescent Psychiatry, 49,* 42–51.

Yasui, M., Dishion, T. J., Stormshak, E., & Ball, A. (2015). Socialization of culture and coping with discrimination among American Indian families: Examining cultural correlates of youth outcomes. *Journal of the Society for Social Work and Research, 6,* 317–341.

Yeates, K. O., Bigler, E. D., Dennis, M., Gerhardt, C. A., Rubin, K. H., Stancin, T., et al. (2007). Social outcomes in childhood brain disorder: A heuristic integration of social neuroscience and developmental psychology. *Psychological Bulletin, 133,* 535–556.

Yee, C. S., Hawken, E. R., Baldessarini, R. J., & Vázquez, G. H. (2019). Maintenance pharmacological treatment of juvenile bipolar disorder: Review and meta-analyses. *International Journal of Neuropsychopharmacology, 22,* 531–540.

Yeganeh, R., Beidel, D. C., Turner, S. M., Pina, A. A., & Silverman, W. K. (2003). Clinical distinctions between selective mutism and social phobia: An investigation of childhood psychopathology. *Journal of the American Academy of Child and Adolescent Psychiatry, 42,* 1069–1075.

Yerys, B. E., Hepburn, S. L., Pennington, B. F., & Rogers, S. J. (2007). Executive function in preschoolers with autism: Evidence consistent with a secondary deficit. *Journal of Autism and Developmental Disorders, 37,* 1068–1079.

Yoshikawa, H., Weisner, T. S., Kalil, A., & Way, N. (2013). Mixing qualitative and quantitative research in developmental science: Uses and methodological choices. *Qualitative Psychology, 1*(S), 3–18.

Young, J. F., Benas, J. S., Schueler, C. M., Gallop, R., Gillham, J. E., & Mufson, L. (2016). A randomized depression prevention trial comparing Interpersonal Psychotherapy–Adolescent Skills Training to group counseling in schools. *Prevention Science, 17,* 314–324.

Young, J. F., Mufson, L., & Davies, M. (2006). Efficacy of Interpersonal Psychotherapy–Adolescent Skills Training: An indicated preventive intervention for depression. *Journal of Child Psychology and Psychiatry, 47,* 1254–1262.

Young, M. H., Brennan, L. C., Baker, R. D., & Baker, S. S. (1996). Functional encopresis. In R. S. Feldman (Ed.), *The psychology of adversity.* Amherst: University of Massachusetts Press.

Young, R. C., Biggs, J. T., Ziegler, V. E., & Meyer, D. A. (1978). A rating scale for mania: Reliability, validity, and sensitivity. *British Journal of Psychiatry, 133,* 429–435.

Young, S. E., Friedman, N. P., Miyake, A., Willcutt, E. G., Corley, R. P., Haberstick, B. C., et al. (2009). Behavioral disinhibition: Liability for externalizing spectrum disorders and its genetic and environmental relation to response inhibition across adolescence. *Journal of Abnormal Psychology, 118,* 117–130.

Youngstrom, E. A. (2010). A developmental psychopathology perspective on the assessment and diagnosis of bipolar disorder. In D. J. Miklowitz & D. Cicchetti (Eds.), *Understanding bipolar disorder: A developmental psychopathology perspective.* New York: The Guilford Press.

Youngstrom, E. A., & Algorta, G. P. (2014). Pediatric bipolar disorder. In E. J. Mash & R. A. Barkley (Eds.), *Child psychopathology.* New York: The Guilford Press.

Youngstrom, E. A., Findling, R. L., & Feeny, N. (2004). Assessment of bipolar spectrum disorders in children and adolescents. In S. L. Johnson & R. L. Leahy (Eds.), *Psychological treatment of bipolar disorder.* New York: Guilford Press.

Youngstrom, E. A., Findling, R. L., Danielson, C. K., & Calabrese, J. R. (2001). Discriminative validity of parent report of hypomanic and depressive symptoms in the General Behavior Inventory. *Psychological Assessment, 13,* 267–276.

Youngstrom, E. A., Frazier, T. W., Demeter, C., Calabrese, J. R., & Findling, R. L. (2008). Developing a ten item mania scale from the parent general behavior inventory for children and adolescents. *The Journal of Clinical Psychiatry, 69,* 831–839.

Youngstrom, E. A., Van Meter, A., Frazier, T. W., Hunsley, J., Prinstein, M. J., Ong, M. L., & Youngstrom, J. K. (2017). Evidence-based assessment as an integrative model for applying psychological science to guide the voyage of treatment. *Clinical Psychology Science and Practice, 24,* 331–363.

Yu, D., Mathews, C. A., Scharf, J. M., Neale, B. M., Davis, L. K., Gamazon, E. R., et al. (2015). Cross-disorder genome-wide analyses suggest a complex genetic relationship between Tourette's Syndrome and OCD. *American Journal of Psychiatry, 172,* 82–93.

Yule, W., Udwin, O., & Murdoch, K. (1990). The "Jupiter" sinking: Effects on children's fears, depression and anxiety. *Journal of Child Psychology and Psychiatry, 31,* 1051–1061.

Yung, A. R., Wood, S. J., Malla, A., Nelson, B., McGorry, P., & Shah, J. (2019). The reality of at risk mental state services: A response to recent criticisms. *Psychological Medicine,* 1–7.

Zahn-Waxler, C., Crick, N. R., Shirtcliffe, E. A., & Woods, K. E. (2006). The origins and development of psychopathology in females and males. In D. Cicchetti & D. J. Cohen (Eds.), *Developmental psychopathology. Vol. 1. Theory and method.* Hoboken, NJ: John Wiley & Sons.

Zahn-Waxler, C., Shirtcliff, E. A., & Marceau, K. (2008). Disorders of childhood and adolescence: Gender and psychopathology. *Annual Review of Clinical Psychology, 4,* 275–303.

Zahran, H. S., Bailey, C. M., Damon, S. A., Garbe, P. L., & Breysse, P. N. (2018). Vital signs: Asthma in children—United States, 2001–2016. *Morbidity and Mortality Weekly Report, 67,* 149–155.

Zalecki, C. A., & Hinshaw, S. P. (2004). Overt and relational aggression in girls with attention deficit hyperactivity

disorder. *Journal of Clinical Child and Adolescent Psychology, 33,* 125–137.

Zalsman, G., Hawton, K., Wasserman, D., van Heeringen, K., Arensman, E., Sarchiapone, M., et al. (2016). Suicide prevention strategies revisited: 10-year systematic review. *The Lancet Psychiatry, 3,* 646–659.

Zalsman, G., Oquendo, M. A., Greenhill, L., Goldberg, P. H., Kamali, M., Martin, A., & Mann, J. J. (2006). Neurobiology of depression in children and adolescents. *Child and Adolescent Psychiatric Clinics of North America, 15,* 843–868.

Zarnegar-Lumley, S., Lange, K. R., Mathias, M. D., Nakajima-Hatano, M., Offer, K. M., Ogu, U. O., et al. (2019). Local anesthesia with general anesthesia for pediatric bone marrow procedures. *Pediatrics, 144,* e20183829.

Zeanah, C. H., & Gleason, M. M. (2015). Attachment disorders in early childhood: Clinical presentation, causes, correlates, and treatment. *Journal of Child Psychology and Psychiatry, 56,* 207–222.

Zeanah, C. H., & Zeanah, P. D. (2019). Infant mental health: The clinical science of early experience. In C. H. Zeanah (Ed.), *Handbook of infant mental health* (4th ed.). New York: The Guilford Press.

Zelazny, J., Melhem, N., Porta, G., Biernesser, C., Keilp, J. G., Mann, J. J., et al. (2019). Childhood maltreatment, neuropsychological function and suicidal behavior. *Journal of Child Psychology and Psychiatry, 60,* 1085–1093.

Zero to Three. (2016). *Diagnostic classification of mental health and developmental disorders of infancy and early childhood: DC: 0–5.* Washington, DC: Author.

Zickgraf, H., & Mayes, S. D. (2019). Psychological, health, and demographic correlates of atypical eating behaviors in children with autism. *Journal of Developmental and Physical Disabilities, 31,* 399–418.

Ziermans, T. B., Schothorst, P. F., Sprong, M., & van Engeland, H. (2011). Transition and remission in adolescents at ultra-high risk for psychosis. *Schizophrenia Research, 126,* 58–64.

Zigler, E., Balla, D., & Hodapp, R. (1984). On the definition and classification of mental retardation. *American Journal of Mental Deficiency, 89,* 215–230.

Zisser, A., & Eyberg, S. M. (2010). Parent-child interaction therapy and the treatment of disruptive behavior disorders. In J. R. Weisz & A. E. Kazdin (Eds.), *Evidence-based psychotherapies for children and adolescents* (2nd ed.). New York: The Guilford Press.

Zisser-Nathenson, A. R., Herschell, A. D., & Eyberg, S. M. (2017). Parent-child interaction therapy and the treatment of disruptive behavior disorders. In J. R. Weisz & A. E. Kazdin (Eds.), *Evidence-based psychotherapies for children and adolescents* (3rd ed.). New York: The Guilford Press.

References

Zito, J. M., Safer, D. J., dos Reis, S., Gardner, J. F., Boles, M., & Lynch, F. (2000). Trends in the prescribing of psychotropic medications to preschoolers. *Journal of the American Medical Association, 283,* 1025–1031.

Zuddas, A., Banaschewski, T., Coghill, D., & Stein, M. A. (2018). ADHD treatment: Psychostimulants. In T. Banaschewski, D. Coghill, & A. Zuddas (Eds.), *Oxford textbook of attention deficit hyperactivity disorder.* Oxford: Oxford University Press.

Zuvekas, S. H., Vitiello, B., & Norquist, G. S. (2006). Recent trends in stimulant medication use among U.S. children. *American Journal of Psychiatry, 163,* 579–585.

Index

Index